Laura Leal-Taixé · Stefan Roth (Eds.)

Computer Vision – ECCV 2018 Workshops

Munich, Germany, September 8–14, 2018
Proceedings, Part III

 Springer

Editors
Laura Leal-Taixé
Technical University of Munich
Garching, Germany

Stefan Roth ⓘD
Technische Universität Darmstadt
Darmstadt, Germany

ISSN 0302-9743   ISSN 1611-3349   (electronic)
Lecture Notes in Computer Science
ISBN 978-3-030-11014-7   ISBN 978-3-030-11015-4   (eBook)
https://doi.org/10.1007/978-3-030-11015-4

Library of Congress Control Number: 2018966826

LNCS Sublibrary: SL6 – Image Processing, Computer Vision, Pattern Recognition, and Graphics

This Springer imprint is published by the registered company Springer Nature Switzerland AG
The registered company address is: Gewerbestrasse 11, 6330 Cham, Switzerland

Lecture Notes in Computer Science 11131

Commenced Publication in 1973
Founding and Former Series Editors:
Gerhard Goos, Juris Hartmanis, and Jan van Leeuwen

Foreword

It was our great pleasure to host the European Conference on Computer Vision 2018 in Munich, Germany. This constituted by far the largest ECCV event ever. With close to 2,900 registered participants and another 600 on the waiting list one month before the conference, participation more than doubled since the last ECCV in Amsterdam. We believe that this is due to a dramatic growth of the computer vision community combined with the popularity of Munich as a major European hub of culture, science, and industry. The conference took place in the heart of Munich in the concert hall Gasteig with workshops and tutorials held on the downtown campus of the Technical University of Munich.

One of the major innovations for ECCV 2018 was the free perpetual availability of all conference and workshop papers, which is often referred to as open access. We note that this is not precisely the same use of the term as in the Budapest declaration. Since 2013, CVPR and ICCV have had their papers hosted by the Computer Vision Foundation (CVF), in parallel with the IEEE Xplore version. This has proved highly beneficial to the computer vision community.

We are delighted to announce that for ECCV 2018 a very similar arrangement was put in place with the cooperation of Springer. In particular, the author's final version will be freely available in perpetuity on a CVF page, while SpringerLink will continue to host a version with further improvements, such as activating reference links and including video. We believe that this will give readers the best of both worlds; researchers who are focused on the technical content will have a freely available version in an easily accessible place, while subscribers to SpringerLink will continue to have the additional benefits that this provides. We thank Alfred Hofmann from Springer for helping to negotiate this agreement, which we expect will continue for future versions of ECCV.

September 2018

Horst Bischof
Daniel Cremers
Bernt Schiele
Ramin Zabih

Foreword

Preface

It is our great pleasure to present these workshop proceedings of the 15th European Conference on Computer Vision, which was held during September 8–14, 2018, in Munich, Germany. We are delighted that the main conference of ECCV 2018 was accompanied by 43 scientific workshops. The ECCV workshop proceedings contain contributions of 36 workshops.

We received 74 workshop proposals on a broad set of topics related to computer vision. The very high quality and the large number of proposals made the selection process rather challenging. Owing to space restrictions, only 46 proposals were accepted, among which six proposals were merged into three workshops because of overlapping themes.

The final set of 43 workshops complemented the main conference program well. The workshop topics presented a good orchestration of new trends and traditional issues, built bridges into neighboring fields, as well as discussed fundamental technologies and novel applications. We would like to thank all the workshop organizers for their unreserved efforts to make the workshop sessions a great success.

September 2018

Stefan Roth
Laura Leal-Taixé

Organization

General Chairs

Horst Bischof	Graz University of Technology, Austria
Daniel Cremers	Technical University of Munich, Germany
Bernt Schiele	Saarland University, Max Planck Institute for Informatics, Germany
Ramin Zabih	CornellNYCTech, USA

Program Chairs

Vittorio Ferrari	University of Edinburgh, UK
Martial Hebert	Carnegie Mellon University, USA
Cristian Sminchisescu	Lund University, Sweden
Yair Weiss	Hebrew University, Israel

Local Arrangement Chairs

Björn Menze	Technical University of Munich, Germany
Matthias Niessner	Technical University of Munich, Germany

Workshop Chairs

Stefan Roth	Technische Universität Darmstadt, Germany
Laura Leal-Taixé	Technical University of Munich, Germany

Tutorial Chairs

Michael Bronstein	Università della Svizzera Italiana, Switzerland
Laura Leal-Taixé	Technical University of Munich, Germany

Website Chair

Friedrich Fraundorfer	Graz University of Technology, Austria

Demo Chairs

Federico Tombari	Technical University of Munich, Germany
Joerg Stueckler	Technical University of Munich, Germany

Publicity Chair

Giovanni Maria   University of Catania, Italy
  Farinella

Industrial Liaison Chairs

Florent Perronnin   Naver Labs, France
Yunchao Gong   Snap, USA
Helmut Grabner   Logitech, Switzerland

Finance Chair

Gerard Medioni   Amazon, University of Southern California, USA

Publication Chairs

Albert Ali Salah   Boğaziçi University, Turkey
Hamdi Dibeklioğlu   Bilkent University, Turkey
Anton Milan   Amazon, Germany

Workshop Organizers

W01 – The Visual Object Tracking Challenge Workshop

Matej Kristan   University of Ljubljana, Slovenia
Aleš Leonardis   University of Birmingham, UK
Jiří Matas   Czech Technical University in Prague, Czechia
Michael Felsberg   Linköping University, Sweden
Roman Pflugfelder   Austrian Institute of Technology, Austria

W02 – 6th Workshop on Computer Vision for Road Scene Understanding and Autonomous Driving

Mathieu Salzmann   EPFL, Switzerland
José Alvarez   NVIDIA, USA
Lars Petersson   Data61 CSIRO, Australia
Fredrik Kahl   Chalmers University of Technology, Sweden
Bart Nabbe   Aurora, USA

W03 – 3D Reconstruction in the Wild

Akihiro Sugimoto   The National Institute of Informatics (NII), Japan
Tomas Pajdla   Czech Technical University in Prague, Czechia
Takeshi Masuda   The National Institute of Advanced Industrial Science
                            and Technology (AIST), Japan
Shohei Nobuhara   Kyoto University, Japan
Hiroshi Kawasaki   Kyushu University, Japan

W04 – Workshop on Visual Learning and Embodied Agents in Simulation Environments

Peter Anderson	Georgia Institute of Technology, USA
Manolis Savva	Facebook AI Research and Simon Fraser University, USA
Angel X. Chang	Eloquent Labs and Simon Fraser University, USA
Saurabh Gupta	University of California, Berkeley, USA
Amir R. Zamir	Stanford University and University of California, Berkeley, USA
Stefan Lee	Georgia Institute of Technology, USA
Samyak Datta	Georgia Institute of Technology, USA
Li Yi	Stanford University, USA
Hao Su	University of California, San Diego, USA
Qixing Huang	The University of Texas at Austin, USA
Cewu Lu	Shanghai Jiao Tong University, China
Leonidas Guibas	Stanford University, USA

W05 – Bias Estimation in Face Analytics

Rama Chellappa	University of Maryland, USA
Nalini Ratha	IBM Watson Research Center, USA
Rogerio Feris	IBM Watson Research Center, USA
Michele Merler	IBM Watson Research Center, USA
Vishal Patel	Johns Hopkins University, USA

W06 – 4th International Workshop on Recovering 6D Object Pose

Tomas Hodan	Czech Technical University in Prague, Czechia
Rigas Kouskouridas	Scape Technologies, UK
Krzysztof Walas	Poznan University of Technology, Poland
Tae-Kyun Kim	Imperial College London, UK
Jiří Matas	Czech Technical University in Prague, Czechia
Carsten Rother	Heidelberg University, Germany
Frank Michel	Technical University Dresden, Germany
Vincent Lepetit	University of Bordeaux, France
Ales Leonardis	University of Birmingham, UK
Carsten Steger	Technical University of Munich, MVTec, Germany
Caner Sahin	Imperial College London, UK

W07 – Second International Workshop on Computer Vision for UAVs

Kristof Van Beeck	KU Leuven, Belgium
Tinne Tuytelaars	KU Leuven, Belgium
Davide Scaramuzza	ETH Zurich, Switzerland
Toon Goedemé	KU Leuven, Belgium

W08 – 5th Transferring and Adapting Source Knowledge in Computer Vision and Second VisDA Challenge

Tatiana Tommasi	Italian Institute of Technology, Italy
David Vázquez	Element AI, Canada
Kate Saenko	Boston University, USA
Ben Usman	Boston University, USA
Xingchao Peng	Boston University, USA
Judy Hoffman	Facebook AI Research, USA
Neela Kaushik	Boston University, USA
Antonio M. López	Universitat Autònoma de Barcelona and Computer Vision Center, Spain
Wen Li	ETH Zurich, Switzerland
Francesco Orabona	Boston University, USA

W09 – PoseTrack Challenge: Articulated People Tracking in the Wild

Mykhaylo Andriluka	Google Research, Switzerland
Umar Iqbal	University of Bonn, Germany
Anton Milan	Amazon, Germany
Leonid Pishchulin	Max Planck Institute for Informatics, Germany
Christoph Lassner	Amazon, Germany
Eldar Insafutdinov	Max Planck Institute for Informatics, Germany
Siyu Tang	Max Planck Institute for Intelligent Systems, Germany
Juergen Gall	University of Bonn, Germany
Bernt Schiele	Max Planck Institute for Informatics, Germany

W10 – Workshop on Objectionable Content and Misinformation

Cristian Canton Ferrer	Facebook, USA
Matthias Niessner	Technical University of Munich, Germany
Paul Natsev	Google, USA
Marius Vlad	Google, Switzerland

W11 – 9th International Workshop on Human Behavior Understanding

Xavier Alameda-Pineda	Inria Grenoble, France
Elisa Ricci	Fondazione Bruno Kessler and University of Trento, Italy
Albert Ali Salah	Boğaziçi University, Turkey
Nicu Sebe	University of Trento, Italy
Shuicheng Yan	National University of Singapore, Singapore

W12 – First Person in Context Workshop and Challenge

Si Liu	Beihang University, China
Jiashi Feng	National University of Singapore, Singapore
Jizhong Han	Institute of Information Engineering, China
Shuicheng Yan	National University of Singapore, Singapore
Yao Sun	Institute of Information Engineering, China

Yue Liao   Institute of Information Engineering, China
Lejian Ren   Institute of Information Engineering, China
Guanghui Ren   Institute of Information Engineering, China

W13 – 4th Workshop on Computer Vision for Art Analysis

Stuart James   Istituto Italiano di Tecnologia, Italy and University College
                           London, UK
Leonardo Impett   EPFL, Switzerland and Biblioteca Hertziana, Max Planck
                           Institute for Art History, Italy
Peter Hall   University of Bath, UK
João Paulo Costeira   Instituto Superior Tecnico, Portugal
Peter Bell   Friedrich-Alexander-University Nürnberg, Germany
Alessio Del Bue   Istituto Italiano di Tecnologia, Italy

W14 – First Workshop on Fashion, Art, and Design

Hui Wu   IBM Research AI, USA
Negar Rostamzadeh   Element AI, Canada
Leonidas Lefakis   Zalando Research, Germany
Joy Tang   Markable, USA
Rogerio Feris   IBM Research AI, USA
Tamara Berg   UNC Chapel Hill/Shopagon Inc., USA
Luba Elliott   Independent Curator/Researcher/Producer
Aaron Courville   MILA/University of Montreal, Canada
Chris Pal   MILA/PolyMTL, Canada
Sanja Fidler   University of Toronto, Canada
Xavier Snelgrove   Element AI, Canada
David Vazquez   Element AI, Canada
Julia Lasserre   Zalando Research, Germany
Thomas Boquet   Element AI, Canada
Nana Yamazaki   Zalando SE, Germany

W15 – Anticipating Human Behavior

Juergen Gall   University of Bonn, Germany
Jan van Gemert   Delft University of Technology, The Netherlands
Kris Kitani   Carnegie Mellon University, USA

W16 – Third Workshop on Geometry Meets Deep Learning

Xiaowei Zhou   Zhejiang University, China
Emanuele Rodolà   Sapienza University of Rome, Italy
Jonathan Masci   NNAISENSE, Switzerland
Kosta Derpanis   Ryerson University, Canada

W17 – First Workshop on Brain-Driven Computer Vision

Simone Palazzo   University of Catania, Italy
Isaak Kavasidis   University of Catania, Italy
Dimitris Kastaniotis   University of Patras, Greece
Stavros Dimitriadis   Cardiff University, UK

W18 – Second Workshop on 3D Reconstruction Meets Semantics

Radim Tylecek   University of Edinburgh, UK
Torsten Sattler   ETH Zurich, Switzerland
Thomas Brox   University of Freiburg, Germany
Marc Pollefeys   ETH Zurich/Microsoft, Switzerland
Robert B. Fisher   University of Edinburgh, UK
Theo Gevers   University of Amsterdam, Netherlands

W19 – Third International Workshop on Video Segmentation

Pablo Arbelaez   Universidad de los Andes, Columbia
Thomas Brox   University of Freiburg, Germany
Fabio Galasso   OSRAM GmbH, Germany
Iasonas Kokkinos   University College London, UK
Fuxin Li   Oregon State University, USA

W20 – PeopleCap 2018: Capturing and Modeling Human Bodies, Faces, and Hands

Gerard Pons-Moll   MPI for Informatics and Saarland Informatics Campus,
                          Germany
Jonathan Taylor   Google, USA

W21 – Workshop on Shortcomings in Vision and Language

Dhruv Batra   Georgia Institute of Technology and Facebook AI
                          Research, USA
Raffaella Bernardi   University of Trento, Italy
Raquel Fernández   University of Amsterdam, The Netherlands
Spandana Gella   University of Edinburgh, UK
Kushal Kafle   Rochester Institute of Technology, USA
Moin Nabi   SAP SE, Germany
Stefan Lee   Georgia Institute of Technology, USA

W22 – Second YouTube-8M Large-Scale Video Understanding Workshop

Apostol (Paul) Natsev   Google Research, USA
Rahul Sukthankar   Google Research, USA
Joonseok Lee   Google Research, USA
George Toderici   Google Research, USA

W23 – Second International Workshop on Compact and Efficient Feature Representation and Learning in Computer Vision

Jie Qin	ETH Zurich, Switzerland
Li Liu	National University of Defense Technology, China and University of Oulu, Finland
Li Liu	Inception Institute of Artificial Intelligence, UAE
Fan Zhu	Inception Institute of Artificial Intelligence, UAE
Matti Pietikäinen	University of Oulu, Finland
Luc Van Gool	ETH Zurich, Switzerland

W24 – 5th Women in Computer Vision Workshop

Zeynep Akata	University of Amsterdam, The Netherlands
Dena Bazazian	Computer Vision Center, Spain
Yana Hasson	Inria, France
Angjoo Kanazawa	UC Berkeley, USA
Hildegard Kuehne	University of Bonn, Germany
Gül Varol	Inria, France

W25 – Perceptual Image Restoration and Manipulation Workshop and Challenge

Yochai Blau	Technion – Israel Institute of Technology, Israel
Roey Mechrez	Technion – Israel Institute of Technology, Israel
Radu Timofte	ETH Zurich, Switzerland
Tomer Michaeli	Technion – Israel Institute of Technology, Israel
Lihi Zelnik-Manor	Technion – Israel Institute of Technology, Israel

W26 – Egocentric Perception, Interaction, and Computing

Dima Damen	University of Bristol, UK
Giuseppe Serra	University of Udine, Italy
David Crandall	Indiana University, USA
Giovanni Maria Farinella	University of Catania, Italy
Antonino Furnari	University of Catania, Italy

W27 – Vision Meets Drone: A Challenge

Pengfei Zhu	Tianjin University, China
Longyin Wen	JD Finance, USA
Xiao Bian	GE Global Research, USA
Haibin Ling	Temple University, USA

W28 – 11th Perceptual Organization in Computer Vision Workshop on Action, Perception, and Organization

Deepak Pathak	UC Berkeley, USA
Bharath Hariharan	Cornell University, USA

W29 – AutoNUE: Autonomous Navigation in Unconstrained Environments

Manmohan Chandraker	University of California San Diego, USA
C. V. Jawahar	IIIT Hyderabad, India
Anoop M. Namboodiri	IIIT Hyderabad, India
Srikumar Ramalingam	University of Utah, USA
Anbumani Subramanian	Intel, Bangalore, India

W30 – ApolloScape: Vision-Based Navigation for Autonomous Driving

Peng Wang	Baidu Research, USA
Ruigang Yang	Baidu Research, China
Andreas Geiger	ETH Zurich, Switzerland
Hongdong Li	Australian National University, Australia
Alan Yuille	The Johns Hopkins University, USA

W31 – 6th International Workshop on Assistive Computer Vision and Robotics

Giovanni Maria Farinella	University of Catania, Italy
Marco Leo	National Research Council of Italy, Italy
Gerard G. Medioni	University of Southern California, USA
Mohan Trivedi	University of California, USA

W32 – 4th International Workshop on Observing and Understanding Hands in Action

Iason Oikonomidis	Foundation for Research and Technology, Greece
Guillermo Garcia-Hernando	Imperial College London, UK
Angela Yao	National University of Singapore, Singapore
Antonis Argyros	University of Crete/Foundation for Research and Technology, Greece
Vincent Lepetit	University of Bordeaux, France
Tae-Kyun Kim	Imperial College London, UK

W33 – Bioimage Computing

Jens Rittscher	University of Oxford, UK
Anna Kreshuk	University of Heidelberg, Germany
Florian Jug	Max Planck Institute CBG, Germany

W34 – First Workshop on Interactive and Adaptive Learning in an Open World

Erik Rodner	Carl Zeiss AG, Germany
Alexander Freytag	Carl Zeiss AG, Germany
Vittorio Ferrari	Google, Switzerland/University of Edinburgh, UK
Mario Fritz	CISPA Helmholtz Center i.G., Germany
Uwe Franke	Daimler AG, Germany
Terrence Boult	University of Colorado, Colorado Springs, USA

Juergen Gall   University of Bonn, Germany
Walter Scheirer   University of Notre Dame, USA
Angela Yao   University of Bonn, Germany

W35 – First Multimodal Learning and Applications Workshop

Paolo Rota   University of Trento, Italy
Vittorio Murino   Istituto Italiano di Tecnologia, Italy
Michael Yang   University of Twente, The Netherlands
Bodo Rosenhahn   Leibniz-Universität Hannover, Germany

W36 – What Is Optical Flow for?

Fatma Güney   Oxford University, UK
Laura Sevilla-Lara   Facebook Research, USA
Deqing Sun   NVIDIA, USA
Jonas Wulff   Massachusetts Institute of Technology, USA

W37 – Vision for XR

Richard Newcombe   Facebook Reality Labs, USA
Chris Sweeney   Facebook Reality Labs, USA
Julian Straub   Facebook Reality Labs, USA
Jakob Engel   Facebook Reality Labs, USA
Michael Goesele   Technische Universität Darmstadt, Germany

W38 – Open Images Challenge Workshop

Vittorio Ferrari   Google AI, Switzerland
Alina Kuznetsova   Google AI, Switzerland
Jordi Pont-Tuset   Google AI, Switzerland
Matteo Malloci   Google AI, Switzerland
Jasper Uijlings   Google AI, Switzerland
Jake Walker   Google AI, Switzerland
Rodrigo Benenson   Google AI, Switzerland

W39 – VizWiz Grand Challenge: Answering Visual Questions from Blind People

Danna Gurari   University of Texas at Austin, USA
Kristen Grauman   University of Texas at Austin, USA
Jeffrey P. Bigham   Carnegie Mellon University, USA

W40 – 360° Perception and Interaction

Min Sun   National Tsing Hua University, Taiwan
Yu-Chuan Su   University of Texas at Austin, USA
Wei-Sheng Lai   University of California, Merced, USA
Liwei Chan   National Chiao Tung University, USA
Hou-Ning Hu   National Tsing Hua University, Taiwan
Silvio Savarese   Stanford University, USA

Kristen Grauman   University of Texas at Austin, USA
Ming-Hsuan Yang   University of California, Merced, USA

W41 – Joint COCO and Mapillary Recognition Challenge Workshop

Tsung-Yi Lin   Google Brain, USA
Genevieve Patterson   Microsoft Research, USA
Matteo R. Ronchi   Caltech, USA
Yin Cui   Cornell, USA
Piotr Dollár   Facebook AI Research, USA
Michael Maire   TTI-Chicago, USA
Serge Belongie   Cornell, USA
Lubomir Bourdev   WaveOne, Inc., USA
Ross Girshick   Facebook AI Research, USA
James Hays   Georgia Tech, USA
Pietro Perona   Caltech, USA
Deva Ramanan   CMU, USA
Larry Zitnick   Facebook AI Research, USA
Riza Alp Guler   Inria, France
Natalia Neverova   Facebook AI Research, France
Vasil Khalidov   Facebook AI Research, France
Iasonas Kokkinos   Facebook AI Research, France
Samuel Rota Bulò   Mapillary Research, Austria
Lorenzo Porzi   Mapillary Research, Austria
Peter Kontschieder   Mapillary Research, Austria
Alexander Kirillov   Heidelberg University, Germany
Holger Caesar   University of Edinburgh, UK
Jasper Uijlings   Google Research, UK
Vittorio Ferrari   University of Edinburgh and Google Research, UK

W42 – First Large-Scale Video Object Segmentation Challenge

Ning Xu   Adobe Research, USA
Linjie Yang   SNAP Research, USA
Yuchen Fan   University of Illinois at Urbana-Champaign, USA
Jianchao Yang   SNAP Research, USA
Weiyao Lin   Shanghai Jiao Tong University, China
Michael Ying Yang   University of Twente, The Netherlands
Brian Price   Adobe Research, USA
Jiebo Luo   University of Rochester, USA
Thomas Huang   University of Illinois at Urbana-Champaign, USA

W43 – WIDER Face and Pedestrian Challenge

Chen Change Loy   Nanyang Technological University, Singapore
Dahua Lin   The Chinese University of Hong Kong, SAR China
Wanli Ouyang   University of Sydney, Australia
Yuanjun Xiong   Amazon Rekognition, USA
Shuo Yang   Amazon Rekognition, USA
Qingqiu Huang   The Chinese University of Hong Kong, SAR China
Dongzhan Zhou   SenseTime, China
Wei Xia   Amazon Rekognition, USA
Quanquan Li   SenseTime, China
Ping Luo   The Chinese University of Hong Kong, SAR China
Junjie Yan   SenseTime, China

Contents – Part III

W16 – 3rd Workshop on Geometry Meets Deep Learning

W17 – 1st Workshop on Brain-Driven Computer Vision

W18 – 3D Reconstruction Meets Semantics

W14 – First Workshop on Fashion, Art and Design

W14 – First Workshop on Fashion, Art and Design

Creative domains render a big part of modern society and have a strong influence on the economy and on cultural life. Much effort within these domains, such as fashion, art or design, centers around the creation, consumption and analysis of creative visual content. In recent years, there has been an explosion of research in applying machine learning and computer vision algorithms to various aspects of the creative domains. This ever-increasing interest is most evident in two important research trends: (1) Computer Vision for Fashion and (2) Visual Content Generation for Creative Applications.

At the First Workshop on Fashion, Art and Design, we brought together researchers, artists, entrepreneurs in this interdisciplinary space to discuss open problems in the two above mentioned areas. The workshop features six invited talks and three tracks of participation: (1) The list of invited speakers was carefully put together to achieve a balance of computer vision research, creative process and industry. (2) The paper track includes 12 accepted papers after a double-blind peer review process, with an acceptance rate of 46%. (3) The art competition track accepted 36 artworks with an acceptance rate of 50%. (4) The challenge track on fashion image generation had 17 participants and received 310 submissions in total.

This workshop was made possible by the contribution of many individuals from the community. We would like to express our gratitude to all the scientists and artists who submitted their work. Our program committee members and art jury members did excellent work in reviewing submitted papers and artworks. We also thank all of the invited speakers for sharing their work and ideas at the workshop. The invited speakers include: Kristen Grauman, Mario Klingemann, Tao Mei, Anna Ridler, Kavita Bala and Aaron Hertzmann. We cordially thank our industry sponsors who allowed us to provide a rich collection of awards to each of the participation track: Element AI, IBM Research, Zalando, Markable.ai, Nvidia, Ssense and Adobe. Lastly, we would like to thank all members of the organizing team for making the workshop happen: Leonidas Lefakis, Joy Tang, Rogerio Feris, Tamara Berg, Luba Elliott, Aaron Courville, Chris Pal, Sanja Fidler, Xavier Snelgrove, David Vazquez, Thomas Boquet and Nana Yamazaki.

We hope you will enjoy the proceedings and we look forward to the next edition!

September 2018

Hui Wu
Negar Rostamzadeh
Julia Lasserre

Deep Learning for Automated Tagging of Fashion Images

Patricia Gutierrez$^{(\boxtimes)}$, Pierre-Antoine Sondag, Petar Butkovic, Mauro Lacy,
Jordi Berges, Felipe Bertrand, and Arne Knudson

Amazon.com, Seattle, USA
{gupatric,pierreas,petarb,lacym,joberges,felipb,knudson}@amazon.com

Abstract. We present 9 deep learning classifiers to predict Fashion attributes in 4 different categories: apparel (dresses and tops), shoes, watches and luggages. Our prediction system hosts several classifiers working at scale to populate a catalogue of millions of products. We provide details of our models as well as the challenges involved in predicting Fashion attributes in a relatively homogeneous problem space.

Keywords: Deep learning · Image recognition · Fashion attributes

1 Introduction

Automatic tagging of products is relevant for online retail applications when dealing with extremely large repositories of products. Given a product image, for instance a dress or a shoe, deep learning models can be generated to predict whether it is a cocktail dress, a black shirt or an stiletto heel. By extracting these tags or attributes from fashion images, queries to the product's catalogue can be generated looking for similar or complementary products, produce recommendations for the user, fill missing metadata, and overall provide an improved search experience, all based exclusively on the product image.

In addition, if a product repository is large enough, it becomes impossible to manually audit or populate missing or mislabeled data. Incorrect labeling makes search results not to match what customers are looking for and sales opportunities are lost when products are labeled incorrectly or are undiscoverable. In such cases, the use of machine learning to scale product classification and data quality becomes a strong alternative to manual processes. Using product images as a source of predictions is extremely powerful as images contain a great detail of information about the product, often larger than the description itself.

In this paper, we present deep learning models to detect fashion attributes and populate a catalogue of millions of products. Our system extracts product information from images, automatically and at scale, doing work equivalent to thousands of manual auditors. We have produced 9 classifiers that predict attributes in 4 different categories: apparel, shoes, watches and luggage over 9 different attributes (sleeve type, boot style, heel type, skirt length, sandal style,

L. Leal-Taixé and S. Roth (Eds.): ECCV 2018 Workshops, LNCS 11131, pp. 3–11, 2019.
https://doi.org/10.1007/978-3-030-11015-4_1

neck style, watches display type, luggage shell type and number of wheels). As a result, we have predicted and tagged 18 million images which are available for search and discoverability in our retail platform. In this paper, we present the details of our models, their accuracy, as well as the challenges involved in predicting attributes in the fashion problem space, which is relatively homogeneous with respect to a given product type.

2   CNN for Fashion Attribute Classification

Convolutional Neural Networks (CNNs) have become the leading technique for many image classification tasks [4, 7, 15]. We trained CNN classifiers using both Resnet [4] and GoogleNet [15] architectures. Resnet gives the flexibility to parameterize the number of layers and thus select the size of the network in correspondence to the size of the training set. GoogleNet, on the other hand, facilitates the use of batch normalization and we performed transfer learning using pre-trained models in this architecture.

Table 1 shows the accuracy of our models and the number of tags predicted and used to update our catalogue in Production. Each model predicts an attribute. Details of each model, their labels, and visual examples are shown in the Appendix (Table 5). Labels were extracted from our fashion catalogue and curated by human auditors. We trained most models using a Resnet-50 or Resnet-101 architecture during 100 epochs. Prior to training, we padded the images with white background to make them square with 500×500 pixels. Then, we resized them to 224×224 pixels for training [6]. We used the raw RGB pixel values as input for the convolutional layers and we trained them end-to-end, using random flipping (with 0.5 probability) to augment the training set. We used a learning rate of 0.01 and a stochastic gradient descent optimizer. We tuned the batch size parameter to maximize the number of images per batch without causing memory overflow. We split the training set, using 70%–80% of images for training and the remaining images for validation. We used transfer learning in 3 of our models (*sleeve type*, *neck style* and *display type*). With transfer learning, we improved accuracies by 1%, 2% and 2% respectively. We applied early stopping when the training accuracy started to deviate strongly from the validation accuracy to reduce the overfitting of the models. The base models used to initialize the weights are in-house GoogleNet classifiers (not public) detecting similar fashion tags but not quite tailored to our labels or product domain. In the case of *display type*, we used as base model a GoogleNet network pre-trained on Imagenet [5].

3   Robustness

Even though CNNs have achieved state-of-the-art performance and even human-level performance, they are still subject to anomalies which affect their robustness. Recent studies [8, 10, 11, 14, 16] have shown that a correctly classified image can be changed by introducing small perturbations -sometimes even imperceptible to the human eye- and yet causing the CNN to misclassify the image into a totally

Table 1. Softlines attributes CNN classifiers

Attribute	Category	Dataset size	Number of classes	Accuracy	Number of tags updated
sleeve type	Apparel	61,702	4	92.90%	8,070,507
boot style	Shoes	19,009	8	89.40 %	8,337,490
display type	Watches	22,288	4	92.62%	782,765
heel type	Shoes	14,127	7	87.93%	584,711
shell type	Luggage	69,535	2	93.77%	347,424
sandal style	Shoes	16,128	7	86.89%	–
skirt length	Apparel	28,109	4	90.78%	–
neck style	Apparel	30,231	12	90.60%	–
number of wheels	Luggage	107,958	3	93.56%	–

different class. Other studies have shown that it is possible to produce synthetic images which are unrecognizable to humans but that state-of-the-art CNNs believe them to be recognizable objects with a 99% confidence [12]. Such images which are visually far from the labeled classes can be considered outliers to the training set.

We have observed issues in the confidence value of our models in alignment with what is discussed above. One of the issues that affected our models performance were small perturbations in the pixels images and the other one was recognizing outliers, as described next.

3.1 Perturbations in Pixel Values

While testing with different libraries to resize the images, we observed that we obtained significative variations in the classifier's predictions when small perturbations to the pixels were performed to the same image. For instance, Fig. 1 shows such effect on a single image, resized with a Python library (Fig. 1(a)) and a Java library (Fig. 1(b)). The resulting compressed images are the same to the human eye, and yet they present small perturbations in their pixels (Fig. 1(c)). When predicting with a Resnet-50 dress classifier trained from scratch, we observe drastic changes in prediction values (dress or not a dress), as shown in Fig. 1 and Table 2.

To improve the robustness of our models, we introduced augmentation parameters to change the brightness, contrast, saturation, hue, pca noise or convert to grayscale the image during training. The goal was to induce certain kinds of variability or noise to the training images. After training with this augmentation parameters, using a pre-trained ImageNet network as base model, and testing different network architectures on a 3971 dress dataset, we were able to make the network more robust, as shown in the experimental results of Table 2, tested on a dress classifier. We can see that by training with a smaller architecture (Alexnet) or regularizing a deeper network (GoogleNet) we were able to increase the accuracy from 83% to 98%. The reason the accuracy suffers no degradation with the Python compression is because this was the resizing library that was used to train.

(a) Resized with Python library. **Prediction: dress**

(b) Resized with Java library. **Prediction: not a dress**

(c) Pixel comparison of both images

Fig. 1. Performance issues related to pixel value perturbations.

Table 2. Accuracy of different models on images resized with different libraries.

Architecture	Accuracy on dataset compressed with Java	Accuracy on dataset compressed with Python
Resnet-18	83%	98%
GoogleNet	93%	99%
Alexnet	98%	98%
GoogleNet with augmentation and base model	98%	98%

3.2 Outliers

We also noticed that images which are incorrectly assigned to the wrong category (e.g. a dress incorrectly stored as a watch) represent outliers for attribute classifiers. If one outlier is presented to the network (e.g. a dress image is presented to a shoe attribute's classifier such as *heel type*), the desirable output would be one where all labels have relatively low confidence values. In this way, we could reject unknown cases by simple thresholding. However, the studies mentioned above and our own empirical results show that thresholding over the confidence value is not enough to identify what is unknown. In fact, as shown in Fig. 2, for each attribute classifier we can always find an outlier image in our product catalogue which is visually far from the training set and yet it produces a high confidence prediction.

One possible explanation for these anomalies related to outliers is the one described in [12]. Classification models create decision boundaries that partition the data into classification regions. Those classification regions can be much larger than the area occupied by the training set. Outliers far from the decision boundary and deep into the classification region may produce high confidence predictions even when they are far from the training set images. This perspective is further investigated in [2]. The effect of uncalibrated networks producing very high confidence predictions is also studied in [3].

item_length	heel_type	sandal_style	sleeve_type	display_type:
mini– 1	flat– 0.99	flatform– 0.99	long– 0.99	analogue_digital – 0,99

Fig. 2. High confidence misclassifications.

To mitigate this risk, we trained Product Type (PT) classifiers as a pre-filtering step prior to attribute prediction (Table 3). Product type classifiers are binary models that predicts whether an image belongs to a given product type or not. Product types have a hierarchical structure and they represent different categories, such as: shoes, boots, tops, shirts, dresses, watches, bracelets, etc. These models act as a pre-validator for our attributes classifiers.

Table 3. Product type CNN classifiers.

Product type	Dataset size	Number of classes	Accuracy
Luggage	185,036	2	99.48%
Watch	45,880	2	97.30%
Shoe	300,000	2	99.24%
Dress	189,975	2	98.38%
Top	119,567	2	98.56%

Notice that product type classifiers achieve a higher accuracy than attribute classifiers. The problem space of product type classification seems to be easier for a CNN than attribute classification. In other words, it is easier to create a model that is able to distinguish a watch from any other product, than it is to create a model that distinguishes between analogue watches and digital watches. In the latter case, the features that the classifier needs to learn are much more specific and there is more overlap between irrelevant features that are shared across classes. Figure 3 shows a representation of images classified by the watch product type model and images classified by the *display type* attribute model for watches. The images correspond to the training set of each model visualized using the t-SNE [9] algorithm. We can observe that the boundary is better defined and the amount of noise is smaller in the watches PT training set than in the *display type* attribute classifier training set.

Therefore, when performing predictions we first check if the image belongs to the correct product type (e.g. is this image a watch?) and then predict the corresponding attribute (e.g. what type of *display type* does this watch contains?). We have observed that, in addition to product type pre-validation, regularizing the network is effective for ruling out outliers. This is shown in Table 4, which depicts experiments performed on 777 watches images containing outliers. We can see how the number of misclassification decreases as the network is regularized (increasing

(a) Product type classifier for (b) *display type* classifier for
watches   watches

Fig. 3. Visual representation of the training sets.

weigh decay and reducing the number of layers). During training, the model was able to fit the training data perfectly and no major accuracy changes were observed by adding regularization. However, when facing an outlier image, the regularized network is able to rule out unknown cases more effectively.

Table 4. Effect of regularizing a network compared to perform PT pre-validation on a noisy set containing outliers. The first column shows the mean confidence value of the predictions. The last three columns show, thresholding by the mean confidence, the percentage of misclassifications, the percentage of misclassifications due to outliers and the overall coverage.

Model	Mean confidence	Errors	Outlier's errors	Coverage
Resnet-50	0.99	47 (7.3%)	22 (3.4%)	82%
Resnet-18, weight decay 0.3	0.93	37 (5.9%)	19 (3.0%)	79.3%
Resnet-18, weight decay 0.5	0.70	31 (5.5%)	9 (1.6%)	71.9%
Resnet-18, weight decay 1	0.40	23 (5.3%)	2 (0.4%)	55.2%
Resnet-50, with PTD validator	0.99	**21 (3.5%)**	**1 (0.1%)**	75.5%

4   Conclusions

From our research, we found that product images can be a valuable source of information to derive fashion attributes to help the customers find the product they are looking for. We showed that CNN based classifiers can reach accuracies around 90 percent extracting attribute's information out of product images. We observed that attribute models have a somewhat reduced training domain which is enclosed to a given category (e.g. shoes, tops, watches, luggages) and provide unreliable predictions when facing an image outside their training scope (outliers). To mitigate such risks, we developed product type classifiers that are able to identify outliers and rule them out. We observed that regularization also provides robustness in these edge cases and in cases where pixel perturbations are introduced in the images as result of pre-processing modifications. As future work, we want to investigate alternatives to the *softmax* function to obtain more effective uncertainty estimates. Some recent studies have proposed approaches in that direction, such as [1, 3, 13, 14]. Overall, we have predicted and tagged 18 million attributes in our fashion catalogue with the values extracted from our most confident predictions, increasing their discoverability.

A Appendix

Table 5. Details of the attributes our classifiers predict.

Attribute	Category	Classes	Examples
sleeve type	Shirts, Blouses, T-Shirts, Dresses	– Long sleeve – Short sleeve – 3/4 sleeve – S leeveless	
boot style	Shoes	– Biker boots – Chelsea boots – Chukka boots – Classic boots – Combat boots – Desert boots – Snow boots – Wellington boots	
display type	Watches	– Analogue – Analogue-Digital – Chronograph – Digital	
heel type	Shoes	– Wedge – Stiletto – Kitten Heel – Cone Heel – Western Heel – Block Heel – Louis Heel – Flat	
shell type	Luggage	– Hard – Soft	

(Continued)

Table 5. *(Continued)*

Attribute	Category	Classes	Examples
skirt length	Dresses, Skirts	– Mini – Knee-Long – Midi – Maxi	
sandal style	Shoes	– Ankle-Strap – Espadrille – Flatform – Gladiator – Platform – Slingback – T-Bar	
neck style	Dresses	– Asymmetric – Collared – Boat Neck – Round Neck – Turtleneck – V-Neck – Halterneck – One-Shoulder – Sweetheart – Square – High Neck – Off the Shoulder	
number of wheels	Luggage	– 0 – 2 – 4	

References

1. Bendale, A., Boult, T.E.: Towards open set deep networks. CoRR abs/1511.06233 (2015)
2. Goodfellow, I., Shlens, J., Szegedy, C.: Explaining and harnessing adversarial examples. In: International Conference on Learning Representations (2015). http://arxiv.org/abs/1412.6572
3. Guo, C., Pleiss, G., Sun, Y., Weinberger, K.Q.: On calibration of modern neural networks. In: ICML 2017 (2017)
4. He, K., Zhang, X., Ren, S., Sun, J.: Deep residual learning for image recognition. In: 2016 IEEE Conference on Computer Vision and Pattern Recognition (CVPR), pp. 770–778 (2016)
5. Deng, J., Dong, W., Socher, R., Li, L.J., Li, K., Fei-Fei, L.: Imagenet: a large-scale hierarchical image database. In: CVPR 2009 (2009)
6. Johnson, J., Li, F.F., Karpathy, A.: Stanford cs231n: convolutional neural networks for visual recognition lectures (2016)
7. Krizhevsky, A., Sutskever, I., Hinton, G.E.: Imagenet classification with deep convolutional neural networks. In: Pereira, F., Burges, C.J.C., Bottou, L., Weinberger, K.Q. (eds.) Advances in Neural Information Processing Systems, vol. 25, pp. 1097–1105. Curran Associates, Inc. (2012). http://papers.nips.cc/paper/4824-imagenet-classification-with-deep-convolutional-neural-networks.pdf
8. Kurakin, A., Goodfellow, I.J., Bengio, S.: Adversarial examples in the physical world. CoRR abs/1607.02533 (2016)
9. van der Maaten, L., Hinton, G.: Visualizing data using t-SNE. J. Mach. Learn. Res. 9, 2579–2605 (2008). http://www.jmlr.org/papers/v9/vandermaaten08a.html
10. Sharif, M., Bhagavatula, S., Bauer, L., Reiter, M.K.: Accessorize to a crime: real and stealthy attacks on state-of-the-art face recognition. In: ACM Conference on Computer and Communications Security, pp. 1528–1540 (2016)
11. Moosavi-Dezfooli, S., Fawzi, A., Fawzi, O., Frossard, P.: Universal adversarial perturbations. CoRR abs/1610.08401 (2016)
12. Nguyen, A.M., Yosinski, J., Clune, J.: Deep neural networks are easily fooled: high confidence predictions for unrecognizable images. In: CVPR, pp. 427–436. IEEE Computer Society (2015)
13. Pereyra, G., Tucker, G., Chorowski, J., Kaiser, L., Hinton, G.E.: Regularizing neural networks by penalizing confident output distributions. CoRR abs/1701.06548 (2017)
14. Subramanya, A., Srinivas, S., Babu, R.V.: Confidence estimation in deep neural networks via density modelling. CoRR abs/1707.07013 (2017)
15. Szegedy, C., et al.: Going deeper with convolutions. In: Computer Vision and Pattern Recognition (CVPR) (2015). http://arxiv.org/abs/1409.4842
16. Szegedy, C., et al.: Intriguing properties of neural networks. CoRR abs/1312.6199 (2013)

Brand > Logo: Visual Analysis of Fashion Brands

M. Hadi Kiapour(✉) and Robinson Piramuthu

eBay, San Francisco, CA 94105, USA
{mkiapour,rpiramuthu}@ebay.com

Abstract. While lots of people may think branding begins and ends with a logo, fashion brands communicate their uniqueness through a wide range of visual cues such as color, patterns and shapes. In this work, we analyze learned visual representations by deep networks that are trained to recognize fashion brands. In particular, the activation strength and extent of neurons are studied to provide interesting insights about visual brand expressions. The proposed method identifies where a brand stands in the spectrum of branding strategy, i.e., from trademark-emblazoned goods with bold logos to implicit no logo marketing. By quantifying attention maps, we are able to interpret the visual characteristics of a brand present in a single image and model the general design direction of a brand as a whole. We further investigate versatility of neurons and discover "specialists" that are highly brand-specific and "generalists" that detect diverse visual features. A human experiment based on three main visual scenarios of fashion brands is conducted to verify the alignment of our quantitative measures with the human perception of brands. This paper demonstrate how deep networks go beyond logos in order to recognize clothing brands in an image.

Keywords: Deep learning · Convolutional networks · Fashion · Brands

1 Introduction

On your walk home, a runner whisks past you. Her feet flying over the concrete and leaves, they make a blur of a small but unmistakable check mark. This remarkably simple logo, dubbed the swoosh, perfectly embodies motion and speed, attributes of the winged Goddess of victory in Greek mythology, Nike.

Fashion is all about identity. From luxury splurges to mass retail sneakers, logos have been considered a key status symbol. Over time however, as buying habits change, the status symbols evolve. Since the rise of the No Logo movement [11], some brands have embraced minimalism. Louis Vuitton made news in 2013 when it pulled back on the use of its iconic LVs on purses. Good branding is more than a logo. It is storytelling; a visual story woven into every piece. Here's a test: if you cover up the logo on a product, can you still tell the brand?

© Springer Nature Switzerland AG 2019
L. Leal-Taixé and S. Roth (Eds.): ECCV 2018 Workshops, LNCS 11131, pp. 12–20, 2019.
https://doi.org/10.1007/978-3-030-11015-4_2

Uniqueness is a vital factor for a successful clothing business. Shoppers not only want to be fashionable, but also want to express themselves. In 1992 Christian Louboutin decided to create a signature style that hints at sensuality and power simultaneously, and they painted the soles of their shoes red! There are a million ways that designers make memorable brand expressions. Sometimes they bring life to a logo, other times they use patterns to make a brand recognizable. Some make eccentric products in shape and geometry and others make name for themselves by unique color combinations, folds and cuts. Figure 1 shows examples drawn from the wide spectrum of visual expressions fashion brands adopt. While some use colorful graphics or repeated logo prints, others design unique patterns or mainly invest on logos.

Fig. 1. Visual brands spectrum. Brands use a wide range of visual expressions. Experts can identify brands even in the absence of logo. While some use colorful graphics, others adopt unique patterns or choose to rely on logo.

With the recent success of computer vision and the rise of online commerce, there is a huge excitement to turn computers into visual experts. The ever-changing landscape of fashion industry has provided a unique opportunity to leverage computational algorithms on large data to achieve the knowledge and expertise unattainable for any individual fashion expert. Previous researchers have worked on clothing parsing [7,22], outfit compatibility and recommendation [20,23], style and trend recognition [2,10], attribute recognition [4,5,14] and retrieval [9,13]. In order to interpret deep visual representations, studies have discovered neurons that can predict semantic attributes shared among categories [6,16] and grand-mother-cell like features [1] and probed the neuron activations to discover concepts [3,21,27]. Another body of research rely on attention paradigm to find parts of the image that are most responsible for the classification [17–19,25]. Our work builds upon the top-down attention mechanism of Zhang et al. [26] to uncover what computer vision models learn in order to distinguish fine-grained fashion brands across a wide variety of products. Specifically, we aim to answer the following questions:

– How can we quantify visual brand representations?
– How do deep networks distinguish between very similar products?
– What are the key visual expressions that brands adopt?
– Which visual representations are shared or unique across brands?
– How well does the learned representations align with human perception?

2   Methodology

Data. We collect a new large dataset of $3,828,735$ clothing product images from 1219 brands taken from a global online marketplace reported in Table 1. The dataset contains diverse images from stock quality photos taken professionally with white background to photos of used products photographed by amateurs in challenging viewpoints and lighting. We grouped the products to fall into five broad categories:*Bags, Footwear, Bottom wear, Outerwear* and *Tops*.

Classification Network. In deep learning, fine-tuning a convolutional network, pretrained on large data, is considered as a simple transfer learning to provide good initialization [24]. We fine-tune the ResNet-50 model on ImageNet [8,12] for classification among the 1219 brands in our dataset and achieve 47.1% top-1 accuracy. Next we use an attention mechanism to generate brand-specific attention maps on the convolution layers. In our experiments, we study *res5b* maps due to its manageable size and proximity to the final classification layer. Our method can be applied to any convolution layer in deep networks.

Table 1. Fashion brands dataset collected from online e-commerce sites.

Category	Subcategories	#Brands	#Train	#Test
Bags	Handbags, Purses	132	$206,232$	18,427
Footwear	Shoes, Heels, Boots	235	$368,846$	37,825
Bottom wear	Pants, Jeans, Skirts	218	$431,568$	44,408
Outer wear	Jackets, Coats	238	$442,950$	42,962
Tops	Tops, Blouses, Dresses	556	$926,033$	89,762
All		1219	$3,480,575$	348,160

Top-Down Excitation Maps. Our goal is to interpret the deep model's predictions in order to explain the visual characteristics of fashion brands. Using the Excitation Backprop method [26], we generate marginal probabilities on intermediate layers for the brand predicted with the maximum posterior probability, hence the name top-down. We assume the response in convolutional layers is positively correlated with their confidence of detection. This probabilistic framework produces well-normalized excitation maps efficiently via a single backward pass down to the target layer. We define two measures to encode the excitations:

Strength. Strength is calculated by computing the maximum over the excitation maps of a convolution layer. For every input image x, we compute excitation map $M_k(x)$ of every internal convolution unit k. We denote the excitation strength of convolutional layer by $S(x) = \max_{s \in h_k w_k} E_s(x)$, where $E_s(x) = \sum_{k=1...K} M_k(x)$ and K is the total number of individual convolution units.

Extent. Extent is a measure to encode the spatial support of high activations in excitation maps. Specifically, we first calculate the excitation map at every location s across all units. Next we compute the ratio of locations where their excitation exceeds the mean value of all the excitations, represented by T. We define excitation extent of input image x by $E(x) = \frac{1}{h_k w_k} \sum_{s \in h_k w_k} \mathbf{1}\left[E_s(x) > T\right]$.

Discriminability. We aim to find units/neurons that often get high excitement values corresponding to a given brand. For every convolutional unit, we calculate the maximum value over the entire excitation map for every image I and compute two distributions for positive P^+ and negative P^- images associated to a brand b. For every unit k, we compute the symmetric KL divergence [21]: $D_k(b|I) = KL(P^+ \| P^-) + KL(P^- \| P^+)$. The units that maximize the distance between the class conditional probabilities are deemed to have higher discriminability.

3 Experiments

3.1 Brand Representations

How do clothing brands make their products stand out among others? What do fashion designers do to appeal to shoppers? In order to answer these questions we begin by exploring two ends of the spectrum of visual branding: brands which make themselves stand out through a localized mark, sign or logo, e.g. Chanel bags or Polo Ralph Lauren Shirts, and brands that convey their message via a spread design using colors and patterns, think colorful Vera Bradley or woven leather Bottega Veneta bags. In the following, we conduct our experiments on the bags category as it depicts a wide range of brand visualization strategies and receives the best classification score among the categories in our dataset.

Strength. Figure 2 depicts brands that obtain the highest excitation strengths. For each brand we compute median of the predicted strength across all samples in the test set. We find that brands such as Fjallraven, Jansport and Coach, design their bags with a unique logo or mark their goods with their brand name.

Extent. What are the brands that are not as invested in logos and instead are interested to convey their message via unique patterns? Figure 2 depicts brands with the highest excitation extent values. For each brand, we find the extent decile to which it belongs to by computing the median of all extent values in the test set. Brands such as For U Designs, print large graphics of animals, nature or galaxy on their bags. Louis Vuitton makes their products remarkably recognizable via a unique checkered pattern or the famous repeated LV monogram. Vera Bradley is filled with colorful floral and paisley patterns and MCM repeats it's logo across a large region of the product. We also see how composition of images in a brand can contributes to large extent levels. The illustrated examples of Supreme brand are photographed in close-up and show the brand name in large size which leads to expanded excitations.

Extent vs. Strength. Next we explore the space of Extent and Strength jointly. We ask, which brands have high extent but no single strong excitation value

Fig. 2. Left: Brands with high Strength. Examples of bags from brands with high excitation strength are shown. All brands show concentrated logos or printed brand names. Right: Brands with high Extent. Examples of bags with high excitation extent are shown. Some brands print a large graphic on their products while other have a repeated pattern or logo. Composition of image can affect the extent signal as shown in the examples in the last column with large, repeated or close-up logos.

in their maps or vice versa? Are there examples that have both high or low extent and strengths? In order to answer these interesting questions, we plot the samples of top and bottom brands with samples falling in the highest and lowest extents in Fig. 3. We find that brands such as Burberry, Gucci or For U Designs are concentrated in the higher half of the spectrum, while logo-heavy brands such as Tommy Hilfiger, Tony Burch and Herschel Supply Co. bags are spread along the strength axis with low extent values. Interestingly, we observe that the model picks up signals, however weak, in the straps of Tommy Hilfiger totes, striped in iconic colors of Tommy Hilfiger. Comparing Tory Burch bags along the spectrum, the logos are hard to capture in the examples falling on the lower side of the strength axis while images of the same brand with high strength show fully visible logos. We also probe the middle region and observe an interesting phenomena. Louis Vuitton and Burberry images that fall in between, show a mix of logo monograms and brand names instead of just patterns.

3.2 Versatility of Convolutional Units

Next, we go one step deeper and rank the convolutional units/neurons of the layer for each brand based on symmetric KL divergence score. We observe some neurons detect complex entangled concepts while others are more interpretable and specialized towards disentangled visual features. Figure 4 left, shows top detection examples of such neurons for two sample brands. Some Adidas neurons detect the logos while others are specialized to detect vertical or horizontal stripes. For Burberry, we find units that detect diagonal or straight patterns, while another unit is more sensitive to the horse rider in the Burberry knight logo.

We further investigate "specialist" vs. "generalist" units. We compute the number of brands activated for each unit. Specialists units are activated for

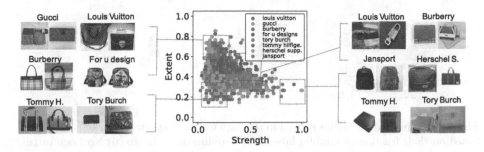

Fig. 3. Extent vs Strength. Depicts the transition of brands across the spectrum. We show samples that fall across the spectrum of extent and strength. Samples with high extent show a repeated texture or a large pattern. Items with high strength show a localized mark, logo or brand name. Hard examples to recognize such as Tommy Hilfiger bags that only show a specific type of stripes require specialized neurons to detect them.

only one or few brands. Figure 4 right, shows examples of specialist units and the brands they activate. Unit 253 is an expert only in detecting the Harley Davidson logo, which is unique and can happen in many locations over the object and requires its own specialized unit. Meanwhile, units 1631 and 770 detect floral and natural patterns that are more general and shared among brands such as Vera Bradley and Mary Frances. Unit 1250 is specialized to detect hobo-shaped bags with a large crescent-shaped bottom and a shoulder strap that represents multiple brands. By analyzing the space of specialist units we can discover unique visual expressions that sets a brand apart. Generalist units point us to features shared by several brands.

Fig. 4. Left: Top activated neurons for Adidas and Burberry brands. Three top neurons specialized in recognizing in (a) Adidas and (b) Burberry. First column show a specialized neuron for recognizing the logo associated with a brand name, second column is specialized for three stripes, last column recognizes the smaller scale logo. First column in (b) recognizes vertical and horizontal stripes, second shows examples for neuron specialized in diagonal patterns and lastly is the logo detector for Louis Vuitton. Right: Specialist vs generalist units.

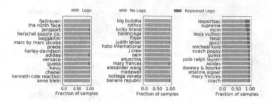 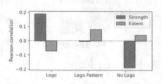

Fig. 5. Left: Individual brands ranked in the logo visibility spectrum. Brands are sorted based on their fraction of samples labeled by humans as (i) Logo, (ii) No Logo or (iii) Repeated Logo. Right: Pearson correlation of Strength and Extent of excitations with brand visibility variations.

3.3 Human Experiment

We conduct a human study asking 5 subjects on Amazon Mechanical Turk to label each product image in the bags category according to the visibility of the logo into one of three groups: (i) Logo (ii) Repeated Logo, when a pattern of repeated logos or monogram and (iii) No Logo. 46% contain a visible logo and 51% contain no logo. This is particularly interesting as a recent study shows that one third of the handbags purchased in the U.S. did not have a visible logo [15]. The classifier correctly predicts 65.01%, 68.67% and 54.46% of the brands in groups (i), (ii) and (iii) respectively. This is significant, given that group (iii) constitutes the majority of the dataset and confirms that deep classifiers learn unique visual characteristics of all three groups.

Logo Visibility in Brands. We further study individual brands by ranking them based on the ratio of samples that fall into each of the three logo visibility groups. Figure 5, shows that brands such as Fjallraven and The North Face are logo-based. On the other hand, Lucky Brand does not depend on logo. Instead, they claim to give your look "the added flare" by embellishments such as fringe and embroidered detailing. Fendi and MCM opt in to repeat their logo in their design. In fact, the "Shopper" totes from MCM are reversible with their logo printed on both inside and outside!

Correlation with Strength and Extent. Finally we compute the Pearson correlation between the predicted strength and extent of the excitation maps and report the results in Fig. 5. We find that excitation strength has strong correlation with samples depicting a logo while extent has a negative correlation with logo-oriented products. Products with repeated logo produce scattered signals with low strength and high extent. For an item with no logo, the network needs to aggregate signals from various spatial locations and hence it is positively correlated with extent and negatively correlated with strength.

Conclusion. In this work, we quantify the deep representations to analyze and interpret visual characteristics of fashion brands. We find units that are specialized to detect specific brands as well as versatile units that detect shared concepts. A human experiment confirms the proposed measures are aligned with human perception.

References

1. Agrawal, P., Girshick, R., Malik, J.: Analyzing the performance of multilayer neural networks for object recognition. In: Fleet, D., Pajdla, T., Schiele, B., Tuytelaars, T. (eds.) ECCV 2014. LNCS, vol. 8695, pp. 329–344. Springer, Cham (2014). https://doi.org/10.1007/978-3-319-10584-0_22
2. Al-Halah, Z., Stiefelhagen, R., Grauman, K.: Fashion forward: forecasting visual style in fashion. In: International Conference on Computer Vision (2017)
3. Bau, D., Zhou, B., Khosla, A., Oliva, A., Torralba, A.: Network dissection: quantifying interpretability of deep visual representations. In: Conference on Computer Vision and Pattern Recognition (2017)
4. Chen, H., Gallagher, A., Girod, B.: Describing clothing by semantic attributes. In: Fitzgibbon, A., Lazebnik, S., Perona, P., Sato, Y., Schmid, C. (eds.) ECCV 2012. LNCS, vol. 7574, pp. 609–623. Springer, Heidelberg (2012). https://doi.org/10.1007/978-3-642-33712-3_44
5. Chen, Q., Huang, J., Feris, R., Brown, L.M., Dong, J., Yan, S.: Deep domain adaptation for describing people based on fine-grained clothing attributes. In: Conference on Computer Vision and Pattern Recognition (2015)
6. Escorcia, V., Niebles, J.C., Ghanem, B.: On the relationship between visual attributes and convolutional networks. In: Conference on Computer Vision and Pattern Recognition (2015)
7. Gong, K., Liang, X., Zhang, D., Shen, X., Lin, L.: Look into person: self-supervised structure-sensitive learning and a new benchmark for human parsing. In: Conference on Computer Vision and Pattern Recognition (2017)
8. He, K., Zhang, X., Ren, S., Sun, J.: Deep residual learning for image recognition. In: Conference on Computer Vision and Pattern Recognition (2016)
9. Kiapour, M.H., Han, X., Lazebnik, S., Berg, A.C., Berg, T.L.: Where to buy it: matching street clothing photos in online shops. In: International Conference on Computer Vision (2015)
10. Kiapour, M.H., Yamaguchi, K., Berg, A.C., Berg, T.L.: Hipster wars: discovering elements of fashion styles. In: Fleet, D., Pajdla, T., Schiele, B., Tuytelaars, T. (eds.) ECCV 2014. LNCS, vol. 8689, pp. 472–488. Springer, Cham (2014). https://doi.org/10.1007/978-3-319-10590-1_31
11. Klein, N.: No Logo: Taking Aim at the Brand Bullies. Random House of Canada, Picador (1999)
12. Krizhevsky, A., Sutskever, I., Hinton, G.E.: Imagenet classification with deep convolutional neural networks. In: Information Processing Systems (2012)
13. Liu, Z., Luo, P., Qui, S., Wang, X., Tang, X.: Deepfashion: powering robust clothes recognition and retrieval with rich annotations. In: Conference on Computer Vision and Pattern Recognition (2016)
14. Liu, Z., Yan, S., Luo, P., Wang, X., Tang, X.: Fashion landmark detection in the wild. In: Leibe, B., Matas, J., Sebe, N., Welling, M. (eds.) ECCV 2016. LNCS, vol. 9906, pp. 229–245. Springer, Cham (2016). https://doi.org/10.1007/978-3-319-46475-6_15
15. Money, C.M.: No logo: why un-branded luxury goods are on the rise (2016). https://www.cnbc.com/2016/11/28/no-logo-why-un-branded-luxury-goods-are-on-the-rise.html
16. Ozeki, M., Okatani, T.: Understanding convolutional neural networks in terms of category-level attributes. In: Cremers, D., Reid, I., Saito, H., Yang, M.-H. (eds.) ACCV 2014. LNCS, vol. 9004, pp. 362–375. Springer, Cham (2015). https://doi.org/10.1007/978-3-319-16808-1_25

17. Ruth, F., Vedaldi, A.: Interpretable explanations of black boxes by meaningful perturbation. In: International Conference on Computer Vision (2017)
18. Selvaraju, R.R., Cogswell, M., Das, A., Vedantam, R., Parikh, D., Batra, D.: Grad-CAM: visual explanations from deep networks via gradient-based localization. In: International Conference on Computer Vision (2017)
19. Springenberg, J.T., Dosovitskiy, A., Borx, T., Riedmiller, M.: Striving for simplicity: the all convolutional net. arXiv preprint arXiv:1412.6806 (2014)
20. Veit, A., Kovacs, B., Bell, S., McAuley, J., Bala, K., Belongie, S.: Learning visual clothing style with heterogeneous dyadic co-occurrences. In: International Conference on Computer Vision (2015)
21. Vittayakorn, S., Umeda, T., Murasaki, K., Sudo, K., Okatani, T., Yamaguchi, K.: Automatic attribute discovery with neural activations. In: Leibe, B., Matas, J., Sebe, N., Welling, M. (eds.) ECCV 2016. LNCS, vol. 9908, pp. 252–268. Springer, Cham (2016). https://doi.org/10.1007/978-3-319-46493-0_16
22. Yamaguchi, K., Kiapour, M.H., Ortiz, L.E., Berg, T.L.: Retrieving similar styles to parse clothing. IEEE Trans. Pattern Anal. Mach. Intell. **37**, 1028–1040 (2014)
23. Yamaguchi, K., Okatani, T., Sudo, K., Murasaki, K., Taniguchi, Y.: Mix and match: joint model for clothing and attribute recognition. In: BMVC (2015)
24. Yosinski, J., Clune, J., Bengio, Y., Lipson, H.: How transferable are features in deep neural networks? In: Advances in Neural Information Processing Systems (2014)
25. Zeiler, M.D., Fergus, R.: Visualizing and understanding convolutional networks. In: Fleet, D., Pajdla, T., Schiele, B., Tuytelaars, T. (eds.) ECCV 2014. LNCS, vol. 8689, pp. 818–833. Springer, Cham (2014). https://doi.org/10.1007/978-3-319-10590-1_53
26. Zhang, J., Lin, Z., Brandt, J., Shen, X., Sclaroff, S.: Top-down neural attention by excitation backprop. In: Leibe, B., Matas, J., Sebe, N., Welling, M. (eds.) ECCV 2016. LNCS, vol. 9908, pp. 543–559. Springer, Cham (2016). https://doi.org/10.1007/978-3-319-46493-0_33
27. Zhou, B., Khosla, A., Lapedriza, A., Oliva, A., Torralba, A.: Object detectors emerge in deep scene CNNs. In: International Conference on Learning Representations (2015)

Tiered Deep Similarity Search for Fashion

Dipu Manandhar$^{(\boxtimes)}$, Muhammet Bastan, and Kim-Hui Yap

Nanyang Technological University, Singapore 639798, Singapore
{dipu002,muhammetbastan,ekhyap}@ntu.edu.sg

Abstract. *How similar are two fashion clothing?* Fashion apparels demonstrate diverse visual concepts with their designs, styles and brands. Hence, there exist a hierarchy of similarities between fashion clothing, ranging from exact instance or brand to similar attributes, styles. An effective search method, thus, should be able to represent the tiers of similarities. In this paper, we present a deep learning based fashion search framework for learning the tiers of similarity. We propose a new attribute-guided metric learning (AGML) with multitask CNNs that jointly learns fashion attributes and image embeddings while taking category and brand information into account. The two tasks in the framework are linked with a guiding signal. The guiding signal, first, helps in mining informative training samples. Secondly, it helps in treating training samples by their importance to capture the tiers of similarity. We conduct experiments in a new BrandFashion dataset which is richly annotated at different granularities. Experimental results demonstrate that the proposed method is very effective in capturing a tiered similarity search space and outperforms the state-of-the-art fashion search methods.

Keywords: Fashion search · Deep metric learning · Multitask learning

1 Introduction

Fashion contributes a significant portion in rapidly growing online shopping and social media [2,9]. With such a growth, visual fashion analysis has received a huge research attention [1,15,16,19,24] and has been successfully deployed in large e-commerce companies and websites [13,23,29] such as *eBay, Amazon, Pinterest, Flipkart,* etc. One of the most important aspects in visual fashion analysis is fashion search. This paper presents a new deep learning based fashion search framework with an interesting fusion of multitask and metric learning.

With the recent advances in deep learning, end-to-end metric learning methods for visual similarity measure have been proposed [3,22]. The main task here is to learn a discriminative feature space for image representation. Particularly for fashion search, the feature space should incorporate various elements of fashion. As fashion domain demonstrates a huge diversity in visual concepts with

---

Electronic supplementary material The online version of this chapter (https://doi.org/10.1007/978-3-030-11015-4_3) contains supplementary material, which is available to authorized users.

L. Leal-Taixé and S. Roth (Eds.): ECCV 2018 Workshops, LNCS 11131, pp. 21–29, 2019.
https://doi.org/10.1007/978-3-030-11015-4_3

their designs, styles, brands, there exist tiers of similarity for fashion clothing. Visual fashion similarity can be defined based on various concepts such as categories (e.g. *dress, hoodie*), brands (e.g. *Adidas, Nike*), attributes (e.g. *color, pattern*) or design (*cropped, zippered*). Figure 1 illustrates tiers of similarity for clothing images. Clothing (A) and the reference clothing (R) are the exact same (brand, model, categories, color etc.) clothing and hence lies closest within the inner circle. Clothing (B) shares the same model as clothing (R) with a different color and hence it is second nearest to (R). Similarly, clothing items (C), (D) & (E) lie farther away. We aim to learn such a tiered feature space, as this provides the desired retrieval outcome for practical fashion search applications.

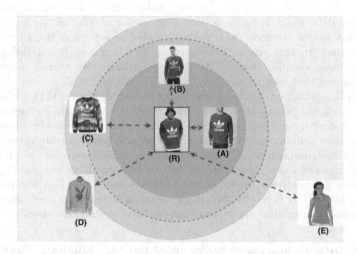

Fig. 1. Example of tiers of similarity in feature space for fashion clothing. Different tiers of similarity are denoted by the dotted concentric circles. Distances between the reference clothing (R) and clothing (A)–(E) represent the degrees of visual similarity.

Deep metric learning has demonstrated huge success in learning visual similarity [3,8,11,22,28]. Siamese networks [5,8,28] and triplet networks [22,27] are the most popular models for metric learning, the latter being reported to be better [10,22]. Although successful, the existing triplet based methods [3,10,22] have few limitations. First, they require exact instance/ID level annotations, and do not perform well with weak label annotations *e.g.*, category labels (shown in Sect. 3). Secondly, these methods employ hard binary decisions during the triplet selection and treat the selected triplets with equal importance, which creates a restriction to learn tiers of similarity.

To learn discriminative feature space, researchers have combined metric learning with auxiliary information using multitask networks which have achieved better performance for face identification and recognition [6,22,30], person re-identification [14,18], clothing search [12]. Particularly for fashion representation, multitask learning with attribute information is used in [12,24].

Where-To-Buy-It (WTBI) [15] used pre-trained features and learned a similarity network using Siamese networks. Recently, *FashionNet* in [19] proposed to jointly optimize classification, attribute prediction and triplet loss for fashion search. However, they do not explore the possible interaction between the tasks and hence do not effectively learn a tiered similarity space required for fashion search.

In view of this, we propose a new *attribute guided metric learning* (AGML) framework using multitask learning for fashion search. The proposed framework utilizes the interactions between the attribute prediction and triplet network, by jointly training them. This has two major advantages over the existing methods. First, it helps in mining informative triplets especially when exact anchor-positive pair annotations are not available. Second, training samples are treated based on their importance in a soft manner which helps in capturing multiple tiers of similarity required for fashion search. We demonstrate its effectiveness for fashion search using a new BrandFashion dataset. Compared to the existing fashion datasets [4,7,19], this dataset is richly annotated with essential elements of fashion including clothing categories, attributes, and brand information which capture different tiers of information in fashion.

2   Proposed Method

The architecture of the proposed framework is shown in Fig. 2. It consists of three identical CNNs with shared parameters θ and accepts image triplets $\{x^a, x^p, x^n\}$ i.e. an anchor image (x^a), a positive image (x^p) from the same class as the anchor, and a negative image (x^n) from a different class. The last fully connected layer has two branches for learning the feature embedding $f(x)$, and the attribute vector $\mathbf{v}$. The guiding signal links two tasks and helps triplet sampling based on the importance of the samples. The network is trained end-to-end using the loss,

$$L_{total}(\theta) = L_{tri}^G(\theta) + \lambda L_{attr}(\theta) \tag{1}$$

where $L_{tri}^G(\theta)$ & $L_{attr}(\theta)$ represent the attribute-guided triplet loss & attribute loss respectively, and λ balances the contribution of the two losses.

2.1   Attribute Prediction Network

We use K semantic attributes to describe the image appearance, denoted $\mathbf{a} = [a_1, a_2, \ldots, a_K]$, where each element $a_i \in \{0, 1\}$ indicates the presence or absence of the ith attribute. The problem of attribute prediction is treated as multilabel classification. We pass the first branch from last fully connected layers into a sigmoid layer to squash the output to $[0, 1]$ and output $\mathbf{v}$. The attribute prediction is optimized using binary-cross entropy loss $L_{attr}(\theta) = -\sum_{i=1}^{K} [a_i \log(v_i) + (1 - a_i) \log(1 - v_i)]$, where a_i is binary target attribute labels for image x, and v_i is a component of $\mathbf{v} = [v_1, v_2, \ldots, v_K]$, which is the predicted attribute distribution.   ·

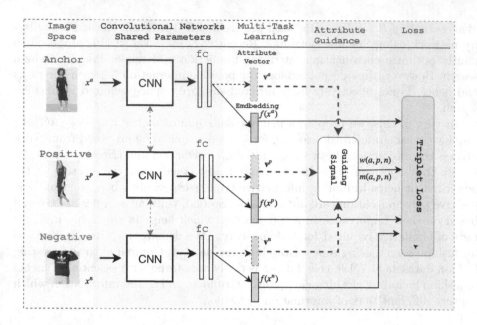

Fig. 2. Architecture of the proposed attribute-guided triplet network.

2.2 Attribute Guided Triplet Training

We use the predicted attribute vectors to guide both triplet mining and triplet loss training.

A. Triplet Mining

Random sampling based on class/ID labels for triplet does not assure the selection of the most informative examples for training. This is especially critical when only category information is available. For effective training, anchor-positive pairs should be reliable. Therefore, we propose to leverage cosine similarity $\langle \mathbf{x}, \mathbf{y} \rangle = \frac{\mathbf{x}^\mathsf{T}\mathbf{y}}{\|\mathbf{x}\|_2 \|\mathbf{y}\|_2}$, between the anchor-positive attribute vectors (outputs of the attribute prediction network) to sample better triplets. In particular, we use a threshold (Φ) such that only the triplets with $\langle \mathbf{v}^a, \mathbf{v}^p \rangle > \Phi$ are selected for the training. This ensures that the anchor-positive pairs are similar in attribute space and hence are reliable.

B. Attribute Guided Triplet Training

We propose two ways to guide the triplet metric learning network. The first weights the whole triplet loss while the second operates on the margin parameter of the loss function. Let $\{x^a, x^p, x^n\}$ be an input triplet sample and $\{f(x^a), f(x^p), f(x^n)\}$ be the corresponding embedding. The proposed attribute-guided triplet loss given by,

$$L_{tri}^G(\theta) = w(a,p,n) \left[\|f(x^a) - f(x^p)\|_2^2 - \|f(x^a) - f(x^n)\|_2^2 + m(a,p,n) \right]_+, \quad (2)$$

where $w(a, p, n)$ and $m(a, p, n)$ are the loss weighting factor and margin factor, which are functions of attribute distributions $\{\mathbf{v}^a, \mathbf{v}^p, \mathbf{v}^n\}$, as explained below.

B1. Soft-Weighted (SW) Triplet Loss

The SW triplet loss operates on the overall loss using the weight factor $w(a, p, n)$. We use $w(a, p, n) = \langle \mathbf{v}^a, \mathbf{v}^p \rangle \langle \mathbf{v}^a, \mathbf{v}^n \rangle$, the product of similarities between attribute vectors of anchor-positive and anchor-negative pairs. The above function adaptively alters the magnitude of the triplet loss. When the anchor-positive pair is similar in attribute space (i.e. $\langle \mathbf{v}^a, \mathbf{v}^p \rangle$ is high), the sample is more confident and reliable. Likewise, when the anchor-negative pair is similar in attribute space (i.e. $\langle \mathbf{v}^a, \mathbf{v}^n \rangle$ is high), it forms a *hard negative example* i.e. high information. Hence, the triplet is given higher priority and more attention during the network update. This is analogous to hard negative mining [22], but we handle them in a soft manner.

B2. Soft-Margin (SM) Triplet Loss

The SM triplet loss operates on the margin parameter using $m(a, p, n)$. The naive triplet loss uses a constant margin m, which treats all triplets equally and restricts learning desired tiered similarity. The soft margin is an adaptive margin $m(a, p, n) = m_0 \log(1 + \langle \mathbf{v}^a, \mathbf{v}^p \rangle \langle \mathbf{v}^a, \mathbf{v}^n \rangle)$, and promotes a tiered similarity space. Similar to SW triplet loss, when both $\langle \mathbf{v}^a, \mathbf{v}^p \rangle$ and $\langle \mathbf{v}^a, \mathbf{v}^n \rangle$ are high, the triplet is more reliable and informative (hard negative), and hence the effective margin becomes larger. In other words, when the negative image and anchor image are very similar in the attribute space, a reliable margin is used to learn the subtle difference and avoid the confusion. Hence, both SW and SM triplet loss explore the importance of the triplets, which helps in learning a tiered similarity space.

3   Experiments

We collected a new BrandFashion dataset with about $10K$ clothing images with distinctive logos from 15 brands. The images are categorized into 16 clothing categories and annotated with 32 semantic attributes. The goal is to demonstrate the tiered similarity space using the category, brand and attribute annotations. There are 50 query images in the dataset. We evaluated the performance for instance search using mean average precision (mAP) and the performance of tiered similarity search using normalized discounted cumulative gain (NDCG) i.e. $NDCG@k = \frac{1}{Z} \sum_i^k \frac{2^{r(i)} - 1}{\log_2(1+i)}$. The relevance score of ith ranked image is calculated based on similarity match considering three levels of information, namely category, brand and attribute i.e. $r(i) = r_i^{cat} + r_i^{brand} + r_i^{attr}$, where $r_i^{cat} \in \{0, 1\}$, $r_i^{brand} \in \{0, 1\}$. The attribute match r_i^{attr} is computed by taking the ratio of the number of matched attributes to the total number of query attributes [12]. Overall, the relevance score summarizes the tiered similarity search performance.

We used VGG16 [25] as the base CNN network, which is trained using the loss defined in Eq. (1), with SGD momentum of 0.5 & learning rate of 0.001. We set λ to 1. The value of margin m_0 is experimentally set to 0.5. For the

SM triplet loss, the value of m_0 set to 0.8 such that the effective margin swings around the original value. We set the threshold (ϕ) to 0.7 and observe that the performance is fairly stable on $\phi \in [0.5, 0.9]$.

Items from the same category and brand are sampled for the anchor-positive pairs, and items from different categories or brands constitute the negative samples. L_2-normalized feature from the last fully connected layer is used as the feature vector. We used PyTorch [20] for the implementation. Similar to [15,19,23], we crop out the clothing region prior to feature extraction. We used Faster-RCNN [21] to jointly detect the brand logo and clothing items in the images.

Table 1. Comparison of the proposed method with state-of-the-art-methods

Method	mAP (%)	NDCG@20(%)
Triplet Loss [22]	33.38	69.92
Multitask Network (Triplet+Attribute)	56.41	76.71
R-MAC [26]	30.03	70.70
Rapid-Clothing [17]	33.17	70.78
Visual-Search@Pinterest [13]	37.11	72.11
VisNet [23]	34.01	63.76
WTBI [15]	41.73	56.43
FashionNet [19]	50.14	80.63
Proposed AGML (SW)	**63.79**	**85.12**
Proposed AGML (SM)	63.71	83.66
Proposed AGML (SW) with Re-ranking	**71.25**	96.16
Proposed AGML (SM) with Re-ranking	71.05	**96.24**

Table 1 compares performance of different methods in terms of mAP and NDCG@20. In terms of mAP, the naive triplet loss achieves 33.8%, while the multitask network (triplet+attribute) achieves 56.4%. This shows that there is a clear benefit of using auxiliary information using multitask metric learning. The proposed method additionally guides the triplet loss using the predicted attributes. The proposed AGML-SW and AGML-SM achieve mAPs of 63.79% and 63.71%. This demonstrates the advantage of attribute guided triplet loss. The proposed method clearly outperforms the deep feature encoding based methods [13,17,26], and state-of-the art metric learning methods [15,19,23].

Similar trend in results can be observed for NDCG in Table 1. The proposed attribute-supervised SW and SM triplet network achieve NDCG@20 of 83.66% and 85.12% respectively. Our method clearly outperforms other state-of-the-art methods which demonstrate the advantage of learning a tiered similarity space. We further take advantage of logo detection to re-rank the retrieval results. The proposed method achieves mAP $\approx$ 71% and NDCG@20 $\approx$ 96% with re-ranking based on detected brand logo information. Figure 3 shows example search results obtained using WTBI [15], FashionNet [19] and the proposed method which further demonstrates the advantage of the proposed method.

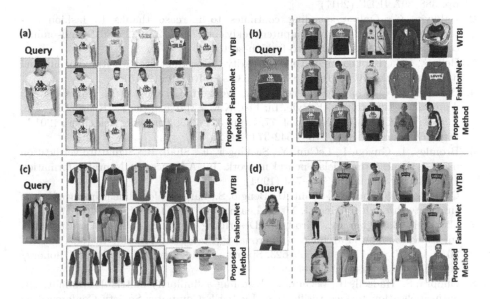

Fig. 3. Sample search results with query images and top-5 retrieved images. Exact same instance matches are highlighted with green borders. Best viewed in color. (Color figure online)

4   Conclusions

We presented a new deep attribute-guided triplet network which explores the importance of training samples and learns a tiered similarity space. The method uses multitask CNN which shares the mutual information among the tasks for better tuning the loss. Using the predicted attributes, the proposed method first mines informative triplets, and then uses them to train the triplet loss in a soft-manner, which helps in capturing the tiered similarity desirable for fashion search. We believe that the tiered similarity search will be appreciated by fashion companies, online retailers as well as customers.

Acknowledgment. This research was carried out at the Rapid-Rich Object Search (ROSE) Lab at the Nanyang Technological University, Singapore. The ROSE Lab is supported by the Infocomm Media Development Authority, Singapore. We gratefully acknowledge the support of NVIDIA AI Technology Center for their donation of GPUs used for our research.

References

1. Al-Halah, Z., Stiefelhagen, R., Grauman, K.: Fashion forward: forecasting visual style in fashion. In: IEEE International Conference on Computer Vision (ICCV), pp. 388–397. IEEE (2017)
2. Baldwin, C.: Online spending continues to increase thanks to fashion sector (2014). https://www.computerweekly.com/news/2240225386/Spend-online-continues-to-increase-thanks-to-fashion-sector
3. Bell, S., Bala, K.: Learning visual similarity for product design with convolutional neural networks. ACM Trans. Graph. (TOG) **34**(4), 98 (2015)
4. Bossard, L., Dantone, M., Leistner, C., Wengert, C., Quack, T., Van Gool, L.: Apparel classification with style. In: Lee, K.M., Matsushita, Y., Rehg, J.M., Hu, Z. (eds.) ACCV 2012. LNCS, vol. 7727, pp. 321–335. Springer, Heidelberg (2013). https://doi.org/10.1007/978-3-642-37447-0_25
5. Bromley, J., Guyon, I., LeCun, Y., Säckinger, E., Shah, R.: Signature verification using a siamese time delay neural network. In: Advances in Neural Information Processing Systems, pp. 737–744 (1994)
6. Chechik, G., Sharma, V., Shalit, U., Bengio, S.: Large scale online learning of image similarity through ranking. J. Mach. Learn. Res. **11**, 1109–1135 (2010)
7. Chen, H., Gallagher, A., Girod, B.: Describing clothing by semantic attributes. In: Fitzgibbon, A., Lazebnik, S., Perona, P., Sato, Y., Schmid, C. (eds.) ECCV 2012. LNCS, vol. 7574, pp. 609–623. Springer, Heidelberg (2012). https://doi.org/10.1007/978-3-642-33712-3_44
8. Chopra, S., Hadsell, R., LeCun, Y.: Learning a similarity metric discriminatively, with application to face verification. In: IEEE Computer Society Conference on Computer Vision and Pattern Recognition, vol. 1, pp. 539–546 (2005)
9. Financial Times: online retail sales continue to soar (2018). https://www.ft.com/content/a8f5c780-f46d-11e7-a4c9-bbdefa4f210b
10. Hermans, A., Beyer, L., Leibe, B.: In defense of the triplet loss for person re-identification. arXiv:1703.07737 (2017)
11. Hu, J., Lu, J., Tan, Y.P.: Discriminative deep metric learning for face verification in the wild. In: IEEE Conference on Computer Vision and Pattern Recognition, pp. 1875–1882 (2014)
12. Huang, J., Feris, R.S., Chen, Q., Yan, S.: Cross-domain image retrieval with a dual attribute-aware ranking network. In: International Conference on Computer Vision, pp. 1062–1070 (2015)
13. Jing, Y., et al.: Visual search at pinterest. In: ACM SIGKDD International Conference on Knowledge Discovery and Data Mining, pp. 1889–1898. ACM (2015)
14. Khamis, S., Kuo, C.-H., Singh, V.K., Shet, V.D., Davis, L.S.: Joint learning for attribute-consistent person re-identification. In: Agapito, L., Bronstein, M.M., Rother, C. (eds.) ECCV 2014. LNCS, vol. 8927, pp. 134–146. Springer, Cham (2015). https://doi.org/10.1007/978-3-319-16199-0_10
15. Kiapour, M.H., Han, X., Lazebnik, S., Berg, A.C., Berg, T.L.: Where to buy it: matching street clothing photos in online shops. In: IEEE International Conference on Computer Vision, pp. 3343–3351 (2015)
16. Kiapour, M.H., Yamaguchi, K., Berg, A.C., Berg, T.L.: Hipster wars: discovering elements of fashion styles. In: Fleet, D., Pajdla, T., Schiele, B., Tuytelaars, T. (eds.) ECCV 2014. LNCS, vol. 8689, pp. 472–488. Springer, Cham (2014). https://doi.org/10.1007/978-3-319-10590-1_31

17. Lin, K., Yang, H.F., Liu, K.H., Hsiao, J.H., Chen, C.S.: Rapid clothing retrieval via deep learning of binary codes and hierarchical search. In: Proceedings of the 5th ACM on International Conference on Multimedia Retrieval, pp. 499–502. ACM (2015)
18. Lin, Y., Zheng, L., Zheng, Z., Wu, Y., Yang, Y.: Improving person re-identification by attribute and identity learning. arXiv:1703.07220 (2017)
19. Liu, Z., Luo, P., Qiu, S., Wang, X., Tang, X.: DeepFashion: powering robust clothes recognition and retrieval with rich annotations. In: IEEE Conference on Computer Vision and Pattern Recognition, pp. 1096–1104 (2016)
20. Paszke, A., et al.: PyTorch. http://pytorch.org
21. Ren, S., He, K., Girshick, R., Sun, J.: Faster R-CNN: towards real-time object detection with region proposal networks. In: Advances in Neural Information Processing Systems (2015)
22. Schroff, F., Kalenichenko, D., Philbin, J.: FaceNnet: a unified embedding for face recognition and clustering. In: IEEE Conference on Computer Vision and Pattern Recognition, pp. 815–823 (2015)
23. Shankar, D., Narumanchi, S., Ananya, H., Kompalli, P., Chaudhury, K.: Deep learning based large scale visual recommendation and search for e-commerce. arXiv:1703.02344 (2017)
24. Simo-Serra, E., Ishikawa, H.: Fashion style in 128 floats: joint ranking and classification using weak data for feature extraction. In: IEEE Conference on Computer Vision and Pattern Recognition, pp. 298–307 (2016)
25. Simonyan, K., Zisserman, A.: Very deep convolutional networks for large-scale image recognition. arXiv:1409.1556 (2014)
26. Tolias, G., Sicre, R., Jégou, H.: Particular object retrieval with integral max-pooling of CNN activations. arXiv:1511.05870 (2015)
27. Wang, J., et al.: Learning fine-grained image similarity with deep ranking. arXiv:1404.4661 (2014)
28. Wang, X., Sun, Z., Zhang, W., Zhou, Y., Jiang, Y.G.: Matching user photos to online products with robust deep features. In: Proceedings of the 2016 ACM on International Conference on Multimedia Retrieval, pp. 7–14. ACM (2016)
29. Yang, F., et al.: Visual Search at eBay. arXiv:1706.03154 (2017)
30. Yi, D., Lei, Z., Liao, S., Li, S.Z.: Learning face representation from scratch. arXiv:1411.7923 (2014)

Deep Fashion Analysis with Feature Map Upsampling and Landmark-Driven Attention

Jingyuan Liu[iD] and Hong Lu[✉][iD]

Shanghai Key Lab of Intelligent Information Processing, School of Computer Science,
Fudan University, Shanghai, People's Republic of China
{jingyuanliu15,honglu}@fudan.edu.cn

Abstract. In this paper, we propose an attentive fashion network to address three problems of fashion analysis, namely landmark localization, category classification and attribute prediction. By utilizing a landmark prediction branch with upsampling network structure, we boost the accuracy of fashion landmark localization. With the aid of the predicted landmarks, a landmark-driven attention mechanism is proposed to help improve the precision of fashion category classification and attribute prediction. Experimental results show that our approach outperforms the state-of-the-arts on the DeepFashion dataset.

Keywords: Fashion analysis · Landmark detection ·
Clothing category classification · Attention mechanism · Deep learning

1 Introduction

Recent years, with the rapid growth of online commerce and fashion-related application, fashion image analysis and understanding have attracted increasing amount of attention in the community. Extensive studies have been conducted in this field, such as category classification, style or attribute prediction, fashion landmark localization, and fashion image synthesis.

In this paper, we study three core problems of fashion image analysis: landmark localization, category classification and attribute prediction. Previous works based on deep learning have shown much success in these fields [3,6,9–11,16,17]. However, most of them fail to further improve fashion analysis accuracy because of the low resolution of the predicted heatmaps after several pooling operations. It limits the prediction accuracy since fashion landmarks usually lie in the sharp corners or edges of clothes. In this paper, we address this problem by using transposed convolution to upsample the feature map. Thus, the predicted heatmaps are high-resolution and have the same size as the input fashion image, which will improve the accuracy of landmark localization.

For enhancing accuracy of category classification and attribute prediction, we also introduce a landmark-driven attention mechanism leveraging the predicted

© Springer Nature Switzerland AG 2019
L. Leal-Taixé and S. Roth (Eds.): ECCV 2018 Workshops, LNCS 11131, pp. 30–36, 2019.
https://doi.org/10.1007/978-3-030-11015-4_4

landmark heatmap. The landmark locations and the convolutional features are combined to form a new attention map, which gives our network a flexible way to focus on the most functional parts of the clothes for category and attribute prediction with the reference to both local landmark positions and global features. Such attention mechanism magnifies the most related information for fashion analysis while filters out unrelated features, thus boosting the category and attribute prediction accuracy. Notably, our whole fashion analysis model is fully differentiable and can be trained end-to-end.

We exert comprehensive evaluations on a large-scale dataset – DeepFashion dataset [9]. Experimental results demonstrate that our fashion analysis model outperforms the state-of-the-arts.
In summary, our **contributions** are:

1. We propose a fashion analysis network: an end-to-end system that addresses category classification and attribute prediction simultaneously, via improving the resolution of heatmaps through upsampling for more accurate landmark localization.
2. We introduce a novel attention mechanism: Landmark heatmaps are used as references to generate a unified attention, so that the network has enough information to enhance or reduce features.
3. Quantitatively, we report, for the first time, our model show improvement over the state-of-the-art on landmark localization, category classification and attribute prediction.

2   Related Work

Fashion analysis has drawn increasing attention in recent years because of its various applications like clothing recognition and segmentation [5,8,17,19], recommendation [4,9,12,13], and fashion landmark localization [10,16,17]. As for landmark localization, some studies utilize regression methods, where convolutional features are directly fed into fully connected layer to fit the coordinate positions of landmarks [9,10]. As shown in [15], this kind of regression is in a highly non-linear and complex form, thus the parameters are difficult to learn. To address this problem, some studies employ fully convolutional networks that produce a position heatmap for each landmark [16,17] but fail to maintain the high resolution of heatmaps during the pipeline, which limits the accuracy. The closest work to our method is [16] whose fashion network is encoded with two attention mechanisms: landmark-aware attention and category-driven attention. Their algorithm was based on two fashion grammars they proposed and was tested on the Deepfashion dataset. [16] suffers from the difficulty of detect landmark in low resolution which is caused by the series of pooling operations. The main differences with our work are that: (i) In our network, we use transposed convolution upsampling to generate more accurate feature maps, which is more suitable for fashion and clothing related tasks and thus improves the accuracy of landmark localization. (ii) Those landmark feature maps will serve as references to generate one unified attention mechanism rather than two for boosting category classification and attribute prediction.

Attention Mechanism has gained popularity in the fields of image recognition [7], image detection [18] and VQA(Visual Question Answering) [2]. Those work demonstrate the efficiency of the attention mechanism that enables the network to learn which parts in an image should be focused on to solve certain tasks. In this paper, a unified attention mechanism is proposed, which avoid of hard deterministic constraints in feature selection and helps our model achieve state-of-the-art results in visual fashion analysis tasks. Besides, in contrast to previous attention-based fashion models [16] with two separate attention branch, our attention has combined those two into one unified branch act as soft constraints and can be learned more easily from data.

3   Methodology

3.1   Problem Formulation

Given a fashion image I, our goal is to predict the landmark position L, category label C and attribute vector A. $L = \{(x_1, y_1), (x_2, y_2)..., (x_{n_l}, y_{n_l})\}$, where x_i and y_i is the coordinate position for each landmark, and n_l is the total number of landmarks. In this paper, we utilize $n_l = 8$ since there are 8 annotated landmarks in the DeepFashion dataset, defined as left/right collar end, left/right sleeve end, left/right waistline, and left/right hem. Category label C satisfies $0 \leq C \leq n_c - 1$, where n_c is the number of all categories. Attribute prediction is treated as a multi-label problem. The label vector $A = (a_1, a_2, ..., a_{n_a}), a_i \in \{0, 1\}$, where n_a is the number of attributes. $a_i = 1$ indicates that the fashion image has the ith attribute.

3.2   Network Architecture

Our main network architecture is based on the VGG-16 networks [14], as shown in Fig. 1. First, we resize the original image to 224×224. Initial convolutional operations are the same as the VGG-16 networks. We add two new branches after the conv4_3 layer. One is the landmark localization branch, the other is a attention branch. Detailed description is as follows.

Landmark Localization Branch. We use several transposed convolution to produce a high-resolution landmark heatmap. In particular, we first utilize 64 1×1 filters to convert the input feature map to $28 \times 28 \times 64$. Then two 3×3 convolutions and one 4×4 transposed convolution are employed to upsample the feature to $56 \times 56 \times 64$. The 3×3 convolution also has a padding of 1 so it does not change the size of the feature map. The stride and padding of the transposed convolution are 2 and 1, respectively. Thus it can upsample the feature map twice its size. In the following, we use the same structure of two convolution and one

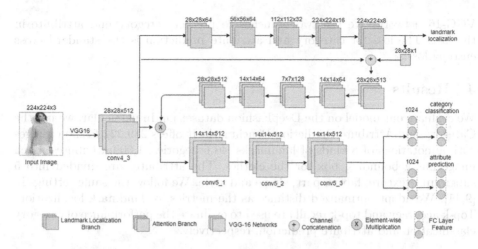

Fig. 1. Our network architecture. The structure is mainly based on the VGG-16 networks, and we add a landmark localization branch and a attention branch. The landmark localization branch produces heatmaps for all landmarks in the original resolution. Predicted heatmaps and the conv4_3 features are then fed into the attention branch, the result of which will be used to gate or magnify the conv4_3 features.

transposed convolution to upsample the feature map to $224 \times 224 \times 16$. Finally, a 1×1 convolution is employed to produce the $224 \times 224 \times 8$ heatmap, denoted as $M' \in R^{224 \times 224 \times 8}$. The ground truth of the landmark heatmap M is generated by adding a Gaussian filter at the corresponding landmark position. We use $L2$ loss to train the landmark localization branch: $l_{landmark} = \frac{1}{N}\|M_{ijk} - M'_{ijk}\|_2^2$, where N is the total number of array elements. By producing heatmaps with the same size as the original image, the landmark localization branch is capable of predicting landmark positions with higher accuracy.

Attention Branch. The attention branch takes the concatenation of the conv4_3 feature and the landmark information as its input. The landmark information is formulated as $M_{ij}^{info} = max\{M''_{ij1}, M''_{ij2}, ..., M''_{ij8}\}$, where M'' $\in R^{28 \times 28 \times 8}$ is the bilinear downsample of M'. It describes the overall landmark positions of the fashion image. We first use one 1×1 convolution to convert the input feature map to $28 \times 28 \times 32$. Then two convolutional layers are employed to squeeze the feature to $7 \times 7 \times 28$. Each layer has one 3×3 convolution and one 2×2 max pooling. Finally we use two transposed convolutions to get the output $A, A \in R^{28 \times 28 \times 512}$. The activation function in the last layer is sigmoid function thus we have $0 < A_{ijk} < 1$.

We denote the conv4_3 feature as F. The output of the attention branch is used to modify F by making $F_{new} = (\frac{1}{2} + A) \circ F$, where $\circ$ stands for element-wise multiplication. We add A by $\frac{1}{2}$ thus the element will be in the range $(\frac{1}{2}, \frac{3}{2})$. Numbers less than 1 will filter out unrelated features, while numbers greater than 1 will magnify important features. The following is the same as the

VGG-16 network. We use two branches to predict category and attribute in the last. The loss for category and attribute prediction is the standard cross entropy loss.

4 Results

We evaluate our model on the DeepFashion dataset [9]. In particular, we use the Category and Attribute Prediction Benchmark. It offers 289,222 fashion images with annotations of 8 kinds of landmarks, 46 categories, 1,000 attributes. Each image has a bounding box for the clothes. The attributes are divided into 5 subgroups: texture, fabric, part, shape and style. We follow the same settings in [9,11]. We adopt normalized distance as the metrics for landmark localization. Top-k accuracy and top-k recall are used to evaluate the performance of category classification and attribute prediction, respectively.

Table 1. Experimental results on the DeepFashion dataset for landmark localization. The best results are marked in **bold**.

Methods	L.Collar	R.Collar	L.Sleeve	R.Sleeve	L.Waistline	R.Waistline	L.Hem	R.Hem	Avg
FashionNet	0.0854	0.0902	0.0973	0.0935	0.0854	0.0845	0.0812	0.0823	0.0872
DFA	0.0628	0.0637	0.0658	0.0621	0.0726	0.0702	0.0658	0.0663	0.0660
DLAN	0.0570	0.0611	0.0672	0.0647	0.0703	0.0694	0.0624	0.0627	0.0643
Wang et al.	0.0415	0.0404	0.0496	**0.0449**	0.0502	0.0523	**0.0537**	**0.0551**	0.0484
Ours	**0.0332**	**0.0346**	**0.0487**	0.0519	**0.0422**	**0.0429**	0.0620	0.0639	**0.0474**

Table 2. Experimental results on the DeepFashion dataset for category classification and attribute prediction. The best results are marked in **bold**.

Methods	Category		Texture		Fabric		Shape		Part		Style		All	
	Top-3	Top-5	Top-3	Top-5	Top-3	Top-5	Top3	Top-5	Top-3	Top-5	Top-3	Top-5	Top-3	Top-5
WTBI [1]	43.73	66.26	24.21	32.65	25.38	36.06	23.39	31.26	26.31	33.24	49.85	58.68	27.46	35.37
DARN [6]	59.48	79.58	36.15	48.15	36.64	48.52	35.89	46.93	39.17	50.14	66.11	71.36	42.35	51.95
FashionNet [9]	82.58	90.17	37.46	49.52	39.30	49.84	39.47	48.59	44.13	54.02	66.43	73.16	45.52	54.61
Lu et al. [11]	86.72	92.51	-	-	-	-	-	-	-	-	-	-	-	-
Corbiere et al. [3]	86.30	92.8	53.60	63.20	39.10	48.80	50.10	59.50	38.80	48.90	30.50	38.30	23.10	30.40
Wang et al. [16]	90.99	95.78	50.31	65.48	40.31	48.23	53.32	61.05	40.65	56.32	68.70	**74.25**	51.53	60.95
Ours	**91.16**	**96.12**	**56.17**	**65.83**	**43.20**	**53.52**	**58.28**	**67.80**	**46.97**	**57.42**	**68.82**	74.13	**54.69**	**63.74**

For landmark localization, we compare our method with 4 recent deep learning models [9,10,16,17]. As shown in Table 1, our model is more accurate and achieves state-of-the-art at 0.0474. For category and attribute prediction, our method is compared with 6 recent top-performing models [1,3,6,9,11,16]. With the aid of the accurate landmark-driven attention, our model outperforms all the competitors, as shown in Table 2.

We also visualize what the attention branch has learned as show in Fig. 2 that it makes the network focus on the related information and ignore the useless information.

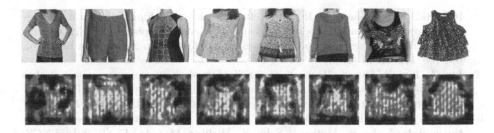

Fig. 2. Attention map visualization

5   Conclusion

In this paper, we design a novel attention-aware model for deep learning-based fashion analysis, leading to a fully differentiable network that can be trained end-to-end. Our model utilizes convolutional upsampling to produce more accurate landmark heatmap. We further introduce an attention mechanism, which takes advantage of the predicted landmark locations for improving the accuracy of category classification and attribute prediction. The experimental results on three benchmarks of the DeepFashion dataset has demonstrated the superior performance of our model, which achieves the state-of-the-art landmark localization, category classification and attribute prediction compared to recent methods.

References

1. Chen, H., Gallagher, A., Girod, B.: Describing clothing by semantic attributes. In: Fitzgibbon, A., Lazebnik, S., Perona, P., Sato, Y., Schmid, C. (eds.) ECCV 2012. LNCS, vol. 7574, pp. 609–623. Springer, Heidelberg (2012). https://doi.org/10.1007/978-3-642-33712-3_44
2. Chen, K., Wang, J., Chen, L.C., Gao, H., Xu, W., Nevatia, R.: ABC-CNN: an attention based convolutional neural network for visual question answering. arXiv preprint arXiv:1511.05960 (2015)
3. Corbiere, C., Ben-Younes, H., Ramé, A., Ollion, C.: Leveraging weakly annotated data for fashion image retrieval and label prediction. arXiv preprint arXiv:1709.09426 (2017)
4. Han, X., Wu, Z., Jiang, Y.G., Davis, L.S.: Learning fashion compatibility with bidirectional LSTMs. In: Proceedings of the 2017 ACM on Multimedia Conference, pp. 1078–1086. ACM (2017)
5. Hidayati, S.C., You, C.W., Cheng, W.H., Hua, K.L.: Learning and recognition of clothing genres from full-body images. IEEE Trans. Cybern. **48**(5), 1647–1659 (2018)
6. Huang, J., Feris, R.S., Chen, Q., Yan, S.: Cross-domain image retrieval with a dual attribute-aware ranking network. In: Proceedings of the IEEE International Conference on Computer Vision, pp. 1062–1070 (2015)
7. Jaderberg, M., Simonyan, K., Zisserman, A., et al.: Spatial transformer networks. In: Advances in Neural Information Processing Systems, pp. 2017–2025 (2015)

8. Kalantidis, Y., Kennedy, L., Li, L.J.: Getting the look: clothing recognition and segmentation for automatic product suggestions in everyday photos. In: Proceedings of the 3rd ACM Conference on International Conference on Multimedia Retrieval, pp. 105–112. ACM (2013)
9. Liu, Z., Luo, P., Qiu, S., Wang, X., Tang, X.: Deepfashion: powering robust clothes recognition and retrieval with rich annotations. In: Proceedings of the IEEE Conference on Computer Vision and Pattern Recognition, pp. 1096–1104 (2016)
10. Liu, Z., Yan, S., Luo, P., Wang, X., Tang, X.: Fashion landmark detection in the wild. In: Leibe, B., Matas, J., Sebe, N., Welling, M. (eds.) ECCV 2016. LNCS, vol. 9906, pp. 229–245. Springer, Cham (2016). https://doi.org/10.1007/978-3-319-46475-6_15
11. Lu, Y., Kumar, A., Zhai, S., Cheng, Y., Javidi, T., Feris, R.: Fully-adaptive feature sharing in multi-task networks with applications in person attribute classification. In: 2017 IEEE Conference on Computer Vision and Pattern Recognition (CVPR), pp. 1131–1140 (2017)
12. Ma, Y., Jia, J., Zhou, S., Fu, J., Liu, Y., Tong, Z.: Towards better understanding the clothing fashion styles: a multimodal deep learning approach. In: AAAI, pp. 38–44 (2017)
13. de Melo, E.V., Nogueira, E.A., Guliato, D.: Content-based filtering enhanced by human visual attention applied to clothing recommendation. In: 2015 IEEE 27th International Conference on Tools with Artificial Intelligence (ICTAI), pp. 644–651. IEEE (2015)
14. Simonyan, K., Zisserman, A.: Very deep convolutional networks for large-scale image recognition. arXiv preprint arXiv:1409.1556 (2014)
15. Tompson, J.J., Jain, A., LeCun, Y., Bregler, C.: Joint training of a convolutional network and a graphical model for human pose estimation. In: Advances in Neural Information Processing Systems, pp. 1799–1807 (2014)
16. Wang, W., Xu, Y., Shen, J., Zhu, S.C.: Attentive fashion grammar network for fashion landmark detection and clothing category classification. In: IEEE Conference on Computer Vision and Pattern Recognition, pp. 4271–4280 (2018)
17. Yan, S., Liu, Z., Luo, P., Qiu, S., Wang, X., Tang, X.: Unconstrained fashion landmark detection via hierarchical recurrent transformer networks. In: Proceedings of the 2017 ACM on Multimedia Conference, pp. 172–180. ACM (2017)
18. Yan, Y., et al.: Unsupervised image saliency detection with gestalt-laws guided optimization and visual attention based refinement. Pattern Recognit. **79**, 65–78 (2018)
19. Yang, W., Luo, P., Lin, L.: Clothing co-parsing by joint image segmentation and labeling. In: Proceedings of the IEEE Conference on Computer Vision and Pattern Recognition, pp. 3182–3189 (2014)

DesIGN: Design Inspiration from Generative Networks

Othman Sbai[1,2], Mohamed Elhoseiny[2], Antoine Bordes[2], Yann LeCun[2,3], and Camille Couprie[2(✉)]

[1] Université Paris Est, Ecole des ponts, Imagine, Marne-la-Vallée, France
[2] Facebook AI Research, Paris, France
{sbaio,elhoseiny,abordes,yann,coupriec}@fb.com
[3] New York University, New York City, USA

Abstract. Can an algorithm create original and compelling fashion designs to serve as an inspirational assistant? To help answer this question, we design and investigate different image generation models associated with different loss functions to boost novelty in fashion generation. The dimensions of our explorations include: (i) different Generative Adversarial Networks architectures that start from noise vectors to generate fashion items, (ii) a new loss function that encourages novelty, and (iii) a generation process following the key elements of fashion design (disentangling shape and texture). A key challenge of this study is the evaluation of generated designs and the retrieval of best ones, hence we put together an evaluation protocol associating automatic metrics and human experimental studies. We show that our proposed creativity loss yields better overall appreciation than the one employed in Creative Adversarial Networks. In the end, about 61% of our images are thought to be created by human designers rather than by a computer while also being considered original per our human subject experiments, and our proposed loss scores the highest compared to existing losses in both novelty and likability.

Keywords: Fashion image generation ·
Generative adversarial networks

1 Introduction

Artificial Intelligence (AI) research has been making huge progress in the machine's capability of human level understanding across the spectrum of perception, reasoning and planning [1–3]. Another key direction yet relatively understudied is creativity where the goal is for machines to generate original items with realistic, aesthetic attributes, usually in artistic contexts. We can indeed imagine AI to serve as inspiration for humans in the creative process and also to act as a sort of assistant able to help with more mundane tasks, especially in the digital domain. Previous work has explored writing pop songs [4], imitating the styles of great painters [5,6] or doodling sketches [7] for instance.

© Springer Nature Switzerland AG 2019
L. Leal-Taixé and S. Roth (Eds.): ECCV 2018 Workshops, LNCS 11131, pp. 37–44, 2019.
https://doi.org/10.1007/978-3-030-11015-4_5

There has also been a growing interest in generating images using GANs, given their ability to generate appealing images unconditionally [8], or conditionally like from text, class labels, and for paired and unpaired image translations [9–11]. However, it is not clear how *creative* such attempts can be considered since most of them mainly tend to mimic training samples without expressing much originality. Creative Adversarial Networks (CANs) [12] have then been proposed to adapt GANs to generate original content (paintings) by encouraging the model to deviate from existing painting styles. Technically, CAN is a Deep Convolutional GAN (DCGAN) model [13] associated with an entropy loss that encourages novelty against known art styles. The specific application domain of CANs (art paintings) allows for very abstract generations to be acceptable but, as a result, does reward originality a lot without judging much how such enhanced creativity can be mixed with realism and standards.

In this paper we study how AI can generate creative samples for fashion. Fashion is an interesting domain because designing original garments requires a lot of creativity but with the constraints that items must be wearable. In contrast to most generative models works [14–16], the originality angle we introduce makes us go beyond replicating images seen during training. Fashion image generation opens the door for breaking creativity into design elements (shape and texture in our case), which is a novel aspect of our work in contrast to CANs. More specifically, this work explores various architectures and losses that encourage GANs to deviate from existing fashion styles covered in the training dataset, while still generating realistic pieces of clothing without needing any image as input. To the best of our knowledge, this work is the first attempt at incorporating creative fashion generation by explicitly relating it to its design elements.

Contributions. (1) We are the first to propose a novelty loss on image generation of fashion items with a specific conditioning of texture and shape, learning a deviation from existing ones. (2) We re-purposed automatic entropy based evaluation criteria for assessment of fashion items in terms of texture and shape; The correlations between the automatic metrics that we proposed and our human study allowed us to *draw some conclusions with useful metrics revealing human judgment.* (3) We proposed a shape conditioned model named Style GAN and a concrete solution to make it work in a non-deterministic way. Trained with creative losses, it results in a *novel and powerful model.* Our best models manage to generate realistic images with high resolution 512×512 using a relatively small dataset (about 4000 images). More than 60% of our generated designs are judged as being created by a human designer while also being considered original, showing that an AI could offer benefits serving as an efficient and inspirational assistant.

2   Models: Architectures and Losses

2.1   Network Architectures

We experiment using two architectures: a modified version of the DCGAN model [13] for higher resolution output images, and our proposed styleGAN model as described below. In addition to its real/fake branch classification, the discriminator in each architecture is augmented with optional classification branches each for shape and texture classes.

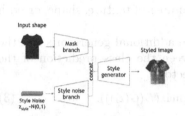

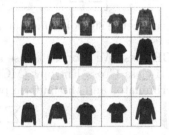

Fig. 1. From the segmented mask of a fashion item and different random vector z, our StyleGAN model generates different styled images.

Fig. 2. From the mask of a product, our StyleGAN model generates different styled image for each style noise.

GANs with Optional Classification Loss. Let $\mathcal{D}$ be a dataset of N images. Following [10], we use shape and texture labels to learn a shape classifier and a texture classifier in the discriminator. Adding these labels improves over the plain model and stabilizes the training for larger resolution. We are adding to the discriminator network either one branch for texture or for shape classification, or two branches for both shape and texture classification and denote the extra classification output of the discriminator D_b. The additional loss is:

$$\mathcal{L}_{D \text{ classif}} = - \sum_{x_i \in \mathcal{D}} \log(\text{softmax}(D_b(x_i))). \tag{1}$$

StyleGAN: Conditioning on Masks. In this model, a generator is trained to compute realistic images from a mask input and noise representing style information (Fig. 1). We use the same discriminator architecture as in DCGAN with classifier branches that learn shape and texture classification on real images on top of real/fake prediction. Training styleGAN with two inputs is difficult, previous approaches of image to image translation such as pix2pix [17] and Cycle-GAN [11] create a deterministic mapping between an input image to a single corresponding one, i.e. edges to handbags for example or from one domain to another. To make sure that no input is being neglected, we add a ℓ_1 loss forcing the generator to output the mask itself in case of null style input z and thus ensure the impact of the shape in the generations as shown in Fig. 1.

2.2   Novelty Losses

Because GANs learn to generate images very similar to the training images, we explore ways to make them deviate from this replication by studying the impact of two additional losses for the generator: the *CAN loss* (as used in [12]), and an *MCE loss* that encourage the generator to confuse the discriminator.

– **CAN loss**: As proposed in [12], the CAN loss is defined as

$$\mathcal{L}_{\text{CAN}} = -\lambda \left[\sum_i \sum_{k=1}^{K} \frac{1}{K} \log(\sigma(D_{b,k}(G(z_i)))) + \frac{K-1}{K} \log(1 - \sigma(D_{b,k}(G(z_i)))) \right], \quad (2)$$

where σ is the sigmoid function, and K the number of texture, shape, or both classes.

– **MCE loss**: We propose to use as alternative additional generator's loss the Multi-class Cross Entropy (MCE) loss between the class prediction of the discriminator and the uniform probability vector.

$$\mathcal{L}_{\text{MCE}} = -\lambda \sum_i \sum_k \frac{1}{K} \log \text{softmax}(D(G(z_i))). \quad (3)$$

Both MCE and sum of binary cross entropy losses encourage deviation from existing categories. However, our MCE criterion considers all classes globally in the softmax unlike the CAN loss which is based on a sum of K independent binary classification losses.

3   Results

Dataset. Unlike similar work focusing on fashion item generation [15,16], we choose a dataset containing fashion items in uniform background allowing the trained models to learn features useful for creative generation without generating wearer faces and backgrounds. We augment the dataset of 4157 images by a factor 5 by jittering images with random scaling and translations. The images are classified into seven clothes categories: jackets, coats, shirts, tops, t-shirts, dresses and pullovers, and 7 textures categories: uniform, tiled, striped, animal skin, dotted, print and graphical pattern.

Automatic Evaluation Metrics. Evaluating the diversity and quality of a set of images has been tackled by scores such as the inception score and variants like the AM score [18]. We adapt both of them for two labels specific to fashion design (shape and texture) and supplement them by a mean nearest neighbor distance. Our final set of automatic scores contains 5 metrics : (1, 2) shape score and texture score, each based on a Resnet-18 classifier [19] of shape or texture respectively. (3, 4) shape AM score and texture AM score, based on the output of the same classifiers. (5) mean distance to 10 nearest neighbors score. We compute the mean distance for each sample to its retrieved k-Nearest Neighbors (NN), with $k = 10$, as the Euclidean distance between the features extracted from a Resnet18 pretrained on ImageNet by removing its last fully connected layer.

Creating Evaluation Sets. We select for each setup (DCGAN or styleGAN trained with texture, shape, both or none novelty criterion) four saved models after a sufficient number of iterations. Our models produce plausible results after training for 15000 iterations with a batch size of 64 images.

Given a set of 10000 generations from a model, we extract different sets of images with particular visual properties such as (ii) high/low texture entropy, (iii) high/low NN distance to real images. We also explore random and mixed sets such as *low shape entropy* and *high nearest neighbors distance*. We expect such a set to contain plausible generations since low shape entropy usually correlates with well defined shapes, while high nearest neighbor distance contains unusual designs. Overall, we have 8 different sets that may overlap. We choose to evaluate 100 images for each set.

Automatic Evaluation Results. We set $\lambda = 5$ for the MCE loss, and $\lambda = 1$ for the CAN loss, as these parameters appeared to work best. All models were trained using the default learning rate 0.002 as in [13]. Our different models take about half a day to train on 4 Nvidia P100 GPUs for 256×256 models and almost 2 days for the 512×512 ones.

Table 1 presents shape and texture scores, AM scores (for shape and texture) and average NN distances computed for each model on 4 selected iterations. Our first observation is that the DCGAN model alone seems to perform worse than all other tested models with the highest NN distance and lower shape and texture scores. The value of the NN distance score may have different meanings.

Table 1. Quantitative automatic evaluation. High scores appear in bold.

Method/Score	Shape	tex.	AM sh	AM tx	NN
Dataset	6.25	3.76	20.4	12.6	5.65
GAN	4.70	2.74	13.3	8.92	14.4
GAN classif	**5.31**	2.86	**14.8**	**9.68**	13.1
CAN shape	5.27	2.77	14.7	8.92	13.1
CAN tex	5.24	3.01	14.4	9.48	13.5
CAN shTex	5.20	**3.24**	14.7	10.0	13.1
MCE shape	5.07	2.80	13.6	8.90	13.0
MCE tex	5.14	**3.33**	14.4	9.30	13.6
MCE shTex	4.98	3.04	13.3	**9.52**	13.2

Table 2. Human evaluation ranked by decreasing overall score (higher is better).

Method/ Human Method	Overall	Shape nov.	Shape comp.	Tex. nov.	Tex. comp.	Real fake
DCGAN MCE shape	**3.78**	**3.58**	**3.57**	**3.64**	**3.57**	60.9
DCGAN MCE tex	**3.72**	**3.57**	3.52	**3.61**	**3.58**	61.1
StyleGAN CANtex	3.65	3.37	3.31	3.44	3.21	49.7
StyleGAN MCE tex	3.61	3.38	3.29	3.50	3.37	53.4
StyleGAN	3.59	3.28	3.21	3.27	3.15	47.2
DCGAN MCEshtex	3.49	3.40	3.24	3.40	3.31	**61.3**
DCGAN CANshtex	3.47	3.28	3.18	3.33	3.16	**63.8**
DCGAN classif	3.42	3.32	3.32	3.37	3.29	52.7
DCGAN CANtex	3.37	3.23	3.12	3.35	3.09	59.7
DCGAN CANshape	3.33	3.28	3.16	3.27	3.12	55.0
DCGAN	3.22	2.95	2.78	3.24	2.83	60.4

A high value could mean an enhanced "creativity" of the model, but also a higher failure rate. The two models having high shape score, AM shape score, AM texture score and NN distances scores are DCGAN with creativity losses models.

Human Evaluation. Each image was rated by 5 persons asked to answer 6 questions: Q1: how do you like this design overall on a scale from 1 to 5? Q2/Q3: rate the novelty of shape (Q2) and texture (Q3) from 1 to 5. Q4/Q5: rate the complexity of shape (Q4) and texture (Q5) from 1 to 5.Q6: Do you think this image was created by a fashion designer or generated by computer? (yes/no).

Table 2 presents the average score obtained by each model on each human evaluation question for the RTW dataset. From this table, we can see that using our novelty loss (MCE shape and MCE tex) performs better than the DCGAN baseline. While the two proposed models with MCE originality loss rank the best on the overall score, we observe that the preferred images have low nearest neighbor distance. This means that generations which are not close to their nearest neighbors are not always pleasant. It is indeed a challenge to obtain models able to generate novel (high nearest neighbor distance) and at the same time pleasant generations. However, we observe that the models that score better in the high nearest neighbors distance set are clearly the ones with our novelty loss(MCE). Figure 3 shows how well our approaches worked on two axis: likability and real appearance. The most popular methods are obtained by the models employing an originality loss and in particular our proposed MCE originality criterion, as they are perceived as the most likely to be generated by designers, and the most liked overall.

We are greatly improving the state-of-the-art here, going from a score of 64 to more than 75 in likeability from classical GANs to our best model with shape creativity. We display images which obtained the best scores for each of the 6 questions in Fig. 4. Our proposed Style GAN (See Fig. 2) is producing competitive scores compared to the best DCGAN setups. In particular, Style-GAN with originality loss is ranked in the top-3.

We computed correlation scores between our automatic metrics and human ratings. The metric that correlates the most with the overall score is the NN distance. There is also a negative correlation of NN dist with real appearance.

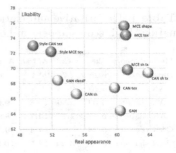

Fig. 3. Evaluation of the different models on the RTW dataset by human annotators on two axis: likability and real appearance. Our models reach nice trade-offs between real appearance and likability.

Fig. 4. Best generations as rated by annotators. Left: Q1: overall score, Q2: shape novelty, Q3: shape complexity; Right: Q4: tex. novelty, Q5: tex. complexity, Q6: Realism.

4   Conclusion

We introduced a specific conditioning of GANs on texture and shape elements for generating fashion design images. While GANs with such classification loss offer realistic results, they tend to reconstruct the training images. Using an MCE originality loss, we learn to deviate from a reproduction of the training set. We also propose a novel architecture named *StyleGAN model*, conditioned on an input mask, enabling shape control while leaving free the creativity space on the inside of the item. All these contributions lead to the best results according to our human evaluation study. We manage to generate accurately 512×512 images, however we seek for better resolution, which is a fundamental aspect of image quality, in our future work. Finally, while our results show visually pleasing textural novelty, it will be interesting to explore larger families of novelty loss functions, and ensure wearability constraints.

References

1. He, K., Gkioxari, G., Dollár, P., Girshick, R.: Mask R-CNN. In: ICCV (2017)
2. Andreas, J., Rohrbach, M., Darrell, T., Klein, D.: Neural module networks. In: CVPR (2016)
3. Silver, D., et al.: Mastering the game of go with deep neural networks and tree search. Nature **529**, 484 (2016)
4. Briot, J.P., Hadjeres, G., Pachet, F.: Deep learning techniques for music generation-a survey. arXiv:1709.01620 (2017)
5. Gatys, L.A., Ecker, A.S., Bethge, M.: Image style transfer using convolutional neural networks. In: CVPR (2016)
6. Dumoulin, V., et al.: A learned representation for artistic style. In: ICLR (2017)
7. Ha, D., Eck, D.: A neural representation of sketch drawings. In: ICLR (2018)
8. Goodfellow, I., et al.: Generative adversarial nets. In: NIPS (2014)
9. Reed, S.E., Akata, Z., Mohan, S., Tenka, S., Schiele, B., Lee, H.: Learning what and where to draw. In: NIPS (2016)
10. Odena, A., Olah, C., Shlens, J.: Conditional image synthesis with auxiliary classifier GANs. In: ICML (2017)
11. Zhu, J.Y., Park, T., Isola, P., Efros, A.A.: Unpaired image-to-image translation using cycle-consistent adversarial networks. In: ICCV (2017)

12. Elgammal, A., Liu, B., Elhoseiny, M., Mazzone, M.: Creative adversarial networks. In: ICCC (2017)
13. Radford, A., Metz, L., Chintala, S.: Unsupervised representation learning with deep convolutional generative adversarial networks. In: ICLR (2016)
14. Date, P., Ganesan, A., Oates, T.: Fashioning with networks: neural style transfer to design clothes. In: KDD ML4Fashion workshop (2017)
15. Zhu, S., Fidler, S., Urtasun, R., Lin, D., Loy, C.C.: Be your own prada: fashion synthesis with structural coherence. In: ICCV (2017)
16. Lassner, C., Pons-Moll, G., Gehler, P.V.: A generative model of people in clothing. In: ICCV (2017)
17. Isola, P., Zhu, J., Zhou, T., Efros, A.A.: Image-to-image translation with conditional adversarial networks. In: CVPR (2017)
18. Zhou, Z., Zhang, W., Wang, J.: Inception score, label smoothing, gradient vanishing and -log(d(x)) alternative. arXiv:1708.01729 (2017)
19. He, K., Zhang, X., Ren, S., Sun, J.: Deep residual learning for image recognition. arXiv:1512.03385 (2015)

FashionSearchNet: Fashion Search with Attribute Manipulation

Kenan E. Ak[1,2(✉)], Ashraf A. Kassim[1], Joo Hwee Lim[2], and Jo Yew Tham[3]

[1] National University of Singapore, Singapore, Singapore
emir.ak@u.nus.edu, ashraf@nus.edu.sg
[2] Institute for Infocomm Research, A*STAR, Singapore, Singapore
joohwee@i2r.a-star.edu.sg
[3] ESP xMedia Pte. Ltd., Singapore, Singapore
thamjy@espxmedia.com

Abstract. The focus of this paper is on retrieval of fashion images after manipulating attributes of the query images. This task is particularly useful in search scenarios where the user is interested in small variations of an image, i.e., replacing the mandarin collar with a button-down. Keeping the desired attributes of the query image while manipulating its other attributes is a challenging problem which is accomplished by our proposed network called FashionSearchNet. FashionSearchNet is able to learn attribute specific representations by leveraging on weakly supervised localization. The localization module is used to ignore the unrelated features of attributes in the feature map, thus improve the similarity learning. Experiments conducted on two recent fashion datasets show that FashionSearchNet outperforms the other state-of-the-art fashion search techniques.

Keywords: CNNs · Fashion retrieval · Similarity learning · Attribute localization

1 Introduction

Recently, there has been a huge interest in fashion-related research. The appearance of deep learning based techniques have boosted the interest in the following areas: fashion/attribute recognition [1–3], fashion retrieval [3–5], attribute discovery [6,7], fashion/human parsing [8–10], recommentation [11–13] and generative adversarial networks [14,15].

Image retrieval is a crucial task as it can significantly lower the time that is required to find the desired item. Most research in image-based fashion retrieval focuses on finding same/similar images in cross-domains [3–5]. In this work, we focus on a search scenario called "fashion search with attribute manipulation" which is illustrated in Fig. 1 where the user would like to search for a similar item as the query image but with a short sleeve instead i.e., the sleeve attribute "sleeveless" needs to be replaced with "short". Until recently [16,17] there wasn't

© Springer Nature Switzerland AG 2019
L. Leal-Taixé and S. Roth (Eds.): ECCV 2018 Workshops, LNCS 11131, pp. 45–53, 2019.
https://doi.org/10.1007/978-3-030-11015-4_6

Fig. 1. Given a query image, the user manipulates the sleeve attribute. The proposed FashionSearchNet utilizes it's feature representations to find images similar to the query image while manipulating the sleeveless attribute.

any published work which allowed to make such modifications on the query image and conduct the fashion retrieval. Our recently introduced FashionSearchNet [17], aims to solve this problem. Different than our prior work [17], we briefly explain the method and share additional experiments.

The proposed FashionSearchNet initially focuses on learning attribute similarities by leveraging weakly supervised localization, i.e., no information is given known about the location of the attributes. The localization module is based on global average pooling (GAP) layer and it is used to generate a several attribute activation maps (AAMs). AAMs are used to extract attribute boundaries and feed attribute relevant features to a set of fully connected layers where the similarity learning is conducted. By using a triplet-based similarity learning process, attributes which share the same value are made to be similar to each other in the feature space. Lastly, another learning mechanism is employed to combine attribute representations into a global representation and used in the fashion search. This mechanism helps the network decide which attribute representation should have higher importance depending on the attribute that is being manipulated.

2   Related Work

Attribute Recognition. Recently, Chen et al. [18] used fine-grained clothing attributes to describe people with a deep domain adaptation network. Mix and match method [19] proposed a joint model for clothing and attribute recognition. Abdulnabi et al. [20] showed that a multi-task CNN model can be used to predict attributes of fashion images. More recently, an approach which combines localization and classification for apparel recognition is proposed by Song et al. [21] but it requires supervision on object boundaries. FashionSearchNet uses the classification loss to learn better attribute representations and in doing so it contributes to its localization ability.

Image Retrieval. Image-based fashion retrieval is an important topic, however, it is mostly based on retrieving the similar/same images [3,5,21,22] which limits the user interaction. In terms of clothing recommendation, both methods proposed in [23, 24] use fashion images from a personal closet to recommend out-fits. However, what if the user does not like a specific attribute of the retrieved image? The idea of fashion search with attribute manipulation comes from Zhao et al. [16] where a CNN is trained (AMNet) by combining the query image with the desired attribute. Different than FashionSearchNet, AMNet [16] does not explore the spatial aspect of attributes, therefore, lacks the ability to conduct the similarity learning on attribute-level. Similar to our method, Singh et al. [25] proposed an end-to-end localization and ranking for relative attributes. However, the fact that they train a new model for each attribute make it infeasible for fashion images.

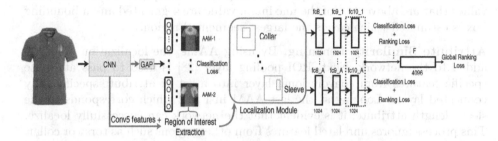

Fig. 2. FashionSearchNet. From each attribute activation maps (AAMs), attribute relevant convolutional features are extracted and pooled to a set of fully connected layers. Both classification and ranking losses are used for similarity learning. Lastly, attribute representations ($fc_{10\_1}, fc_{10\_2}, ...$) are combined into a single representation to conduct fashion search.

3   FashionSearchNet

The proposed FashionSearchNet is based on AlexNet [26] architecture with some modifications. As suggested by [27], 2 more convolutional layers are added after conv5 layer. GAP layer is used to generate AAMs which are then used to extract region of interests. In order to learn attribute similarity, a set of fully connected layers are used and jointly trained with classification and ranking loss. Lastly, a mechanism is employed to help the network decide which attribute representation should have higher importance depending on the attribute manipulation with the global ranking loss.

Attribute Activation Maps. We denote the output of global average pooling as x_I, where I corresponds to the input image. Initially, the network is trained with multi-attribute classification loss function to have reliable AAMs:

$$L_C = -\sum_{I=1}^{N}\sum_{a=1}^{A} log(p(g_{Ia}|x_I w_a)) \tag{1}$$

where g_{Ia} represents the ground truth of the $a'th$ attribute of the $I'th$ image. $x_I w_a{}^1$ calculates weighted linear combination of x_I for attribute a, N is the number of training examples and A is the number of attributes. Next, we define $M_{a_c}(I, i, j)$ as an AAM for class c of an attribute a as follows:

$$M_{a_c}(I, i, j) = \sum_k w_{a_{(k,c)}} conv7_k(I, i, j) \qquad (2)$$

where $w_{a_{(k,c)}}$ is the weight variable of attribute a associated with $k'th$ feature map of class c. c is determined from the class that maximizes the classification confidence. After extracting heatmaps from M_{a_c}, each ROI is estimated with a simple hard threshold technique. Following the technique from [27], the pixel values that are above 20% of the maximum value are segmented and a bounding box is estimated which covers the largest segmented region.

Attribute Similarity Learning. By using AAMs, the localization ability is added to the network. Next, ROI pooling layer [28] is used to pass attribute specific features from convolutional layer into a set of attribute-specific fully connected layers. Looking at the last AAM in Fig. 2 which corresponds to the sleeve length attribute, it is evident that the network can successfully localize. This process ignores unrelated features from other regions such as torso or collar.

At the end of fully connected layers, triplet ranking constraints are imposed to enable attribute similarity learning. Inspired by [29], FashionSearchNet uses the soft-triplet ranking function is utilized which normalizes the distances to the range of (0,1) with a softmax function and formulated as follows:

$$d^+(h(\hat{I}), h(I^+), h(I^-)) = \frac{exp(||h(\hat{I}) - h(I^+)||_2)}{exp(||h(\hat{I}) - h(I^+)||_2) + exp(||h(\hat{I}) - h(I^-)||_2)} \qquad (3)$$

$$d^-(h(\hat{I}), h(I^+), h(I^-)) = \frac{exp(||h(\hat{I}) - h(I^-)||_2)}{exp(||h(\hat{I}) - h(I^+)||_2) + exp(||h(\hat{I}) - h(I^-)||_2)} \qquad (4)$$

Given $||d^+, d^- - 1||_2^2 = d^+$ and $h = fc_{10\_a}$ the ranking loss function becomes:

$$L_T = \sum_{I=1}^{N} \sum_{a=1}^{A} d^+(fc_{10\_a}(\hat{I}), fc_{10\_a}(I^+), fc_{10\_a}(I^-)) \qquad (5)$$

where A is the number of the fully connected layers. The given function aims to minimize $||fc_{10\_a}(\hat{I}), fc_{10\_a}(I^+)||_2$ and maximize $||fc_{10\_a}(\hat{I}), fc_{10\_a}(I^-)||$. We pick triplets from the same mini-batch and the rule is: $\hat{I}$ and I^+ must share the same label while I^- is chosen randomly.

Attribute Manipulation. After the network is trained for the attribute similarities, we extract features from the training images with the same attribute value and average them. These averaged features are stored in a matrix where

---

[1] The dimensions of w_a is [number of feature maps by number of classes associated with a].

each attribute value corresponds to a specific representation so that the "undesired" attribute representations can directly be replaced.

Learning Global Representation. It is evident that some attribute representations should have higher importance when conducting the fashion search. To apply this idea to FashionSearchNet, we use a weight parameter w_{a*} to reduce the concatenated feature length to 4096. Also, we add A number of parameters $\lambda_{a,a*}$ to learn attribute importance. The training is conducted with the following function L_G which we call global ranking loss for a given attribute manipulation a^*:

$$F(I, a^*) = [fc_{10\_1}(I)\lambda_{1,a*}, ..., fc_{10\_A}(I)\lambda_{a,a*}]w_{a*} \tag{6}$$

$$L_G = \sum_{I=1}^{N} \sum_{a^*=1}^{A} d^+(F(\hat{I}, a^*), F(I^+, a^*), F(I^-, a^*)) \tag{7}$$

The rule for picking triplets for the global ranking loss is: $\hat{I}$ and I^+ must be identical in terms of attributes after the attribute manipulation while I^- is chosen randomly.

Collar:
Turndown -> High

Query   Expected Outcomes

Fig. 3. An example of a successful retrieval. Given a query image and attribute manipulation, there are only 2 images in Shopping100k which matches all desired attributes.

4   Experiments

Datasets. We use DeepFashion [2] and Shopping100k [30] datasets to conduct experiments as they contain several attributes. For Shopping100k dataset [30], around 80k images are used for training, 20k images are reserved for the retrieval gallery and 2k images are served as the queries. For DeepFashion dataset [2], we choose to use Attribute Prediction subset and choose the following attributes: category, shape, texture. 90k images are used to train the network, 21k images are reserved for retrieval gallery and 2k images are served as the queries.

Evaluation Metric. We use Top-K retrieval accuracy to perform experiments. Given a query image and an attribute manipulation, the search algorithm finds the "best K" image matches i.e., "Top-K" matches. If the retrieved image matches with all desired attributes after attribute manipulation, it corresponds to a hit (1) or it is a miss (0). We provide a search example in Fig. 3. If a system is able to find one of the expected outcomes in k'th match, Top-k would be equal to 1.

Competing Methods: We compare the performance of FashionSearchNet with "AMNet" [16], an attribute-based method denoted as "Att. Based" which uses AlexNet [26] to predict attributes of query images and substitute the unwanted attributes. To see the effect of AAMs, we remove AAMs from FashionSearchNet and train a network called "FashionSearchNet w/o Loc." in the same fashion but without the extra fully connected layers.

4.1 Fashiong Search with Attribute Manipulation

Average Top-K retrieval accuracy results are presented in Fig. 3 for Shopping100k (a) and DeepFashion (b) datasets. For both datasets, FashionSearchNet achieves the best performance, giving 56.6% and 37.6% Top-30 accuracy respectively. Compared to AMNet, we manage to achieve 16% and 13% improvement. AMNet, on the other hand, is a decent method compared to the basic attribute-based system as AMNet performs 19% and 12% better. The attribute-based method is not a good method as it relies on predicting each of the attributes correctly which is not an easy task. Comparing AMNet [16] with Fashion-SearchNet, there are two drawbacks. Firstly, AMNet ignores the localization aspect of attributes. Secondly, FashionSearchNet conducts similarity learning on attribute-level which is not present in AMNet. Removing the localization ability results in 5.4% and 6.3% performance loss (Fig. 4).

We report the number possible attribute manipulation operations in Table 1. For each attribute, this number varies because for some images as there is no possible attribute manipulation for a certain attribute. Next, we report results depending on an attribute that is being manipulated in Table 2 where Fashion-SearchNet shows a good performance. For Shopping100k dataset, our method

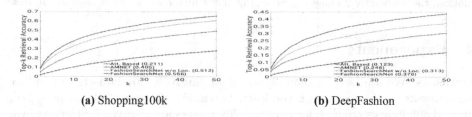

    (a) Shopping100k   **(b)** DeepFashion

Fig. 4. Top-K Retrieval Accuracies for *search by query and attribute manipulation* experiments using (a) Shopping100 k and (b) DeepFashion datasets. The number in the parentheses corresponds to the Top-30 retrieval accuracy.

Fig. 5. Given 2 query images, the user conduct 2 attribute manipulation (collar, sleeve) where the proposed method successfully retrieves images.

Table 1. The number of retrieval instances Shopping100 k and DeepFashion datasets for each attribute.

	Category	Color	Collar	Fabric	Fastening	Fit	Gender	Neckline	Pocket	Pattern	Sleeve	Sport	Category	Shape	Texture
					Shopping100k								DeepFashion		
Count	405	127	1169	544	126	670	313	316	111	835	422	239	1849	1823	1792

Table 2. Top-30 retrieval accuracy for Shopping100 k and DeepFashion Datasets.

	Category	Color	Collar	Fabric	Fastening	Fit	Gender	Neckline	Pocket	Pattern	Sleeve	Sport	Category	Shape	Texture
					Shopping100k								DeepFashion		
Attribute-based	0.095	0.175	0.195	0.320	0.181	0.342	0.089	0.137	0.225	0.299	0.101	0.192	0.118	0.138	0.115
AMNet	0.223	0.433	0.477	0.258	0.248	0.357	0.326	0.350	0.434	0.388	0.360	0.315	0.218	0.249	0.273
FashionSearchNet w/o Loc.	0.339	0.583	0.599	0.330	0.336	0.452	**0.559**	0.494	0.477	0.552	0.524	0.348	0.202	**0.409**	0.330
FashionSearchNet	**0.395**	**0.649**	**0.642**	**0.401**	**0.423**	**0.519**	0.527	**0.532**	**0.531**	**0.575**	**0.640**	**0.436**	**0.380**	**0.409**	**0.338**

outperforms the other methods consistently. We provide 2 examples in Fig. 5 to show the success of the proposed method. For the texture and shape attributes in DeepFashion dataset, the performance is similar to not having the attribute localization module but for the category attribute, AAMs boost the retrieval accuracy. It is especially important to have the localization ability for the category attribute as there might be 2 clothing pieces (pants and shirt) on the wearer. We identify that DeepFashion dataset have many important missing attributes such as sleeve length, collar type etc. which could benefit from the proposed localization method vastly.

5 Conclusion

This paper shows FashionSearchNet's good localization ability enables it to identify the most relevant regions and is able to generate powerful attribute representations. Additionally, FashionSearchNet utilizes a mechanism which helps it to decide which attribute representation should have higher importance depending on the attribute that is being manipulated.

References

1. Dong, Q., Gong, S., Zhu, X.: Multi-task curriculum transfer deep learning of clothing attributes. In: 2017 IEEE Winter Conference on Applications of Computer Vision (WACV), pp. 520–529 (2017)
2. Liu, Z., Luo, P., Qiu, S., Wang, X., Tang, X.: Deepfashion: powering robust clothes recognition and retrieval with rich annotations. In: IEEE Conference Computer Vision Pattern Recognition (CVPR), pp. 1096–1104 (2016)
3. Simo-Serra, E., Ishikawa, H.: Fashion style in 128 floats: joint ranking and classification using weak data for feature extraction. In: IEEE Conference Computer Vision Pattern Recognition (CVPR), pp. 298–307 (2016)
4. Corbiere, C., Ben-Younes, H., Ramé, A., Ollion, C.: Leveraging weakly annotated data for fashion image retrieval and label prediction. arXiv preprint arXiv:1709.09426 (2017)

5. Hadi Kiapour, M., Han, X., Lazebnik, S., Berg, A.C., Berg, T.L.: Where to buy it: matching street clothing photos in online shops. In: Proceedings of the IEEE International Conference on Computer Vision (ICCV), pp. 3343–3351 (2015)

6. Han, X., et al.: Automatic spatially-aware fashion concept discovery. In: Proceedings of the IEEE Conference on Computer Vision and Pattern Recognition, pp. 1463–1471 (2017)

7. Vittayakorn, S., Umeda, T., Murasaki, K., Sudo, K., Okatani, T., Yamaguchi, K.: Automatic attribute discovery with neural activations. In: Leibe, B., Matas, J., Sebe, N., Welling, M. (eds.) ECCV 2016. LNCS, vol. 9908, pp. 252–268. Springer, Cham (2016). https://doi.org/10.1007/978-3-319-46493-0_16

8. Liang, X., et al.: Human parsing with contextualized convolutional neural network. In: Proceedings of the IEEE International Conference on Computer Vision (ICCV), pp. 1386–1394 (2015)

9. Simo-Serra, E., Fidler, S., Moreno-Noguer, F., Urtasun, R.: A high performance CRF model for clothes parsing. In: Cremers, D., Reid, I., Saito, H., Yang, M.-H. (eds.) ACCV 2014. LNCS, vol. 9005, pp. 64–81. Springer, Cham (2015). https://doi.org/10.1007/978-3-319-16811-1_5

10. Yamaguchi, K., Hadi Kiapour, M., Berg, T.L.: Paper doll parsing: retrieving similar styles to parse clothing items. In: Proceedings of the IEEE International Conference on Computer Vision (ICCV), pp. 3519–3526 (2013)

11. Al-Halah, Z., Stiefelhagen, R., Grauman, K.: Fashion forward: Forecasting visual style in fashion. arXiv preprint arXiv:1705.06394 (2017)

12. Han, X., Wu, Z., Jiang, Y.G., Davis, L.S.: Learning fashion compatibility with bidirectional lstms. arXiv preprint arXiv:1707.05691 (2017)

13. Simo-Serra, E., Fidler, S., Moreno-Noguer, F., Urtasun, R.: Neuroaesthetics in fashion: modeling the perception of fashionability. In: Proceedings of the IEEE Conference on Computer Vision and Pattern Recognition, pp. 869–877 (2015)

14. Zhu, S., Fidler, S., Urtasun, R., Lin, D., Loy, C.C.: Be your own prada: fashion synthesis with structural coherence. In: 2017 IEEE International Conference on Computer Vision (ICCV), pp. 1689–1697. IEEE (2017)

15. Han, X., Wu, Z., Wu, Z., Yu, R., Davis, L.S.: Viton: an image-based virtual try-on network. In: The IEEE Conference on Computer Vision and Pattern Recognition (CVPR), June 2018

16. Zhao, B., Feng, J., Wu, X., Yan, S.: Memory-augmented attribute manipulation networks for interactive fashion search. In: IEEE Conference Computer Vision Pattern Recognition (CVPR) (2017)

17. Ak, K.E., Kassim, A.A., Lim, J.H., Tham, J.Y.: Learning attribute representations with localization for flexible fashion search. In: IEEE Conference Computer Vision Pattern Recognition, CVPR, pp. 7708–7717 (2018)

18. Chen, Q., Huang, J., Feris, R., Brown, L.M., Dong, J., Yan, S.: Deep domain adaptation for describing people based on fine-grained clothing attributes. In: Proceedings of the IEEE Conference on Computer Vision and Pattern Recognition, vol. 7, pp. 5315–5324 (2015)

19. Yamaguchi, K., Okatani, T., Sudo, K., Murasaki, K., Taniguchi, Y.: Mix and match: joint model for clothing and attribute recognition. In: BMVC, p. 51–1 (2015)

20. Abdulnabi, A.H., Wang, G., Lu, J., Jia, K.: Multi-task CNN model for attribute prediction. IEEE Trans. Multimedia 17(11), 1949–1959 (2015)

21. Song, Y., Li, Y., Wu, B., Chen, C.Y., Zhang, X., Adam, H.: Learning unified embedding for apparel recognition. arXiv preprint arXiv:1707.05929 (2017)

22. Huang, J., Feris, R.S., Chen, Q., Yan, S.: Cross-domain image retrieval with a dual attribute-aware ranking network. In: Proceedings of the IEEE International Conference on Computer Vision (ICCV), pp. 1062–1070 (2015)
23. Hsiao, W.L., Grauman, K.: Creating capsule wardrobes from fashion images. In: The IEEE Conference on Computer Vision and Pattern Recognition (CVPR), June 2018
24. Tangseng, P., Yamaguchi, K., Okatani, T.: Recommending outfits from personal closet. In: Proceedings of the IEEE Conference on Computer Vision and Pattern Recognition, pp. 2275–2279 (2017)
25. Singh, K.K., Lee, Y.J.: End-to-end localization and ranking for relative attributes. In: Leibe, B., Matas, J., Sebe, N., Welling, M. (eds.) ECCV 2016. LNCS, vol. 9910, pp. 753–769. Springer, Cham (2016). https://doi.org/10.1007/978-3-319-46466-4_45
26. Krizhevsky, A., Sutskever, I., Hinton, G.E.: Imagenet classification with deep convolutional neural networks. In: Advances in neural information processing systems, pp. 1097–1105 (2012)
27. Zhou, B., Khosla, A., Lapedriza, A., Oliva, A., Torralba, A.: Learning deep features for discriminative localization. In: Proceedings of the IEEE Conference on Computer Vision and Pattern Recognition, pp. 2921–2929 (2016)
28. Girshick, R.: Fast R-CNN. In: Proceedings of the IEEE International Conference on Computer Vision, pp. 1440–1448 (2015)
29. Hoffer, E., Ailon, N.: Deep metric learning using triplet network. In: Feragen, A., Pelillo, M., Loog, M. (eds.) SIMBAD 2015. LNCS, vol. 9370, pp. 84–92. Springer, Cham (2015). https://doi.org/10.1007/978-3-319-24261-3_7
30. Ak, K.E., Lim, J.H., Tham, J.Y., Kassim, A.A.: Efficient multi-attribute similarity learning towards attribute-based fashion search. In: 2017 IEEE Winter Conference on Applications of Computer Vision (WACV), pp. 1671–1679. IEEE (2018)

CRAFT: Complementary Recommendation by Adversarial Feature Transform

Cong Phuoc Huynh[(✉)], Arridhana Ciptadi, Ambrish Tyagi, and Amit Agrawal

Amazon Lab126, Sunnyvale, California, USA
{conghuyn,ambrisht,aaagrawa}@amazon.com

Abstract. We propose a framework that harnesses visual cues in an unsupervised manner to learn the co-occurrence distribution of items in real-world images for complementary recommendation. Our model learns a non-linear transformation between the two manifolds of source and target item categories (e.g., tops and bottoms in outfits). Given a large dataset of images containing instances of co-occurring items, we train a generative transformer network directly on the feature representation by casting it as an adversarial optimization problem. Such a conditional generative model can produce multiple novel samples of complementary items (in the feature space) for a given query item. We demonstrate our framework for the task of recommending complementary top apparel for a given bottom clothing item. The recommendations made by our system are diverse, and are favored by human experts over the baseline approaches.

Keywords: Recommender systems ·
Complementary recommendation · Generative adversarial network ·
Unsupervised learning · Adversarial learning

1 Introduction

Recommendation algorithms are central to many commercial applications, particularly for online shopping. In domains such as fashion, customers are looking for clothing recommendations that visually complement their current outfits, styles, and wardrobe. Traditional content-based and collaborative recommendation algorithms [1,18] do not make use of the visual cues to suggest complementary items. Among these, collaborative filtering [16,25] is a commonly used approach, which primarily relies on behavioral and historical data such as co-purchases, co-views, and past purchases to suggest new items to customers. In contrast to these approaches, we address the problem of recommending complementary items for a given query item based on visual cues. Our proposed

---

C. P. Huynh and A. Ciptadi—Equal contributors.

© Springer Nature Switzerland AG 2019
L. Leal-Taixé and S. Roth (Eds.): ECCV 2018 Workshops, LNCS 11131, pp. 54–66, 2019.
https://doi.org/10.1007/978-3-030-11015-4_7

approach is general (modeling visual co-occurrences) and can be applied to different domains such as fashion, home design, etc.

We develop an unsupervised learning approach for Complementary Recommendation using Adversarial Feature Transform (CRAFT), by learning the co-occurrence of item pairs in real images. Here we assume that the co-occurrence frequency of item pairs is a strong indicator of the likelihood of their complementary relationship. We define an adversarial process to train a conditional generative adversarial network that can learn the joint distribution of item pairs by observing samples from the real distribution, i.e., image features of co-occurring items. Instead of direct image synthesis, the generative transformer in CRAFT is trained in the feature space and is able to generate diverse features thanks to the input random vector. The transformed feature vectors are used to recommend images corresponding to the nearest neighbors in the feature space.

The proposed feature transformation approach is novel and unique, with several advantages over existing image and feature generation methods using Generative Adversarial Network (GAN) [8]. While the quality of visual image generation using GANs has improved significantly (especially for faces [13]), it still lacks the realism required for fashion/apparel recommendation. In contrast to image transformation approaches using GAN approach [2,12,27,35], which operate in the image space, CRAFT directly generates features of the recommended items. Therefore, it bypasses the need for generating synthetic images and enables a simpler and more efficient network architecture. This improves the stability of CRAFT during training and avoids common pitfalls such as mode collapse [3]. Another advantage is that our generative model can provide multiple complementary items by learning the joint distribution in the feature space, rather than a fixed mapping provided by image translation approaches.

Table 1. Similarities and differences between our approach and those that use adversarial loss for training.

GAN input	Generative (w/ random seed)	Output	Example
N/A	Yes	Image	Image generation [8]
Image	No	Image	Image-to-image translation [35]
Image + Attribute	No	Image	Image manipulation [17]
Synthetic image	No	Image	Adding realism [27]
Synthetic image	Yes	Image	Adding realism [2]
Image	No	Features	Domain adaptation [29,31]
Features	Yes	Features	Ours

2   Related Work

Generative Adversarial Networks (GAN): The original GAN [8] and variants [7] have been presented as a powerful framework for learning generative models of complex data distributions for various tasks including image generation [13,33], image-to-image translation [12,35], domain adaptation [2,27,29,31], etc. A recent work by Zhu et al. [36] used the GAN framework to generate new clothing on a wearer. Our approach differs from these methods since we do not aim to generate an image of the complementary item. Instead, we use the adversarial training framework to learn the joint distribution between the source and target *features* in an *unsupervised* manner. The GAN paradigm has also found applications in the areas of image manipulation and image transformation [2,12,27,35]. While such an approach can be applied to transform a given image into that of a complementary item, it only provides a fixed mapping. In contrast, our method adopts a generative model that can provide multiple complementary items by learning the joint distribution in the feature space. Further, contrary to methods such as CycleGAN [35] and Zhu et al. [36] that perform image-to-image translation using raw pixels, our approach works directly in the feature space. Feature-based domain adaptation approaches attempt to directly learn a visual encoder for the target domain [29] or a domain-invariant encoder [31] through optimizing an adversarial loss defined on the source, target and augmented features. In contrast, our method learns a generative transformer network that operates in the feature space. Table 1 shows similarities and differences between our approach and those that use adversarial loss for training.

Unsupervised Learning: Recent applications of unsupervised learning for visual tasks include object discovery in videos [4]. In addition, there have been demonstrations of self-supervised learning [6] for the tasks of image colorization, image in-painting, hole filling, jigsaw puzzle solving from image patches, future frame prediction using video data [32], etc. In the fashion domain, annotated data are typically used for predicting fashion-related attributes and matching street-to-catalog images [14,21]. These approaches involve visual search to find *similar* looking items, whereas our approach is focused on finding complementary items. Furthermore, our approach is unsupervised: we only take as input a set of images to learn the feature transformation between complementary objects.

Recommendation: There is a rich body of literature on using behavioral customer data such as browsing and purchasing history to develop recommender systems [16]. Specific to the fashion domain, McAuley et al. [24] employed convolution neural network (CNN) features and non-visual data to build a personalized model of user's preference. In [10,30], the authors proposed to learn visual compatibility via a common embedding across categories. In [9], the authors proposed to learn a bi-directional Long Short Term Memory (LSTM) model in a supervised manner, to suggest items that complement each other in an entire outfit.

The aforementioned recommendation approaches use customer's behavioral data as training labels. Behavioral signals do not necessarily reflect that items viewed or purchased together are visually complementary. In contrast, our unsupervised approach learns item co-occurrences from only visual data. In multiple methods [9,24,30], the recommendation model is non-generative in the sense that it can only evaluate the compatibility between two given items. In [10], the diversity of recommendation is limited by the (fixed) number of embeddings employed. In contrast, our *generative* model is not subject to such a constraint, thanks to its ability to sample an infinite amount of noise vectors.

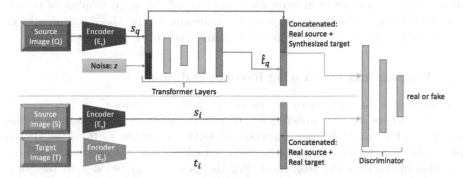

Fig. 1. Architecture for the CRAFT framework. The transformer component is trained to generate the target features conditioned on the source features and a sampled noise vector.

3   Generative Feature Transformer

This section describes our generative recommendation model based on the co-occurrence of item pairs in real-world images. We hypothesize that learning the joint distribution of such pairs can be useful for recommending new items that complement a given query. We adopt an adversarial learning paradigm, where our transformer network learns to generate features of the complementary items conditioned on the query item.

3.1   Network Architecture

Figure 1 depicts the overall architecture of the proposed CRAFT network. The source and the target feature encoders, E_s and E_t, respectively, are fixed and are used to generate feature vectors for training and inference. Typically, it is advisable to use application-specific feature representations, e.g., apparel feature embeddings for clothing recommendations. However, a general representation such as one pre-trained on ImageNet [5] or MS-COCO [20] offer robust alternatives.

Our architecture resembles traditional GAN designs with two main components: a conditional feature transformer and a discriminator. The role of the feature transformer is to transform the source feature s_q into a complementary target feature $\hat{t}_q$. The input to the transformer also consists of a random noise vector z sampled uniformly from a unit sphere in a d_z-dimensional space. By design, the transformer is generative since it is able to sample various features in the target domain.

As discussed, since our approach works in the feature space, we can adopt a simple architecture for the feature transformer and discriminator. The transformer consists of several fully-connected layers, each followed by batch normalization [11] and leaky ReLU [22] activation layers. The discriminator is commensurate to the transformer in capacity, consisting of the same number of layers. This helps balance the power between the transformer and the discriminator in the two-player game, leading to stable training and convergence.

3.2   Training and Generating Recommendations

Our training data consists of N co-occurring feature pairs $\mathcal{C} = \{(s_i, t_i), i = 1, \ldots, N\}$, where $s_i \in \mathbb{R}^{d_s}$ and $t_i \in \mathbb{R}^{d_t}$ denote the features corresponding to the source and the target images, respectively. Given a sample s_q from the source space, the complementary recommendation task is to generate target features $\{\hat{t}_q\}$ that maximizes the likelihood that the pair $(s_q, \hat{t}_q)$ belongs to the joint distribution $p_{\mathcal{C}}$ represented by the training data. Note that the source features fed into the transformer (s_q) and discriminator (s_i) are generally different from each other. To this end, we model the composition of layers in the feature transformer and the discriminator as two functions $T_\phi(s, z) : (s, z) \mapsto \hat{t}$ and $D_\theta(s, t) : (s, t) \mapsto [0, 1]$, respectively. Here, ϕ and θ are the learnable parameters of the two players, transformer and discriminator, respectively, and (s, t) is a pair of source and target feature vectors, and z is a random noise vector.

The training process emulates an adversarial game between the feature transformer and the discriminator, where the discriminator aims to classify feature pairs as real (co-occurring) or synthetic. On the other hand, the feature transformer synthesizes target features $\{\hat{t}_q\}$ conditioned on a given source feature s_q. Its objective is to fool the discriminator into the belief that $\hat{t}_q$ co-occurs with s_q. The feedback from the discriminator encourages the transformer to produce a target feature $\hat{t}_q$ so as to maximize the co-occurrence probability of the synthetic pair.

The adversarial game can be formulated as a mini-max optimization problem. The optimization approach can be implemented by alternating the training of the discriminator and the feature transformer. The overall objective function of the adversarial training process is formulated in Eq. 1.

$$\min_\phi \max_\theta \mathcal{L} \triangleq \mathbb{E}_{(s_i, t_i) \sim p_{\mathcal{C}}} \log D_\theta(s_i, t_i) + \mathbb{E}_{z \sim p_z, s_q \sim p_s} \log(1 - D_\theta(s_q, T_\phi(s_q, z))),$$

$$(1)$$

where p_z and p_s are the probability distribution function (pdf) of the random noise and the source feature.

In the discriminator step (D-step), the discriminator's goal is to assign a binary label, i.e., 0 to the synthesized feature pair $(s_q, \hat{t}_q)$, where $\hat{t}_q = T_\phi(s_q, z)$, and 1 to an actual pair (s_i, t_i). The discriminator's goal is to maximizes the cross entropy loss in Eq. 1. Meanwhile, the feature transformer maximizes the likelihood that the discriminator recognizes synthetic pairs as belonging to the data-generating (joint) distribution $\mathcal{C}$, i.e., assigning a label 1 to such pairs.

Therefore, the transformer step (T-step) aims to minimize the second term on the right-hand side of Eq. 1.

3.3 Generating Recommendations

The recommendation workflow is depicted in Fig. 2. Here, we retain only the transformer's layers shown in Fig. 1 for recommendation. From a given query image, we first extract its features via a pre-trained source encoder, E_s. The query feature, s_q, along with a sampled noise vector, z, is fed to the CRAFT network to generate the feature vector $\hat{t}_q$ for a complementary item. This allows us to generate a diverse set of complementary recommendations by sampling the underlying conditional probability distribution function. We then perform a nearest neighbor search on a pre-indexed candidate subspace with $\hat{t}_q$ as the query vector. Actual recommendation images are retrieved by a reverse lookup that maps the selected features to the original target images.

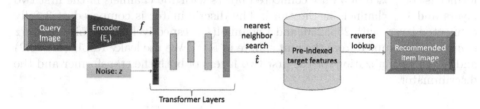

Fig. 2. Generating recommendations using the proposed CRAFT network.

4 Experiments

In this section, we describe the experimental setup and results of applying CRAFT to the problem of complementary apparel recommendation. Specifically, we train the generative transformer network to synthesize features for top clothing items that are visually compatible to a given query bottom item.

4.1 Datasets

We trained the proposed CRAFT network from scratch on unlabeled images, without the need for any human annotation to determine the complementary relationship. To achieve this, we collected 474,184 full-length outfit images of fashion enthusiasts, each containing a top and a bottom item. From each outfit, we extract the regions of interest (ROIs) of co-occurring pairs of tops and bottoms for training. We trained a semantic segmentation network [34] on the "Human Parsing in the Wild" dataset [19] to parse the collected images into top and bottom segments. We consolidate the original labels in the dataset into 15 labels, where top clothing items correspond to the label "upper-clothes" and bottom ones correspond to "pants" and "skirt". Subsequently, we obtained tight bounding boxes/regions of interest (ROIs) around the resulting top and bottom segments. In this manner, the training pairs are obtained automatically without the need for manual annotations of the complementary relationship.

In our experiments, we extract the global averaging pooling feature of the pre-trained Inception-v4 model [28] after performing a forward pass on the top and bottom ROIs. Rather than working in the original 1536-dimensional feature space, we opt for the top 128 PCA components to stabilize the training and reduce the computational load.

4.2   Training and Network Parameters

We use the Adam optimizer [15] with starting learning rate of 0.0002 for both the discriminator and the transformer networks. To improve training stability, we use one-sided label noise [26]. Each minibatch for training the discriminator consists of an equal proportion of synthetic and real feature pairs. The transformer is composed of 3 fully connected layers with 256 channels in the first two layers and 128 channels in the third. The discriminator is composed of 3 fully connected layers with 256, 256, and 1 channel(s), respectively. The noise vector z is uniformly sampled from the unit sphere in $\mathbb{R}^{128}$. We use leaky ReLU ($\alpha = 0.2$) and batch normalization for the first two layers of both the transformer and the discriminator.

4.3   Baseline Algorithms

We compare the CRAFT algorithm with the following baseline methods.

Random recommendations: A trivial baseline generates random recommendations from a given set of candidate options, referred to as *Random*. A random selection can offer a diverse set of target items, but they may not necessarily be complementary to the query item.

Nearest neighbors of source items: In addition, we consider a relevant and good baseline method, which operates by finding nearest neighbors of the query/source feature, and recommend the *corresponding* target items, i.e. the one that co-occurs with the neighboring source items in the training data. We refer to this method as *NN-Source*.

Incompatible recommendations: Lastly, we illustrate that CRAFT not only learns to recommend complementary items, but also the concept of visual incompatibility. The *Incompatible* recommendation method suggests tops that are assigned low discriminator scores by the generative transformer of CRAFT.

4.4   Visualization of the Discriminator Output

In this section, we visualize how the learned transformer network *dynamically* reacts to given queries in terms of assigning compatibility scores for candidate tops. To visualize the space of candidate top items, we projected them to a two-dimensional (2D) subspace using t-SNE [23]. The discriminator output can be

Fig. 3. Each subplot shows a 2D t-SNE embedding of all the candidate tops (left) with the corresponding query image (right). The colors represent the discriminator score for tops conditioned on the query (red: high score, yellow: low score). Note that the discriminator is able to learn that common bottoms such as blue jeans and gray pants are compatible with a wide range of tops as compared to rarer query items such as the patterned skirt shown in the last subplot. (Color figure online)

seen as a proxy for the compatibility score between any top and a given query item. The left-hand side of each subplot in Fig. 3 shows 2D embedding of all the tops in the dataset, color coded by the discriminator/compatibility score for each top with the given bottom item (shown on the right-hand side). Note that the compatibility scores for candidate tops change with the query bottom. The yellow colors in the t-SNE plot denote low compatibility, while shades of orange to red denote high compatibility (see color bar). It is interesting to note how universal items such as blue jeans or gray pants are compatible with a large set of candidate tops, while rare bottoms like the richly textured pattern skirt shown on the bottom row are compatible with only a handful of tops. This illustrates that our network is able to model the distribution of real item pairs.

4.5   Qualitative Results

Figure 4 shows qualitative results of the different recommendation methods for two query items. For this experiment, we generated 8 top recommendations from each algorithm and asked a fashion specialist to identify the top items that complement the given bottom query. While all of the approaches produce visually diverse recommendations, not all of them are compatible with the query. For a common bottom outfit such as dark jeans (Fig. 4(a)), NN-Source perform as well as our algorithm (CRAFT), while for a less common bottom such as bright pink skirt (Fig. 4(b)) they perform worse (see Sect. 4.7 for a more thorough analysis). This is aligned with our intuition that the quality of NN-Source recommendation highly depends on the proximity of the neighbors of the query. Interestingly, the *Incompatible* algorithm demonstrates its ability to learn the concept of visual *incompatibility*: it often produces unusual outfit recommendation (e.g., the fur top as the third item in Fig. 4(a)).

4.6   User Study Design

When recommendations are provided from an open ended set, they are difficult to evaluate in absolute terms. For subjective domains such as fashion, it is preferable

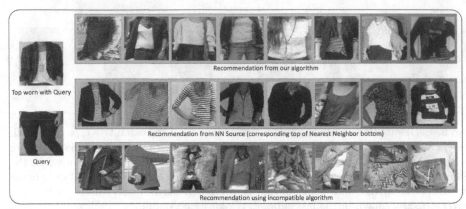

(a) Recommendations for dark jeans

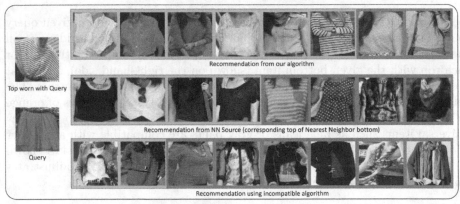

(b) Recommendations for a pink skirt

Fig. 4. Top to bottom: recommendations for two queries by CRAFT, NN-Source and the Incompatible algorithms. Highlighted in green are the items accepted marked by a fashion specialist as complementary to the query input, whereas rejected items are in red. Best viewed in color. Our approach generates better and diverse recommendations. (Color figure online)

to obtain input from domain experts who are familiar with nuances involved in making style-appropriate recommendations. We adopt A/B testing as the main methodology to compare our proposed approach to the baselines. Here, we evaluate the relevance of recommendations generated by each algorithm by measuring their *acceptance* by domain experts.

We approached a panel of four fashion specialists (FS) to provide feedback on recommendations generated by various algorithms. Each FS was presented with 17 recommendations for a given query (bottom) item, for each of the four algorithms. Among these recommendations, the FS were asked to select those that they judge to be complementary to the query. We used a total of 64 different query bottoms in this study, ranging for popular bottoms such as blue jeans to less common bottoms such as richly patterned skirts. The images were presented to FS in a random order to eliminate any bias for the algorithm or query items. Since some FS are in general more selective than others, we need to normalize for their individual bias. To achieve this, we add the *actual* top worn by the user in the query outfit to the set of 17 recommendations at a random location. We normalize the FS acceptance scores by their likelihood of selecting the actual top as an acceptable recommendation. Note that we only perform analysis on the newly recommended tops, and exclude the original top from our results.

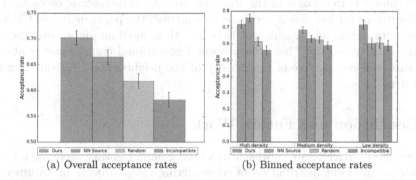

(a) Overall acceptance rates   (b) Binned acceptance rates

Fig. 5. Mean acceptance rate of recommendations by fashion specialists (error bars indicate 95% confidence intervals). (a) Overall acceptance rating for each algorithm. (b) Acceptance ratings binned according to the density (high, medium, low) of query items.

4.7 Quantitative Analysis

Figure 5(a) shows the average rate of acceptance of generated recommendations for all FS for the four algorithms. As discussed, acceptance rates were normalized by the probability of each FS accepting the actual top for the given query bottom. The error bar denotes the 95% confidence interval for each of the results. Non-overlapping error bars indicate that the differences between the two results are statistically significant. The NN-Source algorithm has the overall acceptance score of 66.5 ± 1.4 and outperforms the *Random* and *Incompatible* baseline algorithms as expected. The CRAFT approach generates recommendations with the highest FS acceptance score (70.3 ± 1.4).

Stratification by Feature Space Density. It is even more interesting to break down the analysis of the results in terms of the density of the query items in the feature space. To this end, we approximate the density of each query point by taking the average distance to $K = 25$ nearest neighbors and bin the queries into low, medium, and high density regions, respectively. Figure 5(b) shows the average recommendation acceptance rate provided by FS for each algorithm in each density region. Again, the error bars denote the 95% confidence interval for each result. For queries that fall in the high density regions, the difference between CRAFT and the NN-Source algorithm is statistically insignificant (error bars overlap). This is expected since nearest neighbor search is a good estimator of the joint top-bottom density for high density regions, where a large number of samples are available. This is expected since nearest neighbor search is a good estimator of the conditional distribution of tops given a bottom for high density regions, where a large number of bottoms are available. However, the NN-Source algorithm starts to degrade at the medium density level, and eventually degenerates to similar performance as the *Random* and the *Incompatible* recommendation algorithms for low density regions. In contrast, the performance of CRAFT is consistent across all regions and is better than baseline algorithms for mid and low density regime. Thus, the proposed conditional transformer is able to generalize well irrespective of the density of the neighborhood surrounding the query item.

5   Conclusion and Future Work

We presented CRAFT, an approach to visual complementary recommendation by learning the *joint* distribution of co-occurring visual objects in an unsupervised manner. Our approach does not require annotations or labels to indicate complementary relationships. The feature transformer in CRAFT samples a *conditional* distribution to generate diverse and relevant item recommendations for a given query. The recommendations generated by CRAFT are preferred by the domain experts over those produced by competing approaches.

By modeling the feature level distributions, our framework can potentially enable a host of applications, ranging from domain adaptation to one- or few-shot learning. The current work could be extended to incorporate the end-to-end learning of domain-related encoders as part of the generative framework.

References

1. Adomavicius, G., Tuzhilin, A.: Toward the next generation of recommender systems: a survey of the state-of-the-art and possible extensions. IEEE Trans. Knowl. Data Eng. **17**(6), 734–749 (2005)
2. Bousmalis, K., Silberman, N., Dohan, D., Erhan, D., Krishnan, D.: Unsupervised pixel-level domain adaptation with generative adversarial networks. In: CVPR, pp. 95–104 (2017)
3. Che, T., Li, Y., Jacob, A.P., Bengio, Y., Li, W.: Mode regularized generative adversarial networks. In: ICLR (2017)
4. Croitoru, I., Bogolin, S.V., Leordeanu, M.: Unsupervised learning from video to detect foreground objects in single images. In: ICCV, pp. 4335–4343 (2017)
5. Deng, J., Dong, W., Socher, R., Li, L.J., Li, K., Fei-Fei, L.: ImageNet: a large-scale hierarchical image database. In: CVPR (2009)
6. Doersch, C., Zisserman, A.: Multi-task self-supervised visual learning. In: ICCV (2017)

7. Donahue, J., Krähenbühl, P., Darrell, T.: Adversarial feature learning. In: International Conference on Learning Representations (2017)
8. Goodfellow, I., Pouget-Abadie, J., Mirza, M., Xu, B., Warde-Farley, D., Ozair, S.: Generative adversarial nets. In: NIPS, pp. 2672–2680 (2014)
9. Han, X., Wu, Z., Jiang, Y.G., Davis, L.S.: Learning fashion compatibility with bidirectional LSTMs. In: ACM on Multimedia Conference, pp. 1078–1086 (2017)
10. He, R., Packer, C., McAuley, J.: Learning compatibility across categories for heterogeneous item recommendation. In: IEEE 16th International Conference on Data Mining, ICDM, pp. 937–942 (2016)
11. Ioffe, S., Szegedy, C.: Batch normalization: accelerating deep network training by reducing internal covariate shift. In: ICML, pp. 448–456 (2015)
12. Isola, P., Zhu, J.Y., Zhou, T., Efros, A.A.: Image-to-image translation with conditional adversarial nets. In: CVPR (2017)
13. Karras, T., Aila, T., Laine, S., Lehtinen, J.: Progressive growing of GANs for improved quality, stability, and variation. In: ICLR (2018)
14. Kiapour, M.H., Han, X., Lazebnik, S., Berg, A.C., Berg, T.L.: Where to buy it: matching street clothing photos in online shops. In: ICCV (2015)
15. Kingma, D.P., Ba, J.: Adam: a method for stochastic optimization. In: ICLR (2015)
16. Koren, Y., Bell, R.: Advances in collaborative filtering. In: Ricci, F., Rokach, L., Shapira, B., Kantor, P.B. (eds.) Recommender Systems Handbook, pp. 145–186. Springer, Boston, MA (2011)
17. Lample, G., Zeghidour, N., Usunier, N., Bordes, A., Denoyer, L., Ranzato, M.: Fader networks: manipulating images by sliding attributes. In: Advances in Neural Information Processing Systems, pp. 5963–5972 (2017)
18. Lew, M.S., Sebe, N., Djeraba, C., Jain, R.: Content-based multimedia information retrieval: state of the art and challenges. ACM Trans. Multimed. Comput. Commun. Appl. 2(1), 1–19 (2006)
19. Liang, X., Liu, S., Shen, X., Yang, J., Liu, L., Dong, J., Lin, L., Yan, S.: Deep human parsing with active template regression. IEEE Trans. Pattern Anal. Mach. Intell. 37(12), 2402–2414 (2015)
20. Lin, T.-Y., et al.: Microsoft COCO: common objects in context. In: Fleet, D., Pajdla, T., Schiele, B., Tuytelaars, T. (eds.) ECCV 2014. LNCS, vol. 8693, pp. 740–755. Springer, Cham (2014)
21. Liu, S., Song, Z., Wang, M., Xu, C., Lu, H., Yan, S.: Street-to-shop: cross-scenario clothing retrieval via parts alignment and auxiliary set. In: 2012 IEEE Conference on Computer Vision and Pattern Recognition, Providence, RI, pp. 3330–3337 (2012)
22. Maas, A.L., Hannun, A.Y., Ng, A.Y.: Rectifier nonlinearities improve neural network acoustic models. In: ICML, vol. 30 (2013)
23. van der Maaten, L., Hinton, G.: Visualizing high-dimensional data using t-SNE. J. Mach. Learn. Res. 9, 2579–2605 (2008)
24. McAuley, J.J., Targett, C., Shi, Q., van den Hengel, A.: Image-based recommendations on styles and substitutes. In: SIGIR (2015)
25. Melville, P., Mooney, R.J., Nagarajan, R.: Content-boosted collaborative filtering for improved recommendations. In: Eighteenth National Conference on Artificial Intelligence, pp. 187–192 (2002)
26. Salimans, T., Goodfellow, I., Zaremba, W., Cheung, V., Radford, A., Chen, X.: Improved techniques for training GANs. In: NIPS, pp. 2234–2242 (2016)
27. Shrivastava, A., Pfister, T., Tuzel, O., Susskind, J., Wang, W., Webb, R.: Learning from simulated and unsupervised images through adversarial training. In: CVPR (2017)

28. Szegedy, C., Ioffe, S., Vanhoucke, V.: Inception-v4, inception-resnet and the impact of residual connections on learning. AAAI abs/1602.07261 (2017)
29. Tzeng, E., Hoffman, J., Darrell, T., Saenko, K.: Adversarial discriminative domain adaptation. In: CVPR (2017)
30. Veit, A., Kovacs, B., Bell, S., McAuley, J., Bala, K., Belongie, S.: Learning visual clothing style with heterogeneous dyadic co-occurrences. In: International Conference on Computer Vision (ICCV) (2015)
31. Volpi, R., Morerio, P., Savarese, S., Murino, V.: Adversarial feature augmentation for unsupervised domain adaptation. In: Computer Vision and Pattern Recognition (2018)
32. Vondrick, C., Torralba, A.: Generating the future with adversarial transformers. In: CVPR (2017)
33. Wang, T.C., Liu, M.Y., Zhu, J.Y., Tao, A., Kautz, J., Catanzaro, B.: High-resolution image synthesis and semantic manipulation with conditional gans. In: Computer Vision and Pattern Recognition (2018)
34. Zhao, H., Shi, J., Qi, X., Wang, X., Jia, J.: Pyramid scene parsing network. In: CVPR (2017)
35. Zhu, J.Y., Park, T., Isola, P., Efros, A.A.: Unpaired image-to-image translation using cycle-consistent adversarial networks. In: ICCV (2017)
36. Zhu, S., Fidler, S., Urtasun, R.: Be your own prada: fashion synthesis with structural coherence. In: ICCV (2017)

Full-Body High-Resolution Anime Generation with Progressive Structure-Conditional Generative Adversarial Networks

Koichi Hamada$^{(\boxtimes)}$, Kentaro Tachibana, Tianqi Li, Hiroto Honda, and Yusuke Uchida

DeNA Co., Ltd., Tokyo, Japan
{koichi.hamada,kentaro.tachibana,tianqi.li,
hiroto.honda,yusuke.a.uchida}@dena.com

Abstract. We propose Progressive Structure-conditional Generative Adversarial Networks (PSGAN), a new framework that can generate full-body and high-resolution character images based on structural information. Recent progress in generative adversarial networks with progressive training has made it possible to generate high-resolution images. However, existing approaches have limitations in achieving both high image quality and structural consistency at the same time. Our method tackles the limitations by progressively increasing the resolution of both generated images and structural conditions during training. In this paper, we empirically demonstrate the effectiveness of this method by showing the comparison with existing approaches and video generation results of diverse anime characters at 1024×1024 based on target pose sequences. We also create a novel dataset containing full-body 1024×1024 high-resolution images and exact 2D pose keypoints using Unity 3D Avatar models.

Keywords: Generative adversarial networks · Anime generation · Image generation · Video generation

1 Introduction

Recently automatic image and video generation using deep generative models has been studied [5,10,21]. These are useful for media creation tools such as photo editing, animation production and movie making. Focusing on anime creation, automatic character generation can inspire experts to create new characters, and also can contribute to reducing costs for drawing animation. Jin et al. [9]

Electronic supplementary material The online version of this chapter (https://doi.org/10.1007/978-3-030-11015-4_8) contains supplementary material, which is available to authorized users.

© Springer Nature Switzerland AG 2019
L. Leal-Taixé and S. Roth (Eds.): ECCV 2018 Workshops, LNCS 11131, pp. 67–74, 2019.
https://doi.org/10.1007/978-3-030-11015-4_8

focuses on image generation for anime character faces with GAN architecture. However full-body character generation has not been studied enough. Generation of images for anime characters which only focused on face images was proposed, however, its quality was not satisfactory for animation production requirements [9]. To generate full-body characters automatically and add actions to them with high quality is a great help for making new characters and drawing animations. Therefore, we work on generating full-body character images and adding actions to them (i.e., video generation) with high quality.

There remain two problems to applying full-body character generation to animation production: (i) generation with high-resolution, (ii) generation with specified sequences of poses.

Generative Adversarial Networks (GANs) [5] are one of the most promising candidates as a framework applied to a diverse range of image generation tasks [8,9,14,16,17,25]. Recent progress of GANs with hierarchical and progressive structures has been realizing high-resolution and high-quality image generation [10], text-to-image synthesis [23,24], and image synthesis from label map [22]. However, It is still a challenge for GANs to generate structured objects consistent with global structures [4], such as full-body character generation. On the other hand, GANs with structural conditions, such as pose keypoints and facial landmarks, have also proposed [1,7,13–15,18,19]. However, their image resolution and quality are insufficient.

We propose Progressive Structure-conditional GANs (PSGAN) to tackle these problems by imposing the structural conditions at each scale generation with progressive training. We show that PSGAN is able to generate full body anime characters and animations with target pose sequences at 1024×1024 resolution. As PSGAN generates images with latent variables and structural conditions, PSGAN is able to generate controllable animations for various characters with target pose sequences. Figure 1 shows some example of animation generation results.

2   Proposed Methods

2.1   Progressive Structure-Conditional GANs

Our key idea is to learn image representation with structural conditions progressively. Figure 2 shows generator G and discriminator D architecture of PSGAN. PSGAN increases the resolution of generated images with structural conditions at each scale and generates high-resolution images. We adopt the same architecture of the image generator and discriminator as Progressive GAN [10], except that we impose structural conditions on both the generator and discriminator at each scale by adding pose maps with corresponding resolutions, which significantly stabilizes training. GANs with structural conditions have also been proposed [1,7,13–15,18,19]. They exploit a single-scale condition while we use multi-scale conditions. More specifically, we downsample the full-resolution structural condition map at each scale to form multi-scale condition maps. For each scale,

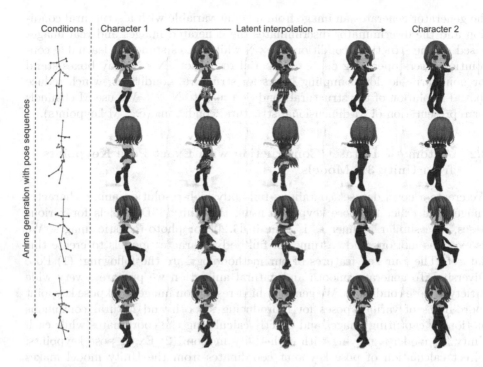

Fig. 1. Generated images of full-body anime characters at 1024×1024 by PSGAN with a test pose sequence. A generated anime at 1024×1024 by PSGAN is at https://youtu.be/bIi5gSITK0E.

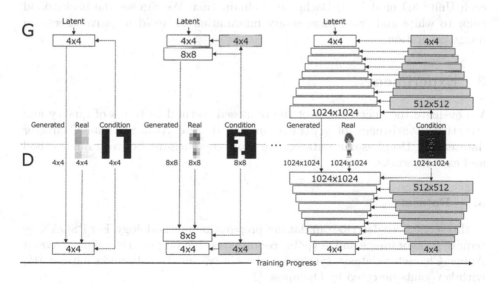

Fig. 2. Generator (G) and Discriminator (D) architecture of PSGAN.

the generator generates an image from a latent variable with a structural condition and the discriminator discriminates the generated images and real images based on the structural conditions. $N \times N$ white boxes stand for learnable convolution layers operating on $N \times N$ spatial resolution. $N \times N$ gray boxes stand for non-learnable downsampling layers for structural conditions, which reduce spatial resolution of the structural condition map to $N \times N$. We use M channels for representation of M-dimensional structural conditions (e.g. M keypoints).

2.2 Automatic Dataset Construction with Exact Pose Keypoints from Unity 3D Models

We create a novel dataset containing full-body high-resolution anime character images and exact 2D pose keypoints using the Unity[1] 3D models for various poses, in a similar manner as is done in [3,20] for photo-realistic images. We use various motions and costumes of full-body character models to create this dataset. The four key features of our methodology are the following: (1) Pose Diversity: To generate smooth and natural animation we prepare a very wide variety of pose conditions. We generate high-resolution images and pose keypoint coordinates of various poses for reproducing smooth and natural continuous motion by capturing images and exactly calculating the coordinates while each Unity 3D model is moving with each Unity motion. (2) Exact pose keypoints: Direct calculation of pose keypoint coordinates from the Unity model makes it possible to calculate the coordinates with no estimation error. (3) Infinite number of training images: An infinite number of synthetic images with keypoint maps are obtained by generating 3D modeled avatars using Unity automatically. Various images with keypoints can be created by replacing detachable items for each Unity 3D model. (4) Background elimination: We can set the background color to white and erase unnecessary information to avoid negative effects on image generation.

3   Experiments

We evaluate the effectiveness of the proposed method in terms of quality and structural consistency of generated images on the Avatar Anime-Character dataset and DeepFashion dataset. We show comparisons between our method and existing works.

3.1   Datasets

In this section, we describe our dataset preparation methodology. For PSGAN we require pairs of image and keypoint coordinates. We prepare the original Avatar Anime-Character dataset synthesized by Unity, and DeepFashion dataset [12] with keypoints detected by Openpose [2].

---

[1] Unity: https://unity3d.com.

Fig. 3. Samples of Avatar Anime-Character dataset.

Avatar Anime-Character Dataset. We create a dataset of full-body 1024 × 1024 high-resolution images with exact 2D pose keypoints from Unity 3D Avatar models based on the above proposed method. We divide several continuous actions of one avatar into 600 poses, and calculate keypoints in each pose. We conduct such process for 69 kinds of costumes, and obtain 47,400 images in total. We also obtain 20 keypoints based on the location of the bones of the 3D model. Figure 3 shows samples of created data. Anime characters (left of pair) and pose images (right of pair) are shown.

DeepFashion Dataset. The DeepFashion dataset (In-shop Clothes Retrieval Benchmark) [12] consists of 52,712 in-shop clothes images, and 200,000 cross-pose/scale pairs. All images are in 256 × 256 resolution and are richly annotated by bounding box, clothing type and pose type. However, none of them has keypoint annotations. Following [14], we use Openpose [2] to extract keypoint coordinates from images. The number of keypoints is 18 and examples with less than 10 detected keypoints are omitted.

3.2 Experimental Setups

We use the same stage design and the same loss function as [10]. We train networks with 600k images and structural conditions for each stage and use WGAN-GP loss [6] with $n_{critic} = 1$. We use a minibatch size 16 at the stage for 4 × 4 – 128 × 128 image generation and gradually decrease it to 12 for 256 × 256, 5 for 512 × 512, and 2 for 1024 × 1024 respectively due to GPU memory constraints. We use M channels of structural conditions as pose keypoints. M is 20 for the Avatar Anime-Character dataset and 18 for DeepFashion dataset. At each scale, the single pixel value at the corresponding keypoint coordinate is set to 1 and -1 elsewhere. For downsampling the condition map, we use max-pooling with kernel size 2 and stride 2 at each scale. We train the networks using Adam [11] with $\beta_1 = 0$, $\beta_2 = 0.99$. We use $\alpha = 0.001$ at the stage for 4 × 4 – 64 × 64 image generation and gradually decrease it to $\alpha = 0.0008$ for 128 × 128, $\alpha = 0.0006$ for 256 × 256, $\alpha = 0.0002$ for 512 × 512, and $\alpha = 0.0001$ for 1024 × 1024 respectively.

3.3 Avatar Anime-Character Generation at 1024 × 1024

We show examples of a variety of anime characters and animations generated at 1024 × 1024 by PSGAN. Figure 1 shows generated results of full-body anime characters at 1024×1024 with a test pose sequence. We can generate new full-body anime characters by interpolating latent variables corresponding to anime characters with different costumes (character 1 and 2) for various poses. By fixing the latent variables and giving continuous pose sequences to the network, we can generate an animation of the specified anime characters[2].

3.4   Comparison of PSGAN, Progressive GAN, and PG2

First, we evaluate structural consistency of PSGAN compared to Progressive GAN [10]. Figure 4 shows generated images on the DeepFashion dataset (256×256) by Progressive GAN and PSGAN. We observe that Progressive GAN is not capable of generating natural images consistent with their global structures (for example, left four images). On the other hand, PSGAN can generate plausible images consistent with their global structures by imposing the structural conditions at each scale.

Fig. 4. Comparison of structural consistency with [10] on DeepFashion dataset.

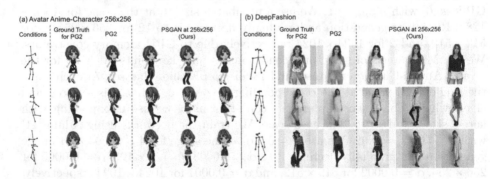

Fig. 5. Comparison of generated image quality based on pose conditions with [14] at 256×256 on (a) Avatar Anime-Character dataset and (b) DeepFashion dataset.

---

[2] An illustration video for adding action to full-body anime characters with PSGAN is at https://youtu.be/0LQlfkvQ3Ok.

Next, we evaluate image quality on pose conditional image generation of PSGAN compared to Pose Guided Person Image Generation (PG2) [14]. PG2 requires a source image and a corresponding target pose to convert the source image to an image with the structure of the target pose. Meanwhile, PSGAN generates an image with the structure of the target pose from latent variables and the target pose and does not need paired training images. Figure 5 shows generated images of PSGAN and PG2 on the 256 × 256 resolution version of the Avatar dataset and DeepFashion dataset. We pick the weight parameter for L1 loss of PG2 (which affects image quality) to 1.0. The input image of PG2 is omitted. We can observe the generated images of PSGAN are less blurry and more detailed than PG2 due to structural conditions imposed at each scale.

4 Conclusion

In this paper, we have demonstrated smooth and high-resolution animation generation with PSGAN. We have shown that the method can generate full-body anime characters and the animations based on target pose sequences at 1024 × 1024 resolution. PSGAN progressively increases the resolution of generated images with structural conditions at each scale during training and generates detailed images for structured objects, such as full-body characters. As PSGAN generates images with latent variables and structural conditions, it is able to generate controllable animations with target pose sequences. Our experimental results demonstrate that PSGAN can generate a variety of high-quality anime characters from random latent variables, and smooth animations by imposing continuous pose sequences as structural conditions. Since the experimental setting still remains limited, such as one avatar and several actions, we plan to conduct experiments and evaluation in various conditions. We plan to make the Avatar Anime-Character dataset available in the near future.

References

1. Balakrishnan, G., Zhao, A., Dalca, A.V., Durand, F., Guttag, J.: Synthesizing images of humans in unseen poses. In: Proceedings of CVPR (2018)
2. Cao, Z., Simon, T., Wei, S.E., Sheikh, Y.: Realtime multi-person 2D pose estimation using part affinity fields. In: Proceedings of CVPR (2016)
3. Chen, W., et al.: Synthesizing training images for boosting human 3D pose estimation. In: Proceedings of 3D Vision (2016)
4. Goodfellow, I.: NIPS 2016 tutorial: generative adversarial networks. arXiv:1701.00160 (2017)
5. Goodfellow, I.J., et al.: Generative adversarial nets. In: Proceedings of NIPS (2014)
6. Gulrajani, I., Ahmed, F., Arjovsky, M., Dumoulin, V., Courville, A.: Improved training of Wasserstein GANs. In: Proceedings of NIPS (2017)
7. Hu, Y., Wu, X., Yu, B., He, R., Sun, Z.: Pose-guided photorealistic face rotation. In: Proceedings of CVPR (2018)
8. Isola, P., Zhu, J.Y., Zhou, T., Efros, A.A.: Image-to-image translation with conditional adversarial networks. In: Proceedings of CVPR (2017)

9. Jin, Y., Zhang, J., Li, M., Tian, Y., Zhu, H.: Towards the high-quality anime characters generation with generative adversarial networks. In: Proceedings of NIPS Workshop on Machine Learning for Creativity and Design (2017)
10. Karras, T., Aila, T., Laine, S., Lehtinen, J.: Progressive growing of GANs for improved quality, and stability, and variation. In: Proceedings of ICLR (2018)
11. Kingma, D.P., Ba, J.: Adam: a method for stochastic optimizations. In: Proceedings of ICLR (2015)
12. Liu, Z., Luo, P., Qiu, S., Wang, X., Tang, X.: DeepFashion: powering robust clothes recognition and retrieval with rich annotations. In: Proceedings of CVPR (2016)
13. Ma, L., Sun, Q., Georgoulis, S., Gool, L.V., Schiele, B., Fritz, M.: Disentangled person image generation. In: Proceedings of CVPR (2018)
14. Ma, L., Sun, Q., Jia, X., Schiele, B., Tuytelaars, T., Gool, L.V.: Pose guided person image generation. In: Proceedings of NIPS (2017)
15. Qiao, F., Yao, N., Jiao, Z., Li, Z., Chen, H., Wang, H.: Geometry-contrastive generative adversarial network for facial expression synthesis. arXiv:1802.01822 (2018)
16. Radford, A., Metz, L., Chintala, S.: Unsupervised representation learning with deep convolutional generative adversarial networks. In: Proceedings of ICLR (2016)
17. Reed, S., Akata, Z., Yan, X., Logeswaran, L., Schiele, B., Lee, H.: Generative adversarial text to image synthesis. In: Proceedings of ICML (2017)
18. Si, C., Wang, W., Wang, L., Tan, T.: Multistage adversarial losses for pose-based human image synthesis. In: Proceedings of CVPR (2018)
19. Siarohin, A., Sangineto, E., Lathuiliere, S., Sebe, N.: Deformable GANs for pose-based human image generation. In: Proceedings of CVPR (2018)
20. Varol, G., et al.: Learning from synthetic humans. In: Proceedings of CVPR (2017)
21. Vondrick, C., Pirsiavash, H., Torralba, A.: Generating videos with scene dynamics. In: Proceedings of NIPS (2016)
22. Wang, T.C., Liu, M.Y., Zhu, J.Y., Tao, A., Kautz, J., Catanzaro, B.: High-resolution image synthesis and semantic manipulation with conditional GANs. In: Proceedings of CVPR (2018)
23. Zhang, H., et al.: Stackgan++: realistic image synthesis with stacked generative adversarial networks. TPAMI (2018)
24. Zhang, Z., Xie, Y., Yang, L.: Photographic text-to-image synthesis with a hierarchically-nested adversarial network. In: Proceedings of CVPR (2018)
25. Zhu, J.Y., Park, T., Isola, P., Efros, A.A.: Unpaired image-to-image translation using cycle-consistent adversarial networks. In: Proceedings of ICCV (2017)

Convolutional Photomosaic Generation via Multi-scale Perceptual Losses

Matthew Tesfaldet[1,2]([✉]), Nariman Saftarli[3]([✉]), Marcus A. Brubaker[1,2]([✉]), and Konstantinos G. Derpanis[2,3]([✉])

[1] Department of Electrical Engineering and Computer Science,
York University, Toronto, Canada
{mtesfald,mab}@eecs.yorku.ca
[2] Vector Institute, Toronto, Canada
[3] Department of Computer Science, Ryerson University, Toronto, Canada
{nsaftarli,kosta}@scs.ryerson.ca

Abstract. Photographic mosaics (or simply *photomosaics*) are images comprised of smaller, equally-sized image tiles such that when viewed from a distance, the tiled images of the mosaic collectively resemble a perceptually plausible image. In this paper, we consider the challenge of automatically generating a photomosaic from an input image. Although computer-generated photomosaicking has existed for quite some time, none have considered simultaneously exploiting colour/grayscale intensity and the structure of the input across scales, as well as image semantics. We propose a convolutional network for generating photomosaics guided by a multi-scale perceptual loss to capture colour, structure, and semantics across multiple scales. We demonstrate the effectiveness of our multi-scale perceptual loss by experimenting with producing extremely high resolution photomosaics and through the inclusion of ablation experiments that compare with a single-scale variant of the perceptual loss. We show that, overall, our approach produces visually pleasing results, providing a substantial improvement over common baselines.

Keywords: Photomosaic · ASCII text · Deep learning · Perceptual loss · Multi-scale analysis

1   Introduction

Photographic mosaics (or simply *photomosaics*) are images comprised of smaller, equally-sized image tiles (or "templates") such that when viewed from a distance, the tiled images of the mosaic collectively resemble a perceptually plausible image. Although the term has existed since the 1990s (specifically for photography), the unique art form of stitching together a series of adjacent pictures to produce a scene has existed since the 1970s. They are inspired from traditional mosaics, an ancient art form dating back at least as far as 1500 BCE, where scenes and patterns were depicted using coloured pieces of glass, stone or

© Springer Nature Switzerland AG 2019
L. Leal-Taixé and S. Roth (Eds.): ECCV 2018 Workshops, LNCS 11131, pp. 75–83, 2019.
https://doi.org/10.1007/978-3-030-11015-4_9

(a) Input   (b) Soft selection   (c) Hard selection
                     (during training)   (during inference)

Fig. 1. Given an input image, (a), and a collection of template images (pictured are 8×8 Apple emoji templates), our convolutional network generates a photomosaic, (c), that is perceptually similar to the input. For training our model, we exploit a continuous relaxation of the non-differentiable discrete template selection process to encourage the "soft" outputs, (b), to be as one-hot as possible for proper evaluation by our multi-scale perceptual metric. Zoom in for details.

other materials. Here we focus on *computer-generated* photomosaics. Computer-generated photomosaicking relies on various algorithms to select suitable combinations of templates from a given collection to compose a photomosaic that is perceptually similar to a target image.

In early work, Harmon and Knowlton experimented with creating large prints from collections of small symbols or images. In their famous artwork, "Studies in Perception I" [6], they created an image of a choreographer by scanning a photograph with a camera and converting the grayscale values into typographic symbols. This piece was exhibited at one of the earliest computer art exhibitions, "The Machine as Seen at the End of the Mechanical Age", held at the Museum of Modern Art in New York City in 1968. Soon after, Harmon [7] investigated how much information is required for recognizing and discriminating faces and what information is the most important for perception. To demonstrate that very little detail was required for humans to recognize a face, he included a mosaic rendering of Abraham Lincoln consisting of varying shades of gray. Based on Harmon's findings, Salvador Dalí, in 1976, created the popular photomosaic, "Gala Contemplating the Mediterranean Sea" [4]. This was among the first examples of photomosaicking, and one of the first by a recognized artist.

Generally, there are two methods of photomosaicking: *patch-wise* (*e.g.*, [14]) and *pixel-wise* (*e.g.*, [18]). Patch-wise photomosaicking involves matching each tiled region with a template consisting of the closest average colour. In pixel-wise photomosaicking the matching is done on a per-pixel level between the pixels of the target image and the templates. This is computationally more expensive but generally produces more visually pleasing results since the per-pixel matching allows a rudimentary matching of structure.

Computer-generated photomosaicking has mostly been explored in the context of matching colour/grayscale intensities and, in an extremely limited sense, structures. Pixel-wise methods are limited to matching the colour of individual pixels, while patch-wise methods typically use simple similarity metrics that may miss important structural information, *e.g.*, edges, curves, etc. Both are limited to analysis at a single scale and generally ignore overall image semantics when producing a photomosaic. In contrast, our proposed approach involves a holistic analysis of colour, structure, and semantics across multiple scales.

Jetchev *et al.* [8] experimented with using convolutional networks (ConvNets) to form a perceptually-based mosaicking model; however, their approach was limited to a texture transfer process and consequently was not true photomosaicking, *i.e.*, their outputs did not consist of tiled images. Furthermore, their approach did not account for matching colours between the input and output, only structure, and only at a single scale.

In this paper, we propose a perceptually-based approach to generating photomosaics from images using a ConvNet. We rely on a perceptual loss [9] for guiding the discrete selection process of templates to generate a photomosaic. Inspired by previous work [17], we extend the perceptual loss over multiple scales. Our approach is summarized in Fig. 1.

We make the following contributions. Given a discrete set of template images, we propose a feed-forward ConvNet for generating photomosaics. To the authors' knowledge, we are the first to demonstrate a ConvNet for photomosaicking that utilizes a perceptual metric. We demonstrate the effectiveness of our multi-scale perceptual loss by experimenting with producing extremely high resolution photomosaics and through the inclusion of ablation experiments that compare with a single-scale variant of the perceptual loss. We show that, overall, our approach produces visually pleasing results with a wide variety of templates, providing a substantial improvement over common baselines.

2 Technical Approach

Given an RGB input image, $\mathbf{X} \in \mathbb{R}^{H \times W \times 3}$, our goal is to generate a photomosaic, $\mathbf{Y} \in \mathbb{R}^{H \times W \times 3}$, where H and W denote the image height and width. For every non-overlapping tiled region in the image, we learn a distribution of weightings (or coefficients) for selecting templates. This is represented using a map of one-hot encodings, denoted by $\mathbf{C} \in [0, 1]^{(H/H_T) \times (W/W_T) \times N_T}$, where H_T, W_T, and N_T denote the template height, template width, and the number of templates, respectively. Each spatial position on this map contains a one-hot encoding denoted by $\mathbf{c}_{r,c}$, where r and c correspond to its row and column position on the map. RGB templates, $\mathbf{T} \in \mathbb{R}^{H_T \times W_T \times 3N_T}$, are given and fixed between training and testing. In Sect. 2.1, we outline our encoder-decoder ConvNet architecture. Section 2.2 describes how we exploit a continuous relaxation of the argmax function to make training differentiable. Finally, Sect. 2.3 describes our multi-scale perceptual loss which is used to train the decoder portion of the function.

2.1 Encoder-Decoder Architecture

Our ConvNet is designed as an encoder-decoder network that takes $\mathbf{X}$ as input and produces $\mathbf{Y}$ as the photomosaic output. We adopt the VGG-16 [16] ConvNet pre-trained on the ImageNet dataset [15] as the encoder portion of our network, which is kept fixed. For the purpose of photomosaicking, we find using the layers up to pool3 of VGG-16 to be sufficient. Our decoder is as follows: a $1 \times 1 \times 256$ (corresponding to $height \times width \times num\_filters$) convolution, a ReLU activation, a $3 \times 3 \times N_T$ convolution (3×3 to encourage template consistency among neighbours), and a channel-wise softmax to produce the template coefficients. To keep the range of activations stable, we use layer normalization [2] after each convolution in the decoder. In all convolutional layers we use a stride of 1.

For each tiled region, $\mathbf{y}_{r,c}$, of the final output, $\mathbf{Y}$, let $\mathbf{c}_{r,c}(i)$ be the i-th coefficient of the one-hot encoding corresponding to that region and $\mathbf{T}(i) \in \mathbb{R}^{H_T \times W_T \times 3}$ the i-th template of RGB templates $\mathbf{T}$. The output $\mathbf{y}_{r,c}$ is generated by linearly combining the templates for that region by their respective template coefficients,

$$\mathbf{y}_{r,c} = \sum_{i=1}^{N_T} \mathbf{c}_{r,c}(i)\mathbf{T}(i). \tag{1}$$

The final output, $\mathbf{Y}$, is a composition of each tiled output $\mathbf{y}_{r,c}$.

2.2 Learning a Discrete Selection of Templates

Key to our approach is the *discrete* selection of templates at each tiled region. This is necessary to produce a photomosaic. During training, however, using an argmax to select the template with the maximal coefficient is not possible because the argmax function is non-differentiable. Instead, we exploit a continuous relaxation of the argmax by annealing the softmax that produces the coefficients. In particular, we gradually upscale the softmax inputs during training by $1/\tau$, where τ is the "temperature" parameter that is gradually "cooled" (*i.e.*, reduced) as training progresses. In the limit as $\tau \to 0$, the softmax function approaches the argmax function and Eq. 1 becomes nearly equivalent to a discrete sampler, as desired. Specifically, the softmax distribution of coefficients nears a one-hot distribution. This encourages the network to select a single template for each tiled region. During inference, however, instead of linearly combining templates by their respective coefficients, each tiled region output, $\mathbf{y}_{r,c}$, can be generated by selecting the template corresponding to the argmax of the distribution of coefficients, $\mathbf{c}_{r,c}$.

2.3 Multi-scale Perceptual Loss

So-called "perceptual losses" have previously been used as a representation of salient image content for image stylization tasks, *e.g.*, image style transfer [5,9]. Instead of generating images based on differences between raw colour pixel values, perceptual losses are used to enable high quality generation of images based on differences between low-level to high-level image feature representations extracted from the convolutional layers of a pre-trained ConvNet. To that end, we use a perceptual loss [9] to guide the network to produce photomosaics that are perceptually similar to the input. Specifically, the perceptual loss measures the difference between low-level features (*e.g.*, visual content such as edges, colours, curves) to high-level features (*e.g.*, semantic content such as faces and objects) computed on the input image and the output photomosaic. Like our encoder, we use the VGG-16 [16] ConvNet pre-trained on the ImageNet dataset [15]. However, here it is used as a perceptual metric and layers conv1_1, conv2_1, conv3_1, conv4_1, and conv5_1 are used for computing the perceptual loss. Formally, let $\phi_l(\mathbf{X})$ be the activations of the l-th layer of VGG-16 when processing input $\mathbf{X}$. The perceptual loss is computed as the average Mean Squared Error (MSE) between feature representations of $\mathbf{X}$ and $\mathbf{Y}$,

$$L(\mathbf{X}, \mathbf{Y}) = \frac{1}{L} \sum_l \|\phi_l(\mathbf{X}) - \phi_l(\mathbf{Y})\|_2^2, \tag{2}$$

where L is the number of layers used for computing the perceptual loss.

To produce visually accurate photomosaics, we require the objective to consider the content within each tiled region as well as the content spanning multiple tiled regions. This necessitates analysis across multiple scales. Motivated by prior work [10,17], we compute the perceptual loss (Eq. 2) on a Gaussian pyramid [3] of the input and output. This guides the decoder to select templates that closely match the content within each tiled region, as well as collectively match the overall content of the input. To mitigate the influence of seams between tiled regions, we blur the photomosaic output before feeding it into the loss. Our final objective is as follows:

$$L(\mathbf{X}, B(\mathbf{Y})) = \frac{1}{SL} \sum_s \sum_l \|\phi_l(\mathbf{X}^s) - \phi_l(B(\mathbf{Y}^s))\|_2^2, \tag{3}$$

where input $\mathbf{X}^s$ is taken from the s-th level of a Gaussian pyramid, $B(\mathbf{Y}^s)$ is the blurred photomosaic output taken from the same level, and S is the number of scales used for the pyramid.

Training. For training the weights of our decoder, we use the images from the Microsoft COCO dataset [13]. We train on a merger of the train, test, and validation splits of COCO. We resize each image to 512×512 and train with a batch size of 12 for 2,000 iterations. We use the Adam optimizer [11] with a learning rate of $6e-3$ that is exponentially decayed every 100 iterations at a rate of 0.96. We follow a temperature cooling schedule starting from $\tau = 1$ and gradually decreasing τ every 10 iterations until $\tau = 0.067$. Our network is implemented using TensorFlow [1]. Training roughly takes 20 min on an NVIDIA Titan V GPU. Figure 2 shows results using various 8×8 templates on a 512×512 input.

Fig. 2. Photomosaic results using 8×8 "glyphs" as templates. (left-to-right) Input, Apple emoji icons, sprites from "Super Mario Bros.", ASCII characters, text characters from "The Matrix". Zoom in for details.

3   Experiments

To evaluate our approach, we perform two experiments: a baseline qualitative comparison using nearest neighbour with both a simple L2 metric and with a Structural SIMilarity (SSIM) [19] metric, which is a perception-based metric that attempts to address shortcomings of L2 by taking the local image structure into account; and a qualitative comparison between using a single scale and multiple scales for the perceptual loss. Finally, we experiment with producing extremely high resolution photomosaics. For our full photomosaic results, collection of templates used, and source code, please refer to the supplemental material on the project website: ryersonvisionlab.github.io/perceptual-photomosaic-projpage.

   (a) Input   (b) NN with L2   (c) NN with SSIM   (d) Ours

Fig. 3. Baseline comparisons. Given an input image, (a), photomosaics are generated using nearest neighbour (NN) with an L2 metric, (b), NN with a SSIM metric, (c), and our convolutional approach, (d). From (b) to (d), the top row of photomosaics consist of Apple emoji templates and the bottom row of photomosaics consist of oriented edge templates. Zoom in for details.

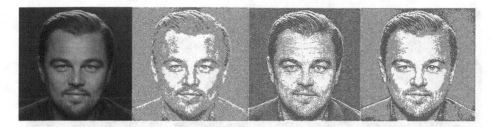

Fig. 4. Photomosaic outputs when using a single vs multi-scale perceptual loss. (left-to-right) Input, single-scale at a fine scale, single-scale at a coarse scale, multi-scale at both fine and coarse scales. Zoom in for details.

Baselines. To demonstrate that our approach improves upon common baselines in capturing colour, structure, and semantics across multiple scales, we compare against nearest neighbour with L2 and SSIM for template selection on two sets of templates: the complete set of emojis from Apple, and a specially-designed set of templates of oriented edges at varying thicknesses and rotations. Photomosaics are generated as follows: for each tiled region, the template with the lowest L2 loss or highest SSIM when compared with the underlying image content (in raw colour pixel values) is selected. Figure 3 shows our results. Nearest neighbour with L2 (Fig. 3b) completely fails in retaining both the colour and structure of the input. With SSIM (Fig. 3c), some structure of the input is preserved, albeit only at small scales, while colour accuracy is generally lacking. Moreover, both methods do not preserve the semantics of the input, such as the subject's hair, nose, and eyes. In contrast, our approach (Fig. 3d) reliably captures the colour, structure, and semantics of the image.

Single vs. Multi-scale. We perform an ablation study on our multi-scale perceptual loss to present the individual contributions of each scale (*i.e.*, fine and coarse) and to motivate the benefit of incorporating information across multiple scales. When the perceptual loss is operating on a single scale, it is restricted to scrutinizing the photomosaic output at that scale. As shown in Fig. 4, when the scale is only at a fine level, the output fails to preserve larger structures like the outline around the subject's jawline and ears. At a coarse level, the reduction in resolution prevents finer details from being captured, such as the orientation of edges in the input image, resulting in a noisier output. However, when using the multi-scale perceptual loss operating on both fine and coarse scales, the output reliably preserves both the finer details and the coarse structure of the image.

High Resolution. To demonstrate the effectiveness of using a multi-scale perceptual loss, we experiment with generating extremely high resolution photomosaics, as shown in Fig. 5. The input is a $5,280 \times 3,960$ image of Vincent Van Gogh's painting, "Starry Night", and the output is a visually compelling $10,560 \times 7,936$ photomosaic. The multi-scale perceptual loss enables the model

Fig. 5. High resolution photomosaics. (left) A $5,280 \times 3,960$ input and (right) a $10,560 \times 7,936$ photomosaic using 32×32 templates from a collection of 17,500 rotated and colour-shifted images taken from the top-100 images from the Hubble Space Telescope [12]. Shown are the downsampled versions of the images to save space; please see the supplemental for the full resolution images.

to capture both the coarse scale and fine scale features of the input. For example, the input image content spanning multiple tiled regions (*e.g.*, the large black tower and the stars) are reliably captured in the photomosaic through the appropriate composition of templates, while the input image content within tiled regions are reliably captured through the appropriate selection of templates that match the underlying image structure, such as the orientation and colour of the brush strokes.

4   Conclusion

In this paper, we presented a ConvNet for generating photomosaics of images given a collection of template images. We rely on a multi-scale perceptual loss to guide the discrete selection process of templates to generate photomosaics that best preserve colour, structure, and semantics of the input across multiple scales. We show that our approach produces visually pleasing results with a wide variety of templates, providing a substantial improvement over common baselines. We demonstrate the benefits of a multi-scale perceptual loss through the inclusion of ablation experiments and by experimenting with generating extremely high resolution photomosaics.

Acknowledgements. MT is supported by a Natural Sciences and Engineering Research Council of Canada (NSERC) Canadian Graduate Scholarship. KGD and MAB are supported by NSERC Discovery Grants. This research was undertaken as part of the Vision: Science to Applications program, thanks in part to funding from the Canada First Research Excellence Fund.

References

1. Abadi, M., et al.: TensorFlow: a system for large-scale machine learning. In: 12th USENIX Symposium on Operating Systems Design and Implementation (OSDI 2016), pp. 265–283 (2016). https://www.usenix.org/system/files/conference/osdi16/osdi16-abadi.pdf
2. Ba, J.L., Kiros, J.R., Hinton, G.E.: Layer normalization. arXiv:1607.06450 (2016)
3. Burt, P.J., Adelson, E.H.: The Laplacian pyramid as a compact image code. IEEE Trans. Commun. **31**, 532–540 (1983)
4. Dalí, S.: Gala Contemplating the Mediterranean Sea which at Twenty Meters Becomes the Portrait of Abraham Lincoln Exhibited in 1976. Guggenheim Museum, New York
5. Gatys, L.A., Ecker, A.S., Bethge, M.: Image style transfer using convolutional neural networks. In: CVPR, pp. 2414–2423 (2016)
6. Harmon, L., Knowlton, K., Hay, D.: Studies in Perception I Exhibited at The Machine as Seen at the End of the Mechanical Age, 27 November 1968– 9 February 1969, The Museum of Modern Art, New York
7. Harmon, L.D.: The recognition of faces. Sci. Am. **229**(5), 70–83 (1973)
8. Jetchev, N., Bergmann, U., Seward, C.: GANosaic: mosaic creation with generative texture manifolds. In: NIPS Workshop (2017)
9. Johnson, J., Alahi, A., Fei-Fei, L.: Perceptual losses for real-time style transfer and super-resolution. In: Leibe, B., Matas, J., Sebe, N., Welling, M. (eds.) ECCV 2016. LNCS, vol. 9906, pp. 694–711. Springer, Cham (2016). https://doi.org/10.1007/978-3-319-46475-6_43
10. Ke, T.W., Maire, M., Yu, S.X.: Multigrid neural architectures. In: CVPR, pp. 6665–6673 (2017)
11. Kingma, D.P., Ba, J.: Adam: a method for stochastic optimization. In: ICLR (2014)
12. Kornmesser, M.: Top 100 images. https://www.spacetelescope.org/images/archive/top100 (2015), images by ESA/Hubble (M. Kornmesser)
13. Lin, T.-Y., et al.: Microsoft COCO: common objects in context. In: Fleet, D., Pajdla, T., Schiele, B., Tuytelaars, T. (eds.) ECCV 2014. LNCS, vol. 8693, pp. 740–755. Springer, Cham (2014). https://doi.org/10.1007/978-3-319-10602-1_48
14. Martins, D.: Photo-mosaic (2014). https://github.com/danielfm/photo-mosaic. Accessed 15 July 2018
15. Russakovsky, O., et al.: ImageNet large scale visual recognition challenge. IJCV **115**(3), 211–252 (2015)
16. Simonyan, K., Zisserman, A.: Very deep convolutional networks for large-scale image recognition. In: ICLR (2015)
17. Snelgrove, X.: High-resolution multi-scale neural texture synthesis. In: SIGGRAPH ASIA Technical Briefs (2017)
18. Tran, N.: Generating photomosaics: an empirical study. In: SAC, pp. 105–109 (1999)
19. Wang, Z., Bovik, A.C., Sheikh, H.R., Simoncelli, E.P.: Image quality assessment: from error visibility to structural similarity. IEEE Trans. Signal Process **13**, 600–612 (2004)

W15 – Anticipating Human Behavior

W15 – Anticipating Human Behavior

In contrast to humans that are very good in anticipating the behavior of other objects, animals, or humans, developing methods that anticipate human behavior from video or other sensor data is very challenging and has just recently received an increase of interest. The purpose of the workshop *Anticipating Human Behavior* was therefore to discuss recent approaches that anticipate human behavior from video or other sensor data, to bring together researchers from multiple fields and perspectives, and to discuss major research problems and opportunities and how we should coordinate efforts to advance the field.

For the workshop, 9 out of 16 submissions were accepted and presented as talks at the workshop. All accepted papers are published in these proceedings and cover the anticipation of trajectories, hands, objects, actions, video frames, and semantic segmentation. In addition, we had two invited keynote talks by Michael S. Ryoo (Indiana University, USA) on *Robots Anticipating Future Scene* and by Dariu M. Gavrila (Delft University of Technology, The Netherlands) on *Vulnerable Road User Path Prediction*. Furthermore, 11 posters were presented which included already published work as well as work in progress:

- Long Zhao et al. *Learning to Forecast and Refine Residual Motion for Image-to-Video Generation*
- Haoye Cai et al. *Deep Video Generation, Prediction and Completion of Human Action Sequences*
- Liang-Yan Gui et al. *Adversarial Geometry-Aware Human Motion Prediction*
- Marcos Baptista-Ríos et al. *Embarrassingly Simple Model for Early Action Proposal*
- Federico Becattini et al. *Am I done? Predicting Action Progress in Video*
- Fatemeh Ziaeetabar et al. *A Novel Semantic Framework for Anticipation of Manipulation Actions*
- Yazan Abu Farha et al. *When will you do what? - Anticipating Temporal Occurrences of Activities*
- Philipp Kratzer et al. *Motion Prediction with Gaussian Process Dynamical Models and Trajectory Optimization*
- Nicholas Rhinehart et al. *R2P2: A ReparameteRized Pushforward Policy for Diverse, Precise Generative Path Forecasting*
- Yuge Shi et al. *Action Anticipation with RBF Kernelized Feature Mapping RNN*
- Camille Couprie et al. *Predicting Future Instance Segmentations by Forecasting Convolutional Features*

We thank all members of the program committee, presenters, and participants of this workshop. We also thank the German Research Foundation for financial support (DFG Research Unit FOR 2535 Anticipating Human Behavior).

September 2018

Juergen Gall
Jan van Gemert
Kris Kitani

Action Anticipation by Predicting Future Dynamic Images

Cristian Rodriguez[1,2](✉) , Basura Fernando[1,2](✉) , and Hongdong Li[1,2](✉)

[1] Australian National University, Canberra, Australia
{cristian.rodriguez,basura.fernando,hongdong.li}@anu.edu.au
[2] Australian Centre for Robotic Vision, Brisbane, Australia

Abstract. Human action-anticipation methods predict what is the future action by observing only a few portion of an action in progress. This is critical for applications where computers have to react to human actions as early as possible such as autonomous driving, human-robotic interaction, assistive robotics among others. In this paper, we present a method for human action anticipation by predicting the most plausible future human motion. We represent human motion using *Dynamic Images* [1] and make use of tailored loss functions to encourage a generative model to produce accurate future motion prediction. Our method outperforms the currently best performing action-anticipation methods by 4% on JHMDB-21, 5.2% on UT-Interaction and 5.1% on UCF 101-24 benchmarks.

Keywords: Action-anticipation · Prediction · Generation · Motion representation · Dynamic image

1 Introduction

When interacting with other people, human beings have the ability to anticipate the behaviour of others and act accordingly. This ability comes naturally to us and we make use of it subconsciously. Almost all human interactions rely on this *action-anticipation* capability. For example, when we greet each other, we tend to anticipate what is the most likely response and act slightly proactively. When driving a car, an experienced driver can often predict the behaviour of other road users. Tennis players predict the trajectory of the ball by observing the movements of the opponent. The ability to anticipate the action of others is essential for our social life and even survival. It is critical to transfer this ability to computers so that we can build smarter robots in the future, with better social interaction abilities that think and act fast.

Electronic supplementary material The online version of this chapter (https:// doi.org/10.1007/978-3-030-11015-4_10) contains supplementary material, which is available to authorized users.

L. Leal-Taixé and S. Roth (Eds.): ECCV 2018 Workshops, LNCS 11131, pp. 89–105, 2019.
https://doi.org/10.1007/978-3-030-11015-4_10

In computer vision, this topic is referred to as *action anticipation* [2–6] or early action prediction [7,8]. Although action anticipation is somewhat similar to *action recognition*, they differ by the information being exploited. Action-recognition processes the entire action within a video and generate a category label, whereas action-anticipation aims to recognise the action *as early as possible*. More precisely, action-anticipation needs to predict the future action labels as early as possible by processing fewer image frames (from the incoming video), even if the human action is still in progress.

Instead of directly predicting action labels [4], we propose a new method that generates future motion representation from partial observations of human action in a video. We argue that the generation of future motion representation is more intuitive task than generating future appearance, hence easier to achieve. A method that is generating future appearance given the current appearance requires to learn a conditional distribution of factors such as colour, illumination, objects and object parts, therefore, harder to achieve. In contrast, a method that learns to predict future motion does not need to learn those factors. Furthermore, motion information is useful for recognising human actions [9,10] and can be presented in various image forms [9,11].

In this paper we propose to predict future motion representation for action anticipation. Our method hallucinates what is in the next motion representation of a video sequence given only a fraction of a video depicting a partial human action. We make use of a convolutional autoencoder network that receives a motion image as input at time t and outputs a motion image for the future (*e.g.* $t+1$). Using Markov assumption, we generate more motion images of the future using already generated motion images (*i.e.* we generate motion images for time $t+1, \cdots, t+k$). Then we process generated motion images using Convolutional Neural Network (CNN) to make action predictions for the future. As we are able to generate future motion images, now we are able to predict human actions only observing few frames of a video containing an action.

We train our action anticipation and motion generation network with several loss functions. These loss functions are specifically tailored to generate accurate representations of future motion and to make accurate action predictions.

Clearly, the motion information depends on the appearance and vice versa. For example, motion representations such as the optical flow relies on two consecutive RGB frames. Similarly, the content of dynamic images [9] relies on the appearance of consecutive frames. The relationship between static appearance and motion information is somewhat surprising and mysterious [12]. Recently, proposed dynamic images has managed to explore this relationship to some degree of success [9]. In particular, dynamic images summarise the temporal evolution of appearance of few frames (*e.g.* 10 frames) into a single image. Therefore, this motion summary image (a.k.a. dynamic image) captures the motion information of those frames. In this work, we hallucinate dynamic images for the future and use them for the task of action anticipation[1].

---

[1] However, the main concept of this paper is applicable for other types of motion images as well (optical flow, motion history images).

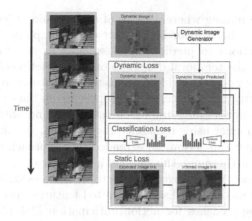

Fig. 1. Training of our generation module using multiple loss functions. **(a)** *Dynamic Loss* evaluates the difference in motion information between predicted and ground truth dynamic image using $\mathcal{L}_2$ norm. **(b)** *Classification Loss* takes care of generating dynamic images that are useful for action anticipation. **(c) Static Loss** computes the $\mathcal{L}_2$ norm between predicted and ground truth RGB information at $t + k$ to evaluate the difference in appearance.

We generate dynamic images using both expected appearance and motion of the future. Specifically, future dynamic images are generated by taking into account both reconstructive loss (coined *dynamic loss*) and future expected appearance which is coined *static loss*. As motion and appearances should adhere to each other, static loss is designed to satisfy expected future appearance in the generated dynamic images. In addition to that our generated dynamic images make use of class information and therefore discriminative. These loss functions are tailored to generate accurate future dynamic images as is depicted in Fig. 1. In a summary, we make the following contributions:

- Using a simple CNN architecture, we demonstrate the effectiveness of dynamic images for future content prediction.
- We design a set of effective loss functions to produce accurate future dynamic images.
- We obtain state-of-the-art performance for early activity recognition on standard benchmarks.

2   Related Work

Action prediction and anticipation literature can be classified into deep learning and non-deep learning-based methods.

Human activity prediction is studied using integral histograms of spatial-temporal bag-of-features coined dynamic bag-of-words in the early days [3]. Yu *et al.* [8] propose to use spatial-temporal action matching for early action prediction task using spatial-temporal implicit shape models. Li *et al.* [13], propose to explore sequence mining where a series of actions and object co-occurrences are encoded as symbolic sequences. Kong et al. [14] explore the temporal evolution of human actions to predict the class label as early as possible. This model [14] captures the temporal dynamics of human actions by explicitly considering all the history of observed features as well as features in smaller temporal segments. More recently, Soomro et al. [6] propose to use binary SVMs to localise and classify video snippets into sub-action categories and obtain the final class label in an online manner using dynamic programming. Because it is needed to train one classifier per sub-action, [5] extended this approach using a structural SVM formulation. Furthermore, this method introduces a new objective function to encourage the score of the correct action to increase as time progresses [5].

While all above methods utilise handcrafted features, most recent methods use deep learning approaches for action anticipation [2,4,15]. Deep learning-based methods can be primarily categorised into two types; 1. methods that rely on novel loss functions for action anticipation [2,4,16] and 2. methods that try to generate future content by content prediction [15].

In this context, [2] propose to use a Long Short-Term Memory (LSTM) with ranking loss to model the activity progression and use that for effective action prediction task. They use Convolutional Neural Network (CNN) features along with a LSTM to model both spatial and temporal information. Similarly, in [16], a new loss function known as the exponentially growing loss is proposed. It tries to penalize errors increasingly over time using a LSTM-based framework. Similarly, in [4], a novel loss function for action anticipation that aims to encourage correct predictions as early as possible is proposed. The method in [4] tries to overcome ambiguities in early stages of actions by preventing false negatives from the beginning of the sequence. Furthermore, a recently online action localisation method is presented which can also be used for online early action predictions [17]. However, this method primarily focuses on online action detection.

Instead of predicting the future class label, in [15], the authors propose to predict the future visual representation. However, the main motivation in [15] is to learn representations using unlabeled videos. Our work is different from [15] as we are predicting the future motion using dynamic images. We make use reconstruction loss, class information loss, and expected future appearance as a guide to predict future motion images. As our generated dynamic images are trained for action anticipation, they are class specific and different from original dynamic images [1]. As demonstrated, our generated dynamic images are more effective than original dynamic images for action anticipation task. Gao et al. [18] propose to generate future appearance using LSTM autoencoder to anticipate actions using both regression loss and classification loss. We argue that predicting future appearance representation is a complex task. We believe that action anticipation can benefit from motion prediction more than challenging appearance prediction.

Predicting the future content has been explored on other related problems in other domains of computer vision. Some of the work focuses on predicting (or forecasting) the future trajectories of pedestrians [19] or predicting motion

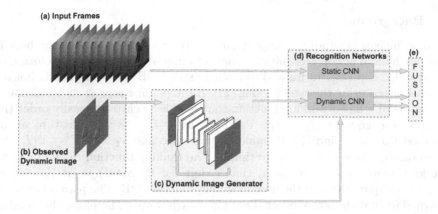

Fig. 2. Overview of our approach. We receive as an input a sequence of RGB video frames (**a**). Then we use RGB images with windows size T to compute the Dynamic Images for seen part of the video (**b**). The last dynamic image of the seen part is used to feed our dynamic image generator and generate $\hat{D}_{t+1}$ (**c**). Next, we feed *Dynamic* CNN with observed dynamic images and generated dynamic images and *Static* CNN with RGB images (**d**). Finally, we fusion all the outputs of our recognition networks (**e**).

from still images [19, 20]. However, we are the first to show the effectiveness of predicting good motion representations for early action anticipation.

3 Method

The objective of our work is to recognise human actions as early as possible from a video sequence depicting human action. We present a method that hallucinates future motion from a partially observed human action sequence (RGB video clip). Then we process these hallucinated future motion representations to make future action predictions a.k.a. action anticipation. Our motion representation is based on dynamic images [1, 9]. Dynamic images model dynamic information of a short video clip and summarise motion information to a single frame. We present a method to hallucinate future dynamic images using a convolutional autoencoder neural network. We process generated dynamic images to predict future human actions using a CNN named *dynamic CNN*. To improve action recognition performance further, we use observed still image appearance information and process them with a *static CNN*. Furthermore, we make use of dynamic images created from observed RGB data and use the same dynamic CNN to make predictions. Therefore, we make use of three kinds of predictions and fuse them to make the final prediction (see Fig. 2). In the following section, we present some background about dynamic images Sect. 3.1 and then we present our dynamic image generation model in Sect. 3.2. Then we discuss loss functions in Sect. 3.3 and how to train our model in Sect. 3.4.

3.1   Background

Dynamic images [1,9] are a compact motion representation of videos which is useful for human action recognition. They summarise the temporal evolution of a short video clip (*e.g.* 10 frames) to a single still RGB image. Dynamic images are constructed using the rank pooling [21]. Rank pooling represents a video as a parameters of a linear ranking function that is able to chronologically order the elements of a sequence $\langle I_1, ..., I_T \rangle$. Precisely, let $\psi(I_t) \in \mathbb{R}^d$ be a feature vector extracted from each individual frame in the video and $V_t = \frac{1}{t} \sum_{\tau=1}^{t} \psi(I_\tau)$ be the average of these features up to time t. The ranking function $S(t|\mathbf{d})$ predicts a ranking score for each frame at time t denoted by $S(t|\mathbf{d}) = \langle \mathbf{d}, V_t \rangle$, where $\mathbf{d} \in \mathbb{R}^d$ is the parameter of the linear ranking function [21]. The parameter set $\mathbf{d}$ is learned so that the score reflect the rank of each frame. Therefore, the ranking score for later frame at time q ($q > t$) is associated with a larger score, *i.e.* $S(q|\mathbf{d}) > S(t|\mathbf{d})$. Learning $\mathbf{d}$ is posed as a convex optimisation problem using the RankSVM [22] formulation given as Eq. 1.

$$\mathbf{d}^* = \rho(I_1, ..., I_t; \psi) = \operatorname*{argmin}_{d} E(\mathbf{d}),$$

$$E(\mathbf{d}) = \frac{\lambda}{2}||\mathbf{d}||^2 + \frac{2}{T(T-1)} \times \sum_{q>t} \max\{0, 1 - S(q|\mathbf{d}) + S(t|\mathbf{d})\}. \qquad (1)$$

Optimising Eq. 1 defines a function $\rho(I_1, ..., I_T; \psi)$ that maps a video sequence of length T to a single vector denoted by $\mathbf{d}$. Since this parameter vector contains enough information to rank all frames in the video clip, it aggregates temporal information from all frames. Therefore, it can be used as a video motion descriptor or a temporal descriptor.

When one applies this technique directly on RGB image pixels, the resulting $\mathbf{d}^*$ is known as the *dynamic image*. The output $\mathbf{d}^*$ has same dimensions as input images. Resulting dynamic image $\mathbf{d}^*$ summarises the temporal information of the RGB video sequence. Bilen *et al.* [1] present an approximation to rank pooling which is faster. This approximate rank pooling is essential for our method to hallucinate future dynamic images. Bilen *et al.* [1] proved that $\mathbf{d}^*$ can be expressed by the following Eq. 2.

$$\mathbf{d}^* = \sum_{t=1}^{T} \alpha_t I_t. \qquad (2)$$

The coefficients α_t are given by $\alpha_t = 2(T - t + 1) - (T + 1)(H_T - H_{t-1})$ where $H_t = \sum_{i=1}^{t} 1/i$ is the t-th Harmonic number and $H_0 = 0$. We construct dynamic images using approximated rank pooling by taking a weighted sum of input image sequence where weights are given by predefined coefficients α.

3.2   Future Motion Prediction Model

Given a collection of videos X with corresponding human action class labels Y, our aim is to predict the human action label as early as possible.

Each video $X_i \in X$ is a sequence of frames $X_i = \langle I_1, I_2, \cdots, I_n \rangle$ of variable length n. We process each sequence of RGB frames to obtain a sequence of dynamic images using Eq. 2. Instead of summarising the entire video with a single dynamic image, we propose to generate multiple dynamic images from a single video sequence using a fixed window size of length T. Therefore, each dynamic image is created using T consecutive frames. We process each training video X_i and obtain a sequence of dynamic images $\langle D_1, D_2, \cdots, D_n \rangle$. Our objective is to train a model that is able to predict the future dynamic image D_{t+k} given the current dynamic images up to time t $i.e.$ $\langle D_1, D_2, \cdots, D_t \rangle$. Therefore, we aim to model the following conditional probability distribution using a parametric model

$$P(D_{t+k}|\langle D_1, D_2, \cdots, D_t \rangle; \Theta) \tag{3}$$

where Θ are the parameters of our generative model ($k \geq 1$). We simplify this probabilistic model using the Markov assumption, hence now $k = 1$ and condition only on the previous dynamic image D_t. Then our model simplifies to following Eq. 4.

$$P(D_{t+1}|D_t; \Theta) \tag{4}$$

The model in Eq. 4 simplifies the training process. Furthermore, it may be possible to take advantage of different kinds of neural machine to implement the model in Eq. 4 such as autoencoders [23], variational conditional autoencoders [24,25] and conditional generative adversarial networks [26].

Now the challenge is to find a good neural technique and loss function to train such a model. We use a denoising convolutional autoencoder to hallucinate future dynamic images given the current ones. Our convolutional autoencoder receives a dynamic image at time t and outputs a dynamic image for next time step $t+1$. In practice, dynamic images up to time t is observed, and we recursively generate dynamic images for time $t + 1, \cdots, t + k$ using Markov assumption. Although we use a denoising convolutional autoencoder, our idea can also be implemented with other generative models. The autoencoder we use has 4 convolution stages. Each convolution has kernels of size 5×5 with a stride of 2 and the number of features maps for the convolution layers are set to 64, 128, 256, and 512 respectively. Then the deconvolution is the inverted mirror of the encoding network (see Fig. 2), which is inspired by the architecture used in DCGAN [27]. Next, we discuss suitable loss functions for training the autoencoder.

3.3   Loss Functions for Training the Autoencoder

First, we propose make use of reconstructive loss coined $Dynamic\ Loss$ to reduce the $\mathcal{L}_2$ distance between predicted dynamic image $\hat{D}_{t+1}$ and the ground truth dynamic image obtained from the training data D_{t+1} as shown in Eq. 5.

$$\mathcal{L}_{DL} = ||\hat{D}_{t+1} - D_{t+1}||_2 \tag{5}$$

Even though this loss function helps us to generate expected future dynamic image, it does not guarantee that the generated dynamic image is discriminative for action anticipation. Indeed, we would like to generate a dynamic image that contains more action class information. Therefore, we propose to explore the teacher-student networks [28] to teach the autoencoder to produce dynamic images that would be useful for action anticipation. First, we train a teacher CNN which takes dynamic images as input and produces the action category label. Let us denote this teacher CNN by $f(D_i; \Theta_{cnn})$ where it takes dynamic image D_i and produces the corresponding class label vector $\hat{y}_i$. This teacher CNN that takes dynamic images as input and outputs labels is called *Dynamic CNN* (see Fig. 2). This teacher CNN is trained with cross-entropy loss [29]. Let us denote our generator network as $g(D_t; \Theta) \rightarrow D_{t+1}$. We would like to take advantage of the teacher network $f(; \Theta_{cnn})$ to guide the student generator $g(D_t; \Theta)$ to produce future dynamic images that are useful for classification. Given a collection of current and future dynamic images with labels, we train the generator with the cross-entropy loss as follows:

$$\mathcal{L}_{CL} = - \sum_t y_i \log f(g(D_t; \Theta); \Theta_{cnn}) \qquad (6)$$

where we fix the CNN parameter Θ_{cnn}. Obviously, we make the assumption that CNN $f(D_i; \Theta_{cnn})$ is well trained and has good generalisation capacity. We call this loss as the *classification loss* which is denoted by $\mathcal{L}_{CL}$. In theory, compared to original dynamic images [1,9], our generated dynamic images are class specific and therefore discriminative.

Motion and appearance are related. Optical flow depends on the appearance of two consecutive frames. Dynamic images depends on the evolution of appearance of several consecutive frames. Therefore, it is important verify that generated future motion actually adhere to future expected appearance. Another advantage of using dynamic images to generate future motion is the ability exploit this property explicitly. We make use of future expected appearance to guide the generator network to produce accurate dynamic images. Let us explain what we mean by this. When we generate future dynamic image D_{t+1}, as demonstrated in Eq. 7, implicitly we also recover the future RGB frame I_{t+1}. Using this Eq. 7, we propose so-called *static loss* (SL) (Eq. 8) that consists of computing the $\mathcal{L}2$ loss between the generated RGB image $\hat{I}_{t+1}$ and real expected image I_{t+1}.

$$D_{t+1} = \sum_{i=1}^{T} \alpha_i I_{t+1+i}$$

$$D_{t+1} = \alpha_T I_{T+t+1} \sum_{i=1}^{T-1} \alpha_i I_{t+1+i}$$

$$I_{T+t+1} = \frac{D_{t+1} - \sum_{i=1}^{T-1} \alpha_i I_{t+1+i}}{\alpha_T} \qquad (7)$$

The applicability of static loss does not limit only to matching the future expected appearance, but also we guide the autoencoder model $g(; \Theta)$ to use all implicitly generated RGB frames from $\hat{I}_{t+2}$ to $\hat{I}_{T+t+1}$ making future dynamic image better by modeling the evolution of appearance of static images. Indeed, this is a better loss function than simply taking the dynamic loss as in Eq. 5.

$$\mathcal{L}_{SL} = ||\hat{I}_{T+t+1} - I_{T+t+1}||_2 \tag{8}$$

3.4 Multitask Learning

We train our autoencoder with multiple losses, the static loss ($\mathcal{L}_{SL}$), the dynamic loss ($\mathcal{L}_{DL}$) and the classification loss ($\mathcal{L}_{CL}$). By doing so, we aim to generate dynamic images that are good for the classification, as well as representative of future motion. With the intention to enforce all these requirements, we propose to train our autoencoder with batch wise multitask manner. Overall, one might write down the global loss function $\mathcal{L} = \lambda_{sl}\mathcal{L}_{SL} + \lambda_{dl}\mathcal{L}_{DL} + \lambda_{cl}\mathcal{L}_{CL}$. However, instead of finding good scalar weights $\lambda_{sl}, \lambda_{dl}$, and λ_{cl}, we propose to divide each batch into three sub-batches, and optimise each loss using only one of those sub batches. Therefore, during each batch, we optimise all losses with different sets of data. We found this strategy leads to better generalisation than optimising a linear combination of losses.

3.5 Inference

During inference, we receive RGB frames from a video sequence as input. Using those RGB frames, we compute *dynamic images* following Eq. 2 with a window size length $T = 10$. In the case that the amount of frames is less that what is needed to compute the dynamic image i.e. 10% of the video is observed, we compute the dynamic image with the available frames according to Eq. 2. We use the last dynamic image (D_t) to predict the following dynamic image ($\hat{D}_{t+1}$). We repeat this process to generate k number of future dynamic images using Markov assumption. We process each observed RGB frame, observed dynamic images and generated dynamic images by respective static and dynamic CNNs that are trained to make predictions (see Fig. 2). Then, we obtain a score vector for each RGB frame, dynamic image and generated dynamic image. We sum them together and use temporal average pooling to make the final prediction.

4   Experiments and Results

In this section, we perform a series of experiments to evaluate our action antic- ipation method. First, we present results for action recognition using the *static CNN* and the *dynamic CNN* in Sect. 4.1. Then, we evaluate the impact of differ- ent loss functions for generating future dynamic images in Sect. 4.2. After that in Sect. 4.3, we compare our method with state-of-the-art techniques for action anticipation. Finally, we present some other additional experiments to further analyse our model in Sect. 4.4.

Datasets. We test our method using three popular datasets for human action analysis JHMDB [30], UT-Interaction [31] and UCF101-24 [32], which have been used for action anticipation in recent prior works [4,6,17].

Table 1. Action recognition performance using dynamic and RGB images over JHMDB and UT-Interaction datasets. Action recognition performance is measured at frame level.

	JHMDB	UT-Interaction
Static CNN	55.0%	70.9%
Dynamic CNN	54.1%	71.8%

JHMDB dataset is a subset of the challenging HMDB51 dataset [33]. JHMDB is created by keeping action classes that involve a single person action. Videos have been collected from different sources such as movies and the world-wide-web. JHMDB dataset consists of 928 videos and 21 action classes. Each video contains one human action which usually starts at the beginning of the video. Following the recent literature for action anticipation [4], we report the average accuracy over the three splits and report results for so called *earliest* setup. For earliest recognition, action recognition performance is measured only after observing 20% of the video. To further understand our method, we also report recognition performance w.r.t. time (as a percentage). **UT-Interaction** dataset (UTI) contains 20 video sequences where the average length of a video is around 1 min. These videos contain complete executions of 6 human interaction classes: shake-hands, point, hug, push, kick and punch. Each video contains at least one execution of an interaction, and up to a maximum of 8 interactions. There are more than 15 different participants with different clothing. The videos are recorded with 30 fps and with a resolution of 720 × 480 which we resize to 320 × 240. To evaluate all methods, we use recommended 10-fold leave-one-out cross-validation per set and report the mean performance over all sets. **UCF101-24** dataset is a subset of the challenging UCF101 dataset. This subset of 24 classes contains spatio-temporal localisation annotation. It has been constructed for THUMOS-2013 challenge[2]. On average there are 1.5 action instances per video, each instance cover approximately 70% of the duration of video. We report the action-anticipation accuracy for set 1, as has been done previously in [17].

4.1 Training of *Static* and *Dynamic* CNNs

In this section, we explain how we train our *static* and *dynamic* CNNs (see Fig. 2). Similar to [1,9], we train a *Static CNN* for RGB frame-based video action recognition and a *Dynamic CNN* for dynamic image-based action recognition. In all our experiments, each dynamic image is constructed using 10 RGB frames (T = 10). We use different data augmentation techniques to reduce the effect of over-fitting. Images are randomly flipped horizontally, rotated by a random amount in a range of −20 to 20°, horizontally shifted in a range of −64 to 64 pixels, vertically shifted in a range of −48 to 48 pixels, sheared in a range of 10° counter-clockwise, zoomed in a range of 0.8 to 1.2 and shifted channels in a range of 0.3.

---

[2] http://crcv.ucf.edu/ICCV13-Action-Workshop/download.html.

Table 2. Results of using multitask learning to generate future dynamic images.

	JHMDB-21	UT-Interaction
$\mathcal{L}_{DL}$	42.8%	64.3%
$\mathcal{L}_{SL}$	49.5%	64.2%
$\mathcal{L}_{DL} + \mathcal{L}_{SL}$	53.4%	66.5%
$\mathcal{L}_{DL} + \mathcal{L}_{CL}$	52.5%	64.5%
$\mathcal{L}_{DL} + \mathcal{L}_{SL} + \mathcal{L}_{CL}$	54.0%	68.4%

We make use of pre-trained Inception Resnet V2 [29] to fine-tune both *Static CNN* and the *Dynamic CNN* using a learning rate of 0.0001. We use a batch size of 32 and a weight decay of 0.00004. We use ADAM [34] optimizer to train these networks using epsilon of 0.1 and beta 0.5. Action recognition performance using these CNNs for JHMDB and UTI datasets are reported in Table 1. Note that the action recognition performance in Table 1 is only at frame level (not video level). We use these trained *Static* and *Dynamic* CNNs in the generation of future motion representation, dynamic images, and action anticipation tasks.

4.2   Impact of Loss Functions

In this section we investigate the effectiveness of each loss function, explained in Sect. 3.3, in the generation process of future dynamic images. We evaluate the quality of the generated dynamic images in a *quantitative* evaluation. Using the dynamic CNN to report action recognition performance over generated dynamic images.

We perform this experiment constructing a sequence of dynamic images using Eq. 2 for each test video in the dataset. Then for each test dynamic image, we generate the future dynamic image using our convolutional autoencoder. Therefore, the number of generated dynamic images is almost equal to real testing dynamic images. Then we use our dynamic CNN (which has been pretrained in previous section) to evaluate the action recognition performance of generated dynamic images (**DIg**). Using this approach we can evaluate the impact of several loss functions in the generation of dynamic images.

We use the first split of JHMDB and the first set of UTI to perform this experiment. We make use of the three proposed losses in Sect. 3.3: dynamic-loss ($\mathcal{L}_{DL}$), class-based loss ($\mathcal{L}_{CL}$) and static-loss ($\mathcal{L}_{SL}$) to train our autoencoder. We train the convolutional autoencoder using ADAM solver with a batch size of 32, a learning rate of 0.0001. We train our model for 30 epochs using the same augmentation process used in Sect. 4.1.

We use the generalisation performance of *real dynamic images* from Table 1 as a reference to estimate the quality of generated dynamic images. Since, we measure the performance of generated dynamic images in the same way.

As can be seen in Table 2, a combination of $\mathcal{L}_{DL}$, $\mathcal{L}_{CL}$ and $\mathcal{L}_{SL}$ gives excellent recognition performance of 54.0% for the generated dynamic images which is

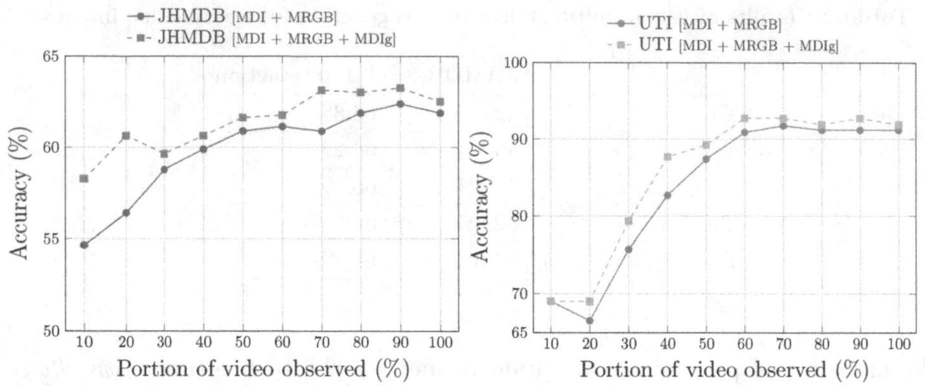

Fig. 3. Action anticipation performance with respect to portion of the video observed on JHMDB *(left)* and UTI *(right)* datasets.

very close to the model performance of single dynamic CNN 54.1% in the case of JHMDB dataset. Indicating that our generative model along with loss functions are capable of generating representative and useful future dynamic images. A similar trend can be seen for UTI dataset. Notice that the $\mathcal{L}_{DL}$ and $\mathcal{L}_{SL}$ already produce good recognition performance on JHMDB and UTI datasets, which suggest that those losses can generated images that understand the human motion. However, those generated images are not class specific. We conclude that convolutional autoencoder model trained with three losses is able to generate robust future dynamic images. These generated dynamic images are effective in action recognition.

4.3 Action Anticipation

Our action anticipation network consist of a *static* CNN and a *dynamic* CNN (see Fig. 2). Our action anticipation baseline uses observed multiple RGB frames and multiple dynamic images similar to [1]. In addition to that our method generates K number of future dynamic images and make use of them with dynamic CNN. Action anticipation performance is evaluated at different time steps after observing fraction of the video (*i.e.*, 10%, 20% of the video). Results are shown in Fig. 3, where we can see the effect of adding generated dynamic images (MDIg) to our pipeline. In the case of JHMDB the most significant improvement is obtained at 20% which is an enhancement of **5.1%** with respect to the baseline. In the UTI dataset, the most significant improvement is obtained at 40% of the video observed with a performance enhancement of **5.0%** with respect to the baseline. Moreover, the less significant improvement are obtained when the video observation approaches the 100% with a 0.62% and 0.71% of improvement with respect to the baseline on JHMDB and UTI dataset respectively.

Another standard practice is to report the action anticipation performance using *earliest* and *latest* prediction accuracies as done in [3,4]. Although, there

Table 3. Comparison of action anticipation methods on **JHMDB** dataset. 20% of video is observed at *Earliest*.

Method	Earliest	Latest
DP-SVM [5]	5%	46%
S-SVM [5]	5%	43%
Where/What [6]	12%	43%
Context-Aware + Loss of [16]	28%	43%
Ranking Loss [2]	29%	43%
Context-Aware + Loss of [2]	33%	39%
E-LSTM [4]	55%	58%
ROAD [17]	57%	68%
Ours	**61%**	63%

Table 5. Comparison of action anticipation methods using **UTI** dataset. 50% of the video is observed at *Earliest*.

Method	Earliest	Latest
S-SVN [5]	11.0%	13.4%
DP-SVM [5]	13.0%	14.6%
CuboidBayes [3]	25.0%	71.7%
CuboidSVM [35]	31.7%	85.0%
Context-Aware+Loss of [16]	45.0%	65.0%
Context-Aware+Loss of [2]	48.0%	60.0%
BP_SVM [36]	65.0%	83.3%
I-BoW [3]	65.0%	81.7%
D-BoW [3]	70.0%	85.0%
E-LSTM [4]	84.0%	90.0%
Ours	89.2%	91.9%

Table 4. Comparison of action anticipation methods on **UCF101-24** dataset. 10% of video is observed at Earliest.

	Earliest	Latest
ROAD (RTF) [17]	81.7%	83.9%
ROAD (AF) [17]	84.2%	85.5%
Ours	89.3%	90.2%

is no agreement of what is the proportion of frames used in earliest configuration through different datasets. We make use of the proportion that has been employed by baselines (20% and 50% of the video for JHMDB and UTI respectively). Therefore, following [4] we report results in Tables 3 and 5 for JHMDB and UTI datasets respectively. We outperform other methods that rely on additional information, such as optical flow [2,5,6] and Fisher vector features based on improved Dense Trajectories [5]. Our approach outperforms the state-of-the-art by **4.0%** on JHMDB and by **5.2%** on UTI datasets in the earliest configuration. Finally, we report results on UCF101-24 dataset for action anticipation. For this dataset, we use 10% of the video to predict the action class in the earliest configuration. As we can see in Table 4, We outperform previous method [17] by **5.1%** on the earliest configuration. A more detailed analysis using UCF101-24 dataset is provided on the supplementary material.

These experiments evidence the benefits of generating future motion information using our framework for action anticipation.

4.4 Further Exploration

In Fig. 4 we observe the influence of generating dynamic images recursively for earliest configuration in JHMDB and UTI datasets. We generate K number of future dynamic images recursively using the very last true dynamic image. As it can be seen in Fig. 4, as we generate more dynamic images into the future, the prediction performance degrades due to the error propagation. We report action recognition performance for each generated future dynamic image (*i.e.* for the generated future dynamic image at K). If we do not generate any dynamic image for the future, we obtain an action recognition performance of 55.9%. If we include generated dynamic images, we obtain a best of 61.0% on JHMDB. A similar trend can be seen for UTI dataset, where without future dynamic image we obtain 87.4% and after generation we obtain an action recognition performance of 89.2%. The influence of generating more future dynamic images is shown in Fig. 4.

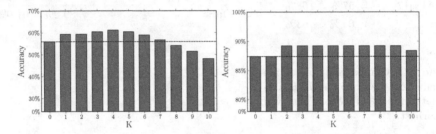

Fig. 4. Impact of generating more future dynamic images recursively on JHMDB *(left)* and UTI *(right)* datasets. K is the number of generated dynamic images based on observed RGB frames. K = 0 means no dynamic image is generated.

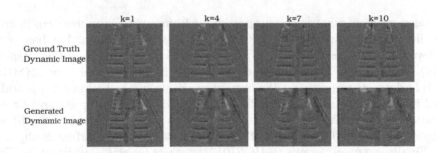

Fig. 5. Visual comparison between generated dynamic image *(bottom)* and ground truth *(top)*. K refers to how many iterations we apply in the generation of dynamic image.

Finally, we visually inspect the recursively generated dynamic images for K equal to 1, 4, 7 and 10 in Fig. 5. Although, we can use our model to generate quite accurate dynamic images, as we predict into the further, the generated dynamic images might contain some artifacts.

5 Discussion

In this paper, we demonstrate how to hallucinate future video motion representation for action anticipation. We propose several loss functions to train our generative model in a multitask scheme. Our experiments demonstrate the effectiveness of our loss functions to produce better future video representation for the task of action anticipation. Moreover, experiments show that made use of the hallucinated future video motion representations improves the action anticipation results of our powerful backbone network. With our simple approach we have outperformed the state-of-the-art in action anticipation in three important action anticipation benchmarks. In the future, we would like to incorporate additional sources of information to hallucinate other dynamics such as optical flow using the same framework. Furthermore, we would like to extend this method to predict dynamic images further into the future.

Acknowledgments. We thank NVIDIA Corporation for the donation of the GPUs used in this work.

References

1. Bilen, H., Fernando, B., Gavves, E., Vedaldi, A., Gould, S.: Dynamic image networks for action recognition. In: CVPR (2016)
2. Ma, S., Sigal, L., Sclaroff, S.: Learning activity progression in LSTMs for activity detection and early detection. In: CVPR (2016)
3. Ryoo, M.S.: Human activity prediction: early recognition of ongoing activities from streaming videos. In: ICCV (2011)
4. Sadegh Aliakbarian, M., Sadat Saleh, F., Salzmann, M., Fernando, B., Petersson, L., Andersson, L.: Encouraging LSTMs to anticipate actions very early. In: ICCV (2017)
5. Soomro, K., Idrees, H., Shah, M.: Online localization and prediction of actions and interactions. arXiv:1612.01194 (2016)
6. Soomro, K., Idrees, H., Shah, M.: Predicting the where and what of actors and actions through online action localization. In: CVPR (2016)
7. Lan, T., Chen, T.-C., Savarese, S.: A hierarchical representation for future action prediction. In: Fleet, D., Pajdla, T., Schiele, B., Tuytelaars, T. (eds.) ECCV 2014. LNCS, vol. 8691, pp. 689–704. Springer, Cham (2014). https://doi.org/10.1007/978-3-319-10578-9_45
8. Yu, G., Yuan, J., Liu, Z.: Predicting human activities using spatio-temporal structure of interest points. In: ACMMM (2012)
9. Bilen, H., Fernando, B., Gavves, E., Vedaldi, A.: Action recognition with dynamic image networks. IEEE Trans. Pattern Anal. Mach. Intell. **PP**(99), 1 (2017)
10. Simonyan, K., Zisserman, A.: Two-stream convolutional networks for action recognition in videos. In: NIPS (2014)

11. Ahad, M.A.R., Tan, J.K., Kim, H., Ishikawa, S.: Motion history image: its variants and applications. Mach. Vis. Appl. **23**(2), 255–281 (2012)
12. Carreira, J., Zisserman, A.: Quo Vadis, action recognition? A new model and the kinetics dataset. In: CVPR (2017)
13. Li, K., Fu, Y.: Prediction of human activity by discovering temporal sequence patterns. IEEE Trans. Pattern Anal. Mach. Intell. **36**(8), 1644–1657 (2014)
14. Kong, Y., Kit, D., Fu, Y.: A discriminative model with multiple temporal scales for action prediction. In: Fleet, D., Pajdla, T., Schiele, B., Tuytelaars, T. (eds.) ECCV 2014. LNCS, vol. 8693, pp. 596–611. Springer, Cham (2014). https://doi.org/10.1007/978-3-319-10602-1_39
15. Vondrick, C., Pirsiavash, H., Torralba, A.: Anticipating visual representations from unlabeled video. In: CVPR (2016)
16. Jain, A., Singh, A., Koppula, H.S., Soh, S., Saxena, A.: Recurrent neural networks for driver activity anticipation via sensory-fusion architecture. In: ICRA (2016)
17. Singh, G., Saha, S., Sapienza, M., Torr, P.H.S., Cuzzolin, F.: Online real-time multiple spatiotemporal action localisation and prediction. In: ICCV (2017)
18. Gao, J., Yang, Z., Nevatia, R.: RED: reinforced encoder-decoder networks for action anticipation. arXiv:1707.04818 (2017)
19. Kitani, K.M., Ziebart, B.D., Bagnell, J.A., Hebert, M.: Activity forecasting. In: Fitzgibbon, A., Lazebnik, S., Perona, P., Sato, Y., Schmid, C. (eds.) ECCV 2012. LNCS, vol. 7575, pp. 201–214. Springer, Heidelberg (2012). https://doi.org/10.1007/978-3-642-33765-9_15
20. Pellegrini, S., Ess, A., Schindler, K., Van Gool, L.: You'll never walk alone: modeling social behavior for multi-target tracking. In: ICCV (2009)
21. Fernando, B., Gavves, E., Oramas, J., Ghodrati, A., Tuytelaars, T.: Rank pooling for action recognition. IEEE Trans. Pattern Anal. Mach. Intell. **39**(4), 773–787 (2017)
22. Smola, A.J., Schölkopf, B.: A tutorial on support vector regression. Stat. Comput. **14**(3), 199–222 (2004)
23. Baldi, P.: Autoencoders, unsupervised learning, and deep architectures. In: ICML (2012)
24. Kingma, D.P., Mohamed, S., Rezende, D.J., Welling, M.: Semi-supervised learning with deep generative models. In: NIPS (2014)
25. Sohn, K., Lee, H., Yan, X.: Learning structured output representation using deep conditional generative models. In: NIPS (2015)
26. Mirza, M., Osindero, S.: Conditional generative adversarial nets. arXiv:1411.1784 (2014)
27. Radford, A., Metz, L., Chintala, S.: Unsupervised representation learning with deep convolutional generative adversarial networks. In: ICLR (2016)
28. Hinton, G., Vinyals, O., Dean, J.: Distilling the knowledge in a neural network. arXiv:1503.02531 (2015)
29. Szegedy, C., Ioffe, S., Vanhoucke, V., Alemi, A.A.: Inception-v4, Inception-ResNet and the impact of residual connections on learning. In: AAAI (2017)
30. Jhuang, H., Gall, J., Zuffi, S., Schmid, C., Black, M.J.: Towards understanding action recognition. In: ICCV (2013)
31. Ryoo, M.S., Aggarwal, J.K.: UT-Interaction Dataset, ICPR contest on Semantic Description of Human Activities (SDHA) (2010). http://cvrc.ece.utexas.edu/SDHA2010/Human_Interaction.html
32. Soomro, K., Zamir, A.R., Shah, M.: UCF101: a dataset of 101 human actions classes from videos in the wild (2012). arXiv:1212.0402

33. Kuehne, H., Jhuang, H., Garrote, E., Poggio, T., Serre, T.: HMDB: a large video database for human motion recognition. In: ICCV (2011)
34. Kingma, D.P., Ba, J.: Adam: a method for stochastic optimization. In: ICLR (2015)
35. Ryoo, M.S., Chen, C.-C., Aggarwal, J.K., Roy-Chowdhury, A.: An overview of contest on semantic description of human activities (SDHA) 2010. In: Ünay, D., Çataltepe, Z., Aksoy, S. (eds.) ICPR 2010. LNCS, vol. 6388, pp. 270–285. Springer, Heidelberg (2010). https://doi.org/10.1007/978-3-642-17711-8_28
36. Laviers, K., Sukthankar, G., Aha, D.W., Molineaux, M., Darken, C., et al.: Improving offensive performance through opponent modeling. In: AIIDE (2009)

Predicting Action Tubes

Gurkirt Singh[✉], Suman Saha, and Fabio Cuzzolin

Oxford Brookes University, Oxford, UK
gurkirt.singh-2015@brookes.ac.uk

Abstract. In this work, we present a method to predict an entire 'action tube' (a set of temporally linked bounding boxes) in a trimmed video just by observing a smaller subset of it. Predicting where an action is going to take place in the near future is essential to many computer vision based applications such as autonomous driving or surgical robotics. Importantly, it has to be done in real-time and in an online fashion. We propose a **T**ube **P**rediction network (TPnet) which jointly predicts the past, present and future bounding boxes along with their action classification scores. At test time TPnet is used in a (temporal) sliding window setting, and its predictions are put into a tube estimation framework to construct/predict the video long action tubes not only for the observed part of the video but also for the unobserved part. Additionally, the proposed action tube predictor helps in completing action tubes for unobserved segments of the video. We quantitatively demonstrate the latter ability, and the fact that TPnet improves state-of-the-art detection performance, on one of the standard action detection benchmarks - J-HMDB-21 dataset.

1 Introduction

Imagine a pedestrian on the sidewalk, and an autonomous car cruising on the nearby road. If the pedestrian stays on the sidewalk and continues walking, they are of no concern for the self-driving car. What, instead, if they start approaching the road, in a possible attempt to cross it? Any future prediction about the pedestrian's action and their possible position on/off the road would crucially help the autonomous car avoid any potential incident. It would suffice to foresee the pedestrian's action label and position half a second early to avoid a major accident. As a result, awareness about surrounding human actions is essential for the robot-car.

We can formalise the problem as follows. We seek to predict both the class label and the future spatial location(s) of an action instance as early as possible, as shown in Fig. 1. Basically, it translates into early spatiotemporal action detection [31], achieved by completing action instance(s) for the unobserved part of the video. As commonly accepted, action instances are here described by 'tubes' formed by linking bounding box detections in time.

Electronic supplementary material The online version of this chapter (https://doi.org/10.1007/978-3-030-11015-4_11) contains supplementary material, which is available to authorized users.

L. Leal-Taixé and S. Roth (Eds.): ECCV 2018 Workshops, LNCS 11131, pp. 106–123, 2019.
https://doi.org/10.1007/978-3-030-11015-4_11

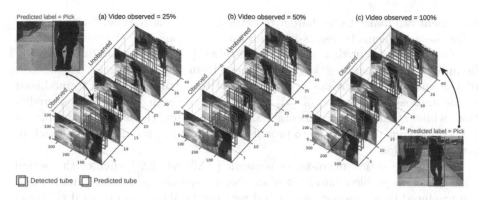

Fig. 1. An Illustration of the action tube prediction problem using an example in which a "pickup" action is being performed on a sidewalk. As an ideal case, we want the system to predict an action tube as shown in (c) (i.e. when 100% of the video has been processed) just by observing 25% of the entire clip (a). We want the tube predictor to predict the action class label (shown in red) alongside predicting the spatial location of the tube. The red shaded bounding boxes denote the detected tube in the observed portion of the input video, whereas, the blue coloured bounding boxes represent the future predicted action tube for the unobserved part of the clip. (Color figure online)

In an existing relevant work by Singh *et al.* [31], early label prediction and online action detection are performed jointly. The action class label for an input video is predicted early on just by observing a smaller portion (a few frames) of it, whilst the system incrementally builds action tubes in an online fashion. In contrast, the proposed approach can predict both the class label of an action and its future location(s) (i.e., the future shape of an action tube). In this work, by *'prediction'* we refer to the estimation of both an action's label and location in *future*, unobserved video segments. We term *'detection'* the estimation of action labels/locations in the observed segment of video up to any given time, i.e., for *present* and *past* video frames.

The computer vision community is witnessing a rising interest in problems such as early action label prediction [2,9,16,20,24,28,31,32,39,40,42], online temporal action detection [6,23,33,39], online spatio-temporal action detection [31,32,38], future representation prediction [16,34] or trajectory prediction [1,15,21]. Although, all these problems are interesting, and definitely encompass a broad scope of applications, they do not entirely capture the complexity involved by many critical scenarios including, e.g., surgical robotics or autonomous driving. In opposition to [31,32], which can only perform early label prediction and online action detection, in this work we propose to predict both future action location and action label. A number of challenges make this problem particularly hard, e.g., the temporal structure of an action is obviously not completely observed; locating human actions is itself a difficult task; the observed part can only provide clues about the future locations. In addition, camera movement can make it even harder to extrapolate an entire tube. We propose to solve these problems by regressing the future locations from the present tube.

The ability to predict *action micro-tubes* (sets of temporally connected bounding boxes spanning k video frames) from pairs of frames [29] or sets of k frames [10,13] provides a powerful tool to extend the single frame-based online approach by Singh *et al.* [31] in order to cope with action location prediction, while retaining its incremental nature. Combining the basic philosophies of [29,31] has thus the potential to provide an interesting and scalable approach to action prediction.

Briefly, the action micro-tubes network (AMTnet, [29]), divides the action tube detection problem into a set of smaller sub-problems. Action 'micro-tubes' are produced by a convolutional neural network (a 3D region proposal network) processing two input frames that are Δ apart. Each micro-tube consists of two bounding boxes belonging to the two frames. When the network is applied to consecutive pairs of frames, it produces a set of consecutive micro-tubes which can be finally linked [31] to form complete action tubes. The detections forming a micro-tube can be considered as implicitly linked, hence reducing the number of linking subproblems. Whereas AMTnet was originally designed to generate micro-tubes using only appearance (RGB) inputs, here we augment it by introducing the feature-level fusion of flow and appearance cues, drastically improving its performance and, as a result, that of TPnet.

Concept: We propose to extend the action micro-tube detection architecture by Saha *et al.* [29] to produce, at any time t, past ($\tau < t$), present, and future ($\tau > t$) detection bounding boxes, so that each (extended) micro-tube contains bounding boxes for both observed and not yet observed frames. All bounding boxes, spanning presently observed frames as well as past and future ones (in which case we call them predicted bounding boxes), are considered to be linked, as shown in blue in Fig. 2.

We call this new deep network 'TPnet'.

Once bounding boxes are regressed, the online tube construction method of Singh *et al.* [31] can be incrementally applied to the observed part of the video to generate one or more 'detected' action tubes at any time instant t.

Further, in virtue of TPnet and online tube construction, the temporally linked micro-tubes forming each currently detected action tube (spanning the observed segment of the video) also contain past and future estimated bounding boxes. As these predicted boxes are implicitly linked to the micro-tubes which compose the presently detected tube, the problem of linking to the latter the future bounding boxes, leading to a whole action tube, is automatically addressed.

The proposed approach provides two main benefits: (i) future bounding box predictions are implicitly linked to the present action tubes; (ii) as the method relies only on two consecutive frames separated by a constant distance Δ, it is efficient enough to be applicable to real-time scenarios.

Contributions: In Summary we present a Tube Predictor network (TPnet) which:

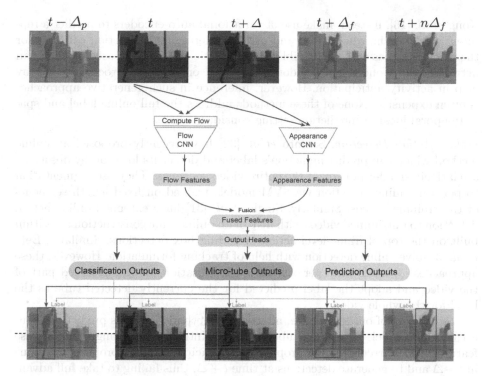

Fig. 2. Workflow illustrating the application of TPnet to a test video at a time instant t. The network takes frames f_t and $f_{t+\Delta}$ as input and generates classification scores, the micro-tube (in red) for frames f_t and $f_{t+\Delta}$, and prediction bounding boxes (in blue) for frames $f_{t-\Delta_p}$, $f_{t+\Delta_f}$ up to $f_{t+n\Delta_f}$. All bounding boxes are considered to be linked to the micro-tube. Note that predictions also span the past: a setting called smoothing in the estimation literature. Δ_p, Δ_f and n are network parameters that we cross-validate during training. (Color figure online)

- given a partially observed video, can (early) predict video long action tubes in terms of both their classes and the constituting bounding boxes;
- demonstrates that training a network to make predictions also helps in improving action detection performance;
- demonstrates that feature-based fusion works better than late fusion in the context of spatiotemporal action detection.

2   Related Work

Early Label Prediction. Early, online action label prediction has been studied using dynamic bag of words [28], structured SVMs [9], hierarchical representations [20], LSTMs [39] and Fisher vectors [6]. Recently, Yeung *et al.* [39,40] have proposed a variant of long short-term memory (LSTM) deep networks for modelling these temporal relations via multiple input and output connections.

Kong *et al.* [16], instead, make use of variational auto-encoders to predict a representation for the whole video and use it to determine the action category for the whole video as early as possible. Probabilistic approaches based on Bayesian networks [24], Conditional Random Fields [17] or Gaussian processes [12] may help in activity anticipation. However, inference in such generative approaches is often expensive. None of these methods address the full online label and spatiotemporal location prediction setting considered here.

Online Action Detection. Soomro *et al.* [32] have recently proposed an online method which can predict an action's label and detect its location by observing a relatively smaller portion of the entire video sequence. They use segmentation to perform online detection via SVM models trained on fixed length segments of the training videos. Similarly, Singh *et al.* [31] have extended online action detection to untrimmed videos with help of an online tube construction algorithm built on the top of frame-level action bounding box detections. Similarly, Behl *et al.* [3] solve online detection with help of tracking formulation. However, these approaches [3,31,32] only perform action localisation for the observed part of the video and adopt the label predicted for the currently detected tube as the label for the whole video.

To the best of our knowledge, no existing method generates predictions concerning both labels and action tube geometry. Interestingly, Yang *et al.* [38] use features from current, frame t proposals to 'anticipate' region proposal locations in $t + \Delta$ and to generate detections at time $t + \Delta$, thus failing to take full advantage of the anticipation trick to predict the future spatiotemporal extent of the action tubes.

Advances in action recognition are always going to be helpful in action prediction from a general representation learning point of view. For instance, Gu *et al.* [8] have recently improved on [13,25] by plugging in the inflated 3D network proposed by [5] as a base network on multiple frames. Although they use a very strong base network pre-trained on the large "Kinetics" [14] dataset, they do not handle the linking process within the network as the AVA [8] dataset's annotations are not temporally linked. Analogously, learning to predict future representation [34] can be useful in general action prediction (cfr. e.g. [16]).

Recently, inspired by the record-breaking performance of CNN-based object detectors [22,26,27], a number of scholars [3,7,25,30,31,35,37,41] have tried to extend frame-level object detectors to videos for spatio-temporal action localisation. These approaches, however, fail to tackle spatial and temporal reasoning jointly at the network level, as spatial detection and temporal association are treated as two disjoint problems. More recent works have attempted to address this problem by reducing the amount of linking required with the help of 'micro-tubes' [29] or 'tubelets' [10,13] for small sets of frames taken together, where micro-tube boxes from different frames are considered to be linked together. AMTnet [29] by Saha *et al.* is particularly interesting, because of its compact (GPU memory-wise) and flexible nature, as it can exploit pairs of successive frames Δ sampling intervals apart, that it can also leverage sparse annotations [36] as well. For these reasons in this work we build on AMTnet as base network, improving its feature representation by feature-level fusion of motion and appearance cues.

3   Methodology

In this section, we describe our tube prediction framework for the problem formulation described in Sect. 3.1. Our approach has four main components. Firstly, we tie the future action tube prediction problem (Sect. 3.1) with action micro-tube [29] detection. Secondly, we devise our tube prediction network (TPnet) to predict future bounding boxes along with current micro-tubes, and describe its training procedure in Sect. 3.3. Thirdly, we use TPnet in a sliding window fashion (Sect. 3.4) in the temporal direction while generating micro-tubes and corresponding future predictions. These, eventually, are fed to a tube prediction framework (Sect. 3.4) to generate the future of any current action tube being built using micro-tubes.

3.1   Problem Statement

We define an *action tube* as a connected sequence of detection boxes in time without interruptions and associated with a same action class c, starting at first frame f_1 and ending last frame f_T, in trimmed video: $T_c = \{b_1, ...b_t, ...b_T\}$. Tubes are constrained to span the entire video duration, like in [7]. At any time point t, a tube is divided into two parts, one needs to be detected $T_c^d = \{b_1, ...b_t\}$ up to f_t and another part needs to be predicted/estimated $T_c^p = \{b_{t+1}, ...b_T\}$ from frame f_{t+1} to f_T along with its class c. The observed part of the video is responsible for generating T_c^d (red in Fig. 1), while we need to estimate the future section of the tube T_c^p (blue in Fig. 1) for the unobserved segment of the video. The first sub-problem, the online detection of T_c^d, is explained in Sect. 3.2. The second sub-problem (the estimation of the future tube segment T_c^p) is tackled by a tube prediction network (TPnet, Sect. 3.3) in a novel tube prediction framework (Sect. 3.4).

3.2   From Micro-tubes to Full Action Tubes

Saha *et al.* [29] introduced *micro-tubes* in their action micro-tube network (AMTnet) proposal, shown in Fig. 3. AMTnet decomposes the problem of detecting T_c into a set of smaller problems, detecting micro-tubes $m_t = \{b_t, b_{t+\Delta}\}$ at time t along with their classification scores for $C + 1$ classes, using two successive frames f_t and $f_{t+\Delta}$ as an input (Fig. 3(a)). Subsequently, the detection micro-tubes $\{m_1...m_{t-\Delta}\}$ are linked up in time to form action tube T_c^d. Similar to [22], one background class is added to the class list which takes the number classes to $C + 1$.

AMTnet employs two parallel CNN streams (Fig. 3(b)), one for each frame, which produce two feature maps (Fig. 3(c)). These feature maps are stacked together into one (Fig. 3(d)). Finally, convolutional heads are applied in a sliding window (spatial) fashion over predefined 3×3 anchor regions [22], which correspond to P prior [22] or anchor [27] boxes. Convolutional heads produce a $P \times 8$ output per micro-tube (Fig. 3(f)) and $P \times (C + 1)$ corresponding classification scores (Fig. 3(g)). Each micro tube has 8 coordinate, 4 for the bounding box b_t in frame f_t and 4 for bounding box $b_{t+\Delta}$ in frame $f_{t+\Delta}$. As shown in Fig. 3(f), the pair of boxes can be considered as implicitly linked together, hence the name micro-tube.

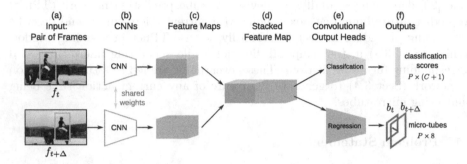

Fig. 3. Overview of the action micro-tube detection network (AMTnet). As it only predicts micro-tubes and their scores, here we modify it to predict the future locations associated with the given micro-tubes, as shown in Fig. 2.

Originally, Saha *et al.* [29] employed FasterRCNN [27] as base detection architecture. Here, however, we switch to Single Shot Detector (SSD) [22] as a base detector for efficiency reasons. Singh *et al.* [31] used SSD to propose an online and real-time action tube generation algorithm, while Kalogeiton *et al.* [13] adapted SSD to detect micro-tubes (or, in their terminology, 'tubelets') k frames long.

More importantly, we make two essential changes to AMTnet. Firstly, we enhance its feature representation power by fusing appearance features (based on RGB frames) and flow features (based on optical flow) at the feature level (see the fusion step shown in Fig. 4), unlike the late fusion approach of [13,31]. Note that the original AMTnet framework does not make use of optical flow at all. We will show that feature-level fusion dramatically improves its performance. Secondly, the AMTnet-based tube detection framework proposed in [29] is offline, as micro-tube linking is done recursively in an offline fashion [7]. Similar to Kalogeiton *et al.* [13], we adapt the online linking method of [31] to link micro-tubes in to a tube $\mathcal{T}_c^d$.

Micro-tube Linking Details: Let B_t be the set of detection bounding boxes from frame f_t, and B_{t+1} the corresponding set from f_{t+1}, generated by a frame-level detector. Singh *et al.* [31] associate boxes in B_t to boxes in B_{t+1}, whereas, in our case, we need to link micro-tubes $m_t \in M_t \doteq B_t^1 \times B_{t+\Delta}^2$ from a pair of frames $\{f_t, f_{t+\Delta}\}$ to microtubes $m_{t+\Delta} \in M_{t+\Delta} \doteq B_{t+\Delta}^1 \times B_{t+2\Delta}^2$ from the next set of frames $\{f_{t+\Delta}, f_{t+2\Delta}\}$. This happens by associating elements of $B_{t+\Delta}^2$, coming from M_t, with elements of $B^1_{t+\Delta}$, coming from $M_{t+\Delta}$. Interestingly, the latter is a relatively easier sub-problem, as all such detections are generated based on the same frame, unlike the across frame association problem considered in [31]. The association is achieved based on Intersection over Union (IoU) and class score, as the tubes are built separately for each class in a multi-label scenario. For more details, we refer the reader to [31].

Since we adopt the online linking framework of Singh *et al.* [31], we follow most of the linking setting used by them, e.g.: linking is done for every class separately; the non-maximal threshold is set to 0.45. As shown in Fig. 5(a) to (b), the last box of the first micro-tube (red) is linked to the first box of next micro-tube (red). So, the first set of micro-tubes is produced at f_1, the following one at f_Δ the one after that at $f_{2\Delta}$, and so on. As a result, the last micro-tube is generated at $f_{t-\Delta}$ to cover the observable video duration up to time t. Finally, we solve for the association problem as described above.

3.3   Training the Tube Prediction Network (TPnet)

AMTnet allow us to detect current tubes $\mathcal{T}^d_c$ by generating a set of successive micro-tubes $\{m_1...m_{t-\Delta}\}$, where $m_{t-\Delta} = \{b_{t-\Delta}, b_t\}$. However, our aim is to predict the future section $\mathcal{T}^p_c$ of the tube using the latter linked micro-tubes, up to time t.

To address this problem, we propose a tube prediction framework aimed at simultaneously estimating a micro-tube m_t, a set $z_t = \{b_{t-\Delta_p}, b_{t+\Delta_f}, ...b_{t+n\Delta_f}\}$ of *past and future detections*, and the classification scores for the $C + 1$ classes. Δ_p measures how far in the past we are looking into, whereas Δ_f is a future step size, and n is the number of future steps. This is performed by a new Tube Prediction network (TPnet).

The underlying architecture of TPnet is shown in Fig. 4. TPnet takes two successive frames from time t and $t+\Delta$ as input. The two input frames are fed to two parallel CNN streams, one for appearance and one for optical flow. The resulting feature maps are fused together, either by concatenating or by element-wise summing the given feature maps. Finally, three types of convolutional output heads are used for P prior boxes as shown in Fig. 4. The first one produces the $P \times (C + 1)$ classification outputs; the second one regresses the $P \times 8$ coordinates of the micro-tubes, as in AMTnet; the last one regresses $P \times (4(1 + n))$ coordinates, where 4 coordinates correspond to the frame at $t - \Delta_p$, and the remaining $4n$ are associated with the n future steps. The training procedure of the new architecture is illustrated below.

Multi-task Learning. TPnet is designed to strive for three objectives, for each prior box p. The first task (i) is to classify the P prior boxes; the second task (ii) is to regress the coordinates of the micro-tubes; the last (iii) is to regress the coordinates of the past and future detections associated with each micro-tube.

Given a set of P anchor boxes and the respective outputs we compute a loss following the training objective of SSD [22]. Let $x^c_{i,j} = \{0, 1\}$ be the indicator for matching the i-th prior box to the j-th ground truth box of category c. We

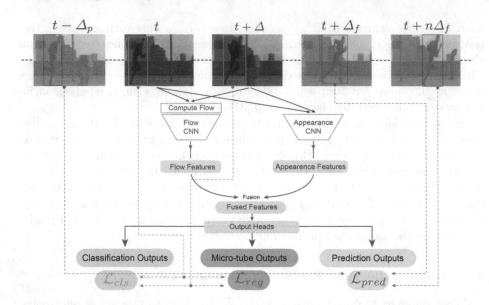

Fig. 4. Overview of the tube prediction network (TPnet) architecture at training time.

use the bipartite matching procedure described in [22] for matching the ground truth micro-tubes $G = \{g_t, g_{t+\Delta}\}$ to the prior boxes, where g_t is a ground truth box at time t. The overlap is computed between a prior box p and micro-tube G as the mean IoU between p and the ground truth boxes in G. A match is defined as positive ($x_{i,j}^c = 1$) if the overlap is more than or equal to 0.5.

The overall loss function $\mathcal{L}$ is the following weighted sum of classification loss ($\mathcal{L}_{cls}$), micro-tube regression loss ($\mathcal{L}_{reg}$) and prediction loss ($\mathcal{L}_{pred}$):

$$\mathcal{L}(x, c, m, G, z, Y) = \frac{1}{N}\big(\mathcal{L}_{cls}(x, c) + \alpha\mathcal{L}_{reg}(x, m, G) + \beta\mathcal{L}_{pred}(x, z, Y)\big), \quad (1)$$

where N is the number of matches, c is the ground truth class, m is the predicted micro-tube, G is the ground truth micro-tube, z assembles the predictions for the future and the past, and Y is the ground truth of future and past bounding boxes associated with the ground truth micro-tube G. The values of α and β are both set to 1 in all of our experiments: different values might result in better performance.

The classification loss $\mathcal{L}_{cls}$ is a softmax cross-entropy loss; a hard negative mining strategy is also employed, as proposed in [22]. The micro-tube loss $\mathcal{L}_{reg}$ is a Smooth L1 loss [27] between the predicted (m) and the ground truth (G) micro-tube. Similarly, the prediction loss $\mathcal{L}_{pred}$ is also a Smooth L1 loss between the predicted boxes (z) and the ground truth boxes (Y). As in [22,27], we regress the offsets with respect to the coordinates of matched prior box p matched to G for both m and z. We use the same offset encoding scheme as used in [22].

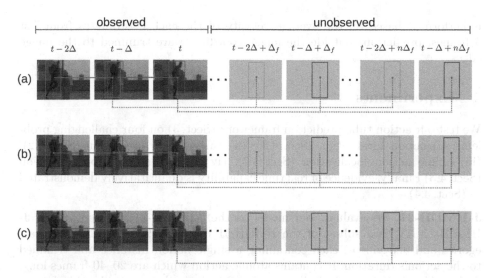

Fig. 5. Overview of future tube ($\mathcal{T}_c^p$) prediction using the predictions that are linked to micro-tubes. The first row (a) shows two output micro-tubes in light red and red and their corresponding predictions in future in light blue and blue. In row (b) two micro-tubes are linked together, after which they are shown in the same colour (red). By induction on the previous step, in row (c) we show that the predictions associated with two micro-tubes are linked together as well, hence forming one single tube. The observed segment is shown in red, while the predicted segment for the part of the video yet to observe is shown in blue. (Color figure online)

3.4 Tube Prediction Framework

TPnet is shown in Fig. 2 at test time. As in the training setting, it observes only two frames that are Δ apart at any time point t. The outputs of TPnet at any time t are linked to a micro-tube, each micro-tube containing a set of bounding boxes $\{m_t = \{b_t, b_{t+\Delta}\}; z_t = \{b_{t-\Delta_p}, b_{t+\Delta_f}, ..., b_{t+\Delta_f}\}\}$, which are considered as linked together.

As explained in Sect. 3.2, given a set of micro-tubes $\{m_1...m_{t-\Delta}\}$ we can construct $\mathcal{T}_c^d$ by online linking [31] of the micro-tubes. As a result, we can use predictions for $t + \Delta_f$ up to $t + n\Delta_f$ to generate the future of $\mathcal{T}_c^d$, thus extending it further into the future as shown in Fig. 5. More specifically, as it is indicated in Fig. 5(a), a micro tube at $t - 2\Delta$ is composed by $n + 2$ bounding boxes ($\{b_{t-2\Delta}, b_{t-\Delta}, b_{t-2\Delta+\Delta_f}, ...b_{t-\Delta+n\Delta_f}\}$) linked together. The last micro-tube is generated from $t - \Delta$. In the same fashion, putting together the predictions associated with all the past micro-tubes ($\{m_1...m_{t-\Delta}\}$) yields a set of linked future bounding boxes ($\{b_{t+1}, ..., b_{t+\Delta+\Delta_f}, ..., b_{t-\Delta+n\Delta_f}\}$) for the current action tube $\mathcal{T}_c^d$, thus outputting a part of the desired future $\mathcal{T}_c^p$.

Now, we can generate future tube $\mathcal{T}_c^p$ from the set of linked future bounding boxes ($\{b_{t+1}, ...b_{t-\Delta+\Delta_f}, ...b_{t-\Delta+n\Delta_f}\}$) from $t+1$ to $t-\Delta+n\Delta_f$ and simple linear extrapolation of bounding boxes from $t - \Delta + n\Delta_f$ to T. Linear extrapolation is performed based on the average velocity of the each coordinates from last 5 frames, predictions outside the image coordinate are trimmed to the image edges.

4 Experiments

We test our action tube prediction framework (Sect. 3) on four challenging problems: (i) action localisation (Sect. 4.1), (ii) early action prediction (Sect. 4.2), (iii) online action localisation (Sect. 4.2), (iv) future action tube prediction (Sect. 4.3) Finally, evidence of real time capability is quantitatively demonstrated in (Sect. 4.4).

J-HMDB-21. We evaluate our model on the J-HMDB-21 [11] benchmark. J-HMDB-21 [11] is a subset of the HMDB-51 dataset [19] with 21 action categories and 928 videos, each containing a single action instance and trimmed to the action's duration. It contains atomic action which are 20–40 frames long. Although, videos are of short duration (max 40 frames), we consider this dataset because tubes belong to the same class and we think it is a good dataset to start with for action prediction task.

Evaluation Metrics. Now, we define the evaluation metrics used in this paper. (i) We use a standard mean-average precision metric to evaluate the detection performance when the whole video is observed.
(ii) Early label prediction task is evaluated by video classification accuracy [31, 32] as early as when only 10% of the video frames are observed.
(iii) Online action localisation (Sect. 4.2) is set up based on the experimental setup of [31], and use mAP (mean average precision) as metric for online action detection i.e. it evaluates present tube $(\mathcal{T}_c^d)$ built in online fashion.
(iv) The future tube prediction is a new task; we propose to evaluate its performance in two ways. Firstly, we evaluate the quality of the whole tube prediction from the start of the videos to the end as early as when only 10% of the video is observed. The entire tube predicted (by observing only a small portion (%) of the video) is compared against the ground truth tube for the whole video. Based on the detection threshold we can compute mean-average-precision for the complete tubes, we call this metric *completion-mAP* (c-mAP). Secondly, we measure how well the future predicted part of the tube localises. In this measure, we compare the predicted $(\mathcal{T}_c^p)$ tube with the corresponding ground truth future tube segment. Given the ground truth and the predicted future tubes, we can compute the mean-average precision for the predicted tubes, we call this metric *prediction-mAP* (p-mAP).

We report the performance of previous three tasks (i.e. task ii to iv) as a function of *Video Observation Percentage*, i.e., the portion (%) of the entire video observed.

Baseline. We modified AMTnet to fuse flow and appearance features Sect. 3.2. We treat it as a baseline for all of our tasks. Firstly, we show how feature fusion helps AMTnet in Sect. 4.1, and compare it with other action detection methods

Table 1. Action localisation results on JHMDB dataset. The table is divided into four parts. The first part lists approaches which takes a single frame as input; the second part presents approaches which takes multiple frames as input; the third part contemplates different fusion strategies of our feature-level fusion (based on AMTnet); lastly, we report the detection performance of our TPnet by ignoring the future and past predictions and only use the detected micro-tubes to produce the final action tubes.

Methods	$\delta = 0.2$	$\delta = 0.5$	$\delta = 0.75$	$\delta = .5:.95$	Acc %
MR-TS Peng et al. [25]	74.1	73.1	–	–	–
FasterRCNN Saha et al. [30]	72.2	71.5	43.5	40.0	–
OJLA Behl et al. [3][a]	–	67.3	–	36.1	–
SSD Singh et al. [31][a]	73.8	72.0	44.5	41.6	–
AMTnet Saha et al. [29] rgb-only	57.7	55.3	–	–	–
ACT kalogeiton et al. [13][a]	74.2	73.7	52.1	44.8	61.7
T-CNN (offline) Hou et al. [10]	**78.4**	76.9	–	–	67.2
MR-TS [25] + I3D [5] Gu et al. [8]	–	**78.6**	–	–	–
AMTnet-LateFusion[a]	71.7	71.2	49.7	42.5	65.8
AMTnet-FeatFusion-Concat[a]	73.1	72.6	59.8	48.3	68.4
AMTnet-FeatFusion-Sum[a]	73.5	72.8	59.7	48.1	69.6
Ours TPnet$_{053}$[a]	72.6	72.1	58.0	46.7	67.5
Ours TPnet$_{453}$[a]	73.8	73.0	59.1	47.3	68.2
Ours TPnet$_{051}$[a]	74.6	73.1	60.5	49.0	**69.8**
Ours TPnet$_{451}$[a]	74.8	74.1	**61.3**	**49.1**	68.9

TPnet$_{abc}$ represents our TPnet where $a = \Delta_p$, $b = \Delta_f$ and $c = n$; [a]means online methods.

along with our TPnet. Secondly in Sect. 4.3, we linearly extrapolate the detection from AMTnet to construct the future tubes, and use it as a baseline for tube prediction task.

Implementation Details. We train all of our networks with the same set of hyper-parameters to ensure the fair comparison and consistency, including TPnet and AMTnet. We use an initial learning rate of 0.0005, and the learning rate drops by a factor of 10 after $5K$ and $7K$ iterations. All the networks are trained up to $10K$ iterations. We implemented AMTnet using pytorch (https://pytorch.org/). We initialise AMTnet and TPnet models using the pretrained SSD network on J-HMDB-21 dataset on its respective train splits. The SSD network training is initialised using image-net trained VGG network. For, optical flow images, we used optical flow algorithm of Brox et al. [4]. Optical flow output is put into a three channel image, two channels are made of flow vector and the third channel is the magnitude of the flow vector.

TPnet$_{abc}$. The training parameters of our TPnet are used to define the name of the setting in which we use our tube prediction network. The network name TPnet$_{abc}$ represents our TPnet where $a = \Delta_p$, $b = \Delta_f$ and $c = n$, if Δ_p is set to

0 it means network doesn't learn to predict the past bounding boxes. In all of our settings, we use $\Delta = 1$.

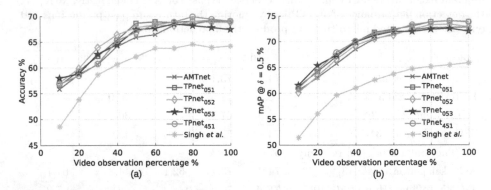

Fig. 6. Early label prediction results (video-level label prediction accuracy) on J-HMDB-21 dataset in sub-figure (a). Online action detection results (mAP with detection threshold $\delta = 0.5$) on J-HMDB-21 dataset are shown in sub-figure (b). TPnet$_{abc}$ represents our TPnet where $a = \Delta_p$, $b = \Delta_f$ and $c = n$.

4.1 Action Localisation Performance

Table 1 shows the traditional action localisation results for the whole action tube detection in the videos of J-HMBD-21 dataset.

Feature fusion compared to the late fusion scheme in AMTnet shows (Table 1) remarkable improvement, at detection threshold $\delta = 0.75$ the gain with feature level fusion is 10%, as a result, it is able to surpass the performance of ACT [13], which relies on set of 6 frames as compared to AMTnet which uses only 2 successive frames as input. Looking at the average-mAP ($\delta = 0.5 : 95$), we can see that the fused model improves by almost 8% as compared to single frame SSD model of Singh *et al.* [31]. We can see that concatenation and sum fusion perform almost similar for AMTnet. Sum fusion is little less memory intensive on the GPUs as compared to the concatenation fusion; as a result, we use sum fusion in our TPnet.

TPnet for detection is shown in the last part of the Table 1, where we only use the detected micro-tubes by TPnet to construct the action tubes (Sect. 3.2). We train TPnet to predict future and past (i.e. when $\Delta_p > 0$) as well as present micro-tubes. We think that predicting bounding boxes for both the past and future video segments acts as a regulariser and helps improving the representation of the whole network. Thus, improving the detection performance (Table 1 TPNet$_{051}$ and TPNet$_{451}$). However, that does not mean adding extra prediction task always help when a network is asked to learn prediction in far future, as is the case in TPNet$_{053}$ and TPNet$_{453}$, we have a drop in the detection performance. We think there might be two possible reasons for this, (i) network might starts to focus more on prediction task, and (ii) videos in J-HMDB-21 are short and number of training samples decreases drastically ($19K$ for TPNet$_{051}$ and $10K$ for TPNet$_{453}$), because we can not use edge frames of the video in training samples as we need a ground truth bounding box which is 15 frames in the future, as $\Delta_f = 5$ and $n = 3$ for TPNet$_{053}$. However, in Sect. 4.3, we show that the TPNet$_{053}$ model is the best to predict the future very early.

4.2   Early Label Prediction and Online Localisation

Figure 6(a) and (b) show the early prediction and online detection capabilities of Singh et al. [31], AMTnet-Feature Fusion-sum and our TPnet.

Soomro et al. [32]'s method also perform early label prediction on J-HMDB-21; however, their performance is deficient, as a result the plot would become skewed (Fig. 6(a)), so we omit theirs from the figure. For instance, by observing only the initial 10% of the videos in J-HMDB-21, TPnet$_{453}$ able to achieve a prediction accuracy of 58% as compared to 48% by Singh et al. [31] and 5% by Soomro et al. [32], which is in fact higher than the 43% accuracy achieved by [32] after observing the entire video. As more and more video observed, all the methods improve, but TPnet$_{451}$ show the most gain, however, TPnet$_{053}$ observed the least gain from all the TPnet settings shown. Which is in-line with action localisation performance discussed in the previous Sect. 4.1. We can observe the similar trends in online action localisation performance shown in Fig. 6(b). To reiterate, TPnet$_{053}$ doesn't get to see the training samples from the end portion of the videos, as it needs a ground truth bounding box from 15 frames ahead. So, the last frame it sees of any training video is $T - 15$, which is almost half the length of the most extended video (40 frames) in J-HMDB-21. This effect magnifies when online localisation performance measured at $\delta = 0.75$, we provide the evidence of it in the supplementary material.

4.3   Future Action Tube Prediction

Our main task of the paper is to predict the future of action tubes. We evaluate it using two newly proposed metrics ($p\text{-}mAP$ and $c\text{-}mAP$) as explained earlier at the start of the experiment Sect. 4. Result are shown in Fig. 7 for future tube prediction (Fig. 7(a)) with p-mAP metric and tube completion with c-mAP as metric.

Although, the TPnet$_{053}$ is the worst setting of TPnet model for early label prediction (Fig. 6(a)), online detection (Fig. 6(b)) and action tube detection (Table 1), but as it predicts furthest in the future (i.e. 15 frame away from the present time), it is the best model for early future tube prediction (Fig. 7(a)). However, it does not observe as much appreciation in performance as other settings as more and more frames are seen, owing to the reduction in the number of training samples. On the other hand, TPnet$_{451}$ observed large improvement as compared to TPnet$_{051}$ as more and more portion of the video is observed for

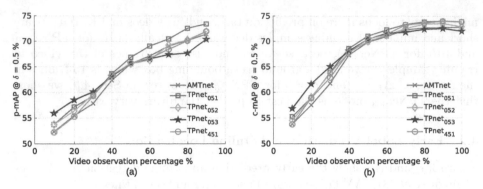

Fig. 7. Future action tube prediction results (a) (prediction-mAP (p-mAP)) for predicting the tube in unobserved part of the video. Action tube prediction results (b) (completion-mAP (c-mAP)) for predicting video long tubes as early as possible on J-HMDB-21 dataset in sub-figure (b). We use p-mAP (a) and c-mAP (b) with detection threshold $\delta = 0.5$ as evaluation metrics on J-HMDB-21 dataset. $TPnet_{abc}$ represents our TPnet where $a = \Delta_p$, $b = \Delta_f$ and $c = n$.

tube completion task (Fig. 7(b)), which strengthen our arguement that predicting not only the future but also the past is useful to achieve more regularised predictions.

Comparision with the Baseline. As explained above, we use AMTnet as a baseline, and its results can be seen in all the plots and the Table. We can observe that our TPnet performs better than AMTnet in almost all the cases, especially in our desired task of early future prediction (Fig. 7(a)) $TPnet_{043}$ shows almost 4% improvement in p-mAP (at 10% video observation) over AMTnet.

Discussion. Predicting further into the future is essential to produce any meaningful predictions (seen in $TPnet_{053}$), but at the same time, predicting past is helpful to improve overall tube completion performance. One of the reasons for such behaviour could be that J-HMDB-21 tubes are short (max 40 frames long). We think training samples for a combination of $TPnet_{053}$ and $TPnet_{451}$, i.e. $TPnet_{453}$ are chosen uniformly over the whole video while taking care of absence of ground truth in the loss function could give us better of both settings. We show the result of $TPnet_{453}$ in current training setting in supplementary material. The idea of regularising based on past prediction is similar to the one used by Ma et al. [23].

4.4   Test Time Detection Speed

Singh et al. [31] showcase their method's online and real-time capabilities. Here we use their online tube generation method for our tube prediction framework to inherit those properties. The only question mark is TPnet's forward pass speed. We thus measured the average time taken for a forward pass for a batch size of 1 as compared to 8 by [31]. A single forward pass takes 46.8 ms to process one text example, showing that it can be run in almost real-time at 21 fps with two streams on a single 1080Ti GPU. One can improve speed even further by testing TPnet with Δ equal to 2 or 4 and obtain a speed improvement of 2× or 2×. However, use of dense optical flow [4], which is slow, but as in [31], we can always switch to real-time optical [18] with small drop in performance.

5   Conclusions

We presented TPnet, a deep learning framework for future action tube prediction in videos which, unlike previous online tube detection methods [31,32], generates future of action tubes as early as when 10% of the video is observed. It can cope with the future uncertainty better than the baseline methods while remaining state-of-the-art in action detection task. Hence, we provide a scalable platform to push the boundaries of action tube prediction research; it is implicitly scalable to multiple action tube instances in the video as future prediction is made for each action tube separately. We plan to scale TPnet for action prediction in temporally untrimmed videos in the future.

References

1. Alahi, A., Goel, K., Ramanathan, V., Robicquet, A., Fei-Fei, L., Savarese, S.: Social LSTM: human trajectory prediction in crowded spaces. In: Proceedings of the IEEE Conference on Computer Vision and Pattern Recognition, pp. 961–971 (2016)
2. Aliakbarian, M.S., Saleh, F.S., Salzmann, M., Fernando, B., Petersson, L., Andersson, L.: Encouraging LSTMs to anticipate actions very early. In: IEEE International Conference on Computer Vision (ICCV), vol. 1 (2017)
3. Behl, H.S., Sapienza, M., Singh, G., Saha, S., Cuzzolin, F., Torr, P.H.: Incremental tube construction for human action detection. arXiv preprint arXiv:1704.01358 (2017)
4. Brox, T., Bruhn, A., Papenberg, N., Weickert, J.: High accuracy optical flow estimation based on a theory for warping. In: Pajdla, T., Matas, J. (eds.) ECCV 2004. LNCS, vol. 3024, pp. 25–36. Springer, Heidelberg (2004). https://doi.org/10.1007/978-3-540-24673-2_3
5. Carreira, J., Zisserman, A.: Quo vadis, action recognition? A new model and the kinetics dataset. In: 2017 IEEE Conference on Computer Vision and Pattern Recognition (CVPR), pp. 4724–4733. IEEE (2017)
6. De Geest, R., Gavves, E., Ghodrati, A., Li, Z., Snoek, C., Tuytelaars, T.: Online action detection. arXiv preprint arXiv:1604.06506 (2016)
7. Gkioxari, G., Malik, J.: Finding action tubes. In: IEEE International Conference on Computer Vision and Pattern Recognition (2015)
8. Gu, C., et al.: Ava: a video dataset of spatio-temporally localized atomic visual actions. arXiv preprint arXiv:1705.08421 (2017)
9. Hoai, M., De la Torre, F.: Max-margin early event detectors. Int. J. Comput. Vis. 107(2), 191–202 (2014)
10. Hou, R., Chen, C., Shah, M.: Tube convolutional neural network (T-CNN) for action detection in videos. In: IEEE International Conference on Computer Vision (2017)

11. Jhuang, H., Gall, J., Zuffi, S., Schmid, C., Black, M.: Towards understanding action recognition (2013)
12. Jiang, Y., Saxena, A.: Modeling high-dimensional humans for activity anticipation using Gaussian process latent CRFs. In: Robotics: Science and Systems, RSS (2014)
13. Kalogeiton, V., Weinzaepfel, P., Ferrari, V., Schmid, C.: Action tubelet detector for spatio-temporal action localization. In: IEEE International Conference on Computer Vision (2017)
14. Kay, W., et al.: The kinetics human action video dataset. arXiv preprint arXiv:1705.06950 (2017)
15. Kitani, K.M., Ziebart, B.D., Bagnell, J.A., Hebert, M.: Activity forecasting. In: Fitzgibbon, A., Lazebnik, S., Perona, P., Sato, Y., Schmid, C. (eds.) ECCV 2012. LNCS, vol. 7575, pp. 201–214. Springer, Heidelberg (2012). https://doi.org/10. 1007/978-3-642-33765-9_15
16. Kong, Y., Tao, Z., Fu, Y.: Deep sequential context networks for action prediction. In: Proceedings of the IEEE Conference on Computer Vision and Pattern Recognition, pp. 1473–1481 (2017)
17. Koppula, H.S., Gupta, R., Saxena, A.: Learning human activities and object affordances from RGB-D videos. Int. J. Robot. Res. 32(8), 951–970 (2013)
18. Kroeger, T., Timofte, R., Dai, D., Van Gool, L.: Fast optical flow using dense inverse search. arXiv preprint arXiv:1603.03590 (2016)
19. Kuehne, H., Jhuang, H., Garrote, E., Poggio, T., Serre, T.: HMDB: a large video database for human motion recognition. In: 2011 IEEE International Conference on Computer Vision (ICCV), pp. 2556–2563. IEEE (2011)
20. Lan, T., Chen, T.-C., Savarese, S.: A hierarchical representation for future action prediction. In: Fleet, D., Pajdla, T., Schiele, B., Tuytelaars, T. (eds.) ECCV 2014. LNCS, vol. 8691, pp. 689–704. Springer, Cham (2014). https://doi.org/10.1007/ 978-3-319-10578-9_45
21. Lee, N., Choi, W., Vernaza, P., Choy, C.B., Torr, P.H., Chandraker, M.: Desire: distant future prediction in dynamic scenes with interacting agents. In: Proceedings of the IEEE Conference on Computer Vision and Pattern Recognition, pp. 336–345 (2017)
22. Liu, W., et al.: SSD: single shot multibox detector. arXiv preprint arXiv:1512.02325 (2015)
23. Ma, S., Sigal, L., Sclaroff, S.: Learning activity progression in LSTMs for activity detection and early detection. In: Proceedings of the IEEE Conference on Computer Vision and Pattern Recognition, pp. 1942–1950 (2016)
24. Nazerfard, E., Cook, D.J.: Using Bayesian networks for daily activity prediction. In: AAAI Workshop: Plan, Activity, and Intent Recognition (2013)
25. Peng, X., Schmid, C.: Multi-region two-stream R-CNN for action detection. In: Leibe, B., Matas, J., Sebe, N., Welling, M. (eds.) ECCV 2016. LNCS, vol. 9908, pp. 744–759. Springer, Cham (2016). https://doi.org/10.1007/978-3-319-46493-0_45
26. Redmon, J., Farhadi, A.: Yolo9000: better, faster, stronger. arXiv preprint arXiv:1612.08242 (2016)
27. Ren, S., He, K., Girshick, R., Sun, J.: Faster R-CNN: towards real-time object detection with region proposal networks. In: Advances in Neural Information Processing Systems, pp. 91–99 (2015)
28. Ryoo, M.S.: Human activity prediction: early recognition of ongoing activities from streaming videos. In: IEEE International Conference on Computer Vision, pp. 1036–1043. IEEE (2011)

29. Saha, S., Singh, G., Cuzzolin, F.: AMTnet: action-micro-tube regression by end-to-end trainable deep architecture. In: IEEE International Conference on Computer Vision (2017)
30. Saha, S., Singh, G., Sapienza, M., Torr, P.H.S., Cuzzolin, F.: Deep learning for detecting multiple space-time action tubes in videos. In: British Machine Vision Conference (2016)
31. Singh, G., Saha, S., Sapienza, M., Torr, P., Cuzzolin, F.: Online real-time multiple spatiotemporal action localisation and prediction. In: IEEE International Conference on Computer Vision (2017)
32. Soomro, K., Idrees, H., Shah, M.: Predicting the where and what of actors and actions through online action localization (2016)
33. Tahmida Mahmud, M.H., Roy-Chowdhury, A.K.: Joint prediction of activity labels and starting times in untrimmed videos. In: IEEE International Conference on Computer Vision, vol. 1 (2017)
34. Vondrick, C., Pirsiavash, H., Torralba, A.: Anticipating the future by watching unlabeled video. arXiv preprint arXiv:1504.08023 (2015)
35. Weinzaepfel, P., Harchaoui, Z., Schmid, C.: Learning to track for spatio-temporal action localization. In: IEEE International Conference on Computer Vision and Pattern Recognition (2015)
36. Weinzaepfel, P., Martin, X., Schmid, C.: Human action localization with sparse spatial supervision. arXiv preprint arXiv:1605.05197 (2016)
37. Weinzaepfel, P., Martin, X., Schmid, C.: Towards weakly-supervised action localization. arXiv preprint arXiv:1605.05197 (2016)
38. Yang, Z., Gao, J., Nevatia, R.: Spatio-temporal action detection with cascade proposal and location anticipation. In: BMVC (2017)
39. Yeung, S., Russakovsky, O., Jin, N., Andriluka, M., Mori, G., Fei-Fei, L.: Every moment counts: dense detailed labeling of actions in complex videos. arXiv preprint arXiv:1507.05738 (2015)
40. Yeung, S., Russakovsky, O., Mori, G., Fei-Fei, L.: End-to-end learning of action detection from frame glimpses in videos. In: CVPR (2016)
41. Zolfaghari, M., Oliveira, G.L., Sedaghat, N., Brox, T.: Chained multi-stream networks exploiting pose, motion, and appearance for action classification and detection. In: IEEE International Conference on Computer Vision, pp. 2923–2932. IEEE (2017)
42. Zunino, A., Cavazza, J., Koul, A., Cavallo, A., Becchio, C., Murino, V.: Predicting human intentions from motion cues only: a 2D+ 3D fusion approach. In: Proceedings of the 2017 ACM on Multimedia Conference, pp. 591–599. ACM (2017)

Forecasting Hands and Objects
in Future Frames

Chenyou Fan[✉], Jangwon Lee, and Michael S. Ryoo

Indiana University, Bloomington, IN 47401, USA
{fan6,leejang,mryoo}@indiana.edu

Abstract. This paper presents an approach to *forecast* future presence and location of human hands and objects. Given an image frame, the goal is to predict what objects will appear in the future frame (e.g., 5 s later) and where they will be located at, even when they are not visible in the current frame. The key idea is that (1) an intermediate representation of a convolutional object recognition model abstracts scene information in its frame and that (2) we can predict (i.e., regress) such representations corresponding to the future frames based on that of the current frame. We present a new two-stream fully convolutional neural network (CNN) architecture designed for forecasting future objects given a video. The experiments confirm that our approach allows reliable estimation of future objects in videos, obtaining much higher accuracy compared to the state-of-the-art future object presence forecast method on public datasets.

Keywords: Future location forecast · Activity prediction · Object forecast

1 Introduction

The ability to forecast future scene is very important for intelligent agents. The idea is to provide them an ability to infer future objects, similar to humans predicting how the objects in front of them will move and what objects would newly appear. This is particularly necessary for interactive/collaborative systems, including robots, autonomous cars, surveillance systems, and wearable devices. For instance, a robot working on a collaborative task with a human needs to predict what objects the human is expect to move and how they will move; a surgery robot needs to forecast what surgical instruments a human surgeon will need in a few seconds to better support the person. Similarly, forecasting will enable an autonomous driving agent to predict when and where pedestrians or other vehicles are likely to appear even before they are within the view. The forecasting is also necessary for more natural human-robot interaction as well as better real-time surveillance, since this will allow faster reaction of such systems in response to humans and objects.

In the past 2–3 years, there has been an increasing number of works on 'forecasting' in computer vision. Researchers studied forecasting trajectories

© Springer Nature Switzerland AG 2019
L. Leal-Taixé and S. Roth (Eds.): ECCV 2018 Workshops, LNCS 11131, pp. 124–137, 2019.
https://doi.org/10.1007/978-3-030-11015-4_12

[6,19], convolutional neural network (CNN) representations [17], optical flows and human body parts [9], and video frames [4,8]. However, none of these approaches were optimized for forecasting explicit locations of objects appearing in videos. Vondrick et al. [17] only forecast presence of objects without giving their future locations. The method of Luo et al. [9] requires the person to be already in the scene in order to forecast his/her future pose, also it does not consider objects. [4,8] were designed for forecasting direct image frames, instead of doing object-level estimations of locations. To our knowledge, an end-to-end approach to learn the forecast model optimized for future object location estimation has been lacking.

This paper introduces a new approach to forecast presence and location of hands and objects in future frames (e.g., 5 s later). Given an image frame, the objective is to predict future bounding boxes of appearing objects even when they are not visible in the current frame (e.g., Fig. 1). Our key idea is that (1) an intermediate CNN representation of an object recognition model abstracts scene/motion information in its frame and that (2) we can model how such representation changes in the future frames based on the training data. For (1), we design a new two-stream CNN architecture with an auto-encoder by extending the state-of-the-art convolutional object detection network (SSD [7]). For (2), we present a fully convolutional regression network that allows us to infer future CNN representations. These two networks are combined to directly predict future locations of human hands and objects, forming a deeper network that could be trained in an end-to-end fashion (Fig. 2).

Current frame   1 second future   5 second future   Current frame   1 second future   5 second future

Fig. 1. Example object location forecasts on the ADL dataset. Both 1 s and 5 s future bounding box forecasts are presented, overlaid on the actual future frames. The approach only uses the current frame as an input to forecast future boxes. Three types of objects, oven, tap, and person, are predicted in the two examples.

We evaluate our proposed approach with two first-person video datasets and one urban street scene dataset. Hands and objects dynamically appear and disappear in first-person videos taken with wearable cameras, making them suitable for the evaluation of our approach. Notably, in our experiments with the public ADL dataset [12], our accuracy was higher than the previous state-of-the-art [17] by more than 0.25 mean average precision (AP).

2   Related Work

Researchers are increasingly focusing on 'forecasting' of future scene. This work includes early recognition of ongoing human activities [5,14] as well as more explicit forecasting of human trajectories and future locations [6,10,11,19,21]. There are also works forecasting future features or video frames themselves [4,9,17].

Kitani et al. [6] presented an approach to predict human trajectories in surveillance videos. [10,19] also focused on forecasting trajectories. However, most of these trajectory-based works are limited in the sense that they assume the person/object to be forecasted is already present in the scene. This is particularly limited when dealing with objects recorded in wearable/robot cameras, since objects often go out of the scene and return as the camera and the body parts move. Park et al. [11] tried to predict the future location of the person, while using egocentric videos. Rhinehart and Kitani [13] used egocentric videos to learn a reinforcement learning model of the tasks, in order to forecast semantic states and goals. However, their forecasts were done without explicit modeling of when/where the objects need to appear.

Recently, Vondrick et al. [17] showed that forecasting fully connected layer outputs of a convolutional neural network (e.g., VGG [16]) is possible. The paper further demonstrated that such representation forecast can be used to predict the future presence of objects (i.e., whether a particular object will appear within 5 s later or not). However, due to the limited dimensionality of the representation (i.e., 4K-D), the approach was not directly applicable for predicting 'locations' of objects in the scene. Similarly, Luo et al. [9] used CNN regression to forecast optical flow fields, and used such optical flows to predict how human body part will move. It requires the human to be present in the scene initially and his/her body pose is correctly estimated. Finn et al. [4] predicted future video frames by learning dynamics from training videos, but it also assumed the objects to be already present in the scene.

We believe this is the first paper to present a method to explicitly forecast location of objects in future frames using a fully convolutional network. The contribution of this paper is in (1) introducing the concept of future object forecast using fully convolutional regression of intermediate CNN representations, and (2) the design of the two-stream SSD model to consider both appearance and motion optimized for video-based future forecasting. There were previous works on pixel-level forecasting of future frames including [4,9,18,20], but they were limited to pixel-level motion prediction instead of doing object-level predictions. Our approach does not assume hand/object to be in the scene for their future location prediction, unlike prior works based on tracking (e.g., trajectory-based estimation) or pixel motion (e.g., optical flow estimation). For example, Fig. 1 shows our model forecasting an oven to appear 5-s later, which is not visible in the current frame.

3   Approach

The objective of our approach is to predict hands and objects in the future scene given the current image frame. We propose a new two-stream convolutional neural network architecture, with a fully convolutional future representation

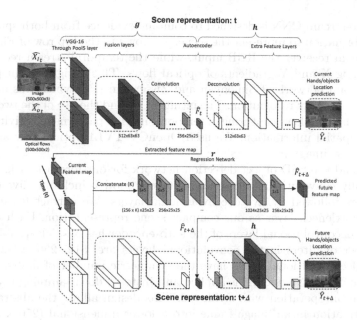

Fig. 2. Overview of our approach: It consists of two fully convolutional neural networks: The first network is the two-stream object detection network (the 1st row and the 3rd row of the figure). The 1st row and the 3rd row are the duplicates of the same model. The second network is the fully convolutional regression network to predict the future intermediate scene representation (the 2nd row). Only the colored layers are used in the actual testing/inference stage.

regression module (Fig. 2). The proposed model consists of two CNNs: (1) an extended two-stream video version of the Single Shot MultiBox Detector (SSD) [7] also with a convolutional auto-encoder, and (2) a future regression network to predict the intermediate scene representation corresponding to the future frame.

The key idea of our approach is that we can forecast scene configurations of the near future (e.g., 5 s later) by predicting (i.e., regressing) its intermediate CNN representation. Inside our fully convolutional hand/object detection network, we abstract scene/motion information of the input frame as its intermediate representation (i.e., $\hat{F}_t$ in Fig. 2) using convolutional auto-encoder. Our approach estimates the intermediate representation of the 'future frame' (i.e., $\hat{F}_{t+\Delta}$) from it, and combines it with the later layers of the object detection network to obtain their future bounding boxes.

3.1   Two-Stream Network for Scene Representation

In this subsection, we introduce our two-stream CNN extending the previous fully convolutional object detection network. The objective of this component is to abstract the scene at time t into a lower dimensional representation, so that estimation of hand and object locations becomes possible.

Our two-stream CNN is designed to combine evidence from both spatial and motion information to represent the scene, as shown in the top row of Fig. 2. The spatial stream receives the RGB input, while the temporal stream receives the corresponding X and Y gradients of optical flows. This design was inspired by the two-stream network of Simonyan and Zisserman [15], which was originally proposed for activity recognition. The intuition behind the use of the two-stream network is that it allows capturing of temporal motion patterns in activity videos as well as spatial information. We used OpenCV TVL1 optical flow algorithm to extract flow images.

We extend the SSD object detection network for our forecast task. We first insert a fully convolutional auto-encoder to our model, including five convolutional layers followed by five deconvolutional layers. We extract feature maps from the bottleneck layer as our compact scene representation. Each convolutional and deconvolutional layers of the auto-encoder has 5×5 learnable filters. The number of filters in the convolutional layers are: 512, 256, 128, 64, and 256. The deconvolutional layers have the symmetric number of filters: 256, 64, 128, 256, and 512. No pooling is applied and instead, downsampling is achieved by convolution operation with stride $= 2$. This design allows the abstraction of scene information in an image frame into a lower dimensional ($256 \times 25 \times 25$) intermediate representation.

We design our object-based scene representation network to have both the spatial-steam and temporal-stream part. Instead of using a late-fusion to combine spatial and temporal streams at the end of network as was done in [15], we design an early-fusion by combining two streams' feature maps before the encoder-decoder component. Specifically, at the conv5 layers, two $256 \times 25 \times 25$ feature blobs from both streams are combined to form a single $256 \times 25 \times 25$ blob by learning one-by-one kernels.

In addition, since our future regression component (to be described in Subsect. 3.2) handles combining representations of multiple past frame, we reduce the amount of computations in our temporal stream by making it receive only one optical flow image instead of stacked optical flows from multiple frames.

Let f denote the proposed two-stream CNN to estimate object locations given a video frame at time t. This function has two input variables $\hat{\mathbf{X}}_{\mathbf{I}t}$ and $\hat{\mathbf{X}}_{\mathbf{O}t}$, which represent the given image frame and the corresponding optical flow image at time t respectively. Note that $\hat{\mathbf{X}}_{\mathbf{O}t}$ is calculated from image I_{t-1} and I_t, so no future information after time t is used. Then, we can decompose this function into two sub functions, $f = g \circ h$:

$$\hat{\mathbf{Y}}_t = f(\hat{\mathbf{X}}_{\mathbf{I}t}, \hat{\mathbf{X}}_{\mathbf{O}t}) = h(\hat{\mathbf{F}}_t) = h(g(\hat{\mathbf{X}}_{\mathbf{I}t}, \hat{\mathbf{X}}_{\mathbf{O}t})), \tag{1}$$

where a function $g : (\hat{\mathbf{X}}_{\mathbf{I}}, \hat{\mathbf{X}}_{\mathbf{O}}) \to \hat{\mathbf{F}}$ denotes convolutional layers to extract compressed visual representation (feature map) $\hat{\mathbf{F}}$ from $\hat{\mathbf{X}}_{\mathbf{I}t}$ and $\hat{\mathbf{X}}_{\mathbf{O}t}$, and $h : \hat{\mathbf{F}} \to \hat{\mathbf{Y}}$ indicates the remaining part of the proposed network that uses the compressed feature map as an input for predicting hands and object locations $\hat{\mathbf{Y}}_t$ at time t. The first row and the last row of Fig. 2 shows such architecture.

The loss function used for the training is identical to the original SSD [7], which is a combination of localization and confidence losses.

3.2   Future Regression Network

Our objective is to forecast the locations of objects in the future frame $\hat{\mathbf{Y}}_{t+\Delta}$ based on current frame $\hat{\mathbf{Y}}_t$. We formulate this as a regression task of forecasting future intermediate representation $\hat{\mathbf{F}}_{t+\Delta}$ of the proposed two-stream network based on its current intermediate representation $\hat{\mathbf{F}}_t$. The main idea is that the intermediate representation of our proposed network abstracts spatial and motion information of hands and objects, and that we can learn a convolutional network modeling how such representation changes over time. Importantly, once we obtain the future intermediate representation $\hat{\mathbf{F}}_{t+\Delta}$, we pass the predicted future representation to the decoder part of the auto-encoder as well as the remaining part of the SSD backbone network to explicitly forecast future hand/object bounding boxes. By feeding the regressed future intermediate representation, the SSD network will give the predicted coordinates of objects as if it has "seen" the future scene.

Let r denote our future regression network to predict the future intermediate scene representation $\hat{\mathbf{F}}_{t+\Delta}$ given a current scene representation $\hat{\mathbf{F}}_t$.

$$\hat{\mathbf{F}}_{t+\Delta} = r_w(\hat{\mathbf{F}}_t). \tag{2}$$

The regression network consist of nine convolutional layers, each having 256 channels of 5×5 filters except the last two layers. We use dilated convolution with 1024 filters to cover a large receptive field of 13×13 for the 8th layer, and 256 1×1 filters are used for the last layer.

A desirable property of this formulation is that it allows training of the weights (w) of the regression network with unlabeled videos using the reconstruction loss as shown below:

$$w^* = \arg \min_w \sum_{i,t} \|r_w(g(\hat{\mathbf{X}}_{\mathbf{I}t}^i, \hat{\mathbf{X}}_{\mathbf{O}t}^i)) - g(\hat{\mathbf{X}}_{\mathbf{I}t+\Delta}^i, \hat{\mathbf{X}}_{\mathbf{O}t+\Delta}^i)\|_2^2 \tag{3}$$

where $\hat{\mathbf{X}}_t^i$ indicates the frame or flow image at time t from video i. Once we get the future scene representation $\hat{\mathbf{F}}_{t+\Delta}$, it is fed to h to forecast hand/object locations corresponding to the future frame:

$$\hat{\mathbf{Y}}_{t+\Delta} = h(\hat{\mathbf{F}}_{t+\Delta}). \tag{4}$$

Figure 2 shows data flow of our proposed approach during the inference (i.e., testing) phase. Given a video frame $\hat{\mathbf{X}}_{\mathbf{I}t}$ and its corresponding optical flow image $\hat{\mathbf{X}}_{\mathbf{O}t}$ at time t, (1) we first extract the intermediate representation (g), and (2) give it to the future regression network (r) to obtain future scene representation $\hat{\mathbf{F}}_{t+\Delta}$. Finally, (3) we predict future location of hands/objects $\hat{\mathbf{Y}}_{t+\Delta}$ by providing the predicted future scene representation to the remaining part of the proposed two-stream CNN (h) at time t.

$$\hat{\mathbf{Y}}_{t+\Delta} = h(\hat{\mathbf{F}}_{t+\Delta}) = h(r(\hat{\mathbf{F}}_t)) = h(r(g(\hat{\mathbf{X}}_{\mathbf{I}t}, \hat{\mathbf{X}}_{\mathbf{O}t}))). \tag{5}$$

In addition to the above basic formulation, our proposed approach is extended to use previous K frames to obtain $\hat{\mathbf{F}}_{t+\Delta}$ as illustrated in Fig. 2.

$$\hat{\mathbf{Y}}_{t+\Delta} = h(r([g(\hat{\mathbf{X}}_{\mathbf{I}t}, \hat{\mathbf{X}}_{\mathbf{O}t}), ..., g(\hat{\mathbf{X}}_{\mathbf{I}t-(K-1)}, \hat{\mathbf{X}}_{\mathbf{O}t-(K-1)})])). \qquad (6)$$

Our future representation regression network allows predicting future objects while considering the implicit scene/object/motion context in the scene. The intermediate representation $\hat{\mathbf{F}}_t$ abstracts spatial/motion information in the current scene, and our fully convolutional future regressor takes advantage of it for the forecast.

4   Experiments

We conducted three sets of experiments to confirm the forecast ability of our approach using the fully convolutional two-stream regression architecture. In the first experiment, we use a first-person video dataset to predict future human hand locations. In the second and third experiments, we use one public egocentric video dataset and one street scene dataset with object annotations to evaluate our methods of predicting future object locations and presences.

4.1   Dataset

Human Interaction Videos: We collected an in-house dataset which contains 47 first-person videos of human-human collaboration scenarios with a wearable camera. The dataset contains videos with two types of collaborative scenarios: (1) a person wearing the camera cleaning up objects on a table as another person approaches the table while holding a large box (i.e., making a room to put the box), and (2) the camera wearer pushes a trivet on a table as another person with a cooking pan approaches. The duration of each video clip is between 4 and 10 s. In our future location forecast task, we fix the SSD backbone including the auto-encoder part, and train the regressor part based on Sect. 3.2.

Activities of Daily Living (ADL): This first-person video dataset [12] contains 20 videos of 18 daily activities, such as making tea and doing laundry. This is a challenging dataset since frames display a significant amount of motion blur caused by the camera wearer's movement. This dataset also suffers from noisy annotations. Object bounding boxes were provided as ground truth annotations. Although there are 43 types of objects in the dataset, we trained our model (and the baselines) for the 15 most common categories, following the setting used in [17]. We split the ADL dataset into four sets, using three sets for the training and the remaining set for the testing, following the setting.

Cityscapes: This dataset [2,3] is a benchmark dataset for semantic segmentation of objects in urban street scenes, which has 30 different classes of objects/scenes (e.g., person, car, sidewalk, ...) with both pixel-level and instance level annotations. For each video, the 20th image of every 30 frame video snippet has been annotated. That is, the time interval between two adjacent frames is 1.8 s. We split 27 videos with fine-grained segmentation masks into 17/5/5 as our training/validation/test sets following the standard setting. We chose seven 'object' classes with sufficient number of training instances in the dataset: bike, traffic sign, traffic light, rider, bus, car, and person. We evaluated forecasting future locations and presences of these objects as they are major moving objects in the scenes and also have enough numbers of occurrences in both train and testing sets (i.e., more than 200 samples). The original annotations are in forms of polygons as instance-level segmentation masks. We convert those polygons to bounding boxes to make our setting similar to the ADL forecast setting described above. Forecasting objects in the next annotated frame (1.8 s later) and the next third annotated frame (5.4 s later) was evaluated.

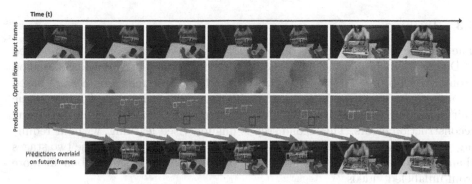

Fig. 3. Examples of hand location forecast. The first row shows the input frames and the second row shows the optical flows. The third row shows our future hand forecast results and we overlaid our predictions on 'future' frames in the last row. Red boxes correspond to the predicted 'my left hand' locations, blue boxes correspond to 'my right hand', green boxes correspond to the opponent's left hand, and the cyan boxes correspond to the opponent's right hand. In the first frame, the model forecasts that the right hand 'will appear', before it actually sees the hand. (Color figure online)

4.2 Baselines

In order to confirm the benefits of our proposed approach quantitatively, we created multiple baselines.

(i) SSD trained with future annotations is the original SSD model [7] for object bounding box estimation, which was trained to forecast future hands/objects. Instead of providing current-frame object bound boxes as ground truths in the training step, we provided 'future' ground truth hand/object locations. This enables the model to directly regress future object boxes given the current frame. We also implemented a **(ii) two-stream version of SSD**, making the SSD architecture to also consider optical flows.

(iii) Hands only is the baseline only using estimated hand locations in the current frame to predict their future locations. The idea is to confirm whether the detection of hand locations is sufficient to infer their future locations. A set of fully connected layers were used for the future location estimation, taking the current frame hand locations as its input representation.

In addition, we implemented simpler versions of our approach, **(iv) one-stream networks**, which use the same CNN architecture as our proposed approach except that it only has the spatial stream (taking RGB input) without the temporal stream (taking optical flow input). We constructed this baseline to confirm how much the temporal-stream of our network helps predicting future hand/object locations. We also compare ours against [17] for future object presence forecast. Finally, we are comparing our approach with the **(v) Vondrick et al.'s method** [17] designed for the object presence forecast. This was done by evaluating our approach on the ADL dataset with the same experimental setup as [17].

4.3 Training

The training of our models was done in two stages. We first finetune the modified SSD network including the auto-encoder part (for scene representation) based on ground-truth object locations. Next, we train the future regressor (i.e., r) based on intermediate representations extracting from any *current and future* frame pair in training videos, with the L2 loss (between $r(\hat{\mathbf{F}}_t)$ and $\hat{\mathbf{F}}_{t+\Delta}$) for measuring reconstruction errors. The second step is unsupervised learning, without requiring additional annotations. We found it more stable to separate these two stages than end-to-end training the entire model, since the 2nd stage can benefit more from unlabeled videos.

4.4 Evaluation

Hand Location Forecast: We first evaluated the performance of our approach to predict future hand locations using our unlabeled human interaction dataset. This is a less noisier dataset than the ADL dataset. Here, we use hand detection results (from the original SSD model trained on the EgoHands dataset [1]) as the ground truth hand labels for the evaluation, since the interaction videos do not have any human annotations. We randomly split the dataset into the training set and the test set; we used 32 videos for the training and the remaining 15 videos for the testing. We used the precision and recall as our evaluation measure. Whether the forecasted bounding boxes are true positives or not was decided based on the intersection over union (IoU) ratio between areas of each predicted box and the (future) ground truth box. The IoU threshold was 0.5.

Table 1 shows quantitative results of 1-s future hand prediction. Since our network may use previous K frames as an input for the future regression, we reported the performances of our approach with $K = 1,5,10$ frames. We observe that our proposed approaches significantly outperform the original SSD trained with future hand locations. The one-stream model performed better than the SSD baseline, suggesting the effectiveness of our concept of future regression. Note that our one-stream $K = 1$ takes the exactly same amount of input as the SSD baseline. Our two-stream models performed better than the one-stream

Table 1. Future hand *location* forecasts measured with Human Interaction dataset.

Method	Evaluation		
	Precision	Recall	F-measure
Hands only	4.78 ± 3.70	5.06 ± 4.06	4.87 ± 3.81
SSD w/future Annot.	27.53 ± 23.36	9.09 ± 8.96	13.23 ± 12.62
Ours (one-stream): K = 1	27.04 ± 16.50	21.71 ± 14.71	23.45 ± 14.99
Ours (one-stream): K = 5	29.97 ± 15.37	23.89 ± 16.45	25.40 ± 15.51
Ours (one-stream): K = 10	36.58 ± 16.91	28.78 ± 17.96	30.90 ± 17.02
Ours (two-stream): K = 1	37.21 ± 22.49	26.69 ± 14.28	30.21 ± 16.07
Ours (two-stream): K = 5	37.41 ± 22.97	26.19 ± 14.93	30.06 ± 17.16
Ours (two-stream): K = 10	**42.89** ± 23.61	**30.46** ± 13.08	**34.18** ± 16.48

models, indicating the temporal stream is helpful to predict future locations. Our proposed model with $K = 10$ yields the best performance in terms of all three metrics, at about 34.18 score in F-measure. Figure 3 shows example hand forecast results.

Object Location Forecast: We used the ADL dataset [12] to evaluate future object location forecast performances. Both 1-s and 5-s future bounding box locations are predicted, and the performances were measured in terms of mean average precision (mAP). The IoU ratio of 0.5 was used to determine whether a predicted bounding box is correct compared to the ground truth. Note that ADL dataset is a challenging dataset for future prediction, since the videos were taken from the first-person view displaying strong egocentric motion. Further, appearing objects are not evenly distributed across different videos. Many objects appear and disappear from the scene even within the 5 s window due to the camera ego-motion.

Table 2 shows average precision (AP) of each object category. We show that our approach significantly outperforms the SSD baseline. While only taking advantage of the same amount of information (i.e., a single frame), our approach (one-stream $K = 1$) achieved a superior performance. By using additional temporal information, our approach (two-stream $K = 1,10$) outperforms its one-stream version by 2–5% in mAP. This indicates that motion information is helpful in predicting the right location of objects in future frames, especially in first-person videos with strong ego-motion. Figure 1 shows example object predictions in 1-s and 5-s future. Based on RGB and optical flow information in the frames, our approach is able to predict future objects even when they are not visible in the current scene.

Object Presence Forecast: In this experiment, we used the ADL dataset to evaluate our approach in forecasting 'presence' of objects in future frames. Specifically, we decide whether the objects will *exist* (in the future frame) or not, regardless their locations. Similar to our object location forecast experiment, we obtained

Table 2. Future object *location* forecast evaluation using the ADL dataset.

	Method	dish	door	utensil	cup	oven	person	soap	tap	tbrush	tpaste	towel	trashc	tv	remote	mAP
	SSD with future annotation	0	0.5	0	0	0	0.2	0	1.3	0	0	0	0	0	0	0.1
	SSD (two-stream)	1.6	12.4	0	0.9	5.1	9.6	0	2.8	0	0	0	0	29.8	1.3	4.5
1 sec	Ours (one-stream K=1)	0.4	15.0	1.2	2.6	13.8	43.4	4.4	19.0	0	0	0.3	0	16.0	18.8	9.6
	Ours (one-stream K=10)	0.4	14.0	0	0.7	16.1	45.8	5.4	22.9	0	0	0.9	0	20.5	6.8	9.5
	Ours (two-stream K=1)	7.3	19.6	1.9	1.8	37.2	26.2	11.6	33.8	0.0	1.4	1.5	0.8	11.0	11.9	11.9
	Ours (two-stream K=10)	3.8	10.1	1.8	5.5	19.0	59.6	2.8	41.8	0.0	0.0	3.4	0.0	15.9	45.2	**14.9**
	SSD with future annotation	0	0	0	0	0.2	0	0	0	0	0	0	0	3.0	0	0.2
	SSD (two-stream)	2.0	11.7	0	3.2	10.2	0.5	3.2	0	0	0	0	0	20.0	0	3.7
5 sec	Ours (one-stream K=1)	0.5	10.8	0	0.3	16.5	10.4	3.2	8.2	0	0	0.7	0	3.9	1.7	4.0
	Ours (one-stream K=10)	0.2	10.7	0	0.2	0.7	35.7	1.3	5.6	0	0	0.5	0	3.8	1.2	4.7
	Ours (two-stream K=1)	1.5	9.8	0.4	0.4	24.1	17.0	8.6	15.8	0.0	0.0	1.6	0.2	7.5	5.8	6.6
	Ours (two-stream K=10)	0.7	4.7	0.0	5.0	9.7	35.6	0.7	10.5	0.0	0.0	1.4	0.0	15.0	24.8	**7.7**

Table 3. Future object *presence* forecast (5 s) evaluation using the ADL dataset.

	Method	dish	door	utensil	cup	oven	person	soap	tap	tbrush	tpaste	towel	trashc	tv	remote	mAP
	Vondrick [17]	4.1	22.2	5.7	16.4	17.5	8.4	19.5	20.6	9.2	5.3	5.6	4.2	8.0	2.6	10.7
	SSD with future annotation	18.9	17.6	0	28.1	7.1	23.0	0	37.7	0	0	0	0	20.4	0	10.9
	SSD (two-stream)	13.5	22.4	0	15.2	4.1	14.3	39.8	21.4	0	0	0	0.4	48.4	0	12.8
5 sec	Ours (one-stream K=1)	34.4	37.0	18.9	19.2	24.3	75.1	70.0	55.0	23.8	6.7	16.6	2.1	57.5	61.7	35.9
	Ours (one-stream K=10)	35.1	42.4	22.2	29.9	37.9	69.9	68.0	67.6	21.7	47.7	17.7	5.2	30.5	36.4	38.0
	Ours (two-stream K=1)	38.2	44.1	23.8	29.1	37.2	73.1	67.1	60.6	12.2	38.0	13.7	4.4	37.2	58.5	38.4
	Ours (two-stream K=10)	35.7	44.0	24.2	29.3	39.6	75.7	68.9	63.2	20.4	47.2	18.2	4.6	40.4	60.3	**40.8**

Fig. 4. Examples of street scene object forecast. Left column shows current frames, while right column shows frames after 1.8 s.

PR-curves and calculated AP of each object category. We trained our model to predict presence of objects in 5-s-future frames. This experiment makes it possible to directly compare our approach with the results of [17]'s AlexNet based architecture, following the same standard setting used in their experiments.

Table 3 compares different versions of our proposed approach with the baselines. We observe that that our approaches significantly outperform the results reported in [17] while following the same setting. Our two-stream K = 10 version obtained the mean AP of 40.8%, which is higher than the previous state-of-the-art by the margin of 30%. In addition, our one-stream $K = 1$ version that only uses one single RGB frame as an input obtained higher accuracy than the SSD baseline and [17] while using the same input. Their performances were 35.9 vs. 10.9 vs. 10.7. We also confirmed that our two-stream $K = 1$ version performs better than the two-stream version of SSD.

Table 4 shows additional experimental results on Cityscapes dataset, measured for both the location and presence forecast tasks. In this dataset, frames are annotated with 1.8 s gaps; the annotation frame rate is low. We thus only trained $K = 1$ versions of our methods in this experiment. We compare our methods (both the one-stream version and the two-stream version) with the SSD two-stream baseline. We observe that our future regression models perform superior to the baseline two-stream SSD, by benefiting from their explicit future representation regression capability. This is consistent in both 1.8 s and 5.4 s forecast tasks, and in both the future location and presence prediction tasks (Fig. 4).

Table 4. Future object forecast evaluation using the Cityscapes dataset. Per-class AP varies a lot depending on what object class the CNN model decides to fire more frequently (i.e., learned prior/bias), but the mean AP results show more consistent trend.

(a): Future object location								
Method	bike	sign	light	rider	bus	car	person	mAP
1.8 s SSD (two-stream)	3.6	2.3	0.0	0.2	0.2	14.8	12.8	4.9
Ours (one-stream $K = 1$)	4.5	3.5	0.6	1.9	0.0	13.0	15.4	5.6
Ours (two-stream $K = 1$)	7.8	2.6	0.3	7.2	0.0	11.6	15.1	6.4
5.4 s SSD (two-stream)	2.3	1.4	0.1	0.3	0.3	15.2	7.4	3.9
Ours (one-stream $K = 1$)	3.2	2.1	0.1	0.5	0.4	15.4	14.2	5.1
Ours (two-stream $K = 1$)	7.2	2.3	0.9	5.1	1.0	11.3	10.0	5.4
(b): Future object presence								
Method	bike	sign	light	rider	bus	car	person	mAP
1.8 s SSD (two-stream)	77.3	95.9	39.1	28.8	15.2	22.9	83.9	51.9
Ours (one-stream $K = 1$)	74.7	94.2	55.4	45.6	7.8	20.6	88.0	55.2
Ours (two-stream $K = 1$)	75.6	92.1	54.0	64.8	6.8	14.9	84.0	56.1
5.4 s SSD (two-stream)	79.1	95.6	26.8	24.2	9.7	22.9	76.3	47.8
Ours (one-stream $K = 1$)	73.8	93.4	45.5	60.3	9.6	15.0	77.8	53.6
Ours (two-stream $K = 1$)	77.7	91.6	34.4	32.7	13.5	31.4	75.5	51.0

5   Conclusion

We presented a new approach to explicitly *forecast* human hands and objects using a fully convolutional future representation regression network. The key idea was to forecast scene configurations of the near future by predicting (i.e., regressing) intermediate CNN representations of the future scene. We presented a new two-stream model to represent scene information of the given image frame, and experimentally confirmed that we can learn a function (i.e., a network) to model how such intermediate scene representation changes over time. The experimental results confirmed that our object forecast approach significantly outperforms the previous work on the public ADL dataset.

References

1. Bambach, S., Lee, S., Crandall, D.J., Yu, C.: Lending a hand: detecting hands and recognizing activities in complex egocentric interactions. In: IEEE International Conference on Computer Vision (ICCV), December 2015
2. Cordts, M., et al.: The cityscapes dataset for semantic urban scene understanding. In: Proceedings of the IEEE Conference on Computer Vision and Pattern Recognition (CVPR) (2016)
3. Cordts, M., et al.: The cityscapes dataset. In: CVPR Workshop on the Future of Datasets in Vision (2015)
4. Finn, C., Goodfellow, I., Levine, S.: Unsupervised learning for physical interaction through video prediction. In: Advances in Neural Information Processing Systems (NIPS), pp. 64–72 (2016)
5. Hoai, M., De la Torre, F.: Max-margin early event detectors. In: IEEE Conference on Computer Vision and Pattern Recognition (CVPR) (2012)
6. Kitani, K.M., Ziebart, B.D., Bagnell, J.A., Hebert, M.: Activity forecasting. In: Fitzgibbon, A., Lazebnik, S., Perona, P., Sato, Y., Schmid, C. (eds.) ECCV 2012. LNCS, vol. 7575, pp. 201–214. Springer, Heidelberg (2012). https://doi.org/10.1007/978-3-642-33765-9_15
7. Liu, W., et al.: SSD: single shot multibox detector. In: Leibe, B., Matas, J., Sebe, N., Welling, M. (eds.) ECCV 2016. LNCS, vol. 9905, pp. 21–37. Springer, Cham (2016). https://doi.org/10.1007/978-3-319-46448-0_2
8. Lotter, W., Kreiman, G., Cox, D.: Deep predictive coding networks for video prediction and unsupervised learning. arXiv preprint arXiv:1605.08104 (2016)
9. Luo, Z., Peng, B., Huang, D.A., Alahi, A., Fei-Fei, L.: Unsupervised learning of long-term motion dynamics for videos. arXiv preprint arXiv:1701.01821 (2017)
10. Ma, W., Huang, D., Lee, N., Kitani, K.M.: A game-theoretic approach to multi-pedestrian activity forecasting. arXiv preprint arXiv:1604.01431 (2016)
11. Park, H.S., Hwang, J.J., Niu, Y., Shi, J.: Egocentric future localization. In: IEEE Conference on Computer Vision and Pattern Recognition (CVPR) (2016)
12. Pirsiavash, H., Ramanan, D.: Detecting activities of daily living in first-person camera views. In: IEEE Conference on Computer Vision and Pattern Recognition (CVPR), pp. 2847–2854. IEEE (2012)
13. Rhinehart, N., Kitani, K.M.: First-person activity forecasting with online inverse reinforcement learning. In: IEEE International Conference on Computer Vision (ICCV) (2017)
14. Ryoo, M.S.: Human activity prediction: early recognition of ongoing activities from streaming videos. In: IEEE International Conference on Computer Vision (ICCV) (2011)
15. Simonyan, K., Zisserman, A.: Two-stream convolutional networks for action recognition in videos. In: Advances in Neural Information Processing Systems (NIPS), pp. 568–576 (2014)

16. Simonyan, K., Zisserman, A.: Very deep convolutional networks for large-scale image recognition. In: ICLR (2015)
17. Vondrick, C., Pirsiavash, H., Torralba, A.: Anticipating visual representations with unlabeled video. In: IEEE Conference on Computer Vision and Pattern Recognition (CVPR) (2016)
18. Walker, J., Doersch, C., Gupta, A., Hebert, M.: An uncertain future: forecasting from static images using variational autoencoders. In: Leibe, B., Matas, J., Sebe, N., Welling, M. (eds.) ECCV 2016. LNCS, vol. 9911, pp. 835–851. Springer, Cham (2016). https://doi.org/10.1007/978-3-319-46478-7_51
19. Walker, J., Gupta, A., Hebert, M.: Patch to the future: unsupervised visual prediction. In: IEEE Conference on Computer Vision and Pattern Recognition (CVPR), pp. 3302–3309 (2014)
20. Xue, T., Wu, J., Bouman, K.L., Freeman, W.T.: Visual dynamics: probabilistic future frame synthesis via cross convolutional networks. In: Advances in Neural Information Processing Systems (NIPS) (2016)
21. Yagi, T., Mangalam, K., Yonetani, R., Sato, Y.: Future person localization in first-person videos. In: IEEE Conference on Computer Vision and Pattern Recognition (CVPR) (2018)

RED: A Simple but Effective Baseline Predictor for the *TrajNet* Benchmark

Stefan Becker[⊠][iD], Ronny Hug[iD], Wolfgang Hübner[iD], and Michael Arens[iD]

Fraunhofer Institute for Optronics, System Technologies, and Image Exploitation
IOSB, Gutleuthausstr. 1, 76275 Ettlingen, Germany
stefan.becker@iosb.fraunhofer.de

Abstract. In recent years, there is a shift from modeling the tracking problem based on Bayesian formulation towards using deep neural networks. Towards this end, in this paper the effectiveness of various deep neural networks for predicting future pedestrian paths are evaluated. The analyzed deep networks solely rely, like in the traditional approaches, on observed tracklets without human-human interaction information. The evaluation is done on the publicly available *TrajNet* benchmark dataset [39], which builds up a repository of considerable and popular datasets for trajectory prediction. We show how a Recurrent-Encoder with a Dense layer stacked on top, referred to as RED-predictor, is able to achieve top-rank at the *TrajNet* 2018 challenge compared to elaborated models. Further, we investigate failure cases and give explanations for observed phenomena, and give some recommendations for overcoming demonstrated shortcomings.

Keywords: Trajectory forecasting · Path prediction · Trajectory-based activity forecasting

1 Introduction

The prediction of possible future paths is a central building block for an automated risk assessment. The applications cover a wide range from mobile robot navigation, including autonomous driving, smart video surveillance to object tracking. Dividing the many variants of forecasting approaches can be roughly done by asking how the problem is addressed or what kind of information is provided. Firstly, addressing this problem reaches from traditional approaches such as the Kalman filter [25], linear [34] or Gaussian regression models [42], auto-regressive models [2], time-series analysis [37] to optimal control theory [27], deep learning combined with game theory [32], or the application of deep convolutional networks [21] and recurrent neural networks (RNNs) as a sequence generation problem [3,4,23]. Secondly, the grouping can be done by using the provided information. On the one hand, the approaches can solely rely on observations of

---

S. Becker and R. Hug—Equal contribution.

L. Leal-Taixé and S. Roth (Eds.): ECCV 2018 Workshops, LNCS 11131, pp. 138–153, 2019.
https://doi.org/10.1007/978-3-030-11015-4_13

consecutive positions extracted by visual tracking or on the other hand, by using richer context information. This can be for example human-human interactions or human-space interactions or general additional visual extracted information such as pedestrian head orientation [28] or head poses [17]. For some representative approaches which model human-human interactions, one should mention the works of Helbing and Molnár [19] and Coscia et al. [10] or approaches in combination with RNNs such as the works of Alahi et al. [3,4]. The spatial context of motion can in principle be learned by training a model on observed positions of a particular scene, but it is not guaranteed that the model successfully captures spatial points of interest and does not only implicitly keep spatial information by performing path integration in order to predict new positions. Nevertheless, here we distinguish such approaches from approaches where scene context is provided as further cue for example by semantic labeling [6] or scene encoding [44]. The challenges of *Trajectory Forecasting Benchmarking* (*TrajNet* 2018) [39] are designed to cover some inherent properties of human motion in crowded scenes. The *World H-H TrajNet* challenge in particular looks at predicting motions in world plane coordinates of human-human interactions. The aim of this paper is to find an effective baseline predictor only based on the partial history and find the maximum potential achievable prediction accuracy for this challenge. Achieving this objective involves an evaluation of different deep neural networks for trajectory prediction and analysis of the datasets properties. Further, we propose small changes and pre-processing steps to modify a standard RNN prediction model to result in a simple but effective RNN architecture that obtains comparable performance to more elaborated models, which additionally captures the interpersonal aspect of human-human interaction.

The paper is structured as follows. Firstly, the properties of the *TrajNet* benchmark dataset are analyzed in Sect. 2. Then, some basic deep neural networks are shortly described and evaluated (Sect. 3). Further, the modifications in order to increase the prediction performance are presented in Sect. 4. The achieved results and an additional failure analysis are discussed in Sect. 5. Finally, a conclusion is given in Sect. 6.

2   *TrajNet* Benchmark Dataset Analysis

The trajectory forecasting challenges *TrajNet* [39] provide the community with a defined and repeatable way of comparing path prediction approaches as well as a common platform for discussions in the field. In this section some properties of the current repository for the *World H-H TrajNet* challenge of popular datasets for trajectory-based activity forecasting are analyzed and thereby design choices for the proposed predictor are deduced.

In most datasets, the scene is observed from a bird's eye view, but there are also scenarios where the scene is observed under a higher depression angle. The selected surveillance datasets cover real world scenarios with a varying crowd densities and varying complexity of trajectory patterns. Details of the datasets are summarized in Table 1 (adapted from *TrajNet* website). The selection includes the following datasets. The *BIWI Walking Pedestrians Dataset* [36]

Table 1. Training (green) and test (cyan) dataset of the world plane human-human dataset challenge (adapted from the *TrajNet* website [39]).

Name	Resolution	#Pedestrian	Framerate	Reference
BIWI Hotel	720 × 576	389	2.5	[36]
Crowds Zara	720 × 576	204	2.5	[30]
Crowds Students	720 × 576	415	2.5	[30]
Crowds Arxiepiskopi	720 × 576	24	2.5	[30]
PETS 2009	768 × 576	19	2.5	[14]
Stanford Drone Dataset (SDD)	595 × 326	3295	2.5	[38]
BIWI ETH	640 × 480	360	2.5	[36]
Crowds Zara	720 × 576	148	2.5	[30]
Crowds Uni Examples	720 × 576	118	2.5	[30]
Stanford Drone Dataset (SDD)	595 × 326	3297	2.5	[38]

also sometimes referenced as *ETH Walking Pedestrians (EWAP)*, which is split into two sets (*ETH* and *Hotel*). The *Crowds* dataset also called *UCY "Crowds-by-Example"* dataset [30] contains three scenes from an oblique view, where the first (Zara) shows a part of a shopping street, the second (*Students/Uni Examples*) captures a part of the uni campus and the third scene (*Arxiepiskopi*) captures a different part of the campus. Then, the *Stanford Drone Dataset (SDD)* [38] consists of multiple aerial images capturing different locations around the Stanford campus. And finally the *PETS 2009* dataset [14], where different outdoor crowds activities are observed by multiple static cameras. Sample images with full trajectories and tracklets are shown in Fig. 1.

Fig. 1. Example trajectories from the *BIWI ETH* dataset and example tracklets from the sequence *Hyang_07* from the *Stanford Drone Dataset (SDD)*.

It is common and good practice to apply cross-validation. For the TajNet challenge, it is done by omitting complete datasets for testing. Because the behavior of humans in crowds is scene-independent and for measuring the generalization capabilities of various approaches across datasets this is very reasonable, in particular for providing a benchmark for human-human interactions. Nevertheless, by combining all training sets the spatial context of scene specific motion and the reference systems are lost. When only relying on observed motion trajectories positional information is crucial in order to learn spatio-temporal variation. For example, the sidewalks in the *Hyang* sequences (see Fig. 1) lead to a spatially depending change in the curvature of a trajectory. Since our focus is on deep neural networks including RNNs, the shift from position information to higher order motion helps to overcome some drawbacks. Before RNNs were successfully applied for tracking pedestrians in a surveillance scenario, they gained attention due to their success in tasks such as speech recognition [9,15] and caption generation [11,43]. Since these domain are particularly different to trajectory prediction in certain aspects, their position-dependent movement is not important. Accordingly, RNNs can benefit from conditioning on previous offsets for scene independent motion prediction. This insight is not new, yet utilizing offsets really helps not only stabilizing the learning process but also improves the prediction performance for the evaluated networks. This shift to offsets or rather velocities has been also successfully applied for example for the prediction of human poses based on RNNs [33]. In the context of deep networks the same effect can also be achieved by adding residual connections, which have been shown to improve performance on deep convolutional networks [18] Presumably due to the limitation of the input and output spaces, for applying on the *TrajNet* challenge instead of prediction of the next position (where will the person be next) predicting the following offsets (where will the person go next) [23,24] also contributed to increased prediction accuracy. This becomes immediately apparent by looking at the complete tracklets of the training and test set (see Fig. 2). Firstly, it takes a considerably higher modeling effort to represent all possible positions instead of modeling particular velocities. Further, input data outside the training range can lead to undefined states in the deep network, which result in an unreasonably random output. Some of the initialization tracklets clearly lie outside the training input space. Also, approaches with profit from human-human interaction such as [3,4,16,17] in combination with deep networks lack here information about surrounding persons to interact, so that the decoding of relative distances is not possible because of a reduced person density.

Another factor for improving the prediction performance is becoming apparent when contemplating the offset distribution of the data. Figure 3 shows the offsets histograms for x and y separately. Due to the loss of the reference system, it is impossible to assume a reasonable location distribution a-priori. In contrast, the offset and magnitude distribution clearly reflects the preferred walking speeds in the data. The histograms also show that a large amount of persons is standing. In the recent work of Hasan et al. [17], it was emphasized that forecasting

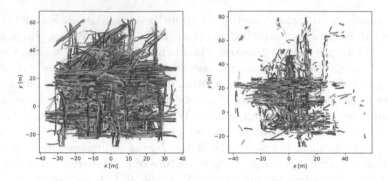

Fig. 2. (Left) Visualization of all tracklets of the training set from the *TrajNet* dataset collection. (Right) Visualization of all initialization tracklets of the test set.

errors are in general higher when the speed of persons is lower and argued that when persons are walking slowly their behavior becomes less predictable, due to physical reasons (less inertia). During our testing we discovered the same phenomenon. In particular RNN based networks tend to overestimate slow velocities and do sometimes not accurately identify the standing behavior. Despite this problem, the range of offsets is very limited compared to the location distribution and shows a clear tendency towards expected a-priori values. Common techniques for sequence prediction problems are normalization and standardization of the input data. Whereby normalization has a similar role on the position data, applying standardization on position input data shows no benefit. In our experiments, standardization worked slightly better than normalization or an embedding layer for input encoding. Although the effect on the performance is quite low for the *TrajNet* challenge, our best result is achieved using standardized offsets as input. It is rarely strictly necessary to standardize the inputs, but there are practical reasons such as accelerating the training or reducing the chances of getting stuck in local optima [7]. Predicting offsets also guarantees that the output directly conforms better with the range of common activation functions.

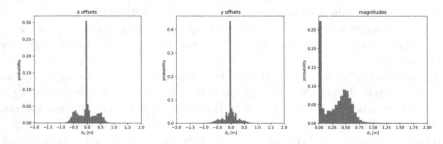

Fig. 3. (Left, Middle) Offset histograms of the training set. (Right) Magnitude histogram of the offsets.

Without discretization artifacts, the dynamic of humans is smooth and persistent. The trajectory data from the *TrajNet* dataset includes varying discretization artifacts or noise levels resulting from different methods with which ground truth data was generated. Part of the ground truth trajectories are generated by a visual tracker or manually annotated.

For approximating the amount of noise in the datasets, the distance between a smoothed spline fit through the complete tracklets is compared to the provided ground truth tracklet points. The spline fitting is done with a polynom of degree $k = 4$ independent for the x and y values. If the smoothing is too strong, it can drift too far away from the actual data. Nevertheless, the achieved fitted trajectories form a smooth and natural path and are used as rough assessment for the noise levels in the ground truth trajectory data. The results for the training set are summarized in Table 2.

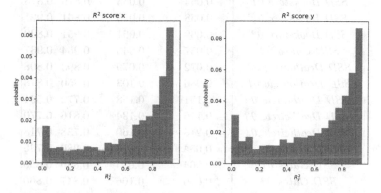

Fig. 4. Coefficient of determination R^2 for x and y for all training tracklets of the *World H-H TrajNet* challenge.

The approximated noise levels clearly show the variation in the ground truth data. In order to outperform a linear baseline predictor the learned model must be able to successfully model different velocity profiles and capture curved paths out of input data with different noise levels. Due to the varying noise levels, initial experiments to solely train on smoothed fitted trajectories with synthetic noise performed worse. Nevertheless, for the prediction of the future steps the best performing predictor is trained to forecast smoothed paths. Before the different evaluated models are introduced, the last data analysis of the training set is intended to assess the complexity in terms of the non-linearity of the trajectories. Therefore, the coefficient of determination R^2 for a linear interpolation is calculated separately for the x and y values. This linear interpolation serves as baseline predictor for the *TrajNet* challenge. The histograms of R^2 for the training set are shown in Fig. 4. R^2 is the percentage of the variation that is explained by the model and is used to determine the suitability of the regression fit as a linearity measure [12]. The average R^2 values are summarized in Table 2. It can be seen that for most tracklets a linear interpolation works very

Table 2. Standard deviation of the distance between a smoothed spline fit and the ground truth trajectory data. The average R^2 score for all tracklets in the subsets.

Name	$\sigma_{x,\text{spline}}$ [m]	$\sigma_{y,\text{spline}}$ [m]	$\bar{R}^2_x$	$\bar{R}^2_y$
Overall	0.067	0.069	0.889	0.811
BIWI Hotel	0.042	0.031	0.637	0.876
Crowds Zara_02	0.029	0.035	0.952	0.758
Crowds Zara_03	0.026	0.031	0.935	0.716
Crowds Students_01	0.033	0.029	0.868	0.852
Crowds Students_03	0.039	0.040	0.915	0.76
Crowds Arxiepiskopi_01	0.050	0.027	0.959	0.677
PETS 2009 S2L1	0.037	0.026	0.781	0.877
SSD Bookstore_00	0.060	0.063	0.889	0.844
SSD Bookstore_01	0.054	0.053	0.879	0.878
SSD Bookstore_02	0.068	0.073	0.861	0.921
SSD Bookstore_03	0.069	0.061	0.951	0.830
SSD Coupa_03	0.057	0.043	0.954	0.937
SSD Deathcircle_00	0.072	0.079	0.893	0.808
SSD Deathcircle_01	0.086	0.103	0.850	0.818
SSD Deathcircle_02	0.151	0.158	0.772	0.591
SSD Deathcircle_03	0.116	0.134	0.816	0.770
SSD Deathcircle_04	0.215	0.160	0.738	0.713
SSD Gates_00	0.054	0.073	0.980	0.735
SSD Gates_01	0.064	0.084	0.859	0.890
SSD Gates_03	0.086	0.106	0.847	0.860
SSD Gates_04	0.071	0.155	0.820	0.906
SSD Gates_05	0.069	0.067	0.858	0.904
SSD Gates_06	0.077	0.072	0.840	0.905
SSD Gates_07	0.084	0.126	0.908	0.817
SSD Gates_08	0.076	0.088	0.922	0.820
SSD Hyang_04	0.048	0.050	0.829	0.842
SSD Hyang_05	0.059	0.081	0.872	0.740
SSD Hyang_06	0.070	0.066	0.875	0.811
SSD Hyang_07	0.040	0.079	0.879	0.894
SSD Hyang_09	0.036	0.088	0.998	0.652
SSD Nexus_00	0.076	0.082	0.886	0.742
SSD Nexus_01	0.067	0.095	0.929	0.771
SSD Nexus_02	0.069	0.074	0.934	0.726
SSD Nexus_03	0.188	0.113	0.786	0.572
SSD Nexus_04	0.097	0.073	0.847	0.724
SSD Nexus_07	0.053	0.069	0.935	0.764
SSD Nexus_08	0.067	0.070	0.926	0.681
SSD Nexus_09	0.052	0.094	0.913	0.816

well. In order to outperform the linear interpolation baseline, it is crucial to not only cover a variety of complex observed motions, but to also produce robust results in simpler situations. As mentioned above, the person velocity has to be effectively captured by the model.

3   Models and Evaluation

The goal of this work is by using a sort of coarse to fine searching strategy to reach the maximum achievable prediction accuracy without further cues such as human-human interaction or human-space interaction based on basic networks. Towards this end, we started with a set of networks with a limited set of hyper-parameters to narrow it down to one network, in order to then extend the hyper-parameter set for a more exhaustive tuning. The multi-modal aspect of trajectory prediction is hardly considerable when there is no fixed reference system. Thus, the performance is compared in accordance to the community with the two error metrics of the average displacement error (ADE) and the final displacement error (FDE) (see for example [3,16,17,36,41,44]). The average of both combined values are then used as overall average to rank the approaches. The ADE is defined as the average L2 distance between ground truth and the prediction over all predicted time steps and the FDE is defined as the L2 distance between the predicted final position and the true final position. For the *World H-H TrajNet* challenge the unit of the error metrics is meter. For all experiments, 8 (3.2 s) consecutive positions are observed, before predicting the next 12 (4.8 s) positions.

Besides the provided approaches of the *World H-H TrajNet* challenge, the following basic neural networks for a coarse evaluation are selected:

Multi-Layer-Perceptron (MLP): The MLP is tested with different linear and non-linear activation functions. One variation concatenates all inputs and predicts 24 outputs directly. Further, cascaded architectures with a step-wise prediction are examined. We vary between different coordinate system of Euclidean and polar coordinates. As mentioned in Sect. 2, positions and offsets (also orientation normalized) are considered as inputs and outputs.

RNN-MLP: RNNs extend feed-forward networks or rather the MLP model due to their recurrent connections between hidden units. Vanilla RNNs produce an output at each time step. For the evaluation of the RNN-MLP, we vary only the MLP layer which is used for the decoding of the positions and offsets.

RNN-Encoder-MLP: In contrast to the RNN-MLP network, the complete initialization tracklet is used to generate the internal representation before a prediction is done. The RNN-Encoder-MLP is varied by alternating activation functions for the MLP and by alternatively predicting the complete future path/offsets instead of only next steps. As a further alternative, the full path is predicted as offsets to one reference point instead of applying path integration in order to predict the final position.

RNN-Encoder-Decoder-Model (Seq2Seq): In addition to RNN-Encoder-MLPs, Seq2Seqs include a second network. This second decoder network takes the internal representation of the encoder and then starts predicting the next steps. The different settings for the evaluation of this model where due to alternating activation functions for the MLP on top of the decoder RNN.

Temporal Convolutional Networks (TCN): As an alternative to RNNs and based on *WaveNets* [35], Bai et al. [5] introduced a general convolution architecture for sequence prediction. We tested their standard and extended architecture with a gating mechanism (GTCN). For a more detailed description, we refer to the original papers.

All networks were trained with varying number of layers (1 to 5) and hidden units (4 to 64) using stochastic gradient descent with a fixed learning rate of 0.005. The models are trained for 100 epochs using ADAM optimizer [26] and have been implemented in *Tensorflow* [1]. Firstly, only standard RNN cells are used for the experiments. Later, we also tested with RNNs variants Long Short-Term Memory [20] (LSTM) and Gated Recurrent Unit [8] (GRU). As loss the mean squared error between the predicted and the ground truth position or offsets over all time steps is used.

In order to emphasize trends a part from the result of the first experiments are summarized in Table 3 (highlighted in gray). The best results were achieved with the RNN-Encoder-MLP. However, in most cases the different architectures perform very similar. These initial result also show that the best performing networks lie close to the result achieved with linear interpolation. Outlier weak performances are due some strong overestimation of slow person velocities and some undefined random predictions when using positions. Hasan et al. reduced this effect by integrating head pose information. We can only remark for the tested networks that this effect can also differ for different runs. Naturally it is important that during training the networks see enough samples from standing of slow moving situations. Excluding such samples through heuristic or probabilistic filtering only helps during application.

There is no network that is clearly performing best, thus the gap between a MLP predictor and a Seq2Seq model is very narrow in the test scenarios. However, besides the factors derived from the data analysis, a prediction of the full path instead of step-wise prediction helps to overcome an accumulation of errors that are fed back into the networks. For the *TrajNet* challenge with a fixed prediction horizon, we thus prefer the RNN-Encoder-MLP over a Seq2Seq model. In the domain of human pose prediction based on RNNs, Li et al. [31] reduced this problem with an Auto-Conditioned RNN Network and Martinez et al. [33] propose using a Seq2Seq model along with a sampling-based loss. The TCNs perform here similar to RNNs. Since RNNs are more common, also as part of architectures which model interactions (see [3,4,17,44]) to represent single motion, we keep the RNN-Encoder-MLP as our favored model.

Table 3. Results for the world plane human-human dataset challenge (*World H-H TrajNet* challenge).

Approach	Overall Average ↓	FDE [m] ↓	ADE [m] ↓	Reference
RED	**0.797**	1.229	0.364	Ours
Social Forces (EWAP)	**0.819**	1.266	0.371	[19]
Predictor SUL	**0.887**	1.374	0.399	
Social Forces (ATTR)	0.904	1.395	0.412	[19]
OSG	1.385	2.106	0.664	
Social LSTM	1.387	2.098	0.675	[3]
Vanilla LSTM	2.107	3.114	1.100	
Occupancy LSTM	2.111	3.12	1.101	
Interactive Gaussian Processes	1.642	1.038	2.245	[13]
Linear Interpolation	0.894	1.359	0.429	
Linear MLP (Pos)	1.041	1.592	0.491	
Linear MLP (Off)	0.896	1.384	0.407	
Non-Linear MLP (Off)	2.103	3.181	1.024	
Linear RNN	0.951	1.482	0.420	
Non-Linear RNN	**0.841**	1.300	0.381	
Linear RNN-Encoder-MLP	0.892	1.381	0.404	
Non-Linear RNN-Encoder-MLP	**0.827**	1.276	0.377	
Linear Seq2Seq	0.923	1.429	0.418	
Non-Linear Seq2Seq	**0.860**	1.331	0.390	
TCN	**0.841**	1.301	0.381	[5]
Gated TCN	0.947	1.468	0.426	[5]

Results highlighted in blue are taken from the *TrajNet* website [39]
(http://trajnet.stanford.edu/, accessed 22.06.2018)

4 RNN-Encoder-MLP: RED-predictor

According to the training set analysis and the comparison of architectures the selected model for the *TrajNet* challenge modeling only single human motion is a RNN-Encoder-MLP. In this section, the final design choices, which lead to the submitted predictor which achieved top-rank at the *World H-H TrajNet* challenge, are summarized. The RNN-Encoder as favored model can generalize to deal with varying noisy inputs and is thus able to better capture the person motion compared to the linear interpolation baseline. The main insight is that motion continuity is easier to express in offsets or velocities, because it takes considerably more modeling effort to represent all possible conditioning positions. Especially for the *World H-H TrajNet* challenge, with the different range for positions in the training and test set, this has significant influence on whether a good performance can be obtained. Instead of using the given input sequence $\mathcal{X}^T = \{(x^t, y^t) \in \mathbb{R}^2 | t = 1, \ldots, t_{obs}\}$ of t_{obs} consecutive pedestrian positions along a trajectory, here the offsets are used for conditioning the network $\mathcal{X}^T = \{(\delta_x^t, \delta_y^t) \in \mathbb{R}^2 | t = 2, \ldots, t_{obs}\}$. Apart from the smaller modeling effort to represent conditioned offsets and the prevention of undefined states due to a suitable data range this domain shift makes data-preprocessing such as the used standardization more reasonable. Since the offset or rather velocity distribution follows a normal distribution around the expected walking speeds of pedestrians compared to the position distribution. In order to deal with the varying discretization artefacts of the ground truth trajectories and make further training easier, smoothed trajectories are used as desired output. Since the prediction length is fixed, the effect of error accumulation during a step-wise prediction is reduced by not feeding back RNN output and applying a full path prediction. Full path integration worked similarly well, but here offsets to the reference positions (last observed position) are predicted. In order to increase the amount of training data, data augmentation is done by reverting all training tracklets. With the combination of all listed factors the proposed simple but effective baseline predictor for the *TrajNet* challenge is ready. In its core the architecture is a Recurrent-Encoder with a dense MLP layer stacked on top. Hence, the predictor is referred to as RED-predictor and can be defined by:

$$h_{encoder}^t = \text{RNN}(h_{encoder}^{t-1}, \delta_{(x,y)}^t; W_{encoder})$$
$$\mathcal{Y}^T = \{(\delta_x^{t+k}, \delta_y^{t+k}) + (x^t, y^t) \in \mathbb{R}^2 | k = 1, \dots, t_{pred}\} = \text{MLP}(h_{encoder}^t; W_{MLP})$$

Here, $RNN(\cdot)$ is the recurrent network, $h_{encoder}$ the hidden state of the RNN-Encoder with corresponding weight and biases $W_{encoder}$, which is used to generate the full, smoothed path. The multilayer perceptron $MLP(\cdot)$ including the conforming weights and biases W_{MLP} maps the vector $h_{encoder}$ to the coordinate space. The overall architecture is visualized in Fig. 5.

The best achieved result is highlighted in red in Table 3. After a fine search for this network, the shown result is produced with a LSTM cell (state size of 32) and one recurrent layer. The proposed predictor was able to produce sophisticated results compared to elaborated models which additionally rely on interaction information such as the model from Helbing and Molnár [19] and

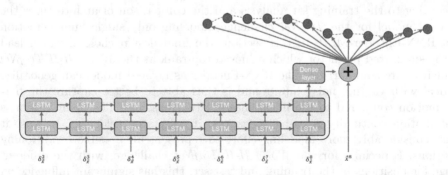

Fig. 5. Visualization of the RED architecture. The conditioning is done for the full initialization sequence $\mathcal{X}^T = \{(\delta_x^t, \delta_y^t) \in \mathbb{R}^2 | t = 2, \dots, t_8\}$. The internal representation is then used to predict the desired path at once (all 12 positions) using the last observed position (x^8, y^8) as reference for localization.

the Social-LSTM [3]. Compared to all submitted approaches of the *World H-H TrajNet* 2018 challenge, the RED predictor achieved the best result. All results highlighted in blue were either also officially submitted or provided by the organizers. Nevertheless, the Social-LSTM is one of the first proposed RNN-based architectures which includes human-human interaction and laid the basis for architectures such as presented in the work of Hasan et al. [17] or Xue et al. [44]. Single motion is modeled with an LSTM network. By applying some of the proposed factors to the model, it is expected that the model and equity accordingly model extensions are able to outperform the proposed single motion predictor.

5   Discussion and Failure Cases

After emphasizing the factors needed in order to achieve sophisticated results based on standard neural networks in the above sections, in this section we discuss some failure cases.

Without exploiting scene-specific knowledge for trajectory prediction, some particular changing behavior in the human motion is not predictable. For example, in the shown tracklet from *SSD Hyang* (see Fig. 6), there is no cue for a turning maneuver in the initialization tracklet. In order to correct the prediction, new observations are required. All methods tend to predict in such a situation a relatively straight line, resulting in a high prediction error. A scene-independent motion representation is pursuant to better generalize, but for overcoming some limitation in the achievable prediction accuracy, the spatial context is required. The sample tracklet also illustrates the multi-modal nature of the prediction problem. While the person is making a left turn, it is also possible to make a right turn. By using a single maximum-likelihood path the multi-modality of a motion and the uncertainty in the prediction is not covered. The prediction uncertainty can be considered by using the normalized estimation error square (nees) [22], also known as Mahalanobis distance, which corresponds to a weighted Euclidean distance of the errors. But most methods are designed as a regression model, thus for a unified evaluation system the Mahalanobis distance is not applicable. As mentioned, there are a few approaches which include the multi-modal aspect of the problem [24,27,29]. Without additional cues of the current scene, these approaches are limited to a fixed scene.

Independent of the question how to include all aspects of a problem in a unified benchmarking, they strongly influence the possible achievable results. The results presented in Sect. 3 show that independent from the model complexity approaches restricted to observing only information from one trajectory are in range to their reachable performance limit on the current dataset repository. Of course due to the fast development in the field of deep neural networks there is still space for improvement, but the current benchmark cannot be completely solved. However, the *TrajNet* challenges also provides human-human and human-space information and recent work such as the approaches of Gupta et al. [16] (human-human) or Xua et al. [44] and Sadeghian et al. [40] (human-human, human-space) show possibilities of how to further improve the performance accuracy.

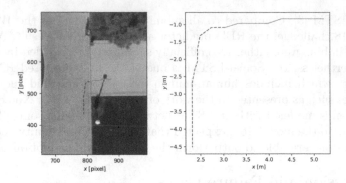

Fig. 6. Example where the scene context strongly influences the person trajectory. The initialization tracklet (solid line) delivers no evidence for a turning maneuver at the intersection. This also shows the multi-modal nature of the prediction problem.

6   Conclusion

In this paper, we presented an evaluation of deep learning approaches for trajectory prediction on *TrajNet* benchmark dataset. The initial results showed that without further cues such as human-human interaction or human-space interaction most basic networks achieve similar results in small range close to a maximum achievable prediction accuracy. By modifying a standard RNN prediction model, we were able to provide a simple but effective RNN architecture that achieves a performance comparable to more elaborated models and achieved the top-rank on the *World H-H TrajNet* 2018 challenge.

Acknowledgements. The authors thank the organizers of the *TrajNet* challenge for providing a framework towards a more meaningful, standardized trajectory prediction benchmarking.

References

1. Abadi, M., et al.: TensorFlow: large-scale machine learning on heterogeneous systems (2015). https://www.tensorflow.org/, software available from tensorflow.org
2. Akaike, H.: Fitting autoregressive models for prediction. Ann. Inst. Stat. Math. **21**(1), 243–247 (1969). http://EconPapers.repec.org/RePEc:spr:aistmt:v:21:y:1969:i:1:p:243-247
3. Alahi, A., Goel, K., Ramanathan, V., Robicquet, A., Fei-Fei, L., Savarese, S.: Social LSTM: human trajectory prediction in crowded spaces. In: Conference on Computer Vision and Pattern Recognition (CVPR), pp. 961–971. IEEE (2016)
4. Alahi, A., et al.: Learning to predict human behaviour in crowded scenes. In: Group and Crowd Behavior for Computer Vision. Elsevier (2017)
5. Bai, S., Kolter, J.Z., Koltun, V.: An empirical evaluation of generic convolutional and recurrent networks for sequence modeling. arXiv preprint abs/1803.01271 (2018). http://arxiv.org/abs/1803.01271

6. Ballan, L., Castaldo, F., Alahi, A., Palmieri, F., Savarese, S.: Knowledge transfer for scene-specific motion prediction. In: Leibe, B., Matas, J., Sebe, N., Welling, M. (eds.) ECCV 2016. LNCS, vol. 9905, pp. 697–713. Springer, Cham (2016). https://doi.org/10.1007/978-3-319-46448-0_42

7. Brownlee, J.: Introduction to time series forecasting with python: how to prepare data and develop models to predict the future (2017). https://books.google.de/books?id=bA5ItAEACAAJ

8. Cho, K., et al.: Learning phrase representations using rnn encoder-decoder for statistical machine translation. In: Conference on Empirical Methods in Natural Language Processing (EMNLP), pp. 1724–1734. Association for Computational Linguistics, Doha, Qatar (2014). http://www.aclweb.org/anthology/D14-1179

9. Chung, J., Kastner, K., Dinh, L., Goel, K., Courville, A., Bengio, Y.: A recurrent latent variable model for sequential data. In: Advances in Neural Information Processing Systems (NIPS) (2015)

10. Coscia, P., Castaldo, F., Palmieri, F.A., Alahi, A., Savarese, S., Ballan, L.: Long-term path prediction in urban scenarios using circular distributions. Image Vis. Comput. **69**, 81–91 (2018). https://doi.org/10.1016/j.imavis.2017.11.006. http://www.sciencedirect.com/science/article/pii/S0262885617301853

11. Donahue, J., et al.: Long-term recurrent convolutional networks for visual recognition and description. In: Conference on Computer Vision and Pattern Recognition. IEEE (2015)

12. Draper, N.R., Smith, H.: Applied Regression Analysis. Wiley Series in Probability and Mathematical Statistics. Wiley, New York (1966)

13. Ellis, D., Sommerlade, E., Reid, I.: Modelling pedestrian trajectory patterns with Gaussian processes. In: International Conference on Computer Vision Workshops (ICCVW), pp. 1229–1234. IEEE (2009). https://doi.org/10.1109/ICCVW.2009.5457470

14. Ferryman, J., Shahrokni, A.: Pets 2009: dataset and challenge. In: IEEE International Workshop on Performance Evaluation of Tracking and Surveillance (PETS), pp. 1–6 (2009). https://doi.org/10.1109/PETS-WINTER.2009.5399556

15. Graves, A., Mohamed, A., Hinton, G.: Speech recognition with deep recurrent neural networks. In: International Conference on Acoustics, Speech and Signal Processing, pp. 6645–6649 (2013). https://doi.org/10.1109/ICASSP.2013.6638947

16. Gupta, A., Johnson, J., Fei-Fei, L., Savarese, S., Alahi, A.: Social GAN: socially acceptable trajectories with generative adversarial networks. In: Conference on Computer Vision and Pattern Recognition (CVPR). IEEE (2018)

17. Hasan, I., Setti, F., Tsesmelis, T., Bue, A.D., Galasso, F., Cristani, M.: MX-LSTM: mixing tracklets and vislets to jointly forecast trajectories and head poses. In: Conference on Computer Vision and Pattern Recognition (CVPR). IEEE (2018)

18. He, K., Zhang, X., Ren, S., Sun, J.: Deep residual learning for image recognition. In: Conference on Computer Vision and Pattern Recognition (CVPR), pp. 770–778 (2016). https://doi.org/10.1109/CVPR.2016.90

19. Helbing, D., Molnár, P.: Social force model for pedestrian dynamics. Phys. Rev. E **51**, 4282–4286 (1995). https://doi.org/10.1103/PhysRevE.51.4282. https://link.aps.org/doi/10.1103/PhysRevE.51.4282

20. Hochreiter, S., Schmidhuber, J.: Long short-term memory. Neural Comput. **9**(8), 1735–1780 (1997). https://doi.org/10.1162/neco.1997.9.8.1735

21. Huang, S., et al.: Deep learning driven visual path prediction from a single image. IEEE Trans. Image Process. **25**(12), 5892–5904 (2016). https://doi.org/10.1109/TIP.2016.2613686

22. Huber, M.: Nonlinear Gaussian filtering: theory, algorithms, and applications. Ph.D. thesis, Karlsruhe Institute of Technology (KIT) (2015)
23. Hug, R., Becker, S., Hübner, W., Arens, M.: On the reliability of LSTM-MDL models for predicting pedestrian trajectories. In: Representations, Analysis and Recognition of Shape and Motion from Imaging Data (RFMI), Savoie, France (2017)
24. Hug, R., Becker, S., Hübner, W., Arens, M.: Particle-based pedestrian path prediction using LSTM-MDL models. In: IEEE International Conference on Intelligent Transportation Systems (ITSC) (2018). http://arxiv.org/abs/1804.05546
25. Kalman, R.E.: A new approach to linear filtering and prediction problems. ASME J. Basic Eng. **82**, 35–45 (1960)
26. Kingma, D.P., Ba, J.: Adam: a method for stochastic optimization. In: International Conference for Learning Representations (ICLR) (2015)
27. Kitani, K.M., Ziebart, B.D., Bagnell, J.A., Hebert, M.: Activity forecasting. In: Fitzgibbon, A., Lazebnik, S., Perona, P., Sato, Y., Schmid, C. (eds.) ECCV 2012. LNCS, vol. 7575, pp. 201–214. Springer, Heidelberg (2012). https://doi.org/10.1007/978-3-642-33765-9_15
28. Kooij, J.F.P., Schneider, N., Flohr, F., Gavrila, D.M.: Context-based pedestrian path prediction. In: Fleet, D., Pajdla, T., Schiele, B., Tuytelaars, T. (eds.) ECCV 2014. LNCS, vol. 8694, pp. 618–633. Springer, Cham (2014). https://doi.org/10.1007/978-3-319-10599-4_40
29. Lee, N., Choi, W., Vernaza, P., Choy, C.B., Torr, P.H.S., Chandraker, M.: Desire: distant future prediction in dynamic scenes with interacting agents. In: Conference on Computer Vision and Pattern Recognition (CVPR). IEEE (2017)
30. Lerner, A., Chrysanthou, Y., Lischinski, D.: Crowds by example. Comput. Graph. Forum **26**(3), 655–664 (2007)
31. Li, Z., Zhou, Y., Xiao, S., He, C., Li, H.: Auto-conditioned LSTM network for extended complex human motion synthesis. arXiv preprint abs/1707.05363 (2017). http://arxiv.org/abs/1707.05363
32. Ma, W., Huang, D., Lee, N., Kitani, K.M.: Forecasting interactive dynamics of pedestrians with fictitious play. In: Conference on Computer Vision and Pattern Recognition (CVPR), pp. 4636–4644. IEEE (2017). https://doi.org/10.1109/CVPR.2017.493
33. Martinez, J., Black, M.J., Romero, J.: On human motion prediction using recurrent neural networks. In: Conference on Computer Vision and Pattern Recognition (CVPR), pp. 4674–4683. IEEE (2017). https://doi.org/10.1109/CVPR.2017.497
34. McCullagh, P., Nelder, J.A.: Generalized Linear Models. Chapman & Hall, CRC, London (1989)
35. van den Oord, A., et al.: Wavenet: a generative model for raw audio. arXiv preprint abs/1609.03499 (2016). http://arxiv.org/abs/1609.03499
36. Pellegrini, S., Ess, A., Schindler, K., van Gool, L.: You'll never walk alone: modeling social behavior for multi-target tracking. In: International Conference on Computer Vision, pp. 261–268. IEEE (2009). https://doi.org/10.1109/ICCV.2009.5459260
37. Priestley, M.B.: Spectral Analysis and Time Series. Academic Press, London, New York (1981)
38. Robicquet, A., Sadeghian, A., Alahi, A., Savarese, S.: Learning social etiquette: human trajectory understanding in crowded scenes. In: Leibe, B., Matas, J., Sebe, N., Welling, M. (eds.) ECCV 2016. LNCS, vol. 9912, pp. 549–565. Springer, Cham (2016). https://doi.org/10.1007/978-3-319-46484-8_33
39. Sadeghian, A., Kosaraju, V., Gupta, A., Savarese, S., Alahi, A.: Trajnet: towards a benchmark for human trajectory prediction. arXiv preprint (2018)

40. Sadeghian, A., Kosaraju, V., Sadeghian, A., Hirose, N., Savarese, S.: SoPhie: an attentive GAN for predicting paths compliant to social and physical constraints. arXiv preprint arXiv:1806.01482 (2018)
41. Vemula, A., Muelling, K., Oh, J.: Modeling cooperative navigation in dense human crowds. In: International Conference on Robotics and Automation (ICRA), pp. 1685–1692. IEEE, May 2017. https://doi.org/10.1109/ICRA.2017.7989199
42. Williams, C.K.I.: Prediction with Gaussian processes: from linear regression to linear prediction and beyond. In: Jordan, M.I. (ed.) Learning in Graphical Models. NATO ASI Series, pp. 599–621. Springer, Dordrecht (1998). https://doi.org/10.1007/978-94-011-5014-9_23
43. Xu, K., et al.: Show, attend and tell: neural image caption generation with visual attention. In: Bach, F., Blei, D. (eds.) International Conference on Machine Learning. Proceedings of Machine Learning Research, vol. 37, pp. 2048–2057. PMLR, Lille, France (2015)
44. Xue, H., Huynh, D.Q., Reynolds, H.M.: SS-LSTM: a hierarchical LSTM model for pedestrian trajectory prediction. In: Winter Conference on Applications of Computer Vision (WACV). IEEE (2018)

Joint Future Semantic and Instance Segmentation Prediction

Camille Couprie[1]([✉]), Pauline Luc[1,2], and Jakob Verbeek[2]

[1] Facebook AI Research, 75002 Paris, France
{coupriec,paulineluc}@fb.com
[2] Univ. Grenoble Alpes, Inria, CNRS, Grenoble INP, LJK, 38000 Grenoble, France
jakob.verbeek@inria.fr

Abstract. The ability to predict what will happen next from observing the past is a key component of intelligence. Methods that forecast future frames were recently introduced towards better machine intelligence. However, predicting directly in the image color space seems an overly complex task, and predicting higher level representations using semantic or instance segmentation approaches were shown to be more accurate. In this work, we introduce a novel prediction approach that encodes instance and semantic segmentation information in a single representation based on distance maps. Our graph-based modeling of the instance segmentation prediction problem allows us to obtain temporal tracks of the objects as an optimal solution to a watershed algorithm. Our experimental results on the Cityscapes dataset present state-of-the-art semantic segmentation predictions, and instance segmentation results outperforming a strong baseline based on optical flow.

1 Introduction

Video prediction appears as a natural objective to develop smarter strategies towards the acquisition of a visual common sense of machines. In the near future, it could help for planning and robotic applications, for instance by anticipating human behavior. Predicting future frames has known many developments in the color space [11,14,21,25,28]. Luc *et al.* [20] proposed to predict future semantic segmentations instead of color intensities. They showed that this space was more relevant, obtaining better results and directly usable high level information.

Recently, Luc *et al.* [19] introduced the more challenging task of forecasting future instance segmentation. In addition to the prediction of the semantic category of every single pixel, instance level segmentation also requires the specification of an object identifier, i.e. the delineation of every object. More specifically, [19] developed a predictive model in the space of convolutional features of the state-of-the-art Mask R-CNN segmentation approach. Although this method leads to the first instance prediction results outperforming a strong optical flow baseline, it has an extensive training time of about six days, and requires the

---

Grenoble INP—Institute of Engineering Univ. Grenoble Alpes.

© Springer Nature Switzerland AG 2019
L. Leal-Taixé and S. Roth (Eds.): ECCV 2018 Workshops, LNCS 11131, pp. 154–168, 2019.
https://doi.org/10.1007/978-3-030-11015-4_14

setting of multiple hyperparameters. In addition, the predictions of this feature-based approach are not temporally consistent, i.e. there is no matching or correspondence between the object instances at time t and $t + 1$.

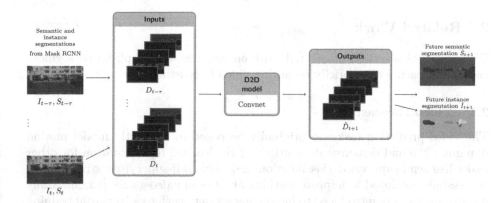

Fig. 1. Our representation enables both future semantic and instance segmentation prediction, based on distance maps from the different objects contours. For each channel of an input segmentation, corresponding to a specific class, the segmentation is decomposed into zeros for background, ones for objects and high values for contours. Then a convnet is trained to predict the future representation. Taking its argmax lets us recover the future semantic segmentation, and computing a watershed from it leads to the future instance segmentation.

We extend semantic segmentation forecasting by proposing a novel representation that encodes both semantic and instance information, with low training requirements and temporally consistent predictions. More specifically, from Mask R-CNN outputs and for each semantic category, we produce a map indicating the objects' presence at each spatial position, and boundaries of instances using distance transforms. An arg-max on the prediction leads to the future semantic segmentation, and the instance segmentation can be obtained by any seeded segmentation approach, such as a watershed for instance. In the following, we use "seeds" or "markers" to denote a set of pixels that mark each of the objects to be segmented. The choice to rely on seeds to obtain the final segmentation maps is a strength of our approach, allowing us to track the instance prediction in time, constituting a novel feature in comparison to [19]. In this work, we show that defining the seeds as a simple linear extrapolation of the centroids' position of past objects leads to satisfying results. Our approach is summarized in Fig. 1. Our contributions are the following:

1. We introduce a simple and memory efficient representation that encodes both the semantic and the instance-level information for future video prediction.
2. We model the prediction of the final instance segmentation as a graph optimization problem that we solve with a watershed with optimality guarantees. We show that the proposed solution produces good results compared to a

strong optical flow baseline, and note that the formulation allows the use of other seeded graph-based methods.

3. The use of seeds in our final instance segmentation prediction allows us to incorporate tracking of the objects in a very natural way.

2   Related Work

We focus in this section on related work on instance and graph based segmentation approaches after briefly reviewing video forecasting.

2.1   Video Forecasting

The video prediction task was originally proposed to efficiently model motion dynamics [25] and demonstrate a utility of the learned representation for other tasks like semi-supervised classification [28]. This self-supervised strategy was successfully employed to improve learning abilities in video games [13,23]. Many improvements were introduced to handle uncertainty such as adversarial training [21], or VAE modeling [3,12,31].

Diverse spaces of prediction have been considered besides the color intensities: for instance, flow fields [31], actions [30], poses [32], or bounding boxes of objects [6]. Choosing the semantic segmentation space like in [20] allows us to significantly reduce the complexity of the predictions in contrast to RGB values while reaching a very detailed level of spatial information about the scene. Exploiting in addition instance segmentations as in [19] is semantically richer and leads to better anticipated trajectories.

We may notice a complementarity of information arising in forecasting tasks. For instance, the authors of [18] perform joint semantic segmentation and optical flow future prediction. In an orthogonal direction, we leverage here the complementarity of instance and semantic segmentation tasks.

2.2   Instance Segmentation

Among different instance segmentation methods, some are based on recurrent networks [27], others on watershed transformation [4], or on CRFs [2]. The most successful ones are based on object proposals [17,24]. In particular, the state-of-the-art for instance segmentation was recently set by the Mask R-CNN approach proposed by He *et al.*[17]. Mask R-CNN essentially extends the successful framework of Faster R-CNN for object detection [26] to instance segmentation by adding an extra branch that segments most confidently detected objects.

Distance map based representations were employed for instance segmentation in [33] but differ from our encoding. While they compute distances from object centroids, we instead compute distances from the object contours. Distance maps are also computed in [4], entirely from contours in semantically segmented objects. Again, our case is different, as we are only keeping the distance information in the contour area. Once provided future contour information, our method relies on seeded graph-based segmentation, that we review below.

2.3 Seeded Graph Based Segmentation

Given weighted graphs, Graph Cuts [7] aim to find a minimum cut between foreground and background seeds and were extended to multi-label segmentation in [8]. Random walker relaxes the Graph Cut problem, by considering the combinatorial Dirichlet problem [15]. Shortest Paths [5] assign each pixel to a given label if there is a shorter path from it to this label's seed than to any other label seed. After links between Graph cuts, Random walker and Shortest Paths were established by Sinop and Grady [16], and links between Graph Cuts and watershed by [1], the unified Power watershed segmentation framework was introduced [10]. It presents a novel watershed algorithm that optimizes an energy function similarly to previously cited works, while having a quasi-linear complexity and being robust to seed sizes. In this work, we take advantage of these properties (speed, accuracy, robustness to seeds size) to compute future instance maps as the solution to an optimization problem.

3 Joint Future Instance and Segmentation Prediction

In this section we detail the principle of our approach, after introducing how to infer future semantic segmentation prediction as in [19].

3.1 Background: Future Semantic Segmentation Prediction

Given a sequence of images $X_{t-\tau}$ to X_t, Luc *et al.* [19] propose a baseline for predicting future semantic segmentation that encodes the corresponding segmentations $S_{t-\tau}$ to S_t, as computed by the Mask R-CNN network [17]. Given the outputs of Mask R-CNN as lists of instance predictions, composed of a confidence score, a class k, and a binary mask, a semantic segmentation label map is created to form the inputs and targets of a convolutional network. Specifically, the encoding $S_t^{(k)}$ to feed their model, denoted $S2S$, is built as follows: If any instances have been detected in X_t, instances are sorted by order of ascending confidence. For each instance mask, if its confidence score is high enough (in practice above 0.5), the semantic segmentation spatial positions corresponding to the object are updated with label $k \in \{1, ..., K\}$. These semantic segmentation input and target maps are of resolution 128×256, i.e. downsampled by a factor 8 with respect to the original input image's resolution.

A convolutional model is then trained with 4 inputs S_{t-3} to S_t to predict S_{t+1}. This model $S2S$ constitutes a strong baseline for our work. However, this encoding does not take advantage of the instance information.

3.2 Predicting Distance Map Based Representations

Architecture. For the previously described baseline $S2S$ and our proposed $D2D$ model, we adopt the convolutional network architecture proposed in [20]. It is a single scale convnet composed of 7 layers of convolutions, three of them dilated, and each of them followed by a ReLU, except for the last one. We use the same feature map scale parameter $q = 1.25$ that allows an efficient training. For the prediction of multiple frames, the single frame prediction model is applied auto-regressively, using its prediction for the previous time step as input to predict the next time step, and so on.

Distance Based Encoding. We now introduce a new method for representing the instance and semantic information together. As illustrated in Fig. 1, our method defines a new encoding of the semantic and instance representation at time t called D_t. Our convolutional network will be trained with inputs D_{t-3} to D_t to output the future representation $\hat{D}_{t+1}$. The algorithm to obtain our representation $D_t^{(k)}$ for class k at time t is defined as follows.

We denote each boolean array forming a segmentation mask of instance m in image X_t as $I_t^{(m)}$. The instance segmentation predictions are given by Mask R-CNN outputs, and are downsampled by a factor 8 with respect to the original input image's resolution, similarly to the previously described baseline.

Let us denote the size of a mask $I_t^{(m)}$ by $n \times p$, and (x, y) the integer coordinates of the image pixels. For each instance m of class k, we compute a truncated Euclidean distance map $d_t^{(k,m)}(x, y)$ to the background pixels as described in [22]. More formally,

$$d_t^{(k,m)}(x,y) = \min_{i,j:0\leq i<n \text{ and } 0\leq j<p \text{ and } I_t^{(m)}(i,j)=0} \lfloor((x-i)^2 + (y-j)^2)^{\frac{1}{2}}\rfloor. \quad (1)$$

The distance maps of all instances of same class k are merged in $d_t^{(k)}$:

$$d_t^{(k)} = \max_m d_t^{(k,m)}. \quad (2)$$

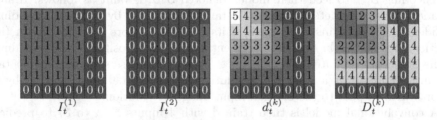

Fig. 2. Illustration of different steps building our distance map based encoding $D_t^{(k)}$ at time t given a class k from individual instance segmentations $I^{(1)}$ and $I^{(2)}$ for class k.

An illustration of this step is shown in Fig. 2. For the special case of the background class, the distance is computed relatively to the set of all instances.

We are mostly interested in keeping the contour information in our representation, the distance map in the center of the objects is irrelevant for our task. However, the distance information in a close neighborhood of the objects contours may be useful to introduce some flexibility in the penalization of the prediction errors that are frequent in contours area. The smoothness introduced by the distance information in the contour area allows small mistakes without too much penalization. Therefore, to eliminate the unnecessary distance values of object centers, we bound $d_t^{(k)}$ to θ to flatten the distance values located in the centers of the instances. In practice, we set $\theta = 4$.

As we also want to encode the semantic segmentation information in a way to obtain it from an argmax operation, we transform $d_t^{(k)}$ to indicate objects by ones, and background by zeros: our final action on $d_t^{(k)}$ is therefore to invert its value by multiplying by -1 and adding $(\theta + 1)$ in the areas of objects. In summary, from the merged distance map $d_t^{(k)}$ of Eq. 2, our encoding is defined as

$$D_t^{(k)} = -\min(d_t^{(k)}, \theta) + \mathbb{1}(d_t^{(k)})(\theta + 1), \qquad (3)$$

where $\mathbb{1}()$ is the indicator function, equal to 1 when $d_t^{(k)} > 0$ and 0 otherwise.

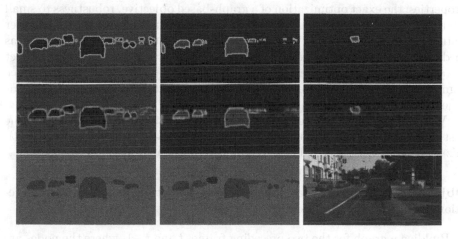

Fig. 3. Distance map inputs for one image. First line: last input distance maps for classes background, car and truck. Second line: short term predictions for the same classes. Last line: prediction of the baseline $S2S$, distance-based prediction, and distance-based prediction superimposed with future RGB frame.

Examples of such a representation D_t are displayed in Figs. 2 and 3. Given inputs $D_{t-\tau}, ..., D_t$, the convolutional network described in the previous section is trained to predict the future D_{t+1}. We denote its output by $\hat{D}_{t+1}$. The final segmentation $\hat{S}_{t+1}$ is then retrieved by computing the argmax over the different classes:

$$\hat{S}_{t+1} = \operatorname*{argmax}_{k \in \{1, ..., K\}} \hat{D}_{t+1}^{(k)}. \qquad (4)$$

The map of maximum elements may then be exploited to lead to individual object instance segmentations as presented in the next section.

3.3   Forecasting Instance Segmentation

The obtained map of maxima of our distance based representation contains object contour information as high values, resembling image gradient. As the background class map also contains meaningful object contour information, we add it to the map of maxima to straighten the contour map. We note this contour map

$$W = \max_{k \in \{1,...,K\}} \hat{D}_{t+1}^{(k)} + \hat{D}_{t+1}^{(background)}. \tag{5}$$

By construction, its minima form seeds to object instances and background. It is therefore very natural to apply a watershed algorithm on the obtained map. Seeing the map as a topological relief, this method simulates water growing from minima, and builds a watershed line every time different water basins merge.

As studied in [1,10], the watershed transform [29] may be seen as part of a family of graph based optimization methods that includes Graph Cuts, Shortest Paths, Random Walker. The Power watershed algorithm [10] is an optimization algorithm for seeded segmentation that arose from these findings, gathering nice properties: the exact optimization of a graph-based objective, robustness to small seeds and a quasi-linear complexity. These reasons justify the use of the Power watershed approach. In our experiments, we present results using minima as seeds, but also propose a better strategy that allows us to track each object instance. To that end, we identify object tracks from the two preceding instance segmentations and linearly extrapolate their centroid positions, to obtain our object seed.

We now describe the two steps of our instance segmentation method. The first one consists in the extraction of seeds, and the second in graph-based optimization given these seeds. The two steps are illustrated in Fig. 4.

Object Trajectory Forecasting for Seed Selection. Specifically, the creation of our list of seed coordinates z involves:

- Building a graph for the two preceding frames t and $t-1$, where the nodes are the objects centroids, linked by an edge when they are of the same semantic class. Each edge is weighted by a similarity coefficient w depending on the sizes s and average RGB intensities, denoted $c^{(1)}, c^{(2)}, c^{(3)}$ of its nodes:

$$w_{t,t-1} = \frac{|s_t - s_{t-1}|}{\max{(s_t, s_{t-1})}} + \frac{\sum_{i=1}^{3} \log(\|c_t^{(i)} - c_{t-1}^{(i)}\|^2 + 1)}{3 \log(255^2)}. \tag{6}$$

Objects of similar appearance are therefore linked by an edge of small weight.
- For each object of frame t: compute the shortest edge to objects of frame $t-1$ when possible. Store the matched centroids trajectory. Remove the edge and its nodes from the graph, and repeat.
- Linear extrapolation of future centroids' coordinates.

This procedure is illustrated in Fig. 4a.

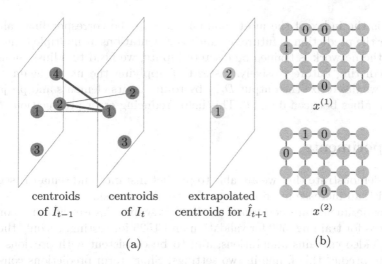

centroids of I_{t-1} centroids of I_t extrapolated centroids for $\hat{I}_{t+1}$

$x^{(1)}$

$x^{(2)}$

(a)   (b)

Fig. 4. Computing the future instances. (a) First step: compute the coordinates of future instance centroids positions by selection of shortest paths in the blue graph weighted by w (Eq. 6). (b) Second step: computing the solution $x^{(1)}, x^{(2)}$ to two subproblems defined in the red graph by Power-watershed optimization (Eq. 7), corresponding to continuous labelings of instances 1 and 2. After the computation of the background labeling, given by $x^{(3)} = 1-(x^{(1)}+x^{(2)})$, the final future instance prediction is given by $\hat{I}_{t+1} = \mathrm{argmax}\,(x^{(1)}, x^{(2)}, x^{(3)})$. (Color figure online)

Final Segmentation Step via Seeded Graph Based Optimization. The Power watershed algorithm is then used with its default parameters ($q = 2, p \to \infty$) to compute an optimal watershed segmentation map.

Formally, a new graph (V, E) is built where the set of nodes V corresponds to instance pixel labels to discover, and edges from E are linking neighboring nodes in a 4 connected setting. The weights W are given by maxima of the network prediction computed from Eq. 5. Given a set of L identified instance centroids whose node positions are stored in a vector z, L labelings $x^{(l)}$ on the graph are computed as the solution of

$$\underset{x^{(l)}}{\mathrm{argmin}} \lim_{p\to\infty} \sum_{e_{ij}\in E} (W_i + W_j)^p (x_i^{(l)} - x_j^{(l)})^2, \qquad (7)$$

subject to $x_{z_i}^{(l)} = 1$ if $i = l$ and $x_{z_i}^{(l)} = 0$ for all $i \neq l$. For the background segmentation, we define background seeds by a set of two points placed at the middle of the top and bottom halves of the frame. These seeds positions are added to the vector z and therefore enforced in the computation of the $x^{(l)}$. A solution $x^{(l+1)}$ is computed as $x^{(l+1)} = 1 - \sum_{l=1}^{L} x^{(l)}$. An illustration is provided in Fig. 4b. The labeling of the graph leads us to our map of future predictions $\hat{I}_{t+1}$ at each pixel i given by

$$\hat{I}_{t+1}(i) = \delta \underset{l}{\mathrm{argmax}}\, x_i^{(l)}, \qquad (8)$$

where δ is the index of the most common class in the corresponding values of $\hat{S}_{t+1}$. For the prediction of future semantic segmentations at multiple time steps, because the network is trained on discrete inputs, we need to adjust the inputs when predicting autoregressively. Instead of applying the model again on the outputs, we discretize the output D_{t+1} by rounding its elements and projecting back the values between 0 and θ. This helps reducing error propagation.

4   Experiments

We now demonstrate that we are able to predict instance and semantic segmentation with an increase in performance for the latter task.

Our experiments are performed on the Cityscapes dataset [9], that contains 2975 videos for training, 500 for validation and 1525 for testing. As only the 20th frame of video contains annotations, and to be consistent with previous work, we aim to predict this frame in two settings. Short term predictions consist in predicting frame 20 using frames $8, 11, 14, 17$ and mid term, computing frames $14, 17, 20$ from $2, 5, 8, 11$. The mid term prediction setting is therefore more challenging, as it aims to forecast a 0.5 s future. As in [19,20], our models are validated using the IoU SEG metric on the validation set, which corresponds to the mean Intersection over Union computed between the predictions and the segmentation obtained via Mask R-CNN. As Mask R-CNN is an object-based segmentation method, it only outputs segmentations for the 8 classes that correspond to moving object instances: person, rider, car, truck, bus, train, motorcycle, and bicycle. We also report results of the same copy and flow baseline. The copy approach simply provides the last input as future segmentation. The flow baseline is based on pixel warping using optical flow computed between the last two frames. $D2D$ was trained using stochastic gradient descent with a momentum of 0.9, and a learning rate of 0.02.

The semantic segmentation accuracy is computed via the mean intersection over union with the ground truth. The instance segmentation accuracy is provided by computing the AP and AP-50. As our instance predictions are not associated with classifiers scores, we set the confidence equal to 1 everywhere. Mask R-CNN, $F2F$ [19], and the optical flow baseline all produce a list of instance maps that may overlap with each other. As argued in [2], the AP measures favor this category of methods to the detriment of approaches that output a unique answer at each spatial position. Since the former methods in fact eventually threshold their results at the confidence parameter 0.5 for visualization purposes, we compute AP and AP-50 on the segments formed by a non-overlapping segmentation map.

Specifically, for each method, we compute a superimposition of instance segments by filling a map with segments ranked by ascending confidence. In the AP and AP-50 computations, there is a step where segment proposals are matched with ground truth segments. For each proposal segment, if less than half of their pixels overlap with any object of the superimposed map, this segment is discarded in the evaluation. Then we compute AP and AP-50 scores on ground truth segments and remaining segments. We note the obtained scores "Non Overlapping AP": NO-AP and NO-AP-50. In the particular case of our $D2D$ results, AP and NO-AP are equivalent.

Table 1. Short and mid term semantic segmentation of moving objects (8 classes) performance on the Cityscapes validation dataset.

	Short term (0.17 s)	Mid term (0.50 s)
	IoU	IoU
Oracle [20]	64.7	64.7
S2S [20]	55.3	40.8
Oracle [19]	73.3	73.3
Copy [19]	45.7	29.1
Flow [19]	58.8	41.4
S2S [19]	55.4	42.4
F2F [19]	**61.2**	41.2
D2D	56.0	**43.0**

Flow $F2F$ $D2D$ (ours)

Fig. 5. Mid term future instance segmentation results. The flow baseline produces large distortions of objects subject to large displacements.

Our future semantic segmentation performance is reported in Table 1. While the $F2F$ and flow baseline results lead to high mean IoU in the short term, their performance are lower than $D2D$ in the mid term term setting. $D2D$ also slightly improves over the $S2S$ baseline that was state-of-the-art for future semantic segmentation prediction.

We compare our results with the $S2S$ baseline, optical flow baseline and the $F2F$ approach in Figs. 6 and 5. We observe that our method is fairly accurate in a number of situations where $F2F$ and the Flow baseline meet difficulties for mid term predictions.

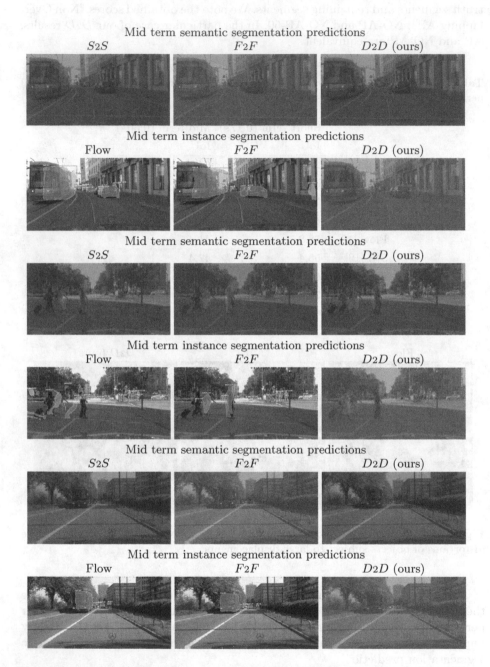

Fig. 6. Additional mid term comparative results. The flow baseline produces large distortions of small objects, in particular pedestrians. The F_2F predictions may be very inaccurate for large objects.

Table 2 provides quantitative results of instance segmentation accuracies of proposed methods. Our *D2D* approach does not compare favorably with the other baselines for short term predictions. However, for mid term ones, it clearly outperforms the copy baseline, and performs slightly better than the flow baseline. We experiment using three different sets of seeds for model *D2D*: minima of the predictions $\hat{S}$, extrapolated object centroids, and centroids of the oracle future segmentation, to provide an upper bound for our method's performance. We observe that $F2F$ does lead to superior results, but at a much higher training cost. Learning in the pyramidal feature space of Mask R-CNN requires indeed to train and then finetune four networks, fixing each time an adequate learning rate. As summarized in Table 3, our approach is much lighter with less than 1M parameters, leads to superior semantic segmentation results, and comprises a built-in object tracking mechanism.

Table 2. Instance segmentation performance on the Cityscapes validation dataset, in terms of "Non-overlapping" AP measures. To avoid the bias of the standard AP and AP-50 measure in favor of proposal based methods, where several overlapping solutions are evaluated, we propose the "Non-overlapping" AP metrics, which consists in AP with a specific change in the matching step with ground truth segments. We first create a superimposed map for each proposal based methods (here the oracle, copy, F2F, optical flow baselines). For each proposal segment, if less than half of their pixels overlap with any object of the superimposed map, this segment is discarded in the evaluation. Then we compute AP and AP-50 scores on ground truth segments and remaining segments.

	Short term		Mid term	
	NO-AP-50	NO-AP	NO-AP-50	NO-AP
Mask R-CNN oracle	57.7	33.0	57.7	33.0
Copy last input	19.8	8.9	5.8	1.5
Optical flow baseline	30.8	14.1	9.5	3.6
F2F	**30.8**	**15.5**	**16.1**	**6.6**
D2D future centroids (oracle)	18.9	8.8	11.7	4.4
D2D pred. (seeds: minima)	14.2	6.5	7.1	2.9
D2D linear extrapolation	14.9	6.7	10.2	3.7

Figure 7 presents mid term segmentation results that illustrate the effectiveness of the proposed built-in tracking strategy of instances.

Table 3. Comparative overview of future segmentation methods based on Mask R-CNN. Our $D2D$ approach cumulates state-of-the-art semantic segmentation performance, inference and training speed, and temporally consistent results.

	Feature based	Optical	Distance based
	$F2F$	Flow baseline	$D2D$ (ours)
Mid term sem. segm (IoU)	41.2	41.4	**43.0**
Mid term inst. segm (NO-AP-50)	**16.1**	9.5	10.2
Tracking included	No	**Yes**	**Yes**
Training time	6 days	-	**1.5 day**
Network size	65M	-	0.8M
Training hyperparam. to tune	8	-	2
Inference time	**Some sec.**	2 min	**Some sec.**
Post-processing	Threshold	Hole filling, thresh.	Optimization

Our prediction of frame 14   Our prediction of frame 17   Our prediction of frame 20

Fig. 7. Mid term instance segmentation results produced by our $D2D$ model. Most forecasted instances are consistent in a 0.5 s future.

5   Conclusion

We introduced a novel approach for predicting both future instance and semantic segmentation. Our distance map based encoding allows us to recover both information by a simple argmax or a graph-based optimization algorithm.

We improve in term of mean IoU over the state-of-the-art method for future semantic segmentation prediction while also allowing future instance prediction efficiently. While obtaining a lower performance in terms of instance segmentation performance compared to feature level prediction, we improve over a strong optical flow baseline. Furthermore, relying on seeded segmentation allows us to incorporate tracking into our results and obtain an optimal solution.

Ultimately, we hope to employ our representation as a light, simple and effective building block to develop more sophisticated and better performing forecasting methods.

Acknowledgment. We thank Piotr Dollárd and anonymous reviewers for their precious comments.

References

1. Allène, C., Audibert, J.Y., Couprie, M., Keriven, R.: Some links between extremum spanning forests, watersheds and min-cuts. Image Vis. Comput. **28**, 1460–1471 (2009)
2. Arnab, A., Torr, P.H.S.: Pixelwise instance segmentation with a dynamically instantiated network. In: CVPR (2017)
3. Babaeizadeh, M., Finn, C., Erhan, D., Campbell, R.H., Levine, S.: Stochastic variational video prediction. In: ICLR (2018)
4. Bai, M., Urtasun, R.: Deep watershed transform for instance segmentation. In: CVPR (2017)
5. Bai, X., Sapiro, G.: A geodesic framework for fast interactive image and video segmentation and matting. In: ICCV (2007)
6. Bhattacharyya, A., Fritz, M., Schiele, B.: Long-term on-board prediction of people in traffic scenes under uncertainty. In: CVPR (2018)
7. Boykov, Y., Jolly, M.P.: Interactive graph cuts for optimal boundary & region segmentation of objects in N-D images. In: ICCV (2001)
8. Boykov, Y., Veksler, O., Zabih, R.: Fast approximate energy minimization via graph cuts. PAMI **23**, 1222–1239 (2001)
9. Cordts, M., et al.: The cityscapes dataset for semantic urban scene understanding. In: CVPR (2016)
10. Couprie, C., Grady, L., Najman, L., Talbot, H.: Power watershed: a unifying graph-based optimization framework. PAMI **33**(7), 1384–1399 (2011)
11. Denton, E., Birodkar, V.: Unsupervised learning of disentangled representations from video. In: NIPS (2017)
12. Denton, E., Fergus, R.: Stochastic video generation with a learned prior. In: ICML (2018). http://proceedings.mlr.press/v80/denton18a.html
13. Dosovitskiy, A., Koltun, V.: Learning to act by predicting the future. In: ICLR (2017)
14. Finn, C., Goodfellow, I., Levine, S.: Unsupervised learning for physical interaction through video prediction. In: NIPS (2016)
15. Grady, L.: Random walks for image segmentation. PAMI **28**(11), 1768–1783 (2006)
16. Grady, L., Sinop, A.K.: Fast approximate random walker segmentation using eigenvector precomputation. In: CVPR (2008)
17. He, K., Gkioxari, G., Dollár, P., Girshick, R.: Mask R-CNN. In: ICCV (2017)
18. Jin, X., et al.: Predicting scene parsing and motion dynamics in the future. In: NIPS (2017)
19. Luc, P., Couprie, C., Verbeek, J., LeCun, Y.: Predictive learning in feature space for future instance segmentation. In: ECCV (2018)
20. Luc, P., Neverova, N., Couprie, C., Verbeek, J., LeCun, Y.: Predicting deeper into the future of semantic segmentation. In: ICCV (2017)

21. Mathieu, M., Couprie, C., LeCun, Y.: Deep multi-scale video prediction beyond mean square error. In: ICLR (2016)
22. Meijster, A., Roerdink, J.B.T.M., Hesselink, W.H.: A general algorithm for computing distance transforms in linear time. In: Goutsias, J., Vincent, L., Bloomberg, D.S. (eds.) Mathematical Morphology and its Applications to Image and Signal Processing, pp. 331–340. Springer, Boston (2000). https://doi.org/10.1007/0-306-47025-X_36
23. Oh, J., Guo, X., Lee, H., Lewis, R.L., Singh, S.P.: Action-conditional video prediction using deep networks in Atari games. arXiv:1507.08750 (2015)
24. Pinheiro, P.O., Lin, T.-Y., Collobert, R., Dollár, P.: Learning to refine object segments. In: Leibe, B., Matas, J., Sebe, N., Welling, M. (eds.) ECCV 2016. LNCS, vol. 9905, pp. 75–91. Springer, Cham (2016). https://doi.org/10.1007/978-3-319-46448-0_5
25. Ranzato, M., Szlam, A., Bruna, J., Mathieu, M., Collobert, R., Chopra, S.: Video (language) modeling: a baseline for generative models of natural videos. arXiv:1412.6604 (2014)
26. Ren, S., He, K., Girshick, R., Sun, J.: Faster R-CNN: towards real-time object detection with region proposal networks. In: NIPS (2015)
27. Romera-Paredes, B., Torr, P.H.S.: Recurrent instance segmentation. In: Leibe, B., Matas, J., Sebe, N., Welling, M. (eds.) ECCV 2016. LNCS, vol. 9910, pp. 312–329. Springer, Cham (2016). https://doi.org/10.1007/978-3-319-46466-4_19
28. Srivastava, N., Mansimov, E., Salakhutdinov, R.: Unsupervised learning of video representations using LSTMs. In: ICML (2015)
29. Vincent, L., Soille, P.: Watersheds in digital spaces: an efficient algorithm based on immersion simulations. PAMI **13**(6), 583–598 (1991)
30. Vondrick, C., Pirsiavash, H., Torralba, A.: Anticipating the future by watching unlabeled video. In: CVPR (2016)
31. Walker, J., Doersch, C., Gupta, A., Hebert, M.: An uncertain future: forecasting from static images using variational autoencoders. In: Leibe, B., Matas, J., Sebe, N., Welling, M. (eds.) ECCV 2016. LNCS, vol. 9911, pp. 835–851. Springer, Cham (2016). https://doi.org/10.1007/978-3-319-46478-7_51
32. Walker, J., Marino, K., Gupta, A., Hebert, M.: The pose knows: video forecasting by generating pose futures. In: ICCV (2017)
33. Watanabe, T., Wolf, D.: Distance to center of mass encoding for instance segmentation. arXiv:1711.09060 (2017)

Context Graph Based Video Frame Prediction Using Locally Guided Objective

Prateep Bhattacharjee$^{(\boxtimes)}$ ⓘ and Sukhendu Das ⓘ

Department of Computer Science and Engineering,
Indian Institute of Technology Madras, Chennai, Tamil Nadu, India
prateepb@cse.iitm.ac.in, sdas@iitm.ac.in

Abstract. This paper proposes a feature reconstruction based approach using pixel-graph and Generative Adversarial Networks (GAN) for solving the problem of synthesizing future frames from video scenes. Recent methods of frame synthesis often generate blurry outcomes in case of long-range prediction and scenes involving multiple objects moving at different velocities due to their holistic approach. Our proposed method introduces a novel pixel-graph based context aggregation layer (Pix-Graph) which efficiently captures long range dependencies. PixGraph incorporates a weighting scheme through which the internal features of each pixel (or a group of neighboring pixels) can be modeled independently of the others, thus handling the issue of separate objects moving in different directions and with very dissimilar speed. We also introduce a novel objective function, the Locally Guided Gram Loss (LGGL), which aides the GAN based model to maximize the similarity between the intermediate features of the ground-truth and the network output by constructing Gram matrices from locally extracted patches over several levels of the generator. Our proposed model is end-to-end trainable and exhibits superior performance compared to the state-of-the-art on four real-world benchmark video datasets.

1 Introduction

Although video understanding has been one of the key areas of computer vision, the problem of predicting frames from natural video scenes has not been explored till recently. Compared to image reconstruction tasks, generation of multiple video frames requires understanding of non-trivial spatio-temporal feature representations. Past approaches in this area involve the use of Long Short Term Memory (LSTM) networks [1,2], recurrent neural networks [3] and action conditional deep networks [4]. Majority of the recent approaches [5–7] focus on predicting the semantics which is useful in decision making problems. Mathieu

Electronic supplementary material The online version of this chapter (https://doi.org/10.1007/978-3-030-11015-4_15) contains supplementary material, which is available to authorized users.

© Springer Nature Switzerland AG 2019
L. Leal-Taixé and S. Roth (Eds.): ECCV 2018 Workshops, LNCS 11131, pp. 169–185, 2019.
https://doi.org/10.1007/978-3-030-11015-4_15

et al. [8] proposed a frame prediction model based on Generative Adversarial Networks (GAN). Contrary to the semantic based approaches, this multi-scale GAN uses the future frames (during training) as target from large amount of natural video scenes to produce crisp and clear output. This method also overcomes the issue of producing blurry output when the L2 penalty is used as the objective function, by introducing a gradient based loss (GDL). Recently, Villegas *et al.* [9] incorporates different encoding streams for motion and content by using LSTM based encoders. Another approach in synthesizing frames is to use pixel-autoregressive models [10,11]. Also, latent variable models *viz.* Variational Auto-encoders (VAE) [12] have been used for both single [13] and multi-frame predictions [14]. Although these approaches (also [15–18]) offer improvement in the quality of the produced frames over the semantic based models, they often fail to perform satisfactorily in environments differing greatly from the training set and in case of faraway predictions. Very recently, [19] used a two-stage GAN based framework and introduces two novel objective functions based on cross-correlation and a distance based divergence measure. This work captures the spatial as well as temporal information through the use of a cross-correlation based loss. Although this improves the scores over the state-of-the-art, it often fails on situations where multiple objects having very different velocity are present in the scene simultaneously. We overcome this issue by modeling the internal features corresponding to the pixels (or a group of pixels) using graph based structures which capture contextual dependencies in spatio-temporal regions.

Our proposed work incorporates two GAN based models: (a) feature generating GAN (F-GAN) and (b) reconstruction GAN (R-GAN). These two networks act in an encoder-decoder arrangement and are trained together end-to-end. F-GAN learns to generate intermediate feature representations, while R-GAN reconstructs the future frames from the generated feature space. The PixGraph layer sits on top of the convolutional part of F-GAN. The learning process of F-GAN is aided by a Locally Guided Gram Loss (LGGL) function. This minimizes the distance between the intermediate feature maps of the ground truth frames, produced by another auxiliary network and the feature maps from the F-GAN itself, by forming soft "local guidance" regions. The auxiliary network is trained simultaneously along with the two generators. The raison d'être of the feature generating network is to break the process of frame prediction from a direct coarse strategy into a finer multi-step method. The reconstruction network minimizes the L1 loss along with a gradient based objective function, Gradient Divergence Loss (GDL) [8]. The salient parts of our work are: (a) graph based context aggregation layer (PixGraph) with a novel weighting scheme for context aggregation, (b) novel encoder-decoder type GAN based architecture in the domain of video frame prediction and (c) a novel feature based objective function (LGGL) for bridging the gap between the predicted and target outputs efficiently. We quantitatively and qualitatively evaluate the proposed method using four popular real world video datasets: (a) KTH [20], (b) Weizmann [21], (c) UCF-101 [22] and (d) KITTI [23].

2   Proposed Architecture

The overall proposed system for predicting future frames mimics an encoder-decoder like arrangement via an amalgamation of two GANs [24]. Overall, these are composed of two sub-networks: (a) the Generator (G) and (b) the Discriminator (D). The generator (G) is trained to produce realistic outputs by learning the underlying true data distribution p_{data} and consequently making the job of differentiating between true and synthetic outputs by the discriminator harder. In contrast, the discriminator D learns to distinguish between the real data and the synthetic outputs produced by the generator. In short, GANs use an alternating two player min-max game-like learning strategy [24] to achieve the mixed equilibrium of generating better synthetic outputs. The objective function minimized by the GANs [24] is given by

$$\min_G \max_D v(D, G) = \mathbb{E}_{x \sim p_{data}}[log(D(x))] + \mathbb{E}_{z \sim p_z}[log(1 - D(G(z)))] \quad (1)$$

where, x is a sample from the true distribution p_{data} and vector z is sampled from a uniform (or Gaussian) noise distribution p_z. As our work deals with videos instead of arbitrary data distributions, the input to F-GAN is a sequence of video frames (discussed in Sect. 2.2), while R-GAN receives a collection of 2D intermediate context aggregated feature map(s) (refer Fig. 1). The following sub-sections describe the working principles of the proposed PixGraph module along with the feature generation and reconstruction stages.

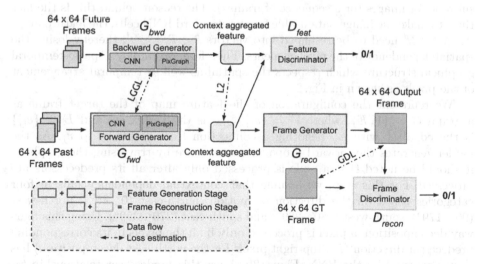

Fig. 1. The proposed GAN based network architecture for video frame prediction

2.1   PixGraph Module

The feature generation stage comprises of two generators, G_{fwd} and G_{bwd} and a discriminator D_{feat}. The main purpose of this feature generating stage is to incorporate the idea of context aggregation and local region representation. We propose PixGraph, a graph based Recurrent Neural Network (RNN) [25] layer to perform context aggregation in this paper. In the setting of video frame prediction, it is natural to assume that nearby pixels are dependent to each other and graph based RNN models this contextual dependency in a elegant way.

Forward Pass Through PixGraph. Mathematically, the working principle of RNNs [25] is expressed as:

$$h^{(t)} = f(W_{IH}x^{(t)} + W_H h^{(t-1)} + b)$$
$$y^{(t)} = g(W_{HO}h^{(t)} + c) \tag{2}$$

where, the hidden layer $h^{(t)}$ at step t is represented as a non-linear function f over the current input $x^{(t)}$ and the hidden layer at the previous time step $h^{(t-1)}$; W_{IH} is the weight matrix between the input and hidden layers, W_H among the hidden layer themselves and W_{HO} is the output matrix connecting the hidden and output layers; b, c are the bias vectors; $y^{(t)}$ is the output layer and $g(.)$, a non-linear activation function.

Although the standard RNN [25] captures temporal dependencies in sequential data such as sentences, where a chain-structure is present, they are not suitable for images (or a sequence of frames). The reason behind this is the fact that, to make the image data usable for the standard RNN cells, the feature maps $x \in \mathbb{R}^{h \times w \times d}$ need to be reshaped into vectors $\hat{x} \in \mathbb{R}^{(h.w) \times d}$, thereby losing the spatial dependency of the pixel elements. Therefore, we employ a spatio-temporal graphical structure which respects the spatial as well as temporal arrangement of the pixels as shown in Fig. 2.

We represent the configuration of the feature map of the target frame as a graph $G = \{V, E\}$, where $V = \{v_i\}_{i=1:N}$ is the vertex set and $E = \{e_{ij}\}$ is the edge set with e_{ij} denoting a connection from vertex v_i to v_j. As the model generates the forward propagation sequence by traversing the graph G, it should be noted that a node is processed only after all its predecessors are processed. For this step, we assume that contextual dependency falls in four categories based on the direction of motion: north-east $(0°–89°)$, north-west $(90°–179°)$, south-west $(180°–269°)$ and south-east $(270°–359°)$. Using this four-way decomposition, a pixel is processed only if all the pixels in its corresponding predecessor direction (*i.e.* top-right pixels for the north-east decomposition) has been processed by the RNN. Figure 2b shows this predecessor relationship for the north-west decomposition graph.

For representing the aforementioned decomposition more formally, let the set of four direction based graphs be $\hat{G} = \{G_1, G_2, G_3, G_4\}$. The graph based RNN is applied simultaneously and independently on each of these decompositions to generate four corresponding hidden layer feature maps h_i, i = 1:4.

These are finally weight-aggregated to form the final hidden layer feature map h. Mathematically, these operations are expressed as:

$$h_i^{(v_j)} = f(W_{IH}^i x^{(v_j)} + \sum_{v_k \in \mathcal{P}_{G_i}(v_j)} W_{HH}^i h_i^{(v_k)} + b_i) \tag{3}$$

$$o^{(v_j)} = g(\sum_{G_i \in \hat{G}} \lambda_i W_{HO}^i h_i^{(v_j)} + c) \tag{4}$$

where, $\mathcal{P}_{G_i}(v_j)$ is the set of parent or predecessor pixel units of v_j in the component graph G_i and λ_i are the corresponding weights for each of the components.

Equations 3–4 consider the spatially contextual relations only for the current time-step. This is extended to multiple time-steps in the past for capturing the temporal context by considering a set of component graph sets $\hat{\mathbf{G}} = \{\hat{G}_{t-3}, \hat{G}_{t-2}, \hat{G}_{t-1}, \hat{G}_t\}$. Also, we assume that the motion is smooth such that each pixel (or a set of pixels) is only dependent on a small neighborhood around it in the previous step. Following this, we restrict the valid predecessor units to a small 3×3 neighborhood region in the corresponding direction of the component. This local region is gradually grown to a 9×9 patch for $\hat{G}_{t-3}$ to capture the motion efficiently over a short time-period. Considering the fact that each of the graphs $\hat{G}_{t-i}$ is broken into 4 directional components, a 9×9 local window practically captures information from a 17×17 neighborhood centered around the currently processing pixel unit. Under this framework, Eq. 3 is re-written as:

$$h_i^{(v_j)} = f(W_{IH}^i x^{(v_j)} + \sum_{\substack{v_l \in \mathcal{P}_{G_{t-a}^i}(v_j) \\ a \in \{0,1,2,3\}}} W_{PH}^{t-a,i} x^{(v_l)} + \sum_{v_k \in \mathcal{P}_{G_i}(v_j)} W_{HH}^i h_i^{(v_k)} + b_i) \tag{5}$$

where, the first and last summation terms capture the contextual information from the previously processed pixel features whereas, the second summation involving $W_{PH}^{t-a,b}$ captures motion information from the local regions of the feature maps of the previous frames with $t - a$ denoting the time-step and i representing the corresponding directional component as discussed before. Equation 4 remains unchanged as the weighted-aggregation logic stays the same under this framework.

Computing the Gradients. To facilitate the learning process using back-propagation algorithm the derivatives are calculated for the PixGraph module in the backward pass. In this case, each of the vertices are processed in the reverse order of the previous forward propagation sequence. Hence, instead of considering the predecessor set $\mathcal{P}(v_j)$ as discussed before, a successor set $\mathcal{S}(v_j)$ is calculated. Using this, the error accumulated to the hidden unit for vertex v_j

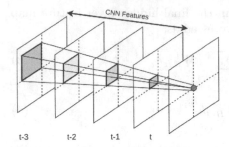

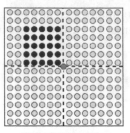

PixGraph Hidden Units

(a) The hidden state of the current processing unit (in red) is connected to all the parent input units in the shaded regions of previous time-steps (denoted by t). The dimension of this valid predecessor region grows as we go further into the past

(b) The hidden state of the current processing unit (in red) is also connected to the hidden states of the already processed units. To limit influence from far-away sections, the predecessor set of vertices is restricted to a small neighborhood (black units)

Fig. 2. The PixGraph module. Both (a) and (b) illustrates the north-west component of the context graph. Similar logic applies for the other directions (Color figure online)

is broken into two components: (a) errors from v_j: $\frac{\partial o^{(v_j)}}{\partial h^{(v_j)}}$ and (b) sum of errors from the successor set: $\sum_{v_k} \frac{\partial o^{(v_k)}}{\partial h^{(v_j)}} = \sum_{v_k} \frac{\partial o^{(v_k)}}{\partial h^{(v_k)}} \frac{\partial h^{(v_k)}}{\partial h^{(v_j)}}$. This way, the derivatives are calculated as:

$$
\begin{aligned}
dh_i^{(v_j)} &= \frac{\partial o^{(v_j)}}{\partial h_i^{(v_j)}} + \sum_{v_k} \frac{\partial o^{(v_k)}}{\partial h_i^{(v_k)}} \frac{\partial h_i^{(v_k)}}{\partial h^{(v_j)}} \\
&= \lambda_i (W_{HO}^i)^T g'(o^{(v_j)}) + \sum_{v_k \in S_{G_i}(v_j)} (W_{HH}^i)^T dh_i^{(v_k)} \circ f'(h_i^{(v_k)})
\end{aligned}
\tag{6}
$$

where, S is the successor set of vertex v_j and $\circ$ represents the Hadamard product. Similarly, the gradients of the other learned parameters are computed as:

$$
\nabla W_{HO}^i = g'(\lambda_i W_{HO}^i h^{(v_j)} + c)(\lambda_i h_i^{(v_j)})^T
\tag{7}
$$

$$
\nabla W_{HH}^i = \sum_{v_k \in S_{G_i}(v_j)} dh_i^{(v_k)} \circ f'(h_i^{(v_k)}) h_i^{(v_j)}
\tag{8}
$$

$$
\nabla W_{IH}^i = dh_i^{(v_j)} \circ f'(h_i^{(v_j)})(x^{(v_j)})^T
\tag{9}
$$

$$
\nabla W_{PH}^{t-a,i} = \sum_{v_l \in S_{G_{t-a}^i}(v_j)} dh_i^{(v_j)} \circ f'(h_i^{(v_l)})(x^{(v_j)})^T
\tag{10}
$$

where, the symbols bear the usual notation as mentioned before.

Apart from the derivatives of the weight matrices, the λ parameter can be fixed at some predefined value (viz. $\lambda_1 = \lambda_2 = \lambda_3 = \lambda_4 = \frac{1}{4}$ to give equal importance to the features from all the direction based contexts), or can be learned as well. To give our model the maximum flexibility, we chose to learn the λ_i values and compute the derivatives as follows:

$$\nabla \lambda_i(v_j) = g'(\lambda_i W^i_{HO} h^{(v_j)} + c)(W^i_{HO} h^{(v_j)}_i)^T \tag{11}$$

Learning the λ_i values instead of giving equal weight to all the components helps to model situations where multiple close-by objects move in different directions *e.g.* a busy road-crossing where pedestrians are moving in all sorts of directions.

2.2 Stage-1: Feature Generation Using PixGraph

As shown in Fig. 1, two similar generators, G_{fwd} and G_{bwd} are used to generate an intermediate representation of the target frame(s). For ease of discussion, we will assume that the network takes as input a sequence of M frames and generates a single frame at the next time-step. All the input and output frames have the same dimension $W \times H$ ($W = H$ for simplicity). G_{fwd} is used to output the internal representation of the target frame at time-step $t+1$ with a sequence of M frames at time-steps $T = t - M + 1, t - M + 2, ..., t$ as input. On the other hand, G_{bwd} also creates another feature representation of the same target frame at time-step $t + 1$ from a sequence of N consecutive frames at time-steps $T = t + 2, t + 3, ..., t + N + 1$. Essentially, G_{fwd} creates a representation in the forward direction while G_{bwd} does the same in the backward direction. From Fig. 1, the initial part of both the networks are standard convolutional networks with the last layer being the PixGraph module as discussed in the previous subsection. Note that, G_{bwd} is only used in the training phase for future frame generation. Although, the same model can be used for interpolation of frames as well, in which case we retain the G_{bwd} in the evaluation stage also. Thus, using this forward-backward encoding of intermediate features, the model serves a dual purpose of interpolation as well as extrapolation of video frames. The outputs from both these networks are fed to the feature discriminator (D_{feat}). As the motivation of using the feature generator is to bring the intermediate feature maps of the forward and backward generators closer in the feature space, D_{feat} is trained to distinguish between the synthesized feature maps produced by G_{fwd} and G_{bwd}. The target labels chosen for features fed to D_{feat} are: '0' for the feature maps generated by G_{fwd} and '1' for that from G_{bwd}. Apart from minimizing the adversarial objective of GAN, the model also minimizes the L2 distance of the intermediate feature maps produced by G_{fwd} and G_{bwd}.

Although GANs are notorious for their training instability, our proposed model of simultaneous learning of the discriminator along with the forward and backward generators is elegant and successful due to: *(a)* Although minimizing the sum squared distance (L2) is a traditional method used in optimization literature, it results in production of blurry frames. This shortcoming is evaded in our work by minimizing the L2 distance between a large number of high-dimensional feature maps instead of the pixels in the generated frames and *(b)* Projecting the past and future frames to a shared space of context aggregated features using PixGraph and a novel non-linear objective function (described in Sect. 3) increases separability for better discrimination.

2.3   Stage-2: Reconstruction

The reconstruction phase of the frame prediction framework is essentially another Generative Adversarial Network fine-tuned to produce sharp, high-quality sequence of frames. This phase consists of two networks: (a) frame generator (G_{recon}) and (b) frame discriminator (D_{recon}). The context-aggregated internal feature map produced by the PixGraph module on top of G_{fwd} of dimension $W_{int} \times H_{int}$ is fed as input to G_{recon}, which in turn produces the final output frame at time-step $t+1$. For simplicity, we keep the number of frames generated to 1. The discriminator, (D_{recon}), at this stage is trained to distinguish between the synthetic and true data in the RGB image space.

Exploration of different architectures for the feature generation and reconstruction stages led to an observation that using residual blocks in the reconstruction stage produces comparatively better outputs at less training time. Also, the same helps in diminishing the effect of vanishing gradients through by-passing higher level features using identity pathways.

3   Locally Guided Gram Loss (LGGL)

The joint problem of projecting the input video frame sequence in an intermediate feature space shared by the features from the future frames and optimizing the discriminator to differentiate between them simultaneously is a non-trivial problem. For these situations, we use feature maps from several layers of G_{fwd} and G_{bwd}. By breaking the feature maps into local regions, the proposed objective function guides the neurons of G_{fwd} to transform the original input data to the targeted feature space.

Let $FM_k^{fwd}(X)$ and $FM_k^{bwd}(Y)$ denote the feature representations of the past and future frame sequences X and Y used as input to G_{fwd} and G_{bwd} respectively at layer k of G_{fwd} and G_{bwd} respectively. Also, each of the columns of FM_k^{fwd} and FM_k^{bwd} are vectorized $i.e.$ $FM_k \in \mathbb{R}^{W_k \times H_k \times N_k}$ where, W_k, H_k and N_k are the width, height and number of feature maps at layer k respectively. Our aim is to transform each small local (spatially) region of the feature maps from G_{fwd}, at several layers by using those from G_{bwd}. We divide the feature maps into R non-overlapping square regions and use the concept of Gaussian Guidance Maps (GGM). GGMs are essentially normalized ($[0,1]$) image maps and specifies how much weightage is given to a specific neuron in the guiding policy. We noticed that the neurons near the border of all the R regions contribute almost equally to capture an intermediate feature; whereas, those near the center are often mutually exclusive in their role. Armed with this intuition, we assign a higher weightage for the center neurons in the GGM and lower it near the borders. This is modeled with the help of a Gaussian distribution. Note that the guidance maps have zero values for areas outside the boundaries of a particular region, thereby suppressing unwanted effects from those (*e.g. sky*) far away from the current one (*e.g. road*).

The feature maps of each of the K layers are multiplied with R GGM to compute the Locally Guided Gram matrix (LGG) $\mathcal{G}$. This is defined as:

$$[FM_k^{fwd}]_r = [GGM]_r \circ FM_k^{fwd} \tag{12}$$

$$[\mathcal{G}_k^{fwd}]_r = [FM_k^{fwd}]_r^T [FM_k^{fwd}]_r \tag{13}$$

where, $r \in R$, $\circ$ represents element-wise multiplication, $[GGM]_r$ is the normalized GGM for region r and $[\mathcal{G}_k^{fwd}]_r$ is the LGG of the same. We compute the values for the feature maps of the backward network simultaneously, using analysis similar to Eqs. 12 and 13.

Each of the LGG matrices now becomes the target for optimization for the corresponding regions in the feature space. This way, the objective function for LGGL is expressed in Sum of Squared Distance (SSD) form as:

$$\mathcal{L}_{LGGL} = \frac{1}{K} \sum_{k=1}^{K} \frac{1}{R^2(N_k)^2} \sum_{r=1}^{R} \left[[\mathcal{G}_k^{fwd}]_r - [\mathcal{G}_k^{bwd}]_r \right]^2 \tag{14}$$

As the granularity of the extracted features vary proportionally with the depth of CNNs, $\mathcal{L}_{LGGL}$ minimizes the feature distance in a hierarchical fashion and greatly enhances the stability of the feature generating stage.

4   Overall Objective Function

We integrate the objective functions described in Sect. 3 with the traditional adversarial loss function [24] as well as the well-known $L1$ and $L2$ metrics for the proposed frame prediction network. The generator (G_{fwd}) in the feature generation stage thus optimizes the following weighted function:

$$\mathcal{L}_{comb}^{fwd} = \lambda_{adv}^{fwd} \mathcal{L}_{adv}^{G_{fwd}}(X) + \lambda_{LGGL} \mathcal{L}_{LGGL}(X, Y) + \lambda_{L2}^{fwd} \mathcal{L}_{L2}(X_{int}, Y_{int}) \tag{15}$$

where, the symbols bear the standard notations as mentioned in the previous sections. The optimal values for the co-efficients $\lambda_{adv}^{fwd}, \lambda_{L2}^{fwd}$ and λ_{LGGL} are empirically found to be $0.10, 0.45$ and 0.45. Similarly, the objective function for the backward generator G_{bwd} is:

$$\mathcal{L}_{comb}^{bwd} = \lambda_{adv}^{bwd} \mathcal{L}_{adv}^{G_{bwd}}(X) + \lambda_{LGGL} \mathcal{L}_{LGGL}(X, Y) + \lambda_{L2}^{bwd} \mathcal{L}_{L2}(X_{int}, Y_{int}) \tag{16}$$

where, the co-efficients are kept equal to their forward generator counterparts. On the other hand, the combined loss function for the reconstruction phase generator (G_{recon}) includes the Gradient Divergence Loss (GDL) [8] for enhancing the sharpness of the generated frame(s) and is represented as:

$$\mathcal{L}_{comb}^{recon} = \lambda_{adv}^{recon} \mathcal{L}_{adv}^{G_{recon}}(X_{int}) + \lambda_{L1}^{recon} \mathcal{L}_{L1}(Y, Y') + \lambda_{GDL} \mathcal{L}_{GDL}(Y, Y') \tag{17}$$

In all our experiments, we keep the weights λ_{adv}^{recon}, λ_{L1}^{recon} and λ_{GDL} as $0.10, 0.25$ and 0.65 respectively (determined empirically for best performance).

These combined objectives in Eqs. 15–17 when minimized simultaneously, reduce the gap in the intermediate and RGB features spaces of the target (GT) and generated frame(s), thereby generating better results.

5   Experiments

We evaluate our frame prediction network on four popular benchmark datasets: (a) KTH [20], (b) Weizmann [21], (c) UCF-101 [22] and (d) KITTI [23]. Among these, KTH and Weizmann contain various simple human actions in a predominantly static background. The UCF-101 dataset comprises of scenes with 101 different complex human actions. Although it contains much complex scenes than the KTH and Weizmann, it still suffers from the problem of static background which can lead the network to just learn to copy pixel values. To overcome this issue, we use Sports-1M [26], a large database of natural sports videos, for training. Lastly, KITTI contains street view scenes taken from a car mounted camera and generally does not suffer from the static background problem.

Quantitative studies with recent state-of-the-art and other methods have been carried out using two image quality measurement metrics: (a) Peak Signal to Noise Ratio (PSNR) [27] and (b) Structural Similarity Index Measure (SSIM) [28].

5.1   Results on KTH and Weizmann

The KTH dataset comprises of 6 different human actions from 25 subjects. Videos in this dataset have rather simplistic motions which are periodic and predominantly exhibit a static background. Following [9], we use persons 1–16 for training and the rest for testing purpose. Apart from these, we also selected walking, running, one and two hands waving classes from the Weizmann database. All the experiments are done using 64×64 dimension input and target frames. The network is trained using a set of 10 consecutive frames to predict up-to 10

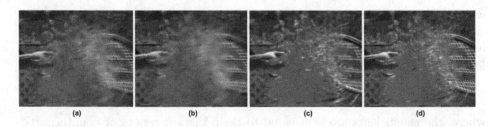

Fig. 3. Effect of layer selection in the feature generation stage. Zoomed-in patches of outputs from models optimized with LGGL taking into account: (a) early, (b) terminal and (c) optimum choice (mixed) of layers from G_{fwd} and G_{bwd} networks. The same patch from the ground-truth frame is shown in (d). Observe the trade-off between blurriness and sharpness in each of the cases (Best viewed in color)

frames in the future. For a fair comparison with [9], clips from the running and jogging classes are sampled every 3rd frame while for the rest of the classes the sample period is one in every 10 frames. As our network predicts 10 frames in the future, the sampling rate is chosen to be 10 instead of 20 (as in [9]). Additional results for deeper prediction are shown the supplementary document. The layers conv_2, conv_4, conv_6, conv_9 and conv_10 of G_{fwd} and G_{bwd} were found to be the optimum choice for the Locally Guided Gram Loss (LGGL) in the feature generation stage (refer Sects. 1 & 2 in supplementary document for architecture). Choosing only the early layers for LGGL produced features which forced G_{recon} to predict output frames having sharp edges with overall color and texture informations intact, but lacking in finer details (e.g. cloth patterns). A reverse effect was observed (sharper details but blurry edges) when features were chosen from later parts of the feature generation network (see Fig. 3).

From the quantitative results presented in Table 1, it is evident that the proposed framework is superior to its closest competitor MCNet both in terms of PSNR and SSIM quality measures. Also note that the drop in reconstruction quality is substantially less than other methods, as we go deeper into the future. This can be attributed to the weighted context aggregation of the Pix-Graph module which captures the temporal information in locally restricted areas. MCNet uses LSTMs as well as two separate networks for capturing both the temporal and spatial information. While the complex framework of MCNet learns periodic motions, it often fails to perform in case of complex scenes with highly non-periodic motion. Also, as our method learns an intermediate feature representation that is explicitly trained to fuel the prediction quality, the output frames look much more photo-realistic (refer to supplementary figures for additional illustrations).

Table 1. Comparison of performance for KTH and Weizmann datasets using PSNR/SSIM scores. GDL stands for Gradient Divergence Loss [8]. Best results in bold.

Methods	Frame-1		Frame-4	
	Weizmann	KTH	Weizmann	KTH
ConvLSTM + RES [9]	36.2/0.97	33.8/0.94	29.8/0.92	27.9/0.86
MCNet + RES [9]	36.8/0.97	33.9/0.94	31.9/0.94	28.3/0.88
Adv + L1 (w/o PixGraph)	27.3/0.83	25.2/0.82	22.4/0.78	21.3/0.72
Adv + L1 + LGGL (w/o PixGraph)	30.1/0.85	29.9/0.85	24.8/0.79	23.5/0.73
Adv + L1 (PixGraph)	38.4/0.95	35.1/0.93	33.7/0.94	30.8/0.89
Adv + L1 + LGGL (PixGraph)	41.8/0.97	39.8/0.96	38.2/0.95	36.1/0.91
Adv + L1 + LGGL + GDL (PixGraph)	**42.5/0.98**	**40.8/0.96**	**38.8/0.96**	**36.7/0.91**

5.2 Results on UCF-101

The UCF-101 dataset contains realistic scenes of 101 types of human actions collected from YouTube. Compared to KTH and Weizmann, this database is

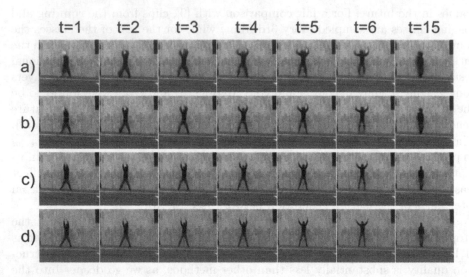

Fig. 4. Qualitative result for Weizmann dataset. The combination of models used are (a) L1 + LGGL, (b) L1 + LGGL (PixGraph) and (c) GDL [8] + L1 + LGGL (Pix-Graph). The last row represents ground-truth frames

Table 2. Quantitative comparison of performance of different methods for the UCF-101 and KITTI datasets using PSNR/SSIM scores. (*) indicates that models are fine tuned on patches of size 64×64 [8]. ($\dagger$) represents model trained on 2 frames as input. (-) denotes unavailability of performance results. GDL stands for Gradient Divergence Loss [8]. Last 5 rows report the scores obtained using the proposed method. Best results are given in bold.

Methods	Frame-1		Frame-2	
	UCF-101	KITTI	UCF-101	KITTI
GDL L1* [8]	29.9/0.90	-	26.4/0.87	-
Adv + GDL fine-tuned* [8]	32.0/0.92	-	28.9/0.89	-
Optical flow [8]	31.6/0.93	-	28.2/0.90	-
ConvLSTM [9]	27.3/0.87	-	23.3/0.78	-
ConvLSTM + RES [9]	29.8/0.90	-	25.1/0.82	-
MCNet [9]	27.9/0.87	-	23.8/0.80	-
MCNet + RES UCF101 [9]	30.5/0.91	-	27.7/0.86	-
Deep Voxel Flow† [29]	35.8/0.96	-	-	-
SNCCL + PCDL + L1 [19]	38.2/0.95	40.2/0.94	36.8/0.93	37.7/0.91
Adv + L1 (w/o PixGraph)	24.2/0.82	28.3/0.81	23.5/0.81	26.8/0.80
Adv + L1 + LGGL (w/o PixGraph)	27.5/0.86	30.1/0.86	26.7/0.84	28.1/0.83
Adv + L1 (PixGraph)	34.2/0.93	36.3/0.92	33.5/0.92	35.9/0.91
Adv + L1 + LGGL (PixGraph)	38.8/0.95	41.2/0.95	37.6/0.94	39.3/0.93
Adv + L1 + LGGL + GDL (PixGraph)	**40.1/0.96**	**42.3/0.96**	**39.2/0.95**	**40.1/0.94**

complex and larger in size. Following [8], we train our models using 4 consecutive frames as input and the 5th as target at the training phase. As the scenes from this dataset contain many frames having static background, we train using random 64×64 (patches) exhibiting motion, estimated using the $L2$ distance between frames in consecutive time-steps. Apart from the UCF-101 frames, Sports-1M [26] is also used for reasons similar to the experimental settings described in [8]. We sampled one in every 10 videos of the test split of UCF-101 for the evaluation phase and identified regions containing significant motion by calculating optical flow features (using [30]). The architecture is kept the same as that used for predicting frames from KTH and Weizmann dataset. Also, we again use the combination of features from convolutional layers $2, 4, 5$ and 7 of the feature generation stage for calculating LGGL. Notice the substantial increase in the PSNR/SSIM values of the PixGraph based proposed model over the basic one in Table 2. Similar to the results obtained in case of KTH and Weizmann datasets, the trend of a slower rate of degradation (measured using PSNR and SSIM) of the output (produced) frames is also evident in the UCF-101 ablation studies due to the efficient context aggregation power of PixGraph. Qualitative results are shown in Figs. 3 and 4 of the supplementary document and also in Fig. 5. Inclusion of residual blocks in the reconstruction stage generator plays a more involved role in UCF-101 predictions than in KTH and Weizmann datasets.

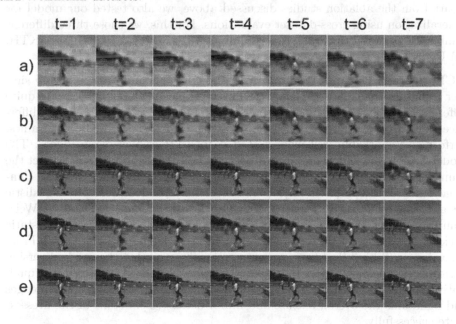

Fig. 5. Qualitative results for UCF-101 on a scene involving high amount of camera motion. The combination of models used are (a) L1, (b) NCCL + PCDL + L1 [19], (c) Deep Voxel Flow [29] and (d) LGGL + L1 (PixGraph). The last row represents GT frames

5.3   Results on KITTI

KITTI is a traffic scene database containing videos captured from a camera mounted on cars. In contrast to KTH, Weizmann and UCF-101, the videos from this dataset do not generally suffer from the issue of static background. Hence, we did not use any auxiliary dataset such as Sports-1M for training. For all our experimental studies, videos from (a) road and (b) city have been used. The models were trained using four consecutive frames as input and the subsequent four as target. For quantitative evaluation, we selected one among every five videos from the above mentioned classes to predict 8 frames in the future. Table 2 provides the quantitative comparison of several of our models for KITTI. Interesting to note that, the bare model with only $L1$ objective and the adversarial losses fail to reconstruct realistic versions of KITTI scenes. This is due to the fact that the model seems to reconstruct by averaging between every two consecutive frames producing ghost image type artifacts. This issue is almost entirely subdued by the use of PixGraph and LGGL (see Table 2), thereby confirming once again its role in guiding the feature generation network into building a rich context aggregated intermediate feature space.

5.4   Cross-Dataset Evaluation

Apart from the ablation studies discussed above, we also tested our model for generalization using cross-dataset evaluations. For this, we chose three different combinations of datasets (listed as training → testing): (a) UCF-101 → KTH, (b) UCF-101 → Weizmann and (c) UCF-101 → KITTI.

UCF-101 → KTH and Weizmann. Although KTH and Weizmann are simpler in nature than UCF-101 and KITTI, the scenes in these datasets are quite different in style, color and motion pattern. In spite of these inherent differences, our proposed models when trained with UCF-101 for predicting frames, performed remarkably well when tested with KTH or Weizmann videos. The model without any of our proposed objectives failed miserably to reconstruct the frames. Inclusion of LGGL greatly helps to generate legible scenes whereas, combination of all the proposed objectives successfully produce near photo-realistic images. The quantitative results for UCF-101 → KTH and UCF-101 → Weizmann are shown in Table 3. As both KTH and Weizmann have a large static background, the color patterns were easy to predict (simple pixel copy). From the values in Table 3 (last two rows), it can be observed that the residual version performs significantly better than the other models. This is evident in the qualitative results also (see Fig. 1 in the supplementary) as it produces sharp edges and maintains the overall texture and minor details (*e.g.* details of the dresses) quite successfully.

UCF-101 → KITTI. We also tested our models trained for UCF-101 on the KITTI dataset by feeding 6 input frames to produce 8 future frames. The PSNR/SSIM values in Table 4 indicate the generalizability of our proposed models in this cross-dataset arrangement. Note that, in this particular case, the

Table 3. Comparison of UCF-101 → KTH and Weizmann cross-dataset performance using PSNR/SSIM measures for different adversarial models. Best results in bold.

Methods	Frame-1		Frame-4		Frame-10	
	Weizmann	KTH	Weizmann	KTH	Weizmann	KTH
L1 + LGGL (w/o PixGraph)	28.7/0.84	28.2/0.85	23.4/0.78	22.3/0.72	19.8/0.73	19.6/0.70
L1 + LGGL (PixGraph)	**40.2/0.96**	**38.2/0.95**	**36.4/0.94**	**33.9/0.90**	**31.2/0.90**	**28.9/0.84**

Table 4. Comparison of UCF-101 → KITTI cross-dataset performance using PSNR/SSIM measures for different adversarial models. Best results in bold.

Methods	Frame-1	Frame-2	Frame-4	Frame-8
L1 + LGGL (w/o PixGraph)	29.2/0.85	26.9/0.82	24.7/0.80	20.8/0.78
L1 + LGGL (PixGraph)	**38.6/0.94**	**37.5/0.91**	**34.2/0.86**	**31.1/0.83**

PSNR values decrease (with increasing frame number) a bit faster compared to that for other databases, while the trend of slow rate in decrease of the SSIM value remains unaltered. As PSNR is a pixel-wise difference measure, small changes in a large number of pixels result in a far worse value despite being perceptually acceptable. As SSIM uses features for measuring the similarity, it does not get affected by this undesired phenomenon. Figure 2 in the supplementary shows qualitative results of this cross-dataset experimentation.

6   Conclusion

This paper proposes a 2-stage encoder-decoder type GAN for predicting photo-realistic future frames with a novel graph based context aggregation layer, PixGraph. Further, for diminishing the issues of instability and building a meaningful intricate intermediate feature space, we employed a novel region based guidance objective: the Locally Guided Gram Loss (LGGL). Extensive evaluation on popular benchmark datasets and KITTI, a database previously not quite explored in the genre of frame prediction, reveal the superiority of our proposed model, especially the PixGraph module, over the recent state-of-the-art methods.

References

1. Srivastava, N., Mansimov, E., Salakhudinov, R.: Unsupervised learning of video representations using LSTMs. In: International Conference on Machine Learning, pp. 843–852 (2015)
2. Hochreiter, S., Schmidhuber, J.: Long short-term memory. Neural comput. 9(8), 1735–1780 (1997)
3. Ranzato, M., Szlam, A., Bruna, J., Mathieu, M., Collobert, R., Chopra, S.: Video (language) modeling: a baseline for generative models of natural videos. arXiv preprint arXiv:1412.6604 (2014)

4. Oh, J., Guo, X., Lee, H., Lewis, R.L., Singh, S.: Action-conditional video prediction using deep networks in Atari games. In: Advances in Neural Information Processing Systems, pp. 2863–2871 (2015)
5. Vondrick, C., Pirsiavash, H., Torralba, A.: Generating videos with scene dynamics. In: Advances in Neural Information Processing Systems, pp. 613–621 (2016)
6. Lan, T., Chen, T.-C., Savarese, S.: A hierarchical representation for future action prediction. In: Fleet, D., Pajdla, T., Schiele, B., Tuytelaars, T. (eds.) ECCV 2014. LNCS, vol. 8691, pp. 689–704. Springer, Cham (2014). https://doi.org/10.1007/978-3-319-10578-9_45
7. Walker, J., Gupta, A., Hebert, M.: Patch to the future: unsupervised visual prediction. In: Proceedings of the IEEE Conference on Computer Vision and Pattern Recognition, pp. 3302–3309 (2014)
8. Mathieu, M., Couprie, C., LeCun, Y.: Deep multi-scale video prediction beyond mean square error. In: International Conference on Learning Representations (ICLR) (2016)
9. Villegas, R., Yang, J., Hong, S., Lin, X., Lee, H.: Decomposing motion and content for natural video sequence prediction. In: ICLR, vol. 1, no. 2 (2017)
10. Oord, A.v.d., Kalchbrenner, N., Kavukcuoglu, K.: Pixel recurrent neural networks. arXiv preprint arXiv:1601.06759 (2016)
11. Kalchbrenner, N., et al.: Video pixel networks. In: International Conference on Machine Learning, pp. 1771–1779 (2017)
12. Kingma, D.P., Welling, M.: Auto-encoding variational bayes. arXiv preprint arXiv:1312.6114 (2013)
13. Xue, T., Wu, J., Bouman, K., Freeman, B.: Visual dynamics: probabilistic future frame synthesis via cross convolutional networks. In: Advances in Neural Information Processing Systems, pp. 91–99 (2016)
14. Babaeizadeh, M., Finn, C., Erhan, D., Campbell, R.H., Levine, S.: Stochastic variational video prediction. arXiv preprint arXiv:1710.11252 (2017)
15. Vondrick, C., Torralba, A.: Generating the future with adversarial transformers. In: IEEE Conference on Computer Vision and Pattern Recognition (CVPR) (2017)
16. Lu, C., Hirsch, M., Schölkopf, B.: Flexible spatio-temporal networks for video prediction. In: Proceedings of the IEEE Conference on Computer Vision and Pattern Recognition, pp. 6523–6531 (2017)
17. Zhou, Y., Berg, T.L.: Learning temporal transformations from time-lapse videos. In: Leibe, B., Matas, J., Sebe, N., Welling, M. (eds.) ECCV 2016. LNCS, vol. 9912, pp. 262–277. Springer, Cham (2016). https://doi.org/10.1007/978-3-319-46484-8_16
18. Liang, X., Lee, L., Dai, W., Xing, E.P.: Dual motion GAN for future-flow embedded video prediction. arXiv preprint (2017)
19. Bhattacharjee, P., Das, S.: Temporal coherency based criteria for predicting video frames using deep multi-stage generative adversarial networks. In: Advances in Neural Information Processing Systems, pp. 4268–4277 (2017)
20. Schuldt, C., Laptev, I., Caputo, B.: Recognizing human actions: a local SVM approach. In: Proceedings of the 17th IEEE International Conference on Pattern Recognition, vol. 3, pp. 32–36 (2004)
21. Blank, M., Gorelick, L., Shechtman, E., Irani, M., Basri, R.: Actions as space-time shapes. In: Tenth IEEE International Conference on Computer Vision, vol. 2, pp. 1395–1402 (2005)
22. Soomro, K., Zamir, A.R., Shah, M.: UCF101: a dataset of 101 human actions classes from videos in the wild. arXiv preprint arXiv:1212.0402 (2012)

23. Geiger, A., Lenz, P., Stiller, C., Urtasun, R.: Vision meets robotics: the KITTI dataset. Int. J. Robot. Res. **32**(11), 1231–1237 (2013)
24. Goodfellow, I., et al.: Generative adversarial nets. In: Advances in Neural Information Processing Systems, pp. 2672–2680 (2014)
25. Elman, J.L.: Finding structure in time. Cogn. Sci. **14**(2), 179–211 (1990)
26. Karpathy, A., Toderici, G., Shetty, S., Leung, T., Sukthankar, R., Fei-Fei, L.: Large-scale video classification with convolutional neural networks. In: IEEE International Conference on Computer Vision and Pattern Recognition (2014)
27. Bovik, A.C.: The Essential Guide to Video Processing, 2nd edn. Academic Press, Cambridge (2009)
28. Wang, Z., Bovik, A.C., Sheikh, H.R., Simoncelli, E.P.: Image quality assessment: from error visibility to structural similarity. IEEE Trans. Image Process. (TIP) **13**(4), 600–612 (2004)
29. Liu, Z., Yeh, R., Tang, X., Liu, Y., Agarwala, A.: Video frame synthesis using deep voxel flow. In: International Conference on Computer Vision (ICCV), vol. 2 (2017)
30. Brox, T., Bregler, C., Malik, J.: Large displacement optical flow. In: IEEE Conference on Computer Vision and Pattern Recognition, pp. 41–48 (2009)

Convolutional Neural Network
for Trajectory Prediction

Nishant Nikhil[1,2](✉) and Brendan Tran Morris[2](✉) (iD)

[1] Indian Institute of Technology Kharagpur, Kharagpur, India
nishantnikhil@iitkgp.ac.in
[2] University of Nevada, Las Vegas, USA
brendan.morris@unlv.edu

Abstract. Predicting trajectories of pedestrians is quintessential for autonomous robots which share the same environment with humans. In order to effectively and safely interact with humans, trajectory prediction needs to be both precise and computationally efficient. In this work, we propose a convolutional neural network (CNN) based human trajectory prediction approach. Unlike more recent LSTM-based moles which attend sequentially to each frame, our model supports increased parallelism and effective temporal representation. The proposed compact CNN model is faster than the current approaches yet still yields competitive results.

Keywords: Convolutional neural network · Trajectory prediction · Anticipating human behavior

1 Introduction

Autonomous robots like self-driving cars on a road or a food-delivery robot in a restaurant must share the same space with humans. In order to do so in a safe and acceptable manner, these robots must be able to understand and cooperate with humans. One task of paramount importance for avoiding collisions and for smooth maneuvering is to accurately predict the future trajectories of humans in their shared space. Further, given the wide diversity of platforms and environments for which prediction may be required (e.g. small robots with limited computing capabilities or without connectivity to cloud computing resources), simple models with better time complexity are desired.

Traditionally, hand-crafted features were used for trajectory prediction and modeling motion of pedestrians' trajectory with respect to others surrounding them. [1] propose a discrete choice framework for pedestrian dynamics, modeling short-term behavior of individuals as a response to the presence of other pedestrians. The Social Force model [2] incorporates two interactive forces for microsimulation of crowds. Attractive forces guiding the pedestrians towards their goal and repulsive forces for encouraging collision avoidance in-between

© Springer Nature Switzerland AG 2019
L. Leal-Taixé and S. Roth (Eds.): ECCV 2018 Workshops, LNCS 11131, pp. 186–196, 2019.
https://doi.org/10.1007/978-3-030-11015-4_16

the pedestrians and in-between a pedestrian and environmental obstacles. Yamaguchi et al. [3] solves the same problem as an energy minimization problem. While successful, hand-crafted features are hard to scale since influencing factors must be described explicitly.

In recent years, Deep Neural Networks (DNN) have been utilized for the trajectory prediction task since they utilize a data-driven approach to tease out relationships and influences which may not have been apparent. These DNN-based approaches [4–7] have demonstrated impressive results. Almost all of these approaches are based on Recurrent Neural Networks (RNNs) [8] since a trajectory is a temporal sequence. As RNNs share parameters across time, they are capable of conditioning the model on all previous positions of a trajectory. Although theoretically, RNNs can retain information from all previous words of a sentence, practically they fail at handling long-term dependencies. Also, RNNs are prone to the vanishing and exploding gradient problems when dealing with long sequences.

Long Short-Term Memory (LSTM) networks [9], a special kind of RNN architecture, were designed to address these problems. Although LSTMs have been found to address the sequence based problems effectively but they need quite a bit of task-specific engineering like clipping gradients. Also in RNNs, predictions for later time-steps must wait for the predictions from preceding time-steps and hence can't be parallelized during training or inference time.

Recently, Convolutional Neural Network (CNN) based architectures have provided encouraging results in sequence-to-sequence tasks [10] like machine translation [11,12], image generation [13] and Image Captioning [14]. Inspired by these, we study CNNs for the task of trajectory prediction. This is the first work we are aware of to use an end-to-end convolutional architecture for trajectory prediction (Deo and Trivedi [15] used convolutional pooling for incorporating social context from hidden states of the LSTM network). We believe the CNN is superior to LSTM for temporal modeling since trajectories are continuous in nature, do not have complicated "state", and have high spatial and temporal correlation which can be exploited by computationally efficient convolution operations.

The major contribution of the work can be summarized as proposing a fast CNN-based model for trajectory prediction that is competitive with more complicated state-of-the-art LSTM-based techniques which require more contextual information. We discuss our CNN architecture in Sect. 2. Section 3 provides an experimental evaluation to highlight the efficacy of our approach and value due to simplicity. Finally, in Sect. 4, we conclude the paper with closing remarks.

2   Trajectory Prediction Method

Recent work in prediction has utilized recurrent networks to model temporal dependencies and sequence-like nature of trajectories using LSTMs. Most efforts in this area look to augment position input with social [4,5] or scene [6,16] context resulting in more complicated architectures. In contrast, our work seeks to simplify the network architecture and make more direct use of trajectory structure (spatio-temporal consistency) by using highly efficient convolutions temporal support.

2.1 Problem Setup

For trajectory prediction, we are given the trajectory of all the pedestrians. It is assumed that each scene is pre-processed and we have the spatial coordinates of every i-th pedestrian at time t as $X_t = (x_t^i, y_t^i)$. That is, we have the pedestrian trajectory data as $X = \{X_1, X_2, X_3, X_4, \ldots, X_n\}$ for time steps $t = 1, 2, \ldots, T_{obs}$. Note: for simplicity the pedestrian superscript i is not listed. We have to predict the future trajectories of all the pedestrians for time steps $t = T_{obs+1}, \ldots, T_{pred}$ as $\hat{Y} = \{\hat{Y}_1, \hat{Y}_2, \hat{Y}_3, \hat{Y}_4, \ldots, \hat{Y}_m\}$ all at once.

2.2 LSTM-Based Frameworks

Most current research in trajectory prediction has utilized LSTM cells for handling temporal dependencies. The working of LSTM cells are governed by the following equations:

$$f_t = \sigma_g(W_f X_t + U_f h_{t-1} + b_f) \tag{1}$$

$$i_t = \sigma_g(W_i X_t + U_i h_{t-1} + b_i) \tag{2}$$

$$o_t = \sigma_g(W_o X_t + U_o h_{t-1} + b_o) \tag{3}$$

$$c_t = f_t \circ c_{t-1} + i_t \circ \sigma_c(W_c x_t + U_c h_{t-1} + b_c) \tag{4}$$

$$h_t = o_t \circ \sigma_h(c_t) \tag{5}$$

In these equations, X_t is the input vector to the LSTM unit, f_t is the forget gate's activation vector, i_t is the input gate's activation vector, o_t is the output gate's activation vector, h_t is the output vector of the LSTM unit and c_t is the cell state vector. w, u, B are the parameters of weight matrices and bias vectors which are learned during the training.

The basic LSTM formulation has been extended to add more complicated LSTM units by adding more contextual information such as social cues (influence of neighboring humans) [4,5] or environmental cues (influence of scene) [6,16]. While these have been effective in improving prediction performance, they still utilize the LSTM which has hidden state h_t dependent on previous time-steps and can not be parallelized. Sequential evaluation limits the speed of any LSTM-based architecture.

2.3 CNN-Based Framework

In contrast with LSTM-based networks, our proposed network (Fig. 1) utilizes highly parallelizable convolutional layers to handle temporal dependencies. The CNN-network is actually a simple sequence-to-sequence architecture. Trajectory

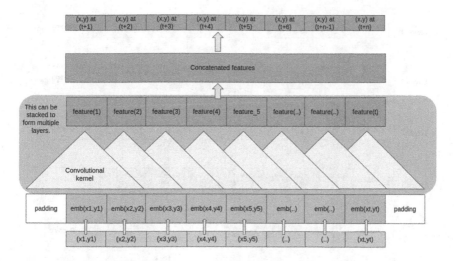

Fig. 1. Our convolutional model for trajectory prediction. Note that all operations are feed-forward in nature and hence can be parallelized.

histories are used as input and embedded to a fixed size through a fully connected layer. Convolutional layers are stacked and used to enforce temporal consistency. Finally, the features from the final convolutional layer are concatenated and passed through a fully connected layer to generate all predicted positions $(x^t, y^t)_{t=t+1}^{t+t_{pred}}$ at once.

The model is inspired by the work of [14] which has to predict a discrete output for the neural machine translation task. In that setting, the output at the next time step is highly dependent on the current time step for grammatical coherency and CNNs performed well. The major differences between this work and theirs are that trajectory prediction provides continuous output rather than discrete items and our architecture predicts all future time steps at once. We constantly pad the input to convolution layer such that output from the convolutional layer is of the same size as input to the layer. This way, we can build a neural network as deep as we want. We build the network deep enough to capture the context from every time step of the observed trajectory. We discuss more in the next subsection.

Through an ablation study (Sect. 3.2), we found that predicting one time step at a time leads to worse results than all future times at once. We believe this is due to error of the current prediction being propagated forward in time in a highly correlated fashion. Also, unlike LSTM-based architectures which utilize a recurrent function to compute sequentially, all the computation in the proposed model are feed-forward in nature resulting in a significant performance boost with respect to inference time. Additionally, the convolutions can be easily parallelized.

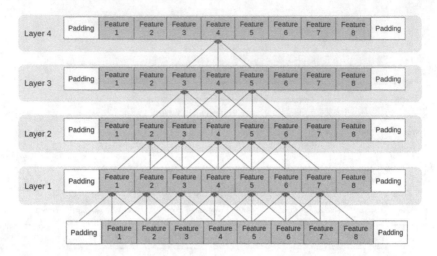

Fig. 2. For an input having eight temporal dimension and convolutional layers having kernel size of three, we need at least four layer to capture the context from all time-steps.

2.4 Implementation Details

We use a kernel size of 3 for all the kernels, by ablation study we found that it works better than other odd kernel sizes when we apply symmetric padding. As the observed trajectory length is eight for all the experiments we conduct, we use a four-layered convolutional network. As shown in Fig. 2, All the features in layer 4 capture context from all eight trajectory observations. Unlike temporal convolutional networks (TCNs), we do not use dilated convolutions because we do not want to lose information on such a small temporal dimension. Additionally, we use full rather than causal kernels since the output is a prediction. The embedding layer which converts the geometrical coordinates to embeddings has a dimension of 32, and the subsequent convolution layers produce outputs of the same dimensions. For optimization, we use Adam [17] with a learning rate of 0.001. We use a batch size of 32. The model is trained until the validation loss (L2 loss) stops decreasing.

3 Experiments

Following common practice in literature (e.g. [4]), experimental evaluation is conducted on publically available pedestrian trajectory datasets. Evaluation utilizes eight historical samples (3.2 s) to give a long-term prediction of the next 12 samples (4.8 s).

3.1 Datasets and Evaluation Criteria

Two publicly available datasets which provide over 1500 pedestrian trajectories in varied crowd settings are utilized in our experiments. The ETH dataset [18] consists of the ETH and HOTEL scenes while the UCY dataset [19] has the UNIV, ZARA1, and ZARA2 scenes. The trajectories are rich with challenging human-human interaction scenarios such as group behavior, non-linear trajectories, people crossing paths, collision avoidance, and group formation and dispersion. All trajectory data has been converted from image to real-world coordinates and interpolated at 2.5 Hz.

As with prior work [5, 20], we use two metrics for computing prediction error:

1. Average Displacement Error (ADE): Computes the mean of euclidean distance between the points in predicted trajectory and the corresponding points in ground truth for all predicted time steps.

$$ADE = \frac{\sum_{t=obs+1}^{T_{pred}} \left\| Y_t - \hat{Y}_t \right\|}{T_{pred} - T_{obs}}$$

2. Final Displacement Error (FDE): The Euclidean distance between final destination as per the ground truth and the predicted destination at end of the prediction period T_{pred}.

$$FDE = \left\| Y_{T_{pred}} - \hat{Y}_{T_{pred}} \right\|$$

Similar to [4, 5], we follow leave-one-out approach. We train on four of the five crowd scenes and test on the remaining set. The trajectory is observed for 8-time steps (3.2 s), then the model makes the prediction for 12-time steps (4.8 s).

Table 1. Quantitative ADE/FDE for the task of predicting 12 future time steps given 8 previous time steps. More contextual information is provided from left to right ([+]social, [++]raw scene image)

Dataset	Ours	LSTM	S-GAN[+]	S-LSTM[+]	S-GAN-P[+]	SoPhie[++]
ETH	1.04/2.07	1.09/2.41	0.81/1.52	1.09/2.35	0.87/1.62	**0.70/1.43**
HOTEL	**0.59/1.17**	0.86/1.91	0.72/1.61	0.79/1.76	0.67/1.37	0.76/1.67
UNIV	0.57/1.21	0.61/1.31	0.60/1.26	0.67/1.40	0.76/1.52	**0.54/1.24**
ZARA1	0.43/0.90	0.41/0.88	0.34/0.69	0.47/1.00	0.35/0.68	**0.30/0.63**
ZARA2	**0.34/0.75**	0.52/1.11	0.42/0.84	0.56/1.17	0.42/0.84	0.38/0.78
AVG	0.59/1.22	0.70/1.52	0.58/1.18	0.72/1.54	0.61/1.21	**0.54/1.15**

3.2 Quantitative Evaluation

In Table 1, we compare prediction results against five different architectures:

1. LSTM: A simple Long Short-Term Memory architecture without any pooling mechanism, i.e. it doesn't consider any social context.

2. S-LSTM [5]: This model combines LSTMs with a social pooling mechanism to provide social context in a fixed rectangular grid.
3. S-GAN [4]: This model uses LSTM and variable social max-pooling mechanism in a Generative Adversarial Network (GAN) architecture to generate multiple plausible trajectories. The S-GAN-P variant also uses a social pooling mechanism.
4. SoPhie [6]: Apart from having LSTM and pooling for features in a GAN setting, this model applies a scene attention mechanism over the features extracted from images of the scene to augment trajectory information.

The results are organized by increasing contextual information (e.g. social pooling or raw images for scene information) from left to right. Note: that LSTM, S-LSTM, and S-GAN results in Table 1 were reported in [4].

We find that our model consistently outperforms the LSTM baseline even though they are utilizing the same basic position inputs. We speculate that this is because the CNNs do a better job at handling long-term dependencies than the LSTM specifically for continuous numerical regression where the notion of state is not complicated. Interestingly, ours is the best performing architecture for the HOTEL scene even without the use of social or environmental cues. This is likely due to the simplicity of the scene since even a simple linear regressor provides better results (0.39/0.72) than all reported here [4]. However, the simple CNN still performs very well even in more complicated scenarios (UNIV and ZARA2) and actually beats techniques that utilize social context. The UNIV result is most surprising since it is the most complicated scene with large crowds of people. In these situations, social context may not be relevant (Fig. 4(b)). In fact, the average performance is quite similar to S-GAN (provides many plausible trajectories), better than S-GAN-P (multiple trajectories with social pooling), and competitive with SoPhie even though those techniques use social context and scene image context (in the case of SoPhie).

Table 2. Speed comparison with other architectures

	LSTM	S-GAN	S-GAN-P	Ours
Time (s)	0.009	0.022	0.067	0.002
Speed-Up	7.44×	3.0×	1×	33.5×

The main advantage of our proposed CNN prediction architecture is the computational efficiency of convolution operations which can be highly parallelized. A speed comparison is provided in Table 2 which reports inference time in seconds and speed up factor with respect to the baseline S-GAN-P. The high speed of our method makes it well suited for mobile robot applications which need to make predictions in real-time.

Furthermore, to decide the number of layers we trained our architecture with different numbers of convolutional layers. Table 3 indicates that four layers

Table 3. CNN layer ablation study

Layers	Three	Four	Five
ADE	0.60	0.58	0.70
FDE	1.30	1.20	1.40

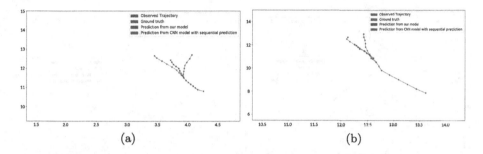

(a)   (b)

Fig. 3. Multi vs. Sequential Output. Trajectory prediction sequentially point-by-point performs poorly due to error propogation to future time-steps (trajectory curves off). Our multi-output model tends to be more resistant to such error accumulation.

performed the best. We believe this happens because three-layered networks are not able to capture context from all time-steps and five-layered networks are over-parametrized.

3.3 Qualitative Evaluation

In Figs. 3 and 4, we examine the quality of trajectories produced by the CNN architecture. One important finding was that sequential prediction (similar to LSTM-based models) performed very poorly (Fig. 3). Prediction error for the maroon curve was propagated forward resulting in trajectories that "curved off" over time. In contrast, the multi-output CNN architecture was more resistant to this type of error accumulation.

Figure 4 provides a comparison between the CNN (blue) and S-GAN (maroon). (a) provides an example when the CNN has a better prediction than S-GAN. In (b), S-GAN's social pooling causes poor prediction since it thinks all five pedestrians should be moving as a group. Their prediction of the two right moving pedestri6ans is strongly pulled to the left resulting in large error. In contrast, the CNN is able to independently predict with better results. The UNIV scene in particular is quite dense making the pooling operation challenging. In (c), both CNN and S-GAN fail as seen in the center. In particular, three pedestrians seem to move in unison to avoid something in the scene and therefore neither algorithm is aware. Finally, (d) shows an example of S-GAN performing better than CNN. It is interesting to note that for both (a) and (d), neither technique is actually working that well. Also, it is difficult to fully understand what is happening without overlaying the trajectories on the image frame. This strongly

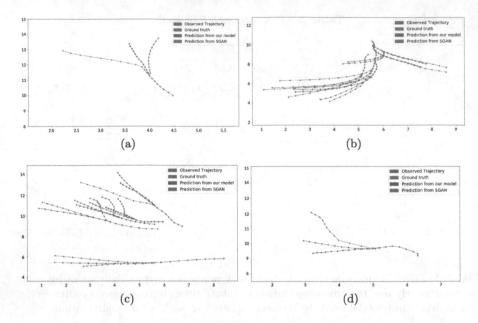

Fig. 4. Qualitative Comparison on UNIV. (a) CNN model is better able to interpolate while the S-GAN model seems to accumulate error in subsequent time-steps. (b) Social pooling erroneously combines all five pedestrians and thinks they all should be moving left. Without pooling, the CNN model is able to better predict the two pedestrians moving right. (c) Both models do a poor job of prediction, especially in the center. (d) SGAN provides a better prediction than CNN. (Color figure online)

hints that trajectories alone (even with social pooling) is not sufficient to make robust prediction.

Note that unlike state-of-the-art architectures (e.g. S-GAN and SoPhie), our CNN prediction architecture does not include any context outside of individual trajectory information. Similar social pooling schemes could be added and further improvements are expected. Additionally, S-GAN reported a 49× speed up over S-LSTM which would make our CNN architecture 500× S-LSTM.

4   Conclusions

We present a convolutional architecture based neural network model for trajectory prediction. The simple model gives competitive results with the current state-of-art LSTM-based models while providing better inference time performance. We hope that following this work, more people would be interested in utilizing clever convolutional architectures for trajectory prediction. Given the current architecture is quite simple, future work will examine the use of dilated convolutions to decrease the number of layers while maintaining the same receptive field and incorporating social context into the model.

References

1. Antonini, G., Bierlaire, M., Weber, M.: Discrete choice models of pedestrian walking behavior. Transp. Res. Part B: Methodol. **40**(8), 667–687 (2006)
2. Helbing, D., Molnar, P.: Social force model for pedestrian dynamics. Phys. Rev. E **51**, 4282–4286 (1998)
3. Yamaguchi, K., Berg, A.C., Ortiz, L.E., Berg, T.L.: Who are you with and where are you going? In: CVPR 2011, pp. 1345–1352 (2011)
4. Gupta, A., Johnson, J., Fei-Fei, L., Savarese, S., Alahi, A.: Social GAN: socially acceptable trajectories with generative adversarial networks. In: IEEE Conference on Computer Vision and Pattern Recognition (CVPR). Number CONF (2018)
5. Alahi, A., Goel, K., Ramanathan, V., Robicquet, A., Fei-Fei, L., Savarese, S.: Social LSTM: human trajectory prediction in crowded spaces. In: The IEEE Conference on Computer Vision and Pattern Recognition (CVPR), June 2016
6. Sadeghian, A., Kosaraju, V., Sadeghian, A., Hirose, N., Savarese, S.: SoPhie: an attentive GAN for predicting paths compliant to social and physical constraints. arXiv preprint arXiv:1806.01482 (2018)
7. Fernando, T., Denman, S., Sridharan, S., Fookes, C.: Soft + hardwired attention: an LSTM framework for human trajectory prediction and abnormal event detection. CoRR abs/1702.05552 (2017)
8. Mikolov, T., Karafiát, M., Burget, L., Černocký, J., Khudanpur, S.: Recurrent neural network based language model. In: Eleventh Annual Conference of the International Speech Communication Association (2010)
9. Hochreiter, S., Schmidhuber, J.: Long short-term memory. Neural Comput. **9**(8), 1735–1780 (1997)
10. Bai, S., Kolter, J.Z., Koltun, V.: An empirical evaluation of generic convolutional and recurrent networks for sequence modeling. CoRR abs/1803.01271 (2018)
11. Gehring, J., Auli, M., Grangier, D., Yarats, D., Dauphin, Y.N.: Convolutional sequence to sequence learning. CoRR abs/1705.03122 (2017)
12. Vaswani, A., et al.: Attention is all you need. CoRR abs/1706.03762 (2017)
13. van den Oord, A., Kalchbrenner, N., Vinyals, O., Espeholt, L., Graves, A., Kavukcuoglu, K.: Conditional image generation with PixelCNN decoders. In: Proceedings of the 30th International Conference on Neural Information Processing Systems. NIPS 2016, USA, pp. 4797–4805. Curran Associates Inc. (2016)
14. Aneja, J., Deshpande, A., Schwing, A.: Convolutional image captioning. In: Computer Vision and Pattern Recognition (2018)
15. Deo, N., Trivedi, M.M.: Convolutional social pooling for vehicle trajectory prediction. CoRR abs/1805.06771 (2018)
16. Xue, H., Huynh, D.Q., Reynolds, M.: SS-LSTM: a hierarchical LSTM model for pedestrian trajectory prediction. In: 2018 IEEE Winter Conference on Applications of Computer Vision (WACV), pp. 1186–1194, March 2018
17. Kingma, D.P., Ba, J.: Adam: a method for stochastic optimization. CoRR abs/1412.6980 (2014)
18. Pellegrini, S., Ess, A., Van Gool, L.: Improving data association by joint modeling of pedestrian trajectories and groupings. In: Daniilidis, K., Maragos, P., Paragios, N. (eds.) ECCV 2010. LNCS, vol. 6311, pp. 452–465. Springer, Heidelberg (2010). https://doi.org/10.1007/978-3-642-15549-9_33

19. Leal-Taixé, L., Fenzi, M., Kuznetsova, A., Rosenhahn, B., Savarese, S.: Learning an image-based motion context for multiple people tracking. In: IEEE Conference on Computer Vision and Pattern Recognition (CVPR) (2014)
20. Lee, N., Choi, W., Vernaza, P., Choy, C.B., Torr, P.H.S., Chandraker, M.K.: DESIRE: distant future prediction in dynamic scenes with interacting agents. In: 2017 IEEE Conference on Computer Vision and Pattern Recognition (CVPR), pp. 2165–2174 (2017)

Action Alignment from Gaze Cues in Human-Human and Human-Robot Interaction

Nuno Ferreira Duarte[1][✉], Mirko Raković[1,2], Jorge Marques[1], and José Santos-Victor[1]

[1] Vislab, Institute for Systems and Robotics, Instituto Superior Técnico, Universidade de Lisboa, Lisbon, Portugal
{nferreiraduarte,rakovicm,jsm,jasv}@isr.tecnico.ulisboa.pt
[2] Faculty of Technical Sciences, University of Novi Sad, Novi Sad, Serbia
rakovicm@uns.ac.rs

Abstract. Cognitive neuroscience experiments show how people intensify the exchange of non-verbal cues when they work on a joint task towards a common goal. When individuals share their intentions, it creates a social interaction that drives the mutual alignment of their actions and behavior. To understand the intentions of others, we strongly rely on the gaze cues. According to the role each person plays in the interaction, the resulting alignment of the body and gaze movements will be different. This mechanism is key to understand and model dyadic social interactions.

We focus on the alignment of the leader's behavior during dyadic interactions. The recorded gaze movements of dyads are used to build a model of the leader's gaze behavior. We use of the follower's gaze behavior data for two purposes: (i) to determine whether the follower is involved in the interaction, and (ii) if the follower's gaze behavior correlates to the type of the action under execution. This information is then used to plan the leader's actions in order to sustain the leader/follower alignment in the social interaction.

The model of the leader's gaze behavior and the alignment of the intentions is evaluated in a human-robot interaction scenario, with the robot acting as a leader and the human as a follower. During the interaction, the robot (i) emits non-verbal cues consistent with the action performed; (ii) predicts the human actions, and (iii) aligns its motion according to the human behavior.

Keywords: Action anticipation · Gaze behavior · Action alignment · Human-robot interaction

Work supported by EU H2020 project 752611 - ACTICIPATE, FCT project UID/EEA/50009/2013 and RBCog-Lab research infrastructure.

Electronic supplementary material The online version of this chapter (https://doi.org/10.1007/978-3-030-11015-4_17) contains supplementary material, which is available to authorized users.

L. Leal-Taixé and S. Roth (Eds.): ECCV 2018 Workshops, LNCS 11131, pp. 197–212, 2019.
https://doi.org/10.1007/978-3-030-11015-4_17

1   Introduction

Humans can interact with the environment, objects, or with other humans. Interacting with the environment and objects requires visually adjusting our movements in order to correctly perform the intended action. The interaction with other humans requires the contribution of different components. Humans use verbal communication to express motion and intent to others. However, since verbalizing every step of the interaction would be time-consuming and cognitively expensive, humans use the body as a communication tool. This means that while we are executing our intended action, we are also communicating to others the exact action we are performing. This capacity is referred to as non-verbal communication and involves all the motion degrees of freedom in our bodies: from pointing a finger expressing a direction of interest, to a saccadic eye movement to specify a place that attracted our attention.

The work described in [6] investigates how the non-verbal communication cues of one human allows the others to read his action intentions. The non-verbal communication of the actor was recorded using a motion tracking system for the motion of the body, and a head mounted eye tracker for the gaze behavior of the eyes. The scenario involved one actor, interacting with 3 humans, and performing one of two actions: *placing* of an object on a table, or *giving* the object to one of the humans facing him. These actions were chosen as they fall into two categories of actions defined in micro-sociological studies [3]. The *placing* action is an instance of an *individual action*, while the *giving* action is part of the category *action-in-interaction*, that requires for communications between the interaction partners.

The focus of [6] was on the importance of the different non-verbal communication cues: arm movement, head movement, and eye movement. A human study was performed in which subjects watched short fragments of videos of the actor performing one of two possible actions. These fragments contain different amounts of information concerning the non-verbal cues, and the objective was to analyze the impact of each cue on the capacity to "read" the intentions of the actor. The data collected was used to model the arm behavior for the two types of actions, and to propose a gaze controller that, combined with the arm movement, is able to generate human-like movements, just like those observed in the Human-human interaction (HHI) experiments. This was corroborated by building a robotic controller that, when applied to a humanoid robot to perform the same actions, allows human subjects to understand the robot's intentions from the video fragments, with an accuracy similar to the case of a human actor.

Nevertheless, the work was incomplete as it only studied the behavior of one of the parts of the interaction. So the logical step was to study not only the non-verbal communication of the human performing the action, but also the communication cues emitted by the second participant in the interaction. The focal point of Raković et al. paper [23] was on the eyes' non-verbal communication, and the "gaze dialogue" model derived to couple the agent's gaze behavior. Each agent's behavior was modeled as a Hidden Markov Model (HMM), where the states were the gaze fixations, and the observations the gaze fixations of the other agent. However, the approach discusses the prediction of one agent's action from his gaze fixations in order to adapt the gaze behavior of the second agent for an improved collaboration.

We adopt the terminology of [10] concerning the interaction roles, where one agent can be viewed as the leader and the other one as the follower, in the sense that the follower adapts his/her behavior to the leader, but not the other way around. Hence, in a human-robot interaction (HRI) scenario, a robotic follower will adapt to a human leader. However, when the robot is the leader, the model behaves deterministically and it does not adapt to the behavior of the human follower. In this case, the robot (leader) does not take the speed of the human participant into account, and it is not concerned with the human's understanding of the action. The contribution of the current paper is on tackling this issue.

In [23] the leader's gaze behavior was pre-defined as the average, most likely behavior observed from the HHI scenario. Although this behavior may work on average for most interactions, an HRI is never deterministic since humans are naturally unpredictable and stochastic. As such, a reliable model for the leader's behavior needs to take the feedback of the follower's behavior into account. In this way, it becomes possible to achieve the third level of interaction [10], where both agents, the leader and the follower, adapt to each other in order to achieve a mutual alignment. The focus of this work is on closing the loop of the mutual alignment, by adapting the behavior of the actor performing the action (leader), to the behavior of the actor observing and eventually participating in the interaction (follower).

Section 2 discusses the relevant work done in the quest of understanding non-verbal communication, as well as on human action anticipation, when humans interact with other humans or objects. Section 3 describes the dataset and the HHI scenario used in this work, and the analysis of the data collected from the head mounted gaze tracker. The modeling of the gaze behavior is included in Sect. 4 and the HRI implementation with the results are shown in Sect. 5. The paper ends with a discussion of the results obtained, followed by an overall conclusion and delineating future work challenges.

2   Related Work

HRI requires the human and the robot to understand each other [27]. Modeling the interaction between agents has been tackled in several fields, including robotics, computer vision, and cognitive and behavioral science. Lukic et al. [18] presented the intrapersonal model for manipulating objects based on Gaussian Mixture Models to generate human-like behavior of the hand, arm, and eyes. This was later adapted to human-robot interaction in [6] to yield human-like behavior when involving non-verbal communication. Furthermore, the model was adapted in [23] to describe the non-verbal cues of the eyes of two agents using a cross-agent HMM.

There have been other approaches for modeling the eye gaze behavior over the years [7]. Ivaldi et al. [12] developed a robotic controller that uses the head gaze orientation to understand which object the human is gazing at. One drawback is the use of head orientation as a proxy to estimate the eye gaze. In [5], the eye gaze estimates are used to understand the fixation point of humans. This combines eye tracking data with pointing gestures extracted from RGB-depth cameras, to estimate eye gaze fixation. The limitation with this approach is that all the processing is done off-line, and not during the interaction. Andrist et al. [2] studied the gaze interaction of a human with a virtual agent in a sandwich-making task based on HHI experiments to improve the speed of the collaboration. However, this work only applies to the 'instructor role', that we designate as the leader's perspective, and lacks generality.

Palinko et al. [20] identify the pupil position in the eye in order to estimate the gaze direction. Despite not requiring any additional hardware to track the gaze orientation, they are constrained by the limited resolution of the iCub robot cameras and the accuracy will depend on lighting conditions. As for detecting joint attention, [28] describes work on the extraction of the gaze direction from the head pose of the human. Instead, we intend to extract the visual information collected with the two eye trackers during the HHI experiment scenario, that is publicly available from the Raković et al. [24].

Regarding action anticipation, there has been research on the understanding of human motion [15], modeling the human motion to infer the executed action [29] and predicting human trajectories to trace a path of least collision for the robot, [22]. The prediction algorithm takes into account the human-environment and human-human natural adaptation to calculate the optimal path for the robot. Farhan et al. [8] instead focus on predicting the action happening in the long future, instead of anticipating the ongoing action, using pre-recorded videos trained in large datasets of humans performing several different actions.

Koppula et al. [16] include a rich dataset of human poses and objects to classify the action. However, it does not take advantage of the gaze behavior of humans to predict the action sooner and with higher accuracy. There are several papers presenting the use of human body coordinates, and only very few have gaze information, often limited to a couple of example scenarios [1,9,11].

Schydlo et al. [26] developed a learning based action anticipation model using motion and gaze fixation data of the human-human interaction experiment from the publicly available dataset of [6]. The model can quite accurately perform an early anticipation of the ongoing action, using a combination of the body and gaze coordinates. This action anticipation model uses a recurrent neural network to learn the non-verbal cues that the body and gaze behavior provide in order to distinguish between two actions: a *giving* or *placing* action. Although it can accurately predict the action at an early stage, the information given to the network can not be generalized to different HHI or HRI scenarios. Additionally, it does not provide the robot with any information on how to behave after the action is predicted, thus breaking any possibility of mutual understanding and alignment. Moreover, the results in [26] were deterministic, meaning it would give the same output when given the same data. Instead, the human behavior is stochastic and mutual alignment requires the robot to adapt to a specific participant and not to an average behavior of a group of humans. In this paper, we discuss the importance of the two agents aligning with each other, and an approach where the agents exchange information from each other in order to predict the other's action, and adapt his/her own behavior.

3   Dyad Interaction Experiment

The dyad interaction experiment is composed of two actors participating in a joint task (Fig. 1). The two actors have to perform a turn-taking task of *placing* an object on the table, or *giving* the object to the other person. From this experiment we collect the gaze fixations of 6 participants, i.e. 3 dyads. We get a total of 72 actions seen from two perspectives. Out of 72 actions, 36 actions were *giving* and 36 were *placing*. The gaze fixations are tracked using the Pupil Labs eye tracker [13]. These sensors are connected through an LSL Network [17] which synchronizes and collects the data together with cameras recording the interaction - the egocentric view camera gives the subject's perspective. The gaze behavior of all 144 actions are labeled with identified relevant fixations and events throughout the action. The fixations are object (i.e. brick), team-mates' face (TM face), team-mates' hand (TM hand), own hand, team-mates' tower (TM tower), and own tower; and the events are object picked, object handed over, and object placed. Object handed over exists only in the *giving* action. In [24] it can be found a detail description of the experimental set-up and the data acquisition procedure. The focus of this paper is two-fold: (i) the gaze behavior of the leader during the *giving* action, more specifically on how he/she behaves before and after the handover, and (ii) follower's gaze fixation behavior when the action is *giving* or *placing*.

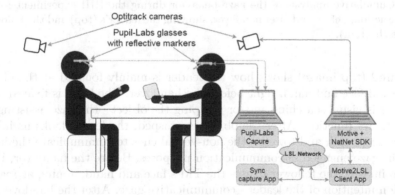

Fig. 1. Representation of the HHI experimental set-up and all the different communication systems. The image is taken from [24].

Figure 2 shows the time spent on each of these gaze fixation states, throughout the whole action, and for the two perspectives. In addition to the total amount of time spent on each state, we distinguish the gaze behavior before and after the handover. For these experiments, the handover time is defined as the moment when the leader's hand releases the object, and it is identified by the change in the fingers acceleration with respect to the brick.

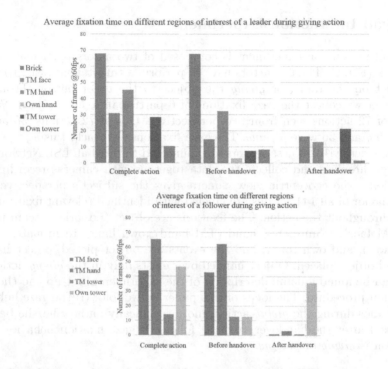

Fig. 2. Cumulative analysis of the gaze behavior during the HHI experiment for the complete action, before and after handover, showing the leader's (top) and the follower's fixations (bottom).

Figure 2 (top image) shows how the leader is mainly focused at the object, and the TM face and hand, right before the handover. The brick is fixated when the leader is visual searching and/or grasping the object - the gaze assisting the motor control function. After the object is grasped, the leader looks mainly at the TM face, hand, and towers - the non-verbal cues to communicate the intention - the gaze engaged in communication purposes. Before the handover, Fig. 2 (bottom image), the follower fixates the TM's face and hand, aiming at reading the action intention of the leader - communicative gaze. After the handover, the non-verbal cues serve purely functional goals. As the object is already in the follower's possession, the remainder of the action requires the follower to fixate his own tower and controlling the arm towards the goal - the functional role of gaze to assist the motor control.

In the next section, the information from the HHI dataset is used to model the leader's behavior. The leader's gaze data will be used to model the stochastic behavior of the human that is different before and after the handover. The follower's gaze behavior will be used to retrieve his/her own understanding of the action, which is then provided to the leader to assess the follower's engagement in the interaction.

4   Modeling of the Leader's Behavior

Figure 3 shows the block diagram for modeling the gaze behavior and aligned motion planning of agents P_1 and P_2. The state of each agent is defined as the gaze fixation S_k and type of action A_k. The fixations $[S_1(k), S_1(k-1), ...]$ are emitted by agent P_1, which are from the perspective of agent P_2, represented as observations $[O_1(k), O_1(k-1), ...]$. Simultaneously, fixations $[S_2(k), S_2(k-1), ...]$ are emitted by agent P_2, and represented as observations $[O_2(k), O_2(k-1), ...]$ of agent P_1.

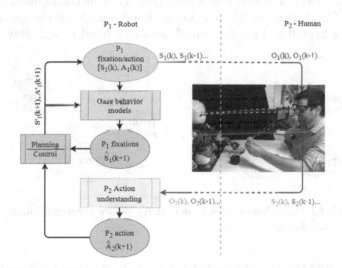

Fig. 3. Block diagram of the proposed leader's gaze behavior and alignment model. Agent P_1 emits fixations S_1 which corresponds to a particular action A_1. From the 'Gaze behavior models' it is generated the next fixation, $\hat{S}_1(k+1)$, from the previous knowledge, $S_1(k)$ and $A_1(k)$. The $\hat{S}_1(k+1)$ is the next fixation without the influence of agent P_2 in the interaction, i.e. without mutual alignment. Agent P_1 observation, $O_2(k)$, is used to calculate the understanding of agent P_2, $\hat{A}_2(k+1)$. This is then fed to the 'Planning/Control' block, together with the next fixation $\hat{S}_1(k+1)$, to estimate the new fixation and action of agent P_1, $S_1'(k+1)$ and $A_1'(k+1)$, respectively. (Color figure online)

The central parts on Fig. 3 correspond to the gaze behavior models (blue block) and human action understanding (yellow block) and will be detailed in Sects. 4.1 and 4.2, respectively. The 'Gaze behavior models' encode the leader's gaze stochastic behavior, that depends on the type of action (in this paper the focus is on modeling the *giving* action, i.e. action-in-interaction) and can change over time after a significant event (i.e. object handover). Action understanding uses the gaze fixation of the human to estimate the probabilities of *giving* versus *placing* action. This is fed back to the 'Planning/Control' block for the motion planning of the agent and selection of appropriate gaze behavior model.

4.1 Gaze Behavior of the Leader

The leader's gaze behavior is modeled with Discrete-Time Markov Chains (DTMC) [4]. A DTMC represents the evolution of a system that stochastically switches from one state to another, at discrete time instances. The model has an associated internal state variable: $S_k \in \{U_1, ..., U_N\}$ where $U_1, ..., U_N$ denotes admissible state values, i.e. fixations, and $k \in \{1, ..., T\}$ denotes the discrete time instants. In the case of a *giving* action, the leader has six admissible states before the handover, and four states after (Fig. 4). This corresponds to the top image from Fig. 2 with six fixations before handover. After the handover, the brick is never fixated and the fixation of one's own hand is negligibly small.

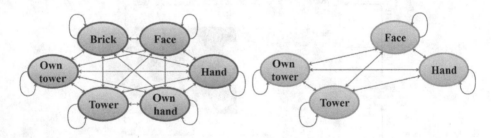

Fig. 4. DTMC for the behavior of a leader: (left) before the brick handover; (right) after the brick handover.

The two DTMCs (for the period before and after the handover) are represented by transition matrices learned from the HHI data, which has labeled fixations of the dyad throughout all the actions. Transitions of the fixations for *giving* before and after handover are counted, and the obtained transition matrices are given in Table 1.

The admissible states that correspond to the indexes of the rows and columns of the transition matrices are: 1 - Brick, 2 - TM Face, 3 - TM Hand, 4 - Own hand, 5 - TM tower and 6 - Own tower, before handover; and 1 - TM Face, 2 - TM Hand, 3 - TM tower and 4 - Own tower, after handover. To illustrate the output behavior that can be obtained with the DTMCs, we generated the fixation sequence of 400 samples (Fig. 5), the first 200 samples using the DTMC before handover and 200 samples using the DTMC after handover. Figure 5 show that the fixations before handover are the brick, follower's face, and hand. After the handover, the fixations are the follower's face, hand, and tower, with very

Table 1. Transition matrix before handover A^L_{bhon} and after handover A^L_{ahon} for the *giving* action

Handover	Leader		
Before	$A^L_{bhon} =$	$\begin{bmatrix} 0.9861 & 0.0016 & 0.0045 & 0.0016 & 0.0041 & 0.0020 \\ 0.0038 & 0.9505 & 0.0438 & 0.0019 & 0 & 0 \\ 0.0018 & 0.0211 & 0.9718 & 8.81e^{-04} & 0.0044 & 0 \\ 0 & 0 & 0.0571 & 0.933 & 0.0095 & 0 \\ 0.0072 & 0.0145 & 0.0435 & 0.0036 & 0.9239 & 0.0072 \\ 0.0566 & 0.0031 & 0.0031 & 0.0126 & 0 & 0.9245 \end{bmatrix}$	
After	$A^L_{ahon} =$	$\begin{bmatrix} 0.9623 & 0.0205 & 0.0154 & 0.0017 \\ 0.0309 & 0.9423 & 0.0247 & 0.0021 \\ 0.0196 & 0.0039 & 0.9712 & 0.0052 \\ 0.0179 & 0.0179 & 0 & 0.9643 \end{bmatrix}$	

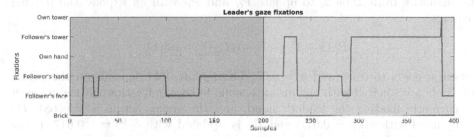

Fig. 5. Leader's fixations when is applied the DTMC before handover (blue section) and DTMC after handover (green section). (Color figure online)

short fixation of the own tower. The leader's fixation are given in the top image of Fig. 2.

4.2   Human Action Understanding

Referring to Fig. 3, the robot (agent P_1) has access to the fixations of the human (agent P_2) which are represented as observations $O_2(k) \in \{V_1, ..., V_M\}$. The admissible fixations of the human are denoted by $V_1, ..., V_M$. The type of action is inferred from the HHI data of the follower's gaze fixations, by calculating the (average) empirical probabilities for *giving* versus *placing* conditioned to the follower's fixation, see Table 2.

When the follower looks at the leader's face, the probabilities for *giving* and *placing* are respectively 49.5% and 50.5%, meaning that it is not a strong cue for the action. Instead, when the follower looks at the leader's hand or at his own tower, it signals that the follower understood that the leader intends to give him the brick. Finally, if the follower fixates the leader's tower, this is a strong signal that the follower understood that the leader will perform a *placing* action.

Table 2. Average probabilities for the *giving* and *placing* actions, with respect to the follower's gaze fixations

	Giving	Placing
Leader's face	0.495	0.505
Leader's hand	0.617	0.383
Leader's tower	0.294	0.706
Own tower	0.844	0.156

To select which action is being performed, we estimate the an action probability by combining the information related to the instantaneous follower's fixations, with the past history of that probability. These probability signals are denoted as P_G and P_P, respectively for the *giving* and *placing* actions.

Based on the current instantaneous follower's fixation, we use the action probabilities from Table 2, to update P_G and P_P with an exponential moving average:

$$P_G(k+1) = (1-\alpha)P_G(k) + \alpha\delta(k)$$

where k refers to time, and $\alpha = 0.05$. The update $\delta(k)$ depends on the values of Table 2, evaluated with the instantaneous follower's fixations. If the follower is currently fixating the leader's hand, and the *giving* action is selected, P_G is updated with $\delta(k) = 0.617$, and P_P is updated with $\delta(k) = -0.617$. If the *placing* action is selected, P_G is updated with $\delta(k) = -0.383$, and P_P is updated with $\delta(k) = 0.383$. This mechanism ensures a smooth evolution of the action probabilities and filters out spurious noisy measurements.

An example of human fixation, and the output of action understanding block are given in Figs. 7 and 9. In Fig. 7, the human is engaged in the action and the probability of *giving* is always higher than the probability for *placing*. However, in the second example, during a certain period of time, the human fixates the leader's tower, communicating that he is understanding that the agent will perform a *placing* action. In this period, the probability for *placing* grows, until the human switches the fixations to the agent's hand or its own tower. The second example will illustrate on-line alignment of the leader's action planning from the follower's gaze cues.

5   Human Robot Interaction Experiment

We used the iCub robotic platform [19] for our experiments. As a humanoid robot, the iCub has a body structure that is similar to the human body, so that humans can more easily understand the robot's motor behavior and, hence, its intentions [6,14]. The eyes of the robot are 2 cameras capable of vergence and version movements, as in the human oculomotor system.

We used the same HRI experiment scheme as in [23], with the objective to track the gaze fixations of the human as a follower, while (s)he interacts with the robot. The gaze fixations are tracked with the Pupil Labs tracker, see Sect. 3.

A Cartesian-based gaze controller [25] was used to control the robot's eyes when fixating 3D coordinate points. The motor control of the torso, arm, hand, and fingers was done with a minimum jerk Cartesian controller [21], which is responsible for guiding the movement of the robot to grasp the object, as well as to move the object to the handover location, and return to the resting position.

Figure 6 shows a robot performing a *giving* action. The HRI experiment starts with the human not attending to the robot, and looking at his notebook. During that time, the robot is continuing the non-verbal communication described in Sect. 4. This is an attempt of reaching action alignment with the human through the robot's gaze behavior. Since the robot does get any information from the human, i.e. no important cue provided by the eye tracker, the robot assumes the human did not yet understand the interaction intention, and will not complete the *giving* action. After the robot manages to catch the attention of the human, i.e. the human is looking at important cues of the interaction - states S_2 of the gaze behavior - the robot realizes the human understood the interaction intent, and proceeds to complete the handover action, see Fig. 7.

Fig. 6. The first experiment of a robot interacting with a human initially disengaged from the interaction. The green hallow circle in the top row images is the human gaze fixation. The red dots mark the important interaction cues (robot's face, robot's hand, robot's tower, own tower). When the green circle is in the region of interest of the red dot, then it is classified as the human looking at that cue. (Color figure online)

In the second experiment, we test the alignment of the robot, when the human misunderstands the action. Figure 8 shows the human initially looking at the robot's face and hand. This implies that the human understands the on-going action, as it is seen from the action prediction outcome in Fig. 9.

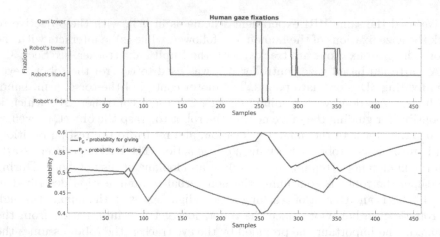

Fig. 7. Top: Human gaze fixations during the first HRI experiment. Bottom: The prediction of the understood action, i.e. the robot's understanding of the human behavior based on his gaze cues.

Fig. 8. The second experiment of a robot interacting with a human that misunderstands the robot's action. The interaction starts with an engaged human with the correct action, then the human misunderstands the robot's action, i.e. the action alignment, and hence, mutual alignment is broken. Only after looking at the robot, the human finally understands the actual robot action.

The human then switches to fixate the robot's tower, see human gaze fixations in the top plot of Fig. 9 (samples [190–310]). This changes the prediction of the robot, concerning what the human understands, to a *placing* action. This results in the robot retracting the arm, signaling that there is no action alignment, and that the interaction needs to adapt. The human then looks again at the robot's face and hand, giving the robot the correct prediction of the action. The robot resumes the interaction and finally hands over the object. Supplementary video material is included for both interaction scenarios.

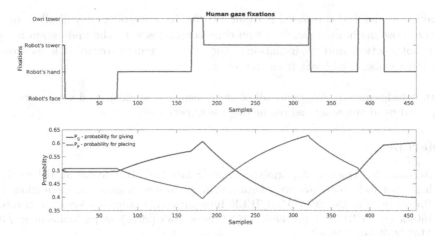

Fig. 9. Top: Human gaze fixations for the second HRI experiment. Bottom: Robot predictions of the human actions, updated over time. The robot adapts the arm movement in response to the human gaze behavior (Fig. 8).

6   Conclusion and Future Work

This work describes a model of the stochastic gaze behavior of a leader, in a leader-follower social interaction. The gaze fixations are used as an instrument for non-verbal communication, to achieve transparency of the intended actions of an artificial agent. Simultaneously, the agent also reads the human partner's gaze cues to understand the action (s)he performs. Based on this feedback, an agent can plan its motion to align its behavior to the current conditions of the social interaction. The proposed models for gaze behavior and action understanding, were integrated in the iCub's robot controller and validated in a HRI scenario with a human in the loop.

The iCub's gaze behavior was modeled with two discrete-time Markov chains, to drive the gaze before and after handover. The outcome of the models correlates to the analysis obtained from the HHI experiment data.

Inferring the level of understanding of the action by a human is also based on the HHI experiment data. From these data, an instantaneous probability of the two types of action (*giving* and *placing*) is built. These instantaneous probabilities integrated over time, are used to decide if the human understands the robot's action. Our experiments illustrate how the understanding of the action changes from the correct to the wrong action, and back again to the correct one. When the inferred action is misunderstood, it signals the robot to stop moving the arm toward the handover location, and to go back to the resting position. During that period, the gaze behavior continued to emit cues to communicate the intention of the interaction.

Future work will involve more thorough evaluation of the impact of the gaze behavior controller and motion planning alignment in the quality of HRI. We aim to enroll a group of naive subjects in a HRI with the iCub running the gaze behavior model and compared it to an alternative controller. It will allow us to analyze how the human gaze reaction time correlates with the understanding of the robot's action, and the initiation of the arm movement towards the handover location to take the object from the robot.

Acknowledgements. We thank all of our colleagues, students and volunteers that supported us in preparing and conducting the experiments.

References

1. Admoni, H., Dragan, A., Srinivasa, S.S., Scassellati, B.: Deliberate delays during robot-to-human handovers improve compliance with gaze communication. In: Proceedings of the 2014 ACM/IEEE International Conference on Human-robot Interaction, HRI 2014, pp. 49–56. ACM, New York (2014). http://doi.acm.org/10.1145/2559636.2559682
2. Andrist, S., Gleicher, M., Mutlu, B.: Looking coordinated: Bidirectional gaze mechanisms for collaborative interaction with virtual characters. In: Proceedings of the 2017 CHI Conference on Human Factors in Computing Systems, CHI 2017, pp. 2571–2582. ACM, New York (2017). http://doi.acm.org/10.1145/3025453.3026033
3. Bassetti, C.: Chapter 2 - social interaction in temporary gatherings: A sociological taxonomy of groups and crowds for computer vision practitioners. In: Murino, V., Cristani, M., Shah, S., Savarese, S. (eds.) Group and Crowd Behavior for Computer Vision, pp. 15–28. Academic Press (2017). https://doi.org/10.1016/B978-0-12-809276-7.00003-5, http://www.sciencedirect.com/science/article/pii/B9780128092767000035
4. Biagini, F., Campanino, M.: Discrete time Markov chains. In: Elements of Probability and Statistics, pp. 81–87. Springer, Cham (2016). https://doi.org/10.1007/978-3-319-07254-8_6
5. Domhof, J., Chandarr, A., Rudinac, M., Jonker, P.: Multimodal joint visual attention model for natural human-robot interaction in domestic environments. In: 2015 IEEE/RSJ International Conference on Intelligent Robots and Systems (IROS), pp. 2406–2412, September 2015. https://doi.org/10.1109/IROS.2015.7353703
6. Duarte, N.F., Rakovic, M., Tasevski, J., Coco, M.I., Billard, A., Santos-Victor, J.: Action anticipation: reading the intentions of humans and robots. IEEE Robot. Autom. Lett. **3**(4), 4132–4139 (2018). https://doi.org/10.1109/LRA.2018.2861569
7. Duchowski, A.T.: Gaze-based interaction: A 30 year retrospective, vol. 73, pp. 59–69 (2018). https://doi.org/10.1016/j.cag.2018.04.002, http://www.sciencedirect.com/science/article/pii/S0097849318300487
8. Farha, Y.A., Richard, A., Gall, J.: When will you do what? - anticipating temporal occurrences of activities. arXiv preprint arXiv:1804.00892 (2018)
9. Fathi, A., Ren, X., Rehg, J.M.: Learning to recognize objects in egocentric activities. In: Proceedings of the 2011 IEEE Conference on Computer Vision and Pattern Recognition, CVPR 2011, pp. 3281–3288. IEEE Computer Society, Washington, DC (2011). https://doi.org/10.1109/CVPR.2011.5995444, http://dx.doi.org/10.1109/CVPR.2011.5995444
10. Gallotti, M., Fairhurst, M., Frith, C.: Alignment in social interactions. Conscious. Cogn. **48**, 253–261 (2017)
11. Gottwald, J.M., Elsner, B., Pollatos, O.: Good is upspatial metaphors in action observation. Front. Psychol. **6**, 1605 (2015). https://doi.org/10.3389/fpsyg.2015.01605. https://www.frontiersin.org/article/10.3389/fpsyg.2015.01605

12. Ivaldi, S., Anzalone, S., Rousseau, W., Sigaud, O., Chetouani, M.: Robot initiative in a team learning task increases the rhythm of interaction but not the perceived engagement. Front. Neurorobotics **8**, 5 (2014)

13. Kassner, M., Patera, W., Bulling, A.: Pupil: an open source platform for pervasive eye tracking and mobile gaze-based interaction. In: Proceedings of the 2014 ACM International Joint Conference on Pervasive and Ubiquitous Computing: Adjunct Publication, pp. 1151–1160. ACM (2014)

14. Kelley, R., Tavakkoli, A., King, C., Nicolescu, M., Nicolescu, M.: Understanding activities and intentions for human-robot interaction (2010). https://doi.org/10.5772/8127

15. Kitani, K.M., Ziebart, B.D., Bagnell, J.A., Hebert, M.: Activity forecasting. In: Fitzgibbon, A., Lazebnik, S., Perona, P., Sato, Y., Schmid, C. (eds.) ECCV 2012. LNCS, vol. 7575, pp. 201–214. Springer, Heidelberg (2012). https://doi.org/10.1007/978-3-642-33765-9_15

16. Koppula, H.S., Saxena, A.: Anticipating human activities using object affordances for reactive robotic response. IEEE Trans. Pattern Anal. Mach. Intell. **38**(1), 14–29 (2016). https://doi.org/10.1109/TPAMI.2015.2430335

17. Kothe, C.: Lab streaming layer (LSL) (2018). https://github.com/sccn/labstreaminglayer. Accessed 26 Feb 2015

18. Lukic, L., Santos-Victor, J., Billard, A.: Learning robotic eye-arm-hand coordination from human demonstration: a coupled dynamical systems approach. Biol. Cybern. **108**(2), 223–248 (2014)

19. Metta, G., et al.: The iCub humanoid robot: an open-systems platform for research in cognitive development. Neural Networks **23**(8–9), 1125–1134 (2010)

20. Palinko, O., Rea, F., Sandini, G., Sciutti, A.: Eye gaze tracking for a humanoid robot. In: 2015 IEEE-RAS 15th International Conference on Humanoid Robots (Humanoids), pp. 318–324, November 2015. https://doi.org/10.1109/HUMANOIDS.2015.7363561

21. Pattacini, U., Nori, F., Natale, L., Metta, G., Sandini, G.: An experimental evaluation of a novel minimum-jerk cartesian controller for humanoid robots. In: 2010 IEEE/RSJ International Conference on Intelligent Robots and Systems (IROS), pp. 1668–1674. IEEE (2010)

22. Pfeiffer, M., Schwesinger, U., Sommer, H., Galceran, E., Siegwart, R.: Predicting actions to act predictably: Cooperative partial motion planning with maximum entropy models. In: 2016 IEEE/RSJ International Conference on Intelligent Robots and Systems (IROS), pp. 2096–2101, October 2016. https://doi.org/10.1109/IROS.2016.7759329

23. Rakovic, M., Duarte, N.F., Marques, J., Santos-Victor, J.: Modelling the gaze dialogue: non-verbal communication in human-human and human-robot interaction. Paper Under Revis. **1**(1), 1–12 (2018)

24. Raković, M., Duarte, N., Tasevski, J., Santos-Victor, J., Borovac, B.: A dataset of head and eye gaze during dyadic interaction task for modeling robot gaze behavior. In: MATEC Web of Conferences, vol. 161, p. 03002. EDP Sciences (2018)

25. Roncone, A., Pattacini, U., Metta, G., Natale, L.: A cartesian 6-dof gaze controller for humanoid robots. In: Robotics: Science and Systems (2016)

26. Schydlo, P., Rakovic, M., Jamone, L., Santos-Victor, J.: Anticipation in human-robot cooperation: a recurrent neural network approach for multiple action sequences prediction. In: IEEE International Conference on Robotics and Automation, ICRA 2018 (2018)

27. Sciutti, A., Mara, M., Tagliasco, V., Sandini, G.: Humanizing human-robot interaction: on the importance of mutual understanding. IEEE Technol. Soc. Mag. **37**(1), 22–29 (2018). https://doi.org/10.1109/MTS.2018.2795095
28. Ycel, Z., Salah, A.A., Meriçli, Ç., Meriçli, T., Valenti, R., Gevers, T.: Joint attention by gaze interpolation and saliency. IEEE Trans. Cybern. **43**(3), 829–842 (2013). https://doi.org/10.1109/TSMCB.2012.2216979
29. Zhang, J., Li, W., Ogunbona, P.O., Wang, P., Tang, C.: Rgb-d-based action recognition datasets: a survey. Pattern Recognit. **60**, 86–105 (2016). https://doi.org/10.1016/j.patcog.2016.05.019. http://www.sciencedirect.com/science/article/pii/S0031320316301029

Group LSTM: Group Trajectory Prediction in Crowded Scenarios

Niccoló Bisagno[1]([✉]), Bo Zhang[2], and Nicola Conci[1]

[1] University of Trento, Trento, Italy
{niccolo.bisagno,nicola.conci}@unitn.it
[2] Dalian Maritime University, Dalian, China
bzhang@dlmu.edu.cn

Abstract. The analysis of crowded scenes is one of the most challenging scenarios in visual surveillance, and a variety of factors need to be taken into account, such as the structure of the environments, and the presence of mutual occlusions and obstacles. Traditional prediction methods (such as RNN, LSTM, VAE, etc.) focus on anticipating individual's future path based on the precise motion history of a pedestrian. However, since tracking algorithms are generally not reliable in highly dense scenes, these methods are not easily applicable in real environments. Nevertheless, it is very common that people (friends, couples, family members, etc.) tend to exhibit coherent motion patterns. Motivated by this phenomenon, we propose a novel approach to predict future trajectories in crowded scenes, at the group level. First, by exploiting the motion coherency, we cluster trajectories that have similar motion trends. In this way, pedestrians within the same group can be well segmented. Then, an improved social-LSTM is adopted for future path prediction. We evaluate our approach on standard crowd benchmarks (the UCY dataset and the ETH dataset), demonstrating its efficacy and applicability.

Keywords: Group prediction · Crowd analysis ·
Trajectory clustering · Social-LSTM

1 Introduction

Crowd analysis is a hot topic in computer vision, covering a wide range of applications in visual surveillance. The main challenges in crowd analysis include: crowd dynamics modeling [5,43]; crowd segmentation [4]; crowd activity classification [33]; abnormal behavior detection [16,25]; density estimation [30]; and crowd behavior anticipation [2].

Among them, crowd behavior anticipation is an emerging task, which has drawn a fair amount of attentions, due to the rapid development in machine learning, and particularly the deep learning techniques applied to time series analysis (such as RNN [34], GRU [9], LSTM [18], and VAE [22]).

Different from crowd behavior recognition, the prediction task has its distinguished characteristics, which is generally addressed by observing the motion

© Springer Nature Switzerland AG 2019
L. Leal-Taixé and S. Roth (Eds.): ECCV 2018 Workshops, LNCS 11131, pp. 213–225, 2019.
https://doi.org/10.1007/978-3-030-11015-4_18

histories of the subjects moving in the scene. In some specific applications (i.e., early warning, abnormal event detection, collision avoidance), prediction plays a more relevant role comparing to activity recognition, as dangerous behaviors should be warned in advance. Traditional methods can merely make one-step forecasting (e.g., Kalman filter, particle filter, Markov chains); thanks to deep learning, long term prediction is becoming applicable gradually.

At the beginning, researchers merely focused on anticipating individual's future path. The corresponding models highly rely on the precise motion history of a pedestrian, thus being generally intractable in very dense environments, due to the instability of object tracking algorithms in presence of frequent mutual occlusions.

However, continuous and precise frame-based tracking might not be essential. In fact, in most cases, people pay more attention on the whole dynamics of the scene. People gathering and behaving together will generate and exhibit macro-scopic salient features, which are instead worth being observed. Such coarse-level information usually maps densely and sparsely populated areas, including direction and flow characteristics, as well as the final destinations. Therefore, in such scenarios, it makes more sense to focus on group activities instead of individuals. It is well known that people moving in the crowds usually tend to follow a series of implicit social rules [28]. For instance, individuals tend to speed up or slow down their paces in order to avoid collisions when a vehicle or another group of people is approaching; people prefer to preserve personal space, thus keeping a certain distance from their neighbors; pedestrians tend to follow people in their front especially in presence of crowded situations, to prevent collisions.

Focusing on grouping, it is very common that friends/couples/families tend to move in accordance with a coherent motion pattern. Based on this assumption, we propose a novel approach to predict future trajectories at the group level, in order to further analyze crowded scenes from a holistic point of view. Firstly, by exploiting the motion coherency, we cluster trajectories that have similar motion trends. In this way, pedestrians within the same group can be highlighted and segmented. Finally, an improved social-LSTM is proposed to estimate the future path prediction.

The main contributions of this work are summarized as follows:

- we propose a novel framework for group behavior prediction;
- we exploit an improved coherent filtering to enhance the trajectory clustering performance;
- we propose a strategy for long term prediction of pedestrians, which leverages on group dynamics.

The rest of the paper is organized as follows: Sect. 2 briefly reviews the related work in the field of crowd analysis. The proposed framework, called Group LSTM for conciseness, is described in Sect. 3, including the steps of trajectory clustering and group path prediction. The experimental results are provided in Sect. 4. Conclusions and future work are summarized in Sect. 5.

2   Related Work

A detailed literature on the recent works in crowd analysis, especially regarding the topics of crowd dynamic modeling, social activity forecasting, and group segmentation, can be found in some recent surveys [13,20,24]. In the next paragraphs, we will concentrate on two specific sub-topics, namely, group analysis and forecasting.

2.1   Group Analysis in Crowds

In the early approaches, trajectories were adopted to represent low level motion features in the crowd. By clustering trajectories with similar motion trends, pedestrians can be gathered into different groups. In [42], the traditional k-means algorithm was exploited to learn different motion modalities in the scene. In [21], support vector clustering was exploited to group pedestrians. In [44], coherent filtering was presented to detect coherent motion patterns in a crowded environment [40].

As far as the representation of collective activities is concerned, Ge et al. [12] worked on the automatic detection of small individual groups who are traveling together. Ryoo et al. [31] introduced a probabilistic representation of group activities, for the purpose of recognizing different types of high-level group behaviors. Yi et al. [41] investigated the interactions between stationary crowd groups and pedestrians to analyze pedestrian's behaviors, including walking path prediction, destination prediction, personality classification, and abnormal event detection. Shao et al. [32] proposed a series of scene-independent descriptors to quantitatively describe group properties, such as collectiveness, stability, uniformity, and conflict. Bagautdinov et al. [7] presented a unified end-to-end framework for multi-person action localization and collective activity recognition using deep recurrent networks.

2.2   Social Activity Forecasting

Forecasting social activities has lately gained a relevant amount of attentions, especially as far as crowd analysis is concerned. This research domain is rather diversified and it involves trajectory prediction, interaction modeling, and contextual modeling. Among the pioneering research in social activity analysis, Helbing et al. [17] introduced the well known Social Force Model (SFM), which is able to describe social interactions between humans [23,27]. Other models, such as the continuum crowds model [36] and the Reciprocal Collision Avoidance [37], are capable to reproduce human interactions using priors. In [3], the Social Affinity Maps (SAM) features and the Origin and Destination (OD) priors were proposed to forecast pedestrians' destinations using multi-view surveillance cameras. Robicquet et al. [29] introduced a large scale dataset that contains various types of targets (pedestrians, bikers, skateboarders, cars, buses, and golf carts) using aerial cameras, in order to evaluate trajectory forecasting performance in real outdoor environments. In [1,26], contextual information is taken into account as well, to model the static configuration and the dynamic evolution of the scene.

More recently, neural networks have been employed to predict events in crowded videos. In particular, with the emerging of deep generative models (such as RNN, LSTM, VAE), the sequence-to-sequence generation problem can be solved properly, making it possible to handle the long-term prediction task directly. Alahi et al. [2] proposed the so-called social-LSTM to model the interactions among people in a neighborhood by adding a new social pooling layer; In [22], Lee et al. presented a deep stochastic IOC RNN encoder-decoder framework to predict the future paths of multiple interacting agents in dynamic scenes. Ballan et al. [8] considered both the dynamics of moving agents and the scene semantics to predict scene-specific motion patterns.

Social activities are often ruled not only by the motion dynamics, but are also driven by human factors. Jain et al. [19] adopted a structural RNN that combines spatio-temporal graphs and recurrent neural networks to model motion and interactions in the scene. Fernando et al. [38] applied both the soft attention and the hard-wired attention on the social LSTM, and significantly promote the trajectory prediction performance. Varshneya et al. [6] presented a soft attention mechanism to forecast individual's path, which exploits the spatially aware deep attention model. Vemula et al. [39] proposed a novel social attention model that can capture the relative importance of each person when navigating in the scene.

3   Group LSTM

The motion of pedestrians in crowded scenes is highly influenced by the behavior of other people in the surroundings and their mutual relationships. Stationary groups, groups of pedestrians walking together, people coming from opposite directions, will exert different effects on the action that one pedestrian takes. Thus, it becomes necessary to take people in the neighborhood into account when forecasting the behavior of an individual in the crowd.

To achieve this goal, we propose a framework, which is able to consider whether the subject of interest is walking coherently with the pedestrians in his surroundings or not. By exploiting the coherent filtering approach [44], we first detect people moving coherently in a crowd, and then adopt the Social LSTM to predict future trajectories. In this way, we are able to improve the prediction performance, accounting for the interactions between socially related and unrelated pedestrians in the scene.

3.1   Pedestrian Trajectory Clustering

Coherent motion describes the collective movements of particles in a crowd. The coherent filtering studies a prior meant to describe the coherent neighbor invariance, which is the local spatio-temporal relation between particles moving coherently. The algorithm is based on two steps. First, it detects the coherent motion of pedestrians in the scene. Then, points moving coherently are associated to the same cluster. Point clusters will continue to evolve, and new clusters will emerge over time. Finally, each pedestrian i is assigned to a cluster s_i. The outputs of the coherent filtering are consist of the sets s_i $(i = 1, 2, \cdots, n)$ of people moving in a coherent manner. If a pedestrian is not moving or it does not belong to any coherent group, it is considered as belonging to its own set.

The coherent filtering originally relies on the KLT tracker [35], aiming at detecting candidate points for tracking and generating trajectories, which will then be used as the input of the algorithm. The KLT tracker may detect many key points for each pedestrian, thus there is no clear correspondence between the number of key points and the number of pedestrians. Our objective is to cluster pedestrians into groups, where each individual in a group is represented using a single point, as shown in Fig. 1. For this purpose, and without loss of generality, we apply the coherent filtering algorithm directly on the ground truth of pedestrian trajectories.

Fig. 1. Each pedestrian is represented by a single keypoint. Pedestrians walking in the same direction are clustered into one group s_i. In this example, two sets of pedestrians going in opposite directions are identified.

3.2   Group Trajectory Prediction

We extend the work of Alahi et al. [2], which models the relationships of pedestrians in the neighborhood by introducing a so-called social pooling layer. In the Social LSTM model, the pedestrian is modeled using an LSTM network as displayed in Fig. 2. Furthermore, each pedestrian is associated with other people in his neighborhood via a social pooling layer. The social pooling layer allows pedestrians to share their hidden states, thus enabling each network to predict the future positions of an individual based on his own hidden state and the hidden states in the neighborhood.

The ith pedestrian at time instance t in the scene is represented by the hidden state h_t^i in an LSTM network. We set the hidden-state dimension to D and the neighborhood size to N_0, respectively. The neighborhood of the ith agent ped^i is described using a tensor H_t^i as in Eq. 1, with dimensions of $N_0 \times N_0 \times D$:

$$H_t^i(m,n,:) = \sum_{j \in N} 1_{mn}[x_t^j - x_t^i, y_t^j - y_t^i] 1_{ij}[s_i \neq s_j] h_{t-1}^j \qquad (1)$$

where $1_{mn}[x,y]$ is an indicator function to select pedestrians in the neighborhood. It is defined as in Eq. 2:

$$1_{mn}[x,y] = \begin{cases} 0 & \text{if } [x,y] \notin \text{cell mn} \\ 1 & \text{if } [x,y] \in \text{cell mn} \end{cases} \qquad (2)$$

If two pedestrians i and j belong to the same coherent set s_i, they will not be taken into account when computing the social pooling layer for each of them. The function $1_{ij}[i \in s_i, j \in s_i]$ is an indicator function defined as in Eq. 3:

$$1_{ij}[s_i \neq s_j] = \begin{cases} 0 & \text{if } i \in s_i, j \in s_i \\ 1 & \text{if } i \in s_i, j \notin s_i \end{cases} \qquad (3)$$

Doing so, the social pooling layer of each pedestrian contains information only about pedestrians, which are not moving coherently with him.

Once computed, the social hidden-state tensor is embedded into a vector a_t^i. The output coordinates are embedded in the vector e_t^i. Following the recurrence defined in [2], we can predict our trajectories gradually.

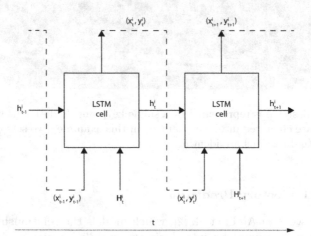

Fig. 2. The figure represents the chain structure of the LSTM network between two consecutive time steps, t and $t+1$. At each time step, the inputs of the LSTM cell are the previous position (x_{t-1}^i, y_{t-1}^i) and the Social pooling tensor H_t^i. The output of the LSTM cell is the current position (x_t^i, y_t^i).

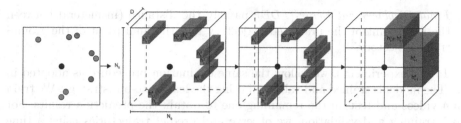

Fig. 3. Representation of the Social hidden-state tensor H_t^i. The black dot represents the pedestrian of interest ped_i. Other pedestrians ped_j ($\forall j \neq i$) are shown in different color codes, namely green for pedestrians belonging to the same set, and red for pedestrians belonging to a different set. The neighborhood of ped_i is described by $N_0 \times N_0$ cells, which preserves the spatial information by pooling spatially adjacent neighbors. Pedestrians belonging to the same set are not used for the final computation of the pooling layer H_t^i.

4   Results

4.1   Implementation Details

In the first place, we need to configure the coherent filtering to cluster pedestrians. To this aim, we use $K = 10$, $d = 1$ and $\lambda = 0.2$ according to the original implementation.

For our LSTM network, we adopt the following configuration. The embedding dimension for the spatial coordinates is set to 64. The spatial pooling size, which corresponds to an area of $4 \times 4\,\mathrm{m}^2$, is set to 32. The pooling operation is performed using a sum pooling window of size 8×8 with no overlaps. The hidden state dimension is 128. The learning rate is set to 0.003, and RMS-prop [11] is used as the optimizer. The model is trained on a single GPU using a PyTorch[1] implementation.

4.2   Quantitative Results

Our experiments are carried out on two publicly available datasets, commonly used as the standard benchmarks for crowded scenarios, namely, the UCY dataset [23] and the ETH dataset [27].

The two datasets present a rather large set of real-world trajectories covering a variety of complex crowd behaviors that are particularly interesting for our research.

In the same way as other works [2,27], we evaluate our results with the following two metrics:

- *Average Displacement Error (ADE)*, namely the average displacement error (in meters) between each point of the predicted path with respect to the ground truth path.

---

[1]   http://pytorch.org.

– *Final Displacement Error (FDE)*, namely the distance (in meters) between the final point of the predicted trajectory and the final point of the ground truth trajectory.

In our experiments, we follow the same evaluation procedure as adopted in [2]. The model is trained and validated using the leave-one-out strategy. We train on 4 videos and test on the remaining one to obtain the prediction results. For both training and validation, we observe and predict trajectories using a time interval of 0.4 s. We observe trajectories for 8 time steps and predict for the next 12 time steps, meaning that we observe trajectories for $t_{obs} = 3.2$ s and predict for the next $t_{pred} = 4.8$ s. In the training phase, only trajectories that remain in the scene for at least 8 s are considered.

We compare our method with the Social LSTM model [2] and its most recent variant [14]. We also compare our model with a linear model, which uses the Kalman filter to predict future trajectories under the assumption of linear acceleration, as also reported in [2]. The numerical results are shown in Table 1.

Our method performs on average better or equal than other methods, especially on the UCY dataset. This is due to the characteristics of crowd flows in the scene, which usually consist of easily identifiable groups walking in opposite directions. However, for the ETH dataset, the motion patterns are more varied and chaotic.

Our results show that the prediction performance can be improved when considering pedestrians that are not moving coherently. We argue that the change

Table 1. Quantitative results using our Group-LSTM and the mentioned baseline approaches on the UCY and ETH datasets, respectively. Two error metrics, namely, the Average Displacement Error (ADE) and the Final Displacement Error (FDE) are reported (in meters) for an observation interval $t_{obs} = 3.2$ s and a prediction of subsequent $t_{pred} = 4.8$ s. Our model outperforms other approaches, especially in terms of average error.

Metric	Dataset	Lin.[2]	Social-LSTM[14]	Social-GAN[14]	Group-LSTM
ADE	ETH [27]	1.33	1.09	0.81	0.28
	HOTEL [27]	0.39	0.86	0.72	0.28
	ZARA1 [23]	0.62	0.41	0.34	0.23
	ZARA2 [23]	0.77	0.52	0.42	0.34
	UCY [23]	0.82	0.61	0.60	0.56
	AVERAGE	0.79	0.70	0.58	0.34
FDE	ETH [27]	2.94	2.41	1.52	1.12
	HOTEL [27]	0.72	1.91	1.61	0.89
	ZARA1 [23]	1.21	1.11	0.84	0.91
	ZARA2 [23]	1.48	1.31	1.26	1.49
	UCY [23]	1.59	0.88	0.69	1.48
	AVERAGE	1.59	1.52	1.18	1.18

of motion and the evolution of trajectories are mainly influenced by pedestrians which move in different directions with respect to the pedestrian of interest. People walking together, instead, loosely influence each other, as they behave as in a group.

4.3   Qualitative Results

In Sect. 4.2 we have shown that considering only pedestrians not moving coherently can improve the prediction precision. In this section we will further evaluate the consistency of the predicted trajectories.

As a general rule, the LSTM-based approaches for trajectory prediction follow a data-driven approach. Furthermore, the future planning of pedestrians in a crowd are highly influenced by their goals, their surroundings, and their past motion histories. Pooling the correct data in the social layer can promote the prediction performance in a significant way.

In order to guarantee a reliable prediction, we not only need to account for spatio-temporal relationships, but also need to preserve the social nature of behaviors. According to the studies in interpersonal distances [10,15], socially correlated people tend to stay closer in their personal space and walk together in crowded environments as compared to pacing with unknown pedestrians. Pooling only unrelated pedestrians will focus more on macroscopic inter-group interactions rather than intra-group dynamics, thus allowing the LSTM network to improve the trajectory prediction performance. Collision avoidance influences the future motion of pedestrians in a similar manner if two pedestrians are walking together as in a group.

In Tables 2, 3 and Fig. 4, we display some demos of predicted trajectories which highlight how our Group-LSTM is able to predict pedestrian trajectories with better precision, showing how the prediction is improved when we pool in the social tensor of each pedestrian only pedestrians not belonging to his group.

In Table 2, we show how the prediction of two pedestrians walking together in the crowd improves when they are not pooled in each other's pooling layer. When the two pedestrians are pooled together, the network applies on them the typical repulsion force to avoid colliding with each other. Since they are in the same group, they allow the other pedestrian to stay closer in they personal space.

Table 2. ETH dataset: the prediction is improved when pooling in the social tensor of each pedestrian only pedestrians not belonging to his group. The green dots represent the ground truth trajectories; the blue crosses represent the predicted paths.

Name	Scene	Our Group-LSTM	Social-LSTM
ETH Univ Frame 2425			

In Fig. 4 we display the sequences of two groups walking toward each other. In Table 3, we show how the prediction for the two groups is improved with respect to the Social LSTM. While both prediction are not very accurate, our Group LSTM perform better because it is able to forecast how pedestrian belonging to the same group will stay together when navigating the environment.

| (a) | (b) | (c) | (d) |

Fig. 4. Sequences taken from the UCY dataset. It displays an interaction example between two groups, which will be further analyzed in Table 3.

Table 3. We display how the prediction is improved for two groups walking in opposite directions. The green dots represent the ground truth trajectories, while the blue crosses represent the predicted paths.

Name	Scene	Our Group-LSTM	Social-LSTM
UCY Univ Frame 1025			

5   Conclusion

In this work, we tackle the problem of pedestrian trajectory prediction in crowded scenes. We propose a novel approach, which combines the coherent filtering algorithm with the LSTM networks. The coherent filtering is used to identify pedestrians walking together in a crowd, while the LSTM network is used to predict the future trajectories by exploiting inter and intra group dynamics. Experimental results show that the proposed Group LSTM outperforms the Social LSTM in the prediction task on two public benchmarks (the UCY and ETH datasets). For the future work, we plan to further investigate social relationships and how fixed obstacles will influence the behaviors of other pedestrians.

Acknowledgement. This work is partly supported by the National Natural Science Foundation of China (Grant No. 61702073), and the Fundamental Research Funds for the Central Universities (Grant No. 3132018190).

References

1. Context-aware trajectory prediction in crowded spaces. In: Proceedings of the
2. Alahi, A., Goel, K., Ramanathan, V., Robicquet, A., Fei-Fei, L., Savarese, S.: Social LSTM: human trajectory prediction in crowded spaces. In: Proceedings of the International Conference on Computer Vision and Pattern Recognition, pp. 961–971. IEEE (2016)
3. Alahi, A., Ramanathan, V., Li, F.F.: Socially-aware large-scale crowd forecasting. In: Proceedings of the International Conference on Computer Vision and Pattern Recognition, pp. 2203–2210. IEEE (2014)
4. Ali, S., Shah, M.: A lagrangian particle dynamics approach for crowd flow segmentation and stability analysis. In: Proceedings of the International Conference on Computer Vision and Pattern Recognition, pp. 1–6. IEEE (2007)
5. Allain, P., Courty, N., Corpetti, T.: Crowd flow characterization with optimal control theory. In: Zha, H., Taniguchi, R., Maybank, S. (eds.) ACCV 2009. LNCS, vol. 5995, pp. 279–290. Springer, Heidelberg (2010). https://doi.org/10.1007/978-3-642-12304-7_27
6. Vemula, A., Muelling, K., Oh, J.: Social attention: modeling attention in human crowds. https://arxiv.org/abs/1710.04689 (2017)
7. Bagautdinov, T., Alahi, A., Fleuret, F., Fua, P., Savarese, S.: Social scene understanding: end-to-end multi-person action localization and collective activity recognition. In: Proceedings of the International Conference on Computer Vision and Pattern Recognition, pp. 3425–3434. IEEE (2016)
8. Ballan, L., Castaldo, F., Alahi, A., Palmieri, F., Savarese, S.: Knowledge transfer for scene-specific motion prediction. In: Leibe, B., Matas, J., Sebe, N., Welling, M. (eds.) ECCV 2016. LNCS, vol. 9905, pp. 697–713. Springer, Cham (2016). https://doi.org/10.1007/978-3-319-46448-0_42
9. Chung, J., Gulcehre, C., Cho, K., Bengio, Y.: Empirical evaluation of gated recurrent neural networks on sequence modeling. arXiv preprint arXiv:1412.3555 (2014)
10. Conci, N., Bisagno, N., Cavallaro, A.: On modeling and analyzing crowds from videos. In: Computer Vision for Assistive Healthcare, pp. 319–336. Elsevier (2018)
11. Dauphin, Y., de Vries, H., Bengio, Y.: Equilibrated adaptive learning rates for non-convex optimization. In: Advances in Neural Information Processing Systems (NIPS), pp. 1504–1512 (2015)
12. Ge, W., Collins, R.T., Ruback, R.B.: Vision-based analysis of small groups in pedestrian crowds. IEEE Trans. Pattern Anal. Mach. Intell. 34(5), 1003–1016 (2012)
13. Grant, J., Flynn, P.: Crowd scene understanding from video: a survey. ACM Trans. Multimedia Comput. Commun. Appl. 13(2), 19 (2017)
14. Gupta, A., Savarese, S., Alahi, A., et al.: Social gan: Socially acceptable trajectories with generative adversarial networks. In: IEEE Conference on Computer Vision and Pattern Recognition (CVPR), No. CONF (2018)
15. Hall, E.T., et al.: Proxemics [and comments and replies]. Curr. Anthropol. 9(2/3), 83–108 (1968)
16. Hassner, T., Itcher, Y., Kliper-Gross, O.: Violent flows: Real-time detection of violent crowd behavior. In: Proceedings of the International Conference on Computer Vision and Pattern Recognition Workshops, pp. 1–6. IEEE (2012)
17. Helbing, D., Molnar, P.: Social force model for pedestrian dynamics. Phys. Rev. E 51(5), 4282 (1995)

18. Hochreiter, S., Schmidhuber, J.: Long short-term memory. Neural Comput. **9**(8), 1735–1780 (1997)
19. Jain, A., Zamir, A., Savarese, S., Saxena, A.: Structural-RNN: deep learning on spatio-temporal graphs. In: Proceedings of the International Conference on Computer Vision and Pattern Recognition, pp. 5308–5317. IEEE (2015)
20. Kok, V., Mei, K., Chan, C.: Crowd behavior analysis: a review where physics meets biology. Neurocomputing **177**, 342–362 (2016)
21. Lawal, I., Poiesi, F., Aguita, D., Cavallaro, A.: Support vector motion clustering. IEEE Trans. Circuits Syst. Video Technol. **27**(11), 2395–2408 (2017)
22. Lee, N., Choi, W., Vernaza, P., Choy, C., Torr, P., Chandraker, M.: Desire: Distant future prediction in dynamic scenes with interacting agents. In: Proceedings of the International Conference on Computer Vision and Pattern Recognition, pp. 2165–2174. IEEE (2017)
23. Lerner, A., Chrysanthou, Y., Lischinski, D.: Crowds by example, vol. 26, pp. 655–664. Wiley Online Library (2007)
24. Li, T., Chang, H., Wang, M., Ni, B., Hong, R., Yan, S.: Crowded scene analysis: a survey. IEEE Trans. Circuits Syst. Video Technol. **25**(3), 367–386 (2015)
25. Li, W., Mahadevan, V., Vasconcelos, N.: Anomaly detection and localization in crowded scenes. IEEE Trans. Pattern Anal. Mach. Intell. **36**(1), 18–32 (2013)
26. Ma, W., Huang, D., Lee, N., Kitani, K.M.: A game-theoretic approach to multi-pedestrian activity forecasting (2016)
27. Pellegrini, S., Ess, A., Schindler, K., Van Gool, L.: You'll never walk alone: modeling social behavior for multi-target tracking. In: Proceedings of the International Conference on Computer Vision, pp. 261–268. IEEE (2009)
28. Robicquet, A., Sadeghian, A., Alahi, A., Savarese, S.: Learning social etiquette: human trajectory understanding in crowded scenes. In: Leibe, B., Matas, J., Sebe, N., Welling, M. (eds.) ECCV 2016. LNCS, vol. 9912, pp. 549–565. Springer, Cham (2016). https://doi.org/10.1007/978-3-319-46484-8_33
29. Robicquet, A., et al.: Forecasting social navigation in crowded complex scenes (2016)
30. Stewart, R., Andriluka, M., Ng, A.: End-to-end people detection in crowded scenes. In: Proceedings of the International Conference on Computer Vision and Pattern Recognition, pp. 2325–2333. IEEE (2016)
31. Ryoo, M., Aggarwal, J.: Stochastic representation and recognition of high-level group activities. Int. J. Comput. Vis. **93**(2), 183–200 (2011)
32. Shao, J., Loy, C.C., Wang, X.: Learning scene-independent group descriptors for crowd understanding. IEEE Trans. Circuits Syst. Video Technol. **27**(6), 1290–1303 (2017)
33. Solmaz, B., Moore, B.E., Shah, M.: Identifying behaviors in crowd scenes using stability analysis for dynamical systems. IEEE Trans. Pattern Anal. Mach. Intell. **34**(10), 2064–2070 (2012)
34. Sutskever, I., Vinyals, O., Le, Q.: Sequence to sequence learning with neural networks. In: Advances in Neural Information Processing Systems, pp. 3104–3112 (2014)
35. Tomasi, C., Kanade, T.: Detection and tracking of point features (1991)
36. Treuille, A., Cooper, S., Popović, Z.: Continuum crowds. ACM Trans. Graphics (TOG) **25**, 1160–1168 (2006)
37. Van Den Berg, J., Guy, S.J., Lin, M., Manocha, D.: Reciprocal n-body collision avoidance. In: Pradalier, C., Siegwart, R., Hirzinger, G. (eds.) Robot. Res., pp. 3–19. Springer, Berlin (2011)

38. Varshneya, D., Srinivasaraghavan, G.: Human trajectory prediction using spatially aware deep attention models. https://arxiv.org/abs/1705.09436 (2017)
39. Vemula, A., Muelling, K., Oh, J.: Social attention: Modeling attention in human crowds. arXiv:1710.04689 (2017)
40. Yamaguchi, K., Berg, A.C., Ortiz, L.E., Berg, T.L.: Who are you with and where are you going? In: Proceedings of the International Conference on Computer Vision and Computer Vision, pp. 1345–1352. IEEE (2011)
41. Yi, S., Li, H., Wang, X.: Understanding pedestrian behaviors from stationary crowd groups. In: Proceedings of the International Conference on Computer Vision and Pattern Recognition, pp. 3488–3496. IEEE (2015)
42. Zhong, J., Cai, W., Luo, L., Yin, H.: Learning behavior patterns from video: a data-driven framework for agent-based crowd modeling. In: Proceedings of the International Conference on Autonomous Agents and Multiagent Systems, pp. 801–809 (2015)
43. Zhou, B., Tang, X., Wang, X.: Learning collective crowd behaviors with dynamic agent. Int. J. Comput. Vis. **111**(1), 50–68 (2015)
44. Zhou, B., Tang, X., Wang, X.: Coherent filtering: detecting coherent motions from crowd clutters. In: Fitzgibbon, A., Lazebnik, S., Perona, P., Sato, Y., Schmid, C. (eds.) ECCV 2012. LNCS, pp. 857–871. Springer, Heidelberg (2012). https://doi.org/10.1007/978-3-642-33709-3_61

W16 – 3rd Workshop on Geometry Meets Deep Learning

W16 – 3rd Workshop on Geometry Meets Deep Learning

Welcome to the Proceedings for the 3rd Workshop on Geometry Meets Deep Learning (GMDL), held in conjunction with the European Conference on Computer Vision (ECCV) on September 14th 2018 in Munich, Germany.

The goal of this workshop series is to encourage the interplay between geometric vision and deep learning. Deep learning has emerged as a common approach to learning data-driven representations. While deep learning approaches have achieved remarkable performance improvements in most 2D vision problems, such as image classification and object detection, they cannot be directly applied to geometric vision problems due to the fundamental differences between 2D and 3D vision problems, including the non-Euclidean nature of geometric objects, higher dimensionality, and the lack of large-scale annotated 3D datasets. To address these shortcomings, developing methods that integrate geometric components with deep neural networks is a promising research direction. This workshop series aims to bring together experts from both the areas of 3D vision and deep learning to summarize recent advances, exchange ideas, and inspire new directions.

We received a total number of 26 full-paper submissions that covered a wide range of topics, such as 3D object/human pose estimation, structure from motion, 3D segmentation, and image synthesis. Each submission was sent to at least two independent reviewers who were senior researchers in the related area. According to the reviewers' suggestions and internal discussions among the workshop chairs, 18 papers were accepted to the workshop, five of which were accepted as oral presentations and the rest as poster presentations. The workshop chairs did not submit any paper to avoid conflicts in the review process.

We thank all of the reviewers and authors for their hard work. The 3rd GMDL workshop would not have been such a great success without them. We had a record attendance at the workshop, with an impressive 200 attendees filling the room during the sessions! Judging by the large attendance and enthusiasm at the workshop, there is indeed a growing awareness and interest in approaches that combine deep learning with geometric vision, and we anticipate continued growth in the area.

Best regards,
Xiaowei Zhou
Emanuele Rodolà
Jonathan Masci
Kosta Derpanis

Scene Coordinate Regression
with Angle-Based Reprojection Loss
for Camera Relocalization

Xiaotian Li[1(✉)], Juha Ylioinas[1], Jakob Verbeek[2], and Juho Kannala[1]

[1] Aalto University, Espoo, Finland
{xiaotian.li,juha.ylioinas,juho.kannala}@aalto.fi
[2] Univ. Grenoble Alpes, Inria, CNRS, Grenoble INP, LJK, 38000 Grenoble, France
jakob.verbeek@inria.fr

Abstract. Image-based camera relocalization is an important problem
in computer vision and robotics. Recent works utilize convolutional neural networks (CNNs) to regress for pixels in a query image their corresponding 3D world coordinates in the scene. The final pose is then solved
via a RANSAC-based optimization scheme using the predicted coordinates. Usually, the CNN is trained with ground truth scene coordinates,
but it has also been shown that the network can discover 3D scene geometry automatically by minimizing single-view reprojection loss. However,
due to the deficiencies of the reprojection loss, the network needs to be
carefully initialized. In this paper, we present a new angle-based reprojection loss, which resolves the issues of the original reprojection loss. With
this new loss function, the network can be trained without careful initialization, and the system achieves more accurate results. The new loss
also enables us to utilize available multi-view constraints, which further
improve performance.

Keywords: Camera relocalization · Scene coordinate regression ·
Deep neural networks

1 Introduction

Image-based camera relocalization is the problem of estimating the 6 DoF camera
pose in an environment from a single image. It plays a crucial role in computer
vision and robotics, and is the key component for a wide range of applications,
such as pedestrian localization and navigation of autonomous robots [8], simultaneous localization and mapping (SLAM) [9], and augmented reality [5,25].

Many conventional localization methods proposed in the literature [31–33] are
based on hand-crafted local image features, such as SIFT, ORB, or SURF [1,24,
30]. These methods usually require a 3D point cloud model where each 3D point
is associated with the image features from which it was triangulated. Given a
query image, its 6D camera pose is recovered by first finding a large set of matches
between 2D image features and 3D points in the model via descriptor matching,

© Springer Nature Switzerland AG 2019
L. Leal-Taixé and S. Roth (Eds.): ECCV 2018 Workshops, LNCS 11131, pp. 229–245, 2019.
https://doi.org/10.1007/978-3-030-11015-4_19

and then using a RANSAC-based [10] strategy to reject outlier matches and estimate the camera pose on inliers. However, these local image features are limited by their hand-crafted feature detectors and descriptors. They are not robust enough for localization in challenging scenarios, and thus limit the use of these conventional methods.

Neural network based localization approaches have been recently explored. For example, PoseNet [19] utilizes a convolutional neural network that takes a single RGB image as input and directly regresses the 6 DoF camera pose relative to a scene. Since these methods formulate the camera pose estimation task as a regression problem, which is solved using neural networks, no conventional hand-crafted features are required. These methods can successfully predict camera pose in challenging environments where the conventional methods fail, but their overall accuracy still lags behind the conventional ones. An alternative neural network based solution is to keep the two-stage pipeline of conventional methods and formulate the first stage of the pipeline for generating 2D-3D correspondences as a learning problem. For example, the recently presented DSAC pipeline [2] predicts the 6 DoF pose by first regressing for image patches their 3D positions in the scene coordinate frame, and then determining the camera pose via a RANSAC-based scheme using the produced correspondences. The regression step in the first stage is the so-called scene coordinate regression and the 3D positions are the scene coordinates. Results have shown that these methods achieve state-of-the-art localization accuracy.

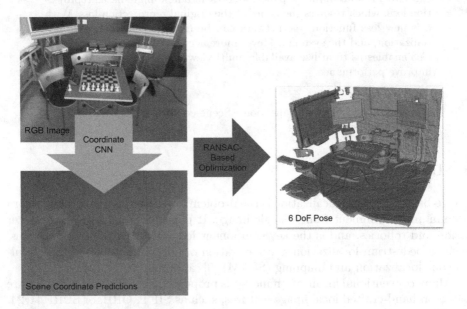

Fig. 1. Localization pipeline. In this two-stage pipeline, a coordinate CNN first produces scene coordinate predictions from an RGB image, and then the predicted correspondences are fed into a RANSAC-based solver to determine the camera pose.

As the improved version of DSAC, DSAC++ [4] has demonstrated that scene coordinate regression can be learned even without ground truth scene coordinates. A new 3-step training strategy is proposed for training the DSAC++ pipeline. When there are no ground truth scene coordinates available, the first training step is to initialize the network using approximate scene coordinates. In the second training step, the network is further trained via optimizing reprojection loss which is measured by the sum of residuals between projected 3D points in a 2D image plane. Finally, an end-to-end optimization step is performed. The second step is crucial for the network to discover scene geometry and the first step is also necessary for the second step to work. However, initializing the network using approximate scene coordinates that are far from the ground truth ones might also degenerate localization accuracy.

In order to train the network without an initialization step, we propose in this work a novel loss function for learning scene coordinate regression. We call this new loss angle-based reprojection loss. This new loss function has better properties compared to the original reprojection loss, and thus careful initialization is not required. In addition, this new loss allows us to additionally exploit multi-view constraints.

The contributions of this paper can be summarized as follows:

- We present a novel angle-based reprojection loss, which enables the training of coordinate network without careful initialization and improves localization accuracy.
- We show that based on this new loss function, we can incorporate multi-view constraints to further improve the accuracy.

2   Related Work

Image-based camera localization in large-scale environments is often addressed as an image retrieval problem [46]. These methods rely on efficient and scalable retrieval approaches to determine the location of a query image. Typically, the query image is matched to a database of geotagged images and the most similar images to it are retrieved. The location of the query image is then estimated according to the known locations of the retrieved images. These approaches can scale to extremely large urban environments and even entire cites. However, all these methods can only produce an approximate location of the camera and are unable to output an exact estimate of 6 DoF camera pose.

To directly obtain 6 DoF camera pose with respect to a scene, approaches based on sparse local features such as SIFT [24] have been proposed. Instead of matching a query image to geotagged database images, these methods usually use a reconstructed 3D point cloud model obtained from Structure-from-Motion [38] to represent the scene. Each 3D point in the model is associated with one or more local image feature descriptors. Thus, a set of 2D-3D correspondences can be established by matching local image features to 3D points in the model. Based on the 2D-3D correspondences, the camera pose of the query image can be determined by a Perspective-n-Point [21] solver inside a RANSAC [10] loop.

To scale up these methods to large environments, an efficient and effective descriptor matching step is needed. Therefore, techniques such as prioritized matching [31], intermediate image retrieval [15,34], geometric outlier filtering [45], and co-visibility filtering [32] have been proposed. However, due to limitations of the hand-crated features, these approaches can fail in challenging scenarios.

PoseNet [19] was the first approach to tackle the problem of 6 DoF camera relocalization with deep learning. PoseNet demonstrates the feasibility of directly regressing the 6 DoF camera pose from a query RGB image via a deep CNN. Later works have been proposed to extend this method for better accuracy. For example, in [17], the authors explore Bayesian Neural Networks to produce relocalization uncertainty of the predicted pose. LSTM-Pose [42] utilizes LSTM units [14] on the output of CNN to extract better features for localization. Another variant, Hourglass-Pose [27], makes use of the encoder-decoder hourglass architecture which can preserve the fine-grained information of input image. Moreover, [18] demonstrates that PoseNet performance can be improved by leveraging geometric loss functions. However, these methods are still outperformed by conventional sparse feature based methods. More recently, two multitask models VlocNet [40] and VlocNet++ [29] have been introduced. These models operate on consecutive monocular images and utilize auxiliary learning during training. Remarkably, they can offer promising localization performance that surpasses the sparse feature based methods.

Unlike PoseNet, Laskar *et al.* introduce a deep learning based localization framework, which relies on image retrieval and relative camera pose estimation [22]. This method requires no scene-specific training and can generalize well to previously unseen scenes. Similarly, Taira *et al.* put forth an image retrieval based localization system for large-scale indoor environments [39]. After retrieval of candidate poses, the pose is estimated based on dense matching. A final pose verification step via virtual view synthesis can further improve the robustness of the system. To achieve robust visual localization under a wide range of viewing conditions, semantic information has also been exploited in [36].

Our work is most closely related to methods based on the scene coordinate regression framework. The original scene coordinate regression pipeline is proposed for RGB-D camera relocalization [37]. This method formulates descriptor matching as a regression problem and applies a regression forest [7] to produce 2D-3D correspondences from an RGB-D input image. Similarly to a sparse feature based pipeline, the final camera pose is recovered from the correspondences via a RANSAC-based solver. Since generating correspondences is directly achieved by the regression forest, no traditional feature extraction, feature description, or feature matching processes are required. This method has been further extended in later works [6,13,41]. Currently, practical low-cost devices are usually equipped with RGB cameras only. However, these methods still require a depth signal at both training and test time.

To localize RGB-only images, an auto-context random forest is adopted in the pipeline in [3]. In [26], Massiceti *et al.* explored random-forest-to-neural-network mapping strategy. Recently, Brachmann et al. proposed a differentiable version of RANSAC (DSAC) [2] and presented a localization system based on it. In the DSAC pipeline, two CNNs are adopted for predicting scene coordinates and for scoring hypotheses respectively. Since the entire pipeline is differentiable, an end-to-end optimization step can be performed using ground truth camera poses. In contrast to DSAC, which adopts a patch-based network for scene coordination regression, a full-frame network considering global image appearance is presented in [23] and a data augmentation strategy is proposed to ensure the accuracy. However, all of these methods require ground truth scene coordinates for training. DSAC++ [4], the successor version of DSAC, demonstrates the feasibility of learning scene coordinate regression without scene coordinate ground truth. This is achieved by first initializing the predictions with approximate scene coordinates and then optimizing reprojection errors. This method is the current state-of-the-art on the 7-Scenes dataset [37] and the Cambridge Landmarks dataset [19].

3   Method

In this work, we follow the two-stage pipeline of DSAC and DSAC++ for RGB-only camera relocalization. In the first stage, given an RGB image, a coordinate CNN is adopted to generate dense 3D scene coordinate predictions to form 2D-3D correspondences. In the second stage, a RANSAC-based scheme is performed to generate pose hypotheses with their scores and determine the final pose estimate which can be further refined. The overall pipeline is illustrated in Fig. 1.

DSAC first demonstrates how to incorporate CNNs into the two-stage pipeline and achieves state-of-the-art results. DSAC++ further addresses the main shortcomings of the DSAC pipeline and achieves substantially more accurate results. More importantly, unlike previous works which require scene coordinate ground truth generated using RGB-D training images or available 3D model during training, DSAC++ is able to discover 3D scene geometry automatically. That is, the coordinate CNN can be trained from RGB images only with their ground truth camera poses, and no ground truth scene coordinates or depth information is needed. This is achieved by first using approximate scene coordinates to initialize the network and then optimizing reprojection loss, which is calculated using the ground truth poses. In the initialization step, the approximate scene coordinates are generated to have a constant distance d from the camera plane and serve as the dummy ground truth for training. The reprojection loss can then help the network to recover the scene geometry, but it may not work without the initialization step, even though the initialization step itself provides poor localization performance. However, the DSAC++ pipeline still has a main drawback. That is, a proper value for constant distance d should be selected carefully, since a value that is far off the actual range of distances can result in poor accuracy [4].

In the following, we present a new angle-based reprojection loss that allows us to train the coordinate CNN without careful initialization. We explain the deficiencies of the original reprojection loss and present our new loss function in Sect. 3.1. This new loss function also enables us to utilize available multi-view reprojection and photo-consistency constraints, which we discuss in Sects. 3.2 and 3.3 respectively.

3.1 Angle-Based Reprojection Loss

For a training image I_i, the reprojection loss is calculated using the scene coordinate predictions and the ground truth pose. It can be written as[1]:

$$\mathcal{L}_{rep} = \sum_{k \in P_i} \|Ch_i^{-1}y_k(I_i; w) - p_k^i\| \tag{1}$$

where C is the intrinsic matrix, h_i is the camera pose for image I_i, P_i is the set of all points in image I_i, $y_k(I_i; w)$ is the scene coordinate prediction for point k with input image I_i and learnable parameters w, p_k^i is the 2D position of point k in image I_i.

As mentioned above, the DSAC++ pipeline requires a carefully selected distance d for generating approximate scene coordinates when training without ground truth scene coordinates. However, improper selection of d may also lead to poor performance. Therefore, one may wonder if it is possible to train the network without an initialization step. Unfortunately, if we train the network directly using the reprojection loss without the initialization step, the training might not converge due to unstable gradients. The unstable gradients are caused by minimizing the reprojection loss at the beginning of training when the predictions of the network could be behind the camera or close to the camera center.

The shortcomings of the reprojection loss are illustrated in Fig. 2. As we can see, the reprojection loss does not constrain the predictions to be in front of the camera, and the loss could be 0 even when the predictions are behind the camera. Therefore, in such cases, the reprojection loss cannot help the network to discover the true geometry of the scene. In addition, when the z coordinate of a prediction in the camera coordinate frame is close to zero, the corresponding projected point in the image plane could be extremely far away from the ground truth one, resulting in extremely large loss value and exploding gradients. More importantly, we believe the ability of the network to discover the scene geometry automatically comes from the patch-based nature of the predictions. The output neurons of the fully-convolutional network used in the DSAC++ pipeline have a limited receptive field. Since local patch appearance is relatively invariant w.r.t. to viewpoint change, the explicitly applied single-view reprojection loss could be considered as implicit multi-view constraints. However, when the predictions are behind camera, minimizing reprojection loss to fulfill multi-view constraints could lead to inconsistent gradients. This again prevents the network from discovering the true geometry of a scene.

---

[1] We omit the conversions between homogeneous coordinates and Cartesian coordinates for simplicity. This also applies to equations in the rest of the paper.

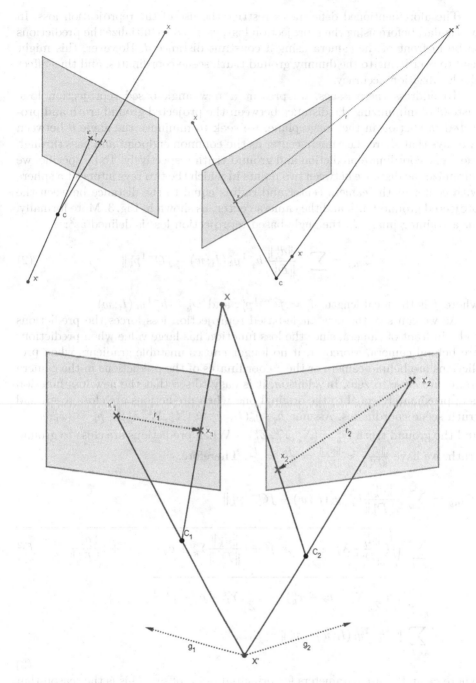

Fig. 2. Top left: when predictions are behind the camera, loss can still be 0. Top right: reprojected predictions can be easily far from the ground truth. Bottom: predictions behind the camera can cause inconsistent gradients.

The aforementioned deficiencies restrict the use of the reprojection loss. In particular, before using the reprojection loss, we need to initialize the predictions to be in front of the camera using a constant distance d. However, this might lead to overfitting to the dummy ground truth scene coordinates, and thus affect the localization accuracy.

To address these issues, we present a new angle-based reprojection loss. Instead of minimizing the distance between the projected ground truth and projected prediction in the image plane, we seek to minimize the angle θ between two rays that share the camera center as the common endpoint and pass through the scene coordinate prediction and ground truth respectively. To be specific, we minimize the distance between two points in which the two rays intersect a sphere with center at the camera center and radius equal to the distance between the projected ground truth and the camera center, as shown in Fig. 3. More formally, for a training image I_i, the angle-based reprojection loss is defined as[2]:

$$\mathcal{L}_{ang} = \sum_{k \in P_i} \| \frac{\|d_k^i\|}{\|D_k^i\|} h_i^{-1} y_k(I_i; w) - fC^{-1} p_k^i \| \tag{2}$$

where f is the focal length, $d_k^i = fC^{-1}p_k^i$, and $D_k^i = h_i^{-1}y_k(I_i; w)$.

As we can see, the new angle-based reprojection loss forces the predictions to be in front of camera, since the loss function has large value when predictions are behind camera. Moreover, it no longer causes unstable gradients when predictions are behind camera or the z coordinates of the predictions in the camera frame are close to zero. In addition, it is easy to see that the new loss function is approximately equal to the original one when predictions are close to ground truth scene coordinates. Assume $h_i^{-1}y_k(I_i; w) = (X_k^i, Y_k^i, Z_k^i)^T$, $p_k^i = (x_k^i, y_k^i)^T$, and the ground truth $\dot{D}_k^i = (\dot{X}_k^i, \dot{Y}_k^i, \dot{Z}_k^i)^T$. When predictions are close to ground truth, we have $\frac{\|d_k^i\|}{\|D_k^i\|} \approx \frac{\|d_k^i\|}{\|\dot{D}_k^i\|} = \frac{f}{\dot{Z}_k^i} \approx \frac{f}{Z_k^i}$. Therefore:

$$\mathcal{L}_{ang} = \sum_{k \in P_i} \| \frac{\|d_k^i\|}{\|D_k^i\|} h_i^{-1} y_k(I_i; w) - fC^{-1} p_k^i \|$$

$$= \sum_{k \in P_i} \sqrt{(\frac{\|d_k^i\|}{\|D_k^i\|} X_k^i + c_x - x_k^i)^2 + (\frac{\|d_k^i\|}{\|D_k^i\|} Y_k^i + c_y - y_k^i)^2 + (\frac{\|d_k^i\|}{\|D_k^i\|} Z_k^i - f)^2}$$

$$\approx \sum_{k \in P_i} \sqrt{(\frac{f}{Z_k^i} X_k^i + c_x - x_k^i)^2 + (\frac{f}{Z_k^i} Y_k^i + c_y - y_k^i)^2}$$

$$= \sum_{k \in P_i} \|Ch_i^{-1} y_k(I_i; w) - p_k^i\| = \mathcal{L}_{rep}$$

$$\tag{3}$$

where c_x and c_y are parameters for principal point offset. This is the reason that we call the new loss function angle-based reprojection loss.

---

[2] We assume $f_x = f_y = f$ in this paper, but the loss function is also applicable when $f_x \neq f_y$.

Note that in order to minimize the angle θ, one may also maximize the dot product of the two unit vectors of the two rays, but the resulting loss function no longer has the property to be approximately equal to the reprojection loss when predictions are close to ground truth scene coordinates.

3.2   Multi-view Reprojection Loss

Although with only single-view reprojection loss, the network can already approximately recover the scene geometry, sometimes it is still difficult for the network to learn accurate scene coordinate predictions, e.g., when ground truth poses are erroneous or there are ambiguities in the scene. Therefore, if we could exploit explicitly multi-view constraints during training, we might achieve more accurate localization performance.

One way to incorporate multi-view constraints is to utilize available multi-view correspondences to form multi-view reprojection loss. The correspondences might come from a reconstructed 3D model or can be directly generated by correspondence matching.

Since the original reprojection loss is problematic when predictions are behind camera, it is more likely to cause problem in the multi-view cases. Therefore, we formulate the multi-view reprojection loss based on our new angle-based reprojection loss. For one training image, the loss function can be written as:

$$
\mathcal{L}_{multi} = \sum_{k \in P_i^-} \| \frac{\|d_k^i\|}{\|D_k^i\|} h_i^{-1} y_k(I_i; w) - fC^{-1} p_k^i \|
$$
$$
+ \lambda \sum_{k \in P_i^*} \sum_{j \in \mathcal{I}_k \cup \{I_i\}} \| \frac{\|d_k^j\|}{\|D_k^j\|} h_j^{-1} y_k(I_i; w) - fC^{-1} p_k^j \|
$$

(4)

where λ is the balance weight, P_i^- is the set of all points in image I_i which have no corresponding points, P_i^* is the set of points in image I_i which have corresponding points in other training images, $\mathcal{I}_k$ is the set of images in which point k has a corresponding point. As we can see, $\sum_{k \in P_i^-} \| \frac{\|d_k^i\|}{\|D_k^i\|} h_i^{-1} y_k(I_i; w) - fC^{-1} p_k^i \|$ encodes single-view constraints, and $\sum_{k \in P_i^*} \sum_{j \in \mathcal{I}_k \cup \{I_i\}} \| \frac{\|d_k^j\|}{\|D_k^j\|} h_j^{-1} y_k(I_i; w) - fC^{-1} p_k^j \|$ encodes multi-view constraints.

3.3   Photometric Reconstruction Loss

If training data consists of sequences of images, it is also possible to constrain the scene coordinate predictions using photometric reconstruction loss. Photometric reconstruction loss has recently become a dominant strategy for solving many geometry related learning problems. It enables neural networks to learn many tasks, such as monocular depth [11,12], ego-motion [47], and optical flow [44], in a self-supervised manner.

For learning scene coordinate regression, given a training image I_i and a neighboring image I_j, we can reconstruct the training image by sampling pixels

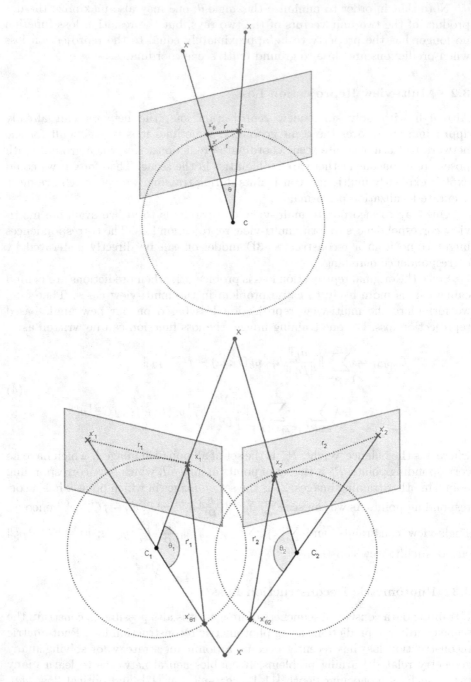

Fig. 3. Top: to minimize θ, we minimize r'. Bottom: the new loss enforces predictions to be in front of the camera and causes no unstable gradients.

from the neighboring image based on the scene coordinate predictions and the pose of the neighboring image. Specifically, for a point k in the training image I_i, we can project it to the neighboring image and obtain its 2D coordinates in the neighboring image:

$$p_k^j = Ch_j^{-1} y_k(I_i; w) \tag{5}$$

Then, the pixel value for point k in the reconstructed image $\hat{I}_i$ can be sampled using bilinear sampler based on the coordinates p_k^j. That is, the sampled pixel value is the weighted sum of the values of the four neighboring pixels of p_k^j.

Following [12], our photometric reconstruction loss is a combination of an $L1$ loss term and a simplified SSIM loss term with a 3×3 block filter:

$$\mathcal{L}_{pr} = \sum_{k \in P_i} (1 - \alpha) \mid \hat{I}_i^k - I_i^k \mid + \alpha \frac{1 - SSIM(\hat{I}_i^k, I_i^k)}{2} \tag{6}$$

where $\alpha = 0.85$.

Since in the beginning of training, the scene coordinate predictions could be quite far from the ground truth ones, the projected 2D coordinates of points in the neighboring image might also be far from valid pixels. In other words, we are unable to obtain valid gradients by minimizing the photometric recon- struction loss. Therefore, using only photometric reconstruction loss for learning scene coordinate regression may not work. Thus, we pair it with our angle-base reprojection loss, and the final loss function can be written as:

$$\mathcal{L}_{ang+pr} = \mathcal{L}_{ang} + \lambda \mathcal{L}_{pr} \tag{7}$$

4   Experiments

We evaluate the performance of our approach on the 7-Scenes dataset [37] and the Cambridge Landmarks dataset [19], which are described in Sect. 4.1. The implementation details are explained in Sect. 4.2 and the results are given in Sect. 4.3.

4.1   Evaluation Dataset

The 7-Scenes dataset [37] is a widely used RGB-D dataset provided by Microsoft Research. It consists of seven different indoor environments, and exhibits sev- eral challenges, such as motion blur, illumination changes, textureless surfaces, repeated structures, reflections, and sensor noise. Each scene contains multiple sequences of tracked RGB-D camera frames and these sequences are split into training and testing data. The RGB-D images are captured using a handheld Kinect camera at 640×480 resolution and associated with 6 DoF ground truth camera poses obtained via the KinectFusion system [16,28].

The Cambridge Landmarks [19] is an outdoor RGB relocalization dataset, which consists of six scenes from around Cambridge University. Each scene is composed of hundreds or thousands of frames, which are divided into training and test sequences. The 6 DoF ground truth camera poses of the images are generated with structure from motion techniques [43].

In contrast to some previous works, ground truth scene coordinates are not necessary for learning scene coordinate regression in this work. Therefore, we use only RGB images at both training and test time.

4.2 Implementation Details

Note that the following implementation details are for the experiments on the 7-Scenes dataset. For the experiments on the Cambridge Landmarks dataset, we simply follow DSAC++ [4] except that we train the network with our angle-based reprojection loss only for $450K$ iterations, we halve the learning rate every $50K$ iterations after $250K$ iterations, and we perform no gradient clipping.

We adopt the FCN network architecture used in the DSAC++ pipeline which takes a 640×480 image as input and produces 80×60 scene coordinate predictions. For implementation simplicity, unlike DSAC++, in the second stage of the pipeline, we use a non-differentiable version of the RANSAC-based scheme for pose estimation, which scores hypotheses using inlier count instead of soft inlier count. The details of the used pose estimation algorithm are explained in [23]. In this paper, we mainly focus on the loss functions for learning scene coordinate regression in the first stage of the pipeline, and thus the entire pipeline is not required to be end-to-end trainable. However, it is also straightforward to adopt the differentiable optimization strategy and perform an extra end-to-end optimization step at the end of the training as described in [4].

We train the network from scratch without the scene coordinate initialization training step for $600K$ iterations with a batch size of 1 using the Adam [20] optimizer where $\beta_1 = 0.9$, $\beta_2 = 0.999$, and $\epsilon = 10^{-8}$. The initial learning rate is set to 0.0001 and is halved after $180K$, $360K$, $420K$, $480K$ and $540K$ iterations. Following [4], training images are randomly shifted by a maximum of 8 pixels, horizontally and vertically, to make full use of the training data, since the network produces one prediction for each 8×8 image block.

When training the network using the multi-view reprojection loss, for efficiency, we do not use all the correspondences to calculate the latter term of the loss. In particular, we calculate $\sum_{k \in P_i^*} \sum_{j \in \{I_i, I_m\}} \| \frac{\|d_k^j\|}{\|D_k^j\|} h_j^{-1} y_k(I_i; w) - fC^{-1}p_k^j \|$ instead of $\sum_{k \in P_i^*} \sum_{j \in \mathcal{I}_k \cup \{I_i\}} \| \frac{\|d_k^j\|}{\|D_k^j\|} h_j^{-1} y_k(I_i; w) - fC^{-1}p_k^j \|$ where I_m is an image randomly selected from $\mathcal{I}_k$. The co-visibility information used to form the multi-view constraints is extracted from a sparse model constructed with Colmap [35]. Moreover, we set the balance weight $\lambda = 60$.

When computing the photometric reprojection loss, the neighboring image is randomly selected from the same sequence with difference in index less or equal to 10. Since the network produces 80×60 scene coordinate predictions, we resize both the training images (after shifting) and the neighboring images to 80×60, and the camera intrinsic parameters are also adjusted accordingly. The balance weight λ is set to 20.

4.3   Results

The experimental results of our method on the 7-Scenes dataset and the Cambridge Landmarks dataset are given in Table 1. For the Cambridge Landmarks dataset, we report median localization errors of our method trained with single-view constraints only. For the 7-Scenes dataset, we report both median localization errors and accuracy measured as the percentage of query images for which the camera pose error is below 5° and 5 cm, as the latter one can better represent the localization performance. Our method is compared to the state-of-the-art DSAC++ method trained without an accurate 3D scene model.

Table 1. Results of our method on the 7-Scenes dataset and the Cambridge Landmarks dataset. We compare the performance of our method to DSAC++. Note that Complete denotes the accuracy measured by the 5°, 5 cm criterion on the combined set of the test frames (17000) of all scenes for the 7-Scenes dataset.

	5°, 5 cm (Median Error)			
Scene	DSAC++ [4]	Ours	Ours+multi-view	Ours+photometric
Chess	93.8% (2 cm, 0.7°)	95.1% (2 cm, 0.6°)	96.1% (2 cm, 0.6°)	96.0% (2 cm, 0.6°)
Fire	75.6% (3 cm, 1.1°)	84.0% (3 cm, 1.0°)	88.6% (2 cm, 1.0°)	86.4% (2 cm, 1.0°)
Heads	18.4% (12 cm, 6.7°)	80.5% (2 cm, 1.1°)	86.9% (2 cm, 1.0°)	83.2% (2 cm, 1.1°)
Office	75.4% (3 cm, 0.8°)	80.4% (3 cm, 0.8°)	80.6% (3 cm, 0.8°)	81.6% (3 cm, 0.8°)
Pumpkin	55.9% (5 cm, 1.1°)	56.8% (4 cm, 1.1°)	60.3% (4 cm, 1.1°)	59.2% (4 cm, 1.1°)
Red kitchen	50.7% (5 cm, 1.3°)	59.9% (4 cm, 1.2°)	61.9% (4 cm, 1.2°)	60.0% (4 cm, 1.2°)
Stairs	2.0% (29 cm, 5.1°)	2.9% (25 cm, 4.5°)	11.3% (13 cm, 3.4°)	4.7% (22 cm, 4.9°)
Complete	60.4%	69.2%	71.8%	70.4%
Great court	(66 cm, 0.4°)	(51 cm, 0.3°)	-	-
K. College	(23 cm, 0.4°)	(18 cm, 0.3°)	-	-
Old Hospital	(24 cm, 0.5°)	(19 cm, 0.4°)	-	-
Shop Facade	(9 cm, 0.4°)	(7 cm, 0.3°)	-	-
St M. Church	(20 cm, 0.7°)	(25 cm, 0.7°)	-	-

According to the results, for the 7-Scenes dataset, when training the network using our new angle-based reprojection loss without initializing the network predictions with constant distance value, the fraction of accurately localized test images is improved by 8.8 % points compared to DSAC++. Similarly, for the Cambridge Landmarks dataset, our method achieves better median pose accuracy on four out of five scenes. Moreover, for the 7-Scenes dataset, the accuracy can be further improved by utilizing either multi-view correspondences or photometric reconstruction metric. Compared to using single-view constraints only, we observed that the additional loss terms could make the network produce more accurate scene coordinate predictions during training. This means that incorporating multi-view constraints could help the network better discover scene geometry, and thus leads to improved localization performance.

We also attempted to train the network using the original reprojection loss without the scene coordinate initialization step. However, we found that for most of the scenes, training could not converge in both single-view and multi-view cases. In addition, when using the photometric reconstruction loss, for all the scenes, we observed that the training of the network without the angle-based reprojection loss term would always get stuck in a local minimum with large scene coordinate prediction error, resulting in a completely failed localization system.

When training with either the multi-view reprojection loss or the photometric reconstruction loss, the balance weight λ is important for achieving good localization results. If the weight is set too small, the multi-view constraints will have no effect on training. However, if it is set too large, we found that the localization accuracy could also drop. For example, when training with the photometric reconstruction loss with $\lambda = 50$, test accuracy for Office decreases to 79.5%. It would be interesting to explore learnable weighting strategy presented in [18] in future work.

Note that our method is still less accurate compared to the DSAC++ method trained with a 3D model (76.1%), as our method is trained without access to adequate scene geometry information. When training with the multi-view reprojection loss, only a sparse set of points have corresponding points in other images (typically about 1000 points for a 640×480 image). That is, the multi-view constraints are active for only a small portion of the points in a training image. We believe that with denser correspondence information, our method could achieve better results. For the photometric reconstruction loss, adding an additional loss term similar to the left-right consistency proposed in [12], which enforces predictions to be consistent between different views, might be also helpful to further improve the accuracy, but we did not explore it.

5   Conclusion

In this work, we have presented a new angle-based reprojection loss for learning scene coordinate regression for image-based camera relocalization. Our novel loss function makes it possible to train the coordinate CNN without a scene coordinate initialization step, resulting in improved localization accuracy. Moreover, this novel loss function allows us to explore available multi-view constraints, which can further improve performance.

Acknowledgements. Authors acknowledge funding from the Academy of Finland (grant numbers 277685, 309902). This work has also been partially supported by the grant "Deep in France" (ANR16-CE23-0006) and LabEx PERSYVAL (ANR-11-LABX0025-01).

References

1. Bay, H., Tuytelaars, T., Van Gool, L.: SURF: speeded up robust features. In: Leonardis, A., Bischof, H., Pinz, A. (eds.) ECCV 2006. LNCS, vol. 3951, pp. 404–417. Springer, Heidelberg (2006). https://doi.org/10.1007/11744023_32
2. Brachmann, E., et al.: DSAC - differentiable RANSAC for camera localization. In: CVPR (2017)
3. Brachmann, E., Michel, F., Krull, A., Yang, M.Y., Gumhold, S., Rother, C.: Uncertainty-driven 6D pose estimation of objects and scenes from a single RGB image. In: CVPR (2016)
4. Brachmann, E., Rother, C.: Learning less is more - 6D camera localization via 3D surface regression. In: CVPR (2018)
5. Castle, R.O., Klein, G., Murray, D.W.: Video-rate localization in multiple maps for wearable augmented reality. In: ISWC (2008)
6. Cavallari, T., Golodetz, S., Lord, N.A., Valentin, J.P.C., di Stefano, L., Torr, P.H.S.: On-the-fly adaptation of regression forests for online camera relocalisation. In: CVPR (2017)
7. Criminisi, A., Shotton, J.: Decision Forests for Computer Vision and Medical Image Analysis. Springer, London (2013). https://doi.org/10.1007/978-1-4471-4929-3
8. Cummins, M., Newman, P.: FAB-MAP: probabilistic localization and mapping in the space of appearance. Int. J. Rob. Res. **27**(6), 647–665 (2008)
9. Eade, E., Drummond, T.: Scalable monocular SLAM. In: CVPR (2006)
10. Fischler, M.A., Bolles, R.C.: Random sample consensus: a paradigm for model fitting with applications to image analysis and automated cartography. Commun. ACM **24**(6), 381–395 (1981)
11. Garg, R., Vijay Kumar, B.G., Carneiro, G., Reid, I.: Unsupervised CNN for single view depth estimation: geometry to the rescue. In: Leibe, B., Matas, J., Sebe, N., Welling, M. (eds.) ECCV 2016. LNCS, vol. 9912, pp. 740–756. Springer, Cham (2016). https://doi.org/10.1007/978-3-319-46484-8_45
12. Godard, C., Mac Aodha, O., Brostow, G.J.: Unsupervised monocular depth estimation with left-right consistency. In: CVPR (2017)
13. Guzmán-Rivera, A., et al.: Multi-output learning for camera relocalization. In: CVPR (2014)
14. Hochreiter, S., Schmidhuber, J.: Long short-term memory. Neural Comput. **9**(8), 1735–1780 (1997)
15. Irschara, A., Zach, C., Frahm, J.M., Bischof, H.: From structure-from-motion point clouds to fast location recognition. In: CVPR (2009)
16. Izadi, S., et al.: KinectFusion: real-time 3D reconstruction and interaction using a moving depth camera. In: UIST (2011)
17. Kendall, A., Cipolla, R.: Modelling uncertainty in deep learning for camera relocalization. In: ICRA (2016)
18. Kendall, A., Cipolla, R.: Geometric loss functions for camera pose regression with deep learning. In: CVPR (2017)
19. Kendall, A., Grimes, M., Cipolla, R.: PoseNet: a convolutional network for real-time 6-DOF camera relocalization. In: ICCV (2015)
20. Kingma, D.P., Ba, J.: Adam: a method for stochastic optimization. In: ICLR (2015)
21. Kneip, L., Scaramuzza, D., Siegwart, R.: A novel parametrization of the perspective-three-point problem for a direct computation of absolute camera position and orientation. In: CVPR (2011)

22. Laskar, Z., Melekhov, I., Kalia, S., Kannala, J.: Camera relocalization by computing pairwise relative poses using convolutional neural network. In: ICCVW (2017)
23. Li, X., Ylioinas, J., Kannala, J.: Full-frame scene coordinate regression for image-based localization. In: RSS (2018)
24. Lowe, D.G.: Distinctive image features from scale-invariant keypoints. Int. J. Comput. Vis. **60**(2), 91–110 (2004)
25. Lynen, S., Sattler, T., Bosse, M., Hesch, J.A., Pollefeys, M., Siegwart, R.: Get out of my lab: large-scale, real-time visual-inertial localization. In: RSS (2015)
26. Massiceti, D., Krull, A., Brachmann, E., Rother, C., Torr, P.H.S.: Random forests versus neural networks - what's best for camera relocalization? In: ICRA (2017)
27. Melekhov, I., Ylioinas, J., Kannala, J., Rahtu, E.: Image-based localization using hourglass networks. In: ICCVW (2017)
28. Newcombe, R.A., et al.: KinectFusion: real-time dense surface mapping and tracking. In: ISMAR (2011)
29. Radwan, N., Valada, A., Burgard, W.: VlocNet++: deep multitask learning for semantic visual localization and odometry. CoRR abs/1804.08366 (2018)
30. Rublee, E., Rabaud, V., Konolige, K., Bradski, G.R.: ORB: an efficient alternative to SIFT or SURF. In: ICCV (2011)
31. Sattler, T., Leibe, B., Kobbelt, L.: Fast image-based localization using direct 2D-to-3D matching. In: ICCV (2011)
32. Sattler, T., Leibe, B., Kobbelt, L.: Improving image-based localization by active correspondence search. In: Fitzgibbon, A., Lazebnik, S., Perona, P., Sato, Y., Schmid, C. (eds.) ECCV 2012. LNCS, vol. 7572, pp. 752–765. Springer, Heidelberg (2012). https://doi.org/10.1007/978-3-642-33718-5_54
33. Sattler, T., Leibe, B., Kobbelt, L.: Efficient effective prioritized matching for large-scale image-based localization. IEEE Trans. Pattern Anal. Mach. Intell. **39**(9), 1744–1756 (2017)
34. Sattler, T., et al.: Are large-scale 3D models really necessary for accurate visual localization? In: CVPR (2017)
35. Schönberger, J.L., Frahm, J.: Structure-from-motion revisited. In: CVPR (2016)
36. Schönberger, J.L., Pollefeys, M., Geiger, A., Sattler, T.: Semantic visual localization. In: CVPR (2018)
37. Shotton, J., Glocker, B., Zach, C., Izadi, S., Criminisi, A., Fitzgibbon, A.W.: Scene coordinate regression forests for camera relocalization in RGB-D images. In: CVPR (2013)
38. Snavely, N., Seitz, S.M., Szeliski, R.: Modeling the world from internet photo collections. Int. J. Comput. Vis. **80**(2), 189–210 (2008)
39. Taira, H., et al.: InLoc: indoor visual localization with dense matching and view synthesis. In: CVPR (2018)
40. Valada, A., Radwan, N., Burgard, W.: Deep auxiliary learning for visual localization and odometry. In: ICRA (2018)
41. Valentin, J.P.C., Nießner, M., Shotton, J., Fitzgibbon, A.W., Izadi, S., Torr, P.H.S.: Exploiting uncertainty in regression forests for accurate camera relocalization. In: CVPR (2015)
42. Walch, F., Hazirbas, C., Leal-Taixe, L., Sattler, T., Hilsenbeck, S., Cremers, D.: Image-based localization using lstms for structured feature correlation. In: ICCV (2017)
43. Wu, C.: Towards linear-time incremental structure from motion. In: 3DV (2013)

44. Yu, J.J., Harley, A.W., Derpanis, K.G.: Back to basics: unsupervised learning of optical flow via brightness constancy and motion smoothness. In: Hua, G., Jégou, H. (eds.) ECCV 2016. LNCS, vol. 9915, pp. 3–10. Springer, Cham (2016). https://doi.org/10.1007/978-3-319-49409-8_1
45. Zeisl, B., Sattler, T., Pollefeys, M.: Camera pose voting for large-scale image-based localization. In: ICCV (2015)
46. Zhang, W., Kosecka, J.: Image based localization in urban environments. In: 3DPVT (2006)
47. Zhou, T., Brown, M., Snavely, N., Lowe, D.G.: Unsupervised learning of depth and ego-motion from video. In: CVPR (2017)

Deep Normal Estimation for Automatic Shading of Hand-Drawn Characters

Matis Hudon[✉] [ID], Mairéad Grogan [ID], Rafael Pagés [ID], and Aljoša Smolić [ID]

V-SENSE, Trinity College Dublin, Dublin, Ireland
{hudonm,mgrogan,pagesscr,smolica}@scss.tcd.ie
https://v-sense.scss.tcd.ie/

Abstract. We present a new fully automatic pipeline for generating shading effects on hand-drawn characters. Our method takes as input a single digitized sketch of any resolution and outputs a dense normal map estimation suitable for rendering without requiring any human input. At the heart of our method lies a deep residual, encoder-decoder convolutional network. The input sketch is first sampled using several equally sized 3-channel windows, with each window capturing a local area of interest at 3 different scales. Each window is then passed through the previously trained network for normal estimation. Finally, network outputs are arranged together to form a full-size normal map of the input sketch. We also present an efficient and effective way to generate a rich set of training data. Resulting renders offer a rich quality without any effort from the 2D artist. We show both quantitative and qualitative results demonstrating the effectiveness and quality of our network and method.

Keywords: Cartoons · Non-photorealistic rendering ·
Normal estimation · Deep learning

1 Introduction

Despite the proliferation of 3D animations and artworks, 2D drawings and hand-drawn animations are still important art communication media. This is mainly because drawing in 2D is not tied to any constraining tools and brings the highest freedom of expression to artists. Artists usually work in three steps: firstly, they create the raw animation or drawing which includes finding the right scene composition, character posture, and expression. Secondly, they refine the artwork, digitalise it and clean the line-art. Finally, they add color or decorative textures, lights and shades. When working on numerous drawings some of these steps can become quite tedious. To help with these time-consuming and repetitive tasks, scientists have tried to automate parts of the pipeline, for example, by cleaning the line-art [36,37], scanning [24], coloring [42,52], and by developing image registration and inbetweening techniques [41,49,50].

© Springer Nature Switzerland AG 2019
L. Leal-Taixé and S. Roth (Eds.): ECCV 2018 Workshops, LNCS 11131, pp. 246–262, 2019.
https://doi.org/10.1007/978-3-030-11015-4_20

Fig. 1. Our method takes as input a drawing of any resolution and estimates a plausible normal map suitable for creating shading effects. From left to right: Input drawing and flat colors, normal estimation and two renderings with different lighting configurations.

In this paper, we consider the shading task. Besides bringing appeal and style to animations, shades and shadows provide important visual cues about depth, shape, movement and lighting [19,29,48]. Manual shading can be challenging as it requires not only a strong comprehension of the physics behind the shades but also, in the case of an animation, spatial and temporal consistency within and between the different frames. The two basic components required to calculate the correct illumination at a certain point are the light position with respect to the point and the surface normal. These normals are unknown in hand-drawn artwork. Several state-of-the-art approaches have tried to reconstruct normals and/or depth information directly from line-drawing [9,12,14,17,26,29,40,43], however, most of these works seem to be under-constrained or require too many user inputs to really be usable in a real-world artistic pipeline.

We propose a method to estimate high-quality and high-resolution normal maps suitable for adding plausible and consistent shading effects to sketches and animations (Fig. 1). Unlike state-of-the-art methods, our technique does not rely on geometric assumptions or additional user inputs but works directly, without any user interaction, on input line-drawings. To achieve this, we have built a rich dataset containing a large number of training pairs. This dataset includes different styles of characters varying from cartoon ones to anime/manga. To avoid tedious and labor intensive manual labelling we also propose a pipeline for efficiently creating a rich training database. We introduce a deep Convolutional Neural Network (CNN) inspired by Lun et al. [26] and borrow ideas from recent advances such as symmetric skipping networks [32]. The system is able to efficiently predict accurate normal maps from any resolution input line drawing. To validate the effectiveness of our system, we show qualitative results on a rich variety of challenging cases borrowed from real world artists. We also compare our results with recent state-of-the-art and present quantitative validations. Our contributions can be summarized as follows:

- We propose a novel CNN pipeline tailored for predicting high-resolution normal maps from line-drawings.
- We propose a novel tiled and multi-scale representation of input data for efficient and qualitative predictions.

– We propose a sampling strategy to generate high-quality and high resolution normal maps and compare to recent CNNs including a fully convolutional network.

2   Related Work

Before introducing our work, we first review existing methods on shape from sketches. They can be classified into two categories: geometry-based methods and learning-based methods.

2.1   Inferring 3D Reconstruction from Line Drawings

Works like Teddy [15] provide interactive tools for building 3D models from 2D data by "inflating" a drawing into a 3D model. Petrovic's work [29] applies this idea to create shades and shadows for cel animation. While this work reduces the labor of creating the shadow mattes compared to traditional manual drawing, it also demonstrates that a simple approximation of the 3D model is sufficient for generating appealing shades and shadows for cel animation. However, it still requires an extensive manual interaction to obtain the desired results. Instead of reconstructing a 3D model, Lumo [17] assumes that normals at the drawing outline are coplanar with the drawing plane and estimates surface normals by interpolating from the line boundaries to render convincing illumination. Olsen et al. [27] presented a very interesting survey for the reconstruction of 3D shapes from drawings representing smooth surfaces. Later, further improvements were made such as handling T-junctions and cups [18], also using user drawn hatching/wrinkle strokes [6,16] or cross section curves [35,46] to guide the reconstruction process. Recent works exploit geometric constraints present in specific types of line drawings [28,34,51], however, these sketches are too specific to be generalized to 2D hand-drawn animation. In TexToons [40], depth layering is used to enhance textured images with ambient occlusion, shading, and texture rounding effects. Recently, Sýkora et al. [43] apply user annotation to recover a bas-relief with approximate depth from a single sketch, which they use to illuminate 2D drawings. This method clearly produces the best results, though it is still not fully automatic and still requires some user input. While these state-of-the-art methods are very interesting, we feel that the bas-relief ambiguity has not yet been solved. High-quality reconstructions require considerable user effort and time, whereas efficient methods rely on too many assumptions to be generalized to our problem. Although the human brain is still able to infer depth and shapes from drawings [5,7,21], this ability still seems unmatched in computer graphics/vision using geometry-based methods.

2.2   Learning Based Methods

As pure geometric methods fail to reconstruct high-quality 3D from sketches or images without a large number of constraints or additional user input, we are not the first to think that shape synthesis is fundamentally a learning problem. Recent works approach the shape synthesis problem by trying to predict surface depth and normals from real pictures using CNNs [8,31,47]. While these works show very promising results, their inputs provide much more information about the scene than drawn sketches, such as textures, natural shades and colors. Another considerable line of work employs parametric models (such as existing or deformed cars, bikes, containers, jewellery, trees, etc.) to guide shape reconstruction through CNNs [3,13,30]. Recently, Han et al. [11] presented a deep learning based sketching system relying on labor efficient user inputs to easily model 3D faces and caricatures. The work of Lun et al. [26], inspired by that of Tatarchenko et al. [44], is the closest to our work. They were the first to use CNNs to predict shape from line-drawings. While our method and network were inspired by their work, it differs in several ways: their approach makes use of multi-view input line-drawings whereas ours operates on a single input drawing, which allows our method to also be used for hand-drawn animations. Moreover, we present a way of predicting high-resolution normal maps directly, while they only show results for predicting 256×256 sized depth and normal maps and then fusing them into a 3D model. They provide a detailed comparison between view-based and voxel-based reconstruction. More recently Su et al. [39] proposed an interactive system for generating normal maps with the help of deep learning. Their method produces relatively high quality normal maps from sketch input combining a Generative Adversarial Network framework together with user inputs. However, the reconstructed models are still low resolution and lack details. The high-quality and high-resolution of our results allow us to qualitatively compete with recent work, including animation and sketch inflation, for high quality shading (see Sect. 2.1).

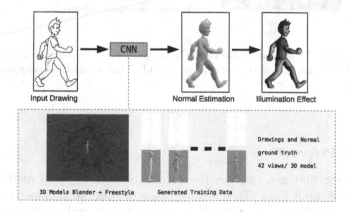

Fig. 2. System overview.

3   Proposed Technique

Figure 2 illustrates our proposed pipeline. The input to our system is a single arbitrary digital sketch in the form of a line drawing of a character. The output is an estimated normal map suitable for rendering effects, with the same resolution as the input sketch. The normals are represented as 3D vectors with values in the range $[-1, 1]$. The normal estimation relies on a CNN model trained only once offline.

The high resolution input image is split into smaller tiles/patches of size $256 \times 256 \times 3$, which are then passed through the CNN normal prediction and finally combined into a full resolution normal map. The training phase of the CNN requires a large dataset of input drawings and corresponding ground truth normal maps. As normal maps are not readily available for 2D sketches or animations, such a dataset cannot be obtained manually, and we therefore make use of 3D models and sketch-like renderings (Freestyle plugin in Blender ©) to generate the training dataset.

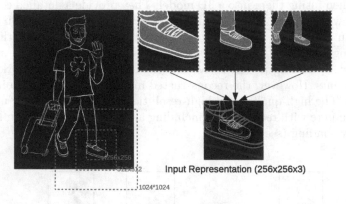

Input Representation (256x256x3)

Fig. 3. Structure of the input data. Here the target normal reconstruction scale is the blue channel. The two other channels provide additional multi-scale representation of the local area

3.1   Input Preparation

One key factor that can improve the success of a CNN-based method is the preparation of input data. To take advantage of this, we propose a new data representation to feed to our network. Instead of simply feeding tiles of our input line drawing to the encoder, we feed in many multi-scale tile representations to the CNN, with each tile capturing a local area of interest of the sketch. This multi-scale representation prevents our network from missing important higher scale details. A multi-scale tile example is shown in Fig. 3. Each channel of the tile is used to represent the lines of the sketch in a local area at one of 3 different scales. In each channel, pixels on a line are represented by a value of 1. The first channel in each tile (blue channel in Fig. 3) represents the scale at which the normal vectors will be estimated.

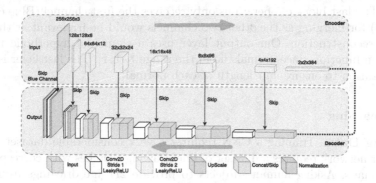

Fig. 4. Overall structure of the proposed network.

3.2 CNN Model

Our main requirements for the CNN is that the output has to be of the same size as the input and that extracted normals have to be aligned pixel-wise with the input line drawing. This is why a U-net based CNN is an appropriate choice. A typical pixel-wise CNN model is composed of two parts: an encoding branch and a decoding branch. Our proposed network is represented in Fig. 4, the top branch being the encoding network and the bottom branch the decoding network.

Encoder. The encoder, inspired by Lun et al. [26], compresses the input data into feature vectors which are then passed to the decoder. In the proposed network, this feature extraction is composed of a series of 2D convolutions, down-scaling and activation layers. The size of every filter is shown in Fig. 4. Rather than using max-pooling for down-scaling, we make use of convolution layers with a stride of 2 as presented by Springenberg et al. [38]. As our aim is to predict the normals, which take values in the range $[-1, 1]$, our activation functions also need to let negative values pass through the network. Therefore, each group of operations (convolution/down-scale), is followed by leaky ReLUs (slope 0.3), avoiding the dying ReLUs issue when training.

Decoder. The decoder is used to up-sample the feature vector so that it has the original input resolution. Except for the last block, the decoder network is composed of a series of block operations composed of up-sampling layers (factor of 2), 2D convolutions (stride 1, kernel 4) and activation layers (Leaky ReLUs with slope = 0.3). Similarly to U-Net [32] we make use of symmetric skipping between layers of the same scale (between the encoder and the decoder) to reduce the information loss caused by successive dimension reduction. To do so, each level of the decoder is merged (channel-wise) with the block of the corresponding encoder level. Input details can then be preserved in the up-scaling blocks. The last block of operations only receives the first channel (Blue channel in Fig. 3) for merging as the other two channels would be irrelevant at this final level of reconstruction. Our output layer uses a sigmoidal hyperbolic tangent activation function since normals lie in the range $[-1, 1]$. The last layer is an L_2 normalization to ensure unit length of each normal.

3.3   Learning

Training Data. Training a CNN requires a very considerable dataset. In our case, our network requires a dataset of line drawing sketches with corresponding normal maps. Asking human subjects to provide 2D line drawings from a 3D model would be too labour-intensive and time consuming. Instead we apply an approach similar to Lun et al. [26], automatically generating line drawings from 3D models using different properties such as silhouette, border, contour, ridge and valley or material boundary. We use the Freestyle software implemented for Blender©[10] for this process. Using Blender©scripts we were able to automatically create high-resolution drawings from 3D models (42 viewpoints per 3D model), along with their corresponding normal maps. As we generate our normal maps from 3D models alone, all background pixels have the same background normal value of $[-1, 0, 0]$. This will be used in the loss function computation (see Sect. 3.3). Tiling the input full resolution image into 256×256 tiles also provides a tremendous data augmentation. We extract 200 randomly chosen tiles from every drawing, making sure that every chosen tile contains sufficient drawing information. Therefore our relatively small dataset of 420 images (extracted from ten 3D models) is augmented to an 84000 elements training dataset.

Loss Function. During the training, as we are only interested in measuring the similarity of the foreground pixels, we use a specific loss function:

$$L = \sum_p (1 - N_e(p) \cdot N_t(p)) \times \delta_p, \tag{1}$$

where $N_e(p)$ and $N_t(p)$ are the estimated and ground truth normals at pixel p respectively, and δ_p ensures that only foreground pixels are taken into account in the loss computation, being 0 whenever p is a background pixel (i.e. whenever $N_t = [-1, 0, 0]$) and 1 otherwise.

We train our model with the ADAM solver [20] (learning rate $= 0.001$) against our defined loss function. Finally, the learning process ends when the loss function converges.

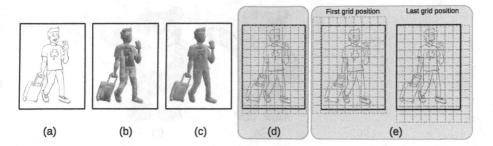

Fig. 5. Normal map reconstruction of the input sketch (a) using a direct naive sampling (b) and our multi-grid diagonal sampling (c). Sampling grids used in direct naive sampling (d) and multi-grid diagonal sampling (e).

3.4 Tile Reconstruction

As the network is designed to manage $256 \times 256 \times 3$ input elements, high-resolution drawings have to be sampled into $256 \times 256 \times 3$ tiles. These tiles are then passed through the network and outputs have to be combined together to form the expected high-resolution normal map. However, the deep reconstruction of normal maps is not always consistent across tile borders, and may be inaccurate when a tile misses important local strokes, as can be seen in Fig. 5(b). Direct naive tile reconstructions can therefore lead to inconsistent, blocky normal maps, which are not suitable for adding high-quality shading effects to sketches.

In order to overcome this issue, we propose a multi-grid diagonal sampling strategy as shown in Fig. 5(e). Rather than processing only one grid of tiles, we process multiple overlapping grids, as shown in Fig. 5(e). Each new grid is created by shifting the original grid (Fig. 5(d)) diagonally, each time by a different offset. Then at every pixel location, the predicted normals are averaged together to form the final normal map, as shown in Fig. 5(c). The use of diagonal shifting is an appropriate way to wipe away the blocky (mainly horizontal and vertical) sampling artifacts seen in Fig. 5(b) when computing the final normal map. Increasing the number of grids also improves the accuracy of the normal estimation, however, the computational cost also increases with the number of grids. We therefore measured the root mean squared error (RMSE) of the output normal map versus ground truth depending on the number of grids and found that using 10 grids is a good compromise between quality of estimation and efficiency (<1 s for a $1K \times 2K$ px input image).

3.5 Texturing and Rendering

Since only the normal maps are predicted, and the viewing angle remains the same, properties from the input image such as flat-colors or textures can be directly used for rendering. Once textured or colorized, any image based rendering can be applied to the sketch, as in Fig. 6(c), such as diffuse lighting, specular

Fig. 6. Different types of shading: One can also employ a stylized toon shader such as [2,4,23,45], or classic non-photorealistic technique imitating global illumination such as diffuse and/or specular, Fresnel effect etc.

lighting or Fresnel effect (as presented in [33]). For a more stylized effect one can also apply a toon shader, as in Fig. 6(b).

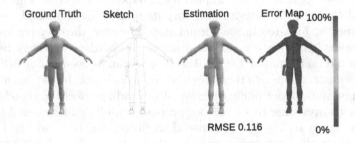

Fig. 7. Comparison of our normal estimation versus ground truth normal of a 3D model. From left to right: the ground truth normal map, the estimated sketch from the 3D model, our estimated normal map and finally the error map. This 3D model was not part of the training database.

4   Results and Discussion

In this section, we evaluate the full system using both qualitative and quantitative analysis. All the experiments are performed using line-drawings that are not included in our training database. Furthermore, as the training database only contains drawings with a line thickness of one pixel, we pre-process our input drawings using the thinning method proposed by Kwot [22].

We have implemented our deep normal estimation network using Python and Tensorflow [1]. The whole process takes less than 2.5 s for a 1220 × 2048 image running on an Intel Core i7 with 32 GB RAM and an Nvidia TITAN Xp. See Table 1 for a timing breakdown of each individual stage.

Table 1. Timings

Pre-processing	0.114 s
Single grid creation	0.012 s
Single grid prediction	0.054 s
Assembling grids	<0.1 s
Total time 1220 × 2048 - 10 Grids	2.328 s

Table 2. Tests results: Average error with L1, L2 and Angular metrics using our test database of 126 1K × 2K images, (FullyConv) Fully convolutional networks, (S2N) sketch to normals [39] with no user input on 256 × 256 images, (OursNoMS) our method without multi-scale input, (OursMS) our method.

Metric	FullyConv	S2N (256 × 256)	OursNoMS	OursMS
L1	0.244	0.227	0.208	**0.199**
L2	0.282	0.266	0.241	**0.231**
Angular	28.770	27.236	24.40	**23.468**

4.1 Quantitative Evaluation

We measure the accuracy of our method using a test database composed of 126 1K × 2K images, created with 3D models which are converted into sketches with the same non-photorealistic rendering technique we used to create our training database (see Sect. 3.3). This way, we can compare the result of our technique with the original normal ground truth of the 3D model which, of course, was not included in the training database.

Table 2 shows the numerical results of our different quantitative tests including our network with (OursMS) and without (OursNOMS) the multi-scale input, a fully convolutional network (FullyConv) trained on our database with patchwise training [25]. We also trained the network from [39] with our database, however with the code provided we were only able to process images at low resolution. The results shown in Table 2 for this method (S2N) are for 256 × 256 images, hence input images and ground truth normal maps had to be re-sized beforehand. For every metric, our method (with multi-scale input) was the most accurate. Also note that using our network in a fully convolutional way to process images of high resolution is not as accurate as using our tiling technique.

Figure 7 shows a test sketch along with the ground truth normal map, our reconstructed normal map with 10 grids and a visual colored error map. While the overall root mean square error measured on the normal map is relatively low, the main inaccuracies are located on the feet and details of the face and the bag (which might be because there are no similar objects to the bag in our database). Also, as the reconstruction depends highly on the sketch strokes, minor variations and/or artistic choices in the input drawings can lead to different levels of accuracy. For example, artists commonly draw very simplified face details with very few strokes rather than realistic ones, which is especially visible in the nose, ears and eyes. In fact, the non-photorealistic method used to generate the sketches is already an estimation of what a sketch based on a 3D model could look like. We see this effect, for example, looking at the difference between the ground truth and predicted normals at the bottom of the jacket in Fig. 7, as some lines are missing on the sketch estimation; an artist might make different drawing choices.

Fig. 8. Shading effects with different light configurations.

4.2 Visual Results

To show the versatility of our method we test it with a set of sketches with very different styles. Figure 12 presents results for four of these sketches: column (a) shows the original sketch, (b) the estimated normal map, (c) the flat-shaded sketch, and (d) shows the sketch after applying shading effects. As shown in column (b), normal maps present extremely fine details, which are correctly predicted in difficult areas such as fingers, cloth folds or faces; even the wrench, in the third row, is highly detailed. Column (d) shows the quality of shading that can be obtained using our system: final renders produce believable illumination and shading despite the absence of depth information. Once the normals are predicted, the user is able to render plausible shading effects consistently from any direction. This can be seen in Fig. 8, where we show several shading results using the same input drawing, by moving a virtual light around the cat.

Fig. 9. Normals obtained with our method (top) and possible shading (bottom).

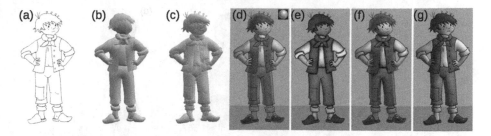

Fig. 10. Comparison with state-of-the-art methods. Input drawing (a), normals from the 3D reconstruction by [43] (b), our predicted normals (c), normal map based shading using Lumo [17] (d), 3D-like shading used in TexToons [40] (e), 3D reconstruction with global illumination effects [43] (e), Our approach (f). (3D model, line drawing and shading results from [43] kindly provided by the authors. Source drawing ©Anifilm. All rights reserved.)

Moreover, our method can be applied to single drawings as well as animations, without the need of any additional tools, as our method can directly and automatically generate normal maps for each individual frame of an animation. Our normal prediction remains consistent across all frames without the need to explicitly address temporal consistency or add any spatiotemporal filters. Figure 9 shows how shading is consistent and convincing along the animated sequence. As our normal vectors are estimated using training data, errors can occur in areas of sketches that are not similar to any object found in the database, such as the folded manual in the third row of Fig. 12. Such artifacts can be minimised by increasing the variety of objects captured by the training data. Furthermore, when boundary conditions are only suggested rather than drawn in the input drawing, it can result in unwanted smooth surface linking elements. An example of this effect can be seen between the cat's head and neck (Fig. 12, third row). The Ink-and-Ray approach presented in [43] handles such C^0 and C^1 boundary conditions (sparse depth inequalities, grafting, etc.) at the cost of additional user input. Finally, while most strokes in the sketch enhance the normal vector estimation, such as those around cloth folds, others only represent texture, and *texture copying* artifacts may appear when these are considered for normal estimation. However, an artist using our tool could easily avoid such unnecessary texture copying artifacts by drawing texture on a sepa-

Fig. 11. Line-drawing of the Utah teapot (left), normal obtained with our method (middle), shading effect (right).

Fig. 12. Our algorithm takes as input the artist line-art (a) and estimates a high-resolution and quality normal map (b). Flat colours (c) can now be augmented with shading effects (d).

rate layer. In Fig. 10, we compare our method to other state-of-the-art geometry based approaches: Lumo [17], TexToons [40] and the Ink-and-Ray pipeline [43]. We created shading effects using our own image-based render engine and tried to match our result as closely as possible to the lighting from [43] for an accurate qualitative comparison. While both Lumo [17] and our technique create 2D normal maps to generate shades, Lumo requires significant user interaction to generate their results. As neither our technique nor Lumo create a full 3D model, neither can add effects such as self-shadowing or inter-reflections. TexToons and

Ink-and-Ray are capable of producing such complex lighting effects, however, again at the cost of significant user interaction. Relative depth ordering added in TexToons via user input, allows for the simulation of ambient occlusion, while Ink-and-Ray requires a lot of user input to reconstruct a sufficient 3D model to allow for the addition of global illumination effects. However, in Fig. 10 we can observe that even without a 3D model, our technique can create high quality shading results without any user interaction, while also being very fast. Furthermore, also shown in Fig. 10, the normal map estimated by Ink-and-Ray is missing many of the finer details of the sketch. Our normal estimation in comparison is more accurate in areas such as folds, facial features, fingers, and hair.

The tiling method used to train the CNN has the effect that we learn normals of primitives rather than of full character shapes. Therefore we can also estimate normals for more generalised input data. Examples of this are shown in Fig. 12 (third row, wrench) and in Fig. 11: even though these objects are not represented in the training database, normals are correctly estimated, allowing us to render high-quality shading effects.

5   Conclusion and Future Work

In this paper we presented a CNN-based method for predicting high-quality and high-resolution normal maps from single line drawing images of characters. We demonstrated the effectiveness of our method for creating plausible shading effects for hand-drawn characters and animations with different types of rendering techniques. As opposed to recent state-of-the-art works, our method does not require any user annotation or interaction, which drastically reduces the labor that is drawing shades by hand. Our tool could be easily incorporated into the animation pipelines used nowadays, to increase efficiency of high quality production. We also showed that using a network in a fully convolutional way does not necessarily produce the most accurate results even when using patch-wise training. We believe and have proven that CNNs further push the boundaries of 3D reconstruction, and remove the need for laborious human interaction in the reconstruction process. While this work only focuses on reconstructing high fidelity normal maps, the CNN could be further extended to also reconstruct depth as in [26] and therefore full 3D models as in [43]. While we created a substantial training database we strongly believe that the predictions could be further improved and applicability extended by simply extending the training database. Other types of drawings could be added to the database such as everyday life objects. Dedicated CNNs could be pre-trained and made available for different types of objects (such as characters in our example here) if better customization is required.

Acknowledgements. The authors would like to thank David Revoy and Ester Huete, for sharing their original creations. This publication has emanated from research conducted with the financial support of Science Foundation Ireland (SFI) under the Grant Number 15/RP/2776. We gratefully acknowledge the support of NVIDIA Corporation with the donation of the Titan Xp GPU used for this research.

References

1. Abadi, M., et al.: Tensorflow: large-scale machine learning on heterogeneous distributed systems. arXiv preprint arXiv:1603.04467 (2016)
2. Anjyo, K.i., Wemler, S., Baxter, W.: Tweakable light and shade for cartoon animation. In: Proceedings of the 4th International Symposium on Non-photorealistic Animation and Rendering, pp. 133–139. ACM (2006)
3. Bansal, A., Russell, B., Gupta, A.: Marr revisited: 2D–3D alignment via surface normal prediction. In: Proceedings of the IEEE Conference on Computer Vision and Pattern Recognition, pp. 5965–5974 (2016)
4. Barla, P., Thollot, J., Markosian, L.: X-Toon: an extended toon shader. In: Proceedings of the 4th International Symposium on Non-photorealistic Animation and Rendering, pp. 127–132. ACM (2006)
5. Belhumeur, P.N., Kriegman, D.J., Yuille, A.L.: The bas-relief ambiguity. Int. J. Comput. Vis. **35**(1), 33–44 (1999)
6. Bui, M.T., Kim, J., Lee, Y.: 3D-look shading from contours and hatching strokes. Comput. Graph. **51**, 167–176 (2015)
7. Cole, F., et al.: How well do line drawings depict shape? In: ACM Transactions on Graphics (ToG), vol. 28, p. 28. ACM (2009)
8. Eigen, D., Fergus, R.: Predicting depth, surface normals and semantic labels with a common multi-scale convolutional architecture. In: Proceedings of the IEEE International Conference on Computer Vision, pp. 2650–2658 (2015)
9. Feng, L., Yang, X., Xiao, S., Jiang, F.: An interactive 2D-to-3D cartoon modeling system. In: El Rhalibi, A., Tian, F., Pan, Z., Liu, B. (eds.) Edutainment 2016. LNCS, vol. 9654, pp. 193–204. Springer, Cham (2016). https://doi.org/10.1007/978-3-319-40259-8_17
10. Grabli, S., Turquin, E., Durand, F., Sillion, F.X.: Programmable rendering of line drawing from 3D scenes. ACM Trans. Graph. (TOG) **29**(2), 18 (2010)
11. Han, X., Gao, C., Yu, Y.: DeepSketch2Face: a deep learning based sketching system for 3D face and caricature modeling. arXiv preprint arXiv:1706.02042 (2017)
12. Henz, B., Oliveira, M.M.: Artistic relighting of paintings and drawings. Vis. Comput. **33**(1), 33–46 (2017)
13. Huang, H., Kalogerakis, E., Yumer, E., Mech, R.: Shape synthesis from sketches via procedural models and convolutional networks. IEEE Trans. Vis. Comput. Graph. **23**(8), 2003–2013 (2017)
14. Hudon, M., Pagés, R., Grogan, M., Ondřej, J., Smolić, A.: 2D shading for cel animation. In: Expressive The Joint Symposium on Computational Aesthetics and Sketch Based Interfaces and Modeling and Non-photorealistic Animation and Rendering (2018)
15. Igarashi, T., Matsuoka, S., Tanaka, H.: Teddy: A sketching interface for 3D freeform design. In: SIGGRAPH 1999 Conference Proceedings. ACM (1999)
16. Jayaraman, P.K., Fu, C.W., Zheng, J., Liu, X., Wong, T.T.: Globally consistent wrinkle-aware shading of line drawings. IEEE Trans. Vis. Comput. Graph. **24**(7), 2103–2117 (2017)
17. Johnston, S.F.: Lumo: illumination for cel animation. In: Proceedings of the 2nd International Symposium on Non-photorealistic Animation and Rendering, pp. 45–ff. ACM (2002)
18. Karpenko, O.A., Hughes, J.F.: Smoothsketch: 3D free-form shapes from complex sketches. In: ACM Transactions on Graphics (TOG), vol. 25, pp. 589–598. ACM (2006)

19. Kersten, D., Mamassian, P., Knill, D.C.: Moving cast shadows induce apparent motion in depth. Perception **26**(2), 171–192 (1997)
20. Kingma, D., Ba, J.: Adam: a method for stochastic optimization. arXiv preprint arXiv:1412.6980 (2014)
21. Koenderink, J.J., Van Doorn, A.J., Kappers, A.M.: Surface perception in pictures. Atten. Percept. Psycho. **52**(5), 487–496 (1992)
22. Kwok, P.: A thinning algorithm by contour generation. Commun. ACM **31**(11), 1314–1324 (1988)
23. Lee, Y., Markosian, L., Lee, S., Hughes, J.F.: Line drawings via abstracted shading. In: ACM Transactions on Graphics (TOG), vol. 26, p. 18. ACM (2007)
24. Li, C., Liu, X., Wong, T.T.: Deep extraction of manga structural lines. ACM Trans. Graph. (TOG) **36**(4), 117 (2017)
25. Long, J., Shelhamer, E., Darrell, T.: Fully convolutional networks for semantic segmentation. In: Proceedings of the IEEE Conference on Computer Vision and Pattern Recognition, pp. 3431–3440 (2015)
26. Lun, Z., Gadelha, M., Kalogerakis, E., Maji, S., Wang, R.: 3D shape reconstruction from sketches via multi-view convolutional networks. arXiv preprint arXiv:1707.06375 (2017)
27. Olsen, L., Samavati, F.F., Sousa, M.C., Jorge, J.A.: Sketch-based modeling: a survey. Comput. Graph. **33**(1), 85–103 (2009)
28. Pan, H., Liu, Y., Sheffer, A., Vining, N., Li, C.J., Wang, W.: Flow aligned surfacing of curve networks. ACM Trans. Graph. (TOG) **34**(4), 127 (2015)
29. Petrović, L., Fujito, B., Williams, L., Finkelstein, A.: Shadows for cel animation. In: Proceedings of the 27th Annual Conference on Computer Graphics and Interactive Techniques, pp. 511–516. ACM Press/Addison-Wesley Publishing Co. (2000)
30. Pontes, J.K., Kong, C., Sridharan, S., Lucey, S., Eriksson, A., Fookes, C.: Image2Mesh: a learning framework for single image 3D reconstruction. arXiv preprint arXiv:1711.10669 (2017)
31. Rematas, K., Ritschel, T., Fritz, M., Gavves, E., Tuytelaars, T.: Deep reflectance maps. In: Proceedings of the IEEE Conference on Computer Vision and Pattern Recognition, pp. 4508–4516 (2016)
32. Ronneberger, O., Fischer, P., Brox, T.: U-Net: convolutional networks for biomedical image segmentation. In: Navab, N., Hornegger, J., Wells, W.M., Frangi, A.F. (eds.) MICCAI 2015. LNCS, vol. 9351, pp. 234–241. Springer, Cham (2015). https://doi.org/10.1007/978-3-319-24574-4_28
33. Schlick, C.: An inexpensive BRDF model for physically-based rendering. In: Computer Graphics Forum, vol. 13, pp. 233–246. Wiley Online Library (1994)
34. Schmidt, R., Khan, A., Singh, K., Kurtenbach, G.: Analytic drawing of 3D scaffolds. In: ACM Transactions on Graphics (TOG), vol. 28, p. 149. ACM (2009)
35. Shao, C., Bousseau, A., Sheffer, A., Singh, K.: CrossShade: shading concept sketches using cross-section curves. ACM Trans. Graph. **31**(4) (2012). https://doi.org/10.1145/2185520.2185541. https://hal.inria.fr/hal-00703202
36. Simo-Serra, E., Iizuka, S., Ishikawa, H.: Mastering sketching: adversarial augmentation for structured prediction. arXiv preprint arXiv:1703.08966 (2017)
37. Simo-Serra, E., Iizuka, S., Sasaki, K., Ishikawa, H.: Learning to simplify: fully convolutional networks for rough sketch cleanup. ACM Trans. Graph. (TOG) **35**(4), 121 (2016)
38. Springenberg, J.T., Dosovitskiy, A., Brox, T., Riedmiller, M.: Striving for simplicity: the all convolutional net. arXiv preprint arXiv:1412.6806 (2014)

39. Su, W., Du, D., Yang, X., Zhou, S., Hongbo, F.: Interactive sketch-based normal map generation with deep neural networks. In: ACM SIGGRAPH Symposium on Interactive 3D Graphics and Games (i3D 2018). ACM (2018)

40. Sỳkora, D., Ben-Chen, M., Čadík, M., Whited, B., Simmons, M.: Textoons: practical texture mapping for hand-drawn cartoon animations. In: Proceedings of the ACM SIGGRAPH/Eurographics Symposium on Non-photorealistic Animation and Rendering, pp. 75–84. ACM (2011)

41. Sỳkora, D., Dingliana, J., Collins, S.: As-rigid-as-possible image registration for hand-drawn cartoon animations. In: Proceedings of the 7th International Symposium on Non-photorealistic Animation and Rendering, pp. 25–33. ACM (2009)

42. Sỳkora, D., Dingliana, J., Collins, S.: Lazybrush: flexible painting tool for hand-drawn cartoons. In: Computer Graphics Forum, vol. 28, pp. 599–608. Wiley Online Library (2009)

43. Sỳkora, D., et al.: Ink-and-ray: bas-relief meshes for adding global illumination effects to hand-drawn characters. ACM Trans. Graph. (TOG) **33**(2), 16 (2014)

44. Tatarchenko, M., Dosovitskiy, A., Brox, T.: Multi-view 3D models from single images with a convolutional network. In: Leibe, B., Matas, J., Sebe, N., Welling, M. (eds.) ECCV 2016. LNCS, vol. 9911, pp. 322–337. Springer, Cham (2016). https://doi.org/10.1007/978-3-319-46478-7_20

45. Todo, H., Anjyo, K.I., Baxter, W., Igarashi, T.: Locally controllable stylized shading. ACM Trans. Graph. (TOG) **26**(3), 17 (2007)

46. Tuan, B.M., Kim, J., Lee, Y.: Height-field construction using cross contours. Comput. Graph. **66**, 53–63 (2017)

47. Wang, X., Fouhey, D., Gupta, A.: Designing deep networks for surface normal estimation. In: Proceedings of the IEEE Conference on Computer Vision and Pattern Recognition, pp. 539–547 (2015)

48. Wanger, L.R., Ferwerda, J.A., Greenberg, D.P.: Perceiving spatial relationships in computer-generated images. IEEE Comput. Graph. Appl. **12**(3), 44–58 (1992)

49. Whited, B., Noris, G., Simmons, M., Sumner, R.W., Gross, M., Rossignac, J.: BetweenIT: an interactive tool for tight inbetweening. In: Computer Graphics Forum, vol. 29, pp. 605–614. Wiley Online Library (2010)

50. Xing, J., Wei, L.Y., Shiratori, T., Yatani, K.: Autocomplete hand-drawn animations. ACM Trans. Graph. (TOG) **34**(6), 169 (2015)

51. Xu, B., Chang, W., Sheffer, A., Bousseau, A., McCrae, J., Singh, K.: True2Form: 3D curve networks from 2D sketches via selective regularization. ACM Trans. Graph. **33**(4), 131 (2014)

52. Zhang, L., Ji, Y., Lin, X.: Style transfer for anime sketches with enhanced residual U-Net and auxiliary classifier GAN. arXiv preprint arXiv:1706.03319 (2017)

3D Surface Reconstruction by Pointillism

Olivia Wiles$^{(\boxtimes)}$ and Andrew Zisserman

Visual Geometry Group, Department of Engineering Science,
University of Oxford, Oxford, UK
{ow,az}@robots.ox.ac.uk

Abstract. The objective of this work is to infer the 3D shape of an object from a single image. We use sculptures as our training and test bed, as these have great variety in shape and appearance.

To achieve this we build on the success of multiple view geometry (MVG) which is able to accurately provide *correspondences* between images of 3D objects under varying viewpoint and illumination conditions, and make the following contributions: first, we introduce a new loss function that can harness image-to-image correspondences to provide a supervisory signal to train a deep network to infer a depth map. The network is trained end-to-end by differentiating through the camera. Second, we develop a processing pipeline to automatically generate a large scale multi-view set of correspondences for training the network. Finally, we demonstrate that we can indeed obtain a depth map of a novel object from a single image for a variety of sculptures with varying shape/texture, and that the network generalises at test time to new domains (e.g. synthetic images).

1 Introduction

Humans are able to effortlessly perceive 3D shape of a previously unseen object from a single image – or at least we have the impression that we do this. For example for a piecewise smooth sculpture such as the one by Henry Moore in Fig. 1, we know where there are concavities, convexities and saddles, as well as where there are holes and sharp points. *How* this is achieved has long been studied in computer vision in terms of geometric cues from the silhouette [1], the texture [2–4], self-shadows, specularities [5], shading [6,7], chiaroscuro [8], etc.

In this paper our objective is to be able to reconstruct such objects from a single image. Deep learning has significantly boosted progress in 3D reconstruction from single images, but so far methods have mostly depended on the availability of synthetic 3D training examples, or using a single class, or pre-processing the data using SfM and MVS to extract depth. In contrast, our self-supervised approach is to learn directly from real images, capitalizing on many years of research

Electronic supplementary material The online version of this chapter (https:// doi.org/10.1007/978-3-030-11015-4_21) contains supplementary material, which is available to authorized users.

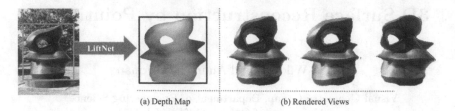

(a) Depth Map   (b) Rendered Views

Fig. 1. Given this image of the *Spindle Piece* by *Henry Moore*, LiftNet predicts the 3D shape of the sculpture via a depth map (a), where blue is further away and yellow nearer, and thereby enables new views to be rendered (b). LiftNet is trained self-supervised on real images using correspondences *without* any knowledge of depth or camera parameters. (Color figure online)

on MVG [9–12] that is able to automatically determine matching views of a 3D object and generate point correspondences, without requiring any explicit 3D information as supervision.

The key idea is to use image-to-image point correspondences to provide a *training* loss on the depth map predicted by a CNN, called *LiftNet*. This is illustrated in Fig. 2. Suppose we are attempting to infer the depth of the object in a *source* view, and there are a number of image point correspondences available between the *source* view and a *target* view (where a correspondence is defined by the projection of a 3D surface point into the source and target views). A correspondence can be computed in two ways. First, it can be computed using matching methods from MVG (such as SIFT, and epipolar geometry). This method does not involve using the depth of the surface and we treat these correspondences as ground truth. Second, it can be computed by inferring the depth of the point in the *source* view and projecting the 3D point into the *target* view. If the CNN correctly predicts the depth of the points in the *source* view, then the projected points will coincide with the ground truth correspondences in the *target* view; however, if the depth prediction is incorrect, then the distance between the projected and corresponding points – the re-projection error – defines a loss that can be used to train the network.

Of course, the correspondences between two views of a particular sculpture only provide constraints at those points on the surface – and correspondences will mainly be found at surface texture, surface discontinuities, and boundaries [13], i.e. not uniformly across the surface. However, for each sculpture there are multiple pairs of images; and each pair can 'probe' (and constrain) different points on the surface according to its correspondences. Finally, and most importantly, the network must learn to predict correspondences not just for a particular sculpture, but for *all* the sculptures (and all their view pairs) in the training set – and we have 170K training pairs and around 31M training correspondences. The only way it can solve this task is to infer 3D shape for each image.

To this end, we formulate a new deep learning framework for extracting 3D shape which is similar to the artistic *pointillist* style. Analogously to how pointillists build up colour variation in an image from dots of discrete colour, we use points in correspondence between images of an object in order to train a network over time to learn the 3D shape of the object.

Contributions. This work presents three contributions: first, to use corresponding points to formulate a differentiable loss on the object shape that can be used to train a network from scratch (Sect. 3). The formulation includes differentiating through the camera to train the network end-to-end.

The second contribution is a pipeline based on MVG for automatically extracting robust correspondences between multiple pairs of images of a sculpture (Sect. 4). We use these correspondences to train the network on real images, *without* ground truth 3D depth information. This is done entirely automatically and is the first system to our knowledge to learn to predict shape end-to-end for a set of objects by using correspondences and geometry in this manner.

The final contribution is our experimental results in Sect. 5, which demonstrate that the trained network can not only predict depth for the given domain but also generalises to synthetic data, allowing its generalisation capability to be evaluated quantitatively.

2 Related Work

Depth Prediction. The ability to learn depth using a deep learning framework was introduced by [14], who use a dataset of ground truth depth and RGB image pairs to train a network to predict depth. This has been improved on with better architectures in [15,16] and generalised to ordinal relationships in [17,18].

A recent set of works have considered how to extract the 3D depth of a scene between pairs of images without knowing the camera motion or depth [19–22]. This is done by predicting both depth and cameras in the network. This information is then used to transform one view and the photometric error between the generated image and the ground truth is used to train the network. These works require that the two images be very similar, such that the photometric error gives a robust and sensible loss. As a result, the images come from stereo datasets or consecutive video frames, such that the relative appearance change is small. On the other hand, our approach uses point correspondences directly, and consequently the images can vary dramatically in illumination, texture, size, position, etc. and our loss is robust to these changes.

3D Shape Prediction. Going beyond depth prediction, which is view based, the entire 3D shape of the object can be reconstructed from multiple views by using strong supervision from the known 3D geometry to predict a voxel [23,24] or point cloud [25–27] representation. Alternatively, the supervision can be from photo consistency or silhouette constraints [28–32]. However, these methods require knowledge of the camera parameters in order to enforce the geometric constraints.

These methods have been extended to deal with natural images in the work of [33–35], but [33] still requires a synthetic dataset on which to train their network which is then fine-tuned on real images. [34] uses structure from motion

(SfM)/multi-view stereo (MVS) [9] from a video sequence as the ground truth 3D shape on which to train their network for reconstructing a finite set of classes; [35] extends this idea to unordered image collection of historic landmarks by using many images of the given landmark. In our case, we are not restricted to a finite set of classes, and do not require a video sequence or many images of the same scene in order to obtain a dense reconstruction, but instead train from the available correspondences directly, and these correspondences only need to exist over a handful of images. As a result, our approach can be used with far fewer samples of each landmark or sculpture.

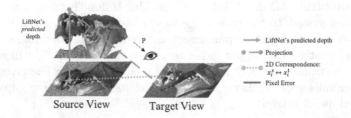

Fig. 2. An illustration of the training loss: $\mathcal{L}_{\text{corr}}$. Given $\mathbf{x}_i^s \leftrightarrow \mathbf{x}_i^t$ and the best camera P, we minimise the error between $\mathbf{PX}_i$ and $\mathbf{x}_i^t$. The depth d_i value of $\mathbf{X}_i$ is LiftNet's predicted depth for the *source* view at $\mathbf{x}_i^s$. If d_i were correctly predicted by LiftNet there would be no error as $\mathbf{X}_i$ would project to $\mathbf{x}_i^t$; the image distance between the projected point and $\mathbf{x}_i^t$ provides the training loss. As the network's prediction improves, the distance reduces to zero.

3   Approach

The goal is to recover 3D structure from a single image by predicting a depth map, but *without* requiring ground truth 3D information in training. In this section we first define the loss functions used to train the network. Then the LiftNet architecture is described in Sect. 3.3. In the following we assume that correspondences between images are available (as described in Sect. 4).

As introduced in Sect. 1, the depth predicted by the LiftNet CNN in the *source* view is supervised by using point correspondences as follows: (i) let the set of correspondences be denoted as $\mathbf{x}_i^s \leftrightarrow \mathbf{x}_i^t$, where $\mathbf{x}_i^s$ are the points in the *source* view, and $\mathbf{x}_i^t$ the points in the *target* view. (ii) Then in the *source* view we can determine the 3D points $\mathbf{X}_i$ that project to $\mathbf{x}_i^s$ (since the network gives the depth of each point). (iii) Since we know the correspondence between $\mathbf{X}_i$ and $\mathbf{x}_i^t$ we can compute the best camera that projects the 3D points $\mathbf{X}_i$ into the *target* view. (iv) If the 3D shape has been predicted perfectly, then the 3D points $\mathbf{X}_i$ will project perfectly onto $\mathbf{x}_i^t$. If they do not, then this *reprojection error* provides a loss that can be minimized to train the network. The resulting loss is defined as:

$$\mathcal{L}_{\text{corr}} = \frac{1}{N} \sum_{i=1}^{N} d_R(\mathbf{PX}_i, \mathbf{x}_i^t); \tag{1}$$

where $d_R(.,.)$ denotes the Euclidean (L_2) pixel distance between vectors subject to a robustness function R.

This loss is a useful constraint, as it enforces important properties of the object, such as concavities and convexities. Moreover, this can be done for any pair of images for which correspondences can be obtained. There is no requirement that the images be photometrically consistent – e.g. lighting, texture, position etc. can vary dramatically between views.

Finally, a robustness term R is added (Sect. 3.2), as the 2D correspondences may be noisy (as explained in Sect. 4).

3.1 Point Correspondence Loss $\mathcal{L}_{\text{corr}}$

We minimise the projection error between $\mathbf{X}_i$ and $\mathbf{x}_i^t$ using the best camera $P: \frac{1}{N}\sum_{i=1}^{N} d_R(P\mathbf{X}_i, \mathbf{x}_i^t)$. The steps are as follows:

A. Choose the Camera. This work assumes an affine camera and an orthogonal coordinate system in the *source* view, which is why $\mathbf{X}_i = [x_i^s, y_i^s, d_i, 1]^T$ projects to $\mathbf{x}_i^s = (x_i^s, y_i^s)$ in the *source* view. As has been noted previously [9,36,37], the affine case is a very stable and useful approximation to perspective projection. The reader is referred to the supplementary material for a detailed review of this camera model. However, we note that the ideas presented here (e.g. the method of differentiating the camera) generalise in a straight forward manner to the perspective case.

B. Determine the Camera. We first determine the camera matrix P by solving the system of equations $\mathbf{x}_i^t = P\,\mathbf{X}_i$ for P. We know which values $\mathbf{X}_i$ and $\mathbf{x}_i^t$ should correspond because LiftNet's prediction is simply a depth map, so $\mathbf{x}_i^s = (x_i^s, y_i^s)$ in pixels maps to $\mathbf{X}_i = [x_i^s, y_i^s, d_i, 1]^T$ (d_i is the depth prediction at that point) and we know, via the correspondences, that $\mathbf{x}_i^s \leftrightarrow \mathbf{x}_i^t$, so $\mathbf{X}_i$ maps to $\mathbf{x}_i^t$. This gives the following system of equations:

$$\begin{bmatrix} x_1^t \dots x_N^t \\ y_1^t \dots y_N^t \end{bmatrix} = P \begin{bmatrix} x_1^s \dots x_N^s \\ y_1^s \dots y_N^s \\ d_1 \dots d_N \\ 1 \dots 1 \end{bmatrix}. \tag{2}$$

However, directly solving the system of equations would be problematic due to the effect of outliers, (e.g. noise in the data). A standard approach to deal with noise is to make use of RANSAC [38]. This method solves a system of equations by finding a solution that satisfies the most constraints. The satisfied constraints are called inliers, the others outliers. In our case, we want to find P such that the maximum number of pairs $\mathbf{X}_i$ and $\mathbf{x}_i^t$ satisfy the condition $|\mathbf{x}_i^t - P\mathbf{X}_i|_2 < T$ for some threshold T. Given the set of inliers $\mathbf{X}_{i_{\text{inliers}}}, \mathbf{x}_{i_{\text{inliers}}}^t$, a new system of linear equations is constructed: $\mathbf{x}_{i_{\text{inliers}}}^t = P\mathbf{X}_{i_{\text{inliers}}}$.

C. Compute the Loss. Given P, all points $\mathbf{X}_i$ are projected into the *target* view and the error between their projection and known location $\mathbf{x}_i^t$ is computed. The loss is then as given in (1).

D. Differentiate Through the Camera. In order to train the network end to end, it is necessary to compute the derivative $\frac{\partial P}{\partial d_i}$. To do this, we re-write the system of equations such that P is explicitly a function of $x^t_{i_{\text{inliers}}}/X_{i_{\text{inliers}}}$ such that computing the derivative is straightforward. For ease of notation, the matrix of inliers $X_{i_{\text{inliers}}}$ is referred to as X and of inliers $x_{i_{\text{inliers}}}$ as x from now on. The pseudo-inverse X^+ is computed using the singular value decomposition (SVD) [39]. (If the SVD of a matrix A is $A = U\Sigma V^T$ then its pseudo inverse can be written as $A^+ = V\Sigma^+ U^T$.) Then the system of equations can be re-written as:

$$x = PX \tag{3}$$

$$x^T = X^T P^T \tag{4}$$

$$(X^T)^+ x^T \approx (X^T)^+ X^T P^T \approx P^T \tag{5}$$

$$(V\Sigma^+ U^T) x^T = P^T \tag{6}$$

Note that because the system of equations in (2) is over-constrained then of course this is not an exact solution, but the pseudo-inverse solves the system of equations in the least-squares sense [39] which is what we require. Also, note that because the outliers are ignored when computing P due to RANSAC, we can ignore them in this computation and only consider the inliers. This gives the forward pass.

To perform the backward pass, it is necessary to compute the derivative $\frac{\partial P}{\partial d_i}$. This is a straight-forward application of the product and chain rule, except for the computation of the SVD. However, previous work (e.g. [40]) has demonstrated how to compute these derivatives. As a result we can back-propagate through the computation of P to the estimation of the height values d_i. This is achieved in practice using standard layers in a neural network library (e.g. PyTorch [41]). Note that computing the gradients for U, V could lead to potential instability if X^T is not full rank or has repeated singular values; however, this was not a problem in practice.

Discussion. We note that our method computes **d** up to an overall affine ambiguity. This amounts to a scaling and shearing in the depth prediction. This ambiguity is seen in human vision, as humans have been shown to reconstruct objects (such as vases) up to an affine transformation in depth [42,43]. It is hypothesised that this difficulty arises from the fact that, assuming Lambertian reflectance and given a single image, the surface of an object can only be recovered up to a generalized bas-relief ambiguity [44].

3.2 Robustness

As the correspondences and segmentations will be noisy, it is necessary that the loss function is robust to these errors. To do this we use a smooth function to weight the errors [45] so that errors above a threshold τ are given a constant cost:
$$\mathcal{R}(x) = \begin{cases} \frac{1}{2}x^2(1 - \frac{x^2}{2\tau^2}), & \text{if } x^2 \leq \tau^2 \\ \tau^2/4, & \text{otherwise} \end{cases}.$$

3.3 Architecture

The architecture used is based on the U-Net [46] variant of pix2pix [47]. This architecture includes skip connections in order to maintain high level detail. However, we incorporate two modifications. First the last activation is replaced by a tanh layer to enforce that the output lies between $[-1, 1]$. We impose this range so that the predicted depth does not grow too large, making training unstable. As LiftNet learns depth up to a scaling factor in depth, this in no way constrains the types of surfaces that LiftNet can describe. Second, the nearest neighbour upsampler is replaced by a bilinear upsampler. This mitigates against pixelated effects [48,49]. Please refer to the supp. material for full details.

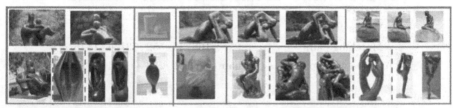

(a) The images are organised by artist (solid lines) into clusters (dashed lines). Note the variety and complexity of the sculptures: in shape, materials, lighting, and viewpoint.

(b) Sample correspondences for pairs of images. The images may be taken at different times of year, in different contexts/illumination conditions and the material itself may change over time due to weather.

Fig. 3. The Sculpture dataset. Note that this is only a tiny subset of the clusters and a fraction of the number of images within a cluster. Please refer to the supp. material for more examples.

4 The Sculpture Dataset

We assemble a large scale dataset of images of sculptures for training and testing by combining multiple public datasets [13,50–52] and downloading additional images from the web. The dataset incorporates a wide variety of artists, styles and materials. It is divided at the artist level to prevent any information bleeding between the sets. Table 1 gives the number of artists and works used as well as the train/val/test splits.

The dataset includes multiple works (sculptures) by different artists (sculptors) organised into a set of clusters. Within a cluster, the images are of the same sculpture (shape), but there may be multiple instances of the sculpture, some made of different material. The utility of the dataset is that within a cluster there are many point correspondences between image pairs that can be used for training the network. Figure 3 shows a sample of sculptures, correspondences and an example cluster.

Table 1. Dataset statistics for the Sculpture dataset. Note the large number of artists and works. This results in a large variety of styles and shapes that LiftNet must contend with. A total of 31M point correspondences ($\approx$181 correspondences $\times 169K$ pairs) are automatically generated and used to train LiftNet.

	Train	Val	Test	All
#Artists	138	7	1	143
#Works	1031	27	129	1187
#Matching pairs	168726	552	13166	182K
Avg # correspondences per pair	181	223	174	181

The remainder of this section describes the steps used to download, prepare, and obtain the image pair correspondences of the dataset. Additional details are given in the supplementary material.

Image Extraction. We combine multiple sculpture datasets: [13,50–52] and download additional images from the web.

Obtaining Segmentations. To segment the images, RefineNET [53] is trained on 2000 hand-labelled sculptures by artists *Rodin* and *Henry Moore*. It achieves a 0.94 IoU score and 0.97 accuracy on the validation dataset. This is used for a wide variety of images and it generalises well to new sculptures.

Obtaining Correspondences. The final step is to determine a valid set of correspondences. The OpenMVG pipeline [54] is used to extract an initial dense list of correspondences between pairs of images. The segmentation from RefineNET above is then used to mask out correspondences from the irrelevant background parts of the image. Additionally those correspondences that do not satisfy the affine fundamental matrix, which is computed using RANSAC, are removed. Finally, those image pairs that can be mapped by an affine homography (i.e. a 2D transformation between images) are thrown out, as they will not provide a constraint on 3D structure.

Despite these post-processing steps, there will still be noise in the correspondences, motivating the use of a robust cost in our losses explained in Sect. 3.

5   Experiments

A challenge of our framework is to determine its prediction quality, as there is *no* ground truth depth information for the automatically collected Sculpture

dataset. To this end, LiftNet is evaluated in multiple environments and scenarios. *First*, we use a realistic synthetic dataset of sculptures SketchFab [55]
and ShapeNet [56] for which we can determine ground truth information and
thereby correspondences between views; these are introduced below. LiftNet is
then trained using these generated correspondences and compared to a baseline trained to explicitly regress depth on Sects. 5.3 and 5.4. *Second*, we train
LiftNet on real data: the Sculpture dataset. This network is then compared to
a number of self-supervised and supervised methods in Sect. 5.5. This evaluation is performed on two datasets: first it is performed on Scanned, a dataset of
scanned objects. Second, the evaluation is performed on SketchFab (despite the
domain gap between real and synthetic images the network generalises to this
new domain). Finally, it is evaluated qualitatively on the Sculpture dataset in
Sect. 5.6.

5.1   Datasets, Evaluation Metrics, and Baselines

The SketchFab and ShapeNet Datasets. SketchFab is a large dataset of synthetic 3D models of sculptures generated using photogrammetry. There are 425
sculptures divided into 372/20/33 train/val/test sculptures. ShapeNet consists
of multiple semantic classes, each of which is divided into train/val/test using
the given splits. For evaluation, five views of each SketchFab object and 10 views
of each ShapeNet object are rendered in Blender [57] using orthographic projection and the ground truth depth extracted. The SketchFab objects are viewed
with azimuth $\in [0°, 120°]$, elevation $0°$ whereas ShapeNet objects are viewed
with azimuth $\in [0°, 360°]$ and elevation $\in [-45°, 45°]$. As the depth and cameras
of the renders are known, the ground truth correspondences between images can
be determined by projecting the depth in the *source* view into the *target* view.

Scanned. Additional data is collected from the 80 sculpture videos of [58]. These
are taken 'in-the-wild' with a hand-held camera. Of these videos, 11 objects are
chosen and the sculpture region segmented. This gives 208 images for testing.

Evaluation Metrics. The results are reported using multiple metrics: the
L_1 error, root mean squared error, relative L_1 error, and squared rel. difference [14]. To evaluate the depth prediction, it is necessary to take into account
the ambiguity in the z axis (the depth prediction). This is done by allowing
for a scaling/translation in depth. Thus for all models (including those trained
on ground truth depth), when reporting results, the depth prediction d_{pred} for
an image is first normalised by $d^*_{\text{pred}} = \alpha(d_{\text{pred}} - \beta_1) + \beta_2$ where β_1 is the
median of d_{pred}, β_2 is the median of d_{gt} and α allows for a scaling in depth:
$\alpha = \sum_{xy}(d_{\text{pred}} * d_{gt})/\sum_{xy}(d^2_{\text{pred}})$. ($d_{gt}$ denotes ground truth and $\sum_{xy}$ denotes
summation over pixel locations.)

Baselines. In the evaluation on synthetic data, we compare against a supervised baseline, explicitly trained to regress depth. We use the same network (e.g.

pix2pix) as LiftNet. The MSELoss is used but after first accounting for a scaling and translation in depth as follows. If the depth predicted is d_{pred} then the normalised depth is $d_{\mathrm{pred}}^* = \alpha(d_{\mathrm{pred}} - \beta_1) + \beta_2$, which is computed as described above for the evaluation metrics. The loss is then $|d_{\mathrm{pred}}^* - d_{gt}|_2$.

5.2 Training

The network is trained as follows. Two images with correspondences are sampled from the dataset; one is designated *source*, the other *target*. The *source* view is then input to LiftNet, which predicts the depth at all pixels. The predicted depth of the foreground pixels d_i, concatenated with the x_i, y_i position of the pixel in the image give the 3D points in the *source* view $\mathbf{X}_i = [x_i, y_i, d_i, 1]^T$. The correspondence loss – $\mathcal{L}_{\mathrm{corr}}$ – is then imposed on these 3D points.

At *test* time (visualised in Fig. 4), an image is simply input to the network. This gives the depth prediction for all pixels. For visualisation purposes, the sculpture (the foreground pixels) are segmented from the background and only the depth values at these foreground pixels is shown.

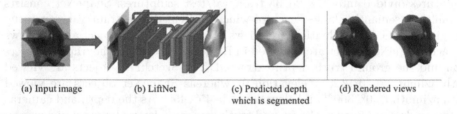

(a) Input image   (b) LiftNet   (c) Predicted depth   (d) Rendered views
                                                which is segmented

Fig. 4. The test time pipeline for LiftNet. (a) An image is selected from the test dataset and input to LiftNet (Sect. 3.3). (b) LiftNet gives a depth map prediction at all points. (c–d) The rendered depth is then segmented and visualised at new views. (This is a sample result on the test set.)

The models are trained on a single Titan GPU in PyTorch [59]. They take about half a day to train. All models trained on the Sculpture dataset are trained as follows. The models are trained with SGD, a learning rate of $1e^{-5}$, and momentum of 0.9. The gradients are clamped to ± 5. These models are trained until the correspondence error on the Sculpture dataset's validation set stops decreasing. When trained on SketchFab or ShapeNet, models are trained with SGD a learning rate of $1e^{-3}$, and momentum of 0.9. The gradients are clamped to ± 5. They are trained until the correspondence error on the validation set stops decreasing or a maximum of 200 epochs.

5.3 Quantitative Results on ShapeNet

In this section, we evaluate LiftNet on ShapeNet. In order to test the correspondence loss, 50 correspondences per pair of images of an object are randomly chosen and fixed using the known depth and camera transformation. This gives the training set.

The results are reported in Table 2 and LiftNet is compared to training the same network architecture (i.e. pix2pix) but directly regressing the ground truth depth up to a scaling and translation in depth as described above.

Table 2. Comparison of 'LiftNet trained on ShapeNet correspondences' to 'pix2pix trained using a MSE loss on ShapeNet'. The error measure is RMSE ($\times$ 100).

	rif.	boo.	bus	bed	spe.	cab.	lam.	cha.	tra.	pla.	tab.	dis.	mot.	car	wat.	pho.	sofa
pix2pix	**1.71**	2.14	**1.89**	2.16	1.66	1.76	1.44	1.87	**1.71**	**0.90**	2.52	2.28	**1.71**	1.33	**1.36**	1.56	2.19
LiftNet	2.03	**1.94**	2.11	**1.21**	**1.29**	**1.21**	**1.38**	**0.94**	2.06	1.05	**1.51**	**1.66**	1.92	**1.12**	1.51	**1.52**	**1.34**

These results are perhaps surprising, as LiftNet does better on multiple classes and comparably on most. Thus, training with a limited number of correspondences can yield comparable results to training with dense depth.

5.4   Quantitative Results on SketchFab

In this section, LiftNet is evaluated on a synthetic dataset of sculptures, Sketch-Fab, which has more varied shapes than ShapeNet. LiftNet is trained using ground truth correspondences for SketchFab for every pixel (i.e. dense points). LiftNet's performance is then compared with the baseline methods trained with depth. As demonstrated in Table 4, our method performs similarly to the supervised method trained explicitly to regress depth. Qualitative results are given in the supplementary material.

While here we have used all points, for ShapeNet only 50 correspondences was sufficient. Consequently, we additionally investigate in Table 3 the performance as a function of the number of training correspondences used per image and demonstrate that using a fraction of the available number of correspondences gives comparable results to using all. For example, using 100 correspondences gives similar results – 0.175/0.254 L1/RMSE error versus 0.175/0.255; we can use 1.1% of the correspondences and achieve comparable results to using all.

5.5   Quantitative Results Using Real World Data

Given the initial experiments on ShapeNet and SketchFab, which demonstrate that our loss is sufficient to learn about 3D and that using sparse correspondences is powerful, we turn our attention to using real-world, noisy data. The model is trained on the real-world images from the Sculpture dataset. However, as there is no large dataset of ground truth 3D sculptures, we evaluate on two datasets. First, we evaluate on real images using the Scanned dataset. Second we evaluate the model's generalisation capabilities by evaluating on SketchFab. To perform well, the model must generalise to a new, synthetic domain which may require a

Table 3. Evaluation of LiftNet's robustness to the number of training correspondences. Lower is better. These results demonstrate that using only 50 correspondences per training pair gives similar results to using all. Thus, sparse correspondences are sufficient for training LiftNet.

# Correspondences per image	L_1	RMSE	$\frac{d^* - d_{gt}}{d_{gt}}$	$\frac{(d^* - d_{gt})^2}{d_{gt}}$
10	0.183	0.263	0.0673	0.0253
50	0.178	0.261	0.0650	0.0242
100	0.175	0.254	0.0640	0.0233
≈9000	0.175	0.255	0.0641	0.0233

Table 4. The performance of LiftNet evaluated on the SketchFab dataset. Across all metrics, lower is better.

Method	Trained with	Training dataset	L_1	RMSE	$\frac{d^* - d_{gt}}{d_{gt}}$	$\frac{(d^* - d_{gt})^2}{d_{gt}}$
COLMAP [60]	Depth from SfM	Sculptures	0.195	0.284	0.0760	0.0291
LiftNet: $\mathcal{L}_{Corr}$ (no R)	Correspondences	Sculptures	0.190	0.277	0.0690	0.0269
LiftNet: $\mathcal{L}_{Corr}$	Correspondences	Sculptures	**0.186**	**0.270**	**0.0677**	**0.0256**
Zhou et. al. [21]	Photometric error	Sculptures	0.202	0.291	0.0732	0.0297
Chen et al. [17]	Ground truth ordinal depth	Depth-in-the-wild	0.186	0.269	0.0680	0.0258
LiftNet: $\mathcal{L}_{Corr}$	Correspondences	SketchFab	0.175	**0.254**	0.0641	0.0233
pix2pix	Depth	SketchFab	**0.173**	**0.254**	**0.0628**	**0.0226**

challenging domain shift. However, in practice, the model seems robust enough to generalise to this domain.

Training. When training, the loss on the validation set decreases from ≈4.0 to ≈3.4, converging in $40K$ iterations.

Ablation Studies. The first step is to ensure that our loss does indeed enforce that LiftNet learns about depth. To perform this check, we evaluate LiftNet on the test set of SketchFab and evaluate the effect of adding each component: the correspondence loss $\mathcal{L}_{corr}$ and the robustness term R.

The results are reported in Table 4. From these results, it is clear that the correspondence loss provides a strong constraint on the predicted depth, which is improved by the robustness term.

Comparison to SfM. The benefit of our approach is that we do not require videos of the same object but instead can use unordered image collections and a small number of images per object. To demonstrate this, we compare to COLMAP [60]. COLMAP is run on the clusters and the recovered 3D used to train a model to explicitly regress depth. COLMAP failed for 77% of the clusters, as there are not sufficient images/correspondences for it to converge to a global solution. Tables 4 and 5 compares the performance of the two methods. The proposed pipeline and LiftNet training are superior, due to (we assume): (1) more data for training, as no correspondences are thrown out; and (2) that the depth from COLMAP may be incorrect due to the small number of images per cluster, which may lead to an incorrect solution.

This experiment suggests that our method is additionally useful when fine-tuning a pre-trained model (e.g. with ground truth depth) on a new domain with only a few images per instance (e.g. lesser known landmarks, sculptures, etc.) as a SfM approach would fail given the sparse amount of information.

Table 5. The performance of LiftNet evaluated on the Scanned dataset. Across all metrics, lower is better.

Method	Trained with	Training dataset	L_1 (cm)	RMSE (cm)	$\frac{d^* - d_{gt}}{d_{gt}}$	$\frac{(d^* - d_{gt})^2}{d_{gt}}$
COLMAP [60]	Depth from SfM	Sculptures	9.5	11.8	**0.0741**	18.1
LiftNet: $\mathcal{L}_{Corr}$	Correspondences	Sculptures	**9.4**	**11.6**	**0.0741**	16.6
Zhou et. al. [21]	Photometric error	Sculptures	9.8	12.1	0.0761	18.7
Chen et al. [17]	Ground truth ordinal depth	Depth-in-the-wild	9.3	11.7	0.0722	17.1

Comparison to Other Self-supervised Approaches. The second hypothesis to test is whether our method is more robust than other self-supervised methods which rely on photometric consistency. We compare to the work of [21] by running their model on our dataset. However, we note that their method requires knowledge of the intrinsic camera parameters which we do not have. As a result, we assume the intrinsic camera parameters have focal length 0.7*W, and the principal point is (0.5W, 0.5H) (W/H are the width/height of the image). The results are reported in Table 4. As can be seen their model does poorly: this is presumably due to a number of challenging characteristics of the Sculpture dataset. First, as mentioned above the intrinsic camera parameters are not known and may change from image to image. Second, there are large changes in illumination, changes in context, changes in weather, etc. All of these characteristics make using a photometric loss not robust and lead to worse results.

Comparison to Supervised Approaches. Despite LiftNet doing better than comparable self-supervised approaches, as reported above, the next question is how does LiftNet compare to a method [17] trained with depth supervision. [17] is pre-trained on the NYU depth dataset [61] which contains 795 densely annotated images and fine-tuned on the depth-in-the-wild [17] which contains 5M images with ordinal relationships. As demonstrated in Tables 4 and 5, LiftNet does comparably or better than this *supervised* baseline.

5.6   Qualitative Results on the Sculpture Dataset

We demonstrate in Fig. 5 the predictions of LiftNet on the testing portion of the Sculpture dataset and compare them visually to two other methods: COLMAP and the supervised method [17]. We note that COLMAP performs poorly, presumably as there are very few training points. [17] produces reasonable results, as it is trained on a large dataset of outdoors images with supervision on relative

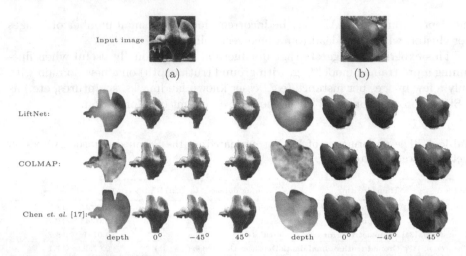

Fig. 5. Reconstruction results for LiftNet (top), COLMAP (middle) and Chen *et al.* [17] (bottom), visualised using Open3D [62]. The input image is shown at the top, then the predicted depth (blue is further away, yellow nearer), and rendered 3D at multiple viewpoints. Zoom in for details. From these images, the following are demonstrated. First, Chen *et al.* learns a prior over the image that the bottom of the image is nearer and the top further away. This is demonstrated in (a) and further examples in the supp. material. Second, COLMAP's depth predictions are noisy. Finally, LiftNet produces convincing depth maps which can be rendered at new views. (Color figure online)

depth in addition to NYU, but it has certain priors over the image (e.g. that points in the bottom of the image are always nearer than those in the top – as for most images the foreground is at the bottom of the image and sky at the top). Please see the supplementary material for more results.

6   Discussion

In this paper, we have introduced a framework for learning 3D shape using easily attainable sparse correspondences *without* depth supervision. Our insight is that we can make use of sparse correspondences, which can be obtained in much less constrained environments than approaches requiring photometric consistency. Given enough sparse correspondences across many instances, the network learns a dense depth prediction. The approach has been demonstrated on a challenging sculpture dataset of real images and a synthetic sculpture dataset with known ground truth information.

It is interesting to consider why this training scenario based on real images, and sculptures in particular, produces a network that performs well on real images and also generalizes to synthetic image. It is probably in part because the training data has natural augmentation – instances of a sculpture with the same shape may be made from different materials (bronze, marble) or have different texturing and appearance due to different weathering or illumination conditions. The network must learn to produce the same shape, irrespective of these multifarious conditions. This is a challenging learning problem but, if successful, then the network has correctly learnt to disentangle the material/appearance from the shape, and to pick out cues to shape from appearance. Thus it can generalize to objects with different materials, e.g. synthetic ones.

Acknowledgements. The authors would like to thank Fatma Guney for helpful feedback and suggestions. This work was funded by an EPSRC studentship and EPSRC Programme Grant Seebibyte EP/M013774/1.

References

1. Koenderink, J.J.: What does the occluding contour tell us about solid shape? Perception **13**, 321–330 (1984)
2. Witkin, A.P.: Recovering surface shape and orientation from texture. Artif. Intell. **17**(1–3), 17–45 (1981)
3. Malik, J., Rosenholtz, R.: Computing local surface orientation and shape from texture for curved surfaces. IJCV **23**(2), 149–168 (1997)
4. Blake, A., Marinos, C.: Shape from texture: estimation, isotropy and moments. Artif. Intell. **45**(3), 323–380 (1990)
5. Fleming, R.W., Torralba, A., Adelson, E.H.: Specular reflections and the perception of shape. J. Vis. **4**(9), 798–820 (2004)
6. Zhang, R., Tsai, P.S., Cryer, J.E., Shah, M.: Shape-from-shading: a survey. IEEE PAMI **21**(8), 690–706 (1999)
7. Barron, J.T., Malik, J.: Shape, illumination, and reflectance from shading. IEEE PAMI **37**, 1670–1687 (2015)
8. Koenderink, J.J., van Doorn, A.J.: Photometric invariants related to solid shape. Optica Acta **27**(7), 981–996 (1980)
9. Hartley, R.I., Zisserman, A.: Multiple View Geometry in Computer Vision, 2nd edn. Cambridge University Press, Cambridge (2004). ISBN 0521540518
10. Lowe, D.: Distinctive image features from scale-invariant keypoints. IJCV **60**(2), 91–110 (2004)
11. Snavely, N., Seitz, S., Szeliski, R.: Photo tourism: exploring photo collections in 3D. In: Proceedings of the ACM SIGGRAPH, vol. 3, pp. 835–846 (2006)
12. Schaffalitzky, F., Zisserman, A.: Multi-view matching for unordered image sets, or "How do I organize my holiday snaps?". In: Heyden, A., Sparr, G., Nielsen, M., Johansen, P. (eds.) ECCV 2002. LNCS, vol. 2350, pp. 414–431. Springer, Heidelberg (2002). https://doi.org/10.1007/3-540-47969-4_28
13. Arandjelović, R., Zisserman, A.: Name that sculpture. In: ACM International Conference on Multimedia RetrievalD (2012)
14. Eigen, D., Puhrsch, C., Fergus, R.: Depth map prediction from a single image using a multi-scale deep network. In: NIPS (2014)
15. Laina, I., Rupprecht, C., Belagiannis, V., Tombari, F., Navab, N.: Deeper depth prediction with fully convolutional residual networks. In: 2016 Fourth International Conference on 3D Vision (3DV) (2016)
16. Eigen, D., Fergus, R.: Predicting depth, surface normals and semantic labels with a common multi-scale convolutional architecture. In: Proceedings of the CVPR (2015)

17. Chen, W., Fu, Z., Yang, D., Deng, J.: Single-image depth perception in the wild. In: NIPS (2016)
18. Zoran, D., Isola, P., Krishnan, D., Freeman, W.T.: Learning ordinal relationships for mid-level vision. In: Proceedings of the ICCV (2015)
19. Vijayanarasimhan, S., Ricco, S., Schmid, C., Sukthankar, R., Fragkiadaki, K.: SfM-Net: learning of structure and motion from video. arXiv preprint arXiv:1704.07804 (2017)
20. Godard, C., Aodha, O.M., Brostow, G.J.: Unsupervised monocular depth estimation with left-right consistency. In: Proceedings of the CVPR (2017)
21. Zhou, T., Brown, M., Snavely, N., Lowe, D.G.: Unsupervised learning of depth and ego-motion from video. In: Proceedings of the CVPR (2017)
22. Ummenhofer, B., et al.: DeMoN: depth and motion network for learning monocular stereo. In: Proceedings of the CVPR (2017)
23. Choy, C.B., Xu, D., Gwak, J.Y., Chen, K., Savarese, S.: 3D-R2N2: a unified approach for single and multi-view 3D object reconstruction. In: Leibe, B., Matas, J., Sebe, N., Welling, M. (eds.) ECCV 2016. LNCS, vol. 9912, pp. 628–644. Springer, Cham (2016). https://doi.org/10.1007/978-3-319-46484-8_38
24. Girdhar, R., Fouhey, D.F., Rodriguez, M., Gupta, A.: Learning a predictable and generative vector representation for objects. In: Leibe, B., Matas, J., Sebe, N., Welling, M. (eds.) ECCV 2016. LNCS, vol. 9910, pp. 484–499. Springer, Cham (2016). https://doi.org/10.1007/978-3-319-46466-4_29
25. Fan, H., Su, H., Guibas, L.: A point set generation network for 3D object reconstruction from a single image. In: Proceedings of the CVPR (2017)
26. Sinha, A., Unmesh, A., Huang, Q., Ramani, K.: SurfNet: generating 3D shape surfaces using deep residual networks. In: Proceedings of the CVPR (2017)
27. Wu, J., Zhang, C., Xue, T., Freeman, B., Tenenbaum, J.: Learning a probabilistic latent space of object shapes via 3D generative-adversarial modeling. In: NIPS, pp. 82–90 (2016)
28. Soltani, A.A., Huang, H., Wu, J., Kulkarni, T.D., Tenenbaum, J.B.: Synthesizing 3D shapes via modeling multi-view depth maps and silhouettes with deep generative networks. In: Proceedings of the CVPR (2017)
29. Tulsiani, S., Zhou, T., Efros, A., Malik, J.: Multi-view supervision for single-view reconstruction via differentiable ray consistency. In: Proceedings of the CVPR (2017)
30. Rezende, D., Eslami, S.M.A., Mohamed, S., Battaglia, P., Jaderberg, M., Heess, N.: Unsupervised learning of 3D structure from images. In: NIPS, pp. 4997–5005 (2016)
31. Yan, X., Yang, J., Yumer, E., Guo, Y., Lee, H.: Perspective transformer nets: Learning single-view 3D object reconstruction without 3D supervision. In: NIPS (2016)
32. Gadelha, M., Maji, S., Wang, R.: 3D shape induction from 2D views of multiple objects. arXiv preprint arXiv:1612.05872 (2016)
33. Zhu, R., Kiani, H., Wang, C., Lucey, S.: Rethinking reprojection: closing the loop for pose-aware shape reconstruction from a single image. In: Proceedings of the ICCV (2017)
34. Novotny, D., Larlus, D., Vedaldi, A.: Learning 3D object categories by looking around them. In: Proceedings of the ICCV (2017)
35. Li, Z., Snavely, N.: MegaDepth: Learning single-view depth prediction from internet photos. In: Proceedings of the CVPR (2018)

36. Hong, J.H., Zach, C., Fitzgibbon, A., Cipolla, R.: Projective bundle adjustment from arbitrary initialization using the variable projection method. In: Leibe, B., Matas, J., Sebe, N., Welling, M. (eds.) ECCV 2016. LNCS, vol. 9905, pp. 477–493. Springer, Cham (2016). https://doi.org/10.1007/978-3-319-46448-0_29
37. Hong, J.H., Zach, C., Fitzgibbon, A.: Revisiting the variable projection method for separable nonlinear least squares problems. In: Proceedings of the CVPR (2017)
38. Fischler, M.A., Bolles, R.C.: Random sample consensus: a paradigm for model fitting with applications to image analysis and automated cartography. Commun. ACM **24**(6), 381–395 (1981)
39. Strang, G.: Linear Algebra and Its Applications, 2nd edn. Academic Press, Inc., Cambridge (1980)
40. Papadopoulo, T., Lourakis, M.I.A.: Estimating the Jacobian of the singular value decomposition: theory and applications. In: Vernon, D. (ed.) ECCV 2000. LNCS, vol. 1842, pp. 554–570. Springer, Heidelberg (2000). https://doi.org/10.1007/3-540-45054-8_36
41. Paszke, A., et al.: Automatic differentiation in PyTorch (2017)
42. Todd, J.T.: The visual perception of 3D shape. Trends Cogn. Sci. **8**(3), 115–121 (2004)
43. Koenderink, J.J., Van Doorn, A.J., Kappers, A.M.: Surface perception in pictures. Percept. Psychophys. **52**(5), 487–496 (1992)
44. Belhumeur, P.N., Kriegman, D.J., Yuille, A.L.: The bas-relief ambiguity. IJCV **35**(1), 33–44 (1999)
45. Liwicki, S., Zach, C., Miksik, O., Torr, P.H.S.: Coarse-to-fine planar regularization for dense monocular depth estimation. In: Leibe, B., Matas, J., Sebe, N., Welling, M. (eds.) ECCV 2016. LNCS, vol. 9906, pp. 458–474. Springer, Cham (2016). https://doi.org/10.1007/978-3-319-46475-6_29
46. Ronneberger, O., Fischer, P., Brox, T.: U-Net: convolutional networks for biomedical image segmentation. In: Navab, N., Hornegger, J., Wells, W.M., Frangi, A.F. (eds.) MICCAI 2015. LNCS, vol. 9351, pp. 234–241. Springer, Cham (2015). https://doi.org/10.1007/978-3-319-24574-4_28
47. Isola, P., Zhu, J.Y., Zhou, T., Efros, A.A.: Image-to-image translation with conditional adversarial networks. In: Proceedings of the CVPR (2017)
48. Odena, A., Dumoulin, V., Olah, C.: Deconvolution and Checkerboard Artifacts. Distill (2016)
49. Chen, Q., Koltun, V.: Photographic image synthesis with cascaded refinement networks. In: Proceedings of the ICCV (2017)
50. Arandjelović, R., Zisserman, A.: Smooth object retrieval using a bag of boundaries. In: Proceedings of the ICCV (2011)
51. Fouhey, D.F., Gupta, A., Zisserman, A.: 3D shape attributes. In: Proceedings of the CVPR (2016)
52. Knapitsch, A., Park, J., Zhou, Q.Y., Koltun, V.: Tanks and temples: benchmarking large-scale scene reconstruction. ACM Trans. Graph. **36**(4) (2017)
53. Lin, G., Milan, A., Shen, C., Reid, I.: RefineNet: multi-path refinement networks with identity mappings for high-resolution semantic segmentation. In: Proceedings of the CVPR (2017)
54. Moulon, P., Monasse, P., Marlet, R., Others: OpenMVG. An open multiple view geometry library. https://github.com/openMVG/openMVG
55. Wiles, O., Zisserman, A.: SilNet: single- and multi-view reconstruction by learning from silhouettes. In: Proceedings of the BMVC (2017)
56. Chang, A.X., et al.: ShapeNet: an information-rich 3D model repository. Technical report arXiv:1512.03012 [cs.GR] (2015)

57. Blender Online Community: Blender - a 3D modelling and rendering package (2017)
58. Choi, S., Zhou, Q.Y., Miller, S., Koltun, V.: A large dataset of object scans. arXiv:1602.02481 (2016)
59. Pytorch
60. Schönberger, J.L., Frahm, J.M.: Structure-from-motion revisited. In: Proceedings of the CVPR (2016)
61. Silberman, N., Hoiem, D., Kohli, P., Fergus, R.: Indoor segmentation and support inference from RGBD images. In: Fitzgibbon, A., Lazebnik, S., Perona, P., Sato, Y., Schmid, C. (eds.) ECCV 2012. LNCS, vol. 7576, pp. 746–760. Springer, Heidelberg (2012). https://doi.org/10.1007/978-3-642-33715-4_54
62. Zhou, Q.Y., Park, J., Koltun, V.: Open3D: a modern library for 3D data processing. arXiv:1801.09847 (2018)

Detecting Parallel-Moving Objects in the Monocular Case Employing CNN Depth Maps

Nolang Fanani[1(✉)], Matthias Ochs[1], and Rudolf Mester[1,2]

[1] Visual Sensorics and Information Processing Lab, Goethe University Frankfurt, Frankfurt, Germany
nolang.fanani@vsi.cs.uni-frankfurt.de
[2] Computer Vision Laboratory, ISY, Linköping University, Linköping, Sweden

Abstract. This paper presents a method for detecting independently moving objects (IMOs) from a monocular camera mounted on a moving car. We use an existing state of the art monocular sparse visual odometry/SLAM framework, and specifically attack the notorious problem of identifying those IMOs which move parallel to the ego-car motion, that is, in an 'epipolar-conformant' way. IMO candidate patches are obtained from an existing CNN-based car instance detector. While crossing IMOs can be identified as such by epipolar consistency checks, IMOs that move parallel to the camera motion are much harder to detect as their epipolar conformity allows to misinterpret them as static objects in a wrong distance. We employ a CNN to provide an appearance-based depth estimate, and the ambiguity problem can be solved through depth verification. The obtained motion labels (IMO/static) are then propagated over time using the combination of motion cues and appearance-based information of the IMO candidate patches. We evaluate the performance of our method on the KITTI dataset.

1 Introduction

Identifying moving objects is one of the main challenges in the context of autonomous driving. While the advancement of deep learning has shown convincing results to generate semantic segmentation of objects associated with moving objects (e.g. cars, bicycles, pedestrians, etc.), it is still a challenging task to verify whether such object is independently moving or in a static mode. We summarize such moving objects under the term *independently moving objects (IMOs)*.

We propose to combine the deep learning method and the classical geometry approach to identify IMOs using monocular camera (see Fig. 1). It is well known that the frame-to-frame egomotion induces the *epipolar constraint* which all

---

Electronic supplementary material The online version of this chapter (https://doi.org/10.1007/978-3-030-11015-4_22) contains supplementary material, which is available to authorized users.

L. Leal-Taixé and S. Roth (Eds.): ECCV 2018 Workshops, LNCS 11131, pp. 281–297, 2019.
https://doi.org/10.1007/978-3-030-11015-4_22

corresponding points in two images have to obey to. Points or areas which do not move conformant to the epipolar geometry are obviously candidates for belonging to independently moving objects. However, IMOs can also be *epipolar-conformant*, when they move parallel to the camera motion (for an illustration and a formal definition, see Fig. 2 and Sect. 4.1).

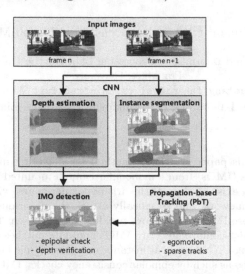

Fig. 1. The scheme of the our novel proposed method to identify IMOs. The *IMO detection* and *depth estimation* blocks are the new contributions.

How to detect IMOs which do not move parallel to the camera motion using monocular camera has been discussed in many papers [1–3]. The present paper focuses on the more challenging problem of detecting epipolar-conformant IMOs. The proposed method is built on top of the *propagation-based tracking (PbT)* framework [4], a recently proposed sparse monocular odometry scheme, made available to us by its authors. PbT is one of the leading published monocular visual odometry methods in the KITTI visual odometry benchmark.

The main contribution of our approach is to solve the inherently hard problem for the sparse monocular visual odometry: detecting moving objects which move parallel (or anti-parallel) to the camera motion, such as cars in the same or adjacent lanes, including oncoming traffic. As illustrated in see Fig. 2, due to its epipolar consistency, a parallel-moving point visually appears exactly as an static point, but in a different (pseudo)distance.

The approach presented here is to employ two CNNs: one that provides a car instance segmentation [5], also used in [4], and a new one designed for and described in this paper that provides depth estimates for single monocular images. In the decoder part of this residual encoder-decoder network, we introduce the new upsampling block. The depth map from the CNN allows us to compare distances obtained from geometric triangulation with such obtained from appearance, and thus supports the detection of epipolar-conformant IMOs also for the monocular case.

We emphasise that the system component presented here, a module that discriminates real moving objects from objects that could be moving ones but are actually standing still currently, is built upon an existing and properly working visual odometry system (PbT/PMO, [4]). This visual odometry (VO) system could be replaced by any other one that works properly and which is (like PMO/PbT) not disturbed by moving objects. In other words, the component we focus on in this paper is independent of the choice of the visual odometry platform it is attached to, as long as this platform fullfils certain functional requirements.

2   Related Work

As we focus on the detection of moving cars from a moving ego-vehicle, the scenario is very different to others such as handheld cameras or general robot vision [1,2], because the motion is strongly constrained by the car dynamics. In the area of advanced driver assistance systems (ADAS), many approaches work with additional information such as using a stereo system [6–9] to identify IMOs. In contrast to these approaches, we want to show that it is possible to reliably detect IMOs from a monocular camera only.

Previously published monocular algorithms on moving vehicle detection can be differentiated into two categories: appearance-based approaches (e.g. [1,10]) and motion-based approaches (e.g. [11,12]). We aim at providing an approach that combines both approaches, in a way similar to [13], using the following cues to determine the presence of an independently moving object and to track it: (a) the appearance of a car (in terms of a CNN-based car instance detector) as well as (b) motion cues from sparse optical flow, considering the epipolar geometry. Our approach shares some similarities with [14] who use two separate CNNs to determine visual odometry and object localization and fuse their results to obtain object localizations. Our method is also related to [15] where CNNs are used to obtain a rigidity score for each object and this is combined with motion cues from optical flow. Bai et al. [16] estimate the dense optical flow fields from each IMO candidate using an approach similar to ours, by employing a CNN to provide the car region candidates. However, they focus only on obtaining the optical flow and do not identify whether the car patches are moving in 3D or not.

Crossing IMOs can be identified because the crossing motions induce inconsistency w.r.t. the epipolar geometry, as discussed in [9]. However, parallel-moving IMOs are epipolar conformant. Klappstein et al. [17] proposed a positive height and depth constraint, but IMOs moving in opposite direction to the ego-car were only detected using a heuristic approach. Wong et al. [18] utilized the size and contours of cars to detect parallel-moving IMOs.

Appearance based dense depth estimate from a single monocular image is one of the key components of our proposed monocular framework, similar to the work by Ranftl et al. [19]. We use an encoder-decoder architecture for our CNN. The encoder of our network consists of the ResNet-50 architecture, which was proposed by He et al. [20]. To retrieve the origin size of the input image from last layer of the encoder, we use a decoder, which follows the ideas of the fully convolutional networks [21]. A quite similar encoder-decoder architecture for dense depth map estimation has recently been proposed by Laina et al. [22], but they do not add long skip connections to refine the output.

Those networks can be trained in an unsupervised or supervised way [23] or by a combination of both. The drawback of supervised learning is always the lack of much good labeled training data. To avoid the downside of supervised learning, the authors of [24–26] introduced an (semi-)unsupervised approach for estimating monocular depth maps, where they use stereo images during training to learn the disparity between both images.

Our depth estimation approach belongs to the category of supervised learning. During the training phase (only), we use LIDAR measurements and fuse them to with depth maps, which are computed by SGM [27]. Combining this training idea and our new decoder architecture, we are capable to generate state-of-the-art appearance based depth maps from a single image, which we need to identify for IMO candidates to fully solve the task of detection of parallel moving objects detection through depth verification.

3   Framework Overview

The proposed IMO detection scheme builds on a monocular visual odometry framework, the *propagation based tracking (PbT)* scheme [4], which was made available to us by its authors. An important principle of PbT is that each new relative camera pose for a new frame $n + 1$ is *predicted* using the car ego-dynamics. This prediction is used for a soft epipolar tracking (excluding gross deviations from the epipolar structure). Subsequently, a *refined* relative pose is computed only on the basis of keypoints that have been tracked at least twice, this means: keypoints which already passed a stringent test of belonging to the epipolar-conformant environment. All keypoints, including the new ones generated in sparsely covered areas of a new frame, are tracked in an epipolar-guided manner as discussed in more detailed way in Sect. 3.1. All IMO candidate patches in image n are to be classified in one of the three states: static, IMO, or undetermined.

We tackle the problem of IMO detection by classifying the IMOs into two categories: epipolar-conformant IMOs and non-epipolar-conformant IMOs. The keypoints on non-epipolar-conformant IMOs cannot be tracked by the PbT framework, because PbT restricts the matches to be along the epipolar lines. Not finding a photometric consistent match on or close to the epipolar line is thus the basis of labeling keypoints as *'cannot belong to static background'*. This fact serves as the basis of our strategy to detect non-epipolar-conformant IMOs. Failure to track a majority or even all keypoints on an IMO candidate indicates that the IMO candidate is highly likely an IMO.

Detecting epipolar-conformant IMOs, i.e. parallel-moving IMOs, is much more challenging. Monocular camera has an inherent limitation to identify objects moving parallel to the camera. Both static keypoints and parallel-moving

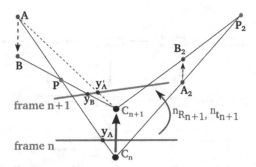

Fig. 2. Bird-eye view. A camera moves from C_n to C_{n+1}. A keypoint which moves parallel to the camera, from A to B, is visually identical to a static point P for the camera. This parallel-moving keypoint is epipolar-conformant. See text for details.

keypoints can be tracked using epipolar-style PbT and they look exactly the same by the monocular camera as illustrated in Fig. 2. This means, a keypoint correspondence from a parallel-moving IMO could lead also to an ambiguous static point.

We employ a CNN to provide depth map estimates. With the depth map in hand, we can now detect epipolar-conformant IMOs using a depth verification scheme, consisting of the following two steps:

- Comparison of the depth information between triangulated depth by PbT and CNN depth map on the tracked keypoints observed on IMO candidates.
- Comparison of the relative depth difference extracted from two time-consecutive CNN depth maps of IMO candidates and the egomotion estimates from PbT.

3.1 PbT Framework

The principle of keypoint tracking from PbT is used also during IMO detection, thus we give some details in the following. The egomotion of the ego-car is estimated using keypoints which have been confirmed to be static (=belonging to the static environment). These keypoints are the union of keypoints which are not in a CNN-detected car patch, and keypoints from car patches that have been classified as static. In addition, PbT with its epipolar constraint is able to propagate the static label of a car patch on subsequent frames as long as the keypoints inside that car patch are successfully tracked.

As the matching and tracking processes used in the present paper are guided by the epipolar geometry, patches which have a local structure with only one dominant orientation (e.g. lines and straight edges) can be matched as long as the dominant orientation is sufficiently well inclined relative to the epipolar line under consideration. In order to track the keypoint on subsequent frames, we employ an iterative differential matching which minimizes the photometric error between the patch correspondences. A keypoint is finally accepted and used for

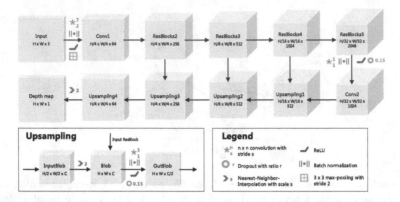

Fig. 3. The proposed network architecture for the depth map estimation. The decoder part is built upon a ResNet-50. We have replaced the fully connected and the global average pooling layer from the original ResNet-50 with our new upsampling block, which takes long skip connection into account. The output of our network has the same size as the input.

pose estimation when it has been tracked on at least three consecutive frames which reflects its 3D consistency.

3.2   CNN-Based IMO Candidate Patches

IMO candidate patches are obtained by a instance-level segmentation CNN which detects vehicles. We employ the *deep contours* approach, proposed in [5]. The CNN has been trained to label individual vehicles using the Cityscapes dataset [28]. The output of this CNN are 5 channels: one for the semantic label of vehicles and four channels representing the left, right, top, and bottom contours of each vehicle. Based on these information the instances of the vehicles are separated as independent patches, which we use as IMO candidate patches in our proposed framework.

3.3   Propagation of Label Information

We track the IMO labels over frames by using a dynamic motion model and simple image patch descriptors. Each IMO patch is represented by a feature vector consisting of its center of mass, its size (pixel count), its mean gray value and the gray value standard deviation. We predict the position of the car patch at the next frame using the information of the three last positions based on the assumption of constant 2D acceleration.

The association between the 'old' patches in the image n and a new patch in the image $n+1$ is performed in a looping greedy manner (forward and backward), whenever car patches are observed in both image n and image $n + 1$, subjecting each potential association between a patch in image n and a patch in image

$n + 1$. An association match between two car patches is accepted only when the pair of car patches reciprocally chooses each other as the best match.

3.4 CNN-Based Depth Image

For generating the appearance based dense depth maps, a second CNN takes as input an RGB image and estimates the inverse depth $\rho(x) = d(x)^{-1} \in [0, 1]$ for each pixel location $x \in \Omega$. Thus, the output size of the encoder-decoder network must be the same as for the input. The architecture of the depth estimation network is depicted in Fig. 3.

The structure of the encoder part from our network is adopted from the ResNet-50, which was proposed by He et al. [20]. The original ResNets were designed to classify images into different object categories. Hence, their last layers consist of a global average pooling and a fully connected layer to predict the class labels. We replace these layers with our novel upsampling blocks, which act as the decoder. Following the remarks of Odena et al. [29], we do not use unpooling or strided convolution operations to increase the size of the feature maps. Instead, we use nearest-neighbor interpolation to magnify the feature maps. If we increased only the size of the feature maps in this way, the predicted depth maps could not resolve fine structured elements of the image. To solve this problem, we add the output of some residual blocks of the encoder network via long skip connections to the interpolated feature maps. In this way, we allow the network to estimate the depth for fine details in the image. Afterwards, we apply a convolution layer with a kernel size of 3×3 and striding of 1, followed by batch normalization, ReLU and a dropout layer with a dropout ratio of 0.15. The structure of such a upsampling block is shown in the bottom of Fig. 3.

Our supervised loss function $\mathcal{L}$ is only based on the absolute difference of the estimated inverse depth $\rho_{CNN}(x)$ and a measured one $\rho_{GT}(x)$, which acts as ground truth. We evaluate the loss only on pixel positions $x \in \Omega_{GT}$, where $\rho_{GT}(x)$ is available by a valid measurement. The number of valid measurements is denoted as N.

$$\mathcal{L} = \frac{1}{N} \sum_{x \in \Omega_{GT}} |\rho_{CNN}(x) - \rho_{GT}(x)| \tag{1}$$

As training data, we use the raw KITTI data from [30]. We take the KITTI split of [25], which separates the data into a training, validation and testing set. The training set consists of 29000 images. For the ground truth inverse depth map, we fuse for each image the sparse LIDAR measurements from KITTI with the inverse depth map, which is computed with corresponding stereo image by SGM [27]. This allows us to evaluate the loss on many more positions than by only using the sparse LIDAR data. Furthermore, SGM builds a coherency between the image and the depth map, which is crucial for training a CNN. The LIDAR data do not cover this issue, because they are not necessarily synchronized with the camera and the center of the sensors do not coincide, which can lead to unwanted ambiguities.

The encoder part of the network is initialized with pretrained weights from ImageNet. The weights of the decoder part are randomly initialized with the proposed method of [20]. To avoid overfitting, we include dropout layers into the decoder network. We trained our network with a mini-batch size of 4 and use the ADAM optimizer. The network converged after 90 epochs.

4   Detection of Epipolar-Conformant IMOs

In the monocular case, assuming rigidity for the complete set of points, epipolar-conformant point sets on moving objects will be assigned wrong distance values. Therefore, if we have some information about the depth of a candidate point set, we can design a test on conformity to the static background. The depth map which is needed as side information for this purpose is provided by the described CNN. We detect an epipolar-conformant IMO by showing that the depth of the IMO candidate car, as provided by the depth map, would not fit to the predicted depth calculated with the assumption that the car is static.

The triangulated depth of the target car, with the assumption that the car is static, can be provided by the PbT framework as long as there are some keypoint correspondences on the target car patch. However on some occasions, such as in a fast highway scene where long displacement occurs, no matched keypoint is available on the target car patch. Without tracked keypoints, no triangulation can be done, hence there is no depth prediction.

In order to handle the case when there are no tracked keypoints on a car patch, the predicted depth of the car is obtained from the depth information on the previous frame, and then shifted by the estimated egomotion of the ego-car. We name the above two approaches as keypoint-based and keypoint-free depth verifications.

In this section, first we will prove that parallel-moving objects are consistent to the epipolar constraint. Second, we show that the speed ratio of a parallel-moving point w.r.t. the ego-car speed directly determines the depth of the triangulated ambiguous static point. Then we explain the keypoint-based and keypoint-free depth verifications to detect parallel-moving IMOs.

We assume that the egomotion estimates, more precisely: the relative pose between frames n and $n+1$, are already provided by PbT. We denote $\mathbf{R}$ and t as the relative rotation and relative translation to transform a fixed point z in the world of the camera coordinate system at frame n (CCS_n) to frame $n+1$ (CCS_{n+1}),

$$z_{n+1} = \begin{pmatrix} {}^n\mathbf{R}_{n+1} & {}^nt_{n+1} \end{pmatrix} \cdot \begin{pmatrix} z_n \\ 1 \end{pmatrix} = {}^n\mathbf{R}_{n+1} \cdot z_n + {}^nt_{n+1} \tag{2}$$

4.1   Proof That a Parallel-Moving Keypoint Is Epipolar-Conformant

We refer to Fig. 2. Let $z_{A(n)}$ be the 3D coordinate of a position A in CCS_n. The corresponding 3D coordinate in CCS_{n+1} is denoted by $z_{A(n+1)}$ and is given by

$$z_{A(n+1)} = {}^n\mathbf{R}_{n+1} \cdot z_{A(n)} + {}^nt_{n+1}. \tag{3}$$

Let $\boldsymbol{y}_A$ and $\boldsymbol{y}_A'$ be respectively the normalized image coordinate of $\boldsymbol{z}_{A(n)}$ and $\boldsymbol{z}_{A(n+1)}$ such that,

$$\boldsymbol{z}_{A(n)} = d_{A(n)} \cdot \boldsymbol{y}_A \tag{4}$$

$$\boldsymbol{z}_{A(n+1)} = d_{A(n+1)} \cdot \boldsymbol{y}_A' \tag{5}$$

where d_A is the depth of position A from the camera center. If $\mathbf{E}$ is the essential matrix between the two frames, the epipolar relation can be written as,

$$\boldsymbol{y}_A'^T \cdot \mathbf{E} \cdot \boldsymbol{y}_A = 0 \tag{6}$$

where the essential matrix is given by

$$\mathbf{E} = [{}^n t_{n+1}]_\times \cdot {}^n \mathbf{R}_{n+1}. \tag{7}$$

In general, Eq. (6) applies to every static point. In other words, every static point is epipolar-conformant.

Now, let us consider a moving point which starts at position A at frame n to position B at frame $n + 1$. It is important to note that the movement is parallel to the camera motion from frame n to frame $n + 1$, as shown in Fig. 2. The new position at position B after the parallel motion, denoted as $\boldsymbol{z}_{B(n+1)}$, can be expressed as the old position at A plus a shift along the translation direction

$$\boldsymbol{z}_{B(n+1)} = \boldsymbol{z}_{A(n+1)} - v \cdot {}^n t_{n+1}, \tag{8}$$

where v is a scale parameter describing the speed ratio of the point w.r.t. the ego-car speed. As the relative translation ${}^n t_{n+1}$ defined in Eq. (2) actually describes how the world relatively moves w.r.t. the camera, we need the minus sign in front of v.

Let $\boldsymbol{y}_B$ be the normalized image coordinate of $\boldsymbol{z}_{B(n+1)}$ and d_B is the depth of position B such that the following applies

$$\boldsymbol{z}_{B(n+1)} = d_B \cdot \boldsymbol{y}_B. \tag{9}$$

Now, we can check the epipolar conformity of the moving point

$$
\begin{aligned}
& \boldsymbol{y}_B^T \cdot \mathbf{E} \cdot \boldsymbol{y}_A \\
& = \frac{(d_{A(n+1)} \cdot \boldsymbol{y}_A' - v \cdot {}^n t_{n+1})^T}{d_B} \cdot \mathbf{E} \cdot \boldsymbol{y}_A \\
& = \frac{d_{A(n+1)}}{d_B} \underbrace{\cdot \boldsymbol{y}_A'^T \cdot \mathbf{E} \cdot \boldsymbol{y}_A}_{0} - \frac{v}{d_B} \cdot \underbrace{{}^n t_{n+1}^T \cdot \mathbf{E} \cdot \boldsymbol{y}_A}_{0} = 0.
\end{aligned}
\tag{10}
$$

We show in Eq. (10) that a parallel-moving keypoint also satisfies the epipolar constraint from frame n to frame $n+1$. That means, we have shown that a point moving parallel to the camera motion is epipolar-conformant.

4.2   Depth Relation Between Parallel-Moving Points and Ambiguous Static Points

As illustrated by Fig. 2, a keypoint correspondence y_A in frame n and y_B in frame $n + 1$ can represent both a moving point from A to B, and an ambiguous triangulated static point P. Let z_P be the 3D coordinate at position P. We investigate the relation between the motion of the parallel-moving point (see Eq. (8)) and the position of the ambiguous triangulated static point z_P.

We compute the intersection of two rays, one from the camera center at CCS_n crossing z_A and another one from the camera center at CCS_{n+1} crossing z_B. We transform all coordinates into CCS_{n+1}, thus having the following two equations representing the rays:

$$z_P^{(1)} = 0 + \alpha \cdot (z_{B(n+1)} - 0) = \alpha \cdot z_{B(n+1)} = \alpha(1 - v) \cdot {}^n t_{n+1} + \alpha \cdot ({}^n R_{n+1} \cdot z_{A(n)}) \quad (11)$$

$$z_P^{(2)} = {}^n t_{n+1} + \beta \cdot (z_{A(n+1)} - {}^n t_{n+1}) = {}^n t_{n+1} + \beta \cdot ({}^n R_{n+1} \cdot z_{A(n)}). \quad (12)$$

By comparing Eqs. (11) and (12), as long as ${}^n R_{n+1} \cdot z_{A(n)}$ is not a multiple of ${}^n t_{n+1}$, we come to the conclusion that

$$\alpha(1 - v) = 1 \quad \rightarrow \quad \alpha = \frac{1}{1 - v} \quad (13)$$

applies. It is important to note that α is also the depth ratio between positions B and P (see Eq. (11)), denoted as d_B and d_P.

$$\frac{d_P}{d_B} = \frac{1}{1 - v} \quad \rightarrow \quad (1 - v)d_P = d_B \quad (14)$$

Hence, we can identify several cases of parallel-moving points based on the analysis of v:

- If the point moves on the opposite direction w.r.t. camera motion ($v < 0$), then the ambiguous static point is nearer than the moving point ($d_P < d_B$).
- If the point moves at the same direction w.r.t. camera motion with lower speed ($0 < v < 1$), then the ambiguous static point is farther than the moving point ($d_P > d_B$).
- If the point moves at the same direction w.r.t. camera motion with the same speed ($v = 1$), then the ambiguous static point is at infinity ($d_P \to \infty$).
- If the point moves at the same direction w.r.t. camera motion with higher speed ($v > 1$), then the ambiguous static point z_P is found behind the camera.

4.3   Keypoint-Based Depth Verification

Let $Q(n)$ and $Q(n + 1)$ be two associated car patches corresponding to the same car from two consecutive frames n and $n + 1$. We employ epipolar matching within $Q(n)$ and $Q(n + 1)$ to obtain keypoint correspondences $x_i(n)$ and $x_i(n + 1)$, for $i = 1, 2, .., m$. This approach is considered only when the number of correspondences is at least τ_{mc}. Then, we triangulate the correspondences to obtain the 3D coordinates z_{Pi}.

We compute the relative difference Δd_i between the triangulated depth d_{Pi} and the depth information from the CNN depth map d_{Bi}:

$$\Delta d_i = \frac{|d_{Bi} - d_{Pi}|}{d_{Pi}} = \frac{|(1-v)d_{Pi} - d_{Pi}|}{d_{Pi}} = |v|. \tag{15}$$

The keypoint x_i on the car patch Q is recognized as a moving point, if the relative depth difference exceeds τ_v. Hence, τ_v also describes the maximum speed ratio w.r.t. the ego-car speed that can be detected as a moving point.

$$\Delta d_i > \tau_v \rightarrow \text{moving point} \tag{16}$$

Let m_i be the number of moving points found in patch Q. The car patch Q is identified as an IMO, if the ratio of moving keypoints exceeds τ_{rm}:

$$\frac{m_i}{m} > \tau_{rm} \rightarrow \text{IMO}. \tag{17}$$

4.4   Keypoint-Free Depth Verification

For keypoint-free depth comparison, we look into the car patches $Q(n)$ and $Q(n+1)$. Combining the 2D pixel position of the patches and the depth information from the CNN, each car patch can be represented by a single 3D point derived from the 2D center of mass of the patch and the median of the depth values.

The 2D center of masses of the patches $Q(n)$ and $Q(n+1)$ are given by $c(n)$ and $c(n+1)$, respectively. The median depth of patches $Q(n)$ and $Q(n+1)$ are denoted as $d(n)$ and $d(n+1)$. Hence, each patch can be represented by a 3D point z whose x and y positions are defined by the center of mass c and the z position is given by the median depth d.

$$z = d \cdot \mathbf{K}^{-1} \cdot \begin{pmatrix} c \\ 1 \end{pmatrix}, \tag{18}$$

where $\mathbf{K}$ is the intrinsic camera matrix.

Now, the patch $Q(n)$ and $Q(n+1)$ are represented by the 3D points $z(n)$ and $z(n+1)$. However, both 3D points are measured based on their respective camera coordinate systems (CCS). In order to compare them, we transform $z(n)$ into CCS_{n+1},

$$z(n \rightarrow n+1) = {}^n\mathbf{R}_{n+1} \cdot z(n) + {}^n t_{n+1}. \tag{19}$$

Now, we can calculate the absolute distance between the 3D points representing patches $Q(n)$ and $Q(n+1)$:

$$\Delta z = |z(n+1) - z(n \rightarrow n+1)|. \tag{20}$$

If both 3D points $z(n \rightarrow n+1)$ and $z(n+1)$ are similar, it indicates that the patch Q corresponds to a static car. However, if they significantly differ, we identify the car as an IMO.

As we deal with parallel-moving cars, the relative position of these cars change only in one axis corresponding to the depth value (z-axis in our setup), hence the depth consistency is the focus to analyze. The x and y components of $z(n \rightarrow n + 1)$ and $z(n + 1)$ are almost always the same. We set τ_{xy} as the maximum value for both x and y components of Δz to be classified as a static car.

Let $d_m(n)$ and $d_m(n + 1)$ be the depth (z) components of $z(n \rightarrow n + 1)$ and $z(n + 1)$. We compute the relative depth difference r_{dm} by

$$r_{dm} = \frac{|d_m(n) - d_m(n + 1)|}{\min(d_m(n), d_m(n + 1))}. \tag{21}$$

The car patch is categorized as an IMO, if the relative depth difference is more than $\tau_{dm,IMO}$ and as a static car, if it is less than $\tau_{dm,static}$.

5   Experiments

We tested our method on the KITTI dataset [30]. Since KITTI does not provide IMO labels for the KITTI odometry dataset, we have created our own dataset to evaluate our approach. We also used KITTI MoSeg dataset [31] to compare our results with competing method.

5.1   IMO Candidates Dataset

For our new dataset, we used the 11 training sequences from the KITTI visual odometry dataset, which consists of 23201 images. The proposed CNN from van den Brand et al. [5] was utilized to generate candidate labels for the vehicle instances. In the current state of the dataset, we have limited the detected objects to vehicles only. This can be further extended to other objects, like pedestrians or bicycle in future work.

Given these segmented candidate labels, we manually assign to each candidate patch in all images one of the following class labels: 0 - background (non-vehicles), 1 - independently moving vehicle, 2 - static (non-moving) vehicle, 3 - far away vehicles (median distance greater than 50m) and 4 - undetermined. We labeled a candidate as undetermined, if the patch does not show a vehicle or if the patch is stretched over more than one vehicles, which do not fall into same category, like static or IMO. Some examples of this dataset are shown in Fig. 4.

5.2   Evaluation of IMO Detection

In our experiments, we used the following values: $\tau_{mc} = 3$, $\tau_v = 0.3$, $\tau_{rm} = 0.4$, $\tau_{xy} = 0.1$, $\tau_{dm,IMO} = 0.05$, $\tau_{dm,static} = 0.01$. As the CNN-based IMO candidate patches can reliably detect IMOs up to a distance of 50 m, the proposed IMO detection is also evaluated for the same maximum distance. We combine our method with a method from [3] which handles detection for non-parallel-moving objects.

Fig. 4. Examples from our new IMO candidates dataset. The colored overlay encoding is as follows: red ↔ IMO (class 0), green ↔ static (class 1), blue ↔ too far away (class 2) and yellow ↔ undetermined (class 3). (Color figure online)

The performance of the IMO classification is expressed by recall R, specificity S, and accuracy A. We also measure the decisiveness of the proposed method to give definite output (IMO/static) as compared to undetermined. We define the decisiveness level D as

$$D = \frac{n_{IMO} + n_{static}}{n_{IMO} + n_{static} + n_{undetermined}} \tag{22}$$

where n_{IMO}, n_{static}, and $n_{undetermined}$ are respectively the number of outputs as IMO, static, and undetermined.

Accuracy on the KITTI MoSeg Dataset. Table 1 presents the precision of the IMO detection using our method and using MODNet [31]. The precision of our method is better on both identifying static cars and moving cars. The average precision of our method is 0.79 as compared to 0.66 of MODNet. Figure 5 shows the exemplary results of the IMO detection using our method and using MODNet.

Fig. 5. Exemplary results of the car classification into static and IMO labels on KITTI MoSeg dataset: using our method (**left**) and using MODNet (**right**). Red color represents IMO, green color represents static car, and yellow color represents undetermined. The comparison shows that our method correctly identifies a static parked car while MODNet wrongly classifies it as an IMO. (Color figure online)

Table 1. Accuracy of IMO detection on the KITTI MoSeg dataset.

Method	P static	P moving	P average
MODNet [31]	0.65	0.67	0.66
Ours	**0.74**	**0.84**	**0.79**

Accuracy on the KITTI Odometry Dataset. The results of the proposed IMO detection on the KITTI odometry dataset are presented in Table 2. The overall decisiveness level is 91%. That means, the undetermined outputs only happen in about 9% of the total car appearances and they mostly occur when the cars are first time observed in the scene. The recall rate, or the true positive rate, has an overall value of 87% which reflects the high accuracy of the IMO detection. The overall specificity rate, or the true negative rate, is 83%, while the overall accuracy is 84%.

Sequence 01 and sequence 04 are notably full of epipolar-conformant IMOs, both parallel and anti-parallel cases. The results in Table 2 for both sequences indicate that the proposed IMO detection is able to identify almost all IMOs. Figure 6 (left image) shows the IMO detection for KITTI sequence 09. The parallel-moving cars are correctly detected and marked with red colors. The static cars are also correctly identified in green colors.

The accuracy level is directly influenced by the user-defined threshold τ_v (see Eq. (16)) that describes the maximum detectable speed ratio of the moving car w.r.t. the ego-car speed. The threshold τ_v should be low enough in order to be able to detect even slow moving objects, while at the same it cannot be too low to anticipate measurement errors. If an IMO moves very slowly below τ_v, the proposed framework cannot identify it as a moving object, as happened in KITTI sequence 10, when a truck moves backward slowly (see the right image of Fig. 6). Similarly, if the error in determining triangulated 3D position is too high (e.g. from matching error or egomotion error), it could lead to false positive or false negative classifications.

Fig. 6. Exemplary results of the car classification into static and IMO labels on the KITTI odometry dataset sequence 09 (left) and sequence 10 (right). Red color represents IMO while green color represents static car. (Color figure online)

Table 2. Accuracy of IMO detection on KITTI dataset.

Sequence	D	R	S	A
0	0.90	0.41	0.81	0.81
1	0.84	0.97	n.a.	0.97
2	0.90	0.71	0.82	0.82
3	0.89	1.00	0.86	0.91
4	0.96	1.00	1.00	1.00
5	0.90	0.95	0.86	0.86
6	0.86	1.00	0.86	0.86
7	0.93	0.87	0.89	0.89
8	0.93	0.61	0.81	0.81
9	0.92	0.76	0.90	0.90
10	0.95	0.68	0.97	0.92
Overall	0.91	0.87	0.83	0.84

6 Conclusion

This paper presents an IMO detection method for the case of a moving monocular camera. The proposed method employs a CNN to provide IMO candidates, and a novel CNN that estimates depth maps from single images. While crossing IMOs can be detected by an epipolar consistency check, we focussed here on the parallel-moving IMOs which are identified through the proposed depth verification scheme. The motion labels (IMO/static) are propagated over time by establishing patch label association between two consecutive frames based on the cue combination of motion and appearance. Experiments on the new KITTI IMO label dataset we created show encouraging performance of the proposed method.

References

1. Jung, B., Sukhatme, G.S.: Detecting moving objects using a single camera on a mobile robot in an outdoor environment. In: International Conference on Intelligent Autonomous Systems, pp. 980–987 (2004)
2. Kundu, A., Jawahar, C.V., Krishna, K.M.: Realtime moving object detection from a freely moving monocular camera. In: IEEE International Conference on Robotics and Biomimetics, pp. 1635–1640 (2010)
3. Fanani, N., Ochs, M., Stürck, A., Mester, R.: CNN-based multi-frame IMO detection from a monocular camera. In: Intelligent Vehicles Symposium (IV). IEEE (2017)
4. Fanani, N., Stürck, A., Ochs, M., Bradler, H., Mester, R.: Predictive monocular odometry (PMO): what is possible without RANSAC and multiframe bundle adjustment? Image Vis. Comput. **68**, 3–13 (2017)

5. van den Brand, J., Ochs, M., Mester, R.: Instance-level segmentation of vehicles by deep contours. In: Chen, C.-S., Lu, J., Ma, K.-K. (eds.) ACCV 2016. LNCS, vol. 10116, pp. 477–492. Springer, Cham (2017). https://doi.org/10.1007/978-3-319-54407-6_32

6. Wedel, A., Meißner, A., Rabe, C., Franke, U., Cremers, D.: Detection and segmentation of independently moving objects from dense scene flow. In: Cremers, D., Boykov, Y., Blake, A., Schmidt, F.R. (eds.) EMMCVPR 2009. LNCS, vol. 5681, pp. 14–27. Springer, Heidelberg (2009). https://doi.org/10.1007/978-3-642-03641-5_2

7. Lenz, P., Ziegler, J., Geiger, A., Roser, M.: Sparse scene flow segmentation for moving object detection in urban environments. In: IEEE Intelligent Vehicles Symposium (IV), pp. 926–932 (2011)

8. Ošep, A., Mehner, W., Mathias, M., Leibe, B.: Combined image- and world-space tracking in traffic scenes. In: ICRA (2017)

9. Zhou, D., Frémont, V., Quost, B., Dai, Y., Li, H.: Moving object detection and segmentation in urban environments from a moving platform. Image Vis. Comput. **68**, 76–87 (2017)

10. López-Rubio, F.J., López-Rubio, E.: Foreground detection for moving cameras with stochastic approximation. Pattern Recogn. Lett. **68**, 161–168 (2015)

11. Yamaguchi, K., Kato, T., Ninomiya, Y.: Vehicle ego-motion estimation and moving object detection using a monocular camera. In: 18th International Conference on Pattern Recognition (ICPR 2006), vol. 4, pp. 610–613 (2006)

12. Jazayeri, A., Cai, H., Zheng, J.Y., Tuceryan, M.: Vehicle detection and tracking in car video based on motion model. IEEE Trans. Intell. Transp. Syst. **12**(2), 583–595 (2011)

13. Ramirez, A., Ohn-Bar, E., Trivedi, M.M.: Go with the flow: improving multi-view vehicle detection with motion cues. In: 22nd International Conference on Pattern Recognition, pp. 4140–4145 (2014)

14. Oliveira, G.L., Radwan, N., Burgard, W., Brox, T.: Topometric localization with deep learning. ArXiv preprint arXiv:1706.08775 (2017)

15. Wulff, J., Sevilla-Lara, L., Black, M.J.: Optical flow in mostly rigid scenes. arXiv preprint arXiv:1705.01352 (2017)

16. Bai, M., Luo, W., Kundu, K., Urtasun, R.: Exploiting semantic information and deep matching for optical flow. In: Leibe, B., Matas, J., Sebe, N., Welling, M. (eds.) ECCV 2016. LNCS, vol. 9910, pp. 154–170. Springer, Cham (2016). https://doi.org/10.1007/978-3-319-46466-4_10

17. Klappstein, J., Stein, F., Franke, U.: Monocular motion detection using spatial constraints in a unified manner. In: Intelligent Vehicles Symposium, pp. 261–267. IEEE (2006)

18. Wong, C.C., Siu, W.C., Jennings, P., Barnes, S., Fong, B.: A smart moving vehicle detection system using motion vectors and generic line features. IEEE Trans. Consum. Electron. **61**(3), 384–392 (2015)

19. Ranftl, R., Vineet, V., Chen, Q., Koltun, V.: Dense monocular depth estimation in complex dynamic scenes. In: Proceedings of the IEEE Conference on Computer Vision and Pattern Recognition, pp. 4058–4066 (2016)

20. He, K., Zhang, X., Ren, S., Sun, J.: Deep residual learning for image recognition. In: Conference on Computer Vision and Pattern Recognition (CVPR), pp. 770–778 (2016)

21. Long, J., Shelhamer, E., Darrell, T.: Fully convolutional networks for semantic segmentation. In: Conference on Computer Vision and Pattern Recognition (CVPR), pp. 3431–3440 (2015)

22. Laina, I., Rupprecht, C., Belagiannis, V., Tombari, F., Navab, N.: Deeper depth prediction with fully convolutional residual networks. In: International Conference on 3D Vision (3DV), pp. 239–248 (2016)
23. Eigen, D., Puhrsch, C., Fergus, R.: Depth map prediction from a single image using a multi-scale deep network. In: Conference on Neural Information Processing Systems (NIPS), pp. 2366–2374 (2014)
24. Garg, R., B.G., V.K., Carneiro, G., Reid, I.: Unsupervised CNN for single view depth estimation: geometry to the rescue. In: Leibe, B., Matas, J., Sebe, N., Welling, M. (eds.) ECCV 2016. LNCS, vol. 9912, pp. 740–756. Springer, Cham (2016). https://doi.org/10.1007/978-3-319-46484-8_45
25. Godard, C., Mac Aodha, O., Brostow, G.J.: Unsupervised monocular depth estimation with left-right consistency. In: Conference on Computer Vision and Pattern Recognition (CVPR) (2017)
26. Kuznietsov, Y., Stückler, J., Leibe, B.: Semi-supervised deep learning for monocular depth map prediction. In: Conference on Computer Vision and Pattern Recognition (CVPR) (2017)
27. Hirschmuller, H.: Stereo processing by semiglobal matching and mutual information. Trans. Pattern Anal. Mach. Intell. (PAMI) 30(2), 328–341 (2008)
28. Cordts, M., et al.: The cityscapes dataset for semantic urban scene understanding. In: Conference on Computer Vision and Pattern Recognition (CVPR), pp. 3213–3223 (2016)
29. Odena, A., Dumoulin, V., Olah, C.: Deconvolution and checkerboard artifacts. Distill 1(10), e3 (2016)
30. Geiger, A., Lenz, P., Stiller, C., Urtasun, R.: Vision meets robotics: the KITTI dataset. Int. J. Robot. Res. 32(11), 1231–1237 (2013)
31. Siam, M., Mahgoub, H., Zahran, M., Yogamani, S., Jagoroand, M., El-Sallab, A.: Modnet: Moving object detection network with motion and appearance for autonomous driving. arXiv preprint arXiv:1709.04821 (2017)

Object Pose Estimation from Monocular Image Using Multi-view Keypoint Correspondence

Jogendra Nath Kundu🆔, M. V. Rahul(✉)🆔, Aditya Ganeshan🆔, and R. Venkatesh Babu🆔

Indian Institute of Science, Bengaluru, India
`rahulmv.cs14@rvce.edu.in`

Abstract. Understanding the geometry and pose of objects in 2D images is a fundamental necessity for a wide range of real world applications. Driven by deep neural networks, recent methods have brought significant improvements to object pose estimation. However, they suffer due to scarcity of keypoint/pose-annotated real images and hence can not exploit the object's 3D structural information effectively. In this work, we propose a data-efficient method which utilizes the geometric regularity of intraclass objects for pose estimation. First, we learn pose-invariant local descriptors of object parts from simple 2D RGB images. These descriptors, along with keypoints obtained from renders of a fixed 3D template model are then used to generate keypoint correspondence maps for a given monocular real image. Finally, a pose estimation network predicts 3D pose of the object using these correspondence maps. This pipeline is further extended to a multi-view approach, which assimilates keypoint information from correspondence sets generated from multiple views of the 3D template model. Fusion of multi-view information significantly improves geometric comprehension of the system which in turn enhances the pose estimation performance. Furthermore, use of correspondence framework responsible for the learning of pose invariant keypoint descriptor also allows us to effectively alleviate the data-scarcity problem. This enables our method to achieve *state-of-the-art* performance on multiple real-image viewpoint estimation datasets, such as Pascal3D+ and ObjectNet3D. To encourage reproducible research, we have released the codes for our proposed approach (Code: https://github.com/val-iisc/pose_estimation).

Keywords: Pose estimation · 3D structure · Keypoint estimation · Correspondence network · Convolutional neural network

---

J.N. Kundu, M.V. Rahul and A. Ganeshan—Equal contribution.

Electronic supplementary material The online version of this chapter (https://doi.org/10.1007/978-3-030-11015-4_23) contains supplementary material, which is available to authorized users.

L. Leal-Taixé and S. Roth (Eds.): ECCV 2018 Workshops, LNCS 11131, pp. 298–313, 2019.
https://doi.org/10.1007/978-3-030-11015-4_23

1 Introduction

Estimating 3D pose of an object from a given RGB image is an important and challenging task in computer vision. Pose estimation can enable AI systems to gain 3D understanding of the world from simple monocular projections. While ample variation is observed in the design of objects of a certain type, say chairs, the intrinsic structure or skeleton is observed to be mostly similar. Moreover, in case of 3D objects, it is often possible to unite information from multiple 2D views, which in succession can enhance 3D perception of humans as well as artificial vision systems. In this work, we show how intraclass structural similarity of objects along with multi-view 3D interpretation can be utilized to solve the task of fine-grained 3D pose estimation.

By viewing instances of an object class from multiple viewpoints over time, humans gain the ability to recognize sub-parts of the object, independent of pose and intra-class variations. Such viewpoint and appearance invariant comprehension enables human brain to match semantic sub-parts between different instances of same object category, even from simple 2D perspective projections (RGB image). Inspired from human cognition, an artificial model with similar matching mechanism can be designed to improve final pose estimation results. In this work, we consider a single template model with known keypoint annotations as a 3D structural reference for the object category of interest. Subsequently, Key-point correspondence maps are obtained by matching keypoint-descriptors of synthetic RGB projections from multiple viewpoints, with respect to the spatial descriptors from a real RGB image. Such keypoint-correspondence maps can provide the geometric and structural cues useful for pose estimation.

The proposed pose estimation system consists of two major parts; (1) A Fully Convolutional Network which learns pose-invariant local descriptors to obtain keypoint-correspondence, and (2) A pose estimation network which fuses information from multiple correspondence maps to output the final pose estimation result. For each object class, we annotate a single template 3D model with sparse 3D keypoints. Given an image, in which the object's pose is to be estimated, first it is paired with multiple rendered images from different viewpoints of the template 3D model (see Fig. 1). Projections of the annotated 3D keypoints is tracked on the rendered synthetic images to provide ground-truth for learning of efficient key-point descriptor. Subsequently, keypoint-correspondence maps are generated for each image pair using correlation of individual keypoint descriptor (from rendered image) to the spatial descriptors obtained from the given image.

Recent works [10,12,21] show that deep neural networks can effectively merge information from multiple 2D views to deliver enhanced view estimation performance. These approaches require multi-view projections of the given input image to exploit the multi-view information. But in the proposed approach, we attempt to take advantages of multi-view cue by generating correspondence map from the single-view real RGB image by comparing it against multiview synthetic renders. This is achieved by feeding the multi-view keypoint correspondence maps through a carefully designed fusion network (convolutional neural network) to obtain the final pose estimation results. Moreover, by fusing information from multiple viewpoints, we show significant improvement in pose estimation, making our pose estimation approach *state-of-the-art* in competitive real-image datasets, such as Pascal3D+ [32] and ObjectNet3D [31]. In Fig. 1, a diagrammatic overview of our approach is presented.

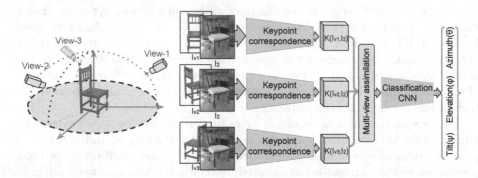

Fig. 1. Illustration of the proposed pipeline. Given a real image I_2, it is paired with multiple 2D views of a template 3D model with annotated keypoints. For each pair of images, keypoint correspondence maps are generated, represented by $K(I_{vk}, I_2)$. Finally, the pose estimator network assimilates information from all correspondence maps to predicts the pose parameters.

Many recent works [8,29,32], have utilized deep neural networks for 3D object understanding and pose estimation. However, these approaches have several drawbacks. Works such as [25,30] achieve improved pose estimation performance by utilizing a vast amount of synthetic data. This can be a severe bottleneck when an extensive repository of diverse 3D models for a specific category is unavailable (as in case of novel object-classes, such as mechanical parts, abstract 3D models etc.). Additionally, 3D-INN [30] require a complex keypoint-refinement module that, while being remarkable at keypoint estimation, shows sub-optimal performance for viewpoint estimation, when compared against current state-of-the-art models. We posit that it is essential to explore and exploit strong 3D-structural object priors to alleviate various general issues, such as data-bottleneck and partial-occlusion, which are observed in object viewpoint estimation. Moreover, our approach has two crucial advantages. Firstly, our keypoint correspondence map captures relation between the keypoint and the entire 2D spatial view of the object in a given image. That is, the correspondence map not only captures information regarding spatial location of keypoint in the given image, but also captures various relations between the keypoint and other semantic-parts of the object. In Fig. 2, we show the obtained correspondence map for varied keypoints, and provide evidence for this line of reasoning. Secondly, our network fuses the correspondence map of each keypoint from multiple views.

To summarize, our main contributions in this work include: (1) a method for learning pose-invariant local descriptors for various object classes, (2) a keypoint correspondence map formulation which captures various explicit and implicit relations between the keypoint, and a given image, (3) a pose estimation network which assimilates information from multiple viewpoints, and (4) state-of-the-art performance on real-image object pose estimation datasets for indoor object classes such as 'Chair', 'Sofa', 'Table' and 'Bed'.

2   Related Work

Local Descriptors and Keypoint Correspondence: A multitude of work propose formulations for local discriptors of 3D objects, as well as 2D images. Early methods employed hand-engineered local descriptors like SIFT or HOG [2,3,15,27] to represent semantic part structures useful for object comprehension. With the advent of deep learning, works such as [5,9,23,33] have proposed effective learning methods to obtain local descriptor correspondence in 2D images. Recently, Huang et al. [11] propose to learn local descriptors for 3D objects following deep multi-view fusion approach. While this work is one of our inspirations, our method differs in many crucial aspects. We do not require extensive multi-view fusion of local descriptors as performed by Huang et al. for individual local points. Moreover we do not rely on a large repository of 3D models with surface segmentation information for generalization. For effective local descriptor correspondence, Universal Correspondence Network [5] formulate an optimization strategy for learning robust spatial correspondence, which is used in coherence with an active hard-mining strategy and a convolutional spatial transformer (STN). While [5] learn geometric and spatial correspondence for task such as semantic part matching, we focus on the learning procedure of their approach and adapt it for learning our pose-invariant local descriptors.

Multi-view Information Assimilation: Borotschnig et al. [4], and Paletta et al. [18] were one of the earliest works to show the utility of multi-view information for improving performance on tasks related to 3D object comprehension. In recent years, multiple innovative network architectures, such as [10,21] have been proposed for the same. One of the earliest works to combine deep learning with multi-view information assimilation, [24] showed that 2D image-based approaches are effective for general object recognition tasks, even for 3D models. They proposed an approach for 3D object recognition based on multiple 2D projections of the object, surpassing previous works which were based on other 3D object representations such as voxel and mesh format. In [20], Qi et al. give a comprehensive study on the voxel-based CNN and multi-view CNN for 3D object classification. Apart from object classification, multi-view approach is seen to be useful for a wide variety of other tasks, such as learning local features for 3D models [11], 3D object shape prediction [28] etc. In this work, we use multi-view information assimilation for object pose estimation in a given monocular RGB image using multiple views of a 3D template model.

Object Viewpoint Estimation: Many recent works [17,19] use deep convolutional networks for object viewpoint estimation. While works such as [29] attempt pose estimation along with keypoint estimation, an end-to-end approach solely for 3D pose estimation was first proposed by RenderForCNN [25]. Su *et al.* [25] proposed to utilize vast amount of synthetic rendered data from 3D CAD models with dataset specific cues for occlusion and clutter information, to combat the lack of pose annotated real data. In contrast, 3D Interpreter Network (3D-INN) [30] propose an interesting approach where 3D keypoints and view is approximated by minimizing a novel re-projection loss on the estimated 2D keypoints. However, the requirement of vast amount of synthetic data is a significant bottleneck for both the works. In comparison, our method relies on the presence of a single synthetic template model per object category, making our method significantly data efficient and far more scalable. This is an important pre-requisite to incorporate the proposed approach for novel object classes, where multiple 3D models may not exists. Recently, Grabner *et al.* [8] estimate object pose by predicting the vertices of a 3D bounding box and solving a perspective-n-point problem. While achieving state-of-the-art performance in multiple object categories, they could not surpass performance of [25] on the challenging indoor object classes such as 'chair','sofa', and 'table'. It is essential to provide stronger 3D structural priors to learn pose estimation under data scarcity scenario for such complex categories. The structural prior is effectively modeled in our case by keypoint correspondence and multi-view information assimilation.

3   Approach

This section consist of 3 main parts: in Sect. 3.1, we present our approach for learning pose invariant local descriptors, Sect. 3.2 explains how the keypoint correspondence maps are generated, and Sect. 3.3 explains our regression network, along with various related design choices. Finally, we briefly describe our data generation pipeline in Sect. 3.4.

3.1   Pose-Invariant Local Descriptors

To effectively compare given image descriptors with the keypoint descriptors from multi-view synthetic images, our method must identify various sub-parts of the given object, invariant to pose and intra-class variation. To achieve this we train a convolutional neural network (CNN), which takes an RGB image as input and gives a spatial map of local descriptors as output. That is, given an image I_1 of size $h \times w$, our network predicts a spatial local descriptor map L_{I_1} of size $h \times w \times d$, where the d-dimensional vector at each spatial location is treated as the corresponding local descriptor.

Following the approach of other established method [5,11], we use the CNN to form two branches of a Siamese architecture with shared convolutional parameters. Now, given a pair of images I_1 and I_2 with annotated keypoints, we pass them through the siamese network to get the spatial local descriptor maps L_{I_1} and L_{I_2} respectively. The annotated keypoints are then used to generate positive and negative correspondence pairs, where a positive correspondence pair refers to a pair of points $I_1(x_k, y_k), I_2(x'_k, y'_k)$ such that they represent a certain semantic keypoint. In [5], authors present the correspondence contrastive loss, which is used to reduce the distance between the local descriptors of positive correspondence pairs, and increase the distance for the negative pairs. Let $\mathbf{x_i} = (x_k, y_k)$ and $\mathbf{x'_i} = (x'_k, y'_k)$ represent spatial locations on I_1 and I_2 respectively. The correspondence contrastive loss can be defined as,

$$Loss = \frac{1}{2N} \sum_i^N \{ s_i \| L_{I_1}(\mathbf{x}) - L_{I_2}(\mathbf{x'}) \|^2 +$$

$$(1 - s_i) \max (0, \, m - \| L_{I_1}(\mathbf{x}) - L_{I_2}(\mathbf{x'}) \|^2) \} \tag{1}$$

where N is the total number of pairs, $s_i = 1$ for positive correspondence pairs, and $s_i = 0$ for negative correspondence pairs.

Chief benefit of using a correspondence network is its utility to combat data-scarcity. Given N samples with keypoint annotation, we can generate $^NC_2$ training samples for training the local descriptor representations. The learned local descriptors do most of the heavy lifting by providing useful structural cues for 3D pose estimation. This helps us avoid extensive usage of synthetic data and the common pitfalls associated with it, such as domain shift [14] while testing on real samples. Compared to state-of-the-art works [25,30], where millions of synthetic data samples were used for effecting training, we use only 8k renders of a single template 3D model per class (which is less than 1% of the data used by [25,30]). Another computational advantage we observe is in terms of run-time efficiency. Given a single image, we estimate the local descriptors for all the visible points on the object. This is in stark contrast to Huang et al. [11], where multiple images were used for generating local descriptors for each point of the object.

In most cases such as in [30], objects are represented by a sparse set of keypoints. Learning feature descriptors for only a few sparse semantic keypoints has many disadvantages. In such case, the models fails to learn efficient descriptors for spatial regions away from the defined semantic keypoint locations. However, information regarding parts away from these keypoints can also be useful for pose estimation. Hence, we propose to learn proxy-dense local descriptors to obtain more effective correspondence maps (see Fig. 3b and c). This also allows us to train the network more efficiently by generating enough amount of positive and negatives correspondence pairs. For achieving this objective, we generate dense keypoints for all images, details of which are presented in Sect. 3.3.

Correspondence Network Architecture: The siamese network contains two branches with shared weights. It is trained on the generated key-point annotations (details in Sect. 3.3) using the loss, Eq. 1 described above. For the Siamese network, we employ a standard Googlenet [26] architecture with imagenet pre-trained weights. Further, to obtain spatially aligned local features L_I, we use a convolutional spatial transformation layer after *pool4* layer of googlenet architecture, as proposed in UCN [5]. The use of convolutional spatial transformation layer is found to be very useful for semantic part correspondence in presence of reasonably high pose and intra-class variations.

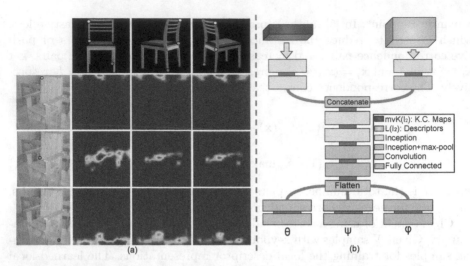

Fig. 2. (a) The Keypoint Correspondence map generated by our approach. The top row shows the template 3D model from 3 Views where 3 different keypoints are highlighted. First column shows the real image where pose has to be estimated. As we can see, Keypoints have lesser ambiguity when looked from views where they are clearly visible (For eg., back-leg keypoint, View 2 and 3). (b) The architecture of our pose estimator network.

3.2 Keypoint Correspondence Maps

The CNN introduced in the previous section provides a spatial local descriptor map L_{I_1} for a rendered synthetic image I_1. Now, using the keypoint annotations rendered from the 3D template model, we want to generate a spatial map, which can capture the location of corresponding keypoint in a given real image, I_2. To achieve this we propose to utilize pairwise descriptor correlation between both the images. Let, L_{I_1} is of size $h \times w \times d$, and x_k represents a keypoint in I_1. Now our goal is to estimate a correspondence map of keypoint x_k for the real image I_2. By taking correlation of the local descriptor at x_k, $L_{I_1}(x_k)$ with all locations (i', j') of the spatial local descriptor for image I_2, i.e. L_{I_2}, correspondence maps are obtained for each keypoint, x_k. Using max-out Hadamard product H, we compute the pairwise descriptor correlation for any (i', j') in I_2 and x_k in I_1 as follows:

$$H(x_k, (i, j)) = \max(0, L_{I_1}(x_k)^T L_{I_2}(i', j'))$$

$$C_{x_k, I_2}(L_{I_1}(x_k), \ L_{I_2}(i', j')) = \frac{\exp^{H(x_k, i, j)}}{\sum_{p,q} \exp^{H(x_k, p, q)}}$$

As the learned local descriptors are unit normalized, the max-out Hadamard product $H(x_k, (i, j))$ represents only positive correlation between local descriptor at x_k with local descriptors of all locations (i, j) in image I_2. By applying softmax on the entire map of rectified Hadamard product, multiple high correlation

values will be suppressed by making the highest correlation value more prominent in the final correspondence map. Such normalization step is in line with
the traditionally used second nearest neighbor test proposed by Lowe *et al.* [16].
Using the above formulation, keypoint correspondence maps C_{x_k, I_2} is generated
for a set of sparse structurally important keypoints $x_k, for k = 1, 2, ..., N$ in
image I_1. The structurally important keypoints that we use for each object class
are the same as the ones used by [30]. Finally, We use the structurally important
keypoint set for individual object category as defined by Wu *et al.* [30]. Finally
the stacked correspondence map for all structural keypoints of I_1 computed for
image I_2 is represented by $K(I_1, I_2)$. Here $K(I_1, I_2)$ is of size $N \times h \times w$, where
N is the number of keypoints.

As explained earlier, our keypoint correspondence map computes the relation
between the keypoint x_k in I_1 and all the points (i, j) in I_2. In comparison
to [30], where a location heatmap is predicted for each keypoint, our keypoint
correspondence map captures the interplay between different keypoints as well.
This in turn acts as an important cue for final pose estimation. Figure 1 shows
keypoint correspondence maps generated by our approach, which clearly provide
evidence of our claims.

3.3   Multi-view Pose Estimation Network

With the structural cues for object in image I_2 provided by the keypoint correspondence set $K(I_1, I_2)$, we can estimate pose of the object more effectively. In
our setup, I_1 is a synthetically rendered image of the template 3D model with the
tracked 2D keypoint annotations, and I_2 is the image of interest where the pose
has to be estimated. It is important to note, that $K(I_1, I_2)$ contains information
regarding relation between the keypoints $x_k, k = 1, 2, ..., N$ in I_1 with respect to
the image I_2. However, as I_1 is a 2D projection of the 3D template object, it
is possible that some keypoints are self occluded, or only partially visible. For
such keypoints C_{x_k, I_2} would contain noisy and unclear correspondence. As mentioned earlier, the selected keypoints are structurally important and hence lack
of information of any of them can hamper the final pose estimation performance.

To alleviate this issue, we propose to utilize a multi-view pose estimation
approach. We first render the template 3D model from multiple viewpoints
$I_{v1}, I_{v2}, ... I_{vm}$ considering m viewpoints. Then, the keypoint correspondence set
is generated for each view by pairing I_{vk} with I_2 for all k. Finally, information from multiple views is combined together by concatenating all the correspondence sets to form a fused Multi-View Correspondence set, represented by
$mvK(I_2)$. Here, $mvK(I_2)$ is of size $(m \times N, h, w)$; where m is the number of
views, and N is the number of structurally important keypoints. subsequently,
$mvK(I_2)$ is supplied as an input to our pose estimation network which effectively combines information from multiple-views of the template object to infer
the required structural cues. For a given m, we render $I_{v1}, I_{v2}, ... I_{vm}$ from fixed
viewpoints, $v_k = (360/m \times k, 10, 0)$ for $k = 1, 2, ... m$; where v_k represents a tuple
of azimuth, elevation and tilt angles in degree.

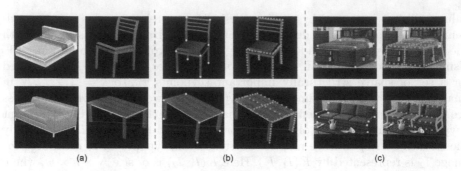

Fig. 3. (a) The single 3D template model selected for each class. (b) Template models are annotated with sparse 3D keypoints, which are projected to 2D keypoints in each rendered image. From these keypoints, dense keypoint annotation is generated by sampling along the skeleton. (c) Similar process is used on real image datasets where sparse 2D keypoint annotation has been provided.

In Fig. 2b, the architecture of our pose estimation network is outlined. Empirically, we found Inception Layer to be most efficient in terms of performance for memory footprint. We believe, multiple receptive fields in the inception layer help the network to learn structural relations at varied scales, which later improves pose estimation performance. For effective modeling, we consider deeper architecture with reduced number of filters per convolutional layer. Here, the pose estimation network classifies the three Euler angles, namely azimuth (θ), elevation (ϕ), and tilt (ψ). Following [25], we use the Geometric Structure Aware Classification Loss for effective estimation of all the three angles.

As a result of proxy-dense correspondence, Pose-Invariant local descriptor $L(I_2)$ has information about dense keypoints. But $mvK(I_2)$ leverages information only from the sparse set of structurally important keypoints. Therefore, we also explore whether $L(I_2)$ can also be utilized to improve the final pose estimation performance. To achieve this, we concatenate convolution-processed feature map of $L(I_2)$ with inception-processed features of $mvK(I_2)$ to form the input to our pose-estimation network. This brings us to our final state-of-the-art architecture. Various experiments are performed in Sect. 4.1, which outline the benefits of each of the design choices.

3.4   Data Generation for Local Descriptors

Learning an efficient pose-invariant keypoint descriptor requires presence of ground-truth positive correspondence pair in sufficient amount. For each real image, we generate an ordered set of dense keypoints by forming a skeletal frame of the object from the available sparse keypoint annotations provided in Keypoint-5 dataset [30]. To obtain dense positive keypoint pairs, we sample additional points along the structural skeleton lines obtained from the semantic sparse keypoints for both real and synthetic image. Various simple keypoint pruning methods based on seat presence, self-occlusion etc. are used to remove noisy keypoints (more detail in supplementary). Figure 3(c) shows some real images where dense keypoint annotation is generated from available sparse keypoint annotation as described above.

For our synthetic data, a single template 3D model (per category) is manually annotated with a sparse set of 3D keypoints. These models are shown in Fig. 3a. Using a modified version of the rendering pipeline presented by [25], we render the template 3D model and project sparse 2D keypoints from multiple views to generate synthetic data required for the pipeline. Similar skeletal point sampling mechanism as mentioned earlier is used to from dense keypoint annotation for each synthetic image as shown in Fig. 3b (more details in supplementary).

4   Experiments

In this section, we evaluate the proposed approach with other state-of-the-art models for multiple tasks related to viewpoint estimation. Additionally, multiple architectural choices are validated by performing various ablation on the proposed multi-view assimilation method.

Datasets: We empirically demonstrate *state-of-the-art* or competitive performance when compared to several other methods on two public datasets. *Pascal3D+* [32]: This dataset contains images from Pascal [6] and ImageNet [22] set labeled with both detection and continuous pose annotations for 12 rigid object categories. *ObjectNet3D* [31]: This dataset consists of 100 diverse categories, 90,127 images with 201,888 objects. Due to the requirement of keypoints, keypoint-based methods can be evaluated only on object-categories with available keypoint annotation. Hence, we evaluate our method on 4 categories from these dataset namely, Chair, Bed, Sofa and Dining-table (3 on Pascal3D+, as it does not contain Bed category). We evaluate our performance for the task of object viewpoint estimation, and joint detection and viewpoint estimation.

Metrics: Performance in object viewpoint estimation is measured using *Median Error* (*MedErr*) and *Accuracy atθ* (*Acc$_\theta$*), which were introduced by Tulsiani *et al.* [29]. *MedErr* measures the median geodesic distance between the predicted pose and the ground-truth pose (in degree) and *Acc$_\theta$* measures the % of images where the geodesic distance between the predicted pose and the ground-truth pose is less than θ (in radian). While previous works evaluate *Acc$_\theta$* with $\theta = \pi/6$ only, we evaluate *Acc$_\theta$* with smaller θ as well (i.e. for $\theta = \pi/8$ and $\pi/12$) to highlights our models ability to deliver more accurate pose estimates. Finally, to evaluate performance on joint detection and viewpoint estimation, we use *Average Viewpoint Precision at 'n' views* (*AVP-n*) metric as introduced in [32].

Training details: We use ADAM optimizer [13] having a learning rate of 0.001 with minibatch-size 7. For each object class, we assign a *single* 3D model from Shapenet Repository as the object template. The local feature descriptor network is trained using 8,000 renders of the template 3D model (per class), along with real training images from Keypoint-5 and Pascal3D+. Dense correspondence annotations are generated for this segment of the training (refer Sect. 3.4).

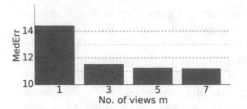

Fig. 4. $Acc_{\pi/6}$ vs number for views 'm' used for the multi-view information assimilation in our method.

Table 1. Ablation on our model for validating the utility of $L(I_2)$ in improving pose estimation.

Ours$_N$	$MedErr$	$Acc_{\pi/6}$
w/o $L(I_2)$	11.51	0.74
with $L(I_2)$	**9.52**	**0.80**

Finally, the pose estimation network is trained using Pascal3D+ or ObjectNet3D datasets. This training regime provides us our normal model, labeled **Ours$_N$**. Additionally, to compare against RenderForCNN [25] in the presence of synthetic data, we construct a separate training regime, where the synthetic data provided by RenderForCNN [25] is also utilized for training the pose estimation network. The model trained in this regime is labeled **Ours$_D$**.

4.1   Ablative Analysis

In this section, we focus on evaluating the utility of various components of our method for object viewpoint estimation. Our ablative analysis focuses on the Chair category. The Chair category, having high intra-class variation, is considered one of the most challenging classes and provides minimally biased dataset for evaluating ablations of our architecture. For all the ablations, the network is trained on the train-subset of ObjectNet3D and Pascal-3D+ dataset. We report our ablation statistics on the easy-test-subset of Pascal3D+ for chair category, as introduced by [29].

First, we show the utility of the Multi-view information assimilation by performing ablations on the number of views 'm'. In Fig. 4, we evaluate the $MedErr$ for our method with 'm' varying from 1 to 7. Note that we do not utilize the local descriptors $L(I_2)$ in this setup and the pose estimator uses only the multi-view keypoint correspondence maps $mvK(I_2)$ as input. As the figure shows, additional information from multiple views is crucial. For having an computationally efficient yet effective system, we use $m = 3$ for all the following experiments. Next, it is essential to ascertain the utility of local descriptors $L(I_2)$ in improving our performance. In Table 1, we can clearly observe increment in performance due to usage of $L(I_2)$ along with $mvK(I_2)$. Hence, in our final pipeline, the pose estimator network is designed to include the $L(I_2)$ as an additional input.

4.2   Object Viewpoint Estimation

In this section, we evaluate our method against other *state-of-the-art* approaches for the task of viewpoint estimation. Similar to other keypoint-based pose estimation works, such as 3D-INN [30], we conduct our experiments on all object classes where 2D-keypoint information is available.

Pascal3D+: Table 2 compares our approach to other *state-of-the-art* methods, namely Grabner *et al.* [8] and RenderForCNN [25]. The table shows, our best performing method **Ours$_D$** clearly outperform other established approaches on pose estimation task.

Table 2. Performance for object viewpoint estimation on PASCAL 3D+ [32] using ground truth bounding boxes. Note that *MedErr* is measured in degree.

Category	Su *et al.* [25]		Grabner *et al.* [8]		**Ours$_D$**	
	$Acc_{\pi/6}$	*MedErr*	$Acc_{\pi/6}$	*MedErr*	$Acc_{\pi/6}$	*MedErr*
Chair	0.86	9.7	0.80	13.7	0.83	**8.84**
Sofa	0.90	**9.5**	0.87	13.5	**0.90**	10.74
Table	0.73	10.8	0.71	11.8	**0.87**	**6.00**
Average	0.83	10.0	0.79	13.0	**0.87**	**8.53**

ObjectNet3D: As none of the existing works have shown results on Object-Net3D dataset, we trained RenderForCNN using the synthetic data and code provided by the authors Su *et al.* [25] for ObjectNet3D. Table 3 compares our method against RenderForCNN on various metrics for viewpoint estimation. RenderForCNN, which is trained using 500,000 more samples of synthetic images, still shows poor performance than the proposed method **Ours$_N$**.

Table 3. Evaluation on viewpoint estimation based tasks on the ObjectNet3D dataset. Note that **Ours$_N$** is trained with no synthetic data, where as Su *et al.* is trained with 500,000 synthetic images (for all 4 classes).

Method	Metric	Chair	Sofa	Table	Bed	Avg.
Object viewpoint estimation						
MedErr	Su *et al.* [25]	9.70	8.45	4.50	7.21	7.46
	Ours$_N$	**7.94**	**3.55**	**3.33**	**7.10**	**5.48**
$Acc_{\pi/6}$	Su *et al.* [25]	0.75	0.90	0.77	0.77	0.80
	Ours$_N$	**0.81**	**0.92**	**0.90**	**0.82**	**0.86**
$Acc_{\pi/8}$	Su *et al.* [25]	0.71	0.89	0.72	0.75	0.76
	Ours$_N$	**0.78**	**0.90**	**0.88**	**0.79**	**0.83**
$Acc_{\pi/12}$	Su *et al.* [25]	0.64	0.80	0.68	0.72	0.71
	Ours$_N$	**0.72**	**0.86**	**0.84**	**0.74**	**0.79**
Joint object detection and pose estimation						
AVP-4	Su *et al.* [25]	**23.9**	69.8	53.5	65.1	53.1
	Ours$_N$	22.1	**71.9**	**65.7**	**71.6**	**57.8**

4.3   Joint Object Detection and Viewpoint Estimation

Now, for this task, our pipeline is used along with object detection proposal from R-CNN [7] using MCG [1] object proposals to estimate viewpoint of objects in each detected bounding box, as also followed by V&K [29]. Note that the performance of all models in this task is affected by the performance of the underlying Object Detection module, which varies significantly among classes.

Pascal3D+: In Table 4, we compare our approach against other *state-of-the-art* keypoint-based methods, namely, 3D-INN [30] and V&K [29]. The metric comparison shows superiority of our method, which in turn highlights ours' ability to predict pose even with noisy object localization.

Table 4. Comparison of **Ours$_D$** with other keypoint-based pose estimation approaches for the task of joint object detection and viewpoint estimation on Pascal3D+ dataset.

AVP−4	Chair	Sofa	Table	Avg.
V&K [29]	25.1	43.8	24.3	31.1
3D-INN [30]	23.1	**45.8**	–	–
Ours$_D$	**26.0**	41.9	**26.5**	**31.5**

ObjectNet3D: Here, we trained RenderForCNN using the synthetic data and code provided by the authors Su *et al.* [25]. Table 3 compares our method against RenderForCNN on the *AVP-n* metric.

Table 3 clearly demonstrates sub-optimal performance of RenderForCNN on ObjectNet3D. This is due to the fact that, the synthetic data provided by the authors Su *et al.* [25] is overfitted to the distribution of Pascal3D+ dataset. This leads to a lack of generalizability in RenderForCNN, where a mismatch in the synthetic and real data distribution can significantly lower its performance. Moreover, Table 3 not only presents our superior performance, but also highlights the poor generalizability of RenderForCNN.

4.4   Analysis

Here, we present analysis of results on additional experiments to highlight the chief benefits of the proposed approach.

Effective Data Utilization: To highlight the effective utilization of data in our method, we compare **Ours$_N$** against other methods trained without utilizing any synthetic data. For this experiment, we trained RenderForCNN without utilizing synthetic data and compare it to **Ours$_N$** in Table 5. The Table not only provides evidence for high data dependency of RenderForCNN, it also highlights our superior performance against Grabner *et al.* [8] even in limited data scenario.

Table 5. Performance for object viewpoint estimation on PASCAL 3D+ [32] using ground truth bounding boxes.

Category	Su et al. [25]		Grabner et al. [8]		Ours$_N$	
	$Acc_{\pi/6}$	MedErr	$Acc_{\pi/6}$	MedErr	$Acc_{\pi/6}$	MedErr
Chair	0.70	11.30	0.80	13.70	**0.80**	**9.52**
Sofa	0.65	14.45	**0.87**	13.50	0.80	**9.96**
Table	0.70	**5.80**	0.71	11.80	**0.83**	6.00
Average	0.68	10.51	0.79	13.0	**0.81**	**8.49**

Higher Precision of Our Approach: Table 6 compares **Ours$_N$** to Render-ForCNN [25] on stricter metrics, namely $Acc_{\pi/8}$ and $Acc_{\pi/12}$. Further, we show a plot of Acc_θ vs θ in Figs. 5 and 6 for multiple classes in both Pascal3D+ and ObjectNet3D dataset. Compared to the previous state-of-the-art model, we are able to substantially improve the performance with harsher θ bounds, indicating that our model is more precise on estimating the pose of objects on both 'Chair' and 'Table' category. This firmly establishing the superiority of our approach for the task of fine-grained viewpoint estimation.

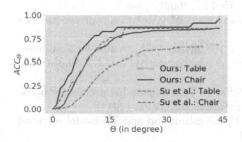

Fig. 5. Acc_θ vs θ in Pascal3D+.   **Fig. 6.** Acc_θ vs θ in ObjectNet3D.

Table 6. Comparison of our approach to existing *state-of-the-art* methods for stricter metrics (On Pascal3D). For evaluating RenderForCNN on pascal3D+, the model provided by the authors Su et al. has been used. The best value has been highlighted in **bold**, and the second best has been colored red.

Metric	Method	Chair	Sofa	Table	Avg.
$Acc_{\pi/8}$	Su et al. [25]	0.59	0.79	0.68	0.68
	Ours$_N$	0.78	0.77	0.83	0.79
	Ours$_D$	**0.81**	**0.85**	**0.86**	**0.84**
$Acc_{\pi/12}$	Su et al. [25]	0.42	0.69	0.60	0.57
	Ours$_N$	0.69	0.67	0.83	0.73
	Ours$_D$	**0.72**	**0.75**	**0.83**	**0.76**

5   Conclusions

In this paper, we present a novel approach for object viewpoint estimation, which combines keypoint correspondence maps from multiple views, to achieve state-of-the-art results on standard pose estimation datasets. Being data-efficient, our method is suitable for large-scale or novel-object based real world applications. In future work, we would like to make the method weakly-supervised as obtaining keypoint annotations for novel object categories is non-trivial. Finally, the pose-invariant local descriptors show a promise of usability in other tasks, which will also be explored in the future.

References

1. Arbeláez, P., Pont-Tuset, J., Barron, J.T., Marques, F., Malik, J.: Multiscale combinatorial grouping. In: CVPR (2014)
2. Aubry, M., Maturana, D., Efros, A.A., Russell, B.C., Sivic, J.: Seeing 3D chairs: exemplar part-based 2D-3D alignment using a large dataset of cad models. In: CVPR (2014)
3. Berg, A.C., Berg, T.L., Malik, J.: Shape matching and object recognition using low distortion correspondences. In: CVPR (2005)
4. Borotschnig, H., Paletta, L., Prantl, M., Pinz, A.: Appearance-based active object recognition. Image Vis. Comput. **18**(9), 715–727 (2000)
5. Choy, C.B., Gwak, J., Savarese, S., Chandraker, M.: Universal correspondence network. In: NIPS (2016)
6. Everingham, M., Eslami, S.A., Van Gool, L., Williams, C.K., Winn, J., Zisserman, A.: The pascal visual object classes challenge: a retrospective. Int. J. Comput. Vis. **111**(1), 98–136 (2015)
7. Girshick, R., Donahue, J., Darrell, T., Malik, J.: Rich feature hierarchies for accurate object detection and semantic segmentation. In: CVPR (2014)
8. Grabner, A., Roth, P.M., Lepetit, V.: 3D pose estimation and 3D model retrieval for objects in the wild. In: CVPR (2018)
9. Han, K., et al.: SCNet: learning semantic correspondence. In: ICCV (2017)
10. He, X., Zhou, Y., Zhou, Z., Bai, S., Bai, X.: Triplet-center loss for multi-view 3D object retrieval. In: CVPR (2018)
11. Huang, H., Kalogerakis, E., Chaudhuri, S., Ceylan, D., Kim, V.G., Yumer, E.: Learning local shape descriptors from part correspondences with multiview convolutional networks. ACM Trans. Graph. **37**(1), 6 (2017)
12. Kanezaki, A., Matsushita, Y., Nishida, Y.: RotationNet: joint object categorization and pose estimation using multiviews from unsupervised viewpoints. In: CVPR (2018)
13. Kingma, D.P., Ba, J.: Adam: a method for stochastic optimization. In: ICLR (2015)
14. Kundu, J.N., Uppala, P.K., Pahuja, A., Babu, R.V.: Adadepth: unsupervised content congruent adaptation for depth estimation. In: CVPR (2018)
15. Liu, C., Yuen, J., Torralba, A.: SIFT flow: dense correspondence across scenes and its applications. In: Hassner, T., Liu, C. (eds.) Dense Image Correspondences for Computer Vision, pp. 15–49. Springer, Cham (2016). https://doi.org/10.1007/978-3-319-23048-1_2
16. Lowe, D.G.: Distinctive image features from scale-invariant keypoints. Int. J. Comput. Vis. **60**(2), 91–110 (2004)

17. Mahendran, S., Ali, H., Vidal, R.: 3D pose regression using convolutional neural networks. In: ICCV (2017)
18. Paletta, L., Pinz, A.: Active object recognition by view integration and reinforcement learning. Robot. Auton. Syst. **31**(1), 71–86 (2000)
19. Poirson, P., Ammirato, P., Fu, C.Y., Liu, W., Kosecka, J., Berg, A.C.: Fast single shot detection and pose estimation. In: 3DV (2016)
20. Qi, C.R., Su, H., Niessner, M., Dai, A., Yan, M., Guibas, L.J.: Volumetric and multi-view CNNs for object classification on 3D data. In: CVPR (2016)
21. Rhodin, H., et al.: Learning monocular 3D human pose estimation from multi-view images. In: CVPR (2018)
22. Russakovsky, O., et al.: Imagenet large scale visual recognition challenge. Int. J. Comput. Vis. **115**(3), 211–252 (2015)
23. Schmidt, T., Newcombe, R., Fox, D.: Self-supervised visual descriptor learning for dense correspondence. IEEE Robot. Autom. Lett. **2**, 420 (2017)
24. Su, H., Maji, S., Kalogerakis, E., Learned-Miller, E.: Multi-view convolutional neural networks for 3D shape recognition. In: ICCV (2015)
25. Su, H., Qi, C.R., Li, Y., Guibas, L.J.: Render for CNN: viewpoint estimation in images using CNNs trained with rendered 3D model views. In: CVPR (2015)
26. Szegedy, C., et al.: Going deeper with convolutions. In: CVPR (2015)
27. Taniai, T., Sinha, S.N., Sato, Y.: Joint recovery of dense correspondence and cosegmentation in two images. In: CVPR (2016)
28. Tulsiani, S., Efros, A.A., Malik, J.: Multi-view consistency as supervisory signal for learning shape and pose prediction. In: CVPR (2018)
29. Tulsiani, S., Malik, J.: Viewpoints and keypoints. In: CVPR (2015)
30. Wu, J., et al.: Single image 3D interpreter network. In: Leibe, B., Matas, J., Sebe, N., Welling, M (eds.) ECCV 2016. LNCS, vol. 9910, pp. 365–382. Springer, Cham (2016). https://doi.org/10.1007/978-3-319-46466-4_22
31. Xiang, Y., et al.: ObjectNet3D: a large scale database for 3D object recognition. In: Leibe, B., Matas, J., Sebe, N., Welling, M. (eds.) ECCV 2016. LNCS, vol. 9912, pp. 160–176. Springer, Cham (2016). https://doi.org/10.1007/978-3-319-46484-8_10
32. Xiang, Y., Mottaghi, R., Savarese, S.: Beyond PASCAL: a benchmark for 3D object detection in the wild. In: WACV (2014)
33. Yu, W., Sun, X., Yang, K., Rui, Y., Yao, H.: Hierarchical semantic image matching using CNN feature pyramid. Comput. Vis. Image Underst. **169**, 40–51 (2018)

3DContextNet: K-d Tree Guided Hierarchical Learning of Point Clouds Using Local and Global Contextual Cues

Wei Zeng[✉] and Theo Gevers[✉]

Computer Vision Lab, University of Amsterdam, Amsterdam, Netherlands
{w.zeng,th.gevers}@uva.nl

Abstract. Classification and segmentation of 3D point clouds are important tasks in computer vision. Because of the irregular nature of point clouds, most of the existing methods convert point clouds into regular 3D voxel grids before they are used as input for ConvNets. Unfortunately, voxel representations are highly insensitive to the geometrical nature of 3D data. More recent methods encode point clouds to higher dimensional features to cover the global 3D space. However, these models are not able to sufficiently capture the local structures of point clouds.

Therefore, in this paper, we propose a method that exploits *both* local and global contextual cues imposed by the k-d tree. The method is designed to learn representation vectors progressively along the tree structure. Experiments on challenging benchmarks show that the proposed model provides discriminative point set features. For the task of 3D scene semantic segmentation, our method significantly outperforms the state-of-the-art on the Stanford Large-Scale 3D Indoor Spaces Dataset (S3DIS).

Keywords: Point clouds · K-d tree structure · Contextual cues · Hierarchical learning

1 Introduction

Over the past few years, ConvNets have achieved excellent performance in different computer vision tasks such as image classification [16,17,27], object detection [10,11,25] and semantic segmentation [3,11,18,21].

3D imaging technology has also experienced a major progress. In parallel, a number of annotated large-scale 3D datasets have become publicly available, which are crucial for supervised 3D deep learning models. For example, ModelNet [32] and ShapeNet [7] provide object-level man-made 3D models, whereas Stanford Large-Scale 3D Indoor Spaces Dataset [2] and ScanNet [8] are available as real 3D scene datasets.

Most of the traditional work convert the irregular 3D data (point clouds) to regular formats like 2D projection images [23,29,30] or 3D voxel grids [20,23,32]

© Springer Nature Switzerland AG 2019
L. Leal-Taixé and S. Roth (Eds.): ECCV 2018 Workshops, LNCS 11131, pp. 314–330, 2019.
https://doi.org/10.1007/978-3-030-11015-4_24

as a pre-processing step. Methods that employ 2D image projections of 3D models as their input, such as [29,30], are well suited as inputs to 2D ConvNet architectures. However, the intrinsic 3D geometrical information is distorted by the 3D-to-2D projection. Hence, this type of methods are limited by the exploitation of 3D spatial connections between regions. While it might seem straightforward to extend 2D CNNs to process 3D data by utilizing 3D convolutional kernels, data sparsity and computational complexity are the restrictive factors of this type of approaches [5,20,28,32].

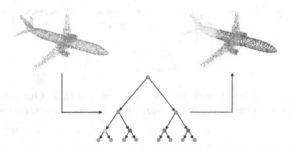

Fig. 1. Example of the implicit 3D space partition of a k-d tree. Colors of different local parts indicate different corresponding nodes in the k-d tree structure (Color figure online)

To fully exploit the 3D nature of point clouds, in this paper, the goal is to use the k-d tree structure [4] as the 3D data representation model, see Fig. 1. Our method consists of two parts: *feature learning* and *aggregation*. The model exploits both local and global contextual information and aggregates point features to obtain discriminative 3D signatures in a hierarchical manner. In the feature learning stage, local patterns are identified by the use of an adaptive feature recalibration procedure, and global patterns are calculated as non-local responses of different regions at the same level. Then, in the feature aggregation stage, point features are merged hierarchically corresponding to the associated k-d tree structure in bottom-up fashion.

Our main contributions are as follows: (1) a novel 3D context-aware neural network is proposed for 3D point cloud feature learning by exploiting the implicit partition space of the k-d tree structure, (2) a novel method is presented to incorporate both local and global contextual information for point cloud feature learning, (3) for semantic segmentation, our method significantly outperforms the state-of-the-art on the challenging Stanford Large-Scale 3D Indoor Spaces Dataset(S3DIS) [2].

2   Related Work

Previous work on ConvNets and volumetric models use different rasterization strategies. Wu et al. propose 3DShapeNets [32] using 3D binary voxel grids as

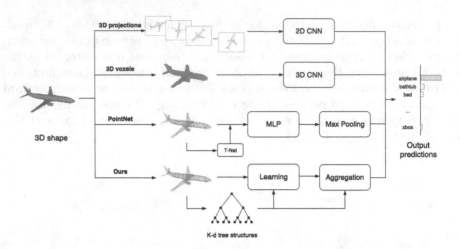

Fig. 2. Comparison to related work for the classification task. Our model is based on hierarchical feature learning and aggregation using the k-d tree structure

input of a Convolutional Deep Belief Network. This is the first work to use deep ConvNets for 3D data processing. VoxNet [20] proposes a 3D ConvNet architecture to integrate the 3D volumetric occupancy grid. ORION [28] exploits the 3D orientation to improve the results of voxel nets for 3D object recognition. Based on the ResNet [12] architecture, Voxception-ResNet (VRN) [5] proposes a very deep architecture. OctNet [26] exploits the sparsity in the input data by using a set of unbalanced octrees where each leaf node stores a pooled feature representation. However, most of the volumetric models are limited by their resolution, data sparsity, and computational cost of 3D convolutions.

Other methods rely on 2D projection images to represent the original 3D data and then apply 2D ConvNets to classify them. MVCNN [30] uses 2D rendered images of 3D shapes to learn representations of multiple views of a 3D model and then combines them to compute a compact descriptor. Deep-Pano [29] converts each 3D shape to a panoramic view and uses 2D ConvNets to build classifiers directly from these panoramas. With well-designed ConvNets, this type of methods (2D projections from 3D) performs successfully in different shape classification and retrieval tasks. However, due to the 3D-to-2D projection, these methods are limited in exploring the full 3D nature of the data. In addition, [6,19] exploits ConvNets to process non-Euclidean geometries. Moreover, Geodesic Convolutional Neural Networks (GCNN) [19] apply linear and non-linear transformations to polar coordinates in a local geodesic system. However, these methods are limited to manifold meshes.

Only recently, a number of methods are proposed that apply deep learning directly to the raw 3D data (point clouds). PointNet [22] is the pioneering work that directly processes 3D point sets in a deep learning setting. Nonetheless, since every point is treated equally, this approach fails in retaining the full 3D information. The modified version of PointNet, PointNet++ [24], abstracts local patterns by sampling representative points and recursively applies Point-Net [22] as a learning component to obtain the final representation. However, it directly discards the unselected points after each layer, and needs to sample points recursively at different scales which may yield relatively slow inference speed. Another recent work, Kd-Network [15] uses a 3D indexing structure to perform the computation. The method employs parameter sharing and calculates representations from the leaf nodes to the roots. However, this method needs to sample the point clouds and to construct k-d trees for every iteration. Further, the method employs multiple k-d trees to represent a single object. It is split-direction-dependent and is negatively influenced by a change in rotation (3D object classification) and viewpoint (3D scene semantic segmentation).

In contrast to previous methods, our model is based on a hierarchical feature learning and aggregation pipeline. Our neural network structure exploits the local and global contextual cues which are inferred by the implicit space partition of the k-d tree. In this way, our model learn features, and calculates the representation vectors progressively using the associated k-d tree. Figure 2 shows a comparison of related methods to our work for the classification task.

3   Method

In this section, we describe our architecture, *3DContextNet*, see Fig. 3. First, the choice of the tree structure is motivated to subdivide the 3D space. Then, the feature learning stage is discussed that uses both local and global contextual cues to encode the point features. Finally, the feature aggregation stage is described that computes representation vectors progressively along the k-d trees.

3.1   K-d Tree Structure: Implicit 3D Space Partition

Our method is designed to capture both the local and global context by learning and aggregating point features progressively and hierarchically. Therefore, a representation model is required to partition 3D point clouds to encapsulate the latent relations between regions. To this end, the k-d tree structure [4] is chosen.

A k-d tree is a space partitioning structure which is constructed by recursively computing axis-aligned hyperplanes to divide point sets. In this paper, we choose the standard k-d tree construction to obtain balanced k-d trees from the 3D input point clouds/sets. The latent region subdivisions of the constructed k-d tree are used to capture the local and global contextual information of point sets. Each node, at a certain level, represents a local region at the same scale, whereas nodes at different levels represent subdivisions at corresponding scales. In contrast to the k-d network of [15], splitting directions and positions are not used for the tree construction. In this way, our method is more robust to jittering and rotation than [15] which trains different affine transformations depending on the splitting directions of the nodes.

The k-d tree structure can be used to search for k-nearest neighbors for each point to determine the local point adjacency and neighbor connectivity.

Our approach uses the implicit local partitioning obtained by the k-d tree structure to determine the point adjacency and neighbor connectivity.

In general, conventional ConvNets learn and merge nearby features at the same time enlarging the receptive fields of the network. Because of the non-overlapping partitioning of the k-d tree structure, in our method, learning and merging at the same time would decrease the size of the remaining points too fast. This may lead to a lack of fine geometrical cues which are factored out during the early merging stages. To this end, our approach divides the network architecture into two parts: *feature learning* and *aggregation*.

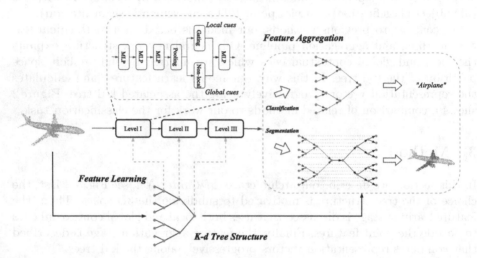

Fig. 3. 3DContextNet architecture. 3D object point clouds are used to illustrate that our method is suitable for both 3D classification and segmentation tasks. The corresponding nodes of the k-d tree determine the receptive fields at different levels. For feature learning, both local and global contextual information is encoded for each level. The associated k-d tree forms the computational graph to compute the representation vectors progressively for feature aggregation

3.2   Feature Learning Stage

Given as input is a 3D point set with the corresponding k-d tree. The tree leaves contain the individual (raw) 3D points with their representation vectors, denoted by $X = \{x_1, \ldots, x_n\} \subseteq R^F$. For example, $F = 3$ denotes the initial vectors containing the 3D point coordinates. Features are directly learned from the raw point clouds without any pre-processing step. According to [36], a function $S(X)$ is permutation invariant to the elements in X, if and only if it can be decomposed in the form of $\rho(\sum_{x \in X} \varphi(x))$, for a suitable transformation of ρ and φ. We follow PointNet [22], where a point set is mapped to a discriminative vector as follows:

$$f(\{x_1, \ldots, x_n\}) \approx g(h(x_1), \ldots, h(x_n)), \tag{1}$$

where $f : 2^{\mathbb{R}^N} \to \mathbb{R}$, $h : \mathbb{R}^N \to \mathbb{R}^K$ and $g : \underbrace{\mathbb{R}^K \times \ldots \times \mathbb{R}^K}_{n} \to \mathbb{R}$ is a symmetric function.

In the feature learning stage, point features are computed at different levels hierarchically. For a certain level, we first process each point using shared multilayer perceptron networks (MLP) as function h in Eq. (1). Then, different local region representations are computed by a symmetric function, max pooling in our work, for the subdivision regions at the same level, as function g in Eq. (1). Then, local and global contextual cues are calculated in parallel based on the local region representations. Note that both the local and global features are concatenated with the corresponding points to retain the number of points.

Local Contextual Cues: Adaptive Feature Recalibration. To model the inter-dependencies between point features in the same region, we use the local region representations obtained from the symmetric function to perform adaptive feature recalibration [13]. All operations are adaptive to each local region, represented by a certain node in the k-d tree. The local region representation obtained by the symmetric function can be interpreted as a feature descriptor for the corresponding local region. A gating function is used with a sigmoid activation to capture the feature-wise dependencies. Point features in this local region are then rescaled by the activations to obtain the adaptive recalibrated output:

$$\tilde{y}_i = \sigma(g(Y)) \cdot y_i, \qquad i = 1, ..., m \qquad (2)$$

where σ denotes the sigmoid activation and g is the symmetric function to obtain the local region representation. $Y = \{y_1, \ldots, y_m\}$ is the point feature set of the local region and m is the number of points in that region. In this way, feature dependencies are consolidated for each local region by enhancing informative features. As a result, we can obtain more discriminative local patterns. Note that the activations act as feature weights and adaptively recalibrate point features for different local regions.

Global Contextual Cues: Non-local Responses. Global contextual cues are based on the non-local responses to capture a greater range of dependencies. Intuitively, a non-local operation computes the response for one position as a weighted sum over the features for all positions in the input feature maps. A generic non-local operation [31] in deep neural networks is calculated by:

$$z_i = \frac{1}{C(x)} \sum_{\forall j} G(x_i, x_j) H(x_j), \qquad (3)$$

where i is the index of the output position and j is the index that enumerates all possible positions. In our case, i represents a local region at a certain level and j enumerates the number of local regions at the same level. Function G denotes the relationships between i and j. Further, function H computes a representation of the input signal at position j. Then, the response is normalized by a factor $C(x)$.

The k-d tree divides the input point set into different local regions. These are represented by different nodes of the tree. Larger range dependencies for different local regions at the same level are computed as non-local responses of the corresponding nodes of the tree. We consider H as an MLP, and the pairwise function G as an embedded Gaussian function:

$$G(x_i, x_j) = e^{\theta(x_i)^T \phi(x_j)}, \tag{4}$$

where $\theta(x_i)$ and $\phi(x_j)$ are two MLPs representing two embeddings. In this paper, the relationships between different nodes at the same level should be undirected, and hence $G(x_i, x_j) = G(x_j, x_i)$. Therefore, the two embeddings are the same i.e. $\theta = \phi$. The normalization factor is calculated by $C(x) = \sum_{\forall j} G(x_i, x_j)$. Note that this operation is different from a fully-connected layer. The non-local responses are based on the connections between different local regions, whereas fully-connected layers use learned weights.

Due to our input format and architecture, the receptive fields of the convolutional kernels are always 1×1 in the feature learning stage. Following DenseNet [14], to strengthen the information flow between layers, layers at the same level are connected (in the feature learning stage) with each other by concatenating all corresponding point features together. Such connections also lead to an implicit deep supervision which makes the network easier to train. The output of the feature learning stage has the same number of points as the input point set.

3.3   Feature Aggregation Stage

In the feature aggregation stage, the associated k-d tree structure is used to form the computational graph to progressively abstract over larger regions. For the classification task, the global signature is computed for the entire 3D model. For the semantic segmentation task, the outputs are the point labels. Instead of aggregating the information once over all points, the more discriminative features are computed in a bottom-up manner. The representation vector of a non-leaf node at a certain level is computed from its children nodes by MLPs and the symmetric function. To that end, max pooling is used as the symmetric function.

For classification, by using this bottom-up and hierarchical approach, more discriminative global signatures are obtained. This procedure corresponds to a ConvNet in which the representation of a certain location is computed from the representations of nearby locations at the previous layers by a series of convolutions and pooling operations. Our architecture is able to progressively capture features at increasingly larger scales. Features at lower levels have smaller receptive fields, whereas features at higher levels have larger receptive fields. That is due to the data-dependent partition of the k-d tree structure. Additionally, our model is invariant to the input order of the point sets, because the aggregating direction is along the k-d tree structure, which is invariant to input permutations.

For the semantic segmentation task, the k-d tree structure is used to represent an encoder-decoder architecture with skip connections to link the related layers.

The input of the feature aggregation stage is the point feature set in which the representation of each point encapsulates both local and global contextual information at different scales. The output is a semantic label for each point.

In conclusion, our architecture fully utilizes the local and global contextual cues in the feature learning stage. It calculates the representation vectors hierarchically in the feature aggregation stage. Hence, with k-d tree guided hierarchical learning, our 3DContextNet can obtain discriminative features for point clouds.

3.4 Discussion

Our method is related to PointNet [22] which encodes the coordinates of each point to higher dimensional features. However, by its design, this method is not able to sufficiently capture the local patterns in 3D space. More recently, PointNet++ [24] is proposed which abstracts local patterns by selecting representative points in a metric space and recursively applies PointNet as a local feature learner to obtain features of the whole point set. In fact, the method handles the non-uniform point sampling problem. However, the set of abstraction layers need to sample the point sets multiple times at different scales which leads to a relative slow inference speed. Further, only the selected points are preserved. Others are directly discarded after each layer which causes the loss of fine geometric details. Another recent work, K-d network [15] performs linear and non-linear transformations and share the transformation parameters corresponding to the splitting directions of each node in the k-d tree. The input of this method is the constructed k-d trees. It needs to calculate the representation vectors for all the nodes of the associated tree structure. For each node at a certain level, the input is the representation vectors of the two previous nodes. The method heavily depends on the splitting direction of each node to train different multiplicative transformations at each level. Hence, the method is not invariant to rotation. Furthermore, point cloud sampling and k-d tree fitting during every iteration lead to slow training and inference speed.

3.5 Implementation Details

Our 3DContextNet model deals with point clouds of a fixed size $N = 2^D$ where D is the depth of the corresponding balanced k-d tree. Point clouds of different sizes can be converted to the same size using sub- or oversampling. In our experiments, not all the levels of the k-d tree are used. For simplicity and efficiency reasons, this number is $L = 3$ for both the feature learning and aggregation stage. The receptive fields (number of points) for each level in the feature learning stage are 32 - 64 - 128 for the classification tasks and 32 - 128 - 512 for the segmentation tasks.

In the feature learning stage, the sizes of the shared MLPs are (64, 64, 128, 128) - (64, 64, 256, 256) - (64, 64, 512, 512) for the three levels, respectively. The size of MLPs for θ and H are 64 - 128 - 256 and 128 - 256 - 512, respectively. Dense connections are applied within each level before the max-pooling layer. In the feature aggregation stage, the MLPs and pooling operations are used

Table 1. 3D semantic segmentation results on the Stanford Large-Scale 3D Indoor Spaces Dataset (S3DIS). Our method outperforms previous state-of-the-art methods by a large margin

	Mean IoU	Overall accuracy	Avg. class accuracy
Baseline [22]	20.1	53.2	-
PointNet [22]	47.6	78.5	66.2
MS + CU(2) [9]	47.8	79.2	59.7
G + RCU [9]	49.7	81.1	66.4
PointNet++ [24]	53.2	83.0	70.5
Ours	**55.6**	**84.9**	**74.5**

recursively to progressively abstract the discriminative representations. For the classification task, the sizes of the MLPs are (1024) - (512) - (256), respectively. For the segmentation task, like the hourglass shape, the sizes of the MLPs are (1024) - (512) - (256) - (256) - (512) - (1024), respectively. The output is then processed by two fully-connected layers with size 256. Dropout is applied after each fully-connected layer with a ratio of 0.5.

4 Experiments

In this section, we evaluate our 3DContextNet on different 3D point cloud datasets. First, it is shown that our model significantly outperforms state-of-the-art methods for the task of semantic segmentation on the Stanford Large-Scale 3D Indoor Spaces Dataset [2]. Then, it is shown that our model provides competitive results for the task of 3D object classification on the ModelNet40 dataset [32] and the task of 3D object part segmentation on the ShapeNet part dataset [7].

4.1 3D Semantic Segmentation of Scenes

Our network is evaluated on the *Stanford Large-Scale 3D Indoor Spaces* (S3DIS) dataset [1,2] for 3D semantic segmentation task. The dataset contains 6 large scale indoor areas and each point is labeled with one of the 13 semantic categories, including 5 types of furniture (*board, bookcase, chair, sofa* and *table*) and 7 building elements (*ceiling, beam, door, wall, window, column* and *floor*) plus *clutter*. We follow the same setting as in [22] and use a 6-fold cross validation over all the areas.

Our method is compared with the baseline by PointNet [22] and the recently introduced MS+CU and G+RCU models [9]. We also produce the results of PointNet++ [24] for this dataset. During training, we use the same pre-processing as in [22]. We first split rooms into blocks of $1\,m \times 1\,m$ and represent each point by a 9-dimensional vector containing coordinates (x, y, z), the

Table 2. IoU per semantic class for the S3DIS dataset with $XYZ - RGB$ as input. It can be derived that our method obtains the state-of-the-art results in mean IoU and for most of the individual classes

	Mean IoU	Ceiling	Floor	Wall	Beam	Column	Window	Door	Table	Chair	Sofa	Bookcase	Board	Clutter
PointNet [22]	47.6	88.0	88.7	69.3	42.4	23.1	47.5	51.6	54.1	42.0	9.6	38.2	29.4	35.2
MS + CU(2) [9]	47.8	88.6	**95.8**	67.3	36.9	24.9	48.6	52.3	51.9	45.1	10.6	36.8	24.7	37.5
G + RCU [9]	49.7	90.3	92.1	67.9	44.7	24.2	52.3	51.2	58.1	47.4	6.9	39.0	30.0	41.9
PointNet++ [24]	53.2	90.2	91.7	73.1	42.7	21.2	49.7	42.3	62.7	**59.0**	19.6	**45.8**	**48.2**	45.6
Ours	**55.6**	**92.6**	93.1	**73.9**	**52.9**	**35.0**	**55.8**	**57.5**	**62.9**	49.0	**22.0**	42.8	39.8	**45.8**

Table 3. IoU per semantic class for the S3DIS dataset using only XYZ input features (no color/appearance). It is shown that our method provides comparable results in mean IoU and for all individual classes even without color/appearance information

	Mean IoU	Ceiling	Floor	Wall	Beam	Column	Window	Door	Table	Chair	Sofa	Bookcase	Board	Clutter
PointNet [22]	40.0	84.0	87.2	57.9	37.0	19.6	29.3	35.3	51.6	42.4	11.6	26.4	12.5	25.5
MS + CU(2) [9]	43.0	86.5	**94.9**	58.8	37.7	25.6	28.8	36.7	47.2	46.1	18.7	30.0	16.8	31.2
PointNet++ [24]	47.0	88.0	92.4	**64.7**	37.7	16.8	31.0	**41.1**	**59.6**	52.0	**29.4**	**42.2**	**19.2**	36.9
Ours	**48.6**	**90.5**	92.8	63.6	**49.4**	**31.2**	**44.2**	37.8	**59.6**	50.6	17.7	38.7	17.3	**37.9**

color information RGB and the normalized position (x', y', z'). The baseline extracts the same 9-dim local features and three additional ones: local point density, local curvature and normals. The standard MLP is used as the classifier. PointNet [22] computes the global point cloud signature and feeds it back to per point features. In this way, each point representation incorporates both local and global information. Recent work by [9] proposes two models that enlarge the receptive field over the 3D scene. The motivation is to incorporate both the input-level context and the output-level context. MS+CU represents the multi-scale input block with a consolidation unit model, while G+RCU stands for the grid-blocks in combination with a recurrent consolidation block model. Point-Net++ [24] exploits metric space distances to build a hierarchical grouping of points and abstracts the features progressively. Results are shown in Table 1. A significance test is conducted between our results and the state-of-the-art results obtained by PointNet++ [24]. The p-value equals to 0.0122 in favor of our method.

We also compare the mean IoU for each semantic class with $XYZ - RGB$ and only with XYZ as input, see Tables 2 and 3 respectively. We obtain state-of-the-art results in mean IoU and for most of the individual classes for both $XYZ - RGB$ and XYZ input. The reason of obtaining comparable results with PointNet++ [24] for furnitures is that the k-d tree structure is computed along the axes. Therefore, it may be inefficient for precise prediction near the splitting boundaries, especially for relatively small objects. Note that our model using only geometry information (i.e. XYZ) achieves better results than the original PointNet method using both geometry and color/appearance information.

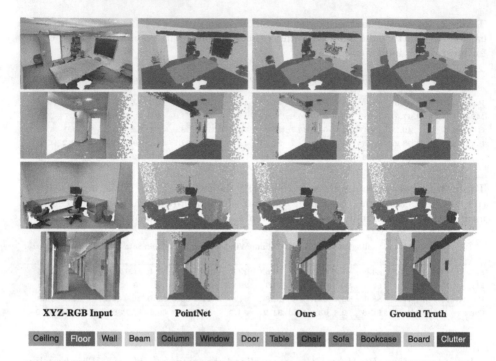

XYZ-RGB Input   **PointNet**   **Ours**   **Ground Truth**

| Ceiling | Floor | Wall | Beam | Column | Window | Door | Table | Chair | Sofa | Bookcase | Board | Clutter |

Fig. 4. Qualitative results for 3D indoor semantic segmentation. Results for the S3DIS dataset with $XYZ - RGB$ as input. From left to right: the input point cloud, the results of PointNet, our results, and the ground truth semantic labels. Our model obtains more consistent and less noisy predictions (Color figure online)

A number of qualitative results are presented in Fig. 4 for the 3D indoor semantic segmentation task. It can be derived that our method provides more precise predictions for local structures. It shows that our model exploits both local and global contextual cues to learn discriminative features to achieve proper semantic segmentation. Moreover, our model size is less than 160 MB and average inference time is less than 70 ms per block, which makes our method suitable for large scale point cloud analysis.

Ablation Study. In this section, experiments are conducted to validate the effects of the different components of our proposed architecture for 3D semantic segmentation task. The baseline is the model corresponding to the vanilla PointNet, but utilizing the k-d tree partitioning to guide the feature learning stage. For a certain level, max-pooling is used to obtain different local region representations which are concatenated with the corresponding point features. We also trained models with different sets of components to test the effectiveness of our approach. We use the sixth fold setting of [24] for S3DIS as our experiment setting (i.e. we test on Area 6 and train on the rest). Results are reported in Table 4. Experimental results show that: (1) with k-d tree guided

Table 4. Effectiveness of different components of our architecture. We use the sixth fold setting of [24] for S3DIS as our training/testing split

	Mean IoU	Overall accuracy
PointNet	63.9	86.0
PointNet++	69.1	90.1
Baseline with k-d tree guided	68.1	89.2
Only progressively aggregation	68.3	88.9
Only global cues	68.7	88.9
Only local cues	69.9	89.8
Global cues and progressively aggregation	69.8	89.9
Local cues and progressively aggregation	71.2	90.4
Local and global cues	71.5	90.1
All	**72.0**	**90.6**

hierarchical feature learning, the baseline obtains better results than PointNet. Hence, local structures do help, (2) local contextual cues boost the performance the most, indicating that local neighborhoods of points contain fine-grained structure information, (3) any single combination of two components increases the performance and combining all of them provides state-of-the-art 3D semantic segmentation results.

4.2   3D Object Classification and Part Segmentation

We evaluate our method on the ModelNet40 shape classification benchmark [32]. The dataset contains a collection of 3D CAD models of 40 categories. We use the official split consisting of 9843 examples for training and 2468 for testing. Using the same experimental settings of [22], we convert the CAD models to point sets by uniformly sampling (1024 points in our case) over the mesh faces. Then, these points are normalized to have zero mean and unit sphere. We also randomly rotate the point sets along the z-axis and jitter the coordinates of each point by Gaussian noise for data augmentation during training.

It can be derived from Table 5, that our model outperforms PointNet [22]. Our model has competitive performance compared to PointNet++. However, our method is much faster in inference time. Table 6 summarizes the comparison of time and space computations between PointNet, PointNet++ and our proposed method. We measure forward pass time with a batch size of 8 using TensorFlow 1.1. PointNet has the best time efficiency, but our model is faster than PointNet++ while keeping a comparable classification performance.

We also evaluate our method on the ShapeNet part dataset [7]. The dataset contains 16881 CAD models of 16 categories. Each category is annotated with 2 to 6 parts. There are 50 different parts annotated in total. We use the official split for training and testing. In this dataset, both the number of shapes and

Table 5. 3D object classification results on ModelNet40. The result of our model outperforms PointNet and is comparable to PointNet++

Method	Input	Accuracy (%)
DeepPano [29]	Image	77.6
MVCNN [30]	Image	90.1
MVCNN-MultiRes [23]	Image	91.4
3DShapeNets [32]	Voxel	77
VoxNet [20]	Voxel	83
Subvolume [23]	Voxel	89.2
PointNet (vanilla) [22]	Point cloud	87.2
PointNet [22]	Point cloud	89.2
K-d network [15]	Point cloud	90.6
PointNet++ [24]	Point cloud	90.7
PointNet++ (with normal) [24]	Point cloud	91.9
Ours	Point cloud	90.2
Ours (with normal)	Point cloud	91.1

Table 6. Comparison of the model sizes and the inference time for the classification task. Our model is faster than PointNet++ while keeping comparable classification performance

	PointNet [22]	PointNet++ (SSG) [24]	PointNet++ (MSG) [24]	PointNet++ (MRG) [24]	3DContextNet
Model size (MB)	40	8.7	12	24	56.8
Forward time (ms)	25.3	82.4	163.2	87.0	45.9

the parts within categories are highly imbalanced. Therefore, many previous methods train their network on every category separately. Our network is trained across categories.

We compare our model with two traditional learning based techniques Wu [33] and Yi [34], the volumetric deep learning baseline (3DCNN) in Point-Net [22], as well as state-of-the-art approaches of SSCNN [35] and Point-Net++ [24], see Table 7. The point intersection over union for each category as well as the mean IoU are reported. In comparison to PointNet, our approach performs better on most of the categories, which proves the importance of local and global contextual information. See Fig. 5 for a number of qualitative results for the 3D object part segmentation task.

Table 7. 3D object part segmentation results on ShapeNet part dataset

	mean	airplane	bag	cap	car	chair	earphone	guitar	knife	lamp	laptop	motor	mug	pistol	rocket	skateboard	table
#shapes		2690	76	55	898	3758	69	787	392	1547	451	202	184	283	66	152	5271
Wu [33]	-	63.2	-	-	-	73.5	-	-	-	74.4	-	-	-	-	-	-	74.8
K-d Networks [15]	77.2	79.9	71.2	80.9	68.8	88.0	72.4	88.9	86.4	79.8	94.9	55.8	86.5	79.3	50.4	71.1	80.2
3DCNN [22]	79.4	75.1	72.8	73.3	70.0	87.2	63.5	88.4	79.6	74.4	93.9	58.7	91.8	76.4	51.2	65.3	77.1
Yi [34]	81.4	81.0	78.4	77.7	75.7	87.6	61.9	92.0	85.4	82.5	95.7	70.6	91.9	85.9	53.1	69.8	75.3
PointNet [22]	83.7	83.4	78.7	82.5	74.9	89.6	73.0	91.5	85.9	80.8	95.3	65.2	93.0	81.2	57.9	72.8	80.6
SSCNN [35]	84.7	81.6	81.7	81.9	75.2	90.2	74.9	93.0	86.1	84.7	95.6	66.7	92.7	81.6	60.6	82.9	82.1
PointNet++ [24]	85.1	82.4	79.0	87.7	77.3	90.8	71.8	91.0	85.9	83.7	95.3	71.6	94.1	81.3	58.7	76.4	82.6
Ours	84.3	83.3	78.0	84.2	77.2	90.1	73.1	91.6	85.9	81.4	95.4	69.1	92.3	81.7	60.8	71.8	81.4

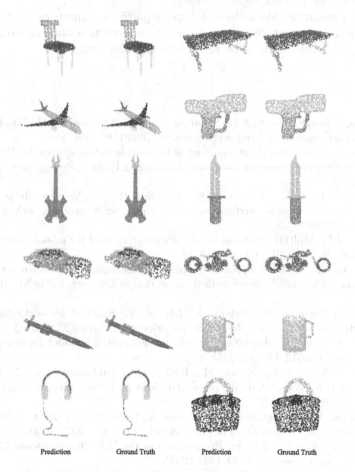

     Prediction   Ground Truth   Prediction   Ground Truth

Fig. 5. Qualitative results for the 3D object part segmentation task. For each group from left to right: the prediction and the ground truth

5   Conclusion

In this paper, we proposed a deep learning architecture that exploits the local and global contextual cues imposed by the implicit space partition of the k-d tree for feature learning, and calculate the representation vectors progressively along the associated k-d tree for feature aggregation. Large scale experiments showed that our model outperformed existing state-of-the-art methods for semantic segmentation task. Further, the model obtained comparable results for 3D object classification and 3D part segmentation.

In the future, other hierarchical 3D space partition structures can be studied as the underlying structure for the deep net computation and the non-uniform point sampling issue needs to be taken into consideration.

References

1. Armeni, I., Sax, S., Zamir, A.R., Savarese, S.: Joint 2D–3D-semantic data for indoor scene understanding. arXiv preprint arXiv:1702.01105 (2017)
2. Armeni, I., et al.: 3D semantic parsing of large-scale indoor spaces. In: Proceedings of the IEEE Conference on Computer Vision and Pattern Recognition, pp. 1534–1543 (2016)
3. Badrinarayanan, V., Kendall, A., Cipolla, R.: SegNet: a deep convolutional encoder-decoder architecture for image segmentation. arXiv preprint arXiv:1511.00561 (2015)
4. Bentley, J.L.: Multidimensional binary search trees used for associative searching. Commun. ACM **18**(9), 509–517 (1975)
5. Brock, A., Lim, T., Ritchie, J.M., Weston, N.: Generative and discriminative voxel modeling with convolutional neural networks. arXiv preprint arXiv:1608.04236 (2016)
6. Bruna, J., Zaremba, W., Szlam, A., LeCun, Y.: Spectral networks and locally connected networks on graphs. arXiv preprint arXiv:1312.6203 (2013)
7. Chang, A.X., et al.: ShapeNet: an information-rich 3D model repository. arXiv preprint arXiv:1512.03012 (2015)
8. Dai, A., Chang, A.X., Savva, M., Halber, M., Funkhouser, T., Nießner, M.: ScanNet: richly-annotated 3D reconstructions of indoor scenes. arXiv preprint arXiv:1702.04405 (2017)
9. Engelmann, F., Kontogianni, T., Hermans, A., Leibe, B.: Exploring spatial context for 3D semantic segmentation of point clouds. In: ICCV 2017 Workshop (2017)
10. Girshick, R.: Fast R-CNN. In: Proceedings of the IEEE International Conference on Computer Vision, pp. 1440–1448 (2015)
11. Girshick, R., Donahue, J., Darrell, T., Malik, J.: Rich feature hierarchies for accurate object detection and semantic segmentation. In: Proceedings of the IEEE Conference on Computer Vision and Pattern Recognition, pp. 580–587 (2014)
12. He, K., Zhang, X., Ren, S., Sun, J.: Deep residual learning for image recognition. In: Proceedings of the IEEE Conference on Computer Vision and Pattern Recognition, pp. 770–778 (2016)
13. Hu, J., Shen, L., Sun, G.: Squeeze-and-excitation networks. arXiv preprint arXiv:1709.01507 (2017)

14. Huang, G., Liu, Z., Weinberger, K.Q., van der Maaten, L.: Densely connected convolutional networks. arXiv preprint arXiv:1608.06993 (2016)
15. Klokov, R., Lempitsky, V.: Escape from cells: deep kd-networks for the recognition of 3D point cloud models. arXiv preprint arXiv:1704.01222 (2017)
16. Krizhevsky, A., Sutskever, I., Hinton, G.E.: ImageNet classification with deep convolutional neural networks. In: Advances in Neural Information Processing Systems, pp. 1097–1105 (2012)
17. LeCun, Y., Bottou, L., Bengio, Y., Haffner, P.: Gradient-based learning applied to document recognition. Proc. IEEE **86**(11), 2278–2324 (1998)
18. Long, J., Shelhamer, E., Darrell, T.: Fully convolutional networks for semantic segmentation. In: Proceedings of the IEEE Conference on Computer Vision and Pattern Recognition, pp. 3431–3440 (2015)
19. Masci, J., Boscaini, D., Bronstein, M., Vandergheynst, P.: Geodesic convolutional neural networks on Riemannian manifolds. In: Proceedings of the IEEE International Conference on Computer Vision Workshops, pp. 37–45 (2015)
20. Maturana, D., Scherer, S.: Voxnet: A 3D convolutional neural network for real-time object recognition. In: 2015 IEEE/RSJ International Conference on Intelligent Robots and Systems (IROS), pp. 922–928. IEEE (2015)
21. Noh, H., Hong, S., Han, B.: Learning deconvolution network for semantic segmentation. In: Proceedings of the IEEE International Conference on Computer Vision, pp. 1520–1528 (2015)
22. Qi, C.R., Su, H., Mo, K., Guibas, L.J.: PointNet: deep learning on point sets for 3D classification and segmentation. arXiv preprint arXiv:1612.00593 (2016)
23. Qi, C.R., Su, H., Nießner, M., Dai, A., Yan, M., Guibas, L.J.: Volumetric and multi-view CNNs for object classification on 3D data. In: Proceedings of the IEEE Conference on Computer Vision and Pattern Recognition, pp. 5648–5656 (2016)
24. Qi, C.R., Yi, L., Su, H., Guibas, L.J.: PointNet++: deep hierarchical feature learning on point sets in a metric space. In: Advances in Neural Information Processing Systems, pp. 5099–5108 (2017)
25. Ren, S., He, K., Girshick, R., Sun, J.: Faster R-CNN: towards real-time object detection with region proposal networks. In: Advances in Neural Information Processing Systems, pp. 91–99 (2015)
26. Riegler, G., Ulusoy, A.O., Geiger, A.: OctNet: learning deep 3D representations at high resolutions. In: Proceedings of the IEEE Conference on Computer Vision and Pattern Recognition, vol. 3 (2017)
27. Russakovsky, O., et al.: Imagenet large scale visual recognition challenge. Int. J. Comput. Vis. **115**(3), 211–252 (2015)
28. Sedaghat, N., Zolfaghari, M., Brox, T.: Orientation-boosted voxel nets for 3D object recognition. arXiv preprint arXiv:1604.03351 (2016)
29. Shi, B., Bai, S., Zhou, Z., Bai, X.: DeepPano: deep panoramic representation for 3-D shape recognition. IEEE Sig. Process. Lett. **22**(12), 2339–2343 (2015)
30. Su, H., Maji, S., Kalogerakis, E., Learned-Miller, E.: Multi-view convolutional neural networks for 3D shape recognition. In: Proceedings of the IEEE International Conference on Computer Vision, pp. 945–953 (2015)
31. Wang, X., Girshick, R., Gupta, A., He, K.: Non-local neural networks (2017)
32. Wu, Z., et al.: 3D shapeNets: a deep representation for volumetric shapes. In: Proceedings of the IEEE Conference on Computer Vision and Pattern Recognition, pp. 1912–1920 (2015)
33. Wu, Z., Shou, R., Wang, Y., Liu, X.: Interactive shape co-segmentation via label propagation. Comput. Graph. **38**, 248–254 (2014)

34. Yi, L., et al.: A scalable active framework for region annotation in 3D shape collections. ACM Trans. Graph. (TOG) **35**(6), 210 (2016)
35. Yi, L., Su, H., Guo, X., Guibas, L.: SyncSpecCNN: synchronized spectral CNN for 3D shape segmentation. In: Computer Vision and Pattern Recognition (CVPR) (2017)
36. Zaheer, M., Kottur, S., Ravanbakhsh, S., Poczos, B., Salakhutdinov, R., Smola, A.: Deep sets (2017)

Evaluation of CNN-Based Single-Image Depth Estimation Methods

Tobias Koch[1]([✉]), Lukas Liebel[1], Friedrich Fraundorfer[2,3], and Marco Körner[1]

[1] Chair of Remote Sensing Technology,
Technical University of Munich, Munich, Germany
{tobias.koch,lukas.liebel,marco.koerner}@tum.de
[2] Institute of Computer Graphics and Vision,
Graz University of Technology, Graz, Austria
fraundorfer@icg.tugraz.at
[3] Remote Sensing Technology Institute,
German Aerospace Center (DLR), Oberpfaffenhofen, Germany

Abstract. While an increasing interest in deep models for *single-image depth estimation (SIDE)* can be observed, established schemes for their evaluation are still limited. We propose a set of novel quality criteria, allowing for a more detailed analysis by focusing on specific characteristics of depth maps. In particular, we address the preservation of edges and planar regions, depth consistency, and absolute distance accuracy. In order to employ these metrics to evaluate and compare state-of-the-art SIDE approaches, we provide a new high-quality RGB-D dataset. We used a *digital single-lens reflex (DSLR)* camera together with a *laser scanner* to acquire high-resolution images and highly accurate depth maps. Experimental results show the validity of our proposed evaluation protocol.

Keywords: Single-image depth estimation · Deep learning · CNN · RGB-D · Benchmark · Evaluation · Dataset · Error metrics

1 Introduction

With the emergence of *deep learning* methods within the recent years and their massive influence on the computer vision domain, the problem of SIDE got addressed as well by many authors. These methods are in high demand for manifold scene understanding applications like, for instance, autonomous driving, robot navigation, or augmented reality systems. In order to replace or enhance traditional methods, *convolutional neural network (CNN)* architectures have been most commonly used and successfully shown to be able to infer geometrical information solely from presented monocular RGB or intensity images, as exemplary shown in Fig. 1.

While these methods produce nicely intuitive results, proper evaluating the estimated depth maps is crucial for subsequent applications, *e.g.*, their suitability for further 3D understanding scenarios [30]. Consistent and reliable relative

© Springer Nature Switzerland AG 2019
L. Leal-Taixé and S. Roth (Eds.): ECCV 2018 Workshops, LNCS 11131, pp. 331–348, 2019.
https://doi.org/10.1007/978-3-030-11015-4_25

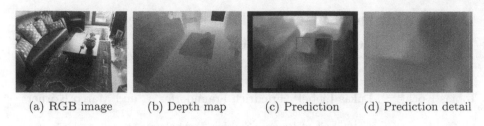

(a) RGB image   (b) Depth map   (c) Prediction   (d) Prediction detail

Fig. 1. Sample image pair from our dataset and depth prediction using a state-of-the-art algorithm [7]. Although the quality of the depth map seems reasonable, the prediction suffers from artifacts, smoothing, missing objects, and inaccuracies in textured image regions

depth estimates are, for instance, a key requirement for path planning approaches in robotics, augmented reality applications, or computational cinematography.

Nevertheless, the evaluation schemes and error metrics commonly used so far mainly consider the overall accuracy by reporting global statistics of depth residuals which does not give insight into the depth estimation quality at salient and important regions, like planar surfaces or geometric discontinuities. Hence, fairly reasonable reconstruction results, as shown in Fig. 1c, are probably positively evaluated, while still showing evident defects around edges. At the same time, the shortage of available datasets providing ground truth data of sufficient quality and quantity impedes precise evaluation.

As these issues were reported by the authors of recent SIDE papers [12,19], we aim at providing a new and extended evaluation scheme in order to overcome these deficiencies. In particular, as our main contributions, we

(i) present a new evaluation dataset acquired from diverse indoor scenarios containing high-resolution RGB images aside highly accurate depth maps from laser scans[1] *(ii)* introduce a set of new interpretable error metrics targeting the aforementioned issues *(iii)* evaluate a variety of state-of-the-art methods using these data and performance measures.

2   Related Work

In this section, we introduce some of the most recent learning-based methods for predicting depth from a single image and review existing datasets used for training and evaluating the accuracy of these methods.

2.1   Methods

Most commonly, stereo reconstruction is performed from multi-view setups, *e.g.*, by triangulation of 3D points from corresponding 2D image points observed by distinct cameras (*cf. multi-view stereo (MVS)* or *structure from motion*

---

[1] This dataset is freely available at www.lmf.bgu.tum.de/ibims1.

(SfM) methods) [27]. Nevertheless, for already many decades, estimating depth or shape from monocular setups or single views is under scientific consideration [2] in psychovisual as well as computational research domains. After several RGB-D datasets were released [4,5,11,25,28], data-driven learning-based approaches outperformed established model-based methods. Especially deep learning-based methods have proven to be highly effective for this task and achieved current state-of-the-art results [3,7,9,10,13,15–18,20–22,24,31–33]. One of the first approaches using CNNs for regressing dense depth maps was presented by Eigen et al. [8] who employ two deep networks for first performing a coarse global prediction and refine the predictions locally afterwards. An extension to this approach uses deeper models and additionally predicts normals and semantic labels [7]. Liu et al. [22] combine CNNs and *conditional random field (CRFs)* in a unified framework while making use of superpixels for preserving sharp edges. Laina et al. [15] tackle this problem with a fully convolutional network consisting of a feature map up-sampling within the network. While Li et al. [17] employ a novel set loss and a two-streamed CNN that fuses predictions of depth and depth gradients, Xu et al. [32] propose to integrate complementary information derived from multiple CNN side outputs using CRFs.

2.2   Existing Benchmark Datasets

In order to evaluate SIDE methods, any dataset containing corresponding RGB and depth images can be considered, which also comprises benchmarks originally designed for the evaluation of MVS approaches. Strecha et al. [29] propose a MVS benchmark providing overlapping images with camera poses for six different outdoor scenes and a ground truth point cloud obtained by a laser scanner. More recently, two MVS benchmarks, the ETH3D [26] and the Tanks & Temples [14] datasets, have been released. Although these MVS benchmarks contain high resolution images and accurate ground truth data obtained from a laser scanner, the setup is not designed for SIDE methods. Usually, a scene is scanned from multiple aligned laser scans and images acquired in a sequential matter. However, it cannot be guaranteed that the corresponding depth maps are dense. Occlusions in the images result in gaps in the depth maps especially at object boundaries which are, however, a key aspect of our metrics. Despite the possibility of acquiring a large number of image pairs, they mostly comprise only a limited scene variety and are highly redundant due high visual overlap. Currently, SIDE methods are tested on mainly three different datasets. Make3D [25], as one example, contains 534 outdoor images and aligned depth maps acquired from a custom-built 3D scanner, but suffers from a very low resolution of the depth maps and a rather limited scene variety. The Kitti dataset [11] contains street scenes captured out of a moving car. The dataset contains RGB images together with depth maps from a Velodyne laser scanner. However, depth maps are only provided in a very low resolution which furthermore suffer from irregularly and sparsely spaced points. The most frequently used dataset is the NYU depth v2 dataset [28] containing 464 indoor scenes with aligned RGB and depth images from video sequences obtained from a Microsoft Kinect v1 sensor. A subset of this dataset is mostly used for training deep networks, while another 654 image and depth pairs serve for evaluation. This large number of image pairs and the various indoor scenarios facilitated the fast progress of SIDE methods. However, active RGB-D sensors, like the Kinect, suffer from a short operational range, occlusions, gaps, and erroneous specular surfaces. The recently released `Matterport3D` [4] dataset provides an even larger amount of indoor scenes collected from a custom-built 3D scanner consisting of three RGB-D cameras. This dataset is a valuable addition to the `NYU-v2` but also suffers from the same weaknesses of active RGB-D sensors.

3   Error Metrics

This section describes established metrics and our new proposed ones allowing for a more detailed analysis.

3.1   Commonly Used Error Metrics

Established error metrics consider global statistics between a predicted depth map Y and its ground truth depth image Y^* with T depth pixels. Beside visual inspections of depth maps or projected 3D point clouds, the following error metrics are exclusively used in all relevant recent publications [7,8,15,19,32]:

Threshold: percentage of y such that $\max(\frac{y_i}{y_i^*}, \frac{y_i^*}{y_i}) = \sigma < thr$

Absolute relative difference: $\mathrm{rel} = \frac{1}{T} \sum_{i,j} |y_{i,j} - y_{i,j}^*| / y_{i,j}^*$

Squared relative difference: $\mathrm{srel} = \frac{1}{T} \sum_{i,j} |y_{i,j} - y_{i,j}^*|^2 / y_{i,j}^*$

RMS (linear): $\mathrm{RMS} = \sqrt{\frac{1}{T} \sum_{i,j} |y_{i,j} - y_{i,j}^*|^2}$

RMS (log): $\log_{10} = \sqrt{\frac{1}{T} \sum_{i,j} |\log y_{i,j} - \log y_{i,j}^*|^2}$

Even though these statistics are good indicators for the general quality of predicted depth maps, they could be delusive. Particularly, the standard metrics are not able to directly assess the planarity of planar surfaces or the correctness of estimated plane orientations. Furthermore, it is of high relevance that depth discontinuities are precisely located, which is not reflected by the standard metrics.

3.2   Proposed Error Metrics

In order to allow for a more meaningful analysis of predicted depth maps and a more complete comparison of different algorithms, we present a set of new quality measures that specify on different characteristics of depth maps which are crucial for many applications. These are meant to be used in addition to the traditional error metrics introduced in Sect. 3.1. When talking about depth maps, the following questions arise that should be addressed by our new metrics:

How is the quality of predicted depth maps for different absolute scene depths? Can planar surfaces be reconstructed correctly? Can all depth discontinuities be represented? How accurately are they localized? Are depth estimates consistent over the whole image area?

Distance-Related Assessment. Established global statistics are calculated over the full range of depth comprised by the image and therefore do not consider different accuracies for specific absolute scene ranges. Hence, applying the standard metrics for specific range intervals by discretizing existing depth ranges into discrete bins (*e.g.*, one-meter depth slices) allows investigating the performance of predicted depths for close and far ranged objects independently.

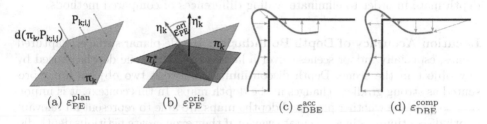

(a) ε_{PE}^{plan} (b) ε_{PE}^{orie} (c) ε_{DBE}^{acc} (d) ε_{DBE}^{comp}

Fig. 2. Visualizations of the proposed error metrics for *planarity errors* (a and b) and *depth boundary errors* (c and d)

Planarity. Man-made objects, in particular, can often be characterized by planar structures like walls, floors, ceilings, openings, and diverse types of furniture. However, global statistics do not directly give information about the shape correctness of objects within the scene. Predicting depths for planar objects is challenging for many reasons. Primarily, these objects tend to lack texture and only differ by smooth color gradients in the image, from which it is hard to estimate the correct orientation of a 3D plane with three-degrees-of-freedom. In the presence of textured planar surfaces, it is even more challenging for a SIDE approach to distinguish between a real depth discontinuity and a textured planar surface, *e.g.*, a painting on a wall. As most methods are trained on large indoor scenes, like `NYU-v2`, a correct representation of planar structures is an important task for SIDE, but can hardly be evaluated using established standard metrics. For this reason, we propose to use a set of annotated images defining various planar surfaces (walls, table tops and floors) and evaluate the flatness and orientation of predicted 3D planes $\pi_k = (\eta_k, o_k)$ compared to ground truth 3D planes $\pi_k{}^* = (\eta_k^*, o_k^*)$. Each plane is specified by a normal vector η and an offset to the plane o. In particular, a masked depth map Y_k of a particular planar surface is projected to 3D points $P_{k;i,j}$ where 3D planes π_k are robustly fitted to both the ground truth and predicted 3D point clouds $\mathcal{P}_k^* = \left\{ P_{k;i,j}^* \right\}_{i,j}$ and $\mathcal{P}_k = \left\{ P_{k;i,j} \right\}_{i,j}$, respectively. The planarity error

$$\varepsilon_{\text{PE}}^{\text{plan}}(\boldsymbol{Y}_k) = \mathbb{V}\left[\sum_{\boldsymbol{P}_{k;i,j}\in\mathcal{P}_k} d\left(\boldsymbol{\pi}_k, \boldsymbol{P}_{k;i,j}\right)\right] \tag{1}$$

is then quantified by the standard deviation of the averaged distances d between the predicted 3D point cloud and its corresponding 3D plane estimate. The orientation error

$$\varepsilon_{\text{PE}}^{\text{orie}}(\boldsymbol{Y}_k) = \text{acos}\left(\boldsymbol{\eta}_k^\top \cdot \boldsymbol{\eta}_k^*\right) \tag{2}$$

is defined as the 3D angle difference between the normal vectors of predicted and ground truth 3D planes. Figures 2a and b illustrate the proposed planarity errors. Note that the predicted depth maps are scaled w.r.t. the ground truth depth map, in order to eliminate scaling differences of compared methods.

Location Accuracy of Depth Boundaries. Beside planar surfaces, captured scenes, especially indoor scenes, cover a large variety of scene depths caused by any object in the scene. Depth discontinuities between two objects are represented as strong gradient changes in the depth maps. In this context, it is important to examine whether predicted depths maps are able to represent all relevant depth discontinuities in an accurate way or if they even create fictitious depth discontinuities confused by texture. An analysis of depth discontinuities can be best expressed by detecting and comparing edges in predicted and ground truth depth maps. Location accuracy and sharp edges are of high importance for generating a set of ground truth depth transitions which cannot be guaranteed by existing datasets acquired from RGB-D sensors. Ground truth edges are extracted from our dataset by first generating a set of tentative edge hypotheses using *structured edges* [6] and then manually selecting important and distinct edges subsequently. In order to evaluate predicted depth maps, edges $\boldsymbol{Y}_{\text{bin}}$ are extracted using structured edges and compared to the ground truth edges $\boldsymbol{Y}_{\text{bin}}^*$ via *truncated chamfer distance* of the binary edge images. Specifically, an *Euclidean distance transform* is applied to the ground truth edge image $\boldsymbol{E}^* = DT(\boldsymbol{Y}_{\text{bin}}^*)$, while distances exceeding a given threshold θ ($\theta = 10\,\text{px}$ in our experiments) are ignored in order to evaluate predicted edges only in the local neighborhood of the ground truth edges. We define the *depth boundary errors (DBEs)*, comprised of an accuracy measure

$$\varepsilon_{\text{DBE}}^{\text{acc}}(\boldsymbol{Y}) = \frac{1}{\sum_i \sum_j y_{\text{bin};i,j}} \sum_i \sum_j e_{i,j}^* \cdot y_{\text{bin};i,j} \tag{3}$$

by multiplying the predicted binary edge map with the distance map and a subsequent accumulation of the pixel distances towards the ground truth edge. As this measure does not consider any missing edges in the predicted depth image, we also define a completeness error

$$\varepsilon_{\text{DBE}}^{\text{comp}}(\boldsymbol{Y}) = \frac{1}{\sum_i \sum_j y_{\text{bin};i,j}^*} \sum_i \sum_j e_{i,j} \cdot y_{\text{bin};i,j}^* \tag{4}$$

by accumulating the ground truth edges multiplied with the distance image of the predicted edges $E = DT(Y_{\text{bin}})$. A visual explanation of the DBEs are illustrated in Figs. 2c and d.

Directed Depth Error. For many applications, it is of high interest that depth images are consistent over the whole image area. Although the absolute depth error and squared depth error give information about the correctness between predicted and ground truth depths, they do not provide information if the predicted depth is estimated too short or too far. For this purpose, we define the *directed depth errors (DDEs)*

$$\varepsilon_{\text{DDE}}^{+}(Y) = \frac{\left|\{y_{i,j}|d_{\text{sgn}}(\pi, P_{i,j}) > 0 \wedge d_{\text{sgn}}(\pi, P_{i,j}^{*}) < 0\}\right|}{T} \tag{5}$$

$$\varepsilon_{\text{DDE}}^{-}(Y) = \frac{\left|\{y_{i,j}|d_{\text{sgn}}(\pi, P_{i,j}) < 0 \wedge d_{\text{sgn}}(\pi, P_{i,j}^{*}) > 0\}\right|}{T} \tag{6}$$

as the proportions of too far and too close predicted depth pixels $\varepsilon_{\text{DDE}}^{+}$ and $\varepsilon_{\text{DDE}}^{-}$. In practice, a reference depth plane π is defined at a certain distance (*e.g.*, at 3 m, *cf.* Fig. 7c) and all predicted depths pixels which lie in front and behind this plane are masked and assessed according to their correctness using the reference depth images.

4 Dataset

As described in the previous sections, our proposed metrics require extended ground truth which is not yet available in standard datasets. Hence, we compiled a new dataset according to these specifications.

4.1 Acquisition

For creating such a reference dataset, high-quality optical RGB images and depth maps had to be acquired. Practical considerations included the choice of suitable instruments for the acquisition of both parts. Furthermore, a protocol to calibrate both instruments, such that image and depth map align with each other, had to be developed. An exhaustive analysis and comparison of different sensors considered for the data acquisition was conducted, which clearly showed the advantages of using a laser scanner and a DSLR camera compared to active sensors like RGB-D cameras or passive stereo camera rigs. We therefore used the respective setup for the creation of our dataset.

In order to record the ground truth for our dataset, we used a highly accurate Leica HDS7000 laser scanner, which stands out for high point cloud density and very low noise level. We acquired the scans with 3 mm point spacing and 0.4 mm RMS at 10 m distance. As our laser scanner does not provide RGB images along with the point clouds, an additional camera was used in order to capture optical imagery. The usage of a reasonably high-quality camera sensor and lens allows for capturing images in high resolution with only slight distortions and a high stability regarding the intrinsic parameters. For the experiments, we chose and calibrated a Nikon D5500 DSLR camera and a Nikon AF-S Nikkor 18–105 mm lens, mechanically fixed to a focal length of approximately 18 mm.

Using our sensor setup, synchronous acquisition of point clouds and RGB imagery is not possible. In order to acquire depth maps without parallax effects, the camera was mounted on a custom panoramic tripod head which allows to freely position the camera along all six degrees of freedom. This setup can be interchanged with the laser scanner, ensuring coincidence of the optical center of the camera and the origin of the laser scanner coordinate system after a prior calibration of the system. It is worth noting, that every single RGB-D image pair of our dataset was obtained by an individual scan and image capture with the aforementioned strategy in order to achieve dense depth maps without gaps due to occlusions.

4.2   Registration and Processing

The acquired images were undistorted using the intrinsic camera parameters obtained from the calibration process. In order to register the camera towards the local coordinate system of the laser scanner, we manually selected a sufficient number of corresponding 2D and 3D points and estimated the camera pose using EPnP [23]. This registration of the camera relative to the point cloud yielded only a minor translation, thanks to the pre-calibrated platform. Using this procedure, we determined the 6D pose of a virtual depth sensor which we use to derive a matching depth map from the 3D point cloud. In order to obtain a depth value for each pixel in the image, the images were sampled down to two different resolutions. We provide a high-quality version with a resolution of 1500 × 1000 px and a cropped NYU-v2-like version with a resolution of 640 × 480 px. 3D points were projected to a virtual sensor with the respective resolution. For each pixel, a depth value was calculated, representing the depth value of the 3D point with the shortest distance to the virtual sensor. It is worth highlighting that depth maps were derived from the 3D point cloud for both versions of the images separately. Hence, no down-sampling artifacts are introduced for the lower-resolution version. The depth maps for both, the high-quality and the NYU-v2-like version, are provided along with the respective images.

4.3   Contents

Following the described procedure, we compiled a dataset, which we henceforth refer to as the *independent Benchmark images and matched scans v1 (iBims-1)* dataset. The dataset is mainly composed of reference data for the direct evaluation of depth maps, as produced by SIDE methods. As described in the previous sections, pairs of images and depth maps were acquired and are provided in two different versions, namely a high-quality version and a NYU-v2-like version.

Example pairs of images and matching depth maps from iBims-1 are shown in Figs. 1a and b and Figs. 3a and b, respectively.

(a) Camera image   (b) Ground truth   (c) Masks   (d) Distinct edges

Fig. 3. Sample from the main part of the proposed iBims-1 dataset with (a) RGB image, (b) depth map, (c) several masks with semantic annotations (*i.e.*, walls (■), floor (■), tables (■), transparent objects (■), and invalid pixels (■)), and (d) distinct edges (▬) (Color figure online)

Additionally, several manually created masks are provided. Examples for all types of masks are shown in Fig. 3c, while statistics of the plane annotations are listed in Table 1. In order to allow for evaluation following the proposed DBE metric, we provide distinct edges for all images. Edges have been detected automatically and manually selected. Figure 3d shows an example for one of the scenes from iBims-1.

This main part of the dataset contains 100 RGB-D image pairs in total. So far, the NYU-v2 dataset is still the most comprehensive and accurate indoor dataset for training data-demanding deep learning methods. Since this dataset has most commonly been used for training the considered SIDE methods, iBims-1 is designed to contain similar scenarios. Our acquired scenarios include various indoor settings, such as office, lecture, and living rooms, computer labs, a factory room, as well as more challenging ones, such as long corridors and potted plants. A comparison regarding the scene variety between NYU-v2 and iBims-1 can be seen in Fig. 4b. Furthermore, iBims-1 features statistics comparable to NYU-v2, such as the distribution of depth values, shown in Fig. 4a, and a comparable field of view.

Table 1. Number and statistics of manually labeled plane masks in iBims-1

Plane type	Images	Instances	Pixels (for NYUv2 res.)
Floor	47	51	1163499
Table	46	54	832984
Wall	82	140	6557108

Additionally, we provide an *auxiliary dataset* which consists of four parts: (1) Four outdoor RGB-D image pairs, containing vegetation, buildings, cars and

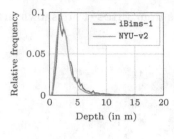 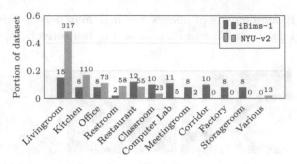

(a) Distribution of depth values   (b) Distribution of samples for each scene type. Absolute numbers are given above

Fig. 4. `iBims-1` dataset statistics compared to the `NYU-v2` dataset. Distribution of depth values (a) and scene variety (b)

larger ranges than indoor scenes. (2) Special cases which are expected to mislead SIDE methods. These show 85 RGB images of printed samples from the `NYU-v2` and the `Pattern` dataset [1] hung on a wall. Those could potentially give valuable insights, as they reveal what kind of image features SIDE methods exploit. Figure 9a shows examples from both categories. No depth maps are provided for those images, as the region of interest is supposed to be approximately planar and depth estimates are, thus, easy to assess qualitatively. (3) 28 different geometrical and radiometrical augmentations for each image of our core dataset to test the robustness of SIDE methods. (4) Up to three additional handheld images for most RGB-D image pairs of our core dataset with viewpoint changes towards the reference images which allows to validate MVS algorithms with high-quality ground truth depth maps.

5   Evaluation

In this section, we evaluate the quality of existing SIDE methods using both established and proposed metrics for our reference test dataset, as well as for the commonly used `NYU-v2` dataset. Furthermore, additional experiments were conducted to investigate the general behavior of SIDE methods, *i.e.*, the robustness of predicted depth maps to geometrical and color transformations and the planarity of textured vertical surfaces. For evaluation, we compared several state-of-the-art methods, namely those proposed by Eigen and Fergus [8], Eigen et al. [7], Liu et al. [21], Laina et al. [15], and Li et al. [19]. It is worth mentioning that all of these methods were solely trained on the `NYU-v2` dataset. Therefore, differences in the results are expected to arise from the developed methodology rather than the training data.

5.1 Evaluation Using Proposed Metrics

In the following, we report the results of evaluating SIDE methods on both NYU-v2 and iBims-1 using our newly proposed metrics. Please note, that due to the page limit, only few graphical results can be displayed in the following sections.

Distance-Related Assessment. The results of evaluation using commonly used metrics on iBims-1 unveil lower overall scores for our dataset (see Table 2). In order to get a better understanding of these results, we evaluated the considered methods on specific range intervals, which we set to 1 m in our experiments. Figure 5 shows the error band of the relative and RMS errors of the method proposed by Li et al. [19] applied to both datasets. The result clearly shows a comparable trend on both datasets for the shared depth range. This proves our first assumption, that the overall lower scores originate from the huge differences at depth values beyond the 10 m depth range. On the other hand, the results reveal the generalization capabilities of the networks, which achieve similar results on images from another camera with different intrinsics and for different scenarios. It should be noted that the error bands, which show similar characteristics for different methods and error metrics, correlate with the depth distributions of the datasets, shown in Fig. 4a.

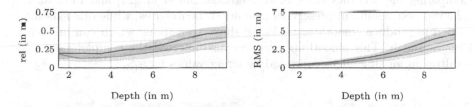

Fig. 5. Distance-related global errors (left: relative error and right: RMS) for NYU-v2 (mean: ▬, ±0.5 std: ▉) and iBims-1 (mean: ▬, ±0.5 std: ▉) using the method of Li et al. [19] (Color figure online)

Planarity. To investigate the quality of reconstructed planar structures, we evaluated the different methods with the planarity and orientation errors ε_{PE}^{plan} and ε_{PE}^{orie}, respectively, as defined in Sect. 3.2, for different planar objects. In particular, we distinguished between horizontal and vertical planes and used masks from our dataset. Figure 6 and Table 2 show the results for the iBims-1 dataset. Beside a combined error, including all planar labels, we separately computed the errors for the individual objects as well. The results show different performances for individual classes, especially orientations of floors were predicted in a significantly higher accuracy for all methods, while the absolute orientation error for walls is surprisingly high. Apart from the general performance of all methods, substantial differences between the considered methods can be determined. It is notable that the method of Li et al. [19] achieved much better results in predict-ing orientations of horizontal planes but also performed rather bad on vertical surfaces.

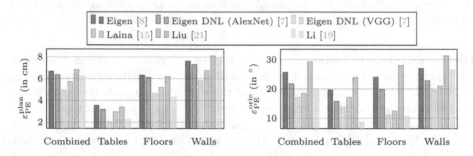

Fig. 6. Results for the planarity metrics $\varepsilon_{\mathrm{PE}}^{\mathrm{plan}}$ (left) and $\varepsilon_{\mathrm{PE}}^{\mathrm{orie}}$ (right) on `iBims-1`

Location Accuracy of Depth Boundaries. The high quality of our refer-ence dataset facilitates an accurate assessment of predicted depth discontinuities. As ground truth edges, we used the provided edge maps from our dataset and computed the accuracy and completeness errors $\varepsilon_{\mathrm{DBE}}^{\mathrm{acc}}$ and $\varepsilon_{\mathrm{DBE}}^{\mathrm{comp}}$, respectively, introduced in Sect. 3.2. Quantitative results for all methods are listed in Table 2. Comparing the accuracy error of all methods, Liu et al. [21] and Li et al. [19] achieved best results in preserving true depth boundaries, while other methods tended to produce smooth edges losing sharp transitions which can be seen in Figs. 7a and b. This smoothing property also affected the completeness error, resulting in missing edges expressed by larger values for $\varepsilon_{\mathrm{DBE}}^{\mathrm{comp}}$.

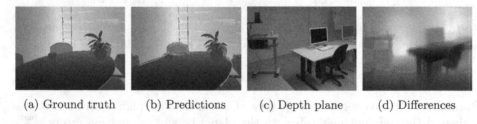

(a) Ground truth   (b) Predictions   (c) Depth plane   (d) Differences

Fig. 7. Visual results after applying DBE (a + b) and DDE (c + d) on `iBims-1`: (a) ground truth edge (—). (b) Edge predictions using the methods of Li et al. [19] (—) and Laina et al. [15] (—). (c) Ground truth depth plane at $d = 3\,\mathrm{m}$ separating foreground from background (■). (d) Differences between ground truth and predicted depths using the method of Li et al. [19]. Color coded are depth values that are either estimated too short (■) or too far (■) (Color figure online)

Directed Depth Error. The DDE aims to identify predicted depth values which lie on the correct side of a predefined reference plane but also distinguishes between overestimated and underestimated predicted depths. This measure could be useful for applications like 3D cinematography, where a 3D effect is generated by defining two depth planes. For this experiment, we defined a reference plane at 3 m distance and computed the proportions of correct ε_{DDE}^0, overestimated ε_{DDE}^+, and underestimated ε_{DDE}^- depth values towards this plane according to the error definitions in Sect. 3.2. Table 2 lists the resulting proportions for iBims-1, while a visual illustration of correctly and falsely predicted depths is depicted in Figs. 7c and d. The results show that the methods tended to predict depths to a too short distance, although the number of correctly estimated depths almost reaches 85% for iBims-1.

Table 2. Quantitative results for standard metrics and proposed PE, DBE, and DDE metrics on iBims-1 applying different SIDE methods

Method	Standard metrics ($\sigma_i = 1.25^i$)						PE (cm/°)		DBE (px)		DDE (%)		
	Rel	$\log_{10}$	RMS	σ_1	σ_2	σ_3	ε_{PE}^{plan}	ε_{PE}^{orie}	ε_{DBE}^{acc}	ε_{DBE}^{comp}	ε_{DDE}^0	ε_{DDE}^-	ε_{DDE}^+
Eigen [8]	0.32	0.17	1.55	0.36	0.65	0.84	6.65	25.62	5.48	70.31	72.06	25.71	2.23
Eigen (AlexNet) [7]	0.30	0.15	1.38	0.40	0.73	0.88	6.34	21.74	4.57	46.52	78.24	17.86	3.90
Eigen (VGG) [7]	0.25	0.13	1.26	0.47	0.78	0.93	**4.93**	**17.18**	4.51	43.64	80.73	17.47	**1.80**
Laina [15]	0.25	0.13	1.20	0.50	0.78	0.91	5.71	18.49	6.89	40.48	81.65	15.91	2.43
Liu [21]	0.30	0.13	1.26	0.48	0.78	0.91	6.82	29.22	3.57	**31.75**	80.46	13.26	6.28
Li [19]	**0.22**	**0.11**	**1.07**	**0.59**	**0.85**	**0.95**	6.22	20.17	3.68	36.27	**84.13**	**12.49**	3.38

Table 3. Quantitative results on the augmented iBims-1 dataset exemplary listed for the global relative distance error. Errors showing relative differences for various image augmentations towards the predicted original input image (Ref)

Method	Ref.	Geometric		Contrast			Ch. Swap		Hue		Saturation	
		LR	UD	$\gamma = 0.2$	$\gamma = 2$	Norm.	BGR	BRG	+9°	+90°	×0	×0.9
Eigen [8]	0.322	−0.003	0.087	0.056	0.015	0.000	0.017	0.018	0.001	0.021	0.003	0
Eigen (AlexNet) [7]	0.301	0.006	0.147	0.105	0.023	−0.002	0.017	0.008	0.002	0.017	0.007	0
Eigen (VGG) [7]	0.254	0.003	0.150	0.109	0.008	0.000	0.010	0.013	0.000	0.012	0.009	0
Laina [15]	0.255	−0.004	0.161	0.078	0.022	−0.001	0.007	0.009	0.000	0.007	0.003	0

5.2   Further Analyses

Making use of our *auxiliary dataset*, a series of additional experiments were conducted to investigate the behavior of SIDE methods in special situations. The challenges cover an augmentation of our dataset with various color and geometrical transformations and an auxiliary dataset containing images of printed patterns and NYU-v2 images on a planar surface.

Data Augmentation. In order to assess the robustness of SIDE methods w.r.t. simple geometrical and color transformation and noise, we derived a set of augmented images from our dataset. For geometrical transformations we flipped the input images horizontally—which is expected to not change the results significantly—and vertically, which is expected to expose slight overfitting effects. As images in the NYU-v2 dataset usually show a considerable amount of pixels on the floor in the lower part of the picture, this is expected to notably influence the estimated depth maps. For color transformations, we consider swapping of image channels, shifting the hue by some offset h and scaling the saturation by a factor s. We change the gamma values to simulate over- and under-exposure and optimize the contrast by histogram stretching. Blurred versions of the images are simulated by applying gaussian blur with increasing standard deviation σ. Furthermore, we consider noisy versions of the images by applying gaussian additive noise and salt and pepper noise with increasing variance and amount of affected pixels, respectively.

Table 3 shows results for these augmented images using the global relative error metric for selected methods. As expected, the geometrical transformations yielded contrasting results. While the horizontal flipping did not influence the results by a large margin, flipping the images vertically increased the error by up to 60%. Slight overexposure influenced the result notably, underexposure seems to have been less problematic. Histogram stretching had no influence on the results, suggesting that this is already a fixed or learned part of the methods. The methods also seem to be robust to color changes, which is best seen in the results for $s = 0$, *i.e.*, greyscale input images which yielded an equal error to the reference. The results for blurring the input images with a gaussian kernel of various sizes, as well as adding a different amount of gaussian and salt and pepper noise to the input images are depicted in Fig. 8.

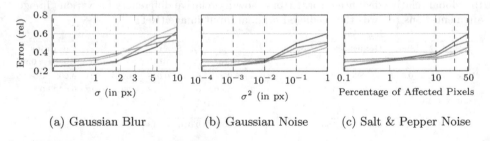

(a) Gaussian Blur   (b) Gaussian Noise   (c) Salt & Pepper Noise

Fig. 8. Quality of SIDE results, achieved using the methods proposed by Eigen et al. [8] (—), Eigen and Fergus [7] (AlexNet —, VGG —), and Laina et al. [15] (—) for augmentations with increasing intensity. Vertical lines (- -) correspond to discrete augmentation intensities

Textured Planar Surfaces. Experiments with printed patterns and NYU-v2 samples on a planar surface exploit which features influence the predictions of SIDE methods. As to be seen in the first example in Fig. 9, gradients seem

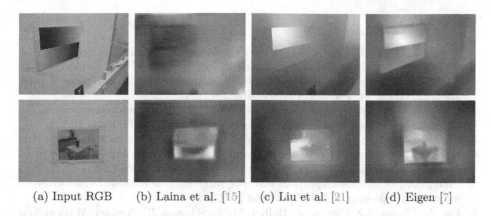

(a) Input RGB   (b) Laina et al. [15]   (c) Liu et al. [21]   (d) Eigen [7]

Fig. 9. Predicted depth for a sample from the auxiliary part of the proposed `iBims-1` dataset showing printed samples from the Patterns [1] dataset (top) and the `NYU-v2` dataset [28] (bottom) on a planar surface

to serve as a strong hint to the network. All of the tested methods estimated incorrectly depth in the depicted scene, none of them, however, identified the actual planarity of the picture.

6   Conclusions

We presented a novel set of quality criteria for the evaluation of SIDE methods. Furthermore, we introduced a new high-quality dataset, fulfilling the need for an extended ground truth of our proposed metrics. Using this test protocol we evaluated and compared state-of-the-art SIDE methods. In our experiments, we were able to assess the quality of the compared approaches w.r.t. to various meaningful properties, such as the preservation of edges and planar regions, depth consistency, and absolute distance accuracy. Compared to commonly used global metrics, our proposed set of quality criteria enabled us to unveil even subtle differences between the considered SIDE methods. In particular, our experiments have shown that the prediction of planar surfaces, which is crucial for many applications, is lacking accuracy. Furthermore, edges in the predicted depth maps tend to be oversmooth for many methods. We believe that our dataset is suitable for future developments in this regard, as our images are provided in a very high resolution and contain new sceneries with extended scene depths.

The `iBims-1` dataset can be downloaded at www.lmf.bgu.tum.de/ibims1.

Acknowledgements. This research was funded by the German Research Foundation (DFG) for Tobias Koch and the Federal Ministry of Transport and Digital Infrastructure (BMVI) for Lukas Liebel. We thank our colleagues from the Chair of Geodesy for providing all the necessary equipment and our student assistant Leonidas Stöckle for his help during the data acquisition campaign.

References

1. Asuni, N., Giachetti, A.: TESTIMAGES: a large-scale archive for testing visual devices and basic image processing algorithms. In: Smart Tools and Apps for Graphics - Eurographics Italian Chapter Conference. The Eurographics Association (2014). https://doi.org/10.2312/stag.20141242
2. Bülthoff, H.H., Yuille, A.L.: Shape from X: psychophysics and computation. In: Computational Models of Visual Processing, pp. 305–330. MIT Press (1991)
3. Chakrabarti, A., Shao, J., Shakhnarovich, G.: Depth from a single image by harmonizing overcomplete local network predictions. In: Proceedings of Advances in Neural Information Processing Systems (NIPS), pp. 2658–2666 (2016)
4. Chang, A., et al.: Matterport3D: learning from RGB-D data in indoor environments. arXiv preprint arXiv:1709.06158 (2017)
5. Dai, A., Chang, A.X., Savva, M., Halber, M., Funkhouser, T., Nießner, M.: ScanNet: richly-annotated 3D reconstructions of indoor scenes. In: Proceedings of the IEEE Conference on Computer Vision and Pattern Recognition (CVPR) (2017)
6. Dollár, P., Zitnick, C.L.: Fast edge detection using structured forests. IEEE Trans. Pattern Anal. Mach. Intell. **37**(8), 1558–1570 (2015)
7. Eigen, D., Fergus, R.: Predicting depth, surface normals and semantic labels with a common multi-scale convolutional architecture. In: Proceedings of the IEEE International Conference on Computer Vision (ICCV), pp. 2650–2658 (2015). https://doi.org/10.1109/ICCV.2015.304
8. Eigen, D., Puhrsch, C., Fergus, R.: Depth map prediction from a single image using a multi-scale deep network. In: Proceedings of Advances in Neural Information Processing Systems (NIPS), vol. 2, pp. 2366–2374 (2014)
9. Fu, H., Gong, M., Wang, C., Batmanghelich, K., Tao, D.: Deep ordinal regression network for monocular depth estimation. In: Proceedings of the IEEE Conference on Computer Vision and Pattern Recognition (CVPR), pp. 2002–2011 (2018)
10. Garg, R., Vijay Kumar, B.G., Carneiro, G., Reid, I.: Unsupervised CNN for single view depth estimation: geometry to the rescue. In: Leibe, B., Matas, J., Sebe, N., Welling, M. (eds.) ECCV 2016. LNCS, vol. 9912, pp. 740–756. Springer, Cham (2016). https://doi.org/10.1007/978-3-319-46484-8_45
11. Geiger, A., Lenz, P., Urtasun, R.: Are we ready for autonomous driving? The kitti vision benchmark suite. In: Proceedings of the IEEE Conference on Computer Vision and Pattern Recognition (CVPR), pp. 3354–3361. IEEE (2012)
12. Hu, J., Ozay, M., Zhang, Y., Okatani, T.: Revisiting single image depth estimation: toward higher resolution maps with accurate object boundaries. arXiv preprint arXiv:1803.08673 (2018)
13. Kim, S., Park, K., Sohn, K., Lin, S.: Unified depth prediction and intrinsic image decomposition from a single image via joint convolutional neural fields. In: Leibe, B., Matas, J., Sebe, N., Welling, M. (eds.) ECCV 2016. LNCS, vol. 9912, pp. 143–159. Springer, Cham (2016). https://doi.org/10.1007/978-3-319-46484-8_9
14. Knapitsch, A., Park, J., Zhou, Q.Y., Koltun, V.: Tanks and temples: benchmarking large-scale scene reconstruction. ACM Trans. Graph. **36**(4) (2017)
15. Laina, I., Rupprecht, C., Belagiannis, V., Tombari, F., Navab, N.: Deeper depth prediction with fully convolutional residual networks. In: Proceedings of the Fourth International Conference on 3D Vision (3DV), pp. 239–248 (2016)
16. Lee, J.H., Heo, M., Kim, K.R., Kim, C.S.: Single-image depth estimation based on fourier domain analysis. In: Proceedings of the IEEE Conference on Computer Vision and Pattern Recognition (CVPR), pp. 330–339 (2018)

17. Li, B., Dai, Y., Chen, H., He, M.: Single image depth estimation by dilated deep residual convolutional neural network and soft-weight-sum inference. arXiv preprint arXiv:1705.00534 (2017)
18. Li, B., Shen, C., Dai, Y., van den Hengel, A., He, M.: Depth and surface normal estimation from monocular images using regression on deep features and hierarchical CRFs. In: Proceedings of the IEEE Conference on Computer Vision and Pattern Recognition (CVPR), pp. 1119–1127 (2015)
19. Li, J., Klein, R., Yao, A.: A two-streamed network for estimating fine-scaled depth maps from single RGB images. In: Proceedings of the IEEE International Conference on Computer Vision (ICCV), pp. 22–29 (2017)
20. Liu, C., Yang, J., Ceylan, D., Yumer, E., Furukawa, Y.: PlaneNet: piece-wise planar reconstruction from a single RGB image. In: Proceedings of the IEEE Conference on Computer Vision and Pattern Recognition (CVPR), pp. 2579–2588 (2018)
21. Liu, F., Shen, C., Lin, G.: Deep convolutional neural fields for depth estimation from a single image. In: Proceedings of the IEEE Conference on Computer Vision and Pattern Recognition (CVPR), pp. 5162–5170 (2015)
22. Liu, F., Shen, C., Lin, G., Reid, I.: Learning depth from single monocular images using deep convolutional neural fields. IEEE Trans. Pattern Anal. Mach. Intell. **38**(10), 2024–2039 (2016)
23. Moreno-Noguer, F., Lepetit, V., Fua, P.: Accurate non-iterative o(n) solution to the PnP problem. In: Proceedings of the IEEE International Conference on Computer Vision (ICCV), pp. 1–8 (2007)
24. Roy, A., Todorovic, S.: Monocular depth estimation using neural regression forest. In: Proceedings of the IEEE Conference on Computer Vision and Pattern Recognition (CVPR), pp. 5506–5514 (2016) https://doi.org/10.1109/cvpr.2016.594
25. Saxena, A., Sun, M., Ng, A.Y.: Make3D: learning 3D scene structure from a single still image. IEEE Trans. Pattern Anal. Mach. Intell. **31**(5), 824–840 (2009)
26. Schöps, T., et al.: A multi-view stereo benchmark with high-resolution images and multi-camera videos. In: Proceedings of the IEEE Conference on Computer Vision and Pattern Recognition (CVPR) (2017)
27. Seitz, S.M., Curless, B., Diebel, J., Scharstein, D., Szeliski, R.: A comparison and evaluation of multi-view stereo reconstruction algorithms. In: Proceedings of the IEEE Conference on Computer Vision and Pattern Recognition (CVPR), vol. 1, pp. 519–528 (2006). https://doi.org/10.1109/CVPR.2006.19
28. Silberman, N., Hoiem, D., Kohli, P., Fergus, R.: Indoor segmentation and support inference from RGBD images. In: Fitzgibbon, A., Lazebnik, S., Perona, P., Sato, Y., Schmid, C. (eds.) ECCV 2012. LNCS, vol. 7576, pp. 746–760. Springer, Heidelberg (2012). https://doi.org/10.1007/978-3-642-33715-4_54
29. Strecha, C., Von Hansen, W., Van Gool, L., Fua, P., Thoennessen, U.: On benchmarking camera calibration and multi-view stereo for high resolution imagery. In: Proceedings of the IEEE Conference on Computer Vision and Pattern Recognition (CVPR), pp. 1–8 (2008)
30. Tateno, K., Tombari, F., Laina, I., Navab, N.: CNN-SLAM: real-time dense monocular slam with learned depth prediction. arXiv preprint arXiv:1704.03489 (2017)
31. Wang, P., Shen, X., Lin, Z., Cohen, S., Price, B., Yuille, A.L.: Towards unified depth and semantic prediction from a single image. In: Proceedings of the IEEE Conference on Computer Vision and Pattern Recognition (CVPR), pp. 2800–2809 (2015)

32. Xu, D., Ricci, E., Ouyang, W., Wang, X., Sebe, N.: Multi-scale continuous CRFs as sequential deep networks for monocular depth estimation. arXiv preprint arXiv:1704.02157 (2017)
33. Xu, D., Wang, W., Tang, H., Liu, H., Sebe, N., Ricci, E.: Structured attention guided convolutional neural fields for monocular depth estimation. In: Proceedings of the IEEE Conference on Computer Vision and Pattern Recognition (CVPR), pp. 3917–3925 (2018)

A Simple Approach to Intrinsic Correspondence Learning on Unstructured 3D Meshes

Isaak Lim[1]([✉]), Alexander Dielen[1], Marcel Campen[2], and Leif Kobbelt[1]

[1] Visual Computing Institute, RWTH Aachen University, Aachen, Germany
isaak.lim@cs.rwth-aachen.de
[2] Osnabrück University, Osnabrück, Germany

Abstract. The question of representation of 3D geometry is of vital importance when it comes to leveraging the recent advances in the field of machine learning for geometry processing tasks. For common unstructured surface meshes state-of-the-art methods rely on patch-based or mapping-based techniques that introduce resampling operations in order to encode neighborhood information in a structured and regular manner. We investigate whether such resampling can be avoided, and propose a simple and direct encoding approach. It does not only increase processing efficiency due to its simplicity – its direct nature also avoids any loss in data fidelity. To evaluate the proposed method, we perform a number of experiments in the challenging domain of intrinsic, non-rigid shape correspondence estimation. In comparisons to current methods we observe that our approach is able to achieve highly competitive results.

Keywords: Shape correspondence estimation · Learning on graphs

1 Introduction

The representation of 3D geometry is a key issue in the context of machine learning in general and deep learning in particular. A variety of approaches, from point clouds over voxel sets to range images, have been investigated. When the input geometry is in the common form of a surface mesh, conversion to such representations typically comes with losses in fidelity, accuracy, or conciseness. Hence, techniques have been introduced to more or less directly take such discrete surface data as input to machine learning methods. Examples are graph-based [4,13] and patch-based approaches [3,17,18]. While graph-based techniques rely on fixed mesh connectivity structures, patch-based techniques provide more flexibility. However, they crucially rely on some form of (re)sampling of the input mesh data, so as to achieve consistent, regular neighborhood encodings, similar to the regular pixel structures exploited for learning on image data.

In this paper we consider the question whether such resampling can be avoided, taking the mesh data as input even more directly. The rationale for

© Springer Nature Switzerland AG 2019
L. Leal-Taixé and S. Roth (Eds.): ECCV 2018 Workshops, LNCS 11131, pp. 349–362, 2019.
https://doi.org/10.1007/978-3-030-11015-4_26

our interest is twofold: the avoidance of resampling would increase the efficiency of inference (and perhaps training) and could possibly increase precision. The increase in efficiency would be due to not having to perform the (typically non-trivial) resampling (either as a preprocess or online). One could hypothesize an increase in precision based on the fact that resampling is, in general, accompanied by some loss of data fidelity.

We propose a resampling and conversion free input encoding strategy for local neighborhoods in manifold 3D surface meshes. In contrast to many previous approaches for learning on surface meshes, we then make use of RNNs and fully-connected networks instead of CNNs, so as to be able to deal with the non-uniform, non-regular structure of the input. Though simple, this raw input encoding is rich enough that our networks could, in theory, learn to emulate common patch resampling operators based on it. Nevertheless, hand-crafting such resampling operators and preprocessing the input accordingly, as previously done, could of course be of benefit in practice. Hence it is important to evaluate practical performance experimentally.

We apply and benchmark our technique in the context of *non-rigid shape correspondence estimation* [29]. The computation of such point-to-point (or shape) correspondences is of interest for a variety of downstream shape analysis and processing tasks (e.g. shape interpolation, texture transfer, etc.). The inference of these correspondences, however, is a challenging task and topic of ongoing investigation. Our experiments in this context reveal that the preprocessing efforts can indeed be cut down significantly by our approach without sacrificing precision. In certain scenarios, as hypothesized, precision can even be increased relative to previous resampling-based techniques.

Contribution. In this work we propose and investigate a novel form of using either fully-connected layers or LSTMs (Hochreiter and Schmidhuber [9]) for point-to-point correspondence learning on manifold 3D meshes. By serializing the local neighborhood of vertices we are able to encode relevant information in a straightforward manner and with very little preprocessing. We experimentally analyze the practical behavior and find that our approach achieves competitive results and outperforms a number of current methods in the task of shape correspondence prediction.

2   Related Work

Several data- and model-driven approaches for finding correspondences between shapes have been proposed in previous works.

Functional Maps. Ovsjanikov et al. [23] approach the problem of finding point-to-point correspondences by formulating a function correspondence problem. They introduce functional maps as a compact representation that can be used for point-to-point maps. Various (model- and data-driven) improvements have been suggested [5,6,8,10,14,21,22,24,25]. Most closely related to our approach, Litany et al. [15] use deep metric learning to optimize input descriptors for the functional maps framework. However, point-to-point correspondence inference in all cases requires the computation of a functional map for each pair of shapes. This possibly costly computation can be avoided with our approach. Once trained, our model can be applied directly for inference.

Generalized CNNs for 3D Meshes. Several data-driven methods that do not rely on functional maps were proposed in recent years. Masci et al. [17] generalize convolution operations in modern deep learning architectures to non-Euclidean domains. To this end they define geodesic disks (patches) around each vertex. Based on a local polar coordinate system the patches can be resampled with a fixed number and fixed pattern of samples (cf. Fig. 1a). This predefined sampling pattern allows to construct a convolution operation on these patches by computing weighted sums of features at sample positions. In order to transfer the information (i.e. descriptors) available discretely at the vertices to the continuous setting of the geodesic disks for the purpose of resampling, they are blended by means of appropriate kernels. Boscaini et al. [3] propose to use anisotropic kernels in this context, while aligning the local coordinate systems with the principal curvature directions. Monti et al. [18] generalize the construction of these blending kernels to Gaussian Mixture Models, which avoids the hand-crafting of kernels in favor of learning them.

Ezuz et al. [7] and Maron et al. [16] both propose forms of global (instead of local patch-wise) structured resampling of the surface, which can then be used as input to well-known CNN architectures used in computer vision.

Similar in spirit to our work is the method introduced by Kostrikov et al. [13]. They apply Graph Neural Networks (cf. [4,20,27]) in the domain of 3D meshes. A key difference is that their network's layers see neighborhood information in reduced blended form (via Laplace or Dirac operators) rather than natively like our approach.

In comparison to these approaches we require very little preprocessing, no heavy online computation, and no resampling. Per-vertex descriptors are exploited directly rather than taking blended versions of them as input.

3   Resampling-Free Neighborhood Encoding

We assume that the input domain is represented as a manifold triangle mesh $\mathcal{M}$. Some form of input data (e.g. positions, normals, or geometry descriptors) is specified or can be computed at the vertices of $\mathcal{M}$. We denote the information (*feature*) at a vertex v by f(v). As in previous work [3,17,18], for the task of correspondence estimation, we would like to collect this information f from a local neighborhood around a vertex a. As mentioned above, we intend to encode this relevant information in a very direct manner, essentially by a notion of serialization of the per-vertex features f in local neighborhoods, without any alterations.

3.1   Spiral Operator

To this end we make the observation that, given a center vertex, the surrounding vertices can quite naturally be enumerated by intuitively following a spiral, as illustrated in Fig. 1b. The only degrees of freedom are the orientation (clockwise or counter-clockwise) and the choice of 1-ring vertex marking the spiral's starting direction. We fix the orientation to clockwise here. The choice of starting direction is arbitrary, and a different sequence of vertices will be produced by the spiral operator depending on this choice. This rotational ambiguity is a common issue in this context, and has been dealt with, for instance, by max-pooling over multiple choices [17], or by making the choice based on additional, e.g. extrinsic, information [3]. We avoid this by instead making a random choice in each iteration during training, enabling the network to learn to be robust against this ambiguity, assuming a sufficient number of parameters in the network.

Given a starting direction (i.e. a chosen 1-ring vertex), the spiral operator produces a sequence enumerating the center vertex, followed by the 1-ring vertices, followed by the 2-ring vertices, and so forth. Thus, for a given k, it is possible to trace the spiral until we have enumerated all vertices up to and including the k-ring. In Fig. 1b this is illustrated for the case $k = 2$, where the sequence reads $[a, b, c, d, e, f, g, \ldots]$. Alternatively, for a given N, we can of course trace until we have enumerated exactly N vertices, thereby producing fixed length sequences – in contrast to the variable length sequences up to ring k.

While the definition and practical enumeration of a spiral's vertices is really simple locally, some care must be taken to support the general setting, in

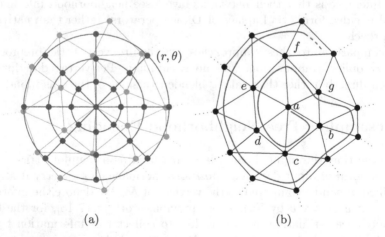

(a)   (b)

Fig. 1. The black graph represents a patch of a triangle mesh. (a) For generalized CNNs on 3D meshes [3,17,18], we would have to compute a blended $f(r, \theta)$ for each node of the magenta polar grid in order to provide a fixed number and pattern of samples for a convolution kernel. (b) Instead, we enumerate the neighborhood vertices of a center vertex a by following a spiral pattern (magenta). For a given feature $f(\cdot)$ we encode the local neighborhood information feeding $[f(a), f(b), f(c), f(d), f(e), f(f), f(g), \ldots]$ into a LSTM Cell.

particular with large k or large N (when k-rings are not necessarily simple loops anymore) or on meshes with boundary (where k-rings can be partial, maybe consisting of multiple components). The following concise definition of the spiral operator handles also such cases.

Let k-ring and k-disk be defined as follows:

$$0\text{-ring}(v) = \{v\},$$
$$(k{+}1)\text{-ring}(v) = N(k\text{-ring}(v)) \setminus k\text{-disk}(v),$$
$$k\text{-disk}(v) = \cup_{i=0\ldots k} \, i\text{-ring}(v),$$

where $N(V)$ is the set of all vertices adjacent to any vertex in set V.

The $\mathrm{spiral}(v, k)$ is defined simply as the concatenation of the *ordered* rings:

$$\mathrm{spiral}(v, k) = (0\text{-ring}(v) \ldots k\text{-ring}(v)).$$

The fixed-length $\mathrm{spiral}(v, N)$ is obtained by truncation to a total of N vertices.

The required order $<$ on the vertices of a k-ring is defined as follows: The 1-ring vertices are ordered clockwise, starting at a random position. The ordering of the $(k{+}1)$-ring vertices is induced by their k-ring neighbors in the sense that vertices v_1 and v_2 in the $(k{+}1)$-ring being adjacent to a common vertex v^* in the k-ring are ordered clockwise around v^*, while vertices v_1 and v_2 having no common k-ring neighbor are sorted in the same order as (any of) their k-ring neighbors.

3.2   Learning

With the (either variable length or fixed length) vertex sequence $[a, b, c, d, e, f, g, \ldots]$ produced for a given center vertex, one easily serializes the neighborhood features as the sequence $[\mathrm{f}(a), \mathrm{f}(b), \mathrm{f}(c), \mathrm{f}(d), \mathrm{f}(e), \mathrm{f}(f), \mathrm{f}(g), \ldots]$.

For the purpose of correspondence estimation our goal is to learn a compact high-level representation of these sequences. This can be done in a straightforward and intuitive way using recurrent neural networks. More specifically, we feed our vertex sequences into an LSTM cell as proposed by Hochreiter and Schmidhuber [9] and use the last cell output as representation. This representation is thus computed using the following equations:

$$f_t = \sigma(W_f \cdot [x_t, h_{t-1}] + b_f),$$
$$i_t = \sigma(W_i \cdot [x_t, h_{t-1}] + b_i),$$
$$o_t = \sigma(W_o \cdot [x_t, h_{t-1}] + b_o),$$
$$c_t = f_t \odot c_{t-1} + i_t \odot \tanh(W_c \cdot [x_t, h_{t-1}] + b_c),$$
$$h_t = o_t \odot \tanh(c_t),$$

where the learnable parameters are the matrices W_f, W_i, W_o, W_c with their respective biases b_f, b_i, b_o, b_c. $[x_t, h_{t-1}]$ is the concatenation of the input x_t (e.g. $\mathrm{f}(a)$) and the previous hidden state h_{t-1}, while c_t and h_t are the current cell- and hidden-state respectively. We denote the Hadamard product as $\odot$.

This generation of a representation of the local neighborhood of a vertex via a LSTM cell is, in an abstract sense, comparable to the generalized convolution operation of previous patch-based approaches. However, the resampling of neighborhoods and computation of blended features $f(r, \theta)$ for each sample (r, θ) (see Fig. 1a) is avoided by our approach. Here r and θ are geodesic polar coordinates of some local coordinate system located at each center vertex. $f(r, \theta)$ is then computed based on a weighted combination of f at nearby vertices (e.g. $f(r, \theta) = w_c f(c) + w_d f(d) + \cdots$). Depending on the nature of f this linear blending can be lossy.

For the case of a fixed length serialization, the use of an RNN supporting variable length input is not necessary. A fully-connected layer (combined with some non-linearity) can be used instead. Naturally, we apply these neighborhood encoding operations repeatedly in multiple layers in a neural network to facilitate the mapping of input features to a higher level feature representation. This is detailed in the following section.

Tessellation Dependence. Our simple method of encoding the neighborhood obviously is not independent of the tessellation of the input. By augmenting the features f with metric information (i.e. by appending length and angle information), we can mitigate this and essentially enable the network to possibly *learn* to be independent. In Sect. 4.1 we investigate the effects of this.

Concretely, we concatenate to the input feature $f(c)$ the distance of the current vertex c to the center vertex a as well as the angle at a between the previous vertex b and c.

3.3   Architecture Details

To evaluate and compare our proposed methods (with variable or fixed length sequences) in the context of shape correspondence estimation, we construct our network architectures in a manner similar to the GCNN3 model proposed by Masci et al. [17]. We replace the convolution layers in GCNN3 by the ones presented above, as detailed below. For the sake of comparability, we use the SHOT descriptor proposed by Salti et al. [26] with 544 dimensions and default parameter settings computed at each vertex as input, following [3, 18].

The original GCNN3 [17] network is constructed as FC16 + GC32 + GC64 + GC128 + FC256 + FC6890. FCx refers to a fully connected layer with output size x, which is applied to each vertex separately. GCx is the geodesic convolution operation followed by angular max-pooling, producing x-dimensional feature vectors for every vertex.

LSTM-NET. Our network (LSTM-NET) for sequences with varying length replaces the GC layers and is constructed as FC16 + LSTM150 + LSTM200 + LSTM250 + FC256 + FC6890. LSTMx is the application of a LSTM cell to a sequence consisting of the input vertex and its neighborhood. In this manner we compute a new feature vector with dimensionality x (encoding neighborhood information) for every vertex, similar to a convolution operation.

Table 1. Number of parameters used in the different network architectures. FCS-NET (20) refers to FCS-NET applied to sequences with length 20, while GCNN3 is our implementation of GCNN3 [17] with the SHOT descriptor

Network	Number of parameters
GCNN3 (SHOT)	2,672,634
LSTM-NET	2,675,706
FCS-NET (20)	2,763,356

FCS-NET. For fixed-length sequences we make use of a network (FCS-NET) constructed as FC16 + FCS100 + FCS150 + FCS200 + FC256 + FC6890. FCSx refers to a fully-connected layer, which takes the concatenated features of a sequence as input and produces a x-dimensional output for every vertex, analogously to the LSTMx operation above.

We apply ReLU [19] to all layer outputs except for the output of the final layer to which we apply softmax. As regularization we apply dropout [28] with $p = 0.3$ after FC16 and FC256. For fair comparison, the layers of our LSTM-NET and FCS-NET were chosen such that the total number of learnable parameters is roughly equal to that of GCNN3 (cf. Table 1). Our networks are implemented with TensorFlow [1].

4 Experiments

For our experiments we used the FAUST dataset (consisting of 100 shapes) [2]. This allows for comparisons to related previous methods, which have commonly been evaluated on this dataset. Following common procedure, for training we used the first 80 shapes (10 of which were used for validation). All experiment results were computed on the last 20 shapes (our test set). We optimized all networks with Adam [12] ($lr = 0.001$, $\beta_1 = 0.9$, $\beta_2 = 0.999$), where each batch consisted of the vertices of one mesh.

In order to evaluate the performance of our LSTM-NET we restrict ourself to sequences of fixed length as input (even though it would be capable of dealing with variable length input). This is because the mesh connectivity is the same over all meshes of the dataset. For varying length sequences (e.g. the 1- and 2-ring of each vertex) the network would potentially be able to learn the valence distribution and use connectivity information as an (unfair) prediction help.

Following Kim et al. [11] we compute point-to-point correspondences and plot the percentage of correct correspondences found within given geodesic radii. For the evaluation no symmetry information is taken into account. We compare to the results from [3,17,18]. In addition we also implemented GCNN3 (using the SHOT instead of the GEOVEC descriptor as input) after Masci et al. [17] and evaluated the method in our setting. We used the parameters and loss proposed in the original paper. As shown in Fig. 2(a) our method outperforms current patch-based approaches with both LSTM-NET and FCS-NET for a sequence length of 30. Note that, by contrast, the average number of interpolated vertices in a patch for GCNN3 is 80. Furthermore, we do not perform any post-processing or refinement on the network predictions. An evaluation of the effect of different sequence lengths is visualized in Fig. 3(a–b). Even with shorter sequence lengths (15) our method achieves competitive results. Qualitative results are visualized in Fig. 6. We show the geodesic distance to the ground truth target vertices on four shapes from the test set. Correspondence errors of relative geodesic distance > 0.2 are clamped for an informative color coding.

4.1   Tessellation Dependence

An important, but often overlooked detail is the fact that the shapes in the FAUST dataset are meshed compatibly, i.e. the mesh connectivity is identical across shapes, and identical vertices are at corresponding points. Unless a correspondence estimation method is truly tessellation-oblivious, this naturally has the potential to incur a beneficial bias in this artifical benchmark, as in any realistic correspondence estimation application scenario, the tessellation will of course be incompatible. We thus repeat our experiments with a remeshed version of the FAUST dataset (see Fig. 4), where each shape was remeshed individually and incompatibly.

Quantitative results are shown in Fig. 2(b). Here (++) denotes the additional relative information that we concatenate to the SHOT descriptor vectors. On

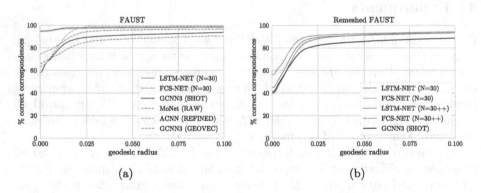

(a)   (b)

Fig. 2. Here the percentage of correct point-to-point correspondence predictions included in varying geodesic radii is shown. (a) shows a comparison of our approaches (FCS-NET, LSTM-NET) on sequences of length N = 30 to current approaches. Dashed lines refer to results reported in previous work. For GCNN3 [17] we compare against the original version that uses the GEOVEC descriptor (dashed) as well as our implementation of GCNN3 (black), which takes the more advanced SHOT descriptor as input. ACNN [3] shows the results after a correspondence map refinement step. For the sake of fair comparison we show the raw (w/o refinement) performance of MoNet [18], as we do not perform any refinement for the output of FCS- and LSTM-NET either. (b) visualizes the results on the remeshed FAUST dataset (cf. Sect. 4.1). As expected, the addition of relative angles and distances (++) is beneficial.

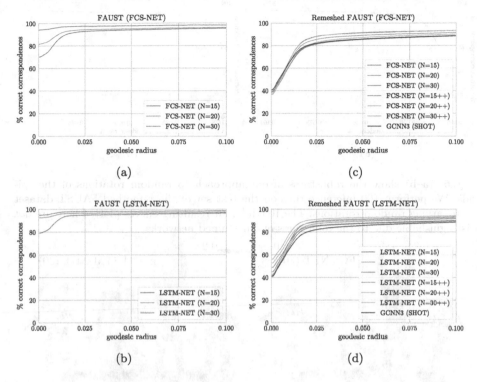

(a)   (c)

(b)   (d)

Fig. 3. Here the percentage of correct point-to-point correspondence predictions included in varying geodesic radii is shown. (a–b) show the effect of different sequence lengths (N = 15, 20, 30) for the FAUST dataset. Even with relatively short sequences (15) we achieve competitive results. (c–d) visualize the results on the remeshed FAUST dataset. For comparison we also show the performance of the GCNN3 [17] network with the SHOT descriptor. (++) denotes the usage of additional metric information.

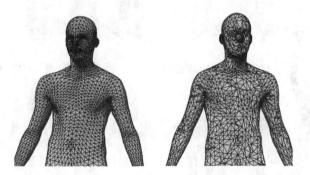

Fig. 4. Left: triangulation of a shape from the original FAUST dataset. Right: independently remeshed version.

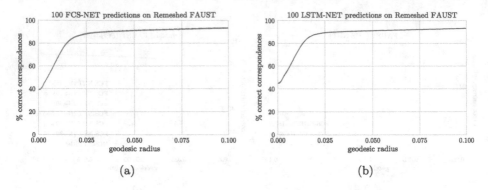

Fig. 5. (a–b) show the robustness of our approach to random rotations of the spirals. We perform 100 inference runs on the test set of the remeshed FAUST dataset with varying random rotations. The 100 different resulting curves plotted here are not distinguishable due to the robustness of our trained networks.

Fig. 6. Geodesic error for 4 shapes from the test set of the FAUST dataset.

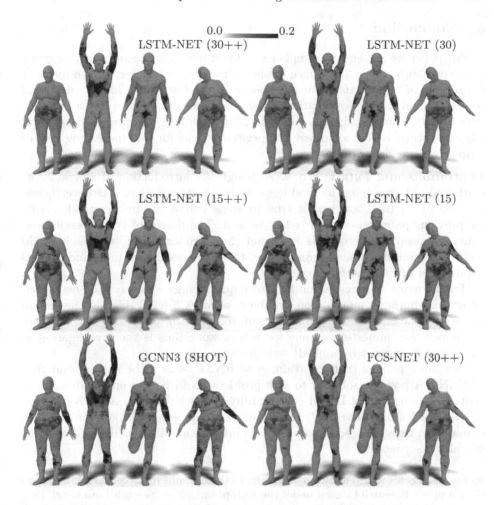

Fig. 7. Geodesic error for 4 shapes from the test set of the remeshed FAUST dataset.

this more challenging dataset we likewise achieve competitive results. Especially the additional information (++) enables our networks to encode less tessellation-dependent representations of neighborhoods for better performance. The effect of different sequence lengths is shown for this dataset in Fig. 3(c–d). For the sake of comparison to the performance of FCS-NET we also restrict LSTM-NET to sequences of fixed length. See Fig. 7 for qualitative results.

Furthermore, we test the robustness of our network predictions to random starting points after the center vertex in our sequences (random rotations of the spiral). To this end we perform 100 predictions with different random rotations on the remeshed FAUST dataset with both FCS-NET and LSTM-NET. As shown in Fig. 5 our networks are highly robust to these random orientations, such that the curves of separate predictions are not discernible.

5   Conclusion

In this paper we presented a simple resampling free input encoding strategy for local neighborhoods in 3D surface meshes. Previous approaches rely on forms of resampling of input features in neighborhood patches, which incurs additional computational and implementational costs and can have negative effects on input data fidelity. Our experiments show that our approach, despite its simple and efficient nature, is able to achieve competitive results for the challenging task of shape correspondence estimation.

Limitations and Future Work. Although the introduction of metric information aims to make our method less sensitive to tessellation, it is nevertheless affected by it; this, however, is true to some extent in any practical setting for previous patch-based approaches as well. The design of truly tessellation-oblivious encoding strategies is a relevant challenge for future work, as it would relieve the training process from having to *learn* tessellation independence, as required for optimal performance.

Furthermore, high resolution meshes require longer sequences to encode relevant neighborhood information. In the case of FCS-NET this also means an increase in the number of parameters required to learn, which can lead to memory issues. An interesting avenue for future work thus is the investigation of sub-sampled (but not resampled) serialization.

A related issue is that the training of RNNs tends to be slower than that of CNNs. A possible solution to this problem could be the application of 1D convolutions instead of LSTM cells or fully connected layers. An investigation into feature learning, given only raw input data (e.g. lengths, angles, or positions of mesh elements) instead of preprocessed information like the SHOT descriptor will also be of interest.

Acknowledgements. The research leading to these results has received funding from the European Research Council under the European Union's Seventh Framework Programme (FP7/2007-2013)/ERC grant agreement n° [340884]. We would like to thank the authors of related work [3,17] for making their implementations available, as well as the reviewers for their insightful comments.

References

1. Abadi, M., et al.: TensorFlow: large-scale machine learning on heterogeneous systems (2015). https://www.tensorflow.org/, software available from tensorflow.org
2. Bogo, F., Romero, J., Loper, M., Black, M.J.: FAUST: dataset and evaluation for 3D mesh registration. In: Proceedings IEEE Conference on Computer Vision and Pattern Recognition (CVPR). IEEE, Piscataway, NJ, USA, June 2014 (2014)
3. Boscaini, D., Masci, J., Rodolà, E., Bronstein, M.: Learning shape correspondence with anisotropic convolutional neural networks. In: Advances in Neural Information Processing Systems, pp. 3189–3197 (2016)
4. Defferrard, M., Bresson, X., Vandergheynst, P.: Convolutional neural networks on graphs with fast localized spectral filtering. In: Advances in Neural Information Processing Systems, pp. 3844–3852 (2016)

5. Eynard, D., Kovnatsky, A., Bronstein, M.M., Glashoff, K., Bronstein, A.M.: Multimodal manifold analysis by simultaneous diagonalization of laplacians. IEEE Trans. Pattern Anal. Mach. Intell. **37**(12), 2505–2517 (2015)
6. Eynard, D., Rodola, E., Glashoff, K., Bronstein, M.M.: Coupled functional maps. In: 2016 Fourth International Conference on 3D Vision (3DV), pp. 399–407. IEEE (2016)
7. Ezuz, D., Solomon, J., Kim, V.G., Ben-Chen, M.: GWCNN: a metric alignment layer for deep shape analysis. In: Computer Graphics Forum, vol. 36, pp. 49–57. Wiley Online Library (2017)
8. Gehre, A., Bronstein, M., Kobbelt, L., Solomon, J.: Interactive curve constrained functional maps. Comput. Graph. Forum **37**(5), 1–12 (2018)
9. Hochreiter, S., Schmidhuber, J.: Long short-term memory. Neural Comput. **9**(8), 1735–1780 (1997)
10. Huang, Q., Wang, F., Guibas, L.: Functional map networks for analyzing and exploring large shape collections. ACM Trans. Graph. (TOG) **33**(4), 36 (2014)
11. Kim, V.G., Lipman, Y., Funkhouser, T.: Blended intrinsic maps. ACM Trans. Graph. (TOG) **30**, 79 (2011)
12. Kingma, D.P., Ba, J.: Adam: a method for stochastic optimization. arXiv preprint arXiv:1412.6980 (2014)
13. Kostrikov, I., Jiang, Z., Panozzo, D., Zorin, D., Bruna, J.: Surface networks. In: The IEEE Conference on Computer Vision and Pattern Recognition (CVPR), June 2018 (2018)
14. Kovnatsky, A., Bronstein, M.M., Bronstein, A.M., Glashoff, K., Kimmel, R.: Coupled quasi-harmonic bases. In: Computer Graphics Forum, vol. 32, pp. 439–448. Wiley Online Library (2013)
15. Litany, O., Remez, T., Rodola, E., Bronstein, A.M., Bronstein, M.M.: Deep functional maps: structured prediction for dense shape correspondence. In: Proceedings of ICCV, vol. 2, p. 8 (2017)
16. Maron, H., et al.: Convolutional neural networks on surfaces via seamless toric covers. ACM Trans. Graph **36**(4), 71 (2017)
17. Masci, J., Boscaini, D., Bronstein, M., Vandergheynst, P.: Geodesic convolutional neural networks on riemannian manifolds. In: Proceedings of the IEEE International Conference on Computer Vision Workshops, pp. 37–45 (2015)
18. Monti, F., Boscaini, D., Masci, J., Rodola, E., Svoboda, J., Bronstein, M.M.: Geometric deep learning on graphs and manifolds using mixture model CNNs. In: Proceedings of CVPR, vol. 1, p. 3 (2017)
19. Nair, V., Hinton, G.E.: Rectified linear units improve restricted Boltzmann machines. In: Proceedings of the 27th International Conference on Machine Learning (ICML 2010), pp. 807–814 (2010)
20. Niepert, M., Ahmed, M., Kutzkov, K.: Learning convolutional neural networks for graphs. In: International Conference on Machine Learning, pp. 2014–2023 (2016)
21. Nogneng, D., Melzi, S., Rodolà, E., Castellani, U., Bronstein, M., Ovsjanikov, M.: Improved functional mappings via product preservation. In: Computer Graphics Forum, vol. 37, pp. 179–190. Wiley Online Library (2018)
22. Nogneng, D., Ovsjanikov, M.: Informative descriptor preservation via commutativity for shape matching. In: Computer Graphics Forum, vol. 36, pp. 259–267. Wiley Online Library (2017)
23. Ovsjanikov, M., Ben-Chen, M., Solomon, J., Butscher, A., Guibas, L.: Functional maps: a flexible representation of maps between shapes. ACM Trans. Graph. (TOG) **31**(4), 30 (2012)

24. Pokrass, J., Bronstein, A.M., Bronstein, M.M., Sprechmann, P., Sapiro, G.: Sparse modeling of intrinsic correspondences. In: Computer Graphics Forum, vol. 32, pp. 459–468. Wiley Online Library (2013)
25. Rodolà, E., Cosmo, L., Bronstein, M.M., Torsello, A., Cremers, D.: Partial functional correspondence. In: Computer Graphics Forum, vol. 36, pp. 222–236. Wiley Online Library (2017)
26. Salti, S., Tombari, F., Di Stefano, L.: SHOT: unique signatures of histograms for surface and texture description. Comput. Vis. Image Underst. **125**, 251–264 (2014)
27. Scarselli, F., Gori, M., Tsoi, A.C., Hagenbuchner, M., Monfardini, G.: The graph neural network model. IEEE Trans. Neural Netw. **20**(1), 61–80 (2009)
28. Srivastava, N., Hinton, G., Krizhevsky, A., Sutskever, I., Salakhutdinov, R.: Dropout: a simple way to prevent neural networks from overfitting. J. Mach. Learn. Res. **15**(1), 1929–1958 (2014)
29. Van Kaick, O., Zhang, H., Hamarneh, G., Cohen-Or, D.: A survey on shape correspondence. In: Computer Graphics Forum, vol. 30, pp. 1681–1707. Wiley Online Library (2011)

Learning Structure-from-Motion from Motion

Clément Pinard[1,2], Laure Chevalley[2], Antoine Manzanera[1(✉)],
and David Filliat[1]

[1] Computer Science and System Engineering Department,
ENSTA ParisTech, Palaiseau, France
{clement.pinard,antoine.manzanera,david.filliat}@ensta-parsitech.fr
[2] Parrot, Paris, France
{clement.pinard,laure.chevalley}@parrot.com

Abstract. This work is based on a questioning of the quality metrics used by deep neural networks performing depth prediction from a single image, and then of the usability of recently published works on unsupervised learning of depth from videos. These works are all predicting depth from a single image, thus it is only known up to an undetermined scale factor, which is not sufficient for practical use cases that need an absolute depth map, i.e. the determination of the scaling factor. To overcome these limitations, we propose to learn in the same unsupervised manner a depth map inference system from monocular videos that takes a pair of images as input. This algorithm actually learns structure-from-motion *from motion*, and not only structure from context appearance. The scale factor issue is explicitly treated, and the absolute depth map can be estimated from camera displacement magnitude, which can be easily measured from cheap external sensors. Our solution is also much more robust with respect to domain variation and adaptation via fine tuning, because it does not rely entirely on depth from context. Two use cases are considered, unstabilized moving camera videos, and stabilized ones. This choice is motivated by the UAV (for Unmanned Aerial Vehicle) use case that generally provides reliable orientation measurement. We provide a set of experiments showing that, used in real conditions where only speed can be known, our network outperforms competitors for most depth quality measures. Results are given on the well known KITTI dataset [5], which provides robust stabilization for our second use case, but also contains moving scenes which are very typical of the in-car road context. We then present results on a synthetic dataset that we believe to be more representative of typical UAV scenes. Lastly, we present two domain adaptation use cases showing superior robustness of our method compared to single view depth algorithms, which indicates that it is better suited for highly variable visual contexts.

© Springer Nature Switzerland AG 2019
L. Leal-Taixé and S. Roth (Eds.): ECCV 2018 Workshops, LNCS 11131, pp. 363–376, 2019.
https://doi.org/10.1007/978-3-030-11015-4_27

1   Introduction

Scene understanding from vision, in particular depth estimation, is a core problem for autonomous vehicles.

One could train a system for depth from vision with supervised learning on an offline dataset which features explicit depth measurement, such as KITTI [5], but even setting up such recording devices can be costly and time demanding, which can limit the amount of data the system can be trained on.

As a consequence, in this paper we are specifically interested in **unsupervised** learning of depth from images using machine learning optimization techniques.

Training to infer the depth of a scene and one's ego-motion is a problem for which recent work has been successfully done with no supervision, leveraging uncalibrated data solely from RGB cameras, but to our knowledge, all of them infer depth from a single image [6,10,20,23,25]. On the contrary, our methods tries to deduce it from multiple frames, using motion instead of context.

UAV navigation, which is one of our favorite use cases, is very specific compared to other ego motion videos. Its two main characteristics are the availability of orientation and the high variability of the visual context:

- An UAV relies on inertial data to maintain its position and the current market for UAVs allows to get high quality video stabilization even for consumer products. As such, orientation of any frame can be assumed to be well estimated.
- Compared to videos acquired from any other vehicle, UAV scenes are very heterogeneous. Unlike a camera fixed to a car, altitude can vary widely and quickly, along with velocity, orientation, and scene visual layout, which context can be hard to figure out with only one frame.

Hence, we propose an unsupervised scene geometry learning algorithm that aims at inferring a depth map from a sequence of images. Our algorithm works with stabilized *and* unstabilized videos, the latter requiring in addition to the depth estimator network an orientation estimator that can bring back digital stabilization.

Our algorithm outputs a depth map assuming a constant displacement, this solves the scale factor incertitude simply by knowing ego-motion speed. This allows a straightforward real conditions depth inference process for any camera with a known speed such as the one of the supporting cars or UAVs.

2   Related Work

First works trying to compute a depth map from images using machine learning can be found as early as 2009 [17]. Whether from multiple frames or a single frame, these techniques have shown great generalization capabilities, especially using end-to-end learning methods such as convolutional neural networks.

2.1   Supervised Depth Networks

Most studied problems for supervised depth learning use a stereo rig along with corresponding disparity [8,24], thanks to dedicated datasets [5,12]. For unconstrained monocular sequences, DepthNet and DeMoN [14,19] are probably the works closest to ours. Using depth supervision, these networks aim to compute a depth map with a pair of images from a monocular video.

The first network explicitly assumes a fixed displacement magnitude and a stabilized video, and only outputs depth, while the second one also outputs a pose, from which translational component is trained to be of constant magnitude. Both methods easily solve the scale factor problem when the camera speed is known. Our main goal here is to achieve the same operation, but with unsupervised training.

2.2   Unsupervised Depth Learning

Most recent works on unsupervised training networks for computing depth maps use differentiable bilinear warping techniques, first introduced in [7]. The main idea is trying to match two frames using a depth map and a displacement. The new loss function to be minimized is the photometric error between the reference frame and the projected one. Depth is then indirectly optimized. Although sensitive to errors coming from occlusions, non Lambertian surfaces and moving objects, this optimization shows great potential, especially when considering how little calibrated data is needed.

For instance [4,6,22] use stereo views and try to reconstruct one frame from the other. This particular use case for depth training allows to always consider the same displacement and rigid scenes since both images are captured at the same time and their relative poses are always the same. However, it constraints the training set to stereo rigs, which are not as easy to set up as a monocular camera.

When trying to estimate both depth and movement, [10,16,23,25] also achieved decent results on completely unconstrained ego-motion video. One can note that some methods [25] are assuming rigid scenes although the training set does not always conform to this assumption. The other ones try to do without this assumption by computing a residual optical flow to resolve the uncertainty from moving objects.

[20] explicitly considered non rigid scenes by trying to estimate multiple objects movements in the scene, to begin with the motion of the camera itself, which allowed them to deduce a flow map, along with the depth map. The reader is referred to the work of Zhou et al. [25] for a more complete vision of the field, as all other works are actually built on this fundamental basis.

3   Single Frame Prediction *vs* Reality

As already mentioned, in the current state of the art of learning from monocular footage, depth is always inferred by the network using a single image. Indeed, it is mentioned in [25] that feeding multiple frames to a network did not yield better results. This may be due to the fact that for particular scenarii with very typical geometric and photometric contexts such as in-car view of the road, depth seems easier to get from the visual layout than from the motion.

Because of the single frame context, current depth quality measurements, originally introduced by Eigen *et al.* [3], expects a relative depth map up to a scale factor. This is problematic, as they completely ignore the scale factor uncertainty, and thus rely on estimating the scale factor as the ratio of the medians of network's output and groundtruth. This is then representative to an ideal use case where the median of an unknown depth map has to be available, which is clearly unrealistic.

One can try to overcome these limitations by figuring out the scale factor with several solutions:

- Measuring depth, at least in one point, with additional sensor such as LiDAR, Time-of-Flight or stereo cameras. This is not a trivial solution and it needs integration, as well as precise calibration.
- Assuming depth consistency across training and testing dataset. This can be particularly useful in datasets like KITTI [5], where the camera is always at the same height and looking at the floor from the same angle, but it is irrelevant on a dataset with high pose variability, *e.g.* UAV videos, and such assumptions will fail.

Thankfully, those techniques do not only predict depth, but also ego-motion. An other network tries to compute poses of frames in a sequence. Considering that the uncertainties about depth in one hand and pose in the other hand are consistent, the scale factors for depth and pose are theoretically the same. As a consequence, depth scale factor can be determined from the ratio between translation estimation, and actual translation measurement, which is already available on cars and UAVs.

A new quality measurement can then be designed, by slightly modifying the already prevalent ones. This new measurement is not relative anymore, it computes actual depth errors, and is more representative of a real application case. This will be denoted in Tables 1, 2 and 3 by the scale factor column. When using standard relative depth measurement, the indication *GT* (for *Ground Truth*) is used, when using translation magnitude, the letter P (for *Pose*) is used.

4   Approach

Inspired from both [14, 25], we propose a framework for training a network similar to DepthNet, but from unlabeled video sequences. The approach can be decomposed into three tasks, as illustrated by Fig. 1:

- From a certain sequence of frames $(I_i)_{0 \leq i < N}$, randomly choose one target frame I_t and one reference frame I_r, forming a pair to feed to DepthNet.
- For each $i \in [\![0, N[\![$, estimate pose $\widehat{T}_{t \to i} = (\widehat{R}_i, t_i)$ of each frame I_i relative to the target frame I_t, and compensate rotation of reference frame I_r to I_r^{STAB} before feeding it to DepthNet, leading to the same situation as original DepthNet, fed with stabilized inputs in [14]. As discussed in Sect. 1, when considering UAV footage, rotation can be supervised.

- Compute the depth map which for presentation purpose will be denoted ζ. DepthNet$(I_r^{\text{STAB}}, I_t) = \zeta(I_r^{\text{STAB}}, I_t)$
- Normalize the translation to constrain it so that the displacement magnitude t_r with respect to I_r, is always the same throughout the training. This point is very important, in order to guarantee the equivariance between depth and motion, imposed by the original DepthNet training procedure.
- As the problem is now made equivalent to the one used in [25], perform a photometric reprojection of I_t to every other frame I_i, thanks to depth ζ_t of I_t and poses $\widehat{T}_{t \to i}$ computed before, and compute loss from photometric dissimilarity with I_i.

The whole reprojection process can be summarized by Eq. 1. Where K denotes the camera intrinsic, p_t homogeneous coordinates of a pixel in frame I_t and $\zeta_t(p_t)$ is the depth value of the pixel outputted by DepthNet. p_t^i are homogeneous coordinates of that very pixel in frame I_i. To get the equivalent pixel in coordinate p_t^i, I_i pixels are bilinearly interpolated.

Our algorithm, although relying on very little calibration, needs to get consistent focal length. This is due to the frame difference being dependent to focal length. However, this problem is easily avoided when training on sequences coming from the same camera. Also, as shown by Eq. 1, camera intrinsic matrix K needs to be known to compute warping and subsequent photometric reprojection loss properly. In practice, assuming optical center in the center of the focal plane worked for all our tests; this is corroborated by tests done by [10] where they used uncalibrated camera, only knowing approximate focal length.

$$\forall i \in [\![0, N]\![, p_t^i = K\widehat{T}_{t \to i}\left(\zeta_t(p_t)K^{-1}p_t\right)$$
$$\widehat{T}_{t \to i}\begin{cases} \mathbb{R}^3 \to \mathbb{R}^3 \\ X \mapsto \widehat{R}_i X + t_i \end{cases} \tag{1}$$

4.1 Pose Estimation

PoseNet, as initially introduced by Zhou et al. [25] is a classic fully convolutional neural Network that outputs 6 DoF transformation pose descriptor for each frame. Output poses are initially relative to the last frame, and then compensated to be relative to the pose of the target frame. This way, PoseNet output is not dependent on the index of the target frame. Besides, computing by default with respect to the last frame makes the inference much more straightforward, as in real condition, target frame on which depth is computed should be the last of the sequence, to reduce latency.

4.2 Frame Stabilization

In order to cancel rotation between target and reference frame, we can apply a warping using rotation estimation from PoseNet. When considering a transformation with no translation, Eq. 1 no longer depends on the depth of each

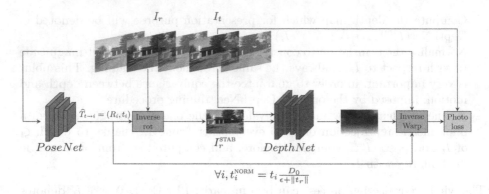

$$\forall i, t_i^{\text{NORM}} = t_i \frac{D_0}{\epsilon + \|t_r\|}$$

Fig. 1. General workflow architecture. *target* and *ref* indices (t and r) are chosen randomly for each sequence (even within the same batch); output transformations of PoseNet are compensated so that $\widehat{T}_{t \to t}$ is identity. D_0 is a fixed nominal displacement.

pixel, and becomes Eq. 2. As such, we can warp the frame to stabilize it using orientation estimation from PoseNet, before computing any depth.

$$p_t^r = K R_r K^{-1} p_t \tag{2}$$

As mentioned in Sect. 1, UAV footages are either stabilized or with a reliable estimated orientation from inertial sensors. This information can be easily leveraged in our training workflow to supervise pose rotation, giving in the end only translation to estimate to PoseNet. In addition, when running in inference, no pose estimation is needed, and only DepthNet is used. A similar algorithm as Pinard *et al.* [15] can then be used to estimate absolute depth maps at a relatively low computational cost.

4.3   Depth Computing and Pose Normalization

Thanks to the close relation between distance and optical flow for stabilized frames, [14] proposed a network to compute depth from stabilized videos. As depth is then provided assuming a constant displacement magnitude, the pose of the reference frame must be normalized to correspond to that magnitude. As such, to get consistent poses throughout the whole sequence, we apply the same normalization ratio, as shown in Fig. 1:

$$\forall i, t_i^{\text{NORM}} = t_i \frac{D_0}{\epsilon + \|t_r\|} \tag{3}$$

The main drawback of normalizing translations is the lack of guarantee about absolute output values. Since we only consider translations relatively to the reference, translations are estimated up to a scale factor that could be - when they are very large - leading to potential errors for rotation estimation, or - when they are very close to 0 - leading to float overflow problems. To overcome these possible issues, along with classic L_2 regularization to avoid high values, we add a constant value ϵ to the denominator. The normalization is then valid only when $\epsilon \ll \|t_r\|$.

4.4 Loss Functions

Let us denote $\widehat{I}_i$ as the inverse warped image from I_i to target image plane by p_t^i and $\| \cdot \|_1$ the L_1 norm operator (corresponding here to the mean absolute value over the array). For readability, we contract $\zeta(I_r, I_t)$ into simply ζ.

The optimization will then try to minimize the dissimilarities between the synthesized view $\widehat{I}_i$ and original frame I_t. As suggested by [6], raw pixel difference can be coupled with structural similarity (SSIM) [21] maximization, in order to be robust to luminosity changes, either from camera auto-exposition or from non Lambertian surfaces. SSIM computation is detailed Eq. 4, where μ and σ are the local mean and variance operators, estimated by convolving the image with Gaussian kernels of size 3×3. $C_1 = 0.01$ and $C_2 = 0.09$ are two constants. Note that the use of convolution in SSIM increases the receptive field of the loss function with respect to the L_1 distance.

$$\text{SSIM}(I_t, I_i) = \frac{(2\mu_{I_t}\mu_{I_i} + C_1) + (2\sigma_{I_t I_i} + C_2)}{(\mu_{I_t}^2 + \mu_{I_i}^2 + C_1)(\sigma_{I_t}^2 + \sigma_{I_i}^2 + C_2)} \tag{4}$$

Our photometric loss $\mathcal{L}_p$ is then a mixture of the two, α being an empirical weight.

$$\mathcal{L}_p = \sum_i \|\widehat{I}_i - I_t\|_1 - \alpha \text{SSIM}(\widehat{I}_i, I_t) \tag{5}$$

Along with frames dissimilarity, in order to avoid divergent depth values in occluded or low textured areas, we add a geometric smooth loss that tries to minimize depth relative Laplacian, weighted by image gradients. Also, contrary to single frame network, depthnet output ζ here is not normalized. Thus, we must scale it according to its mean value. The fraction here represents pixel wise division, ∇ and Δ are the gradient and Laplacian operators respectively, obtained by 3×3 convolutions.

$$\mathcal{L}_g = \left\| \frac{|\Delta\zeta|}{\|\nabla I_t\|} \right\|_1 \times \frac{1}{\|\zeta\|_1} \tag{6}$$

Finally, we apply this loss to multiple scales s of DepthNet outputs, multiplied by a factor giving more importance to high resolution, and our final loss becomes

$$\mathcal{L} = \sum_s \frac{1}{2^s} \left(\mathcal{L}_p^s + \lambda \mathcal{L}_g^s \right) \tag{7}$$

where λ denotes an empirical weight.

Input	Ground truth	Zhou *et al* [25]	Ours

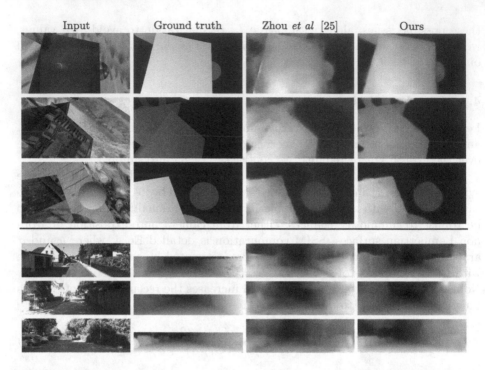

Fig. 2. Comparison between our method and Zhou *et al.* [25] on updated Still Box [14] and KITTI [5].

5   Experiments

5.1   Training Datasets

Our experiments were made on three different datasets. KITTI is one of the most well known datasets for training and evaluating algorithms on multiple computer vision tasks such as odometry, optical flow or disparity. It features stereo vision, LiDAR depth measures and GPS/RTK coupled with IMU for camera poses. During training we only used monocular frames and IMU values when supervising with orientation. We used LiDAR for evaluation. We applied the same training/validation/test split as [25]: about 40k frames for training and 4k for evaluation. We also discarded of the whole set scenes containing the 697 test frames from the Eigen [3] split. We also constructed a filtered test set with the same frames as Eigen, but discarding 69 frames whose GPS position uncertainty was above 1 m. This set was used when displacement data was needed.

We also conducted experiments on an updated version of Still Box, used in [14], in which we added random rotations (*i.e.* we draw an initial rotation speed that remains the same through the sequence). This dataset features synthetic rigid scenes, composed of basic 3d primitives (cubes, spheres, cones and tores) randomly textured using images scrapped from *Flickr*. In this dataset, depth is

Input	Zhou *et al* [25]	Ours

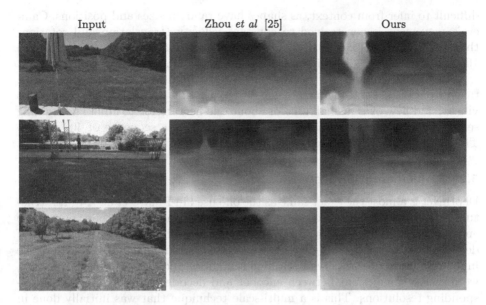

Fig. 3. Subjective comparison of disparity maps between Zhou [25] and our method on a small UAV dataset.

Fig. 4. Some failure cases of our method on KITTI. First column is a detail of a larger image. The foreground car is moving forward and it's detected as far away, while the background car is moving toward us and is detected as close. Second column is a poorly textured road.

difficult to infer from context, as shapes have random sizes and positions. Camera's movement is constrained to constant velocity (translation and rotation) throughout scenes of 20 pictures. The dataset contains 1500 training scenes and 100 test scenes, *i.e.* 30k training frames and 2k validation frames (Fig. 2).

Finally, we trained our network on a very small dataset of UAV videos, taken from the same camera the same day. We used a Bebop2 drone, with 30 fps videos, and flew over a small area of about one hectare for 15 min. The training set contains around 14k frames while the test set is a sequence of 400 frames. This dataset is not annotated, and only subjective evaluation can be done.

5.2 Implementation Details

DepthNet is almost the exact same as the one used in Pinard *et al.* [14]. Its structure mainly consists of two components: the encoder and the decoder parts. The encoder follows the basic structure of VGG [18]. The decoder is made up of deconvolution layers to bring back the spatial feature maps up to a fourth of the input resolution. To preserve both high semantics and rich spatial information, we use skip connections between encoder and decoder parts at different corresponding resolutions. This is a multi-scale technique that was initially done in [2]. The main difference between DepthNet and our network is the ELU function [1] applied to last depth output instead of identity.

PoseNet is the same as [25] which contains 8 convolutional with a stride of 2 layers followed by a global average pooling layer before final prediction. Every layer except the last one are post processed with ReLU activation [11].

We used PyTorch [13] for all tests and trainings, with empirical weights $\lambda = 3$ and $\alpha = 0.075$. We used Adam optimizer [9] with learning rate of 2×10^{-4} and $\beta_1 = 0.9$, $\beta_2 = 0.999$.

5.3 Quality Measurements and Comparison with Other Algorithms

In addition to using standard measurements from [3], our goal is to measure how well a network would perform in real conditions. As stated in Sect. 3, depth map scale factor must be determined from reasonable external data and not from explicit depth ground truth.

We thus compare our solution to [25] where the output is multiplied by the ratio between estimated displacement from PoseNet and actual values. For KITTI, displacement is determined by GPS RTK, but as we only need magnitude, speed from wheels would have been sufficient. When training was done with orientation supervision, we stabilized the frames before feeding them to DepthNet. To test our method on our small UAV dataset, we first did a training on updated Still Box, then an unsupervised fine tuning. Likewise, when using Zhou *et al.* method [25], we pretrained on KITTI before fine tuning on our video.

5.4 Quantative Training Results

Table 1 presents quantitative results compared to prior works. We tried 5 different versions of our network. The first one is the exact same as [14], only trained

Table 1. Quantitative tests on KITTI [5] Eigen split [3]. Measures are the same as in Eigen *et al.* [3]. For blue measures, lower is better, for red measures, higher is better. For training, K is the KITTI dataset [5], S is the Still Box dataset [14]. For scale factor, GT is ground truth, P is pose. When scale was determined with pose, we discarded frames where GPS uncertainty was greater than 1 m. For supervision, D is depth and O is orientation. → denotes fine tuning.

Method	training set	scale factor	supervision	Abs Rel	Sq Rel	RMSE	RMSE log	$\delta < 1.25$	$\delta < 1.25^2$	$\delta < 1.25^3$
Eigen *et al* [3] Coarse	K	GT	D	0.214	1.605	6.563	0.292	0.673	0.884	0.957
Eigen *et al* [3] Fine	K	GT	D	0.203	1.548	6.307	0.282	0.702	0.890	0.958
Zhou *et al* [25]	K	GT	-	0.183	1.595	6.709	0.270	0.734	0.902	0.959
Mahjourian *et al* [10]	K	GT	-	0.163	1.240	6.220	0.250	0.762	0.916	0.968
Zhichao *et al* [23]	K	GT	-	0.155	1.296	5.857	0.233	0.793	0.931	**0.973**
Ranjan *et al* [16]	K	GT	-	**0.148**	**1.149**	**5.464**	**0.226**	**0.815**	**0.935**	0.973
Pinard *et al* [14]	S	P	D + O	0.5071	7.1540	9.6209	0.5032	0.3960	0.6600	0.8138
Zhou *et al*	K	P	-	0.2786	**2.7059**	7.2956	0.3552	0.5816	0.8082	0.8982
Ours	K	P	-	0.3124	5.0302	8.4985	0.4095	0.5919	0.7961	0.8821
Ours	S → K	P	D+O → -	0.2940	3.9925	7.5727	0.3756	0.6092	0.8336	0.9090
Ours	K	P	O	0.2756	3.9335	**7.2939**	0.3539	0.6417	0.8457	0.9179
Ours	S → K	P	D+O → O	**0.2706**	4.4947	7.3119	**0.3452**	**0.6778**	**0.8564**	**0.9242**

Table 2. Quantitative tests on StillBox, no pretraining has been done. The supervised Pinard *et al.* [14] method is here to give an hint on a theoritical limit since it uses the same network, but with depth supervision

Method	scale factor	supervision	Abs Rel	Sq Rel	RMSE	RMSE log	$\delta < 1.25$	$\delta < 1.25^2$	$\delta < 1.25^3$
Pinard *et al* [14]	P	D + O	**0.2120**	**2.0644**	**7.0669**	**0.2959**	**0.7091**	**0.8810**	**0.9460**
Zhou *et al* [25]	GT	-	0.5005	11.4189	15.7207	0.6012	0.4969	0.6767	0.7671
Zhou *et al* [25]	P	-	0.8109	11.9956	17.2740	0.6928	0.3475	0.5733	0.7136
Ours	P	-	0.4684	10.9247	15.7560	0.5440	0.4524	0.6772	0.8037
Ours	P	O	**0.2970**	**5.2827**	**10.5090**	**0.4041**	**0.6684**	**0.8405**	**0.9058**

on StillBox. It serves as a baseline purpose, without finetuning. The other four configurations are training from scratch or finetuning from StillBox, and training with orientation supervision or not.

As we might expect, on KITTI our method fails to converge as well as single image methods using classic relative depth quality measurement. However, when scale factor is determined from poses, we match the performance of the adapted method from [25]. It can also be noted that finetuning provides a better starting point for our network, and that when available on a training set, orientation supervision is very advantageous.

When trying to train a Depth network with stabilized videos, it is then strongly recommended to do a first supervised training on a synthetic dataset such as StillBox.

Some failed test cases can be seen on Fig. 4. The main sources of error are moving objects and poorly textured areas (especially concrete roads), even though we applied depth smooth geometric loss. Our attempt at explaining this failure is the large optical flow value compared to low textured area, meaning matching spatial structures is difficult. However, as KITTI acquisition rate is only 10 fps, we believe this problem would be less common on regular cameras, with typical rates of 30 fps or higher.

Table 2 presents results on the updated Still Box dataset. Zhou *et al.* [25] performs surprisingly well given the theoretical lack of visual context in this dataset. However, our method performs better, whether from orientation supervision or completely unsupervised. We also compare it to supervised DepthNet from [14]. This can be considered a theoretical limit for training DepthNet on Still Box since [14] is completely supervised, and our training method is very close to it, indicating the good convergence of our model and thus our training algorithm and loss design validity.

5.5   Domain Adaptation Results

Finally, Fig. 3 (left) compares Zhou *et al.* [25] and our method on some test frames of our small UAV dataset. Our methods shows much better domain adaptation when fine tuning in a few-shot learning fashion. Especially for foreground objects, as Zhou *et al.* [25] blends it with the trees near the horizon, which is very problematic for navigation. A video with result comparison is provided as supplementary material[1] to this paper.

Table 3 compares domain robustness without any training: we tried inference on an upside-down KITTI test set, with ground up and sky down, and our method performs much better than Zhou *et al.* [25], which is completely lost and performs worse than inferring a constant plane. However, our method is not as performing as Pinard *et al.* [14] which score was expected to be the same as in Table 1, since it has not been trained on any KITTI frames, whether regular or reversed. This shows that our network may have learned to infer depth from both motion and context, which can be considered as a compromise between our two competitors, Zhou *et al.* [25] relying only on context and Pinard *et al.* [14] only on motion.

Table 3. Quantitative tests on upside-down KITTI [5]: sky is down and ground is up. No training has been done. Constant Plane outputs the same depth for every pixel

Method	training set	scale factor	supervision	Abs Rel	Sq Rel	RMSE	RMSE log	$\delta < 1.25$	$\delta < 1.25^2$	$\delta < 1.25^3$
Pinard *et al* [14]	S	P	D + O	**0.4622**	**6.0229**	**9.2277**	**0.4807**	**0.4149**	**0.6863**	**0.8349**
Constant Plane	-	GT	-	0.4568	4.8516	12.0848	0.6000	0.2962	0.5488	0.7524
Zhou *et al* [25]	K	GT	-	0.5931	7.5410	12.9943	0.7340	0.2223	0.4342	0.6263
Zhou *et al* [25]	K	P	-	1.5879	62.1068	21.1424	0.9579	0.1688	0.3260	0.4744
Ours	S → K	P	-	**0.6484**	**15.3906**	**12.4324**	0.6245	0.3820	0.6168	0.7607
Ours	S → K	P	O	0.7158	18.8145	12.5424	**0.5987**	**0.4024**	**0.6370**	**0.7723**

6   Conclusion and Future Work

We have presented a novel method for unsupervised depth learning, using not only depth from context but also from motion. This method leverages the context

---

[1] https://youtu.be/ZDgWAWTwU7U.

of stabilized videos, which is a midway between common use cases of stereo rigs and unconstrained ego-motion. As such, our algorithm provides a solution with embedded deployment in mind, especially for UAVs navigation, and requires only video and inertial data to be used.

Our method is also much more robust to domain changes, which is an important issue when dealing with deployment in large scale consumer electronics on which it is impossible to predict all possible contexts and situations, and our method outperforms single frame systems on unusual scenes.

The greatest limitation of our algorithm is the necessity of rigid scenes *even in inference*. This is one of our goals for a future work.

References

1. Clevert, D.A., Unterthiner, T., Hochreiter, S.: Fast and accurate deep network learning by exponential linear units (ELUs). arXiv preprint arXiv:1511.07289 (2015)
2. Dosovitskiy, A., et al.: FlowNet: learning optical flow with convolutional networks. In: IEEE International Conference on Computer Vision (ICCV) (2015). http://lmb.informatik.uni-freiburg.de/Publications/2015/DFIB15
3. Eigen, D., Puhrsch, C., Fergus, R.: Depth map prediction from a single image using a multi-scale deep network. In: Advances in Neural Information Processing Systems, pp. 2366–2374 (2014)
4. Garg, R., Vijay Kumar, B.G., Carneiro, G., Reid, I.: Unsupervised CNN for single view depth estimation: geometry to the rescue. In: Leibe, B., Matas, J., Sebe, N., Welling, M. (eds.) ECCV 2016. LNCS, vol. 9912, pp. 740–756. Springer, Cham (2016). https://doi.org/10.1007/978-3-319-46484-8_45
5. Geiger, A., Lenz, P., Stiller, C., Urtasun, R.: Vision meets robotics: the KITTI dataset. Int. J. Robot. Res. **32**(11), 1231–1237 (2013)
6. Godard, C., Mac Aodha, O., Brostow, G.J.: Unsupervised monocular depth estimation with left-right consistency. In: CVPR (2017)
7. Jaderberg, M., Simonyan, K., Zisserman, A., et al.: Spatial transformer networks. In: Advances in Neural Information Processing Systems, pp. 2017–2025 (2015)
8. Kendall, A., et al.: End-to-end learning of geometry and context for deep stereo regression. CoRR abs/1703.04309 (2017)
9. Kingma, D.P., Ba, J.: Adam: a method for stochastic optimization. CoRR abs/1412.6980 (2014). http://arxiv.org/abs/1412.6980
10. Mahjourian, R., Wicke, M., Angelova, A.: Unsupervised learning of depth and ego-motion from monocular video using 3D geometric constraints. CoRR abs/1802.05522 (2018). http://arxiv.org/abs/1802.05522
11. Nair, V., Hinton, G.E.: Rectified linear units improve restricted Boltzmann machines. In: Proceedings of the 27th International Conference on Machine Learning (ICML 2010), pp. 807–814 (2010)
12. Mayer, N., et al.: A large dataset to train convolutional networks for disparity, optical flow, and scene flow estimation. In: IEEE International Conference on Computer Vision and Pattern Recognition (CVPR) (2016). http://lmb.informatik.uni-freiburg.de/Publications/2016/MIFDB16. arXiv:1512.02134
13. Paszke, A., et al.: Automatic differentiation in PyTorch. In: NIPS-W (2017)

14. Pinard, C., Chevalley, L., Manzanera, A., Filliat, D.: End-to-end depth from motion with stabilized monocular videos. In: ISPRS Annals of Photogrammetry, Remote Sensing and Spatial Information Sciences IV-2/W3, pp. 67–74 (2017). https://doi.org/10.5194/isprs-annals-IV-2-W3-67-2017. https://www.isprs-ann-photogramm-remote-sens-spatial-inf-sci.net/IV-2-W3/67/2017/

15. Pinard, C., Chevalley, L., Manzanera, A., Filliat, D.: Multi range Real-time depth inference from a monocular stabilized footage using a Fully Convolutional Neural Network. In: European Conference on Mobile Robotics. ENSTA ParisTech, Paris, France, September 2017. https://hal.archives-ouvertes.fr/hal-01587658

16. Ranjan, A., Jampani, V., Kim, K., Sun, D., Wulff, J., Black, M.J.: Adversarial collaboration: joint unsupervised learning of depth, camera motion, optical flow and motion segmentation. CoRR abs/1805.09806 (2018). http://arxiv.org/abs/1805.09806

17. Saxena, A., Sun, M., Ng, A.Y.: Make3D: learning 3D scene structure from a single still image. IEEE Trans. Pattern Anal. Mach. Intell. **31**(5), 824–840 (2009). https://doi.org/10.1109/TPAMI.2008.132

18. Simonyan, K., Zisserman, A.: Very deep convolutional networks for large-scale image recognition. CoRR abs/1409.1556 (2014)

19. Ummenhofer, B., et al.: DeMon: depth and motion network for learning monocular stereo. In: IEEE Conference on Computer Vision and Pattern Recognition (CVPR) (2017). http://lmb.informatik.uni-freiburg.de//Publications/2017/UZUMIDB17

20. Vijayanarasimhan, S., Ricco, S., Schmid, C., Sukthankar, R., Fragkiadaki, K.: SfM-Net: learning of structure and motion from video. CoRR abs/1704.07804 (2017). http://arxiv.org/abs/1704.07804

21. Wang, Z., Bovik, A.C., Sheikh, H.R., Simoncelli, E.P.: Image quality assessment: from error visibility to structural similarity. IEEE Trans. Image Process. **13**(4), 600–612 (2004)

22. Xie, J., Girshick, R., Farhadi, A.: Deep3D: fully automatic 2D-to-3D video conversion with deep convolutional neural networks. In: Leibe, B., Matas, J., Sebe, N., Welling, M. (eds.) ECCV 2016. LNCS, vol. 9908, pp. 842–857. Springer, Cham (2016). https://doi.org/10.1007/978-3-319-46493-0_51

23. Yin, Z., Shi, J.: GeoNet: unsupervised learning of dense depth, optical flow and camera pose. In: CVPR (2018)

24. Zbontar, J., LeCun, Y.: Stereo matching by training a convolutional neural network to compare image patches. J. Mach. Learn. Res. **17**, 1–32 (2016)

25. Zhou, T., Brown, M., Snavely, N., Lowe, D.G.: Unsupervised learning of depth and ego-motion from video. In: CVPR (2017)

Learning Spectral Transform Network on 3D Surface for Non-rigid Shape Analysis

Ruixuan Yu, Jian Sun$^{(\boxtimes)}$, and Huibin Li

Xi'an Jiaotong University, Xi'an 710049, China
yuruixuan123@stu.xjtu.edu.cn, {jiansun,huibinli}@xjtu.edu.cn

Abstract. Designing a network on 3D surface for non-rigid shape analysis is a challenging task. In this work, we propose a novel spectral transform network on 3D surface to learn shape descriptors. The proposed network architecture consists of four stages: raw descriptor extraction, surface second-order pooling, mixture of power function-based spectral transform, and metric learning. The proposed network is simple and shallow. Quantitative experiments on challenging benchmarks show its effectiveness for non-rigid shape retrieval and classification, e.g., it achieved the highest accuracies on SHREC'14, 15 datasets as well as the "range" subset of SHREC'17 dataset.

Keywords: Non-rigid shape analysis · Spectral transform ·
Shape representation

1 Introduction

3D shape analysis has become increasingly important with the advances of shape scanning and processing techniques. Shape retrieval and classification are two fundamental tasks of 3D shape analysis, with diverse applications in archeology, virtual reality, medical diagnosis, etc. 3D shapes generally include rigid shapes, e.g., CAD models, and non-rigid shapes such as human surfaces with non-rigid deformations.

A fundamental problem in non-rigid shape analysis is shape representation. Traditional shape representation methods are mostly based on local artificial descriptors such as shape context [4], mesh-sift [22,39], spin images [19], etc., and they have shown effective performance especially for shape matching and recognition. These descriptors are further modeled as middle level shape descriptors by Bag-of-Words model [21], VLAD [18], etc., and then applied to shape classification and retrieval. For shapes with non-rigid deformations, the model in [11] generalize shape descriptors from Euclidean metrics

Electronic supplementary material The online version of this chapter (https://doi.org/10.1007/978-3-030-11015-4_28) contains supplementary material, which is available to authorized users.

© Springer Nature Switzerland AG 2019
L. Leal-Taixé and S. Roth (Eds.): ECCV 2018 Workshops, LNCS 11131, pp. 377–394, 2019.
https://doi.org/10.1007/978-3-030-11015-4_28

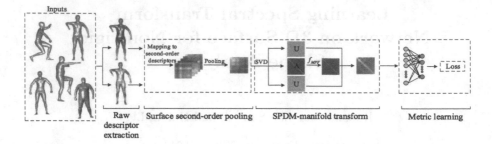

Fig. 1. Architecture of our proposed ST-Net. It consists of four stages, i.e., raw descriptor extraction, surface second-order pooling, SPDM-manifold transform and metric learning.

to non-Euclidean metrics. The spectral descriptors, which are built on spectral decomposition of Laplace-Beltrami operator defined on 3D surface, are popular in non-rigid shape representation. Typical spectral descriptors include diffusion distance [20], heat kernel signature (HKS) [41], wave kernel signature (WKS) [2] and scale invariant heat kernel signature (SIHKS) [6]. In [8], spectral descriptors of SIHKS and WKS using a Large Margin Nearest Neighbor (LMNN) embedding achieved state-of-the-art results for non-rigid shape retrieval. Spectral descriptors are commonly intrinsic and invariant to isometric deformations, therefore effective for non-rigid shape analysis.

Recently, a promising trend in non-rigid shape representation is the learning-based methods on 3D surface for tasks of non-rigid shape retrieval and classification. Many learning-based methods take low-level shape descriptors as inputs and extract high-level descriptors by integrating over the entire shape. In the work of [8], they first extract SIHKS and WKS, and then integrate them to form a global descriptor followed by LMNN embedding. Global shape descriptors are learned by Long-Short Term Memory (LSTM) network in [45] based on spectral descriptors. The eigen-shape and Fisher-shape descriptors are learned by a modified auto-encoder based on spectral descriptors in [12]. These works have shown impressive results in learning global shape descriptors. Though these advances have been achieved, designing learning-based methods on 3D surface is still an emerging and challenging task, including how to design feature aggregation and feature learning on 3D surface for non-rigid shape representation.

In this work, we propose a novel learning-based spectral transform network on 3D surface to learn discriminative shape descriptor for non-rigid shape retrieval and classification. *First*, we define a second-order pooling operation on 3D surface which models the second-order statistics of input raw descriptors on 3D surfaces. *Second*, considering that the pooled second-order descriptors lie on a manifold of symmetric positive definite matrices (SPDM-manifold), we define a novel manifold transform for feature learning by learning a *mixture of power function* on the singular values of the SPDM descriptors. Third, by concatenating the stages of raw descriptor extraction, surface second-order pooling, transform on SPDM-manifold and metric learning, we propose a novel network architecture, dubbed as *spectral transform network* as shown in Fig. 1, which can learn discriminative shape descriptors for non-rigid shape analysis.

To the best of our knowledge, this is the first paper that learns second-order pooling-based shape descriptors on 3D surfaces using a network architecture. Our network structure is simple and easily to be trained, and is justified to be able to significantly improve the discriminative ability of input raw descriptors. It is adaptive to various non-rigid shapes such as watertight meshes, partial meshes and point cloud data. It achieved competitive results on challenging benchmarks for non-rigid shape retrieval and classification, e.g., 100% accuracy on SHREC'14 [32] dataset and the state-of-the-art accuracy on the "range" subset of SHREC'17 [28] in metric of NN [38].

2   Related Works

2.1   Learning Approach for 3D Shapes

Deep learning is a powerful tool in computer vision, speech recognition, natural language processing, etc. Recently, it has also been extended to 3D shape analysis and achieves impressive progresses. One way for the extension is to represent the shapes as volume data [35,44] or multi-view data [3] and then send them to deep neural networks. The voxel and multi-view based shape representation have been successful in rigid shape representation [35,40] relying on a large training dataset. Due to the operations of voxelization and 3D to 2D projection, it may lose shape details especially for non rigid shapes with large deformations, e.g., human bodies with different poses. An alternative way is to define the networks directly on 3D surface based on spectral descriptors as in [5,12,27,45]. These models benefit from the intrinsic properties of spectral descriptors, and utilize surface convolution or deep nueral networks, e.g., LSTM, auto-encoder, to further learn discriminative shape descriptors. PointNet [34,36] is another interesting deep learning approach that directly build network using the point cloud representation of 3D shapes, which can also handle the non-rigid 3D shape classification using non-Euclidean metric. Compared with them, we build a novel network architecture on 3D surface from the perspectives of second-order descriptor pooling and spectrum transform on the pooled descriptors. It is justified to be able to effectively learn surface descriptors on SPDM-manifold.

2.2   Second-Order Pooling of Shape Descriptors

Second-order pooling operation was firstly proposed in [7] showing outstanding performance in 2D vision tasks such as recognition [16] and segmentation [7]. The pooled descriptors lie on a Riemannian SPDM-manifold. Due to non-Euclidean structure of this manifold, many traditional machine learning methods based on Euclidean metrics can not be used directly. As discussed in [1,31], two popular metrics on SPDM-manifold are affine-invariant metric and log-Euclidean metric. Considering the complexity, the log-Euclidean metric and its variants

[15,17] that embed data into Euclidean space are more widely used [7,43]. The power-Euclidean transform [10] has achieved impressive results which theoretically approximates the log-Euclidean metric when its power index approaches zero. The most related shape descriptors to ours for 3D shape analysis are the covariance-based descriptors [9,43]. In [9], they encoded the point descriptors such as angular and texture within a 3D point neighbourhood by a covariance matrix. In [43], the covariance descriptors were further incorporated into the Bag-of-Words model to represent shapes for retrieval and correspondence. In our work, we present a formal definition of second-order pooling of shape descriptors on 3D surface, and define a learning-based spectral transform on SPDM-manifold, which can effectively boost the performance of the pooled descriptors for 3D non-rigid shape analysis.

In the following sections, we first introduce our proposed spectral transform network in Sect. 3. Then, in Sect. 4, we experimentally justify the effectiveness of the proposed network on benchmark datasets for non-rigid shape retrieval and classification. We finally conclude this work in Sect. 5.

3   Spectral Transform Network on 3D Shapes

We aim to learn discriminative shape descriptors for 3D shape analysis by designing a *spectral transform network (ST-Net)* on 3D surface. As illustrated in Fig. 1, our approach consists of four stages: raw descriptor extraction, surface second-order pooling, SPDM-manifold transform and metric learning. In the followings, we will give detailed descriptions of these stages.

3.1   Raw Descriptor Extraction

Let S denote the surface (either mesh or point cloud) of a given shape, in this stage, we extract descriptors from S. For watertight surface, we select spectral descriptors, i.e., SIHKS [6] and WKS [2] as inputs, which are intrinsic and robust to non-rigid deformations. For partial surface and point cloud, we choose local geometric descriptors such as Localized Statistical Features (LSF) [29]. All of them are dense descriptors representing multi-scale geometric features of the shape. Note that our framework is generic, and other shape descriptors can also be used such as normals and curvatures.

Spectral Descriptors. Spectral descriptors are mostly dependent on the spectral (eigenvalues and/or eigenfunctions) of the Laplace-Beltrami operator, and they are well suited for the analysis of non-rigid shapes. Popular spectral descriptors include HKS [41], SIHKS [6] and WKS [2]. Derived from heat diffusion process, HKS [41] reflects the amount of heat remaining at a point after certain time. SIHKS [6] is derived from HKS and it is scale-invariant. Both of them are intrinsic but lack spatial localization capability. WKS [2] is another intrinsic spectral descriptor stemming from Schrödinger equation. It evaluates the probability of a quantum particle on a shape to be located at a point under a certain energy distribution, and it is better for spatial localization.

Local Geometric Descriptors. Another kind of raw shape descriptor is local geometric descriptor, which encodes the local geometric and spatial information of the shape. We select LSF [29] as input for partial and point cloud non-rigid shape analysis, and it encodes the relative positions and angles locally on the shape. Assuming the selected point is s_1, its position and normal vector are $\mathbf{p_1}$ and $\mathbf{n_1}$, another point s_2 with associated position and normal vector as $\mathbf{p_2}$ and $\mathbf{n_2}$ is within the sphere of influence in a radius r of s_1. Then a 4-tuple $(\beta_1, \beta_2, \beta_3, \beta_4)$ is computed as:

$$\beta_1 = \arctan(\mathbf{w} \cdot \mathbf{n_1}, \mathbf{u} \cdot \mathbf{n_2}), \quad \beta_2 = \mathbf{v} \cdot \mathbf{n_2},$$
$$\beta_3 = \mathbf{u} \cdot (\mathbf{p_2} - \mathbf{p_1})/\|\mathbf{p_2} - \mathbf{p_1}\|, \quad \beta_4 = \|\mathbf{p_2} - \mathbf{p_1}\|. \tag{1}$$

where $\mathbf{u} = \mathbf{n_1}, \mathbf{v} = (\mathbf{p_2} - \mathbf{p_1}) \times \mathbf{u}/\|(\mathbf{p_2} - \mathbf{p_1}) \times \mathbf{u}\|, \mathbf{w} = \mathbf{u} \times \mathbf{v}$. For a local shape of N points, a set of $(N - 1)$ 4-tuples are computed for the center point, which are collected into a 4-dimensional joint histogram. By dividing the histogram to 5 bins for each dimension of the tuple, we have a 625-d descriptor for the center point, which encodes the local geometric information around it.

Given the surface S, we extract either spectral or geometric shape descriptors called as raw descriptors for each point $s \in S$, denoted as $\{\mathbf{h}(s)\}_{s \in S}$, which are taken as the inputs of the following stage.

3.2   Surface Second-Order Pooling

In this stage, we generalize the second-order average-pooling operation [7] from 2D image to 3D surface, and propose a surface second-order pooling operation. Given the extracted shape descriptors $\{\mathbf{h}(s)\}_{s \in S}$, the *surface second-order pooling* is defined as:

$$H = \frac{1}{|S|} \int_S \mathbf{h}^{O_2}(s) ds, \quad \mathbf{h}^{O_2}(s) = \mathbf{h}(s)\mathbf{h}(s)^\top, \tag{2}$$

where $|S|$ denotes the area of the surface, $\mathbf{h}^{O_2}(s)$ is the *second-order descriptor* for a point s, and H is a matrix of the pooled second-order descriptor on S, which is taken as the output of this stage.

For the surface represented by discretized irregular triangular mesh, the integral operation in Eq. (2) can be descretized considering the Voronoi area around each point:

$$H = \sum_{s \in S} \pi(s)\mathbf{h}(s)\mathbf{h}(s)^\top, \pi(s) = \frac{a(s)}{\sum_{p \in S} a(p)}, \tag{3}$$

where s denotes a discretized point on S with its Voronoi area as $a(s)$. In our work, we compute $a(s)$ as in [33]. For the shapes composed of point cloud, Eq. (2) can be descretized as average pooling of the second-order information:

$$H = \frac{1}{|S|} \sum_{s \in S} \mathbf{h}(s)\mathbf{h}(s)^\top, \tag{4}$$

where $|\mathcal{S}|$ denotes the number of points on the surface.

The pooled second-order descriptors represent 2nd-order statistics of raw descriptors over the 3D surfaces. It is obvious that H is a symmetric positive definite matrix (SPDM), which lies on a non-Euclidean manifold of SPDM.

3.3   SPDM-Manifold Transform

This stage, i.e., SPDM-T stage, performs non-linear transform on the singular values of the pooled second-order descriptors, and it is in fact a spectral transform on the SPDM-manifold. This transform will be discriminatively learned for specific task enforced by the loss in the next metric learning stage.

Forward Computation. Assuming that we have a symmetric positive definite matrix H, by singular value decomposition, we have:

$$H = U\Lambda U^\top. \tag{5}$$

We first normalize the singular values of H, i.e., the diagonal values of Λ, by $\mathcal{L}_2$-normalization, achieving $\{\tilde{\Lambda}_{ii}\}_{i=1}^{N_\Lambda}$, where N_Λ is the number of singular values, then perform non-linear transform on $\{\tilde{\Lambda}_{ii}\}_{i=1}^{N_\Lambda}$. Inspired by polynomial function, we propose the following transform:

$$\Lambda' = \mathrm{diag}\{f_{MPF}(\tilde{\Lambda}_{11}), \cdots, f_{MPF}(\tilde{\Lambda}_{N_\Lambda N_\Lambda})\}, \tag{6}$$

where $\mathrm{diag}\{\cdot\}$ is a diagonal matrix with input elements as its diagonal values, $f_{MPF}(\cdot)$ is a *mixture of power function*:

$$f_{MPF}(x) = \sum_{i=0}^{N_m} \gamma_i x^{\alpha_i}, \ \alpha_i \in [0,1], \tag{7}$$

where $\{\alpha_i\}_{i=0}^{N_m}$ are $N_m + 1$ samples with uniform intervals in range of $[0,1]$, $\Gamma = (\gamma_0, \gamma_1, \cdots, \gamma_{N_m})^\top$ is a vector of combination coefficients and required to satisfy:

$$\Gamma^\top \mathbf{1} = 1, \ \Gamma \geq \mathbf{0}. \tag{8}$$

To meet these requirements, the coefficients are defined as:

$$\gamma_i = \frac{e^{\omega_i}}{\sum_{j=0}^{N_m} e^{\omega_j}}, \ i = 0, 1, \cdots, N_m. \tag{9}$$

Then we instead learn the parameters in $\Omega = (\omega_0, \omega_1, \cdots, \omega_{N_m})^\top$ to determine Γ.

After this transform, a new singular value matrix Λ' is derived. Combining it with the original singular vector matrix U, we get the transformed descriptor H' as:

$$H' = U\Lambda'U^\top = U\mathrm{diag}\{f_{MPF}(\tilde{\Lambda}_{11}), \cdots, f_{MPF}(\tilde{\Lambda}_{N_\Lambda N_\Lambda})\}U^\top. \tag{10}$$

H' is also a symmetric positive definite matrix. Due to the symmetry of H', the elements of its upper triangular $g(H')$ are kept as the output of this stage, where $g(\cdot)$ is an operator vectorizing the upper triangular elements of a matrix.

Backward Propagation. As proposed in [17], matrix back-propagation can be performed for SVD decomposition. Let $(\cdot)_{diag}$ denote an operator on matrix that sets all non-diagonal elements to 0, $(\cdot)_{Gdiag}$ be an operator of vectorizing the diagonal elements of a matrix, $g^{-1}(\cdot)$ be the inverse operator of $g(\cdot)$, $\odot$ be the Hadamard product operator. For backward propagation, assuming the partial derivative of loss L with respect to $g(H')$ as $\frac{\partial L}{\partial g(H')}$, we have:

$$\frac{\partial L}{\partial \Lambda'} = (U^\top g^{-1}(\frac{\partial L}{\partial g(H')})U)_{diag}, \tag{11}$$

$$(\frac{\partial L}{\partial \Gamma})_i = (\tilde{\Lambda}^{\alpha_i}\frac{\partial L}{\partial \Lambda'})_{Gdiag}^\top \mathbf{1}, \ i = 0, 1, ..., N_m, \tag{12}$$

$$\frac{\partial L}{\partial \Omega} = (\frac{\partial L}{\partial \Gamma} - \Gamma^\top\frac{\partial L}{\partial \Gamma}) \odot \Gamma. \tag{13}$$

The partial derivative of loss function L with respect to the parameter Ω can be derived by successively computing Eqs. (11), (12), (13). Please refer to supplementary material for gradient computations.

Analysis of SPDM-T Stage. The pooled second-order descriptor H lies on the SPDM-manifold, and the popular transform on this manifold is log-Euclidean transform [10], i.e., $H' = \log(H)$. However, it is unstable when the singular values of H are near or equal to zero. The logarithm-based transforms such as $H' = \log(H + \epsilon I)$ [17] and $H' = \log(\max\{H, \epsilon I\})$ [15] are proposed to overcome this instability, but they need a positive constant regularizer ϵ which is difficult to set. The power-Euclidean metric [10] theoretically approximates the log-Euclidean metric when its power index approaches zero while being more stable. Our proposed mixture of power function $f_{MPF}(\cdot)$ is an extension of power-Euclidean transform that takes it as a special case. The SPDM-T stage learns an effective transform in the space spanned by the power functions adaptively using a data-driven approach. Furthermore, the mixture of power function $f_{MPF}(\cdot)$ is constrained to be nonlinear and retains non-negativeness and order of the eigenvalues (i.e., singular values of a symmetric matrix).

From a statistical perspective, H can be seen as a covariance matrix of input descriptors on 3D surface. Geometrically, its eigenvectors in columns of U construct a coordinate system, its eigenvalues reflect feature variances projected to eigenvectors. By transforming these projected variances (eigenvalues), $f_{MPF}(\cdot)$ implicitly tunes the statistics distribution of input raw descriptors in pooling region when training. Since the entropy of Gaussian distribution with covariance $H \in R^{d \times d}$ is $\mathcal{E}(H) = \frac{1}{2}(d + \log(2\pi) + \log\prod_i \Lambda_{ii})$, transforming eigenvalues Λ_{ii} by $f_{MPF}(\cdot)$ implicitly tune the entropy of distribution of raw descriptors on 3D surface.

3.4   Metric Learning

With the transformed descriptors $g(H')$ as input, we embed them into a low-dimensional space where the descriptors are well grouped or separated with the guidance of labels. To prove the effectiveness of the SPDM-T stage, we design a shallow neural network to achieve the metric learning stage. We first normalize the input $g(H')$ by $\mathcal{L}_2$-normalization, achieving $\tilde{g}(H')$, then add a fully connected layer:

$$F = W\tilde{g}(H'), \tag{14}$$

where W is a matrix in size of $D_m \times D_p$. F is the descriptor of the whole shape. We further send F into loss function for specific shape analysis task to enforce the discriminative ability of shape descriptor. In this work, we focus on shape retrieval and classification. We next discuss the loss functions.

Shape Retrieval. Given a training set of shapes, the loss for shape retrieval is defined on all the possible triplets of shape descriptors $\mathcal{T}_R = \{F_i, F_i^{Pos}, F_i^{Neg}\}$, where i is the index of triplet, F_i^{Pos} and F_i^{Neg} are two shape descriptors with same and different labels w.r.t. the target shape descriptor F_i respectively:

$$L = \sum_{i=1}^{|\mathcal{T}_R|} (\mu + ||F_i - F_i^{Pos}|| - ||F_i - F_i^{Neg}||)_+^2 + \eta ||F_i - F_i^{Pos}||, \tag{15}$$

where $|\mathcal{T}_R|$ is the number of triplets in $\mathcal{T}_R$, $|| \cdot ||$ is $\mathcal{L}_2$-norm, μ is the margin, $(\cdot)_+ = \max\{\cdot, 0\}$ and η is a constant to balance these two terms.

Shape Classification. We construct the cross-entropy loss for shape classification. Given the learned descriptor $\{F_i\}$ with their corresponding labels as $\{y_i\}$, we first add a fully connected layer after F_i to map the features to scores for different categories, and then followed by a softmax layer to predict the probability of a shape belonging to different categories, and the probabilities of all training shapes are denoted as $\mathcal{T}_C = \{\widetilde{F}_i\}$. The loss function is defined as:

$$L = \sum_{i=1}^{|\mathcal{T}_C|} \sum_{j=1}^{M} y_i^j \log(\widetilde{F}_i^j) + (1 - y_i^j)\log(1 - \widetilde{F}_i^j) \tag{16}$$

where $|\mathcal{T}_C|$ is the number of training shapes, i and j indicate the shape and category respectively, and M is the total number of categories.

The combination of fully connected layer and loss function results in a metric learning problem. Minimizing the loss function embeds the shape descriptors into a lower-dimensional space, in which the learned shape descriptors are enforced to be discriminative for specific shape analysis task.

3.5   Network Training

For the task of shape retrieval, each triplet of shapes $\{F_i, F_i^{Pos}, F_i^{Neg}\}$ is taken as a training sample and multiple triplets are taken as a batch for training with mini-batch stochastic gradient descent optimizer (SGD). For shape classification, the network is also trained by mini-batch SGD. To train the network, the raw descriptor extraction and second-order pooling stage as well as the SVD decomposition can be computed off-line, and the learnable parameters in ST-Net are Ω in SPDM-T stage and W in metric learning stage and the later fully connected layer (for classification). For the non-linear transform in SPDM-T stage, we set $N_m = 10$, $\alpha_i = \frac{i}{10}$, $i \in \{0, 1, ..., 10\}$. The gradients of loss are back-propagated to the SPDM-T stage.

4 Experiments

In this section, we evaluate the effectiveness of our ST-Net, especially the surface second-order pooling and SPDM-T stages, for 3D non-rigid shape retrieval and classification. We test our model on watertight and partial mesh datasets as well as point cloud dataset. We will successively introduce the datasets, evaluation methodologies, quantitative results and the evaluation of our SPDM-T stage.

4.1 Datasets and Evaluation Methodologies

Considering that our network is designed for non-rigid shape analysis, we evaluate it for shape retrieval on SHREC'14 [32] and SHREC'17 [28] datasets, and we test our architecture for shape classification on SHREC'15 [23] dataset. All of them are composed of non-rigid shapes with various deformations.

SHREC'14. This dataset includes two datasets of Real and Synthetic human data respectively, both of which are composed of watertight meshes. The Real dataset comprises of 400 meshes from 40 human subjects in 10 different poses. The Synthetic dataset consists of 15 human subjects with 20 poses, resulting in a dataset of 300 shapes. We will try three following experimental settings, which will be refered as "setting-i" ($i = 1, 2, 3$). In setting-1, 40% and 60% shapes are used for training and test respectively as in [8]. In setting-2, an independent training set[1] including unseen shape categories is taken as training set and the Real dataset of SHREC'14 is used for test. In setting-3, 30% of the classes are randomly selected as the training classes and remaining 70% classes are used for test as in Litman [32]. Both setting-2 and 3 are challenging because the shapes in training and test sets are disjoint in shape categories.

SHREC'15. This dataset includes 1200 watertight shapes of 50 categories, each of which contains 24 shapes with various poses and topological structures. To compare with the state-of-the-art PointNet++ [36] on the dataset, we use the experimental setting in [36], i.e., treating the shapes as point cloud data, and using 5-fold cross-validation to test the accuracy for shape classification.

---

[1] http://www.cs.cf.ac.uk/shaperetrieval/download.php.

SHREC'17. This dataset is composed of two subsets, i.e., "holes" and "range", which contain meshes with holes and range data respectively. We use the provided standard splits for training/test. The "holes" subset consists of 1216 training and 1078 test shapes, and the "range" subset consists of 1082 training and 882 test shapes.

Evaluation Methodologies. For non-rigid shape retrieval, we evaluate results by NN (Nearest Neighbor), 1-T (First-Tier), 2-T (Second-Tier), and DCG (Discounted Cumulative Gain) [38]. For non-rigid shape classification, the results are evaluated by classification accuracy, i.e., the percentage of correctly classified shapes.

Table 1. Retrieval results on SHREC'14 Synthetic and Real dataset in setting-1 (in %). We show the results of ST-Net as well as the baselines and state-of-the-art CSDLMNN [8].

Method	Synthetic				Real			
	NN	1-T	2-T	DCG	NN	1-T	2-T	DCG
CSDLMNN [8]	99.7	98.0	99.9	99.6	97.9	92.8	98.7	97.6
Surf-O_1	82.7	77.1	84.3	83.6	54.2	52.6	57.9	55.0
Surf-O_2	87.3	84.2	89.2	87.8	61.1	57.2	64.0	63.2
Surf-O_1-ML	**100**	96.9	99.9	99.7	96.7	91.9	98.3	96.9
Surf-O_2-ML	**100**	**100**	**100**	**100**	98.8	96.1	99.6	99.9
ST-Net	**100**	**100**	**100**	**100**	**100**	**99.8**	**100**	**99.9**

4.2 Results for Non-rigid Shape Retrieval on Watertight Dataset

For non-rigid shape retrieval on SHREC'14 datasets, we select SIHKS and WKS as input raw descriptors. We discretize the Laplace-Beltrami operator as in [33], and compute 50-d SIHKS and 100-d WKS. In the surface second-order pooling stage, the descriptors are computed by Eq. (3). When training the ST-Net for shape retrieval, the batch size, learning rate and margin μ are set as 5, 20 and 60 respectively. The descriptor of every shape is 100-d, i.e., $D_m = 100$. In the loss function, η is set as 1.

To justify the effectiveness of our architecture, we compare the following different variants of descriptors for shape retrieval. (1) *Surf-O_1*: pooled raw descriptors on surfaces. (2) *Surf-O_2*: pooled second-order descriptors on surfaces. (3) *Surf-O_1-ML*: descriptors of Surf-O_1 followed by a metric learning stage. (4) *Surf-O_2-ML*: descriptors of Surf-O_2 followed by a metric learning stage. For retrieval task, the descriptors of *Surf-O_1* and *Surf-O_2* are directly used for retrieval based on Euclidean distance. In Table 1, we report the results in experimental setting-1 of these descriptors as well as state-of-the-art CSDLMNN [8] method. As shown in the table, the increased accuracies from Surf-O_1 to Surf-O_2, and that from Surf-O_1-ML to Surf-O_2-ML indicate the effectiveness of the surface second-order pooling stage. The improvements from Surf-O_2-ML to ST-Net demonstrate the advantage of the SPDM-T stage. Our full ST-Net achieves 100% accuracy in NN (i.e., the percentage of retrieved nearest neighbor shapes belonging to the same class as queries) on SHREC'14 Synthetic and Real datasets. Compared with state-of-the-art CSDLMNN [8] method, the competitive accuracies justify the effectiveness of our method.

Table 2 presents results in mean average precision (mAP) on SHREC'14 Real and Synthetic datasets in setting-1 compared with RMVM [14], CSDLMNN [8], in which CSDLMNN is a state-of-the-art approach for this task. For our proposed ST-Net, we randomly split the training and test subsets five times and report the average mAP with standard deviations shown in brackets. In the table, we also present the baseline results of our ST-Net to justify the effectiveness of our architecture. Our ST-Net achieves highest mAP on both datasets, demonstrating its effectiveness for watertight non-rigid shape analysis. In Table 3, we also show the results on SHREC'14 Real dataset using setting-2 and setting-3, which are more challenging since the training and test sets have disjoint shape categories. ST-Net still significantly outperforms the baselines of Surf-O_1-ML and Surf-O_2-ML, and achieves high accuracies. Our ST-Net significantly outperforms Litman [32] using the experimental setting-3.

Table 2. Results for shape retrieval in setting-1 evaluated by mAP in % on SHREC'14 Synthetic and Real datasets. Our ST-Net performs best on both datasets.

Dataset	RMVM[14]	CSDLMNN[8]	Surf-O_1	Surf-O_2	Surf-O_1-ML	Surf-O_2-ML	ST-Net
Synthetic	96.3	99.7	82.7	85.3	93.6	97.1	**100**(0)
Real	79.5	97.9	50.8	50.4	90.5	95.3	**99.9**(0.1)

4.3 Results for Non-rigid Shape Retrieval on Partial Dataset

We now evaluate our approach on non-rigid partial shapes in subsets of "holes" and "range" of SHREC'17 dataset. Considering that the shapes are not watertight surface, we use local geometric descriptors as raw descriptors. We select 3000 points uniformly as in [30] for every shape and compute 625-d LSF as inputs. In the surface second-order pooling stage, the descriptors are computed by Eq. (4). When training the ST-Net for shape retrieval, the batch size, learning rate and margin μ are set as 5, 100 and 60 respectively. The descriptor of every shape is 300-d, i.e., $D_m = 300$. In the loss function, the constant η is set as 1.

In Table 4, we first compare our ST-Net with the baselines, i.e., Surf-O_1, Surf-O_2, Surf-O_1-ML and Surf-O_2-ML to show the effectiveness of our network architecture. The raw LSF descriptors after second-order pooling without learning, i.e., Surf-O_2, produces the accuracy of 69.0% and 71.7% in NN on "holes" and "range" subsets respectively. With the metric learning stage, the results are increased to 75.9% and 77.6% for these two subsets. The ST-Net with both SPDM-T stage and metric learning stage increases the accuracies to be 96.1% and 97.3% respectively, with around 20 percent improvement than the results of Surf-O_2-ML. This clearly shows the effectiveness of our defined SPDM-T stage for enhancing the discriminative ability of shape descriptors.

Moreover, the performance increases from Surf-O_1 to Surf-O_2 and from Surf-O_1-ML to Surf-O_2-ML justify the effectiveness of surface second-order pooling stage over the traditional first-order pooling (i.e., average pooling) on surfaces.

In Table 4, we also compare our results with the methods that participate to the SHREC'17 track, i.e., DLSF [13], 2VDI-CNN, SBoF [25], and BoW+RoPS, BoW+HKS, RMVM [14], DNA [37], etc., and the results of their methods are from [28]. In DLSF [13], they design their deep network by first training a E-block and then training a AC-block. The method of 2VDI-CNN is based on multi-view projections of 3D shapes and deep GoogLeNet [42] for shape descriptor learning. The method of SBoF [25] trains a bag-of-features model using sparse coding. The methods of BoW+RoPS, BoW+HKS combine BoW model with shape descriptors of RoPS and HKS for shape retrieval. As shown in the table, our ST-Net ranks second on the "holes" subset and achieves the highest accuracy in NN, 2-T and DCG on the "range" subset, demonstrating its effectiveness for partial non-rigid shape analysis. Compared with the deep learning-based methods of DLSF [13], 2VDI-CNN, our network architecture is shallow and simple to implement but achieves competitive performance.

In Fig. 2, we show the top retrieved shapes with interval of 5 in ranking index given query shapes on the leftmost column, and the examples in sub-figures (a) and (b) are respectively from SHRES'17 "holes" and "range" subsets. These shapes are with large non-rigid deformations. The examples show that ST-Net enables to effectively retrieve the correct shapes even when the shapes are range data or with large holes.

Table 3. Results for shape retrieval on SHREC'14 Real dataset in setting-2 and -3 (in %). ST-Net achieves the best performance.

	Method	NN	1-T	2-T	EM	DCG
Setting-2	Surf-O_1-ML	45.75	35.25	59.08	34.76	63.84
	Surf-O_2-ML	80.25	63.94	78.39	40.94	80.21
	ST-Net	**85.75**	**71.33**	**88.92**	**43.20**	**88.29**
Setting-3	Litman [32]	79.3	72.7	91.4	43.2	89.1
	Surf-O_1-ML	54.29	46.67	70.91	37.60	71.71
	Surf-O_2-ML	88.76	82.01	96.47	42.82	90.75
	ST-Net	**92.53**(1.49)	**84.78**(2.43)	**96.93**(1.17)	**43.86**(0.36)	**93.85**(1.63)

4.4 Results for Non-rigid Shape Classification on Point Cloud Data

In this section, we mainly aim to compare our approach with state-of-the-art deep network of PointNet++ [36] for non-rigid shape classification by point cloud representation. We compare on SHREC'15 non-rigid shape dataset for classification, and PointNet++ reported state-of-the-art results on this dataset. For every shape, we uniformly sample 3000 points as [30], and take the 625-d

(a) Retrieval results for a shape with "holes"

(b) Retrieval results for a range data

Fig. 2. Instances of retrieved top ranked shapes with interval of 5 in ranking index. The wrongly retrieved shapes are shown in red. (Color figure online)

LSF as raw descriptors. The second-order descriptors are pooled by Eq. (4). When training the ST-Net, the batch size, learning rate are set as 15 and 1.

We compare ST-Net with baseline architectures of Surf-O_1, Surf-O_2, Surf-O_1-ML, Surf-O_2-ML in Table 5. For the ST-Net, we perform 5-fold cross-validation for 6 times (each time using a different train/test split), and the average accuracy is reported with standard deviation shown in bracket. For classification task, the descriptors are sent to classification loss (see Sect. 3.4) for classifier training. The raw descriptors using average pooling, i.e., Surf-O_1, achieves 85.58% in classification accuracy. Our ST-Net achieves 97.37% accuracy, which shows the effectiveness of our network architecture.

In Table 5, we also present the classification accuracies of deep learning-based methods of DeepGM [26] and PointNet++ [36]. DeepGM [26] learns deep features from geodesic moments by stacked autoencoder. PointNet++ [36] is pioneering work for deep learning on point clouds based on a well designed PointNet [34] recursively on a nested partition of the input point set. Compared with the state-of-the-art method of PointNet++ [36], the classification accuracy of our ST-Net is higher.

4.5 Evaluation for SPDM-Manifold Transform

SPDM-T is an essential stage in our ST-Net. Besides the analysis in Sect. 3.3, we evaluate and visualize the learned SPDM-manifold transform in this subsection.

We first evaluate the effects of different transforms in the SPDM-T stage quantitatively on SHREC'14 Real dataset in setting-3. These transforms include power-Euclidean (1/2-pE) [10], i.e., $y = \sqrt{x}$, and logarithm-based transforms: $y = \log(x)$ (L-E) [10], $y = \log(x + \epsilon)$ (L-R) [17] and $y = \log(\max\{x, \epsilon\})$

Table 4. Shape retrieval results on SHREC'17 non-rigid datasets. The deep learning-based methods are signed with "*". The values are formatted as percentage.

(a) The "holes" subset

Meshod	NN	1-T	2-T	DCG
DLSF* [13]	**100**	**97.1**	**99.9**	**99.8**
2VDI-CNN*	90.6	81.8	93.7	95.4
SBoF [25]	81.5	32.6	49.4	78.0
BoW+HKS	57.8	26.1	43.6	72.5
BoW+RoPS	60.7	91.8	97.0	96.8
RMVM[14]	39.2	22.6	40.2	67.9
DNA [37]	7.8	16.3	34.8	63.2
Surf-O_1	66.8	23.6	37.5	71.3
Surf-O_2	69.0	24.0	38.8	71.7
Surf-O_1-ML	73.2	29.4	46.7	75.4
Surf-O_2-ML	75.9	49.4	72.3	83.2
ST-Net	96.1	85.8	95.7	97.7

(b) The "range" subset

Meshod	NN	1-T	2-T	DCG
2VDI-CNN*	96.9	90.6	97.7	98.0
SBoF [25]	81.1	31.7	51.0	76.9
BoW+RoPS	51.5	**91.5**	95.9	96.0
BoW+HKS	51.9	32.6	53.7	73.6
DNA [37]	13.0	18.3	36.6	64.0
Surf-O_1	69.8	26.1	39.4	71.3
Surf-O_2	71.7	25.7	40.2	71.3
Surf-O_1-ML	75.6	27.8	47.7	73.8
Surf-O_2-ML	77.6	58.2	79.7	87.2
ST-Net	**97.3**	86.2	**97.9**	**98.4**

Table 5. Results for shape classification (in %) on SHREC'15. For ST-Net, we repeat 5-fold cross-validation for 6 times and report the average accuracy with standard deviation in bracket.

	DeepGM [26]	PointNet++ [36]	Surf-O_1	Surf-O_2	Surf-O_1-ML	Surf-O_2-ML	ST-Net
Acc	93.03	96.09	85.58	89.84	91.00	93.08	**97.37**(0.97)

(L-M-R) [15]. Besides the transforms mentioned above, we also present the results of $\mathcal{L}_2$- Normalization ($\mathcal{L}_2$-N) and Signed Squareroot $+\mathcal{L}_2$- Normalization (SSN) [24]. These compared results in Table 6 are produced by ST-Net with $f_{MPF}(\cdot)$ fixed as these transforms. The results are measured by NN and 1-T. It is shown that our learned transform achieves the best results. Some of these compared transforms, such as L-E, L-R, L-M-R, perform well in the training set but worse in the test set, and our proposed transform prevents overfitting.

We then visually show the learned transform function $f_{MPF}(\cdot)$ in Fig. 3. We draw the curves of learned $f_{MPF}(\cdot)$ and show examples of pooled second-order descriptors before and after transform using $f_{MPF}(\cdot)$ on SHREC'14 Real dataset for retrieval (Fig. 3(a)) and SHREC'15 dataset for classification (Fig. 3(b)). As shown in the curves, our learned $f_{MPF}(\cdot)$ increases the eigenvalues and increases more on the smaller eigenvalues of the pooled second-order descriptors. According to the analysis in Sect. 3.3, the learned transform $f_{MPF}(\cdot)$ increases the entropy of distribution of input raw descriptors, resulting in more discriminative shape descriptors using metric learning as shown in the experiments. In each sub-figure of Fig. 3, compared with traditional fixed transforms, our net can adaptively learn transforms $f_{MPF}(\cdot)$ for different tasks by discriminative learning. We also show the pooled second-order descriptors before (upper-right images) and after (lower-right images) the transform of $f_{MPF}(\cdot)$ in the sub-figures, and the values around diagonal elements are enhanced after transform.

Table 6. Results for shape retrieval on SHREC'14 Real dataset in setting-3 (in %). Our transform performs the best in both of the training and test sets.

Metric		L-E [10]	L-R [17]	L-M-R [15]	$\mathcal{L}_2$-N	SSN [24]	1/2-pE [10]	Proposed
NN	Train	100	93.33	95.00	95.83	97.50	99.17	98.33
	Test	61.07	65.00	65.36	82.14	84.64	88.57	**92.50**
1-T	Train	93.15	82.04	83.61	87.69	95.37	96.48	96.67
	Test	53.17	49.40	50.36	70.20	75.32	77.30	**85.20**

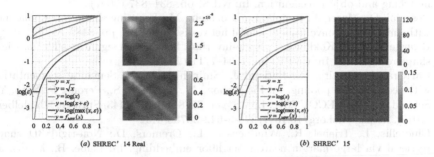

(a) SHREC' 14 Real   (b) SHREC' 15

Fig. 3. Illustrations of learned $f_{MPF}(\cdot)$ in SPDM-T stage. Each sub-figure shows transform curves including our learned $f_{MPF}(\cdot)$ and an example of pooled second-order descriptors before (upper-right images) and after (lower-right images) transform using learned $f_{MPF}(\cdot)$.

5   Conclusion

In this paper, we proposed a novel spectral transform network for 3D shape analysis based on surface second-order pooling and spectral transform on SPDM-manifold. The network is simple and shallow. Extensive experiments on benchmark datasets show that it can significantly boost the discriminative ability of input shape descriptors, and generate discriminative global shape descriptors achieving or matching state-of-the-art results for non-rigid shape retrieval and classification on diverse benchmark datasets.

In the future work, we are interested to design an end-to-end learning framework including the raw descriptor extraction on 3D meshes or point clouds. Furthermore, we can also possibly pack the surface second-order pooling stage, SPDM-T stage and fully connected layer as a block, and add multiple blocks for building a deeper architecture.

Acknowledgement. This work is supported by National Natural Science Foundation of China under Grants 11622106, 61711530242, 61472313, 11690011, 61721002.

References

1. Arsigny, V., Fillard, P., Pennec, X., Ayache, N.: Geometric means in a novel vector space structure on symmetric positive-definite matrices. SIAM J. Matrix Anal. Appl. **29**(1), 328–347 (2007)
2. Aubry, M., Schlickewei, U., Cremers, D.: The wave kernel signature: a quantum mechanical approach to shape analysis. In: ICCV, pp. 1626–1633 (2011)
3. Bai, S., Bai, X., Zhou, Z., Zhang, Z., Tian, Q., Latecki, L.J.: Gift: towards scalable 3D shape retrieval. IEEE Trans. Multimed. **19**(6), 1257–1271 (2017)
4. Belongie, S., Malik, J., Puzicha, J.: Shape context: a new descriptor for shape matching and object recognition. In: NIPS, pp. 831–837 (2001)
5. Boscaini, D., Masci, J., Rodolà, E., Bronstein, M.: Learning shape correspondence with anisotropic convolutional neural networks. In: NIPS, pp. 3189–3197 (2016)
6. Bronstein, M.M., Kokkinos, I.: Scale-invariant heat kernel signatures for non-rigid shape recognition. In: CVPR, pp. 1704–1711 (2010)
7. Carreira, J., Caseiro, R., Batista, J., Sminchisescu, C.: Semantic segmentation with second-order pooling. In: Fitzgibbon, A., Lazebnik, S., Perona, P., Sato, Y., Schmid, C. (eds.) ECCV 2012. LNCS, vol. 7578, pp. 430–443. Springer, Heidelberg (2012). https://doi.org/10.1007/978-3-642-33786-4_32
8. Chiotellis, I., Triebel, R., Windheuser, T., Cremers, D.: Non-rigid 3D shape retrieval via large margin nearest neighbor embedding. In: Leibe, B., Matas, J., Sebe, N., Welling, M. (eds.) ECCV 2016. LNCS, vol. 9906, pp. 327–342. Springer, Cham (2016). https://doi.org/10.1007/978-3-319-46475-6_21
9. Cirujeda, P., Mateo, X., Dicente, Y., Binefa, X.: MCOV: a covariance descriptor for fusion of texture and shape features in 3D point clouds. In: 3DV, pp. 551–558 (2015)
10. Dryden, I.L., Koloydenko, A., Zhou, D.: Non-euclidean statistics for covariance matrices, with applications to diffusion tensor imaging. Ann. Appl. Stat. **3**(3), 1102–1123 (2009)
11. Elad, A., Kimmel, R.: On bending invariant signatures for surfaces. IEEE TPAMI **25**(10), 1285–1295 (2003)
12. Fang, Y., et al.: 3D deep shape descriptor. In: CVPR, pp. 2319–2328 (2015)
13. Furuya, T., Ohbuchi, R.: Deep aggregation of local 3D geometric features for 3D model retrieval. In: BMVC, pp. 121.1–121.12 (2016)
14. Gasparetto, A., Torsello, A.: A statistical model of Riemannian metric variation for deformable shape analysis. In: CVPR, pp. 1219–1228 (2015)
15. Huang, Z., Van Gool, L.: A Riemannian network for SPD matrix learning. In: AAAI (2017)
16. Ionescu, C., Carreira, J., Sminchisescu, C.: Iterated second-order label sensitive pooling for 3D human pose estimation. In: CVPR, pp. 1661–1668 (2014)
17. Ionescu, C., Vantzos, O., Sminchisescu, C.: Matrix backpropagation for deep networks with structured layers. In: ICCV, pp. 2965–2973 (2015)
18. Jegou, H., Douze, M., Schmid, C., Perez, P.: Aggregating local descriptors into a compact image representation. In: CVPR, pp. 3304–3311 (2010)
19. Johnson, A.E., Hebert, M.: Using spin images for efficient object recognition in cluttered 3D scenes. IEEE TPAMI **21**(5), 433–449 (1999)
20. Lafon, S., Keller, Y., Coifman, R.R.: Data fusion and multicue data matching by diffusion maps. IEEE TPAMI **28**(11), 1784–1797 (2006)
21. Li, B., Lu, Y., Li, C., et al.: A comparison of 3D shape retrieval methods based on a large-scale benchmark supporting multimodal queries. CVIU **131**(c), 1–27 (2015)

22. Li, H., Huang, D., Morvan, J., Wang, Y., Chen, L.: Towards 3D face recognition in the real: a registration-free approach using fine-grained matching of 3D keypoint descriptors. IJCV **113**(2), 128–142 (2015)
23. Lian, Z., Zhang, J., et al.: Shrec'15 track: non-rigid 3D shape retrieval. In: Eurographics 3DOR Workshop (2015)
24. Lin, T.Y., RoyChowdhury, A., Maji, S.: Bilinear CNN models for fine-grained visual recognition. In: ICCV, pp. 1449–1457 (2015)
25. Litman, R., Bronstein, A., Bronstein, M., Castellani, U.: Supervised learning of bag-of-features shape descriptors using sparse coding. CGF **33**(5), 127–136 (2014)
26. Luciano, L., Hamza, A.B.: Deep learning with geodesic moments for 3D shape classification. Pattern Recogn. Lett. **83**, 339–348 (2017)
27. Masci, J., Boscaini, D., Bronstein, M., Vandergheynst, P.: Geodesic convolutional neural networks on Riemannian manifolds. In: ICCV, pp. 832–840 (2015)
28. Masoumi, M., Rodola, E., Cosmo, L.: Shrec'17 track: Deformable shape retrieval with missing parts. In: Eurographics 3DOR Workshop (2017)
29. Ohkita, Y., Ohishi, Y., Furuya, T., Ohbuchi, R.: Non-rigid 3D model retrieval using set of local statistical features. In: IEEE International Conference on Multimedia and Expo Workshops, pp. 593–598 (2012)
30. Osada, R., Funkhouser, T., Chazelle, B., Dobkin, D.: Shape distributions. ACM TOG **21**(4), 807–832 (2002)
31. Pennec, X., Fillard, P., Ayache, N.: A Riemannian framework for tensor computing. IJCV **66**(1), 41–66 (2006)
32. Pickup, D., Sun, X., Rosin, P.L., et al.: Shrec'14 track: shape retrieval of non-rigid 3D human models. In: Eurographics 3DOR Workshop (2014)
33. Pinkall, U., Polthier, K.: Computing discrete minimal surfaces and their conjugates. Exp. Math. **2**(1), 15–36 (1993)
34. Qi, C.R., Su, H., Mo, K., Guibas, L.J.: Pointnet: deep learning on point sets for 3D classification and segmentation. In: CVPR, pp. 77–85 (2017)
35. Qi, C.R., Su, H., Nießner, M., Dai, A., Yan, M., Guibas, L.J.: Volumetric and multi-view CNNs for object classification on 3D data. In: CVPR, pp. 5648–5656 (2016)
36. Qi, C.R., Yi, L., Su, H., Guibas, L.J.: Pointnet++: deep hierarchical feature learning on point sets in a metric space. In: NIPS, pp. 5099–5108 (2017)
37. Reuter, M., Wolter, F., Peinecke, N.: Laplace-Beltrami spectra as 'Shape-DNA' of surfaces and solids. Comput. Aided Des. **38**(4), 342–366 (2006)
38. Shilane, P., Min, P., Kazhdan, M., Funkhouser, T.: The Princeton shape benchmark. In: IEEE International Conference on Shape Modeling and Applications, pp. 167–178 (2004)
39. Smeets, D., Keustermans, J., Vandermeulen, D., Suetens, P.: meshSIFT: local surface features for 3D face recognition under expression variations and partial data. CVIU **117**(2), 158–169 (2013)
40. Su, H., Maji, S., Kalogerakis, E., Learnedmiller, E.G.: Multi-view convolutional neural networks for 3D shape recognition. In: ICCV, pp. 945–953 (2015)
41. Sun, J., Ovsjanikov, M., Guibas, L.: A concise and provably informative multi-scale signature based on heat diffusion. In: CGF, pp. 1383–1392 (2009)
42. Szegedy, C., et al.: Going deeper with convolutions. In: CVPR, pp. 1–9 (2015)
43. Tabia, H., Laga, H., Picard, D., Gosselin, P.H.: Covariance descriptors for 3D shape matching and retrieval. In: CVPR, pp. 4185–4192 (2014)

44. Wu, Z., et al.: 3D shapenets: a deep representation for volumetric shapes. In: CVPR, pp. 1912–1920 (2015)
45. Zhu, F., Xie, J., Fang, Y.: Heat diffusion long-short term memory learning for 3D shape analysis. In: Leibe, B., Matas, J., Sebe, N., Welling, M. (eds.) ECCV 2016. LNCS, vol. 9911, pp. 305–321. Springer, Cham (2016). https://doi.org/10.1007/978-3-319-46478-7_19

Know What Your Neighbors Do: 3D Semantic Segmentation of Point Clouds

Francis Engelmann[✉], Theodora Kontogianni, Jonas Schult, and Bastian Leibe

RWTH Aachen University, Aachen, Germany
{engelmann,kontogianni,schult,leibe}@vision.rwth-aachen.de

Abstract. In this paper, we present a deep learning architecture which addresses the problem of 3D semantic segmentation of unstructured point clouds (Fig. 1). Compared to previous work, we introduce grouping techniques which define *point neighborhoods* in the initial world space and the learned feature space. Neighborhoods are important as they allow to compute local or global point features depending on the spatial extend of the neighborhood. Additionally, we incorporate dedicated loss functions to further structure the learned point feature space: the *pairwise distance loss* and the *centroid loss*. We show how to apply these mechanisms to the task of 3D semantic segmentation of point clouds and report state-of-the-art performance on indoor and outdoor datasets.

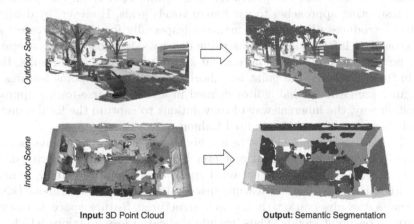

Fig. 1. We present a deep learning framework that predicts a semantic label for each point in a given 3D point cloud. The main components of our approach are *point neighborhoods* in different feature spaces and dedicated *loss functions* which help to refine the learned feature spaces. *Left*: point clouds from indoor and outdoor scenes. *Right*: semantic segmentation results produced by the presented method.

© Springer Nature Switzerland AG 2019
L. Leal-Taixé and S. Roth (Eds.): ECCV 2018 Workshops, LNCS 11131, pp. 395–409, 2019.
https://doi.org/10.1007/978-3-030-11015-4_29

1   Introduction

In the field of 3D scene understanding, semantic segmentation of 3D point clouds becomes increasingly relevant. Point cloud analysis has found its application in indoor scene understanding and more recently has become an essential component of outdoor applications [8]. This is due to the increasing availability and affordability of 3D sensors such as LiDAR or the Matterport scanner.

In the 2D image domain, for many tasks (including semantic segmentation) convolutional neural networks dominate the field. 2D convolutions allow processing large datasets with high resolution images by taking advantage of the locality of the convolutional operator. They reduce the number of model parameters allowing for deeper and more complex models while being efficient [3,17,19,30].

However point clouds have no inherent order, such as pixel neighborhoods. They are generally sparse in 3D space and the density varies with the distance to the sensor. Moreover, the number of points in a cloud can easily exceed the number of pixels in a high resolution image by multiple orders of magnitude. All these properties make it difficult to process point clouds directly with traditional convolutional neural networks.

Recently, a lot of effort has been put into bridging the success from 2D scene understanding into the 3D world [7,16,20–25,27]. In this work, we aim to further narrow down the gap between 2D and 3D semantic scene understanding. The straightforward approach of applying CNNs in the 3D space is implemented by preprocessing the point cloud into a voxel representation first in order to apply 3D convolutions on that new representation [21]. However 3D convolutions have drawbacks. Memory and computational time grows cubicly on the number of voxels, restricting approaches to use coarse voxels grids. However, by doing so, one then introduces discretization artifacts (especially for thin structures) and loose geometric information such as point density. Methods directly operating on the point cloud representation (e.g. [20,22]) produce promising results. However, in these methods, the point neighborhoods over which point features are aggregated are either global [20] or defined in a static coarse-to-fine approach [22]. Either way, the inherent way of convolutions to capture the local structure has only been transferred in a limited fashion.

In this work, we propose to define neighborhoods in an adaptive manner that is primarily sensitive to the local geometry by using K-means clustering on the input point cloud features in the world space and secondly defining dynamic neighborhoods in the learned feature space using k nearest neighbors (kNN). Next comes the observation that a well structured feature space is essential for learning on point clouds. Thus, we add dedicated loss functions which help shaping the feature space at multiple locations in the network.

We showcase the effectiveness of our approach on the task of semantic segmentation of 3D point clouds. We present a comprehensive ablation study evaluating all introduced mechanisms. We apply our method in different scenarios: indoor data from the Stanford 3D Indoor Scene dataset [14] and ScanNet dataset [5] as well as outdoor data from the Virtual KITTI 3D dataset [7,9].

2   Related Work

Before the introduction of deep learning methods, there have been numerous traditional approaches [10,15,18,32] applied to the task of semantically labelling 3D point clouds. Since then, methods relying on deep learning can be roughly split into two groups: methods that impose structure on the unstructured 3D point cloud (by voxelization or projection) followed by standard convolutions, and methods that operate directly on the 3D point clouds:

Voxelized Methods. Up until recently, the standard method to perform semantic segmentation of 3D data involved *voxelization*. Voxelization approaches transform the unstructured 3D point clouds into regular volumetric 3D grids (*voxels*). By doing so, 3D convolutions can be directly applied to the voxels [6,29]. Alternatively, *projection* approaches map the 3D points into 2D images as seen by virtual cameras. Then, 2D convolutions are applied on the projections [2,21]. These methods suffer from major disadvantages: the mapping from a sparse representation to a dense one leads to an increased memory footprint. Moreover, the fixed grid resolution results in discretization artifacts and loss of information.

Point Cloud Methods. A new set of methods started with the work of Point-Net [20]. PointNet operates directly on 3D points. The key idea is the extraction of point features through a sequence of MLPs processing the points individually (point features) followed by a max-pooling operation that describes the points globally (global features). Point- and global-representations are fused (concatenation + MLP) before making the final label predictions. Many methods followed the PointNet paradigm to operate directly on point clouds. Where PointNet partitions the space into cuboidal blocks of fixed arbitrary size, others use octrees [26] or kd-trees [24] to partition the space in a more meaningful way. Furthermore, PointNet does not take into consideration the local geometry and surface information. Clustering has been used in many classical approaches as a way of imposing structure, mostly as a prepossessing step [31,32]. So [22,24] were introduced trying to apply hierarchical grouping of the points and incorporate local structure information. The former used farthest point sampling and the latter kd-trees. The authors of [25] generalize the convolution operator on a spatial neighborhood. Taking it further from local neighborhoods, [16] organizes the points into superpoints of homogeneous elements and defines relationships between them with the use of graph neural networks on their so-called superpoint graph. In [7] also cuboidal blocks are used, which act as superpoints and update their respective global features based on the surrounding blocks in space or scale using GRUs.

We now compare our method to the recent PointNet++ [22] which is an hierarchical extension of the original PointNet [22]. PointNet (PN) globally aggregates point features using max-pooling. PN++ forms local groups (or neighborhoods) based on the metric world space and collapses each group onto a single

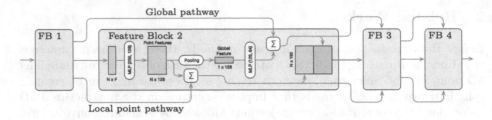

Fig. 2. The first component of our model is a *feature network*, depicted above. It learns high-dimensional features using a series of *feature blocks*. The details of a feature block are shown for feature block 2, the others are equal. Further details and a motivation for the architecture are given in Sect. 3.1. Our complete model is shown in Fig. 5.

representative point. This technique is repeated to increase the receptive field in each iteration. In our work, we follow a similar approach by iteratively applying feature-space neighborhoods (N_F-modules, introduced later): In every N_F iteration, each point is updated with the aggregated feature information from its kNNs. Repeating this procedure allows the information to flow over many points, one hop per iteration. Unlike [22], we build the neighborhood based on the feature space, this allows the network to learn the grouping. In PN++, neighborhoods are statically defined by a metric distance.

Feature Networks. As a first step on our network, we learn strong features using a dedicated feature network. The idea of extracting initial strong features is prominent in the field: In [23], features are learned in 2D image space using CNN for the task of 2.5 semantic segmentation. For the task of object detection, VoxelNet [33] uses a cascade of PointNet like architectures named *Voxel Feature Encoding* to obtain a more meaningful feature representation.

3   Our Approach

In the following, we describe the main components of our network. Starting from the initial point features (e.g. position and color), we learn more powerful feature representations using a new *Feature Network* as described in Sect. 3.1. Next, we define two kinds of neighborhoods (Sect. 3.2) within the point cloud, one defined on the learned feature space and one on the input world space. Based on these groupings, we learn regional descriptors which we use to inform the feature points about their neighborhood. Finally, we further enforce structure on the learned feature space by defining two dedicated loss functions (Sect. 3.3).

3.1   Feature Network

In this section, we describe our simple yet powerful architecture to learn point features. The goal of this component is to transform input features - such as position and color - into stronger learned features. It can be seen as the distilation of important elements from previous works, in particular *PointNet* [20] and *Consolidation Units* [7]. A schematic visualization is shown in Fig. 2.

The network is built from a sequence of *feature blocks*. Each feature block performs the following tasks: Starting from a set of N points, each with feature dimension F, it produces refined *point features* by passing the incoming features F through a multi layer perceptron (MLP). Then, a global representation is computed by aggregating all point features using max-pooling. This *global feature* is again passed through an MLP. Finally, after vertically stacking the global feature N times, it is concatenated with the point features. Thus, a single feature block corresponds to a simplified PointNet. An important distinction is that feature blocks can be stacked to arbitrary depth.

In addition to the feature blocks, we introduce pathway connections which allow the individual feature blocks to consult features from previous layers. We distinguish between the point features (local point pathway) and global features (global pathway). Inspired by DenseNet [12] and ResNet [11], these features can be combined either by concatenation or summation. Our findings are that concatenation gives slightly inferior results over addition with the cost of a higher memory footprint. At the same time, increasing the number of feature blocks in the network is even more important. Thus, in the interest of scalability, in our final feature network we prefer addition over concatenation and use 17 *feature blocks*. Our experiments on different number of feature blocks and aggregation functions are summarized in Table 6. As a result, the feature network provides us with strong features required for the subsequent components.

3.2 Neighborhoods

We employ two different grouping mechanism to define neighborhoods over the point cloud: The *feature space neighborhood* $\mathcal{N}_F$ is obtained by computing the k nearest neighbors (kNN) for each point in the learned feature space, and the *world space neighborhood* $\mathcal{N}_W$ is obtained by clustering points using K-means in the world space. In this context, the world space corresponds to the features of the input point cloud, such as position and color. In the following, we explain the two neighborhoods in more detail and show how they are used to update each point feature.

Feature Space Neighborhood $\mathcal{N}_F$ (See Fig. 3). From the set of N input features of dimensionality F, we compute an $N \times N$ similarity matrix based on the pairwise L_1-distance between the feature points $\mathbf{x}$. We concatenate the features of each point with the features of its k nearest neighbors to construct a kNN tensor. Each slice in the tensor corresponds to an $\mathcal{N}_F$-neighborhood of a feature point $\mathbf{x}_i$. Next, we learn a representation of this neighborhood using an MLP and we generate the updated feature point by applying max-pooling. This procedure is equivalent for each input feature and can be efficiently implemented using convolutions. We will refer to this architecture as an $\mathcal{N}_F$-module.

As such, an $\mathcal{N}_F$-module updates the local feature of a point based on its neighborhood in the feature space. By concatenating multiple $\mathcal{N}_F$-modules, we

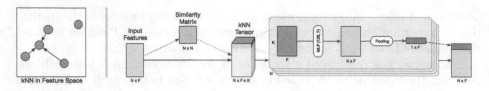

Fig. 3. The *feature space neighborhood* $\mathcal{N}_F(\mathbf{x})$ of a point $\mathbf{x} \in \mathbb{R}^F$ in a F-dimensional feature space is defined as the k *nearest neighbors* (kNN) in the feature space. *Left:* Example for $k = 3$. The point features $\mathbf{x}$ (blue) are updated based on the point features in the $\mathcal{N}_F$ neighborhood. *Right:* Details of a $\mathcal{N}_F$-module for learning point features. (Color figure online)

can increase the receptive field of the operation, one hop at a time, which is comparable to applying multiple convolutions in the image space.

World Space Neighborhood $\mathcal{N}_W$. Unlike kNN, K-means assigns a variable number of points to a neighborhood. K-means clustering is an iterative method, it alternatively assigns points to the nearest mean which represents the cluster center. Then it recomputes the means based on the assigned points. When applied to the world space, K-means can be seen as a pooling operation which reduces the input space and increases the receptive field by capturing long-range dependencies. Additionally, we are offered a feature point representative per cluster by averaging over all cluster members in the feature space.

We use this functionality in the $\mathcal{N}_W$-module: we perform K-means clustering in the world space, and represent each cluster by the average over all feature points in the cluster. Next, we concatenate this average to all the feature points within the same cluster. We then again apply max-pooling which produces a regional descriptor for this cluster. A visualization is shown in Fig. 5.

3.3 Loss Functions

In this section, we define the loss function $\mathcal{L}$ that is minimized during the training of our network. The classification loss $\mathcal{L}_{class}$ at the end of our network is realized as the cross entropy between predicted per-class probabilities and one-hot encoded ground truth semantic labels. Beside the classification loss, we introduce two additional losses $\mathcal{L}_{pair}$ and $\mathcal{L}_{cent}$ which further help to shape the feature space. The final loss is computed as the sum: $\mathcal{L} = \mathcal{L}_{class} + \mathcal{L}_{pair} + \mathcal{L}_{cent}$.

Pairwise Similarity Loss $\mathcal{L}_{pair}$. So far, we assumed that points from the same semantic class are likely to be nearby in the feature space. The *pairwise similarity loss*, described in this section, explicitly enforces this assumption. Similar to [4], we notice that semantic similarity can be measured directly as a distance in the feature space. By minimizing pairwise distances, we can learn an embedding where two points sampled from the same object produce nearby points in the feature space. Equivalently, two points originating from different objects have a large pairwise distance in the feature space. This goal is illustrated with a 2D embedding in Fig. 4.

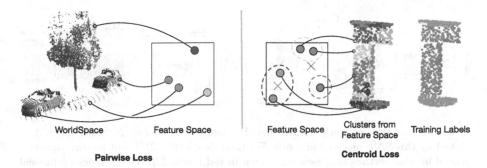

WorldSpace   Feature Space   Feature Space   Clusters from   Training Labels
                                                        Feature Space

Pairwise Loss   **Centroid Loss**

Fig. 4. *Left:* The pairwise distance loss $\mathcal{L}_{pair}$ minimizes the distance in the feature space between points of the same semantic class while it increases the distance between points of different classes. *Right:* The centroid loss $\mathcal{L}_{cent}$ minimizes the distance between features and their corresponding centroids, shown as crosses. The feature space is sketched as a 2D embedding. The point colors in the feature space represent training labels. To demonstrate the quality of our embedding, we further show clustering results (dashed lines) and their projection into world space (middle). See Sect. 3.3 for details. (Color figure online)

All we need is a pairwise distance matrix, which we already compute in the $\mathcal{N}_F$-module (Sect. 3.2). Hence, the distance loss is a natural extension of our network and comes at almost no additional memory cost. For a pair of points (i, j) with features $\mathbf{x}_i$ and $\mathbf{x}_j$, the loss is defined as follows:

$$\ell_{i,j} = \begin{cases} \max(||\mathbf{x}_i - \mathbf{x}_j|| - \tau_{\text{near}}, 0) & \text{if } \mathcal{C}_i = \mathcal{C}_j \\ \max(\tau_{\text{far}} - ||\mathbf{x}_i - \mathbf{x}_j||, 0) & \text{if } \mathcal{C}_i \neq \mathcal{C}_j \end{cases} \tag{1}$$

where τ_{near} and τ_{far} are threshold values and $\mathcal{C}_i$ is the semantic class of point i. Finally, the loss $\mathcal{L}_{pair}$ is computed as the sum over all pairwise losses $\ell_{i,j}$.

Centroid Loss $\mathcal{L}_{cent}$. This loss reduces the within-class distance by minimizing the distance between point features $\mathbf{x}_i$ and a corresponding representative feature $\overline{\mathbf{x}}_i$ (centroid). It makes the features in the feature space more compact. During training, the representative feature can be computed as the mean feature over all points from the same semantic class. An illustration is shown in Fig. 4. We define the centroid loss as the sum over all $(\mathbf{x}_i, \overline{\mathbf{x}}_i)$ pairs:

$$\mathcal{L}_{cent} = \sum_{i \in [1..N]} ||\mathbf{x}_i - \overline{\mathbf{x}}_i|| \tag{2}$$

where N is the total number of points. As distance measure $|| \cdot ||$, we found the cosine distance to be more effective than the L_1 or L_2 distance measures.

4   Implementation Details

In this section, we describe the integration of the aforementioned components into a deep learning architecture. The complete model is depicted in Fig. 5. We

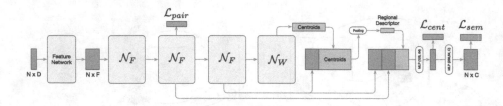

Fig. 5. Our complete network architecture. It consists of a *Feature Network* (Sect. 3.1), followed by three $\mathcal{N}_F$-modules and one $\mathcal{F}_W$-module (Sect. 3.2). Point features are represented by blue rectangles, losses are shown in red (Sect. 3.3). Green blocks represent features computed over clusters in the world space. (Color figure online)

start by learning strong features using our *Feature Network* (Sect. 3.1) producing F-dimensional features. See Table 6 for an evaluation and discussion on the architecture. We then feed these features into three stacked $\mathcal{N}_F$-modules. The subsequent $\mathcal{N}_W$-module computes a regional descriptors for each cluster (based on world space with descriptors form the feature space). We concatenate the regional descriptors to its corresponding feature points of the second and third $\mathcal{N}_F$-module. The concatenated features are passed through another MLP after which we compute the centroid loss. Finally, we reduce the feature points to 13 dimensions corresponding to the number of semantic classes in our datasets. The pairwise distance loss is computed in the beginning in the network. This informs the networks as early as possible which points should have similar features. This provides early layers a stronger signal of what should be learned and simplifies gradient propagation as the gradient is passed through fewer layers [1]. Although the distance loss could be appended at each point where a similarity matrix is computed, we found it most effective to add it to the second $\mathcal{N}_F$-module. An ablation study is provided in Table 1 and shows the contribution of each component in the performance.

Table 1. Ablation study highlighting the contribution of the individual components of our pipeline. The reported numbers refer to our validation set

Components	oAcc	mAcc	mIoU
Feature Network (FN) (Sect. 3.1)	82.43	56.96	47.25
$\mathcal{N}_F$*3 (Sect. 3.2)	81.70	55.14	47.37
$\mathcal{N}_F$*3 + $\mathcal{L}_{pair}$ (Sect. 3.3)	82.51	58.20	49.41
FN + $\mathcal{N}_F$*3 + $\mathcal{L}_{pair}$	83.84	58.29	50.56
FN + $\mathcal{N}_F$*3 + $\mathcal{N}_W$ + $\mathcal{L}_{pair}$ (Sect. 3.2)	84.31	59.18	50.95
FN + $\mathcal{N}_F$*3 + $\mathcal{N}_W$ + $\mathcal{L}_{pair}$ + $\mathcal{L}_{cent}$ (Sect. 3.3)	84.19	60.59	51.56

Table 2. Stanford Large-Scale 3D Indoor Spaces. 6-fold cross validation results. We can present state-of-the-art results in the more difficult CV and slightly inferior results on Area 5.

S3DIS [14]: 6-fold CV	oAcc	mAcc	mIoU
PointNet [20]	78.62	–	47.71
G+RCU [7]	81.1	66.4	49.7
SPG [16]	82.90	64.45	54.06
DGCNN [28]	**84.1**	–	56.1
PointNet++ [22]	81.03	67.05	54.49
RSN [13]	-	66.45	56.47
Ours	83.95	**67.77**	**58.27**

5 Evaluation

In this section, we evaluate the performance of our approach on the task of 3D semantic segmentation. We show qualitative and quantitative results and compare them to previous methods. We evaluate our method on multiple datasets: two indoor and one outdoor dataset showing the versatility of our approach. For each dataset, we report the *overall accuracy* (oAcc), the *mean class accuracy* (mAcc) and the *mean class intersection-over-union* (mIoU).

5.1 Indoor Datasets

We evaluate our model on the *Stanford Large-Scale 3D Indoor Spaces* (S3DIS) dataset [14] and the *ScanNet* dataset [5]. Both datasets have recently become popular to evaluate 3D semantic segmentation methods. The S3DIS dataset consists of 6 different indoor areas, totaling to 272 rooms. Each point is labeled as one of 13 semantic classes as shown in Fig. 6. The ScanNet dataset contains 1523 RGB-D scans labeled with 20 different semantic classes.

5.2 Outdoor Dataset

We apply our approach to the vKITTI3D dataset, a large-scale outdoor data set in an autonomous driving setting. Introduced in [7], this dataset is an adaptation of the synthetic *Virtual KITTI* dataset [9] for the task of semantic segmentation of 3D point clouds. It is split in 6 different sequences containing 13 semantic classes listed in Fig. 7.

5.3 Training Details

For the experiments on the S3DIS dataset, we follow a similar training procedure as [20] i.e. we split the rooms in blocks of 1 m^2 on the ground plane. From each block we randomly sample 4096 points. During evaluation, we predict class labels

Table 3. Stanford Large-Scale 3D Indoor Spaces. Results on Area 5

S3DIS [14]: Area 5	oAcc	mAcc	mIoU
PointNet [20]	–	48.98	41.09
MS + CU(2) [7]	-	52.11	43.02
G + RCU [7]	-	54.06	45.14
SEGCloud [27]	–	57.35	48.92
SPG [16]	**85.14**	**61.75**	**54.67**
Ours	84.15	59.10	52.17

Table 4. IoU per semantic class on the S3DIS dataset. We compare our model against the original PointNet and other recent methods. On average our method outperforms the current state-of-the-art by a large margin, specifically on 'bookcase' and 'board' while being slightly worse on 'beam' and 'sofa'

Method	mIoU	Ceiling	Floor	Wall	Beam	Column	Window	Door	Table	Chair	Sofa	Bookcase	Board	Clutter
PointNet [20]	47.6	88.0	88.7	69.3	42.4	23.1	47.5	51.6	54.1	42.0	9.6	38.2	29.4	35.2
MS+CU(2) [7]	47.8	88.6	95.8	67.3	36.9	24.9	48.6	52.3	51.9	45.1	10.6	36.8	24.7	37.5
SegCloud [27]	48.9	90.1	**96.1**	69.9	0.0	18.4	38.4	23.1	**75.9**	**70.4**	**58.4**	40.9	13.0	42.0
G+RCU [7]	49.7	90.3	92.1	67.9	**44.7**	24.2	**52.3**	51.2	58.1	47.4	6.9	39.0	30.0	41.9
SPG [16]	54.1	**92.2**	95.0	72.0	33.5	15.0	46.5	60.9	65.1	69.5	56.8	38.2	6.9	51.3
Ours	**58.3**	92.1	90.4	**78.5**	37.8	**35.7**	51.2	**65.4**	64.0	61.6	25.6	**51.6**	**49.9**	**53.7**

for all points. Additionally, we add translation augmentation to the block positions. Each point is represented by a 9D feature vector $[x, y, z, r, g, b, x', y', z']$ consisting of the position $[x, y, z]$, color $[r, g, b]$ and normalized coordinates $[x', y', z']$ as in [20]. The hyperparameters of our method are set as follows: for the kNN-clustering, we set $k = 30$ and use the L_1-distance measure. For K-means we dynamically set $K = \lfloor N/52 \rfloor$ where N is the number of points per block. We report scores on a 6-fold cross validation across all areas in Table 2 along with the detailed scores of per class IoU in Table 4. Additionally, we provide scores for Area 5 in Table 3 to compare ourself to [16, 27].

On the ScanNet dataset [5], we use the reference implementation of PointNet++ to train and evaluate our model. This approach allows us to focus on the comparison of the models while abstracting from the training procedures. All hyperparameters remain the same. The results are shown in Table 5.

Table 5. ScanNet. Overall point accuracy (oAcc), mean semantic class accuracy (mAcc), mean Intersection-over-Union (mIoU). ScanNet dataset using the official training and test split from [5], scores are shown on a per-point basis as computed by the PN++ reference implementation. To train on our hardware, we set the batch size to 32 and number of points to 1024

ScanNet [5]	oAcc	mAcc
PointNet++ [22]	71.40	24.51
Our method	**75.53**	**25.39**

Table 6. Study on the feature network. We evaluate the number of layers and compare feature fusion using concatenation or addition. Deeper networks perform better, in general feature addition is slightly stronger while being more memory efficient than concatenation

# Layers	Fusion	mIoU
3	additive	42.15
12	additive	44.46
17	additive	**45.15**
17	concat	44.23
12	concat	43.35
3	concat	41.73

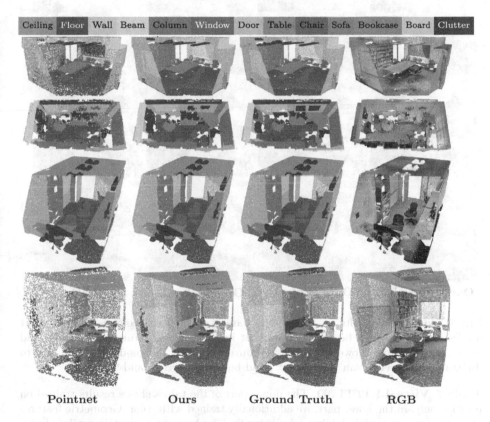

Ceiling Floor Wall Beam Column Window Door Table Chair Sofa Bookcase Board Clutter

Pointnet   Ours   Ground Truth   RGB

Fig. 6. Qualitative results on S3DIS dataset. We show three exemplary rooms. Our method provides segmentations of objects with minimal noise and clear boundaries. As pointed out in the qualitative results, our method performs quite well in challenging objects like 'board' and 'bookcase'. (Color figure online)

On the VKITTI3D dataset, we follow again the same training procedure as on the S3DIS dataset. The scenes are split into blocks of 9 m^2 on the ground plane. Since the dataset is much sparser, we set the number of points sampled per block to N = 256. Training on a 6-fold cross validation is performed as in [7]. We use the same input features as in the indoor dataset and additionally, we analyze how well our method performs if we take into consideration only geometric features (xyz-position) while leaving out color information. This is an interesting experiment, as color is not always imminently available e.g. point clouds from laser scanners. We show quantitative results in Table 7. Qualitative results are shown in Fig. 7.

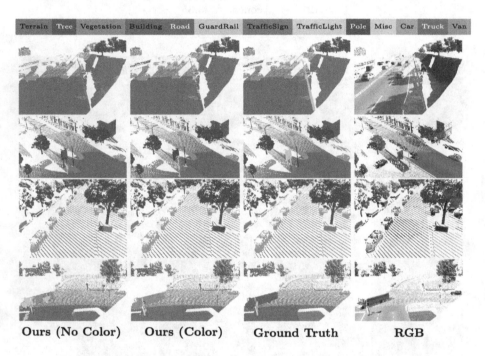

| Terrain | Tree | Vegetation | Building | Road | GuardRail | TrafficSign | TrafficLight | Pole | Misc | Car | Truck | Van |

Ours (No Color)   Ours (Color)   Ground Truth   RGB

Fig. 7. Qualitative results on VKITTI3D dataset. In general, color is an important attribute to distinguish between shapes that have similar structure e.g. 'terrain' and 'road'. The last row shows a failure case, during training our model was not able to differentiate between 'Van' and 'Truck', and between 'Terrain' and 'Road'.

Table 7. Virtual KITTI 3D. The upper part of the tables shows results trained on position only. In the lower part, we additionally trained with color. Geometric features alone are quite powerful. Adding color helps to differ between geometric similar classes

VKITTI3D [7]: 6-fold CV	oAcc	mAcc	mIoU
PointNet [20] from [7]	63.3	29.9	17.9
MS+CU(2) [7]	73.2	40.9	26.4
Ours	**78.19**	**56.43**	**33.36**
Ours (+ color)	**79.69**	**57.59**	**35.59**

6   Conclusion

We have presented a deep learning framework for 3D semantic segmentation of point clouds. Its main components are $\mathcal{N}_F$- and $\mathcal{N}_W$-modules. They allow to incorporate neighborhood information from the feature space and from the world space. We have also introduced the pairwise distance loss $\mathcal{L}_{pair}$ and the centroid loss $\mathcal{L}_{cent}$ in the context of 3D semantic segmentation. The presented method produces state-of-the-art results on current indoor and outdoor datasets.

Acknowledgement. This project was funded by the ERC Consolidator Grant DeeViSe (ERC-2017-CoG-773161).

References

1. Harley, A.W., Konstantinos, G., Derpanis, I.K.: Segmentation-aware convolutional networks using local attention masks. In: IEEE International Conference on Computer Vision (ICCV) (2017)
2. Boulch, A., Saux, B.L., Audebert, N.: Unstructured point cloud semantic labeling using deep segmentation networks. In: Eurographics Workshop on 3D Object Retrieval (2017)
3. Chen, L., Papandreou, G., Kokkinos, I., Murphy, K., Yuille, A.L.: DeepLab: semantic image segmentation with deep convolutional nets, atrous convolution, and fully connected CRFs. arXiv preprint arXiv:1606.00915 (2016)
4. Chopra, S., Hadsell, R., LeCun, Y.: Learning a similarity metric discriminatively, with application to face verification. In: IEEE Conference on Computer Vision and Pattern Recognition (CVPR) (2005)
5. Dai, A., Chang, A.X., Savva, M., Halber, M., Funkhouser, T., Nießner, M.: ScanNet: richly-annotated 3D reconstructions of indoor scenes. In: Proceding of Computer Vision and Pattern Recognition (CVPR). IEEE (2017)
6. Maturana, D., Scherer, S.: VoxNet: a 3D convolutional neural network for real-time object recognition. In: IEEE/RSJ International Conference on Intelligent Robots and Systems (IROS) (2015)
7. Engelmann, F., Kontogianni, T., Hermans, A., Leibe, B.: Exploring spatial context for 3D semantic segmentation of point clouds. In: IEEE International Conference on Computer Vision, 3DRMS (ICCV) Workshop (2017)
8. Engelmann, F., Stückler, J., Leibe, B.: SAMP: shape and motion priors for 4d vehicle reconstruction. In: IEEE Winter Conference on Applications of Computer Vision, WACV (2017)
9. Gaidon, A., Wang, Q., Cabon, Y., Vig, E.: Virtual worlds as proxy for multi-object tracking analysis. In: IEEE Conference on Computer Vision and Pattern Recognition (CVPR) (2016)
10. Hackel, T., Wegner, J.D., Schindler, K.: Fast semantic segmentation of 3D points clouds with strongly varying density. ISPRS **3**(3), 177–184 (2016)
11. He, K., Zhang, X., Ren, S., Sun, J.: Deep residual learning for image recognition. In: IEEE Conference on Computer Vision and Pattern Recognition (CVPR) (2016)
12. Huang, G., Liu, Z., van der Maaten, L., Weinberger, K.Q.: Densely connected convolutional networks. In: IEEE Conference on Computer Vision and Pattern Recognition (CVPR) (2017)

13. Huang, Q., Wang, W., Neumann, U.: Recurrent slice networks for 3D segmentation on point clouds. In: IEEE Conference on Computer Vision and Pattern Recognition (CVPR) (2018)
14. Iro, A., et al.: 3D Semantic Parsing of Large-Scale Indoor Spaces. In: IEEE International Conference on Computer Vision and Pattern Recognition (CVPR) (2016)
15. Lai, K., Bo, L., Fox, D.: Unsupervised feature learning for 3D scene labeling. In: IEEE International Conference on Robotics and Automation (ICRA) (2014)
16. landrieu, L., Simonovsky, M.: Large-scale point cloud semantic segmentation with superpoint graphs. In: IEEE Conference on Computer Vision and Pattern Recognition (CVPR) (2018)
17. Long, J., Shelhamer, E., Darrell, T.: Fully convolutional networks for semantic segmentation. In: IEEE Conference on Computer Vision and Pattern Recognition (CVPR) (2015)
18. Munoz, D., Vandapel, N., Hebert, M.: Directional associative Markov network for 3-D point cloud classification. In: International Symposium on 3D Data Processing, Visualization and Transmission (2008)
19. Noh, H., Hong, S., Han, B.: Learning deconvolution network for semantic segmentation. In: IEEE International Conference on Computer Vision (ICCV) (2015)
20. Qi, C.R., Su, H., Mo, K., Guibas, L.J.: PointNet: deep learning on point sets for 3D classification and segmentation. In: IEEE Conference on Computer Vision and Pattern Recognition (CVPR) (2017)
21. Qi, C.R., Su, H., Niener, M., Dai, A., Yan, M., Guibas, L.J.: Volumetric and multi-view CNNs for object classification on 3D data. In: IEEE Conference on Computer Vision and Pattern Recognition (CVPR) (2016)
22. Qi, C.R., Yi, L., Su, H., Guibas, L.J.: PointNet++: deep hierarchical feature learning on point sets in a metric space. In: Conference on Neural Information Processing Systems (NIPS) (2017)
23. Qi, X., Liao, R., Ya, J., Fidler, S., Urtasun, R.: 3D graph neural networks for RGBD semantic segmentation. In: IEEE International Conference on Computer Vision (ICCV) (2017)
24. Roman, K., Victor, L.: Escape from cells: deep Kd-networks for the recognition of 3D point cloud models. In: IEEE Conference on Computer Vision and Pattern Recognition (CVPR) (2017)
25. Simonovsky, M., Komodakis, N.: Dynamic edge-conditioned filters in convolutional neural networks on graphs. IEEE Conference on Computer Vision and Pattern Recognition (CVPR) (2017)
26. Tatarchenko, M., Dosovitskiy, A., Brox, T.: Octree generating networks: efficient convolutional architectures for high-resolution 3D outputs (2017)
27. Tchapmi, L.P., Choy, C.B., Armeni, I., Gwak, J., Savarese, S.: SEGCloud: semantic segmentation of 3D point clouds. In: International Conference on 3D Vision (3DV) (2017)
28. Wang, Y., Sun, Y., Liu, Z., Sarma, S.E., Bronstein, M.M., Solomon, J.M.: Dynamic graph CNN for learning on point clouds. arXiv preprint arXiv:1801.07829 (2018)
29. Wu, Z., et al.: 3D ShapeNets: a deep representation for volumetric shape modeling. In: IEEE Conference on Computer Vision and Pattern Recognition (CVPR) (2015)
30. Wu, Z., Shen, C., van den Hengel, A.: High-performance semantic segmentation using very deep fully convolutional networks. arXiv preprint arXiv:1604.04339 (2016)
31. Xiong, X., Munoz, D., Andrew, J., Hebert, B.M.: 3-D scene analysis via sequenced predictions over points and regions. In: IEEE International Conference on Robotics and Automation (ICRA) (2011)

32. Xiong, X., Munoz, D., Bagnell, J.A., Hebert, M.: 3-D scene analysis via sequenced predictions over points and regions. In: IEEE International Conference on Robotics and Automation (ICRA) (2011)

33. Zhou, Y., Tuzel, O.: VoxelNet: end-to-end learning for point cloud based 3D object detection. In: IEEE Conference on Computer Vision and Pattern Recognition (CVPR) (2018)

Deep Learning for Multi-path Error Removal in ToF Sensors

Gianluca Agresti and Pietro Zanuttigh$^{(\boxtimes)}$

Department of Information Engineering, University of Padova, Padova, Italy
{gianluca.agresti,zanuttigh}@dei.unipd.it

Abstract. The removal of Multi-Path Interference (MPI) is one of the major open challenges in depth estimation with Time-of-Flight (ToF) cameras. In this paper we propose a novel method for MPI removal and depth refinement exploiting an ad-hoc deep learning architecture working on data from a multi-frequency ToF camera. In order to estimate the MPI we use a Convolutional Neural Network (CNN) made of two sub-networks: a coarse network analyzing the global structure of the data at a lower resolution and a fine one exploiting the output of the coarse network in order to remove the MPI while preserving the small details. The critical issue of the lack of ToF data with ground truth is solved by training the CNN with synthetic information. Finally, the residual zero-mean error is removed with an adaptive bilateral filter guided from a noise model for the camera. Experimental results prove the effectiveness of the proposed approach on both synthetic and real data.

Keywords: ToF sensors · Denoising · Multi-path interference · Depth acquisition · Convolutional Neural Networks

1 Introduction

Time-of-Flight (ToF) cameras are active range imaging systems able to estimate the depth of a scene by illuminating it with a periodic amplitude modulated light signal and measuring the phase displacement between the transmitted and received signal [1]. These sensors achieved a wide popularity thanks to their ability to acquire reliable 3D data at video frame rate. In this paper we propose a method for ToF data denoising that focus on the removal of the Multi-Path Interference (MPI) corruption and of the zero-mean error caused by photon shot and sensor thermal noise. ToF acquisitions rely on the key assumption that the received light signal has been reflected only once inside the scene. Unfortunately this is not true in practice and the projected light can be reflected multiple times before going back to the ToF sensor: this issue is called Multi-Path Interference

Electronic supplementary material The online version of this chapter (https://doi.org/10.1007/978-3-030-11015-4_30) contains supplementary material, which is available to authorized users.

© Springer Nature Switzerland AG 2019
L. Leal-Taixé and S. Roth (Eds.): ECCV 2018 Workshops, LNCS 11131, pp. 410–426, 2019.
https://doi.org/10.1007/978-3-030-11015-4_30

(MPI) and it is one of the main sources of error in ToF data acquisition. The MPI leads to a depth overestimation and this phenomenon is scene dependent, indeed it is related to both the geometry and the properties of the materials inside the scene. The removal of MPI is an ill posed problem with standard single frequency ToF acquisitions but since MPI depth distortion is related to the modulation frequency of the ToF signal, multi-frequency ToF (MF-ToF) sensors can be used for MPI estimation. Some approaches [2–4] following this rationale have been proposed even if with not completely satisfactory results.

Convolutional Neural Networks (CNN) have been widely employed for tasks like denoising and super resolution of image and video data. The application of CNNs to data acquired with ToF cameras for denoising and MPI removal has been investigated only in few works [5–9] due to the difficulty of acquiring the depth ground truth information needed for supervised learning. Here we exploit the information acquired with MF-ToF sensors as input for a deep network architecture able to estimate the unknown MPI corruption. We designed an ad-hoc CNN for this task made of two parts, a coarse one able to understand the global structure of the scene and to globally locate MPI, and a fine one that takes in input the output of the coarse network and allows us to remove the MPI while preserving the small details. Furthermore, an ad-hoc pre-processing step combines the information about the depth and amplitude at multiple frequencies into novel representations that allows the network to learn key clues to estimate the MPI. The critical task of training the deep network has been solved by constructing a synthetic dataset and generating the MF-ToF data using a ToF simulator. The MPI corruption is then removed by subtracting the CNN estimation of the interference. Finally an adaptive bilateral filter guided by an estimation of the ToF noise is used to remove also the zero-mean error. The experimental evaluation has been done on both synthetic and real data, proving how the training on synthetic data can generalize to real world scenes.

2 Related Works

Many different approaches for MPI removal in continuous wave ToF systems employing sinusoidal waveforms have been proposed [2,3,10,11] and an extensive review can be found in [12]. This task is particularly complex since it is an ill-posed problem regarding the retrieval of the sinusoidal light waves related to the shortest paths linking the ToF pixels to the scene points. This is due to various reasons: first of all, the light rays which are interfering are sinusoidal waves at the same modulation frequency and the MPI effects can not be directly detected only by looking at the received waveform in the single frequency case. Moreover since the MPI is scene dependent, the scene geometry is needed to solve the problem but the MPI needs to be removed to estimate the geometry thus creating a chicken-and-egg problem. There are four main families of approaches for MPI correction: methods that use *single frequency ToF data and scene geometry*, methods based on *ray separation*, methods based on *direct and global light separation* and those based on *machine learning* approaches.

The methods which use single frequency ToF data exploit some reflection models in order to estimate the geometry of the scene and correct MPI as done by Fuchs et al. in [13], where reflections with a maximum of 2 bounces are considered. This method is further extended in [14] where multiple albedo and reflections are taken in account. Jimenez et al. [15] proposed a radiometric model to simulate ToF acquisitions and the reflection phenomenon and then correct MPI through non linear optimization.

In methods based on *ray separation*, the light is described as a summation of single sinusoidal waves which are interfering one another in case of MPI. The ray with the shortest path is assumed to be the one carrying the correct depth information (direct light). The method proposed by Freedman et al. in [2] uses 3 modulation frequencies and exploits MPI *frequency diversity* and an L_1 *optimization* to find the light backscattering vector that is assumed to be sparse. In [3], a closed form solution for MPI removal using multi-frequency ToF data is proposed. A method based on the backscattering vector estimation by using random on-off codes instead of standard sinusoidal waveforms for light modulation is proposed in [10].

In the third family of approaches the light is described as the summation of only two sinusoidal waves, one related to the direct component while the other groups together all the sinusoidal waves related to global light (the summation of all the interfering rays). Gupta et al. [11] proposed to use an high modulation frequency to cancel out the sinusoidal global component of the light. The methods proposed by Naik et al. [16], Whyte et al. [17] and Agresti et al. [18] are inspired by the work presented by Nayar in [19]. These methods use an external projector to illuminate the scene with spatial high frequency patterns modulated by the ToF sinusoidal signal to separate the global and direct component of the light and correct MPI.

Only recently, methods based on deep learning have been used on ToF data for denoising purpose. This is due to the fact that depth ground truth is difficult to collect. In [5], ToF data is acquired from a robotic arm setup and the depth ground truth is estimated with a Structured Light system. In [6], an auto-encoder CNN is used with a 2 phase training, in the first phase real depth data without ground truth is used, then the encoder part is kept fix and the decoder part is trained with a synthetic dataset in order to learn how to correct MPI. These methods have in input data taken from single-frequency ToF cameras while our proposal rely on data acquired with multi-frequency ToF cameras. We will show that this choice will improve the MPI correction performance as also done very recently by Su et al. in [8] and Guo et al. in [9]. The first presents an end-to-end deep learning approach to directly estimate a denoised depth map from raw correlation frames. In the second the motion blur is taken in account.

It is possible to find in literature many applications of CNN for 3D estimation from monocular and stereo RGB images [20–22]. An example is the monocular estimation method proposed by Eigen in [21], that exploits a Coarse-Fine network, and its improvement proposed in [22] where a multi-scale CNN is used.

3   Proposed Method

The task of the proposed method is to obtain accurate ToF depth data by removing MPI corruption and reducing zero-mean error related to shot noise. The MPI is estimated by exploiting a CNN whose input are data extracted from a MF-ToF camera, while for the zero-mean error reduction instead we use an adaptive bilateral filter guided by the noise statistic estimated on the input data.

ToF camera pixels are able to compute the correlation function between the received light sinusoidal waves and a reference signal: the computed correlation function appears to be a sinusoidal wave that can be modeled as:

$$c(\theta_i) = B + A\cos\left(\theta_i - \frac{4\pi f_m \cdot d}{c_l}\right) = B + A\cos\left(\theta_i - Kd\right) \qquad (1)$$

where $\theta_i \in [0; 2\pi)$ is the phase sample of the correlation function that is captured by the ToF pixels (nowadays ToF cameras use 4 samples), f_m is the modulation frequency of the light signal, B and A are respectively proportional to the intensity and the amplitude of the received signal, c_l is the speed of light. The depth d of the observed scene point can then be estimated from the 4 correlation samples [1]. This model is correct if each camera pixel receives only one ray from the scene, the direct one. If the pixels receive the summation of light rays reflected multiple times, we have the MPI phenomenon. In this case the ToF correlation function can be modeled as

$$c(\theta_i) = B + A_d\cos\left(\theta_i - Kd_d\right) + \int_{d_d+\epsilon}^{\infty} A'_x\cos\left(\theta_i - Kx\right)dx = B + A_{FF}\cos(\theta_i - Kd_{FF})$$

$$(2)$$

where A_d and d_d are respectively the amplitude and the depth related to the direct light, instead the integral models the global light as the superposition of the rays that are reflected more than once inside the scene. Each interfering ray has its own phase offset and amplitude. In case of MPI, i.e., when $\exists x : A'_x \neq 0$, the depth estimated from Eq. 1, d_{FF}, will be bigger than the correct depth d_d. The phase offsets of the interfering rays are frequency dependent and by changing f_m also the estimated depth d_{FF} and the amplitude A_{FF} will be different. This *frequency diversity* can be used to understand if MPI is acting on MF-ToF cameras and can give us cues for its correction as discussed in [2,3].

In this paper we are going to use data from a ToF camera that captures the scene using the modulation frequencies of 20, 50 and 60 MHz. We will extract some features that are meaningful for MPI analysis directly exploiting the *frequency diversity* on the acquired depth and amplitude images. Moreover, we are going to use also information about the geometry of the scene to estimate the MPI as done in some approaches using single frequency data as [6,13,14]. We devised a CNN for the prediction of the MPI corruption to use all these aspects together. The general architecture of the proposed approach for ToF depth denoising is shown in Fig. 1.

The data acquired by the MF-ToF system is first pre-processed in order to extract a representation that contains relevant information about the MPI

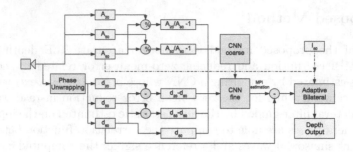

Fig. 1. Architecture of the proposed approach.

presence and strength. As detailed in Sect. 4, where also the motivation for the selection of each input source is presented, the deep network has 5 different input channels containing the ToF depth extracted from the phase at 60 MHz, the difference between the depth maps at different frequencies and the ratio of the amplitudes also at different frequencies.

The CNN architecture of Sect. 5 is made of two main blocks, a coarse network that takes in input the 5 representations and estimates the MPI at low resolution and a fine network that takes in input the 5 representations and the output of the coarse network in order to estimate the MPI interference at full resolution. The estimated multi-path error is then directly subtracted from the ToF depth map (at 60 MHz), thus obtaining a depth map free from multi-path distortion (but still affected by other zero-mean error sources).

The resulting depth map is first filtered with a 3×3 median filter in order to remove depth outliers, then the final output of the proposed method is obtained by further filtering it with an adaptive version of the bilateral filter [23] because of its capability of reducing noise while preserving edges. Bilateral filters have been already used on ToF data [24,25], specially to denoise and upsample the depth map using information from a standard video camera. In our implementation the bilateral filter is guided by the noise information estimated from the received signal amplitude and intensity from which the error variance related to shot noise can be estimated. As suggested in [26], we fixed the spatial smoothing parameter σ_d to a constant value, while the range parameter σ_r is taken proportional to the level of noise. We made the bilateral filter adaptive by using a per pixel noise model for σ_r. In particular we took $\sigma_r = c_r \cdot \tilde{\sigma}_n$, where $\tilde{\sigma}_n$ is an estimate of the depth noise standard deviation due to shot noise. This can be estimated from the amplitude A_{ph} and the intensity I_{ph} of the received light signal [27]:

$$\sigma_n(k, h) = \frac{c_l}{4\sqrt{2}\pi f_m} \frac{\sqrt{I_{ph}(k, h)}}{A_{ph}(k, h)}. \tag{3}$$

A_{ph} and I_{ph} are proportional to the intensity and the amplitude of the correlation function estimated by the ToF pixels. In our experiments we computed $\tilde{\sigma}_n$ from the correlation data and we optimized the values of σ_d and c_r on a subset of the synthetic training dataset. Then we used the selected values ($\sigma_d = 3$ and $c_r = 3.5$) in the evaluation phase.

4 ToF Data Representation

As mentioned before, we used a CNN to estimate the MPI corruption on the ToF depth map at 60 MHz that is phase unwrapped by using the 20 MHz and 50 MHz ToF data. Notice that these frequency values have been selected since they resemble the ones used in real world ToF cameras. We also investigated the possibility of performing the phase unwrapping using the CNN of Sect. 5, but the disambiguation using the MF data proved to be reliable and the deep network optimization is more stable if already phase unwrapped data is fed to it. A critical aspect is the selection of input data that should be informative about the MPI phenomenon. We decided to use as input the following elements:

- The first input $C_1 = d_{60}$ is the ToF depth map at 60 MHz. It is required not only because it is the corrupted input that needs to be denoised but also because the geometry of the scene influences the MPI error and the ToF depth represents the best estimate of the geometry available before the MPI removal process. We selected the depth captured at 60 MHz since the higher the modulation frequency, the more accurate the depth estimation.
- The difference between the depth maps estimated at the different modulation frequencies, used since the MPI corruption changes with the frequency (generally the higher the modulation frequency, the smaller is MPI [11]). We used the differences between the depths at 20 Mhz and 60 Mhz, and between the ones at 50 Mhz and 60 Mhz, i.e., $C_2 = d_{20} - d_{60}$ and $C_3 = d_{50} - d_{60}$.
- The ratio of the amplitudes of the received light signal at different modulation frequencies. In presence of MPI the light waves experiences destructive interferences and in ToF data acquired in presence of MPI the higher the modulation frequency, the lower the resulting amplitude. For this reason, comparing the amplitudes at different frequencies gives us a hint about the MPI presence and strength. We used the ratios between the amplitudes at 20 Mhz and 60 Mhz, and between the ones at 50 Mhz and 60 Mhz, i.e., $C_4 = (A_{20}/A_{60}) - 1$ and $C_5 = (A_{50}/A_{60}) - 1$ (the "-1" term has been introduced to center the data around 0 in case of MPI absence).

The proposed CNN aims at estimating the MPI corruption on the 60 MHz depth map: the targets for the training procedure have been computed by taking a filtered version of the difference between d_{60} and the ground truth depth d_{GT} (the filtering is used to remove the zero mean error, notice that MPI is a low frequency noise). We decided to use this set of inputs for the proposed *Coarse-Fine CNN* since depth and amplitude are data which are generally accessible from commercial ToF cameras. Moreover, by taking the ratio between the amplitudes we are canceling out the gain of the sensor, that can be different for different sensors, making the method more robust to hardware changes. We have tried to use subsets of the input data, but this reduced the performance in MPI esti-mation. Notice that other techniques based on multi-frequency approaches as [2,3] use a per pixel model based on the sparsity of the backscattering vector A'_x of Eq. 2, while in our proposal we are implementing a data-driven model that will suit the diffuse reflection case and thanks to the CNN receptive fields we are capturing the geometrical structure of the scene in addition to the *frequency diversity*. We decided to pre-filter the CNN inputs with a 5×5 median filter to obtain a more stable input and reduce their zero-mean variation.

As aforementioned, it is difficult to collect a real world dataset big enough for CNN training with ToF data and the related depth ground truth. For this reason, we decided to exploit a dataset composed by synthetic scenes, for which the true depth is known. The ToF acquisitions have been performed with the *ToF Explorer* simulator realized by Sony EuTEC starting from the work of Meister et al. [28] which is able to faithfully reproduce ToF acquisition issues like the shot and thermal noise, the read-out noise, artifacts due to lens effects, mixed pixels and specially the multi-path interference. This simulator uses as input the scene data generated by *Blender* [29] and *LuxRender* [30]. In order to build the synthetic dataset we started from the set of *Blender* scenes used in [7]. We used 40 scenes for the training set, while the other 14 different scenes have been used for testing. Each scene has been rendered from a virtual viewpoint with the ToF simulator in order to acquire the ToF raw data (amplitude, intensity and depth image) at the modulation frequencies of 20, 50 and 60 MHz. We also used the Blender rendering engine to acquire the scene depth ground truth. The dataset is publicly available at http://lttm.dei.unipd.it/paper_data/MPI_CNN. The various scenes contain surfaces and objects of different shapes and texture and correspond to very different environments. They also have a very wide depth acquisition range from about 50 cm to 10 m and various corners and structures in which the multi-path phenomenon is critical.

We collected also a set of real scenes with related depth ground truth in order to validate the proposed method for ToF depth refinement. We used a *SoftKinetic* ToF camera in combination with an active stereo system for the acquisitions. The stereo system and the ToF camera have been jointly calibrated and ground truth depth estimated with the active stereo system has been reprojected on the ToF sensor viewpoint. We set up a wooden box (see Fig. 2) that is about 1.5 m wide and 1 m high and composed by a 90° and a 135° angle. The real world dataset is composed by 8 scenes, each captured by looking at the box from different viewpoints and by placing in it objects made of wood, polystyrene and ceramic. Since the acquired dataset is quite small we used it only for testing purposes, while we used the synthetic data for the training of the network. By looking at the scene in Fig. 2, it is possible to see how some critical situations for MPI are present, e.g., the surface angles that are the typical cases where MPI corruption can be clearly observed.

Fig. 2. Wooden box used for the real world acquisition and examples of amplitude images of the acquired scenes. The wooden box has been captured from different viewpoints and with different objects inside.

5   Proposed Deep Learning Architecture

The architecture of the proposed *Coarse-Fine CNN* is shown in Fig. 3: the network is made of two main parts, a coarse sub-network and a fine one.

Since the MPI phenomenon depends on reflections happening in different locations, a proper estimation of its presence needs a relatively wide receptive field of the CNN in order to understand the geometrical structure of the scene. Following this rationale, the coarse network performs an analysis of the input data by applying downsampling with pooling layers increasing the receptive field as a consequence. The coarse network takes in input the 5 data channels described in Sect. 4 and is made of a stack of 5 convolutional layers each followed by a ReLU with the exception of the last one. The first 2 convolutional layers are also followed by a max-pooling stage reducing the resolution of a factor of 2. All the layers perform 3×3 pixels convolutions and have 32 filters, except the last one that has a single filter, producing as output a low resolution estimate of the MPI. The estimated MPI error is finally upsampled of a factor of 4 using a bilinear interpolation in order to bring it back to the original input resolution. This network allows us to obtain a reliable estimate of the regions affected by MPI but, mostly due to the pooling operations, the localization of the interference is not precise and directly subtracting the output of this network to the acquired data would lead to artifacts specially in proximity of the edges. For this reason, we used a second network working at full resolution to obtain a more precise localization of the error. This second network also has 5 convolutional layers with 3×3 convolutions and ReLU activation functions (except the last as before). It has instead 64 filters for each layer and no pooling blocks. The input of the first layer is the same of the previous network but the fourth layer takes as input not only the output of the third layer but also the upsampled output of the coarse network. This allows us to combine the low resolution estimation with a wide receptive field of the previous network with the more detailed but local estimation done by the fine network and to obtain an MPI estimation that captures both the scene global structure and the fine details.

The network has been trained using the synthetic dataset of Sect. 4. Even if it is one of the largest ToF dataset with multi-frequency data and ground truth information, its size is still quite small if compared to datasets typically used for CNNs training. In order to deal with this issue and avoid over-fitting we applied data augmentation techniques on the training data as random sampling

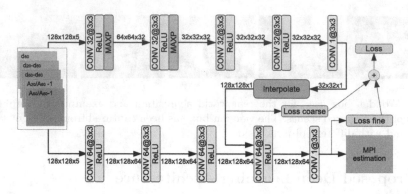

Fig. 3. Architecture of the Coarse-Fine CNN used for MPI estimation in ToF data

of patches, rotation and flipping operations. We extracted 10 random patches of size 128×128 pixels from each of the 40 scenes, then we applied to each of them a rotation of $\pm 5°$ and horizontal and vertical flipping. This leads to a total of about $40 \times 10 \times 5 = 2000$ patches (invalid patches with non complete covering on rotated images have been excluded), that represents a good amount of data for the training of the proposed deep network. The number of patches could be increased by using smaller patches, but this would weaken the ability of the network to understand the geometrical structures of the scenes and to retrieve the MPI corruption.

Due to the small amount of data we have used *K-fold validation* with $K = 5$ on the training set to validate the hyper-parameters of the CNN and of the training procedure as the architecture of the network, the number and depth of the layers, the learning rate and the regularization constant. We have selected the CNN hyper-parameters in order to avoid overfitting and obtain the minimum mean validation MAE among the 5 folds. Once the hyper-parameters have been selected, the CNN has been trained on the whole training set.

For the training we minimized a combined loss made by the sum of two loss functions, one computed on the interpolated output of the coarse network and the other computed on the output of the fine network. This approach allowed to obtain better performances than the separate training of the two sub-networks. Each of the two loss functions is the l_1 *norm* of the difference between the MPI error estimated by the corresponding network and the MPI error computed by comparing the ToF depth at 60 MHz with true depth as described in Sect. 4. The l_1 *norm* is more robust to outliers in the training process if compared with the l_2 *norm* and had more stable results in the validation of the network hyper-parameters. Furthermore the use of l_1 *norm* proved to be more efficient for image denoising [31]. During the training, we exploited the *ADAM* optimizer [32] and a batch size of 16. We started the training with an initial set of weight values derived with Xavier's procedure [33], a learning rate of 10^{-4} and a l_2 regularization with a weighting factor of 10^{-4} for the *norm* of the CNN weights. Figure 4 shows the mean training and validation error across all the epochs of the *K-fold validation*: we trained the network for 150 epochs, that in our case proved to be enough for the validation error to stabilize. The network has been implemented using the *TensorFlow* framework and the training took about 30 minutes on a desktop PC with an Intel i7-4790 CPU and an *NVIDIA Titan X (Pascal)* GPU. The evaluation of a single frame with the proposed network takes instead just 9.5 ms.

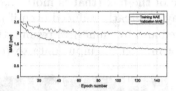

Fig. 4. Mean training (blue) and validation (red) error at each epoch of the *K-fold validation*. (Color figure online)

6   Experimental Results

In order to evaluate the proposed approach we used the two different datasets presented in Sect. 4. The first is the synthetic dataset, that has been used both for the training of the CNN and for the evaluation of the performances of the proposed method. The second one is a smaller real world dataset that has been used only for evaluation purposes due to its limited size.

6.1   Results on Synthetic Data

As already pointed out, we kept 14 synthetic scenes for evaluation purposes only. The scenes used for testing are shown in Fig. 5, notice how they include various types of settings with different sizes, types of textures and several situations where the multi-path error can arise. Figure 6 shows the results of the application of the proposed approach on a subset of the scenes used for testing. It shows the input depth map from the ToF camera at 60 MHz (with phase unwrapping), the depth map after the application of the adaptive bilateral filter and the final result of the proposed approach with their related errors map and the depth ground truth information. By looking at the third and fourth columns it is possible to notice how the adaptive bilateral filter is able to reduce the zero-mean error by preserving the fine details in the scenes, e.g., the small moon in the *castle* is preserved by the filtering process, but the depth overestimation due to MPI is still present. From the fifth and sixth columns it is possible to see how both the multi-path error and the zero-mean noise have been widely reduced by the complete version of the proposed approach. For example in the first 3 scenes there is a very strong multi-path distortion on the walls in the back that has been almost completely removed by the proposed approach for MPI correction. The multi-path estimation is very accurate on all the main surfaces of the scenes, even if the task proved to be more challenging on some small details like the top

of the pots in row 1 or the stairs in row 2. However notice that thanks to the usage
of the Coarse-Fine network the small details of the various scenes are preserved
and there is no blurring of the edges. This can be seen for example another time
from the details of the castle (e.g., the moon shape) in row 3. The box scene (row
4) is another example of the MPI removal capabilities. Notice how the multi-path
on the edges between the floor and the walls is correctly removed. Also the error
on the slope in the middle of the box (that is more challenging due to bounces
from locations farther away) is greatly reduced even if not completely removed.
This evaluation is confirmed also by numerical results, the Mean Absolute Error
(MAE) is reduced from 156 mm on the input data to 70 mm.

Fig. 5. Synthetic test set used for evaluating the proposed approach. The figure shows
a color view for each scene in the dataset. (Color figure online)

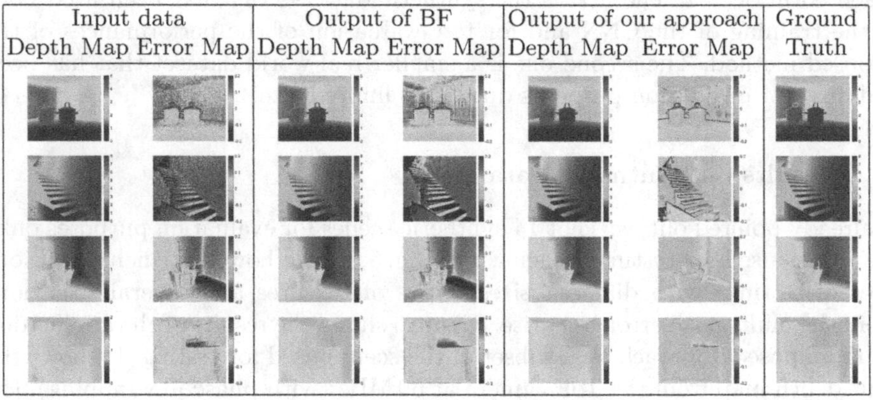

Input data		Output of BF		Output of our approach		Ground
Depth Map	Error Map	Depth Map	Error Map	Depth Map	Error Map	Truth

Fig. 6. Input depth map at 60 MHz, output of the adaptive bilateral filter (BF) and
output of the proposed approach (with MPI correction) on same sample synthetic
scenes with the corresponding error maps. All the values are measured in meters.

Figure 7 compares the error at 60 MHz with its estimation made by the proposed CNN architecture. The second column shows the estimation taken from
the interpolated output of the coarse network: notice how the general distribution of the MPI is correctly estimated but the edges and details (e.g., the moon
over the castle) are lost in this estimation due to the pooling operations that
reduce the resolution. The last column shows instead the output of the Coarse-
Fine architecture and it is possible to notice how the general MPI distribution is
maintained but there is a much higher precision on boundaries and small details.

The second row shows the same data for the *stairs* scene, also in this case notice how the general structure is the same but the estimation follows more accurately the shape of the stairs in the Coarse-Fine output.

Error map (60 MHz)	Coarse CNN estimation	Coarse-Fine CNN estimation

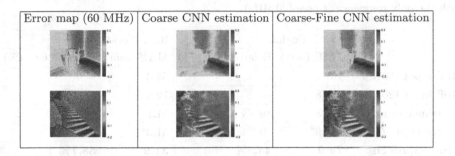

Fig. 7. Estimation of the MPI performed by the proposed approach using only the coarse network or the complete Coarse-Fine architecture.

We also compared the proposed approach with some competing approaches from the literature. In particular we considered the MF-ToF MPI correction scheme proposed by Freedman [2] and the approach based on deep learning presented by Marco in [6] that takes in input the depth map at 20 MHz to remove MPI. The method proposed by Freedman was adapted to use the same triple of frequencies used by the proposed approach. The first column of Table 1 shows the MAE obtained by comparing the output of the 3 methods with the ground truth data on the synthetic dataset. Our approach is able to reduce the error from 156 to 70 mm, reducing it to less than half of the original error. It outperforms with a wide margin both competing approaches. The Freedman method [2] is able to remove only about 10% of the error in the source data obtaining an accuracy of 140 mm. The method of [2] works under the hypothesis that the light backscattering vector is sparse and this is not true in scenes where diffuse reflections are predominant as the considered ones. For this reason, its effectiveness is limited. The method of [6] works under the assumption that the reflections are diffuse and it achieves better results removing about 20% of the original error, but it is still far from the performances of the proposed approach. This is due to the fact that the CNN proposed in [6] uses single frequency ToF data, instead we have shown that the multi-frequency approach can achieve much higher performance using a less complex CNN. The additional material contains also a detailed analysis of the different methods behavior in proximity of corners.

6.2   Results on Real World Data

After evaluating the proposed approach on synthetic data we preformed also some experiments on real world data. For this evaluation we used the real test set introduced in Sect. 4 that is composed by 8 scenes. It has a more limited

Table 1. Mean MAE for competing schemes from the literature and for the proposed approach on synthetic and real world data. The table shows the MAE in millimeters and the relative error between the output of the various methods and the error on input data. Our approach and [2] are multi-frequency methods and are compared with the highest employed frequency (60 MHz) for the relative error, instead [6] (*) is compared with the only frequency it uses (20 MHz).

	Synthetic data		Real World data	
	MAE (*mm*)	Relative Err. (%)	MAE (*mm*)	Relative Err. (%)
ToF input (60 Mhz)	167.3	-	54.3	-
ToF input (20 Mhz)	327.8	-	72.8	-
Freedman et al. [2]	149.8	89.5%	51.1	94.1%
Marco et al. [6]	260.9*	79.6%	51.3*	70.5%
Our approach	**74.9**	**44.8%**	**31.9**	**58.7%**

variety of settings with respect to the synthetic data but still the scenes contain objects of different sizes, types of material and surfaces with different orientations where the MPI can arise. The Coarse-Fine CNN was trained on the synthetic dataset that is composed by scenes with ideal properties, e.g., the reflections are perfectly diffuse, and due to some limitations of the simulator, the synthetic data, even if quite accurate, does not exactly model all the issues of real data.

Figure 8 shows the results of the application of the proposed approach to the set of real world scenes. As before, it shows the input depth map from the ToF camera at 60 MHz and the depth map resulting after the application of the proposed approach with their corresponding error maps and ground truth information. By looking at the images, it is possible to see how the MPI interference is reduced by the application of the proposed approach even if some MPI error remains in the scenes. It is possible to notice how the MPI is almost completely removed on the vertical walls, in particular in proximity of edges between facing surfaces. The reduction is strong also on the small objects like the sphere, the cone or the deer even if some multi-path in proximity of boundaries remains on these objects. On the other side the MPI error is under-estimated on surfaces with a strong inclination, in particular the floor in the various scenes, where the approach is able to reduce only part of the multi-path. By comparing Figs. 6 and 8 it is possible to notice how the strong MPI on these surfaces (e.g., the floors) is not present in the synthetic scenes. This is probably due to the fact that reflections happening on the considered real materials are not ideally diffuse when the light rays are strongly inclined and the ToF simulator does not model this phenomenon. Our approach, as any other machine learning scheme, learns from the training data and is not able to correct issues not present in the training examples.

We compared our approach with [2] and [6] also on the real world data. The results are in the third and fourth column of Table 1. On real data our approach is able to reduce the error from 54.3 to 31.9 mm, i.e., to 58.7% of

| Input data | | Output of our approach | | Ground |
Depth Map	Error Map	Depth Map	Error Map	Truth

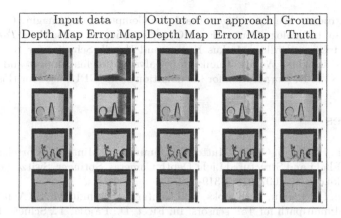

Fig. 8. Input depth map at 60 MHz and output of the proposed approach on same sample real world scenes with the corresponding error maps.

the original error, a very good performance outperforming both the compared approaches even if lower than the one achieved on synthetic data. In particular the proposed method was able to improve the accuracy of the depth estimation on all the considered scenes: in the worst case scene the error reduction is around 29%. Recall that the training is done on synthetic information only, as pointed out in the visual evaluation the issues on the floor reduce the performances. The error removal capability of [2] is limited also in this case, it removes about 6.5% of the error. The method of [6] removes about 30% of the error and gets a bit closer to ours in this experiment, but there is still a gap of more than 10%.

7 Conclusions

In this paper we proposed a novel method for MPI removal and denoising in ToF data. We extracted from MF-ToF data multiple clues based on depth differences and amplitude ratios that proved to be very informative about the MPI presence. Furthermore, by using a Coarse-Fine deep network we were able both to capture the general structure of the MPI interference and to preserve the small details and edges of the scene. Finally, we dealt with the critical issue of ground truth for training data by using synthetic information. Experimental results demonstrated how the proposed approach is able to remove the MPI interference and to remove the ToF data noise without introducing artifacts on both synthetic and real world scenes. Results are impressive on synthetic data and good on real data, but in the second case there are still some limitations due to the differences between the simulated training data and real world acquisitions. For this reason further research will be devoted at improving the results on real data both by improving the realism of the synthetic data and by trying multi-stage training procedures using together synthetic and real data. Semi-supervised learning strategies and Generative Adversarial Networks (GANs) will also be investigated.

Acknowledgment. We would like to thank the Computational Imaging Group at the Sony European Technology Center (EuTEC) for allowing us to use their *ToF Explorer* simulator and Oliver Erdler, Markus Kamm and Henrik Schaefer for their precious comments and insights. We also thank prof. Calvagno for his support and gratefully acknowledge NVIDIA Corporation for the donation of the GPUs used for this research.

References

1. Zanuttigh, P., Marin, G., Dal Mutto, C., Dominio, F., Minto, L., Cortelazzo, G.M.: Time-of-Flight and Structured Light Depth Cameras. Springer, Switzerland (2016). https://doi.org/10.1007/978-3-319-30973-6

2. Freedman, D., Smolin, Y., Krupka, E., Leichter, I., Schmidt, M.: SRA: fast removal of general multipath for ToF sensors. In: Fleet, D., Pajdla, T., Schiele, B., Tuytelaars, T. (eds.) ECCV 2014. LNCS, vol. 8689, pp. 234–249. Springer, Cham (2014). https://doi.org/10.1007/978-3-319-10590-1_16

3. Bhandari, A., et al.: Resolving multipath interference in time-of-flight imaging via modulation frequency diversity and sparse regularization. Optics Lett. **39**(6), 1705–1708 (2014)

4. Peters, C., Klein, J., Hullin, M.B., Klein, R.: Solving trigonometric moment problems for fast transient imaging. ACM Trans. Graph. (TOG) **34**(6), 220 (2015)

5. Son, K., Liu, M.Y., Taguchi, Y.: Learning to remove multipath distortions in time-of-flight range images for a robotic arm setup. In: Proceedings of IEEE International Conference on Robotics and Automation (ICRA), pp. 3390–3397 (2016)

6. Marco, J., et al.: Deeptof: off-the-shelf real-time correction of multipath interference in time-of-flight imaging. ACM Trans. Graph. (TOG) **36**(6), 219 (2017)

7. Agresti, G., Minto, L., Marin, G., Zanuttigh, P.: Deep learning for confidence information in stereo and ToF data fusion. In: Geometry Meets Deep Learning ICCV Workshop, pp. 697–705 (2017)

8. Su, S., Heide, F., Wetzstein, G., Heidrich, W.: Deep end-to-end time-of-flight imaging. In: Proceedings of the IEEE Conference on Computer Vision and Pattern Recognition, pp. 6383–6392 (2018)

9. Guo, Q., Frosio, I., Gallo, O., Zickler, T., Kautz, J.: Tackling 3D ToF artifacts through learning and the FLAT dataset. In: Ferrari, V., Hebert, M., Sminchisescu, C., Weiss, Y. (eds.) ECCV 2018. LNCS, vol. 11205, pp. 381–396. Springer, Cham (2018). https://doi.org/10.1007/978-3-030-01246-5_23

10. Kadambi, A., et al.: Coded time of flight cameras: sparse deconvolution to address multipath interference and recover time profiles. ACM Trans. Graph. (TOG) **32**(6), 167 (2013)

11. Gupta, M., Nayar, S.K., Hullin, M.B., Martin, J.: Phasor imaging: a generalization of correlation-based time-of-flight imaging. ACM Trans. Graph. (TOG) **34**(5), 156 (2015)

12. Whyte, R., Streeter, L., Cree, M.J., Dorrington, A.A.: Review of methods for resolving multi-path interference in time-of-flight range cameras. In: IEEE Sensors, pp. 629–632. IEEE (2014)

13. Fuchs, S.: Multipath interference compensation in time-of-flight camera images. In: 2010 20th International Conference on Pattern Recognition (ICPR), pp. 3583–3586. IEEE (2010)

14. Fuchs, S., Suppa, M., Hellwich, O.: Compensation for multipath in ToF camera measurements supported by photometric calibration and environment integration.

In: Chen, M., Leibe, B., Neumann, B. (eds.) ICVS 2013. LNCS, vol. 7963, pp. 31–41. Springer, Heidelberg (2013). https://doi.org/10.1007/978-3-642-39402-7_4

15. Jiménez, D., Pizarro, D., Mazo, M., Palazuelos, S.: Modeling and correction of multipath interference in time of flight cameras. Image Vis. Comput. **32**(1), 1–13 (2014)

16. Naik, N., Kadambi, A., Rhemann, C., Izadi, S., Raskar, R., Bing Kang, S.: A light transport model for mitigating multipath interference in time-of-flight sensors. In: Proceedings of the IEEE Conference on Computer Vision and Pattern Recognition, pp. 73–81 (2015)

17. Whyte, R., Streeter, L., Cree, M.J., Dorrington, A.A.: Resolving multiple propagation paths in time of flight range cameras using direct and global separation methods. Opt. Eng. **54**(11), 113109 (2015)

18. Agresti, G., Zanuttigh, P.: Combination of spatially-modulated ToF and structured light for MPI-free depth estimation. In: Leal-Taixé, L., Roth, S. (eds.) ECCV 2018 Workshops. LNCS, vol. 11129, pp. 355–371. Springer, Cham (2018)

19. Nayar, S.K., Krishnan, G., Grossberg, M.D., Raskar, R.: Fast separation of direct and global components of a scene using high frequency illumination. ACM Trans. Graph. (TOG) **25**(3), 935–944 (2006)

20. Luo, W., Schwing, A.G., Urtasun, R.: Efficient deep learning for stereo matching. In: Proceedings of the IEEE Conference on Computer Vision and Pattern Recognition, pp. 5695–5703 (2016)

21. Eigen, D., Puhrsch, C., Fergus, R.: Depth map prediction from a single image using a multi-scale deep network. In: Advances in Neural Information Processing Systems, pp. 2366–2374 (2014)

22. Eigen, D., Fergus, R.: Predicting depth, surface normals and semantic labels with a common multi-scale convolutional architecture. In: Proceedings of the IEEE International Conference on Computer Vision, pp. 2650–2658 (2015)

23. Tomasi, C., Manduchi, R.: Bilateral filtering for gray and color images. In: Proceedings of International Conference on Computer Vision (ICCV), pp. 839–846. IEEE (1998)

24. Chan, D., Buisman, H., Theobalt, C., Thrun, S.: A noise-aware filter for real-time depth upsampling. In: Workshop on Multi-camera and Multi-modal Sensor Fusion Algorithms and Applications-M2SFA2 2008 (2008)

25. Marin, G., Zanuttigh, P., Mattoccia, S.: Reliable fusion of ToF and stereo depth driven by confidence measures. In: Leibe, B., Matas, J., Sebe, N., Welling, M. (eds.) ECCV 2016. LNCS, vol. 9911, pp. 386–401. Springer, Cham (2016). https://doi.org/10.1007/978-3-319-46478-7_24

26. Zhang, M., Gunturk, B.K.: Multiresolution bilateral filtering for image denoising. IEEE Trans. Image Process. **17**(12), 2324–2333 (2008)

27. Lange, R., Seitz, P., Biber, A., Lauxtermann, S.C.: Demodulation pixels in CCD and CMOS technologies for time-of-flight ranging. In: Sensors and Camera Systems for Scientific, Industrial, and Digital Photography Applications, vol. 3965, pp. 177–189. International Society for Optics and Photonics (2000)

28. Meister, S., Nair, R., Kondermann, D.: Simulation of time-of-flight sensors using global illumination. In: Bronstein, M., Favre, J., Hormann, K. (eds.) Vision, Modeling and Visualization. The Eurographics Association, Goslar (2013)

29. The Blender Foundation: Blender website. https://www.blender.org/. Accessed 14 Mar 2018

30. The LuxRender Project: Luxrender website. http://www.luxrender.net. Accessed 14 Mar 2018

31. Zhao, H., Gallo, O., Frosio, I., Kautz, J.: Loss functions for image restoration with neural networks. IEEE Trans. Comput. Imaging **3**(1), 47–57 (2017)
32. Kingma, D.P., Ba, J.: Adam: a method for stochastic optimization. arXiv preprint arXiv:1412.6980 (2014)
33. Glorot, X., Bengio, Y.: Understanding the difficulty of training deep feedforward neural networks. In: Proceedings of the Thirteenth International Conference on Artificial Intelligence and Statistics, pp. 249–256 (2010)

PosIX-GAN: Generating Multiple Poses Using GAN for Pose-Invariant Face Recognition

Avishek Bhattacharjee[✉][iD], Samik Banerjee[iD], and Sukhendu Das[iD]

Visualization and Perception Lab, Department of Computer Science and Engineering,
IIT Madras, Chennai, India
{avi,samik}@cse.iitm.ac.in, sdas@iitm.ac.in

Abstract. Pose-Invariant Face Recognition (PIFR) has been a serious challenge in the general field of face recognition (FR). The performance of face recognition algorithms deteriorate due to various degradations such as pose, illuminaton, occlusions, blur, noise, aliasing, etc. In this paper, we deal with the problem of 3D pose variation of a face. for that we design and propose PosIX Generative Adversarial Network (PosIX-GAN) that has been trained to generate a set of nice (high quality) face images with 9 different pose variations, when provided with a face image in any arbitrary pose as input. The discriminator of the GAN has also been trained to perform the task of face recognition along with the job of discriminating between real and generated (fake) images. Results when evaluated using two benchmark datasets, reveal the superior performance of PosIX-GAN over state-of-the-art shallow as well as deep learning methods.

Keywords: Face recognition · Pose · GAN · Multi-task Learning

1 Introduction

Deep learning (DL) has attracted several researchers in the field of computer vision due to its ability to perform face and object recognition tasks with high accuracy than the traditional shallow learning systems. The convolutional layers present in the deep learning systems help to successfully capture the distinctive features of the face [19,30]. For biometric authentication, face recognition (FR) has been preferred due to its passive nature. Most solutions for FR fail to perform well in cases involving extreme pose variations as in such scenarios, the convolutional layers of the deep models are unable to find discriminative parts of the face for extracting information.

Most of the architectures proposed earlier deal with the scenarios where the face images used for training as well as testing the deep learning models [3,15,25] are frontal and near-frontal. Further, the recent use of convolutional neural network (CNN) based models [6,7,15,19,23,25,29], which provide very

© Springer Nature Switzerland AG 2019
L. Leal-Taixé and S. Roth (Eds.): ECCV 2018 Workshops, LNCS 11131, pp. 427–443, 2019.
https://doi.org/10.1007/978-3-030-11015-4_31

high accuracies for FR applications even in the wild scenarios, fail to provide acceptable recognition rates in scenarios with pose variations in faces. These models fail to perform well when the face images provided during testing are at extreme poses due to the inability of the models to find discriminative features in the images provided. On the contrary, our model uses a limited number of face images at different poses to train a GAN model (PosIX-GAN), where nine separate generator models learn to map a single face image at any arbitrary pose to nine specific poses and the discriminator performs the task of face recognition along with discriminating a synthetic face from a real-world sample. In the following, we present brief review of work done on face recognition using CNNs, generative adversarial networks (GANs) as well as shallow methods for head pose estimation and face recognition (FR).

The method proposed by [37] learns a new face representation: the face identity-preserving (FIP) features. Unlike conventional face descriptors, the FIP features can significantly reduce intra-identity variances, while maintaining discriminativeness between identities. The work by Zhu et al. [38] proposes a novel deep neural net, named multi-view perceptron (MVP), which can untangle the identity and view features, and in the meanwhile infer a full spectrum of multi-view images, given a single 2D face image. Kan et al. [14] proposed a multi-view deep network (MvDN), which seeks for a non-linear discriminant and view-invariant representation shared between multiple views. The method proposed by Yin et al. [35] study face recognition as a multi-task problem where identity classification is the main task with pose, illumination and expression estimations being the side tasks. The goal is to leverage the side tasks to improve the performance of face recognition. Yim et al. [34] proposes a new deep architecture based on a novel type of multitask learning, which achieves superior performance by rotating a face from an arbitrary pose and illumination image to a target-pose face image (target pose controlled by the user) while preserving identity. The method proposed by Wu et al. [32] studies a Light CNN framework to learn a deep face representation from the large-scale data with massive noisy labels The method makes use of a Max-Feature-Map (MFM) operation to obtain a compact representation and perform feature filter selection. The method proposed by Tran et al. [30] utilizes an encoder-decoder structured generator that can frontalize or rotate a face with an arbitrary pose, even upto the extreme profile. It explicitly disentangles the representation learning from the pose variation through the pose code in generator and the pose estimation in discriminator. It also adaptively fuses multiple faces to a single representation based on the learnt coefficients. The TP-GAN method proposed by Huang et al. [13] performs photorealistic frontal view synthesis by simultaneously perceiving global structures and local details. It makes use of four landmark located patch networks to attend to local textures in addition to the commonly used global encoder-decoder network. The method proposed by Liu et al. [17] present a novel multi-task adversarial network based on an encoder-discriminator-generator architecture where the encoder extracts a disentangled feature representation for the factors of interest and the discriminators classify each of the factors as individual tasks. Yang et al. [33] proposes a novel recurrent convolutional encoder-decoder network that is trained end-to-end on the task of rendering rotated objects starting from a single image.

The method proposed by Gourier *et al.* [10] addresses the problem of estimating head pose over a wide range of angles from low-resolution images. It uses grey-level normalized face images for linear auto-associative memory where one memory is computed for each pose using a Widrow-Hoff learning rule. Huang *et al.* [12] use Gabor feature based random forests as the classification technique since they naturally handle such multi-class classification problem and are accurate and fast. The two sources of randomness, random inputs and random features, make random forests robust and able to deal with large feature spaces. The method proposed by Tu *et al.* [31] localizes the nose-tip of the faces and estimate head poses in studio quality pictures. After the nose-tip in the training data are manually labeled, the appearance variation caused by head pose changes is characterized by tensor model which is used for head pose estimation.

The works proposed in [27,29,39] mainly deal with multi-stage complex systems, which take the convolutional features obtained from their model and then use PCA (Principal Component Analysis) for dimensionality reduction, followed by classification using SVM. Zhu *et al.* [39] tries to "warp" faces into a canonical frontal view using a deep network, for efficient classification. PCA on the network output in conjunction with an ensemble of SVMs is used for the face verification task. Taigman *et al.* [29] propose a multi-stage approach that aligns faces to a general 3D shape model combining with a multi-class (deep) network which is trained to perform the FR task. The compact network proposed by Sun *et al.* [26 28] uses an ensemble of 25 of these networks, each operating on a different face patch. The FaceNet proposed by Schroff *et al.* [23] uses a deep CNN to directly optimize the embedding itself, based on the triplet loss formulated by a triplet mining method.

Deep Convolutional GAN [20] (DCGAN) first introduced as a convolutional architecture led to improved visual quality in Computer Vision (CV) applications. More recently, Energy Based GANs [36] (EBGANs) were proposed as a class of GANs that aim to model a discriminator $D(x)$ as an energy function. This variant converges in a more stable manner and is both easy to train and robust to hyper-parameter variations. Some of these benefits were attributed to the larger number of targets in the discriminator. EBGAN also implements its discriminator as an auto-encoder with a per-pixel error. While earlier variants of GAN lacked an analytical measure of convergence, Wasserstein GANs [1] (WGANs) recently introduced a loss function that acts as a measure of convergence. However, in their implementation, this comes at the expense of slow training, but with the benefits of stability and better mode of coverage [1]. The BEGAN model [4] utilizes a new equilibrium enforcing method paired with a loss derived from the Wasserstein distance for training auto-encoder based Generative Adversarial Networks. It also provides a new approximate convergence measure, fast and stable training and high visual quality.

Most of the methods of FR/FV discussed above do not show results on Head Pose Image [9] and MultiPIE [11] datasets which have high degree of pose variation in the query faces. Drawbacks of recent GAN based methods are blur, deformities as well as inaccuracy in the synthesis process, as well as instability during training. The contribution of our work on PosIX-GAN model includes synthesis of face images at various poses given an input face image at any arbitrary pose, without much of the aforementioned drawbacks. Apart from this, the proposed model simultaneously performs face recognition with high accuracy. Results are reported using 2 benchmark face datasets with pose variation.

In the rest of the paper, Sect. 2 gives an overview of Generative Adversarial Networks (GANs), Sect. 3 describes the proposed network architecture, along with details about the loss functions used for training. Section 4 provides information about the various datasets used for evaluation of our model. Section 5 reports quantitative as well as qualitative results obtained from experiments performed and observations. Finally, Sect. 6 concludes the paper.

2   Generative Adversarial Network (GAN)

Generative Adversarial Networks (GAN) [8] are based on the adversarial training of two CNN-based models: (i) a generative model (G), which captures the true data distribution, p_{data} and generates images sampled from a distribution p_z, the distribution of the training data provided as input; and (ii) a discriminator model (D), which discriminates between the original images, sampled from p_{data}, and the images generated by G. G maps p_z from a latent space to the data distribution p_{data} of interest, while D discriminates between instances from p_{data} and those generated by G. The adversarial training adopted for GAN, derived from Schmidhuber [22], involves the formulation of an optimization function G to maximize the error in D (*i.e.*, "fool" D by producing novel synthesized instances that appear to have come from p_{data}). Thus the adversarial training procedure followed for GAN, resembles a two player minimax gaming strategy between D and G of a zero-sum game [5] with the value function $V(G, D)$. The overall objective function minimized by GANs [8], is given as:

$$\min_G \max_D V(G, D) = \mathbb{E}_{x \sim p_{data}}[\log D(x)] + \mathbb{E}_{x \sim p_z}[\log(1 - D(G(z)))] \quad (1)$$

To learn p_z over data x, a mapping to data space is represented as $G(z; \theta_g)$, where G is a differentiable function represented by a CNN with parameter set θ_g. Another CNN based deep network represented by $D(x; \theta_d)$ outputs a single scalar [0/1]. $D(x)$ represents the probability that x is generated from the true data rather than p_z.

The major drawback of such an adversarial system is that GANs fail to capture the categorical information, when all the pixels of the image samples obtained from two distributions, p_{data} and p_z are largely different from each other. We aim to overcome the two drawbacks specified above, in addition to the severe degradation in performance of the FR algorithms under severe pose variations, thus forming the underlying motivation of the work presented in this paper.

3   The Proposed Network

The proposed architecture of PosIX-GAN deals with generating faces at nine different poses from an input face (at any arbitrary pose), along with the task of pose invariant face recognition (PIFR) with the help of nine categorical discriminators which produce an output vector $\in \mathbb{R}^{N+1}$ for every image where N signifies the number of categories and 1 signifies whether the input to the network D_i is real or fake. For experimentation, we resized the images across all datasets to 64×64 pixels, to be provided as input to the generator module of PosIX-GAN. The overall architecture is detailed in Fig. 1, with the individual generator (G) and the discriminator (D) are illustrated in Figs. 2 and 3.

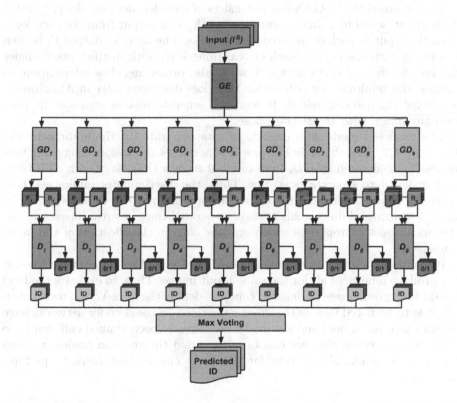

Fig. 1. The proposed architecture of PosIX-GAN, used in our work for PIFR. GE denotes the shared encoder of the generator network, GD_i; $i = \{1, 2, \ldots, 9\}$ denotes nine decoder networks connected to GE. F_i and R_i refers to the set of fake and original images. ID refers to the class IDs generated by the set of nine discriminator D_i; $i = \{1, 2, \ldots, 9\}$ which also generates 0/1 to indicate a real or fake image. (best viewed in color)

3.1   Architecture Details

Figure 1 shows an overview of the architecture of PosIX-GAN. The network consists of two parts, generator and discriminator. The generator itself has two components: a shared encoder network GE and nine decoder networks GD_i; $i = \{1, 2, \ldots, 9\}$ and G_i is defined as $(GE + GD_i)$. The components are described as follows:

The encoder is a deep-CNN based architecture, shown in Fig. 2(a), which takes input images with resolution of 64×64 pixels and outputs a vector $\in \mathbb{R}^{256}$. This encoder architecture has been adopted from that proposed in BEGAN model [4]. The encoder maps the input images to a latent space to produce an encoded vector, which acts as an input to each of the nine decoder networks.

The proposed PosIX-GAN model consists of nine decoder modules (Fig. 2(b)) which are attached to a single encoder network. The output from the encoder is fed as the input to each of the decoder networks. The decoder output F_i is then used along with a separate batch of real images R_i with distinct poses angles (different for every decoder network), while also preserving class information, to evaluate and minimize the patch-wise MSE loss described later in Algorithm 1. This helps the decoder module to learn to generate images at a specific pose given any image with an arbitrary pose.

The proposed model also consists of nine separate discriminator networks D_i; $i = \{1, 2, \ldots, 9\}$, shown in Fig. 3, which performs two tasks, recognizing fake images (F_i) generated by GD_i from original images (R_i) along with classifying input images into separate categories. Thus, the discriminator minimizes three loss components, the loss occurred when an original image is classified as a fake image, loss incurred due classification of generated image as real image and the categorical cross entropy loss which ensures correct classification of the input images.

It may be noted that as the model consists of nine discriminator modules, it may produce nine class-ids for the same input image. Thus, to evaluate the final class-id for a given image during test time, we deploy the Max-Voting mechanism [16]. It is to be noted that as the images provided to the decoder networks have a small variation in pose and the model has already been trained sufficiently to discriminate between different classes with varied tilt and pan angles, a group of decoder networks always vote for the same class, which helps to perform max-voting.

3.2   Loss Functions

The loss functions which have been employed in the proposed PosIX-GAN model are defined as follows:

Patch-Wise MSE Loss. Patch-wise MSE (PMSE) loss is derived from the mean-squared error between two images. Let p_1 and p_2 be the two patches

---

Algorithm 1. Conceptual steps for Patch-wise MSE loss evaluation

---

> **function** PMSE(im_1, im_2)
>   // PATCH_SIZE $\leftarrow$ 11 $\times$ 11 px
>   // stride $\leftarrow$ 3 $\times$ 3 px
> $mse^{(1)} \leftarrow 0; mse^{(2)} \leftarrow 0; mse^{(3)} \leftarrow 0$
>   **foreach** patch $\{p_1, p_2\}$ in $\{im_1, im_2\}$ **do**
>
> $mse^{(1)} := mse^{(1)} + \text{MSE}(p_1^{(1)}, p_2^{(1)})$
>
> $mse^{(2)} := mse^{(2)} + \text{MSE}(p_1^{(2)}, p_2^{(2)})$
>
> $mse^{(3)} := mse^{(3)} + \text{MSE}(p_1^{(3)}, p_2^{(3)})$
>
>   // $\alpha^{(i)} \leftarrow i^{th}$ channel of α
>   // $MSE(a, b)$: as in equation 2
> $loss := 0.2989 \times mse^{(1)} + 0.5870 \times mse^{(2)} 0.1141 \times mse^{(3)}$
> $P\_avg_{loss} := \frac{loss}{|p_1|}$
>   // $|p_i| \leftarrow$ total number of patches
>   **return** P_avg_{loss}

---

extracted from a pair: $image_1$ and $image_2$. The PMSE between $image_1$ and $image_2$, is calculated as:

$$\mathcal{L}_{pmse}(image_1, image_2) = \sum_{i=1}^{|C|} \frac{\lambda_i}{|p|} \sum_{j=1}^{|p|} \|p_1^{(i,j)} - p_2^{(i,j)}\|^2 \tag{2}$$

where, $|C|$ & $|p|$ specifies the number of channels and patches in the image, while the subscript k in p_k represents the image from which the patch is extracted and λ_i's are the weights of each channel in the image ($\lambda = \{0.2989, 0.5870, 0.1141\}$ as used in our experimentations). A weighted linear combination of the three MSE's components is then used to estimate the overall MSE for each patch as given in Algorithm 1. PMSE is the average MSE over all the patches.

Categorical Cross Entropy Loss. Categorical cross-entropy [24] is a loss function used effectively in the field of deep learning (DL) for multi-class classification problems and sigmoid output units. The loss function is given as:

$$\mathcal{L}_{cce}(X, Y) = -\frac{1}{n} \sum_{i=1}^{n} y^{(i)} \ln a(x^{(i)}) \tag{3}$$

where, $X = \{x^{(1)}, \ldots, x^{(n)}\}$ is the set of input examples in the training dataset, and $Y = \{y^{(1)}, \ldots, y^{(n)}\}$ is the corresponding set of labels for those input examples. The function $a(x)$ represents the output of the neural network (perceptron) given input x.

3.3 Training using Multi-objective Adversarial Loss Function

Adversarial training has been used for the training of PosIX-GAN, which minimizes the loss functions within generator ($\mathcal{L}_G^{adv}$) and discriminator ($\mathcal{L}_D^{adv}$). The encoder network transforms the input image into a 256-dimensional vector which is then fed to each of the nine decoder networks, producing nine 64×64 px. images at different poses. Thus, the adversarial loss corresponding to G is given as:

$$\mathcal{L}_G^{adv} = \mathcal{L}_{cce}(D(G(I^B)), 1) + \mathcal{L}_{cce}(D(G(I^B)), y) + \mathcal{L}_{pmse}(I_r^B, G(I^B)) \qquad (4)$$

where, I^B are the real-world face images and B indicates the batch, while r represents nine specific pose angles (see Sect. 4 for further details.), y are the class labels. $\mathcal{L}_{pmse}$ and $\mathcal{L}_{cce}$ are defined earlier in Eqs. 2 and 3. The three components of Eq. 4 are described subsequently. To ensure that the generated images are similar to the original image, the first component is formulated as:

$$\mathcal{L}_{cce}(D(G(I^B)), 1) = \sum_{i=1}^{9} \mathcal{L}_{cce}(D_i(G_i(I^B)), 1) \qquad (5)$$

The following loss function captures the class information and helps to ensure that the generated images resemble the real images of the same class:

$$\mathcal{L}_{cce}(D(G(I^B)), y) = \sum_{i=1}^{9} \mathcal{L}_{cce}(D_i(G_i(I^B)), y) \qquad (6)$$

Finally, the PMSE loss function is given as:

$$\mathcal{L}_{pmse}(I_r^B, G(I^B)) = \sum_{i=1}^{9} \mathcal{L}_{pmse}((I_r^B)_i, G_i(I^B)) \qquad (7)$$

It is to be noted that $(I_r^B)_i$ corresponds to R_i as shown in Fig. 1, for each decoder GD_i. Each of the decoder modules of the generator is fed with the generated images. The decoder modules make use of corresponding real images of the same class at a predefined pose along with these generated images to find a mapping between any arbitrary image and the generated image at a certain pose, while also preserving class-information by minimizing the patch-wise MSE loss which is described in Sect. 3.2.

Post generation of images by G_i, the discriminators D_i (shown in Fig. 3) perform two tasks: (a) it discriminates the images that are generated by G from the original images, and (b) also classifies the images to provide their class-IDs. The training of D is also based on the adversarial loss, described as:

$$\mathcal{L}_D^{adv} = \mathcal{L}_{cce}(D(I_r^B), 1) + \mathcal{L}_{cce}(D(G(I^B)), 0) + \mathcal{L}_{cce}(D(G(I^B)), y) \qquad (8)$$

where, $\mathcal{L}_{cce}(D(G(I^B)), y)$ is the categorical cross-entropy loss. The three terms of Eq. 8 are further described subsequently. The first loss component helps the

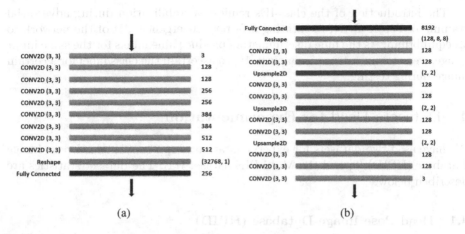

Fig. 2. The architecture of the Generator module G_i which contains a (a) shared encoder module, and a set of nine (b) decoder modules (best viewed in color). (Color figure online)

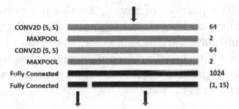

Fig. 3. The architectural details of a single Discriminator module (D_i) (see Fig. 1) (best viewed in color). (Color figure online)

discriminator network to learn to correctly classify the original images as real, given as:

$$\mathcal{L}_{cce}(D(I_r^B), \mathbf{1}) = \sum_{i=1}^{9} \mathcal{L}_{cce}(D_i(I_r^B), \mathbf{1}) \tag{9}$$

The following loss component ensures that the images generated by the generator network are correctly identified as fake images by the discriminator network:

$$\mathcal{L}_{cce}(D(G(I^B)), \mathbf{0}) = \sum_{i=1}^{9} \mathcal{L}_{cce}(D_i(G_i(I^B)), \mathbf{0}) \tag{10}$$

Finally, the last term of the loss function (Eq. 8) given below helps the discriminator network to correctly classify each face image.

$$\mathcal{L}_{cce}(D(G(I^B)), y) = \sum_{i=1}^{9} \mathcal{L}_{cce}(D_i(G_i(I^B)), y) \tag{11}$$

The introduction of the class-IDs reinforces stabilization during adversarial training of PosIX-GAN, facilitating a faster convergence [21] of the network to an equilibrium. As the nine discriminators produce nine labels for the same input image, we use max voting mechanism [16] to ascertain the class label for a certain image during testing.

4   Datasets Used for Experimentation

We have used two datasets for experimentation purposes, viz. Head pose Image Database (HPID) [9] and the Multi-PIE dataset [11]. The dataset statistics are described below:

4.1   Head Pose Image Database (HPID)

The head pose image database is a benchmark of 2790 monocular face images of 15 persons with variations of pan and tilt angles from -90 to $+90°$. Two series of images were captured for each person, having 93 images (each having a distinct pose) in each series. The purpose of having 2 series per person is to be able to train and test algorithms on known and unknown faces. People in the database wear glasses or not and have various skin color. Background is willingly neutral and uncluttered in order to focus on face operations. Figure 4 shows the pose variations present in the dataset where the values represented as $(\cdot, \cdot)$ on top of the images indicate the (tilt, pan) angles.

Fig. 4. A few samples from the Head Pose Image Dataset (HPID) [10] showing the pose variations that are present in the dataset (best viewed in color). The values represented as $(\cdot, \cdot)$ on top of the images indicate the (tilt, pan) angles.

For the purpose of our experimentation, we make use of the complete series 1 and 40% of series 2 for training the PosIX-GAN and use the rest for testing purposes. For the patch-wise MSE loss, we separate a few images per subject from the training set itself and group them into nine sets by the nine tilt angles present across the dataset while clubbing together images at different pan angles under each category, as shown above in Fig. 4. These faces are then utilized by the decoder network to evaluate the patch-wise MSE loss.

4.2   Multi-PIE Dataset

To systematically capture images with varying poses and illuminations a system of 15 cameras and 18 flashes connected to a set of Linux PCs was used. Thirteen cameras were located at head height, spaced at 15° intervals, and two additional cameras were located above the subject, simulating a typical surveillance view. During a recording session 20 images were captured for each camera: one image without any flash illumination, 18 images with each flash firing individually, and then another image without any flash. Taken across all cameras a total of 300 images was captured within 0.7 seconds. Figure 5 shows a few samples from the Multi-PIE dataset where the values on top of the images indicate the corresponding pan angles.

Fig. 5. A few samples from the Multi-PIE dataset [11] showing the pose variations present in the dataset (best viewed in color). The values on top of the images indicate the corresponding pan angles. (Color figure online)

Subjects were seated in front of a blue background in close proximity of the camera. The resulting images are 3072 × 2048 in size with the inter-pupil distance of the subjects typically exceeding 400 pixels. The part of the dataset with neutral expression was only used for experimentation purposes.

Images across Sessions 1–4 with neutral facial expressions was used for experimentation purposes. As our method does not deal with low illumination images, we only used well illuminated face images (file names ending with 06–09) at all pose variations, except Sections 08_1 and 19_1, for experimentation. The filtered data, thus obtained, was randomly partitioned into training (70%) and test (30%) data. As in the case of HPID, a few samples were seperated out from the training set (specifically, from the following nine Sections 04_1, 05_0, 05_1, 08_0, 09_0, 13_0, 14_0, 19_0, 20_0; for the nine decoder networks) and divided into the nine pan angles as shown above in Fig. 5. These nine set of images were then provided as input to the nine decoder networks in G for evaluation of the PMSE loss, thus enabling each of the networks to learn a mapping between any arbitrary pose to a predefined pose (separate for every decoder GD_i).

5 Experimental Results and Observations

The experimentations are performed on a machine with Dual-Xeon processor and 256 GB RAM, having 4 GTX-1080 Ti GPUs. The implementations are all coded in *Keras* platform using *tensorflow*-backend. The model weights were all randomly initialized and was trained on GPU for 5–6 hours. The batch size was kept to 10 and the input size of the network is kept to 64 × 64 pixels.

In the following sections, we report the quantitative results (using Rank-1 recognition rates) as well as qualitative results (faces generated at various poses). We also provide with results where patch-wise MSE loss is not incorporated using the training phase to show the effectiveness of the PMSE loss to obtain crisp result.

Table 1. Rank-1 Recognition Rate for different state-of-the-art methods on the Multi-PIE [11] dataset (in %). Results in bold shows the best performance. All the results except the last row (ours) have been directly reported from [13,30,32].

Sl.	Algorithm	±15°	±30°	±45°	±60°	±75°	±90°
1	Zhu et al. [37]	90.7	80.7	64.1	45.9	-	-
2	Zhu et al. [38]	92.8	83.7	72.9	60.1	-	-
3	Kan et al. [14]	100	100	90.6	85.9	-	-
4	Yin et al. [35]	99.2	98.0	90.3	92.1	-	-
5	Yim et al. [34]	76.64	79.1	78.4	79.2	-	-
6	Wu et al. [32]	100	99.9	99.6	95.0	32.3	9.0
7	Tran et al. [30]	94.0	90.1	86.2	83.2	-	-
8	Liu et al. [17]	95.3	89.7	87.9	84.1	-	-
9	Huang et al. [13]	98.7	98.0	95.4	87.7	77.4	64.6
10	Ours	**100**	**100**	**100**	**97.8**	**85.3**	**80.6**

5.1 Quantitative Results

Table 1 reports the experimental findings of our proposed method, compared with eight state-of-the-art methods, using the Multi-PIE dataset [11]. All the images were cropped using Chehra [2] to discard the background. The Rank-1 recognition rates of the methods listed in Table 1 have been directly reported from [13,30,32] for the dataset. The missing values in the table are not reported by the respective authors in their paper. Although, for lower pose variations the method proposed by Wu et al. [32] performs the 2nd best, but it fails at major pose variations like $\pm 75 - 90°$, where the TP-GAN [13] performs the 2nd best. Comparing all the results reported in Table 1, it may be noted that our method outperforms all other techniques by a considerable margin.

Experiments have also been carried out on the Head Pose Images Dataset [9] where the dataset partition strategy mentioned in Sect. 4.1 has been followed for evaluating the proposed method. The preprocessing procedure in this case remains the same as that done for Multi-PIE dataset. Table 2 reports the Rank-1 recognition rates of the proposed method along with a few classical methods on this dataset. From Table 2, it can be seen that our method outperforms all other compared methods by a large margin. The method proposed by Huang et al. [13] again provides the 2nd best performance.

5.2 Qualitative Results

In this section, we show a few synthetic images generated by PosIX-GAN and also compare our performance with a hybrid BEGAN [4] model implemented without the PMSE loss. Figure 6 shows the generated result by our proposed model PosIX-GAN. The second set of images shown in Fig. 7, which are generated without the use of PMSE loss, exhibit lack the crispness compared to that in

Table 2. Rank-1 Recognition Rate for different state-of-the-art methods on the Head Pose Image Dataset [9] dataset. Results in bold shows the best performance. All the results except the last row (ours) have been directly reported from [12].

Sl.	Algorithm	Classification accuracy
Gourier experimental settings see Table 2 of [18]		
1	Human Performance [10]	59.0
2	Associative Memories [10]	43.9
3	VRF+LDA [12]	66.9
Jilin Tu experimental settings see Table 2 of [18]		
4	High-order SVD [31]	54.8
5	PCA [31]	57.9
6	LEA [31]	50.6
7	VRF+LDA [12]	62.6
Proposed experimental settings (see Sect. 4.1)		
8	Huang et. al [13]	81.8
9	Ours	**92.1**

Fig. 6. The first set of images have good clarity and are closer to the ground truth compared to the second of images which are blurry with aliasing effects throughout. The numerical values at the end of each row in Figs. 6 and 7 indicate the average PSNR/SSIM values for those in each row.

Further, we also compare the synthesis results of DR-GAN [30], MTAN [17] and RNN [33] methods with the proposed PosIX-GAN. Figures 8 and 9 show a few face images generated along with the corresponding PSNR and SSIM values for every image (grayscale version used here) compared $w.r.t.$ ground truth given in top row.

The PSNR/SSIM values estimated for the images indicates the superiority of our method compared to the existing state-of-the-art methods. A noticeable drawback among all methods is their inability to produce crisp images without deformities at extreme poses. The faces generated by PosIX-GAN are devoid of any such deformities and are quite crisp even at extreme pose.

The images generated by the DR-GAN method [30], shown in Fig. 8, exhibit deformities as well as inaccuracies in the generated faces (beard not present in the generated images of Multi-PIE [11], while being present in the ground-truth). The output generated by the MTAN method [17] (Fig. 9; right) is blurry and the quality of synthesis deteriorates with larger values of the pan angle as evident from the PSNR/SSIM values. The RNN method [33] performs the 2nd best in face generation task, which can be verified visually, as well as, from the PSNR/SSIM values reported for each image in Fig. 9 (left). However, this method can only generate images upto a pan angle of $\pm 45°$.

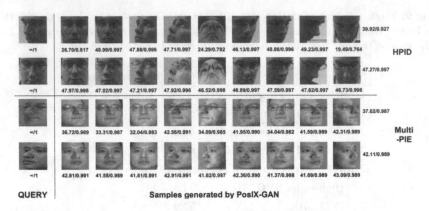

Fig. 6. Images generated by our proposed PosIX-GAN model along with the PSNR/SSIM values (best viewed in color). The numerical values at the end of each row indicate the average PSNR/SSIM values for the complete row. (Color figure online)

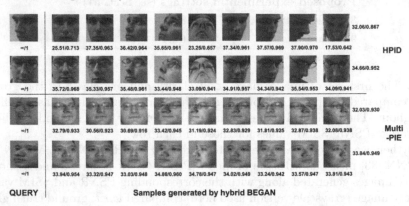

Fig. 7. Images generated by the hybrid BEGAN model (without PMSE loss) along with the PSNR/SSIM values for each image (best viewed in color). The numerical values at the end of each row indicate the average PSNR/SSIM values for the complete row. (Color figure online)

Fig. 8. Comparison of images generated with DR-GAN [30] with the proposed PosIX-GAN for Multi-PIE dataset [11] (best viewed in color). (Color figure online)

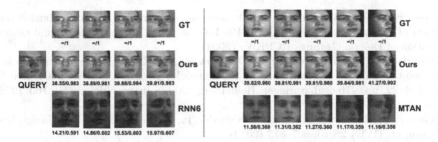

Fig. 9. Comparison of images generated with RNN [33] (left) and MTAN [17] (right) with the proposed PosIX-GAN for Multi-PIE dataset [11] (best viewed in color). (Color figure online)

6   Conclusion

This paper proposes a single-encoder, multi-decoder based generator model as a modified GAN boosted by multiple supervised discriminators for generating face images at different poses, when presented with a face at any arbitrary pose. The supervised PosIX GAN can act as a pre-processing tool for 3-D face synthesis. The qualitative as well as the quantitative results reveal the superiority of our proposed technique over few recent state-of-the-art techniques, using two benchmark datasets for PIFR. The PosIX model is capable of handling extreme pose variations for generation as well as recognition tasks, which most of the state-of-the-art techniques fail to achieve. This method also provides a basis for multiple image 3D face reconstruction, which can be explored in the near future for generating faces with dense set of pose values.

References

1. Arjovsky, M., Chintala, S., Bottou, L.: Wasserstein GAN. arXiv preprint arXiv:1701.07875 (2017)
2. Asthana, A., Zafeiriou, S., Cheng, S., Pantic, M.: Incremental face alignment in the wild. In: IEEE Conference on Computer Vision and Pattern Recognition (CVPR), pp. 1859–1866 (2014)
3. Banerjee, S., Das, S.: Mutual variation of information on Transfer-CNN for face recognition with degraded probe samples. Neurocomputing **310**, 299–315 (2018)
4. Berthelot, D., Schumm, T., Metz, L.: Began: Boundary equilibrium generative adversarial networks. arXiv preprint arXiv:1703.10717 (2017)
5. Binmore, K.: Playing for Real: A Text on Game Theory. Oxford University Press, Oxford (2007)
6. Chen, J.C., Zheng, J., Patel, V.M., Chellappa, R.: Fisher vector encoded deep convolutional features for unconstrained face verification. In: IEEE International Conference on Image Processing (ICIP), pp. 2981–2985 (2016)
7. Chen, M., Xu, Z., Weinberger, K., Sha, F.: Marginalized denoising autoencoders for domain adaptation. arXiv preprint arXiv:1206.4683 (2012)
8. Goodfellow, I., et al.: Generative adversarial nets. In: Advances in Neural Information Processing Systems (NIPS), pp. 2672–2680 (2014)

9. Gourier, N., Hall, D., Crowley, J.L.: Estimating face orientation from robust detection of salient facial features. In: ICPR International Workshop on Visual Observation of Deictic Gestures (ICPRW) (2004)

10. Gourier, N., Maisonnasse, J., Hall, D., Crowley, J.L.: Head pose estimation on low resolution images. In: Stiefelhagen, R., Garofolo, J. (eds.) CLEAR 2006. LNCS, vol. 4122, pp. 270–280. Springer, Heidelberg (2007). https://doi.org/10.1007/978-3-540-69568-4_24

11. Gross, R., Matthews, I., Cohn, J., Kanade, T., Baker, S.: Multi-PIE. Image Vis. Comput. (IVC) 28(5), 807–813 (2010)

12. Huang, C., Ding, X., Fang, C.: Head pose estimation based on random forests for multiclass classification. In: International Conference on Pattern Recognition (ICPR), pp. 934–937 (2010)

13. Huang, R., Zhang, S., Li, T., He, R., et al.: Beyond face rotation: Global and local perception GAN for photorealistic and identity preserving frontal view synthesis. arXiv preprint arXiv:1704.04086 (2017)

14. Kan, M., Shan, S., Chen, X.: Multi-view deep network for cross-view classification. In: Proceedings of the IEEE Conference on Computer Vision and Pattern Recognition (CVPR), pp. 4847–4855 (2016)

15. Krizhevsky, A., Sutskever, I., Hinton, G.E.: ImageNet classification with deep convolutional neural networks. In: Advances in Neural Information Processing Systems (NIPS), pp. 1097–1105 (2012)

16. Lam, L., Suen, S.: Application of majority voting to pattern recognition: an analysis of its behavior and performance. IEEE Trans. Syst. Man Cybern. Part A Syst. Hum. 27(5), 553–568 (1997)

17. Liu, Y., Wang, Z., Jin, H., Wassell, I.: Multi-task adversarial network for disentangled feature learning. In: Proceedings of the IEEE Conference on Computer Vision and Pattern Recognition (CVPR), pp. 3743–3751 (2018)

18. Murphy-Chutorian, E., Trivedi, M.M.: Head pose estimation in computer vision: a survey. IEEE Trans. Pattern Anal. Mach. Intell. 31(4), 607–626 (2009)

19. Parkhi, O.M., Vedaldi, A., Zisserman, A.: Deep face recognition. In: British Machine Vision Conference (BMVC), vol. 1, p. 6 (2015)

20. Radford, A., Metz, L., Chintala, S.: Unsupervised representation learning with deep convolutional generative adversarial networks. In: International Conference on Learning Representations (ICLR) (2015)

21. Salimans, T., Goodfellow, I., Zaremba, W., Cheung, V., Radford, A., Chen, X.: Improved techniques for training GANs. In: Advances in Neural Information Processing Systems (NIPS), pp. 2234–2242 (2016)

22. Schmidhuber, J.: Learning factorial codes by predictability minimization. Neural Comput. 4(6), 863–879 (1992)

23. Schroff, F., Kalenichenko, D., Philbin, J.: FaceNet: a unified embedding for face recognition and clustering. In: Proceedings of the IEEE Conference on Computer Vision and Pattern Recognition (CVPR), pp. 815–823 (2015)

24. Shore, J., Johnson, R.: Axiomatic derivation of the principle of maximum entropy and the principle of minimum cross-entropy. IEEE Trans. Inf. Theory 26(1), 26–37 (1980)

25. Simonyan, K., Zisserman, A.: Very deep convolutional networks for large-scale image recognition. arXiv preprint arXiv:1409.1556 (2014)

26. Sun, Y., Liang, D., Wang, X., Tang, X.: Deepid3: Face recognition with very deep neural networks. arXiv preprint arXiv:1502.00873 (2015)

27. Sun, Y., Wang, X., Tang, X.: Deep learning face representation from predicting 10,000 classes. In: IEEE Conference on Computer Vision and Pattern Recognition (CVPR), pp. 1891–1898 (2014)
28. Sun, Y., Wang, X., Tang, X.: Deeply learned face representations are sparse, selective, and robust. In: IEEE Conference on Computer Vision and Pattern Recognition (CVPR), pp. 2892–2900 (2015)
29. Taigman, Y., Yang, M., Ranzato, M., Wolf, L.: DeepFace: closing the gap to human-level performance in face verification. In: IEEE Conference on Computer Vision and Pattern Recognition (CVPR), pp. 1701–1708 (2014)
30. Tran, L., Yin, X., Liu, X.: Disentangled representation learning GAN for pose-invariant face recognition. In: Proceedings of the IEEE Conference on Computer Vision and Pattern Recognition (CVPR), vol. 3, p. 7 (2017)
31. Tu, J., Fu, Y., Hu, Y., Huang, T.: Evaluation of head pose estimation for studio data. In: Stiefelhagen, R., Garofolo, J. (eds.) CLEAR 2006. LNCS, vol. 4122, pp. 281–290. Springer, Heidelberg (2007). https://doi.org/10.1007/978-3-540-69568-4_25
32. Wu, X., He, R., Sun, Z., Tan, T.: A light cnn for deep face representation with noisy labels. IEEE Trans. Inf. Forensics Secur. **13**(11), 2884–2896 (2018)
33. Yang, J., Reed, S.E., Yang, M.H., Lee, H.: Weakly-supervised disentangling with recurrent transformations for 3D view synthesis. In: Advances in Neural Information Processing Systems (NIPS), pp. 1099–1107 (2015)
34. Yim, J., Jung, H., Yoo, B., Choi, C., Park, D., Kim, J.: Rotating your face using multi-task deep neural network. In: Proceedings of the IEEE Conference on Computer Vision and Pattern Recognition (CVPR), pp. 676–684 (2015)
35. Yin, X., Liu, X.: Multi-task convolutional neural network for pose-invariant face recognition. IEEE Trans. Image Process. (2017)
36. Zhao, J., Mathieu, M., LeCun, Y.: Energy-based generative adversarial network. arXiv preprint arXiv:1609.03126 (2016)
37. Zhu, Z., Luo, P., Wang, X., Tang, X.: Deep learning identity-preserving face space. In: Proceedings of the IEEE International Conference on Computer Vision (ICCV), pp. 113–120 (2013)
38. Zhu, Z., Luo, P., Wang, X., Tang, X.: Multi-view perceptron: a deep model for learning face identity and view representations. In: Advances in Neural Information Processing Systems (NIPS), pp. 217–225 (2014)
39. Zhu, Z., Luo, P., Wang, X., Tang, X.: Recover canonical-view faces in the wild with deep neural networks. arXiv preprint arXiv:1404.3543 (2014)

Semi-supervised Semantic Matching

Zakaria Laskar$^{(\boxtimes)}$ and Juho Kannala

Aalto University, Helsinki, Finland
{zakaria.laskar,juho.kannala}@aalto.fi

Abstract. Convolutional neural networks (CNNs) have been successfully applied to solve the problem of correspondence estimation between semantically related images. Due to non-availability of large training datasets, existing methods resort to self-supervised or unsupervised training paradigm. In this paper we propose a semi-supervised learning framework that imposes cyclic consistency constraint on unlabeled image pairs. Together with the supervised loss the proposed model achieves state-of-the-art on a benchmark semantic matching dataset.

Keywords: Semantic-matching · Geometric matching · Deep-learning

1 Introduction

The task of estimating correspondences across different images is one of the challenging problems in computer vision. Some popular lines of work include optical flow estimation [1], tracking [2] or stereo fusion [3] that all require estimating pixel-wise correspondences between an image pair. However, such problems deal with images of the same scene or object without much change in appearance or geometry of the scene. Such variations are challenges usually observed in semantic matching, where the objective is to estimate correspondences between semantically similar but different instances of the same object or scene.

The current approaches, like other fields in computer vision, can be broadly categorized into hand-crafted [4–6] and deep learning based methods. Hand-crafted methods employ features such as HOG,SURF or SIFT descriptors [7–9] in association with a geometric regularizer to establish spatially consistent correspondences. The deep learning based methods can be divided into following: (*i*)direct methods: that directly learn the correspondence as a matching function [10,11] and (*ii*)indirect methods: that first learn an embedding where representations from similar image patch are mapped close to each other in Euclidean space [12,13] followed by correspondence estimation using nearest neighbor search. However, this involves computationally heavy pairwise matching between putative image patches (or regions) from each image.

One of the problems with training deep learning models is the requirement of large amount of labeled data [14]. Using deep models to solve the semantic matching problem also faces a similar issue, where popular datasets like Proposal Flow [15] consists of about only 1400 image pairs with sparse ground-truth

© Springer Nature Switzerland AG 2019
L. Leal-Taixé and S. Roth (Eds.): ECCV 2018 Workshops, LNCS 11131, pp. 444–455, 2019.
https://doi.org/10.1007/978-3-030-11015-4_32

key-point correspondences, with 700 image pairs used for training. Generating datasets with ground-truth transformations for semantic matching is a challenging task. Sampling images and transformations from a 3D model is feasible for a single object but is not straightforward for multiple objects with intra-class variations. Recent deep learning approaches have addressed this issue using the self-supervised [10,16] and unsupervised paradigm [11]. On the other hand obtaining image pairs with sparse ground-truth point correspondences is relatively simple for small-sized datasets (e.g. Proposal Flow). However, it is even simpler to obtain larger datasets with only image level correspondence. In this paper we explore the semi-supervised semantic correspondence learning framework where only a subset of the training image pairs are labeled with ground-truth correspondences and the rest are unlabeled (or weakly labeled) i.e. only image level correspondence information is available. In particular, we make the following key contributions: *(i)* we show that extending [10] to the supervised setting brings significant increase in semantic matching performance, *(ii)* we propose a novel loss function based on geometric re-projection error via cycle consistency that better complements the above supervised loss to make use of weakly-labeled data.

2   Related Work

Semantic Matching. Much of the earlier decade until recently has seen hand-crafted features and descriptors like SIFT [7], DAISY [8] being used in matching cross-instances of semantically related objects in images. SIFTFlow [17] uses dense SIFT descriptors in an optimization pipeline that minimizes the matching energy. More recently, Ham et al [15] introduced proposal flow that generates dense correspondence by finding putative matches between object proposals. This work along with Taniai et al [18] propose the use of HOG descriptors. With the success of deep learning, CNN representations were used instead of hand-crafted descriptors to establish correspondences. However, [15] shows that the performance still lags behind hand-designed descriptors. This performance gap is attributed to lack of fine-tuning the CNN representations for the target task of semantic matching.

Deep Learning for Dense Correspondence. The success of learning deep features in related problems like optical flow [1], stereo fusion has motivated similar application for semantic matching. Choy et al [19] propose a universal correspondence network for learning fine-grained high resolution feature representation using metric learning. The representations are then used to establish correspondences after geometric verification. Similarly, [12] uses correspondences between region proposals that pass a geometric verification check to fine tune the representations of the network. Kim et al [20] introduce a CNN descriptor termed fully convolutional self-similarity which are then combined with the proposal flow based geometric consistency check. The proposed CNN based approaches are at the same level or better than hand-engineered features, but, include costly pairwise matching between candidate regions. On the other hand, [10,11,21] learn the correspondence and feature representation in an end-to-end framework.

Unsupervised Correspondence Learning. It is common knowledge that neural networks are data hungry models. Transfer learning alleviates the problem to certain extent, but the main challenge lies in the effective use of large amount of unlabeled data. Zhou *et al* [22] propose a training procedure for their network that can learn to predict relative camera motion and depth without supervision using large amount of videos. Similarly, [23] propose to learn homography transformation between an image pair without using ground-truth transformation information. [24] introduced a semi-supervised paradigm based on GAN that learns optical flow from both labeled synthetic datasets and unlabeled real videos. The key recipe in all these algorithms is the idea of photometric consistency. However, in the field of semantic matching, due to large appearance variations, this color constancy constraint does not hold.

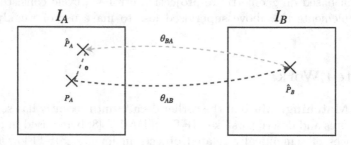

Fig. 1. Cycle consistency. Under cycle consistency constraint transfer error, e of pixel P_A, under the transformations $\theta_{AB} \circ \theta_{BA}$ should be close to zero.

Rocco *et al* [10] propose learning a set of transformations in an iterative manner using synthetically generated ground-truth transformations. As a follow up [11] an unsupervised transformation learning method is proposed that uses feature similarity score at pixel positions consistent with the predicted transformation.

Cycle Consistency Loss. Cycle consistency has been used to learn correspondence in a variety of settings [25,26] where images are defined as nodes and the pairwise flow fields define the edges. The main idea is to minimize the net distance between the key-points in source image and its estimated position obtained by traversing the cycle using respective flow fields. Zhou *et al* [21] extends the idea to the framework of CNNs by leveraging 3D models to create cyclic graphs between the rendered synthetic views and pairs of images. The network is made to predict transformations for image-image and image-synthetic pairs. Using the 4-cycle constraint, the synthetic-synthetic transformation is estimated and compared with the ground-truth to generate gradients. However, the method necessitates the availability of 3D models and sampling appropriate synthetic views.

3   Proposed Method

3.1   Background

In this section we give the reader a brief background of the correspondence estimation via geometric transformation. In [10] a CNN based architecture is proposed, which given two images I_A, I_B, estimates the parameters θ_{AB} of the geometric transformation $\mathbb{T}_{AB}$ between them. The network consists of three sequential stages as explained next.

Feature extraction layer that extracts feature representation for each image f_A, f_B, where $f \in \mathbb{R}^{w \times h \times d}$ is a tensor. This can be interpreted as d dimensional representations at $w \times h$ locations. The tensor representations are then L2 normalized.

Correlation layer computes the correlation between the normalized features resulting in a tensor $c_{AB} \in \mathbb{R}^{w \times h \times (w \times h)}$.

Regression layer is the final stage of the geometry estimation network consisting of a series of convolutional layers and a fully connected layer that finally outputs the parameters of the geometric transformation. Two types of geometric transformations are considered, affine and thine-plate spline (tps). The transformation estimates are computed in an iterative manner. In the first iteration the network outputs affine parameters. Then, I_A is warped using the estimated transformation and feed-forwarded through the second geometry estimation network which outputs the tps parameters. The only difference between the networks in both iteration is in the final fully connected layer which outputs 6 estimates for affine transformation and 18 for thin-plate spline. The final transformation is a composition of the estimated transformations.

Loss function that the network parameters are optimized on is a novel grid loss unlike traditional approaches which directly minimizes the L2 error between the estimated and ground truth transformation parameters. A fixed grid of points $G = \{g_i\}$, where $g \in \mathbb{R}^2$ and $N = |G|$, is defined on I_B is transformed using the estimated and ground truth transformations, $\hat{\theta}$ and θ, to obtain $\mathbb{T}_{\hat{\theta}}$ and $\mathbb{T}_{\theta}$ respectively. The self-supervised grid loss is then computed as the L2 error between the transformed grid locations :

$$L_{ss} = \frac{1}{N} \sum_{i=1}^{N} \|\mathbb{T}_{\hat{\theta}}(G) - \mathbb{T}_{\theta}(G)\|_2 \tag{1}$$

3.2   Semi-supervised Learning

We now proceed to show how the above self-supervised geometric transformation network can be trained in a semi-supervised manner. In semi-supervised learning, we assume to have a dataset of image pairs, D_l labeled with the information of corresponding keypoints. In addition, we have a unlabeled (or weakly labeled) dataset, D_{ul} of image pairs with only image level correspondence.

Supervised Learning. In [22], the authors propose a training procedure to learn relative camera pose and monocular depth estimation by providing supervision only at the meta-task of view synthesis. Thereby, without explicit supervision the network learns to solve intermediate tasks of relative camera pose and depth estimation. The only requirement is that the intermediate tasks should be differentiable w.r.t meta-task to allow back-propagation. Equation 1 has a similar formulation, where the network is forced to learn accurate geometric transformations to better solve the meta-task of minimizing the grid loss. Thereby in a supervised setting with ground-truth pixel correspondences P_A and P_B between I_A and I_B, where $P = \{p_j\}, p \in \mathbb{R}^{2 \times M}$ represents the M corresponding pixel locations in each image, Eq. 1 can be re-written as:

$$L_s = \frac{1}{M} \sum_{i=1}^{M} ||\mathbb{T}_{\hat{\theta}_{BA}}(P_B) - P_A||_2 \qquad (2)$$

Although there are multiple geometric transformations that can fit to a given set of sparse correspondences, the intuition here is that the network will learn to generalize as it observes a diverse set of image pairs and pixel correspondences(e.g. image pairs arising from different object categories have a different distribution of keypoints in correspondence).

Unsupervised Learning. In order to learn geometric transformation from unlabeled image pairs, we propose a self-consistent grid loss. We consider an unlabeled image pair as a directed 2-cycle graph, where the edge represents forward flow/transformation. Cycle consistency [25] states that pixels or points defined in one image, when transferred through the composition of transformations along the edges, should have a zero net displacement as shown in Fig. 1. To accommodate this constraint, we compute both the forward and backward geometric transformations. Thereafter instead of computing the error in the space of the transformed grid positions, we compute the self-consistent grid loss that measures the loss in the original grid locations. Equation 1 can now be written for the unsupervised case as:

$$L_{us} = \frac{1}{N} \sum_{i=1}^{N} ||\mathbb{T}_{\hat{\theta}_{AB}}(\mathbb{T}_{\hat{\theta}_{BA}}(G)) - G||_2 \qquad (3)$$

Converging to the true solution using the proposed loss is not trivial as an identity transformation completely satisfies the constraints of the proposed loss function. However, in the semi-supervised setting, this will not be the case as identity transformation will produce high loss for the labeled image pairs. The semi-supervised objective has the following formulation:

$$L = \sum_{I \in D_l} L_s(I) + \beta \sum_{I' \in D_{ul}} L_{us}(I'), \qquad (4)$$

where β balances the supervised and unsupervised loss functions and is obtained using validation data.

4   Experimental Results

In this section we present the experimental settings to test the proposed method.

4.1   Datasets

In line with previous work [10–12,15], we train the transformation estimation model using the PF-PASCAL dataset [15]. The dataset consists of 1400 image pairs with corresponding key-point annotations. Training,validation and test sets are obtained using the split proposed in [11] resulting in about 700, 300 and 300 image pairs respectively. The image pairs are also classified into 20 object categories.

Labeled Data. We increase the size of the training set to about 2500 using random flipping of image pairs and represent it by D_l. This results in repetitions of image pairs. It is also ensured all test or validation image pairs are removed from D_l.

Unlabeled Data. The total number of all possible image pairs that can be generated from PF-PASCAL dataset is around 33000. However, there is a class imbalance in terms of number of images per object category. This implies the number of possible pairs is also quadratically disproportionate across categories. In order to avoid this class imbalance, we upper bound the number of pairs per category to 100. To this set of image pairs we further add the labeled set D_l, but, remove the correspondence information. The combined set forms our unlabeled set D_{ul} with 7400 image pairs.

Evaluation Criteria. We evaluate the proposed approach using the probability of correctly matched key-points (PCK) metric. This metric counts the number of key-points in the source image whose projection on the target image based on the correspondence prediction lies within a given threshold. As recommended in practice, the key-point coordinates are normalized in the range [0,1] using the respective image width and height. A distance threshold of 0.1 is used to count the correctly transferred keypoints.

4.2   Baselines

We compare our proposed semi-supervised method with the recent state-of-the-art methods: SCNet [12] and its variants,CNNGeo [10] and CNNGeo2 [11]. CNNGeo trained using the loss functions defined in Eqs. 2, 3 are termed CNNGeoS and CNNGeoU respectively. The combination CNNGeoS + CNNGeoU (Eq. 4) is the proposed method. In order to evaluate the performance of our semi-supervised model, we create a baseline model CNNGeoS + CNNGeo2. This baseline model, referred as CNNGeoS2, is also trained using Eq. 4 where the unsupervised loss is now driven by CNNGeo2 instead of the proposed CNNGeoU. We guide the reader to Table 1 for a more comprehensive understanding.

4.3   Implementation Details

Network Architecture. Recent methods [11,27,28] have shown that architectures from the ResNet family [29] are well suited to the task of estimating transformations. We proceed with the ResNet-101 architecture truncated at the *conv4-23* layer. This forms the feature extraction layer (c.f. Sect. 3.1). The correlation and regression layer has the same architecture as in [10,11]. The network is pre-trained end to end using [10].

Training Details. The network is based on PyTorch [30] framework and is trained and evaluated on PF-PASCAL dataset using the split detailed in Sect. 4.1. All training images are resized to 240 × 240 resolution. Back-propagation is done using Adam [31] optimizer with a batch size of 16. These settings are shared by all the geometric transformation methods listed in Table 1. The learning rate is set to 5.10^{-8} for CNNGeo, CNNGeo2 and CNNGeoS2. Particularly, for CNNGeoS2 increasing the learning rate led to drastic drop in key-point transfer accuracy. CNNGeoS and our proposed model are trained with a higher learning rate of 5.10^{-6} as it produced better results on the validation set. β is set to 1 for the proposed semi-supervised method and the baseline CNNGeoS2.

Table 1. Comparison of supervisory methods for baseline methods. The table shows the various baseline geometric transformation methods and the nature of the objective function. The models CNNGeoS and CNNGeoS2 (CNNGeoS + CNNGeo2) are the baseline models. It is compared to our proposed model (CNNGeoS + CNNGeoU).

Methods	Self-supervised	Supervised	Unsupervised
CNNGeo	X		
CNNGeo2			X
CNNGeoS		X	
CNNGeoS2		X	X
CNNGeoU			X
Proposed		X	X

4.4   Results

We evaluated the baselines and existing methods on the PF-PASCAL test set and present our results in Table 2. Overall, the proposed semi-supervised approach outperforms the existing methods and the baseline geometric transformation models. The comparison with SCNet is not direct as we use ResNet-101 architecture which learns powerful representation than VGG-16 used by SCNet. However, the proposed approach and the baseline models (CNNGeo* in Table 2) were trained using a similar training setup and hence the comparison is fair and direct. Supervised model CNNGeoS clearly performs better than the

Table 2. Per class PCK on **PF-PASCAL** dataset. PCK threshold, $\alpha = 0.1$. The proposed model outperforms the existing methods. However, our model uses more supervisory data than the current state-of-the-art CNNGeo2. Nevertheless, baseline models CNNGeoS and CNNGeoS2 based on the recent state-of-the-art are outperformed by our proposed model.

	Aero	Bike	Bird	Boat	Bottle	Bus	Car	Cat	Chair	Cow	D.Table	Dog	Horse	M.Bike	Person	P.Plant	Sheep	Sofa	Train	TV	Mean
LOM[15]	73.3	74.4	54.4	50.9	49.6	73.8	72.9	63.6	46.1	79.8	42.5	48	68.3	66.3	42.1	62.1	65.2	57.1	64.4	58	62.5
SCNet-A	67.6	72.9	69.3	59.7	74.5	72.7	73.2	59.5	51.4	78.2	39.4	50.1	67	62.1	69.3	68.5	78.2	63.3	57.7	59.8	66.3
SCNet-AG	83.9	81.4	70.6	62.5	60.6	81.3	81.2	59.5	53.1	81.2	62	58.7	65.5	73.3	51.2	58.3	60	69.3	61.5	80	69.7
SCNet-AG+	85.5	84.4	66.3	70.8	57.4	82.7	82.3	71.6	54.3	95.3	55.2	59.5	68.6	75	56.3	60.4	60	73.7	66.5	76.7	72.2
CNNGeo	82.4	80.9	85.9	47.2	57.8	83.1	92.8	86.9	43.8	91.7	28.1	76.4	70.2	76.6	68.9	65.7	80	50.1	46.3	60.6	71.9
CNNGeo2	83.7	88	83.4	58.3	68.8	90.3	92.3	83.7	47.4	91.7	28.1	76.3	77	76	71.4	76.2	80	59.5	62.3	63.9	75.8
CNNGeoS	87.6	88.0	87.4	79.2	75.0	93.8	93.1	77.0	60.0	87.5	60.9	67.6	70.9	78.7	72.2	80.0	100.0	80.9	73.3	70.6	79.5
CNNGeoS2	85.3	88.0	78.9	54.2	78.1	88.4	92.8	79.9	51.5	85.4	28.1	72.8	67.9	75.1	66.4	75.7	100.0	59.5	63.3	62.8	74.8
Proposed	89.3	87.4	90.4	66.7	76.6	91.7	95.1	72.1	72.9	87.5	76.6	78.1	80.1	84.2	68.4	86.7	100.0	84.5	86.0	93.9	83.7

self-supervised CNNGeo and unsupervised model CNNGeo2 as expected. This implies the model is able to learn valid geometric transformations using only sparse correspondences.

We now compare the baseline model CNNGeoS2 and our proposed method, which were trained in a semi-supervised framework. The proposed model sets the state-of-the-art in semantic matching across multiple object categories. This also shows that the proposed unsupervised loss (Eq. 3) is complementary to the supervised loss function. Also, both the supervised and unsupervised loss in our model operate in the space of normalized pixel space unlike CNNGeoS2 where the unsupervised loss operates directly on feature representations.

Figures 2, 3 and 4 shows some qualitative results where the source image is warped using the estimated transformations from the baselines (CNNGeoS and CNNGeoS2) and the proposed method respectively.

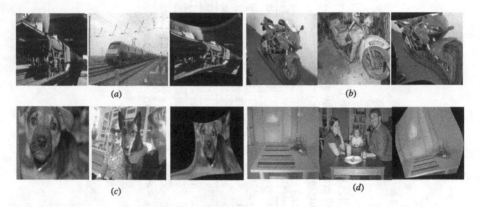

Fig. 2. Qualitative results of image warps as estimated by CNNGeoS. Each figure has 3 columns represented by the source image, target image and the warped source image according to the estimated tps transformation.

Fig. 3. Qualitative results of image warps as estimated by CNNGeoS2. Each figure has 3 columns represented by the source image, target image and the warped source image according to the estimated tps transformation.

Fig. 4. **Qualitative results of image warps as estimated by the proposed method.** Each figure has 3 columns represented by the source image, target image and the warped source image according to the estimated tps transformation.

5   Conclusion

We presented a semi-supervised learning paradigm to address the problem of semantic matching. In particular, we demonstrated that cycle consistency can be integrated with supervised methods to learn correspondence from unlabeled data. Results show that our proposed approach outperforms the state-of-the-art semantic matching methods.

References

1. Fischer, P., et al.: FlowNet: Learning optical flow with convolutional networks. arXiv preprint arXiv:1504.06852 (2015)
2. Engel, J., Schöps, T., Cremers, D.: LSD-SLAM: large-scale direct monocular SLAM. In: Fleet, D., Pajdla, T., Schiele, B., Tuytelaars, T. (eds.) ECCV 2014. LNCS, vol. 8690, pp. 834–849. Springer, Cham (2014). https://doi.org/10.1007/978-3-319-10605-2_54
3. Hosni, A., Rhemann, C., Bleyer, M., Rother, C., Gelautz, M.: Fast cost-volume filtering for visual correspondence and beyond. IEEE Trans. Pattern Anal. Mach. Intell. **35**(2), 504–511 (2013)
4. Bristow, H., Valmadre, J., Lucey, S.: Dense semantic correspondence where every pixel is a classifier. In: Proceedings of the IEEE International Conference on Computer Vision, pp. 4024–4031 (2015)
5. Hur, J., Lim, H., Park, C., Ahn, S.C.: Generalized deformable spatial pyramid: geometry-preserving dense correspondence estimation. In: 2015 IEEE Conference on Computer Vision and Pattern Recognition (CVPR)
6. Kim, J., Liu, C., Sha, F., Grauman, K.: Deformable spatial pyramid matching for fast dense correspondences. In: Proceedings of the 2013 IEEE Conference on Computer Vision and Pattern Recognition, pp. 2307–2314. IEEE Computer Society (2013)

7. Lowe, D.G.: Distinctive image features from scale-invariant keypoints. Int. J. Comput. Vis. **60**(2), 91–110 (2004)
8. Tola, E., Lepetit, V., Fua, P.: DAISY: an efficient dense descriptor applied to wide-baseline stereo. IEEE Trans. Pattern Anal. Mach. Intell. **32**(5), 815–830 (2010)
9. Dalal, N., Triggs, B.: Histograms of oriented gradients for human detection. In: 2005 IEEE Computer Society Conference on Computer Vision and Pattern Recognition, CVPR 2005, vol. 1, pp. 886–893. IEEE (2005)
10. Rocco, I., Arandjelović, R., Sivic, J.: Convolutional neural network architecture for geometric matching. In: CVPR 2017-IEEE Conference on Computer Vision and Pattern Recognition (2017)
11. Rocco, I., Arandjelović, R., Sivic, J.: End-to-end weakly-supervised semantic alignment. arXiv preprint arXiv:1712.06861 (2017)
12. Han, K., et al.: SCNet: learning semantic correspondence. In: International Conference on Computer Vision (2017)
13. Thewlis, J., Zheng, S., Torr, P.H., Vedaldi, A.: Fully-trainable deep matching. arXiv preprint arXiv:1609.03532 (2016)
14. Deng, J., Dong, W., Socher, R., Li, L.J., Li, K., Fei-Fei, L.: ImageNet: a large-scale hierarchical image database. In: CVPR 2009 (2009)
15. Ham, B., Cho, M., Schmid, C., Ponce, J.: Proposal flow. In: CVPR 2016-IEEE Conference on Computer Vision and Pattern Recognition, pp. 3475–3484. IEEE (2016)
16. Novotný, D., Albanie, S., Larlus, D., Vedaldi, A.: Self-supervised learning of geometrically stable features through probabilistic introspection. CoRR (2018)
17. Liu, C., Yuen, J., Torralba, A., Sivic, J., Freeman, W.T.: SIFT flow: dense correspondence across different scenes. In: Forsyth, D., Torr, P., Zisserman, A. (eds.) ECCV 2008. LNCS, vol. 5304, pp. 28–42. Springer, Heidelberg (2008). https://doi.org/10.1007/978-3-540-88690-7_3
18. Taniai, T., Sinha, S.N., Sato, Y.: Joint recovery of dense correspondence and cosegmentation in two images. In: Proceedings of the IEEE Conference on Computer Vision and Pattern Recognition, pp. 4246–4255 (2016)
19. Choy, C.B., Gwak, J., Savarese, S., Chandraker, M.: Universal correspondence network. In: Advances in Neural Information Processing Systems, pp. 2414–2422 (2016)
20. Kim, S., Min, D., Ham, B., Jeon, S., Lin, S., Sohn, K.: FCSS: fully convolutional self-similarity for dense semantic correspondence. In: Proceedings of the IEEE Conference on Computer Vision and Pattern Recognition (2017)
21. Zhou, T., Krahenbuhl, P., Aubry, M., Huang, Q., Efros, A.A.: Learning dense correspondence via 3D-guided cycle consistency. In: Proceedings of the IEEE Conference on Computer Vision and Pattern Recognition, pp. 117–126 (2016)
22. Zhou, T., Brown, M., Snavely, N., Lowe, D.G.: Unsupervised learning of depth and ego-motion from video. In: 2017 IEEE Conference on Computer Vision and Pattern Recognition (CVPR), pp. 6612–6619. IEEE (2017)
23. Nguyen, T., Chen, S.W., Skandan, S., Taylor, C.J., Kumar, V.: Unsupervised deep homography: a fast and robust homography estimation model. IEEE Robot. Autom. Lett. (2018)
24. Lai, W.S., Huang, J.B., Yang, M.H.: Semi-supervised learning for optical flow with generative adversarial networks. In: Advances in Neural Information Processing Systems, pp. 353–363 (2017)
25. Zhou, T., Jae Lee, Y., Yu, S.X., Efros, A.A.: FlowWeb: joint image set alignment by weaving consistent, pixel-wise correspondences. In: Proceedings of the IEEE Conference on Computer Vision and Pattern Recognition, pp. 1191–1200 (2015)

26. Zhou, X., Zhu, M., Daniilidis, K.: Multi-image matching via fast alternating minimization. In: Proceedings of the IEEE International Conference on Computer Vision, pp. 4032–4040 (2015)
27. Laskar, Z., Melekhov, I., Kalia, S., Kannala, J.: Camera relocalization by computing pairwise relative poses using convolutional neural network
28. Melekhov, I., Ylioinas, J., Kannala, J., Rahtu, E.: Image-based localization using hourglass networks
29. He, K., Zhang, X., Ren, S., Sun, J.: Deep residual learning for image recognition. In: Proceedings of the IEEE Conference on Computer Vision and Pattern Recognition, pp. 770–778 (2016)
30. Paszke, A., et al.: Automatic differentiation in PyTorch. In: NIPS-W (2017)
31. Kingma, D.P., Ba, J.: Adam: A method for stochastic optimization. arXiv preprint arXiv:1412.6980 (2014)

Multi-kernel Diffusion CNNs
for Graph-Based Learning
on Point Clouds

Lasse Hansen[1]($\boxtimes$), Jasper Diesel[2], and Mattias P. Heinrich[1]

[1] Institute of Medical Informatics, University of Lübeck, Lübeck, Germany
`hansen@imi.uni-luebeck.de`
[2] Drägerwerk AG & Co. KGaA, Lübeck, Germany

Abstract. Graph convolutional networks are a new promising learning approach to deal with data on irregular domains. They are predestined to overcome certain limitations of conventional grid-based architectures and will enable efficient handling of point clouds or related graphical data representations, e.g. superpixel graphs. Learning feature extractors and classifiers on 3D point clouds is still an underdeveloped area and has potential restrictions to equal graph topologies. In this work, we derive a new architectural design that combines rotationally and topologically invariant graph diffusion operators and node-wise feature learning through 1×1 convolutions. By combining multiple isotropic diffusion operations based on the Laplace-Beltrami operator, we can learn an optimal linear combination of diffusion kernels for effective feature propagation across nodes on an irregular graph. We validated our approach for learning point descriptors as well as semantic classification on real 3D point clouds of human poses and demonstrate an improvement from 85% to 95% in Dice overlap with our multi-kernel approach.

Keywords: Graph convolutional networks ·
Point descriptor learning · Point cloud segmentation

1 Introduction

The vast majority of image acquisition and analysis has so far focused on reconstructing and processing dense images or volumetric data. This is mainly motivated by the simplicity of representing data points and their spatial relationships on regular grids and storing or visualising them using arrays. In particular convolutional operators for feature extraction and pooling have seen increased importance for denoising, segmentation, registration and detection due to the rise of deep learning techniques. Learning spatial filter coefficients through backpropagation is well understood and computationally efficient due to highly optimised matrix multiplication routines for both CPUs and GPUs.

L. Leal-Taixé and S. Roth (Eds.): ECCV 2018 Workshops, LNCS 11131, pp. 456–469, 2019.
https://doi.org/10.1007/978-3-030-11015-4_33

However, many alternative imaging devices such as time-of-flight based 3D scanners or ultrasound that is based on reflectance measurements are not necessarily optimally represented on dense 3D grids. Instead these sparse measurements can be stored and processed more naturally and effectively using point clouds that are connected by edges forming an irregular graph. Moreover, 3D data from multiple sources can be easily combined if represented as point clouds.

The supervised feature learning and further analyses on these irregular domains is a research area that is still in its early stage, in particular in the context of deep learning. The main limitations of previous approaches are their dependency on an equal number of nodes in all graphs (e.g. derived from point clouds) and the same topology, i.e. ordering of nodes and edge connections. Furthermore, some operations on irregular graphs are inefficient for parallel hardware, which limits their usefulness in real world scenarios.

1.1 Related Work

Of all hierarchical feature learning models, convolutional neural networks have shown to be one of the most successful approaches for a wide variety of tasks [24]. Attempts to transfer the concepts from the two dimensional image domain directly to a sparsely sampled 3D space include e.g. volumetric CNNs [19] and multi-view CNNs [27]. However, due to the sparseness of the observed space both techniques lack computational efficiency.

Another class of works addresses this problem more generally by studying the intrinsic structure of data on non-Euclidean and irregular domains. Noteworthy are in particular spectral descriptors that are based on the eigenfunctions and eigenvalues of the Laplace-Beltrami operator. The proposed methods include heat kernel signatures (HKS) [28], wave kernel signatures (WKS) [2] and learnable optimal spectral descriptors (OSD) [17]. Spectral CNNs, defined on graphs, were first introduced in [7]. The main drawback of this method is that it relies on prior knowledge of the graph structure to define a local neighborhood for weight sharing. Consequently, the idea of graph convolutions has been extended in [11,14] by limiting the support size of the learned spectral filters, making them independent of graph topology. In [5,18,20] another approach is presented, which defines a new form of local intrinsic patches on point clouds and general graphs, where the weights parameterizing the construction of patches are learned. Graph attention networks [29] learn a functional mapping to define pairwise weights based on the concatenated features of the involved nodes. The localized spectral CNN (LSCNN) [4], which derives local patches from the windowed Fourier transform, can be seen as a combination of the spectral and the spatial method. [6] provides a comprehensive review of current research on this topic.

Deep learning applied directly on unordered point sets is considered in the PointNet framework [22,23]. The input point set is recursively partitioned into smaller subsets and max pooling is used as a symmetric function to aggregate information regardless of point ordering.

Closest to our approach is the work of [1], that uses a power series of the transition matrix on a graph as diffusion operation to capture local node behavior, while we additionally employ multiple diffusion constants to build the filter kernels based on different variants of the normalized Laplacian. Moreover, we found it critically to build our network in a multi-layer fashion which was not considered in [1].

1.2   Contribution

In this work, we propose a simplified architecture that helps to overcome the limitations stated above, i.e. it can be employed for both grid and irregular graphs, has a comparable or better computational performance than classic CNNs and is theoretically connected to research on mean field inference approaches for graphical models in computer vision. As detailed in Sect. 2, we propose multi-kernel diffusion convolutional neural networks (mkdCNNs) based on two simple building blocks: isotropic, rotationally-invariant graph diffusion operators that propagate information across edges (on the graph) and trainable 1×1 convolutions that manipulate features for each node individually. When employing multiple diffusion constants for the information propagation, which are linearly combined with the following 1×1 convolution, powerful regional features, e.g. curvature, can be learned. A random walk approach is considered to further simplify the diffusion process. In Sect. 3 we successfully validate the proposed multi-kernel diffusion convolutional network on the tasks of learning pointwise correspondences between point clouds of different human poses as well as segmenting body parts.

2   Multi-kernel Diffusion CNNs for Point Clouds

Input to our network is a matrix $\mathbf{P} \in \mathbb{R}^{n \times f}$, where the i-th row corresponds to one of n points $\mathbf{p}_i \in \mathbb{R}^f$ of a point cloud in an f-dimensional feature space.

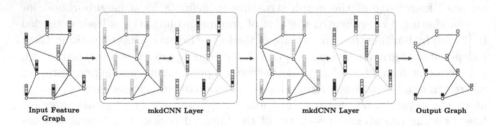

Input Feature   mkdCNN Layer   mkdCNN Layer   Output Graph
Graph

Fig. 1. Example of a two layer multi-kernel Diffusion CNN for node classification: Given an arbitrary input graph with f-dimensional features (left), we employ alternating layers of topology-independent diffusion operators with multiple isotropic kernels that propagate information across the graph, followed by 1×1 convolutions and activations that act on nodes individually and learn abstract representations of features (middle). In the end class predictions for each node a determined by a final 1×1 convolution (right).

2.1   Network Architecture

Figure 1 visualizes our proposed mkdCNN composed of the building blocks described below in detail. The layer input is a feature map defined on a graph. The weighted edges of the graph determine the feature propagation between nodes implemented as diffusion operation. The feature learning step consists of 1×1 convolutions followed by non-linear activations. Therefore, its support is limited to each individual node. Stacked mkdCNN layers can be used in networks for global classification, with a final symmetric pooling function (e.g. max or average pooling), or for semantic node-wise segmentation in a fully convolutional manner.

2.2   Input Feature Graph

The simplest way to capture and represent local geometry in a point cloud is via a k-nearest neighbor graph G_k, where $\mathcal{N}_k(\mathbf{p}_i)$ denotes the set of the k-nearest neighbors of a point $\mathbf{p}_i$ and edge weights are defined by a distance metric $dist_{ij}$ between two points $\mathbf{p}_i$ and $\mathbf{p}_j$. An adjacency matrix $\mathbf{A}$ for the graph is constructed with entries

$$a_{ij} = \begin{cases} \frac{\exp(-dist_{ij}^2)}{2 \cdot \sigma^2}, & \text{if } \mathbf{p}_j \in \mathcal{N}_k(\mathbf{p}_i) \\ 0, & \text{otherwise} \end{cases},$$

where σ denotes a scalar diffusion coefficient. In our work we employ multiple diffusion constants yielding different weighting schemes for the same graph. Spectral graph analysis [9] allows us to extract further geometric properties from the point cloud, e.g. an intrinsic order of points, via the symmetric normalized graph Laplacian $\mathbf{L}_{\text{sym}} = \mathbf{I} - \mathbf{D}^{-1/2} \mathbf{A} \mathbf{D}^{-1/2}$. $\mathbf{I}$ denotes the identity matrix. The degree Matrix $\mathbf{D}$ is solely defined by its diagonal elements $d_{ii} = \sum_j a_{ij}$. For large point clouds it may be necessary to approximate the highly sparse matrix $\mathbf{L}_{\text{sym}}$ to maintain the computational efficiency of deep networks on GPUs. For this purpose, we can perform an eigendecomposition using only the first $m \ll n$ eigenvalues, such that

$$\mathbf{L}_{\text{sym}} = \mathbf{Q} \mathbf{\Lambda} \mathbf{Q}^{\mathsf{T}},$$

where the diagonal matrix $\mathbf{\Lambda}$ holds the m eigenvalues and $\mathbf{Q}$ the corresponding eigenvectors. An alternative to the symmetric Laplacian is the random walk normalized Laplacian $\mathbf{L}_{\text{rw}} = \mathbf{I} - \mathbf{D}^{-1} \mathbf{A}$.

Input point features can be arbitrarily defined depending on the application and additional given information. For graphs derived from or based on regular grids like 2D images and 3D volumes such features may be simple grayscale values/patches or more suitable approaches, e.g. extraction of BRIEF descriptors [8]. Real world coordinates and surface normals can be extracted from 3D point clouds from stereo vision or time-of-flight systems. Once a graph is defined, the spectrum of the Laplacian itself can be used for feature extraction, e.g. B-spline based geometry vectors [17]. Furthermore, the construction of the mkdCNN makes it possible to learn meaningful information with no input features at all. In this case point features are simply initialized with ones.

2.3   mkdCNN Layer

Each of our proposed mkdCNN layers consists of two seperated steps: the diffusion operation and the feature learning.

To propagate features across the graph the Laplacian is used, thus making the propagation step for features independent of employed graph topologies and applicable to graph datasets with varying numbers of nodes. Essential to our mkdCNN layer is the use of multiple isotropic diffusion kernels as visualized in Fig. 2. Together with the following node-wise feature learning, expressive regional features with different local support can be extracted from the non-linear combination of all kernels. The diffused point cloud values $\mathbf{P}'$ can be computed as the solution of the diffusion process

$$\mathbf{P}' = (\lambda \mathbf{L}_{\mathrm{sym}} + \mathbf{I})^{-1}\mathbf{P},$$

where λ denotes the diffusion time [10]. Approximating $\mathbf{L}_{\mathrm{sym}}$ with few eigenvectors as mentioned above yields an efficient computation, as

$$\mathbf{P}' = \mathbf{Q}(\lambda \mathbf{\Lambda} + \mathbf{I})^{-1}\mathbf{Q}^{\mathsf{T}}\mathbf{P}.$$

Therefore, diffusion is mainly affected by the parameters k, σ and λ, that give control over the locality of the feature propagation. As our network can be trained in an end-to-end manner those parameters can either be learned or determined on a holdout validation set. As an alternative diffusion operation, that does not involve the costly matrix inversion, we also considered a random walker, such that

$$\mathbf{P}' = (\mathbf{I} - \mathbf{L}_{\mathrm{rw}})^{t}\mathbf{P}.$$

In this case the diffusion parameters are k, σ and the number of diffusion steps t. Parallels to conditional random fields (CRFs) can be drawn. Our diffusion operation corresponds to one message passing step with the difference that the approximate mean and variance of features are propagated instead of an exact inference of all variables as in CRFs. In [16] a similar approach for efficient and approximate inference on grid-graphs is proposed that involves convolving a downsampled set of message variables with truncated Gaussian kernels.

In our proposed network, features are solely learned through 1×1 convolutions followed by a non-linearity. Besides adding depth to the network this choice is based on the analogy of our design with CRFs, where a label compatibility function is learned to penalize the assignment of different labels to nodes with similar properties [16]. Note that in CRFs the dimensionality of signals residing on each node is limited to the number of output labels and thus the compatibility function is restricted to only learn interactions across few classes, whereas in our approach the compatibility is established between feature maps. Furthermore, the exclusive use of 1×1 convolutions would make it conceptually easy to incorporate well studied building blocks from recent deep learning literature such as dense or residual connections into our network. Instance normalization and dropout are used to stabilize training and we employ a block of two 1×1 kernels each.

$\sigma = .025$ $\sigma = .1$ $\sigma = .25$ $\sigma = 1$

Fig. 2. Visualization of multiple isotropic diffusion kernels (for one point on the chest of a subject) employed in a single feature propagation step of our mkdCNN Layer.

3 Experiments

Our new method is evaluated in two experiments: point descriptor learning and semantic body parts segmentation. We make use of the publicly available FAUST dataset [3], which consists of 100 surface meshes of 10 different subjects, each scanned in 10 different poses. The 3D meshes have a resolution of 6890 vertices and point-wise correspondences between the shapes have been semi-automatically established for all points. As we are only interested in the scanned point clouds, we do not consider the given triangulations in our experiments. Following [4] we split the dataset in a disjoint training (subjects 1–7, 70 shapes), validation (subject 8, 10 shapes) and test set (subjects 9–10, 20 shapes).

3.1 Point Descriptor Learning

The random walk normalized Laplacian for all point clouds was computed using $k = 100$ nearest neighbors. We employed a four layer mkdCNN using the random walk diffusion operation with parameters $\sigma = \{0.0125, 0.025, 0.05, 0.1, 0.125, 0.25, 0.5, 1\}$, $t = 7$ and a constant signal of ones as features on the input graph. All parameters were chosen according to automatic hyperparameter optimization on the validation set. To train the descriptors we used a triplet hinge loss function - i.e. given a point on a randomly sampled shape its normalized Euclidean distance in the descriptor space to a non-corresponding point (on another random sampled shape) should be larger by a margin (here empirically set to 0.2) than its distance to a corresponding point (on another randomly sampled shape). The descriptor dimension was set to 16. Training was performed for 50 epochs with the Adam optimizer [13] and an initial learning rate of 10^{-4}. For each optimization step we considered 6890 triplets. We implemented our architecture in PyTorch [21] and train a model (0.15 million free parameters) on a Nvidia GTX 1070 8 GB in around five hours. At test time the extraction of all 6890 descriptors for one shapes takes approximately 5 s. This time is dominated by the computation of the diffusion operation. Given precomputed diffusion operators our system is able to produce a throughput of 100k points per second.

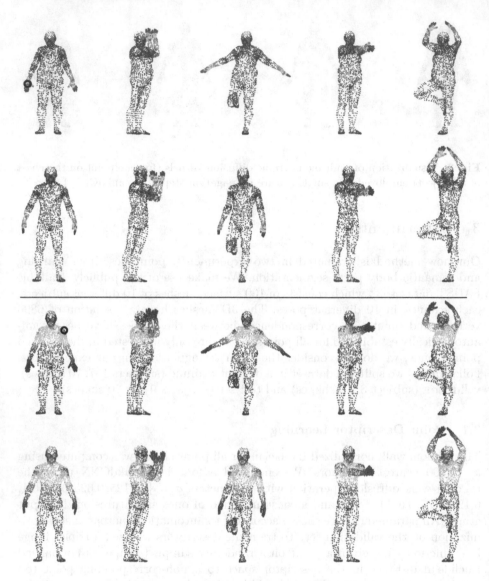

Fig. 3. Visualization of distances in the descriptor space between all points on a selection of shapes from the FAUST test set and a single point **O** on a reference shape (upper left). Cold colors correspond to small distances. Distances are saturated at the median. (Color figure online)

We compare the mkdCNN to four other spectral descriptor approaches, namely HKS [28], WKS [2], OSD [17] and LSCNN [4]. Publicly available implementations of the approaches were used and parameters (e.g. k for the computation of the graph Laplacian) optimized on the validation set.

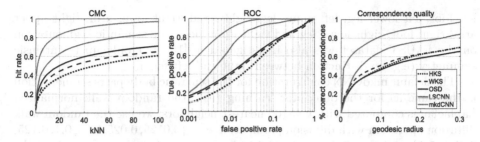

Fig. 4. Comparison of descriptor performances on the FAUST test set. For four comparison methods ■ ■ and our approach ■ we report the cumulative match characteristic (CMC), receiver operating characteristic (ROC) and the correspondence quality, which measures the distance between matched and ground truth points on the underlying mesh of the point cloud. (Color figure online)

Results. Figure 4 shows different evaluation results for all approaches on the FAUST test set. First, the cumulative match characteristic (CMC) is shown. It evaluates the retrieval performance by testing if the correct corresponding point on one shape can be found inside the next k-nearest neighbors from the set of all points of another shape. The k-nearest neighbors are determined by Euclidean distances in the descriptor space and the mean over all points and over all shapes is reported. The hit rate @kNN $= 10$ improved from 0.29 (HKS), 0.35 (WKS), 0.41 (OSD) and 0.52 (LSCNN) to 0.73 (mkdCNN). The receiver operating characteristic (ROC) plots the true positive rate against the false positive rate of point pairs at several distance thresholds in the descriptor space. For a better distinction between the approaches, we plot the ROC curve in semilogarithmic scale. The measurements for the correspondence quality follow [12]. The ground truth meshes are used to compute the geodesic distances between all points on a shape and the percentage of point pair matches that are at most r-geodesically apart from their corresponding ground truth points are reported. For the mkd-CNN this means that over 80% of point matches have a geodesic distance to their ground truth points of 10 cm or less.

Figure 3 visualizes qualitative results of descriptors learned with the mkd-CNN. A point is selected on a reference shape (on the right hand and left shoulder, respectively) and its distance in the descriptor space to all other points on the same and other shapes of the test set is computed. The distances are color-coded, where cold colors correspond to small distances. For most of the shapes distinct peaks around the ground truth are observable.

3.2 Semantic Body Parts Segmentation

The FAUST dataset does not include point-wise semantic labels for human body parts. Therefore, we labeled the points manually on a reference shape and transfered the labels to all other shapes via the known point correspondences. An exemplary ground truth labeling can be seen in Fig. 7 (left). The 15 labels correspond to the head, thorax, abdomen, left hand, left lower arm, left upper arm, left foot, left lower leg, left upper leg, right hand, right lower arm, right upper arm, right foot, right lower leg and right upper leg. The semantic segmentation on the FAUST dataset was also investigated in [15], but only up to intrinsic symmetry (e.g. no distinction between right and left foot).

The default mkdCNN configuration for the semantic body parts segmentation is the same as for the descriptor learning task: the random walk normalized Laplacian is computed with $k = 100$ nearest neighbors; we use the random walk diffusion operation with diffusion parameters $\sigma = \{0.0125, 0.025, 0.05, 0.1, 0.125, 0.25, 0.5, 1\}$ and $t = 7$; a constant signal of ones as features are used on the input graph. For the classification task another 1×1 convolution is employed after the fourth mkdCNN layer producing softmax scores. The model is trained with a cross-entropy loss weighted with the root of inverse label frequencies and the Adam optimizer (initial learning rate: 10^{-4}). Training is stopped after 50 epochs.

General Results. Figure 5 depicts segmentation results for a selection of point clouds from the FAUST test set. The mkdCNN produces accurate and precise point cloud labels, even for challenging poses (fourth column: touching hands, fifth column: right foot touches left knee). A Dice overlap of 0.95 ± 0.04 (averaged over all labels and all shapes of the test set) confirms the good visual impression.

Fig. 5. Visualization of segmentation results on a selection of shapes from the FAUST test set. While the segmentation is visually convincing for most 3D point clouds, small inconsistencies can be observed. On the third shape in the top row points of the right lower arm ■ , right upper arm ■ , left lower arm ■ and left upper arm ■ are not always assigned to the correct side of the body. The same applies for points of the right upper leg ■ and left upper leg   on the fourth shape in the top row. (Color figure online)

Ablation Study Results. To understand the effect of different parameter and architectural choices in the mkdCNN, we perform several ablation experiments on the segmentation task. The default configuration for all experiments is the one described above. Using the exact diffusion process instead of the random walk approach yields a slightly improved Dice (0.96 ± 0.03 vs 0.95 ± 0.04) at the cost of a much higher inference time (approximately 20 s and 5.5 s, respectively) due to the costly matrix inversion. Further evaluation results are shown as box-plots of Dice coefficients in Fig. 6 (top row). In our first ablation experiment we study the effect of different number of diffusion kernels, i.e. the number of employed weighting schemes for the diffusion operation, on the segmentation results. Increasing the number of different σ values from one to eight (and thus also increasing the total number of trainable weights of subsequent 1×1 convolution layers from 40k to 150k) improves the mean Dice from 0.85 ± 0.11 to 0.95 ± 0.04. Particular interesting is the decreased standard deviation which implies a gain in robustness with respect to the variability between shapes. For the second experiment the number of mkdCNN Layers was set to 1, 2, 4 and 8, respectively. With an increased number of layers the size of the feature maps was reduced in order to keep the number of free parameters approximately the same for each configuration. Thus, the performance gain is introduced through a deeper mkdCNN architecture and not attributed to an increased capacity of the network. A difference in Dice overlap is especially recognizable between a one-layer and a two-layer mkdCNN. Another parameter that is not directly connected to the mkdCNN architecture but has a notable effect on the segmentation outcome is the number of nearest neighbors k for the creation of the graph

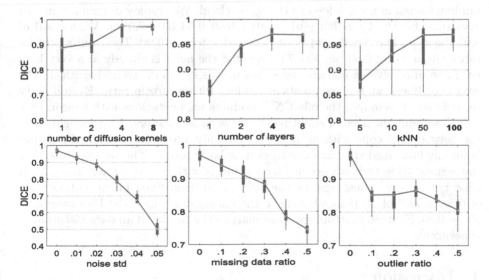

Fig. 6. Body parts segmentation results on the FAUST test set studying different parameter settings and data disturbances. Default configuration parameters are highlighted in bold.

Laplacian from a given point cloud. For the mkdCNN it seems to be an advantage to be build on top of a graph with many locally highly interconnected nodes. The mean Dice coefficient increases from 0.88 ± 0.04 ($k = 5$) to 0.95 ± 0.04 ($k = 100$).

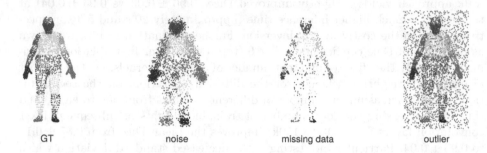

GT   noise   missing data   outlier

Fig. 7. Examples of our different data disturbance experiments. In this Figure Gaussian noise with a standard deviation of 0.03 is added to the ground truth points. The ratio for missing data points as well as added outliers is 0.3.

Robustness Tests Results. A desirable property of a point cloud processing network is robustness against any disturbances of the input data. In a number of experiments we investigate the effect of different data disturbances on the segmentation results. Network parameters were not adapted for the robustness experiments. Figure 7 depicts the impact of the studied point perturbations on an exemplary ground truth point cloud. Robustness against noise is tested with random Gaussian noise added to the input cloud. We employ different standard deviations for the Gaussian (std = $\{0.01, 0.02, 0.03, 0.04, 0.05\}$). With a std of 0.02 the mean Dice coefficient is still approximately at 0.90. The results deteriorates with a std of 0.03 but Fig. 7 shows that the noise is already at a very high level and unresolvable ambiguities exists in this synthetic ground truth. In the next experiment we remove points at random with a certain ratio. Even if every second point is removed the mkdCNN produces segmentations with a mean Dice of 0.75 without the need of adapting the network parameters. To investigate how the network can cope with outliers we randomly add points within the shapes bounding box. Added points are labeled as background. The results show that the segmentation task has become more difficult with the additional background class but is very robust against the ratio of outliers. Even for an outlier ratio of 0.5, i.e. half of all points belong to the background class, the Dice overlap is above 0.80. Figure 6 (bottom row) summarizes the results of all data disturbance experiments.

4   Discussion

Overall the results for both tasks are very promising and demonstrate a substantial improvement over both hand-crafted spectral features and graph convolution approaches. Especially the proposed use of multiple kernels and the consistent employment of mkdCNN layers in a multi-layer fashion helped to decrease error rates for Dice coefficients (i.e. 1–Dice) in our investigated segmentation task by 66% when using eight instead of a single diffusion kernel and by 52% when increasing the depth from one to four layers. This is a significant improvement to the simple diffusion CNN in the work of [1], which is related to our mkdCNN in a configuration with only one kernel and a single layer. Despite using only topology-invariant and isotropic kernels, the learned non-linear combination in our proposed multi-kernel network help to create expressive and highly discriminative filters that enable accurate graph node classification.

When visually inspecting the point descriptor similarity in Fig. 3 it appears that the learned 16-dimensional feature vectors do not differentiate well between symmetric structures (e.g. left and right shoulder). However, the semantic labeling tasks demonstrated that the subtle global differences in the human pose are sufficient to correctly label and distinguish between the right and left half of the body. For some rare cases the evident errors are indeed the inconsistent assignment of points to the correct side of the body (see Fig. 5 top row, third and fourth column).

5 Conclusion

We have presented a new, simple architecture for descriptor learning and semantic segmentation on point clouds. By decoupling the graph propagation and feature learning step the mkdCNN overcomes the limitations of topology dependent approaches. Using the Laplacian and its approximation enables an efficient implementation of the diffusion of feature maps defined on sparse nodes that is transferable to different graphs and we showed that by providing multiple different kernels stronger features can be learned in each subsequent Layer. For the task of descriptor learning on point clouds from the FAUST dataset the mkd-CNN (without any input features) shows better performance than a number of other spectral descriptors and learning approaches. Experiments on manually labeled body parts on the point clouds demonstrate the general feasibility of our approach for the task of semantic segmentation, even for highly noisy input (Gaussian noise, missing points, outliers). We validated several choices for our network architecture in ablation experiments and showed that a multi-layer mkdCNN with a high number of diffusion kernels build on top of a locally highly interconnected graph gives the best segmentation results in terms of Dice overlap. Visual inspection of the segmented point clouds expose rare failure cases due to ambiguities in the symmetry of the human body.

6 Outlook

Our mkdCNN framework provides some straightforward potential extensions for further improvements while maintaining its general design and inherent computational efficiency. Until now, we did not consider signals on our input point cloud but features like fast point feature histograms (FPFH) [25], RGB values (acquired with real-world 3D scanners like the Kinect) or spectral features can potentially increase the networks performance.

In this work we investigated the feasibility of the mkdCNN for learning on point clouds. As the diffusion operation is based on the graph Laplacian the network can be easily employed for general graphs. Testing our approach on graph datasets like Cora or PubMed [26] may yield interesting new insights.

An interesting research direction in general is to enable the possibility to not only learn features of a graph but also the connections (edge weights) between nodes and therefore incorporate mkdCNN into graph attention approaches [29].

References

1. Atwood, J., Towsley, D.: Diffusion-convolutional neural networks. In: Advances in Neural Information Processing Systems, pp. 1993–2001 (2016)
2. Aubry, M., Schlickewei, U., Cremers, D.: The wave kernel signature: a quantum mechanical approach to shape analysis. In: 2011 IEEE International Conference on Computer Vision Workshops (ICCV Workshops), pp. 1626–1633. IEEE (2011)
3. Bogo, F., Romero, J., Loper, M., Black, M.J.: FAUST: dataset and evaluation for 3D mesh registration. In: Proceedings of the IEEE Conference on Computer Vision and Pattern Recognition, pp. 3794–3801 (2014)
4. Boscaini, D., Masci, J., Melzi, S., Bronstein, M.M., Castellani, U., Vandergheynst, P.: Learning class-specific descriptors for deformable shapes using localized spectral convolutional networks. In: Computer Graphics Forum, vol. 34, pp. 13–23. Wiley Online Library (2015)
5. Boscaini, D., Masci, J., Rodolà, E., Bronstein, M.: Learning shape correspondence with anisotropic convolutional neural networks. In: Advances in Neural Information Processing Systems, pp. 3189–3197 (2016)
6. Bronstein, M.M., Bruna, J., LeCun, Y., Szlam, A., Vandergheynst, P.: Geometric deep learning: going beyond euclidean data. IEEE Signal Process. Mag. **34**(4), 18–42 (2017)
7. Bruna, J., Zaremba, W., Szlam, A., Lecun, Y.: Spectral networks and locally connected networks on graphs. In: International Conference on Learning Representations (ICLR 2014), CBLS, April 2014
8. Calonder, M., Lepetit, V., Strecha, C., Fua, P.: BRIEF: binary robust independent elementary features. In: Daniilidis, K., Maragos, P., Paragios, N. (eds.) ECCV 2010. LNCS, vol. 6314, pp. 778–792. Springer, Heidelberg (2010). https://doi.org/10.1007/978-3-642-15561-1_56
9. Chung, F.R., Graham, F.C.: Spectral Graph Theory. No. 92, American Mathematical Society (1997)
10. Desbrun, M., Meyer, M., Schröder, P., Barr, A.H.: Implicit fairing of irregular meshes using diffusion and curvature flow. In: Proceedings of the 26th Annual Conference on Computer Graphics and Interactive Techniques, pp. 317–324. ACM Press/Addison-Wesley Publishing Co. (1999)
11. Henaff, M., Bruna, J., LeCun, Y.: Deep convolutional networks on graph-structured data. arXiv preprint arXiv:1506.05163 (2015)
12. Kim, V.G., Lipman, Y., Funkhouser, T.: Blended intrinsic maps. In: ACM Transactions on Graphics (TOG), vol. 30, p. 79. ACM (2011)

13. Kingma, D.P., Ba, J.L.: Adam: A method for stochastic optimization. In: Proceedings of the 3rd International Conference on Learning Representations (2014)
14. Kipf, T.N., Welling, M.: Semi-supervised classification with graph convolutional networks. arXiv preprint arXiv:1609.02907 (2016)
15. Kleiman, Y., Ovsjanikov, M.: Robust structure-based shape correspondence. In: Computer Graphics Forum. Wiley Online Library (2018)
16. Krähenbühl, P., Koltun, V.: Efficient inference in fully connected CRFs with Gaussian edge potentials. In: Advances in neural information processing systems, pp. 109–117 (2011)
17. Litman, R., Bronstein, A.M.: Learning spectral descriptors for deformable shape correspondence. IEEE Trans. Pattern Anal. Mach. Intell. **36**(1), 171–180 (2014)
18. Masci, J., Boscaini, D., Bronstein, M., Vandergheynst, P.: Geodesic convolutional neural networks on Riemannian manifolds. In: Proceedings of the IEEE International Conference on Computer Vision Workshops, pp. 37–45 (2015)
19. Maturana, D., Scherer, S.: VoxNet: A 3D convolutional neural network for real-time object recognition. In: 2015 IEEE/RSJ International Conference on Intelligent Robots and Systems (IROS), pp. 922–928. IEEE (2015)
20. Monti, F., Boscaini, D., Masci, J., Rodola, E., Svoboda, J., Bronstein, M.M.: Geometric deep learning on graphs and manifolds using mixture model CNNs. In: Proceedings of the CVPR, vol. 1, p. 3 (2017)
21. Paszke, A., et al.: Automatic differentiation in PyTorch. In: NIPS-W (2017)
22. Qi, C.R., Su, H., Mo, K., Guibas, L.J.: PointNet: Deep learning on point sets for 3D classification and segmentation. In: Proceedings of the Computer Vision and Pattern Recognition (CVPR), vol. 1(2), p. 4. IEEE (2017)
23. Qi, C.R., Yi, L., Su, H., Guibas, L.J.: PointNet++: deep hierarchical feature learning on point sets in a metric space. In: Advances in Neural Information Processing Systems, pp. 5099–5108 (2017)
24. Ren, S., He, K., Girshick, R., Sun, J.: Faster R-CNN: towards real-time object detection with region proposal networks. In: Advances in Neural Information Processing Systems, pp. 91–99 (2015)
25. Rusu, R.B., Blodow, N., Beetz, M.: Fast point feature histograms (FPFH) for 3D registration. In: 2009 IEEE International Conference on Robotics and Automation, ICRA 2009, pp. 3212–3217. Citeseer (2009)
26. Sen, P., Namata, G., Bilgic, M., Getoor, L., Galligher, B., Eliassi-Rad, T.: Collective classification in network data. AI Mag. **29**(3), 93 (2008)
27. Su, H., Maji, S., Kalogerakis, E., Learned-Miller, E.: Multi-view convolutional neural networks for 3D shape recognition. In: Proceedings of the IEEE International Conference on Computer Vision, pp. 945–953 (2015)
28. Sun, J., Ovsjanikov, M., Guibas, L.: A concise and provably informative multiscale signature based on heat diffusion. In: Computer Graphics Forum, vol. 28, pp. 1383–1392. Wiley Online Library (2009)
29. Velickovic, P., et al.: Graph attention networks. arXiv preprint arXiv:1710.10903 1.2 (2017)

Attaining Human-Level Performance with Atlas Location Autocontext for Anatomical Landmark Detection in 3D CT Data

Alison Q. O'Neil[1(✉)], Antanas Kascenas[1], Joseph Henry[1], Daniel Wyeth[1], Matthew Shepherd[1], Erin Beveridge[1], Lauren Clunie[1], Carrie Sansom[1], Evelina Šeduikytė[1], Keith Muir[2], and Ian Poole[1]

[1] Canon Medical Research Europe, Edinburgh EH6 5NP, UK
alison.oneil@eu.medical.canon
[2] Queen Elizabeth University Hospital, University of Glasgow,
Glasgow G51 4TF, UK

Abstract. We present an efficient neural network method for locating anatomical landmarks in 3D medical CT scans, using atlas location autocontext in order to learn long-range spatial context. Location predictions are made by regression to Gaussian heatmaps, one heatmap per landmark. This system allows patchwise application of a shallow network, thus enabling multiple volumetric heatmaps to be predicted concurrently without prohibitive GPU memory requirements. Further, the system allows inter-landmark spatial relationships to be exploited using a simple overdetermined affine mapping that is robust to detection failures and occlusion or partial views. Evaluation is performed for 22 landmarks defined on a range of structures in head CT scans. Models are trained and validated on 201 scans. Over the final test set of 20 scans which was independently annotated by 2 human annotators, the neural network reaches an accuracy which matches the annotator variability, with similar human and machine patterns of variability across landmark classes.

1 Introduction

By "anatomical landmark detection", we refer to the task of detecting and localising points in the human body which can be uniquely defined in terms of the anatomical landscape, for instance *superior aspect of right eye globe* or *base of pituitary gland*. Landmark identification is an important enabling technology, providing semantic information that can be used to initialise or aid other medical image analysis algorithms, such as volume registration [12,14,33,35], organ segmentation [2,16,17,22], vessel tracking [29], computer aided detection of pathology [24,40], treatment planning [23], and therapy assessment [7].

Taking a machine learning approach to automated detection enables the heterogeneity of appearance of each landmark to be conveniently represented. Fully

© Springer Nature Switzerland AG 2019
L. Leal-Taixé and S. Roth (Eds.): ECCV 2018 Workshops, LNCS 11131, pp. 470–484, 2019.
https://doi.org/10.1007/978-3-030-11015-4_34

convolutional neural networks (FCNs) are particularly well suited to this task, since whole volumes may be efficiently parsed to detect and localise multiple landmark points concurrently using a learned, shared feature representation.

For the purposes of prediction, the concept of a landmark may be modelled in different ways. An intuitive method would be to regress the positions of the landmarks. This can be done by training the network to make voxelwise predictions of the Euclidean offsets of all landmarks, as in [9,34], then using a scheme such as Hough regression to combine the votes. Offset regression carries a heavy learning burden, since the network must learn to recognise every voxel in a scan, or at least sufficient voxels to enable voting by agreement, and make precise, subtly differing long-range spatial predictions, mapping appearance features to distance measures in the process (i.e. "Where am I relative to each landmark of interest?"). An alternative, more lightweight method is the heatmap regression technique of Payer et al. [31] in which the network is trained to predict the presence of Gaussian heat spots centred at the landmark locations; this is mathematically equivalent to learning a nonlinear measure of the Euclidean landmark offset *magnitude* and is a simpler learning task much more akin to straightforward appearance matching (i.e. "How much do I look like each landmark of interest?").

An important element of the landmark detection problem is how to incorporate long-range spatial context, since points in different parts of the body may have similar appearance and thus be confounded. In [31], the initial appearance-based CNN is followed by a "spatial configuration unit" in which each landmark predicts the location of every other landmark by learning the relative Euclidean offset. This is a reasonable approach for the featured problem of hand X-Ray images, however it would not scale well to body parts and scan protocols in which the orientation, scale and acquisition region are variable. Other methods of capturing global context include U-Net [36] (or the similar V-Net [26]), dual-pathway approaches [8,19], dual networks [25], iterative cascaded networks [37], and the reinforcement learning method of Ghesu et al. [11]. These methods describe various mechanisms for learning both local and long-range information. The U-Net and dual-pathway approaches are methods of combining information at different resolutions in a single end-to-end trained network, whilst the dual network approach delegates the learning of global and local context to different networks. The approach of Toshev and Szegedy [37] is similar to Tu and Bai's idea of autocontext [38], in which the network predictions are iteratively fed to subsequent networks along with the image data such that context is gradually learnt, or gathered, into the network model. Finally, Ghesu et al. 's reinforcement learning approach involves the navigation of multiple agents through a scan volume (from different starting points) until they converge on the landmark position. Thus, agents explicitly train to be spatially aware. A drawback of this approach is its lack of scalability and the potential redundancy since each landmark requires a separate model to be trained.

This paper builds on the work of O'Neil et al. [28,30] in which Tu and Bai's idea of autocontext [38] (iteratively feeding the probabilistic output of a model to a subsequent model) was modified to *atlas location* autocontext (iteratively feeding the coordinate in atlas space, according to the output of a model, to a subsequent model). In these previous works, a decision forest was used. In this paper we show that the decision forest can be replaced by a shallow fully convolutional neural network, which outperforms the decision forest method, and attains human-level performance. Since the model is shallow, this system is memory and time efficient. Memory efficiency is particularly important when taking a unified approach for problems with large 3D inputs and many output classes (many landmarks), requiring many kernels throughout the network, including in the final layers.

2   Method

2.1   Landmark Detection System

Atlas Location Autocontext. The landmark detection system consists of a cascade of two models, with the output of the first providing spatial information to the second in the form of estimated x, y and z atlas space coordinates. The second detector can then be trained not only on image intensity features but also on approximate spatial features; this transmission of learned contextual information is what we term atlas location autocontext. The two models have identical architectures, except that the first has 1 input (image) and the second has 4 inputs (image + atlas space coordinates). We choose to train the first model with data at lower resolution (4 mm per voxel) and the second at higher resolution (2 mm per voxel) in order to emphasise learning of spatial context in pass 0, and learning of local appearance in pass 1. See Fig. 1 for illustration.

Coordinates are determined in this paper by affine alignment of the first model's predicted landmark locations to a landmark atlas, using *iterative weighted least squares fitting*. The least squares fit is that which minimises the sum of the squared distances between the atlas landmarks and the mapped detected landmarks. Since the detected landmarks will sometimes be erroneous or innaccurate — hence the need for a second model! — we weight distances by their detection *certainty* values (see Sect. 2.2) to prioritise fitting of the more confident detections, and then we do iterative refinement. Iterative refinement involves removing landmarks one at a time i.e. dropping the landmark with the largest mapping error, and subsequently recomputing the mapping, until all remaining (mapped) detected landmarks are within a distance d_{Atlas} of the corresponding atlas landmarks. In this way a subset of landmark predictions is discovered with a plausible spatial configuration. The value for d_{Atlas} was chosen by parameter sweep to minimise the average mapping error across the training scan results.

Direct Atlas Correction. For additional robustness, we directly leverage the affine atlas mapping to correct outliers, by mapping the atlas landmarks back to the volume and adjusting each landmark's predicted location to be the voxel

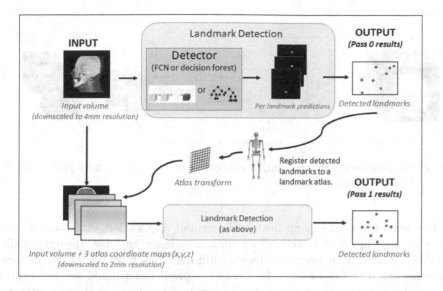

Fig. 1. Landmark detection system using atlas location autocontext

with maximum certainty within a distance d_{Volume} of its mapped atlas counterpart. In other words, we generate spherical regions of interest (ROIs) with radius d_{Volume}, within which the detections must lie. This allows correction of conspicuous outliers and on its own could perhaps be considered a cheap form of "autocontext". For this step we select a generous threshold of $d_{Volume} = 28$ mm.

2.2 Proposed FCN

Model Architecture. The model has a straightforward architecture (see Fig. 2), with 6 layers of $3 \times 3 \times 3$ kernels, where there are 12 kernels in the first layer and the number of kernels doubles in every subsequent layer. The model has 2,661,166 parameters in total. All convolutions are performed using "valid mode" (i.e. the input shrinks at each convolution) and use ReLU activation functions except for the final regression layer which has a linear activation.

Data Pre-processing. Voxel intensities were normalised by first rescaling the HU intensities by 3×10^{-3} since this puts the soft tissue values in the typical $[-1, 1]$ range, and then truncating values to fit the range $[-3, 3]$ (i.e. [-1000HU, 1000HU]). In order to detect landmarks at the edge of the scan, each scan was dilated by the size of the margin required by the network, using pixels with a value equivalent to air (as opposed to zero padding). During training, the data was augmented by left-right reflection of the volume with corresponding switching of the left and right side landmarks. To introduce robustness to acquisition region, scans were randomly cropped with a margin of up to 50 mm. In practice this was done by uniformly sampled translations in the range $+/-50$ mm in x, y and z.

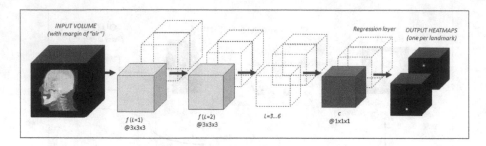

Fig. 2. Our proposed fully convolution network. The number of filters $f(L) = a \times 2^L$, for $a = 12$ and layers $L = 0, 1, 2, ...5$.

Patches were used during both training and application. At training time, this was done in order to control for data imbalance and also (pragmatically) to allow samples from many volumes within each batch without large memory requirements. Patches of $15 \times 15 \times 15$ (i.e. predictions made for the central $3 \times 3 \times 3$ voxels plus the 6-voxel margin required by the model) were extracted at the landmark positions as well as randomly from the remainder of the volume at a ratio of 1:5. At application time, patches of $30 \times 30 \times 30$ (i.e. $42 \times 42 \times 42$ including margin) were tiled to make piecewise predictions covering the whole volume.

Inference. To make the predictions, we use a modified version of the heatmap regression proposed by Pfister *et al.* [32] and applied previously to landmark detection in medical scans by Payer *et al.* [31]. In this scheme each landmark has a separate volumetric output containing a Gaussian heat spot centred at the landmark position. More formally, the temperature t_i of the ith heatmap that we regress against is determined according to distance of the voxel v from the landmark position p_i for landmark i, a standard deviation σ (chosen to be 1 voxel), and a constant k denoting the Gaussian height:

$$t_i = k e^{-\frac{(v-p_i)^2}{2\sigma^2}} \tag{1}$$

We used mean squared error as the loss function and found empirically that the imbalance between background and proximal landmark voxels meant large heights were required for the Gaussian in order to enable training to start (i.e. $k = 1 \times 10^3$ at 4 mm resolution, and $k = 1 \times 10^6$ at 2 mm resolution). This mechanism was chosen for convenience; note that we could have equivalently initialised the network with small kernel weight initialisations, or experimented with weighting of the landmark voxels in the loss function. At prediction time, the predicted position for each landmark is chosen to be simply the output voxel with maximum value t. We divide t by k such that it lies in the range $[0, 1]$, and we term this the landmark *certainty*.

Training Procedure. For each model, kernel weights were initialised using normalised He initialisation [13]. Optimisation of the network was performed using backpropagation with Adam [20], with learning rate $= 0.001$, $\beta_1 = 0.9$ and $\beta_2 = 0.999$. Batches of 32 patches were used, and training was run for 50 epochs (first pass) and 200 epochs (second pass). The weights were retained from the epoch which achieved lowest error on the validation data.

2.3 Benchmarking: Decision Forest Algorithm

As our baseline for comparison, we follow the decision forest approach of Dabbah et al. [4] for which we have a mature C++ implementation. Until the recent popular adoption of CNN solutions, decision forests and their variants were the gold standard for the task of anatomical landmark detection [5,10,12,18,27,27,39,40]. In brief, a decision forest is trained to perform voxelwise classification across $n + 1$ classes, where there are n landmarks and 1 background class. Voxels v_i within 1.5 voxels of the each landmark location p_i are considered to be landmark samples, and are assigned a weight w during training according to Gaussian distribution i.e.:

$$w = ke^{-\frac{(v_i - p_i)^2}{2\sigma^2}} \tag{2}$$

where $k - 1$ and $\sigma = 0.75$ voxels. Voxels outside of these spheres are considered to be background samples. The features for each voxel are the Hounsfield Unit (HU) values of the voxels in the local 100^3 mm neighbourhood (note that scan intensities are not normalised as was done for the FCN), with each tree being given a random sample of 2500 features (random subspace sampling [15]). We trained 100 trees, sampling from $n = 40$ randomly chosen training scans per tree. We further tried using HOG [6] features alongside the intensity features, since these had previously been shown to give improvement over using intensity features alone [28] (note that we used signed rather than unsigned orientations, with no magnitude weighting, as in [28]). In this case we randomly selected 1250 intensity features and 1250 HOG features per tree. Histograms were computed over randomly generated box regions of up to 48 mm in each dimension.

At application time, the novel volume is scanned, and for each landmark, the voxel is selected which has the highest probability of belonging to that landmark class.

3 Experiments

3.1 Data

We demonstrate our method on CT head scan volumes. The data is split into 170 scans for training, 31 scans for validation, and a final (tested once) test set of 20 scans. The data was acquired from a range of scanners (Canon, Siemens, G.E., Philips), scan protocols (both with and without injected arterial contrast), and with a range of resolutions and slice thicknesses. There are approximately equal splits between male and female subjects. Many contain pathology, inclusive of haemorrhage, tumours and age-related change.

A set of 22 landmarks were defined in the head (see Fig. 3). Scan protocols were designed by an in-house clinical analyst (E.B.) with postgraduate-level expertise in anatomy. Three additional observers with education in biological sciences were trained up to perform the annotation. The test set was annotated by two observers, one of whom (observer A, L.C.) has also annotated a large number of the training scans, the second of whom (observer B, E.S.) was independent of the training data. In many scans, only a subset of the landmarks is visible. This may be either because the landmark lies outside of the scan acquisition region, or because the landmark is obscured for some reason, for instance low resolution data, the presence of pathology or the absence of contrast. In the latter case, it is marked as "uncertain" in the ground truth; the 6 landmarks which were marked as uncertain by at least one observer are not included in our metrics.

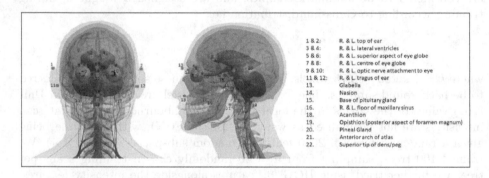

1 & 2:	R. & L. top of ear
3 & 4:	R. & L. lateral ventricles
5 & 6:	R. & L. superior aspect of eye globe
7 & 8:	R. & L. centre of eye globe
9 & 10:	R. & L. optic nerve attachment to eye
11 & 12:	R. & L. tragus of ear
13.	Glabella
14.	Nasion
15.	Base of pituitary gland
16.	R. & L. floor of maxillary sinus
18.	Acanthion
19.	Opisthion (posterior aspect of foramen magnum)
20.	Pineal Gland
21.	Anterior arch of atlas
22.	Superior tip of dens/peg

Fig. 3. Schematic of head landmarks

3.2   Implementation

The FCN was implemented in Python using the Keras library [3], built on top of the Tensorflow library [1]. Parameter exploration was performed on p2.xlarge instances on AWS; these instances have one NVIDIA K80 GPU (2496 cores, 12 GB VRAM). On a computer with an NVIDIA GTX Titan X, run times are of the order of 1 s for the first pass and 2 s for the second (excluding data loading and downscaling, and model loading from disk). In the second pass, we reduce the run time by evaluating only parts of the volume containing the atlas-mapped spherical landmark ROIs identified in the first pass.

The decision forest is implemented in C++. Experiments were run on a computer with two Intel Xeon E5645 (2.4 GHz) processors. Run times are of the order of 1 s for the first pass and 0.5 s for the second pass (excluding data loading and downscaling, and classifier loading from disk). There are a number of optimisations, as described in [4], for instance evaluating only as many trees as required until confident about the prediction, and performing coarse-to-fine scanning of the volume within a pass (i.e. evaluate every second voxel in the volume before evaluating all voxels in the neighbourhood of the maximum-probability landmark positions).

Table 1. Landmark localisation disagreement. The mean, median and max error metrics are computed over for each scan separately and then the mean value is taken across the 20 scans and provided below. Additionally we show the percentage (%) of landmarks with an error greater than 4 mm, computed over all 417 landmarks in the 20 scans. *DF* = Decision Forest with intensity features, *DF (+HOG)* = Decision Forest with intensity + HOG features, *FCN* = proposed fully convolutional network.

Method	Reference							
	Observer A				Observer B			
	Mean	Median	Max	%	Mean	Median	Max	%
Observer A	-	-	-	-	2.20	1.49	9.27	11.0
Observer B	2.20	1.48	9.27	11.0	-	-	-	-
Pass 0 (4 mm)								
DF	4.47	4.03	11.54	50.4	4.58	4.14	11.28	49.2
DF (+HOG)	4.25	3.91	10.07	47.7	4.36	3.92	9.86	46.5
FCN	3.38	2.65	12.20	21.6	3.52	2.71	12.15	23.7
FCN + Atlas Correction	3.03	2.53	10.45	16.1	3.31	2.62	10.89	21.6
Pass 1 (2 mm)								
DF	3.59	2.85	13.73	26.6	3.83	3.02	13.59	27.6
DF (+HOG)	3.30	2.88	**9.77**	24.9	3.47	2.84	**9.69**	26.9
FCN	2.93	1.50	19.98	12.2	3.42	1.84	20.93	17.5
FCN + Atlas Correction	**2.29**	**1.49**	11.41	10.8	**2.77**	**1.78**	12.26	**16.1**
Alternative: Pass 0 (2 mm) + Atlas Correction								
FCN	2.55	1.55	15.08	**10.3**	3.10	1.92	15.38	17.5

3.3   Results

Summary metrics are shown in Table 1 for landmark localisation errors (or disagreements), and some visual results are shown for the FCN in Figs. 4 and 5. The summary metrics show that the FCN outperforms the decision forest methods. The anomalous metric is the mean *max error*, in other words, the mean size of the "worst detected landmark in a scan". This does not appear to improve in the second pass — if anything, the worst error worsens— and the Pass 0 decision forest with HOG features is the best performer. We propose that this occurs because landmarks with atypical appearance (e.g. see the calcified pineal gland example in Fig. 5) are best located by use of spatial context rather than local appearance, hence the efficacy of low resolution HOG features which are aggregated over regions and thus are relatively insensitive to precise changes.

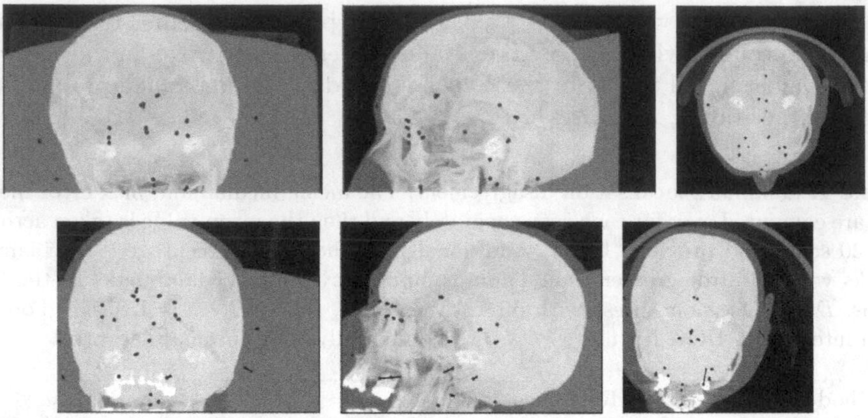

Fig. 4. Coronal, sagittal and axial maximum intensity projections (MIPs) of results for a good case (top) and a poor case (bottom). Green dots = ground truth (observer A), red dots = detected (proposed FCN), and black lines connect corresponding pairs. (Color figure online)

The significance of the improvements of the FCN over the decision forest were verified using a one-tailed paired Student's t-test for the 417 landmark examples, using each observer in turn as the reference, and significance was found to hold for a p-value < 0.01 for all comparisons. However, the results of the FCN model using atlas location autocontext + direct atlas correction were *not* significantly different to those using only the direct atlas correction at 2 mm resolution. It might be that significance could be shown with a larger population of datasets, or for landmarks which vary their relative position more dramatically relative to other structures (e.g. on vessels); in this case the learning could learn the spatial distribution and adapt its localisation to the observed anatomical landscape where explicitly imposed affine constraints could not. What the autocontext system *does* offer is a run time speed-up, since high-resolution processing can be performed selectively, as opposed to over the whole volume (mean run time of approximately 3 s i.e. 1 + 2, as opposed to 5 s for the single-pass system) — however in this case it seems that the atlas channels of the second model have not been conclusively proven to add a benefit.

Regarding human vs. machine performance, the FCN achieves similar mean and median agreement with observer A as the agreement between observers A and B. However, the FCN is less well in agreement with observer B than observer A. There may be two reasons for this. Firstly, the algorithm was trained on annotations from observer A amongst others, so may have learned to mimic the annotation style of observer A. Secondly, since observer A was part of our team for training data annotation, all of her annotations were subject to our selective review process (a percentage of our ground truth observations are reviewed by E.B. for quality control). Therefore mistakes or inconsistencies are more likely

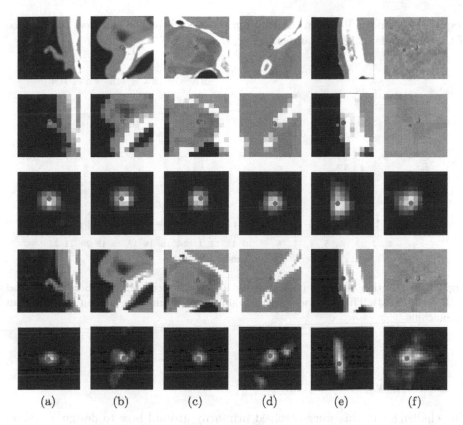

(a)   (b)   (c)   (d)   (e)   (f)

Fig. 5. A few landmark examples: (a) Top of R. ear (b) Acanthion (c) L. optic nerve (d) Opisthion (e) Glabella (f) Pineal gland. The top row shows a comparison of landmark localisations at full resolution, with green and blue denoting observers A and B and red denoting the FCN detected landmark. The next 4 rows show the detected landmark for Pass 0 and Pass 1, at the 4 mm and 2 mm algorithmic operating resolutions respectively, along with MIPs of the FCN heatmaps (black = low certainty and white = high certainty). The direct atlas correction is also used in each pass. Slices are taken at the position of observer A, in the sagittal plane for all but the "Top of R. ear" where a coronal slice is taken. (Color figure online)

to be have been picked up and corrected for observer A (i.e. observer A's ground truth will have some of the characteristics of consensus ground truth).

We further take those errors which are greater than 4 mm, and show the breakdown between observers and between landmarks in Fig. 6. There is a similar pattern to the human vs. human and the human vs. machine disagreement, with most discrepancies arising on surface landmarks (notably 13. = glabella, 3. & 4. = L & R frontal horns of the lateral ventricles). Landmarks on surfaces may be less well defined and inspection of the underlying predictions (see Fig. 5) supports this. Other mistakes by the algorithm are due to landmark appearances less frequently (or never) seen in the training data, such as the calcified appearance of the pineal gland (20.) example in Fig. 5.

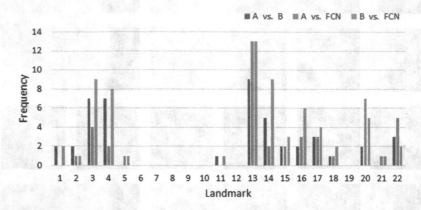

Fig. 6. Distribution of errors (> 4 mm) for all landmarks 1–22 (numbers correspond to those in Fig. 3). The pattern of errors is similar for human vs. human as for human vs. machine.

4   Discussion

The challenges in this work revolved primarily around how to design a system which could detect multiple structures efficiently in a 3D volume. Even with a relatively modest set of 22 landmarks (note that this is just a subset of the hundreds of landmarks that a whole-body system might be expected to learn), the volume of the outputs and the volume of the final layers of the network is large because of the number of classes, the fact that information is generated at the resolution of the data, and the fact that we work with 3D data. This is in contrast to segmentation tasks with a few classes of interest, to which a network such as U-Net might naturally lend itself. Given this requirement, we designed a system that could be both trained and deployed by making patchwise predictions.

It turned out that with our atlas-assisted detection system to enable the learning of spatial context, a fairly straightforward network with a relatively small receptive field gave good results. From the perspective of deployment, a goal was to be robust to "awkward" scan volumes, which might be unusually rotated or cropped, or containing variation due to anatomical or pathological differences. By choosing a model with small receptive field, landmarks are neither reliant nor impacted by spatial context outside of a relatively small neighbourhood. Detection is surprisingly tractable for many landmarks, even with such a limited field of view. Further, so long as we detect sufficient landmarks accurately to compute an accurate affine transform (a minimum of 4 landmarks are required, preferably well spaced i.e. not in a planar arrangement), we can leverage the spatial relationships between landmarks to zone in on landmarks with unusual appearance due to pathology, anatomical or postural variation — albeit without guarantee of precise localisation where pathology has caused an obvious change of appearance. The system also allows mitigation of the time impact of working at higher resolution, by selective evaluation of only the landmark ROIs.

5 Conclusion

Convolutional networks have proven their worth for image recognition tasks in general computer vision tasks [13,21] and in this work, we have shown their efficacy in a medical imaging application, namely the detection of landmarks in head CT volumes. We have benchmarked against a decision forest method (decision forests being the previous gold standard algorithm for this task), for which we have a mature implementation and shown that, given the same system and setup, a neural network significantly outperforms a decision forest, with and without additional feature engineering (i.e. HOG features). Further, we have demonstrated that we are able to attain similar agreement to human observers as that between the human observers, showing accuracy that is approximately equal to a *single* human observer.

By exploiting inter-landmark spatial relationships, we are able to use small CNN models with a small receptive field size, and to apply selectively at high resolution. In fact in this paper, we did not show a significant improvement over the simpler system with direct leveraging of an atlas transform alone (our "atlas correction" step), and this may be enough to correct outliers and achieve good performance, at least for this problem of landmark detection in head scans. Thus, we have trained a system which is nicely scalable — to larger scan volumes and to greater numbers of landmarks — in terms of both GPU memory and run time requirements. The next step is to validate this system on other body parts and other modalities.

Acknowledgements. Many thanks to Queen Elizabeth University Hospital, University of Glasgow, who provided many of the medical scans used for this study, including those shown in the images.

References

1. Abadi, M., et al.: Tensorflow: large-scale machine learning heterogeneous distributed systems. arXiv preprint arXiv:1603.04467 (2016)
2. Chen, C., Xie, W., Franke, J., Grutzner, P.A., Nolte, L.P., Zheng, G.: Automatic X-ray landmark detection and shape segmentation via data-driven joint estimation of image displacements. Med. Image Anal. **18**, 487–499 (2014)
3. Chollet, F.: Keras (2015)
4. Dabbah, M.A., et al.: Detection and location of 127 anatomical landmarks in diverse CT datasets. In: SPIE Medical Imaging, vol. 9034, p. 903415 (2014)

5. Dai, X., Gao, Y., Shen, D.: Online updating of context-aware landmark detectors for prostate localization in daily treatment CT images. Med. Phys. **42**(5), 2594–2606 (2015)

6. Dalal, N., Triggs, B.: Histograms of oriented gradients for human detection. CVPR **1**, 886–893 (2005)

7. Dong, C., Chen, Y.W., Lin, C.L.: Non-rigid registration with constraint of anatomical landmarks for assessment of locoregional therapy. In: IEEE International Conference on Information and Automation (2015)

8. Fan, X., Zheng, K., Lin, Y., Wang, S.: Combining local appearance and holistic view: dual-source deep neural networks for human pose estimation. In: CVPR (2015)

9. Gao, Y., Shen, D.: Context-aware anatomical landmark detection: application to deformable model initialization in prostate CT images. In: Wu, G., Zhang, D., Zhou, L. (eds.) MLMI 2014. LNCS, vol. 8679, pp. 165–173. Springer, Cham (2014). https://doi.org/10.1007/978-3-319-10581-9_21

10. Gao, Y., Shen, D.: Collaborative regression-based anatomical landmark detection. Phys. Med. Biol. **60**(24), 9377–9401 (2016)

11. Ghesu, F.C., Georgescu, B., Grbic, S., Maier, A.K., Hornegger, J., Comaniciu, D.: Robust multi-scale anatomical landmark detection in incomplete 3D-CT data. In: Descoteaux, M., Maier-Hein, L., Franz, A., Jannin, P., Collins, D.L., Duchesne, S. (eds.) MICCAI 2017. LNCS, vol. 10433, pp. 194–202. Springer, Cham (2017). https://doi.org/10.1007/978-3-319-66182-7_23

12. Han, D., Gao, Y., Yaozong, G., Yap, P.T., Shen, D.: Robust anatomical landmark detection with application to MR brain image registration. Comput. Med. Imaging Graph. **46**(3), 277–290 (2015)

13. He, K., Zhang, X., Ren, S., Sun, J.: Delving deep into rectifiers: surpassing human-level performance on imagenet classification. In: ICCV, pp. 1026–1034 (2015)

14. Hellier, P., Barillot, C.: Coupling dense and landmark-based approaches for non-rigid registration. IEEE Trans. Med. Imaging **22**(2), 217–227 (2003)

15. Ho, T.K.: The random subspace method for constructing decision forests. IEEE Trans. Pattern Anal. Mach. Intell. **20**(8), 832–844 (1998). https://ieeexplore.ieee.org/document/709601

16. Ibragimov, B., Likar, B., Pernuš, F., Vrtovec, T.: Shape representation for efficient landmark-based segmentation in 3-D. IEEE Trans. Med. Imaging **33**(4), 861–874 (2014)

17. Ibragimov, B., Likar, B., Pernuš, F., Vrtovec, T.: A game-theoretic framework for landmark-based image segmentation. IEEE Trans. Med. Imaging **31**(9), 1761–1776 (2012)

18. Jimenez-Del-Toro, O., et al.: Cloud-based evaluation of anatomical structure segmentation and landmark detection algorithms: VISCERAL anatomy benchmarks. IEEE Trans. Med. Imaging **35**(11), 2459–2475 (2016)

19. Kamnitsas, K., et al.: Efficient multi-scale CNN with fully connected CRF for accurate brain lesion segmentation. Med. Image Anal. **36**, 61–78 (2017)

20. Kingma, D.P., Ba, J.L.: A method for stochastic optimization. arXiv preprint arXiv:1412.6980 (2014)

21. Krizhevsky, A., Sutskever, I., Hinton, G.E.: Imagenet classification with deep convolutional neural networks. In: Advances in Neural Information Processing Systems, pp. 1097–1105 (2012)
22. Lay, N., Birkbeck, N., Zhang, J., Zhou, S.K.: Rapid multi-organ segmentation using context integration and discriminative models. In: Gee, J.C., Joshi, S., Pohl, K.M., Wells, W.M., Zöllei, L. (eds.) IPMI 2013. LNCS, vol. 7917, pp. 450–462. Springer, Heidelberg (2013). https://doi.org/10.1007/978-3-642-38868-2_38
23. Leavens, C., et al.: Validation of automatic landmark identification for atlas-based segmentation for radiation treatment planning of the head-and-neck region. In: SPIE Medical Imaging, vol. 6914 (2008)
24. Lisowska, A., et al.: Context-aware convolutional neural networks for stroke sign detection in non-contract CT scans. In: Annual Conference on Medical Image Understanding and Analysis, pp. 494–505 (2017)
25. Lu, X., Xu, D., Liu, D.: Robust 3D organ localization with dual learning architectures and fusion. In: Carneiro, G., et al. (eds.) LABELS/DLMIA -2016. LNCS, vol. 10008, pp. 12–20. Springer, Cham (2016). https://doi.org/10.1007/978-3-319-46976-8_2
26. Milletari, F., Navab, N., Ahmadi, S.A.: V-Net: full convolutional neural networks for volumetric medical image segmentation. In: IEEE Fourth International Conference on 3D Vision (3DV), pp. 565–571 (2016)
27. Oktay, O., et al.: Stratified decision forests for accurate anatomical landmark localization. IEEE Trans. Med. Imaging **36**(1), 332–342 (2017)
28. O'Neil, A.: Detection of Anatomical Structures in Medical Datasets. EngD Thesis, September 2016
29. O'Neil, A., Beveridge, E., Houston, G., McCormick, L., Poole, I.: Arterial tree tracking from anatomical landmarks in magnetic resonance angiography scans. In: SPIE Medical Imaging, vol. 9034 (2014)
30. O'Neil, A., Murphy, S., Poole, I.: Anatomical landmark detection in CT data by learned atlas location autocontext. In: MIUA (2015)
31. Payer, C., Štern, D., Bischof, H., Urschler, M.: Regressing heatmaps for multiple landmark localization using CNNs. In: Ourselin, S., Joskowicz, L., Sabuncu, M.R., Unal, G., Wells, W. (eds.) MICCAI 2016. LNCS, vol. 9901, pp. 230 238. Springer, Cham (2016). https://doi.org/10.1007/978-3-319-46723-8_27
32. Pfister, T., Charles, J., Zisserman, A.: Flowing convnets for human pose estimation in videos. In: IEEE ICCV, pp. 1913–1921 (2015)
33. Polzin, T., Rühaak, J., Wernera, R., Handels, H., Modersitzki, J.: Lung registration using automatically detected landmarks. Methods Inf. Med. **53**(4), 250–256 (2014)
34. Riegler, G., Fersti, D., Ruther, M., Bischof, H.: Hough networks for head pose estimation and facial feature localization. In: BMVC (2014)
35. Rohr, K., Stiehl, H.S., Sprengel, R., Buzug, T.M., Weese, J., Kuhn, M.H.: Landmark-based elastic registration using approximating thin-plate splines. IEEE Trans. Med. Imaging **20**(6), 526–534 (2001)
36. Ronneberger, O., Fischer, P., Brox, T.: U-Net: convolutional networks for biomedical image segmentation. In: Navab, N., Hornegger, J., Wells, W.M., Frangi, A.F. (eds.) MICCAI 2015. LNCS, vol. 9351, pp. 234–241. Springer, Cham (2015). https://doi.org/10.1007/978-3-319-24574-4_28
37. Toshev, A., Szegedy, C.: DeepPose: Human pose estimation via deep neural networks. In: CVPR (2014)

38. Tu, Z., Bai, X.: Auto-context and its application to high-level vision tasks and 3D brain segmentation. IEEE Trans. Pattern Anal. Mach. Intell. **32**(10), 1744–1757 (2010)

39. Wang, C.W., et al.: Evaluation and comparison of anatomical landmark detection methods for cephalometric x-ray images: a grand challenge. IEEE Trans. Med. Imaging **34**(9), 1890–1900 (2015)

40. Zhang, J., Gao, Y., Gao, Y., Munsell, B.C., Shen, D.: Detecting anatomical landmarks for fast Alzheimer's disease diagnosis. IEEE Trans. Med. Imaging **35**(12), 2524–2533 (2016)

Deep Fundamental Matrix Estimation Without Correspondences

Omid Poursaeed[1,2](✉), Guandao Yang[1], Aditya Prakash[3], Qiuren Fang[1],
Hanqing Jiang[1], Bharath Hariharan[1], and Serge Belongie[1,2]

[1] Cornell University, Ithaca, USA
op63@cornell.edu
[2] Cornell Tech, New York, USA
[3] Indian Institute of Technology Roorkee, Roorkee, India

Abstract. Estimating fundamental matrices is a classic problem in computer vision. Traditional methods rely heavily on the correctness of estimated key-point correspondences, which can be noisy and unreliable. As a result, it is difficult for these methods to handle image pairs with large occlusion or significantly different camera poses. In this paper, we propose novel neural network architectures to estimate fundamental matrices in an end-to-end manner without relying on point correspondences. New modules and layers are introduced in order to preserve mathematical properties of the fundamental matrix as a homogeneous rank-2 matrix with seven degrees of freedom. We analyze performance of the proposed models using various metrics on the KITTI dataset, and show that they achieve competitive performance with traditional methods without the need for extracting correspondences.

Keywords: Fundamental matrix · Epipolar geometry ·
Deep learning · Stereo

The Fundamental matrix (F-matrix) contains rich information relating two stereo images. The ability to estimate fundamental matrices is essential for many computer vision applications such as camera calibration and localization, image rectification, depth estimation and 3D reconstruction. The current approach to this problem is based on detecting and matching local feature points, and using the obtained correspondences to compute the fundamental matrix by solving an optimization problem about the epipolar constraints [16,27]. The performance of such methods is highly dependent on the accuracy of the local feature matches, which are based on algorithms such as SIFT [28]. However, these methods are not always reliable, especially when there is occlusion, large translation or rotation between images of the scene.

In this paper, we propose end-to-end trainable convolutional neural networks for F-matrix estimation that do not rely on key-point correspondences. The main

---

O. Poursaeed, G. Yang and A. Prakash—Equal contribution.

© Springer Nature Switzerland AG 2019
L. Leal-Taixé and S. Roth (Eds.): ECCV 2018 Workshops, LNCS 11131, pp. 485–497, 2019.
https://doi.org/10.1007/978-3-030-11015-4_35

challenge of directly regressing the entries of the F-matrix is to preserve its mathematical properties as a homogeneous rank-2 matrix with seven degrees of freedom. We propose a reconstruction module and a normalization layer (Sect. 2.2) to address this challenge. We demonstrate that by using these layers, we can accurately estimate the fundamental matrix, while a simple regression approach does not yield good results. Our detailed network architectures are presented in Sect. 2. Empirical experiments are performed on the KITTI dataset [13] in Sect. 3. The results indicate that we can achieve competitive results with traditional methods without relying on correspondences.

1   Background and Related Work

1.1   Fundamental Matrix and Epipolar Geometry

When two cameras view the same 3D scene from different viewpoints, geometric relations among the 3D points and their projections onto the 2D plane lead to constraints on the image points. This intrinsic projective geometry is referred to as the epipolar geometry, and is encapsulated by the fundamental matrix $\mathbf{F}$. This matrix only depends on the cameras' internal parameters and their relative pose, and can be computed as:

$$\mathbf{F} = \mathbf{K_2}^{-T}[\mathbf{t}]_{\times}\mathbf{R}\mathbf{K_1}^{-1} \tag{1}$$

where $\mathbf{K_1}$ and $\mathbf{K_2}$ represent camera intrinsics, and $\mathbf{R}$ and $[\mathbf{t}]_{\times}$ are the relative camera rotation and translation respectively [16]. More specifically:

$$\mathbf{K}_i = \begin{bmatrix} f_i^{-1} & 0 & c_x \\ 0 & f_i^{-1} & c_y \\ 0 & 0 & 1 \end{bmatrix} \tag{2}$$

$$\mathbf{t}_{\times} = \begin{bmatrix} 0 & -t_z & t_y \\ t_z & 0 & -t_x \\ -t_y & t_x & 0 \end{bmatrix} \tag{3}$$

$$\mathbf{R} = \mathbf{R_x}(r_x)\mathbf{R_y}(r_y)\mathbf{R_z}(r_z) \tag{4}$$

in which $(c_x, c_y)^T$ is the principal point of the camera, f_i is the focal length of camera $i = 1, 2$, and t_x, t_y and t_z are the relative displacements along the x, y and z axes respectively. $\mathbf{R}$ is the rotation matrix which can be decomposed into rotations along x, y and z axes. We assume that the principal point is in the middle of the image plane.

While the fundamental matrix is independent of the scene structure, it can be computed from correspondences of projected scene points alone, without requiring knowledge of the cameras' internal parameters or relative pose. If p and q are matching points in two stereo images, the fundamental matrix $\mathbf{F}$ satisfies the equation:

$$q^T\mathbf{F}p = 0 \tag{5}$$

Writing $p = (x, y, 1)^T$ and $q = (x', y', 1)^T$ and $\mathbf{F} = [f_{ij}]$, Eq. 5 can be written as:

$$x'xf_{11} + x'yf_{12} + x'f_{13} + y'xf_{21} + y'yf_{22} + y'f_{23} + xf_{31} + yf_{32} + f_{33} = 0. \quad (6)$$

Let $\mathbf{f}$ represent the 9-vector made up of the entries of $\mathbf{F}$. Then Eq. 6 can be written as:

$$(x'x, x'y, x', y'x, y'y, y', x, y, 1)\mathbf{f} = 0 \quad (7)$$

A set of linear equations can be obtained from n point correspondences:

$$\mathbf{Af} = \begin{bmatrix} x'_1x_1 & x'_1y_1 & x'_1 & y'_1x_1 & y'_1y_1 & y'_1 & x_1 & y_1 & 1 \\ \vdots & \vdots & \vdots & \vdots & \vdots & \vdots & \vdots & \vdots & \vdots \\ x'_nx_n & x'_ny_n & x'_n & y'_nx_n & y'_ny_n & y'_n & x_n & y_n & 1 \end{bmatrix} \mathbf{f} = 0 \quad (8)$$

Various methods have been proposed for estimating fundamental matrices based on Eq. 8. The simplest method is the eight-point algorithm which was proposed by Longuet-Higgins [27]. Using (at least) 8 point correspondences, it computes a (least-squares) solution to Eq. 8. It enforces the rank-2 constraint using Singular Value Decomposition (SVD), and finds a matrix with the minimum Frobenius distance to the computed (rank-3) solution. Hartley [17] proposed a normalized version of the eight-point algorithm which achieves improved results and better stability. The algorithm involves translation and scaling of the points in the image before formulating the linear Eq. 8.

The Algebraic Minimization algorithm uses a different procedure for enforcing the rank-2 constraint. It tries to minimize the algebraic error $\mathbf{A}\|\mathbf{f}\|$ subject to $\|\mathbf{f}\| = 1$. It uses the fact that we can write the singular fundamental matrix as $\mathbf{F} = \mathbf{M}[e]_\times$ where $\mathbf{M}$ is a non-singular matrix and $[e]_\times$ is a skew-symmetric matrix with e corresponding to the epipole in the first image. This equation can be written as $\mathbf{f} = E\mathbf{m}$, where $\mathbf{f}$ and $\mathbf{m}$ are vectors comprised of entries of $\mathbf{F}$ and $\mathbf{M}$, and E is a 9×9 matrix comprised of elements of $[e]_\times$. Then the minimization problem becomes:

$$\text{minimize } \|\mathbf{A}E\mathbf{m}\| \text{ subject to } \|E\mathbf{m}\| = 1 \quad (9)$$

To solve this optimization problem, we can start from an initial estimate of $\mathbf{F}$ and set e as the generator of the right null space of $\mathbf{F}$. Then we can iteratively update e and $\mathbf{F}$ to minimize the algebraic error. More details are given in [16].

The Gold Standard geometric algorithm assumes that the noise in image point measurements obeys a Gaussian distribution. It tries to find the Maximum Likelihood estimate of the fundamental matrix which minimizes the geometric distance

$$\sum_i d(p_i, \hat{p}_i)^2 + d(q_i, \hat{q}_i)^2 \quad (10)$$

in which p_i and q_i are true correspondences satisfying Eq. 5, and $\hat{p}_i$ and $\hat{q}_i$ are the estimated correspondences.

Another algorithm uses RANSAC [11] to compute the fundamental matrix. It computes interest points in each image, and finds correspondences based on proximity and similarity of their intensity neighborhood. In each iteration, it randomly samples 7 correspondences and computes the F-matrix based on them. It then calculates the re-projection error for each correspondence, and counts the number of inliers for which the error is less than a specified threshold. After sufficient number of iterations, it chooses the F-matrix with the largest number of inliers. A generalization of RANSAC is MLESAC [40], which adopts the same sampling strategy as RANSAC to generate putative solutions, but chooses the solution that maximizes the likelihood rather than just the number of inliers. MAPSAC [39] (Maximum A Posteriori SAmple Consensus) improves MLESAC by being more robust against noise and outliers including Bayesian probabilities in minimization. A global search genetic algorithm combined with a local search hill climbing algorithm is proposed in [45] to optimize MAPSAC algorithm for estimating fundamental matrices. [42] proposes an algorithm to cope with the problem of fundamental matrix estimation for binocular vision system used in wild field. It first acquires the edge points using Canny edge detector, and then gets the pre-matched points by the GMM-based point set registration algorithm. It then computes the fundamental matrix using the RANSAC algorithm. [10] proposes to use adaptive penalty methods for valid estimation of Essential matrices as a product of translation and rotation matrices. A new technique for calculating the fundamental matrix combined with feature lines is introduced in [49]. The interested reader is referred to [1] for a survey of various methods for estimating the F-matrix.

1.2   Deep Learning for Multi-view Geometry

Deep neural networks have achieved state-of-the-art performance on tasks such as image recognition [18,24,37,38], semantic segmentation [3,26,43,47], object detection [14,34,35], scene understanding [23,32,48] and generative modeling [15,19,31,33,44] in the last few years. Recently, there has been a surge of interest in using deep learning for classic geometric problems in Computer Vision. A method for estimating relative camera pose using convolutional neural networks is presented in [29]. It uses a simple convolutional network with spatial pyramid pooling and fully connected layers to compute the relative rotation and translation of the camera. An approach for camera re-localization is presented in [25] which localizes a given query image by using a convolutional neural network for first retrieving similar database images and then predicting the relative pose between the query and the database images with known poses. The camera location for the query image is obtained via triangulation from two relative translation estimates using a RANSAC-based approach. [41] uses a deep convolutional neural network to directly estimate the focal length of the camera using only raw pixel intensities as input features. [2] proposes two strategies for differentiating the RANSAC algorithm: using a soft argmax operator, and probabilistic selection. [12] leverages deep neural networks for 6-DOF tracking of rigid objects.

[5] presents a deep convolutional neural network for estimating the relative homography between a pair of images. A more complicated algorithm is proposed

in [8] which contains a hierarchy of twin convolutional regression networks to estimate the homography between a pair of images. [7] introduces two deep convolutional neural networks, MagicPoint and MagicWarp. MagicPoint extracts salient 2D points from a single image. MagicWarp operates on pairs of point images (outputs of MagicPoint), and estimates the homography that relates the inputs. [30] proposes an unsupervised learning algorithm that trains a deep convolutional neural network to estimate planar homographies. A self-supervised framework for training interest point detectors and descriptors is presented in [6]. A convolutional neural network architecture for geometric matching is proposed in [36]. It uses feature extraction networks with shared weights and a matching network which matches the descriptors. The output of the matching network is passed through a regression network which outputs the parameters of the geometric transformation. [22] presents a model which takes a set of images and their corresponding camera parameters as input and directly infers the 3D model.

2   Network Architecture

We leverage deep neural networks for estimating the fundamental matrix directly from a pair of stereo images. Each network consists of a feature extractor to obtain features from the images and a regression network to compute the entries of the F-matrix from the features.

2.1   Feature Extraction

We consider two different architectures for feature extraction. In the first architecture, we concatenate the images across the channel dimension, and pass the result to a neural network to extract features. Figure 1 illustrates the network structure. We use two convolutional layers, each followed by ReLU and Batch Normalization [20]. We use 128 filters of size 3×3 in the first convolutional layer and 128 filters of size 1×1 in the second layer. We limit the number of pooling layers to one in order not to lose the spatial structure in the images.

Location Aware Pooling. As discussed in Sect. 1, the F-matrix is highly dependent on the relative location of corresponding points in the images. However, down-sampling layers such as Max Pooling discard the location information. In order to retain this information, we keep all the indices of where the activations come from in the max-pooling layers. At the end of the network, we append the position of final features with respect to the full-size image. Each location is indexed with an integer in $[1, h \times w \times c]$ normalized to be within the range $[0, 1]$, in which h, w and c are the height, width and channel dimensions of the image respectively. In this way, each feature has a position index indicating from where it comes from. This helps the network to retain the location information and to provide more accurate estimates of the F-matrix.

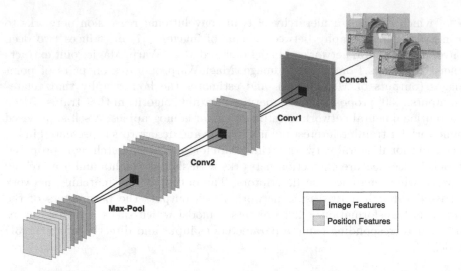

Fig. 1. Single-Stream Architecture. Stereo images are concatenated and passed to a convolutional neural network. Position features can be used to indicate where the final activations come from with respect to the full-size image.

The second architecture is shown in Fig. 2. We first process each of the input images in a separate stream using an architecture similar to the Universal Correspondence Network (UCN) [4]. Unlike the UCN architecture, we do not use Spatial Transformers [21] in these streams since they can remove part of the information needed for estimating relative camera rotation and translation. The resulting features from these streams are then concatenated, and passed to a single-stream network similar to Fig. 1. We can use position features in the single-stream network as discussed previously. These features capture the position of final features the with respect to the concatenated features at the end of the two streams. We refer to this architecture as 'Siamese'. As we show in Sect. 3, this network outperforms the Single-Stream one. We also consider using only the UCN without the single-stream network. The results, however, are not competitive with the Siamese architecture.

2.2 Regression

A simple approach for computing the fundamental matrix from the features is to pass them to fully-connected layers, and directly regress the nine entries of the F-Matrix. We can then normalize the result to achieve scale-invariance. This approach is shown in Fig. 3(left). The main issue with this approach is that the predicted matrix might not satisfy all the mathematical properties required for a fundamental matrix as a rank-2 matrix with seven degrees of freedom. In order to address this issue, we introduce Reconstruction and Normalization layers in the following.

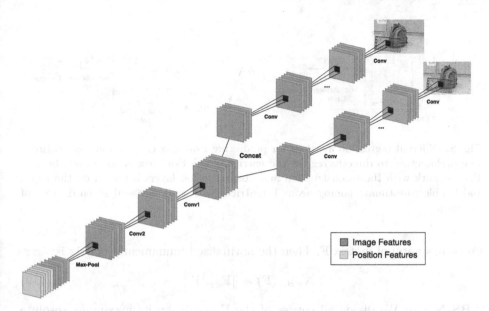

Fig. 2. Siamese Architecture. Images are first passed to two streams with shared weights. The resulting features are concatenated and passed to the single-stream network as in Fig. 1. Position features can be used with respect to the concatenated features.

F-Matrix Reconstruction Layer. We consider Eq. 1 to reconstruct the fundamental matrix:

$$\hat{\mathbf{F}} = \mathbf{K_2}^{-T}[\mathbf{t}]_\times \mathbf{R}\mathbf{K_1}^{-1} \tag{11}$$

we need to determine eight parameters $(f_1, f_2, t_x, t_y, t_z, r_x, r_y, r_z)$ as shown in Eqs. (2–4). Note that the predicted $\hat{\mathbf{F}}$ is differentiable with respect to these parameters. Hence, we can construct a layer that takes these parameters as input, and outputs a fundamental matrix $\hat{\mathbf{F}}$. This approach guarantees that the reconstructed matrix has rank two. Figure 3(right) illustrates the Reconstruction layer.

Normalization Layer. Considering that the F-matrix is scale-invariant, we also use a Normalization layer to remove another degree of freedom for scaling. In this way, the estimated F-matrix will have seven degrees of freedom and rank two as desired. The common practice for normalization is to divide the F-matrix by its last entry. We call this method **ETR-Norm**. However, since the last entry of the F-matrix could be close to zero, this can result in large entries, and training can become unstable. Therefore, we propose two alternative normalization methods.

FBN-Norm: We divide all entries of the F-matrix by its Frobenius norm, so that all the matrices live on a 9-sphere of unit norm. Let $\|\mathbf{F}\|_F$ denote the

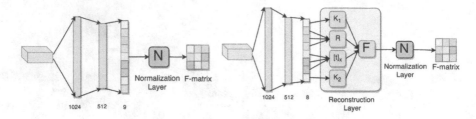

Fig. 3. Different regression methods for predicting F-matrix entries from the features. The architecture to directly regress the entries of the F-matrix is shown on the left. The network with the reconstruction and normalization layers is shown on the right, and is able to estimate homogeneous F-matrices with rank two and seven degrees of freedom.

Frobenius norm of matrix $\mathbf{F}$. Then the normalized fundamental matrix is:

$$\mathcal{N}_{FBN}(\mathbf{F}) = \|\mathbf{F}\|_F^{-1}\mathbf{F} \tag{12}$$

ABS-Norm: We divide all entries of the F-matrix by its maximum absolute value, so that all entries are restricted within $[-1, 1]$ range:

$$\mathcal{N}_{ABS}(\mathbf{F}) = (\max_{i,j}|\mathbf{F}_{i,j}|)^{-1}\mathbf{F} \tag{13}$$

During training, the normalized F-matrices are compared with the ground-truth using both L_1 and L_2 losses. We provide empirical results to study how each of these normalization methods influences performance and stability of training in Sect. 3.

Epipolar Parametrization. Given that the F-matrix has a rank of two, an alternative parametrization is specifying the first two columns $\mathbf{f}_1$ and $\mathbf{f}_2$ and the coefficients α and β such that $\mathbf{f}_3 = \alpha\mathbf{f}_1 + \beta\mathbf{f}_2$. Normalization layer can still be used to achieve scale-invariance. The coordinates of the epipole occur explicitly in this parametrization: $(\alpha, \beta, 1)^T$ is the right epipole for the F-matrix [16]. The corresponding regression architecture is similar to Fig. 3, but we interpret the final eight values differently: the first six elements represent the first two columns and the last two represent the coefficient for combining the columns. The main disadvantage of this method is that it does not work when the first two columns of $\mathbf{F}$ are linearly dependent. In this case, it is not possible to write the third column in terms of the first two columns.

3   Experiments

To evaluate whether our models can successfully learn F-matrices, we train models with various configurations and compare their performance based on the metrics defined in Sect. 3.1. The baseline model (**Base**) uses neither position features nor the reconstruction module. The **POS** model utilizes the position features on top of the **Base** model. Epipolar parametrization (Sect. 2.2) is used for the **EPI** model. **EPI+POS** uses the position features with epipolar parametrization. The **REC** model is the same as **Base** but uses the reconstruction module. Finally, the **REC+POS** model uses both the position features and the reconstruction module.

We use the KITTI dataset for training our models. The dataset has been recorded from a moving platform while driving in and around Karlsruhe, Germany. We use 2000 images from the raw stereo data in the 'City' category, and split them into 1600 train, 200 validation and 200 test images. Ground truth F-matrices are obtained using the ground-truth camera parameters. The same normalization methods are used for both the estimated and the ground truth F-matrices. The feature extractor and the regression network are trained jointly in an end-to-end manner.

3.1 Evaluation Metrics

We use the following metrics to measure how well the F-matrix satisfies the epipolar constraint (Eq. 5) according to the held out correspondences:

EPI-ABS (Epipolar Constraint with Absolute Value):

$$\mathcal{M}_{EPI-ABS}(\mathbf{F}, p, q) = \sum_i |q_i^T \mathbf{F} p_i| \tag{14}$$

EPI-SQR (Epipolar Constraint with Squared Value):

$$\mathcal{M}_{EPI-SQR}(\mathbf{F}, p, q) = \sum_i (q_i^T \mathbf{F} p_i)^2 \tag{15}$$

The first metric is equivalent to the Algebraic Distance mentioned in [9]. We evaluate the metrics based on high-confidence key-point correspondences: we select the key-points for which the Symmetric Epipolar Distance based on the ground-truth F-matrix is less than 2 [16]. This ensures that the point is no more than one pixel away from the corresponding epipolar line.

4 Results and Discussion

Results are shown in Table 1. We compare our method with 8-point, LeMedS and RANSAC algorithms [46]. On average, 60 pairs of keypoints are used per image. As we can observe, the reconstruction module is highly effective, and without it the network is unable to recover accurate fundamental matrices. The position features are also helpful in decreasing the error. The Siamese network outperforms the Single-Stream architecture, and can achieve errors comparable to the ground truth. This shows that the two streams used to process each of the input images are indeed useful. Note that the networks are trained end-to-end

Table 1. Results for Siamese and Single-stream networks on the KITTI dataset. Traditional methods such as 8-point, LeMedS and RANSAC are compared with different variants of our proposed model. Various normalization methods and evaluation metrics are considered.

		Siamese Network		Single-stream Network		
Normalization	Models	EPI-ABS	EPI-SQR	Models	EPI-ABS	EPI-SQR
ETR-Norm	Base	3.77	27.16	Base	4.43	34.34
	POS	4.05	21.90	POS	2.47	9.79
	EPI	0.52	0.28	EPI	1.00	0.99
	EPI + POS	0.88	1.02	EPI + POS	1.00	1.00
	REC	0.56	0.45	REC	0.99	0.99
	REC + POS	0.97	0.98	REC + POS	1.00	0.99
	8-point	1.91	152.83	8-point	1.91	152.83
	LeMedS	1.09	25.50	LeMedS	1.09	25.50
	RANSAC	0.60	3.85	RANSAC	0.60	3.85
	Ground-truth	0.05	0.004	Ground-truth	0.05	0.004
FBN-Norm	Base	1.44	2.58	Base	2.45	9.99
	POS	1.97	5.66	POS	2.78	8.55
	EPI	0.07	0.01	EPI	0.91	0.91
	EPI + POS	0.06	0.005	EPI + POS	0.67	0.58
	REC	0.92	1.11	REC	0.78	1.24
	REC + POS	0.43	0.44	REC + POS	0.87	0.81
	8-point	1.06	11.7	8-point	1.06	11.7
	LeMedS	0.39	0.68	LeMedS	0.39	0.68
	RANSAC	0.27	0.21	RANSAC	0.27	0.21
	Ground-truth	0.05	0.004	Ground-truth	0.05	0.004
ABS-Norm	Base	4.76	30.63	Base	3.55	18.04
	POS	3.74	22.59	POS	2.87	10.4
	EPI	0.18	0.06	EPI	0.92	1.94
	EPI + POS	0.12	0.03	EPI + POS	0.82	0.77
	REC	0.22	0.06	REC	0.77	0.99
	REC + POS	0.28	0.10	REC + POS	0.87	0.81
	8-point	1.17	15.4	8-point	1.17	15.4
	LeMedS	0.72	3.88	LeMedS	0.72	3.88
	RANSAC	0.33	0.39	RANSAC	0.33	0.39
	Ground-truth	0.05	0.004	Ground-truth	0.05	0.004

without the need for extracting point correspondences between the images, yet they are able to achieve competitive results with classic algorithms. The epipolar parametrization generally outperforms the other methods. During the inference time, we just need to pass the images to the feature extraction and regression networks to estimate the fundamental matrices.

5   Conclusion and Future Work

We present novel deep neural networks for estimating fundamental matrices from a pair of stereo images. Our networks can be trained end-to-end without the need for extracting point correspondences. We consider two different network architectures for computing features from the images, and show that the best result is obtained when we first process images in two streams, and then concatenate the features and pass the result to a single-stream network. We show that the simple approach of directly regressing the nine entries of the fundamental matrix does not yield good results. Therefore, a reconstruction module is introduced as a differentiable layer to estimate the parameters of the fundamental matrix. Two different parametrizations of the F-matrix are considered: one based on the camera parameters, and the other based on the epipolar parametrization. We also demonstrate that position features can be used to further improve the estimation. This is due to the sensitivity of fundamental matrices to the location of points in the input images. In the future, we plan to extend the results to other datasets, and explore other parametrizations of the fundamental matrix.

References

1. Armangué, X., Salvi, J.: Overall view regarding fundamental matrix estimation. Image Vis. Comput. **21**(2), 205–220 (2003)
2. Brachmann, E., et al.: DSAC-differentiable RANSAC for camera localization. In: IEEE Conference on Computer Vision and Pattern Recognition (CVPR), vol. 3 (2017)
3. Chen, L.C., Papandreou, G., Kokkinos, I., Murphy, K., Yuille, A.L.: DeepLab: semantic image segmentation with deep convolutional nets, atrous convolution, and fully connected CRFs. IEEE Trans. Pattern Anal. Mach. Intell. **40**(4), 834–848 (2018)
4. Choy, C.B., Gwak, J., Savarese, S., Chandraker, M.: Universal correspondence network. In: Advances in Neural Information Processing Systems, pp. 2414–2422 (2016)
5. DeTone, D., Malisiewicz, T., Rabinovich, A.: Deep image homography estimation. arXiv preprint arXiv:1606.03798 (2016)
6. DeTone, D., Malisiewicz, T., Rabinovich, A.: SuperPoint: self-supervised interest point detection and description. arXiv preprint arXiv:1712.07629 (2017)
7. DeTone, D., Malisiewicz, T., Rabinovich, A.: Toward geometric deep SLAM. arXiv preprint arXiv:1707.07410 (2017)
8. Nowruzi, F.E., Laganiere, R., Japkowicz, N.: Homography estimation from image pairs with hierarchical convolutional networks. In: Proceedings of the IEEE Conference on Computer Vision and Pattern Recognition, pp. 913–920 (2017)
9. Fathy, M.E., Hussein, A.S., Tolba, M.F.: Fundamental matrix estimation: a study of error criteria. Pattern Recognit. Lett. **32**(2), 383–391 (2011)
10. Fathy, M.E., Rotkowitz, M.C.: Essential matrix estimation using adaptive penalty formulations. J. Comput. Vis. **74**(2), 117–136 (2007)
11. Fischler, M.A., Bolles, R.C.: Random sample consensus: a paradigm for model fitting with applications to image analysis and automated cartography. Commun. ACM **24**(6), 381–395 (1981)

12. Garon, M., Lalonde, J.F.: Deep 6-DOF tracking. IEEE Trans. Vis. Comput. Graph. **23**(11), 2410–2418 (2017)
13. Geiger, A., Lenz, P., Stiller, C., Urtasun, R.: Vision meets robotics: the kitti dataset. Int. J. Robot. Res. **32**(11), 1231–1237 (2013)
14. Girshick, R., Donahue, J., Darrell, T., Malik, J.: Rich feature hierarchies for accurate object detection and semantic segmentation. In: Proceedings of the IEEE Conference on Computer Vision and Pattern Recognition, pp. 580–587 (2014)
15. Goodfellow, I., et al.: Generative adversarial nets. In: Advances in Neural Information Processing Systems, pp. 2672–2680 (2014)
16. Hartley, R., Zisserman, A.: Multiple View Geometry in Computer Vision. Cambridge University Press, Cambridge (2003)
17. Hartley, R.I.: In defense of the eight-point algorithm. IEEE Trans. Pattern Anal. Mach. Intell. **19**(6), 580–593 (1997)
18. He, K., Zhang, X., Ren, S., Sun, J.: Deep residual learning for image recognition. In: Proceedings of the IEEE Conference on Computer Vision and Pattern Recognition, pp. 770–778 (2016)
19. Huang, X., Li, Y., Poursaeed, O., Hopcroft, J., Belongie, S.: Stacked generative adversarial networks. In: IEEE Conference on Computer Vision and Pattern Recognition (CVPR), vol. 2, p. 4 (2017)
20. Ioffe, S., Szegedy, C.: Batch normalization: accelerating deep network training by reducing internal covariate shift. arXiv preprint arXiv:1502.03167 (2015)
21. Jaderberg, M., Simonyan, K., Zisserman, A., et al.: Spatial transformer networks. In: Advances in Neural Information Processing Systems, pp. 2017–2025 (2015)
22. Ji, M., Gall, J., Zheng, H., Liu, Y., Fang, L.: SurfaceNet: an end-to-end 3D neural network for multiview stereopsis. arXiv preprint arXiv:1708.01749 (2017)
23. Kendall, A., Badrinarayanan, V., Cipolla, R.: Bayesian SegNet: model uncertainty in deep convolutional encoder-decoder architectures for scene understanding. arXiv preprint arXiv:1511.02680 (2015)
24. Krizhevsky, A., Sutskever, I., Hinton, G.E.: Imagenet classification with deep convolutional neural networks, pp. 1097–1105 (2012)
25. Laskar, Z., Melekhov, I., Kalia, S., Kannala, J.: Camera relocalization by computing pairwise relative poses using convolutional neural network. arXiv preprint arXiv:1707.09733 (2017)
26. Long, J., Shelhamer, E., Darrell, T.: Fully convolutional networks for semantic segmentation. In: Proceedings of the IEEE Conference on Computer Vision and Pattern Recognition, pp. 3431–3440 (2015)
27. Longuet-Higgins, H.C.: A computer algorithm for reconstructing a scene from two projections. Nature **293**(5828), 133–135 (1981)
28. Lowe, D.G.: Object recognition from local scale-invariant features. In: The proceedings of the Seventh IEEE International Conference on Computer Vision, vol. 2, pp. 1150–1157. IEEE (1999)
29. Melekhov, I., Ylioinas, J., Kannala, J., Rahtu, E.: Relative camera pose estimation using convolutional neural networks. In: Blanc-Talon, J., Penne, R., Philips, W., Popescu, D., Scheunders, P. (eds.) ACIVS 2017. LNCS, vol. 10617, pp. 675–687. Springer, Cham (2017). https://doi.org/10.1007/978-3-319-70353-4_57
30. Nguyen, T., Chen, S.W., Skandan, S., Taylor, C.J., Kumar, V.: Unsupervised deep homography: a fast and robust homography estimation model. In: IEEE Robotics and Automation Letters (2018)
31. Poursaeed, O., Katsman, I., Gao, B., Belongie, S.: Generative adversarial perturbations. arXiv preprint arXiv:1712.02328 (2017)

32. Poursaeed, O., Matera, T., Belongie, S.: Vision-based real estate price estimation. arXiv preprint arXiv:1707.05489 (2017)
33. Radford, A., Metz, L., Chintala, S.: Unsupervised representation learning with deep convolutional generative adversarial networks. arXiv preprint arXiv:1511.06434 (2015)
34. Redmon, J., Divvala, S., Girshick, R., Farhadi, A.: You only look once: unified, real-time object detection. In: Proceedings of the IEEE Conference on Computer Vision and Pattern Recognition, pp. 779–788 (2016)
35. Ren, S., He, K., Girshick, R., Sun, J.: Faster R-CNN: towards real-time object detection with region proposal networks. In: Advances in Neural Information Processing Systems, pp. 91–99 (2015)
36. Rocco, I., Arandjelovic, R., Sivic, J.: Convolutional neural network architecture for geometric matching. In: Proceedings of CVPR, vol. 2 (2017)
37. Simonyan, K., Zisserman, A.: Very deep convolutional networks for large-scale image recognition (2014)
38. Szegedy, C., et al.: Going deeper with convolutions. In: Proceedings of the IEEE Conference on Computer Vision and Pattern Recognition, pp. 1–9 (2015)
39. Torr, P.H.S.: Bayesian model estimation and selection for epipolar geometry and generic manifold fitting. Int. J. Comput. Vis. **50**(1), 35–61 (2002)
40. Torr, P.H., Zisserman, A.: MLESAC: a new robust estimator with application to estimating image geometry. Comput. Vis. Image Underst. **78**(1), 138–156 (2000)
41. Workman, S., Greenwell, C., Zhai, M., Baltenberger, R., Jacobs, N.: DEEPFOCAL: a method for direct focal length estimation. In: 2015 IEEE International Conference on Image Processing (ICIP), pp. 1369–1373. IEEE (2015)
42. Yan, N., Wang, X., Liu, F.: Fundamental matrix estimation for binocular vision measuring system used in wild field. In: International Symposium on Optoclectronic Technology and Application 2014: Image Processing and Pattern Recognition, vol. 9301, p. 93010S. International Society for Optics and Photonics (2014)
43. Yu, F., Koltun, V.: Multi-scale context aggregation by dilated convolutions. arXiv preprint arXiv:1511.07122 (2015)
44. Zhang, H., et al.: Stackgan: text to photo-realistic image synthesis with stacked generative adversarial networks. In: IEEE International Conference Computer Vision (ICCV), pp. 5907–5915 (2017)
45. Zhang, Y., Zhang, L., Sun, C., Zhang, G.: Fundamental matrix estimation based on improved genetic algorithm. In: 2016 8th International Conference on Intelligent Human-Machine Systems and Cybernetics (IHMSC), vol. 1, pp. 326–329. IEEE (2016)
46. Zhang, Z.: Determining the epipolar geometry and its uncertainty: a review. Int. J. Comput. Vis. **27**(2), 161–195 (1998)
47. Zhao, H., Shi, J., Qi, X., Wang, X., Jia, J.: Pyramid scene parsing network. In: IEEE Conference on Computer Vision and Pattern Recognition (CVPR), pp. 2881–2890 (2017)
48. Zhou, B., Khosla, A., Lapedriza, A., Torralba, A., Oliva, A.: Places: an image database for deep scene understanding. arXiv preprint arXiv:1610.02055 (2016)
49. Zhou, F., Zhong, C., Zheng, Q.: Method for fundamental matrix estimation combined with feature lines. Neurocomputing **160**, 300–307 (2015)

High Quality Facial Surface and Texture Synthesis via Generative Adversarial Networks

Ron Slossberg[1(✉)], Gil Shamai[2], and Ron Kimmel[1]

[1] Technion CS Department, Haifa, Israel
{ronslos,sgils}@campus.technion.ac.il
[2] Technion EE Department, Haifa, Israel
ron@cs.technion.ac.il

Abstract. In the past several decades, many attempts have been made to model synthetic realistic geometric data. The goal of such models is to generate plausible 3D geometries and textures. Perhaps the best known of its kind is the linear 3D morphable model (3DMM) for faces. Such models can be found at the core of many computer vision applications such as face reconstruction, recognition and authentication to name just a few.

Generative adversarial networks (GANs) have shown great promise in imitating high dimensional data distributions. State of the art GANs are capable of performing tasks such as image to image translation as well as auditory and image signal synthesis, producing novel plausible samples from the data distribution at hand.

Geometric data is generally more difficult to process due to the inherent lack of an intrinsic parametrization. By bringing geometric data into an aligned space, we are able to map the data onto a 2D plane using a universal parametrization. This alignment process allows for efficient processing of digitally scanned geometric data via image processing tools. Using this methodology, we propose a novel face synthesis model for generation of realistic facial textures together with their corresponding geometry. A GAN is employed in order to imitate the space of parametrized human textures, while corresponding facial geometries are generated by learning the best 3DMM coefficients for each texture. The generated textures are mapped back onto the corresponding geometries to obtain new generated high resolution 3D faces.

1 Introduction

In recent years, deep learning has gained popularity in many research fields as well as practical applications. Deep networks are powerful generalization tools

---

R. Slossberg and G. Shamai—Equal contribution.

Electronic supplementary material The online version of this chapter (https://doi.org/10.1007/978-3-030-11015-4_36) contains supplementary material, which is available to authorized users.

© Springer Nature Switzerland AG 2019
L. Leal-Taixé and S. Roth (Eds.): ECCV 2018 Workshops, LNCS 11131, pp. 498–513, 2019.
https://doi.org/10.1007/978-3-030-11015-4_36

which are able to answer complex questions about data samples in a surprisingly effective manner. It has been well established that in order to train highly complex models, it is necessary to obtain extensive amounts of training data which closely approximates the complete data distribution.

Data augmentation is a popular method for extending the size of a given dataset. The idea is to modify the training examples in such a way that keeps their semantic properties intact. For instance, one can apply basic geometric distortions or add noise to a photo of an object in a way that leaves the object recognizable. Though helpful in many cases, these simple data augmentation methodologies often fail to address more complex transformations of the data such as pose, lighting and non-rigid deformations. An example of a more advanced type of data augmentation is demonstrated by [1], who observed that augmenting facial data by applying geometric and photometric transformations increases the performance of facial recognition models.

A different trend in data acquisition and augmentation for training deep networks is to synthesize training examples using a simulator such as [2]. The simulator should be able to model and generate a rich variety of samples which can be constructed under controlled conditions such as pose and lighting. However, synthetically generated examples often look unrealistic and diverge from the distribution of natural data. Methods such as [3] that used unrealistic synthetic data for training their models had to contend with difficulties when applying their models onto real data. A more realistic simulator that captures the real world data statistics more accurately would be expected to allow for easier generalization to real data.

In this line of works, recent papers have focused on making synthetic data more realistic by using *generative adversarial networks* (GANs). Commonly, the simulated data is used as an input to the GAN which can produce a more realistic sample from the synthetic one [2,4]. Taking this approach, the generated samples may appear realistic, however their semantic properties might be altered during the process, even when imposing a loss which penalizes the change in the parameters of the output.

Reducing the scope to modeling photo-geometric data, one of the most commonly used models for representation and synthesis of geometries and textures is the 3DMM [5] (see Sect. 2), originally proposed in the context of 3D human faces. Using a simple linear representation, 3DMM is capable of providing various new samples of the data it is constructed from. However, the generated samples are unrealistic in appearance and since the generation model follows a Gaussian distribution, non-plausible samples may easily result from the generation process.

Here, we propose a new realistic data synthesis approach for human faces. The suggested approach does not suffer from indirect control over various desired attributes such as pose and lighting, yet still produces realistic looking plausible models, in contrast to [5]. Moreover, in contrast to [1,6] the proposed model is not limited to producing new instances of existing individuals, but instead is capable of generating new plausible identities. This synthesis would be beneficial for various applications such as face recognition and biometric verification, as well as face reconstruction [3,7,8].

In particular, we constructed a dataset of 3D facial human scans. by aligning the facial geometries we are able to map the facial textures into 2D images using a universal parametrization. These images form the training data for a GAN of facial textures which is used to produce new plausible textures. Finally, each texture is coupled with a tailored geometry by learning the relation between texture and geometry in the dataset. To the best of our knowledge, the suggested model is the first to realistically synthesize both texture and geometry of human faces. Although in this paper we apply our methodology to human faces, the general framework is not limited to this problem alone.

The rest of the paper is arranged as follows. In Sect. 2 we describe the 3D morphable model (3DMM) which we use throughout the paper. In Sect. 3 we describe our main data processing pipeline. In Sect. 4 we describe the generative adversarial networks we used in the proposed pipeline. In Sect. 5 we describe several methods of generating plausible geometry for a given texture. In Sect. 6 we describe our experimental evaluations of our model. In Sect. 7 we review the main paper contributions as well as discuss our experimental results and their conclusions.

2   3D Morphable Model

In [5] Vetter and Blanz introduced a model by which the geometric structure and the texture of human faces are linearly approximated as a combination of principal vectors. This linear model, known as the *3D Morphable Model* (3DMM), was constructed by 3D scanning of several hundreds of subjects and computing dense registration between them. Classical principal component analysis was applied to the corresponding scans in order to obtain the principal vectors. Then, in order to estimate the 3D face given its 2D projection, they proposed to use an analysis-by-synthesis approach, which alternates between rendering the projection and re-estimating the 3D geometry, texture, and illumination parameters in a gradient descent optimization scheme.

In the 3DMM model, a face is represented by a geometry vector $g = (\hat{x}^1, \hat{y}^1, \hat{z}^1, \hat{x}^2, ...\hat{y}^m, \hat{z}^m) \in \mathbb{R}^{3m}$ and a texture vector $t = (\hat{r}^1, \hat{g}^1, \hat{b}^1, \hat{r}^2, ...\hat{g}^m, \hat{b}^m) \in \mathbb{R}^{3m}$ that contain the coordinates and colors of its m vertices, respectively. Given a set of n faces, each represented by geometry g_i and texture t_i vectors, construct the $3m \times n$ matrices G and T by grouping all geometry and texture vectors into their columns, in the same order. Since all faces are in correspondence, Principal Component Analysis (PCA) [9] can be applied in order to model the data in a basis representation. To that end, denote by V_g and V_t the $3m \times n$ matrices that contain the left singular vectors of $\Delta G = G - \mu_g \mathbb{1}^T$ and $\Delta T = T - \mu_t \mathbb{1}^T$, respectively, where μ_g and μ_t are the average geometry and texture of the faces and $\mathbb{1}$ is a vector of ones.

We assume that the columns of V_g and V_t are ordered by the value of the singular values in a descending manner. The texture and geometry of each face in the model can then be defined by the linear combination

$$g_i = \mu_g + V_g \alpha_{g_i}, \quad t_i = \mu_t + V_t \alpha_{t_i}, \tag{1}$$

where α_{g_i} and α_{t_i} are the coefficients vectors, obtained by $\alpha_{g_i} = V_g^T(g_i - \mu_g)$ and $\alpha_{t_i} = V_t^T(t_i - \mu_t)$. Following this formulation, one can generate new faces in the model by changing the texture and geometry coefficients. In order to obtain plausible faces from the model, the distribution of faces is assumed to follow a multivariate normal distribution, so that the probability for a coefficient vector α is given by

$$P(\alpha) \sim \exp\left\{-\frac{1}{2}\alpha^T \Sigma^{-1} \alpha\right\}, \tag{2}$$

where Σ is a covariance matrix that can be empirically estimated from the data, and for simplicity assumed to be diagonal.

Lastly, in order to obtain robust results when synthesizing new faces, only the first $k \ll n$ basis vectors and corresponding coefficients should be considered in the linear combination. That is, higher order basis vectors, corresponding to smaller PCA singular values, do not have enough data to faithfully estimate their values. Moreover, the number of $3D$ faces in a given dataset is limited and typically cannot cover all high resolution geometries and textures. Taken together, the above linear combination would most likely result in a smooth geometry and texture.

Recently, the 3DMM model was integrated with convolutional neural networks for data augmentation and for recovering pose variations of faces in images [3,4,7,8]. However, faces rendered using the above PCA model tend to be smooth and non-realistic. Using them for data augmentation would require additional steps such as transfer learning or designing additional networks to bridge this gap. Additionally, the multivariate normal distribution assumption rarely follows the true distribution of the data. In Fig. 1a we show examples of faces synthesized using the 3DMM model while considering $k = 200$ basis vectors with corresponding random coefficients for each face. In Fig. 1b, we plot the first two coefficients of real faces, computed by projecting the faces onto the 3DMM basis, and compare them to the coefficients of the synthesized 3DMM faces, showing the gap between the real and the synthesized distributions.

3 Data Acquisition Pipeline

Our main data acquisition pipeline was designed to align 3D scans of human faces vertex to vertex, and map their textures onto a 2D plane using a predefined universal transformation. This process is comprised of four main stages, depicted in Fig. 2: data acquisition, landmark annotation, mesh alignment and texture transfer. In the following section we describe each stage in detail.

Our data construction pipeline begins with the acquisition of high resolution geometric facial scans of human subjects. Due to privacy concerns, we are not permitted to share or display the raw data directly. Motivated by [10,11], we collected roughly 5000 scans from a wide variety of ethnic, gender, and age

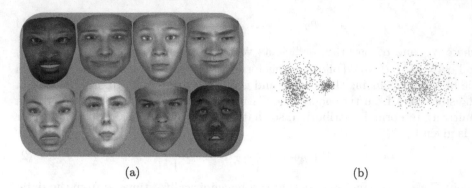

(a)

(b)

Fig. 1. (a) Faces synthesized using the 3DMM linear model. (b) First two PCA coefficients of real and 3DMM generated faces. Left - Real faces distribution. Right - 3DMM faces distribution.

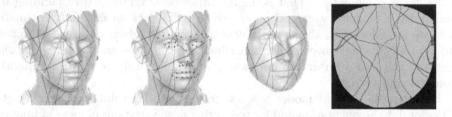

Fig. 2. Data preparation pipeline, left to right: Real scan geometry with demo texture. 3D facial landmarks are added. A template mesh is deformed to fit the scan guided by the landmarks. Texture is transferred onto the deformed template. The texture is mapped to a 2D plane using a universal mapping for the entire dataset.

groups, using a 3DMD^{TM} scanner. Each subject was asked to perform five distinct expressions including a neutral one. The acquired data went through a manual selection process which is intended to filter out corrupted meshes.

Once the data was collected, we proceeded to produce 3D facial landmark annotations in order to guide the subsequent alignment stage. We used Multipie 68 standard facial feature points [12], out of which we discarded the jaw and inner lip due to their instability. The remaining 43 landmarks were added to the meshes semi-automatically by rendering the face and using a pre-trained facial landmark detector [13,14] on the 2D images. The resulting 2D landmarks are back-projected onto the 3D mesh. In order to achieve an even more reliable annotation process, a human annotator manually corrected the erroneous landmarks.

During the alignment stage of the pipeline we performed a vertex to vertex correspondence between each scan and a facial template mesh. The alignment was conducted by deforming a template face mesh according to the geometric structure of each scan, guided by the previously obtained facial landmark points. The deformation process minimizes the energy term in [5]. The energy is made up of 3 terms which contribute to the final alignment. The first term accumulates the distances between the facial landmark points on the target and on the template. The second term aims to minimize the distance between all the mesh points on the template to the target surface. The third term serves as a regularization, and penalizes non-smooth deformations. The energy is minimized using gradient descent until convergence. This alignment process is the cornerstone of our data preparation pipeline.

Once the deformed template is properly aligned with the original scan, the texture is transferred from the scan to the template using a ray casting technique built into the animation rendering toolbox of Blender [15]. The texture is then mapped from the template to a 2D plane using a predefined universal mapping that was constructed once. As a result, the textures of all scans are semantically aligned under a universal mapping. The semantic alignment simplifies the network learning process, since the data is invariant with respect to the locations of the facial parts within the image. In Fig. 3 we show the resulting mapped textures of the dataset.

Fig. 3. Flattened aligned facial textures.

4   GAN

Generative models which are able to mimic examples from a high dimensional data distribution are recently gaining popularity. Such models are tasked with producing novel examples of data from a learned distribution. The first to propose such a model which is based on a deep neural network was [16], who dubbed the term generative adversarial network (GAN). Recent advances in GANs have shown promise in synthesis of audio signals [17], images [18], and image to image translation [19,20]. Here, we use a GAN in a novel way to synthesize high resolution realistic facial textures which can be fitted to 3D facial models. In this section we will describe briefly the main idea and architecture of GANs in general, and more specifically that of [18] which we adopt for our purpose.

A GAN is a special form of convolutional neural network which is designed to generate data samples which are indistinguishable from the training set. The GAN is comprised of two separate networks which are competing against each other. The generator network aims to produce novel examples while the discriminator network aims to distinguish between the generated and real examples. The generator network takes as input a random high dimensional normalized latent code and produces a sample of the same dimension as the data which makes up our training set. Ideally, the implemented loss should penalize deviation from the true data distribution and encourage generated examples which follow it. This loss, however, is highly complex and impractical to design manually. The way to circumvent this problem is to construct the loss function as a dynamic network which continually improves its assessment on how to distinguish between the fake and real data samples. This is why the discriminator network which is used as part of the loss is trained alongside with the generator. The key of the GAN method is that the discriminator produces a gradient which can be used to update the generator weights so that the generated samples are better at confusing the discriminator. This results in a race between the generator and discriminator, constantly improving each other as the training progresses. The typical loss of a GAN can be formulated as the min max loss

$$\min_{G} \max_{D} V(D,G) = \mathbb{E}_{x \sim p_{\text{data}}(x)}[\log D(x)] + \mathbb{E}_{z \sim p_z(z)}[\log(1 - D(G(z)))], \quad (3)$$

where G and D denote the generator and discriminator, x denotes the true data, and z denotes the latent space representation. More sophisticated loss functions have recently shown success in the training process. Some noteworthy examples are Wasserstein loss [21,22] and least squares loss [23], which apply different metrics to the computation of distances between data distributions.

Here we use a successful implementation of GAN dubbed progressive growing GAN [18]. This architecture combines several novel contributions which improve the training stability and the resulting image quality. The core idea is to construct the generator and discriminator as symmetric networks. The generator progressively increases the resolution of the feature maps at each stage until reaching the output image size, while the discriminator gradually reduces the size back to a single output. The training starts from the lowest resolution feature maps, and is guided by low resolution versions of the input data. After a stabilization period, a new layer is added by mixing an up-scaled version of the output emanating from the lower level feature maps, with the higher level output. The mixing coefficient gradually gives more importance to the higher level features at the output, until the contribution of the up-scaled lower layer is discarded completely. At this stage the new layer goes through a stabilization phase, and so on. According to [18], this is the main contribution to the training stabilization and improvement of results. Here, we trained the aforementioned GAN to learn and imitate the previously obtained aligned facial textures. The new synthetic facial textures generated by the GAN are shown in Fig. 4.

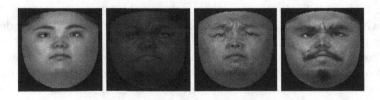

Fig. 4. Facial textures synthesized by GAN.

5   Synthesizing the Geometry

A popular way to deal with 3D textured object representations is to consider a discrete version of their geometry, such as a polygon mesh, while keeping their texture resolution high by mapping the texture from an image to the mesh. The observation that the geometry discretization of the object has a small impact on its appearance can be exploited for the sake of our geometry synthesizer. Figure 5a demonstrates that objects with smooth geometry and high resolution texture appear to be visually similar to their high resolution geometry and texture versions. This shows that the facial texture has a greater influence on perceived appearance than their geometry. Following this assumption, we propose to exploit the 3DMM discussed in Sect. 2 to generate the geometries of our faces as a linear combination of the first $k \ll n$ geometry basis vectors as

$$g = \mu_g + \sum_{i=1}^{k} \alpha_{gi} v_{gi}, \tag{4}$$

where v_{gi} is the i-th vector of the geometry basis V_g and $\{\alpha_{gi}\}_{i=1}^{k}$ are the coefficients that define the geometry.

In this section we explore several possible methods to find plausible geometry coefficients for a given texture. In each subsection we present one of the methods and briefly discuss their strengths and weaknesses. Figure 5b makes a qualitative and quantitative comparison between the various methods. For this comparison, we measure the distance between recovered geometries and the true corresponding geometries on a hold out set of real samples that were not included in the geometry recovery process, using a 10-fold cross validation. The distance is measured by the average of $\|g_r - g_t\|_{L_2}$ for all faces, where g_r and g_t are the recovered and true geometries. The outcome of the comparison is presented for each one of the methods in Fig. 5b.

5.1   Random Geometries

The simplest way to choose the geometry coefficients is by exploiting the multivariate normal distribution assumption of the 3DMM in order to pick random coefficients. Following the formulation in Eq. 2, the probability of the coefficient α_i is

$$P(\alpha_i) \sim \exp\left\{-\frac{\alpha_i^2}{2\sigma_i^2}\right\}, \tag{5}$$

where σ_i^2 is the i-th eigenvalue of the covariance matrix of ΔG, which can be also computed more efficiently as $\sigma_i^2 = \frac{1}{n}\delta_i^2$, where δ_i is the i-th singular value of ΔG. Following that, we compute the singular values $\{\delta_i\}_1^k$ of ΔG and randomize a vector of coefficients from the above probability. The problem with picking a random geometry for each face is that the correlation between the texture and the geometry is ignored. For instance, facial texture could indicate a specific ethnicity or gender which are related to specific geometric traits. The advantage of this method is that it is very simple and fast, and many identities can be created out of a single generated texture.

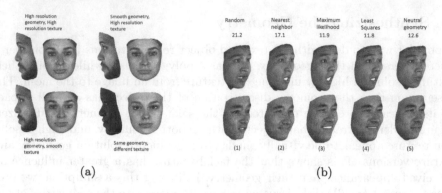

(a)   (b)

Fig. 5. Left: perceptual quality comparison between reduction in geometry detail ($k = 200$ geometry basis vectors) vs reduction in texture detail. Geometric detail loss is very difficult to perceive while texture detail loss is detrimental to the final outcome. Right: two synthesized textures mapped onto different geometries. Each geometry is produced by a method discussed in Sect. 5. (1) random geometry, (2) real geometry from nearest real texture, (3) ML geometry, (4) LS geometry, (5) Neutral geometry. The neutral geometry was obtained using the LS method. The L_2 geometric error tested by 10-fold cross validation is presented for each method at the top.

5.2 Nearest Neighbors

Given a facial texture, a simple way to obtain a geometry that is both plausible and likely to fit the texture is by finding a face in the data with a similar texture and then taking its geometry. Here, given a new facial texture generated by the proposed pipeline, we find the face in the data with the most similar texture, in terms of L_2 norm between the 3DMM texture coefficient, and use its geometry for our synthetic face. This would only require storing the 3DMM coefficients of the training data. The resulting geometry would most likely fit the texture and, moreover, will not loose its high frequencies. Nevertheless, geometries generated in this manner would be constrained to a small set of possible geometries. Additionally, the geometry will indeed retain accurate geometric details, but these will not coincide with the subtle details of the generated texture. For example, a texture of mole in the face would not have a corresponding curved geometry.

5.3 Maximum Likelihood Approach

Returning to the 3DMM formulation, one suitable way to obtain geometry coefficients that most likely fit the texture is by using a maximum likelihood approximation. The mathematical formulation regarding this approach is detailed in the supplementary material.

5.4 Least Squares Approach

The maximum likelihood approach is typically used when a small amount of data is available and one can have some assumptions on the distribution of the data. When sufficient data samples are available, it is usually more beneficial and straightforward to learn or estimate parameters using a least squares minimization scheme. We start from the original 3DMM model defined in Sect. 2. Given a texture coefficient vector α_t, we would like to estimate a plausible geometry coefficient vector α_g. To that end, we group all coefficient vectors α_t and α_g from our data into the columns of the matrices A_g and A_t and search for a matrix W such that

$$\text{loss}(W) = \|W^T A_t - A_g\|_F \tag{6}$$

is minimized. The vanishing gradient of the above least squares minimization problem, yields the solution W given as a closed form by

$$W^* = (A_t A_t^T)^{-1} A_t A_g^T = A_t^+ A_g^T. \tag{7}$$

Given a texture t of a new synthesized face, one can first compute the texture coefficient vector α_t as $\alpha_t = V_t^T (t - \mu_t)$, then compute its geometry coefficient vector α_g as $\alpha_g = W \alpha_t$, and finally compute the geometry as $g = \tilde{V}_g \tilde{\alpha}_g + \mu_g$, where $\tilde{V}_g$ and $\tilde{\alpha}_g$ hold the first k vectors and coefficients of V_g and α_g. It can be seen in Fig. 5b that the LS approach produces the lowest distortion results among our tested methods. For this reason and due to its simplicity, we chose to apply it during all of our subsequent experiments. It is worth mentioning that other applications may benefit from using one of the other methods according to their objective. Our experimental results give another verification to the validity of this approach, in terms of identity distribution and variation as presented in Sect. 6.

5.5 Neutral Face Geometries

The data we have worked with contains faces with a neutral and four other expressions. When estimating the geometry using each of the above methods, we consider all expressions as part of the model. Nevertheless, in some cases one would like to only obtain faces with a neutral expression geometries. One example for the necessity of the neutral pose face model is when the expression is modified using the Blend Shapes [24] (See the Blend Shapes experiment in Sect. 6). The Blend Shapes model takes as input a neutral face and adds linear combinations of facial expressions in order to span the space of possible expressions.

To estimate the geometry for each of the above methods while constraining it to a neutral expression, we suggest to simply replace any geometry g_i in G by the neutral geometry of the same identity in the dataset. Then, repeat the process of any of the above methods. In this manner, we tie each of the textures, regardless of its expression, to the neutral geometry of their identities rather than to the actual geometry which includes the non-neutral expression.

6 Experimental Results

Throughout this section, we use the proposed texture generation model and the Least squares approach described in Subsect. 5.4 for generating the corresponding geometries. The main advantage of our proposed method is that it can be used to create many new identities, and each one of them can be rendered under varying pose, expression and lighting. Given a facial texture synthesized by our system, we extracted its neutral geometry using the method described in Subsect. 5.5. We then used the Blend Shapes model as suggested in [24] to add different expressions to the facial geometry. We changed the pose and lighting and rendered 2D images to obtain numerous examples of the same identity. The resulting images are shown in the supplementary material in figures 1-3.

The sliced Wasserstein distance (SWD) is an efficiently computable randomized approximation to earth-movers distance which can be used to measure statistical similarities between images [25]. A small SWD indicates that the distribution of the patches is similar in both appearance and variation. The authors in [18] used SWD to measure the distance between the training distribution and the generated distribution of their GAN in different scales, and compared them to results produced by various competing methods. More specifically, the SWD between the distributions of patches extracted from the lowest resolution images is indicative of similarity in large-scale image structures, while the high resolution patches encode information about pixel-level attributes. Inspired by this notion, we used the SWD to measure distances between distributions of our training and generated images in different scales. The results of this experiment are shown in Table 1. The table demonstrates that the textures generated by our model are statistically closer to the real data than those generated by 3DMM.

Table 1. Sliced Wasserstein distance (SWD) [25] measured over extracted patches from the real and generated textures. The columns show SWD for patches extracted at different image resolutions, and the final column shows the average SWD over all resolutions.

Resolution	1024	512	256	128	64	32	16	avg
Real	3.53	2.98	3.75	2.6	2.75	2.5	1.63	2.82
Proposed	20.62	10.02	8.52	7.58	7.75	9.89	21.77	12.31
PCA	326	137	42	19.3	11.74	22.86	72.51	90.52

In order to visualize and compare between the distributions of the real and generated data, we used a popular dimensionality reduction process termed T-SNE [26]. We generated textures and geometries according to our model, as well as according to the 3DMM. For 3DMM, we used 200 eigenvectors for both texture and geometry. We then rendered the real and generated faces and fed them into a pre-trained facial recognition network based on [27], which provided an identity descriptor for each rendered face. We used T-SNE to visualize the distribution of obtained identity vectors. We labeled the real data according to race and gender, and found very uniform clusters. We assigned each one of our the faces generated by our proposed model to the closest cluster's center and produced one random example from each cluster. The results of this process are depicted in Fig. 6. The embedding clearly shows that the distribution of identities produced by the proposed pipeline is well matched to the distribution of the real identities included in the training data, and that the pipeline is able to produce data samples from each cluster (race and gender) reliably. On the other hand, the distribution produced by 3DMM, generated by the same training data, is a uniform Gaussian which has no natural clustering.

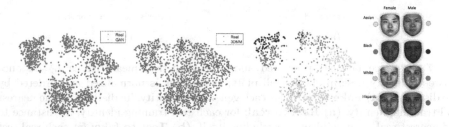

Fig. 6. From left to right: T-SNE [26] embedding of real identities versus GAN synthetic identities, T-SNE embedding of real identities versus 3DMM identities, clusters of real data according to race and gender, and synthetic samples conforming to each cluster.

In the following experiment, we set out to demonstrate that our model is capable of generating novel identities and not just add small variations to the existing training data. To that end, we made use of the identity descriptors extracted previously. We measured the L_2 distance between each generated identity and its closest real identity from the training data, and plotted the ordered distances. We repeated the process within the training data, namely, for each training identity, we measured the L_2 distance to its nearest neighbor within the training set (excluding itself). Figure 7a compares the resulting distances on a normalized axis. It can be seen that the distributions of distances are similar, and that the generated faces are not bounded to small variations in the vicinity of the training samples, in terms of identity. In other words, the variation between generated samples and the existing data is at least as large as the variation of the data itself.

In order to test the ability of our model to generalize to a previously unseen test set of real faces, we held out roughly 5% of the identities during training for evaluation. We measured the L_2 distance between each real test set identity to the closest identity generated by the GAN, as well as to the closest real training set identity. Fig. 7b compares the resulting ordered distances on a normalized axis. It can be seen that the test set identities are closer to the generated identities than those of the training set. Moreover, the "Test to fake" distances are not significantly larger than the "Fake to real" distances in Fig. 7a. This implies that our model is capable of generating samples that diverge significantly from the original training set and may resemble previously unseen data.

Finally, we performed a qualitative evaluation of the ability of our pipeline to generate original data samples. In Fig. 8 we show five textures generated

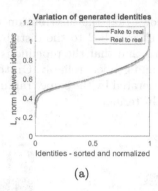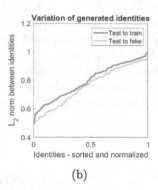

(a)   (b)

Fig. 7. Distance between generated and real identities, measured as L_2 distance between identity descriptors. For all plots, the X axis is normalized and ordered by the distances. **(a) Fake to real:** for each generated identity, its distance to the nearest real training identity. **(a) Real to real:** for each real training identity, its distance to the nearest real training identity, excluding itself. **(b) Test to fake:** for each real test identity, its distance to the nearest generated identity. **(b) Test to train:** for each real test identity, its distance to the nearest real training identity.

by our proposed model, alongside the closest neighbor within the real data in sense of $L2$ norm between identity descriptors. This experiment indicates that the nearest real textures are far enough to be visually distinguished as different people, showing that our model is able to produce novel identities.

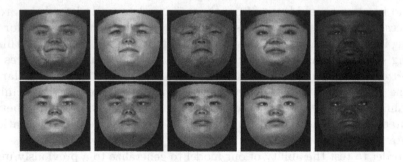

Fig. 8. Top: synthesized facial textures. Bottom: corresponding closest real neighbors in terms of facial identity.

Extended results and illustrations are supplied within the supplementary material.

7   Discussion and Conclusions

In this paper we present a new approach for synthesis of realistic 3D human faces. The proposed model, in contrast to 3DMM [5] is not limited to linear operations, and is able to exhibit more complex relations between the coefficients and the generated samples. In Sect. 2 we show the limitations of the 3DMM model in lack of complexity, realism and ability to correctly sample the true distribution. Namely, its simplified model follows a distribution that could generate non plausible samples. Although 3DMM might be capable of approximating real samples effectively, generating new plausible samples requires the model to conform with the correct data distribution prior.

We base our model on the notion of bringing the dataset into a uniform parametrization space, which allows for easier processing of geometry as images. This step allows to introduce the powerful tools of image processing into our geometric problem such as NN and more specifically, GANs. We use the GAN model in order to closely resemble the distribution of faces in our dataset, which allows to generate new samples that are both plausible and realistic.

The formation of geometries is performed per texture by learning the relation between texture and geometry coefficients of the 3DMM from the real data, following the observation that reducing the resolution of the geometry has negligible effect on the final appearance of the face. In Sect. 5, we explored several methods for this purpose. In our experiments we used the LS method due to its low distortion and simplicity. The resulting geometries take into account expression, gender and race that appear in the texture, making the final result more realistic.

In Sect. 6 we preform several qualitative and quantitative evaluations in order to strengthen our claims. Figure 6 depicts an embedding of real versus generated faces ID's, which demonstrates the ability of our proposed model to span the distribution of identities presented in the real data. It is important to note that the identities cover the same areas while filling the gaps between the real data samples. We also show that the 3DMM model sample distribution unsurprisingly resembles a Gaussian distribution which diverges from the training data distribution, although it was constructed based on this data.

Further experimentation depicted in Fig. 7 shows results of nearest neighbor searches between generated and real samples. It is important to note that Fig. 7b depicts the relation between real and generated samples to test set samples which were held out during training. We were able to show that the distances of real samples to the test set tend to be higher than distances from the generated samples to the same test set. This demonstrates that generated samples do not just produce IDs that are very close to the training set, but also novel IDs that resemble previously unseen examples.

We believe that this general framework for modeling geometry and texture can be useful for many applications. One prominent example is to use our proposed model in order synthesize more realistic facial data which can be used to train face detection, face recognition or face reconstruction models. We also believe that our model can be valuable in cases where many different realistic faces need to be created, such as in film industry or computer games. Note that this does not require to generalize the training samples but only to to produce various different plausible facial samples. This general methodology can also be employed for different various classes of objects where alignment of the data is possible.

Acknowledgements. This research was partially supported by the Israel Ministry of Science, grant number 3-14719 and the Technion Hiroshi Fujiwara Cyber Security Research Center and the Israel Cyber Bureau. We would like to thank Intel Inc for contributing the facial scans used during this research.

References

1. Masi, I., Trần, A.T., Hassner, T., Leksut, J.T., Medioni, G.: Do we really need to collect millions of faces for effective face recognition? In: Leibe, B., Matas, J., Sebe, N., Welling, M. (eds.) ECCV 2016. LNCS, vol. 9909, pp. 579–596. Springer, Cham (2016). https://doi.org/10.1007/978-3-319-46454-1_35
2. Shrivastava, A., Pfister, T., Tuzel, O., Susskind, J., Wang, W., Webb, R.: Learning from simulated and unsupervised images through adversarial training. In: The IEEE Conference on Computer Vision and Pattern Recognition (CVPR), vol. 3, p. 6 (2017)
3. Richardson, E., Sela, M., Or-El, R., Kimmel, R.: Learning detailed face reconstruction from a single image. In: 2017 IEEE Conference on Computer Vision and Pattern Recognition (CVPR), pp. 5553–5562. IEEE (2017)
4. Gecer, B., Bhattarai, B., Kittler, J., Kim, T.K.: Semi-supervised adversarial learning to generate photorealistic face images of new identities from 3D morphable model. arXiv preprint arXiv:1804.03675 (2018)
5. Blanz, V., Vetter, T.: A morphable model for the synthesis of 3D faces. In: Proceedings of the 26th Annual Conference on Computer Graphics and Interactive Techniques, pp. 187–194. ACM Press/Addison-Wesley Publishing Co. (1999)
6. Saito, S., Wei, L., Hu, L., Nagano, K., Li, H.: Photorealistic facial texture inference using deep neural networks. In: IEEE Conference on Computer Vision and Pattern Recognition, CVPR, vol. 3 (2017)
7. Richardson, E., Sela, M., Kimmel, R.: 3D face reconstruction by learning from synthetic data. In: 2016 Fourth International Conference on 3D Vision (3DV), pp. 460–469. IEEE (2016)
8. Sela, M., Richardson, E., Kimmel, R.: Unrestricted facial geometry reconstruction using image-to-image translation. In: 2017 IEEE International Conference on Computer Vision (ICCV), pp. 1585–1594. IEEE (2017)
9. Jolliffe, I.T.: Principal component analysis and factor analysis. In: Jolliffe, I.T. (ed.) Principal Component Analysis. Springer Series in Statistics, pp. 115–128. Springer, New York (1986). https://doi.org/10.1007/978-1-4757-1904-8_7
10. Booth, J., Roussos, A., Ponniah, A., Dunaway, D., Zafeiriou, S.: Large scale 3D morphable models. Int. J. Comput. Vis. **126**(2–4), 233–254 (2018)
11. Booth, J., Roussos, A., Zafeiriou, S., Ponniah, A., Dunaway, D.: A 3D morphable model learnt from 10,000 faces. In: Proceedings of the IEEE Conference on Computer Vision and Pattern Recognition, pp. 5543–5552 (2016)
12. Gross, R., Matthews, I., Cohn, J., Kanade, T., Baker, S.: Multi-pie. Image Vis. Comput. **28**(5), 807–813 (2010)
13. Alabort-i-Medina, J., Antonakos, E., Booth, J., Snape, P., Zafeiriou, S.: Menpo: a comprehensive platform for parametric image alignment and visual deformable models. In: Proceedings of the ACM International Conference on Multimedia, MM 2014, New York, NY, USA, pp. 679–682. ACM (2014)

14. King, D.E.: Dlib-ml: a machine learning toolkit. J. Mach. Learn. Res. **10**, 1755–1758 (2009)
15. Blender Online Community: Blender - a 3D modelling and rendering package. Blender Foundation, Blender Institute, Amsterdam (2017). http://www.blender.org
16. Goodfellow, I., et al.: Generative adversarial nets. In: Advances in Neural Information Processing Systems, pp. 2672–2680 (2014)
17. van den Oord, A., et al.: WaveNet: a generative model for raw audio. arXiv preprint arXiv:1609.03499 (2016)
18. Karras, T., Aila, T., Laine, S., Lehtinen, J.: Progressive growing of GANs for improved quality, stability, and variation. In: International Conference on Learning Representations (ICLR) (2017)
19. Isola, P., Zhu, J.Y., Zhou, T., Efros, A.A.: Image-to-image translation with conditional adversarial networks. arXiv preprint (2017)
20. Zhu, J.Y., Park, T., Isola, P., Efros, A.A.: Unpaired image-to-image translation using cycle-consistent adversarial networks. arXiv preprint arXiv:1703.10593 (2017)
21. Gulrajani, I., Ahmed, F., Arjovsky, M., Dumoulin, V., Courville, A.C.: Improved training of Wasserstein GANs. In: Advances in Neural Information Processing Systems, pp. 5769–5779 (2017)
22. Arjovsky, M., Chintala, S., Bottou, L.: Wasserstein GAN. arXiv preprint arXiv:1701.07875 (2017)
23. Mao, X., Li, Q., Xie, H., Lau, R.Y., Wang, Z., Smolley, S.P.: Least squares generative adversarial networks. In: 2017 IEEE International Conference on Computer Vision (ICCV), pp. 2813–2821. IEEE (2017)
24. Chu, B., Romdhani, S., Chen, L.: 3D-aided face recognition robust to expression and pose variations. In: Proceedings of the IEEE Conference on Computer Vision and Pattern Recognition, pp. 1899–1906 (2014)
25. Rabin, J., Peyré, G., Delon, J., Bernot, M.: Wasserstein barycenter and its application to texture mixing. In: Bruckstein, A.M., ter Haar Romeny, B.M., Bronstein, A.M., Bronstein, M.M. (eds.) SSVM 2011. LNCS, vol. 6667, pp. 435–446. Springer, Heidelberg (2012). https://doi.org/10.1007/978-3-642-24785-9_37
26. van der Maaten, L., Hinton, G.: Visualizing data using t-SNE. J. Mach. Learn. Res. **9**, 2579–2605 (2008)
27. Amos, B., Ludwiczuk, B., Satyanarayanan, M.: OpenFace: a general-purpose face recognition library with mobile applications. Technical report, CMU-CS-16-118, CMU School of Computer Science (2016)

W17 – 1st Workshop on Brain-Driven Computer Vision

W17 – 1st Workshop on Brain-Driven Computer Vision

The 1st Workshop on Brain-Driven Computer Vision, held in Munich (Germany) on 8th September 2018, in conjunction with the European Conference on Computer Vision (ECCV 2018), aimed at inspiring the study and development of paradigms, methods and tools for computer vision driven or inspired by the human brain, both as a computational model and a source of data, and to promote the diffusion of new benchmarks and evaluation protocols to support the scientific community in the pursuing of a better understanding of the brain processes underlying human visual perception and comprehension.

The workshop received 16 submissions, each single-blindly peer-reviewed by at least two members of the Program Committee; 10 submissions were accepted for presentation at the workshop. A discussion paper by the workshop organizers, which did not undergo the reviewing process, was also included in the proceedings.

Prof. John K. Tsotsos, from York University (Toronto, Canada), participated as a keynote speaker, giving a talk titled "Visual Attention: Brain Mechanisms and Computational Models". We would like to thank him for his kind availability.

We also thank the members of the Program Committee:

Antonio Bandera, Malaga University, Spain; Vassilis Belagiannis, Oxford University, UK; Kostas Berberidis, University of Patras, Greece; Kenneth Camilleri, University of Malta, Malta; Silvia Corchs, University of Milano Bicocca, Italy; Konstantinos Derpanis, Ryerson University, Canada; Mariella Dimiccoli, Computer Vision Center, Barcelona, Spain; Francisco Escolano, University of Alicante, Spain; Francesca Gasparini, University of Milano Bicocca, Italy; Georgia Gkioxari, University of California, Berkeley, USA; Daniela Giorgi, CNR, Italy; Sean Holden, University of Cambridge, UK; Leyla Isik, MIT, US; Xiaoyi Jiang, University of Muenster, Germany; Nikos Kolotouros, Penn State University, USA; Sokratis Makrogiannis, Delaware State University, USA; Vassilis Megalooikonomou, University of Patras, Greece; Dimitris Metaxas, Rutgers University, USA; Vittorio Murino, IIT, Italy; Ioannis Patras, Queen Mary, UK; Laurent Perrinet, Aix-Marseille Université, France; Nicolai Petkov, University of Groningen, Netherlands; Panagiotis Petrantonakis, ITI, Greece; Ioannis Rigas, Texas State University, USA; Gemma Roig, MIT, USA; Alessia Saggese, University of Salerno, Italy; Enrique Sanchez-Lozano, University of Nottingham, UK; Mubarak Shah, University of Central Florida, USA; Akihiro Sugimoto, National Institute of Informatics, Japan; Anastasios Tefas,

University of Thessaloniki, Greece; Daniel Thalmann, EPFL, Switzerland; Andreas Tolias, Baylor College of Medicine, USA; Klaus Tonnies, Otto-von-Guericke-Universitaet Magdeburg, Germany.

September 2018

Simone Palazzo
Isaak Kavasidis
Dimitris Kastaniotis
Stavros Dimitriadis

Recent Advances at the Brain-Driven Computer Vision Workshop 2018

Simone Palazzo[1]([✉]), Isaak Kavasidis[1], Dimitris Kastaniotis[2],
and Stavros Dimitriadis[3]

[1] University of Catania, Catania, Italy
{palazzosim,kavasidis}@dieei.unict.it
[2] University of Patras, Patras, Greece
dkastaniotis@upatras.gr
[3] Cardiff University, Cardiff, UK
DimitriadisS@cardiff.ac.uk

Abstract. The 1st edition of the Brain-Driven Computer Vision Workshop, held in Munich in conjunction with the European Conference on Computer Vision 2018, aimed at attracting, promoting and inspiring research on paradigms, methods and tools for computer vision driven or inspired by the human brain. While successful, in terms of the quality of received submissions and audience present at the event, the workshop emphasized some of the factors that currently limit research in this field. In this report, we discuss the success points of the workshop, the characteristics of the presented works, and our considerations on the state of current research and future directions of research in this topic.

Keywords: Brain-Driven Computer Vision ·
Biologically-inspired machine learning

1 Introduction

In recent years, we have witnessed unprecedented advancements in the automatic analysis of visual data by computer algorithms, thanks to a series of factors which unleashed the potential of convolutional neural networks. Part of the reason of their success could be explained by the biologically-inspired design of such models: indeed, while the classic artificial neuron may only by an extreme simplification of the biological neuron, the increasing representational complexity learned by CNNs may be more faithful to the layered structure of the lower areas of the human visual cortex [11, 12]. However, the road towards achieving a degree of artificial emulation of the human visual system high enough to interpret an environment as humans do is still long: while we are able to identify low- to high-level visual patterns from images and videos, artificial models largely miss the human capability to make sense of this information, recognize semantic patterns, correlate to memory and experience, and so on. Additionally, even the kind of neural

L. Leal-Taixé and S. Roth (Eds.): ECCV 2018 Workshops, LNCS 11131, pp. 519–525, 2019.
https://doi.org/10.1007/978-3-030-11015-4_37

computational models that we employ are only loosely based of biological structures and connections: for example, human visual analysis transmits information across cortical brain regions in both feedforward and feedback patterns, with the latter basically missing from current artificial approaches [13–16]. Although some recent works [17] attempted to encode hierarchical predictions [18,19] featuring a combination of feedforward, feedback and recurrent connections, while others explored methods to decode brain visual representations [20–24], we still lack a sufficient understanding of the underlying cognitive processes to emulate and transfer them to physiologically-motivated implementations.

The proposed workshop is inspired by the realization that understanding and speculating on the yet mostly unknown mechanisms used by the brain to process visual information and knowledge may be the key to further advance computer vision beyond the black-box paradigm of training from data in the hope to uncover the very same processes. The daunting yet fascinating challenge presented by this task calls for a largely multidisciplinary effort by research communities in the fields of artificial intelligence, machine learning, cognitive neuroscience, psychology, among others. The aim of the workshop was therefore to excite the study and development of paradigms, methods and tools for computer vision driven or inspired by the human brain, both as a computational model and a source of data, and to promote the diffusion of new benchmarks and evaluation protocols to support the scientific community in the pursuing of a better understanding of the brain processes underlying human visual perception and comprehension.

2   Taxonomy of Workshop Papers

One of the objectives of the Brain-Driven Computer Vision Workshop was to blend research in computer vision with neuroscience, and from this point of view the achieved results were only partly satisfactorily, as many works had a distinct computer-vision–oriented slant, with the "brain-driven" aspect mostly consisting in an algorithmic inspiration.

Hence, our overview of the works presented at the workshop separates them into two categories, based on the perspective of the study regarding the representation of visual information. Papers focusing on representation in biological neurons and on how these neurons respond to different visual stimuli will be discussed in Sect. 2.1; papers focusing on the design of biologically-inspired algorithms for processing digital information will be presented in Sect. 2.2.

2.1   Brain Representation and Human Perception

Visual information processing in human and animal brains is one of the most interesting topics of neuroscience. Traditionally, these studies have revealed significant findings, which in many cases have helped in the development of state of the Computer Vision models [25,26]. In brief, research has been focused on the encoding mechanisms inside visual cortex as well as on the two stream processing hypothesis (hierarchy of processing layers)—namely the ventral (shape processing) and the dorsal (motion processing) systems.

The similarities and differences between biological and artificial neurons is a long-time research topic in computational neuroscience. In [1], the authors discuss the ability of a neural network trained on a particular task to describe the behaviour of neurons that are dedicated to operate on the same task, with a focus on scene-parsing models, that are shown to better explain task-specific brain responses than scene classification models.

In [2], authors focus on the shape information processing (ventral stream) by analyzing the visual stimuli responses in V1 cortex of anesthetized naive Long-Evans rats. To this end, they recorded extracellular potentials and focused on low-level features (position of center of mass and luminosity). Extracellular potentials were initially filtered with a band-pass filter (0.5–11 KHz) followed by an Expectation-Maximization clustering algorithm to differentiate between spikes produced by different neurons. They analyzed these recordings using a number of clustering and classification techniques and concluded that both luminosity and position as well as the combination of the two, are naturally mapped in the V1.

In the spirit of [11], the authors of [3] target the problem of decoding visual representation from fMRI, by analyzing feature correlation through a regressive model trained from brain data and comparing several machine learning methods and similarity measures in order to maximize decoding accuracy. They found that a Multilayer Neural Network is able to best represent the non linear relationship between a Deep CNN and the features of fMRI. Also, features from the whole Visual Cortex surpass the performance of individual cortices. Also, they observed that higher visual cortex areas surpass the lower visual cortex but also, in the lower visual cortex, V4 area surpasses all previous areas—which is quite reasonable as it is an area of the ventral system.

2.2 Brain-Inspired Representation Learning

Researchers in computer vision have traditionally tried to mimic the behavior of the human brain, as it is the most obvious reference model for understanding the visual world.

In this workshop, we had two papers focusing on Capsule Networks [27]. Capsule Networks are inspired by the working mechanism of optic neurons of the human visual system, achieving a significant improvement regarding the ability to efficiently detect presence of a an object in a scene. In [4], the authors presented an architecture for generative adversarial networks (GANs) where the discriminator was modeled as a capsule network and the loss function was adapted to include the standard capsule margin loss. Results evaluated using a Generative Adversarial Metric and a Semi-supervised Classification showed an improvement as compared to GANs working with a regular CNN Discriminator network.

Capsule Nets do not explicitly model the relationship of output vector activations. In this manner in [5], the authors proposed three improvements on the standard capsule network architecture. They proposed a novel routing weight initialization technique, the exploitation of semantic relationships between the primary capsule activations using a densely connected conditional random field (CRF), and a Cholesky transformation–based correlation module to learn a general priority scheme. These modifications gave promising results on the problem of multi-label classification. For the evaluation they incorporated the ADE20K dataset [28], which has 200.000 images from 150 scenes and used the mean Average Precision Metric (mAP) to compare the regular Capsule Networks with the proposed scheme.

Push-pull inhibition is a phenomenon observed in neurons in the V1 area of the visual cortex, which suppresses the response of certain simple cells for stimuli of preferred orientation but of non-preferred contrast, improving the quality of delineation especially in images with spurious texture. The authors of [6] presented a delineation operator that implemented a pull-push inhibition mechanism improving robustness to noise in terms of spurious texture.

In [7], the authors tested the robustness of face recognition models to false positive and, in particular, to simulacra and pareidolia, two categories of psychological phenomena that allow humans to recognize particular objects (such as an arrangement of three points resembling two eyes and a mouth) as faces, and that can be interpreted as false positives triggered by human psychological peculiarities. Their results showed that state-of-the-art models were not robust against these particular types of false positives, confirming the gap between algorithmic and human-level performance.

One of the abilities of animals is to efficiently subitize, i.e., counting the number of objects in a scene. In [8], the authors discussed the intrinsic abilities of deep convolutional neural networks to perform this task. They showed that variational autoencoders were able to spontaneously perform subitizing after training without supervision on a large amount of images. Also, they studied the effect of the size of the object and they concluded that the learned representations are likely invariant to object area. This observation is aligned with recent studies on biological neural networks in cognitive neuroscience.

While it seems trivial for a human subject to identify different temporal segments in a video (i.e., grouping images that belong to the same video scene), it is not so when automated methods are employed. Also, neuroscience findings indicate that stimuli belonging to the same temporal context, are grouped together in clusters of communities formed inside a representational space [29]. Inspired by these findings, in [9], the authors showed a method for learning a representation suitable for the task of temporal video segmentation by using directed graphs that represent how the feature vectors of the images in a video are connected temporally. These temporal edges represent the temporal similarity of the images in the video and then mapped to an automatically learned feature space by employing both LSTM and 'vanilla' neural networks.

In [10], the authors adopted a biological-like pyramidal structure of neuron interconnections to create a model that was able to understand human emotions from sequences of pictures. Given that human facial expressions must be taken in context, the authors opted to consider image sequences instead of single pictures. The image sequences provided the model with more information indicating the actual emotion that the subject displayed. The method was tested on two different datasets obtaining very good results and demonstrating that temporal cues in the expression of emotion play a significant role.

3 Discussion

From an organization point of view, this first edition of the workshop was successful, in terms of both received submissions and, equally important, the number of people attending the workshop. It should be noted that most of the attendees were present at the keynote speech and at the poster session, while fewer participated in the final discussion at the end of the workshop.

As for the quality and content of the accepted submissions, while all were on topic (as defined by the list published in the call for papers[1]), Sect. 2 highlights a certain unbalance between the number of papers tackling the analysis of biological data in the attempt to gain a better understanding of the underlying processes, and those proposing purely-algorithmic approaches with an (sometimes loose) inspiration to neurocognitive mechanisms, with the latter being significantly more numerous. Of course, this might have been expected: working on brain data requires, first and foremost, the availability or accessibility of such data, which is something that not all research groups have, as specific and expensive technology (e.g., EEG and fMRI) are necessary. However, while brain-inspired approaches can certainly be useful, both as practical tools/applications and as a source of architectural ideas for artificial model, we believe that brain activity analysis and the consequent efforts to uncover how visual information is represented and processed in the brain will be the key factor to devising artificial models that fulfill the learning, generalization and adaptation gaps to human performance.

From this point of view, we were hoping to see submissions providing new brain activity datasets to the research community. Given the above-mentioned difficulty in neuroimaging data collection, dataset availability seems to be the main limiting factor in the application of modern machine learning techniques to brain activity understanding, prediction and emulation.

In view of these considerations, the success of this first edition of the workshop will certainly encourage us to continue the series with a new edition; however, we believe that a stricter topic policy will be enforced, trying to attract more submissions that work with and on neuroimaging datasets, in the attempt to push the boundaries of current research in brain visual representation learning, decoding and understanding.

---

[1] http://www.upcv.upatras.gr/BDCV/CFP.html.

List of Workshop Papers

1. Dwivedi, K., Roig, G.: Navigational affordance cortical responses explained by scene-parsing model
2. Vascon, S., Parin, Y., Annavini, E., D'Andola, M., Zoccolan, D., Pelillo, M.: Characterization of visual object representations in rat primary visual cortex
3. Papadimitriou, A., Passalis, N., Tefas, A.: Decoding generic visual representations from human brain activity using machine learning
4. Jaiswal, A., AbdAlmageed, W., Wu, Y., Natarajan, P.: Capsulegan: Generative adversarial capsule network
5. Ramasinghe, S., Athuraliya, C., Khan, S.: A context-aware capsule network for multi-label classification
6. Strisciuglio, N., Azzopardi, G., Petkov, N.: Brain-inspired robust delineation operator
7. Natsume, R., Inoue, K., Fukuhara, Y., Yamamoto, S., Morishima, S., Kataoka, H.: Understanding fake faces
8. Wever, R., Runia, T.F.: Subitizing with variational autoencoders
9. Dias, C., Dimiccoli, M.: Learning event representations by encoding the temporal context
10. Nardo, E.D., Petrosino, A., Ullah, I.: Emop3d: A brain like pyramidal deep neural network for emotion recognition

References

11. Horikawa, T., Kamitani, Y.: Generic decoding of seen and imagined objects using hierarchical visual features. Nat. Commun. **8**, 15037 (2017)
12. Cichy, R.M., Khosla, A., Pantazis, D., Torralba, A., Oliva, A.: Comparison of deep neural networks to spatio-temporal cortical dynamics of human visual object recognition reveals hierarchical correspondence. Sci. Rep. **6**, 27755 (2016)
13. Bullier, J.: Integrated model of visual processing. Brain Res. Brain Res. Rev. **36**(2–3), 96–107 (2001)
14. Kourtzi, Z., Connor, C.E.: Neural representations for object perception: structure, category, and adaptive coding. Annu. Rev. Neurosci. **34**, 45–67 (2011)
15. Kravitz, D.J., Saleem, K.S., Baker, C.I., Mishkin, M.: A new neural framework for visuospatial processing. Nat. Rev. Neurosci. **12**(4), 217–230 (2011)
16. DiCarlo, J.J., Zoccolan, D., Rust, N.C.: How does the brain solve visual object recognition? Neuron **73**(3), 415–434 (2012)
17. Wen, H., Han, K., Shi, J., Zhang, Y., Culurciello, E., Liu, Z.: Deep predictive coding network for object recognition. In: Dy, J., Krause, A., (eds.) Proceedings of the 35th International Conference on Machine Learning. Volume 80 of Proceedings of Machine Learning Research, Stockholmsmässan, Stockholm Sweden, PMLR, 10–15 July 2018, pp. 5266–5275 (2018)
18. Clark, A.: Whatever next? Predictive brains, situated agents, and the future of cognitive science. Behav. Brain Sci. **36**(3), 181–204 (2013)
19. Bastos, A.M., Usrey, W.M., Adams, R.A., Mangun, G.R., Fries, P., Friston, K.J.: Canonical microcircuits for predictive coding. Neuron **76**(4), 695–711 (2012)
20. Spampinato, C., Palazzo, S., Kavasidis, I., Giordano, D., Souly, N., Shah, M.: Deep learning human mind for automated visual classification. In: IEEE Conference on Computer Vision and Pattern Recognition (CVPR), July 2017, pp. 4503–4511 (2017)

21. Palazzo, S., Spampinato, C., Kavasidis, I., Giordano, D., Shah, M.: Generative adversarial networks conditioned by brain signals. In: IEEE International Conference on Computer Vision (ICCV), October 2017, pp. 3430–3438 (2017)
22. Nishimoto, S., Vu, A.T., Naselaris, T., Benjamini, Y., Yu, B., Gallant, J.L.: Reconstructing visual experiences from brain activity evoked by natural movies. Curr. Biol. **21**(19), 1641–1646 (2011)
23. Stansbury, D.E., Naselaris, T., Gallant, J.L.: Natural scene statistics account for the representation of scene categories in human visual cortex. Neuron **79**(5), 1025–1034 (2013)
24. Kavasidis, I., Palazzo, S., Spampinato, C., Giordano, D., Shah, M.: Brain2Image: converting brain signals into images. In: Proceedings of the 2017 ACM on Multimedia Conference, pp. 1809–1817. ACM (2017)
25. Olshausen, B.A., Field, D.J.: Emergence of simple-cell receptive field properties by learning a sparse code for natural images. Nature **381**(6583), 607 (1997)
26. Jhuang, H., Serre, T., Wolf, L., Poggio, T.: A biologically inspired system for action recognition. In: IEEE 11th International Conference on Computer Vision, ICCV 2007, pp. 1–8. IEEE (2007)
27. Sabour, S., Frosst, N., Hinton, G.E.: Dynamic routing between capsules. In: Guyon, I., et al. (eds.) Advances in Neural Information Processing Systems 30, pp. 3856–3866. Curran Associates, Inc. (2017)
28. Zhou, B., Zhao, H., Puig, X., Fidler, S., Barriuso, A., Torralba, A.: Scene parsing through ADE20K dataset. In: Proceedings of the IEEE Conference on Computer Vision and Pattern Recognition (2017)
29. Schapiro, A.C., Rogers, T.T., Cordova, N.I., Turk-Browne, N.B., Botvinick, M.M.: Neural representations of events arise from temporal community structure. Nat. Neurosci. **16**(4), 486 (2013)

CapsuleGAN: Generative Adversarial Capsule Network

Ayush Jaiswal[✉], Wael AbdAlmageed, Yue Wu, and Premkumar Natarajan

USC Information Sciences Institute, Marina del Rey, CA, USA
{ajaiswal,wamageed,yue_wu,pnataraj}@isi.edu

Abstract. We present Generative Adversarial Capsule Network (CapsuleGAN), a framework that uses capsule networks (CapsNets) instead of the standard convolutional neural networks (CNNs) as discriminators within the generative adversarial network (GAN) setting, while modeling image data. We provide guidelines for designing CapsNet discriminators and the updated GAN objective function, which incorporates the CapsNet margin loss, for training CapsuleGAN models. We show that CapsuleGAN outperforms convolutional-GAN at modeling image data distribution on MNIST and CIFAR-10 datasets, evaluated on the generative adversarial metric and at semi-supervised image classification.

Keywords: Capsule networks · Generative adversarial networks

1 Introduction

Generative modeling of data is a challenging machine learning problem that has garnered tremendous interest recently, partly due to the invention of generative adversarial networks (GANs) [5] and its several sophisticated variants[1]. A GAN model is typically composed of two neural networks; (1) a generator that attempts to transform samples drawn from a prior distribution to samples from a complex data distribution with much higher dimensionality, and (2) a discriminator that decides whether the given sample is real or from the generator's distribution. The two components are trained by playing an adversarial game. GANs have shown great promise in modeling highly complex distributions underlying real world data, especially images. However, they are notorious for being difficult to train and have problems with stability, vanishing gradients, mode collapse and inadequate mode coverage [4,16,19]. Consequently, there has been a large amount of work towards improving GANs by using better objective functions [1,2,6], sophisticated training strategies [19], using structural hyperparameters [15,16] and adopting empirically successful tricks[2].

Radford et al. [16] provide a set of architectural guidelines, formulating a class of convolutional neural networks (CNNs) that have since been extensively

---

[1] https://github.com/hindupuravinash/the-gan-zoo.
[2] https://github.com/soumith/ganhacks.

© Springer Nature Switzerland AG 2019
L. Leal-Taixé and S. Roth (Eds.): ECCV 2018 Workshops, LNCS 11131, pp. 526–535, 2019.
https://doi.org/10.1007/978-3-030-11015-4_38

used to create GANs (referred to as Deep Convolutional GANs or DCGANs) for modeling image data and other related applications [10,17]. More recently, however, Sabour et al. [18] introduced capsule networks (CapsNets) as a powerful alternative to CNNs, which learn a more *equivariant* representation of images that is more robust to changes in pose and spatial relationships of parts of objects in images [7] (information that CNNs lose during training, by design). Inspired by the working mechanism of optic neurons in the human visual system, capsules were first introduced by Hinton et al. [7] as locally invariant groups of neurons that learn to recognize visual entities and output activation vectors that represent both the presence of those entities and their properties relevant to the visual task (such as object classification). The training algorithm of CapsNets involves a routing mechanism between capsules in successive layers of the network that imitates hierarchical communication of information across neurons in human brains that are responsible for visual perception and understanding.

The initial intuition behind the design of deep neural networks was to imitate human brains for modeling hierarchical recognition of features, starting from low-level attributes and progressing towards complex entities. CapsNets capture this intuition more effectively than CNNs because they have the aforementioned in-built explicit mechanism that models it. CapsNets have been shown to outperform CNNs on MNIST digit classification and segmentation of overlapping digits [18]. This motivates the question whether GANs can be designed using CapsNets (instead of CNNs) to improve their performance.

We propose Generative Adversarial Capsule Network (CapsuleGAN) as a framework that incorporates capsules within the GAN framework. In particular, CapsNets are used as discriminators in our framework as opposed to the conventionally used CNNs. We show that CapsuleGANs perform better than CNN-based GANs at modeling the underlying distribution of MNIST [13] and CIFAR-10 [12] datasets both qualitatively and quantitatively using the generative adversarial metric (GAM) [9] and at semi-supervised classification using unlabeled GAN-generated images with a small number of labeled real images.

The rest of the paper is organized as follows. Section 2 discusses related work. In Sect. 3 we provide a brief introduction to GANs and CapsNets. Section 4 describes our CapsuleGAN framework along with implementation guidelines. Qualitative and quantitative analyses of our model are presented in Sect. 5. Section 6 concludes the paper and provides directions for future research.

2   Related Work

GANs were originally implemented as feedforward multi-layer perceptrons, which did not perform well on generating complex images like those in the CIFAR-10 dataset [12]. They suffered from mode collapse and were highly unstable to train [16,19]. In an attempt to solve these problems, Radford et al. [16] presented a set of guidelines to design GANs as a class of CNNs, giving rise to DCGANs, which have since been a dominant approach to GAN network architecture design. Im et al. [8] later proposed the use of Recurrent Neural Networks instead of CNNs as generators for GANs, creating a new class of GANs referred to as Generative Recurrent Adversarial Networks or GRANs. On a related note, Odena et al. [15] proposed an architectural change to GANs in the form of a discriminator that also acts as a classifier for class-conditional image generation. This approach for designing discriminators has been a popular choice for conditional GANs [14] recently. Our work is similar in line with [15] in the sense that we propose an architectural change to discriminators. We propose to transition from designing GAN discriminators as CNNs to formulating them as CapsNets, creating a new class of GANs called CapsuleGANs. This idea can be extended to encoder-based GANs like BiGAN [3] where the encoder can be modeled as a CapsNet also.

3   Preliminaries

3.1   Generative Adversarial Networks

Goodfellow et al. [5] introduced GANs as a framework for generative modeling of data through learning a transformation from points belonging to a simple prior distribution ($\mathbf{z} \sim p_z$) to those from the data distribution ($\mathbf{x} \sim p_{data}$). The framework is composed of two models that play an adversarial game: a generator and a discriminator. While the generator attempts to learn the aforementioned transformation $G(\mathbf{z})$, the discriminator acts as a critic $D(\cdot)$ determining whether the sample provided to it is from the generator's output distribution ($G(\mathbf{z}) \sim p_G$) or from the data distribution ($\mathbf{x} \sim p_{data}$), thus giving a scalar output ($y \in \{0, 1\}$). The goal of the generator is to fool the discriminator by generating samples that resemble those from the real data while that of the discriminator is to accurately distinguish between real and generated data. The two models, typically designed as neural networks, play an adversarial game with the objective as shown in Eq. 1.

$$\min_{G} \max_{D} V(D, G) = \mathbb{E}_{\mathbf{x} \sim p_{data}(\mathbf{x})} \left[\log D(\mathbf{x}) \right] + \mathbb{E}_{\mathbf{z} \sim p_z(\mathbf{z})} \left[\log(1 - D(G(\mathbf{z}))) \right] \quad (1)$$

3.2   Capsule Networks

The concept of capsules was first introduced by Hinton et al. [7] as a method for learning robust unsupervised representation of images. Capsules are locally invariant groups of neurons that learn to recognize the presence of visual entities and encode their properties into vector outputs, with the vector length (limited to being between zero and one) representing the presence of the entity. For example, each capsule can learn to identify certain objects or object-parts in images. Within the framework of neural networks, several capsules can be grouped together to form a capsule-layer where each unit produces a vector output instead of a (conventional) scalar activation.

Sabour et al. [18] introduced a routing-by-agreement mechanism for the interaction of capsules within deep neural networks with several capsule-layers, which works by pairwise determination of the passage of information between capsules in successive layers. For each capsule $h_i^{(l)}$ in layer l and each capsule $h_j^{(l+1)}$ in the layer above, a coupling coefficient c_{ij} is adjusted iteratively based on the agreement (cosine similarity) between h_i's prediction of the output of h_j and its actual output given the product of c_{ij} and h_i's activation. Thus, the coupling coefficients inherently decide how information flows between pairs of capsules. For a classification task involving K classes, the final layer of the CapsNet can be designed to have K capsules, each representing one class. Since the length of a capsule's vector output represents the presence of a visual entity, the length of each capsule in the final layer ($\|\mathbf{v_k}\|$) can then be viewed as the probability of the image belonging to a particular class (k). The authors introduce a margin loss L_M for training CapsNets for multi-class classification, as show in Eq. 2:

$$L_M = \sum_{k=1}^{K} T_k \max(0, m^+ - \|\mathbf{v_k}\|)^2 + \lambda(1 - T_k)\max(0, \|\mathbf{v_k}\| - m^-)^2 \quad (2)$$

where T_k represents target labels, $m^+ = 0.9$, $m^- = 0.1$ and $\lambda = 0.5$, a down-weighting factor for preventing initial learning from shrinking the lengths of the capsule outputs in the final layer. The authors also add regularization to the network in the form of a weighted image reconstruction loss, where the vector outputs $\mathbf{v_k}$ of the final layer are presented as inputs to the reconstruction network.

4   Generative Adversarial Capsule Networks

GANs have been mostly used for modeling the distribution of image data and associated attributes, as well as for other image-based applications like image-to-image translation [10] and image synthesis from textual descriptions [17]. The generator and the discriminator have conventionally been modeled as deep CNNs following the DCGAN guidelines [16]. We follow this convention in designing the CapsuleGAN generator as a deep CNN. However, motivated by the stronger intuition behind and the superior performance of CapsNets with respect to CNNs [18], we design the proposed CapsuleGAN framework to incorporate capsule-layers instead of convolutional layers in the GAN discriminator, which fundamentally performs a two-class classification task.

The CapsuleGAN discriminator is similar in architecture to the CapsNet model presented in [18]. CapsNets, in general, have a large number of parameters because, firstly, each capsule produces a vector output instead of a single scalar and, secondly, each capsule has *additional* parameters associated with all the capsules in the layer above it that are used for making predictions about their outputs. However, it is necessary to keep the number of parameters in the CapsuleGAN discriminator low due to two reasons: (1) CapsNets are very powerful models and can easily start harshly penalizing the generator early on in the training process, which will cause the generator to either fail completely or suffer from mode collapse, and (2) current implementations of the dynamic routing algorithm are slow to run. It is important to note that first reason for keeping the number of parameters of the CapsNet low falls in line with the popular design of convolutional discriminators as relatively shallow neural networks with low numbers of relatively large-sized filters in their convolutional layers.

The final layer of the CapsuleGAN discriminator contains a single capsule, the length of which represents the probability whether the discriminator's input is a real or a generated image. We use margin loss L_M instead of the conventional binary cross-entropy loss for training our CapsuleGAN model because L_M works better for training CapsNets. Therefore, the objective of CapsuleGAN can be formulated as shown in Eq. 3.

$$\min_G \max_D V(D, G)$$
$$= \mathbb{E}_{\mathbf{x} \sim p_{data}(\mathbf{x})} \left[-L_M(D(\mathbf{x}), \mathbf{T} = \mathbf{1}) \right] + \mathbb{E}_{\mathbf{z} \sim p_z(\mathbf{z})} \left[-L_M(D(G(\mathbf{z})), \mathbf{T} = \mathbf{0}) \right] \quad (3)$$

In practice, we train the generator to minimize $L_M(D(G(\mathbf{z})), \mathbf{T} = \mathbf{1})$ instead of minimizing $-L_M(D(G(\mathbf{z})), \mathbf{T} = \mathbf{0})$. This essentially eliminates the down-weighting factor λ in L_M when training the generator, which does not contain any capsules.

5   Experimental Evaluation

We evaluate the performance of CapsuleGANs at randomly generating images through a series of experiments as described below, in which we compare CapsuleGANs with convolutional GANs both qualitatively and quantitatively. We implement both the GAN models with the same architecture for their generators. Both convolutional GAN and the proposed CapsuleGAN models are implemented using the publicly available keras-adversarial[3] and CapsNet-Keras[4] packages.

5.1   Data

We provide results of our experiments on MNIST and CIFAR-10 datasets. The MNIST dataset consists of 28×28 sized grayscale images of handwritten digits. The CIFAR-10 dataset contains 32×32 color images grouped into ten classes: airplane, automobile, bird, cat, deer, dog, frog, horse, ship and truck.

5.2   Visual Quality of Randomly Generated Images

We qualitatively compare images generated randomly using both GAN and CapsuleGAN. Figures 1a and b show images generated using the standard convolutional-GAN and CapsuleGAN, respectively, on the MNIST dataset. Qualitatively, both CapsuleGAN and the standard convolutional-GAN produce crisp images of similar quality, that sometimes do not resemble any digit. However, the image-grid generated using GAN seems to have less diversity in terms

---

[3] https://github.com/bstriner/keras-adversarial.
[4] https://github.com/XifengGuo/CapsNet-Keras.

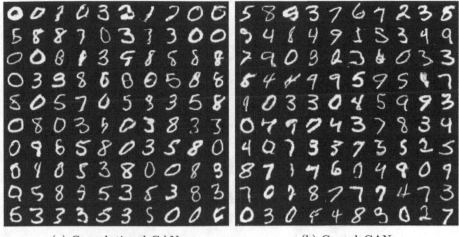

(a) Convolutional GAN   (b) CapsuleGAN

Fig. 1. Randomly generated MNIST images

of generated classes of digits. Figures 2a and b show the results of this experiment on the CIFAR-10 dataset. Both the models produce diverse sets of images but images generated using CapsuleGAN look cleaner and crisper than those generated using convolutional-GAN. We provide results of our quantitative evaluation in the following subsections for deeper analyses of the image generation performance.

5.3 Generative Adversarial Metric

Im et al. [9] introduced the generative adversarial metric (GAM) as a pairwise comparison metric between GAN models by pitting each generator against the opponent's discriminator, i.e., given two GAN models $M_1 = (G_1, D_1)$ and $M_2 = (G_2, D_2)$, G_1 engages in a battle against D_2 while G_2 against D_1. The ratios of their classification errors on real test dataset and on generated samples are then calculated as r_{test} and $r_{samples}$. Following their implementation[5], in practice, the ratios of classification accuracies are calculated instead of errors to avoid numerical problems, as shown in Eqs. 4 and 5

$$r_{samples} = \frac{A(D_{GAN}(G_{CapsuleGAN}(\mathbf{z})))}{A(D_{CapsuleGAN}(G_{GAN}(\mathbf{z})))} \tag{4}$$

$$r_{test} = \frac{A(D_{GAN}(\mathbf{x_{test}}))}{A(D_{CapsuleGAN}(\mathbf{x_{test}}))} \tag{5}$$

Therefore, for CapsuleGAN to win against GAN, both $r_{samples} < 1$ and $r_{test} \simeq 1$ must be satisfied. In our experiments, we achieve $r_{samples} = 0.79$

---

[5] https://github.com/jiwoongim/GRAN/battle.py.

(a) Convolutional GAN   (b) CapsuleGAN

Fig. 2. Randomly generated CIFAR-10 images

Table 1. Results of semi-supervised classification - MNIST

Model	Error rate		
	n = 100	n = 1,000	n = 10,000
Convolutional GAN	0.2900	0.1539	0.0702
CapsuleGAN	**0.2724**	**0.1142**	**0.0531**

and $r_{test} = 1$ on the MNIST dataset and $r_{samples} = 1.0$ and $r_{test} = 0.72$ on the CIFAR-10 dataset. Thus, on this metric, CapsuleGAN performs better than convolutional GAN on the MNIST dataset but the two models tie on the CIFAR-10 dataset.

5.4 Semi-supervised Classification

We evaluate the performance of the convolutional GAN and the proposed CapsuleGAN on semi-supervised classification. In this experiment, we randomly generate $50,000$ images using both GAN and CapsuleGAN. We use the Label Spreading algorithm [20] with the generated images as the unlabeled examples and n real labeled samples, with $n \in \{100, 1000, 10000\}$. We use the scikit-learn[6] package for these experiments. Table 1 shows the results of our experiments on MNIST while Table 2 shows those on CIFAR-10. The error rates are high in most experimental settings because we provide raw pixel values as features to the classification algorithm. However, this allows us to more objectively compare the two models without being biased by feature extraction methods.

---

[6] http://scikit-learn.org/.

Table 2. Results of semi-supervised classification - CIFAR-10

Model	Error rate		
	n = 100	n = 1,000	n = 10,000
Convolutional GAN	0.8305	0.7587	0.7209
CapsuleGAN	**0.7983**	**0.7496**	**0.7102**

The results show that the proposed CapsuleGAN consistently outperforms convolutional GAN for all the tested values of n with a margin of $1.7 - 3.97\%$ points for MNIST and $0.91 - 3.22\%$ points for CIFAR-10. Thus, CapsuleGAN generates images that are more similar to real images and more diverse than those generated using convolutional GAN, leading to better semi-supervised classification performance on the test dataset.

6   Discussion and Future Work

Generative adversarial networks are extremely powerful tools for generative modeling of complex data distributions. Research is being actively conducted towards further improving them as well as making their training easier and more stable. Motivated by the success of CapsNets over CNNs at image-based inference tasks, we presented the generative adversarial capsule network (CapsuleGAN), a GAN variant that incorporates CapsNets instead of CNNs as discriminators when modeling image data. We presented guidelines for designing CapsuleGANs as well as an updated objective function for training CapsuleGANs. We showed that CapsuleGANs outperform convolutional-GANs on the generative adversarial metric and at semi-supervised classification with a large number of unlabeled generated images and a small number of real labeled ones, on MNIST and CIFAR-10 datasets. This indicates that CapsNets should be considered as potential alternatives to CNNs for designing discriminators and other inference modules in future GAN models.

We plan to conduct theoretical analysis of the use of margin loss within the GAN objective. We purposefully did not incorporate many GAN training tricks to fairly evaluate our contributions. The results presented in this paper motivate the use of CapsNets as opposed to CNNs for encoders in GAN variants like BiCoGAN [11]. We see this as an important direction for future research.

Acknowledgements. This work is based on research sponsored by the Defense Advanced Research Projects Agency under agreement number FA8750-16-2-0204. The U.S. Government is authorized to reproduce and distribute reprints for governmental purposes notwithstanding any copyright notation thereon. The views and conclusions contained herein are those of the authors and should not be interpreted as necessarily representing the official policies or endorsements, either expressed or implied, of the Defense Advanced Research Projects Agency or the U.S. Government.

References

1. Arjovsky, M., Chintala, S., Bottou, L.: Wasserstein GAN. arXiv preprint arXiv:1701.07875 (2017)
2. Berthelot, D., Schumm, T., Metz, L.: Began: boundary equilibrium generative adversarial networks. arXiv preprint arXiv:1703.10717 (2017)
3. Donahue, J., Krähenbühl, P., Darrell, T.: Adversarial feature learning. In: International Conference on Learning Representations (2017)
4. Durugkar, I., Gemp, I., Mahadevan, S.: Generative multi-adversarial networks. In: International Conference on Learning Representations (2017)
5. Goodfellow, I., et al.: Generative adversarial nets. In: Advances in Neural Information Processing Systems, pp. 2672–2680 (2014)
6. Gulrajani, I., Ahmed, F., Arjovsky, M., Dumoulin, V., Courville, A.C.: Improved training of Wasserstein GANs. In: Advances in Neural Information Processing Systems, pp. 5769–5779 (2017)
7. Hinton, G.E., Krizhevsky, A., Wang, S.D.: Transforming auto-encoders. In: Honkela, T., Duch, W., Girolami, M., Kaski, S. (eds.) ICANN 2011. LNCS, vol. 6791, pp. 44–51. Springer, Heidelberg (2011). https://doi.org/10.1007/978-3-642-21735-7_6
8. Im, D.J., Kim, C.D., Jiang, H., Memisevic, R.: Generating images with recurrent adversarial networks. arXiv preprint arXiv:1602.05110 (2016)
9. Im, D.J., Kim, C.D., Jiang, H., Memisevic, R.: Generative adversarial metric (2016)
10. Isola, P., Zhu, J.Y., Zhou, T., Efros, A.A.: Image-to-image translation with conditional adversarial networks. In: The IEEE Conference on Computer Vision and Pattern Recognition (CVPR), July 2017
11. Jaiswal, A., AbdAlmageed, W., Wu, Y., Natarajan, P.: Bidirectional Conditional Generative Adversarial Networks. arXiv preprint arXiv:1711.07461 (2017)
12. Krizhevsky, A.: Learning multiple layers of features from tiny images (2009)
13. LeCun, Y., Bottou, L., Bengio, Y., Haffner, P.: Gradient-based learning applied to document recognition. Proc. IEEE **86**(11), 2278–2324 (1998)
14. Mirza, M., Osindero, S.: Conditional Generative Adversarial Nets. arXiv preprint arXiv:1411.1784 (2014)
15. Odena, A., Olah, C., Shlens, J.: Conditional image synthesis with auxiliary classifier GANs. In: Precup, D., Teh, Y.W. (eds.) Proceedings of the 34th International Conference on Machine Learning, Proceedings of Machine Learning Research, vol. 70, pp. 2642–2651. PMLR, International Convention Centre, Sydney, Australia, 06–11 August 2017. http://proceedings.mlr.press/v70/odena17a.html
16. Radford, A., Metz, L., Chintala, S.: Unsupervised representation learning with deep convolutional generative adversarial networks. In: International Conference on Learning Representations (2016)
17. Reed, S., Akata, Z., Yan, X., Logeswaran, L., Schiele, B., Lee, H.: Generative adversarial text-to-image synthesis. In: Proceedings of The 33rd International Conference on Machine Learning (2016)
18. Sabour, S., Frosst, N., Hinton, G.E.: Dynamic routing between capsules. In: Advances in Neural Information Processing Systems, pp. 3859–3869 (2017)

19. Salimans, T., et al.: Improved techniques for training GANs. In: Lee, D.D., Sugiyama, M., Luxburg, U.V., Guyon, I., Garnett, R. (eds.) Advances in Neural Information Processing Systems, vol. 29, pp. 2234–2242. Curran Associates, Inc. (2016). http://papers.nips.cc/paper/6125-improved-techniques-for-training-gans. pdf
20. Zhou, D., Bousquet, O., Lal, T.N., Weston, J., Schölkopf, B.: Learning with local and global consistency. In: Advances in Neural Information Processing Systems, vol. 16. pp. 321–328. MIT Press (2004)

Navigational Affordance Cortical Responses Explained by Scene-Parsing Model

Kshitij Dwivedi[ID] and Gemma Roig[✉][ID]

Singapore University of Technology and Design, Singapore, Singapore
kshitij_dwivedi@mymail.sutd.edu.sg, gemma_roig@sutd.edu.sg

Abstract. Deep Neural Networks (DNNs) are the leading models for explaining the population responses of neurons in the visual cortex. Recent studies show that responses of some task-specific brain regions can also be explained by a DNN trained for classification. In this work, we propose that responses of task-specific brain regions are better explained by DNNs trained on a similar task. We first show that responses of scene selective visual areas like parahippocampal place area (PPA) and Occipital Place Area (OPA) are better explained by a DNN trained for scene classification than one trained for object classification. Next, we consider a particular case of OPA which has been shown to encode navigational affordances. We argue that a scene parsing task, which predicts the class of each pixel in the scene is more related to navigational affordances than scene classification. Our results show that the responses in OPA are better explained by the scene parsing model than the scene classification model.

Keywords: Deep Neural Networks ·
Representational similarity analysis · Occipital Place Area ·
Neural Encoding

1 Introduction

In recent works, DNNs have been shown to explain the responses of the human visual cortex. In several recent works [3,7,8,12,15–17], it has also been demonstrated that responses in visual cortex during perception and neural network activations of different layers of a DNN are highly correlated. Areas from higher visual cortex have been shown to be more correlated with the deeper layers [7,17] and areas of lower visual cortex have been shown to be highly correlated with the initial layers of the DNN [7].

DNNs have also been used to explain responses of brain areas associated with specific visual tasks. In a recent work by Bonner and Epstein [2], they explore the possibility of explaining the navigational affordances with the functional Magnetic Resonance Imaging (fMRI) activation patterns in the OPA. They show that fMRI responses in OPA are associated with the navigational affordances of

© Springer Nature Switzerland AG 2019
L. Leal-Taixé and S. Roth (Eds.): ECCV 2018 Workshops, LNCS 11131, pp. 536–545, 2019.
https://doi.org/10.1007/978-3-030-11015-4_39

the scenes. In a subsequent work [1], they explore if layers of a DNN trained for scene classification can serve as a computational model of navigational affordance related responses in the OPA.

In this work, we investigate if the responses of a brain area performing specific visual tasks are explained better by a computational model performing a similar task rather than a generic classification model. In scene parsing task, the aim is to predict the class labels for all the locations in the image. The output of the scene parsing task can label the free space available for navigation and the obstacles present in the scene. Thus, we argue that a scene parsing model will explain the spatial scene property like navigational affordances, and hence, the OPA responses better than a scene classification model. We investigate this in the following steps:

1. We investigate if a scene classification model better explains the responses in scene-selective areas PPA [6] and OPA [5] better than an object classification model.
2. We investigate if a model trained on a potential task similar to navigational affordance such as scene parsing explains OPA responses and behavioral model for navigational affordances better than a scene classification model.
3. We perform a detailed comparative analysis of the specific class labels with the OPA and PPA responses to gain more insights into the functionality of these areas.

The results from all the experiments above suggest that due to task similarity, scene parsing model explains cortical responses to the navigational affordance in scenes better than a classification model. Our results reinforce the use of models trained to perform similar tasks for explaining responses of task-specific areas in the visual cortex.

2   Methods

In the first section, we describe RSA [9] which is a standard method to compare the correlation of computational and behavioral models with human brain activity. In the second section, we briefly describe the dataset we used in this work and then in the following sections we provide the details of the DNN models used for analysis.

2.1   Representation Similarity Analysis (RSA)

RSA is used to compare the information encoded in brain responses with a computational or behavioral model by computing the correlation of the corresponding Representation Dissimilarity matrices (RDMs). In the case of comparison with DNNs, we compute the correlation of RDMs of the brain responses with the RDM of layer activations of the DNNs.

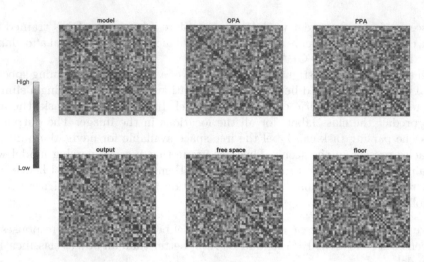

Fig. 1. Top row: RDM of the behavioral model for navigational affordance followed by RDMs of brain responses in OPA and PPA. Bottom row: RDMs of final layer, free space labels, and floor mask output of a scene parsing DNN

Representation Dissimilarity Matrix (RDM). The RDM for a dataset is constructed by computing dissimilarities of all possible pairs of stimulus images. For fMRI data, the RDMs are computed by comparing the fMRI responses while for DNNs the RDMs are computed by comparing the layer activations for each image pair in the dataset. In this work, we consider OPA and PPA RDMs for comparison as these areas have been hypothesized to represent scene affordances [2] and scene layout [6] respectively. We also compare the DNN RDMs with a behavior Navigational Affordance Map (NAM) [1] that represents navigational affordances in a scene. The top row in Fig. 1 shows RDMs of NAM, OPA, PPA obtained from the dataset and bottom row shows the RDMs of the final layer output, combined activation of units corresponding to free space, and activation of the floor unit of the scene parsing DNN.

The dissimilarity metric used in this work is $1 - \rho$ where ρ is the Pearson's correlation coefficient. Although in previous work [1], where a scene classification DNN was compared with the navigational affordance the dissimilarity metric used was the Euclidean distance, we observed that with $1 - \rho$ as the dissimilarity metric, the correlation was higher. Hence, in this work for all the analysis $1 - \rho$ is used as the dissimilarity metric to compute RDMs of layer activations. We did not use PCA on layer activations as done in [1] since the spatial information in the case of convolutional layer outputs is lost by performing PCA.

Statistical Analysis. We use RSA toolbox [13] to compute RDM correlations and corresponding p-values and standard deviation using bootstrap similar to [1]. For determining which RDM better explains the behavioral or neural RDMs, we perform a two-sided statistical comparison. The p-values are estimated as the proportion of bootstrap samples further in the tails than 0. The number of bootstrap iterations for all the analysis was set to 5000.

2.2   Navigational Affordance Dataset and Model

The stimuli images used for analysis consisted of 50 images of indoor environments. The subject's fMRI responses were obtained while they performed a category-recognition task (bathroom or not). In this work, we directly use the precomputed RDMs of the navigational affordance map (NAM), PPA and OPA provided by Bonner and Epstein [1]. Recall that RDMs are constructed by computing dissimilarities of all possible pairs in the dataset as explained in Sect. 2.1.

To obtain NAM, first, an independent group of subjects was asked to indicate the paths in each image starting from the bottom using a computer mouse. The probabilistic maps of paths for each image were created followed by histogram construction of navigational probability in one-degree angular bins radiating from the bottom center of the image. This histogram represents a probabilistic map of potential navigation routes from the viewer's perspective. For further details of the navigational affordance model or dataset, we refer the reader to [1, 2].

2.3   Deep Neural Network Models to Explain Brain Responses

In this section, we describe the architecture of the DNN models used in the analysis.

Object Classification Model. We used Alexnet [10] which we refer as Alexnet$_{object}$, trained on Imagenet [4] dataset (an object classification dataset) as the object classification model. The Alexnet model [10] consists of 5 convolutional layers each followed by a pooling layer and 3 fully connected layers after the last pooling layer.

Scene Classification Models. We used the same model as above (Alexnet) but trained on Places [18] dataset (a scene classification dataset) as the scene classification model (referred as Alexnet$_{scene}$). For comparison with scene parsing model we choose VGG16 [14] trained on Places as the scene classification model (VGG$_{scene-class}$). The reason behind the different choice of scene classification models was that we were unable to find a pretrained scene parsing model with similar architecture as Alexnet. The VGG16 model contains 13 convolutional layers with 5 pooling layer after a convolutional block of either 2 or 3 convolutional layers and 3 fully connected (FC) layers after the last convolutional layer.

Scene Parsing Models. We use fully convolutional modification of VGG16 [11] trained on the scene parsing dataset ADE20k [19,20] as the scene parsing model (referred as $VGG_{scene-parse}$). In $VGG_{scene-parse}$, the FC layers are replaced by convolutional layers to predict pixel-wise spatial mask. We use pyramid scene parsing network ($PSP_{scene-parse}$) for performing analysis of class specific masks as $PSP_{scene-parse}$ outperforms $VGG_{scene-parse}$ on scene parsing task and hence the class masks are more accurate and suitable for this particular analysis. The $PSP_{scene-parse}$ model introduces a pyramid pooling module that fuses features of four different scales to obtain superior performance on scene parsing task.

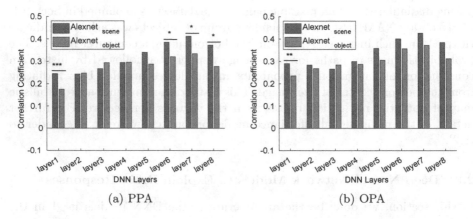

(a) PPA   (b) OPA

Fig. 2. RSA of (a) PPA with layers of DNN trained on scene and object classification.(b) OPA with layers of DNN trained on scene and object classification. The asterisk at the top indicates the significance of difference (*$p < 0.05$, **$p < 0.01$, ***$p < 0.001$)

3   Results

Here, we first report the correlation results of the scene-selective areas (OPA and PPA) with an object classification model ($Alexnet_{object}$) and a scene classification model ($Alexnet_{scene}$). Then, we report the correlation results of the NAM, OPA, and PPA with a scene parsing model ($VGG_{scene-parse}$) and a scene classification model ($VGG_{scene-class}$). Finally, we investigate category specific activations of the scene-parsing model and compare the correlations of NAM, OPA, and PPA with relevant categories.

3.1   Scene vs. Object Classification

We compare the correlation of all pooling and fully connected layer outputs of $Alexnet_{scene}$ and $Alexnet_{object}$ with scene-selective brain areas (OPA and PPA). From the comparison result with PPA, we observe that for all the layers except pool3 the $Alexnet_{scene}$ show a higher correlation (Fig. 2(a)). A similar trend is observed by comparing with OPA (Fig. 2(b)). The results support our hypothesis that a model trained on a related type of images better represents the brain activity.

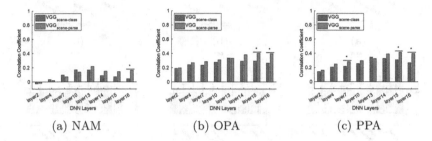

| (a) NAM | (b) OPA | (c) PPA |

Fig. 3. RSA of (a) NAM with layers of DNN trained on scene classification and parsing(b) OPA with layers of DNN trained on scene classification and parsing, and, (c) PPA with layers of DNN trained on scene classification and parsing. The asterisk at the top indicates the significance of difference (*$p < 0.05$, **$p < 0.01$, ***$p < 0.001$)

3.2 Scene-Parsing vs. Scene-Classification

For computing the correlation with OPA, PPA, and NAM, we use the outputs of 5 pooling layer and 3 fully connected layers of VGG$_{\text{scene-class}}$ and 5 pooling layers and convolutionalized version of 3 fully connected layers of VGG$_{\text{scene-parse}}$

In general, from Fig. 3 we observe that deeper layers of VGG$_{\text{scene-parse}}$ model have higher correlation values with the behavioral model and brain responses than the earlier layers. Further, for all three cases, we observe that the difference in correlation values of VGG$_{\text{scene-parse}}$ and VGG$_{\text{scene-class}}$ is more significant in the deeper layers with higher correlation values for VGG$_{\text{scene-parse}}$ layers.

One explanation for these results that supports our hypothesis is that the deeper layers of the DNNs are more task-relevant while earlier layers perform generic feature processing. A related possible explanation might be that since VGG$_{\text{scene-parse}}$ is a fully convolutional model, it's last three layers are convolutional while in VGG$_{\text{scene-class}}$ the last 3 layers are fully connected. This suggests that convolutional layers may better represent a spatial scene property such as navigational affordance. The convolutional layer output has information about the spatial structure of the scene in explicit form while fully connected layers lose the spatial information, and therefore this might be another possible reason for the high difference in the correlation values. This again supports our hypothesis of task-related models being more correlated as compared to a generic model.

The results also suggest that spatial information is preserved in the higher brain areas such as PPA and OPA and the models with the fully connected layers may not represent these areas better than fully convolutional models. The results show navigational affordance related model VGG$_{\text{scene-parse}}$ shows a higher correlation in most of the layers with NAM, PPA, and OPA.

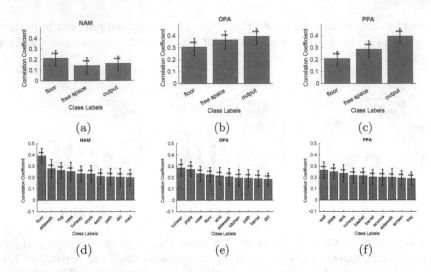

Fig. 4. Top: RSA of final layer output of $VGG_{scene-parse}$, free space, floor labels with (a) NAM,(b) OPA, and (c) PPA. Bottom: Top-10 correlated classes with (d) NAM,(e) OPA, and (f) PPA. Error bars represent bootstrap ± 1 s.e.m. (*$p < 0.05$, **$p < 0.01$, ***$p < 0.001$).

3.3   Floor and Free Space Labels

To investigate further what information is present in the OPA activity, we first separate out labels from the ADE20k dataset which correspond to free space. We found 13 such labels (road, floor, sidewalk, etc.) that correspond to free spaces. Since the images in the dataset were from indoor scenes, we considered one more case with only floor label. The output of $VGG_{scene-parse}$ consists of 151 channels in which 150 channels correspond to a class in the ADE20k dataset, and one channel corresponds to the background. Therefore, we investigated if the output of channels corresponding to free space classes such as roads and floor might have a higher correlation with the NAM and OPA.

Using RSA, we compute the correlation of the final layer of the scene parsing with NAM and OPA and compare it with the output containing only free space labels (13 channels) and floor labels (1 channel). From the results of the comparison, shown in Fig. 4 (top row), we observe that although for RSA analysis with NAM the output with only floor label shows the highest correlation this is not the case with the OPA. The results suggest that OPA might encode information more than just the floor labels which are highly representative of the navigational affordance in the images considered.

Top Correlated Classes. To gain further insights about the information encoded in OPA and PPA we computed the correlation of each class activation from the DNN with place areas OPA and PPA and also with the NAM. From the class activation maps with high correlatison values, we may gain some insights about what is encoded in the place areas. For this analysis, we choose a highly accurate scene-parsing model $PSP_{scene-parse}$ which generates more accurate masks than $VGG_{scene-parse}$ model used in the previous analysis. We take the activations of the last output layers which has 150 channels corresponding to each class in the ADE20k dataset and then compute RDMs corresponding to each channel output for RSA analysis.

For the NAM (Fig. 4(d)), as expected the floor class has the highest correlation. The next few classes that showed the highest correlation values were also indicative of free space such as rug, sidewalk, runway, etc. Surprisingly, the objects such as vase and clock also showed high correlation. This might be because vase and clock are typically placed on floor and wall, respectively.

For OPA (Fig. 4(e)), although 50% of the labels in the top-10 list included labels corresponding to free space, rest of the labels include objects like plate, vase, sink, kitchen, and barrel. One possible explanation for these classes is the experimental design in which the OPA responses were recorded. The subjects were asked to classify whether the room displayed is a bathroom or not. The objects such as sink, plate, and vase are highly indicative of the room type, and OPA responses may be related to the classification task. Therefore, the high correlation of OPA with these objects is explained by assuming that OPA is involved in the classification task. Further, knowing the scene category is also crucial for planning navigation. A related possible explanation is that the objects also suggest the spatial layout of the scene by indicating the presence of obstacles and therefore can be relevant for navigational affordances.

PPA, on the other hand, is hypothesized to represent the spatial layout of the scenes and is insensitive to the navigational affordance as shown in [1]. The results from this analysis (Fig. 4(f)) are consistent with [1] as the majority of the labels with high correlation are objects that are indicative of scene layout and category and only a few of the highly correlated classes correspond to free space.

4   Conclusion

In this work, we demonstrated that task-specific areas in the visual cortex are better explained by a model trained to perform a similar task. In particular, we first showed that responses of scene selective visual areas are better explained by a DNN trained on the similar type of the images. Next, we showed that OPA activity which has been hypothesized to be associated with the navigational affordances shows a higher correlation with task-relevant deeper layers of a scene parsing DNN than a scene classification DNN.

Our results also show that a DNN model trained for scene parsing task may provide more insights about the brain responses associated with navigational affordances (OPA brain area). With the scene parsing model, we were able to perform the detailed analysis with each class activation showing that OPA responses are also highly correlated with the objects that are indicative of the scene type. This suggests that OPA also plays a role in scene classification since knowing scene category is also crucial for planning navigation.

Acknowledgement. This work was funded by the MOE SUTD SRG grant (SRG ISTD 2017 131). Kshitij Dwivedi was also funded by SUTD President's Graduate Fellowship.

References

1. Bonner, M.F., Epstein, R.A.: Computational mechanisms underlying cortical responses to the affordance properties of visual scenes. PLOS Comput. Biol. **14**, e1006111 (2018). https://doi.org/10.1371/journal.pcbi.1006111
2. Bonner, M.F., Epstein, R.A.: Coding of navigational affordances in the human visual system. Proc. Nat. Acad. Sci. **114**(18), 4793–4798 (2017)
3. Cichy, R.M., Khosla, A., Pantazis, D., Torralba, A., Oliva, A.: Comparison of deep neural networks to spatio-temporal cortical dynamics of human visual object recognition reveals hierarchical correspondence. Sci. Rep. **6**(June), 1–13 (2016). https://doi.org/10.1038/srep27755
4. Deng, J., Dong, W., Socher, R., Li, L.J., Li, K., Fei-Fei, L.: Imagenet: a large-scale hierarchical image database. In: 2009 IEEE Conference on Computer Vision and Pattern Recognition. CVPR 2009, pp. 248–255. IEEE (2009)
5. Dilks, D.D., Julian, J.B., Paunov, A.M., Kanwisher, N.: The occipital place area is causally and selectively involved in scene perception. J. Neurosci. **33**(4), 1331–1336 (2013)
6. Epstein, R., Harris, A., Stanley, D., Kanwisher, N.: The parahippocampal place area: recognition, navigation, or encoding? Neuron **23**(1), 115–125 (1999)
7. Horikawa, T., Kamitani, Y.: Generic decoding of seen and imagined objects using hierarchical visual features. Nature Commun. **8**, 15037 (2017)
8. Khaligh-Razavi, S.M., Kriegeskorte, N.: Deep supervised, but not unsupervised, models may explain IT cortical representation. PLoS Comput. Biol. **10**(11), e1003915 (2014). https://doi.org/10.1371/journal.pcbi.1003915
9. Kriegeskorte, N., Mur, M., Bandettini, P.A.: Representational similarity analysis-connecting the branches of systems neuroscience. Front. Syst. Neurosci. **2**, 4 (2008)
10. Krizhevsky, A., Sutskever, I., Hinton, G.E.: ImageNet classification with deep convolutional neural networks. In: Advances in Neural Information Processing Systems, pp. 1097–1105 (2012)
11. Long, J., Shelhamer, E., Darrell, T.: Fully convolutional networks for semantic segmentation. In: Proceedings of the IEEE Conference on Computer Vision and Pattern Recognition, pp. 3431–3440 (2015)
12. Martin Cichy, R., Khosla, A., Pantazis, D., Oliva, A.: Dynamics of scene representations in the human brain revealed by magnetoencephalography and deep neural networks. NeuroImage **153**, 346–358 (2017). https://doi.org/10.1016/j.neuroimage.2016.03.063
13. Nili, H., Wingfield, C., Walther, A., Su, L., Marslen-Wilson, W., Kriegeskorte, N.: A toolbox for representational similarity analysis. PLoS Comput. Biol. **10**(4), e1003553 (2014)
14. Simonyan, K., Zisserman, A.: Very deep convolutional networks for large-scale image recognition. arXiv preprint arXiv:1409.1556 (2014)
15. Tacchetti, A., Isik, L., Poggio, T.: Invariant recognition drives neural representations of action sequences, pp. 1–23 (2016). https://doi.org/10.1371/journal.pcbi.1005859. http://arxiv.org/abs/1606.04698

16. Yamins, D.L.K., Hong, H., Cadieu, C.F., Solomon, E.A., Seibert, D., DiCarlo, J.J.: Performance-optimized hierarchical models predict neural responses in higher visual cortex. Proc. Nat. Acad. Sci. **111**(23), 8619–8624 (2014). https://doi.org/10.1073/pnas.1403112111. http://www.pnas.org/cgi/doi/10.1073/pnas.1403112111

17. Yamins, D.L., DiCarlo, J.J.: Using goal-driven deep learning models to understand sensory cortex. Nat. Neurosci. **19**(3), 356 (2016)

18. Zhou, B., Lapedriza, A., Khosla, A., Oliva, A., Torralba, A.: Places: a 10 million image database for scene recognition. IEEE Trans. Pattern Anal. Mach. Intell. **40**, 1452–1464 (2017)

19. Zhou, B., Zhao, H., Puig, X., Fidler, S., Barriuso, A., Torralba, A.: Semantic understanding of scenes through the ADE20K dataset. arXiv preprint arXiv:1608.05442 (2016)

20. Zhou, B., Zhao, H., Puig, X., Fidler, S., Barriuso, A., Torralba, A.: Scene parsing through ADE20K dataset. In: Proceedings of the IEEE Conference on Computer Vision and Pattern Recognition, pp. 633–641 (2017)

A Context-Aware Capsule Network
for Multi-label Classification

Sameera Ramasinghe[1,2]($\boxtimes$), C. D. Athuraliya[1], and Salman H. Khan[2]

[1] ConscientAI Labs, Colombo, Sri Lanka
[2] Australian National University, Canberra, Australia
sameera.ramasinghe@anu.edu.au

Abstract. Recently proposed Capsule Network is a brain inspired architecture that brings a new paradigm to deep learning by modelling input domain variations through vector based representations. Despite being a seminal contribution, CapsNet does not explicitly model structured relationships between the detected entities and among the capsule features for related inputs. Motivated by the working of cortical network in HVS, we seek to resolve CapsNet limitations by proposing several intuitive modifications to the CapsNet architecture. We introduce, (1) a novel routing weight initialization technique, (2) an improved CapsNet design that exploits semantic relationships between the primary capsule activations using a densely connected Conditional Random Field and (3) a Cholesky transformation based correlation module to learn a general priority scheme. Our proposed design allows CapsNet to scale better to more complex problems, such as the multi-label classification task, where semantically related categories co-exist with various interdependencies. We present theoretical bases for our extensions and demonstrate significant improvements on ADE20K scene dataset.

1 Introduction

After nearly two decades since its inception, convolutional neural networks (CNNs) [1] have eventually become the norm for computer vision tasks. Vision tasks that widely use CNNs include object recognition [2,3], object detection [4,5] and semantic segmentation [6,7]. Despite their popularity and high effectiveness in most vision tasks, previous works have pointed out several limitations of CNNs in vision applications. One major limitation is the notable trade-off between preserved spatial information and the transformation invariance with pooling operations. Furthermore, CNNs marginally tackle rotational invariance.

To overcome aforementioned limitations in CNNs, recently introduced Capsule Networks (CapsNets) [8] propose a novel deep architecture for feature abstraction while preserving underlying spatial information. This architecture is motivated by human brain function and suggests equivariance over invariance while demonstrating comparable performance on digit classification with MNIST dataset [9]. These early results of CapsNet manifest a new direction for future deep architectures. However to our knowledge, CapsNet architecture

L. Leal-Taixé and S. Roth (Eds.): ECCV 2018 Workshops, LNCS 11131, pp. 546–554, 2019.
https://doi.org/10.1007/978-3-030-11015-4_40

has not been used for larger and complex datasets, specifically for multi-label classification tasks where the goal is to tag an input image with multiple object categories. This is due to the reason that original CapsNet does not incorporate contextual information necessary for complex tasks such as multi-label classification. In this work we evaluate the original CapsNet architecture on a large image dataset with over 150 object classes that appear in complex real-world scenes. We then propose a new context-aware CapsNet architecture that makes informed predictions by exploiting semantic relationships of object classes as well as underlying correlations of low-level capsules. Our model is inspired by the working of human brain where contextual and prior information is effectively modeled [10].

To enable faster training on large datasets, we **first** propose a novel weight initialization scheme based on trainable parameters with back-propagation. This update allows initial routing weights to capture low-level feature distributions and improves the convergence rate and accuracy compared to equal routing weight initialization of the original CapsNet. **Second**, we argue that the corresponding elements of primary capsule predictions are interrelated since primary capsule predictions encapsulate the attributes of object classes. In simple terms, this means that the presence of object attributes (such as position, rotation and texture) in one capsule's output are dependent on similar attributes that are detected by neighbouring capsules. This property was not utilized in the original CapsNet architecture. To characterize this, we introduce an end-to-end trainable Conditional Random Field (CRF) to encourage network predictions to be more context specific. **Third**, the original CapsNet captures the priority between primary and decision capsules independently for each data point. We argue that there exists a general priority scheme between decision and primary capsules, which is distributed across the dataset. Therefore, we propose a correlation module to capture the overall priority of primary capsule predictions throughout the dataset that effectively encapsulates broader context.

We apply proposed architecture for multi-label classification on a large scene dataset, ADE20K [11], and report significant improvements over the original CapsNet architecture.

2   Related Work

Hinton et al. [12] first proposed capsule as a new module in deep neural networks by transforming auto-encoders architecture. Capsules were suggested as an alternative to widely adapted subsampling layers of CNNs and to encapsulate more precise spatial relationships. Sabour et al. [8] recently proposed a complete neural network architecture for capsules with dynamic routing and a reconstruction loss. They demonstrated state of the art performance on MNIST dataset [9]. They also outperformed existing CNN architectures on a new dataset, MultiMNIST [8], created by overlaying one digit on top of another digit from a different class. More recently, Hinton et al. [13] proposed an updated capsule architecture with a logistic unit and a new iterative routing procedure between capsule layers based on the Expectation-Maximization (EM) algorithm [14]. This new capsule architecture significantly outperformed baseline CNN models on small-NORB dataset [15] and reported that the new architecture is less vulnerable to white box adversarial attacks. Xi *et al.* [16] extended initial CapsNet work by utilizing it on CIFAR10 classification task. However, CapsNet has not been used before for complex structured prediction tasks and our work is a key step towards this direction.

3   Methodology

A decision capsule is considered to be a complete representation of an object class. That means each of its scalar element describes a certain attribute of an object class such as rotation or position. These attributes may not be semantically meaningful, but an object can be completely reconstructed using the elements of the corresponding capsule. Each corresponding element of different decision capsules represents similar attributes of different objects. For example, the ith scalar element of jth decision capsule may represent the rotation of a chair, while i^{th} scalar element of $(j + 1)^{th}$ decision capsule may describe the rotation of a desk.

The predictions by primary capsules for decision capsules encapsulate the attributes of an object class. Therefore, the corresponding elements of outputs from primary capsules are conditioned upon each other. For example, there may be a hidden condition such that if the primary capsule is in state A, a chair cannot be rotated in α direction when a spatially nearby desk is rotated in β direction. To exploit this behavior we feed primary capsule predictions to an end-to-end trainable CRF module to learn the inter-dependencies among attributes.

Here, CRF module is used as a structured prediction mechanism for each primary capsule to conditionally alter its predictions. Thus the CRF is able to capture semantic relationships across object classes. Moreover, we introduce a correlation module which can prioritize predictions by primary capsules and effectively predict decision capsules. The overall architecture is illustrated in Fig. 1. We first begin with the description of routing weight initialization and then explain the densely connected CRF and the correlation module in subsequent sections.

3.1   Initializing Routing Weights

In the original CapsNet, primary capsules can be interpreted as a set of Z stacked feature maps. Each primary capsule element can be considered as a part of a low-level feature. Following this assumption we rearrange primary capsules as a $N \times N \times D$ grid where $N \times N \times D$ is the total number of primary capsules. Each item in the grid is a capsule with I dimensions. Hence, $D = Z/I$.

Instead of initializing routing weights equally, we modify the initial routing weights as trainable parameters and use backpropagation to train them.

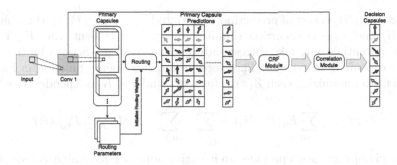

Fig. 1. Proposed CapsNet architecture

This forces the initial routing weights to be dependent on the low-level feature distribution resulting faster convergence.

To this end, we first define a statistical value per capsule to represent its element distribution. Let K and J be the number of primary and decision capsules respectively, and $C = \{c_1, c_2, \ldots, c_K\}$ be the set of primary capsules. Then we map the capsules to a set $S = \{s_1, s_2, \ldots, s_K\}$ where $s_k = \frac{\mu_k}{max(\sigma_k, \epsilon)}, \forall 0 < k < K, 0 < \epsilon << 1$ and μ_k and σ_k are mean and standard deviation of kth primary capsule elements respectively. $max(\sigma_k, \epsilon)$ gives the maximum value between σ_k and ϵ for each k. The operation outputs a real valued $N \times N \times D$ dimensional tensor. Treating this tensor as a stacked set of feature maps and convolving it with a single $f \times f$ kernel with $(f-1)/2$ padding, where f is a positive integer (we use $f - 5$ in our experiments), give a set of feature maps with dimensions $N \times N \times D$. We obtain $K \times J$ dimension matrix B by transforming the elements of the feature maps as a row vector $\hat{b} = (b_1, b_2, \ldots, b_K)$, and then repeating it J times. We use elements of B as initial routing weights between primary and decision capsules.

3.2 CRF Module

CRF is an effective technique for structured prediction where output variables are interdependent. Furthermore, CRFs are capable of discriminative training due to conditional probabilistic modeling. They are widely used in important applications of computer vision, natural language processing and bioinformatics. We propose to use CRFs to model relationships between primary capsules in the CapsNet. The CRF models each element of each primary capsule prediction as a random variable and forms a Markov Random Field when the variables are conditioned upon inputs.

Let $P_{k,j}(i)$ denote the ith element of the prediction by k^{th} primary capsule for the jth decision capsule. Considering predictions for all decision capsules by primary capsules, we define the energy function,

$$Z(x) = \sum_{k=0}^{K}\sum_{i=0}^{I}\sum_{j=0}^{J} E_u(P_{k,j}(i)) + \sum_{k=0}^{K}\sum_{i=0}^{I}\sum_{j'=0}^{J}\sum_{j=0, j\neq j'}^{J} E_p(P_{k,j}(i), P_{k,j'}(i)) \quad (1)$$

where $E_u(P_{k,j}(i))$ is cost of prediction $P_{k,j}(i)$ and $E_p(P_{k,j}(i), P_{k,j'}(i))$ is the cost of $P_{k,j}(i)$ and $P_{k,j'}(i)$ occurring simultaneously. It is evident from Eq. 1 that pairwise potentials only take corresponding elements of predictions by the same primary capsule in to account. Therefore minimizing energy function in Eq. 1 is equivalent to minimizing each $Z(x)_{k,i}$ for $i < I$ and $k < K$ independently where,

$$Z(x)_{k,i} = \sum_{j=0}^{J} E_u(P_{k,j}(i)) + \sum_{j'=0}^{J} \sum_{j=0,j\neq j'}^{J} E_p(P_{k,j}(i), P_{k,j'}(i)) \qquad (2)$$

Mean-field approximation provides an iterative approach to minimize dense CRF energy functions. This technique approximates a total energy function $Z(x)_{k,i}$ as a product of simple marginal energy functions $Z(X)_{k,i} = \prod_l H_{k,i}^l(x_l)$.

Zheng et al. [17] leveraged this idea by formulating a dense CRF as a stack of differentiable layers. They also showed that multiple iterations of this stack of layers can be treated as an RNN. We adapt this technique to minimize the energy function Eq. 2.

Algorithm 1. CRF as a stack of CNN layers

1: $H_{kj}(i) = \frac{1}{X_{ik}} exp(E_u(P_{k,j}(i))) \forall i, j, k$ ▷ **Initialization**
2: **for** $itr = 0$ **to** $MaxItr$ **do**
3:     $\bar{H}_{kj}(i) = \sum_{j'} E_p(H_{kj}(i), H_{kj'}(i))$ ▷ **Calculation of pair-wise potentials**
4:     $\tilde{H}_{kj}(i) = H_{kj}(i) - \bar{H}_{kj}(i)$ ▷ **Addition of pair-wise potentials to unary potentials**
5:     $H_{kj}(i) = \frac{1}{X_{ik}} e^{\tilde{H}_{kj}(i)}$ ▷ **Normalization**
6: **end for**

The first line is the initialization. Here, $X_{i,k} = \sum_{j=0}^{J} e^{P_{ij}^k}$ where J is the number of decision capsules. Since $E_u(P_{k,j}(i))$ is the cost of the ith element of the prediction, we can treat the predicted element as $P_{k,j} = -E_u(P_{k,j}(i))$. This is equivalent to applying the softmax function over each set of ith elements of the predictions by k^{th} primary capsule for j^{th} decision capsules. Line number 3 illustrates the cost of pair-wise potentials. Instead of deriving the pair-wise potential function manually, using back-propagation to find optimum mapping is both effective and efficient. Since all the corresponding element pairs have to be taken into account, we apply a fully connected layer on top of the predictions to learn this pair-wise potential function. Since we are minimizing $Z(x)_{k,i}$ for each i and k independently, these layers are not connected across i or k, which reduces the computational complexity significantly. Line number 4 illustrates adding the unary potentials to pair-wise potentials. Line number 5 is equivalent to applying softmax function over the outputs.

3.3 Correlation Module

In the CapsNet architecture, each primary capsule has a unique prediction for each decision capsule. Since primary capsules are essentially a set of low-level features, this can be viewed as each low level feature estimating the state of the output class. Moreover, each low-level feature priority depends on the output class. For example, a circle detector may perform better in predicting the state of a wheel, while a horizontal edge detector may perform better in predicting the state of a bridge.

The original routing technique tries to capture these varying priorities of primary capsules with respect to decision capsules by a weighted sum of predictions. The routing weights are adjusted in the next iteration according to the similarity between primary capsule predictions and the decision capsule of the current iteration. The magnitude of similarity is estimated by dot product. Following this method the network learns the priorities independently for each data point. However, we argue that there is also a general priority scheme that is distributed across the whole dataset, that can be learned during the training. Therefore, we propose a novel correlation based approach to discover these priorities and estimate final prediction.

Unlike the CRF module, our objective here is to find correlation between the attribute distributions of corresponding predictions of primary capsules and a decision capsule, instead of finding the dependency between each single corresponding attribute of predictions. Given a set of predictions for a specific decision capsule, the goal of the correlation module is to find the decision capsule elements by exploiting priorities of each primary capsule. The correlation coefficients between a decision capsule and a primary capsule predictions are learned throughout the training. Furthermore, these correlation coefficients should depend on the low-level feature distribution and also should be trainable. To this end, we use a property of Cholesky transformation [18] and derive a generic function to achieve this task.

Let two distributions be Q and R. Cholesky transformation ensures,

$$\begin{bmatrix} \bar{Q} \\ \bar{R} \end{bmatrix} = \begin{bmatrix} 0 & 1 \\ \rho_1 & \sqrt{1 - \rho_1{}^2} \end{bmatrix} \begin{bmatrix} Q \\ R \end{bmatrix} \tag{3}$$

$$\bar{Q} = R, \bar{R} = \rho_1 Q + \sqrt{1 - \rho_1{}^2} R \tag{4}$$

and produces two distributions $\bar{Q}$, $\bar{R}$ which are correlated by a factor of ρ_1. Likewise,

$$\begin{bmatrix} \bar{\bar{Q}} \\ \bar{\bar{R}} \end{bmatrix} = \begin{bmatrix} 0 & 1 \\ \rho_2 & \sqrt{1 - \rho_2{}^2} \end{bmatrix} \begin{bmatrix} R \\ Q \end{bmatrix} \tag{5}$$

$$\bar{\bar{Q}} = Q, \bar{\bar{R}} = \rho_2 R + \sqrt{1 - \rho_2{}^2} Q \tag{6}$$

produces two distributions $\bar{\bar{Q}}$, $\bar{\bar{R}}$ which are correlated by a factor of ρ_2. Therefore if we choose,

$$\rho_2 = \sqrt{1 - \rho_1{}^2} \tag{7}$$

we get $T = \bar{R} = \bar{\bar{R}}$, where T and R are correlated by ρ_1 and, T and Q are correlated by ρ_2. Using this property and considering two component distributions $D_1 = P_{k,j}$ and $D_2 = P_{k',j}$, where $P_{k,j}$ is the component distribution of kth

primary capsule prediction for j^{th} decision capsule, we obtain a new distribution $\hat{D}$, satisfying $\rho_{\hat{D},D_1} = \rho_1$, and $\rho_{\hat{D},D_2} = \alpha\rho_1$. Here, ρ_{x_1,x_2} denotes the correlation between the two particular distributions x_1 and x_2. Using Eq. 7,

$$\frac{\rho_1}{\alpha} = \sqrt{1 - \rho_1{}^2}, \rho_1 = \frac{\alpha}{\sqrt{1 + \alpha^2}} \tag{8}$$

$$\hat{D} = [\frac{\alpha}{\sqrt{1+\alpha^2}}D_1 + \frac{1}{\sqrt{1+\alpha^2}}D_2] \tag{9}$$

Using Eq. 9, we define a recursive function f_ρ to obtain a correlated element distribution.

$$f_\rho(P_{1,j}|P_{2,j}\ldots,P_{k,j},\ldots,P_{K,j}) = \frac{\alpha_K}{\sqrt{1+\alpha_K^2}}f_\rho(P_{1,j}|P_{2,j}\ldots,P_{k,j},\ldots,P_{K-1,j})$$

$$+ \frac{P_{K,j}}{\sqrt{1+\alpha_K^2}}, \forall 0 < k \leq K, 0 < j \leq J \tag{10}$$

where $f_\rho(P_{1,j}|P_{2,j}) = [\frac{\alpha_2}{\sqrt{1+\alpha_2^2}}P_{1,j} + \frac{1}{\sqrt{1+\alpha_2^2}}P_{2,j}]$. Using this derivation, we obtain the jth decision capsule $C_j = f_\rho(P_{1,j}|P_{2,j}\ldots,P_{k,j},\ldots,P_{K,j})$. Here, α requires be trainable and dependent on low-level feature distributions. Since the above operation is differentiable, the first criteria is fulfilled. To enforce α to be dependent on low-level features, we use the following method.

Consider a $N \times N$ low-level feature map. Since we need $J(K-1)$ trainable parameters as per Eq. 10, we convolve this particular feature map with a set of $J(K-1)$ kernels with sizes $N \times N$ each. This outputs $J(K-1)$ number of scalar values, which can be used as α parameters.

4   Experiments

We conduct experiments to demonstrate the effectiveness of each of the improvements; new initialization scheme of routing weights, CRF module and the correlation module. We use mean average precision (mAP) as the evaluation metric throughout the experiments with precision threshold 0.5. We use ADE20K dataset to evaluate the proposed architecture given its complex scenes and rich multi-label annotations for training images. ADE20K provides over $20,000$ training and testing images annotated with 150 semantic object categories.

4.1   Importance of Trainable Initial Routing Weights

The goal of replacing the equal initialization of routing weights with trainable weights is faster convergence. In order to test the significance of this, we train the proposed architecture with and without the trainable initial routing scheme and test the validation mAP. The results are illustrated in Fig. 2.

As shown in Fig. 2 the validation mAP stabilizes around 15th epoch for the CapsNet without the proposed routing weight initialization method. On the contrary, the CapsNet with the proposed routing weight initialization method stabilizes around 9th epoch. Therefore it is evident that the proposed method is able to achieve faster convergence compared to equal initial routing weights.

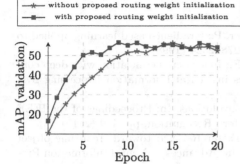

- —✱— without proposed routing weight initialization
- —■— with proposed routing weight initialization

Fig. 2. Evaluation of convergence gain by trainable initial routing weights.

Table 1. Comparison of the proposed architecture with the baseline

Method	mAP
Original CapsNet	42.38
Ours (RW + CRF)	52.50
Ours (RW + CRF + CORR)	**56.71**

4.2 Comparison with the Baseline

We compare the original CapsNet architecture with the proposed one by measuring the mAP measure. Table 1 shows the comparison results. We gain a significant 14.33 mAP gain over total 150 object classes compared to the original architecture. Furthermore, we demonstrate performance gains by CRF and correlation modules, and show that each module provides complementary improvements. We gain an improvement of 10.12 mAP by adding the CRF module and a 4.21 mAP improvement by adding the correlation module on top of the CRF module. All the architectures are trained for 20 epochs.

5 Conclusions

In this work we attempt to overcome several limitations of CapsNet by introducing an improved architecture inspired by the contextual modeling in visual cortex [10]. Our objective is two fold: effectively capture complex interactions between primary capsules and leverage data wide correlations between representations of similar inputs. To this end, we introduced three novel ideas. Firstly, we proposed a new routing weight initialization that can be trained using backpropagation. This replaced existing equal initial routing weights with a more intuitive and efficient technique. Secondly, we introduced a CRF based method to exploit conditional attributes of primary capsule predictions to capture the context of neighbouring objects. Thirdly, we proposed a correlation module to learn dataset-wise priority scheme instead of capturing the priority separately for each data point. As demonstrated through our experiments, these improvements in CapsNet model design contributes to a substantial accuracy improvement of over 33% in multi-label classification on a challenging dataset.

References

1. LeCun, Y., Bottou, L., Bengio, Y., Haffner, P.: Gradient-based learning applied to document recognition. Proc. IEEE **86**, 2278–2324 (1998)
2. Krizhevsky, A., Sutskever, I., Hinton, G.E.: Imagenet classification with deep convolutional neural networks. In: Advances in Neural Information Processing Systems, pp. 1097–1105 (2012)
3. Szegedy, C., et al.: Going deeper with convolutions. In: Proceedings of the IEEE Conference on Computer Vision and Pattern Recognition, pp. 1–9 (2015)
4. Ren, S., He, K., Girshick, R., Sun, J.: Faster R-CNN: towards real-time object detection with region proposal networks. In: Advances in Neural Information Processing Systems 28, pp. 91–99 (2015)
5. Redmon, J., Divvala, S.K., Girshick, R.B., Farhadi, A.: You only look once: unified, real-time object detection. arXiv preprint arXiv:1506.02640 (2015)
6. Long, J., Shelhamer, E., Darrell, T.: Fully convolutional networks for semantic segmentation. In: Proceedings of the IEEE Conference on Computer Vision and Pattern Recognition, pp. 3431–3440 (2015)
7. Badrinarayanan, V., Kendall, A., Cipolla, R.: Segnet: a deep convolutional encoder-decoder architecture for image segmentation. IEEE Trans. Pattern Anal. Mach. Intell. **39**(12), 2481–2495 (2017)
8. Sabour, S., Frosst, N., Hinton, G.E.: Dynamic routing between capsules. In: Advances in Neural Information Processing Systems, pp. 3859–3869 (2017)
9. LeCun, Y., Cortes, C., Burges, C.J.: The MNIST database of handwritten digits (1998)
10. Bar, M.: Visual objects in context. Nature Rev. Neurosci. **5**(8), 617 (2004)
11. Zhou, B., Zhao, H., Puig, X., Fidler, S., Barriuso, A., Torralba, A.: Scene parsing through ADE20K dataset. In: Proceedings of the IEEE Conference on Computer Vision and Pattern Recognition (2017)
12. Hinton, G.E., Krizhevsky, A., Wang, S.D.: Transforming auto-encoders. In: Honkela, T., Duch, W., Girolami, M., Kaski, S. (eds.) ICANN 2011. LNCS, vol. 6791, pp. 44–51. Springer, Heidelberg (2011). https://doi.org/10.1007/978-3-642-21735-7_6
13. Hinton, G.E., Sabour, S., Frosst, N.: Matrix capsules with EM routing. In: International Conference on Learning Representations (2018)
14. Dempster, A.P., Laird, N.M., Rubin, D.B.: Maximum likelihood from incomplete data via the EM algorithm. J. Royal Stat. Soc. Ser. B **39**, 1–38 (1977)
15. LeCun, Y., Huang, F.J., Bottou, L.: Learning methods for generic object recognition with invariance to pose and lighting. In: Proceedings of the IEEE Conference on Computer Vision and Pattern Recognition, pp. 97–104 (2004)
16. Xi, E., Bing, S., Jin, Y.: Capsule network performance on complex data. arXiv preprint arXiv:1712.03480 (2017)
17. Zheng, S., et al.: Conditional random fields as recurrent neural networks. In: Proceedings of the IEEE International Conference on Computer Vision, pp. 1529–1537 (2015)
18. Ramasinghe, S., Rajasegaran, J., Jayasundara, V., Ranasinghe, K., Rodrigo, R., Pasqual, A.A.: Combined static and motion features for deep-networks based activity recognition in videos. IEEE Trans. Circuits Syst. Video Technol., 1 (2017)

Brain-Inspired Robust Delineation Operator

Nicola Strisciuglio[✉], George Azzopardi, and Nicolai Petkov

Bernoulli Institute, University of Groningen, Groningen, The Netherlands
n.strisciuglio@rug.nl

Abstract. In this paper we present a novel filter, based on the existing COSFIRE filter, for the delineation of patterns of interest. It includes a mechanism of push-pull inhibition that improves robustness to noise in terms of spurious texture. Push-pull inhibition is a phenomenon that is observed in neurons in area V1 of the visual cortex, which suppresses the response of certain simple cells for stimuli of preferred orientation but of non-preferred contrast. This type of inhibition allows for sharper detection of the patterns of interest and improves the quality of delineation especially in images with spurious texture.

We performed experiments on images from different applications, namely the detection of rose stems for automatic gardening, the delineation of cracks in pavements and road surfaces, and the segmentation of blood vessels in retinal images. Push-pull inhibition helped to improve results considerably in all applications.

Keywords: COSFIRE filter · Delineation push-pull inhibition

1 Introduction

The delineation of elongated structures is a fundamental process in image processing and computer vision, for various applications: detection of rose stems for automatic gardening robotics, crack delineation in roads or walls, segmentation of blood vessels in medical images, segmentation of roads and rivers in aerial images and so on. In these applications, images usually contain large amounts of background noise and spurious texture, which cause segmentation errors [1–3].

In this paper, we present a novel filter, inspired by the push-pull inhibition that is exhibited by some neurons in area V1 of the primary visual cortex. We construct a filter that has two components, an excitatory and an inhibitory one, based on the existing model of neurons with excitatory receptive fields in area V1, called CORF [4], whose implementation is known as B-COSFIRE and shown to be effective for the delineation of blood vessels in medical images [5,6], also in combination with machine learning techniques [7]. We name the proposed filter RUSTICO, which stands for RobUST Inhibition-augmented Curvilinear Operator, and show how push-pull inhibition contributes to strengthen the robustness

© Springer Nature Switzerland AG 2019
L. Leal-Taixé and S. Roth (Eds.): ECCV 2018 Workshops, LNCS 11131, pp. 555–565, 2019.
https://doi.org/10.1007/978-3-030-11015-4_41

with respect to noise and spurious texture in the delineation of elongated patterns. The aim of this work is to demonstrate how inspiration from neurophysiological findings can be used to design effective algorithms, on which one can build more complex systems.

State-of-the-art approaches for the delineation of curvilinear patterns in images were recently reviewed in [8]. Fundamental methods are based on a parametric formulation of the pattern of interest, namely line-like structures. The Hough transform, for instance, projects an input image onto a parameter space (slope and bias) in which linear segments are easier to detect. The disadvantage of parametric methods is that they require a strict mathematical model of the patterns of interest, and different shapes require different formulations.

Other methods are based on filtering or mathematical morphology, such as the Frangi detector that employs multi-scale local derivatives [9]. Matched filters, which model the profile of the elongated patterns with 2D Gaussian kernels, were proposed in [10]. Combination of different techniques, such as Frangi filters and Gabor Wavelets, was also studied [11]. Mathematical morphology techniques assume *a-priori* knowledge about the geometry of the patterns of interest [12], such as size, orientation and width [13], or concavity [14]. Recently, a method called RORPO, based on morphological path operators was proposed for the delineation of 2D and 3D curvilinear patterns [15].

Point processes were also employed to segment networks of elongated structures, which are considered as complex sets of linear segments [2]. They were also combined with Gibbs models [16], Monte-Carlo simulation [17], and graph-based representations with topological information about the line networks [18]. These methods are computationally very expensive, not being suitable for real-time or high resolution image processing.

Machine learning techniques have also been investigated to perform pixelwise segmentation of elongated patterns. Early approaches in [19,20] constructed pixel-wise feature vectors with multi-scale Gaussian and Gabor wavelet features, respectively, or with the responses of a bank of ridge detectors [21]. Invariant moments were also used to describe the pixel characteristics in [22]. More recently, Convolutional Neural Networks (CNNs) gained particular popularity in computer vision, for many tasks including segmentation. In [23], for instance, image patches containing lines were used to train a CNN for the segmentation of blood vessels in medical images. More general architectures for segmentation were proposed, such as U-Net [24] and SegNet [25]. CNNs are supervised approaches, employ a large amount of filters at different stages and usually achieve high segmentation performance, but require large amounts of labeled training data to learn effective models and are computationally very expensive, requiring GPU hardware.

The approach that we introduce in this work is unsupervised and, hence, it is not appropriate to compare it with the performance of CNNs, but rather to demonstrate how we can make use of neuro-physiological evidence about the functioning of the visual system to improve image processing and computer vision algorithms. We demonstrate the effectiveness of the push-pull inhibition phenomenon and the improved robustness of the proposed filter in three applications were spurious textures are present, namely delineation of rose stems for garden robotics, detection of cracks in road surfaces and segmentation of blood vessels in retinal images.

The paper is organized as follows. In Sect. 2, we describe the proposed implementation of the push-pull inhibition mechanism, and the data sets used for the experiments in Sects. 3. We present the results that we achieved, and provide a discussion of the results and comparison with those obtained by existing methods in Sect. 4. We draw conclusions in Sect. 5.

2   Method

The main idea of RUSTICO is the design of an operator selective for curvilinear patterns with push-pull inhibition. This type of inhibition is known to suppress responses to spurious texture and thus emphasizing more the detection of linear structures. In practice, RUSTICO takes input from two types of COSFIRE filters of the type introduced in [5], one that gives excitatory input and the other that acts as inhibitory component. We compute the response of RUSTICO by subtracting the (weighted) response of the inhibitory component from the excitatory one.

2.1   B-COSFIRE Filter

The COSFIRE filter approach is trainable, in that the selectivity of the filter is determined from an automatic configuration procedure that analyzes a given prototype pattern. In [5], a bar-like synthetic prototype pattern was used and the resulting filter responded strongly to blood vessels in retinal images. In [4], instead, an edge prototype pattern was used for configuration of a COSFIRE filter that was very effective for contour detection.

The automatic configuration of a COSFIRE filter involves two steps: first, the determination of keypoints in the given prototype pattern that we illustrate in Fig. 1 by means of a system of concentric circles and linear filtering with difference-of-Gaussians (DoG) functions and secondly, the description of such keypoints in terms of four parameters. These parameters include the polarity δ and standard deviation σ, which describe the type (center-on or center-off) along with the spread of the outer Gaussian function[1] of the DoG that gives the maximum response in the concerned keypoint. The other two parameters are the distance ρ and polar angle ϕ of the keypoint with respect to the center of the prototype. We define a COSFIRE filter as a set of 4-tuples $B = \{(\delta_i, \sigma_i, \rho_i, \phi_i) \mid i = 1 \dots n\}$.

The response of a B-COSFIRE filter, denoted by $r_B(x, y)$, is computed by first calculating an intermediate feature map for each tuple followed by combining all features maps by geometric mean. The feature map of tuple i is computed

---

[1] The standard deviation of the inner Gaussian function is 0.5σ.

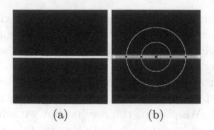

(a)   (b)

Fig. 1. (a) A prototype line and a (b) sketch of the configuration process.

in four steps: firstly, *convolve* the image with a DoG function whose polarity is δ_i and standard deviation σ_i, secondly *rectify* the output by a rectification linear unit (ReLU) that sets to zero all negative responses, thirdly *blur* the thresholded response map by a Gaussian function whose standard deviation $\sigma' = \sigma_0 + \alpha\rho_i$ where σ_0 and α are hyperparameters which we set empirically, and lastly *shift* the blurred responses by the vector $[\rho_i, \pi - \phi_i]$.

To configure a B-COSFIRE filter which is selective for the same prototype but rotated by a given offset ψ, one can construct a new filter B_ψ by manipulating the angular parameter in all tuples of the filter B: $B^\psi = \{(\delta_i, \sigma_i, \rho_i, \phi_i + \psi) \mid \forall \, (\delta_i, \sigma_i, \rho_i, \phi_i) \in B\}$. This mechanism is required to achieve tolerance to rotation. For more details on COSFIRE filters we refer the reader to [5].

2.2 Push-Pull Inhibition

Push-pull inhibition is a phenomenon that has been observed in many simple cells [26]. It is thought that an interneuron inhibits the response of the simple cell to which it is connected. The receptive field of the interneuron is typically larger than that of the simple cell. The effect is that response of the simple cell is suppressed for a stimulus with preferred orientation but with contrast opposite of the preferred one. We model the interneuron by another COSFIRE filter which we denote by $\hat{B}_\lambda$ and define it as $\hat{B}_\lambda = \{-\delta_i, \lambda\sigma_i, \rho_i, \phi_i \mid \forall \, (\delta_i, \sigma_i, \rho_i, \phi_i) \in B\}$ where λ is a weighting factor that controls the size of the afferent DoG functions. The response of the inhibitory COSFIRE filter $r_{\hat{B}_\lambda}(x, y)$ is computed with the same procedure described above.

2.3 RUSTICO

We define an orientation-selective RUSTICO as a pair $R_\lambda(B, \hat{B}_\lambda)$ and compute its response $R(x, y)$ by combining the excitatory and inhibitory inputs with a linear function:

$$R(x, y) = |r_B(x, y) - \xi r_{\hat{B}_\lambda}(x, y)|^+ \tag{1}$$

where ξ is the weighting or strength of the inhibitory component, which we determine experimentally, and $|.|^+$ indicates the ReLU function.

In order to configure a RUSTICO filter that is tolerant to rotations we consider various pairs of excitatory and inhibitory COSFIRE filters that are selective for different orientations and then combine their response maps. Formally, we denote by R_ψ^M a multi-orientation RUSTICO and define it as a set $\tilde{R}_\Psi = \{(B^\psi, \hat{B}_\lambda^\psi) \mid \forall\ \psi \in \Psi\}$. Finally, the multi-orientation RUSTICO response $r_{\tilde{R}_\Psi}(x, y)$ is achieved by taking the maximum superposition of the response maps corresponding to all pairs in the set $\tilde{R}_\Psi$:

$$r_{\tilde{R}_\Psi}(x, y) = \max_{\psi \in \Psi}\{|r_{B^\psi}(x, y) - \xi r_{\hat{B}_\lambda^\psi}(x, y)|^+\} \tag{2}$$

3 Materials

We tested the performance of the proposed operator with push-pull inhibition on different data sets, namely the TB-roses-1, the CrackTree206 [27] and the DRIVE [21] data sets. We show example images from the three data sets, together with the corresponding ground truth delineation maps in Fig. 2.

The TB-roses-1 data set is composed of 100 images, which we recorded in a real garden in the context of the TrimBot2020 project [28]. It is designed for testing algorithms for delineation of rose branches in applications of gardening robotics. The images have resolution of 960×540 pixels and are provided together with two ground truth images, one indicating the centerline of the rose branches and the other marking the whole segmented branches. The data set is publicly available[2].

The CrackTree206 data set is composed of 206 images of road surface, taken with an RGB camera at resolution 800×600 pixels. The images contain spurious texture around the road cracks, due to the intrinsic composition of the asphalt. This makes the delineation of cracks a hard task, since the size and contrast of the cracks are very similar to the one of the textured background. The images are provided with manually labeled images that delineate the center-line of the cracks and serve as ground truth for performance evaluation.

The DRIVE data set of retinal fundus images is divided into a training and a test set, both containing 20 images at resolution 565×584 pixels. The images are recorded with a fundus camera with $30°$ field of view and are provided with manually labeled ground truth images from two different observers. Similar to existing works, we used the ground truth of the first observer as gold standard for the evaluation of our method.

---

[2] http://gitlab.com/nicstrisc/RUSTICO.

4   Experiments

4.1   Evaluation

For the rose stem and road crack center-line detection, we compute the precision (Pr), recall (Re) and F-score (F). For the computation of these metrics, we consider a certain amount of pixel distance d^* to account for tolerance in the position of the detected center-line with respect to the position in the ground truth images [27]. We used $d^* = 3$ for the TB-roses-1 data set and $d^* = 2$ for the CrackTree206 data set (as reported in [27]). We compute the evaluation metrics by thresholding the output of RUSTICO with different values of threshold t, ranging from 0.01 to 1 in steps of 0.01 and report the results for the value t^* of the threshold that contributes to the highest average F-score on the considered data set.

Fig. 2. Example images from the considered data sets, together with the corresponding ground truth images.

In the case of retinal vessel delineation, we evaluate the performance of the proposed method by computing the Matthews correlation coefficient (MCC) and the Connectivity-Area-Length (CAL) measure [29]. The MCC is a reliable measure of accuracy for two-class classification problems where the cardinality of the classes is unbalanced. A value of 1 indicates perfect classification, while 0 and -1 correspond to random and completely wrong classification, respectively.

Pixel-wise comparison of the output of delineation algorithms with respect to ground truth images is subject to various problems. For instance, a displacement of the segmented image of one pixel in any direction would cause a substantial reduction of performance results. Moreover, evaluation of the performance against different ground truth images causes disparate results. The CAL was demonstrated to be robust to such issues and to be in accordance with perceptual quality of the segmentation output [29]. The CAL measure is computed as the product of three measures of connectivity, area and length of the segmented line networks compared with the corresponding ground truths. Each of the single measures has values between 0 and 1, with 0 indicating complete difference, while 1 representing a perfect match with the ground truth. For further details about the computation of the CAL metric we refer the reader to [29].

4.2   Results and Discussions

In Table 1, we report the results achieved by the proposed method, in comparison with those of the original COSFIRE filter. For the three considered applications, the push-pull inhibition mechanism that we embedded in the RUSTICO filter contributed to a substantial improvement of the delineation output. We achieved an increase of the value of the performance measures that is statistical significant (TB-roses: $p < 0.01$; CrackTree206: $p < 0.01$: DRIVE: $p < 0.05$). The improvement of results is evident from Fig. 3, where we show the precision-recall curves achieved by the RUSTICO (solid line) and COSFIRE (dashed line) filters on the TB-roses-1 (Fig. 3a) and the CrackTree206 (Fig. 3b) data sets. The curves show a substantial improvement of performance of RUSTICO with respect to COSFIRE in applications with images containing noise and spurious textures. For the CrackTree206 data set, we report the results achieved by existing methods: COSFIRE [30] ($F = 0.6630$), SegExt ($F = 0.55$), Canny ($F = 0.26$), global pb ($F = 0.44$) and pbCGTG ($F = 0.35$). These results, except for those of the CrackTree [27] algorithm with and without pre-processing ($F = 0.85$ and $F = 0.77$, respectively), although specifically designed to deal with the characteristics of the concerned images, are considerably lower than those of RUSTICO ($F = 0.6846$).

Table 1. Comparison of the performance of the COSFIRE filter (C) and the proposed RUSTICO (R) on the TB-roses, CrackTree206 and DRIVE data sets. As quantitative measurements, for the former two data sets we use the F-score (F), while for the latter data set we use the CAL metric. The filters have different parameters according to the data set (TB-roses: $\sigma = 2.5, \rho = 16, \sigma_0 = 3, \alpha = 0.1, \lambda = 0.5, \xi = 1.5$; CrackTree206: $\sigma = 5.7, \rho = 12, \sigma_0 = 5, \alpha = 0.1, \lambda = 3, \xi = 2$: DRIVE: $\sigma = 2.1, \rho = 10, \sigma_0 = 3, \alpha = 0.2, \lambda = 3, \xi = 1$). The parameters λ and ξ are specific of RUSTICO and not used for COSFIRE.

# images	TB-roses-1		CrackTree206		DRIVE	
	35		206		20	
	F		F		CAL	
	C	R	C	R	C	R
Avg.	0.3385	**0.3822**	0.6630	**0.6846**	0.7213	**0.7280**
p	**<0.01**		**<0.01**		**<0.05**	

In Table 2, we report the quantitative comparison of the results achieved by RUSTICO with respect to those obtained by existing approaches on the DRIVE data set of retinal images. Among the methods based on filtering and mathematical morphology (above the middle line), RUSTICO achieves the best MCC and CAL measures with high statistical significance. We computed the performance of existing methods for which the segmentation output is publicly available. In the case of RORPO, we run experiments by varying the parameters with a grid search and reported the best obtained values. Methods based on machine learning perform generally better on pixel-wise classification, but show lower or comparable performance with that of RUSTICO in terms of CAL.

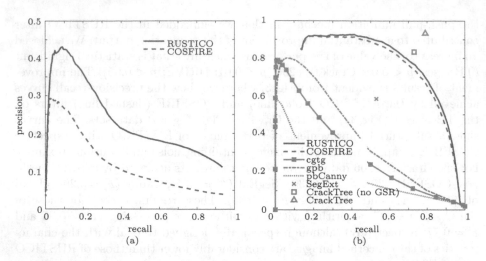

Fig. 3. Precision-Recall curves achieved by RUSTICO (solid line) and COSFIRE (dashed line) on the (a) TB-roses-1 and (b) CrackTree data sets, together with the results achieved by existing approaches.

Table 2. Comparison of the results achieved by RUSTICO on the DRIVE data set with those obtained by existing method. The sign - indicates no statistical difference, while * and ** indicate that the corresponding results are statistically higher than those of RUSTICO with significance level 0.05 and 0.01, respectively.

Method	MCC	p	CAL	p
RUSTICO	**0.7287**	-	**0.7280**	-
COSFIRE [5]	0.7189	<0.01	0.7213	<0.05
Jiang et al. [31]	0.6378	<0.01	0.5178	<0.01
Perez et al. [13]	0.6645	<0.05	0.5673	<0.01
RORPO [15]	0.6871	<0.01	0.6228	<0.01
Zana et al. [32]	0.7258	-	0.6180	<0.01
Staal et al. [21]	0.7378	*	0.7010	<0.05
Niemeijer et al. [19]	0.7222	-	0.6589	<0.01
FC-CRF [33]	**0.7556**	**	**0.7311**	-
UP-CRF [33]	0.7401	*	0.6747	<0.01

5   Conclusions

We presented a new method for the delineation of elongated patterns in images with spurious texture, named RUSTICO, that incorporates a push-pull inhibition mechanism operated by some neurons in area V1 of the visual cortex. RUSTICO takes input from two COSFIRE filters with opposite polarity and responds to elongated patterns also when they are surrounded by noise. We demonstrated how the findings of neuro-physiological studies of the visual system into image processing algorithms can be used to design more robust algorithms. The push-pull inhibition included in RUSTICO contributed to a statistically significant improvement with respect to existing methods in applications of delineation of rose stems for automatic gardening, detection of cracks in road surfaces and segmentation of blood vessels in medical images. We created and made available a data set of 100 labeled images to test algorithm for segmentation of rose stems.

Acknowledgment. This research received funding from the EU H2020 research and innovation framework (grant no. 688007, TrimBot2020).

References

1. Zhang, L., Zhang, Y., Wang, M., Li, Y.: Adaptive river segmentation in sar images. J. Electron. **26**(4), 438–442 (2009)
2. Lacoste, C., Descombes, X., Zerubia, J.: Point processes for unsupervised line network extraction in remote sensing. IEEE Trans. Pattern Anal. Mach. Intell **27**(10), 1568–1579 (2005)
3. Strisciuglio, N., Petkov, N.: Delineation of line patterns in images using B-COSFIRE filters. In: IWOBI, pp. 1–6 (2017)
4. Azzopardi, G., Petkov, N.: A CORF computational model of a simple cell that relies on LGN input outperforms the Gabor function model. Biol. Cybern. **106**(3), 177–189 (2012)
5. Azzopardi, G., Strisciuglio, N., Vento, M., Petkov, N.: Trainable COSFIRE filters for vessel delineation with application to retinal images. Med. Image Anal. **19**(1), 46–57 (2015)
6. Strisciuglio, N., Azzopardi, G., Vento, M., Petkov, N.: Unsupervised delineation of the vessel tree in retinal fundus images. In: VIPIMAGE, pp. 149–155 (2015)
7. Strisciuglio, N., Azzopardi, G., Vento, M., Petkov, N.: Supervised vessel delineation in retinal fundus images with the automatic selection of B-COSFIRE filters. Mach. Vis. Appl. **27**, 1–13 (2016)
8. Bibiloni, P., González-Hidalgo, M., Massanet, S.: A survey on curvilinear object segmentation in multiple applications. Pattern Recognit. **60**, 949–970 (2016)
9. Frangi, A.F., Niessen, W.J., Vincken, K.L., Viergever, M.A.: Multiscale vessel enhancement filtering. In: Wells, W.M., Colchester, A., Delp, S. (eds.) MICCAI 1998. LNCS, vol. 1496, pp. 130–137. Springer, Heidelberg (1998). https://doi.org/10.1007/BFb0056195
10. Al-Rawi, M., Qutaishat, M., Arrar, M.: An improved matched filter for blood vessel detection of digital retinal images. Comput. Biol. Med. **37**(2), 262–267 (2007)
11. Oliveira, W.S., Teixeira, J.V., Ren, T.I., Cavalcanti, G.D.C., Sijbers, J.: Unsupervised retinal vessel segmentation using combined filters. PLoS ONE **11**(2), 1–21 (2016)
12. Mendonca, A.M., Campilho, A.: Segmentation of retinal blood vessels by combining the detection of centerlines and morphological reconstruction. IEEE Trans. Med. Imag. **25**(9), 1200–1213 (2006)
13. Martinez-Pérez, M.E., Hughes, A.D., Thom, S.A., Bharath, A.A., Parker, K.H.: Segmentation of blood vessels from red-free and fluorescein retinal images. Med. Image Anal. **11**(1), 47–61 (2007)

14. Lam, B., Gao, Y., Liew, A.C.: General retinal vessel segmentation using regularization-based multiconcavity modeling. IEEE Trans. Med. Imag. **29**(7), 1369–1381 (2010)
15. Merveille, O., Talbot, H., Najman, L., Passat, N.: Curvilinear structure analysis by ranking the orientation responses of path operators. IEEE Trans. Pattern Anal. Mach. Intell **40**(2), 304–317 (2018)
16. Lafarge, F., Gimel'Farb G.G., Descombes, X.: Geometric feature extraction by a multimarked point process. IEEE Trans. Pattern Anal. Mach. Intell 32(9), 1597–1609 (2010)
17. Verdié, Y., Lafarge, F.: Efficient Monte Carlo sampler for detecting parametric objects in large scenes. In: Fitzgibbon, A., Lazebnik, S., Perona, P., Sato, Y., Schmid, C. (eds.) ECCV 2012. LNCS, vol. 7574, pp. 539–552. Springer, Heidelberg (2012). https://doi.org/10.1007/978-3-642-33712-3_39
18. Türetken, E., Benmansour, F., Andres, B., Gowacki, P., Pfister, H., Fua, P.: Reconstructing curvilinear networks using path classifiers and integer programming. IEEE Trans. Pattern Anal. Mach. Intell. **38**(12), 2515–2530 (2016)
19. Niemeijer, M., Staal, J., van Ginneken, B., Loog, M., Abramoff, M.: Comparative study of retinal vessel segmentation methods on a new publicly available database. In: Proceedings of the SPIE - The International Society for Optical Engineering, pp. 648–656 (2004)
20. Soares, J.V.B., Leandro, J.J.G., Cesar Jr., R.M., Jelinek, H.F., Cree, M.J.: Retinal vessel segmentation using the 2-D Gabor wavelet and supervised classification. IEEE Trans. Med. Imag. **25**(9), 1214–1222 (2006)
21. Staal, J., Abramoff, M., Niemeijer, M., Viergever, M., van Ginneken, B.: Ridge-based vessel segmentation in color images of the retina. IEEE Trans. Med. Imag. **23**(4), 501–509 (2004)
22. Marin, D., Aquino, A., Emilio Gegundez-Arias, M., Manuel Bravo, J.: A new supervised method for blood vessel segmentation in retinal images by using gray-level and moment invariants-based features. IEEE Trans. Med. Imag. **30**(1), 146–158 (2011)
23. Liskowski, P., Krawiec, K.: Segmenting retinal blood vessels with deep neural networks. IEEE Trans. Med. Imag. **35**(11), 2369–2380 (2016)
24. Ronneberger, O., Fischer, P., Brox, T.: U-Net: convolutional networks for biomedical image segmentation. In: Navab, N., Hornegger, J., Wells, W.M., Frangi, A.F. (eds.) MICCAI 2015. LNCS, vol. 9351, pp. 234–241. Springer, Cham (2015). https://doi.org/10.1007/978-3-319-24574-4_28
25. Badrinarayanan, V., Kendall, A., Cipolla, R.: SegNet: a deep convolutional encoder-decoder architecture for image segmentation. IEEE Trans. Pattern Anal. Mach. Intell. (2017)
26. Taylor, M.M., Sedigh-Sarvestani, M., Vigeland, L., Palmer, L.A., Contreras, D.: Inhibition in simple cell receptive fields is broad and off-subregion biased. J. Neurosci. **38**(3), 595–612 (2018)
27. Zou, Q., Cao, Y., Li, Q., Mao, Q., Wang, S.: Cracktree: automatic crack detection from pavement images. Pattern Recognit. Lett. **33**(3), 227–238 (2012)
28. Strisciuglio, N., et al.: Trimbot2020: an outdoor robot for automatic gardening. In: 50th International Symposium on Robotics (2018)
29. Gegundez-Arias, M.E., Aquino, A., Bravo, J.M., Marin, D.: A function for quality evaluation of retinal vessel segmentations. IEEE Trans. Med. Imag. **31**(2), 231–239 (2012)

30. Strisciuglio, N., Azzopardi, G., Petkov, N.: Detection of curved lines with B-COSFIRE filters: a case study on crack delineation. In: Felsberg, M., Heyden, A., Krüger, N. (eds.) CAIP 2017. LNCS, vol. 10424, pp. 108–120. Springer, Cham (2017). https://doi.org/10.1007/978-3-319-64689-3_9

31. Jiang, X., Mojon, D.: Adaptive local thresholding by verification-based multi-threshold probing with application to vessel detection in retinal images. IEEE Trans. Pattern Anal. Mach. Intell. 25(1), 131–137 (2003)

32. Zana, F., Klein, J.: Segmentation of vessel-like patterns using mathematical morphology and curvature evaluation. IEEE Trans. Med. Imag. 10(7), 1010–1019 (2001)

33. Orlando, J.I., Prokofyeva, E., Blaschko, M.B.: A discriminatively trained fully connected conditional random field model for blood vessel segmentation in fundus images. IEEE Trans. Biomed. Eng. 64(1), 16–27 (2017)

Understanding Fake Faces

Ryota Natsume[1(✉)], Kazuki Inoue[1], Yoshihiro Fukuhara[1],
Shintaro Yamamoto[1], Shigeo Morishima[1], and Hirokatsu Kataoka[2]

[1] Waseda University, Shinjuku, Japan
nano.poteto@toki.waseda.jp, {sogew3,f_yoshi}@ruri.waseda.jp,
s.yamamoto@fuji.waseda.jp, shigeo@waseda.jp
[2] National Institute of Advanced Industrial Science and Technology (AIST),
Tsukuba, Japan
hirokatsu.kataoka@aist.go.jp

Abstract. Face recognition research is one of the most active topics in computer vision (CV), and deep neural networks (DNN) are now filling the gap between human-level and computer-driven performance levels in face verification algorithms. However, although the performance gap appears to be narrowing in terms of accuracy-based expectations, a curious question has arisen; specifically, *Face understanding of AI is really close to that of human?* In the present study, in an effort to confirm the brain-driven concept, we conduct image-based detection, classification, and generation using an in-house created fake face database. This database has two configurations: (i) false positive face detections produced using both the Viola Jones (VJ) method and convolutional neural networks (CNN), and (ii) simulacra that have fundamental characteristics that resemble faces but are completely artificial. The results show a level of suggestive knowledge that indicates the continuing existence of a gap between the capabilities of recent vision-based face recognition algorithms and human-level performance. On a positive note, however, we have obtained knowledge that will advance the progress of face-understanding models.

Keywords: Face recognition · False positives · Simulacra

1 Introduction

In the field of computer vision (CV), research on human faces, which includes face detection [1,2], three-dimensional (3D) face reconstruction from images [3,4], and face recognition [5,6] is one of the most active topics. Assisted by the rise of deep neural networks (DNN), vision-based approaches have improved to the point where face verification with DeepFace [7] and face recognition with FaceNet [8] now exceed human performance levels.

R. Natsume and K. Inoue—Equal contribution.

L. Leal-Taixé and S. Roth (Eds.): ECCV 2018 Workshops, LNCS 11131, pp. 566–576, 2019.
https://doi.org/10.1007/978-3-030-11015-4_42

However, a curious question has arisen; specifically; *"Does artificial intelligence (AI) recognize faces the same way humans do?"* For example, vision-based approaches still have some mistaken case that humans don't have (see Fig. 1).

Herein, we consider recent vision-based approaches to human-like face understanding in terms of the two following aspects:

1. False-positive face analysis (Fig. 2(b) and (c)): False-positive human face detections are far more likely with an AI face detector than during human observation, but observations in feature space seem to be similar. Hence, face false-positive detections by representative face detection algorithms can help us gain a better grasp of AI face understanding.
2. Simulacra/pareidolia face analysis (Fig. 2(d)): Simulacra [9] and pareidolia [10] are psychological phenomena that allow humans to recognize particular objects (such as an arrangement of three points resembling two eyes and a mouth) as faces. In other words, simulacra/pareidolia face detections are false positives triggered by human psychological peculiarities.

The analysis of false positives (Fig. 2(b) and (c)) and simulacra faces (Fig. 2(d)) may help us form a perspective concerning human-like face recognition. We define the above-mentioned two aspects as *fake faces*.

In this paper, we confirm human-like face recognition parameters by analyzing fake faces. To carry out our experiments, we collected a fake face database that contains (i) false-positive faces extracted via the Viola Jones method (VJ) [1] and convolutional neural networks (CNN) [11], and (ii) simulacra/pareidolia faces. Since we believe that image classification and generation are required to understand fake faces, we will attempt to implement face classification with CNN and conduct fake face generation with generative adversarial networks (GAN) [12] using our fake face database.

In face classification, we begin by training CNN [to classify fake faces in order to verify the accuracy of real faces; whereas in fake face generation, we train GAN with the fake face database and determine whether the generated images will be recognized as faces by human observers. The results show a level of suggestive knowledge that indicates the continuing existence of a gap between the capabilities of recent vision-based face recognition algorithms and human-level performance. On a positive note, we have obtained knowledge that will advance the progress of current face understanding models.

The main contributions of this work include:

Conceptual Contribution: We confirmed the answer to the question, *"Is AI face understanding actually close to human-level performance?"*, by analyzing performance levels with fake faces. The results of our experiments show that CNN-based approaches have limitations when recognizing human-like faces, and it is thought that a new perspective of joint-understanding with real and fake faces will help facilitate more human-like face understanding.

Database Contribution: We also present a novel database, referred to as the fake face database, which contains false positives produced by face detector and

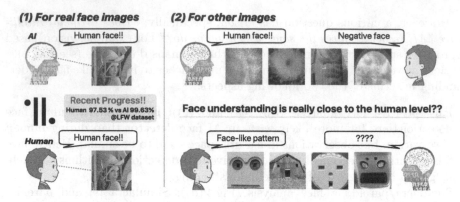

Fig. 1. The recent progress (left) and our curious scenario (right) in face understanding: (left) For real face images, we have achieved significant progress with AI-based systems such as DeepFace [7] and FaceNet [8]. This is especially notable in FaceNet, which outperformed human-level accuracy by 99.63 to 97.53 on the (top-right) Labeled Faces in the Wild (LFW) dataset. For other images, we found that AI-based systems misinterpret some objects as faces even though humans (bottom-right) can correctly identify negative faces. Humans also correctly recognize face-like objects that are described as simulacra faces. In this paper, we verify the curious scenario with CV tools such as CNN image classification and GAN image generation.

simulacra/pareidolia faces. The use of this database helped us to confirm the gap between human- and computer-based face understanding.

2   Fake Faces

2.1   VJ/CNN Fake Faces

Face detection research has a long history [13]. Its fundamental approaches are based on shallow learning involving tools such as support vector machines (SVMs) with handcrafted features [1]. In recent years, object detection has improved along with the recent progress of DNN algorithms [11]. However, neither of these methods have yet achieved 100% accuracy, which means they sometimes detect non face objects, i.e. false positives. As shown in Fig. 2, false positive faces can be totally unlike real faces. Fig. 2(b) and (c) show false positives produced by a handcrafted features-based method (VJ) [1] and a DNN-based method (CNN face detector), [11] respectively. Input images are grayscale in the former and RGB in the latter. Our analysis of these false positive images is expected to help us to understand how AI recognizes faces.

In fact, each of the false positive types have different characteristics because VJ detects faces based on handcrafted features, whereas CNN face detectors detect faces based on millions of learning features. Therefore, in this work, false positives detected by handcrafted features and those detected by deep learning are handled differently. In the next section, we will analyze these two false positive types in an effort to fill the gap between human and AI characteristics.

(a) a real face   (b) a false positive by VJ   (c) a false positive by CNN   (d) a simulacra face

Fig. 2. (a) is a real face, (b) and (c) are false positives identified by a hand-crafted face detector (VJ) [1] and a CNN face detector [11], respectively; whereas (d) consists of simulacra faces, which are false positives produced by human psychological face recognition characteristics. In this work, we refer to (b), (c) and (d) as fake faces, and examine the relationship between fake faces and real faces (a).

Hereafter, we will refer to VJ and CNN false positives as VJ fake faces and CNN fake faces, respectively.

2.2 Simulacra Fake Faces

In this paper, simulacra [9] refer to false positive recognition triggered by the psychological phenomena of human brains that cause us to perceive three points (arranged appropriately) as a face, as shown in Fig. 2(d). One proposed theory posits that human brain face recognition is guided primarily by the identification of two eyes and a mouth. Therefore, in spite of possessing wholly unrealistic texture and shapes, a group of three points located on reversed triangle vertices can trigger human false positive face detection.

Pareidolia [10] is another of the psychological phenomena that causes humans to recognize wall stains or tree bark patterns as faces. Pareidolia faces also have textures that are associated with two eyes and a mouth, much the same as simulacra faces. In this paper, we refer to both simulacra and pareidolia faces as simulacra fake faces. In Fig. 2, it can be seen that, in terms of human perception, simulacra fake faces are more identifiable as faces than VJ/CNN fake faces.

However, previous studies [14,15] have shown that since handcrafted feature-based face detectors cannot recognize simulacra faces, additional algorithms would be necessary if it were desirable to detect simulacra faces in addition to real faces. Since this study suggests that simulacra faces are not sufficiently similar to human faces to be detected by AI algorithms, we will analyze simulacra fake faces in order to reveal how much vision-based face understanding resembles human perception.

3 Approaches to Verify Computer Face Understanding

Next, we analyze VJ, CNN, and simulacra fake faces to verify whether AI algorithms have human-like face understanding. To accomplish this, we conducted three experiments: face detection of simulacra faces, face classification trained with fake faces, and fake face generation. In simulacra fake-face detection, we examined simulacra false positives to gain an understanding of the gap between humans and AI in face recognition characteristics. In face classification with fake faces, we determine how similar AI false positives are to real faces. In addition, we confirm whether an AI can learn real face characteristics from simulacra fake faces. In fake face generation, we compare images generated by GAN trained with each fake face type in order to gain an understanding of fake face characteristics. The overall goal of these experiments is to clarify the gap between human beings and computers in understanding real faces.

3.1   Face Detection to Simulacra Fake Faces

As mentioned in [14,15], we confirmed that face detectors trained with real faces could not detect simulacra fake faces. To accomplish this, we chose two types of face detectors, VJ [1] and CNN [11], and applied them to simulacra fake faces in an in-house created database (see Sect. 4). Next, the simulacra fake face detection accuracy was compared with that of images with and without real faces.

3.2   Face Classification Trained with Fake faces

Here, we discuss our attempt to classify real faces using CNN [16] trained with fake faces. However, it is important to note that real faces are not fed into a CNN classifier during the training period. In the testing phase, we attempted to verify whether the trained CNN could classify real faces and other objects. In this paper, to simplify the experiment, binary classification of fake faces and other objects was conducted. Let $y \in \{0,1\}$ denote a class label including fake faces and other objects, I denote an image from training set, θ denote trainable parameters, and loss function for the CNN $f(I, \theta, y_i)$ is written as:

$$\mathcal{L}_{cl}(f(I, \theta, y_i)) = -\log\left(\frac{e^{f(I,\theta,y_i)}}{\sum_j e^{f(I,\theta,y_j)}}\right) \tag{1}$$

3.3   Fake Face Generation Trained with Fake Faces

In our experiment, we used GAN [12]to visualize the behavior of fake face images. The GAN architecture used in these experiments consists of a generator G and a discriminator D. These networks are trained adversarially as standard GAN. The adversarial loss is defined in the ordinary manner:

$$\mathcal{L}_{GAN} = \mathbb{E}_{\boldsymbol{x} \sim p_{data}(\boldsymbol{x})}[\log D(\boldsymbol{x})] + \mathbb{E}_{\boldsymbol{z} \sim p_z(\boldsymbol{z})}[1 - \log(G(\boldsymbol{z}))]$$

4   Collection of Fake Face Database

4.1   Fake Faces Detected by Face Detectors

To collect fake faces via face detectors, we classified the images in a large-scale database. Databases like ImageNet [17] collect images of numerous kinds of objects such as cats and dogs. As a result of our preliminary experiment, we gathered images with labels that are frequently detected as faces and used those images in our training. To avoid the overfitting specific objects, we collected fake faces from Places365-Challenge [18] using VJ and CNN face detectors.

As mentioned above, VJ detects faces by using thousands of dimensional handcrafted features, while CNN detect faces using millions of features. Thus, we regard VJ and CNN false positives as different objects. The images detected as faces naturally include real as well as fake faces. To remove the real faces from the detected images, we applied semantic segmentation [19].

We obtained the per-pixel labels of entire images using semantic segmentation. Since human faces often appear simultaneously with human bodies, semantic segmentation for an entire image results in better accuracy for human label predictions than for just the detected area. If the per-pixel label map in a detected area does not contain human labels, we regard the image in the detected area as a fake face.

Totally, 26,006 VJ fake faces, and 77,885 CNN fake faces were collected for face detector use.

4.2 Fake Faces in Simulacra and Pareidolia

First, we retrieved images tagged with the word "pareidolia" from Flickr [20] and selected 785 photos that showed simulacra phenomenon. Next, we downloaded 528 images from the site "WHAT THE FACE" [21], which contains numerous simulacra images. In total, we collected 1,313 simulacra images. We then manually annotated the positions of the eyes and mouth. Finally, we cropped each image into a square in order to ensure that its width and height was two times the distance between the eyes and that the center of the eyes was located at (0.5 × width, 0.3 × height). When the cropped region protruded from the original image, the protruding regions were filled with the average color of the image.

5   Experiments

We investigated computer-driven fake face understanding through image detection, classification, and generation. Here, we employed an in-house created fake face database (described in Sect. 4). The settings and results of simulacra fake face detection, face classification, and generation are described in each subsection.

5.1 Analysis for Face Detection to Simulacra Fake Faces

Settings of Face Detection to Simulacra Fake faces. To validate CV methods for recognizing simulacra fake faces, we adapted face detectors to simulacra fake faces, real faces, and images without faces. More specifically, we used 1,313 simulacra fake faces from our fake face database, 50,000 real faces from

CelebA, [22], and 1,313 images without faces obtained from Places365-Challenge. To these images, we adapted VJ and CNN face detectors and then calculated the detection rate for simulacra fake faces, real faces, and the misdetection frequency.

Results and Discussion of Face Detection Using Simulacra Fake faces. As shown in Table 1, VJ and CNN face detectors have far lower detection accuracy for simulacra fake faces than is found for real faces. In particular, we found that VJ face detectors detect simulacra fake faces at the same frequency rate as they do for images that do not contain real faces. This result shows that VJ has the same level of accuracy for simulacra fake face detection as it has for misdetection accuracy, and that VJ considers simulacra fake faces to be extremely different from real faces. Moreover, even though DNN exceeds human performance, they still have low accuracy for recognizing simulacra fake faces. These results not only show that face detectors do not recognize simulacra fake faces as real faces, but that they also do not recognize them as false positive faces. Taken together, they also confirm that existing vision-based methods do not see similarities between simulacra fake faces and real faces.

Table 1. Detection rate for image queries each face detectors.

Method	Simulacra fake faces	Real faces	Images without faces
VJ	1.06	87.4	0.838
CNN	7.09	86.6	1.83

Table 2. Result of real face classification trained with each fake face type.

Measurements	Trained with VJ fake face	Trained with CNN fake face	Trained with simulacra fake face
Precision	0.991	0.987	0.877
Recall	0.997	0.999	0.829
F-measure	0.994	0.993	0.852

5.2 Analysis of Face Classifications Trained with Fake Faces

Face Classification Settings. In this analysis, we trained our classifier to catalogue fake faces as positives, non face objects as negatives and confirmed its ability to assign those classifications correctly during the testing phase.

To analyze current false positives by face detectors, we fine-tuned ResNet-50 [23] with our fake face database in the face classification stage. For negative samples, we collected non face images from MS COCO [24].

We began by cropping images via bounding box annotations and then adapted them to the face detectors. Cropped images in which the face detectors did not detect faces were regarded as negative samples. When conducting testing, we used the face images from CelebA that were cropped by the CNN face detector as true data. Three experiments, VJ, CNN, and simulacra were conducted. Through all our experiments, the positive and negative images used in training were fake faces and non faces, respectively; whereas the positive and negative images used in testing were real faces and non faces, respectively. In the VJ, CNN, and simulacra experiments, the numbers of images used for training were 20,800, 20,800, and 1050 respectively, whereas the images used for testing were 5,206, 5,206, and 263 respectively, and the applied face detectors were VJ, CNN, and VJ, respectively.

Please note that in VJ experiments, images are converted to grayscale, and then input to the classifier. In all experiments, each classifier was trained for 20 epochs.

Face Classification Results and Discussion. As shown in Table 2, classifiers trained with VJ/CNN fake faces can successfully classify real faces as positives. This result suggests that face detectors perceive that fake faces have characteristics that are similar to real faces in feature space. Therefore, we could confirm that CV face detectors recognize fake faces in ways that are similar to those used to detect real faces. However, to human beings, the fake faces identified by face detectors (see Fig. 2(b) and (c)) are extremely different from real faces. This indicates that there is still a gap between humans and AI in face understanding.

Furthermore, Table 2 shows that the classifier trained with simulacra fake faces is reasonably accurate, which tells us that it is capable of discerning some real-face features from simulacra fake faces. Therefore, we can conclude that a better understanding of simulacra fake faces could provide one of the keys to filling the gap between humans and AI in face understanding.

5.3   Analysis for Fake Face Generation Trained with Fake faces

Settings of Fake face Generation. In fake face generation, we use deep convolutional GAN (DCGAN) [25] as our GAN model. The numbers of training images were 26,006, 77,885, and 1,313 for the VJ, CNN, and simulacra experiments, respectively. Due to the small number of simulacra images, we doubled the number of images to 2,616 by flipping them. We then trained our networks with the 2,616 simulacra images over 1,000 epochs. In all our experiments, the images were resized to 64×64 and then trained with DCGAN for 77,000 global steps in mini-batches of 100 data.

Results and Discussion of Fake Face Generation. The results of fake face generation are shown in Fig. 3. Note that we refer to the results generated by our GAN trained with VJ fake faces as VJ results. GAN trained with CNN and simulacra fake faces are referred to as CNN results and simulacra results, respectively. The images shown in Fig. 3(a) and (b) are VJ/CNN results. Here, we can see that those images have something resembling eyes and a mouth as well as facial contours. These results suggest that VJ and CNN fake faces

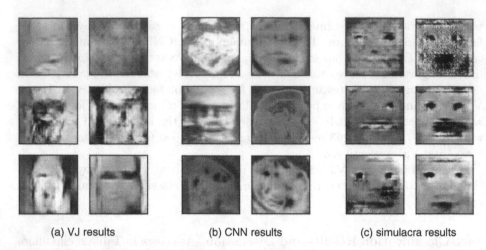

(a) VJ results   (b) CNN results   (c) simulacra results

Fig. 3. Results of fake face generation. (a) and (b) are trained by VJ and CNN images. (c) is trained with simulacra fake faces.

are close to real faces in feature space, whereas most of them do not look like real human faces. Images generated by the generator trained with simulacra fake faces (Fig. 3) show that the eyes and mouth are synthesized more clearly than the VJ/CNN results. Furthermore, in contrast to the VJ/CNN results, the images in simulacra result have no contours. By comparing the false positives of vision-based methods (VJ/CNN) with false positives of humans (simulacra), we find that while humans strongly focus on the eyes and mouths, vision-based methods not only focus on the eyes and mouths, they also note contours when detecting faces.

6   Conclusion

In this paper, we surveyed the face understanding of AI algorithms by creating a novel fake face database that includes AI (face detector [1,11] and human false positives (i.e. pareidolia [10]). We also conducted face detection and generation experiments with our fake face database and found a level of suggestive knowledge that indicates the continuing existence of a gap between the capabilities of recent vision-based face recognition algorithms and human-level performance. On a positive note, however, we also obtained knowledge that will advance the progress of face-understanding models.

Acknowledgments. This study was granted in part by the Strategic Basic Research Program ACCEL of the Japan Science and Technology Agency (JPMJAC1602). Shigeo Morishima was supported by a Grant-in-Aid from Waseda Institute of Advanced Science and Engineering. We have had the support and encouragement of cvpaper.challenege group.

References

1. Viola, P., Jones, M.: Rapid object detection using a boosted cascade of simple features. In: Proceedings of the 2001 IEEE Computer Society Conference on Computer Vision and Pattern Recognition, CVPR 2001, vol. 1, pp. I-511–I-518 (2001)
2. Bai, Y., Zhang, Y., Ding, M., Ghanem, B.: Finding tiny faces in the wild with generative adversarial network. In: The IEEE Conference on Computer Vision and Pattern Recognition (CVPR), June 2018
3. Blanz, V., Vetter, T.: A morphable model for the synthesis of 3D faces. In: Proceedings of the 26th Annual Conference on Computer Graphics and Interactive Techniques, SIGGRAPH 1999, pp. 187–194. ACM Press/Addison-Wesley Publishing Co., New York (1999)
4. Tran, L., Liu, X.: Nonlinear 3D face morphable model. In: The IEEE Conference on Computer Vision and Pattern Recognition (CVPR), June 2018
5. Ahonen, T., Hadid, A., Pietikainen, M.: Face description with local binary patterns: application to face recognition. IEEE Trans. Pattern Anal. Mach. Intell. 28(12), 2037–2041 (2006)
6. Zhao, J., et al.: Towards pose invariant face recognition in the wild. In: The IEEE Conference on Computer Vision and Pattern Recognition (CVPR), June 2018
7. Taigman, Y., Yang, M., Ranzato, M., Wolf, L.: DeepFace: closing the gap to human-level performance in face verification. In: The IEEE Conference on Computer Vision and Pattern Recognition (CVPR), June 2014
8. Schroff, F., Kalenichenko, D., Philbin, J.: FaceNet: a unified embedding for face recognition and clustering. In: The IEEE Conference on Computer Vision and Pattern Recognition (CVPR), June 2015
9. Baudrillard, J.: Simulacra and simulations: disneyland. In: Lemert, Ch. (ed.) Social Theory. The Multicultural and Classic Readings, pp. 524–530. Westview Press, Boulder (1993)
10. Liu, J., Li, J., Feng, L., Li, L., Tian, J., Lee, K.: Seeing Jesus in toast: neural and behavioral correlates of face pareidolia. Cortex 53, 60–77 (2014)
11. Liu, W., et al.: SSD: single shot multibox detector. In: Leibe, B., Matas, J., Sebe, N., Welling, M. (eds.) ECCV 2016. LNCS, vol. 9905, pp. 21–37. Springer, Cham (2016). https://doi.org/10.1007/978-3-319-46448-0_2
12. Goodfellow, I., et al.: Generative adversarial nets. In: Ghahramani, Z., Welling, M., Cortes, C., Lawrence, N.D., Weinberger, K.Q. (eds.) Advances in Neural Information Processing Systems 27, pp. 2672–2680. Curran Associates, Inc. (2014)
13. Zafeiriou, S., Zhang, C., Zhang, Z.: A survey on face detection in the wild: past, present and future. Comput. Vis. Image Underst. 138, 1–24 (2015)
14. Takahashi, K., Watanabe, K.: Seeing objects as faces enhances object detection. I-Perception 6(5), 2041669515606007 (2015)
15. Abaci, B., Akgül, T.: Detecting face-looking images. In: 2015 23rd Signal Processing and Communications Applications Conference (SIU), pp. 2186–2189, May 2015
16. Krizhevsky, A., Sutskever, I., Hinton, G.E.: Imagenet classification with deep convolutional neural networks. In: Pereira, F., Burges, C.J.C., Bottou, L., Weinberger, K.Q. (eds.) Advances in Neural Information Processing Systems 25, pp. 1097–1105. Curran Associates, Inc. (2012)
17. Deng, J., Dong, W., Socher, R., Li, L.J., Li, K., Fei-Fei, L.: Imagenet: a large-scale hierarchical image database. In: 2009 IEEE Conference on Computer Vision and Pattern Recognition, pp. 248–255, June 2009

18. Zhou, B., Lapedriza, A., Khosla, A., Oliva, A., Torralba, A.: Places: a 10 million image database for scene recognition. IEEE Trans. Pattern Anal. Mach. Intell. **40**, 1452–1464 (2017)

19. Long, J., Shelhamer, E., Darrell, T.: Fully convolutional networks for semantic segmentation. In: The IEEE Conference on Computer Vision and Pattern Recognition (CVPR), June 2015

20. Flickr. https://www.flickr.com/ (2018)

21. Face, W.T.: https://www.wtface.com/ (2018)

22. Liu, Z., Luo, P., Wang, X., Tang, X.: Deep learning face attributes in the wild. In: Proceedings of International Conference on Computer Vision (ICCV) (2015)

23. He, K., Zhang, X., Ren, S., Sun, J.: Deep residual learning for image recognition. In: The IEEE Conference on Computer Vision and Pattern Recognition (CVPR), June 2016

24. Lin, T.-Y., et al.: Microsoft COCO: common objects in context. In: Fleet, D., Pajdla, T., Schiele, B., Tuytelaars, T. (eds.) ECCV 2014. LNCS, vol. 8693, pp. 740–755. Springer, Cham (2014). https://doi.org/10.1007/978-3-319-10602-1_48

25. Radford, A., Metz, L., Chintala, S.: Unsupervised representation learning with deep convolutional generative adversarial networks. CoRR abs/1511.06434 (2015)

Characterization of Visual Object Representations in Rat Primary Visual Cortex

Sebastiano Vascon[1,2(✉)] ⓘ, Ylenia Parin[1], Eis Annavini[3] ⓘ,
Mattia D'Andola[3] ⓘ, Davide Zoccolan[3] ⓘ, and Marcello Pelillo[1,2] ⓘ

[1] DAIS, Ca' Foscari University of Venice, Via Torino 155, 30170 Mestre, VE, Italy
`sebastiano.vascon@unive.it`
[2] ECLT, Ca' Foscari University of Venice, San Marco 2940, 30124 Venice, VE, Italy
[3] Visual Neuroscience Lab, International School for Advanced Studies (SISSA),
Via Bonomea 265, Trieste, TS, Italy

Abstract. For most animal species, quick and reliable identification of visual objects is critical for survival. This applies also to rodents, which, in recent years, have become increasingly popular models of visual functions. For this reason in this work we analyzed how various properties of visual objects are represented in rat primary visual cortex (V1). The analysis has been carried out through supervised (classification) and unsupervised (clustering) learning methods. We assessed quantitatively the discrimination capabilities of V1 neurons by demonstrating how photometric properties (luminosity and object position in the scene) can be derived directly from the neuronal responses.

Keywords: Rat's visual system · Core Object Recognition · Objects classification

1 Introduction

For most animals, recognition of visual objects is of paramount importance. The visual system of many species has adapted to quickly and effortlessly detect and classify objects in spite of major variation (or transformation) in their appearance. This set of abilities is called Core Object Recognition [2] and is typical of primate species, where a hierarchy of visual cortical areas, known as the ventral stream, supports shape processing and image understanding [3]. In recent years, some authors [21,22] have investigated whether such core ability also exists in rats, by exploiting machine-learning tools, such as information theory and pattern classifiers, which have proved to be invaluable tools to understand how object vision works in primates [2]. Indeed, rodents have become increasingly interesting model organisms to study the mammalian visual system [8–10,23]. In particular, rodent object-processing abilities are supposed to be located along a

---

S. Vascon, Y. Parin and E. Annavini—Equal contribution.

© Springer Nature Switzerland AG 2019
L. Leal-Taixé and S. Roth (Eds.): ECCV 2018 Workshops, LNCS 11131, pp. 577–586, 2019.
https://doi.org/10.1007/978-3-030-11015-4_43

progression of cortical areas, starting in primary visual cortex (V1), and extending to lateral extrastriate areas LM, LI, and LL [8,20], which are thought to be an homologous of the primate ventral stream. Recent work by [21] has shown that, indeed, visual object representations along this progression become more explicit, i.e.: (1) information about low-level visual properties, such as luminance, is gradually lost; and (2) object identity becomes more easily readable through linear classifiers, even in the presence of changes in object appearance.

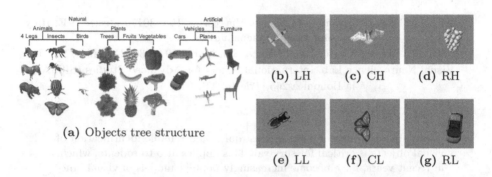

(a) Objects tree structure

(b) LH   (c) CH   (d) RH

(e) LL   (f) CL   (g) RL

Fig. 1. Stimulus set. The image on the left shows the semantic hierarchical structure of the objects belonging to the stimulus set. The images on the right show an example stimulus for each combination of position (first letter of the label) and luminosity (the second letter), e.g., "LH" stands for left and high luminosity, "RL" stands for right and low luminosity, "CL" stands for center and low luminosity, etc.

In this work, we tried to understand at a deeper level what visual properties are encoded in the activity of a population of rat V1 neurons, using both unsupervised and supervised machine learning algorithms. The focus on V1 was motivated by the fact that this cortical area is the entry stage of visual information in cortex (future work will aim at providing a similar characterization in higher-order visual cortical areas).

Specifically, in this study, we applied for the first time the Dominant Set [16] clustering algorithm (DS) to understand the structure of visual object representations in a visual cortical area. The choice of the DS has been driven also by it recent success in related fields, like in brain connectomic [5,6] or neuroscience [17], making it a good candidate for the task at hand. Furthermore, we applied an array of supervised algorithms to show that V1 neuronal responses can be used to predict with great accuracy the photometric information on the scene presented to the rat.

The article is organized as follows: in Sect. 2 we provide a description of the experimental methods that were used to produce the stimulus set and to record the responses of V1 neurons; in Sect. 3 we describe the analysis we carried out to understand the organization of visual stimuli in terms of V1 neuron responses; in Sect. 4 we show how V1 neuronal responses can be used to classify some key visual properties of the stimuli, i.e., their location within the visual field and their luminosity; the Sect. 5 concludes the paper with some future perspectives.

2   Materials and Methods

In this section, we describe the steps that were performed to build the dataset and, whether non-conventional, the methodologies used to analyze the data.

2.1   Stimulus Set and Data Acquisition

For our experiments, we built a rich and ecological stimulus set using a large number of objects, organized in a semantic hierarchy (Fig. 1). To build the stimulus set we used 40 3D models of real world objects[1], both natural and artificial, each rendered in 36 different poses, randomly chosen around four main views (frontal, lateral, top, and 45° in azimuth and elevation), at one of three possible sizes (30–35–40°) chosen at random, in one of three possible positions (0°, ±15°), also chosen at random, and rotated in plane of either 0, 90 or ±45° for a total of 1440 stimuli. To further characterize the stimulus set we extracted a set of low and mid level features (such as position, contrast, and orientation) of the stimuli as they were presented on-screen to the rat: for the scope of the current work we will focus on the *position* of the center of mass, and on the *luminosity*. Stimuli were presented on a gray background to anesthetized naïve Long-Evans rats for 250 ms while collecting extracellular neuronal activity from all the layers of primary visual cortex (V1) using multi-shank, 64-channel silicon electrode arrays[2]. We recorded extracellular potentials using an RZ2 BioAmp signal processor[3] at a sampling frequency of 24.4141 kHz. We characterized the neurons by carefully mapping the positions of each unit's receptive field (RF), rotating the rat afterwards in order to center the RFs on the screen and thus achieve maximal response to the stimuli.

2.2   Data Preprocessing

We filtered the raw extracellular potentials with a band-pass filter (0.5–11 kHz) to extract neurons' spiking activity, and the resulting action potentials (spikes) were extracted using an Expectation-Maximization clustering algorithm [18] that separates the spikes produced by different neurons according to their shape. Then, we estimated the optimal spike count window for each neuron using its firing rate averaged over the 10 best stimuli [1, 21], and we used it to compute the average number of spikes produced by a neuron in response to each stimulus, across its repeated presentations. Finally, we scaled the spike counts of each neuron to zero mean and unitary variance to obtain the population vectors for the stimulus set [12]. This led to a vector of size 177 for each visual stimulus that was used in all unsupervised and supervised analysis, where 177 is the total number of units (single- and multi-unit) obtained through spike sorting.

---

[1] TurboSquid https://www.turbosquid.com/.
[2] NeuroNexus Technologies, Ann Arbor, MI, USA.
[3] Tucker-Davis Technologies, Alachua, FL, USA.

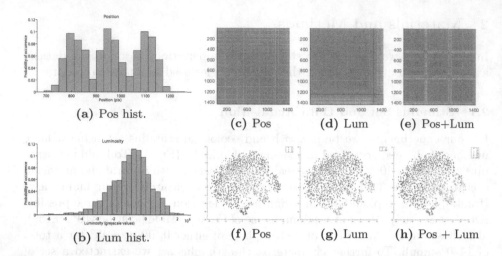

Fig. 2. Feature distribution and binning visualization. Figures a–b report position and luminosity histograms. Figures c–d show distance matrices of neuronal population vectors ordered by position and luminosity. Figure e shows the same distance matrix in which rows and columns are ordered according to the binning of the combined feature. Figures f–h report tSNE [13] 2-dimensional maps where point color refers to the feature binning. (Color figure online)

2.3   Characterization of Visual Features

To quantify the low- and mid-level features of the stimuli, we saved them as they were presented during the experiments and we extracted the position of the center of mass of each stimulus and the total luminosity w.r.t. the background, defined as $L_{tot} = \sum(I(i,j) - 128)$, where $I(i,j)$ is the matrix of pixel intensities in greyscale values. As shown in Fig. 2a, the distribution of the position of the stimuli along the x axis was, as expected from the presentation protocol, trimodal, with the three peaks corresponding to the three main visual field positions used to show the stimuli during the experiment. This naturally leads to partition the set of stimuli in three classes, according to their position: left, right, or center. The luminosity instead shows a unimodal distribution that does not suggest a clear categorization; for this reason we visually inspected the distance matrix of the neuronal population vectors corresponding to each object, ordered according to the luminosity of the objects (see Fig. 2d). We then set a threshold (red lines in Fig. 2d) by hand at the point where the stimuli clearly separate. The final distribution of samples (objects) per class is reported in Table 1.

3   Characterize Object Representations Through Clustering

First, we analyzed the space of neuronal responses obtained from V1 through unsupervised (clustering) methods. The aim was to assess how performing is the

Table 1. Classes distributions.

Pos.		Luminosity		Tot. Pos.
		Low lum.	High lum.	
Pos.	Right	411	69	480
	Center	406	74	480
	Left	407	73	480
Tot. Lum.		1224	216	1440

Table 2. Best Average Silhouette value for each compared clustering method and number of clusters extracted.

Algorithm	K	SIL
DBSCAN eps $= 14.9$ minPts $= 4$	2	0.525
DS $\sigma = 504$	2	**0.565**
K-Means k $= 2$	2	0.448
K-Medoids k $= 2$	2	0.394

rat's neuronal embedding of the visual stimuli in terms of automatic grouping. The rationale is that stimuli having similar photometric characteristics (position and/or luminosity) should lie close to each other in the embedding, while being well separated from those having different properties. To check whether the neuronal mapping was meaningful in this regard, we tested different clustering algorithms, considering their best parameter setting under both internal and external indexes. The performances of each method have been stressed to their limit, so as to provide a guideline for future studies relying on similar methods. To have an intuition of the complexity of this task we first visually inspected the distance matrices of all the stimuli per classes (see Fig. 2c–e). The distance matrix is a symmetric matrix of size $n \times n$ (where $n = 1440$) containing the Euclidean distances of all the neuronal population vectors for each pair of stimuli. Then the matrix is sorted accordingly to the visual feature (position, luminosity and the binned position+luminosity) under exam. As one can note, the matrix relative to the class position resembles a random matrix, and the three classes (left, center, right) are not clearly identifiable. Instead, the other two matrices, related to luminosity and the combination between position and luminosity, clearly report the two and six classes in which features are binned.

3.1 Experiments

The experiments that have been carried out compared the performances of supervised clustering algorithms like k-means [14] and k-medoids [11] (where the number of cluster is known in advance) and unsupervised techniques like *DBSCAN* [7] and *Dominant Set*[16], where no a-priori information on the underlying

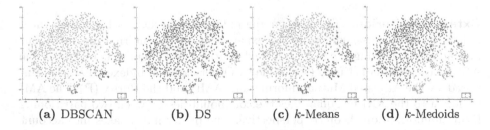

| (a) DBSCAN | (b) DS | (c) k-Means | (d) k-Medoids |

Fig. 3. Best partition according to SIL. Each point of the map is colored according to the cluster it belongs. Clusters are obtained with different methods through Silhouette maximization. (Color figure online)

Table 3. Best ARI value for each compared clustering algorithm and stimulus classes. The best clustering algorithm for each feature and external index is highlighted in bold.

Alg.	Position				Luminosity				Position & luminosity			
	K	AMI	P	ARI	K	AMI	P	ARI	K	AMI	P	ARI
DBSCAN	2	0.008	0.388	0.012	2	0.43	0.924	0.633	2	0.128	0.31	0.136
DS	17	0.179	**0.746**	0.121	2	**0.475**	**0.933**	**0.675**	17	0.268	**0.672**	0.171
Kmeans	6	**0.255**	0.692	**0.233**	2	0.336	0.89	0.534	6	**0.378**	0.638	**0.299**
Kmedoids	3	0.189	0.557	0.179	2	0.257	0.85	0.415	6	0.313	0.543	0.21

structures is available. We performed two different experiments considering on a first instance an internal criterion, the *Silhouette* [19], and later an external one, the *Adjusted Rand Index* (ARI). The silhouette is a specific measure for each object and accounts for how well each object lies within its cluster and how well is separated from the others. In order to provide a global measure, the *overall average silhouette width* (SIL) is taken [19]. The ARI is a measure that accounts for the agreement of two partitions, the predicted from a clustering method and the annotation: the higher its value, the better the algorithm has separated data. For all the clustering methods, the Euclidean metric has been used to compute distances/similarities.

Internal Criterion. For each method we searched in its parameters space the setting that maximizes the SIL. Maximizing the average silhouette means finding the parameters of a partitioning algorithm that separate and merge points in the best way possible provided their similarities or dissimilarities. In case a clustering method collapsed to an unwanted solution (one single cluster), we looked for the highest SIL value which separates the objects into at least two clusters with minimum density equal to the size of the less represented class of objects (in our case 69, see Table 1 for the classes distributions). We amend that this particular selection criterion is not completely fair, because it mixes some prior-information on the structure of the data with an internal index, but has the positive effect to find a reasonable solution for all the clustering algorithms at hand. The quantitative and qualitative results are reported in Table 2 and in Fig. 3 respectively.

External Criterion. The test on the external criteria has been performed following the same schema as in the experiment on the internal measures, but instead of maximizing the SIL we looked for the parameters that maximize the ARI for each class of stimuli (see Table 1). Other external indexes that are computed are the Adjusted Mutual Information (AMI) and the Purity (P). The AMI is similar to the ARI but quantifies the commonalities between two partitioning from an information-theoretic perspective. The purity index takes into account how the labels are organized inside of each cluster. We performed these experiments to understand which method has the potential of grouping as expected the different neuronal mappings with respect to the single classes. The quantitative and qualitative results are reported in Table 3 and in Fig. 4 respectively.

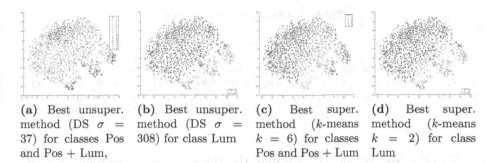

(a) Best unsuper. method (DS σ = 37) for classes Pos and Pos + Lum,

(b) Best unsuper. method (DS σ = 308) for class Lum

(c) Best super. method (k-means k = 6) for classes Pos and Pos + Lum

(d) Best super. method (k-means k = 2) for class Lum

Fig. 4. Best partition according to ARI. For each stimulus feature we selected the best partition produced by supervised (k-means and k-medoids) and unsupervised method (DS and DBSCAN) by maximizing ARI metric. Each point of the map is colored according to the cluster it belongs to. (Color figure online)

3.2   Results

In general the values of SIL, ARI and AMI are quite low indicating that the task is very complex, data is very noisy and visual stimuli are not perfectly mapped to the neuronal response. This can be easily seen in Figs. 2f–h, where the tSNE [13] projection shows a mixing of classes, in particular on the upper part of the projection for the position (Fig. 2f) and position+luminosity (see Fig. 2h). The luminosity classes, instead, are well separated from each other. From both perspectives (internal and external indexes) the embedding found using the responses from V1 was sufficiently able to group the different classes.

Considering the internal index (see Table 2), the method that best performs was the DS, outperforming also the supervised methods like k-means and k-medoids. The motivations are due to the fact that DS only depends on the similarity matrix, which is not the case for the other techniques that also rely on other assumptions (like the number of clusters or global densities). Regarding the results for the external criterion (see Table 3) the best unsupervised clustering method is the DS among all features. The top purity is reached by the DS and this can be explained by the higher number of clusters that are generated. In terms of supervised clustering, the best performing method is k-means in all the considered metrics. These results suggest us that, in case of absent a-priori information on the number of clusters, the DS method can be considered as a more-than-valid alternative to standard approaches (like DBSCAN). Furthermore, knowledge on the number of clusters can be fruitfully used by supervised clustering algorithms (like k-means).

4   Inferring Object Properties with Supervised Learning

As seen in Sect. 3, the analysis of the neuronal embedding was meaningful under different criteria to analyze how the space is partitioned. This lead to a second set of experiments in terms of discrimination power of the features extracted from

Table 4. Classifier performances.

Alg.	Position				Luminosity				Position+luminosity			
	ACC	AUC	mF1	MF1	ACC	AUC	mF1	MF1	ACC	AUC	mF1	MF1
Lin SVM	0.906	0.961	0.859	0.859	0.913	0.922	0.913	0.818	0.756	0.500	0.268	0.181
Ker SVM	**0.942**	**0.979**	**0.912**	**0.912**	**0.939**	**0.970**	**0.939**	**0.877**	0.758	0.536	0.275	0.181
ECOC LSVM	0.908	0.963	0.862	0.862	0.912	0.922	0.912	0.813	**0.937**	**0.966**	**0.810**	**0.778**
k-NN ($k = 9$)	0.913	0.960	0.870	0.870	0.931	0.937	0.931	0.855	0.935	0.944	0.805	0.763

the V1 area. We considered separately the three classes of photometric characteristics *position, luminosity* and *position+luminosity* and carried out several tests by training and testing standard classifiers (Linear/Kernel SVM[4], Error Correcting Output Code Linear SVM[5] [4] and k-NN) on the V1 embedding to confirm its discrimination capability. The rationale is that similar visual stimuli will lie in close proximity and vice-versa different ones will be located far away. With this assumption, a classifier should be able to find a boundary to discriminate between the classes.

4.1 Experiments and Results

Considering a class of visual stimuli (see Table 1 for a details on classes) we performed a 5-fold cross validation to find the best parameter setting of each classifier. The folds have been created in a stratified way ensuring that each class is represented with the same proportion of the dataset. The training and testing have been performed randomly generating 10 different splits of the data and consequently averaging the performances. To evaluate the performances we used four indexes that are common in classification tasks: *accuracy* (ACC), *average area under the ROC curve* (AUC), the *micro F-measure* (mF1) and the *macro F-measure* (MF1) [15]. The results are reported in Table 4. It is evident how the neuronal responses can be used successfully to classify visual stimuli; in fact, we achieved a very high ACC, AUC and (in general) F-score. As expected, due to the class imbalance (see Table 1), the MF1 is a bit lower than the mF1. This is particularly evident for the luminosity and position+luminosity classes, in which a strong imbalance (the larger class is $\simeq$6 times bigger w.r.t. the smaller one) is reported. Regarding the class position and the class luminosity, the best performing method was the Kernel SVM followed by the k-NN. It is worth to note that the simple k-NN is the second best choice for all the three classes; this gives us an indication of the difficulties in finding a linear separator, hence on the non linear separability of the space. This motivates also the fact that the Linear SVM performs poorly w.r.t. the Kernel SVM. Furthermore, in the case of position+luminosity the best performing method was the ECOC L-SVM followed by the k-NN. This is explained by the fact that, in that particular case, we increased the number of classes from 2–3 to 6, needing more hyperplanes

---

[4] Software at https://www.csie.ntu.edu.tw/~cjlin/libsvm/.
[5] Software at https://www.mathworks.com/help/stats/fitcecoc.html.

to separate them. The ECOC is based on an ensemble of Linear SVMs trained in one-vs-one mode which creates all the possible intersecting hyperplanes w.r.t. the classes. For this reason it outperforms the other classifiers, while being not so far from the performances of the Linear SVM for the Position and for the Luminosity, both cases having fewer classes. Concerning the stability of the results we reported a maximum mean standard deviation of $\simeq 1\%$ considering all the 10 runs.

5   Conclusions

In this paper, we investigated how visual stimuli are mapped into the representational space of V1 neurons focusing on two low-level properties (luminosity and position within the visual field). We thus quantified the extent to which these properties were accurately represented in the V1 population space, using supervised and unsupervised learning methods. We found that, indeed, both luminosity and position and their combination are naturally mapped in the V1 representation, and that these features can be accurately extracted using pattern classifiers. Among the clustering methods, DS showed the greatest accuracy at inferring the structure of the representation. Among the classifiers, the SVM with nonlinear kernel achieved the highest accuracy. In both cases, this testifies of the complexity of the representation and of the not complete linear discriminability of the data.

As future work, we will try different distance functions and will test whether other higher-level visual features, e.g. orientation, are encoded. Moreover, the same data processing pipeline will be applied to higher-oder visual areas, e.g. LM-LI-LL, to understand the differences with V1.

Acknowledgement. This work was supported by a European Research Council Consolidator Grant (DZ, project n. 616803-LEARN2SEE).

References

1. Baldassi, C., Alemi-Neissi, A., Pagan, M., DiCarlo, J.J., Zecchina, R., Zoccolan, D.: Shape similarity, better than semantic membership, accounts for the structure of visual object representations in a population of monkey inferotemporal neurons. PLOS Comput. Biol. **9**(8), 1–21 (2013)
2. DiCarlo, J.J., Cox, D.D.: Untangling invariant object recognition. Trends Cogn. Sci. **11**(8), 333–341 (2007)
3. DiCarlo, J.J., Zoccolan, D., Rust, N.C.: How does the brain solve visual object recognition? Neuron **73**(3), 415–434 (2012)
4. Dietterich, T.G., Bakiri, G.: Solving multiclass learning problems via error-correcting output codes. J. Artif. Intell. Res. **2**, 263–286 (1994)
5. Dodero, L., Vascon, S., Giancardo, L., Gozzi, A., Sona, D., Murino, V.: Automatic white matter fiber clustering using dominant sets. In: 2013 International Workshop on Pattern Recognition in Neuroimaging, pp. 216–219, June 2013

6. Dodero, L., Vascon, S., Murino, V., Bifone, A., Gozzi, A., Sona, D.: Automated multi-subject fiber clustering of mouse brain using dominant sets. Front. Neuroinform. **8**, 87 (2015)
7. Ester, M., Kriegel, H.P., Sander, J., Xu, X.: A density-based algorithm for discovering clusters a density-based algorithm for discovering clusters in large spatial databases with noise. In: Proceedings of the Second International Conference on Knowledge Discovery and Data Mining, KDD 1996, pp. 226–231. AAAI Press (1996)
8. Glickfeld, L.L., Olsen, S.R.: Higher-order areas of the mouse visual cortex. Ann. Rev. Vis. Sci. **3**(1), 251–273 (2017)
9. Glickfeld, L.L., Reid, R.C., Andermann, M.L.: A mouse model of higher visual cortical function. Curr. Opin. Neurobiol. **24**, 28–33 (2014)
10. Huberman, A.D., Niell, C.M.: What can mice tell us about how vision works? Trends Neurosci. **34**(9), 464–473 (2011)
11. Kaufman, L., Rousseeuw, P.: Clustering by means of medoids. In: Statistical Data Analysis Based on the L1 Norm and Related Methods, pp. 405–416. North-Holland, Amsterdam (1987)
12. Kiani, R., Esteky, H., Mirpour, K., Tanaka, K.: Object category structure in response patterns of neuronal population in monkey inferior temporal cortex. J. Neurophysiol. **97**(6), 4296–4309 (2007)
13. van der Maaten, L., Hinton, G.: Visualizing data using t-SNE. J. Mach. Learn. Res. **9**, 2579–2605 (2008)
14. MacQueen, J.: Some methods for classification and analysis of multivariate observations. In: Proceedings of the Fifth Berkeley Symposium on Mathematical Statistics and Probability, Volume 1: Statistics, pp. 281–297. University of California Press, Berkeley (1967)
15. Manning, C.D., Raghavan, P., Schütze, H.: Introduction to Information Retrieval. Cambridge University Press, New York (2008)
16. Pavan, M., Pelillo, M.: Dominant sets and pairwise clustering. IEEE Trans. Pattern Anal. Mach. Intell. **29**(1), 167–172 (2007)
17. Pennacchietti, F., et al.: Nanoscale molecular reorganization of the inhibitory post-synaptic density is a determinant of GABAergic synaptic potentiation. J. Neurosci. **37**, 1747–1756 (2017)
18. Rossant, C., et al.: Spike sorting for large, dense electrode arrays. Nat. Neurosci. **19**(4), 634–641 (2016)
19. Rousseeuw, P.J.: Silhouettes: a graphical aid to the interpretation and validation of cluster analysis. J. Comput. Appl. Math. **20**, 53–65 (1987)
20. Sereno, M.I., Allman, J.: Cortical visual areas in mammals. Neural Basis Vis. Funct. **4**, 160–172 (1991)
21. Tafazoli, S., et al.: Emergence of transformation-tolerant representations of visual objects in rat lateral extrastriate cortex. eLife **6**, 1–39 (2017)
22. Vermaercke, B., Gerich, F.J., Ytebrouck, E., Arckens, L., Op de Beeck, H.P., Van den Bergh, G.: Functional specialization in rat occipital and temporal visual cortex. J. Neurophysiol. **112**(8), 1963–1983 (2014)
23. Zoccolan, D.: Invariant visual object recognition and shape processing in rats. Behav. Brain Res. **285**, 10–33 (2015)

Learning Event Representations
by Encoding the Temporal Context

Catarina Dias[1] and Mariella Dimiccoli[2,3(✉)]

[1] Faculty of Engineering, University of Porto,
Rua Doutor Roberto Frias, 4200-465 Porto, Portugal
catfdias@gmail.com
[2] Department of Mathematics and Computer Science, University of Barcelona,
Gran via de les Corts Catalanes 585, 08007 Barcelona, Spain
dimiccolimariella@gmail.com
[3] Computer Vision Center, Campus UAB,
Edifici O, 08193 Cerdanyola del Valles, Barcelona, Spain

Abstract. This work aims at learning image representations suitable for event segmentation, a largely unexplored problem in the computer vision literature. The proposed approach is a self-supervised neural network that captures patterns of temporal overlap by learning to predict the feature vector of neighbor frames, given the one of the current frame. The model is inspired to recent experimental findings in neuroscience, showing that stimuli associated with similar temporal contexts are grouped together in the representational space. Experiments performed on image sequences captured at regular intervals have shown that a representation able to encode the temporal context provides very promising results on the task of temporal segmentation.

Keywords: Representation learning · Event learning · LSTM · Neural networks

1 Introduction

As our sensory system is inherently continuous, we experience the world as an uninterrupted stream of perceptual stimuli. However, sensory information is automatically segmented by our brain into discrete *events* that can be understood, remembered and retrieved from the memory. How these event representations are generated at neural level is a very active area of research in neuroscience [1–5]. Although firstly questioned more than fifty years ago [1], it was only in 2007 that the seminal work of Zacks [2] revealed the key role of uncertainty and surprise in determining event boundaries. Later on, Kurby and Zacks [3] hypothesized that event segmentation might arise as a side effect of integrating information over the recent past to improve predictions about the near future. More recently, Shapiro et al. [4] have shown that neural representation

© Springer Nature Switzerland AG 2019
L. Leal-Taixé and S. Roth (Eds.): ECCV 2018 Workshops, LNCS 11131, pp. 587–596, 2019.
https://doi.org/10.1007/978-3-030-11015-4_44

of events are not tied to predictive uncertainty, but arise from temporal community structures: items that share the temporal context are grouped together in a representational space. Focusing more on a higher level processing, DuBrow and Davachi [5] have argued that event boundaries are generated by changes in our goals and these goals determine how information is stored and retrieved in our brain.

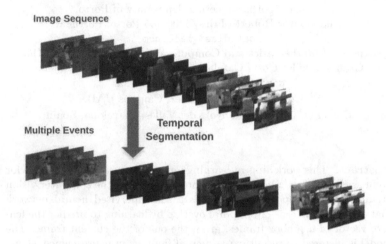

Fig. 1. Example of temporal segmentation of a sequence of images.

Besides neuroscience, event segmentation is also receiving an increasing attention in computer vision [6–10]. Indeed, temporal video segmentation can be considered the first step towards automatic annotation and recognition of digital video sequences (see Fig. 1). The growing size of today's available unconstrained videos on internet raises the need of automatically detecting, recognizing and retrieving the type of complex events occurring in them. Typically, state of the art algorithms for event or action recognition rely on event boundary detection and visual features extracted at image level or at event level such as semantic features or optical flow. Most recent and promising approaches for event detection [11,12] use concept scores as intermediate representation, which are the confidence of the occurrence of the concepts in the video. For example, the event *Having a dinner with friends* can be described as the occurrence of *food, laughing, people, bottles* ... etc. However, the resulting concept-based event representation is highly noisy due to the high variability of concept's appearance on the one hand and to the high variability of the concept representation for a complex event on the other hand. Therefore it is difficult to segment temporally a video based on semantic features.

Given the relevance of the problem, in this paper, we propose to learn a representation for image sequences suitable for the task of temporal segmentation. Inspired by the theory Shapiro et al. [4], our model aims at embedding the temporal context of images via a self-supervised *pretext task* consisting in predicting the feature vector of neighbor frames given the concept vector of the current frame.

The reminder of this paper is as follows. In Sect. 2, we present the proposed approach, while in Sect. 3 we detail and discuss experimental results. We conclude the paper with Sect. 4, summarizing its main contributions and findings.

2   Learning Event Representations

Here, we first introduce the concepts underlying the proposed model. Second, we describe the *pretext task* that we use to learn the temporal representations and subsequently present the *validation task* which is employed to evaluate the quality of the learned representations (see Fig. 2).

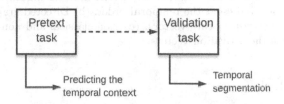

Fig. 2. Modules of the proposed method.

2.1   Underlying Model

Hereafter, we consider a toy example to illustrate the intuition underlying our model. Let us suppose that we are given a sequence of N images and each image is represented by a feature vector as shown in Fig. 3(a).

Relying on the feature vector representation, we built a directed graph, where each vertex corresponds to a feature vector and each direct edge going from, says, A to B indicates that feature vector B temporally follows feature vector A in the image sequence. The resulting graph, shown in Fig. 3(b) indicates that the underlying representation of the image sequence presents two community structures, with many edges joining vertices of the same community and comparatively few edges joining vertices of different communities. Therefore, the directed graph could be regarded as a more intuitive simplified model that represents the temporal context of sequence data.

In the next section, we focus on how to automatically learn a feature space, where temporally nearby frames belonging to the same event lie close to each other.

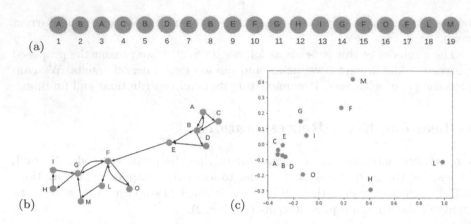

Fig. 3. (a) Image sequence representation: the letters indicate the feature vectors identifier and the numbers represent the temporal order. (b) Directed graph encoding the temporal relations between feature vectors. (c) Non-classical and non-metric multidimensional scaling of the activation vectors.

2.2   Pretext Task

Representation learning aims at building intermediate representations of data useful to solve machine learning tasks. In self-supervised learning, one trains a model to solve a so-called *pretext task* on a dataset without the need for human annotation by exploiting labeling that comes for "free" with the data.

In our case, similarly to *word2vec* models in natural language processing [13], the pretext task is a prediction task, that given a frame, aims at predicting the temporally neighbor frames corresponding to the temporal context. This leads to learn a function from a given frame to the frames surrounding it. We considered two different implementations. The first one is a simple neural network with a single hidden layer that takes as input the feature vector x_i of the frame i and is trained to output the concept vector $x_{i\pm n}$ of the frame $i \pm n$, with $n \in \{1, .., m\}$ by minimizing the Mean Squared Error (MSE) between x_i and the estimation of x_{i+1}, say $\hat{x}_{i+1}$. After training, the new feature vector $\tilde{x}_i$ embedding the temporal context for the image i, is obtained by multiplying x_i to the learned weight matrix W. This procedure is illustrated on Fig. 4.

The second one is a many-to-many encoder-decoder long short term memory (LSTM) recurrent neural network. The model is trained to predict the feature vector of the next frame in a sequence based on the n previous ones. This process is illustrated in Fig. 5. The network is trained by feeding batches of sequential frames of size $n < N$ randomly extracted, where N is the full length of the video sequence. The new family of feature vectors $\tilde{\mathbf{x}}$ are obtained after training, as output of the encoder by feeding it the original feature vectors $\mathbf{x}$.

In the case of the toy example illustrated in the previous section, we used one-hot encoding for the 12 feature vectors and we trained a neural network to predict the feature vector of the image $i + 1$ given the concept vector i.

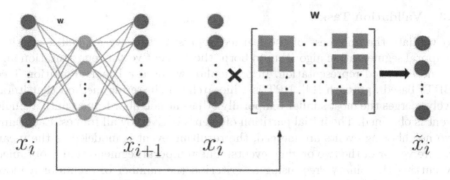

Fig. 4. Left: Training a single layer neural network to predict the concept vector of the image $i + 1$ given the concept vector of the image i as input. Right: Extraction of the new feature vector for the image i by multiplying the original concept vector by the weights of the trained neural network.

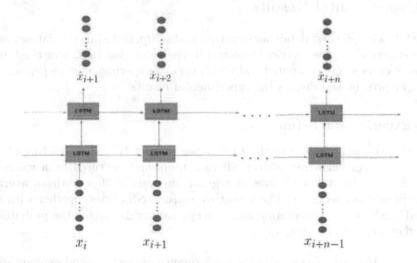

Fig. 5. Encoder-decoder LSTM layer neural network. The new feature vector is obtained as output of the decoder (first layer LSTM) after training.

In Fig. 3(c) is shown the multidimensional scaling of the activation vectors obtained multiplying the original feature vectors by the weight matrix learned with the prediction task. From this figure we can clearly see how the feature vectors that on Fig. 3(b) were linked by numerous edges lie close to each other on this new representational space (A, B, C, D, E on the one side, and G, I, F, M, H, L, O on the other side).

Since the main objective is to transfer the learned representation to target task, in the next section we detail how we validate the goodness of the new learned representation.

2.3   Validation Task

To validate the goodness of the learned representation we applied a classical temporal segmentation algorithm to both, the concept vector representation and the new learned representation. In particular, we used a Binary Partition Tree (BPT) based approach [14]. BPT is a hierarchical clustering method that iteratively merges the most similar temporally adjacent neighbor frames until a single event is obtained. The initial partition of events is given by all frames. Each time two neighboring events are merged, the resulting event is modeled as the mean feature vector of the two original events. The temporal segmentation is obtained by cutting the binary tree, using as criterion the number of events or a more complex function that takes into account the similarity of all the merging. Since the goal of this work is to show that encoding the temporal context is beneficial for temporal segmentation, we used the most simple criterion.

3   Experimental Results

In the following, we first detail our experimental setup, including the dataset used in the experiments, the metrics employed in the validation task, how the initial feature vectors where computed and which type of experiments were performed. Then, we present and discuss the experimental results.

3.1   Experimental Setup

Dataset. We used a subset of the EDUB-Seg dataset [15,16], consisting of ten image sequences belonging to five different users and captured by a wearable photo-camera that takes pictures at regular intervals of 30 s, with an average of 662 images per sequence. The subset we considered, comes together with the ground truth event segmentation and concept vectors describing the probability of each concept in the images.

Evaluation Measure. To evaluate the performance of the temporal segmentation we used the F-measure. In particular, we considered as true positives (TPs) the images that the BPT detects as boundaries of an event and that were manually defined in the GT. The false positives (FPs) are the images detected as events delimiters, but that were not marked in the GT, and the false negatives (FNs) the boundaries not detected but present in the GT. In all cases we considered a tolerance of 5 frames as in [16]. Good event segmentations correspond to F-measure values close to 1.

Feature Extraction. In our experiments, the original feature vectors are obtained as in [16] by firstly detecting concepts independently on each image by means of a concept detector, and then by clustering them in a semantic space by relying on WordNet [17] (see Fig. 6). The number of clusters found determines the size of the vocabulary of concepts. Each element of the feature vector corresponds to the probability of finding a given concept in the image.

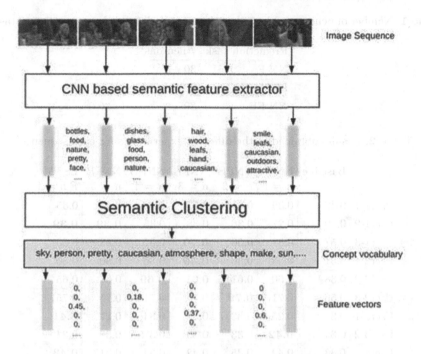

Fig. 6. Semantic feature extraction and generation of concept-based event representation as in [16].

Experiments. We performed three different class of experiments, with slightly different prediction tasks. The first one is the most simple forward prediction (NN forward): given the ith feature vector as input to predict the $(i + 1)^{th}$ feature vector. The second one is a forward prediction that takes into account the previous n feature vectors to predict the next feature vector (LSTM forward). In our experiments we used $n = 50$. The third one is a forward-backward prediction (NN forward-backward): given the ith feature vector as input to predict the neighbor feature vectors inside a window of length n centered at i. We considered $n = \{2, 3, 4, 5\}$. All models were trained by using the MSE of the prediction as loss function and by using Stochastic Gradient Descent (SGD) as optimizer. The results reported on Tables 2 and 3 were achieved by setting the learning rate to 0.1 for the encoder-decoder LSTM model, with momentum to 0.9 for the NN models. The number of neurons used in the hidden layer was different accordingly to the prediction task as shown on Table 1. The size of the original feature vector was 50, extracted following the procedure described in Sect. 2.2. For each sequence the weights that ensured a better performance were saved for later generation of the new learned representation. The BPT based approach described in Sect. 2.3 for event segmentation was applied by relying on both, the original feature vectors and the new learned representation.

Table 1. Number of neurons in the hidden layer used in the different prediction tasks.

Prediction task	#neurons
NN F	30
LSTM F	20
NN FB	30

Table 2. Results obtained in the different experiments for each sequence.

	Baseline	NNF n = 1	NNFB n = 2	NNFB n = 3	NNFB n = 4	NNFB n = 5	LSTM F n = 1
User1-1	0.32	0.39	0.51	0.57	**0.71**	0.47	0.35
User1-2	0.29	0.27	0.36	0.38	0.35	**0.39**	**0.39**
User1-3	0.57	0.58	0.56	**0.70**	0.67	0.53	0.53
User2-1	0.51	0.53	0.56	**0.59**	0.56	0.50	0.50
User2-2	0.38	0.60	0.61	0.64	**0.69**	0.67	0.65
User2-3	0.56	0.71	**0.79**	0.75	0.71	0.75	0.75
User3-1	0.30	0.25	0.33	0.35	0.34	0.27	**0.41**
User3-2	0.39	**0.42**	0.33	0.39	0.37	0.37	0.34
User4	0.33	0.42	0.35	0.42	0.34	0.31	**0.43**
User5	0.38	0.44	0.39	0.42	0.43	0.43	**0.47**

3.2   Results and Discussion

Table 2 shows the results obtained on each sequence and for each prediction task. On Table 3, is reported the average over all sequences for each experiment. As it can be observed on Table 3, the F-measure of the temporal segmentation obtained relying on a representation that encode the temporal context, outperforms the baseline, obtained using the original feature vectors, for all prediction tasks. In particular, the representation learned through the forward-backward prediction achieves the best performance. Furthermore, the performance increases with the size of the temporal window achieving the maximum value for a window of size 3 and then decreases again. These results have shown that, although its simplicity, the proposed approach is very effective to learn event representations, and suggest that encoding the temporal context is crucial for event learning.

Key issues to be investigated, is what features are most suited as basis for the temporal embedding in videos, if they can be learned in an end-to-end fashion and which prediction task would be more effective in the video domain.

Table 3. Average results for each prediction task and baseline performance.

Validation task	F-measure
NN F, n = 1	0.4610
LSTM F	0.4820
NN FB, n = 2	0.4790
NN FB, n = 3	**0.5210**
NN FB, n = 4	0.5170
NN FB, n = 5	0.4690
Baseline	0.4030

4   Conclusions

To the best of our knowledge, this work has presented the first attempt to learn image representations suitable for event segmentation. The proposed approach is inspired to recent experimental findings in neuroscience showing that neural representations of events arise from temporal community structures. To learn the temporal embedding, we proposed a pretext task consisting of predicting the feature vector of neighboring images in a temporal window of fixed size, by using two different approaches: a simple neural network and an encoder-decoder LSTM. Experimental results performed on a dataset of image sequences captured at regular intervals have shown that the new learned representation outperforms the original feature-based representation on the task of temporal segmentation. The generalization of the approach to temporal segmentation of video, would have an important impact in the processing of untrimmed videos.

Acknowledgments. This work was partially founded by TIN2015-66951-C2, SGR 1742, ICREA Academia 2014, Marató TV3 (20141510), Nestore Horizon2020 SC1-PM-15-2017 (769643) and CERCA. The funders had no role in the study design, data collection, analysis, and preparation of the manuscript. The authors gratefully acknowledge NVIDIA Corporation for the donation of the GPU used in this work.

References

1. Newtson, D., Engquist, G.A., Bois, J.: The objective basis of behavior units. J. Pers. Soc. Psychol. **35**(12), 847 (1977)
2. Zacks, J.M., Speer, N.K., Swallow, K.M., Braver, T.S., Reynolds, J.R.: Event perception: a mind-brain perspective. Psychol. Bull. **133**(2), 273 (2007)
3. Kurby, C.A., Zacks, J.M.: Segmentation in the perception and memory of events. Trends Cogn. Sci. **12**(2), 72–79 (2008)
4. Schapiro, A.C., Rogers, T.T., Cordova, N.I., Turk-Browne, N.B., Botvinick, M.M.: Neural representations of events arise from temporal community structure. Nature Neurosci. **16**(4), 486 (2013)
5. DuBrow, S., Davachi, L.: Temporal binding within and across events. Neurobiol. Learn. Memory **134**, 107–114 (2016)

6. Koprinska, I., Carrato, S.: Temporal video segmentation: a survey. Signal Process. Image Commun. **16**(5), 477–500 (2001)
7. Krishna, M.V., Bodesheim, P., Körner, M., Denzler, J.: Temporal video segmentation by event detection: a novelty detection approach. Pattern Recogn. Image Anal. **24**(2), 243–255 (2014)
8. Liwicki, S., Zafeiriou, S.P., Pantic, M.: Online kernel slow feature analysis for temporal video segmentation and tracking. IEEE Trans. Image Process. **24**(10), 2955–2970 (2015)
9. Theodoridis, T., Tefas, A., Pitas, I.: Multi-view semantic temporal video segmentation. In: 2016 IEEE International Conference on Image Processing (ICIP), pp. 3947–3951. IEEE (2016)
10. Iwan, L.H., Thom, J.A.: Temporal video segmentation: detecting the end-of-act in circus performance videos. Multimed. Tools Appl. **76**(1), 1379–1401 (2017)
11. Xu, Z., Yang, Y., Hauptmann, A.G.: A discriminative CNN video representation for event detection. In: Proceedings of the IEEE Conference on Computer Vision and Pattern Recognition, pp. 1798–1807 (2015)
12. Chang, X., Yang, Y., Hauptmann, A.G., Xing, E.P., Yu, Y.L.: Semantic concept discovery for large-scale zero-shot event detection. In: International Joint Conference on Artificial Intelligence (IJCAI) (2015)
13. Mikolov, T., Yih, W.t., Zweig, G.: Linguistic regularities in continuous space word representations. In: Proceedings of the 2013 Conference of the North American Chapter of the Association for Computational Linguistics: Human Language Technologies, pp. 746–751 (2013)
14. Salembier, P., Garrido, L.: Binary partition tree as an efficient representation for image processing, segmentation, and information retrieval. IEEE Trans. Image Process. **9**(4), 561–576 (2000)
15. Talavera, E., Dimiccoli, M., Bolaños, M., Aghaei, M., Radeva, P.: R-clustering for egocentric video segmentation. In: Paredes, R., Cardoso, J.S., Pardo, X.M. (eds.) IbPRIA 2015. LNCS, vol. 9117, pp. 327–336. Springer, Cham (2015). https://doi.org/10.1007/978-3-319-19390-8_37
16. Dimiccoli, M., Bolaños, M., Talavera, E., Aghaei, M., Nikolov, S.G., Radeva, P.: SR-clustering: semantic regularized clustering for egocentric photo streams segmentation. Comput. Vis. Image Underst. **155**, 55–69 (2017)
17. Miller, G.A.: Wordnet: a lexical database for english. Commun. ACM **38**(11), 39–41 (1995)

Decoding Generic Visual Representations from Human Brain Activity Using Machine Learning

Angeliki Papadimitriou(✉)[ID], Nikolaos Passalis[ID], and Anastasios Tefas[ID]

Artificial Intelligence and Information Analysis Laboratory,
Aristotle University of Thessaloniki, 541 24 Thessaloniki, Greece
akpapadim@csd.auth.gr

Abstract. Among the most impressive recent applications of neural decoding is the visual representation decoding, where the category of an object that a subject either sees or imagines is inferred by observing his/her brain activity. Even though there is an increasing interest in the aforementioned visual representation decoding task, there is no extensive study of the effect of using different machine learning models on the decoding accuracy. In this paper we provide an extensive evaluation of several machine learning models, along with different similarity metrics, for the aforementioned task, drawing many interesting conclusions. That way, this paper (a) paves the way for developing more advanced and accurate methods and (b) provides an extensive and easily reproducible baseline for the aforementioned decoding task.

Keywords: Neural decoding · Deep visual representations

1 Introduction

Neural decoding is the process of deciphering human brain activity of subjects performing a specific task. In order to record a subject's brain activity, several functional neuroimaging techniques are available. The term "functional" refers to the temporal aspect that allows these methods to capture the changes of brain activity over time. Such methods are Electroencephalography (EEG) [1] and functional Magnetic Resonance Imaging (fMRI) [2], which have been extensively employed in the literature to study human brain activity during various tasks, such as sleep [3,4], walking [5,6], and dancing [7,8].

Among the most impressive applications of fMRI is the *visual representation decoding* [9]. Visual representation decoding refers to the *prediction* of what a subject sees or imagines by observing *only* his/her neural activity. More specifically, the subject encodes the stimulus as an internal neural representation and the goal is to design a model that can recover that representation by partially observing the brain state (e.g., by observing EEG or fMRI signals) in order to understand or even reconstruct the stimulus that evoked it [9–12].

© Springer Nature Switzerland AG 2019
L. Leal-Taixé and S. Roth (Eds.): ECCV 2018 Workshops, LNCS 11131, pp. 597–606, 2019.
https://doi.org/10.1007/978-3-030-11015-4_45

However, it is not possible to infer the actual internal neural representations of a subject and use them to train models that can perform the aforementioned decoding task. To overcome this limitation, the representation must be supplied from an external source. In [9] it has been shown that the features extracted from various levels of a deep Convolutional Neural Network (CNN) are tightly correlated with the brain activity observed from various brain regions. Therefore, usually the features extracted from a CNN are employed as the intermediate neural representation that can be used to decode what a subject actually sees or imagines [9,12]. Then, the visual representation can be decoded from the observed brain signals using machine learning models [13]. Even though there is an increasing interest in the aforementioned visual representation decoding task, there is no extensive study of the effect of using different machine learning models, as well as of the effect of various hyper-parameters employed during this process, on the decoding accuracy.

The main contribution of this paper is the extensive evaluation of different machine learning models, along with different similarity metrics, for the recently proposed task of decoding visual representations from human brain activity signals. That way, this paper (a) paves the way for developing more advanced and accurate decoding methods and (b) provides an extensive and easily reproducible baseline for the aforementioned task. To this end, all the experiments performed in this paper can be readily reproduced using the code available on-line at https://github.com/angpapadi/Visual-Representation-Decoding-from-Human-Brain-Activity.

Several interesting conclusions are drawn from the results presented in this paper. Even though different models seem to behave differently for the various decoding tasks, using a Multilayer Perceptron (MLP) seems to provide the best decoding accuracy. The choice of the similarity measure for the decoding process can also be of crucial importance for some tasks. Furthermore, several conclusions regarding the actual way that the brain works can be also drawn from the results, e.g., in imagery tasks brain regions that belong to the higher visual cortex seem to exhibit higher predictive power, while lower visual cortex regions seem to encode lower level features that require the use of non-linear models for the decoding, etc.

The rest of this paper is structured as follows. The used decoding method, along with the evaluated machine learning models and similarity metrics are described in Sect. 2, while the experimental protocol and evaluation results are provided in Sect. 3. Finally, conclusions are drawn and future research directions are discussed in Sect. 4.

2   Machine Learning for Visual Representations Decoding

The method used in this paper builds upon the generic brain activity decoding pipeline proposed in [9]. Figure 1 provides an overview of the employed decoding pipeline. First, a subject either views an image or is instructed to imagine a concept (related to a category of images viewed before), while his/her brain activity is monitored using fMRI. Also, a CNN is used to extract a feature representation from the corresponding images (as they are presented to the subject). The use of a CNN layer for this task is not arbitrary. As discussed in [9], the features extracted from various layers of a CNN are tightly associated with the activity of various part of the human visual cortex. This allows for using these representations as an intermediate step for decoding the human brain activity for specific visual tasks, i.e., recognizing the class of an image shown to or imagined by a subject. To this end, a regression model is trained to predict the representation of the viewed image directly using the measured fMRI signals. Then, the class of the image can be inferred by measuring the similarity between the predicted representation to a set of prototype class representations, where each class is represented by the average feature vector extracted by feeding a set of images that belong to a specific class to the used CNN. Note that by regressing the image representation, instead of merely classifying the brain signals into a set of predetermined classes, allows for using the aforementioned pipeline for image categories that were *never presented* to the subject and/or regression model during the training.

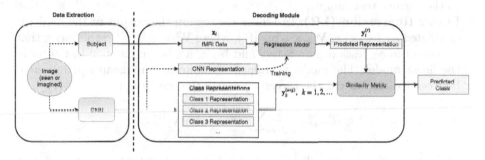

Fig. 1. Pipeline for decoding generic visual representations from human brain activity

The decoding pipeline can be more formally defined as follows. Let $\mathbf{x}_i \in \mathbb{R}^D$ denote a D-dimensional feature vector appropriately extracted from the measured fMRI signals when the i-th experiment is performed [9]. Also, let $\mathbf{y}_i^{(t)} \in \mathbb{R}^L$ be the representation extracted from a layer of a CNN, when the image used for the i-th experiment is fed to the network, and L denote the dimensionality of the extracted feature representation. The prototype class representation for the k-th class is defined as: $\mathbf{y}_k^{(avg)} = \frac{1}{|\mathcal{R}_k|} \sum_{\mathbf{y} \in \mathcal{R}_k} \mathbf{y}$, where $\mathcal{R}_k$ is the set of CNN representations extracted from the images that belong to class k and $|\mathcal{R}_k|$ is the cardinality of this set. Then, a machine learning model $f_{\mathbf{W}}(\mathbf{x})$ is used to regress the aforementioned image representation, where $\mathbf{W}$ denotes the parameters of the employed model. The output of this model is denoted by $\mathbf{y}_i^{(r)} = f_{\mathbf{W}}(\mathbf{x}_i) \in \mathbb{R}^L$ and can be used to infer the class of the corresponding image by measuring the similarity of $\mathbf{y}_i^{(r)}$ with each of the class representations $\mathbf{y}_k^{(avg)}$. Therefore, the predicted class k^* of the object the subject sees or imagines is calculated as:

$$k^* = \arg\max_k S(\mathbf{y}_i^{(r)}, \mathbf{y}_k^{(avg)}) \tag{1}$$

where $S(\mathbf{a}, \mathbf{b})$ is an appropriately defined similarity metric between two vectors $\mathbf{a} \in \mathbb{R}^L$ and $\mathbf{b} \in \mathbb{R}^L$. Note that the CNN representation $\mathbf{y}_i^{(r)}$ is only needed during the training process of the regression model, as also shown in Fig. 1. Then, the class of the object that a subject sees or imagines can be inferred (during the test) without having access to the corresponding image representation, since only the (precomputed) class representation vectors are needed.

As already stated in Sect. 1, the main contribution of this paper is the extensive evaluation of various machine learning models for the task of decoding generic visual representations from human brain activity. To this end, four different regression models are evaluated in this paper. The used models are briefly described bellow:

1. **k-Nearest Neighbor Regression (kNN):** In k-Nearest Neighbor Regression the k nearest neighbors of a data sample are used to regress its target by averaging the (known) target feature vectors of its k neighbors [14]. The contribution of each neighbor is appropriately weighted according to its distance to the current test sample.

2. **Linear Regression (LR):** In Linear Regression the output of the model is calculated as $f_{\mathbf{W}}(\mathbf{x}) = \mathbf{W}_{lr}\mathbf{x} + \mathbf{b}_{lr}$ [15], where $\mathbf{W}_{lr} \in \mathbb{R}^{L \times D}$ is a matrix that contains the regression parameters and $\mathbf{b}_{lr} \in \mathbb{R}^L$ is the independent term in the linear model. The model is trained to minimize the mean squared error between its output and the target representation given by:

$$\mathcal{L}_{mse} = \frac{1}{2N} \sum_i ||f_{\mathbf{W}}(\mathbf{x_i}) - \mathbf{y}_i^{(t)}||_2^2, \tag{2}$$

where $||\mathbf{x}||_2$ denotes the l^2 norm of a vector $\mathbf{x}$ and N is the number of data samples used to fit the regression model. The model can be *regularized* to avoid overfitting, e.g., using the l^2 norm of the regression coefficients as regularizer leads to Ridge Regression (RR) [16].

3. **Kernel Regression (KR):** Kernel Regression is a non-linear variant of LR, where the data are first (non-linearly) projected into a higher-dimensional space, where they can be better separated [17]. KR employs the so-called *kernel trick* to allow for efficiently fitting the regression model, even when the data are projected into an infinite dimensional space.

4. **Multilayer Perceptrons (MLP):** Multilayer Perceptrons are powerful neural network-based methods that can model complex relationships between the input data and their targets through multiple non-linear layers [18]. Several methods have been proposed for training and designing MLP networks. In this work, the networks are trained to minimize the loss function given in (2) using the Adam optimizer [19]. MLPs are often prone to overfitting the data, especially when a small number of training samples is used. To overcome this issue, regularization methods, such as Dropout [20] (also abbreviated as "drop."), can be used.

The selected hyper-parameters for the evaluated models, e.g., number of hidden units in the MLP, regularizer weight, etc., are presented in Sect. 3. Both the input vectors $\mathbf{x}_i$, as well as the extracted representations $\mathbf{y}_i^{(t)}$, are normalized to have zero mean and unit variance (z-score normalization). The output of the regression model is then appropriately "denormalized", using the mean and standard deviation computed on the train set, in order to compute the similarity with the prototype class representation vectors $\mathbf{y}_k^{(avg)}$.

Apart from the model used for the regression process, the accuracy of the proposed decoding pipeline critically relies on employed similarity metric. Three different similarity metrics $S(\mathbf{a}, \mathbf{b})$ are evaluated in this paper:

1. **Euclidean similarity:** The Euclidean similarity is computed as the inverse of Euclidean distance: $S_{euclidean}(\mathbf{a}, \mathbf{b}) = \frac{1}{1 + ||\mathbf{a} - \mathbf{b}||_2}$.
2. **Cosine similarity:** The cosine similarity is defined as the angle between two vectors: $S_{cosine}(\mathbf{a}, \mathbf{b}) = \frac{\mathbf{a}^T \mathbf{b}}{||\mathbf{a}||_2 ||\mathbf{b}||_2}$.
3. **Pearson similarity:** The Pearson similarity (correlation) between two vectors is computed as: $S_{pearson}(\mathbf{a}, \mathbf{b}) = \frac{(\mathbf{a} - \mu_a)^T (\mathbf{b} - \mu_b)}{||\mathbf{a} - \mu_a||_2 ||\mathbf{b} - \mu_b||_2}$, where μ_a and μ_b are the average of the values in vectors $\mathbf{a}$ and $\mathbf{b}$ respectively.

3   Experimental Evaluation

In this paper the dataset provided by the authors of [9] is used, while we also closely follow the experimental setup and evaluation metrics described in their work. More specifically, the dataset contains fMRI data from 5 subjects, where each subject was presented with 1,200 images from 150 object categories to form the train set and 50 additional images from 50 different categories were presented to them to form the test set. It should be stressed that different image categories are contained in the train set and test set, prohibiting the use of traditional classification algorithms for the task of neural decoding. Also, two different types of experiments were conducted: (a) image presentation experiments, where the aforementioned images were presented to the subjects, and (b) imagery experiments, where the subjects were instructed to imagine one image that belongs to one of the 50 categories of the test set. The dataset contains a total of 1,750 test samples for the image presentation experiments and 500 test samples per subject for the imagery experiments. The interested reader is referred to [9] for more details regarding the data collection protocol and experimental setups. Furthermore, for all the conducted experiments, the preprocessed fMRI and CNN feature vectors provided by the authors of [9] were used. Regarding the CNN architecture, an AlexNet with 5 convolutional (CNN1-CNN5) and 3 fully connected layers (FC1-FC3), trained on the Imagenet dataset was used [21]. From each layer 1,000 random units were sampled and used as the extracted feature representation (before applying the activation function). The feature vectors provided by [9] are used, to allow for easily reproducing the conducted experiments.

The hyper-parameters selected for the evaluated models are briefly described bellow. For the k-Nearest Neighbor model the $k = 5$ nearest neighbors were used.

For the Ridge Regression the weight of the regularizer was set to 1, while for the Kernel Regression several different kernels were evaluated. The best results were obtained when a 2nd degree polynomial kernel was used and the regression model was regularized (Kernel Ridge Regression) [22]. The weight of the regularizer was set to 0.005, while the constant term of the kernel was set to 10. Finally, an MLP with one hidden layer with 300 neurons with sigmoid activations was chosen, after experimenting with many different MLP architectures/activation functions and evaluating their regression accuracy. The MLP was also combined with the Dropout method (dropout probability 30% for the input layer). All the MLP models were trained for 100 epochs (batch size 128) with a learning rate of 0.001 (the default hyper-parameters for the Adam algorithm were used). The LR, KR and kNN models were implemented using the scikit-learn library [23], while the MLP models were implemented using the keras library [24].

The evaluation results for the image presentation experiments are reported in Table 1. The models were trained to regress the features vectors extracted from the last (CNN5) convolutional layer of the CNN, since this layer has been shown to provide the best neural decoding accuracy [9]. The features extracted from the CNN are decoded using different regions selected from the fMRI data: the lower visual cortex areas (V1-V4) and higher visual cortex areas, namely the lateral occipital complex (LOC), fusiform face area (FFA) and parahippocampal place area (PPA). Voxels from regions V1-V3 are combined to form the lower visual cortex (LVC) region and voxels from LOC, FFA and PPA form the higher visual cortex (HVC). The whole visual cortex is denoted by "VC". The Pearson similarity is used in the conducted experiments. All the extracted voxels from the corresponding brain regions were used in the conducted experiments, i.e., we did not select only the voxels with the highest correlation, as in [9]. This allows for retaining as much information as possible. The decoding accuracy is measured as proposed in [9]: every possible combination of the correct class against all the classes is considered and the mean decoding accuracy is reported. Note that a random classifier will achieve a decoding accuracy of 50% under this binary evaluation setup.

Several interesting conclusions can be drawn from the results reported in Table 1. First, the non-linear models (KR, MLP) achieve significantly higher decoding accuracy for the lower visual cortex regions (V1-V4, LVC), as well as for the LOC and FFA regions. For example the decoding accuracy from the V2 region increases from 76.29% to 84.68%, when an MLP is used instead of a LR model. This possibly suggests that complex non-linear relationships between the extracted voxels and the corresponding deep features indeed exist for these (individual) regions. On the other hand, when voxels from the whole visual cortex are used as input (VC), then all the evaluated models (except for the kNN) achieve almost the same decoding accuracy, ranging from 93.16% to 93.95%. Also, the differences between the predictive power of the LVC and HVC regions are small. For example, the MLP achieves 89.74% decoding accuracy when using the features extracted from the LVC region and 90.14% decoding accuracy when using the features extracted from the HVC region, demonstrating that can reliably decode the image representations regardless the used region. Using regularization seems to slightly improve the decoding accuracy of linear regression. However, this is not true for the MLP, which achieves the best decoding accuracy without any form of regularization (the differences are small though). Using a non-linear regressor (KR) seems to significantly improve the results over the plain linear regression in most of the cases. However, the kNN model seems to be unable to reliably decode the features. This can be possibly attributed to the highly non-linear nature of the model that mostly relies on the local properties of the input space that prohibits the effective generalization for samples that do not follow the original distribution. Finally, note that the MLP achieves the best decoding accuracy, significantly outperforming the rest of the models.

Table 1. Image Presentation Evaluation: Decoding accuracy for different machine learning models

Model	V1	V2	V3	V4	LVC	LOC	FFA	PPA	HVC	VC
LR	77.49	76.29	83.51	88.55	86.47	83.25	81.93	84.01	88.67	93.16
RR	79.05	78.92	84.47	88.85	86.81	83.82	82.52	84.03	88.83	93.17
kNN	74.58	73.97	72.94	75.82	75.12	75.17	75.33	74.66	76.29	77.70
KR	80.64	83.32	87.14	89.06	89.63	85.33	84.77	82.71	89.81	93.45
MLP	81.95	84.68	87.73	90.68	89.74	86.47	86.13	84.29	90.14	93.95
MLP (drop.)	82.10	83.56	86.54	88.90	88.73	85.73	85.10	82.92	90.01	93.75

The corresponding results for the imagery experiments are reported in Table 2. For the imagery experiments it seems that the HVC region provides significantly better decoding accuracy than the LCV region. For example, the MLP using dropout achieves 71.04% decoding accuracy when using the HVC features as input, while the accuracy drops to 63.63% when using the LVC as input. This can be possibly attributed to the lack of physical stimulus for the imagery evaluation, and can possibly hint that the imagery tasks are mostly related to the areas of the higher visual cortex. Even though for the imagery tasks the MLP is the second best performing model, the kNN achieves the best decoding accuracy for almost every brain region. This highlights the importance of using a machine learning model that fits the problem at hand, i.e., the imagery-based decoding is significantly harder than the image presentation-based decoding, requiring significantly more powerful and non-linear models. Nonetheless, it should be stressed that MLPs (when combined with the appropriate regularizer) seem to be able to handle this task especially well, compared to the rest of the models.

In the previous experiments, the Pearson correlation was used as similarity metric. The effect of three different similarity metrics on the accuracy of the best model for the image presentation (MLP) and imagery experiments (knn) is evaluated in Table 3. For the image presentation experiments (denoted by "(IP)") the differences are quite small, even though the Pearson similarity achieves the best accuracy in most of the cases. On the other hand, the Euclidean similarity seems to perform significantly better than the other two similarity measures for the imagery task (denoted by "(I)"). Again, this highlights the importance of using the appropriate model, along with an appropriately selected similarity metric, for tasks with different characteristics.

Table 2. Imagery Evaluation: Decoding accuracy for different machine learning models

Model	V1	V2	V3	V4	LVC	LOC	FFA	PPA	HVC	VC
LR	59.45	57.36	62.91	64.94	60.2	61.87	61.41	68.21	62.87	65.19
RR	59.32	58.4	63.15	65.32	60.64	62.12	61.81	68.26	63.27	65.18
kNN	**67.87**	**66.68**	**67.49**	**70.18**	**67.51**	**70.66**	**69.62**	69.32	<u>70.63</u>	**69.99**
KR	57.29	59.2	65.1	68.28	61.37	65.06	63.27	66.63	65.32	65.00
MLP	60.20	<u>63.98</u>	66.07	68.93	63.45	69.24	68.33	**70.39**	67.89	65.73
MLP (drop.)	<u>62.50</u>	62.05	<u>66.74</u>	<u>70.00</u>	<u>63.63</u>	<u>70.38</u>	<u>69.26</u>	<u>69.79</u>	**71.04**	<u>68.14</u>

Table 3. Evaluating the effect of different similarity metrics on the decoding accuracy

Model	V1	V2	V3	V4	LVC	LOC	FFA	PPA	HVC	VC
MLP+Eucl.(IP)	81.86	83.78	86.17	88.30	88.13	84.79	84.42	82.87	88.11	92.47
MLP+Cos.(IP)	**84.39**	83.98	82.58	87.66	81.25	83.48	85.94	**88.05**	87.81	92.36
MLP+Pear.(IP)	81.95	**84.68**	**87.73**	**90.68**	**89.74**	**86.47**	**86.13**	84.29	**90.14**	**93.95**
knn+Eucl.(I)	**71.38**	**70.57**	**70.98**	**72.85**	**71.01**	**73.11**	**72.56**	**72.38**	**73.17**	**72.75**
knn+Cos.(I)	70.66	69.81	70.20	72.01	70.39	72.39	71.67	71.54	72.32	71.88
knn+Pear.(I)	67.87	66.68	67.49	70.18	67.51	70.66	69.62	69.32	70.63	69.99

4 Conclusions

In this paper an extensive evaluation of different machine learning models and similarity measures for the task of decoding deep visual representations from human brain activity signals was presented and several interesting conclusions were drawn. For example, different models seem to behave differently for the various decoding tasks, while using a Multilayer Perceptron (MLP) seems to provide the best decoding accuracy for most of the tasks. Furthermore, the choice of an appropriate similarity measure was shown to be of crucial importance for some tasks. Finally, observations regarding how the brain actually works can also be possibly deduced from the results reported in this paper.

There are many interesting future research directions. Metric learning methods can be used to learn the optimal similarity measure, further increasing the decoding accuracy. Convolutional Neural Networks can be used to better model the spatial relationships between voxels [21], while Recurrent Neural Networks can be used to model the temporal behavior of brain activity [25]. Finally, transfer learning [26] and cross-modal knowledge transfer methods [27] can be employed to appropriately transfer the knowledge that can be shared among different subjects, leading to the development of effective subject-agnostic decoding models.

References

1. Niedermeyer, E., da Silva, F.L.: Electroencephalography: Basic Principles, Clinical Applications, and Related Fields. Lippincott Williams & Wilkins, Philadelphia (2005)
2. Huettel, S.A., Song, A.W., McCarthy, G., et al.: Functional Magnetic Resonance Imaging, vol. 1. Sinauer Associates Sunderland, MA (2004)
3. Tagliazucchi, E., Laufs, H.: Decoding wakefulness levels from typical fMRI resting-state data reveals reliable drifts between wakefulness and sleep. Neuron 82(3), 695–708 (2014)
4. Horikawa, T., Tamaki, M., Miyawaki, Y., Kamitani, Y.: Neural decoding of visual imagery during sleep. Science 340(6132), 639–642 (2013)
5. Gwin, J.T., Gramann, K., Makeig, S., Ferris, D.P.: Removal of movement artifact from high-density EEG recorded during walking and running. J. Neurophysiol. 103(6), 3526–3534 (2010)
6. Presacco, A., Goodman, R., Forrester, L., Contreras-Vidal, J.L.: Neural decoding of treadmill walking from noninvasive electroencephalographic signals. J. Neurophysiol. 106(4), 1875–1887 (2011)
7. Fink, A., Graif, B., Neubauer, A.C.: Brain correlates underlying creative thinking: EEG alpha activity in professional vs. novice dancers. NeuroImage 46(3), 854–862 (2009)
8. Cruz-Garza, J.G., Hernandez, Z.R., Nepaul, S., Bradley, K.K., Contreras-Vidal, J.L.: Neural decoding of expressive human movement from scalp electroencephalography (EEG). Front. Hum. Neurosci. 8, 188 (2014)
9. Horikawa, T., Kamitani, Y.: Generic decoding of seen and imagined objects using hierarchical visual features. Nature Commun. 8, 15037 (2017)
10. Wen, H., Shi, J., Zhang, Y., Lu, K.H., Cao, J., Liu, Z.: Neural encoding and decoding with deep learning for dynamic natural vision. Cerebral Cortex 1–25
11. Güçlütürk, Y., Güçlü, U., Seeliger, K., Bosch, S., van Lier, R., van Gerven, M.A.: Reconstructing perceived faces from brain activations with deep adversarial neural decoding. In: Proceedings of the Advances in Neural Information Processing Systems, pp. 4246–4257 (2017)
12. Wen, H., Shi, J., Chen, W., Liu, Z.: Transferring and generalizing deep-learning-based neural encoding models across subjects. NeuroImage 176, 152–163 (2018)
13. Nasrabadi, N.M.: Pattern recognition and machine learning. J. Electron. Imaging 16(4), 049901 (2007)
14. Hastie, T., Tibshirani, R.: Discriminant adaptive nearest neighbor classification and regression. In: Proceedings of the Advances in Neural Information Processing Systems, pp. 409–415 (1996)
15. Mosteller, F., Tukey, J.W.: Data Analysis and Regression: A Second Course in Statistics. Addison-Wesley Series in Behavioral Science: Quantitative Methods. Addison-Wesley, Mass (1977)
16. Hoerl, A.E., Kennard, R.W.: Ridge regression: biased estimation for nonorthogonal problems. Technometrics 12(1), 55–67 (1970)
17. Shawe-Taylor, J., Cristianini, N., et al.: Kernel Methods for Pattern Analysis. Cambridge University Press, New York (2004)
18. Haykin, S.S.: Neural Networks and Learning Machines, vol. 3. Pearson Education, Upper Saddle River (2009)
19. Kingma, D., Ba, J.: Adam: a method for stochastic optimization. In: Proceedings of the International Conference on Learning Representations (2014)

20. Srivastava, N., Hinton, G., Krizhevsky, A., Sutskever, I., Salakhutdinov, R.: Dropout: a simple way to prevent neural networks from overfitting. J. Mach. Learn. Res. **15**(1), 1929–1958 (2014)
21. Krizhevsky, A., Sutskever, I., Hinton, G.E.: Imagenet classification with deep convolutional neural networks. In: Proceedings of the Advances in Neural Information Processing Systems, pp. 1097–1105 (2012)
22. Vovk, V.: Kernel ridge regression. In: Empirical Inference, pp. 105–116 (2013)
23. Pedregosa, F., et al.: Scikit-learn: machine learning in python. J. Mach. Learn. Res. **12**, 2825–2830 (2011)
24. Chollet, F., et al.: Keras (2015). https://keras.io
25. Graves, A., Mohamed, A.-r., Hinton, G.: Speech recognition with deep recurrent neural networks. In: Proceedings of the IEEE International Conference on Acoustics, Speech and Signal Processing, pp. 6645–6649 (2013)
26. Pan, S.J., Yang, Q., et al.: A survey on transfer learning. IEEE Trans. Knowl. Data Eng. **22**(10), 1345–1359 (2010)
27. Passalis, N., Tefas, A.: Learning deep representations with probabilistic knowledge transfer. In: Ferrari, V., Hebert, M., Sminchisescu, C., Weiss, Y. (eds.) ECCV 2018. LNCS, vol. 11215, pp. 283–299. Springer, Cham (2018). https://doi.org/10.1007/978-3-030-01252-6_17

EmoP3D: A Brain Like Pyramidal Deep Neural Network for Emotion Recognition

Emanuel Di Nardo[1], Alfredo Petrosino[1], and Ihsan Ullah[2]([⊠])

[1] CVPR Lab, University of Naples Parthenope, Napoli, Italy
{emanuel.dinardo,alfredo.petrosino}@uniparthenope.it
[2] Data Mining and Machine Learning Group, Discipline of Information Technology,
National University of Ireland Galway, Galway, Ireland
ihsan.ullah@nuigalway.ie

Abstract. The paper reports a new model based on the understanding and encompassing intelligence from brain i.e. biological pyramidal neurons, tailored for emotion recognition. Our objective is to introduce and utilize usage of non-Convolutional layers in models and show comparable or state-of-the-art performance for multi-class emotion recognition problem. We open-sourced the optimized code for researchers. Our model shows state-of-the-art performance on two emotion recognition datasets (eNTERFACE and Youtube) enhancing previous best result by 9.47% and 20.8%, respectively.

Keywords: Emotion recognition · Pyramidal neural network · 3DPyraNet · Convolutional neural network

1 Introduction

Despite wide applicability and success of deep neural networks, understanding the human visual system for emotion recognition (ER) needs more study about the representation and processing of visual information in the brain. Indeed, human emotion recognition from sensors such as speech, heartbeat, breathing, muscle tension, etc. are not as successful in real-time as of visual sensors. Emotion recognition shows the mood, personality, motivation, and intentions of a person. For example, it can help in maintaining law and order situation in a crowded scenario by identifying the force behind the positive or negative intentions of a person in the scene which can be controlled before getting out of control. Humans can easily read and understand the facial expression of a person. However, it is not the same for machines. Recognition of human emotions (e.g. happy, sad, tensed) from speech can be wrongly classified due to the noise in the scene. Whereas, one can not have implanted sensors over the human body all the time. Therefore, human facial expression recognition in the videos is a highly researched area of computer vision (CV) and machine learning (ML). Psychology divide human emotions in six i.e. anger, disgust, fear, happy, sad,

© Springer Nature Switzerland AG 2019
L. Leal-Taixé and S. Roth (Eds.): ECCV 2018 Workshops, LNCS 11131, pp. 607–616, 2019.
https://doi.org/10.1007/978-3-030-11015-4_46

and surprise. Our model utilized the visual features of humans to classify among these six categories.

The applications of emotion recognition are not limited to surveillance. It is widely used for video summarization, e-commerce, normalizing facial images by removing emotions, and helping people with neurological disorder [25]. For example, research has shown that people affected by multiple sclerosis disease can face difficulty in understanding the features or expression that help in understanding the emotions of others [3].

The traditional CV approach is to use spatio–temporal features extracted with handcrafted descriptors and then classifying them with a state-of-the-art classifier. ML approaches try to automatically learn features from the training samples and give accurate predictions based on the trained model. In this paper, we will enhance a recently introduced deep neural network called 3D pyramidal neural network (3DPyraNet) [22,24], already proposed by the authors. The model is based on the motivation from pyramidal neurons in the brain. It uses a pyramidal structure and introduces a new layer called correlation layer as well as a new weighting scheme that helps in better learning and reduction of the number of parameters as compared to other state-of-the-art deep models. In this paper, we enhance the model introducing per frame normalization in the normalization layer as well as increased size of the model. The model is evaluated on two challenging datasets for emotion recognition, i.e eNTERFACE, created in a laboratory mimicking real-world emotions, and Youtube, collected from real-world YouTube videos.

The paper is organized as follows: Sect. 2 provides an overview of the work being done until now. Section 3 provides a motivational background behind the proposed model. Further, its sub-sections explain the details about existing techniques that are modified, combined and enhanced for our proposed models. Datasets and data preparation are discussed in Sect. 4. Section 5 provides details about the used benchmark datasets and achieved results. Finally, Sect. 6 concludes this paper.

2   Background

ER from videos is a challenging task. Prior approaches [12,16] use to define face landmarks in order to extract important features that are specific to face elements and their position. Later, other CV approaches such as [1] integrate time motion image and the quantized image matrix to extract visual features. In [26], a kernel-based technique identifies optimal transformations that represent the coupled patterns between features from multiple modalities. One example is [15], that was developed to work on audio-visual features. It performs a multi-class classification. However, it expects that only one emotion at a time can be recognized. Visual input is not fully raw information hence relevant key-frames that are the most representative frames in an image sequence with emotions are extracted using a clustering-based strategy. Out of these, geometric features, metric distances, angles, and others are learned by an Inception network.

MARN model [28] tries to discover relations between multiple modalities using a Recurrent Neural Network with a hybrid long-short-term memory architecture (LSTHM). Each input is processed by the proposed LSTHM. The output of each network is concatenated and used as input for a multi-attention block. All features are concatenated and a deep neural network is used with K softmax layers to output coefficients for each modality. Chen et al. [4] proposed a model based on reinforcement learning that utilizes word-level fusion and uses LSTM with Temporal Attention to predict human emotion. One of the most efficient technique is [25] that also works on multi-modality. Visual features are extracted using 2D and 3D convolutional neural networks. 2D model uses VGG-16 architecture [17] and 3D features are extracted with C3D [5]. In both cases, a feature vector of 4096 dimensions is extracted. Each model performs a temporal fusion using scores produced by softmax layer and low dimensional vectors of 297 and 394 features are extracted. All modalities are combined to get the resulting feature vector. Definitely, temporal fusion is done using a length variable LSTM in order to take all the descriptor as inputs obtaining a VGG-LSTM and a C3D-LSTM network.

The most recent approach is proposed in [8] where many architectures are adopted at one time. It uses HoloNet [27], pre-trained DenseNet [9] and ResNet [7]. At each epoch, the models are fine-tuned by many supervised support networks that help to generalize the emotional states. This deep and mixed model takes advantage of multi-modal handcrafted features and shows promising results.

Pyramid structure has a deep role in improving the performance of neural network models. Both Neural Network & Image Pyramids have similar structure i.e. exponential reduction and coarse to fine refinement. Pyramidal ImageNet (gradual decreasing) Vs. the non-Pyramidal ImageNet model showed equal or better performance despite fewer parameters [22]. PyramidNet enhanced ResNet by similar concept as [22] but in reverse order (gradually increasing) [6]. Literature review shows that different models uses different datasets which make it hard to benchmark one model with others. Our model will be evaluated on a dataset called eNTERFACE, that is used by many researchers, and on ICT Youtube. In next section, the enhanced 3DPyraNet model is explained.

3 Proposed Model

The proposed model (EmoP3D) is an enhancement of 3D pyramidal neural network (3DPyraNet) proposed in [22]. The proposed 3D pyramidal architecture was based on the concept of coarse to fine refinement or the decision making in a pyramidal structure inside the brain. More specifically, similar to the pyramidal neurons in a biological brain [21]. Pyramidal neurons exist in cortical layers. They communicate with each other as well as with sub-cortical regions of the brain through their long axonal projections forming a pyramid structure before taking a decision and transferring to higher layers. The cortical layers in the mammalian cerebral cortex perform a major role in important cognitive functions, perception and motor control. In [21], the role of pyramidal neurons at layer 2, 3 and 5 is compared and it is shown how it affects the motor skill learning of mice. Further, it is in human nature to work and decide based on the course to fine refinement (pyramid structure) e.g. shopping in a market. Similarly, traditional feature subset selection technique has the same concept of selecting the most relevant features out of a large set of ambiguous and redundant features.

3DPyraNet was further inspired by pyramidal structures in [2], weighting scheme in [18], and 3D spatio-temporal structure from 3D Convolutional Neural Network (3DCNN) [10]. It works on utilizing spatio-temporal features in a video as input. 3DCNN and CNN do reduce spatial resolution, however, increase the number of maps in each higher layer which avoids the strict pyramid structure of the network.

On the contrary, [23] adopted a strict pyramidal architecture. This topology tends to reduce the dimensions of the input layer by layer, in order to obtain fine non-ambiguous high-quality features. It uses *Weighted Sum* (WS), or more commonly the cross-correlation product for each receptive field. It is the basic network operation in this model instead of convolution. The most fundamental property is that the number of weights in a layer is equal to the input image or feature map size. The sliding kernel and then WS results in a partial weight sharing scheme. This means that each neuron has a unique local weight that is updated at each iteration inside the receptive field of specific output neurons. This reduces the burden on each weight parameter and enhances the performance of the network. The pyramidal structure and weighting scheme has a "sparse-to-influence" effect. It helps to remove irrelevant features and preserves the most discriminative and relevant features during the training process. Therefore, it can learn complex structure even with fewer feature maps and hidden layers.

The strict structure preserves the number of feature maps for each layer. The weight matrix and input mask have equal size. After each weighted sum operation, it is reduced as it goes to a higher layer. This helps in reduction of features as well as in maintaining and reducing the number of learn-able parameters as compared to recent deep networks with a large number of parameters. In order to maintain pyramid structure and extract more features, three 3d weight matrices are incorporated to extract more temporal information at the first hidden layer, as shown in Fig. 1. This approach fuses the local weights connectivity with weight sharing because 3DWS layers preserve the local connectivity on 2D space, but working on small temporal region weights are shared on depth, repeating the same weights volume on each time-depth step. Temporal extension extracts correlation among objects and actions in adjacent frames. The output in a layer l of a neuron $N_{u,v,z}^l$ for a receptive field $R_{u,v,z}^l$ using 3D weighted sum operation become:

$$y_{u,v,z}^l = f_l \left(\sum_{i \in R_{u,v,z}^l} \sum_{j \in R_{u,v,z}^l} \sum_{k \in R_{u,v,z}^l} [W_{i,j,k}^l \circ x_{i,j,k}^{l-1}] + b_{u,v,z}^l \right) \tag{1}$$

As it is possible to see the bias term b^l has the same shape as the output neuron map, it means that each neuron has an own bias term to be learned. It is different from the standard bias concept of other network models where it has the size of

Table 1. Network structure per layer for both datasets (eNTERFACE and YouTube)

Dataset	Input-size	WS1	L3P	WS5	FC
Both	$16 \times 100 \times 100 \times 1$	$14 \times 97 \times 97 \times 1 \times 3$	$12 \times 48 \times 48 \times 1 \times 3$	$10 \times 45 \times 45 \times 1 \times 3$	60750

the output feature maps. The adopted 3D temporal pooling layer is different from any other kind of pooling layer because it not only reduces spatial and temporal dimensions but also performs a data transformation on previous weighted sum layer to avoid scale and translation problems. Mathematically it is defined as:

$$y_{u,v,z}^{l} = f_l(W_{u,v,z}^{l} \times \max_{i,j,k \in R_{u,v,z}^{l}} y_{i,j,k}^{l-1} + b_{u,v,z}^{l}) \tag{2}$$

3.1 Model Structure

A general description about the key layers i.e. WS layer and a max-pooling layer of the proposed model is given in previous Sect. 3. Further, it consists of the activation layer, a normalization layer, and fully connected layer. The model is composed of two 3DWS layers linked together by a 3D max pooling layer. In normalization layer, each frame is normalized individually with zero mean unit variance. Each 3DWS layer is followed by an activation layer which is followed by the normalization layer. Similarly, each 3D-Max-Pooling layer is followed by activation and normalization layers. To preserve the strict property, each correlation layer uses three feature maps. To ensure a fast convergence and avoid gradients problems a *Leaky ReLU* activation function [11] is used. Complete structure can be seen in Fig. 1. Finally an output layer, a softmax classifier is used for class probability estimation. Each 3DWS layer reduces the number of feature maps by two as well as reduces the spatial size of feature maps based on the size of receptive field and stride used at that layer. Similarly, in pooling layer, not only pooling reduces the spatial resolution but the 3D structure reduces the feature maps by two. Hence it maintains a continuous constant reduction in both spatial and temporal dimensions forming a pyramid structure that helps in providing most discriminative features at the final layer. The model takes an input clip of size $16 \times 100 \times 100 \times 1$ (depth, height, width, channels). We have taken this to make it similar to the work done in [29]. However, the network is not restrictive to the input size and this can be changed according to the application. This change of input size changes the structure of the network resulting in a different number of parameters to train.

A total of three weight matrices are used with a receptive field of $3 \times 4 \times 4$ for depth, height and width dimensions in weighted sum layers. It is also adopted a valid max pooling structure with a receptive field of 2 with a step of 2 in order to halves the spatial dimensions and reduce the temporal domain in a progressive, soft manner. Back-propagation algorithm is used to train the network. Mini-batch gradient descends with a batch size of 100 samples for each dataset is used with Momentum optimization algorithm [20]. Table 1 shows the size of each layer of the network. It shows that the network reduces its size gradually and resulting in an FC layer of size 60750.

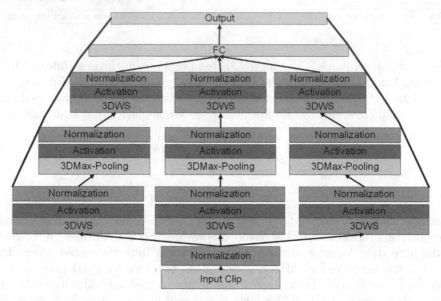

Fig. 1. 3DPyraNet architecture

4   Dataset and Data Preparation

There are many datasets for ER, but they are for the most compatible only with 2D methods. Since we propose a method that is able to capture temporal features across multiple frames, it is mandatory to use a dataset that allow to model this behavior. Two datasets in the literature that are mostly used are eNTERFACE'05 [13] and Youtube [14]. eNTERFACE'05 dataset adopts 42 subjects from 14 different countries. Each subject reacted to a story told to catch real emotions from them. They express 6 different emotions and, for each of them, there are five reactions. There is a total of 1166 video sequence. Youtube dataset starts with the fact that people express emotions in different ways. It contains videos of people from different age and gender in various topics. Furthermore, these are not recorded in a "controlled" environment because an emotion recognition system should be able to work in many contexts. There are 20 female subjects and 27 male subjects with age in the range 14–60. It provides three polarity classes i.e anger, worried, and happiness. Each video sequence is pre-processed to detect and extract the subject's face. It is done using a "Multitask CNN" proposed in [29] and available in [19]. Some sample facial images are shown in Fig. 2. In this paper, each image is gray-scaled and re-sized to have 100×100 height and width dimensions. A sequence of 16 consecutive frames with an overlap of 8 frames is used as input clip. In the Youtube dataset, each clip is a mix of emotions so the most prevalent one is chosen if there is an emotion overlap in a sequence.

Fig. 2. Sample images from eNTERFACE (First row) and YouTube (Second Row)

5   Results and Discussion

Using the proposed architecture, we adopted a 10-Fold cross-validation approach to evaluate the performance on each dataset. Comparing our model with state-of-the-art methods, it is possible to see in Table 2 that our model outperforms previous techniques on both datasets. The most important comparison is done with [4, 15, 28] that is the most recent end-to-end approach proposed for emotion recognition on the same dataset. Our model outperforms the previous best result provided by a CNN based model (AVER-CNN) by more than 9% enhancement in the accuracy over eNTERFACE emotion recognition dataset. Whereas, EmoP3D outperformed previous models i.e. LSTM(A) and MARN by more than 20% increase in accuracy. A confusion matrix over a single run is also shown to inspect per class influence. We can observe from the left matrix of Fig. 3 that overall performance is good over the whole dataset, only two classes that are *Sadness* and *Surprise* shows to be more difficult to understand by the network. Both of them are even hard for a normal human being to recognize. From Fig. 3 right matrix, the most confusing class is the neutral sentiment, it is clear that "neutral" isn't a true defined and distinguished sentiment and it is also difficult for human understanding to identify it. We also optimized the code and open-sourced the cuda based code of EmoP3D implementation for researchers. The code is available on Github[1]. Table 3 shows comparison of the time taken by new code vs old code. It gave us more than 79% speedup.

---

[1] https://github.com/CVPRLab-UniParthenope/EmoP3D/projects.

Table 2. Comparison in-terms of accuracy with other state-of-the-art models

Approach	eNTERFACE	Youtube
AVER-Geometric [15]	41.59%	–
KCMFA [26]	58%	–
AVER-CNN [15]	62%	–
LSTM(A) (Binary) [4]	–	52.3%
MARN [28]	–	54.2%
EmoP3D (Ours)	**71.47%**	**75%**

Table 3. Processing time comparison of 3DPyraNet implementation vs. EmoP3D

	Sample size	Time (s) for a batch of 100 samples	Time (s) for a single input	Speedup
3DPyraNet	$13 \times 80 \times 100$	105	1.05	–
Ours EmoP3D	$16 \times 100 \times 100$	1.32	0.0132	**~79%**

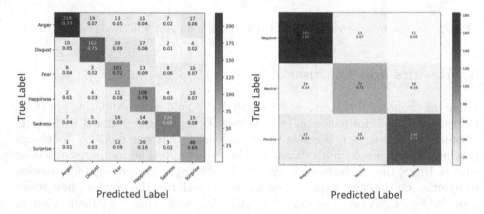

Fig. 3. Confusion matrices for eNTERFACE (left) and YouTube (right) result

6   Conclusion

Our biological pyramidal neurons inspired architecture is able to outperform other models used for ER. It demonstrates that the temporal domain has an important role in the expression of emotion. It is a process that involves many temporal stages that need to be well defined. This work opens the way to many scenarios that can help to identify emotions deeply. For example, it is possible to extend this work to multiple domains using also information provided by voice or where possible from what a person is telling. This information can be used together in a multimodal approach to enhance the ability of a machine to identify, understand and maybe reproduce human emotions. The proposed architecture shows its generalization power by showing good results in both control (eNTERFACE) and uncontrolled (YouTube) environment datasets. In the future, we intend to further increase the network depth and use ResNet structure with 3DWS layers.

References

1. Bejani, M., Gharavian, D., Charkari, N.M.: Audiovisual emotion recognition using anova feature selection method and multi-classifier neural networks. Neural Comput. Appl. **24**(2), 399–412 (2014)
2. Cantoni, V., Petrosino, A.: Neural recognition in a pyramidal structure. IEEE Trans. Neural Netw. **13**(2), 472–480 (2002). https://doi.org/10.1109/72.991433
3. Cecchetto, C., et al.: Facial and bodily emotion recognition in multiple sclerosis: the role of alexithymia and other characteristics of the disease. J. Int. Neuropsychol. Soc. **20**(10), 1004–1014 (2014). https://doi.org/10.1017/S1355617714000939
4. Chen, M., Wang, S., Liang, P.P., Baltrušaitis, T., Zadeh, A., Morency, L.P.: Multimodal sentiment analysis with word-level fusion and reinforcement learning. In: Proceedings of the 19th ACM International Conference on Multimodal Interaction, pp. 163–171. ACM (2017)
5. Fan, Y., Lu, X., Li, D., Liu, Y.: Video-based emotion recognition using CNN-RNN and C3D hybrid networks. In: Proceedings of the 18th ACM International Conference on Multimodal Interaction, pp. 445–450. ACM (2016)
6. Han, D., Kim, J., Kim, J.: Deep pyramidal residual networks. In: Proceedings - 30th IEEE Conference on Computer Vision and Pattern Recognition, CVPR 2017, 2017 January, pp. 6307–6315 (2017). https://doi.org/10.1109/CVPR.2017.668
7. He, K., Zhang, X., Ren, S., Sun, J.: Deep residual learning for image recognition. CoRR abs/1512.03385 (2015). http://arxiv.org/abs/1512.03385
8. Hu, P., Cai, D., Wang, S., Yao, A., Chen, Y.: Learning supervised scoring ensemble for emotion recognition in the wild. In: Proceedings of the 19th ACM International Conference on Multimodal Interaction, pp. 553–560. ACM (2017)
9. Huang, G., Liu, Z., Weinberger, K.Q.: Densely connected convolutional networks. CoRR abs/1608.06993 (2016). http://arxiv.org/abs/1608.06993
10. Ji, S., Xu, W., Yang, M., Yu, K.: 3D convolutional neural networks for human action recognition. IEEE Trans. Pattern Anal. Mach. Intell. **35**(1), 221–231 (2013). https://doi.org/10.1109/TPAMI.2012.59
11. Maas, A.L., Hannun, A.Y., Ng, A.Y.: Rectifier nonlinearities improve neural network acoustic models. In: Proceedings of ICML, vol. 30, p. 3 (2013)
12. Mansoorizadeh, M., Charkari, N.M.: Multimodal information fusion application to human emotion recognition from face and speech. Multimedia Tools Appl. **49**(2), 277–297 (2010)
13. Martin, O., Kotsia, I., Macq, B., Pitas, I.: The enterface'05 audio-visual emotion database. In: 22nd International Conference on Data Engineering Workshops, Proceedings, p. 8. IEEE (2006)
14. Morency, L.P., Mihalcea, R., Doshi, P.: Towards multimodal sentiment analysis: harvesting opinions from the web. In: Proceedings of the 13th International Conference on Multimodal Interfaces, pp. 169–176. ACM (2011)
15. Noroozi, F., Marjanovic, M., Njegus, A., Escalera, S., Anbarjafari, G.: Audio-visual emotion recognition in video clips. IEEE Trans. Affect. Comput. (2017)
16. Paleari, M., Huet, B.: Toward emotion indexing of multimedia excerpts. In: International Workshop on Content-Based Multimedia Indexing, CBMI 2008, pp. 425–432. IEEE (2008)

17. Parkhi, O.M., Vedaldi, A., Zisserman, A.: Deep face recognition. In: BMVC, vol. 1, p. 6 (2015)
18. Phung, S.L., Bouzerdoum, A.: A pyramidal neural network for visual pattern recognition. IEEE Trans. Neural Netw. **18**(2), 329–343 (2007). https://doi.org/10.1109/TNN.2006.884677
19. Schroff, F., Kalenichenko, D., Philbin, J.: FaceNet: a unified embedding for face recognition and clustering. In: Proceedings of the IEEE Conference on Computer Vision and Pattern Recognition, pp. 815–823 (2015)
20. Sutton, R.S.: Two problems with backpropagation and other steepest-descent learning procedures for networks. In: Proceedings of Eighth Annual Conference of the Cognitive Science Society (1986)
21. Tjia, M., Yu, X., Jammu, L.S., Lu, J., Zuo, Y.: Pyramidal neurons in different cortical layers exhibit distinct dynamics and plasticity of apical dendritic spines. Front. Neural Circuits **11**, 43 (2017)
22. Ullah, I., Petrosino, A.: About pyramid structure in convolutional neural networks. In: Proceedings of the International Joint Conference on Neural Networks 2016-October, pp. 1318–1324 (2016). https://doi.org/10.1109/IJCNN.2016.7727350
23. Ullah, I., Petrosino, A.: Spatiotemporal features learning with 3DPyraNet. In: Blanc-Talon, J., Distante, C., Philips, W., Popescu, D., Scheunders, P. (eds.) ACIVS 2016. LNCS, vol. 10016, pp. 638–647. Springer, Cham (2016). https://doi.org/10.1007/978-3-319-48680-2_56
24. Ullah, I., Petrosino, A.: A ssatio-temporal feature learning approach for dynamic scene recognition. In: Shankar, B.U., Ghosh, K., Mandal, D.P., Ray, S.S., Zhang, D., Pal, S.K. (eds.) PReMI 2017. LNCS, vol. 10597, pp. 591–598. Springer, Cham (2017). https://doi.org/10.1007/978-3-319-69900-4_75
25. Vielzeuf, V., Pateux, S., Jurie, F.: Temporal multimodal fusion for video emotion classification in the wild. In: Proceedings of the 19th ACM International Conference on Multimodal Interaction, pp. 569–576. ACM (2017)
26. Wang, Y., Guan, L., Venetsanopoulos, A.N.: Kernel cross-modal factor analysis for information fusion with application to bimodal emotion recognition. IEEE Trans. Multimedia **14**(3), 597–607 (2012). https://doi.org/10.1109/TMM.2012.2189550
27. Yao, A., Cai, D., Hu, P., Wang, S., Sha, L., Chen, Y.: HoloNet: towards robust emotion recognition in the wild. In: Proceedings of the 18th ACM International Conference on Multimodal Interaction, ICMI 2016, pp. 472–478. ACM, New York (2016). https://doi.org/10.1145/2993148.2997639
28. Zadeh, A., Liang, P.P., Poria, S., Vij, P., Cambria, E., Morency, L.P.: Multi-attention recurrent network for human communication comprehension. arXiv preprint arXiv:1802.00923 (2018)
29. Zhang, K., Zhang, Z., Li, Z., Qiao, Y.: Joint face detection and alignment using multitask cascaded convolutional networks. IEEE Signal Process. Lett. **23**(10), 1499–1503 (2016)

Subitizing with Variational Autoencoders

Rijnder Wever[✉] and Tom F. H. Runia[ID]

Intelligent Sensory Information Systems,
University of Amsterdam, Amsterdam, Netherlands
rien334@gmail.com

Abstract. Numerosity, the number of objects in a set, is a basic property of a given visual scene. Many animals develop the perceptual ability to *subitize*: the near-instantaneous identification of the numerosity in small sets of visual items. In computer vision, it has been shown that numerosity emerges as a statistical property in neural networks during unsupervised learning from simple synthetic images. In this work, we focus on more complex natural images using unsupervised hierarchical neural networks. Specifically, we show that *variational autoencoders* are able to spontaneously perform subitizing after training without supervision on a large amount of images from the Salient Object Subitizing dataset. While our method is unable to outperform supervised convolutional networks for subitizing, we observe that the networks learn to encode numerosity as a basic visual property. Moreover, we find that the learned representations are likely invariant to object area; an observation in alignment with studies on biological neural networks in cognitive neuroscience.

Keywords: Object counting · Numerosity · Variational autoencoders

1 Introduction

The ability to answer the question "How many?" is an important capability of our visual recognition system. Animals use *visual number sense* to rank, quantify and label objects in a scene [29]. There is evidence [2,28,32] that the human brain uses at least two distinct mechanisms for non-verbal representation of number: one for large quantity *estimation* and a *subitizing* faculty for near-instantaneous identification of a small number of objects (1–4). In this work, we propose a brain-inspired approach for learning to subitize from large image datasets.

The concepts of visual number sense and instance counting are well studied in computer vision [1,4,13,24,27,36,41,43,45]. Most recent work relies on supervised learning using deep convolutional neural networks (CNNs) [22] to assess the instance count in a given scene. While existing methods perform admirably on various counting tasks, the number of visual classes and the availability of labeled image datasets is decisive for their performance. Motivated by these observations and our visual cognition system, this paper explores hierarchical representation learning for visual numerosity in an *unsupervised* setting.

© Springer Nature Switzerland AG 2019
L. Leal-Taixé and S. Roth (Eds.): ECCV 2018 Workshops, LNCS 11131, pp. 617–627, 2019.
https://doi.org/10.1007/978-3-030-11015-4_47

Our work is inspired by the observation of Stoianov and Zorzi [38] that visual numerosity emerges as a statistical property of images in artificial neural networks trained in an unsupervised manner. Specifically, the authors train Restricted Boltzmann Machines (RBMs) on synthetic images containing a random number of objects and show that neural response distributions correlate with number discriminability. Their observations are intriguing but the simple synthetic images do not capture the complexity of natural visual scenes. In this work, we focus on unsupervised learning of numerosity representations from natural images containing diverse object classes (see example images in Fig. 1).

The contributions of this work are the following. We explore the emergence of visual number sense in deep networks trained in an unsupervised setting on natural images. Specifically, we propose the use of variational autoencoders with both the encoder and decoder parametrized as CNNs to effectively handle complex images and maintain spatial organization. For optimization, we include the recently proposed feature perceptual loss [14] instead of the pixel-to-pixel distance metric to aid representation learning. Finally, we present preliminary quantitative and qualitative results on unsupervised representation learning for numerosity from the Salient Object Subitizing dataset [45].

Fig. 1. Example images from the Salient Object Subitizing dataset [45]. Although the ability to *subitize* should allow people to identify the number of instances in each image at a glance, these scenes pose a challenge to computer vision models due to variety in appearance, saliency ambiguity, scene clutter and occlusion.

2   Related Work

Numerical Cognition. Non-verbal numerical competence is implicitly developed across humans [7,9,10,21] and animal species [6,12,28]. These abilities possibly arise from numerosity being an integral part of the sensory world [40]. Interestingly, humans have developed the ability to *subitize* [18,19] for near-instantaneous numerosity identification of small visual sets (1–4 items). The near-instantaneous character of subitizing and its spontaneous neural development are possibly caused by the visual system's limited but automatic capability to process spatial configurations of salient objects [7,17,32]. Whereas visual number sense relates to object area and density, the neural responses of numerosity-selective cognitive systems were found to be invariant to all visual features except numerosity [12,28]. Furthermore, studies on cognitive neuroscience have shown that the perception of number functions independently from mathematical reasoning [12,33]. All these findings suggest that visual number sense is a perceptual property that emerges directly from the visual sensory input.

Numerosity in Computer Vision. Instance counting in visual scenes has received substantial interest from the deep vision community, notably in object counting [4,13,24,27,30], crowd-size estimation [15,43], animal population estimation [1] and video repetition [25,34]. The shared similarity between most of these recent works is their use of CNNs for supervised representation learning from large image datasets. Of these approaches, the recent work of Zhang et al. [45] is most similar to ours as we also evaluate on the task of instance counting and use their Salient Object Subitizing dataset. While these methods are effective on specific domains, they require large amounts of labeled data and are limited to a predefined set of visual classes and numerosity range. Therefore, we here study brain-inspired unsupervised representation learning for visual number sense.

Stoianov and Zorzi [38] discovered the emergence of neural populations in artificial neural networks sensitive to numerosity while invariant to object size. Their observations align with object size invariance for visual number sense in the human brain [28]. In this work we emphasize on learning visual number representations from realistic natural images rather than the simple binary images studied in [38]. As a consequence, representation learning becomes significantly more challenging, making RBMs difficult to train. We propose variational autoencoders [20] to learn visual numerosity representations in an unsupervised setting.

3 Methods

Inspired by Stoianov and Zorzi [38] we propose an unsupervised generative model to learn visual numerosity representations from natural and synthetic image datasets. Specifically, we use a variational autoencoder for encoding and reconstructing training images. The underlying principle is that numerosity is a key characteristic in the images and the network learns to encode visual numerosity in the latent representation.

3.1 Variational Autoencoder

We use the original definition of the variational autoencoder (VAE) as introduced by Kingma and Welling [20]. VAEs are among the most popular approaches for unsupervised representation learning due to their generative nature and the fact that the encoder and decoder can be parameterized by neural networks trainable with stochastic gradient descent. For an excellent overview of VAEs we refer the reader to the tutorial of Doersch [8] as we here only outline the core idea.

VAEs learn to map data samples X to a posterior distribution $Q(z \mid X)$ rather than a deterministic latent representation as used in conventional autoencoders. Inputs can be reconstructed by sampling latent vector z from the posterior distribution and passing it through a decoder network. To make sampling feasible, the posterior distribution is parametrized by a Gaussian distribution with its mean and variance predicted by the encoder. In addition to a reconstruction loss, the posterior $Q(z \mid X)$ is regularized with its Kullback Leibler divergence from a prior distribution $P(z)$ which is typically also Gaussian with zero mean and unit variance such that the KL divergence can be computed in closed form [20]. Together, the VAE's objective function is the summation of a reconstruction term (negative log-likelihood of the data) and the KL regularization:

$$\mathcal{L}_{VAE} = E[\log P(X \mid z)] - \mathcal{D}_{KL}[Q(z \mid X) \parallel P(z)] \tag{1}$$

We use this formulation with both encoder and decoder parametrized as convolutional neural network to learn visual representations from a large collection of images displaying scenes with a varying number of salient objects.

Fig. 2. Top: original images from the Salient Object Subitizing dataset [45]. **Center:** VAE reconstructions using traditional loss. **Bottom:** VAE reconstructions using feature perceptual loss. Note the improved ability to reconstruct salient objects and contour sharpness, likely beneficial for object subitizing.

3.2 Feature Perceptual Loss

VAEs are known to produce blurry reconstructions [11]. In our preliminary experiments we observed difficulties with reconstructing multiple salient objects, negatively affecting the ability to subitize. Therefore, we employ the recent feature perceptual loss of Hou et al. [14] which uses intermediate layer representations in the objective function of the autoencoder. The authors use a VGG-19 network [37] pretrained on ImageNet [35] denoted as Φ and define a set of layers $l_i \in L$ for computing the perceptual loss. Specifically, during the training the mean squared error between the hidden representations of input image X and the reconstruction $\widetilde{X}$ is added to the loss for the predefined layers:

$$\mathcal{L}_{rec}^{L} = \sum_{l \in L} \text{MSE}(\Phi(X)^l, \Phi(\widetilde{X})^l) \tag{2}$$

The intuition is that responses of layers l_i should be retained in reconstruction $\widetilde{x}$ as they represent important visual characteristics. Following their recommendations and our own findings, we use $L = \{\texttt{relu1\_1}, \texttt{relu2\_1}, \texttt{relu3\_1}\}$ from the pretrained VGG-19 network to compute the loss. The feature perceptual loss and original VAE objective are weighed according to $\mathcal{L}_{total} = \alpha\mathcal{L}_{kl} + \beta\mathcal{L}_{rec}$ in which α and β are hyperparameters. We found this extension to our autoencoder to improve visual saliency and representation learning compared to plain pixel-by-pixel reconstruction loss (see Fig. 2 for a visual comparison).

4 Experiments

4.1 Datasets

Salient Object Subitizing Dataset. Proposed by Zhang et al. [45], the Salient Object Subitizing (SOS) dataset contains 14K images for the purpose of instance counting. The images originate from MS-COCO [26], ImageNet [35] and SUN [42]. Each image is annotated with an instance count label: 0, 1, 2, 3 or 4+ salient objects. The final image collection is biased towards centered dominant objects and backgrounds scenes as the authors observe [45]. In practice, the class imbalance may pose training difficulties. See Fig. 1 for some examples.

Synthetic Data. To counter class imbalance and increase dataset size we follow Zhang et al. [45] in pretraining our model with synthetic images and gradually adding images from the SOS dataset. The images are synthesized by cut-pasting objects from the THUS10000 dataset [5] onto backgrounds from the SUN dataset [42]. Following [45] we apply random image transforms to each object to increase diversity in appearance. For example images we refer to Fig. 7 in [45].

4.2 Implementation Details

Network Architecture. Our models are implemented in PyTorch [31]. The VAE's encoder and decoder are parameterized as CNNs. Denoting a convolutional layer as $N @ K_w \times K_h - S$ with N filters of size $K_w \times K_h$ and stride S, the encoder architecture is as follows: $64 @ 4 \times 4 - 1 \rightarrow 64 @ 4 \times 4 - 2 \rightarrow 128 @ 4 \times 4 - 2 \rightarrow 768 @ 4 \times 4 - 2$. Final spatial features are fed in two fully-connected layers encoding the μ and Σ parameters of the posterior distribution for sampling latent vectors using the reparametrization trick [20]. The Σ layer uses softplus activation to ensure a positive output. The decoder uses transposed convolutions [44] to upsample latent representations and is implemented by the following architecture: $768 @ 3 \times 3 - 1 \rightarrow 768 @ 3 \times 3 - 2 \rightarrow 256 @ 3 \times 3 - 2 \rightarrow 64 @ 3 \times 3 - 2$. All convolutional blocks are followed by Leaky ReLU activation and batch normalization [16]. The feature perceptual loss parameters are set to $\alpha = 1.0$ and $\beta = 0.03$. The size of the latent dimension is set to 180.

Optimization. Data augmentation of random horizontal flips, crops and color shifts is applied to all images. Preprocessed images are of 161×161 size when fed into the network. We warm-up by pretraining on 80K synthetic images and gradually start adding natural images beyond 20 epochs. The initial learning rate is set to 0.0015 and is divided by 5 when the loss on the test set plateaus for more than 4 epochs. The VAE is trained for a total of 140 epochs. To remedy the class imbalance we follow [23] by randomly removing 10% examples from the most frequent classes (and loss weighting for the softmax classifier in Sect. 4.3).

Table 1. Comparison of our unsupervised approach to existing supervised approaches for *instance counting* over the Salient Object Subitizing dataset. We report the count average precision (%) over the entire test set. Results from existing methods (rows 2–4) were reported in [45]. Our method is unable to outperform the fully-supervised CNN of [45] but performs well given that our visual representations are trained unsupervised.

Count label →	0	1	2	3	4+	Mean
Chance	27.5	46.5	18.6	11.7	9.7	22.8
GIST [39]	67.4	65.0	32.3	17.5	24.7	41.4
SIFT+IFV [3]	83.0	68.1	35.1	26.6	38.1	50.1
CNN_FT [45]	93.6	93.8	75.2	58.6	71.6	78.6
VAE + softmax (ours)	76.0	49.0	40.0	27.0	30.0	44.4

4.3 Evaluating the Visual Numerosity Representation

In this experiment we evaluate the strength of the representations learned by the VAE in unsupervised setting. As the visual reconstructions are hard to compare and do not conceal the sense visual numerosity, we perform a quantitative comparison with the state-of-the-art [3,39,45] by training a softmax classifier on top of the visual representations learned without supervision. The task is to predict the instance count (classification). Specifically, we fix the VAE parameters and feed the latent representations for a given image to the softmax classifier referred to as **VAE + softmax**. The softmax classifier is modeled as a two-layer perceptron with 160 units per layer and ReLU activations. It predicts the instance count from the VAE's latent representations. We use the SOS train set *with* count labels to minimize cross-entropy loss. Note that this count classifier uses supervision on top of the unsupervised visual representations. We compare the subitizing performance with existing work: handcrafted GIST features with SVM classifier [39], a SIFT-based representation with Improved Fisher Vectors (IFV) [3] and the fully-supervised CNN specifically designed for subitizing [45].

Table 1 reports the performance of both our method and existing work on the SOS test set [45]. The subitizing performance of our softmax classifier is comparable to the performance of the GIFT and SVM classifier [39] and SIFT+IFV [3]. Our method is unable to surpass the fully-supervised CNN of [45]. This is not surprising as their network is significantly larger, pretrained on millions of images from ImageNet and uses full supervision from the SOS count labels. Our visual representations are trained in unsupervised setting without ImageNet pretraining. The quantitative results indicate that unsupervised learning of a representation of visually complex images by a VAE discovered that numerosity in the subitizing range is a key characteristic of natural scenes.

4.4   Size-Invariant Numerosity Detectors

We investigate whether the learned visual representations for numerosity estimation are invariant to *object area*, as found in [38] for simple synthesized data and observed in cognitive studies [12,28]. Our methodology is similar to Stoianov and Zorzi [38]: we search for a relationship between the VAE's latent representations and both cumulative object area and instance count in synthesized images.

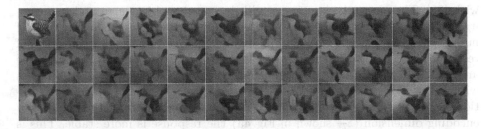

Fig. 3. Top Left: original image with a single salient instance from SOS. **Remaining Images:** reconstructions of the VAE by slightly increasing the response at individual dimensions in the latent representation. A single value in the latent space can correspond to multiple image characteristics such as lighting, color, numerosity and object size.

To this end, we create a dataset with synthetic images containing $N \in [0, 4]$ copies of the same object (with N sampled uniformly at random) and their corresponding cumulative area values A (measured in the number of pixels). We fix the VAE parameters and create a set of latent vectors Z from 35K synthetic images with 15 object classes from the THUS10000 dataset [5]; the size between objects in each image varies modestly. To reduce noise in the representations created by the VAE we make sure objects are not overlapping (interestingly, overlapping objects hinder our brain's ability to subitize [7]). Although not natural images, their appearance is more diverse than the binary images of [38].

Using all latent vectors z from Z, we search for latent dimensions z_i that serve as either numerosity or area encoders by means of a linear regression suggested in [38]. Following their approach, we fit the following relationship between z_i and the variables A and N across the entire dataset (all variables normalized):

$$z_i = \beta_1 \log(N) + \beta_2 \log(A) + \varepsilon \tag{3}$$

Stoianov and Zorzi [38] formulate two criteria for which an individual dimension z_i significantly responds to changes in object size or numerosity. First, the dimension should explain at least 10% of the variance ($R^2 \geq 0.1$) in the activity, and secondly, the regression coefficient of the complementary property has an absolute value smaller than 0.1. Here, we slightly loosen the first criteria of [38] by setting the threshold to 5% variance because the visual complexity of our training images is significantly higher. More specifically, in our VAE the individual latent dimensions z_i can be responsible for encoding more than one visual characteristic. This is observed in Fig. 3, where a slight change in the latent dimension can change more than one visual characteristic in the reconstruction. Due to this fact, the responses of z_i will inherently be noisier.

From the regression over 35K synthetic images we found one or two reoccurring dimensions that responded to area A or numerosity N with regression error $R^2 > 0.06 \pm 0.020$. Interestingly, we also found that whenever the regression showed multiple dimensions responding to object area, the two dimensions always changed in opposite direction (different sign) which is in agreement with [38]. Therefore, the latent space likely encodes object area and numerosity as independent properties of images, consistent with coding properties of numerosity-selective neurons [12]. Finally, in Fig. 4 we plot the characteristics of response profiles of the dimensions z_i that were found to encode either cumulative area or visual numerosity. For the area dimension (z_{88} shown in Fig. 4b), images with either very small or large cumulative area push the mean response distribution significantly upward or downward. On the other hand, for the numerosity encoding dimension (z_{77} shown in Fig. 4a) the response is more stable. This is evidence for dimension z_{77} encoding visual number sense while being invariant to object size.

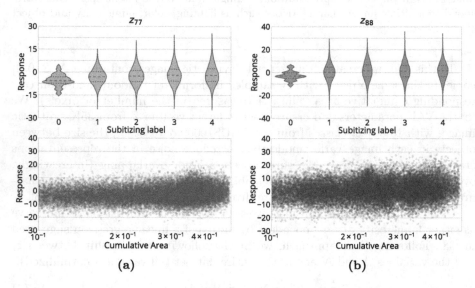

(a)   (b)

Fig. 4. Response distribution of two latent dimensions when feeding synthetic images of different subitizing label and cumulative object area. (a) z_{77} responds to numerosity (subitizing label) whereas being invariant to object size ($R^2 = 0.055$ for the fit of Eq. (3)). (b) z_{88} shows a typical response profile of a dimension sensitive to cumulative object count ($R^2 = 0.056$). The cumulative object area A is shown on logarithmic scale.

5 Conclusion

We have proposed unsupervised representation learning for visual number sense on natural images. Specifically, we propose a convolutional variational autoencoder to learn the concept of number from both synthetic and natural images without supervision. In agreement with previous findings on numerosity in artificial multi-layer perceptrons [38] and biological neuronal populations [12,28], a representation with the ability to encode numerosity within the subitizing range invariant to object area and appearance has been learned. Therefore, we present additional evidence that the concept of visual number sense emerges as a statistical property in variational autoencoders when presented a set of images displaying a varying number of salient objects.

Acknowledgements. The authors would like to thank the Intelligent Sensory Information Systems Institute and the Informatics Institute of the University of Amsterdam for their financial contribution to the travel expenses.

References

1. Arteta, C., Lempitsky, V., Zisserman, A.: Counting in the wild. In: Leibe, B., Matas, J., Sebe, N., Welling, M. (eds.) ECCV 2016. LNCS, vol. 9911, pp. 483–498. Springer, Cham (2016). https://doi.org/10.1007/978-3-319-46478-7_30
2. Burr, D., Ross, J.: A visual sense of number. Curr. Biol. **18**(6), 425–428 (2008)
3. Chatfield, K., Lempitsky, V.S., Vedaldi, A., Zisserman, A.: The devil is in the details: an evaluation of recent feature encoding methods. In: BMVC (2011)
4. Chattopadhyay, P., Vedantam, R., Selvaraju, R.R., Batra, D., Parikh, D.: Counting everyday objects in everyday scenes. In: CVPR (2017)
5. Cheng, M.-M., Mitra, N.J., Huang, X., Torr, P.H., Hu, S.-M.: Global contrast based salient region detection. PAMI **37**(3), 569–582 (2015)
6. Davis, H., Pérusse, R.: Numerical competence in animals: definitional issues, current evidence, and a new research agenda. Behav. Brain Sci. **11**(4), 561–579 (1988)
7. Dehaene, S.: The Number Sense: How the Mind Creates Mathematics. OUP, New York (2011)
8. Doersch, C.: Tutorial on variational autoencoders. arXiv preprint arXiv:1606.05908 (2016)
9. Feigenson, L., Dehaene, S., Spelke, E.: Core systems of number. Trends Cognit. Sci. **8**(7), 307–314 (2004)
10. Franka, M.C., Everettb, D.L., Fedorenkoa, E., Gibsona, E.: Number as a cognitive technology: evidence from pirahã language and cognition. Cognition **108**, 819–824 (2008)
11. Goodfellow, I., Bengio, Y., Courville, A., Bengio, Y.: Deep Learning, vol. 1. MIT Press, Cambridge (2016)
12. Harvey, B.M., Klein, B.P., Petridou, N., Dumoulin, S.O.: Topographic representation of numerosity in the human parietal cortex. Science **341**(6150), 1123–1126 (2013)
13. He, S., Jiao, J., Zhang, X., Han, G., Lau, R.W.: Delving into salient object subitizing and detection. In: ICCV (2017)

14. Hou, X., Shen, L., Sun, K., Qiu, G.: Deep feature consistent variational autoencoder. In: WACV (2017)
15. Hu, Y., Chang, H., Nian, F., Wang, Y., Li, T.: Dense crowd counting from still images with convolutional neural networks. J. Vis. Commun. Image Represent. **38**, 530–539 (2016)
16. Ioffe, S., Szegedy, C.: Batch normalization: accelerating deep network training by reducing internal covariate shift. In: ICML (2015)
17. Jansen, B.R., Hofman, A.D., Straatemeier, M., Bers, B.M., Raijmakers, M.E., Maas, H.L.: The role of pattern recognition in children's exact enumeration of small numbers. Br. J. Dev. Psychol. **32**(2), 178–194 (2014)
18. Jevons, W.S.: The power of numerical discrimination. Nature **3**, 281–282 (1871)
19. Kaufman, E.L., Lord, M.W., Reese, T.W., Volkmann, J.: The discrimination of visual number. Am. J. Psychol. **62**(4), 498–525 (1949)
20. Kingma, D.P., Welling, M.: Auto-encoding variational Bayes. In: ICLR (2014)
21. Lakoff, G., Núñez, R.E.: Where mathematics comes from: how the embodied mind brings mathematics into being. AMC **10**, 12 (2000)
22. LeCun, Y., Bengio, Y., Hinton, G.: Deep learning. Nature **521**(7553), 436 (2015)
23. Lemaître, G., Nogueira, F., Aridas, C.K.: Imbalanced-learn: a Python toolbox to tackle the curse of imbalanced datasets in machine learning. JMLR **18**(17), 1–5 (2017)
24. Lempitsky, V., Zisserman, A.: Learning to count objects in images. In: NIPS (2010)
25. Levy, O., Wolf, L.: Live repetition counting. In: ICCV (2015)
26. Lin, T.-Y., et al.: Microsoft COCO: common objects in context. In: Fleet, D., Pajdla, T., Schiele, B., Tuytelaars, T. (eds.) ECCV 2014. LNCS, vol. 8693, pp. 740–755. Springer, Cham (2014). https://doi.org/10.1007/978-3-319-10602-1_48
27. Liu, X., Wang, Z., Feng, J., Xi, H.: Highway vehicle counting in compressed domain. In: CVPR (2016)
28. Nieder, A.: The neuronal code for number. Nat. Rev. Neurosci. **17**(6), 366–382 (2016)
29. Nieder, A., Dehaene, S.: Representation of number in the brain. Ann. Rev. Neurosci. **32**, 185–208 (2009)
30. Noroozi, M., Pirsiavash, H., Favaro, P.: Representation learning by learning to count. In: ICCV (2017)
31. Paszke, A., et al.: Automatic differentiation in pytorch. In: NIPS Workshops (2017)
32. Piazza, M., Izard, V.: How humans count: numerosity and the parietal cortex. Neuroscientist **15**(3), 261–273 (2009)
33. Poncet, M., Caramazza, A., Mazza, V.: Individuation of objects and object parts rely on the same neuronal mechanism. Sci. Rep. **6**, 38434 (2016)
34. Runia, T.F.H., Snoek, C.G.M., Smeulders, A.W.M.: Real-world repetition estimation by div, grad and curl. In: CVPR, June 2018
35. Russakovsky, O., et al.: Imagenet large scale visual recognition challenge. IJCV **115**(3), 211–252 (2015)
36. Seguí, S., Pujol, O., Vitria, J.: Learning to count with deep object features. In: CVPR Workshops (2015)
37. Simonyan, K., Zisserman, A.: Very deep convolutional networks for large-scale image recognition. In: ICLR (2015)
38. Stoianov, I., Zorzi, M.: Emergence of a "visual number sense" in hierarchical generative models. Nat. Neurosci. **15**(2), 194 (2012)
39. Torralba, A., et al.: Context-based vision system for place and object recognition. In: ICCV (2003)

40. Viswanathan, P., Nieder, A.: Neuronal correlates of a visual "sense of number" in primate parietal and prefrontal cortices. Proc. Natl. Acad. Sci. **110**(27), 11187–11192 (2013)
41. Walach, E., Wolf, L.: Learning to count with CNN boosting. In: Leibe, B., Matas, J., Sebe, N., Welling, M. (eds.) ECCV 2016. LNCS, vol. 9906, pp. 660–676. Springer, Cham (2016). https://doi.org/10.1007/978-3-319-46475-6_41
42. Xiao, J., Hays, J., Ehinger, K.A., Oliva, A., Torralba, A.: Sun database: large-scale scene recognition from abbey to zoo. In: CVPR (2010)
43. Xiong, F., Shi, X., Yeung, D.-Y.: Spatiotemporal modeling for crowd counting in videos. In: ICCV (2017)
44. Zeiler, M.D., Krishnan, D., Taylor, G.W., Fergus, R.: Deconvolutional networks. In: CVPR (2010)
45. Zhang, J., et al.: Salient object subitizing. IJCV **124**(2), 169–186 (2017)

W18 – 3D Reconstruction Meets Semantics

W18 – 3D Reconstruction Meets Semantics

The goal of our second workshop on 3D Reconstruction meets Semantics (3DRMS) was to explore and discuss new ways for integrating techniques from 3D reconstruction with recognition and learning. Invited talks by renowned experts gave an overview of the current state of the art: **Andrew Davison** (Professor at Imperial College London, Dyson Robotics Lab) was speaking about how SLAM evolves into spatial AI systems, which allow devices to interact usefully with their environment. **Thomas Funkhouser** (Professor at the Princeton University) explained how we can help RGB-D cameras understand their 3D environment by means of semantic scene or depth completion and extrapolation. **Christian Häne** (Google) presented his work on semantics and learning for dense 3D reconstruction of objects done at UC Berkeley and ETH Zurich. All of the speakers also engaged in an interesting panel discussion.

At the same time, we provided authors a platform to present novel approaches towards answering questions such as: How can semantic information be used to improve the dense matching process in 3D reconstruction techniques? How valuable is 3D shape information for the extraction of semantic information?

We received 21 submissions tackling those problems, of which 18 were regular papers and 3 extended abstracts (up to 6 pages). Thanks to 12 external reviewers each regular paper got at least two reviews. Based on the recommendations from the reviewers, the papers were discussed by the workshop organizers in a second meta-review round. As a result of this discussion 7 regular papers (39%) were accepted. Extended abstracts were not peer-reviewed to allow authors future publications on these topics and 2 of them (66%) were selected based on their fit to the workshop and the potential to lead to interesting discussions (thus creating valuable feedback for the authors). Subsequently 9 spotlights presentations were given by the authors, followed by a poster session. We are glad the workshop attracted its audience, especially during the invited talks and the panel discussion at the end of the program (see gallery on our website).

Part of the workshop was a challenge on combining 3D and semantic information in complex scenes. To this end, a challenging outdoor dataset was released, consisting of both synthetic and real images of gardens. Given a set of images and their known camera poses, the goal for the challenge participants was to create a semantically annotated 3D model of the scene. Three challenge submissions were received and two of them presented at the workshop, showing some state-of-the-art performance. More details can be found in a discussion paper, which is a part of the proceedings (has not been not peer-reviewed).

September 2018

Radim Tyleček
Torsten Sattler
Thomas Brox
Marc Pollefeys
Robert B. Fisher
Theo Gevers

The Second Workshop on 3D Reconstruction Meets Semantics: Challenge Results Discussion

Radim Tylecek[1(✉)], Torsten Sattler[2], Hoang-An Le[3], Thomas Brox[4], Marc Pollefeys[2,5], Robert B. Fisher[1], and Theo Gevers[4]

[1] University of Edinburgh, Edinburgh, Scotland
rtylecek@inf.ed.ac.uk
[2] Department of Computer Science, ETH Zurich, Zurich, Switzerland
[3] University of Amsterdam, Amsterdam, Netherlands
[4] University of Freiburg, Freiburg im Breisgau, Germany
[5] Software Development Centre, Microsoft, Zurich, Switzerland

Abstract. This paper discusses a reconstruction challenge held as a part of the second 3D Reconstruction meets Semantics workshop (3DRMS). The challenge goals and datasets are introduced, including both synthetic and real data from outdoor scenes, here represented by gardens with a variety of bushes, trees, other plants and objects. Both qualitative and quantitative evaluation of the challenge participants' submissions is given in categories of geometric and semantic accuracy. Finally, comparison of submitted results with baseline methods is given, showing a modest performance increase in some of the categories.

Keywords: 3D reconstruction · Semantic segmentation · Challenge · Dataset

1 Introduction

Over the last decades, we have seen tremendous progress in the area of 3D reconstruction, enabling us to reconstruct large scenes at a high level of detail in little time. However, the resulting 3D representations only describe the scene at a geometric level. They cannot be used directly for more advanced applications, such as a robot interacting with its environment, due to a lack of semantic information. In addition, purely geometric approaches are prone to fail in challenging environments, where appearance information alone is insufficient to reconstruct complete 3D models from multiple views, for instance, in scenes with little texture or with complex and fine-grained structures.

At the same time, deep learning has led to a huge boost in recognition performance, but most of this recognition is restricted to outputs in the image plane or, in the best case, to 3D bounding boxes, which makes it hard for a robot to act based on these outputs. Integrating learned knowledge and semantics

© Springer Nature Switzerland AG 2019
L. Leal-Taixé and S. Roth (Eds.): ECCV 2018 Workshops, LNCS 11131, pp. 631–644, 2019.
https://doi.org/10.1007/978-3-030-11015-4_48

with 3D reconstruction is a promising avenue towards a solution to both these problems. For example, the semantic 3D reconstruction techniques proposed in recent years, e.g. [9], jointly optimize the 3D structure and semantic meaning of a scene and semantic SLAM methods add semantic annotations to the estimated 3D structure. Another recent step in this direction [5] shows that semantic and geometric relationships can be learned end-to-end from data as variational priors. Learning formulations of depth estimation, such as in [6], show the promises of integrating single-image cues into multi-view reconstruction and, in principle, allow the integration of depth estimation and recognition in a joint approach.

The goal of the 3DRMS workshop was to explore and discuss new ways for integrating techniques from 3D reconstruction with recognition and learning. In order to support work on questions related to the integration of 3D reconstruction with semantics, the workshop featured a semantic reconstruction challenge[1].

In this paper we will first present the challenge objectives and introduce datasets available for training, testing and validation of considered semantic reconstruction methods. Next, received submissions will be described, performance evaluation criteria defined and finally quantitative results will be compared and discussed.

2   Reconstruction Challenge

The challenge dataset was rendered from a drive through a semantically-rich virtual garden scene with many fine structures. Virtual models of the environment allowed us to provide exact ground truth for the 3D structure and semantics of the garden and rendered images from virtual multi-camera rig, enabling the use of both stereo and motion stereo information. The challenge participants submitted their result for benchmarking in one or more categories: the quality of the 3D reconstructions, the quality of semantic segmentation, and the quality of semantically annotated 3D models. Additionally, a dataset captured in a real garden from moving robot was available for validation.

2.1   Objectives

Given a set of images and their known camera poses, the goal of the challenge was to create a semantically annotated 3D model of the scene. To this end, it was necessary to compute depth maps from the images and then fuse them together (potentially while incorporating information from the semantics) into a single 3D model.

What we consider particularly challenging is the complex geometric structure of objects in the outdoor scenes we ask participants to reconstruct in 3D. Unlike scenes of man-made environments (indoor, urban, road-side) with certain degree of regularity of seen surfaces, a typical outdoor scene will have trees and plants with fine structures such as leaves, stems or branches, which are thin and notoriously hard to represent accurately. In real conditions those are also inherently

---

[1] http://trimbot2020.webhosting.rug.nl/events/3drms/challenge.

non-rigid objects, e.g. grass moving in wind, which requires robust matching procedures to cope with small moving object parts. We hoped the participants would come up with representations or priors that will adapt to different objects' geometry based on their semantic class to handle such difficulties.

3   Garden Dataset

Three groups of data were provided for the challenge, see Fig. 3 for sample images.

Synthetic training sequences consist of 20k calibrated images with their camera poses, ground truth semantic annotations, and a semantically annotated 3D point cloud of 4 different virtual gardens.

Synthetic testing sequence consists of 5k calibrated images with their camera poses from 1 virtual garden.

Real-world validation sequence consists of 300 calibrated images with their camera poses from 1 real garden.

Semantic labels of objects distinguished are the following, with color code in brackets: *Grass* (light green), *Ground* (brown), *Pavement* (grey), *Hedge* (ochre), *Topiary* (cyan), *Rose* (red), *Obstacle* (blue), *Tree* (dark green), *Background* (black).

All data are available from the git repository https://gitlab.inf.ed.ac.uk/ 3DRMS/Challenge2018, where also details on the file formats can be found.

3.1   Synthetic Garden Data

We have randomly generated 5 virtual gardens (square $12\,\mathrm{m} \times 12\,\mathrm{m}$) and rendered them using Blender, similar to Nature dataset [14]. The camera trajectories were generated to simulate a robot moving through the garden, moving on smooth trajectories, occasionally stopping and turning on spot, as shown in Fig. 1. At each waypoint 10 views were rendered from a virtual camera rig, which has pentagonal shape, with a stereo camera pair on each side as in Fig. 2. Fine-grained details, such as grass and leaves, were generated on the fly during rendering. Details on dataset generation can be found in [2].

3.2   Real Garden Data

The real dataset for the the 3DRMS challenge was collected in a test garden at Wageningen University Research Campus, Netherlands, which was built specifically for experimentation in robotic gardening. A validation sequence based on test_around_garden scenario with 124 frames from the previous year dataset was adopted for this year.

Calibrated Images. Image streams from four cameras (0, 1, 2, 3) were provided. Figure 2 shows these are mounted in a pairwise setup, the pair 0–1 is oriented to the front and the pair 2–3 to the right side of the robot vehicle.

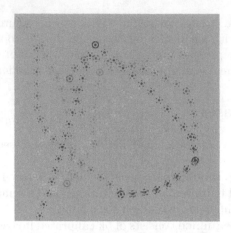

Fig. 1. Randomly generated trajectories for the test scene (unique color for each sequence)

Resolution of the images is 752×480 (WVGA), cameras 0 and 2 are color while cameras 1 and 3 are greyscale (but sharper). All images were undistorted with the intrinsic camera parameters, calibration was performed with Kalibr toolbox [7]. The camera poses were estimated with COLMAP [17] and manually aligned to the coordinate system of the laser point cloud.

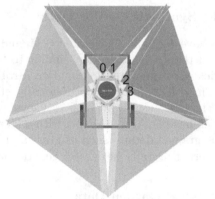

Fig. 2. Pentagonal camera rig mounted on the robot (left). First four cameras were included in the real challenge data (right, green). (Color figure online)

Semantic Image Annotations. Manual pixel-wise ground truth (GT) annotations (Fig. 3) produced with semantic annotation tool [20] are provided for frames from cameras 0 and 2.

Color image (undistorted)   Semantic annotation

Fig. 3. Synthetic and real images of a garden from front camera mounted on a moving robot.

Semantic Point Cloud. The geometry of the scene was acquired by *Leica ScanStation P15*, which achieves accuracy of 3 mm at 40 m. Its native output merged from 20 individual scans (Fig. 4) was sub-sampled with a spatial filter to achieve a minimal distance between two points of 10 mm, which becomes the effective accuracy of the GT. For some dynamic parts, like leaves and branches, the accuracy can be further reduced due to movement by the wind, etc.

Fig. 4. Point cloud of the real garden from laser scanner (height-colored).

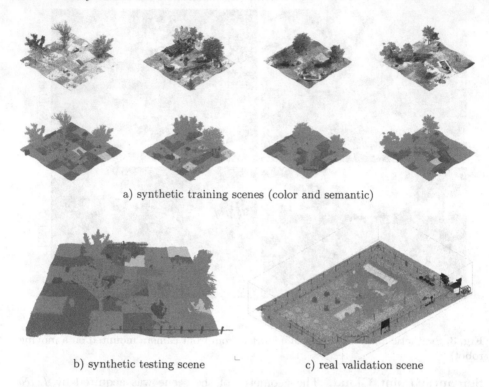

a) synthetic training scenes (color and semantic)

b) synthetic testing scene   c) real validation scene

Fig. 5. GT semantic point cloud of virtual and real gardens with color-coded labels.

Semantic labels were assigned to the points with multiple 3D bounding boxes drawn around individual components of the point cloud belonging to the garden objects or terrain using the Rosemat[2] annotation tool [20]. Ultimately the point cloud was split into segments corresponding to train and test sequences as shown in Fig. 5.

4   Submitted Results

Three submission were received fort this challenge:

DTIS [3] *(ONERA, Université Paris Saclay, France):* In their pipeline, initial SGM stereo results are fed to FuseNet [11], which jointly predicts a 2D semantic segmentation map and refined depth. Those are fused using TSDF in a 3D volumetric representation with colors and labels. Ultimately MC [15] extracts a surface mesh with labels assigned by voting.

HAB [10] *(Video Analytics Lab, Indian Institute of Science, Bangalore, India):* Their approach starts with ELAS stereo [8] producing a dense point cloud labeled

---

[2] Rosbag Semantic Annotation Tool for Matlab. https://github.com/rtylecek/rosemat.

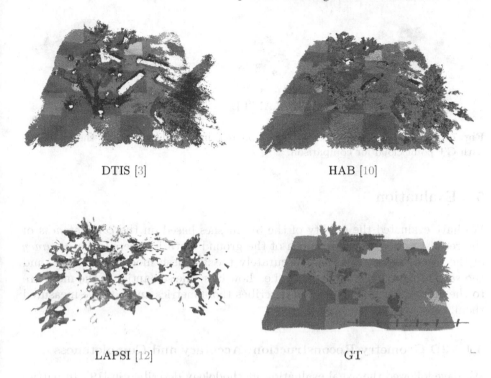

DTIS [3]   HAB [10]

LAPSI [12]   GT

Fig. 6. Semantic and color meshes based on synthetic images submitted to the challenge with GT point cloud for comparison.

with 2D semantic segmentation from DeepLabV3 [4]. The resulting point cloud is denoised with class-specific filters and similarly mesh reconstruction is using PSR [13] for flat surface classes and ball-pivoting for fine structures.

LAPSI [12] *(LaPSI, UFRGS, Brazil):* Only the geometric mesh was generated, in two variants: LAPSI360 using all 10 cameras and LAPSI4 using only 4 cameras. We omit the latter variant from some comparisons as it was generally performing just slightly worse than the former.

In addition to the three submitted results we have also compared to current state-of-the-art methods in both reconstruction [17] and classification [1] tasks.

COLMAP [16] *(3D Reconstruction baseline):* A general-purpose Structure-from-Motion (SfM) and Multi-View Stereo (MVS) pipeline with a graphical and command-line interface. It offers a wide range of features for reconstruction of ordered and unordered image collections.

SegNet [1] *(Semantic baseline):* For comparison with the 2D state-of-the-art a SegNet architecture [1] is adapted for the given garden semantics.

DTIS [3]   LAPSI [12]   GT

Fig. 7. Semantic and color meshes based on real images submitted to the challenge with GT point cloud for comparison.

5   Evaluation

We have evaluated the quality of the 3D meshes based on the *completeness* of the reconstruction, i.e., how much of the ground truth is covered, the *accuracy* of the reconstruction, i.e., how accurately the 3D mesh models the scene, and the *semantic accuracy* of the mesh, i.e., how close the semantics of the mesh are to the ground truth. This section describes those metrics and how we measured them.

5.1   3D Geometry Reconstruction: Accuracy and Completeness

We have followed the usual evaluation methodology described in [19]. In particular, *accuracy* is distance d (in m) such that 90% of the reconstruction is within d of the ground truth mesh and *completeness* is the percent of points in the GT point cloud that are within 5 cm of the reconstruction.

The distances between the reconstruction and GT are calculated using a point-to-mesh metric for completeness and vertex-to-point for accuracy. The faces of submitted meshes were subdivided to have a same maximum edge length. The difference between the evaluated results is shown in Fig. 8, which all use the same color scale for accuracy or completeness. Cold colors indicate well reconstructed segments while hot colors indicate hallucinated surface (accuracy) or missing parts (completeness).

The evaluation was limited to the space delimited by the bounding box of the test area plus 2 m margin. Following [18] we also plot cumulative histograms of distances in Fig. 9.

5.2   Semantic Classification Accuracy

The accuracy of semantic labels assigned to vertices or faces of the 3D model (Figs. 6 and 7) was evaluated by its projection to all test images with known poses (denoted '3D' below). Some submissions also directly included image segmentation results (denoted '2D'), which were also compared.

Visual comparison of the results in a selected frame is given in Fig. 10. In the error mask the red pixels indicate incorrectly classified pixels, grey were correct and black were not evaluated. Quantitative results are presented by confusion

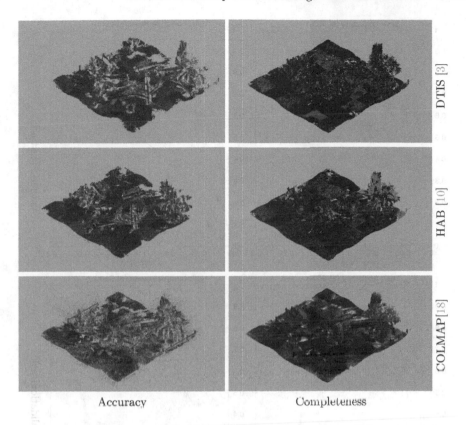

Fig. 8. Visual comparison of submitted geometry and test scene GT point cloud. Distances [0–1 m]: cold colors indicate well reconstructed segments, hot colors indicate noisy surface (accuracy) or missing parts (completeness).

matrices for all images in the test set in Fig. 11, where semantic accuracy is the percentage of correctly predicted pixels across all test images, and similarly in Fig. 12 for real images.

5.3   Results and Discussion

The quantitative comparison in all performance categories is given in Table 1 for synthetic data and in Table 2 for real validation data.

The baseline Structure-from-Motion method COLMAP [17] was outperformed by HAB submission by 3 cm in terms of accuracy on synthetic data, but at the cost of lower completeness (Table 1). The COLMAP result could be potentially improved by filtering out outliers seen in Fig. 8, still the class-specific filters used in HAB would likely work for its advantage.

While DTIS submission was lacking good geometry, its joint depth and semantic segmentation resulted in a slight boost of 1% in 2D semantic segmentation accuracy over the SegNet baseline [1], which did not have access to depths.

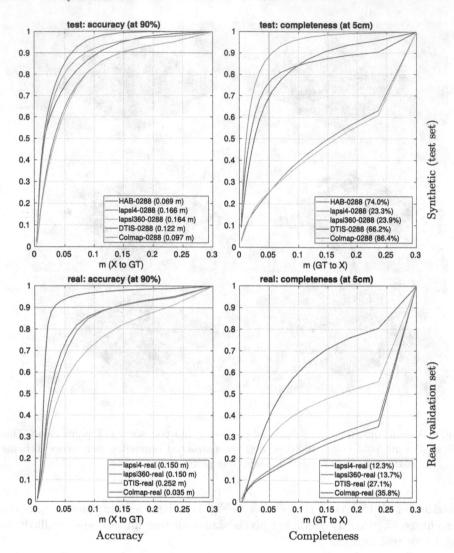

Fig. 9. Quantitative comparison of geometry with cumulative histograms of distances between GT and submissions.

This however did not translate to 3D semantic accuracy, where the change of representation to less accurate mesh resulted in 12% drop in performance. Further inspection of the results shows that most object instances are correctly classified, and the 10–20% error appears near object boundaries or contours.

The real dataset proved to be more challenging Table 2, where the deep network employed by DTIS would apparently need more data for fine-tuning.

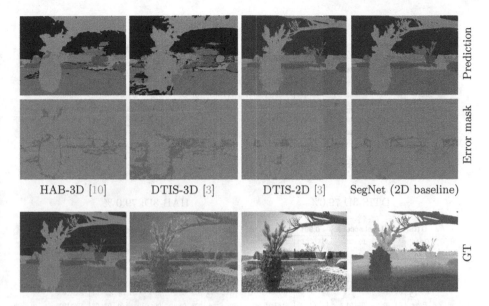

Fig. 10. Comparison of predicted semantic maps for a sample synthetic frame (above) and GT semantics with color image, overlay and depth map (below). Error mask: *red* marks incorrect pixels, *grey* correct. (Color figure online)

This probably allowed the classic MVS baseline to prevail in both accuracy and completeness. Among the challenge participants, LAPSI was slightly better on accuracy, but their mesh was otherwise very sparse as low completeness suggests, probably resulting from overly conservative setting of the method.

In summary, best performers for synthetic data were HAB in 3D Geometry category and DTIS in the semantic category. On real data DTIS also scored better than the other submissions.

Table 1. Comparison of submitted results on synthetic test set.

Method	3D reconstruction		Semantic	
	Accuracy	Completeness	Accuracy-2D	Accuracy-3D
DTIS [3]	0.122 m	66.2%	**91.1%**	79.0%
HAB [10]	**0.069 m**	**74.0%**		79.0%
LAPSI [12]	0.164 m	23.9%		
Baseline	*0.097 m*	*86.4%*	*90.2%*	

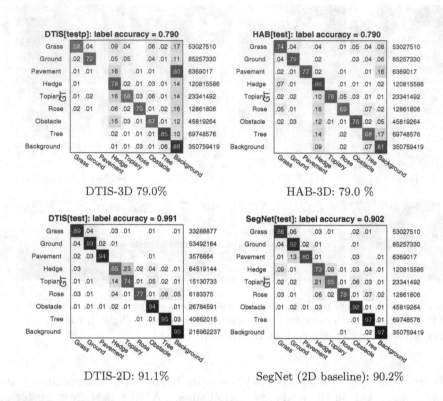

Fig. 11. Evaluation of predicted semantic labels on test set. Confusion matrix: *dark* on diagonal indicates good match of the prediction with GT labels. Semantic accuracy: pixel-wise ratio of correct predictions over all test images.

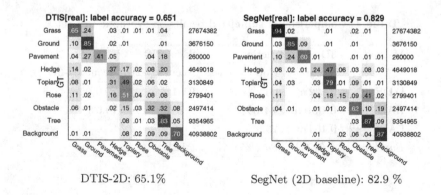

Fig. 12. Evaluation of predicted semantic labels on real set.

Table 2. Comparison of submitted results on real validation set.

Method	3D reconstruction		Semantic
	Accuracy	Completeness	Accuracy-2D
DTIS [3]	0.25 m	**27.1%**	**65.1%**
HAB [10]			
LAPSI [12]	**0.15 m**	13.7%	
Baseline	*0.035 m*	*35.8%*	*82.9%*

6   Conclusion

The workshop challenge competitors have shown that in some cases the joint semantic and 3D information reasoning can improve results. The performance gain was however rather marginal, suggesting that further optimization and design changes are needed to fully unlock the potential that such approaches offer and come up with methods giving overall balanced improvements. For this purpose, we will continue to support new authors in evaluating their methods on the garden dataset.

Acknowledgements. The workshop, reconstruction challenge and acquisition of datasets was supported by EU project TrimBot2020.

References

1. Badrinarayanan, V., Kendall, A., Cipolla, R.: SegNet: a deep convolutional encoder-decoder architecture for image segmentation. IEEE Trans. Pattern Anal. Mach. Intell. **39**, 2481–2495 (2017)
2. Baslamisli, A.S., Groenestege, T.T., Das, P., Le, H.-A., Karaoglu, S., Gevers, T.: Joint learning of intrinsic images and semantic segmentation. In: Ferrari, V., Hebert, M., Sminchisescu, C., Weiss, Y. (eds.) ECCV 2018. LNCS, vol. 11210, pp. 289–305. Springer, Cham (2018). https://doi.org/10.1007/978-3-030-01231-1_18
3. Carvalho, M., Ferrera, M., Boulch, A., Moras, J., Saux, B.L., Trouvé-Peloux, P.: Co-learning of geometry and semantics for online 3D mapping. In: 3DRMS Workshop Challenge, ECCV (2018)
4. Chen, L.C., Papandreou, G., Schroff, F., Adam, H.: Rethinking atrous convolution for semantic image segmentation. arXiv preprint arXiv:1706.05587 (2017)
5. Cherabier, I., Schönberger, J.L., Oswald, M.R., Pollefeys, M., Geiger, A.: Learning priors for semantic 3D reconstruction. In: Ferrari, V., Hebert, M., Sminchisescu, C., Weiss, Y. (eds.) ECCV 2018. LNCS, vol. 11216, pp. 325–341. Springer, Cham (2018). https://doi.org/10.1007/978-3-030-01258-8_20
6. Eigen, D., Fergus, R.: Predicting depth, surface normals and semantic labels with a common multi-scale convolutional architecture. In: Proceedings of ICCV, pp. 2650–2658 (2015)
7. Furgale, P., Rehder, J., Siegwart, R.: Unified temporal and spatial calibration for multi-sensor systems. In: International Conference on Intelligent Robots and Systems, pp. 1280–1286, November 2013

8. Geiger, A., Roser, M., Urtasun, R.: Efficient large-scale stereo matching. In: Kimmel, R., Klette, R., Sugimoto, A. (eds.) ACCV 2010. LNCS, vol. 6492, pp. 25–38. Springer, Heidelberg (2011). https://doi.org/10.1007/978-3-642-19315-6_3
9. Häne, C., Zach, C., Cohen, A., Pollefeys, M.: Dense semantic 3D reconstruction. Trans. Pattern Anal. Mach. Intell. **39**(9), 1730–1743 (2017)
10. Haque, S.M., Arora, S., Babu, V.: 3D semantic reconstruction using class-specific models. In: 3DRMS Workshop Challenge, ECCV (2018)
11. Hazirbas, C., Ma, L., Domokos, C., Cremers, D.: FuseNet: incorporating depth into semantic segmentation via fusion-based CNN architecture. In: Lai, S.-H., Lepetit, V., Nishino, K., Sato, Y. (eds.) ACCV 2016. LNCS, vol. 10111, pp. 213–228. Springer, Cham (2017). https://doi.org/10.1007/978-3-319-54181-5_14
12. Ilha, G., Waszak, T., Pereira, F.I., Susin, A.A.: Lapsi-360. In: 3DRMS Workshop Challenge, ECCV (2018)
13. Kazhdan, M., Hoppe, H.: Screened poisson surface reconstruction. ACM Trans. Graph. (ToG) **32**(3), 29 (2013)
14. Le, H.A., Baslamisli, A.S., Mensink, T., Gevers, T.: Three for one and one for three: flow, segmentation, and surface normals. In: Proceedings of BMVC (2018)
15. Lorensen, W.E., Cline, H.E.: Marching cubes: a high resolution 3D surface construction algorithm. ACM SIGGRAPH Comput. Graph. **21**, 163–169 (1987)
16. Schönberger, J.L., Zheng, E., Frahm, J.-M., Pollefeys, M.: Pixelwise view selection for unstructured multi-view stereo. In: Leibe, B., Matas, J., Sebe, N., Welling, M. (eds.) ECCV 2016. LNCS, vol. 9907, pp. 501–518. Springer, Cham (2016). https://doi.org/10.1007/978-3-319-46487-9_31
17. Schönberger, J.L., Frahm, J.M.: Structure-from-motion revisited. In: Proceedings of CVPR (2016)
18. Schöps, T., et al.: A multi-view stereo benchmark with high-resolution images and multi-camera videos. In: Proceedings of CVPR (2017)
19. Seitz, S.M., Curless, B., Diebel, J., Scharstein, D., Szeliski, R.: A comparison and evaluation of multi-view stereo reconstruction algorithms. In: Proceedings of CVPR, pp. 519–528. IEEE Computer Society, Washington (2006)
20. Tylecek, R., Fisher, R.B.: Consistent semantic annotation of outdoor datasets via 2D/3D label transfer. Sensors **18**(7), 2249 (2018)

A Deeper Look at 3D Shape Classifiers

Jong-Chyi Su$^{(\boxtimes)}$, Matheus Gadelha, Rui Wang, and Subhransu Maji

University of Massachusetts, Amherst, USA
{jcsu,mgadelha,ruiwang,smaji}@cs.umass.edu

Abstract. We investigate the role of representations and architectures for classifying 3D shapes in terms of their computational efficiency, generalization, and robustness to adversarial transformations. By varying the number of training examples and employing cross-modal transfer learning we study the role of initialization of existing deep architectures for 3D shape classification. Our analysis shows that multiview methods continue to offer the best generalization even without pretraining on large labeled image datasets, and even when trained on simplified inputs such as binary silhouettes. Furthermore, the performance of voxel-based 3D convolutional networks and point-based architectures can be improved via cross-modal transfer from image representations. Finally, we analyze the robustness of 3D shape classifiers to adversarial transformations and present a novel approach for generating adversarial perturbations of a 3D shape for multiview classifiers using a differentiable renderer. We find that point-based networks are more robust to point position perturbations while voxel-based and multiview networks are easily fooled with the addition of imperceptible noise to the input.

1 Introduction

Techniques for analyzing 3D shapes are becoming increasingly important due to the vast number of sensors that are capturing 3D data, as well as numerous computer graphics applications. In recent years a variety of deep architectures have been approached for classifying 3D shapes. These range from multiview approaches that render a shape from a set of views and deploy image-based classifiers, to voxel-based approaches that analyze shapes represented as a 3D occupancy grid, to point-based approaches that classify shapes represented as collection of points. However, there is relatively little work that studies the tradeoffs offered by these modalities and their associated techniques.

This paper aims to study three of these tradeoffs, namely the ability to generalize from a few examples, computational efficiency, and robustness to adversarial transformations. We pick a representative technique for each modality. For multiview representation we choose the Multiview CNN (MVCNN) architecture [31]; For voxel-based representation we choose the VoxNet [17,37] constructed using

Electronic supplementary material The online version of this chapter (https://doi.org/10.1007/978-3-030-11015-4_49) contains supplementary material, which is available to authorized users.

L. Leal-Taixé and S. Roth (Eds.): ECCV 2018 Workshops, LNCS 11131, pp. 645–661, 2019.
https://doi.org/10.1007/978-3-030-11015-4_49

convolutions and pooling operations on a 3D grid; For point-based representation we choose the PointNet architecture [32]. The analysis is done on the widely-used ModelNet40 shape classification benchmark [37].

Some of our analysis leads to surprising results. For example, with deeper architectures and a modification in the rendering technique that renders with black background and better centers the object in the image the performance of a vanilla MVCNN can be improved to **95.0%** per-instance accuracy on the benchmark, outperforming several recent approaches. Another example is that while it is widely believed that the strong performance of MVCNN is due to the use of networks pretrained on large image datasets (e.g., ImageNet [26]), we find that even without such pretraining the MVCNN obtains **91.3%** accuracy, outperforming several voxel-based and point-based counterparts that also do not rely on such pretraining. Furthermore, the performance of MVCNN remains at **93.6%** even when trained with binary silhouettes (instead of shaded images) of shapes, suggesting that shading offer relatively little extra information on this benchmark for MVCNN.

We then systematically analyze the generalization ability of the models. First we analyze the accuracy of various models by varying the number of training examples per category. We find that the multiview approaches generalize faster obtaining near optimal performance with far fewer examples compared to the other approaches. We then analyze the role of initialization of these networks. As 3D shape datasets are currently lacking in comparison to large image datasets, we employ cross-modal distillation techniques [7,10] to guide learning. In particular we use representations extracted from pretrained MVCNNs to guide learning of voxel-based and point-based networks. Cross-modal distillation improves the performance of VoxNet and PointNet, especially when training data is limited.

Finally we analyze the robustness of these classifiers to adversarial perturbations. While generating adversarial inputs to VoxNet and PointNet is straightforward, it is not the case for multiview methods due to the rendering step. To this end we design an end-to-end differentiable MVCNN that takes an input a voxel representation and generates a set of views using a differentiable renderer. We analyze the robustness of these networks by estimating the amount of perturbation needed to obtain a misclassification. We find that PointNet is more robust, while MVCNN and VoxNet are both easily fooled by adding a small amount of noise. This is similar to the observations in prior work of adversarial inputs for image-based networks [6,16,33]. Somewhat surprisingly ImageNet pretraining reduces the robustness of the MVCNNs to adversarial perturbations.

In summary, we performed a detailed analysis of several recently proposed approaches for 3D shape classification. This resulted in a new state-of-the-art of **95.0%** on the ModelNet40 benchmark. The technical contributions include the use of cross-modal distillation for improving networks that operate on voxel-based and point-based representations and a novel approach for generating adversarial inputs for 3D shape classification for multiview approaches using a differentiable renderer. This allows us to directly compare and generate adversarial inputs for voxel-based and view-based methods using gradient-based techniques. The conclusion is that while PointNet architecture is less accurate, the use of orderless aggregation mechanism likely makes it more robust to adversarial perturbations compared to VoxNet and MVCNN, both of which are easily fooled.

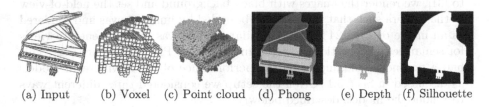

(a) Input   (b) Voxel   (c) Point cloud   (d) Phong   (e) Depth   (f) Silhouette

Fig. 1. Different representations of the input shape. From the left (a) the shapes in the database are represented as triangle meshes, (b) the shape converted to a 30^3 voxel grid, (c) point cloud representation with 2048 points, and (d–f) the model rendered using Phong shading, and as depth and binary silhouette images respectively.

2 Method

This Section describes the protocol for evaluating the performance of various classifiers. We describe the dataset, performance metrics, and training setup in Sect. 2.1, followed by the details of the deep classifiers we consider in Sect. 2.2, and the approach for generating adversarial examples in Sect. 2.3.

2.1 3D Shape Classification

Classification Benchmark. All our evaluation is done on the ModelNet40 shape classification benchmark [37] following the standard training and test splits provided in the dataset. There are 40 categories with 9483 training models and 2468 test models. The numbers of models are not equal across classes hence we report both the per-instance and per-class accuracy on the test set. While most of the literature report results by training on the entire training set, some earlier work, notably [31] reports results on training and evaluation on a subset consisting of 80 training and 20 test examples per category.

Input Representations. The dataset presents each shape as a collection of triangles, hence it is important to describe the exact way in which these are converted to point clouds, voxels, and images for input to different network architectures. These inputs are visualized in Fig. 1 and described below:

- **Voxel representation.** To get voxel representations we follow the dataset from [23] where models are discretized to a $30 \times 30 \times 30$ occupancy grid. The data is available from the author's page.
- **Point cloud.** For point cloud representation we use the data from the Point-Net approach [32] where 2048 points are uniformly sampled for each model.

- **Image representation.** To generate multiple views of the model we use a setup similar to [31]. Since the models are assumed to be upright oriented a set of virtual cameras are placed at 12 radially symmetric locations, i.e. every 30°, facing the object center and at an elevation of 30°. Comparing to [31], we render the images with black background and set the field-of-view of the camera such that the object is bounded by image canvas and rendered as an image of size 224 × 224. A similar scheme was used to generate views for semantic segmentation of shapes in the Shape PFCN approach [12]. This had a non-negligible impact on the performance of the downstream models as discussed in Sect. 3.1. Given the setup we considered three different ways to render the models described below:
  1. Phong shading, where images are rendered with the Phong reflection model [21] using Blender software [2]. The light and material setup is similar to the approach in [31].
  2. Depth rendering, where only the depth value is recorded.
  3. Silhouette rendering, where images are rendered as binary images for pixels corresponding to foreground.

Data Augmentation. Models in the dataset are upright oriented, but not consistently oriented along the axis, i.e., models could be rotated arbitrarily along the upright direction. Models that rely on voxel or point cloud input often benefit from rotation augmentation along the upright axis during training and testing. Similar to the multiview setting we consider models rotated by 30° increments as additional data during training, and optionally aggregating votes across these instances at test time.

2.2 Classification Architectures

We consider the following deep architectures for shape classification.

Multiview CNN (MVCNN). The MVCNN architecture [31] uses rendered images of the model from different views as input. Each image is fed into a CNN with shared weights. A max-pooling layer across different views is used to perform an orderless aggregation of the individual representations followed by several non-linear layers for classification. While the original paper [31] used the VGG-M network [30] we also report results using:

- The VGG-11 network, which is the model with configuration A from [30]. The view-pooling layer is added before the first `fc` layer.
- Variants of residual networks proposed in [8] such as ResNet18, ResNet34, and ResNet50. The view-pooling layer is added before the final `fc` layer.

Voxel Network (VoxNet). The VoxNet was first proposed in several early works [17,37] that uses convolution and pooling layers defined on 3D voxel grids. The early VoxNet models [17] used two 3D convolutional layers and 2 fully-connected layers. In our initial experiments we found the capacity of this network is limited. We also experimented with the deeper VoxNet architecture proposed in [32] which has five blocks of (`conv3d-batchnorm-LeakyReLU`) and includes batch normalization [11]. All `conv3d` layers have kernel size 5, stride 1 and channel size 32. The `LeakyReLU` has slope 0.1. Two fully-connected layers (`fc-batchnorm-ReLU-fc`) are added on top to obtain class predictions.

VoxMVCNN. We also consider a hybrid model that takes voxels as input and uses a MVCNN approach for classification using a differentiable renderer. To achieve this we make two simplifications. First, only six renderings are considered corresponding to viewing directions along six dimensions ($\pm x, \pm y, \pm z$). Second, the rendering is approximated using the approach suggested in PrGAN [5] where line integrals are used to compute pixel shading color. For example the line integral of a volume occupancy grid V along the axis k is given by $P((i,j),V) = 1 - \exp(-\sum_k V(i,j,k))$. The idea is that the higher the sum of occupancy values along the axis, the closer the integral is to 1. The generated views for two models are shown in Fig. 2. The renderings generated this way approximate silhouette renderings as described earlier. The primary advantage of this rendering method is that it's differentiable, and hence we use this model to analyze the robustness of the MVCNN architecture to adversarial inputs (described in Sect. 2.3).

Point Network (PointNet). We follow the same architecture as PointNet [32] that operates on point cloud representations of a model. The architecture applies a series of non-linear mappings individually to each input point and performs orderless aggregations using max-pooling operations. Thus the model is invariant to the order in which the points are presented and can directly operate on point clouds without additional preprocessing such as spatial partitioning, or graph construction. Additionally, some initial layers are used to perform spatial transformations (rotation, scaling, etc.) Despite its simplicity the model and its variants have been shown to be effective at shape classification and segmentation tasks [22,32].

Training Details. All the MVCNN models are trained in two stages as suggested in [31]. The model is first trained as a single-image classification task where the view-pooling layer is removed, then trained to jointly classify all the views with view-pooling layer in the second stage. We use the Adam optimizer [14] with learning rate 5×10^{-5} and 1×10^{-5} for first and second stage respectively and each stage is trained with 30 epochs. The batch size is set to 64 and 96 (eight models with twelve views) for each stage and the weight decay parameter is set to 0.001. The VoxNet is trained with Adam optimizer with learning rate 1×10^{-3} for 150 epochs. The batch size is set to 64 and weight decay parameter is 0.001. The VoxMVCNN is trained using the same procedure as MVCNN. For PointNet [32] we use the publicly available implementation released by the authors.

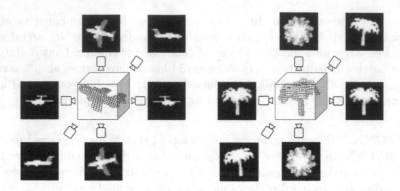

Fig. 2. Examples of rendered images for the VoxMVCNN architecture. The voxel input is rendered using the simplified technique described in Sect. 2.2 to generate 6 images which are processed using the MVCNN architecture [31] for classification.

2.3 Generating Adversarial Inputs

Adversarial examples to image-based deep neural networks have been thoroughly explored in the literature [6,16,19,33]. However, there is no prior work that addresses adversarial examples to deep neural networks based on 3D representations. Here we want to investigate if adversarial shapes can be obtained from different 3D shape recognition models, and perhaps more importantly which 3D representation is more robust to adversarial examples. We define an adversarial example as follows. Consider $\phi(\mathbf{s}, y)$ as the score that a classifier ϕ gives to an input $\mathbf{s}$ belonging to a class y. An adversarial example $\mathbf{s}'$ is a sample that is perceptually similar to $\mathbf{s}$, but $\text{argmax}_y \phi(\mathbf{s}, y) \neq \text{argmax}_y \phi(\mathbf{s}', y)$. It is known from [33] that an effective way to compute adversarial examples to image-based models is the following. Given a sample from the dataset $\mathbf{s}$ and a class y' that one wishes to maximize the score, an adversarial example $\mathbf{s}'$ can be computed as follows

$$\mathbf{s}' = \mathbf{s} + \alpha \nabla_{\mathbf{s}} \phi(\mathbf{s}, y')$$

where $\nabla_{\mathbf{s}}$ is the gradient of the classifier with respect to the input $\mathbf{s}$, and α is the learning rate. For many image models, this single step procedure is able to generate perceptually indistinguishable adversarial examples. However, for some of the examples we experimented, a single step is not enough to generate a misclassification. Thus, we employ the following iterative procedure based on [16]:

$$\mathbf{s}'_0 = \mathbf{s}, \quad \mathbf{s}'_{t+1} = clip_{\mathbf{s}, \epsilon} \{\mathbf{s}_t + \alpha \nabla_{\mathbf{s}} \phi(\mathbf{s_t}, y')\} \tag{1}$$

where $clip_{\mathbf{s}, \epsilon}\{x\}$ is an operator that clips the values of x to make sure the result will be in the L_∞ ϵ-neighborhood of $\mathbf{s}$. Notice that this procedure is agnostic to the representation used by the input data $\mathbf{s}$. Thus, we use the same method to generate adversarial examples for multiple modalities of 3D representation: voxels, point clouds, multi-view images. For voxel grids, we also clip the values of **s** to make sure their values are in $[0, 1]$. For multi-view representations, we need to make sure that all views are consistent with each other. We address this issue by using the VoxMVCNN architecture that generates multiple views from the same object through a differentiable renderer, i.e. line integral, as described in Sect. 2.2.

3 Experiments

We begin by investigating the model generalization in Sect. 3.1. Section 3.2 analyzes the effect of different architectures and renderings for the MVCNN. Section 3.3 uses cross-modal distillation to improve the performance of VoxNet and PointNet. Section 3.4 compares the tradeoffs between different representations. Section 3.5 compares the robustness of different classifiers to adversarial perturbations. Finally, Sect. 3.6 puts the results presented in this paper in the context of prior work.

3.1 Learning from a Few Examples

One of the most desirable properties of a classifier is its ability to generalize from a few examples. We test this ability by evaluating the accuracy of different models as a function of training set size. We select the first M_k models in the training set for each class, where

$$M_k = \min(N_k, \{10, 20, 40, 80, 160, 320, 889\}),$$

and N_k is the number of models in class k. The maximum number of models per-class in the training set of ModelNet40 is 889. Figure 3 shows the per-class and per-instance accuracy for three different models as a function of the training set size. The MVCNN with the VGG-11 architecture has better generalization than VoxNet and PointNet across all training set sizes. MVCNN obtains 77.8% accuracy using only 10 training models per class, while PointNet and VoxNet obtain 62.5% and 57.9% respectively. The performance of MVCNN is near optimal with 160 models per class, far fewer than PointNet and VoxNet. When using the whole dataset for training, MVCNN (95.0%) outperforms PointNet (89.1%) and VoxNet (85.6%) by a large margin.

Several improvements have been proposed for both point-based and voxel-based architectures. The best performing point-based models to the best of our knowledge is the Kd-Networks [15] which achieves 91.8% per-instance accuracy. For voxel-based models, O-CNN [35] uses sparse convolutions to handle higher resolution with Octave trees [18] and achieves 90.6% per-instance accuracy. However, all of them are far below the MVCNN approach. More details and comparison to the state-of-the-art are in Sect. 3.6.

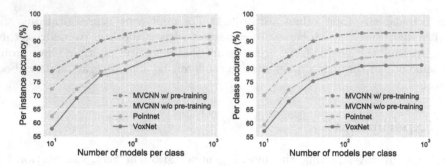

Fig. 3. Classification accuracy as a function of training set size. MVCNN generalizes better than the other approaches. The two MVCNN curves correspond to variants with and without ImageNet pretraining.

3.2   Dissecting the MVCNN Architecture

Given the high performance of MVCNN we investigate what factors contribute to its performance as described next.

Effect of Model Architecture. The MVCNN model in [31] used VGG-M architecture. However a number of different image networks have since been proposed. We used different CNN architectures for MVCNN and report the accuracies in Table 1. All models have similar performance suggesting that MVCNN is robust across different CNN architectures. In Table 3 we also compare with the results using VGG-M and AlexNet. With the same shaded images and training subset, VGG-11 achieves 89.1% and VGG-M has 89.9% accuracy.

Table 1. Accuracy (%) of MVCNN with different CNN architectures. The VGG-11 architectures are on par with the residual network variants.

Model	Per class	Per instance
VGG-11	92.4	95.0
ResNet 18	92.8	95.6
ResNet 34	93.4	95.9
ResNet 50	94.0	95.5

Effect of ImageNet Pretraining. MVCNN benefits from transfer learning from ImageNet classification task. However, even without ImageNet pretraining, the MVCNN achieves 91.3% per-instance accuracy (Table 2). This is higher than several point-based and voxel-based approaches. Figure 3 plots the performance of the MVCNN with VGG-11 network without ImageNet pretraining across training set sizes showing this trend is true throughout the training regime. In Sect. 3.3 we study if ImageNet pretraining can benefit such approaches using cross-modal transfer learning.

Table 2. Effect of ImageNet pretraining on the accuracy (%) of MVCNN. The VGG-11 architecture is used and the full training/test split of the ModelNet40 dataset is used.

Model	Per class	Per instance
VGG-11 w/ ImageNet pretraining	92.4	95.0
VGG-11 w/o ImageNet pretraining	88.7	91.3

Effect of Shape Rendering. We analyze the effect of different rendering approaches for input to a MVCNN model in Table 3. Sphere rendering proposed in [24] refers to rendering each point as a sphere and was shown to improve performance with AlexNet MVCNN architectures. We first compared the tight field-of-view rendering with black background in this work to the rendering in [31]. Since [31] only reported results on the 80/20 training/test split, we first compared the performance of the VGG-11 networks using images from [31]. The performance difference was negligible. However with our shaded images the performance of the VGG-11 network improves by more than 2%.

Using depth images, the per instance accuracy is 3.4% lower than using shaded images, but concatenating shaded images with depth images gives 1.2% improvement. Furthermore, we found the shading information only provides 1.4% improvements over the binary silhouette images. This suggests that most of the discriminative shape information used by the MVCNN approaches lie in the boundary of the object.

Table 3. Accuracy (%) of MVCNN with different rendering methods. The number in the brackets are the number of views used. 12 views are used if not specified.

Model	Rendering	Full training/test		80/20 training/test	
		Per class	Per instance	Per class	Per instance
VGG-M	Shaded from [31]	-	-	89.9	89.9
VGG-M	Shaded from [31] (80×)	-	-	90.1	90.1
VGG-11	Shaded from [31]	-	-	89.1	89.1
VGG-11	Shaded	**92.4**	**95.0**	**92.4**	**92.4**
VGG-11	Depth	89.8	91.6		
VGG-11	Shaded + Depth	94.7	96.2		
VGG-11	Silhouettes	90.7	93.6		
AlexNet	Sphere rendering (20×)	89.7	92.0		
AlexNet-MR	Sphere rendering (20×)	91.4	93.8		

3.3 Cross Modal Distillation

Knowledge distillation [4,10] was proposed for model compression tasks. They showed the performance of the model can be improved by training to imitate the output of a more accurate model. This technique has also been applied on transferring rich representations across modalities. For example, a model trained with images can be used to guide learning of a model for depth images [7], or to a model for sound waves [1]. We investigate such techniques for learning across different 3D representations; Specifically from MVCNN model to PointNet and VoxNet models.

To do this we first train the ImageNet initialized VGG-11 network on the full training set. The logits (the last layer before the softmax) are extracted on the training set. A PointNet (or VoxNet) model is then trained to minimize

$$\sum_{i=1}^{n} \mathcal{L}\left(\sigma(\mathbf{z}_i), y_i\right) + \lambda \sum_{i=1}^{n} \mathcal{L}\left(\sigma\left(\frac{\mathbf{z}_i}{T}\right), \sigma\left(\frac{\mathbf{x}_i}{T}\right)\right) \tag{2}$$

where $\mathbf{x}_i$ and $\mathbf{z}_i$ are the logits from the MVCNN model and from the model being trained respectively, y_i is the class label of the input $\mathbf{s}_i$, $\sigma(x)$ is the softmax function, and $\mathcal{L}$ is the cross-entropy loss $\mathcal{L}(p,q) = -\sum p_i \log q_i$. T is the temperature for smoothing the targets. λ, T are set by grid search for $T \in [1,20], \lambda \in [1,100]$. For example, in PointNet the best hyper-parameters are $T = 20, \lambda = 50$ when training set is small, and $T = 15, \lambda = 10$ when the training set is larger. In VoxNet we set $T = 10, \lambda = 100$ in all cases. Figure 4 shows the result of training VoxNet and PointNet with distillation. For VoxNet the per instance accuracy is improved from 85.6% to 87.4% with whole training set; For PointNet the accuracy is improved from 89.1% to 89.4%. The improvement is slightly bigger when there is less training data.

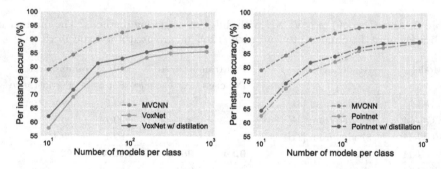

Fig. 4. Model distillation from MVCNN to VoxNet and PointNet. The accuracy is improved by 1.8% for VoxNet and 0.3% for PointNet with whole training set.

3.4   Tradeoffs Between Learned Representations

In this Section we analyze the tradeoffs between the different shape classifiers. Table 4 compares their speed, memory, and accuracy. The MVCNN model has more parameters and is slower, but the accuracy is 5.9% better than PointNet and 9.4% better than VoxNet. Even though the number of FLOPS are far higher for MVCNN the relative efficiency of 2D convolutions results in slightly longer evaluation time compared to VoxNet and PointNet.

We further use an ensemble model combining images, voxels, and point cloud representations. A simple way is to average the predictions from different models. As shown in Fig. 5, the ensemble of VoxNet and PointNet has better performance than using single model. However, the predictions from MVCNN dominate VoxNet and PointNet and gives no benefit for combining the predictions from other models with MVCNN. A more complex scheme where we trained a linear model on top of features extracted from penultimate layers of these networks did not provide any improvements either.

Table 4. Accuracy, speed and memory comparison of different models. Memory usage during training which includes parameters, gradients, and layer activations, for a batch size 64 is shown. Forward-pass time is also calculated with batch size 64 using PyTorch with a single GTX Titan X for all the models. The input resolutions are 224×224 for MVCNN, 32^3 for VoxNet, and 1024 points for PointNet. The accuracy numbers in brackets are for models trained with distillation as described in Sect. 3.3.

Model	Forward-pass time	#params	Memory (GB)	Per class acc. (%)	Per ins. acc. (%)
MVCNN	25.8 ms	128.9M	10.0	92.4	95.0
VoxNet	1.3 ms	1.4M	2.0	81.4 (82.5)	85.6 (87.4)
PointNet	3.1 ms	3.5M	4.4	86.1 (86.7)	89.1 (89.4)

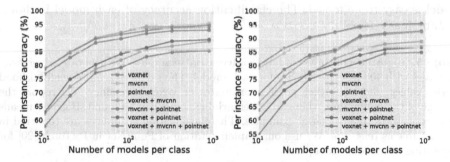

Fig. 5. Accuracy obtained by ensembling models. Left shows results by averaging the predictions while right shows results by training a linear model on the concatenated features extracted from different models.

3.5 Robustness to Adversarial Examples

In this section we analyze and compare the robustness of three shape classification models to adversarial examples. Adversarial examples are generated using the stochastic gradient ascent procedure described in Sect. 2.3. We search the threshold ϵ from 0.001 to 0.9, and find the minimum value of ϵ where we can generate an adversarial example in 1000 iterations with learning rate $\alpha = 1 \times 10^{-6}$.

To make a quantitative analysis between VoxMVCNN and VoxNet, we use the following procedure. Given an input $\mathbf{s}$ and a classifier $\phi(\mathbf{s}, y)$, the "hardest" target class is defined as $y'_{\mathbf{s},\phi(\mathbf{s},y)} = \operatorname{argmin}_y \phi(\mathbf{s}, y)$. We select the first five models for each class from the test set. For each model, we select two target classes $y'_{\mathbf{s},\phi_1(\mathbf{s},y)}$ and $y'_{\mathbf{s},\phi_2(\mathbf{s},y)}$ where ϕ_1 is VoxMVCNN and ϕ_2 is VoxNet. There are total 400 pairs of test cases $(\mathbf{s}, y')$. We say an adversarial example $\mathbf{s}'$ can be found when $y' = \operatorname{argmax}_y \phi(\mathbf{s}', y)$ with $\epsilon \leq 0.9$.

As shown in Table 5, we can generate 399 adversarial examples out of 400 test cases for VoxMVCNN, but only 370 adversarial examples for VoxNet. We then report the minimum ϵ where adversarial examples can be found in each test case. The average ϵ of VoxMVCNN is smaller than VoxNet, which suggests that VoxMVCNN is easier to be fooled by adversarial examples than VoxNet. We also use the VoxMVCNN model trained without ImageNet pre-training. Surprisingly, the model without pre-training is more robust to adversarial examples as the mean of ϵ is bigger than the model with pre-training. As for PointNet, we can generate 379 adversarial examples. Note that the ϵ value here is not comparable with other voxel representations, since in this case we are changing point coordinates instead of occupancy levels.

We also show some qualitative adversarial examples in Figs. 6 and 7. The voxels are scaled according to their occupancy level. In Fig. 6 the input and the target classes are the same for each row, where the target labels are cup, keyboard, bench, and door from top to bottom. In Fig. 7 we use the same input model but set different target class for each column. The differences of adversarial examples for VoxMVCNN are almost imperceptible, as the ϵ is too small and the model is easy to be fooled. The classification accuracy of each model is shown in Table 5 as reference.

Table 5. Robustness of three models to adversarial examples. We generate adversarial examples with 400 test cases $(\mathbf{s}, y')$ for each model. The ϵ defines a L_∞ ϵ-neighborhood of the values that are either point coordinates or voxel occupancy. We report the average of the minimum ϵ where an adversarial example can be found. Bigger ϵ means more robustness to adversarial examples. The classification accuracies are reported in the last row as reference. We use our implementation of PointNet in PyTorch [20] for generating adversarial examples.

	PointNet	VoxNet	VoxMVCNN w/o pre-training	VoxMVCNN w/ pre-training
# Adversarial examples	379	370	290	399
ϵ	0.045 ± 0.054	0.061 ± 0.057	0.041 ± 0.027	0.006 ± 0.006
Per inst. acc. (%)	86.8	85.6	84.4	88.2

3.6 Comparison to Prior Work

We compare our MVCNN result with prior works in Table 6. The results are grouped by the input type. For multi-view image-based models, our MVCNN achieves 95.0% per instance accuracy, which is the best result between all competing approaches. Rotation Net [13], which predicts the object pose and class

Point Cloud	PointNet	Voxels	VoxNet	VoxMVCNN

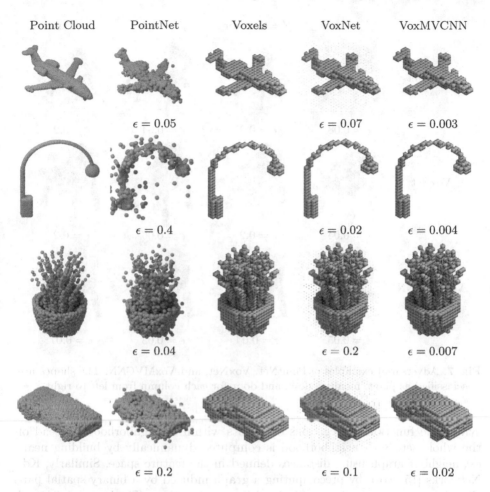

Fig. 6. Adversarial examples of PointNet, VoxNet, and VoxMVCNN. The shapes are misclassified as cup, keyboard, bench, and door for each row from top to bottom. Voxel size represents occupancy level.

labels at the same time, is 0.2% worse than our MVCNN. Dominant Set Clustering [34] works by clustering image features across views and pooling within the clusters. Its performance is 1.0% lower than RotationNet. MVCNN-MultiRes [23] is the most related to our work. They showed that MVCNN with sphere rendering can achieve better accuracy than voxel-based network, suggesting that there is room for improvement in VoxNet. Our VoxNet experiment corroborates to this conclusion. Furthermore, MVCNN-MultiRes uses images in multiple resolutions to boost its performance.

For point-based methods, PointNet [32] and DeepSets [38] use symmetric functions, i.e. max/mean pooling layers, to generate permutation invariant point cloud descriptions. DynamicGraph [36] builds upon PointNet by performing

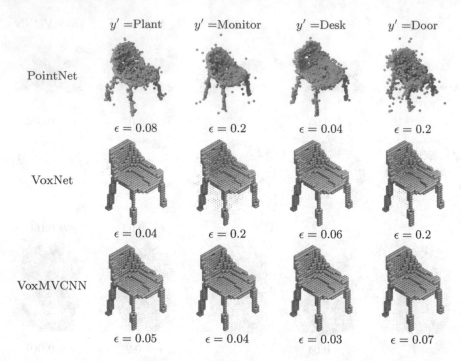

Fig. 7. Adversarial examples of PointNet, VoxNet, and VoxMVCNN. The shapes are misclassified as plant, monitor, desk, and door for each column from left to right.

symmetric function aggregations on points within a neighborhood, instead of the whole set. Such neighborhood is computed dynamically by building nearest neighbor graph using distances defined in the feature space. Similarly, Kd-Networks [15] work by precomputing a graph induced by a binary spatial partitioning tree and use it to apply local linear operations. The best point-based method is 2.8% less accurate then our MVCNN.

For voxel-based methods, VoxNet [17] and 3DShapeNets [37] work by applying 3D convolutions on voxels. ORION [27] is based on VoxNet but predicts the orientation in addition to class labels. OctNet [25] and O-CNN [35] are able to process higher resolution grids by using an octree representation. Fusion-Net [9] combines the voxel and image representations to improve the performance to 90.8%. Our experiments in Sect. 3.4 suggests that since MVCNN already has 95.0% accuracy the benefit of combining different representations is not effective.

Table 6. Accuracy (%) of state-of-the-art methods with different 3D representations. PC refers to point clouds. The order is grouped by input type and sorted by accuracy.

Model	Input	Per class acc.	Per ins. acc.
Our MVCNN	Images	**92.4**	**95.0**
RotationNet [13]		-	94.8
Dominant Set Clustering [34]		-	93.8
MVCNN-MultiRes [23]		91.4	93.8
PANORAMA-NN [28]			90.7
MVCNN [31]		90.1	90.1
DynamicGraph [36]	PC	90.2	92.2
Kd-Networks [15]		-	91.8
LocalFeatureNet [29]		-	90.8
PointNet++ [22]		-	90.7
DeepSets [38]		-	90.0
PointNet [32]		86.2	89.2
VRN Single [3]	Voxels	-	91.3
O-CNN [35]			90.6
ORION [27]		-	89.7
VoxNet [17]		-	83.0
3DShapeNets [37]		77.3	84.7
PointNet++ [22]	PC+Normal	-	91.9
FusionNet [9]	Voxels+Images	-	90.8

4 Conclusion

We investigated on different representations and models for 3D shape classification task, which resulted in a new state-of-the-art on the ModelNet40 benchmark. We analyzed the generalization of MVCNN, PointNet, and VoxNet by varying the number of training examples. Our results indicate that multiview-based methods provide better generalizability and outperform other methods on the full dataset even without ImageNet pretraining or training with binary silhouettes. We also analyzed cross-modal distillation and showed improvements on VoxNet and PointNet by distilling knowledge from MVCNN. Finally, we analyzed the robustness of the models to adversarial perturbations and concluded that point-based networks are more robust to point perturbations, while multiview and voxel-based networks can be fooled by imperceptible perturbations.

Acknowledgment. We acknowledge support from NSF (#1617917, #1749833) and the MassTech Collaborative grant for funding the UMass GPU cluster.

References

1. Aytar, Y., Vondrick, C., Torralba, A.: SoundNet: learning sound representations from unlabeled video. In: Neural Information Processing Systems (NIPS) (2016)
2. Blender Online Community: Blender - a 3D modelling and rendering package. Blender Foundation, Blender Institute, Amsterdam. http://www.blender.org
3. Brock, A., Lim, T., Ritchie, J.M., Weston, N.: Generative and discriminative voxel modeling with convolutional neural networks. arXiv preprint arXiv:1608.04236 (2016)
4. Buciluă, C., Caruana, R., Niculescu-Mizil, A.: Model compression. In: Proceedings of the 12th ACM SIGKDD International Conference on Knowledge Discovery and Data Mining (KDD) (2006)
5. Gadhela, M., Maji, S., Wang, R.: Unsupervised 3D shape induction from 2D views of multiple objects. In: International Conference on 3D Vision 2018 (2017)
6. Goodfellow, I., Shlens, J., Szegedy, C.: Explaining and harnessing adversarial examples. In: International Conference on Learning Representations (ICLR) (2015)
7. Gupta, S., Hoffman, J., Malik, J.: Cross modal distillation for supervision transfer. In: Computer Vision and Pattern Recognition (CVPR) (2016)
8. He, K., Zhang, X., Ren, S., Sun, J.: Deep residual learning for image recognition. In: Computer Vision and Pattern Recognition (CVPR) (2016)
9. Hegde, V., Zadeh, R.: FusionNet: 3d object classification using multiple data representations. arXiv preprint arXiv:1607.05695 (2016)
10. Hinton, G., Vinyals, O., Dean, J.: Distilling knowledge in a neural network. In: Neural Information Processing Systems (NIPS) (2014)
11. Ioffe, S., Szegedy, C.: Batch normalization: accelerating deep network training by reducing internal covariate shift. In: International Conference on Machine Learning (ICML) (2015)
12. Kalogerakis, E., Averkiou, M., Maji, S., Chaudhuri, S.: 3D shape segmentation with projective convolutional networks (2017)
13. Kanezaki, A., Matsushita, Y., Nishida, Y.: RotationNet: joint object categorization and pose estimation using multiviews from unsupervised viewpoints. arXiv preprint arXiv:1603.06208 (2016)
14. Kingma, D.P., Ba, J.: Adam: a method for stochastic optimization. arXiv preprint arXiv:1412.6980 (2014)
15. Klokov, R., Lempitsky, V.: Escape from cells: deep kd-networks for the recognition of 3D point cloud models. In: International Conference on Computer Vision (ICCV) (2017)
16. Kurakin, A., Goodfellow, I.J., Bengio, S.: Adversarial examples in the physical world. arXiv preprint arXiv:1607.02533 (2016)
17. Maturana, D., Scherer, S.: VoxNet: a 3d convolutional neural network for real-time object recognition. In: IEEE International Conference on Intelligent Robots and Systems (IROS) (2015)
18. Meagher, D.J.: Octree encoding: a new technique for the representation, manipulation and display of arbitrary 3-d objects by computer. Electrical and Systems Engineering Department Rensseiaer Polytechnic Institute Image Processing Laboratory (1980)
19. Nguyen, A., Yosinski, J., Clune, J.: Deep neural networks are easily fooled: high confidence predictions for unrecognizable images. In: Computer Vision and Pattern Recognition (CVPR) (2015)
20. Paszke, A., et al.: Automatic differentiation in PyTorch (2017)

21. Phong, B.T.: Illumination for computer generated pictures. Commun. ACM **18**(6), 311–317 (1975)
22. Qi, C.R., Yi, L., Su, H., Guibas, L.J.: Pointnet++: deep hierarchical feature learning on point sets in a metric space. In: Neural Information Processing Systems (NIPS) (2017)
23. Qi, C.R., Su, H., Nießner, M., Dai, A., Yan, M., Guibas, L.: Volumetric and multiview CNNs for object classification on 3d data. In: Computer Vision and Pattern Recognition (CVPR) (2016)
24. Qi, C.R., Su, H., Nießner, M., Dai, A., Yan, M., Guibas, L.: Volumetric andmultiview CNNs for object classification on 3d data. In: Computer Vision and Pattern Recognition (CVPR) (2016)
25. Riegler, G., Ulusoy, A.O., Geiger, A.: OctNet: learning deep 3d representations at high resolutions. In: Computer Vision and Pattern Recognition (CVPR) (2017)
26. Russakovsky, O.: Imagenet large scale visual recognition challenge. Int. J. Comput. Vis. (IJCV) **115**(3), 211–252 (2015)
27. Sedaghat, N., Zolfaghari, M., Amiri, E., Brox, T.: Orientation-boosted voxel nets for 3D object recognition. In: British Machine Vision Conference (BMVC) (2017)
28. Sfikas, K., Theoharis, T., Pratikakis, I.: Exploiting the panorama representation for convolutional neural network classification and retrieval. In: Eurographics Workshop on 3D Object Retrieval (2017)
29. Shen, Y., Feng, C., Yang, Y., Tian, D.: Neighbors do help: deeply exploiting local structures of point clouds. arXiv preprint arXiv:1712.06760 (2017)
30. Simonyan, K., Zisserman, A.: Very deep convolutional networks for large-scale image recognition. arXiv preprint arXiv:1409.1556 (2014)
31. Su, H., Maji, S., Kalogerakis, E., Learned-Miller, E.G.: Multi-view convolutional neural networks for 3D shape recognition. In: International Conference on Computer Vision (ICCV) (2015)
32. Su, H., Qi, C., Mo, K., Guibas, L.: PointNet: deep learning on point sets for 3D classification and segmentation. In: Computer Vision and Pattern Recognition (CVPR) (2017)
33. Szegedy, C., et al.: Intriguing properties of neural networks. arXiv preprint arXiv:1312.6199 (2013)
34. Wang, C., Pelillo, M., Siddiqi, K.: Dominant set clustering and pooling for multiview 3D object recognition. In: British Machine Vision Conference (BMVC) (2017)
35. Wang, P.S., Liu, Y., Guo, Y.X., Sun, C.Y., Tong, X.: O-CNN: octree-based convolutional neural networks for 3D shape analysis. ACM Trans. Graph. (SIGGRAPH) **36**(4), 72 (2017)
36. Wang, Y., Sun, Y., Liu, Z., Sarma, S.E., Bronstein, M.M., Solomon, J.M.: Dynamic graph CNN for learning on point clouds. arXiv preprint arXiv:1801.07829 (2018)
37. Wu, Z., et al.: 3D ShapeNets: a deep representation for volumetric shapes. In: Computer Vision and Pattern Recognition (CVPR) (2015)
38. Zaheer, M., Kottur, S., Ravanbakhsh, S., Poczos, B., Salakhutdinov, R.R., Smola, A.J.: Deep sets. In: Neural Information Processing Systems (NIPS) (2017)

3D-PSRNet: Part Segmented 3D Point Cloud Reconstruction from a Single Image

Priyanka Mandikal$^{(\boxtimes)}$ (ID), K. L. Navaneet (ID), and R. Venkatesh Babu (ID)

Indian Institute of Science, Bangalore, India
priyanka.mandikal@gmail.com, {navaneetl,venky}@iisc.ac.in

Abstract. We propose a mechanism to reconstruct part annotated 3D point clouds of objects given just a single input image. We demonstrate that jointly training for both reconstruction and segmentation leads to improved performance in both the tasks, when compared to training for each task individually. The key idea is to propagate information from each task so as to aid the other during the training procedure. Towards this end, we introduce a *location-aware segmentation loss* in the training regime. We empirically show the effectiveness of the proposed loss in generating more faithful part reconstructions while also improving segmentation accuracy. We thoroughly evaluate the proposed approach on different object categories from the ShapeNet dataset to obtain improved results in reconstruction as well as segmentation. Codes are available at https://github.com/val-iisc/3d-psrnet.

Keywords: Point cloud · 3D reconstruction · 3D part segmentation

1 Introduction

Human object perception is based on semantic reasoning [8]. When viewing the objects around us, we can not only mentally estimate their 3D shape from limited information, but we can also reason about object semantics. For instance, upon viewing the image of an airplane in Fig. 1, we might deduce that it contains four distinct parts - body, wings, tail, and turbine. Recognition of these parts further enhances our understanding of individual part geometries as well as the overall 3D structure of the airplane. This ability to perceive objects driven by semantics is important for our interaction with the world around us and the manipulation of objects within it.

In machine vision, the ability to infer the 3D structures from single-view images has far-reaching applications in the field of robotics and perception. Semantic understanding of the perceived 3D object is particularly advantageous in tasks such as robot grasping, object manipulation, etc.

P. Mandikal and K. L. Navaneet—Equal contribution.

L. Leal-Taixé and S. Roth (Eds.): ECCV 2018 Workshops, LNCS 11131, pp. 662–674, 2019.
https://doi.org/10.1007/978-3-030-11015-4_50

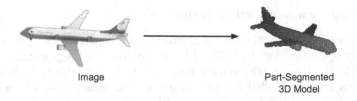

Image   Part-Segmented
                                         3D Model

Fig. 1. Semantic point cloud reconstruction.

Deep neural networks have been successfully employed for tackling the problem of 3D reconstruction. Most of the existing literature propose techniques for predicting the voxelized representation format. However, this representation has a number of drawbacks. First, it suffers from sparsity of information. All the information that is needed to perceive the 3D structure is provided by the surface voxels, while the voxels within the volume increase the representation space with minimal addition of information. Second, the neural network architectures required for processing and predicting 3D voxel maps make use of 3D CNNs, which are computationally heavy and lead to considerable overhead during training and inference. For these reasons, there have been concerted efforts to explore representations that involve reduced computational complexity compared to voxel formats. Very recently, there have been works focusing on designing neural network architectures and loss formulations to process and predict 3D point clouds [3,9,13,14,16]. Since point clouds consist of points being sampled uniformly on the object's surface, they are able to encode maximal information about the object's 3D characteristics. The information-rich encoding and compute-friendly architectures makes it an ideal candidate for 3D shape generation and reconstruction tasks. Hence, we consider the point cloud as our representation format.

In this work, we seek to answer three important questions in the tasks of semantic object reconstruction and segmentation: (1) What is an effective way of inferring an accurate semantically annotated 3D point cloud representation of an object when provided with its two-dimensional image counterpart? (2) How do we incorporate object geometry into the segmentation framework so as to improve segmentation accuracy? (3) How do we incorporate semantic understanding into the reconstruction framework so as to improve the reconstruction of individual parts? We achieve the former by training a neural network to jointly optimize for the reconstruction as well as segmentation losses. We empirically show that such joint training achieves superior performance on both reconstruction and segmentation tasks when compared to two different neural networks that are trained on each task independently. To enable the flow of information between the two tasks, we propose a novel loss formulation to integrate the knowledge from both the predicted semantics and the reconstructed geometry.

In summary, our contributions in this work are as follows:

– We propose 3D-PSRNet, a part segmented 3D reconstruction network, which is jointly optimized for the tasks of reconstruction and segmentation.
– To enable the flow of information from one task to another, we introduce a novel loss function called *location-aware segmentation loss*. We empirically show that the proposed loss function aids in the generation of more faithful part reconstructions, while also resulting in more accurate segmentations.
– We evaluate 3D-PSRNet on a synthetic dataset to achieve state-of-the-art performance in the task of semantic 3D object reconstruction from a single image.

2   Related Work

3D Reconstruction

In recent times, deep learning based approaches have achieved significant progress in the field of 3D reconstruction. The earlier works focused on voxel-based representations [2,4,19]. Girdhar *et al.* [4] map the 3D model and the corresponding 2D representations to a common embedding space to obtain a representation which is both predictable from 2D images and is capable of generating 3D objects. Wu *et al.* [19] utilize variational auto-encoders with an additional adversarial criterion to obtain improved reconstructions. Choy *et al.* [2] employ a 3D recurrent network to obtain reconstructions from multiple input images. While the above works directly utilize the ground truth 3D models in the training stage, [17,18,20,22] try to reconstruct the 3D object using 2D observations from multiple view-points.

Several recent works have made use of point clouds in place of voxels to represent 3D objects [3,5,11]. Fan *et al.* [3] showed that point cloud prediction is not only computationally efficient but also outperforms voxel-based reconstruction approaches. Groueix *et al.* [5] represented a 3D shape as a collection of parametric surface elements and constructed a mesh from the predicted point cloud. Mandikal *et al.* [11] trained an image encoder in the latent space of a point cloud auto-encoder, while also enforcing a constraint to obtain diverse reconstructions. However, all of the above works focus solely on the point cloud reconstruction task.

3D Semantic Segmentation

Semantic segmentation using neural networks has been extensively studied in the 2D domain [6,10]. The corresponding task in 3D has been recently explored by works such as [7,12–15]. Song *et al.* [15] take in a depth map of a scene as input and predict a voxelized occupancy grid containing semantic labels on a per-voxel basis. They optimize for the multi-class segmentation loss and argue that scene completion aids semantic label prediction and vice versa. Our representation format is a 3D point cloud while [15] outputs voxels. This gives rise to a number of differences in the training procedure. Voxel based methods predict an occupancy grid and hence optimize for the cross-entropy loss for both reconstruction as well as segmentation. On the other hand, point cloud based works optimize distance-based metrics for reconstruction and cross-entropy for segmentation. We introduce a location-aware segmentation loss tailored for point cloud representations.

[13,14] introduce networks that take in point cloud data so as to perform classification and segmentation. They introduce network architectures and loss formulations that are able to handle the inherent un-orderedness of the point cloud data. While [3] predicts only the 3D point cloud geometry from 2D images, and [13,14] segment input point clouds, our approach stresses the importance of jointly optimizing for reconstruction and segmentation while transitioning from 2D to 3D.

3   Approach

In this section, we introduce our model, 3D-PSRNet, which generates a part-segmented 3D point cloud from a 2D RGB image. As a baseline for comparison, we train two separate networks for the task of reconstruction and segmentation (Fig. 2(a)). Given an RGB image I as input, the reconstruction network ($baseline_{rec}$) outputs a 3D point cloud $\widehat{X}_p \in \mathbb{R}^{N_p \times 3}$, where N_p is the number of points in the point cloud. Given a 3D point cloud $X_p \in \mathbb{R}^{N_p \times 3}$ as input, the segmentation network ($baseline_{seg}$) predicts the class labels $\widehat{X}_c \in \mathbb{R}^{N_p \times N_c}$, where N_c is the number of classes present in the object category. During inference, image I is passed through $baseline_{rec}$ to obtain $\widehat{X}_p$, which is then passed through $baseline_{seg}$ to obtain $\widehat{X}_c$.

Our training pipeline consists of jointly predicting $(\widehat{X}_p, \widehat{X}_c)$ (Fig. 2(b)). The reconstruction network is modified such that an additional N_c predictions, representing the class probabilities of each point, are made at the final layer. The network is simultaneously trained with reconstruction and segmentation losses, as explained below.

3.1   Loss Formulation

Reconstruction Loss. We require a loss formulation that is invariant to the order of points in the point cloud. To satisfy this criterion, the Chamfer distance between the ground truth point cloud X_p and predicted point cloud $\widehat{X}_p$ is chosen as the reconstruction loss. The loss function is defined as:

$$\mathcal{L}_{rec} = d_{Chamfer}(X_p, \widehat{X}_p) = \sum_{i \in X_p} \min_{j \in \widehat{X}_p} ||i - j||_2^2 + \sum_{i \in \widehat{X}_p} \min_{j \in X_p} ||i - j||_2^2 \qquad (1)$$

Segmentation Loss. We use point-wise softmax cross-entropy loss (denoted by $\mathcal{L}_{ce}$) between the ground truth class labels X_c and the predicted class labels $\widehat{X}_c$. For the training of $baseline_{seg}$, since there is direct point-to-point correspondence

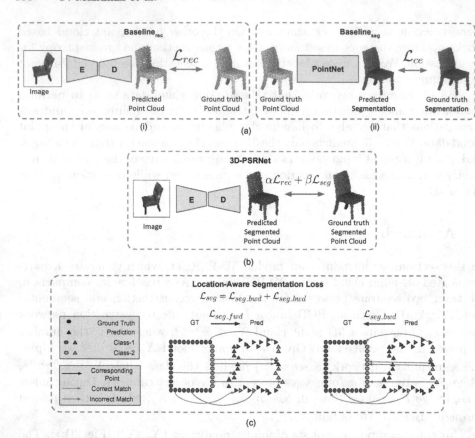

Fig. 2. Semantic point cloud reconstruction approaches. (a) Baseline: (i) A reconstruction network takes in an image input and predicts a 3D point cloud reconstruction of it. (ii) A segmentation network takes in a 3D point cloud as input and predicts semantic labels for every input point. (b) Our approach takes in an image as input and predicts a part segmented 3D point cloud by jointly optimizing for both reconstruction and segmentation, while also additionally propagating information from the semantic labels to improve reconstruction. (c) Point correspondences for location-aware segmentation loss. Incorrect reconstructions and segmentations are both penalized. The overall segmentation loss is the summation of the forward and backward segmentation losses.

between X_p and $\widehat{X}_c$, we directly apply the segmentation loss as the cross-entropy loss between X_c and $\widehat{X}_c$:

$$\mathcal{L}_{ce}(X_c, \widehat{X}_c) = \sum_{\substack{x \in X_c \\ \hat{x} \in \widehat{X}_c}} [x \log(\hat{x}) + (1 - x) \log(1 - \hat{x})] \qquad (2)$$

However, during joint training, there exists no such point-to-point correspondence between the ground truth and predicted class labels. We therefore introduce the *location-aware segmentation loss* to propagate semantic information between matching point pairs (Fig. 2(c)). The loss consists of two terms:

(1) **Forward segmentation loss ($\mathcal{L}_{seg\_fwd}$):** For every point $i \in X_p$, we find the closest point $i' \in \widehat{X}_p$, and apply L_{ce} on their corresponding class labels.

$$\mathcal{L}_{seg\_fwd} = \frac{1}{N_p} \sum_{i \in X_p} \mathcal{L}_{ce}(X_{c_i}, \widehat{X}_{c_{i'}}) \tag{3}$$

(2) **Backward segmentation loss ($\mathcal{L}_{seg\_bwd}$):** For every point $i \in \widehat{X}_p$, we find the closest point $i' \in X_p$, and apply L_{ce} on their corresponding class labels.

$$\mathcal{L}_{seg\_bwd} = \frac{1}{N_p} \sum_{i \in \widehat{X}_p} \mathcal{L}_{ce}(X_{c_{i'}}, \widehat{X}_{c_i}) \tag{4}$$

The overall segmentation loss is then the summation of the forward and backward segmentation losses:

$$\mathcal{L}_{seg} = \mathcal{L}_{seg\_fwd} + \mathcal{L}_{seg\_bwd} \tag{5}$$

The total loss during joint training is then given by,

$$\mathcal{L}_{tot} = \alpha \mathcal{L}_{rec} + \beta \mathcal{L}_{seg} \tag{6}$$

3.2 Implementation Details

For training the baseline segmentation network $baseline_{seg}$, we follow the architecture of the segmentation network of PointNet [13], which consists of ten 1D convolutional layers of filter sizes $[64, 64, 64, 128, 1024, 512, 256, 128, 128, N_c]$, where N_c is the number of class labels. A global maxpool function is applied after the fifth layer and the resulting feature is concatenated with each individual point feature, as is done in the original paper. Learning rate is set to $5e^{-4}$ and batch normalization is applied at all the layers of the network. The networks for the baseline reconstruction network and the joint 3D-PSRNet are similar in architecture. They consist of four 2D convolutional layers with number of filters as $[32, 64, 128, 256]$, followed by four fully connected layers with output dimensions of size $[128, 128, 128, N_p \times 3]$ (reconstruction) and $[128, 128, 128, N_p \times (3 + N_c)]$ (joint), where N_p is the number of points in the point cloud. We set N_p to be 1024 in all our experiments. Learning rate for $baseline_{rec}$ and 3D-PSRNet are set to $5e^{-5}$ and $5e^{-4}$ respectively. We use a minibatch size of 32 in all the experiments. We train the individual reconstruction and segmentation networks for 1000 epochs, while the joint network (3D-PSRNet) is trained for 500 epochs. We choose the best model according to the corresponding minimum loss. In Eq. 6, the values of α and β are set to $1e^4$ and 1 respectively for joint training.

4   Experiments

4.1   Dataset

We train all our networks on synthetic models from the ShapeNet dataset [1] whose part annotated ground truth point clouds are provided by [21]. Our dataset comprises of 7346 models from three exemplar categories - chair, car and airplane. We render each model from ten different viewing angles with azimuth values in the range of $[0°, 360°]$ and elevation values in the range of $[-20°, 40°]$ so as to obtain a dataset of size 73,460. We use the train/validation/test split provided by [21] and train a single model on all the categories in all our experiments.

4.2   Evaluation Methodology

(1) **Reconstruction:** We report both the Chamfer Distance (Eq. 1) as well as the Earth Mover's Distance (or EMD) computed on 1024 points in all our evaluations. EMD between two point sets $\widehat{X}_p$ and X_p is given by:

$$d_{EMD}(X_p, \widehat{X}_p) = \min_{\phi:X_p \to \widehat{X}_p} \sum_{x \in X_p} ||x - \phi(x)||_2 \tag{7}$$

where $\phi : X_p \to \widehat{X}_p$ is a bijection. For computing the metrics, we renormalize both the ground truth and predicted point clouds within a bounding box of length 1 unit.

(2) **Segmentation:** We formulate part segmentation as a per-point classification problem. Evaluation metric is mIoU on points. For each shape S of category C, we calculate the shape mIoU as follows: For each part type in category C, compute IoU between groundtruth and prediction. If the union of groundtruth and prediction points is empty, then count part IoU as 1. Then we average IoUs for all part types in category C to get mIoU for that shape. To calculate mIoU for the category, we take average of mIoUs for all shapes in that category. Since there is no correspondence between the ground truth and predicted points, we use a mechanism similar to the one described in Sect. 3.1 for computing the forward and backward mIoUs, before averaging them out to get the final mIoU as follows:

$$mIoU(X_c, \widehat{X}_c) = \frac{1}{2N_c} \sum_i \frac{N_{ii}}{\sum_j N_{ij} + \sum_j N_{ji} - N_{ii}}$$
$$+ \frac{1}{2N_c} \sum_i \frac{\widehat{N}_{ii}}{\sum_j \widehat{N}_{ij} + \sum_j \widehat{N}_{ji} - \widehat{N}_{ii}} \tag{8}$$

where N_{ij} is the number of points in category i in X_c predicted as category j in $\widehat{X}_c$ for forward point correspondences between X_c and $\widehat{X}_c$. Similarly $\widehat{N}_{ij}$ is for backward point correspondences. N_c is the total number of categories.

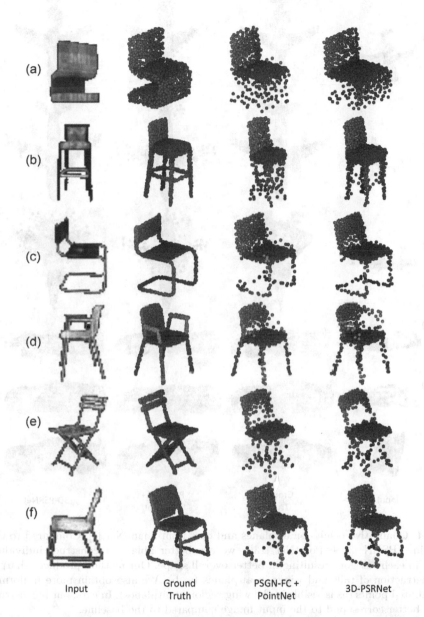

Input	Ground Truth	PSGN-FC + PointNet	3D-PSRNet

Fig. 3. Qualitative results on the chair category from ShapeNet [1]. Compared to the baseline (PSGN [3] + PointNet [13]), we are better able to capture the details present in the input image. Individual parts such as legs (b, e, f) and handles (d) are reconstructed with greater accuracy. Additionally, while outlier points are present in the baseline (a, c), our method produces more uniformly distributed reconstructions.

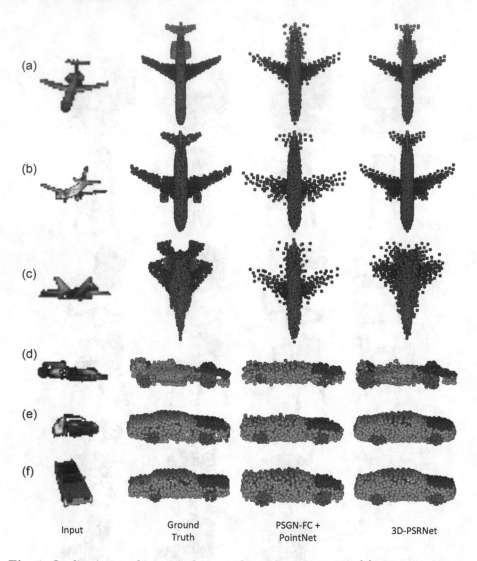

Fig. 4. Qualitative results on airplanes and cars from ShapeNet [1]. Compared to the baseline (PSGN [3] + PointNet [13]), we are better able to reconstruct individual parts in each category resulting in better overall shape. Our method produces sharper reconstruction of tails and wings in airplanes (a, b). We also obtain more uniformly distributed points (as is visible in the wing region of airplanes). In cars, our reconstructions better correspond to the input image compared to the baseline.

4.3   Results

Table 1 presents the quantitative results on ShapeNet for the baseline and joint training approaches. 3D-PSRNet achieves considerable improvement in both the reconstruction (Chamfer, EMD) and segmentation (mIoU) metrics.

Table 1. Reconstruction and Segmentation metrics on ShapeNet [1]. 3D-PSRNet significantly outperforms the baseline in both the reconstruction and segmentation metrics on all categories. Chamfer and EMD metrics are scaled by 100.

Category	Metric	PSGN-FC [3] + PointNet [13]	3D-PSRNet
Chair	Chamfer	6.82	**6.57**
	EMD	11.37	**10.10**
	mIoU	78.09	**81.92**
Car	Chamfer	5.48	**5.14**
	EMD	5.88	**5.53**
	mIoU	59.0	**61.57**
Airplane	Chamfer	**4.06**	4.06
	EMD	7.06	**6.24**
	mIoU	62.86	**68.64**
Mean	Chamfer	5.45	**5.26**
	EMD	8.10	**7.29**
	mIoU	66.65	**70.71**

It outperforms the baseline approach in every metric on all categories. On an average, we obtain **4.1%** improvement in mIoU.

The qualitative results are presented in Figs. 3 and 4. 3D-PSRNet obtains more faithful reconstructions compared to the baseline to achieve better correspondence with the input image. It also predicts more uniformly distributed point clouds. We observe that joint training results in reduced hallucination of parts (for e.g. predicting handles for chairs without handles) and spurious segmentations. We also show a few failure cases of our approach in Fig. 5. The network misses out on some finer structures present in the object (e.g. dual turbines in the case of airplanes). The reconstructions are poorer for uncommon input samples. However, these drawbacks also exist in the baseline approach.

4.4 Relative Importance of Reconstruction and Segmentation Losses

We present an ablative study on the relative weightage of the reconstruction and segmentation losses in Eq. 6. We fix the value of β to one, while α is varied from 10^2 to 10^5. Figure 6 presents the plot of Chamfer, EMD and mIoU metrics for varying values of α. We observe that for very low value of α, both the reconstruction and segmentation metrics are worse off, while there is minimal effect on the average metrics for α greater than 10^3. Based on Fig. 6, we set the value of α to 10^4 in all our experiments.

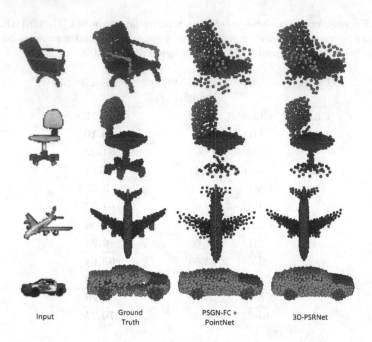

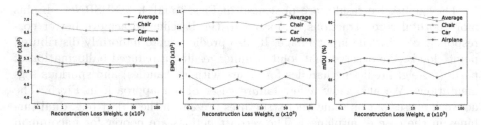

Fig. 5. Failure cases of our method. We notice that our method fails to get finer details in some instances, such as leg details in chairs, dual turbines present in airplanes, and certain car types.

Fig. 6. Ablative study on weight for reconstruction loss, α. Chamfer, EMD and mIOU metrics are calculated for different values of α. Based on the plots, we choose the value of α to be 10^4.

5   Conclusion

In this paper, we highlighted the importance of jointly learning the tasks of 3D reconstruction and object part segmentation. We introduced a loss formulation in the training regime to enable propagating information between the two tasks so as to generate more faithful part reconstructions while also improving segmentation accuracy. We thoroughly evaluated against existing reconstruction and segmentation baselines, to demonstrate the superiority of the proposed approach. Quantitative and qualitative evaluation on the ShapeNet dataset demonstrate the effectiveness in generating more accurate point clouds with detailed part information in comparison to the current state-of-the-art reconstruction and segmentation networks.

References

1. Chang, A.X., et al.: ShapeNet: an information-rich 3D model repository. arXiv preprint arXiv:1512.03012 (2015)
2. Choy, C.B., Xu, D., Gwak, J.Y., Chen, K., Savarese, S.: 3D-R2N2: a unified approach for single and multi-view 3D object reconstruction. In: Leibe, B., Matas, J., Sebe, N., Welling, M. (eds.) ECCV 2016. LNCS, vol. 9912, pp. 628–644. Springer, Cham (2016). https://doi.org/10.1007/978-3-319-46484-8_38
3. Fan, H., Su, H., Guibas, L.: A point set generation network for 3D object reconstruction from a single image. In: Conference on Computer Vision and Pattern Recognition (CVPR), vol. 38 (2017)
4. Girdhar, R., Fouhey, D.F., Rodriguez, M., Gupta, A.: Learning a predictable and generative vector representation for objects. In: Leibe, B., Matas, J., Sebe, N., Welling, M. (eds.) ECCV 2016. LNCS, vol. 9910, pp. 484–499. Springer, Cham (2016). https://doi.org/10.1007/978-3-319-46466-4_29
5. Groueix, T., Fisher, M., Kim, V.G., Russell, B., Aubry, M.: AtlasNet: a papier-Mâché approach to learning 3D surface generation. In: Proceedings IEEE Conference on Computer Vision and Pattern Recognition (CVPR) (2018)
6. He, K., Gkioxari, G., Dollár, P., Girshick, R.: Mask R-CNN. In: 2017 IEEE International Conference on Computer Vision (ICCV), pp. 2980–2988. IEEE (2017)
7. Kalogerakis, E., Averkiou, M., Maji, S., Chaudhuri, S.: 3D shape segmentation with projective convolutional networks. In: CVPR (2017)
8. Koopman, S.E., Mahon, B.Z., Cantlon, J.F.: Evolutionary constraints on human object perception. Cogn. Sci. **41**(8), 2126–2148 (2017)
9. Li, Y., Bu, R., Sun, M., Chen, B.: PointCNN. arXiv preprint arXiv:1801.07791 (2018)
10. Long, J., Shelhamer, E., Darrell, T.: Fully convolutional networks for semantic segmentation. In: Proceedings of the IEEE Conference on Computer Vision and Pattern Recognition, pp. 3431–3440 (2015)
11. Mandikal, P., Navaneet, K.L., Agarwal, M., Babu, R.V.: 3D-LMNet: latent embedding matching for accurate and diverse 3D point cloud reconstruction from a single image. In: Proceedings of the British Machine Vision Conference (BMVC) (2018)
12. Muralikrishnan, S., Kim, V.G., Chaudhuri, S.: Tags2Parts: discovering semantic regions from shape tags. In: Proceedings of the IEEE Conference on Computer Vision and Pattern Recognition, pp. 2926–2935 (2018)
13. Qi, C.R., Su, H., Mo, K., Guibas, L.J.: PointNet: deep learning on point sets for 3D classification and segmentation. Proc. Comput. Vis. Pattern Recogn. (CVPR) **1**(2), 4 (2017)
14. Qi, C.R., Yi, L., Su, H., Guibas, L.J.: PointNet++: deep hierarchical feature learning on point sets in a metric space. In: Advances in Neural Information Processing Systems, pp. 5105–5114 (2017)
15. Song, S., Yu, F., Zeng, A., Chang, A.X., Savva, M., Funkhouser, T.: Semantic scene completion from a single depth image. In: 2017 IEEE Conference on Computer Vision and Pattern Recognition (CVPR), pp. 190–198. IEEE (2017)
16. Su, H., et al.: SplatNet: sparse lattice networks for point cloud processing. arXiv preprint arXiv:1802.08275 (2018)

17. Tulsiani, S., Zhou, T., Efros, A.A., Malik, J.: Multi-view supervision for single-view reconstruction via differentiable ray consistency. In: CVPR, vol. 1, p. 3 (2017)

18. Wu, J., Wang, Y., Xue, T., Sun, X., Freeman, B., Tenenbaum, J.: MarrNet: 3D shape reconstruction via 2.5 d sketches. In: Advances In Neural Information Processing Systems, pp. 540–550 (2017)

19. Wu, J., Zhang, C., Xue, T., Freeman, B., Tenenbaum, J.: Learning a probabilistic latent space of object shapes via 3D generative-adversarial modeling. In: Advances in Neural Information Processing Systems, pp. 82–90 (2016)

20. Yan, X., Yang, J., Yumer, E., Guo, Y., Lee, H.: Perspective transformer nets: learning single-view 3D object reconstruction without 3D supervision. In: Advances in Neural Information Processing Systems, pp. 1696–1704 (2016)

21. Yi, L., et al.: A scalable active framework for region annotation in 3D shape collections. In: SIGGRAPH Asia (2016)

22. Zhu, R., Galoogahi, H.K., Wang, C., Lucey, S.: Rethinking reprojection: closing the loop for pose-aware shape reconstruction from a single image. In: 2017 IEEE International Conference on Computer Vision (ICCV), pp. 57–65. IEEE (2017)

Exploiting Multi-layer Features Using a CNN-RNN Approach for RGB-D Object Recognition

Ali Caglayan[1,2]([⊠]) [iD] and Ahmet Burak Can[2] [iD]

[1] Department of Computer Engineering, Bingol University, Bingol, Turkey
[2] Department of Computer Engineering, Hacettepe University, Ankara, Turkey
{alicaglayan,abc}@cs.hacettepe.edu.tr

Abstract. This paper proposes an approach for RGB-D object recognition by integrating a CNN model with recursive neural networks. It first employs a pre-trained CNN model as the underlying feature extractor to get visual features at different layers for RGB and depth modalities. Then, a deep recursive model is applied to map these features into high-level representations. Finally, multi-level information is fused to produce a strong global representation of the entire object image. In order to utilize the CNN model trained on large-scale RGB datasets for depth domain, depth images are converted to a representation similar to RGB images. Experimental results on the Washington RGB-D Object dataset show that the proposed approach outperforms previous approaches.

Keywords: Convolutional neural network ·
Recursive neural network · Transfer learning ·
RGB-D object recognition

1 Introduction

The prevalence of depth sensors has led to an increasing attention in developing numerous applications in computer vision and robotics. RGB-D object recognition is a challenging fundamental task among these applications. In the meantime, deep learning based methods have surpassed the conventional feature extraction based methods and dominated the field. The breakthrough of convolutional neural networks (CNNs) has enabled to replace hand-engineered feature representations with efficient transferable off-the-shelf features. Deep features have been the focus of various research efforts including object recognition (e.g. [27,29]), detection (e.g. [16,28]), and semantic segmentation (e.g. [15,16]), since they offer biologically-inspired valuable information at hand. A common approach among these methods is to use the features extracted from the final fully-connected layers. The main reason behind this is that these features provide object-specific semantic information with smaller dimensions. However, as moving towards the final layers, it has been observed that these features are

© Springer Nature Switzerland AG 2019
L. Leal-Taixé and S. Roth (Eds.): ECCV 2018 Workshops, LNCS 11131, pp. 675–688, 2019.
https://doi.org/10.1007/978-3-030-11015-4_51

increasingly dependent on the chosen dataset and task [35]. On the other hand, the earlier layers capture distinctive information about the task and provide locally-activated features which are less sensitive to semantics [18,36]. One challenge of the earlier layers is the high dimensionality of features extracted from them. Consequently, features are transformed from general to specific throughout the network and the relational interest information is distributed across the network at different levels [18,35]. However, it is unclear how to exploit the information effectively.

The purpose of this paper is to develop a reliable deep feature learning approach to obtain more accurate classification of RGB-D objects by combining two key insights. The first is to employ a pre-trained CNN as a feature extractor and utilize information at different layers of the network to yield better recognition performance. The second is to apply recursive neural networks (RNNs) to reduce the dimensionality of the features and encode the CNN activations in robust hierarchical feature representations. The idea of combining a trained CNN model with the RNN structure is first presented in [8] for RGB image classification. After carrying out several experiments, the authors find that the activation weights from the 4th layer of the pre-trained network in [9] transformed by RNNs are more suitable and robust for RGB image classification. Our aim in this work is to improve on this idea by gathering feature representations at different levels in a compact and representative feature vector for both RGB and depth data. However, unlike [8], we reshape the activation maps of each layer to give the multiple RNNs in order to reduce the feature dimension. This provides a generic structure for each layer by fixing the tree structure without hurting performance and it allows us to improve recognition accuracy by combining feature vectors at different levels. The incorporation of multiple fixed RNNs together with the pre-trained CNN model allows feature transition at different layers to preserve both semantic and spatial structure of objects. Additionally, we embed depth data into the RGB domain by using surface normals in order to transfer information from a CNN model trained on the ImageNet dataset [12]. To this end, depth maps are colorized by computing three dimensional surface normals and treating each dimension as a color channel. The information from RGB images and depth maps are fused to obtain final RGB-D classification results. The proposed method is then evaluated and compared with the current state-of-the-art methods on the popular Washington RGB-D Object dataset [23] in terms of classification accuracy. The experimental results show the effectiveness of the proposed method both in terms of feature dimensions and classification accuracy. Hence, the contributions of this paper cover the following issues (The source code for our approach is available at: https://github.com/acaglayan/exploitCNN-RNN):

1. We present a novel deep feature learning pipeline which encodes information at different layers by incorporation of RNNs with a pre-trained CNN model for RGB-D object categorization.
2. We investigate features produced by a pre-trained CNN model and our pipeline. We show that RNNs represent activation maps of CNNs in a lower-dimensional space without hurting performance and allows us to encode information at multiple levels to get further hiearchical compact representations.

3. We define a way to allow transfer learning for depth data from a CNN model trained on RGB images. To do that, we compute surface normals from depth maps and normalize them. Despite the characteristic difference between depth and RGB data, the results suggest that a pre-trained CNN on RGB images can effectively capture information from depth images in this way.
4. We provide experimental evidence showing our method improves the state-of-the-art results on the Washington RGB-D Object dataset for category recognition.

2 Method

Encouraged by the recent tremendous advances in deep learning techniques, in this work, we explore the effectiveness of using a pre-trained CNN model together with RNNs to recognize object categories for RGB-D data. Specifically, we employ the pre-trained CNN model in [9] called VGG-f, which has been widely used for object recognition (e.g. [8,36]). In order to leverage the power of CNNs pre-trained over the large-scale RGB datasets such as ImageNet [12] for depth data, we pre-process the depth inputs to encode three color channels at each pixel. We first compute the three-dimensional surface normals from depth maps in which each dimension represents a color channel. Then, the channels are scaled to map values to the 0–255 range.

The structure of our approach is shown in Fig. 1. The proposed approach includes a two-step hierarchical feature learning procedure. In the first step, activation maps are extracted from the pre-trained CNN model at different levels to capture useful translational invariant features. Then, these activation maps are reshaped to reduce dimensions and given to the multiple fixed-tree RNNs to learn hierarchical high-level features of the images. To learn these features, we adapt the proposed work by Bui et al. [8]. They use RNNs with a pre-trained CNN model for feature extraction in an RGB-D object benchmark using only RGB images. The key of their approach is giving the output activation maps of a single intermediate layer as is to the recursive network structure. In contrast to this setting, we however want to efficiently combine features at multiple levels to obtain complementary different feature patterns for both RGB and depth images. Therefore, we modify the baseline framework in several ways. We first reshape the activation maps of the CNN model to cope with the high dimensionality of the produced feature vector of RNNs. This allows us to capture information at different layers for further classification performance. As such, multiple layers provide a compact and representative feature vector for each object class. Secondly, we compute surface normals from depth maps and encode to the RGB color modality to make use of the large-scale RGB dataset of ImageNet for depth modality by transfer learning. Finally, we combine the final feature vector of RGB and depth streams to build highly accurate RGB-D object category recognition method.

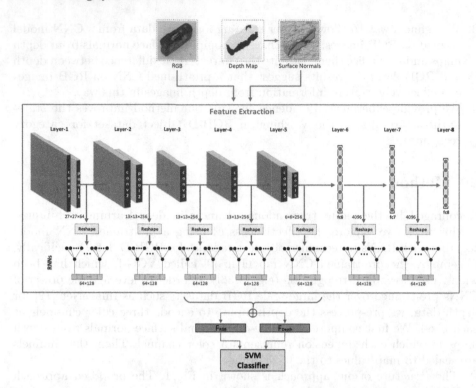

Fig. 1. Overview of the proposed method. The inputs of our approach are RGB images and colorized surface normal images. A pre-trained CNN [9] is employed to extract raw features at different layers. The multiple RNNs are used to learn higher level representations on a fixed tree structure. The learned representations at different layers are fused for final feature vectors of RGB and depth domains and given to a linear SVM classifier.

We use the pre-trained VGG-f model as a feature extractor without fine-tuning. Therefore, the procedure requires no training at feature extraction stage and works fast. The network consists of 5 successive convolutional layers (each might have sub-modules including convolution, pooling, and local contrast normalization operations) followed by 3 fully-connected layers and produces a distribution over the ImageNet dataset [12]. The dimensions of activation maps obtained from each layer are $27 \times 27 \times 64$, $13 \times 13 \times 256$, $13 \times 13 \times 256$, $13 \times 13 \times 256$, $6 \times 6 \times 256$, 4096, 4096, and 1000. The final fully-connected output is the feature representations over the 1000-classes of the ImageNet. For other layers, we reshape the activations by fixing the number of filter bank sizes to 64. Thus, for example, the outputs of fully-connected layers are formed into $8 \times 8 \times 64$ dimensions, and the convolution layers with the same size are converted into $26 \times 26 \times 64$. In this way, the new structures provide a generic ease of use and reduce the size of feature vectors generated by RNNs without sacrificing performance. We refer the readers to [9] for further details of the pre-trained network structure.

After computing activations by forward propagating input images through the pre-trained CNN model, we employ RNNs, whose inputs are the outputs of the CNN, to learn compact global feature representations. RNNs are well-studied models [26,32,33] that can learn higher level representations by applying the same operations recursively on a tree structure. Each layer merges blocks of adjacent vectors into a parent vector with tied weights where the goal is to map inputs $X \in \mathbb{R}^{K \times r \times r}$ into a lower dimensional space $p \in \mathbb{R}^K$ through multiple layers in the end. Then, the parent vector is passed through a nonlinear squash function. In this work, we use the $tanh$ function in order to preserve the original work but any squash function that provides an adequate nonlinearity may be used (e.g. the hyperbolic tangent sigmoid or the elliot sigmoid functions. See Sect. 4.1). A single RNN structure produces a K-dimensional vector, where K is the length of a given input (filter bank size). We use multiple randomly initialized N RNNs in our work. Therefore, a total of $(N \times K)$-dimensional final matrix is produced in the end.

The role of RNN in the process is twofold. First, it reduces the feature space dimensionality and maximizes classification performance. Thus, it allows us to transfer information from multiple layers effectively. Second, intuitively, the semantic content of the child nodes is recursively aggregated into the parent node through the structure. In this way, the resulting information represents the contextual description of the entire image. Moreover, RNNs are random weight based architectures without requiring back-propagation. Unlike CNNs, RNNs use non-overlapping receptive fields. Specifically, the RNNs in this study are of one-level with a single parent vector. Thus, they are computationally fast.

3   Related Work

The currently dominant object recognition solutions are based on deep feature learning techniques. The key enabling factors behind this are that these techniques rely on biologically-inspired learning models that can automatically obtain relevant information from the very low tier of the inputs and the ability to optimize them for the problem at hand. Recent works have shown that a trained CNN on a large-scale dataset can effectively be used to generate good generic representations for other visual recognition tasks [2,25,29,35]. Gupta et al. [17] encode the depth information in three channels using the camera parameters of the inputs in order to utilize a pre-trained CNN model on large-scale RGB images and focus on RGB-D object detection. Schwarz et al. [27] present an approach for RGB-D object recognition and pose estimation using the $fc7$ and $fc8$ activations of the pre-trained CNN of Krizhevsky et al. [22]. A different related approach is proposed by Eitel et al. [13]. They employ a two-stream CNN, one for each modality of RGB and depth channels which are finally combined with a late fusion network. They initialize both streams with weights from a pre-trained network on the ImageNet [12] and fine-tune for the final classification.

The recent work of [36] uses a spatial pyramid pooling strategy at different layers of the network to encode activations of all layers before feature concatenation. Their approach of aggregating information at different levels has inspired us in this work. Asif et al. extract *fc7* features from the pre-trained VGGnet model [31] for five different feature maps to encode the appearance and structural information of objects.

Other methods based on deep feature learning have also been developed. The convolutional k-means descriptor (CKM) [5] is proposed to learn features around SURF [4] interest points. The pioneer work of Socher et al. [32] has been employed for the semi-supervised method of Cheng et al. [11] to utilize grayscale images and surface normals in addition to RGB and depth images. The same work also has been used in the subset based method of Bai et al. [3] to extract patches from several subsets for filter learning. The method of convolutional fisher kernels (CFK) [10] is proposed to integrate CNNs with Fisher Kernel encoding for RGB-D object recognition. Despite its success in terms of accuracy performance, it appears to suffer from a very high-dimensional final feature vector for classification. Zia et al. [38] propose a method that learns RGB information using the pre-trained model of VGGnet [31] and depth information using 3D CNNs to fully exploit the 3D spatial information in depth images. They also propose a hybrid 2D/3D CNN model initialized with pre-trained 2D CNNs and fine-tuned later. They finally concatenate the features from this hybrid structure with the features learnt from depth-only and RGB-only architectures to feed the resulting vector to a classifier for overall recognition performance.

Recursive neural networks (RNNs) [26,33] process structured information by graphs transformed into recursive tree structures to learn distributed representations and have been used in conjuction with other architectures for various research purposes [3,11,21,30,32,33]. In [32], Socher et al. have first introduced an RGB-D object recognition method using the collaboration of CNN with RNN to first learn RGB and depth features in a separate stage and then merge for final classification. Later, this idea has been extended to replace the single CNN layer with a pre-trained CNN model by Bui et al. in [8] for RGB images. The achievement of the AlexNet-RNN [8] shows that transforming features extracted from a pre-trained CNN model by a recursive network structure can greatly increase classification accuracy in RGB object recognition. In this paper, we adapt the pipeline of [8] for RGB-D object recognition with a new structure and follow the idea of [18,36] to utilize information extracted from multi-layers. In this respect, the proposed approach learns robust representations of objects. The empirical evaluation reveals the effectiveness of the proposed approach for RGB-D object recognition by improving the accuracy performance significantly while reducing the feature dimension on the widely used Washington RGB-D Object dataset [23].

4 Evaluation

We evaluate the proposed method on the Washington RGB-D Object dataset [23]. The dataset contains 41, 877 RGB-D images of 51 household object categories and 300 instances of these categories. The experiments are carried out using the 10 train/test splits provided in [23]. For each split, there are roughly 35, 000 training images and 7, 000 test images. From each category, one instance is used for testing and all the remaining instances are used for training. All the inputs are resized to 224 × 224 pixels for convenience to the VGG-f model. The dataset also provides object segmentation masks. Since the background of images is fixed and simple with no cluttered view, we do not extract the background as an extra preprocessing step. Our pipeline could easily handle the background. We first evaluate experimental results with model analysis. Then, we compare the category recognition performance of our approach with several the state-of-the-art methods. We use the open-source MatConvNet toolbox [34] and the provided pre-trained CNN model with it. The obtained feature representations are classified by using a linear SVM classifier (Liblinear [14]).

4.1 Model Analysis

We analyze our approach through several model variations. We first experimentally investigate the effect of squashing functions for the RNN on accuracy performance. To this end, we use four different nonlinearities including *ReLU*, *tanh*, *tansig*, and *elliotsig* functions. We use the same random weights to ensure a valid comparison of non-linearities. As shown in Fig. 2, the results are close to each other in general. However, there is a slight difference between the ReLU and the other nonlinearities. While the ReLU function gives better results for depth data, the others acquire better success for RGB data. Since the difference is negligible, we use the *tanh* nonlinearity function in this study in order to preserve the original RNN work [32].

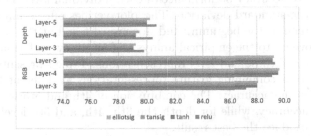

Fig. 2. Effects of different squashing functions for the RNN in terms of classification accuracy (%).

We then evaluate the effect of the RNNs on intermediate layers (*conv*3, *conv*4, and *pool*5). As can be seen from Fig. 3, the RNNs improve classification performance by significantly reducing the feature size (more than ×5 times for layers 3 and 4). The accuracy performance increases for RGB, while for depth it decreases slightly (∼1%). Nevertheless, the compact representation of the RNNs is preferable as it reduces the computational cost significantly and allows us to fuse the output of multiple layers to gain superior performance. We have chosen one of the splits as our development fold for our experiments until now. We use the all 10 splits in the rest of the experiments.

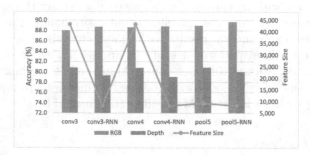

Fig. 3. Effects of RNNs in terms of accuracy performance and feature size on the mid-level raw features of the pre-trained CNN.

In our experiments, we particularly focus on the intermediate layers. The reason for this is our intuitive assumption that the outputs of the middle layers will be the optimal representations. Because it has been shown that features are eventually transformed from general to specific through deep networks [29,37]. While early layers response to low-level raw features such as corners and edges, late layers extract more object-specific features of the trained datasets. Thus, intermediate levels of the network present the optimal representations. Figure 4 shows the average accuracy performance of each individual layer on the 10 splits together with the standard deviation. The plot verifies our assumption with a clear upward trend at the beginning and downward trend at the end.

We now move on to the empirical analysis of accuracy performance on various combinations of these mid-level representations. Table 1 presents the results demonstrating that combining feature representations at different levels significantly improves the accuracy. The combination of 4th and 5th levels for RGB gives the best accuracy, while for depth the 3th, 4th, and 5th level representations together produce the best result.

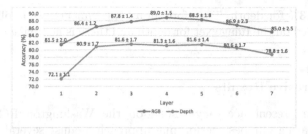

Fig. 4. Accuracy performance of our approach for individual layers.

Table 1. Accuracy performance for different combinations of the mid-level layer fusions (%).

	RGB	Depth	Feature size
Layer3 + Layer4	89.0 ± 1.4	83.0 ± 1.7	16,384
Layer3 + Layer5	89.4 ± 1.5	83.5 ± 1.7	16,384
Layer4 + Layer5	**89.9 ± 1.6**	83.4 ± 1.7	16,384
Layer3 + Layer4 + Layer5	89.8 ± 1.5	**84.0 ± 1.8**	24,576

Finally, we fuse RGB and depth features together to evaluate combined RGB-D accuracy performance. To this end, we first consider the fusion of single layer representations that give the best results for RGB and depth separately. We then evaluate the fusion of the two layers that together provide the optimal results for RGB and depth based on the analysis in Table 1. The average accuracy results with standard deviations are reported in Table 2. Considering fusion of more layers increases the dimensionality of the feature space, which makes classification intractable with limited computational resources. Therefore, we do not consider more layers since the high accuracy advantage of our approach might fade with larger number of features.

Table 2. Combinations of RGB and depth data together for the final RGB-D accuracy results (RGB_4 denotes the result of 4th layer for RGB domain, $RGB_{(4+5)}$ shows the fusion of 4th and 5th layers).

	Accuracy (%)	Feature size
RGB_4 + $Depth_5$	92.0 ± 1.3	16,384
$RGB_{(4+5)}$ + $Depth_{(4+5)}$	92.5 ± 1.2	32,768

In our experiments, we have observed that there is a slight difference between performing image normalization and non-normalization. When we apply image normalization, our best accuracy average drops by 0.2% for RGB, while it increases by 0.3% for depth. Therefore, in all experiments, we apply image normalization based on the ImageNet for depth and there is no image normalization for RGB.

4.2 Comparative Results

In Table 3, we present accuracy results on the Washington RGB-D Object dataset, comparing our best-performing approach against several the state-of-the-art methods. The proposed method achieves the highest recognition accuracy for RGB and the combination of RGB and depth (RGB-D) data. The feature size of the AlexNet-RNN [8], which produces the closest results to our result for RGB, is twice as big as ours. As for the depth data, our approach gives quite competitive results and outperforms all the other methods except that of [36] and [10]. The Hypercube [36] utilizes color information for point cloud embedding. Thus, unlike other methods, the reported result of this method does not rely on pure depth information. The CFK [10] generates a feature set with a size of $1,568,000$ which is about $\times 64$ times larger than that of our method. On the other hand, one reason for the lower success of depth modality comparing to RGB might be that we employ a CNN model trained on the RGB dataset of ImageNet as the underlying feature extractor. This makes sense because these two data modalities have different characteristics. As a result, the proposed method learns effective discriminative deep feature representations in a fast way without requiring training and produces superior accuracy performance results.

We also present the accuracy performance of the individual object categories in Fig. 5. The results demonstrate that our approach gives high performance for most of the object categories. In general, the categories with lower results are *mushroom, peach*, and *pitcher* classes. The main reason for this seems to be that these categories only contain three instances, which is the minimum instance number in the dataset. Hence, this imbalance of the dataset may have biased the learning to favor of categories with more examples. In addition, intra-class variations and inter-class similarity of the object categories may make the classification difficult. In particular, the similarity of many categories in the Washington RGB-D Object dataset leads to confusion in classification. For example, the presence of many geometrically similar categories in the dataset leads to lower depth accuracy in classes such as *ball, lightbulb, lime, pear, potato*, and *tomato*. Also the depth accuracy is low in the *camera* category, whose shiny surfaces may cause corruptions in depth information. As for the RGB data, the success rate is lower in some classes, where texture information is weak in addition to the above common problems (e.g. *bowl* and *plate*).

Table 3. Accuracy comparison of our approach with the related methods on the Washington RGB-D Object dataset (%).

Method	RGB	Depth	RGB-D
Kernel SVM [23]	74.5 ± 3.1	64.7 ± 2.2	83.9 ± 3.5
HKDES [6]	76.1 ± 2.2	75.7 ± 2.6	84.1 ± 2.2
KDES [7]	77.7 ± 1.9	78.8 ± 2.7	86.2 ± 2.1
CKM [5]	-	-	86.4 ± 2.3
CNN-RNN [32]	80.8 ± 4.2	78.9 ± 3.8	86.8 ± 3.3
Subset-RNN [3]	82.8 ± 3.4	81.8 ± 2.6	88.5 ± 3.1
CNN Features [27]	83.1 ± 2.0	-	89.4 ± 1.3
MM-LRF-ELM [24]	84.3 ± 3.2	82.9 ± 2.5	89.6 ± 2.5
CNN-SPM-RNN [11]	85.2 ± 1.2	83.6 ± 2.3	90.7 ± 1.1
Hypercube [36]	87.6 ± 2.2	85.0 ± 2.1	91.1 ± 1.4
CFK [10]	86.8 ± 2.7	**85.8 ± 2.3**	91.2 ± 1.4
AlexNet-RNN [8]	89.7 ± 1.7	-	-
Fus-CNN [13]	84.1 ± 2.7	83.8 ± 2.7	91.3 ± 1.4
Fusion 2D/3D CNNs [38]	89.0 ± 2.1	78.4 ± 2.4	91.8 ± 0.9
STEM-CaRFs [1]	88.8 ± 2.0	80.8 ± 2.1	92.2 ± 1.3
This work	**89.9 + 1.6**	84.0 ± 1.8	**92.5 ± 1.2**

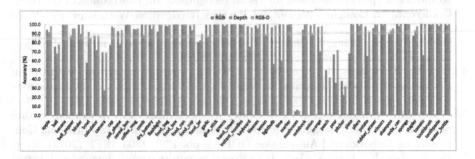

Fig. 5. Per-category success performances of our approach on the Washington RGB-D Object dataset.

5   Conclusion

We have presented a reliable deep feature learning approach using a pre-trained CNN model together with multiple-fixed RNNs to provide more accurate classification performance for RGB-D object recognition. The incorporation of RNNs with the CNN model allows us to deal with high-dimensional features and aggregate information at different layers to further leverage accuracy performance. In order to utilize the CNN models trained on large-scale RGB datasets for depth data, we colorize depth images by computing surface normals from depth maps and treat each dimension of normals as a color channel. We provide extensive experimental analysis of various parameters and comparative results on the popular Washington RGB-D Object dataset. The proposed approach produces promising performances both in terms of reduced feature dimension and high classification accuracy. There is a great potential for further improvement of the proposed approach. One potential factor that was not investigated here is fine-tuning the CNN before integrating the RNNs. Specifically, domain-specific fine-tuning might be effective for depth modality. Also, noting that the VGG-f is used as the underlying pre-trained CNN model in our approach, employing other models such as ResNet [19], DenseNet [20], etc. would be a possible future research direction to further improve accuracy performance. Training RNNs is another potential route for further improvement. Lastly, other depth colorization methods and effective feature fusion techniques could also be studied in the future.

Acknowledgment. We appreciate the generous donation of graphics card by NVIDIA Corporation to support our research.

References

1. Asif, U., Bennamoun, M., Sohel, F.A.: RGB-D object recognition and grasp detection using hierarchical cascaded forests. IEEE Trans. Robot. **33**(3), 547–564 (2017)
2. Azizpour, H., Sharif Razavian, A., Sullivan, J., Maki, A., Carlsson, S.: From generic to specific deep representations for visual recognition. In: Proceedings of the IEEE Conference on Computer Vision and Pattern Recognition Workshops, pp. 36–45 (2015)
3. Bai, J., Wu, Y., Zhang, J., Chen, F.: Subset based deep learning for RGB-D object recognition. Neurocomputing **165**, 280–292 (2015)
4. Bay, H., Tuytelaars, T., Van Gool, L.: SURF: speeded up robust features. In: Leonardis, A., Bischof, H., Pinz, A. (eds.) ECCV 2006. LNCS, vol. 3951, pp. 404–417. Springer, Heidelberg (2006). https://doi.org/10.1007/11744023_32
5. Blum, M., Springenberg, J.T., Wülfing, J., Riedmiller, M.: A learned feature descriptor for object recognition in RGB-D data. In: 2012 IEEE International Conference on Robotics and Automation (ICRA), pp. 1298–1303. IEEE (2012)
6. Bo, L., Lai, K., Ren, X., Fox, D.: Object recognition with hierarchical kernel descriptors. In: 2011 IEEE Conference on Computer Vision and Pattern Recognition (CVPR), pp. 1729–1736. IEEE (2011)
7. Bo, L., Ren, X., Fox, D.: Depth kernel descriptors for object recognition. In: 2011 IEEE/RSJ International Conference on Intelligent Robots and Systems, pp. 821–826. IEEE (2011)
8. Bui, H.M., Lech, M., Cheng, E., Neville, K., Burnett, I.S.: Object recognition using deep convolutional features transformed by a recursive network structure. IEEE Access **4**, 10059–10066 (2016)
9. Chatfield, K., Simonyan, K., Vedaldi, A., Zisserman, A.: Return of the devil in the details: delving deep into convolutional nets. arXiv preprint arXiv:1405.3531 (2014)
10. Cheng, Y., Cai, R., Zhao, X., Huang, K.: Convolutional fisher kernels for RGB-D object recognition. In: 2015 International Conference on 3D Vision (3DV), pp. 135–143. IEEE (2015)

11. Cheng, Y., Zhao, X., Huang, K., Tan, T.: Semi-supervised learning and feature evaluation for RGB-D object recognition. Comput. Vis. Image Underst. **139**, 149–160 (2015)
12. Deng, J., Dong, W., Socher, R., Li, L.J., Li, K., Fei-Fei, L.: Imagenet: a large-scale hierarchical image database. In: IEEE Conference on Computer Vision and Pattern Recognition, CVPR 2009, pp. 248–255. IEEE (2009)
13. Eitel, A., Springenberg, J.T., Spinello, L., Riedmiller, M., Burgard, W.: Multimodal deep learning for robust RGB-D object recognition. In: 2015 IEEE/RSJ International Conference on Intelligent Robots and Systems (IROS), pp. 681–687. IEEE (2015)
14. Fan, R.E., Chang, K.W., Hsieh, C.J., Wang, X.R., Lin, C.J.: Liblinear: a library for large linear classification. J. Mach. Learn. Res. **9**, 1871–1874 (2008)
15. Farabet, C., Couprie, C., Najman, L., LeCun, Y.: Learning hierarchical features for scene labeling. IEEE Trans. Pattern Anal. Mach. Intell. **35**(8), 1915–1929 (2013)
16. Girshick, R., Donahue, J., Darrell, T., Malik, J.: Rich feature hierarchies for accurate object detection and semantic segmentation. In: Proceedings of the IEEE Conference on Computer Vision and Pattern Recognition, pp. 580–587 (2014)
17. Gupta, S., Girshick, R., Arbeláez, P., Malik, J.: Learning rich features from RGB-D images for object detection and segmentation. In: Fleet, D., Pajdla, T., Schiele, B., Tuytelaars, T. (eds.) ECCV 2014. LNCS, vol. 8695, pp. 345–360. Springer, Cham (2014). https://doi.org/10.1007/978-3-319-10584-0_23
18. Hariharan, B., Arbeláez, P., Girshick, R., Malik, J.: Hypercolumns for object segmentation and fine-grained localization. In: Proceedings of the IEEE Conference on Computer Vision and Pattern Recognition, pp. 447–456 (2015)
19. He, K., Zhang, X., Ren, S., Sun, J.: Deep residual learning for image recognition. In: Proceedings of the IEEE Conference on Computer Vision and Pattern Recognition, pp. 770–778 (2016)
20. Huang, G., Liu, Z., Weinberger, K.Q., van der Maaten, L.: Densely connected convolutional networks. In: Proceedings of the IEEE Conference on Computer Vision and Pattern Recognition, vol. 1, p. 3 (2017)
21. Kim, J., Kwon Lee, J., Mu Lee, K.: Deeply-recursive convolutional network for image super-resolution. In: Proceedings of the IEEE Conference on Computer Vision and Pattern Recognition, pp. 1637–1645 (2016)
22. Krizhevsky, A., Sutskever, I., Hinton, G.E.: Imagenet classification with deep convolutional neural networks. In: Advances in Neural Information Processing Systems, pp. 1097–1105 (2012)
23. Lai, K., Bo, L., Ren, X., Fox, D.: A large-scale hierarchical multi-view RGB-D object dataset. In: 2011 IEEE International Conference on Robotics and Automation (ICRA), pp. 1817–1824. IEEE (2011)
24. Liu, H., Li, F., Xu, X., Sun, F.: Multi-modal local receptive field extreme learning machine for object recognition. Neurocomputing **277**, 4–11 (2018)
25. Oquab, M., Bottou, L., Laptev, I., Sivic, J.: Learning and transferring mid-level image representations using convolutional neural networks. In: 2014 IEEE Conference on Computer Vision and Pattern Recognition (CVPR), pp. 1717–1724. IEEE (2014)
26. Pollack, J.B.: Recursive distributed representations. Artif. Intell. **46**(1–2), 77–105 (1990)
27. Schwarz, M., Schulz, H., Behnke, S.: RGB-D object recognition and pose estimation based on pre-trained convolutional neural network features. In: 2015 IEEE International Conference on Robotics and Automation (ICRA), pp. 1329–1335. IEEE (2015)

28. Sermanet, P., Eigen, D., Zhang, X., Mathieu, M., Fergus, R., LeCun, Y.: Overfeat: integrated recognition, localization and detection using convolutional networks. arXiv preprint arXiv:1312.6229 (2013)
29. Sharif Razavian, A., Azizpour, H., Sullivan, J., Carlsson, S.: CNN features off-the-shelf: an astounding baseline for recognition. In: Proceedings of the IEEE Conference on Computer Vision and Pattern Recognition Workshops, pp. 806–813 (2014)
30. Sharma, A., Tuzel, O., Liu, M.Y.: Recursive context propagation network for semantic scene labeling. In: Advances in Neural Information Processing Systems, pp. 2447–2455 (2014)
31. Simonyan, K., Zisserman, A.: Very deep convolutional networks for large-scale image recognition. arXiv preprint arXiv:1409.1556 (2014)
32. Socher, R., Huval, B., Bath, B., Manning, C.D., Ng, A.Y.: Convolutional-recursive deep learning for 3D object classification. In: Advances in Neural Information Processing Systems, pp. 656–664 (2012)
33. Socher, R., Lin, C.C., Manning, C., Ng, A.Y.: Parsing natural scenes and natural language with recursive neural networks. In: Proceedings of the 28th International Conference on Machine Learning (ICML-11), pp. 129–136 (2011)
34. Vedaldi, A., Lenc, K.: Matconvnet: convolutional neural networks for matlab. In: Proceedings of the 23rd ACM International Conference on Multimedia, pp. 689–692. ACM (2015)
35. Yosinski, J., Clune, J., Bengio, Y., Lipson, H.: How transferable are features in deep neural networks? In: Advances in Neural Information Processing Systems, pp. 3320–3328 (2014)
36. Zaki, H.F., Shafait, F., Mian, A.: Convolutional hypercube pyramid for accurate RGB-D object category and instance recognition. In: 2016 IEEE International Conference on Robotics and Automation (ICRA), pp. 1685–1692. IEEE (2016)
37. Zeiler, M.D., Fergus, R.: Visualizing and understanding convolutional networks. In: Fleet, D., Pajdla, T., Schiele, B., Tuytelaars, T. (eds.) ECCV 2014. LNCS, vol. 8689, pp. 818–833. Springer, Cham (2014). https://doi.org/10.1007/978-3-319-10590-1_53
38. Zia, S., Yuksel, B., Yuret, D., Yemez, Y.: RGB-D object recognition using deep convolutional neural networks. In: 2017 IEEE International Conference on Computer Vision Workshop (ICCVW), pp. 887–894. IEEE (2017)

Temporally Consistent Depth Estimation in Videos with Recurrent Architectures

Denis Tananaev[1,2], Huizhong Zhou[1(✉)], Benjamin Ummenhofer[1], and Thomas Brox[1]

[1] University of Freiburg, Freiburg im Breisgau, Germany
{zhouh,ummenhof,brox}@cs.uni-freiburg.de
[2] Robert Bosch GmbH, Stuttgart, Germany
Denis.Tananaev@de.bosch.com

Abstract. Convolutional networks trained on large RGB-D datasets have enabled depth estimation from a single image. Many works on automotive applications rely on such approaches. However, all existing methods work on a frame-by-frame manner when applied to videos, which leads to inconsistent depth estimates over time. In this paper, we introduce for the first time an approach that yields temporally consistent depth estimates over multiple frames of a video. This is done by a dedicated architecture based on convolutional LSTM units and layer normalization. Our approach achieves superior performance on several error metrics when compared to independent frame processing. This also shows in an improved quality of the reconstructed multi-view point clouds.

Keywords: Convolutional LSTM · Recurrent networks · Depth estimation · Video processing

1 Introduction

Triggered by the seminal work of Eigen et al. [6] the estimation of depth maps from just a single image has become a popular tool in computer vision. Depth estimation in a single image is well known to be highly ambiguous and only works due to strong conditional priors learned from previously seen data. The work from Eigen et al. [6] demonstrated the superiority of deep networks over previous attempts with hand-crafted features [23]. The priors learned by a deep network yield an unprecedented accuracy and generality compared to all previous approaches on single-view depth estimation. Of course, the accuracy is far from being competitive with multi-view reconstruction, which becomes evident when visualizing the depth maps in the form of a point cloud. Nevertheless, estimating the depth from single images is no longer a toy problem but is used in places, where dense multi-view reconstruction is not directly applicable, for instance to initialize a monocular SLAM method [26] or for rough but dense depth estimates in autonomous driving [28].

© Springer Nature Switzerland AG 2019
L. Leal-Taixé and S. Roth (Eds.): ECCV 2018 Workshops, LNCS 11131, pp. 689–701, 2019.
https://doi.org/10.1007/978-3-030-11015-4_52

Often in these applications, an image sequence rather than a single image is available, yet these additional images are typically not exploited. There are two sources of information that are inherent to a sequence of images: (1) the motion parallax by a moving camera; (2) the temporal consistency of successive frames. Exploiting the motion parallax has been approached in Ummenhofer et al. [29] for two frames. The motion parallax was used also in Zhou et al. [32] for unsupervised learning of depth from single image. However, there is no approach yet, that exploits the temporal consistency of successive frames.

In this work, we propose a network architecture based on convolutional LSTMs to capture temporal information from previous frames and to enforce temporally consistent depth estimates in a video. We show that such a network improves over independent frame processing, both relative to a single-frame baseline and relative to the state of the art. While it is well-known that temporal consistency has only relatively small effects on standard performance metrics based on average statistics, the qualitative improvement is much higher due to more stable estimates that do not flicker; see the supplemental video. The temporal consistency is also advantageous when combining multiple depth maps to a joint point cloud. As the depth estimates of successive frames agree more, the resulting point cloud is more consistent, too.

2   Related Work

End-to-end depth estimation from a single image with convolutional neural networks was introduced by Eigen [5,6]. These works were introduced before the today most common convolutional encoder-decoder architectures, such as FCN [19] and U-Net [22] were available. They use a multi-scale architecture for depth estimation at different spatial resolutions. Joint depth and normal prediction improved the depth estimation results.

Liu et al. [18] combined convolutional networks with superpixel-based conditional random fields. Chackrabarti et al. [3] generate a midlevel representation of the depth with a deep network to find the best matches for the depth values in a post processing step. At the present, Laina et al. [16] yields the best results on benchmarks. This was achieved by replacing the standard convolutional encoder by a ResNet-50 architecture [11] and by a set of computationally efficient up-sampling blocks.

The methods above process each frame independently, even when processing a video. We propose the use of LSTM units [9,12] to relate the intermediate representation in the network across frames in order to obtain temporally consistent outputs. In particular, we use a convolutional LSTM architecture [31]. The convolutional version of LSTMs captures the spatial context of the input tensor and keeps the number of parameters limited.

3   Network Architecture

The architecture in Fig. 1 integrates a typical convolutional encoder-decoder structure with convolutional LSTM layers (in brown) to analyze the image at

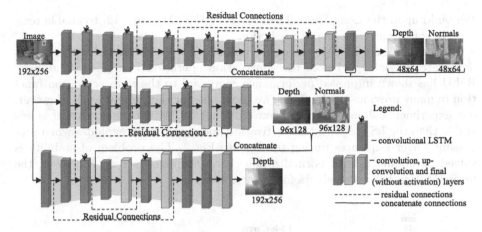

Fig. 1. Overview of the multi-resolution recurrent network architecture. The architecture consists of three encoder-decoder networks that predict the depth at different resolution levels. The low-resolution prediction is fed as input to the next, higher-resolution stream. The first two streams also estimate the normals in addition to the depth. The convolutional LSTM layers carry the state from the previous frame. There are residual connections within each encoder-decoder stream and also between the streams.

various levels of abstraction, where for each level, the state representation from the previous frame is carried over to the present frame. This combination with the previous state enforces the temporal consistency of the states and, consequently, also of the output. Like all common encoder-decoder networks, the architecture has residual connections to directly propagate high-resolution features from the encoder to the respective layer in the decoder. The spatial resolution of all convolutional filters is 3×3. The filters for the up-convolution have size 4×4 and for the LSTM filters we use 5×5 filters.

In addition to the multi-scale analysis due to the encoder-decoder architecture, the architecture includes a coarse-to-fine refinement strategy, which first produces the output depth map at a lower resolution (with a loss applied during training). The low-resolution result is successively refined by the next encoder-decoder stream of the multi-resolution architecture until the resolution of the input image is obtained at the output. This coarse-to-fine strategy efficiently implements the network stacking idea, which has been successful for optical flow estimation [13] and depth from two views [29]. We also added recurrent connections between the layers of the different streams. For the intermediate resolutions, the network also computes the surface normals (with a loss applied during training), which is helpful to learn the depth representation for the surfaces in the scene.

3.1   Convolutional LSTM with Leaky ReLU

Recurrent neural network architectures have shown to be able to leverage temporal data for tasks such as language processing [4] and video captioning [2].

We build upon the Long Short Term Memory (LSTM) unit [12] to enable temporally consistent video depth prediction.

In convolutional LSTMs the input tensor h_t^{l-1} is concatenated with the hidden state tensor h_{t-1}^l before the convolution operation is applied. The leaky ReLU has shown improved performance compared to the tanh activation function in many previous works. Thus, we use it also for the present work. However, our experiments showed that the convolutional LSTM with leaky ReLU is less stable than the LSTM with tanh activation and numerically explodes when processing longer sequences during testing; see Fig. 2. The problem of stability is solved by adding a layer normalization [1] on the cell state c_t^l. Moreover, the normalization layer also allows for faster convergence.

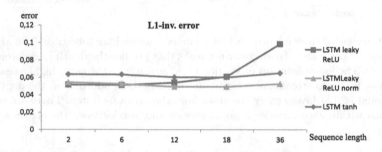

Fig. 2. Network stability at test time with different activation functions used in the LSTM unit. The leaky ReLU activation yields better results than the tanh activation. However, the network becomes unstable over time. Adding layer normalization yields the good performance of the leaky ReLU while being as stable as the tanh activation.

Formally, the convolutional LSTM with leaky ReLU and layer normalization reads:

$$\begin{pmatrix} i \\ f \\ o \\ g \end{pmatrix} = \begin{pmatrix} \sigma \\ \sigma \\ \sigma \\ \text{leakyReLU} \end{pmatrix} \circ W^l * \begin{pmatrix} h_t^{l-1} \\ h_{t-1}^l \end{pmatrix}, \tag{1}$$

$$c_t^l = f \cdot c_{t-1}^l + i \cdot g, \tag{2}$$

$$\hat{c}_t^l = \gamma \left(\frac{c_t^l - \mu(c_t^l)}{\sqrt{\text{var}(c_t^l)}} \right) + \beta, \tag{3}$$

$$h_t^l = o \cdot \text{leakyReLU}(\hat{c}_t^l), \tag{4}$$

where i, f, o, g are the input, forget, output gates and new input, respectively; c_t^l and c_{t-1}^l are the cell states for the current and previous time steps; γ and β are the learned parameters of the layer normalization [1], and μ and var are the mean and variance of the argument over each single data sample.

4   Training Procedure

We train the recurrent network with a batch size of 2 and a sequence length of 7 by unrolling the network. For each frame the network generates a depth map; we apply a loss on each of the outputs.

4.1   Datasets

We train and evaluate our recurrent network on static and dynamic indoor sequences. For the static sequences we use the NYUv2 [24] and SUN3D [30] datasets. Both datasets feature indoor video sequences of offices, living rooms, etc. filmed with a structured light sensor. We use the raw depth from the sensor for NYUv2 and the TSDF fused depth provided by SUN3D. The NYUv2 dataset has 249 training video sequences and 215 test sequences. We use the SUN3D dataset split proposed by Ummenhofer et al. [29] which has 253 sequences for training and 16 for testing.

For dynamic scene experiments we use the Princeton Tracking Benchmark [25]. The dataset consists of indoor scenes with dynamic objects captured with the Kinect sensor. We use 96 sequences for training and four sequences for test.

4.2   Initialization and Training Strategy

We initialize the network weights using Xavier initialization [8] with modifications proposed by [10] for ReLU functions. We normalize the input image values to the range $[-0.5, 0.5]$ and use inverse depth values $\xi = 1/z$ for parameterizing the depth values. Inverse depth emphasizes distances to close objects, yielding more precise predictions for those objects and allows us to represent points at infinity.

For training we use nearest neighbour sampling to resize the ground truth depth maps to 256×192. On NYUv2 we first crop images to 561×427 before downsampling. The output depth has the same resolution as input.

We use ADAM [15] with restarts. The restart technique was proposed for SGD optimization and allows to achieve faster convergence of the network compared to the fixed learning rate schedules [20]. The starting learning rate for each restart is 10^{-4} and it drops to 10^{-6} at the end of each period. The first restart interval is 10000 iterations and it increases by factor 1.5 at each restart.

To avoid overfitting to very long sequences in the training set, we iterate in random order over the set of sequences and sample from each sequence a random segment with 7 frames. This allows the network to see an equal number of training samples from each sequence. Further, we augment the segments by randomly skipping frames with a probability of 0.5.

4.3   Loss Functions

On the depth output, we combine two loss functions. First, we use L1 loss for the inverse depth

$$L_{\text{depth}} = \sum_{i,j} |\xi(i,j) - \hat{\xi}(i,j)|, \tag{5}$$

where $\hat{\xi}(i,j)$ is the ground truth inverse depth. Second, we compute the scale-invariant gradient loss [29] for the inverse depth

$$L_{\text{grad}} = \sum_{h\in 1,2,4,8,16} \sum_{i,j} ||g_h[\xi](i,j) - g_h[\hat{\xi}](i,j)||_2 \tag{6}$$

where $g_h[\xi](i,j)$ is the discrete scale invariant gradient:

$$g_h[f](i,j) = \left(\frac{f(i+h,j)-f(i,j)}{|f(i+h,j)|+|f(i,j)|}, \frac{f(i,j+h)-f(i,j)}{|f(i,j+h)|+|f(i,j)|} \right). \tag{7}$$

In (6) we sum the gradient for five different discretization widths h to cover gradients with different slopes. The gradient loss significantly improves the smoothness of the depth values while preserving sharp depth edges.

The loss on the normals is the non-squared L2 norm

$$L_{\text{normal}} = \sum_{i,j} ||n(i,j) - \hat{n}(i,j)||_2, \tag{8}$$

where $n(i,j)$ is the normal predicted by the network and $\hat{n}(i,j)$ is the ground truth normal, which we derive from the ground truth depth maps.

To balance the importance of the loss functions we use different weights. We assign the weight 300 for the $L1$ depth loss and 1500 for the scale invariant gradient loss and 100 for the loss on the normals. The weights were set empirically.

For the first 10000 iterations we set the weight for the gradient loss to zero, because the scale invariance of L_{grad} can cause instabilities directly after weight initialization. During training and evaluation, we do not consider pixels with invalid depth values.

4.4   Error Metrics

To quantify the quality of the predicted depth maps we compute several common error metrics:

L1 inverse error: $L1 - inv(z,\hat{z}) = \frac{1}{N}\sum_i \left| \frac{1}{z_i} - \frac{1}{\hat{z}_i} \right|$,

The mean root squared error (RMS): $RMS(z,\hat{z}) = \sqrt{\frac{1}{N}\sum_i(z_i - \hat{z}_i)^2}$

Average log_{10} error (log10): $log10(z,\hat{z}) = \frac{1}{N}\sum_i |\log z_i - \log \hat{z}_i|$

Percentage of pixels below a ratio treshold θ: $\max\left(\frac{\hat{z}_i}{z_i}, \frac{z_i}{\hat{z}_i}\right) = \delta(z,\hat{z}) < \theta$.

Here z_i is the depth prediction, $\hat{z}_i$ is the ground truth depth, and N is the number of valid pixels in a depth map.

5   Experiments

5.1   Choice of the Activation Function

To quantify the behaviour of the LSTM with different activation functions and normalization strategies we first ran experiments with a simplified network architecture, which consists of only one encoder with 10 layers and one decoder with 13 layers. We also compared the recurrent network with the LSTM layers removed, i.e., that network does not take information from previous frames into account. Results on SUN3D dataset for a sequence length of 6 are shown in Table 1. The recurrent architecture improves over the single-frame baseline on all metrics, and the leaky ReLU activation unit always outperforms tanh activation. Thus, for the following experiments, we always used leaky ReLU activation with normalization.

Table 1. Comparison of the recurrent architecture to its non-recurrent baseline for two different activation functions in the LSTM unit on the SUN3D dataset. The recurrent architectures improve over the single-frame baseline on all metrics. The leaky ReLU activation unit always outperforms tanh activation.

Metrics	L1-inv	log10	RMS	$\delta < 1.25$	$\delta < 1.25^2$	$\delta < 1.25^3$
Single frame	0.0763	0.170	0.577	73.1%	90.8%	98.2%
LSTM tanh	0.0637	0.156	0.474	80.0%	92.8%	99.1%
LSTM leaky ReLU+norm	**0.0518**	**0.140**	**0.398**	**80.1%**	**94.3%**	**99.6%**

5.2   Comparison to the State of the Art

In Table 2, we compare the full network architecture to the state of the art in depth estimation from single image. We trained the network for the first six restarts on the SUN3D dataset and then fine-tuned it for the last restart on the NYUv2 training data. For the evaluation, we randomly sampled 50 sequences from the NYUv2 test set and evaluated on the first 50 frames of each sequence. We evaluated only in the regions with valid depth values.

The use of temporal consistency with LSTM yields state-of-the-art results in several metrics. Moreover, the version with temporal consistency outperforms the baseline without LSTM units on all metrics. This clearly shows the benefit of taking previous frames into account.

A qualitative comparison is shown in Fig. 3. Our results have sharper boundaries than the single-frame methods, and there is no flickering in the depth maps estimated over time, as can be seen in the supplemental video.

Table 2. Comparison to the state of the art on 50 sequences from the NYUv2 dataset with a length of 50 frames each. The use of temporal consistency with LSTM yields state-of-the-art results on most metrics. The runtime performance of the methods (frames per second) was estimated on the NVidia Geforce Titan X (Maxwell architecture).

Metrics	L1-inv	log10	RMS	$\delta < 1.25$	$\delta < 1.25^2$	$\delta < 1.25^3$	fps
Liu [18]	0.155	0.133	0.995	56.1%	81.1%	88.7%	0.07
Eigen [5]	0.130	0.108	0.885	69.0%	86.9%	91.6%	0.33
Chakrabarti [3]	0.116	0.095	**0.808**	77.1%	88.3%	91.2%	0.04
Laina [16]	0.114	0.093	0.823	77.9%	88.4%	**91.7%**	8.25
Our single-frame	0.119	0.101	0.878	75.4%	87.7%	91.2%	**8.33**
Our LSTM	**0.111**	**0.092**	0.824	**79.6%**	**88.9%**	91.4%	4.54

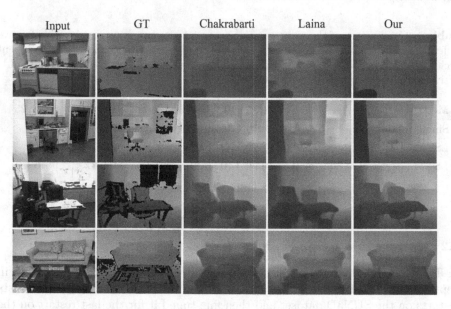

Fig. 3. Qualitative comparison of our LSTM based network to the independent frame processing of Chakrabarti et al. [3] and Laina et al. [16]. The result of the last image in each 50-frame sequence is shown. The proposed architecture with multi-frame processing yields sharper edges and captures more details.

5.3 Temporal Consistency

We show that our LSTM network learns to predict temporally consistent depth maps. We validate this by comparing depth predictions of our LSTM-based architecture with state of the art single-frame depth estimation networks. In Fig. 4 we show the depth trajectory of a point on a 50 frames sequence from the NYUv2 dataset. And in Fig. 5 we further show the temporal consistency comparison with the average depth change over all pixels.

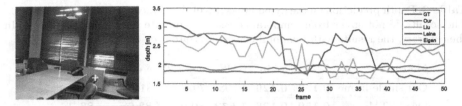

Fig. 4. We track the depth of a single point over time. We use the KLT tracker [21,27] to track the point in the image sequence and plot the depth over time. Our LSTM-based architecture is not only more accurate but also more temporally consistent and therefore suited for processing video streams.

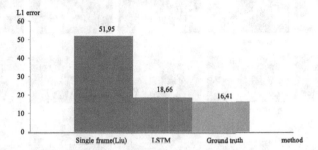

Fig. 5. Comparison of the temporal consistency with single frame Liu et al. [17], our LSTM network, and ground truth. The bars represent the average depth change of corresponding points between consecutive depth frames of a sequence of size 10. In order to compute point correspondences we use Farneback optical flow [7]. Since optical flow estimation introduces additional errors we also show the ground truth results.

Temporal consistency is clearly advantageous in static images. In case of dynamic scenes, temporal consistency, which effectively induces smoothing over time, could have negative effects. It is worth noting, though, that the proposed approach does not smooth the resulting depth map, but the intermediate state representation, i.e., the network can learn to smooth along the point trajectories and consider motion boundaries and occlusion areas. To verify the performance of the recurrent architecture in dynamic scenes we compare it to the single-frame baseline on the Princeton tracking benchmark, which comprises dynamic scenes. We evaluated on four sequences with 50 frames each.

The results in Table 3 show that there is still a small advantage for the LSTM-based architecture, yet it is smaller than in static cases. This indicates that the network cannot learn all of the effects mentioned above, but at least it alleviates most of the negative effects.

A qualitative result is shown in Fig. 6. The single-frame baseline has problems with the shape of the moving object, while the recurrent network can exploit the additional information from previous frames. The effect is strongest when the object gets occluded and is partially not visible in the single frame.

Table 3. Depth prediction on the dynamic scenes of the Princeton tracking benchmark. The results do not suffer from temporal consistency despite the motion of objects. In the contrary, the results with temporal consistency are even a little better.

Metrics	L1-inv	log10	RMS	$\delta < 1.25$	$\delta < 1.25^2$	$\delta < 1.25^3$
Our single-frame	**0.150**	**0.126**	1.698	79.9%	81.8%	82.9%
Our LSTM	**0.150**	**0.126**	**1.672**	**80.0%**	**82.0%**	**83.2%**

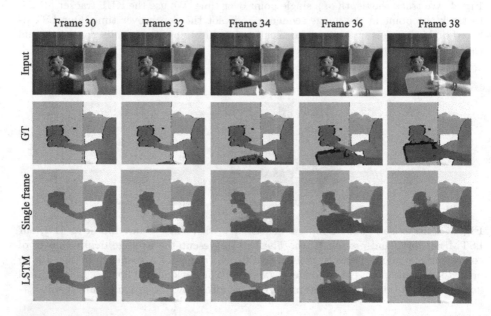

Fig. 6. Dynamic scene from the Princeton tracking benchmark. The temporally consistency due to the LSTM helps to reconstruct the precise depth near boundaries of a moving object.

5.4 3D Reconstruction

We compared the quality of the predicted depth maps also in a full scene reconstruction context, where the depth maps were used as depth channel in an RGB-D SLAM approach [30] to reconstruct a 3D scene from a video sequence. Figure 7 shows the 3D reconstructions.

The temporally consistent depth maps help improve the reconstructed 3D scene, since the variation of the same surface points over time is much reduced. Thus, the point cloud is less noisy which leads to better 3D reconstruction. Also there are less severe misalignments in the scan, since the temporally consistent depth maps are easier to register for the SLAM method.

GT   Eigen   Laina   LSTM

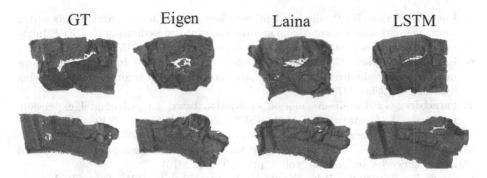

Fig. 7. The result of the RGB-D structure from motion [30] with depth from the neural network of Eigen and Fergus [5], Laina [16] and our recurrent network. For each reconstruction we use a sequence of 25 frames. We use Poisson surface reconstruction to generate the meshes [14]. Inconsistent depth estimates for Eigen and Laina lead to reconstruction artifacts in the surface mesh. The reconstructions from our depth predictions show less artifacts and have more details.

6   Conclusions

In this work, we have introduced the first depth estimation network that optimizes the temporal consistency of the estimated depth map over multiple frames in a video. We have shown that the LSTM with leaky ReLU yields better results than the traditional convolutional LSTM with tanh activation. In this context, we have also shown the importance of layer normalization for the stability of the recurrent network. The experimental results with the proposed multi-frame processing consistently outperformed those with frame-independent processing both in static and dynamic scenes.

Acknowledgements. This project was partially funded by the EU Horizon 2020 project Trimbot2020. We also thank Facebook for their P100 server donation and gift funding.

References

1. Ba, J.L., Kiros, J.R., Hinton, G.E.: Layer normalization. arXiv preprint arXiv:1607.06450 (2016)
2. Ballas, N., Yao, L., Pal, C., Courville, A.: Delving deeper into convolutional networks for learning video representations. In: International Conference on Learning Representations (ICLR 2016) (2016)
3. Chakrabarti, A., Shao, J., Shakhnarovich, G.: Depth from a single image by harmonizing overcomplete local network predictions, pp. 2658–2666 (2016)
4. Cho, K., et al.: Learning phrase representations using RNN encoder-decoder for statistical machine translation. In: Proceedings of the 2014 Conference on Empirical Methods in Natural Language Processing (EMNLP). pp. 1724–1734. Association for Computational Linguistics, Doha, Qatar, October 2014. http://www.aclweb.org/anthology/D14-1179

5. Eigen, D., Fergus, R.: Predicting depth, surface normals and semantic labels with a common multi-scale convolutional architecture. In: Proceedings of the IEEE International Conference on Computer Vision, pp. 2650–2658 (2015)
6. Eigen, D., Puhrsch, C., Fergus, R.: Depth map prediction from a single image using a multi-scale deep network. In: Advances in Neural Information Processing Systems, pp. 2366–2374 (2014)
7. Farnebäck, G.: Two-frame motion estimation based on polynomial expansion. In: Bigun, J., Gustavsson, T. (eds.) SCIA 2003. LNCS, vol. 2749, pp. 363–370. Springer, Heidelberg (2003). https://doi.org/10.1007/3-540-45103-X_50
8. Glorot, X., Bengio, Y.: Understanding the difficulty of training deep feedforward neural networks. In: Aistats, vol. 9, pp. 249–256 (2010)
9. Greff, K., Srivastava, R.K., Koutník, J., Steunebrink, B.R., Schmidhuber, J.: LSTM: a search space odyssey. IEEE Trans. Neural Networks Learn. Syst. **28**(10), 2222–2232 (2017)
10. He, K., Zhang, X., Ren, S., Sun, J.: Delving deep into rectifiers: surpassing human-level performance on imagenet classification. In: Proceedings of the IEEE International Conference on Computer Vision, pp. 1026–1034 (2015)
11. He, K., Zhang, X., Ren, S., Sun, J.: Deep residual learning for image recognition. In: Proceedings of the IEEE Conference on Computer Vision and Pattern Recognition, pp. 770–778 (2016)
12. Hochreiter, S., Schmidhuber, J.: Long short-term memory. Neural Comput. **9**(8), 1735–1780 (1997)
13. Ilg, E., Mayer, N., Saikia, T., Keuper, M., Dosovitskiy, A., Brox, T.: Flownet 2.0: evolution of optical flow estimation with deep networks. In: IEEE Conference on Computer Vision and Pattern Recognition (CVPR), July 2017. http://lmb.informatik.uni-freiburg.de//Publications/2017/IMKDB17
14. Kazhdan, M., Bolitho, M., Hoppe, H.: Poisson surface reconstruction. In: Proceedings of the Fourth Eurographics Symposium on Geometry Processing, SGP 2006, pp. 61–70. Eurographics Association, Aire-la-Ville, Switzerland (2006)
15. Kingma, D.P., Ba, J.: Adam: a method for stochastic optimization. In: Proceedings of the 3rd International Conference on Learning Representations (ICLR 2015) (2015)
16. Laina, I., Rupprecht, C., Belagiannis, V., Tombari, F., Navab, N.: Deeper depth prediction with fully convolutional residual networks. In: 2016 Fourth International Conference on 3D Vision (3DV), pp. 239–248, October 2016. https://doi.org/10.1109/3DV.2016.32
17. Liu, F., Shen, C., Lin, G.: Deep convolutional neural fields for depth estimation from a single image. In: Proceedings of the IEEE Conference on Computer Vision and Pattern Recognition (2015). http://arxiv.org/abs/1411.6387
18. Liu, M., Salzmann, M., He, X.: Structured depth prediction in challenging monocular video sequences. arXiv preprint arXiv:1511.06070 (2015)
19. Long, J., Shelhamer, E., Darrell, T.: Fully convolutional networks for semantic segmentation. In: Proceedings of the IEEE Conference on Computer Vision and Pattern Recognition, pp. 3431–3440 (2015)
20. Loshchilov, I., Hutter, F.: SGDR: stochastic gradient descent with restarts. In: 5th International Conference on Learning Representations (ICLR 2017) (2017)
21. Lucas, B.D., Kanade, T.: An iterative image registration technique with an application to stereo vision. In: Proceedings of the 7th International Joint Conference on Artificial Intelligence, IJCAI 1981, vol. 2, pp. 674–679. Morgan Kaufmann Publishers Inc., San Francisco (1981)

22. Ronneberger, O., Fischer, P., Brox, T.: U-Net: convolutional networks for biomedical image segmentation. In: Navab, N., Hornegger, J., Wells, W.M., Frangi, A.F. (eds.) MICCAI 2015. LNCS, vol. 9351, pp. 234–241. Springer, Cham (2015). https://doi.org/10.1007/978-3-319-24574-4_28
23. Saxena, A., Sun, M., Ng, A.Y.: Make3D: learning 3D scene structure from a single still image. IEEE Trans. Pattern Anal. Mach. Intell. **31**(5), 824–840 (2009)
24. Silberman, N., Hoiem, D., Kohli, P., Fergus, R.: Indoor segmentation and support inference from RGBD images. In: Fitzgibbon, A., Lazebnik, S., Perona, P., Sato, Y., Schmid, C. (eds.) ECCV 2012. LNCS, vol. 7576, pp. 746–760. Springer, Heidelberg (2012). https://doi.org/10.1007/978-3-642-33715-4_54
25. Song, S., Xiao, J.: Tracking revisited using RGBD camera: unified benchmark and baselines. In: 2013 IEEE International Conference on Computer Vision, pp. 233–240, December 2013. https://doi.org/10.1109/ICCV.2013.36
26. Tateno, K., Tombari, F., Laina, I., Navab, N.: CNN-SLAM: real-time dense monocular SLAM with learned depth prediction. In: 2017 IEEE Conference on Computer Vision and Pattern Recognition (CVPR), pp. 6565–6574, July 2017. https://doi.org/10.1109/CVPR.2017.695
27. Tomasi, C., Kanade, T.: Detection and tracking of point features. Int. J. Comput. Vis. **9**(3), 137–154 (1991). Technical report
28. Uhrig, J., Cordts, M., Franke, U., Brox, T.: Pixel-level encoding and depth layering for instance-level semantic labeling. In: Rosenhahn, B., Andres, B. (eds.) GCPR 2016. LNCS, vol. 9796, pp. 14–25. Springer, Cham (2016). https://doi.org/10.1007/978-3-319-45886-1_2
29. Ummenhofer, B., et al.: DeMoN: depth and motion network for learning monocular stereo. In: IEEE Conference on Computer Vision and Pattern Recognition (CVPR) (2017)
30. Xiao, J., Owens, A., Torralba, A.: SUN3D: a database of big spaces reconstructed using SfM and object labels. In: 2013 IEEE International Conference on Computer Vision (ICCV), pp. 1625–1632. IEEE, December 2013. https://doi.org/10.1109/ICCV.2013.458
31. Xingjian, S., Chen, Z., Wang, H., Yeung, D.Y., Wong, W.K., Woo, W.-c.: Convolutional LSTM network: a machine learning approach for precipitation nowcasting. In: Advances in Neural Information Processing Systems, pp. 802–810 (2015)
32. Zhou, T., Brown, M., Snavely, N., Lowe, D.G.: Unsupervised learning of depth and ego-motion from video. In: IEEE Conference on Computer Vision and Pattern Recognition (CVPR) (2017)

End-to-End 6-DoF Object Pose Estimation Through Differentiable Rasterization

Andrea Palazzi[✉], Luca Bergamini, Simone Calderara, and Rita Cucchiara

University of Modena and Reggio Emilia, Modena, Italy
{andrea.palazzi,luca.bergamini24,simone.calderara,
rita.cucchiara}@unimore.it

Abstract. Here we introduce an approximated differentiable renderer to refine a 6-DoF pose prediction using only 2D alignment information. To this end, a two-branched convolutional encoder network is employed to jointly estimate the object class and its 6-DoF pose in the scene. We then propose a new formulation of an approximated differentiable renderer to re-project the 3D object on the image according to its predicted pose; in this way the alignment error between the observed and the re-projected object silhouette can be measured. Since the renderer is differentiable, it is possible to back-propagate through it to correct the estimated pose at test time in an online learning fashion. Eventually we show how to leverage the classification branch to profitably re-project a representative model of the predicted class (i.e. a medoid) instead. Each object in the scene is processed independently and novel viewpoints in which both objects arrangement and mutual pose are preserved can be rendered.

Differentiable renderer code is available at: https://github.com/ndrplz/tensorflow-mesh-renderer.

Keywords: 6-DoF pose estimation · Differentiable rendering

1 Introduction

Inferring the six degrees of freedom (6-DoF) pose (3D rotations + 3D translations) of an object given a single RGB image is extremely challenging. Indeed, this process underlies a deep knowledge of the object itself and of the 3D world that is not easy to distill from a single frame; the kind of object, its 3D shape and the possible 3D transformation that leads to visually plausible outputs must be inferred jointly.

In this work, we show how an approximate differentiable renderer can be exploited to refine the 6-DoF pose estimation prediction using only 2D silhouette information. Keeping the object volume fixed we can back-propagate to the second renderer input, namely the object pose (see Fig. 1). We demonstrate that this differentiable block can be stacked on a 6-DoF pose estimator to significantly

© Springer Nature Switzerland AG 2019
L. Leal-Taixé and S. Roth (Eds.): ECCV 2018 Workshops, LNCS 11131, pp. 702–715, 2019.
https://doi.org/10.1007/978-3-030-11015-4_53

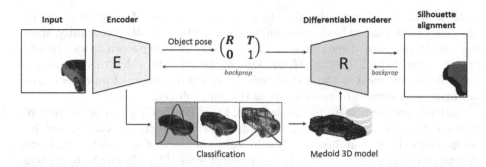

Fig. 1. The overall proposed framework. A deep convolutional encoder is fed with the object mask and predicts both the object's class and 6-DoF pose. By means of a differentiable renderer the predicted cluster medoid can be projected back according to the predicted pose, adding a further online alignment supervision w.r.t. the input mask.

refine the estimated pose using only the 2D alignment information between the input object mask and the rendered silhouette. Leaving aside camera intrinsics, a renderer can be generally thought as a black-box with two inputs and one output. The renderer takes as input (i) a given representation of the 3D object (e.g. voxels, mesh etc.) and (ii) the 6-DoF pose of the object w.r.t. the camera and produces the 2D image of the object or, as in our setting, solely its silhouette.

Typically a rendering algorithm includes many non-differentiable operations (e.g. rounding, hard assignments etc.); it thus cannot be used in a deep learning architecture as it would break the back-propagation chain. Nonetheless, in the context of 3D volume estimation recent works [14,18,24,41,47] have been proposed which exploit approximated differentiable renderers to back-propagate the loss to the first renderer input, namely the 3D representation of the object, but leaving fixed the set of possible camera poses.

Since we rely on an fixed 3D model of the object we can abandon the redundant and expensive voxel representation in favor of meshes, which are lightweight and better tailored to represent 3D models [34]. Also, in contrast w.r.t. previous works, the rendering pipeline is implemented via a *rastering* algorithm, significantly faster than the conventional ray-tracing approach. Eventually, to solve the issue that true 3D model of the object is not usually known at test time, we indicate as a viable solution to perform coarse-grained classification and use a representative 3D model of the object category (*e.g.* a cluster medoid) instead.

We experimentally demonstrate that the proposed pipeline is able to correct the estimated pose effectively even when using surrogate models.

2   Related Works

Beyond all doubt, the ImageNet [10] dataset has been the essential ingredient to many recent advances, since for the first time enough data were available for training very large (deep) models which in turn shook many benchmarks

[6,16,30,33]. More recently the large-scale database of synthetic models ShapeNet [5] dataset is having an analogous impact on the 3D community, showing that, in presence of enough data, 3D geometry and deep learning can be integrated successfully [2,7,22,36,37,46]. One of the areas in which this marriage is being fertile the most is the one of estimating the 3D shape of an object given an image, or to generate novel views of the same object.

Indeed, pre deep learning methods [4,15,20,29,35,42] often need multiple views at test time and rely on the assumption that descriptors can be matched across views [1,13], handling poorly self-occlusions, lack of texture [32] and large viewpoint changes [25]. Conversely, more recent works [2,7,22,36,37,46] are built upon powerful deep learning models trained on virtually infinite synthetic data rendered from ShapeNet [5]. From a high level perspective, we can distinguish methods that learn an implicit representation of object pose and volume and then decode it by means of another deep network [7,11,38,48] from methods that infer from the image a valid 3D representation (e.g. voxel-based) that can be re-projected by means of a differentiable renderer [14,41,44,47] to eventually measure its consistency w.r.t. the input image. Works leveraging the latter approach are strictly related to our proposed method in that they all found different ways to back-propagate through the renderer in order to correct the predicted object volume. Yan *et al.* [47], Gadelha *et al.* [14] and Wiles *et al.* [44] take inspiration from the *spatial transformer network* [18] in the way the predicted volume is sampled to produce the output silhouette, even though they differ in the way the contribution of each voxel is counted for each line of sight. Rendering process proposed in Rezende *et al.* [31] has to be trained via REINFORCE [45] since it is not differentiable. Tulsiani *et al.* [41] frame the rendering phase in a probabilistic setting and define ray potential to enforce consistency. Our method differs substantially from all these works in several features. First, we keep the volume fixed and backpropagate through the renderer to correct the object pose, while the aforementioned works project the predicted 3D volume from a pre-defined set of poses (e.g. 24 azimuthal angles $0°$, $15°$, ... $345°$ around y-axis) and backpropagate the alignment error to correct the volume. Furthermore, while all these works use ray-tracing algorithm for rendering, our work is the first to propose a *differentiable raster-based renderer*. Eventually, all mentioned works represent the volume using voxels, which is inefficient and redundant since almost all valuable information is in the surface [34], while we use its natural parametrization by vertices and faces, i.e. the mesh. Convolutional neural networks (CNNs) have demonstrated analogous effectiveness in the task of object pose estimation, traditionally framed as a Perspective-n-Points (PnP) correspondence problem between the 3D world points and their 2D projections in the image [21,26]. With respect to descriptor-based methods [8,9,25], modern methods relying on CNNs [23,37,40] can solve ambiguities and handle occluded keypoints thanks to their high representational power and composite field of view, and have shown impressive results in specific tasks such as the one of human pose estimation [27,39,43,49]. Building upon this success, recent methods [28,50] combine CNN-extracted keypoints and deformable shape

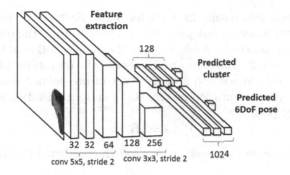

Fig. 2. Architecture of the encoder network. Visual features are extracted from the input image by means of 2D convolutions (first three layers have 5×5 kernel, last two have 3×3 kernel. All convolutional layers have stride 2 and are followed by leaky ReLu non-linearities). The flattened feature vector is fed to two fully connected branch, which estimate the object class and pose respectively.

models in a unique optimization framework to jointly estimate the object pose and shape. Differently from all these works, here we propose a substantially new method to integrate the object shape and pose estimation and model fitting in a unique end-to-end differentiable framework. To the best of our knowledge, this is the first work in which a differentiable renderer is used to correct the 6-DoF object pose estimation just by back-propagating 2D information on silhouette alignment error.

3   Model Description

Given a single RGB image in which one or more objects of interest has already been segmented, we train a deep convolutional encoder to predict the class and the 6-DoF pose (rotation and translation) of each object w.r.t the camera. We then exploit an approximate renderer to re-project the silhouette of object on the image according to the pose predicted by the encoder. As the true object models are not available at test time, for re-projection a representative object (*i.e.* medoid) of the predicted class is used. Also, since the rendering phase is approximated with a differentiable function, we can not only measure the alignment error w.r.t. the input object mask, but also back-propagate it to the encoder weights. Eventually, this allows us to fine-tune the encoder online optimizing just the alignment error. Our overall architecture is depicted in Fig. 1. In what follows both the encoder and the renderer models are detailed.

3.1   Encoder

The deep convolutional encoder network is schematized in Fig. 2. The first part of the network is dedicated to feature extraction and it is shared by the classification and the pose estimation branch. The network has been designed inspired by [38] which showed favorable results in a related task. Features extracted are then used by two fully-connected independent branches to infer the object class and the camera pose respectively. All layers but the last are followed by leaky ReLu activation with $\alpha = 0.2$. Differently from most of the literature [14,44,47] we do not quantize the pose space into a discrete set of pre-defined poses to ease the task. Conversely, given a rotation matrix $\mathbf{R}_{3\times3}$ and a translation vector $\mathbf{t}_{3\times1}$ we regress the object pose

$$\mathbf{P}_{3\times4} = \begin{bmatrix} \mathbf{R} \ \mathbf{t} \end{bmatrix} \tag{1}$$

by optimizing the mean square error between the predicted and the true pose:

$$\mathcal{L}(\mathcal{X}, \mathcal{Y}_p, \theta) = \frac{1}{N} \sum_i \|y_i - f_p(x_i, \theta)\|^2 \quad x_i \in \mathcal{X}, y_i \in \mathcal{Y}_p \tag{2}$$

where $\mathcal{X}$ is the set of RGB images, $\mathcal{Y}_p$ is the set of true $\mathbf{P}_{3\times4}$ pose matrices and $f_p(x_i, \theta)$ is the pose predicted by the encoder for example x_i according to its weights θ. From a technical standpoint, for each X, Y, Z axis the encoder regresses the cosine of the Euler rotation angle and the respective translation. The output roto-translation matrix is then composed following Euler ZYX convention: in this way predicted matrices are guaranteed to be always geometrically consistent. For the classification branch we instead optimize the following categorical cross-entropy function:

$$\mathcal{L}(\mathcal{X}, \mathcal{Y}_c, \theta) = -\frac{1}{N} \sum_i y_i \log f_c(x_i, \theta) \tag{3}$$

where $x_i \in \mathcal{X}$ is an input RGB image, $f_c(x_i, \theta)$ is the encoder predicted distribution over possible clusters for example x_i and y_i in the true one-hot distribution for example x_i.

3.2   Differentiable Renderer

To measure the reliability of the predicted 6-DoF pose and to be able to correct it at test time, we design a fully differentiable renderer for re-projecting the silhouette of the 3D model on the image according to the predicted object pose. This allows to refine the estimated pose by back-propagating the alignment error between the 2D silhouettes. To the best of our knowledge, it is the first time that a fully-differentiable raster-based renderer is used to this purpose. Differently from concurrent works such as [47], our rendering process starts from the raw mesh triangles and not from a 3D voxel representation. While the latter is easier to predict by a neural network since it has a static shape, its footprint scales with the cube of the resolution and forces to use ray-tracing techniques to render the final image, known to be slow and harder to parallelize. Despite rastering does not allow for photo-realistic shaded images, as it does not imply light sources rays tracing, it is still well suited for all tasks which require the object shape silhouette from different point of views as in our case.

Our renderer is composed of two main parts:

- A *rastering algorithm*, which applies the predicted camera to the 3D triangles meshes to obtain 2D projected floating point coordinates of the corners;
- An *in/out test* to determine which projected points lie inside the triangles, *i.e.* which triangles must be filled.

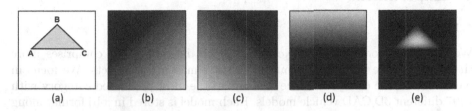

Fig. 3. Exemplification of the approximated rastering process. First each triangle composing the mesh is projected in the 2D image (a) using Eq. 4. The determinant product inside the max of Eq. 5 selects the points which lie on the left side of each edge of the triangle (b), (c), (d). The product of these three terms gives an approximated yet differentiable rendering of the triangle's silhouette (e).

While the first step is fully differentiable, a naive implementation of the latter exploits boolean masks to select the pixels to be filled, which eventually breaks the backpropagation through the network. Inspired by [18], we employed a spatial transformation to assign a value to each pixel based on a relation between its coordinates and those of the triangles corners. While a boolean mask represents hard membership, this approach assigns each pixels a continuous value, thus applying a soft (differentiable) membership. From a more technical standpoint, given all triangles T which compose the mesh of current model, we project the 3D triangle vertices V_{3D} as follows:

$$\begin{bmatrix} V_{2D} \\ 1 \end{bmatrix} = \begin{bmatrix} x/z \\ y/z \\ 1 \end{bmatrix} = \mathbf{K}_{3\times3}\mathbf{P}_{3\times4}^{-1} \begin{bmatrix} V_{3D} \\ 1 \end{bmatrix} \tag{4}$$

where $\mathbf{K}_{3x3}$ is the camera calibration matrix and $\mathbf{P}_{3\times4}^{-1}$.

Then, defined as $E^{(i)} = [(v_1, v_0), (v_2, v_1), (v_0, v_2)]$ the three edges of the i-th projected triangle, the renderer's output for pixel in location (u, v) can be computed as:

$$g_{u,v} = \sum_i^T F_{norm}\left(\prod_{(v_j,v_k)}^{E^{(i)}} \max\left(\left|\begin{matrix} v_j - v_k \\ v_j - (u,v) \end{matrix}\right|\left|\begin{matrix} v_1 - v_0 \\ v_2 - v_1 \end{matrix}\right|, 0\right)\right), \quad (u,v) \in H \times W$$

$$where \quad F_{norm}(x) = \tanh \frac{x - min(x)}{max(x) - min(x)} \tag{5}$$

and H, W indicate the image height and width in pixels. We refer the reader to Fig. 3 for a better intuition of Eq. 5. It is worth noticing that the i-th triangle contributes to the output only if all the three determinant products are positive, meaning that (u, v) point lies on the left side of all three triangle edges $i.e.$ it is inside the triangle.

4   Experiments

4.1   Dataset

We train our model on ShapeNetCore(v2) [5] dataset, which comprises more than 50K unique 3D models from 55 distinct man-made objects. We focus in particular on the car synset since it is one of the most populated category with 7497 different 3D CAD vehicle models. Each model is stored in .obj format along with its materials and textures: dimensions, number of vertices and details vary greatly from one model another.

Data Collection. To collect the data, we first load a random model on the origin $\mathbf{t} = (0, 0, 0)$ of our reference system. We then create a camera in location $\mathbf{t} = (x, y, z)$. While on xy plane the location is randomly sampled in a $q_x \times q_y$ grid, we keep fixed $z = k$ under the assumption that the camera is mounted somewhere at height k on a moving agent (e.g. an unmanned vehicle). We then force the camera to point an empty object e that is randomly sampled at $z = 0$ and x, y sampled as above in a $e_x \times e_y$ grid: in this way we make the object to appear translated in the camera image. Eventually, the camera image is dumped along with the camera pose to constitute an example x_i. We refer the reader to Fig. 4 to get a better insight into the procedure. *Data collection details:* In our experiments we set $q_x = q_y = 10$ and $k = 1.5$, which is the average height of a European vehicle. For the empty object we set $e_x = e_y = 3$. Models are standardized s.t. the major dimension has length 6. For each cluster, the models are split with ratio 0.6-0.2-0.2 into train, validation and test set respectively. Medoids are expected to be known at test-time and do not belong to any of the splits. Models are rendered using Blender CYCLES engine [3] to maximize photo-realism.

Selecting the Representative 3D Model. Since the true 3D object model is hardly available at test time, we want to verify if a surrogate 3D model can be instead successfully employed for the rendering process. Analogously to Du et al. [12] we distinguish three main vehicle clusters, namely (i) *Sedan* passenger cars, (ii) *Sport-utility vehicles* (SUV, which are also passenger cars but have off-road features like raised ground clearance) and (iii) *Cargo* vehicles such as trucks and ambulances. Aligned CAD models for the three clusters are depicted in Fig. 4(c). Following Tatarchenko et al. [38] we selected the representative model for each cluster, by extracting and comparing the HOG descriptors from two standard rendered views of each CAD model (i.e. frontal and side). Eventually we compute the $L2$ distance between descriptors and for each cluster we retain the cluster medoid, *i.e.* the model with the least average distance from all the others.

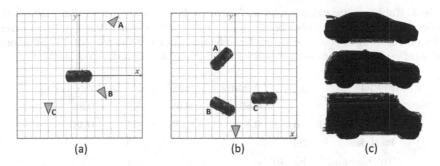

Fig. 4. On the left is depicted how all camera poses predicted by the encoder independently for each object (a) can be roto-translated to a common origin to reconstruct the overall scene (b), also in Fig. 7. On the right, the average silhouette of vehicles belonging to *sedan*, *SUV* and *cargo* is shown (c). For each cluster all 3D meshes are overlaid before taking the snapshot from the side view; the high overlap highlights the low intra-cluster variance.

4.2   Model Evaluation

Metrics. The encoder ability to estimate the 3D pose of the object is measured by means of geodesic distance between predicted and true rotation matrix [17, 40] as:

$$\Delta(\mathbf{R}_{true}, \mathbf{R}_{pred}) = \frac{\|\log(\mathbf{R}_{true}^T \mathbf{R}_{pred})\|_F}{\sqrt{2}} \qquad (6)$$

where $\|\mathbf{A}\|_F = \sqrt{\sum_{i,j} |a_{ij}|^2}$ indicates the Frobenius norm. In particular, we report the median value of the aforementioned distance over all predictions in test set as Median Viewpoint Error (MVE). We also report the percentage of examples in which the pose rotation error is smaller than $\pi/6$ as $Acc_{\frac{\pi}{6}}$. To measure the re-projection alignment error we instead rely on mean intersection over union (mIoU) metric defined over the N test examples as $\frac{1}{N} \sum_i \frac{S_i \cap \tilde{S}_i}{S_i \cup \tilde{S}_i}$ $i = 1, \dots, N$: where S_i is the ground truth silhouette and $\tilde{S}_i = g(f_p(x_i), f_c(x_i), \mathbf{K})$ is the renderer output given the predicted object pose, cluster and camera intrinsics $\mathbf{K}$.

Model Performance. To prove the effectiveness of the proposed method we first train the 6-DoF pose estimation network alone to jointly estimate the object class and its 6-DoF pose. In this way, we get a baseline to measure the successive contribute of the prediction refinement through our differentiable rendering module. State-of-the-art results on test set reported in Table 1 (first row) indicate this to be already a strong baseline. The prediction refinement module is then plugged-in, and the evaluation is repeated. For each example, the medoid of the predicted class is rendered according to the predicted pose, back-propagating the alignment error between the true and the rendered silhouette for 30 optimization steps. Results of this analysis are reported in Table 1 (second row) and indicate a huge performance gain (20%) obtainable by maximizing the 2D alignment between object masks.

Table 1. Table summarizing model performance. It is worth noticing that none of the metrics in the table are explicitly optimized during refinement. Results of concurrent works on the vehicle class are shown for reference, despite the task of [37,40] is only viewpoint estimation (not 6-DoF pose) and all are trained on different dataset.

Model	Accuracy ↑	mIoU ↑	MVE ↓	$Acc_{\frac{\pi}{6}}$ ↑
encoder	0.89	0.59	5.7	0.86
encoder+refinement	**0.89**	**0.72**	**4.5**	**0.90**
Pavlakos *et al.* [28]	-	-	6.9	-
Tulsiani and Malik [40]	-	-	9.1	0.89
Su *et al.* [37]	-	-	6.0	0.88

The significant improvement in all the metrics, despite none of these is optimized explicitly, suggests that the proposed differentiable rendering module is a viable solution for refining the predicted 6-DoF even at test time, requiring minimal information (*i.e.* only the object mask). The process of prediction refinement can be appreciated in Fig. 5.

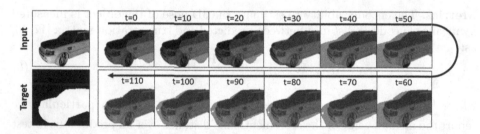

Fig. 5. Online refinement of the estimated pose; We overlay in red the predicted silhouette for each optimization step. Despite the initial estimate (t = 0) was noticeably wrong, the 6-DoF object pose is gradually corrected using only 2D silhouette alignment information. (Color figure online)

Renderer Ablation Study. We measure, at first, the impact of rendering resolution on the optimization process by refining the object 6-DoF estimated pose using different rendering resolutions. Results reported in Table 2 show that working at higher resolution is definitely helpful while very-low resolution are hardly beneficial, if not detrimental, for the optimization process. This supports the need to abandon the voxel-based representation, whose computational footprint increases with the cube of resolution. We then compare our renderer with the publicly available implementation of Perspective Transformer Network (PTN) by Yan *et al.* [47]. Results are shown in Fig. 6(a). Since PTN relies on a fixed $32 \times 32 \times 32$ voxel representation, rendering at higher resolution hardly changes the output's fidelity w.r.t. the true silhouette. Conversely, our mesh-based renderer is able to effectively take advantage of the higher resolution. Comparing our rendering time with PTN [47] in Fig. 6(b), we see that PTN scores favorably only for very-low voxel and image resolutions, while as resolution increases the

Table 2. Gains obtained in pose estimation using different rendering resolutions. Increasing the resolution used for rendering the silhouette is much beneficial to the optimization process. Conversely, for very low resolution this phase is hardly helpful.

Renderer resolution	Δ IoU $\uparrow$	Δ Viewpoint error $\downarrow$	Δ Translation error $\downarrow$
16×16	$+0.00$	$+0.15$	$+0.02$
32×32	$+0.03$	-0.26	$+0.00$
64×64	$+0.05$	-0.57	$+0.00$
128×128	$+0.11$	-1.03	-0.01
256×256	$+0.13$	-1.29	-0.03

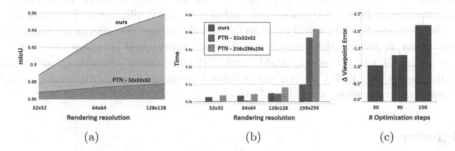

(a)   (b)   (c)

Fig. 6. (a) Intersection over union between rendered silhouette and the ground truth one for both our renderer and Perspective Transformer Networks (PTN) [47], at different rendering resolutions. (b) Rendering time for different image (and PTN voxel) resolutions. (c) Average viewpoint error improvement for different number of optimization steps. See text for details.

PTN rendering time increases exponentially due to the voxel-based representation. Eventually, in Fig. 6(c) we show that our average viewpoint error continues to decrease along with the number of refinement optimization steps.

Training Details. Encoder is trained until convergence with batch size $= 64$ and ADAM optimizer with learning rate 10^{-5} (other hyper-parameters as suggested

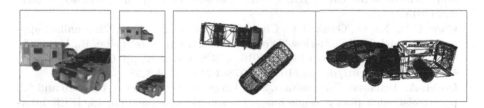

Fig. 7. Qualitative results for multiple object scenes. Since all predicted poses lie in the same reference system (see Fig. 4), different views of the scene can be produced by means of any rendering engine. It is worth noticing that each object has been substituted by the representative model for its predicted class.

in the original paper [19]). Batch size is decreased to 20 and learning rate to 10^{-6} during renderer fine-tuning. We find useful dropout ($p = 0.5$) after all dense layers and $L2$ weight decay over feature extraction for regularization purposes.

5 Conclusions

In this work we introduce a 6-DoF pose estimation framework which allows an *online* refinement of the predicted pose from minimal 2D information (*i.e.* the object mask). A fully differentiable raster-based renderer is developed for re-projecting the object silhouette on the image according to the predicted 6-DoF pose: this allows to correct the predicted pose by simply back-propagating the alignment error between the observed and the rendered silhouette. Experimental results indicate (i) the overall effectiveness of the online optimization phase, (ii) that proxy representative models can be profitably used in place of the true ones in case these are not available and (iii) the benefit of working in higher resolution, well-handled by our raster-based renderer but hardly managed by concurrent ray-tracing, voxel-based algorithms.

References

1. Agarwal, S., et al.: Building Rome in a day. Commun. ACM **54**(10), 105–112 (2011)
2. Aubry, M., Maturana, D., Efros, A.A., Russell, B.C., Sivic, J.: Seeing 3D chairs: exemplar part-based 2D–3D alignment using a large dataset of CAD models. In: Proceedings of the IEEE Conference on Computer Vision and Pattern Recognition, pp. 3762–3769 (2014)
3. Blender Online Community: Blender - a 3D modelling and rendering package. Blender Foundation, Blender Institute, Amsterdam (2017). http://www.blender.org
4. Boyer, E., Franco, J.S.: A hybrid approach for computing visual hulls of complex objects. In: Proceedings of the IEEE Conference on Computer Vision and Pattern Recognition, pp. 695–701. IEEE Computer Society Press (2003)
5. Chang, A.X., et al.: ShapeNet: an information-rich 3D model repository. arXiv preprint arXiv:1512.03012 (2015)
6. Chen, L.C., Papandreou, G., Kokkinos, I., Murphy, K., Yuille, A.L.: DeepLab: semantic image segmentation with deep convolutional nets, atrous convolution, and fully connected CRFs. IEEE Trans. Pattern Anal. Mach. Intell. **40**(4), 834–848 (2018)
7. Choy, C.B., Xu, D., Gwak, J.Y., Chen, K., Savarese, S.: 3D-R2N2: a unified approach for single and multi-view 3D object reconstruction. In: Leibe, B., Matas, J., Sebe, N., Welling, M. (eds.) ECCV 2016. LNCS, vol. 9912, pp. 628–644. Springer, Cham (2016). https://doi.org/10.1007/978-3-319-46484-8_38
8. Collet, A., Berenson, D., Srinivasa, S.S., Ferguson, D.: Object recognition and full pose registration from a single image for robotic manipulation. In: IEEE International Conference on Robotics and Automation, ICRA 2009, pp. 48–55. IEEE (2009)
9. Collet, A., Martinez, M., Srinivasa, S.S.: The moped framework: object recognition and pose estimation for manipulation. Int. J. Robot. Res. **30**(10), 1284–1306 (2011)

10. Deng, J., Dong, W., Socher, R., Li, L.J., Li, K., Fei-Fei, L.: ImageNet: a large-scale hierarchical image database. In: IEEE Conference on Computer Vision and Pattern Recognition, CVPR 2009, pp. 248–255. IEEE (2009)
11. Dosovitskiy, A., Springenberg, J.T., Tatarchenko, M., Brox, T.: Learning to generate chairs, tables and cars with convolutional networks. IEEE Trans. Pattern Anal. Mach. Intell. **39**(4), 692–705 (2017)
12. Du, X., Ang Jr., M.H., Karaman, S., Rus, D.: A general pipeline for 3D detection of vehicles. In: ICRA (2018)
13. Fitzgibbon, A., Zisserman, A.: Automatic 3D model acquisition and generation of new images from video sequences. In: 9th European Signal Processing Conference (EUSIPCO 1998), pp. 1–8. IEEE (1998)
14. Gadelha, M., Maji, S., Wang, R.: 3D shape induction from 2D views of multiple objects. 3D Vision (2017)
15. Gortler, S.J., Grzeszczuk, R., Szeliski, R., Cohen, M.F.: The lumigraph. In: Proceedings of the 23rd Annual Conference on Computer Graphics and Interactive Techniques, pp. 43–54. ACM (1996)
16. He, K., Zhang, X., Ren, S., Sun, J.: Deep residual learning for image recognition. In: Proceedings of the IEEE Conference on Computer Vision and Pattern Recognition, pp. 770–778 (2016)
17. Huynh, D.Q.: Metrics for 3D rotations: comparison and analysis. J. Math. Imaging Vis. **35**(2), 155–164 (2009)
18. Jaderberg, M., Simonyan, K., Zisserman, A., et al.: Spatial transformer networks. In: Advances in Neural Information Processing Systems, pp. 2017–2025 (2015)
19. Kingma, D.P., Ba, J.: Adam: a method for stochastic optimization. arXiv preprint arXiv:1412.6980 (2014)
20. Kolev, K., Klodt, M., Brox, T., Cremers, D.: Continuous global optimization in multiview 3D reconstruction. Int. J. Comput. Vis. **84**(1), 80–96 (2009)
21. Lepetit, V., Moreno-Noguer, F., Fua, P.: EPnP: an accurate O(n) solution to the PnP problem. Int. J. Comput. Vis. **81**(2), 155 (2009)
22. Lim, J.J., Khosla, A., Torralba, A.: FPM: fine pose parts-based model with 3D CAD models. In: Fleet, D., Pajdla, T., Schiele, B., Tuytelaars, T. (eds.) ECCV 2014. LNCS, vol. 8694, pp. 478–493. Springer, Cham (2014). https://doi.org/10.1007/978-3-319-10599-4_31
23. Long, J.L., Zhang, N., Darrell, T.: Do convnets learn correspondence? In: Advances in Neural Information Processing Systems, pp. 1601–1609 (2014)
24. Loper, M.M., Black, M.J.: OpenDR: an approximate differentiable renderer. In: Fleet, D., Pajdla, T., Schiele, B., Tuytelaars, T. (eds.) ECCV 2014. LNCS, vol. 8695, pp. 154–169. Springer, Cham (2014). https://doi.org/10.1007/978-3-319-10584-0_11
25. Lowe, D.G.: Distinctive image features from scale-invariant keypoints. Int. J. Comput. Vis. **60**(2), 91–110 (2004)
26. Moreno-Noguer, F., Lepetit, V., Fua, P.: Accurate non-iterative O(n) solution to the PnP problem. In: IEEE 11th international conference on Computer vision, ICCV 2007, pp. 1–8. IEEE (2007)
27. Newell, A., Yang, K., Deng, J.: Stacked hourglass networks for human pose estimation. In: Leibe, B., Matas, J., Sebe, N., Welling, M. (eds.) ECCV 2016. LNCS, vol. 9912, pp. 483–499. Springer, Cham (2016). https://doi.org/10.1007/978-3-319-46484-8_29
28. Pavlakos, G., Zhou, X., Chan, A., Derpanis, K.G., Daniilidis, K.: 6-DoF object pose from semantic keypoints. In: 2017 IEEE International Conference on Robotics and Automation (ICRA), pp. 2011–2018. IEEE (2017)

29. Pollefeys, M., Koch, R., Vergauwen, M., Van Gool, L.: Metric 3D surface reconstruction from uncalibrated image sequences. In: Koch, R., Van Gool, L. (eds.) SMILE 1998. LNCS, vol. 1506, pp. 139–154. Springer, Heidelberg (1998). https://doi.org/10.1007/3-540-49437-5_10

30. Redmon, J., Divvala, S., Girshick, R., Farhadi, A.: You only look once: unified, real-time object detection. In: Proceedings of the IEEE Conference on Computer Vision and Pattern Recognition, pp. 779–788 (2016)

31. Rezende, D.J., Eslami, S.A., Mohamed, S., Battaglia, P., Jaderberg, M., Heess, N.: Unsupervised learning of 3D structure from images. In: Advances in Neural Information Processing Systems, pp. 4996–5004 (2016)

32. Saponaro, P., Sorensen, S., Rhein, S., Mahoney, A.R., Kambhamettu, C.: Reconstruction of textureless regions using structure from motion and image-based interpolation. In: 2014 IEEE International Conference on Image Processing (ICIP), pp. 1847–1851. IEEE (2014)

33. Simonyan, K., Zisserman, A.: Very deep convolutional networks for large-scale image recognition. arXiv preprint arXiv:1409.1556 (2014)

34. Sinha, A., Unmesh, A., Huang, Q., Ramani, K.: SurfNet: generating 3D shape surfaces using deep residual networks. In: Proceedings of CVPR (2017)

35. Starck, J., Hilton, A.: Model-based human shape reconstruction from multiple views. Comput. Vis. Image Underst. **111**(2), 179–194 (2008)

36. Stark, M., Goesele, M., Schiele, B.: Back to the future: learning shape models from 3D CAD data. In: BMVC, vol. 2, p. 5. Citeseer (2010)

37. Su, H., Qi, C.R., Li, Y., Guibas, L.J.: Render for CNN: viewpoint estimation in images using CNNs trained with rendered 3D model views. In: Proceedings of the IEEE International Conference on Computer Vision, pp. 2686–2694 (2015)

38. Tatarchenko, M., Dosovitskiy, A., Brox, T.: Multi-view 3D models from single images with a convolutional network. In: Leibe, B., Matas, J., Sebe, N., Welling, M. (eds.) ECCV 2016. LNCS, vol. 9911, pp. 322–337. Springer, Cham (2016). https://doi.org/10.1007/978-3-319-46478-7_20

39. Toshev, A., Szegedy, C.: DeepPose: human pose estimation via deep neural networks. In: Proceedings of the IEEE Conference on Computer Vision and Pattern Recognition, pp. 1653–1660 (2014)

40. Tulsiani, S., Malik, J.: Viewpoints and keypoints. In: Proceedings of the IEEE Conference on Computer Vision and Pattern Recognition, pp. 1510–1519 (2015)

41. Tulsiani, S., Zhou, T., Efros, A.A., Malik, J.: Multi-view supervision for single-view reconstruction via differentiable ray consistency. In: CVPR, vol. 1, p. 3 (2017)

42. Vogiatzis, G., Esteban, C.H., Torr, P.H., Cipolla, R.: Multiview stereo via volumetric graph-cuts and occlusion robust photo-consistency. IEEE Trans. Pattern Anal. Mach. Intell. **29**(12), 2241–2246 (2007)

43. Wei, S.E., Ramakrishna, V., Kanade, T., Sheikh, Y.: Convolutional pose machines. In: Proceedings of the IEEE Conference on Computer Vision and Pattern Recognition, pp. 4724–4732 (2016)

44. Wiles, O., Zisserman, A.: SilNet: single-and multi-view reconstruction by learning from silhouettes. In: British Machine Vision Conference (2017)

45. Williams, R.J.: Simple statistical gradient-following algorithms for connectionist reinforcement learning. Mach. Learn. **8**, 5–32 (1992)

46. Wu, J., Zhang, C., Xue, T., Freeman, B., Tenenbaum, J.: Learning a probabilistic latent space of object shapes via 3D generative-adversarial modeling. In: Advances in Neural Information Processing Systems, pp. 82–90 (2016)

47. Yan, X., Yang, J., Yumer, E., Guo, Y., Lee, H.: Perspective transformer nets: learning single-view 3D object reconstruction without 3D supervision. In: Advances in Neural Information Processing Systems, pp. 1696–1704 (2016)
48. Yang, J., Reed, S.E., Yang, M.H., Lee, H.: Weakly-supervised disentangling with recurrent transformations for 3D view synthesis. In: Advances in Neural Information Processing Systems, pp. 1099–1107 (2015)
49. Zhou, X., Zhu, M., Leonardos, S., Derpanis, K.G., Daniilidis, K.: Sparseness meets deepness: 3D human pose estimation from monocular video. In: Proceedings of the IEEE Conference on Computer Vision and Pattern Recognition, pp. 4966–4975 (2016)
50. Zhu, M., Zhou, X., Daniilidis, K.: Single image pop-up from discriminatively learned parts. In: Proceedings of the IEEE International Conference on Computer Vision, pp. 927–935 (2015)

YOLO3D: End-to-End Real-Time 3D Oriented Object Bounding Box Detection from LiDAR Point Cloud

Waleed Ali(iD), Sherif Abdelkarim(iD), Mahmoud Zidan(iD),
Mohamed Zahran$^{(\boxtimes)}$(iD), and Ahmad El Sallab(iD)

Valeo AI Research, Cairo, Egypt
{waleed.ali,sherif.abdelkarim,
mahmoud.ismail-zidan.ext,mohamed.zahran,
ahmad.el-sallab}@valeo.com

Abstract. Object detection and classification in 3D is a key task in Automated Driving (AD). LiDAR sensors are employed to provide the 3D point cloud reconstruction of the surrounding environment, while the task of 3D object bounding box detection in real time remains a strong algorithmic challenge. In this paper, we build on the success of the one-shot regression meta-architecture in the 2D perspective image space and extend it to generate oriented 3D object bounding boxes from LiDAR point cloud. Our main contribution is in extending the loss function of YOLO v2 to include the yaw angle, the 3D box center in Cartesian coordinates and the height of the box as a direct regression problem. This formulation enables real-time performance, which is essential for automated driving. Our results are showing promising figures on KITTI benchmark, achieving real-time performance (40 fps) on Titan X GPU.

Keywords: 3D object detection · LiDAR · Real-time

1 Introduction

Automated Driving (AD) success is highly dependent on efficient environment perception. Sensors technology is an enabler to environment perception. LiDAR-based environment perception systems are essential components for homogeneous (same sensor type) or heterogeneous (different sensors types) fusion systems. The key feature of LiDAR is its physical ability to perceive depth at high accuracy.

Among the most important tasks of the environment perception is Object Bounding Box (OBB) detection and classification, which may be done in the 2D (bird-view) or the 3D space. Unlike camera-based systems, LiDAR point clouds are lacking some features that exist in camera RGB perspective scenes, like colors. This makes the classification task from LiDAR only more complicated.

W. Ali and S. Abdelkarim—Contributed equally.

© Springer Nature Switzerland AG 2019
L. Leal-Taixé and S. Roth (Eds.): ECCV 2018 Workshops, LNCS 11131, pp. 716–728, 2019.
https://doi.org/10.1007/978-3-030-11015-4_54

On the other hand, depth is given as a natural measurement by LiDAR, which enables 3D OBB detections. The density of the LiDAR point cloud plays a vital role in the efficient classification of the object type, especially small objects like pedestrians and animals.

Real-time performance is essential in AD systems. While Deep Learning (DL) has a well-known success story in camera-based computer vision, such approaches suffer high latency in their inference path, due to the expensive convolution operations. In the context of object detection, rich literature exists that tackles the problem of real-time performance. Single shot detectors, like YOLO [1] and SSD [2] are some of the best in this regard.

In this paper, we extend YOLO V2 [3] to perform 3D OBB detection and classification from 3D LiDAR point cloud (PCL). In the input phase, we feed the bird-view of the 3D PCL to the input convolution channels. The network architecture follows the meta-architecture of YOLO with architecture adaptation and tuning to match the nature of the sparse LiDAR input. The predictions include 8 regression outputs + classes (versus 5 regressors + classes in case of YOLO V2): the OBB center in 3D (x, y, z), the 3D dimensions (length, width and height), the orientation in the bird-view space, the confidence, and the object class label. Following the one-shot regression theme, we do not depend on any region proposal pipelines, instead, the whole system is trained end to end.

The main contributions of this work can be summarized as follows:

1. Extending YOLO V2 [3] to include orientation of the OBB as a direct regression task.
2. Extending YOLO V2 [3] to include the height and 3D OBB center coordinates (x, y, z) as a direct regression task.
3. Real-time performance evaluation and experimentation with Titan X GPU, on the challenging KITTI benchmark, with recommendations of the best grid-map resolution, and operating IoU threshold that balances speed and accuracy.

The results evaluated on KITTI benchmark shows a clear advantage of the proposed approach, in terms of real-time efficiency (40 fps), and a promising accuracy. The rest of the paper is organized as follows: first, we discuss the related works, followed by a description of the proposed approach, and the combined one-shot loss for the 3D OBB, then we present, and discuss the experimental results on the KITTI benchmark dataset. Finally, we provide concluding remarks in Sect. 5.

2   Related Work

In this section, we summarize 3D object detection in autonomous driving for LiDAR point clouds. We then summarize related works in orientation prediction, which we use to predict the real angle of the vehicle. Finally, we discuss the implications of 3D object detection on the real-time performance.

Fig. 1. Sample of the output shown in 3D and projected on the top view map

2.1   3D Object Detection

There are three ways to do 3D object detection in terms of sensor type. Firstly, it is the LIDAR-only paradigm, which benefits from accurate depth information. Overall, these paradigms differ in data preprocessing. Some approaches project point cloud in 2D view (Bird-View, Front-View) such as [4,5]; and some [6] convert the point cloud to a front view depth map. Others like [7,8], convert the point cloud to voxels producing a discrete square grid.

The Second one is the camera-only paradigm; which works by adding prior knowledge about the objects' sizes, and trying to predict 3D bounding box using monocolor camera. [9,10] can produce highly accurate 3D bounding boxes using only camera images. [11] uses stereo vision to produce high-quality 3D object detection.

The LIDAR-camera fusion comes at the last. This paradigm tries to utilize the advantages of both paradigms mentioned above. The LIDAR produces accurate depth information, and the camera produces rich visual features; if we combine the output of the two sensors, we can have more accurate object detection and recognition. MV3D [5] fuses bird view, front view and the RGB camera to produce 3D vehicle detection. F-pointnet [12] combines raw point cloud with RGB camera images. Object detection on RGB image produces a 2D bounding box which maps to a frustum in the point cloud. Then, 3D object detection is performed directly on frustum to produce accurate bounding boxes. However, fusing lidar data with camera suffers from adding more time complexity to the problem.

In this work, we are following the first paradigm of using only lidar point cloud projected as special bird view grid to keep the 3D information, more details will be discussed in Sect. 3.1.

2.2 Orientation Prediction

One approach in finding the orientation is introduced by MV3D [5], where the orientation vector is assumed to be in the direction of the longer side of the box. This approach fails in regards to pedestrians because they don't obey this rule.

Another approach is to convert the orientation vector to its component, as shown in [13,14]. AVOD [13] converts the orientation vector to sine and cosine. Complex YOLO [14] converts the orientation vector to real and imaginary values. The problem with this is that the regression does not guarantee, or preserve any type of correlation between the two components of the angle.

2.3 Real Time Performance

Object detection is fundamental to automated driving, yet it suffers from computational complexity. There is a need to make the models as efficient as possible in terms of size and inference time maintaining a good accuracy.

Some work has been done to tackle the efficiency of models, such as Squeeze-Net [15], Mobile-Net [16], and Shuffle-Net [17], and for object detection, there is Tiny YOLO and Tiny SSD [18]. All these architectures are optimized for camera images, and they cannot easily be adapted to work on images produced from LiDAR point clouds. The reason is that, unlike camera images, LiDAR images consist of very sparse information. Vote3Deep [19] performs 3D sparse convolution to take advantage of this sparsity.

Extending YOLOv2 [3], we include the orientation of the OBB as a direct regression task, unlike the work in [14], which suggests two separate losses for the real and imaginary parts of the angle, without explicit nor implicit correlation between them, which may result in wrong or invalid angles in many cases.

In addition, in [14], 3D OBB height and z-center are not a natural or exact output from the network, but rather a heuristic based on statistics and average sizes of the data. In this work, we extend YoLo v2 [3] to include height and 3D OBB center as direct regression tasks. A sample of our output can be seen in Fig. 1, taken from KITTI benchmark test data.

3 Approach

3.1 Point Cloud Representation

We project the point cloud to create a bird's eye view grid map. We create two grid maps from the projection of the point cloud as shown in Fig. 2. The first feature map contains the maximum height, where each grid cell (pixel) value represents the height of the highest point associated with that cell. We use only the maximum height instead of a more complex statistic over the z dimension because we are only interested in the highest point of the object. The second grid map represent the density of points. Which means, the more points are associated with a grid cell, the higher its value would be. The density is calculated using the following equation taken from MV3D paper [5]:

$$min(1.0, \frac{\log(N+1)}{\log(64)})$$ (1)

Where N is the number of points in each grid cell.

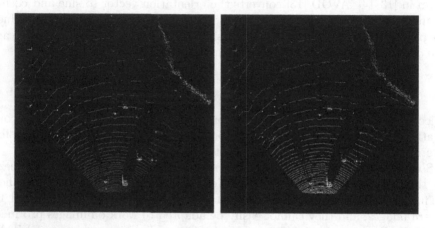

Fig. 2. Sample of the input grid maps. Left: the height map. Right: the density map.

3.2   Yaw Angle Regression

The orientation of the bounding boxes has a range from $-\pi$ to π. We normalized that range to be from -1 to 1, and adapted our model to directly predict the orientation of the bounding box via a single regressed number. In the loss function, we compute the mean squared error between the ground truth and our predicted angle:

$$\sum_{i=0}^{s^2} \sum_{j=0}^{B} L_{ij}^{obj} (\phi_i - \hat{\phi}_i)^2$$ (2)

In our experimentation, we used using tanh as an activation for the angle output yaw (to bound the output between -1 and 1), but it did not offer an improvement over the linear activation.

3.3   3D Bounding Box Regression

We added two regression terms to the original YOLO v2 [3] in order to produce 3D bounding boxes, the z coordinate of the center, and the height of the box.

The regression over the z coordinate in Eq. (5) is done in a way similar to the regression of the x Eq. (3) and y Eq. (4) coordinates via a sigmoid activation function.

While the x and y are regressed by predicting a value between 0 and 1 at each grid cell, locating where the point lies within that cell, the value of z is only mapped to lie within one vertical grid cell as illustrated in Fig. 3. The reason for choosing to map z values to only one grid while x and y are mapped to several grid cells is that the variability of values in the z dimension are much smaller than that of the x and y (most objects have very similar box elevations).

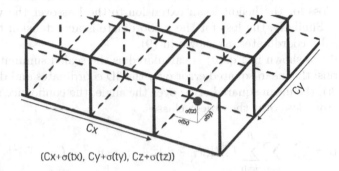

(Cx+σ(tx), Cy+σ(ty), Cz+σ(tz))

Fig. 3. Sample of the grid output when extended to the third dimension where cz equals 0 since the grids are only one level high in the z dimension.

The height of the box h Eq. (8) is also predicted similarly to the width w in Eq. (6) and length l in Eq. (7)

$$b_x = \sigma(t_x) + c_x \tag{3}$$
$$b_y = \sigma(t_y) + c_y \tag{4}$$
$$b_z = \sigma(t_z) + c_z \tag{5}$$
$$b_w = p_w e^{t_w} \tag{6}$$
$$b_l = p_l e^{t_l} \tag{7}$$
$$b_h = p_h e^{t_h} \tag{8}$$

3.4   Anchors Calculation

In YOLO-v2 [3], anchors are calculated using k-means clustering over the width and length of the ground truth boxes. The point behind using anchors, is to find priors for the boxes, onto which the model can predict modifications. The anchors must be able to cover the whole range of boxes that can appear in the data. In [3], the model is trained on camera images, where there is a high variability of box sizes, even for the same object class. Therefore, calculating anchors using clustering is beneficial.

On the other hand, in the case of bird's eye view grid maps, there is no such high variability in box dimensions within the same object class (most cars have similar sizes). For this reason, we chose not to use clustering to calculate the anchors, and instead, calculate the mean 3D box dimensions for each object class, and use these average box dimensions as our anchors.

3.5   Combined Loss for 3D OBB

The loss for 3D oriented boxes is an extension to the original YOLO loss for 2D boxes. The loss for the yaw term is calculated as described in Subsect. 3.2 and Eq. (2). The loss for the height is an extension to the loss over the width and length in (9). Similarly, the loss for the z coordinate is an extension to the loss over the x and y coordinates, as shown in (9).

The total loss shown in Eq. (9) is calculated as the scaled summation of the following terms: the mean squared error over the 3D coordinates and dimensions (x, y, z, w, l, h), the mean squared error over the angle, the confidence score, and the cross entropy loss over the object classes.

$$
\begin{aligned}
L = \lambda_{coor} \sum_{i=0}^{s^2} \sum_{j=0}^{B} L_{ij}^{obj} [(x_i - \hat{x}_i)^2 + (y_i - \hat{y}_i)^2 + (z_i - \hat{z}_i)^2] \\
+ \lambda_{coor} \sum_{i=0}^{s^2} \sum_{j=0}^{B} L_{ij}^{obj} [(\sqrt{w_i} - \sqrt{\hat{w}_i})^2 + (\sqrt{l_i} - \sqrt{\hat{l}_i})^2 \\
+ (\sqrt{h_i} - \sqrt{\hat{h}_i})^2] \\
+ \lambda_{yaw} \sum_{i=0}^{s^2} \sum_{j=0}^{B} L_{ij}^{obj} (\phi_i - \hat{\phi}_i)^2 \\
+ \lambda_{conf} \sum_{i=0}^{s^2} \sum_{j=0}^{B} L_{ij}^{obj} (C_i - \hat{C}_i)^2 \\
+ \lambda_{conf} \sum_{i=0}^{s^2} \sum_{j=0}^{B} L_{ij}^{noobj} (C_i - \hat{C}_i)^2 \\
+ \lambda_{classes} \sum_{i=0}^{s^2} \sum_{j=0}^{B} L_{ij}^{obj} \sum_{c \in classes} (p_i(c) - \hat{p}_i(c))^2
\end{aligned}
\tag{9}
$$

Where: λ_{coor}: the weight assigned to the loss over the coordinates, λ_{conf}: the weight assigned to the loss over predicting the confidence, λ_{yaw}: the weight assigned to the loss over the orientation angle, $\lambda_{classes}$: the weight assigned to the loss over the class probabilities, L_{ij}^{obj}: a variable that takes the values of 0 and 1 based on whether there is a ground truth box in the ith and jth location. 1 if there's a box, and 0 otherwise, L_{ij}^{noobj}: the opposite of the previous variable takes the value of 0 if there's no object, and 1 otherwise, x_i, y_i, z_i: the gound truth coordinates, $\hat{x}_i, \hat{y}_i, \hat{z}_i$: the ground truth and predicted orientation angle, $\phi_i, \hat{\phi}_i$: the ground truth and predicted orientation angle, $C_i, \hat{C}_i$: the ground truth and predicted confidence, w_i, l_i, h_i: the ground truth width, height, and length of the box, $\hat{w}_i, \hat{l}_i, \hat{h}_i$: the predicted width, height, and length of the box and $p_i(c), \hat{p}_i(c)$: The ground truth and predicted class probabilities. B is the number of boxes, and s is the length of one of the sides of the square output grid, thus s^2 is the number of grids in the output.

4   Experiments and Results

4.1   Network Architecture and Hyper Parameters

Our model is based on YOLO-v2 [3] architecture with some changes, as shown in Table 1.

1. We modified one max-pooling layer to change the down-sampling from 32 to 16 so we can have a larger grid at the end; this has a contribution in detecting small objects like pedestrians and cyclists.
2. We removed the skip connection from the model as we found it resulting in less accurate results.
3. We added terms in the loss function for yaw, z center coordinate, and height regressions to facilitate the 3D oriented bounding box detection.
4. Our input consists of 2 channels, one representing the maximum height, and the other one representing the density of points in the point cloud, computed as shown in Eq. (1).

4.2   Dataset and Preprocessing

We used KITTI benchmark dataset. The point cloud was projected in 2D space as a bird view grid map with a resolution of 0.1 m per pixel, same resolution is used by MV3D [5].

The range represented from the LiDAR space by the grid map is 30.4 m to right and 30.4 m to the left, and 60.8 m forward. Using this range with the above mentioned resolution of 0.1 results in an input shape of 608×608 per channel.

The height in the LiDAR space is clipped between $+2$ m and -2 m, and scaled to be from 0 to 255 to be represented as pixel values in the maximum height channel.

Since in KITTI benchmark only the objects that lies on the image plane are labeled, we filter any points from the point cloud that lie outside the image plane. The rationale behind this, is to avoid giving the model contradictory information. Since objects lying on the image plane would need to be detected, while the ones lying outside that plane should be ignored, as they are not labeled. Therefore, we only include the points that lie within the image plane.

Table 1. Network architecture

Layer	Filters	Size	Feature maps
conv2d	32	(3, 3)	$608 \times 608 \times 2$
maxpooling	-	(size 2, stride 2)	
conv2d	64	(3, 3)	
maxpooling	-	(size 2, stride 2)	
conv2d	128	(3, 3)	
conv2d	64	(3, 3)	
conv2d	128	(3, 3)	
maxpooling	-	(size 2, stride 1)	
conv2d	256	(3, 3)	
conv2d	128	(3, 3)	
conv2d	256	(3, 3)	
maxpooling	-	(size 2, stride 2)	
conv2d	512	(3, 3)	
conv2d	256	(1,1)	
conv2d	512	(3, 3)	
conv2d	256	(1,1)	
conv2d	512	(3, 3)	
maxpooling	-	(size 2, stride 2)	
conv2d	1024	(3, 3)	
conv2d	512	(1, 1)	
conv2d	1024	(3, 3)	
conv2d	512	(1, 1)	
conv2d	1024	(3, 3)	
conv2d	1024	(3, 3)	
conv2d	1024	(3, 3)	
conv2d	1024	(3, 3)	
conv2d	1024	(1,1)	$38 \times 38 \times 33$
reshape	-	-	$38 \times 38 \times 3 \times 11$

4.3 Training

The network is trained in an end-to-end fashion. We used stochastic gradient descent with a momentum of 0.9, and a weight decay of 0.0005. We trained the network for 150 epochs, with a batch size of 4.

Our learning rate schedule is as follows: for the first few epochs, we slowly raise the learning rate from 0.00001 to 0.0001. If we start at a high learning rate,

(a) Car   (b) pedestrian   (c) cyclist

Fig. 4. Performance against IOU threshold

our model often diverges due to unstable gradients. We continue training with 0.0001 for 90 epochs, then 0.0005 for 30 epochs, and finally, 0.00005 for the last 20 epochs.

4.4 KITTI Results and Error Analysis

As discussed in [20], and from the results reported in [1,3], YOLO performs very well with the detection metric of mean average precision at IOU threshold of 0.5. This gives us an advantage over the previous work in 3D detection from point cloud in terms of speed with an accepted mAP, as shown in Fig. 4.

However, performance drops significantly as the IOU threshold increases indicating that we struggle to get the boxes perfectly aligned with the object, which is an inherited problem in all YOLO versions [1,3,20]. Figure 4 shows that the model succeeds in detecting the objects but struggles with accurately localizing them.

Compared with the state of the art approaches on 3D object detection, such as MV3D [5], which fails in detecting pedestrians and cyclists despite its relatively large, and complex multi view, multi sensor network, as well as, AVOD [13], which dedicates a separate network for detecting cars, and one for pedestrians and cyclists, our proposed architecture can detect all objects from only a two channel bird view input, and with just one single network, achieving a real time performance of 40 fps, and a 75.3% mAP on 0.5 IOU threshold for moderate cars. The precision and recall scores on our validation set (about 40% of the KITTI training set) are shown in Table 2.

Table 2. Validation results

Label	Precision	Recall
Pedestrian	44.0%	39.2%
Cyclist	65.13%	51.1%
Car	94.07%	83.4%

4.5   Effect of Grid Map Resolution

Grid map resolution is a critical hyper-parameter that affect memory usage, time and performance. For instance, if we want to deploy the model on an embedded target, we have to focus on fast inference time with small input size, and reasonable performance.

The area of the grid map grows proportionally to the length or width of the grid map squared. This means increasing the resolution of the grid map, increases the area of the grid map (and thus the inference time) quadratically. This can be seen in Fig. 5, where there is a rapid increase in the inference time after the 0.15 m/pixel mark, where only increasing the resolution by 0.05 m/pixel (from 0.15 m/pixel to 0.1 m/pixel) causes the inference time to double from 16.9 ms to 30.8 ms.

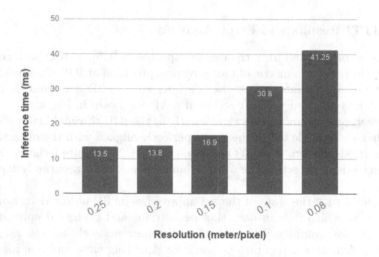

Fig. 5. Inference time at different resolutions

5   Conclusions

In this paper we present real-time LiDAR based system for 3D OBB detection and classification, based on extending YOLO-v2 [3]. The presented approach is trained end to end, without any pipelines of region proposals which ensure real time performance in the inference pass. The box orientation is ensured by direction regression on the yaw angle in bird-view. The 3D OBB center coordinates and dimensions are also formulated as a direct regression task, with no heuristics. The system is evaluated on the official KITTI benchmark at different IoU thresholds, with recommendation of the best operating point to get real time performance and best accuracy. In addition, the real time performance is evaluated at different grid-map resolutions. The results suggest that single shot detectors can be extended to predict 3D boxes while maintaining real-time performance; however this comes with a cost on the localization accuracy of the boxes.

References

1. Redmon, J., Divvala, S., Girshick, R., Farhadi, A.: You only look once: unified, real-time object detection. In: Proceedings of the IEEE Conference on Computer Vision and Pattern Recognition, pp. 779–788 (2016)
2. Liu, W., et al.: SSD: single shot MultiBox detector. In: Leibe, B., Matas, J., Sebe, N., Welling, M. (eds.) ECCV 2016. LNCS, vol. 9905, pp. 21–37. Springer, Cham (2016). https://doi.org/10.1007/978-3-319-46448-0_2
3. Redmon, J., Farhadi, A.: YOLO9000: better, faster, stronger. In: 2017 IEEE Conference on Computer Vision and Pattern Recognition (CVPR), pp. 6517–6525. IEEE (2017)
4. Li, B., Zhang, T., Xia, T.: Vehicle detection from 3D lidar using fully convolutional network. arXiv preprint arXiv:1608.07916 (2016)
5. Chen, X., Ma, H., Wan, J., Li, B., Xia, T.: Multi-view 3D object detection network for autonomous driving. In: IEEE CVPR, vol. 1, p. 3 (2017)
6. Asvadi, A., Garrote, L., Premebida, C., Peixoto, P., Nunes, U.J.: DepthCN: vehicle detection using 3D-LIDAR and ConvNet. In: IEEE ITSC (2017)
7. Li, B.: 3D fully convolutional network for vehicle detection in point cloud. In: 2017 IEEE/RSJ International Conference on Intelligent Robots and Systems (IROS), pp. 1513–1518. IEEE (2017)
8. Zhou, Y., Tuzel, O.: VoxelNet: end-to-end learning for point cloud based 3D object detection. arXiv preprint arXiv:1711.06396 (2017)
9. Mousavian, A., Anguelov, D., Flynn, J., Košecká, J.: 3D bounding box estimation using deep learning and geometry. In: 2017 IEEE Conference on Computer Vision and Pattern Recognition (CVPR), pp. 5632–5640. IEEE (2017)
10. Chabot, F., Chaouch, M., Rabarisoa, J., Teulière, C., Chateau, T.: Deep MANTA: a coarse-to-fine many-task network for joint 2D and 3D vehicle analysis from monocular image. In: Proceedings of IEEE Conference on Computer Vision Pattern Recognition (CVPR), pp. 2040–2049 (2017)
11. Chen, X., Kundu, K., Zhu, Y., Ma, H., Fidler, S., Urtasun, R.: 3D object proposals using stereo imagery for accurate object class detection. IEEE Trans. Pattern Anal. Mach. Intell. 40(5), 1259–1272 (2018)
12. Qi, C.R., Liu, W., Wu, C., Su, H., Guibas, L.J.: Frustum pointnets for 3D object detection from RGB-D data. arXiv preprint arXiv:1711.08488 (2017)
13. Ku, J., Mozifian, M., Lee, J., Harakeh, A., Waslander, S.: Joint 3D proposal generation and object detection from view aggregation. arXiv preprint arXiv:1712.02294 (2017)
14. Simon, M., Milz, S., Amende, K., Gross, H.M.: Complex-YOLO: real-time 3D object detection on point clouds. arXiv preprint arXiv:1803.06199 (2018)
15. Iandola, F.N., Han, S., Moskewicz, M.W., Ashraf, K., Dally, W.J., Keutzer, K.: SqueezeNet: AlexNet-level accuracy with 50x fewer parameters and <0.5mb model size. arXiv preprint arXiv:1602.07360 (2016)
16. Howard, A.G., et al.: MobileNets: efficient convolutional neural networks for mobile vision applications. arXiv preprint arXiv:1704.04861 (2017)

17. Zhang, X., Zhou, X., Lin, M., Sun, J.: ShuffleNet: an extremely efficient convolutional neural network for mobile devices. arXiv preprint arXiv:1707.01083 (2017)
18. Wong, A., Shafiee, M.J., Li, F., Chwyl, B.: Tiny SSD: a tiny single-shot detection deep convolutional neural network for real-time embedded object detection. arXiv preprint arXiv:1802.06488 (2018)
19. Engelcke, M., Rao, D., Wang, D.Z., Tong, C.H., Posner, I.: Vote3Deep: fast object detection in 3D point clouds using efficient convolutional neural networks. In: 2017 IEEE International Conference on Robotics and Automation (ICRA), pp. 1355–1361. IEEE (2017)
20. Farhadi, J.R.A.: YOLOv3: an incremental improvement (2018)

Increasing the Robustness of CNN-Based Human Body Segmentation in Range Images by Modeling Sensor-Specific Artifacts

Lama Seoud[(✉)], Jonathan Boisvert, Marc-Antoine Drouin, Michel Picard, and Guy Godin

National Research Council, 1200 Montreal Road, Ottawa, ON K1A 0R6, Canada
{lama.seoud,jonathan.boisvert,marc-antoine.drouin,michel.picard,
guy.godin}@nrc-cnrc.gc.ca

Abstract. This paper addresses the problem of human body parts segmentation in range images acquired using a structured-light imaging system. We propose a solution based on a fully convolutional neural network trained on realistic synthetic data that were simulated in a way that closely emulates our structured-light imaging system with its inherent artifacts such as occlusions, noise and missing data. The results on synthetic test data demonstrate quantitatively the performance of our method in identifying 33 body parts, with negligible confusion between the front and back sides of the body and between the left and right limbs. Our experiments highlight the importance of sensor-specific data augmentation in the training set to improve the robustness of the segmentation. Most importantly, when applied to range data actually acquired by our system, the method was capable of accurately segmenting the different body parts with inter-frame consistency in real-time.

Keywords: Human body segmentation · Structured-light imaging · Convolutional neural network

1 Introduction

Despite a long history of publications on the matter, human pose estimation and human body segmentation is still a challenging research subject. Challenges come from the large variations in pose, shape, viewpoint, lighting and clothing. Nevertheless, it is a key step in human motion analysis which finds application in a large variety of fields. In advanced manufacturing, robots or machines need postural information on the human they are interacting with in order to collaborate safely and effectively. In healthcare, physiotherapy can be performed remotely by examining the kinematics recorded by a marker-less vision system while a patient is at home doing his/her exercises.

L. Leal-Taixé and S. Roth (Eds.): ECCV 2018 Workshops, LNCS 11131, pp. 729–743, 2019.
https://doi.org/10.1007/978-3-030-11015-4_55

Range sensors have drawn much interest for human activity related research since they provide explicit 3D information about the shape, and that is invariant to clothing color, skin color and illumination changes compared to RGB cameras, and facilitates background subtraction. Among the existing range sensing technologies, structured-light sensors offer the advantages of high resolution combined with high speed, compared to time-of-flight cameras or stereoscopic reconstruction systems, making it more practical for real-time applications. Additionally, structured-light systems are typically more affordable.

However, triangulation-based systems (which include structured-light sensors) generate shadows or occlusions in the image when parts of the scene cannot be seen by both the projector and the camera. Those occlusions depend on the shape of the object being imaged, but also on the structured-light system design characteristics (distance between projector and camera, the triangulation angle, lens focals, *etc.*). Missing points and measurement noise are also dependent both on the object characteristics and on the design of the 3D measuring system. For instance, rapid movements and/or dark or patterned clothes may generate holes or missing data in the images. These artifacts inherent to this kind of sensor add a level of difficulty to the task of human body segmentation that is typically not addressed in the literature.

In this work, we address the problem of real-time human body segmentation from range images acquired by a high resolution structured-light imaging system. The challenge toward this goal is to design a segmentation model that is able to reason about 3D spatial information and, at the same time, is robust to artifacts inherent to the structured-light system, such as occlusions or triangulation shadows, noise and missing data.

To address this challenge, our contributions are as follows. First, we propose a domain-specific data augmentation strategy that closely simulates the actual acquisition scenario with the same intrinsic parameters as our sensor and the artifacts it generates. Second, we adapt the fully convolutional network of [20] to range images of the human body in order for it to transfer its learning toward 3D spatial information instead of light intensities. Third, we quantitatively demonstrate the importance of simulating sensor-specific artifacts in the training set to improve the robustness of the segmentation of actual range images.

2   Related Work

Most previous work on human pose estimation use as input either a single RGB image or a RGB video sequence [5,9,15,19,23,24]. Even though these images contain rich information, the sensitivity of RGB sensors to illumination changes and the presence of texture that interferes with geometric features affect the robustness of RGB image-based human pose estimation. With the advent and wide accessibility of range sensors, research on range image-based or RGBD-based (color and depth) methods [2,7,8,16,21] has become very active.

Furthermore, the literature related to human body pose estimation can be categorized into generative and discriminative methods. Generative methods consist in fitting a human body shape template or prior to the input data points, using some optimization procedures, making them considerably time-consuming. Point clouds obtained by range sensing motivate the use of different variants of the iterative closest point algorithm, such as in [7]. A subclass of generative approaches groups methods that use part-based models where the human body is represented as a skeleton with different body parts connected by joints-imposed constraints or kinematics constraints, such as the popular pictorial structural model [5,19] or some Markov Random Field based graphical model to impose spatial constraints [23].

On the other hand, discriminative methods consist in directly identifying a mapping between the input image and the body parts or joints. Among these methods, some aim at detecting the joints by regression methods [22,24], or identifying and classifying interest points [16], or segmenting the body into its individual parts using a pixel-level classification [2,11,15,21]. Because it does not take into account the kinematic properties of the human body configuration, those methods may result in incoherent body parts segmentation. Nevertheless, machine learning approaches, either random forests [21,22] or deep convolutional neural networks [2,8,9,11,15,24] have proved that, with sufficiently large training datasets, the global distribution of body parts is somehow implicitly learned by the classification model. The biggest advantage of discriminative methods over model-based method is in execution time, making them more suitable for real-time applications.

Machine learning approaches rely heavily on the size and quality of the training data. Several papers have addressed the limited availability of segmented range and RGB images of the human body and proposed datasets of synthetic training data [4,14,21,25,27]. Generally, synthetic range images are generated using some motion capture sequences with retargeting of different body shapes and standard computer graphics techniques. While authors emphasize the importance of having a variety of shapes and poses, they tend to neglect the artifacts introduced by actual range sensing systems, limiting the generalization performance on real data.

However, a better modeling of the sensor characteristics has already been shown to improve performances of a different learning task applied to RGBD image. For instance, Planche et al. [17] demonstrated improved performances in the determination of the position and orientation of isolated rigid objects using this kind of approach. It should therefore provide gains for body segmentation methods as well since those sensor characteristics can significantly alter the appearance of body parts in range images. Furthermore, the complex relationship between occlusions and the changing shape of a deformable object (such as the human body) might provide insight that a CNN (Convolutional Neural Network) can use to boost performances.

3   Method

In this section, we first describe our imaging system based on structured light, the configuration of which is then used to synthetically generate realistic range images from existing 3D human body meshes. For those synthetic images to be realistic, we define and simulate occlusions, noise and missing data. The labeling of the different body parts is then described, followed by the deep neural network configuration and its training. Finally, we provide an overview of our experimental setup for the evaluation of our method on both synthetic and real data.

3.1   Structured-Light Imaging System

Our structured-light imaging system [6] uses a high-resolution projector and a Emergent Vision Technologies camera working at 360 fps. The standoff distance is 2.5 m and the system baseline is 0.75 m. The system was designed to cover the volume of an adult performing large amplitude movements. The focal lengths are respectively 12 and 12.5 mm for the projection and collection lenses. The lateral resolution of the system is 1 mm and the range uncertainty is sub-millimetric.

In our experiments, we configured the system to use 5 phase shift patterns for range measurements and 7 binary patterns for the phase unwrapping. The system can generate 2 M points range images at 30 Hz. The configuration of our system is illustrated in Fig. 1.

Fig. 1. Set-up of our 3D human body imaging system with the structured-light projector (A), the camera (B) and the real-time body part segmentation projected on a large screen (C).

The size of the resulting range images is 1920 × 988 pixels, however, in this work, we down-sampled the images by a factor of 3 for a faster training.

3.2   Building a Realistic Set of Synthetic Data

To generate training data for our model, we used a methodology inspired from the work of [27] but with a particular emphasis on replicating the output of our structured-light imaging system.

We collected 3D meshes of the human body from 3 publicly available datasets: SCAPE [1], MIT [26] and CAESAR [18]. The first one consists of 71 meshes of the same unclothed subject (labeled as A) in different poses. The second one consists of 2 clothed subjects (labeled as B and C) in 4 different motion sequences each (walking, jumping, crane, squatting, bouncing and hand-standing), for a total of 825 and 850 meshes for B and C respectively. The third dataset comprises the meshes of 583 minimally clothed subjects in the same canonical posture.

Posture variability is covered by SCAPE and MIT meshes, while inter-subject variability is mostly covered by CAESAR meshes. Having both clothed and unclothed subjects adds a level of invariance to clothing.

For each 3D mesh, we simulated 54 different range images: the mesh is placed iteratively at 2.15 m, 2.55 m, and 2.95 m from the camera along its focal axis and for each position, the mesh is rendered from 18 different viewpoints around the model (10° rotation between each pair of consecutive views). This enforces an invariance to distance and viewpoint.

In a real acquisition system, range images are affected by artifacts proper to the imaging system itself. Using a structured-light sensor, light occlusions are present when part of the scene is not illuminated by the projector (Fig. 2). On top of that, the acquisition can be affected by noisy range values resulting from the calibration of the system. Finally, because of dark patterned clothes and/or rapid movements, some data might be missing in the range image.

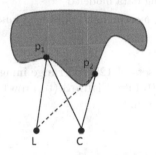

Fig. 2. Light occlusions: top view of a structured-light imaging system with the light projector (L) and the camera (C). Point p_1 is illuminated by L and seen by C, thus it rendered as a foreground pixel in the range image. Point p_2 is seen by C but not illuminated by L, this occlusion results in a background valued pixel in the range image.

In order for our classification model to be robust to those inherent artifacts, we simulated the presence of occlusions, missing data, and measurement noise in our training:

- Light occlusions modeling: For structured-light specific occlusions, we considered two frame buffers, one that emulates the light projector and the other the camera, and we considered only the pixels that are rendered in both buffers.
- Measurement noise modeling: To simulate range measurement noise, additive Gaussian noise is added to the foreground pixels. For each image a standard deviation is randomly selected between 0 mm (noise) and 100 mm (which is considerably more then the expected noise on our real data).

– Missing data modeling: By missing data in range images, we mean pixels that do not correspond to any light occlusions, but whose value was two erroneous due to rapid motion or dark patterned clothes and thus discarded from the range image. To model those "missing data" in a given range image, we randomly removed a random percentage of pixels from the foreground and replaced it by background values. The pixel removal rate is randomly chosen between 0%, 5% and 50%.

To evaluate the effect of each of these artifacts, we created five variations of the dataset, each one modeling a different combination of artifacts (see Table 1).

Table 1. Description of differences between the datasets used in the experiments.

Dataset	Description
X_{none}	No sensor-specific artifacts modeled
X_{occ}	Only occlusions modeled
X_{noise}	Only measurement noise modeled
X_{md}	Only missing data modeled
X_{all}	Occlusions, measurement noise and missing data modeled

In total, we generated 5 sets of 125 766 range images of size 640×329 pixels with the range encoded on 16 bits. Figure 3 (top row) illustrates some examples of the simulated synthetic data.

Fig. 3. Examples of simulated synthetic range images (top row) with their corresponding segmentation into 33 body parts (bottom row). Each color correspond to a distinct body part. Note the presence of occlusions (for instance the self-occlusion of the left leg in the first column or the disconnected leg and head in the second column).

3.3 Annotating the Data

To annotate the different body parts in the range images, we used anatomical landmarks identified as salient points on the 3D meshes. For the meshes in CAESAR, the coordinates of 33 anatomical landmarks are provided with each mesh. For SCAPE and MIT, we manually identified those same landmarks on one mesh for each of the subjects A, B and C; we then used the fact that the meshes of each subject in different postures share the same topology to propagate those landmarks coordinates to the remaining meshes of these subjects.

To define body parts from those anatomical landmarks, we used the fast marching closest neighbor algorithm [12] that aggregates the vertices that are the closest to the landmarks in terms of geodesic distance on the triangular mesh. For each landmark or resulting body part, a distinct label and color are attributed.

Finally, for each simulated range map, an image of the same size is generated with the corresponding labels encoded on 8 bits. The background is set to an arbitrary value that will be ignored in the remaining process. Some examples of segmented images are provided in Fig. 3 (bottom row).

3.4 Network Description

We approach the problem of body parts tracking from range images as a pixel classification problem. Thus, to perform the segmentation, we defined a dense fully convolutional neural network [20] derived from the Alexnet [13]. The architecture of our network is detailed in Fig. 4.

To do so, we first removed the final classification layer of the Alexnet and replaced all the fully connected layers of the Alexnet by convolutional layers with a stride of 1 and a kernel size of 1. At the end of the network, before the final classification, we added *conv8*, a 1×1 convolutional layer with 16 outputs in order to extract for each pixel a 16D features vector and *upfeat*, a backward convolution (deconvolution) layer to bilinearly up-sample the coarse outputs to pixel-wise outputs that are the same size as the input image.

Finally, the last convolutional layer, *score*, provides for each pixel 33 outputs corresponding to the 33 body parts considered in our segmentation problem. Also, because the original Alexnet aims at classifying 3-channel RGB images, we had to modify the first convolutional layer, *conv1* to adapt it so that it takes only one channel (the range).

3.5 Network Training

From each of the 5 datasets of simulated range images, 97 146 images are selected as follows and used for training the network: for subject A, we used the first 57 postures for training and the remaining 14 postures for testing, for subjects B and C, we used the jumping and the squatting sequences respectively for testing and the remaining for training, for the CAESAR dataset, we used the first 467 subjects for training and the remaining for the test. This way, we ensure that

Layers	Parameters	Weight initialisation
score	Convolution (k=1, s=1, o=33)	Gaussian
upfeat	Deconvolution (k=63, s=16, o=16) + Crop	Bilinear
conv8	Convolution (k=1, s=1, o=16) + ReLU	Gaussian
conv7	Convolution (k=1, s=1, o=4096) + ReLU + Dropout	Adapted from Alexnet
conv6	Convolution (k=6, s=1, o=4096) + ReLU + Dropout	Adapted from Alexnet
pool5	Pooling (max, k=3, s=2)	
conv5	Convolution (k=3, s=1, o=256) + ReLU	Alexnet
conv4	Convolution (k=3, s=1, o=384) + ReLU	Alexnet
conv3	Convolution (k=3, s=1, o=384) + ReLU	Alexnet
pool2	Pooling (max, k=3, s=2)	
conv2	Convolution (k=5, s=1, o=256) + ReLU	Alexnet
pool1	Pooling (max, k=3, s=2)	
conv1	Convolution (k=11, s=4, o=96) + ReLU	Adapted from Alexnet

Fig. 4. Architecture of the fully-convolutional neural network trained for body parts segmentation. Starting from the deepest layers at the bottom and going up to shallower layers. k: kernel size, s: stride, o: number of outputs

all the range images generated from one mesh are considered together either for training or for testing the network.

Instead of training our network from scratch, we performed a transfer learning. We started the training with the weights of the Alexnet and we fine-tuned it by applying a gradient of learning rates: for the deepest layers corresponding to more generic filters, we applied a smaller learning rate (0.01 times the learning rate of the last layer), and for the shallowest layers corresponding to application specific features, we gradually increased the learning rate.

For the first layer of our network, *conv1*, we averaged the original weights of the 3-channels in the Alexnet to generate 1-channel filters. And for the additional layers that are not part of the original Alexnet, we initialized the weights using a Gaussian distribution with a standard deviation of 0.01. The deconvolution layer implements a bilinear up-sampling filter and its weights are kept frozen during the training.

The training is performed using the stochastic gradient descent, with a fixed last layer learning rate of 10^{-2}, a momentum of 0.99 and a weight decay of 5×10^{-4}. At each iteration, we used a gradient accumulation across 20 images. We run the training over 70 000 iterations. A softmax loss layer computes the cost function while ignoring all the pixels that belong to the background of the input image.

We used the Caffe framework [10] to implement the training on an 12 GB NVIDIA GeForce GTX TITAN X GPU.

3.6   Experimental Setup

We performed a two-step evaluation of the proposed method. First, to quantify the classification accuracy on simulated data, we considered the remaining 28 620 images of the X_{all} dataset as our synthetic test set. To weigh each body part equally despite their varying sizes, the accuracy is reported as the average per-class segmentation accuracy, as in [21]. Test images always include random additive noise, missing data, and occlusions. We also evaluate the relationship between the confidence probability associated with each classified pixel (obtained by softmax) and the classification accuracy.

In a second step, we applied our method to real data sequences acquired with our structured-light imaging system and we qualitatively evaluated the inter-frame consistency, considering that the processing is performed independently on each frame. We also report the overall processing time.

4   Results and Discussion

In this section, we report and analyze the results obtained on both the synthetic test dataset and the real data acquired by our structured-light 3D imaging system. We also evaluate the robustness to noise and missing data as well as the computational performance of the proposed method.

4.1   Results on the Synthetic Test Set

Over the entire synthetic test set, we report a global average per-class segmentation accuracy of 81.3% when the network is trained using the X_{all} dataset. Figure 5 provide an example of the results. Most of the errors are located at the edges of the segmentation. This is due in part to the ground truth annotations. In fact, when rendering the annotated faces of the meshes, the 2D projection creates triangular patterns at the edges of the body parts. However, when computing

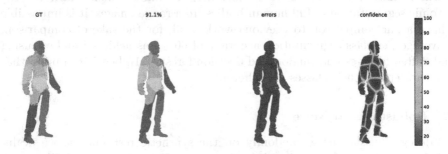

Fig. 5. Confidence in the segmentation. From left to right, the ground truth segmentation (GT), the result of the CNN segmentation, the error image (blue for correct, red for error in the segmentation) and the confidence image computed as a probability using the softmax function and expressed in percentage. (Color figure online)

the confidence in the segmentation using the softmax function at the output of the network for a random test image (Fig. 5), we see that the confidence on the edges of the segmentation is the lowest. Thus, if we apply a threshold of 70% on the confidence values, we get an average per-class segmentation accuracy of 97.8% for this image instead of 91.1%, while discarding only 18% of the pixels in the test set.

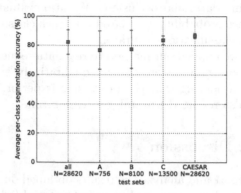

Fig. 6. Average ± one standard deviation per-class segmentation accuracy for the whole test set and the different subsets.

Figure 6 reports the average per-class segmentation accuracy for the whole test set and for the test subsets corresponding to subjects A, B, C separately and the CAESAR test set, as well as the per-class accuracy on the whole test set. The best results are obtained on the CAESAR test set where the variation is essentially in the human shape, the pose being similar for all subjects in the database. On the contrary, the segmentation accuracy for the test set from SCAPE is only of 78.1%, indicating that the model is more robust to inter-subject shape variations than to intra-subject pose variations.

Unfortunately, because there is currently no unified benchmark for the anatomic segmentation of full human bodies from range images, it is impossible to have a fair comparison to previous work. Still, for the sake of comparison, an average per-class segmentation accuracy of 60% was achieved at best using handcrafted features and randomized decision forests [21], bearing in mind that their dataset and their classes are different.

4.2 Robustness to Noise

By adding Gaussian noise randomly on the synthetic test images, we evaluated the robustness of our network to the presence of noise. Figure 7 illustrates the average segmentation accuracy computed on the whole test set for different amounts of simulated Gaussian noise. This result clearly demonstrates that the system is highly robust to Gaussian noise in the range maps, even when its standard deviation reaches 40 mm, which is significantly larger than the

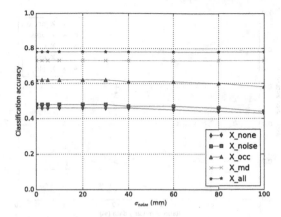

Fig. 7. Robustness to Gaussian noise reported as the average of the segmentation accuracy evaluated on the synthetic test set based on training with each of the five training set variations (see Table 1 for details).

range accuracy of our system ($<1\,\text{mm}$). This robustness to noise is implicitly embedded in the architecture of the CNN itself, particularly at the pooling layers. Furthermore, it appears that simulating sensor-specific artifacts improved performances at varying levels with missing data simulation and occlusions providing the greatest individual gains.

4.3 Robustness to Missing Data

By randomly removing data from the range images in the synthetic test set, we evaluated the robustness of our network to missing data. We trained the network with five variants of the training set presented earlier (see Table 1). Figure 8 illustrates the segmentation accuracy computed on the whole test set for different amounts of missing data. This result clearly demonstrates the importance of simulating missing data and occlusions (to a lesser degree) during the training to increase the robustness of the network. To our knowledge, no previous work has analyzed the effects of missing data on the human body parts segmentation from range and/or RGB images, even though robustness to missing data is an important feature especially when dealing with real range image acquisition where rapid movements and/or dark clothes can generate holes in the image.

4.4 Results on a Real Data Sequence

The results on the synthetic datasets demonstrate quantitatively the performance of the proposed segmentation network. We are also interested in evaluating qualitatively the performance in a real scenario, with real range images acquired using our own structured-light imaging system. The effect of considering the sensor-specific artifacts on real data in practice is illustrated in Fig. 9 for 3 range images acquired with our structured-light imaging system. Qualitatively,

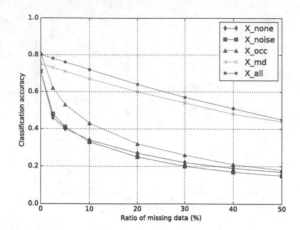

Fig. 8. Robustness to random missing data, reported as the average of the segmentation accuracy evaluated on the synthetic test set. Training was performed using the five training set variations (see Table 1 for details).

the worst segmentation results are obtained when no occlusions and no missing data are considered in the training set. These results on real test data emphasize even more the importance of a good modeling of the sensor's characteristics in the simulation of training data, and hence in the training of the CNN.

A video illustrating the real-time body parts segmentation on a live full motion sequence is available at: https://youtu.be/2aEbHqwKlmg. The subject performs successively a jump, a squat, two 360° rotations, and ends in a final posture with crossing arms on the chest. Qualitatively, the different body parts are accurately segmented in most frames with remarkably little jitter. Even in the two full 360° rotations, the performance in differentiating the front and the back sides of the body, as well as the left and right limbs is very satisfactory, discarding the need for a tracking algorithm as opposed to the conclusions in [21]. During the full rotations, when the subject is perpendicular to the baseline of the system, the arms are correctly segmented even though there is self-occlusion with the rest of the body. However, one evident segmentation error is noted in the crossed arms final posture where the forearms are vanishing in the chest in the segmented images. This particular failure mode has also been raised in previous work [21] and we believe that this is partly due to the lack of similar postures in the training set.

4.5   Processing Time

We evaluated the performance of the network on the same hardware as the training, an 12 GB NVIDIA GeForce GTX TITAN X GPU. We recorded the processing time required to perform a segmentation, considering the data already loaded on the memory. We recorded an average of 61 ms (±1.2 ms) on the whole

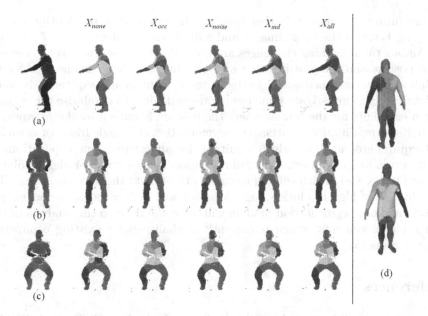

X_{none} X_{occ} X_{noise} X_{md} X_{all}

(a)

(b)

(c)

(d)

Fig. 9. For each image (a, b and c), the results of the segmentation using the CNN trained on each of the 5 training set variations (see Table 1 for details) are illustrated from left to right respectively. In the absence of ground truth for those actual range images, a template body segmentation is provided on the right (d) to qualitatively compare the segmentation results.

test set with the average image size being 640 × 329 pixels. This results shows that method would be suitable for real-time applications.

5 Conclusion

We presented in this paper a deep learning approach for human body parts segmentation from range images. Not only did it yield semantically accurate results in synthetic test data, but we demonstrated its performance in a real scenario with images acquired with a high-resolution structured-light imaging system. We have also demonstrated the importance of having a realistic sensor-specific training set to improve the robustness of the segmentation to artifacts such as occlusions, noise and missing data which affect the range images acquired by a structured-light system in particular.

The proposed data-augmentation strategy is specific to structured-light imaging systems. Of course, depending on the acquisition system, sensor-specific artifacts are quite different. Time-of-flight sensors, for example, suffer from the multiple paths problem, whereas passive stereo systems deal with non-uniform noise depending on the texture of the object being imaged.

Compared to previous work, we considered a segmentation of the body into 33 parts, which is a finer granularity than most of the previous work [2,8,11,15].

In the future, we aim at further refining the granularity to identify a dense mapping between the range images and a 3D body template.

Among the remaining challenges are the self-occlusions, such as the crossed-arms posture and the postures that are very different than the one used for the training. However, since our objective is to segment image sequences, it would be interesting to investigate some temporal constraints to regularize the segmentation especially for the frames where the posture is unseen by the network.

In its current implementation, the segmentation of a single frame of size 640×329 requires around 60 ms which is suitable for almost real-time applications. In future work, we plan on using the full resolution images from our high-resolution sensor (1920×988), which will require more attention to the processing time. The combination of high resolution, high accuracy and high speed of our acquisition system and our segmentation module will open the door to the analysis of tiny and rapid movements, which is currently a challenge for existing commercial range sensors [3].

References

1. Anguelov, D., Srinivasan, P., Koller, D., Thrun, S., Rodgers, J., Davis, J.: SCAPE: shape completion and animation of people. In: ACM Transactions on Graphics - Proceedings of ACM SIGGRAPH 2005, pp. 408–416 (2005)
2. Chandra, S., Tsogkas, S., Kokkinos, I.: Accurate human-limb segmentation in RGB-D images for intelligent mobility assistance robots. In: IEEE International Conference on Computer Vision (ICCV), pp. 44–50 (2015)
3. Chen, L., Wei, H., Ferryman, J.: A survey of human motion analysis using depth imagery. Pattern Recogn. Lett. **34**(15), 1995–2006 (2013)
4. Chen, W., et al.: Synthesizing training images for boosting human 3D pose estimation. In: International Conference on 3D Vision, pp. 479–488 (2016)
5. Dantone, M., Gall, J., Leistner, C.: Human pose estimation using body parts dependent joint regressors. In: IEEE Conference on Computer Vision and Pattern Recognition (CVPR), pp. 3041–3048 (2013)
6. Drouin, M.A., Blais, F., Godin, G.: High resolution projector for 3D imaging. In: International Conference on 3D Vision (3DV), vol. 1, pp. 337–344 (2014)
7. Ganapathi, V., Plagemann, C., Koller, D., Thrun, S.: Real-time human pose tracking from range data. In: Fitzgibbon, A., Lazebnik, S., Perona, P., Sato, Y., Schmid, C. (eds.) ECCV 2012. LNCS, vol. 7577, pp. 738–751. Springer, Heidelberg (2012). https://doi.org/10.1007/978-3-642-33783-3_53
8. Haque, A., Peng, B., Luo, Z., Alahi, A., Yeung, S., Fei-Fei, L.: Towards viewpoint invariant 3D human pose estimation. In: Leibe, B., Matas, J., Sebe, N., Welling, M. (eds.) ECCV 2016. LNCS, vol. 9905, pp. 160–177. Springer, Cham (2016). https://doi.org/10.1007/978-3-319-46448-0_10
9. Jain, A., Tompson, J., LeCun, Y., Bregler, C.: MoDeep: a deep learning framework using motion features for human pose estimation. In: Cremers, D., Reid, I., Saito, H., Yang, M.-H. (eds.) ACCV 2014. LNCS, vol. 9004, pp. 302–315. Springer, Cham (2015). https://doi.org/10.1007/978-3-319-16808-1_21
10. Jia, Y., et al.: Caffe: convolutional architecture for fast feature embedding. In: ACM International Conference on Multimedia, pp. 675–678 (2014)

11. Jiu, M., Wolf, C., Taylor, G., Baskurt, A.: Human body part estimation from depth images via spatially-constrained deep learning. Pattern Recogn. Lett. **50**, 122–129 (2014)
12. Kimmel, R., Sethian, J.A.: Computing geodesic paths on manifolds. In: Proceedings of the National Academy of Sciences of the United States of America, vol. 95, pp. 8431–8435 (1998)
13. Krizhevsky, A., Sutskever, I., Hinton, G.: ImageNet classification with deep convolutional neural networks. In: Advances in Neural Information Processing Systems (NIPS), pp. 1097–1105 (2012)
14. Nishi, K., Miura, J.: Generation of human depth images with body part labels for complex human pose recognition. Pattern Recogn. **71**, 402–413 (2017)
15. Oliveira, G.L., Valada, A., Bollen, C., Burgard, W., Brox, T.: Deep learning for human part discovery in images. In: Proceedings - IEEE International Conference on Robotics and Automation, pp. 1634–1641 (2016)
16. Plagemann, C., Ganapathi, V., Koller, D., Thrun, S.: Real-time identification and localization of body parts from depth images. In: Proceedings - IEEE International Conference on Robotics and Automation, pp. 3108–3113 (2010)
17. Planche, B., et al.: DepthSynth: real-time realistic synthetic data generation from CAD models for 2.5D recognition. In: International Conference on 3D Vision (3DV) (2017)
18. Robinette, K.M., Daanen, H., Paquet, E.: The CAESAR project: a 3-D surface anthropometry survey. In: Second International Conference on 3D Digital Imaging and Modeling, 3DIM, pp. 380–386 (1999)
19. Sapp, B., Taskar, B.: MODEC: multimodal decomposable models for human pose estimation. In: IEEE Conference on Computer Vision and Pattern Recognition (CVPR), pp. 3674–3681 (2013)
20. Shelhamer, E., Long, J., Darrell, T.: Fully convolutional networks for semantic segmentation. IEEE Trans. Pattern Anal. Mach. Intell. **39**(4), 640–651 (2016)
21. Shotton, J., et al.: Real-time human pose recognition in parts from single depth images. Commun. ACM **56**(1), 119–135 (2013)
22. Shotton, J., et al.: Efficient human pose estimation from single depth images. IEEE Trans. Pattern Anal. Mach. Intell. **35**(12), 2821–2840 (2013)
23. Tompson, J., Jain, A., LeCun, Y., Bregler, C.: Joint training of a convolutional network and a graphical model for human pose estimation. In: Advances in Neural Information Processing Systems (NIPS), pp. 1799–1807 (2014)
24. Toshev, A., Szegedy, C.: DeepPose: human pose estimation via deep neural networks. In: IEEE Conference on Computer Vision and Pattern Recognition (CVPR), pp. 1653–1660 (2014)
25. Varol, G., et al.: Learning from synthetic humans. In: IEEE Conference on Computer Vision and Pattern Recognition (CVPR) (2017)
26. Vlasic, D., Baran, I., Matusik, W., Popović, J.: Articulated mesh animation from multi-view silhouettes. ACM Trans. Graph. **27**(3), 1–9 (2008)
27. Wei, L., Huang, Q., Ceylan, D., Vouga, E., Li, H.: Dense human body correspondences using convolutional networks. In: IEEE Conference on Computer Vision and Pattern Recognition (CVPR), pp. 1544–1553 (2016)

Author Index

Printed in the United States
By Bookmasters

Printed in the United States
By Bookmasters